Architect's Legal Handbook

Architect's Legal Handbook
The Law for Architects

Eighth edition

Edited by

Anthony Speaight QC (Editor)
Gregory Stone QC (Consultant Editor)

AMSTERDAM BOSTON HEIDELBERG LONDON NEW YORK OXFORD
PARIS SAN DIEGO SAN FRANCISCO SINGAPORE SYDNEY TOKYO

Architectural Press is an imprint of Elsevier

Architectural
Press

Architectural Press is an imprint of Elsevier
The Boulevard, Langford Lane, Kidlington, Oxford, OX5 1GB
30 Corporate Drive, Suite 400, Burlington, MA 01803, USA

First edition 1973 by the Architectural Press Ltd
Second edition 1978
Third edition 1982
Fourth edition 1985
Reprinted 1987
Reprinted 1989 by Butterworth Architecture
Fifth edition 1990
Sixth edition 1996
Reprinted 1997, 1998, 1999
Seventh edition 2000
Reprinted 2001, 2003 (twice)
Eighth edition 2004
Reprinted 2005, 2007, 2008 (twice)

British Library Cataloguing in Publication Data
A catalogue record for this book is available from the British Library

Library of Congress Cataloging-in-Publication Data
A catalog record for this book is available from the Library of Congress

ISBN: 978-0-7506-6130-0

For information on all Architectural Press publications
visit our website at www.elsevierdirect.com

Printed and bound in *China*

08 09 10 9 8 7 6 5

Working together to grow
libraries in developing countries
www.elsevier.com | www.bookaid.org | www.sabre.org

ELSEVIER   BOOK AID
International   Sabre Foundation

Contents

Editor's Preface

The aim of this book remains to provide within the compass of a single volume a statement of the law relevant to an architect in practice.

No one lawyer could write with authority about so many different aspects of the law. Each chapter is contributed by an expert in the particular field. Our authors come from a range of backgrounds – judges, barristers, solicitors, architects, and building control officers. Many contributors carry on responsibility for a chapter from edition to edition. A few, though, are on the occasion of each new edition unable to continue, sometimes for the most illustrious of reasons. For this 8th edition we welcome several new lawyer and architect authors: Christopher Miers RIBA, chairman of the Society of Construction Law; Oliver Palmer FRIBA, who was responsible for recasting the Building Regulations; Ruth Downing, a barrister expert in employment law; James Leabeater, barrister; Melanie Willems, of the international law firm Lovells; and Sarah Lupton RIBA, of the University of Wales.

The book covers the law of the whole of the United Kingdom. In space terms the law of England and Wales occupies pride of place. But Scots law is also covered in respect of the many areas of law where it is different. In addition Northern Ireland's law is also explained in areas where it diverges from English law. Some fields of law, such as EU law, are common for the whole of the United Kingdom.

I am grateful to Angus Stewart QC, of the Scots Bar, who has advised me as to Scottish authors, and to Sir Richard McLaughlin, now a High Court judge in Northern Ireland, who marshalled the team of authors from Northern Ireland.

Although the pace of change of substantive law has slightly slowed, the years since the last edition have seen a complete revolution in the manner in which disputes are resolved. Formerly if someone wanted to make a claim against another person he went to court or, if there was an arbitration agreement, the dispute was arbitrated. The pace was measured, the emphasis on ensuring that each side had a fair chance to put its case. Today a number of quite new procedures have to be considered. The first step is to serve requisite pieces of paper, of which a prime example is the withholding notice required for some purposes by the Housing Grants Construction and Regeneration Act. Next might come the whirlwind process of a 28-day adjudication. A party dissatisfied with the adjudicator's decision may then refuse to pay and fight the enforcement process in the Technology and Construction Court. Whether enforced or not, the adjudication decision is of only 'temporary finality' and the whole issue can be refought in litigation or arbitration. But by now, if not before, the parties will probably try to reach a mutually acceptable outcome by mediation. The importance of all these procedures is such that there is now a distinct section of the book devoted to them – Part 3: Dispute Resolution. This contains a full chapter devoted to adjudication with its rapidly growing case-law. There is a completely new chapter on mediation. There are also new chapters on dispute resolution in Scotland and Northern Ireland.

This book is not intended to turn architects into fully fledged legal advisers. What we hope is that it will identify for architects the legal issues affecting their work, and alert them to the circumstances in which legal advice is necessary. Unrealistic as many of us may consider the law's standard to be, the hard reality is that judges expect architects either to know a good deal of law themselves, or else regularly to call on legal advice. In *Robert Morgan v Jervis* (2003) the Court of Appeal held that an architect might commit a negligent breach of duty if he failed to inform a client when a Construction Act withholding notice was needed.

It was a similar story in *West Faulkner Associates v London Borough of Newham* (1994). An architect's interpretation of 'regularly and diligently' in the JCT contract was different from that of the judges. The Court of Appeal said he would have been 'fireproof' if he had taken legal advice; but he had not, so he was not, and a heavy judgment against him for professional negligence was the result.

Anthony Speaight
4 Pump Court, Temple

Acknowledgements

Acknowledgement is given to the following bodies for permission to use sample documents and statutory publications:

Architects' Registration Council of the United Kingdom
British Property Federation
Building Employer's Confederation
Her Majesty's Stationery Office
Office for Official Publications of the European Communities
Royal Incorporation of Architects in Scotland
Royal Institute of British Architects
Scottish Building Contracts Committee

Extracts from the JCT documentation are reproduced by kind permission of the copyrights owners, The Joint Contracts Tribunal Limited, and the publishers, RIBA Publications.

The editors would also like to thank Anthony Lavers, Professor of Law at Oxford Brookes University for compiling the Bibliography, and Ben Hughes, barrister for compiling the Table of Statutes and Statutory Instruments, and the Table of Cases.

Information provided in this document its provided 'as is' without warranty of any kind, either express or implied. Every effort has been made to ensure accuracy and conformance to standards accepted at the time of publication. The reader is advised to research other sources of information on these topics.

Contributors

Editor

Anthony Speaight, QC – Barrister, of 4 Pump Court, Temple, London. Bencher of Middle Temple. Co-author of *The Law of Defective Premises*. Co-editor of *Butterworths Professional Negligence Service*. Past member of the Council of the Society of Construction Law. Chairman of the Editorial Board of *Counsel, journal of the Bar of England and Wales* (1990–4). Chairman of the Bar Council's Access to the Bar Committee. Specialises in construction contract and professional negligence work.

Consultant Editor

Gregory Stone, QC – Barrister, of 4–5 Gray's Inn Square, Gray's Inn; co-author of *The Law of Defective Premises*; contributor of articles on legal topics to the *Architect's Journal*; educated in England and France; did postgraduate work in Economics, and worked as Chief Economist to a merchant bank before coming to the Bar; now specializes in planning, administrative and local government work.

Contributors – England & Wales

Andrew Bartlett, QC, Chartered Arbitrator – practises from Crown Office Chambers at 1 Paper Buildings, London both as counsel and as arbitrator in professional negligence, construction and insurance. He is the General Editor of *Emden's Construction Law* and author of numerous articles in legal journals.

Graham Brown, ARB, RIBA, ACArch, FCIArb – Architect, Project Manager, Contract and Practice Consultant, Arbitrator and Mediator; Director of Tindall Brown Architects and Project Managers; Visiting lecturer at schools of architecture in UK and overseas; Part 3 Examiner for Architects Registration Board and Architectural Association; Architectural Practice NVQ test assessor and verifier; Formerly Principal Lecturer in Law and Management and Director of Professional Training at Partsmouth School of Architecture.

Martin Dixon – Fellow and Senior University Lecturer in Law, Queens' College, Cambridge. Visiting Professor of Law, City University, London. Sometime Legal Officer to the United Nations in Vienna. He has written extensively on Land Law, including co-authorship of Ruoff & Roper, The Law of Registered Conveyancing.

Richard Dyton, LLB, MSc, AKC – Solicitor, Partner at Simmons & Simmons; specialist advice to architects and engineers; negotiation and conclusion of international commercial agreements; author of *Eurolegislation in Building Maintenance and Preservation* (2nd edn) and *EC Legislation affecting the Practice of UK Architects and Engineers*. Winner: Legal Business Construction Law Team of the Year (1999)

Kim Franklin, FCIArb – Chartered Arbitrator, Barrister' practises from Crown Office Chambers at 2 Crown Office Row, Temple, London, as counsel, arbitrator and adjudicator in construction disputes. She is joint editor of *Construction Law Journal*, a contributing author of *The Legal Obligations of the Architect* and a regular columnist for the *Architect's Journal*.

Andrew Fraser-Urquhart, MA (Cantab) – Called to the Bar in 1993, having previously been employed by the Bank of England. He practises from 4–5 Gray's Inn Square where he specializes in Town & Country Planning, Local Government and Judicial Review. He has extensive experience both of planning inquiries and Local Plan work.

Andrew Geddes, MA (Oxon) – Called to the Bar in 1972; while at the Bar he specialized in EEC law writing extensively on that topic in the specialist press. Publications include: *Product and Service Liability in the EEC, Protection of Individual Rights under EC Law* and *Public and Utility Procurement*. He was appointed a circuit judge in March 1994 and authorized to sit as a High Court Judge in August 1995.

Muhammed Haque (BA Oxon) – Graduated in Engineering Science before being called to the Bar. He practises from Crown Office Chambers, 2 Crown Office Row, London and specializes in construction litigation, including the professional negligence of architects, engineers and surveyors. He is an Editor of *Emden's Construction Law*.

Alexander Hickey MA (Oxon) – Alexander is a barrister practising from 4 Pump Court, Temple one of the leading set of chambers in the construction and commercial field. Alexander specialises in construction, engineering, computer and technology disputes, as well as professional negligence claims against architects and other construction professionals.

Ann Minogue is a partner in the Construction and Engineering group at Linklaters, solicitors. She specialises in non-contentious construction work on real estate projects particularly acting for a number of key developers. In addition, she has been involved in the procurement of a number of major Arts' Projects. She has a regular column in Building Magazine, sits on the membership committee of the British Counsel for Offices and the Construction Committee at the British Property Federation. She is also a member of the Next Steps' Forum chaired by Sir Michael Latham. She is a council member at City University.

Vincent Moran, MA (Cantab) – Barrister and member of Gray's Inn. He specializes in professional negligence, including architects' and surveyors' negligence. He went to the Bar after studying History at Clare College, Cambridge and working for an American Bank.

Matthew Needham-Laing, RIBA, LLB, MSc, ACIArb – Architect, Solicitor and accredited Adjudicator, Mathew is a Partner in Fenwick Elliot LLP, solicitors specialising in construction and engineering law, acting for architects, employers, contractors and sub-contractors in adjudication, arbitration and litigation, as well as negotiating drafting profession appointments and construction conracts.

Graham North, MRICS, MCIArb – Chartered Building Surveyor and Partner of Anstey Horne & Co., specialises in party wall matters and boundary issues generally; past Chairman of the Boundaries & Party Walls Practice Panel of the RICS and Building Surveyors' Division of the City of London Branch of the RICS. Editor of the Party Wall Surveyors' Manual. He Lectures regularly to the property profession and for RICS and RIBA Branches.

Clare Potter, MA (Oxon) – Solicitor; Partner in the EC & Competition Group of Simmons & Simmons. She has extensive experience of advising on all aspects of EC and competition law with particular experience of advising utilities and utility regulators and has had periods of secondment to the European Commission and the Department of Trade and Industry.

James Leabeater – Barrister, practises from 4 Pump Court, Temple, London, in construction, professional negligence and insurance law.

Clive Thorne – Partner at Denton Hall and Head of the Intellectual Property Litigation Group. He has wide experience of all aspects of Intellectual Property law. He has written widely in numerous publications and is co-author of *Intellectual Property – the New Law* and *The User's Guide to Copyright*. He is also admitted as a solicitor in Hong Kong where he practised in the 1980s and a barrister and solicitor in Victoria, Australia. He is a Fellow of the Chartered Institute of Arbitrators.

Melanie Willems, LLB (Hons), MSc Construction Law and Arbitration – partner at Lovells in the Projects Engineering and Construction group in London. She focuses on contentious construction and engineering matters and has been involved in a number of significant projects, domestically and internationally. Her experience includes UK dispute resolution, international and domestic arbitration, and many forms of Alternative Dispute Resolution, including mediation and expert determination.

Oliver Palmer – AA Dipl, FRIBA, FRSA, MRICS – Architect, principal in private practice 1956–75; RIBA Prize Winner 1974; DOE (now ODPM) Building Regulations Division (Technical Secretary of the Building Regulations Advisory Committee, recasting The Building Regulations) 1975–87; Head of the European Branch of the Construction Directorate 1987–1992; Consultant to the Commission of the European Communities 1992–94. Member or Chairman of BSI, CEN and EC committees. Lecturer. Publications include *HomeBuilder* (HMSO).

Sarah Lupton MA, DipArch, LLM, FCIArb is a **senior lecturer** at the Welsh School of Architecture and a partner in Lupton Stellakis. She is a member of the RIBA Disciplinary Committee, the RIBA President's Advisory Committee on Arbitration and the CIC Liability Committee. She is a member of the RIBA panel of adjudicators, and has acted as expert witness in relation to construction disputes and ARB disciplinary proceedings. She is author of *Architects Guide to Adjudication, Architects Guide to Arbitration*, and a series of guides to standard forms of building contract, including *Guide to JCT98*. She is also the co-author of two books in the *Through the Legislation Maze* series, co-editor of that series and editor of the *Architects's Job Book* and *Architect's Handbook of Practice Management*.

Kim Franklin, FCIArb – Chartered Arbitrator, Barrister, practises from Crown Office Chambers, 2 Crown Office Row, Temple, London, as counsel, arbitrator and adjudicator in construction disputes. She is joint editor of Construction Law Journal, a contributing author of The Legal Obligations of the Architect and a regular columnist for the Architect's Journal.

Rachel Toulson MA (Cantab) – Barrister and member of the Inher Temple. She practices from Crown Office Chambers at 2 Crown Office Row, London in common law and commercial litigation, including professional negligence and construction.

Amanda Telfer – Solicitor at Denton Wilde Sapte, a leading international law firm. She has worked on a wide variety of contentious and non-contentious UK nd international intellectual property work, specifically for media and technology clients. She specialises in IP and media litigation, including copyright, passing off, trade marks, design rights, database rights, confidentiality/contract, defamation, data protection and domain name disputes.

Ruth Downing – Barrister called to the Bar in 1978 – specialises in employment law with interest particularly in equal opportunities and personal injury litigation.

Contributors – Scotland
Consultant Editor

Angus Stewart, QC – Advocate, practising from Parliament House, High Street, Edinburgh; Chairman Faculty of Advocates Committee on Human Rights; formerly Keeper of the Advocates Library Chairman of the Scottish Council of Law Reporting; standing junior counsel to the Department of the Environment in Scotland, 1983–1988; recent publications include articles on local government, civil procedure and professional negligence; litigation specialist with interests in administrative law, construction, contract, land law and negligence.

Peter Franklin, MSc, FCIOB – Building Control and Fire Safety Consultant. Formerly Senior Building Adviser at the Scottish Office involved with building control legislation including acting as an assessor to BSAC. Served on many BSI committees, working parties, official inquiries, etc and Consultant on Scottish Fire Safety codes for hospitals, historic buildings and prisons.

Robert Howie, QC, LLB – Advocate.

Peter McCormack, MA (Oxon), LIB (Edin) – Advocate; previously consultant with Arthur Andersen & Co Management Consultancy Division, London; tutor in Mercantile and Commercial Law, University of Edinburgh, 1991–93; called to the Scottish Bar in 1992.

Steven L. Stuart – Advocate; member of the Scottish Planning, Local Government and Environmental Bar Group; formerly Lecturer in Private Law at the University of Dundee; co-author of *Scottish Civic Government Licensing Law*. He has appeared in a number of major public enquiries in Scotland.

Christopher Miers – BA, DipArch, MSc(Constr.Law), RIBA, FCIArb, MAE. Charted Architect, Chartered Arbitrator and CEDR Accredited Mediator. Member of Council and past Chairman of the Society of Construction Law (1995); member of Board of Editors of the Construction and Engineering Law Journal (1997-). Director of Probyn Miers architects. In addition to his continuing architectural practice Christopher is widely appointed as an adjudicator, arbitrator, expert witness and mediator.

Ferguson Bell LLB (Construction Law) FRICS FCIArb MAE – Belfast based Chartered Surveyor practising mainly as an Arbitrator, Adjudicator, Mediator and Expert Witness in the field of construction Disptues.

Robert White – Barrister at 4-5 Gray's Inn Square, the celebrated public law set of Chambers. He was called to the Bar in 1993, and specializes in Planning, Local Government and Compulsory Purchase Law.

Gordon Gibb, B Arch Dip Arch (Glas), LLM, RIBA, ARIAS – Director, Gibb Architects Ltd., based in Glasgow. Director of Professional Practice at Mackintosh School of Architecture. Project experience includes sports centres, health care, competition-winning commercial developments and Listed Building renovation. He is a part-time lecturer at the Mackintosh School of Architecture, has contributed to the RIBA Part III examination and has acted as a Council member of the RIAS. Using his legal training he has also undertaken planning appeals and Public Inquiries and as an Expert Witness has considerable court experience in contract and negligence claims.

Contributors – Northern Ireland

J. Ronald McDaniel Dip Arch (Sheff), FRIBA – Formerly Hon. Vice-President, Member of Council and Convenor of the Constitution Committee of the Royal Society of Ulster Architects. Trustee of the Architects Benevolent Society in London. Formerly Chief Architect of the DHSS, Northern Ireland.

Jonathan L. Dunlop – Barrister in practice at the Northern Ireland Bar with experience in the fields of contract law, company law, insolvency and planning law. He is currently the Northern Ireland Law Reporter for the Irish Times.

William Orbinson – Northern Irish Barrister who specializes in Planning and Environmental Law, acting primarily for developers and public bodies in planning appeals and inquiries. One of only three N.I. lawyers to hold the Law Society/Royal Town Planning Institute Joint Planning Examination and to qualify as a Legal Associate of the RTPI, Mr Orbinson is also an Affiliate of the Irish Planning Institute and of the Royal Society of Ulster Architects, and the sole N.I. Associate of the Planning and Environment Bar Association: The Specialist Bar Association for Planning, the Environment and Local Government. A founding member and past Chair of EPLANI: The Environmental & Planning Law Association for Northern Ireland, he has also served on the local branch Executive of the RPTI and on the Architecture & Planning and Housing Committees of the Royal Society of Ulster Architects. Mr. Orbinson is the author of most of the leading publications on the Northern Irish planning system, and a contributor on planning and architecturally-related issues to Planning magazine and Perspective, the journal of the Royal Society of Ulster Architects.

Brian Sherrard – Barrister; formerly lecturer in property law at the Queen's University of Belfast, he is now the principal legal assistant to the Lord Chief Justice of Northern Ireland.

Brain H. Speers LLB MCIArb – Solicitor with the Belfast firm of Carnson Morrow Graham, 20 May Street, Belfast whose practice includes construction disputes, arbitration and adjudication. He has a particular interest in mediation and provides a course of approval training to lawyers and surveyors.

Part One
General principles of law

1

Introduction to English law

ANTHONY SPEAIGHT QC

1 The importance of law
Ignorantia juris non excusat

1.01 The well-worn maxim that ignorance of the law is no excuse applies with equal force to everyone, including architects. Everyone who offers a service to others and claims expertise to do what he offers has a responsibility to society in general and to his clients in particular to know the law.

Architects and the law

1.02 Architects like other professional people, have a duty to acquire a working knowledge of the law as it affects their professional work. In the case of an architect the relevant fields of law are notably those of contract, especially the standard forms of building contract, and the various statutory regulations, such as the Building Regulations, planning law, health and safety law, European procurement law, and the like. An architect will also want to know about the areas of law which affect him or her personally. When can he be sued? How can he sue for his fees? When is copyright in his drawings protected? How should he insure? What is the legal relationship between him and his employer, or between him and his employees? An architect is not expected to know all the law in these areas himself. But he is expected to ensure that his client does not suffer from the absence of his own legal knowledge. He is expected to know enough law to be aware of the circumstances in which specialist legal advice is needed. He should then advise his client to obtain legal advice. Alternatively, he should himself instruct a barrister directly.

The legal system – rules of society

1.03 People living in all types of community have one thing in common: mutually agreed rules of conduct appropriate to their way of life, with explicit consequences for failure to observe the rules. This is what law is about. The more varied the activities and the more complex the social structure, the greater is the need for everyone to be aware of the part he or she must play in formulating and observing the rules. In highly developed communities these rules have grown into a complex body of law. In the United Kingdom the law is continually developing and being modified as personal rights and social responsibilities are re-interpreted.

The English 'common law' system

1.04 There are two principal legal systems in the western world. One is the so-called civil law system, which prevails in most parts of continental Europe. It has its origins in Roman law and is today founded on written codes. The other is usually known as the common law system. This originated in England during the Middle Ages. Today it is the basis of law in Canada, Australia, New Zealand,

Hong Kong, Singapore, and almost all former British territories. It is even the basis of law in the United States of America. The international character of English law is not often appreciated by non-lawyers, but is sufficiently alive for cases from other common law jurisdictions to guide English courts on those occasions, which are admittedly rare, when English case law is silent on a point. The courts of other common law more frequently follow English decisions. A Commonwealth Law Conference held every three years, at which the leading lawyers from remarkably diverse national backgrounds discuss legal issues together, serves to reinforce the bonds of the common law world.

2 Sources of law

2.01 English law may be conveniently divided into two main parts – unwritten and written – and there are several branches of these.

Common law

2.02 Common law – the unwritten law – includes the early customary laws assembled and formulated by judges, with modifications of the old law of equity (paragraph 3.09). Common law therefore means all other than enacted law (paragraph 2.06), and rules derived solely from custom and precedent are rules of common law. It is the unwritten law of the land because there is no official codification of it.

Judicial precedent

2.03 The basis of all legal argument and decision in the English courts is founded upon the application of rules announced in earlier decisions and is called *stare decisis* (let the decision stand). From this has evolved the doctrine of judicial precedent, now a fundamental characteristic of common law.

2.04 Two factors contributed to the important position that the doctrine of judicial precedent holds today: the Judicature Acts (paragraph 3.12) and the creation of the Council of Law Reporting, which is responsible for issuing authoritative reports which are scrutinized and revised by judges and which contain a summary of arguments by counsel and of the judgments given. It is essential for the operation of a system of law based on previous cases that well-authenticated records of arguments and decisions be available to all courts and everyone required to advise on the law.

Authority of a judgment

2.05 Legally, the most important part of a judgment is that where the judge explains the principles on which he has based his decision. A judgment is an authoritative lecture on a branch of the law; it includes a *ratio decidendi* (the statement of grounds for the decision)

and one or more *obiter dicta* (things said by the way, often not directly relevant to the matters at issue). It is the *ratio decidendi* which creates precedents for the future. Such precedents are binding on every court with jurisdiction inferior to the court which gave the decision; even courts of equal or superior jurisdiction seldom fail to follow an earlier decision. Until recently even the House of Lords which has been the highest English Court, regarded themselves as bound by their own decisions. The House of Lords now regards itself as free to depart from its previous decisions, but has done so on only a handful of occasions. One of the few occasions was the overruling of *Anns v Merton* [1978] AC728 by *Murphy v Brentwood* [1991] AC398 – a saga well known to architects, and described in Chapter 3 of this book.

Legislation

2.06 Legislation – the written or enacted law – comprises the statutes, Acts and edicts of the sovereign and his advisers. Although historically enacted law is more recent than common law because Parliament has been in existence only since the thirteenth century, legislation by Acts of Parliament takes precedence over all other sources of law and is absolutely binding on all courts while it remains on the statute books. If an Act of Parliament conflicts with a common law rule, it is presumed that Parliament was aware of the fact and that there was a deliberate intention that it should do so.

2.07 All legislation must derive its authority directly or indirectly from Parliament; the only exception being that in cases of national emergency the Crown can still legislate by Royal Proclamation. In its statutes, Parliament usually lays down general principles, and in most legislation Parliament delegates authority for carrying out the provisions of statutes to non-parliamentary bodies. Subordinate legislation is required which may take the form of Orders in Council (made by the government of the day – in theory by the sovereign in Council), regulations, statutory instruments or orders made by government departments, and the by-laws of statutory undertakings and local authorities.

2.08 The courts are required to interpret Acts in accord with the wording employed. They may not question or even discuss the validity of the enactment. Rules have been established to help them interpret ambiguities: there is a presumption that Parliament in legislative matters does not make mistakes, but in general this principle does not apply to statutory instruments unless the governing Act says anything to the contrary. The courts may decide whether rules or orders are made within the powers delegated to the authorised body ordered to make them, or whether they are *ultra vires* (outside the body's power). By-laws must not only be *intra vires* but also reasonable.

European Union law

2.09 Since 1 January 1973 there has been an additional source of law: that is the law of the European Community. By accession treaty Her Majesty's Government undertook that the United Kingdom would accept the obligations of membership of the three original European Communities, that is, the Coal and Steel Community, the Economic Community and the Atomic Energy Community. That commitment was honoured by the enactment of the European Communities Act 1972. Section 2(1) of the 1972 Act provided that all directly applicable provisions of the treaties establishing the European Communities should become part of English law; so, too, would all existing and future Community secondary legislation. Since the terms of the treaties are in the main in very general terms, most detailed Community policy is embodied in secondary legislation. Most major decisions are taken in the form of 'directives', which require member states to achieve stated results but leave it to the member state to choose the form and method of implementation. Other Community decisions, known as 'regulations', have direct effect.

In consequence, there is today an ever-growing corpus of European Union decisions incorporated into English law. This topic is discussed more fully in Chapter 27.

The European Convention on Human Rights

2.10 In 1950, a number of western European countries adopted a Convention for the Protection of Human Rights and Fundamental Freedoms (now invariably referred as the European Convention on Human Rights). It was a symbolic response both to the horrors of Nazism in the recent past and to the curtailment of freedom in the communist states of eastern Europe. A novel feature of this Convention was the creation of a European Court of Human Rights Court in which individual citizens could present grievances against their governments. For many years the Convention and the Court had no standing within the United Kingdom beyond the fact that the United Kingdom government had by a treaty undertaken to accept them. Enthusiasts for the Convention saw it as potentially something which might play a role similar to that of the United States constitution. But this scenario faced a number of problems. Firstly, the process of European integration has not, or at any rate has not yet, reached the point where United Kingdom domestic law is subject to a European federal law. Secondly, any form of entrenchment of fundamental rights in the United Kingdom is hard to reconcile with the democratic doctrine of the supremacy of Parliament, of which a facet is the principle that no parliament can bind its successor. Eventually, a mechanism was adopted in the Human Rights Act 1998, whereby the Convention is accorded some standing in English law, without derogating from the supremacy of Parliament. This has been achieved by enacting that legislation should, so far as possible, be interpreted in accordance with Convention rights. If this is impossible, a court may make a declaration of incompatibility. Despite the interest which has been generated by the Human Rights Act, and the fact that it has been cited in a significant number of cases in recent years, it has had little practical impact on the actual decisions of English courts: it has almost always been held, sometimes after prolonged argument, that existing English law is, in fact, compliant with Convention rights.

3   Legal history
Origins of English law

3.01 One cannot understand English law without an awareness of its history. The seeds of custom and rules planted in Anglo-Saxon and earlier times have developed and grown gradually into a modern system of law. The Normans interfered little with common practices they found, and almost imperceptibly integrated them with their own mode of life. William I did not regard himself as a conqueror, but claimed to have come by invitation as the lawful successor of Edward the Confessor – whose laws he promised to re-establish and enforce.

Feudal system and land law

3.02 The Domesday Book (1086), assembled mainly by itinerant judges for taxation purposes, provided William I with a comprehensive social and economic survey of his newly acquired lands. The feudal system in England was more universally applied than it was on the Continent – a result perhaps of the thoroughness of the Domesday survey. Consequently, in England feudal law was not solely a law for the knights and bishops of the realm, nor of some parts of the country alone: it affected every person and every holding of land. It became part of the common law of England.

3.03 To the knowledge acquired from Domesday, the Normans applied their administrative skills; they established within the framework of the feudal system new rules for ownership of land, new obligations of loyalty to the administration under the Crown, and reorganized arrangements for control of the people and for hearing and judgment of their disputes. These were the true origins of our modern legal system.

3.04 Ultimate ownership of land in England is still, in theory, in the Crown. The lord as 'landowner' merely held an 'estate' or 'interest' in the land, directly or indirectly, as tenant from the king. A person holding an estate of the Crown could, in turn, grant it to another

person, but the ownership still remained in the Crown. The tenant's 'interest' may have been of long or short duration and as varied as the kinds of services that might be given in return for the 'estate'. In other words, many different estates and interests in land existed. Tenure and estate are distinct. 'Tenure' refers to the relation of the landlord to his overlord, at its highest level to the king. 'Estate' refers to the duration of his interest in the land, and has nothing whatever to do with the common use of the word.

Possession not ownership

3.05 English law as a result has never used the concept of ownership of land but instead has concentrated on the fact of 'possession', mainly because ownership can refer to so many things and is ill-fitted to anything so permanent and immovable as a piece of land. A man's title to land in England is based on his being able to prove that he has a better right to possession of it than anyone else who claims it.

Real and personal property

3.06 Law makes a distinction between 'real' and 'personal' property. The former are interests in land other than leasehold interests; the latter includes leasehold interests and applies to movable property (personal property and chattels). A leasehold interest in land is classed as 'personal' rather than 'real' property because in early times it was not possible to recover a leasehold interest by 'real' actions for the return of the thing (*res*). In common law a dispossessed owner of freehold land could bring an action for recovery of possession, and an order would be made for the return to him of his land. For the recovery of personal (tangible or movable) articles his remedy was limited to a personal action in which the defendant had the option of either returning the property or paying its value.

Beginnings of common law

3.07 Foundations of both the common law and the courts of justice were laid by Henry II (1154–1189). In his reign the 'king's justice' began to be administered not only in the King's Court – the *Curia Regis* – where the sovereign usually sat in person and which accompanied him on his travels about the country, but also by justices given commissions of assize directing them to administer the royal justice systematically in local courts throughout the whole kingdom. In these courts it was their duty to hear civil actions which previously had been referred to the central administration at Westminster. It was the judges of assize who created the common law. On completion of their circuits and their return to Westminster they discussed their experiences and judgments given in the light of local customs and systems of law. Thus a single system common to all was evolved; judge-made in the sense that it was brought together and stated authoritatively by judges, but it grew from the people in that it was drawn directly from their ancient customs and practices.

3.08 Under the able guidance of Edward I (1272–1307) many reforms were made, notably in procedures and mainly in the interest of the subject as against the royal officials and the law began to take its characteristic shape. Three great common law courts became established at Westminster:

1   The King's Bench, broadly for cases in which the Crown had interest.
2   Common pleas, for cases between subject and subject.
3   Exchequer, for those having a fiscal or financial aspect.

However, as administered in these courts, the common law was limited in its ability to meet every case. This led to the establishment of the principles of equity.

Equity

3.09 In the Middle Ages the common law courts failed to give redress in certain types of cases where redress was needed, either because the remedy the common law provided (i.e. damages) was unsuitable or because the law was defective in that no remedy existed. For instance, the common law did not recognize trusts and at that time there was no way of compelling a trustee to carry out his obligations. Therefore disappointed and disgruntled litigants exercised their rights of appeal to the king – the 'fountain of all justice'. In due course, the king, through his Chancellor (keeper of his conscience, because he was also a bishop and his confessor), set up a social Court of Chancery to deal with them.

3.10 During the early history of the Court of Chancery, equity had no binding rules. A Chancellor approached his task in a different manner from the common law judges; he gave judgment when he was satisfied in his own mind that a wrong had been done, and he would order that the wrong be made good. Thus the defendant could clear his own conscience at the same time. The remedy for refusal was invariably to be imprisoned until he came to see the error of his ways and agree with the court's ruling. It was not long before a set of general rules emerged in the Chancery Courts which hardened into law and became a regular part of the law of the land. There is, however, another and even more fundamental aspect of equity. Though it developed in the Court of Chancery as a body of law with defined rules, its ideal from earliest times was the simple belief in moral justice, fairness, and equality of treatment for all, as opposed to the strict letter of the law. Equity in that sense has remained to this day a basic principle of English justice.

3.11 Up to the end of the fifteenth century the Chancellor had generally been a bishop, but after the Reformation the position came to be held by professional lawyers (of whom the first was Sir Thomas More) under whom the rules of equity became almost as rigid as those of common law; and the existence of separate courts administering the two different sets of rules led to serious delays and conflicts. By the end of the eighteenth century the courts and their procedures had reached an almost unbelievable state of confusion, mainly due to lack of coordination of the highly technical processes and overlapping jurisdiction. Charles Dickens describes without much exaggeration something of the troubles of a litigant in Chancery in the case of '*Jarndyce v Jarndyce*' (*Bleak House*).

Victorian reforms

3.12 Nineteenth-century England was dominated by a spirit of reform, which extended from slavery to local government. The law and the courts did not escape reform, and the climax came with the passing of the Judicature Acts of 1873 (and much additional and amending legislation in the years that followed) whereby the whole court system was thoroughly reorganized and simplified, by the establishment of a single Supreme Court. The Act also brought to an end the separation of common law and equity; they were not amalgamated and their rules remained the same, but henceforth the

rules of both systems were to be applied by all courts. If they were in conflict, equity was to prevail.

3.13 The main object of the Judicature Act 1873 was an attempt to solve the problems of delay and procedural confusion in the existing court system by setting up a Supreme Court. This consisted of two main parts:

1   The High Court of Justice, with three Divisions, all courts of Common Law and Equity. As a matter of convenience cases concerned primarily with common law questions being heard in the Queen's Bench Division; those dealing with equitable problems in the Chancery Division; and the Probate, Divorce, and Admiralty Division with the three classes indicated by its title.
2   The Court of Appeal – hearing appeals from decisions of the High Court and most appeals from County Courts.

Modern reforms

3.14 By the Courts Act 1971 there was a modest re-organisation of the divisions of the High Court. A Family Division was created to handle child cases as well as divorce and matrimonial property disputes, and the Crown Court was created in place of a confusing array of different criminal courts. During the last decades of the twentieth-century the work of the County Courts was progressively extended, with the financial limit if their jurisdiction being progressively lifted. The present court arrangements in England are more fully discussed in Chapter 13 on Litigation.

4   The legal systems of the United Kingdom

4.01 Within the United Kingdom there are two traditions of law and three principal legal jurisdictions. English law prevails in the jurisdiction which is constituted by England and Wales. The English common law system is also the basis of the law in Northern Ireland, but Northern Ireland has its own statutory provisions and also its own courts. Scotland has not only its own courts, but also its own law and legal traditions. It had its own system at the time of the Union in 1707, and always retained them.

4.02 The one unifying feature of the legal system of the United Kingdom has been the House of Lords which is the supreme court of appeal for all three jurisdictions. It usually has 12 judges, of whom two are by tradition always Scots, and one has recently been from Northern Ireland. They are officially known as lords of appeal in ordinary, and usually referred to as law lords. In 2003, the Government published proposals for a new Supreme Court for the United Kingdom. Whereas the present law lords are all peers with full membership of the upper chamber of Parliament, the proposal is that the judges of the new Supreme Court should have no connection with the legislature. At the time of going to press, the government's bill to establish this new court had been referred to a select committee.

4.03 This edition of this book covers the law in the whole of the United Kingdom. There are certain separate chapters dealing with Scotland and Northern Ireland. In other instances, there are sections at the end of chapters written by English law authors, explaining whether, and to what extent, there are differences in Scotland and Northern Ireland.

5   The scheme of this book

5.01 There are five main sections of the book:

1   In the first section the reader is offered the general principles of the law. This introductory chapter is immediately followed by chapters setting out the principles of the two areas of English law of the greatest importance to architects, namely contract and tort. A third area of basic English law of relevance to architects,

namely land law, is also covered in an early chapter. There are separate chapters providing an introduction to Scots law and to Northern Ireland's legal system.

2 The next main section of the book deals with what is almost certainly the legal subject of greatest day-to-day importance to architects, namely building contracts. This section begins with a general introduction. There is a full commentary on the most important of all standard forms, namely the JCT standard form, 1998 edition, in which the text of every single clause is reproduced. In the next chapter there is a full discussion of nominated sub-contracting under the current JCT documents, and a briefer discussion of some of the other principal standard forms used on building contracts.

3 The third section deals with dispute resolution. The normal method of resolving disputes in most spheres of activity is litigation. But in the construction world there are a number of alternatives which are frequently used. Most construction contracts contain an arbitration clause, by which the parties agree to be bound by the decision of a private dispute resolution mechanism: for many years arbitration was the most common mode of determining construction disputes. Today, however, the most common method is adjudication, which means a quick decision which is binding for only a temporary period. By legislation in 1996 a right to adjudication is now compulsory in almost all construction contracts. Such is the attraction of a quick decision that not only is adjudication today being used with great frequency, but hardly ever are adjudicator's decisions being challenged in subsequent litigation of arbitration. Of growing popularity, too, is mediation, which refers to consensual meetings by parties with a neutral facilitator: the success rate in achieving a settlement at mediations is very high. Separate chapters deal with each of these methods of dispute resolution.

4 The fourth section is concerned with the statutory and regulatory framework. Statutory authorities are described. There follow chapters on statutory regulations in the fields of planning, construction regulations, and health and safety regulations. The chapter on European Union law as it affects architects is also included in this section.

5 The final section of the book concerns the architect in practice. It begins with the law affecting the legal organisation of an architect's office. It covers the contracts which architects make with their own clients for the provision of their professional services, and contracts which architects enter with non-clients to provide them with a cause of action against the architect if his professional work was faulty. The next chapter deals with the liability of architects when faulty professional services are alleged. That is followed by the chapter on professional indemnity insurance to cover architects against such risks. An architect's copyright in his own drawings is dealt with in the chapter on the distinct area of the law of copyright. The ever-changing field of employment law, which affects every architect who employs staff, is the subject of a separate chapter. The chapter on international work does not, by its very nature, deal with English or Scots law, and so in one sense ought not to be part of this book at all: but the information on the practices in other jurisdictions is invaluable to architects who undertake work abroad, and fits more logically here than anywhere else in this book. Finally, this section deals with architects' registration and professional conduct.

2

The English law of contract

ALEXANDER HICKEY

1 Introduction

1.01 The purpose of this chapter is to give an overview of the law of contract: to show both how it relates to other areas of the law, and to describe the general principles on which the English law of contract operates. Although most of the examples are from areas with which architects will be familiar, the principles they illustrate are for the most part general. Other sections of this book deal in detail with specific areas of the law of contract and their own special rules. The general rules described in this chapter may on occasion seem trite and hardly worth stating. Yet it is often with the most fundamental – and apparently simple – principles of law that the most difficult problems arise. Just as it is important to get the foundations of a building right, so also it is necessary to understand the basic rules of contract law, without which detailed knowledge of any particular standard form of contract is of little use. This chapter condenses into a few pages of material which if fully discussed would fill many long books. The treatment is necessarily selective and condensed.

2 Scope of the law of contract

2.01 The criminal law sets out limitations on people's behaviour, and punishes them when they do not conform to those rules. A criminal legal action is between the State (the Crown) and an individual. The civil law is quite different. It determines the rights and liabilities which exist between parties in particular circumstances. The parties to a civil action are known as 'claimant' (until recently the claimant was called 'plaintiff') and 'defendant' and the former claims a remedy for the acts or omissions of the latter. The difference, then, is that unlike criminal law (which is concerned with punishment) the civil law is about providing remedies – the law tries to put things 'back to rights' as best it can. The remedies available are various: the court may award 'damages' as a means of compensating the loss suffered by the claimant, or it may declare what the rights of the parties are, or, in certain circumstances, it will order a party to do or to refrain from doing something.

2.02 Two of the biggest areas of the civil law are contract and tort. In certain factual contexts they can overlap, and in recent years their overlap has caused the courts great problems, but they are conceptually quite distinct, and it is important to understand the distinction.

2.03 A claimant will sue a defendant in contract or tort when he objects to something the defendant has done or failed to do. Sometimes the claimant will not have spared a thought for the defendant – indeed may very well not know the defendant – before the objectionable act or omission occurs. For example: the defendant carelessly runs the claimant over; the defendant's bonfire smoke ruins the claimant's washing; the defendant tramples across the claimant's field; the defendant writes a scurrilous article about the claimant in the local newspaper. All these wrongs are torts, indeed the label 'tort' is an archaic word for 'wrong'. Each of the torts listed above have particular labels, respectively negligence, nuisance, trespass and defamation. It is because the acts of the defendant have brought him into contact or proximity with the claimant the law of torts may impose a liability on the defendant. The law of torts is considered in Chapter 3.

2.04 On other occasions the claimant and defendant are parties to a contract, so that before the objectionable event occurs the parties have agreed what their legal obligations to one another shall be in certain defined circumstances. So, for instance, if the claimant engages the defendant plumber to install a new sink, and it leaks, or retains the defendant architect to design a house which falls down, or employs the defendant builder to build a house and it is not ready on time, the extent of the defendant's liability in a contract claim will depend on the terms and conditions of the contract between them. Of course, there may, in some circumstances, be an identical or similar liability in tort as well for the two are not mutually exclusive. But the conceptual distinction is quite clear.

3 What is a contract?

3.01 A contract is an agreement made between two or more persons which is binding in law, and is capable of being enforced by those persons in court or other tribunal (such as an arbitral tribunal). The people who made the contract are described as being party or 'privy' to it and they are said to enjoy 'privity of contract'. This expression means that the parties are drawn into a close legal relationship with each other which is governed by the agreement that they have made. That legal relationship creates rights and obligations between the parties and binds only between those who are privy to the contract, and not other people who are not parties (often described in law books as 'strangers' or by the misnomer 'third parties') even though those people may be affected by the contract directly or indirectly. The doctrine of privity of contract is examined in more detail later in this chapter. Usually the agreement will contain a promise or set of promises that each party has made to the other: this is known as a bilateral contract because each party promises to do something. For example, X promises to build a house for Y and Y promises to pay X for doing so. Sometimes only one party will make a promise to do something if the other party actually does something stipulated by the former. For example, X promises to pay £100 if Y completes and returns a marketing questionnaire to X. Such a contract is known as an unilateral contract because the promise is one-sided. Although X has promised to pay in the stipulated circumstances, Y is under no obligation to complete and return the marketing questionnaire but if he does the court or arbitral tribunal will recognize a binding agreement that X will pay him £100. In building projects during negotiations for the award of a formal contract one sometimes finds so-called letters of intent expressed in terms such as these: 'Please proceed with the works and if no formal contract is concluded we will pay you your costs and expenses that you have incurred.' It is often not appreciated that a letter in such terms can create a unilateral contract which the court will enforce, albeit not the formal contract which the parties had hoped to finalize. And although one often talks of a 'written' or 'formal' contract it is not really the piece of paper which itself is the contract – the piece of paper merely records what the terms of the contract are. For most types of contract there is no requirement for a written document at all and an oral contract is just as binding in law, although in practice when there is a dispute proving later what was orally agreed at the outset is more difficult. That difficulty is avoided if there is documentary evidence of what was agreed. Indeed, the usual (though not always the inflexible) rule is that the written document containing the agreed terms will be decisive evidence of the contract whatever the parties have said previously: this is sometimes called the 'four corners' rule.

Contracts under seal

3.02 There are some contracts which have to be made or evidenced in writing (such as contracts to transfer interests in land) and some contracts have to be made under seal. Either there is literally a wax seal at the end of the document where the parties sign, or there is some mark representing a seal. But any contract may be made under seal, and the seal provides the consideration for the contract (see below). The most important consequence, and often the reason why parties choose this method of contracting is that the limitation period for making a claim pursuant to a contract under seal is twelve years instead of the usual six (see paragraphs 14.01–14.02).

Basic requirements for establishing whether there is a contract

3.03 To test whether there is a contract the court or arbitral tribunal will look for three essential things: first, the intention of the parties to create legal relations, second, whether there was in fact agreement between the parties and third, whether there was consideration for the agreement. Each of these aspects requires further scrutiny.

4 Intention to create legal relations

4.01 'If you save me my seat I'll buy you a drink.' 'OK.' Such a casual exchange has all the appearances of a contract, but if the thirsty seat saver tried to claim his dues through a court he would probably be disappointed, for the law will not enforce a promise if the parties did not intend their promises to be legally binding. Bargains struck on terms that 'if you sell that car, I'll eat my hat' are not seriously considered to be legally binding. Similarly one hears of people making a 'gentlemen's agreement' where honour dictates the actions between the parties along the lines of 'I'll see you right, if there is anything you need, it will be done'. However, a moral obligation is not enough.

5 Consideration

5.01 It is convenient to deal with consideration next. A simple one-way promise – 'I'll paint your ceiling' – without more is not a contract, because there is neither any element of bargain nor anything done in return. Again a contingent promise such as 'I will pay you £100 if it rains on Tuesday' is not a contract. In such a case the person receiving the windfall of £100 did nothing to deserve or earn the money. It is important to distinguish this situation from a unilateral contract where there is a one-way promise but something is done in return. In the examples given above X completed and returned the marketing questionnaire; the builder proceeded to do the works while negotiations were ongoing. With the exception of contracts under seal, English contract law demands that there must

be consideration for the promise to be enforceable. Consideration is thus the other half of the bargain or, as lawyers used to say, the 'quid pro quo' meaning 'something for something else'. In a unilateral contract the 'something else' is the performance by the party who wants to receive the promised benefit. In a bilateral contract often the promise of one party is exchanged for the promise of the other party. The court has defined consideration like this:

> 'An act or forbearance of one party, or the promise thereof, is the price for which the promise of the other is bought, and the promise thus given for value is enforceable' (*Dunlop v Selfridge* [1951] AC 847 855).

5.02 There are a number of important and well-established rules about consideration. The rules, often expressed in rather antiquated language, are set out in the headings below but are best understood by giving some examples. Some, but not all, of these rules should now be considered with caution because the legal landscape has radically changed with the enactment of the Contracts (Rights of Third Parties) Act 1999. That Act made sweeping changes to the doctrine of privity of contract, and consequently it will affect the closely related doctrine of consideration. The changes brought about by that Act will no doubt take many years to work themselves out. However, while it is all but certain that the doctrine of consideration will remain as a fundamental ingredient to the formation of a contract between parties, the doctrine is unlikely to survive in the long term as a means of preventing 'strangers' to the contract from seeking to enforce that contract where it benefits them.

1 Adequacy of consideration irrelevant

5.03 Although consideration must be given for value this simply means that there must be some intrinsic value no matter how small: a peppercorn rent for a property, for instance, is good consideration. The value of the consideration can be quite disproportionate to the other half of the bargain which it supports. In *Midland Bank Trust Company v Green* [1980] Ch 590, a farm worth £40 000 was sold by a husband to his wife for just £500. £500 was good consideration. The court will not interfere with the level of consideration because to do so would be to adjudicate on the question of whether it was a good or bad deal for one of the parties. The commercial aspects of a contract, the bargain, is best left for the parties to decide.

2 Consideration must move from the promisee

5.04 If A (the promisor) promises B (the promisee) that he will build a wall on B's land and C will pay £1000 to A for doing so, there is no contract between A and B for the consideration of £1000 in return for the wall has not been given by B. B has done nothing to earn or deserve A's promise to build the wall so the court will not assist B in enforcing the promise. Another way of looking at this situation is to say that it is only when a party provides consideration that he is drawn into 'privity of contract'. It has been debated for centuries whether privity of contract and consideration are really the same thing or two sides of the same coin. At the very least it can be said that consideration is the touchstone for privity of contract for without consideration there can be no contract at all. Even if A and B had signed a piece of paper recording the 'agreement' between themselves, although they could say they are parties or privy to the arrangement, they do not enjoy privity of a (legally enforceable) contract. In the situation above, it might be that a contract was actually reached between A and C because each of them provided consideration which drew A and C into privity of contract. But the other essential requirements for a contract would need to be met before it could be said that there was a contract between them.

5.05 The effect of this rule is that if A does not build the wall, or does so but bodges the job, B has no right of recourse against A in contract. (He might, in certain circumstances, be able to sue A in tort if A bodged the building of the wall so that it collapsed and injured someone or if it damaged B's other property. This is no comfort to a peeved B who has no wall at all, or a badly built wall.) With the advent of the Contracts (Rights of Third Parties) Act 1999, however, so long as a contract exists between A and C, B would probably be able to sue A on the basis that a contract between A and C was for B's benefit even though B provided no consideration. B's position is, of course, not changed by the Act if no contract exists between A and C.

3 Consideration need not move to the promisor

5.06 On the other hand if A promises to build the wall if B will pay £1000 to C (a local charity) and if B either pays C or promises A that he will pay C, B will have given consideration for A's promise. A contract will exist between A and B on these facts and B will be able to enforce A's promise. The difference between this situation and the former is that B has earned the right to enforce the agreement even though A does not directly benefit from B's consideration. C, however, is not a party to that contract and under the previous law C would have no right of recourse against B (or A) if B does not pay £1000 because C did not provide consideration. Now, C would be likely to use the 1999 Act to seek to enforce the contract by arguing that contractual promise to pay £1000 was for its benefit.

4 Consideration must not be past

5.07 The general rule (there are some ways around it) is that an act which has already been performed cannot provide consideration to support a contract subsequently entered into. Suppose A gives B £1000 at Christmas, and at Easter B agrees to build a wall for B 'in consideration of the £1000'. A cannot sue B if he does not build the wall, for there is no element of bargain, and no consideration supports the promise to build the wall. Also a past agreement to do something cannot usually be used as consideration for a new promise. However, in an unusual case, *Williams & Roffey Bros. & Nicholls (Contractors) Ltd* [1990] 1 All ER 512, a main contractor had contracted to complete the building of some housing units by a certain time but it became clear that he was unlikely to do so because the sub-contractors were in financial difficulties and the main contractor was potentially exposed to liability for liquidated damages in his contract with the employer. The main contractor promised to pay the sub-contractors more money to ensure completion on time. The Court of Appeal held that that promise was enforceable because the main contractor's promise to pay more to ensure completion on time was supported by consideration from the sub-contractors. This was because the main contractor received the practical benefit of ensuring that he would not be penalized and that the work would continue (even though the sub-contractors were already contractually bound to do the work by that time).

5.08 As between the parties and a contract consideration rarely causes problems, because it is usually abundantly clear what the consideration is: very often in the contracts architects deal with, the consideration for providing works or services will be the fee to be paid for them. But on the rare occasions when consideration is lacking the consequences can be critical for the aggrieved party, who has no contract on which he can sue.

6 'Agreement'

6.01 The existence of agreement between the parties to a contract is in practice the most troublesome of the three essential ingredients.

6.02 The inverted commas around 'agreement' are intentional. The law of contract does not peer into the minds of contracting parties to see what they really intended to contract to do; it contents itself with taking an objective view and, on the basis of what the parties have said and done, and the surrounding context in which they did so, the courts decide what the parties should be taken to have intended. The court asks whether, in the eyes of the law, they should be considered to have been in agreement.

6.03 To perform this somewhat artificial task the courts use a set formula or analytical framework which can be thought of as the recipe which must be followed by parties to a contract. The recipe is simple: offer and acceptance.

George Cruikshank.

Offer

6.04 An offer is a promise, made by the offeror, to be bound by a contract if the offeree accepts the terms of the offer. The offer matures into a contract when it is accepted by the other party.

6.05 The offer can be made to just one person (the usual case) or it can be made to a group of people, or even to the world at large. The case of *Carlill v Carbolic Smoke Ball Company* [1892] 2 QB 484, [1893] 1 QB 256 is an example of an offer to all the world. The defendant company manufactured a device called a carbolic smoke ball, which was intended to prevent its users from catching flu. They advertised it with the promise that they would pay £100 to anybody who used the smoke ball three times a day as directed and still caught flu. The unfortunate claimant caught flu despite using the smoke ball, and not unnaturally felt she was entitled to the £100 offered. The Court of Appeal held that the company's advertisement constituted an offer to contract, and by purchasing the smoke ball the claimant had accepted the offer, so that a contract was created. Accordingly the claimant successfully extracted her £100 from the company.

6.06 Not all pre-contractual negotiations are offers to contract. In deals of any complexity there will often be a lot of exploratory negotiation before the shape of the final contract begins to emerge, and it is not until a late stage that there will be a formal offer to contract by one party to the other.

6.07 Easy to confuse with an offer to contract is an invitation to treat. An invitation to treat is an offer to consider accepting an offer to contract from the other party. Most advertisements 'offering' goods for sale, and also the goods lying on a supermarket shelf with their price labels, are merely invitations to treat. When the prospective purchaser proffers the appropriate sum to the cashier at the desk it is the customer who is making the offer, which can be accepted or rejected by the cashier. It will by now be obvious that the dividing line between an invitation to treat and an offer to contract can be very fine but the distinction is important.

Acceptance

6.08 The acceptance of the offer can be by word – written or oral – or by conduct and the acceptance must be communicated or made known to the offeror. Silence is not sufficient to accept an offer because neither assent nor dissent has been communicated by the offeree. The court is thus not able objectively to see whether there was an 'agreement': it will not peer into the offeree's mind.

6.09 An acceptance must be unequivocal and it must be a complete acceptance of every term of the offer. 'I accept your terms but only if I can have 42 days to pay instead of 28' will not be an acceptance, for it purports to vary the terms of the offer. It is a counter-offer, which itself will have to be accepted by the seller. And such a counter-offer will destroy the original offer which it rejects, and which can therefore no longer be accepted. In the old case of *Hyde v Wrench* [1840] 3 Beav 334, the defendant Wrench offered to sell some land to the plaintiff for £1000. On 8 June Hyde said he would pay £950. On 27 June Wrench refused to sell for £950 and on 29 June Hyde said he would pay £1000 after all. Wrench refused to sell. It was held that there was no contract. Hyde's counter-offer on 8 June had destroyed the initial offer of £1000 and by 29 June it was too late for Hyde to change his mind.

6.10 Sometimes an offer will specify a particular method of acceptance. For instance, A will ask B to signal his acceptance by signing a copy letter and returning it within 21 days. Ordinarily B can only accept by complying with that method of acceptance. However, sometimes the court will decide that an equally effective method of acceptance will suffice if it is clear that both parties understood that there was acceptance and assumed there was a contract.

Revocation of offer and the postal rules

6.11 An offer can be withdrawn or revoked up until such time as it is accepted. An acceptance is of course final – otherwise people would constantly be pulling out of contracts because they had had afterthoughts. Since an offer can be both revoked by its maker and destroyed by a counter-offer, yet matures into a contract when it is accepted, it can be crucial to decide when these events occur.

6.12 An acceptance is generally effective when it is received by the offeror. But if the acceptance is made by posting a letter then the acceptance takes effect when the letter is posted. But revocation by post takes effect when the letter is received by the offeree. The working of these rules is neatly exemplified by the case of *Byrne v Van Tienhoven* [1880] 5 CPD 344. There the defendants made an offer to the claimants by letter on 1 October. The letter was received on 11 October and immediately accepted by telegram. Meanwhile, on 8 October the defendants had thought better of their offer and sent a letter revoking it. This second letter did not reach the claimants until 20 October. There was a binding contract because the acceptance took effect before the revocation. The result would have been the same even if the acceptance had been by letter and the letter had arrived with the defendants after 20 October.

Battle of the forms

6.13 These mostly Victorian rules about offer and acceptance may seem rather irrelevant to modern commercial transactions. But there is one context in which they regularly appear: the so-called 'battle of the forms' which takes place when two contracting parties both deal on their own standard terms of business, typically appearing on the reverse of their estimates, orders, invoices and other business stationery.

6.14 A vendor sends an estimate on his usual business form, with his standard terms and conditions on the reverse, and a note saying that all business is done on his standard terms. The purchaser sends back an order purporting to accept the estimate, but on the back of his acceptance are his standard terms, which are doubtless more favourable to him than the vendor's. The vendor sends the goods, and the purchaser pays for them. Is there a contract, and if there is, whose standard terms is it on?

6.15 The purchaser's 'acceptance' and order is not a true acceptance, because it does not accept all the terms of the vendor's offer, since it purports to substitute the purchaser's standard terms. So the purchaser's order is in legal terms a counter-offer, and this is

accepted – in this example – by the vendor's action in sending the goods.

6.16 If there are long-drawn-out negotiations as to quantities, prices and so on, all on business stationery containing standard terms, the problems are compounded, and the result, best found by working backwards and identifying the last communication on standard terms, is rather artificial and is rather a matter of luck.

6.17 The courts have tried on occasion to substitute a rather less mechanical analysis of offer and acceptance, looking at the negotiations as a whole (see especially Lord Denning in *Butler Machine Tool Co Ltd v Ex-Cell-O Corporation (England) Ltd* [1979] 1 WLR 401 at 405) but this approach has not found universal judicial acceptance, and it seems that whatever the artificiality of a strict analysis in terms of offer and acceptance it is difficult to find an alternative approach which is workable in all cases. However, in many construction and commercial cases in which protracted and complex negotiations result in a situation considered to be binding by the parties, pinpointing a defining moment when an offer and an acceptance was made ignores the modern commercial reality. In such cases, the court and arbitral tribunal tends to adopt an approach suitable to the needs of the business community and will look over the whole course of the negotiations to see whether the parties have agreed on all the essential terms. If they have the court or arbitral tribunal will usually find that there is a contract despite the difficulty of the legal analysis.

6.18 This topic leads on naturally to the next. Once it is established that a contract exists, what are its terms?

7 Terms of a contract

Express terms

7.01 The most obvious terms of a contract are those which the parties expressly agreed. In cases where there is an oral contract there may be conflicting evidence as to what actually was said and agreed, but with the written contracts with which architects will most often deal, construing the express terms is usually less problematic: just read the document evidencing the contract. The 'four corners rule' restricts attention to within the four corners of the document, and even if the written terms misstate the intention of one of the parties – perhaps that party had not read the document carefully before signing it – he will be bound by what is recorded save in exceptional circumstances. This is another manifestation of the objective approach of English contract law discussed above.

7.02 It should be noted at this stage that things said or written prior to making a contract may affect the parties' legal obligations to one another even though they are not terms of the contract. This matter is discussed in the section on misrepresentation.

Implied terms

7.03 Implied terms are likely to catch out the unwary. There are three types of implied term: those implied by statute, those implied by custom, and those implied by the court.

Terms implied by the court

7.04 With unfortunate frequency contracting parties discover too late that their contract has failed to provide for the events which have happened. One party will wish that the contract had included a term imposing liability on the other in the circumstances that have turned out, and will try to persuade the court that such a term in his favour should be implied into the contract, saying, in effect, that the court ought to read between the lines of the contract and find the term there. Obviously one cannot have an implied term which in inconsistent with the express terms.

7.05 There are some particular terms in particular types of contract which the courts will, as a matter of course, imply into contracts of a particular kind. For instance, a contract for the lease of a furnished property will be taken to include a term that it will be reasonably fit for habitation at the commencement of the tenancy.

7.06 More frequently there will be no authority on the particular type of term which is sought to imply. The courts have developed an approach to these problems, based on an early formulation in the case of *The Moorcock* [1889] 14 PD 64. There the owner of the ship *The Moorcock* had contracted with the defendants to discharge his ship at their jetty on the Thames. Both parties must have realized that the ship would ground at low tide; in the event it not only grounded but, settling on a ridge of hard ground, it was damaged. The plaintiff owners said that the defendants should be taken to have given a warranty that they would take reasonable care to ensure that the river bottom was safe for the vessel – and the Court of Appeal agreed. Bowen LJ explained: 'the law[raises] an implication from the presumed intention of the parties, with the object of giving to the transaction such efficacy as both parties must have intended it should have'

This is called the 'business efficacy' test; but it is clear that the term must be necessary for business efficacy, rather than be simply a term which makes better sense of the contract if it is included than if it is not. In *Shirlow v Southern Foundries* [1939] 2 KB 206 at 227, Mackinnon LJ expressed the test in terms of the 'officious bystander' which provides a readily memorable – if not always easy applicable – formulation of the rule:

'Prima facie, that which in any contract is left to be implied and need not be expressed is something which is so obvious it goes without saying; so that, if while the parties were making their bargain an officious bystander were to suggest some express provision for it in their agreement, they would testily suppress him with a common, "Oh, of course".'

The officious bystander test is obviously difficult to pass. Both parties must have taken the term as 'obvious'. The ploy of trying to persuade a court that a term should be read into the contract in favour of one party is tried much more often than it succeeds. The moral for architects as for any other contracting party, is that the proper time to define contractual terms is before the contract is made, not after things have gone wrong.

7.07 Sometimes parties will argue for an implied term to fill in the gaps in an otherwise incomplete agreement or in situations where the parties have opposing arguments as to what was in fact agreed. In those situations the court is likely to say that there was no contract and it is not the court's role to make the contract for the parties.

Terms implied by custom

7.08 The custom of a particular type of business is relevant in construing the express terms of a contract and may on occasion be sufficient to imply into a contract a term which apparently is not there at all. In *Hutton v Warren* [1836] 1 M & W 466, a lease was held to include a term effecting the local custom that when the tenant's tenancy came to an end he would be entitled to a sum representing the seed and labour put into the arable land. There are other examples from the law of marine insurance, many of which are now crystallized in statute law, but

'An alleged custom can be incorporated into a contract only if there is nothing in the express or necessarily implied terms of the contract to prevent such inclusion and, further, that a custom will only be imported into a contract where it can be so imported consistently with the tenor of the document as a whole.' (*London Export v Jubilee Coffee* [1958] 2 All ER 411, at 420.)

The place of terms implied by custom in the modern law is small; but custom as a guide in construing terms of a contract continues to be of some importance.

Terms implied by statute

7.09 For architects there are two very important statutes which may automatically incorporate terms into their contracts: the Sale

of Goods Act 1979 (SOGA) and the Supply of Goods and Services Act 1982 (SOGASA). The principal relevant sections of those Acts are fairly straightforward, but of course they have to be read in their context to see their precise effect (see Extracts 2.1 and 2.2).

Extract 2.1 Sale of Goods Act 1979, as amended by Sale and Supply of Goods Act 1994

14.(1) Except as provided in this section and section 15 below and subject to any other enactment, there is no implied condition or warranty about the quality or fitness for purpose of goods supplied under a contract of sale.

(2) Where the seller sells goods in the course of a business, there is an implied term that the goods supplied under the contract are of satisfactory quality.

(2A) For the purposes of this Act, goods are of satisfactory quality if they meet the standard that a reasonable person would regard as satisfactory, taking account of any description of the goods, the price (if relevant) and all the other relevant circumstances.

(2B) For the purposes of this Act, the quality of goods includes their state and condition and the following (among others) are in appropriate cases aspects of the quality of goods –

    (a) fitness for all the purposes for which goods of the kind in question are commonly supplied,

    (b) appearance and finish,

    (c) freedom from minor defects,

    (d) safety, and

    (e) durability.

(2C) The term implied by subsection (2) above does not extend to any matter making the quality of goods unsatisfactory –

    (a) which is specifically drawn to the buyer's attention before the contract is made,

    (b) where the buyer examines the goods before the contract is made, which that examination ought to reveal, or

    (c) in the case of a contract for sale by sample, which would have been apparent on a reasonable examination of the sample.

(3) Where the seller sells goods in the course of a business and the buyer, expressly or by implication, makes known –

    (a) to the seller, or

    (b) where the purchase price or part of it is payable by instalments and the goods were previously sold by a credit-broker to the seller, to that credit-broker,

any particular purpose for which the goods supplied under the contract are reasonably fit for that purpose, whether or not that is a purpose for which such goods are commonly supplied, except where the circumstances show that the buyer does not rely, or that it is unreasonable for him to rely, on the skill or judgement of the seller or credit-broker.

Extract 2.2 Supply of Goods and Services Act 1982

12.(1) In this Act a 'contract for the supply of a service' means, subject to subsection (2) below, a contract under which a person 'the supplier' agrees to carry out a service.

(2) For the purposes of this Act, a contract of service or apprenticeship is not a contract for the supply of a service.

13. In a contract for the supply of a service where the supplier is acting in the course of a business, there is an implied term that the supplier will carry out the service with reasonable care and skill.

14.(1) Where, under a contract for the supply of a service by a supplier acting in the course of a business, the time for the service to be carried out is not fixed by the contract, left to be fixed in a manner agreed by the contract or determined by the course of dealing between the parties, there is an implied term that the supplier will carry out the service within a reasonable time.

(2) What is a reasonable time is a question of fact.

15.(1) Where, under a contract for the supply of a service, the consideration for the supply of a service is not determined by the contract, but left to be determined in a manner agreed by the contract or determined by the course of dealing between the parties, there is an implied term that the party contracting with the supplier will pay a reasonable charge.

(2) What is a reasonable charge is a question of fact.

7.10 The terms implied by SOGA and SOGASA can be excluded by express provision in the contract (SOGA, Section 55 and SOGASA, Section 16), although in both cases this is subject to the provisions of the Unfair Contract Terms Act 1977.

8 Exclusion clauses, UCTA, and the Unfair Terms in Consumer Contracts Regulations 1999

8.01 A contracting party, particularly a contracting party with a dominant position relative to the other, may try to include in the contract terms which are extremely advantageous to him in the event that he is in breach of some principal obligation under the contract. The commonest way to do this is to exclude or limit his liability in certain circumstances. A carrier might, for example, offer to carry goods on terms including a clause that in the event of loss or damage to the goods being carried his liability should be limited to £100 per each kilo weight of the goods carried. The consignor of a parcel of expensive jewellery would be little assisted by a finding that the carrier was liable for their loss if the damages he could recover were limited to £100 per kilo.

Unfair Contracts Terms Act 1977

8.02 The Unfair Contracts Terms Act 1977 (UCTA) is quite different in ambit from what its title suggests. It should be understood from the outset that the Act is not concerned generally with the fairness of the contractual bargain or the contractual obligations that a party has agreed to. Broadly (although this is an over simplification) the Act is designed to do two things. Firstly, the Act prevents or restricts a person from escaping liability (wholly or in part) for his negligence. Secondly, the Act prevents or restricts a person from escaping liability (wholly or in part) for breach of contract. The rules about which situations the Act covers are more complicated than that but a general summary of the relevant parts of the Act is set out below. Although this rather short Act is far from a model of clarity in the way that it is drafted and arranged, nevertheless it makes a hugely significant contribution to the law of contract and tort. UCTA does not apply to certain types of contract, in particular insurance contracts.

8.03 Section 2(1) of the Act makes it illegal for a person to exclude liability for death or personal injury as a result of his negligence. This section applies both in a contractual and a non-contractual context. For example, if a farmer sets up dangerous booby-traps on his land to dissuade burglars and puts up a notice saying that he will not be responsible for injuries caused to trespassers that notice will be ineffective by UCTA. In the contractual context, a coach operator who makes it a condition of travel that his liability for negligence to passengers is excluded will not escape liability if the coach has been negligently maintained resulting in a crash that injures the passengers. Contract clauses of this sort are becoming rarer but it is surprising how, even today some 25 years after the Act, one can find contracts which contain clauses that attempt to limit this type of liability.

8.04 Section 2(2) of the Act prevents a person from unreasonably excluding or restricting his liability for other loss and damage resulting from negligence (i.e. economic loss). Again, it applies both in a contractual and non-contractual context. It is of course possible, by using an appropriately worded clause, to exclude loss or damage caused by negligence if the test of 'reasonableness' in section 11 is satisfied. The test of reasonableness is that the term should be fair and reasonable having regard to the circumstances which were known, or ought to be known, to the parties when the contract was made. In practice, it is often difficult to satisfy this test. This section applies to all contracts, unlike the next major section of the Act.

8.05 Section 3 of the Act is one of the most important parts of the Act, which applies to ordinary (i.e. non-negligent) breaches of contract. However, it does not apply to all contracts. Instead, it applies

to the following two limited contractual situations:

(1) a contract where one of the parties is a consumer, that is to say, a person who is not acting in the course of business; or
(2) where the contract is made on one party's standard written terms of business. General standard forms of contract, such as JCT or ICE forms will not necessarily be a party's standard written terms. However, if a party regularly uses a particular form (perhaps with his own special amendments) those terms may be held to be his standard written terms, see *British Fermentation Products Ltd v Compair Reavell Ltd* – Technology and Construction Court (1999) 66 Constr LR 1 and *Pegler Ltd v Wang (UK) Ltd* [2000] BLR 218. UCTA was applied to the RIBA Architect's Standard Form of Agreement in *Moores v Yakely Associates Ltd* [1999] 62 Constr LR 76 where it was held that the Architect's limit of liability clause was reasonable, a decision which was subsequently affirmed in the Court of Appeal.

Section 3 provides that unless a party can prove that a contractual term was reasonable within the meaning of section 11 (see above), a party in breach of contract cannot exclude or restrict his liability for that breach of contract nor can a party claim to be entitled to render incomplete, significantly different, or defective performance of his obligations or, even worse, no performance at all.

8.06 Section 13 provides that a party is not permitted to make his liability or enforcement of his liability subject to onerous conditions or to restrict rights and remedies of the other party. This section only appears to apply in circumstances where sections 2 and 3 of the Act already apply.

8.07 In conclusion, where there is a one-off contract between two commercial enterprises, UCTA will not apply. But it seems likely that there may be an increasing likelihood in the future of litigants arguing that UCTA does apply to standard forms, particularly if there is evidence that one party regularly uses a particular standard form. Nevertheless, it is probable that even if UCTA does apply, the terms will satisfy the reasonableness test. The court is likely to say that experienced business men are the best judges of what is commercially fair. However, it is important to bear in mind that in a contractual chain, the party at the bottom may be a consumer who will be able to benefit from UCTA. This can mean that the contractor near the bottom of the chain will not be able to transfer onto the consumer the risk passed down from the top of the chain. The consumer obtains yet further protection from the Unfair Terms in Consumer Contracts Regulations.

Unfair Terms in Consumer Contracts Regulations 1999

8.08 These regulations replaced an earlier set of regulations introduced in 1994 to give effect to an EC directive on unfair terms in consumer contracts. Unlike UCTA, these regulations really are designed to examine whether or not clauses in the contract are unfair to the consumer. The 1999 regulations took effect on 1 October 1999 and apply to contracts made with consumers after that date. As is commonly the case with domestic legislation required by European law, the regulations use expressions and ideas that are unfamiliar or not well established in English law. Indeed, traditionally English law did not generally interfere with the bargain made by the parties to see if it was unfair. The modern era has been marked by a whole raft of Acts and regulations which were introduced to protect the consumer against the superior bargaining power of large commercial entities.

8.09 The regulations apply to contracts with consumers where the other party is a seller or supplier of goods or services: this is interpreted as broadly as possible so that a person will be a seller or supplier wherever that party is acting in the course of his trade profession or business. A consumer must be a natural person rather than a limited company. Certain contracts are excepted from the regulations, notably employment contracts.

8.10 The regulations only apply to terms which have not been individually negotiated between the parties. This upholds the principle that the bargain negotiated between the parties is a matter entirely for the parties. Consistent with that principle, the regulations will not apply to terms regarding the price or the subject matter of the contract provided that such terms are in plain intelligible language.

8.11 The regulations contain a non-exhaustive 'grey-list' of terms which will generally be deemed to be unfair: most of these are the sort of clauses which common sense indicates are unfair to the consumer. Not surprisingly these include the same types of clauses which would fall foul of UCTA. Also included are clauses which impose penalties on consumers, which allow the other party to change the service or goods that it supplies, to interpret or change the terms the contract at his discretion or to terminate the contract early. The regulations also give certain regulatory bodies, such as the Office of Fair Trading, the power to take legal action to prevent the use of such terms.

8.12 The full impact of the regulations remains to be seen. The regulations are likely to prove wider in scope than UCTA so far as consumer contracts are concerned. They have already been held to apply to strike out onerous terms in mortgage lending agreements: see *Falco Finance Ltd v Gough* [1999] CCLR 16. They have also been used to strike out an arbitration agreement under the standard NHBC Buildmark Agreement in *Zealander v Laing Homes Ltd.* (2000) 2 TCLR 724. In that case the home owner brought Court proceedings against Laing Homes for breach of contract alleging that there were defects in the house. The Defendant objected to the court's jurisdiction contending that the dispute was required to go to arbitration. The court held that this arbitration clause only covered matters under the Buildmark agreement not all matters for which the claimant might claim against the Defendant and this created a significant imbalance for the consumer because he would be put to the expense of using two separate proceedings to bring his claims and was financially disadvantaged compared to the Defendant. Care must be taken, particularly when using standard terms of business, or a standard form contract, in agreements with a consumer to make sure that it will satisfy both the regulations and UCTA.

9 Standard term contracts

9.01 Many of the contracts with which architects are involved are standard form contracts. Chapter 9 deals at length with one such contract, the JCT Standard Form of Building Contract, and in other areas other standard form contracts are available. The use of such contracts has a number of advantages. A great deal of experience has gone into drafting these contracts so that many pitfalls of fuzzy or uncertain wording can be avoided. And where the words used are open to different interpretations it may well be that case law has definitively settled their meaning. In effect the user of a standard term contract enjoys the benefit of other people's earlier litigation in sorting out exactly what obligations the standard terms impose. The effects of well-litigated and well-established terms and conditions also have an impact on third parties. Insurers in particular will know where they stand in relation to a contract on familiar terms and therefore the extra premiums inevitable on uncertain risks can be avoided.

9.02 One potential problem with STCs can be minimized if it is appreciated. Just as tinkering with a well-tuned engine can have catastrophic consequences, so 'home-made' modifications of STCs can have far-reaching effects. Many of the provisions and definitions used in STCs interlink, and modifying one clause may have unforeseen and far-reaching ramifications. If parties to an STC want to modify it because it does not seem to achieve exactly the cross-obligations they want to undertake, it is highly advisable to take specialist advice.

10 Misrepresentation

10.01 Pre-contractual negotiations often cover many subjects which are not dealt with by the terms (express or implied) of the

eventual contract. In some circumstances things said or done before the contract is made can lead to liability.

Representations and misrepresentations

10.02 A representation is a statement of existing fact made by one party to the eventual contract (the misrepresentor) to the other (the misrepresentee) which induces the representee to enter into the contract. A misrepresentation is a representation which is false. Two elements of the definition need elaboration.

Statement of existing fact

10.03 The easiest way to grasp what is meant by a statement of existing fact is to see what is not included in the expression. A promise to do something in the future is not a representation – such a statement is essentially the stuff of which contracts are made, and the place for promises is therefore in the contract itself. An opinion which is honestly held and honestly expressed will not constitute an actionable misrepresentation. This is sometimes said to be because it is not a statement of fact and it is perhaps simplest to see this by realizing that it does not make sense to talk of an opinion being false or untrue, so that in any event it cannot be a misrepresentation. But a statement of opinion 'I believe such and such . . .' can be a representation and can therefore be a misrepresentation if the representor does not actually hold the belief, because, as Bowen LJ explained:

> 'The state of a man's mind is as much a fact as the state of his digestion. It is true that it is very difficult to prove what the state of a man's mind at a particular time is, but if it can be ascertained it is as much a fact as anything else. A misrepresentation as to the state of a man's mind is, therefore, a statement of fact.' (*Edgington v Fitzmaurice* [1885] 29 ChD 459 at 483.)

10.04 A somewhat more surprising line of authority holds that 'mere puff' or sales-speak does not constitute a representation. Hence describing land as 'uncommonly rich water meadow' was held not to constitute a representation in *Scott v Hanson* [1829] 1 Russ & M 128. But the courts today are rather less indulgent to exaggerated sales talk and if it can be established that effusive description of a vendor's product is actually untrue it seems that the courts would today be more likely to hold that to be a misrepresentation than would their nineteenth-century predecessors.

10.05 Silence generally does not constitute a representation. A vendor is generally under no obligation to draw to the attention of his purchaser the defects in that which he is selling, and even tacit acquiescence in the purchaser's self-deception will not usually create any liability. However, there are cases in which silence can constitute a misrepresentation. If the representor makes some representation about a certain matter he must not leave out other aspects of the story so that what he says is misleading as a whole: so although a total non-disclosure may not be a misrepresentation, partial non-disclosure may be.

Reliance

10.06 To create any liability the representee must show that the misrepresentation induced him to enter into the contract – the misrepresentation must have been material. Therefore if the misrepresentee knew that the representation was false, or if he was not aware of the representation at all, or if he knew of it but it did not affect his judgement, then he will have no grounds for relief. But the misrepresentation need not be the only, nor even indeed the principal, reason why the misrepresentee entered into the contract.

The three types of misrepresentation

10.07 If the representor making the misrepresentation made it knowing it was untrue, or without believing it was true, or recklessly, not caring whether it was true or false, then it is termed a fraudulent misrepresentation. If, however, the representor made the false statement believing that it was true but had taken insufficient care to ensure that it was true, then it will be a negligent misstatement. Finally, if the misrepresentor had taken reasonable care to ensure that it was true, and did believe that it was true, then it is merely an innocent misrepresentation.

Remedies for misrepresentation

10.08 This is a very difficult area of the law, and the finer details of the effects of the Misrepresentation Act 1967 are still not entirely clear. The summary which follows is extremely brief.

Principal remedy: rescission

10.09 The basic remedy for misrepresentation is rescission, which is the complete termination and undoing of the contract. The misrepresentee can in many circumstances oblige the misrepresentor to restore him to the position he would have been in had the contract never been made.

10.10 Rescission is not available if the misrepresentee has, with knowledge of the misrepresentation, affirmed the contract. A long lapse of time before the misrepresentee opts to rescind is often taken as affirmation. Rescission is not available if a third party has, since the contract was made, himself acquired for value an interest in the subject matter of the contract. Nor is it available, almost by definition, if it is impossible to restore the parties to the status quo before the contract was made.

10.11 The court now has a general power to grant damages in lieu of rescission (Misrepresentation Act 1967, section 2(2)), and may award damages to the victim of a negligent or innocent representation even where the misrepresentee would rather have the contract rescinded instead.

Damages

10.12 The victim of a fraudulent misrepresentation may sue for damages as well as claim rescission, and the measure of damages will be tortious.

10.13 The victim of a negligent misrepresentation may also recover damages (section 1) as well as rescission. It is not entirely clear how damages should be calculated.

10.14 In the case of an innocent misrepresentation there is no right to damages, but, as already explained, the court may in its discretion award damages in lieu of rescission.

The law of negligent misstatement

10.15 Misrepresentation alone is complicated. The matter is compounded by the availability of damages for the tort of negligent misstatement (rather than misrepresentation), which is discussed in Chapter 3. There will be many instances in which an actionable misrepresentation is also an actionable misstatement.

11 Performance and breach

11.01 All the topics considered so far have been concerned with matters up to and including the creation of a contract – matters generally of greater interest to lawyers than to men of business or to architects. But both lawyers and architects have a close interest in whether or not a party fulfils its obligations under a contract and, if it does not, what can be done about it.

The right to sue on partial performance of a complete contract

11.02 Many contracts take the general form of A paying B to perform some work or to provide some service. It is unusual for the party performing the work or providing the service to do nothing at all; the usual case will be that much of the work is done according to

the contract, but some part of the work remains incomplete, undone, or improperly performed. This situation needs to be considered from both sides. We begin with examining whether the incomplete performer can sue his paymaster if no money is forthcoming.

11.03 The general rule of contract law is that a party must perform precisely what he contracted to do. The consequence is that in order to make the other liable in any way under the contract all of that party's obligations must be performed. If the contract is divided up into clearly severable parts each will be treated for these purposes as a separate contract, and virtually all building contracts will of course make provision for stage payments. Nevertheless it is important to be aware of the general rule which applies to a contract where one lump sum is provided for all the works. Non-performance (as opposed to misperformance) of some part will disentitle the partial performer from payment.

11.04 An example is *Bolton v Mahadeva* [1972] 1 WLR 1009. There the claimant agreed to install a hot water system for the defendant for a lump-sum payment of £560. The radiators emitted fumes and the system did not heat the house properly. Curing the defects would cost £174. The defendant was held not liable to pay the claimant anything.

11.05 There is an important exception to this rule, even for entire contracts. If the party performing the works has 'substantially performed' his obligations then he is entitled to the contract sum subject only to a counter-claim for those parts remaining unperformed. In *Hoenig v Isaacs* [1952] 2 All ER 176 there was a lump-sum contract for the decoration and furnishing of the defendant's flat for the price of £750. When the claimant left, one wardrobe door needed replacing and one shelf was too short, and would have to be remade. The Court of Appeal held that although 'near the borderline' on the facts, the claimant had substantially performed his contractual obligations and was therefore able to recover his £750, subject only to the deduction of £56, being the cost of the necessary repairs.

Remedies against the incomplete performer

11.06 The flip-side of the situation of suing on an incompletely performed contract is suing the incomplete performer. Obviously incomplete performance or misperformance gives to the other party, who has so far performed his obligations as they fall due, a right to damages to put him in the position he would have been in had the contract been performed. But in some circumstances another remedy will be available to the aggrieved party, for he will be able to hold himself absolved from any further performance of his obligations under the contract.

11.07 This right to treat the contract as at an end arises in three situations.

Breach of a contractual condition

11.08 The first situation is if the term which the non- or misperforming party has breached is a contractual condition rather than merely a warranty. It used to be thought that all contractual terms were either conditions or warranties. Whether a term was one or the other might be determined by statute, by precedent, or might have to be decided by the court by looking at the contract in the light of the surrounding circumstances. If the term was a condition then any breach of it, however minor, would allow the aggrieved party to treat the contract as at an end. The modern tendency is to adopt a more realistic approach and to escape from the straitjacket dichotomy of conditions and warranties. In *Hong Kong Fir Shipping Co. Ltd v Kawasaki Kisen Kaisha Ltd* [1962] 2 QB 26, at 70 Lord Diplock explained that

'There are, however, many contractual terms of a more complex character which cannot be categorised as being "conditions" or "warranties" . . . Of such undertakings all that can be predicated is that some breaches will and others will not give rise to an event which will deprive the party in default of substantially the whole benefit which it was intended he should obtain from the contract; and the legal consequences of the breach of any such undertaking, unless provided for expressly in the contract, depend on the nature of the event to which the breach gives rise and do not follow automatically from a prior classification of the undertaking as a "condition" or "warranty".'

These terms which are neither conditions nor warranties have been unhelpfully named 'innominate terms' and although their existence decreases the importance of this first type of circumstance in which an aggrieved party can treat its contractual obligations as at an end, it is nevertheless still open for the contracting parties expressly to make a contractual term a condition, in which case any breach of it allows this remedy in addition to a claim for damages.

Repudiatory breach

11.09 If the breach 'goes to the root of the contract' or deprives the party of substantially the whole benefit the contract was intended to confer on him, then he will be entitled to treat the contract as at an end.

Renunciation

11.10 If one party evinces an intention not to continue to perform his side of the contract then the other party may again treat the contract as at an end.

Election

11.11 In all three of the circumstances described above the innocent party has a choice as to whether or not to treat himself as discharged. He may prefer to press for performance of the contract so far as the other party is able to perform it, and to restrict himself to his remedy in damages. But once made, the election cannot unilaterally be changed, unless the matter which gave rise to it is a continuing state of affairs which therefore continues to provide the remedy afresh.

11.12 The rule that the innocent party may, if he prefers, elect to press for performance following (for instance) a renunciation can have a bizarre result. In *White and Carter (Councils) v McGregor* [1962] AC 413 the claimant company supplied litter bins to local councils. The councils did not pay for the bins, but they allowed them to carry advertising, and the claimants made their money from the companies whose advertisements their bins carried. The defendant company agreed to hire space on the claimants' bins for three years. Later the same day they changed their mind and said that they were not going to be bound by the contract. The claimants could have accepted that renunciation, but, perhaps short of work and wanting to keep busy, opted to carry on with the contract, which they proceeded to do for the next three years. They sued successfully for the full contract price: there was no obligation on them to treat the contract as at an end and they were not obliged to sue for damages only.

12 Privity of contract

Privity of contract

12.01 As explained at the beginning of this chapter, the distinguishing feature of contract law is that it defines the rights and obligations of the two or more parties to the contract. That party must have provided consideration in order to be able to enforce his rights or the obligations of the other party: without that consideration he will not have earned the right to the benefits of the contract. The issue of privity of contract really comes into sharp focus when the performance of the contract has not gone according to plan and a person wants to enforce the contract. Whether a person can sue or be sued in respect of a contract depends upon having privity of contract.

12.02 That rule has caused problems for third parties who stand to benefit by the contract, as in examples discussed above. In the

construction industry there are often a number of complex contract chains where benefits extend to someone else at a different point in the chain. The industry is therefore prone to suffer the problems of deprived third parties who can see the benefits they are entitled to but cannot get at them because they depend upon enforcement by the parties to the contract. This can be frustrating for the third party, when the contracting parties do not take steps to secure the benefit either because the contracting party who can enforce the term is unwilling to rock the boat or cause confrontation with the other contracting party with whom he has (or hopes to have) a long-standing relationship, or because there is already some dispute between the third party and the contracting party who can enforce the benefit on his behalf, or, just as commonplace, because of general inefficiency or apathy. A typical example is where a main contractor has contracted with the employer to pass onto the sub-contractor payments for the value of the work done or, from the other perspective, where an employer wants the sub-contract works to be finished but has no direct contract with them and can only badger the main contractor who has engaged the sub-contractors to insist on performance. Such problems become more acute when one of the contracting parties is incapacitated, usually through insolvency. What if the main contractor goes bust and is dissolved, leaving the employer with no recourse to the sub-contractors to secure completion of the sub-contract works? Or similarly, how can the sub-contractor insist on being paid for work done ultimately for the employer, when he was depending upon the (now dissolved) main contractor to secure payment on his behalf?

12.03 Until the Contracts (Rights of Third Parties Act) 1999 the best a non-party could do was attempt to persuade one of the parties to sue the other on his behalf in order to be compensated for the non-party's lack of benefit. Obviously the party may not be willing to incur the cost or take the time and risk involved in suing the other party. Even if he did, the problem was that the party would normally be compensated only for his own loss – which in those circumstances would be no more than nominal – not the non-party's loss which would be substantial.

12.04 The difficulties of a contracting party suing on behalf of the third party are discussed in the important House of Lords case of *Alfred McAlpine Construction Ltd v Panatown Ltd* [2001] 1 AC 518. In that case, a building contractor entered into a contract with the employer for the construction of an office block and car park. The site was actually owned by another company in the same group of companies as the employer, and the owner – rather than the employer – was ultimately going to benefit from the office block and car park. In addition to the contract with the employer, the building contractor also entered into a 'duty of care' deed with the owner of the site. By that deed (which was a contract in itself) the owner acquired a direct remedy against the contractor in respect of any failure by the contractor to exercise reasonable skill, care and attention to any matter within the scope of the contractor's responsibilities under the contract. Serious defects were found in the building and the employer served notice of arbitration claiming damages for defective work and delay. The contractor objected on the basis that that the employer, having suffered no loss, was not entitled to recover substantial damages under the contract. The arbitrator said that the employer could recover substantial damages, based upon one of the exceptions to the privity of contract rule. The High Court allowed the contractor's appeal against that decision and decided that the employer could not recover substantial damages. The Court of Appeal allowed the employer's appeal and the matter ended up in the House of Lords. Their Lordships held (by a 3:2 majority) that the employer was only entitled to nominal damages because it had suffered no loss itself. The House of Lords would not permit the employer to recover losses on behalf of the owner because the owner had a duty of care deed (a collateral contract) which provided him with a direct remedy against the contractor for the losses arising out of the contractor's defective performance. Interestingly, had the protagonists not set up that direct contractual framework by a duty of care deed for the owner, it is possible that the House of Lords might have been prepared to allow the employer to recover full damages (which he would then have to pass onto the owner) in order to fashion an effective remedy where otherwise none existed. If the situation were to arise now, the owner might be able to sue under the employer's contract by using the 1999 Act.

The Contracts (Rights of Third Parties) Act 1999

12.05 In order to resolve the privity problem for the third party stranger who benefits from a contract, Parliament introduced legislation – the Contracts (Rights of Third Parties) Act 1999 – to give that person a direct right to sue on that contract, although of course the stranger still cannot be sued on the contract. The Act is one of the most radical reforms to the law of contract since medieval times. Its effect is not to abolish privity of contract but to create a massive exception to the doctrine. The Act applies to all contracts made after 11 May 2000. The Act also applies to contracts made between 11 November 1999 and 11 May 2000 where the contract states that the Act is specifically to apply. However, it should be noted at the outset that the parties to the contract are free to exclude the Act.

12.06 By section 1 the third party will have a right to enforce a term in the contract made for his benefit if

1 the term in the contract expressly says that he may enforce that term; or
2 if he is expressly identified in the contract by name, class or description (even if not in existence at the time the contract is made) and the term purports to confer a benefit on him.

An example of the first kind would be a contract term which says that X's next-door neighbours can claim compensation from the builder for any damage to their property while the works are carried out on X's land. An example of the second kind would be a contract term which says that compensation is payable by the builder to the next-door neighbours for any damage caused while the builder carries out works on X's land but does not specifically provide for the next-door neighbours to make a claim. A less clear-cut situation is where the builder has contracted not to cause a nuisance to X's neighbours while carrying out the works but says nothing about compensation or other remedy. It is in such a situation that the distinction between the law of contract and the law of tort seems to have become blurred.

12.07 It would appear that it is not only 'positive' rights that can be enforced by a third party (such as a claim to payment) but also a term which contains 'defensive' rights such as a limitation or exclusion clause (section 1(6) of the Act).

12.08 However, the statutory scheme only takes effect subject to the contract between the parties: the party's freedom of contract is preserved (except in the case of a subsequent variation to the contract where the original terms conferred a benefit on a third party which is enforceable by the statutory scheme see paragraph 12.10 below). For this reason a third party will not have the right to enforce a term of someone else's contract if on a proper interpretation of the contract, the contracting parties did not intend that term to be enforceable by the third party (see section 1(2) of the Act). What this means is that the term of the contract sought to be enforced cannot be viewed in isolation from the rest of the contract. It is thus possible to provide an express term conferring a benefit on a third party but precluding the third party from enforcing that benefit or simply to contract out of the statutory provisions altogether.

12.09 It is important to realise that the third party can only enforce the **term** which benefits the third party, not the whole contract. So a next-door neighbour who benefits from a compensation clause cannot enforce a term which obliges the builder to complete the work by a certain date where there has been delay because he is fed up with the duration of the works. However, it will no doubt be possible for the contract to provide that the whole terms of the contract should be for the benefit of the third party and should be enforceable by him.

12.10 In enforcing his right the third party will be able to enjoy all the remedies available to the contracting parties, although one notable exception seems to be the inability of the third party to invoke section 2(2) the Unfair Contract Terms Act (see paragraph 8.04 above). It should be noted that the third party is not similarly prevented from relying upon the Unfair Terms in Consumer Contracts Regulations (see paragraph 8.08 and following). However, the third party will not be put in a better position than the contracting parties and so can only exercise his right in accordance with and subject to the terms and conditions of the contract. Where there are exclusions and limitations they will apply to the third party just as much as the contracting parties. And just as a contracting party has to mitigate his loss where the other party is in breach of contract, so too will a third party have to mitigate his loss. Also the third party's right will be subject to any defence or set-off that the party against whom the term is enforced would have against the other contracting party. Additionally the third party can also expect his right to be subject to counterclaims and set-offs which the other contracting party has against the third party under any separate relationship. For example, if C can sue B for the price of work done under the contract between A and B, B can counterclaim for damages suffered under a separate contract between C and B the previous year when C bodged that job. Of course, the rights of set-off will be subject to the express terms of the contract.

12.11 The Act also places restrictions on the contracting parties to preserve the third party's rights obtained under the statutory scheme. The restrictions apply where the third party has communicated his assent to the benefit/right to the person against whom the benefit/right would be enforced (called 'the promisor'), or if the promisor is aware that the third party has relied on the term, or where the promisor could reasonably have foreseen that the third party would rely upon and has in fact relied upon the term. The restriction upon the contracting parties in section 2, is to prevent the contracting parties from varying the contract terms, or cancelling the contract so as to extinguish or alter the third party's right without the third party's consent. But as has been said already, the statutory scheme is subject to the express terms of the contract and so the third party's consent is not necessary if the contract expressly provides so (but no doubt the court will require clear words dispensing with the need for the third party's consent). In the absence of an express term to this effect the third party's consent can only be waived by the court (not an arbitral tribunal) with or without conditions attached (e.g. the payment of compensation) where the court is satisfied that either

1 the third party's consent cannot be obtained because his whereabouts cannot reasonably be ascertained
2 the third party is mentally incapable of giving his consent or
3 it cannot reasonably be ascertained whether the third party in fact relied upon the term.

12.12 In order to avoid the problem of double liability the court may reduce the award available to the third party in circumstances where one of the parties has already recovered a sum in respect of the third party's loss against the promisor. And of course the Act does not restrict in any way the ability of contracting parties to enforce the terms of the contract nor any other rights that the third party might have outside of the contract (such as a similar claim in tort).

12.13 Certain types of contract are excluded, such as contracts of employment, contracts for the carriage of goods, negotiable instruments or certain contracts under section 14 of the Companies Act 1985.

12.14 The Act is a welcome news for third parties and is sure to take the law of contract in interesting new directions. It is still far too early to say whether all of the problems will be resolved or whether the Act will create its own. There does not appear to be any (reported) case on the impact of the Act as yet. It is worth reiterating that the parties themselves can exclude the Act which means the traditional common law rules will still apply. So the law of contract could develop in different directions depending upon whether the Act applies to the contract or not. A cautious construction industry (as well as other industries) began by excluding the provisions of the Act in its standard forms. Instead the industry prefers for the time being to use the collateral warranty method as seen in *Panatown*. Interestingly, the JCT has recently brought out a new Major Projects Form 2003 which embraces the Act and, if all works well, other forms may follow suit.

13 Agency

13.01 The law of agency has developed as a framework in which the doctrine of privity of contract is often applied, because a common problem is to determine exactly who the parties to a contract are. For A to act as an agent for P his principal is for A to act as P's representative. A's words or actions will create legal rights and liabilities for P who is therefore bound by what A does. It is just as if P had said or done those things himself. The agent's actions might have consequences for P in contract, or tort, or some other area of the law, but in this chapter it is naturally only with contractual liabilities that we are concerned. In general, if A, as P's agent, properly contracts with C, then the resulting contract is a contract between P and C. A is not privy to the contract, and can neither sue or be sued upon it.

13.02 There are two sets of legal obligations which are of interest. The first is those between the principal and his agent. That relationship of agency may, but need not, itself be the subject of a contract – the contract of agency. For instance, A may be rewarded by a percentage commission on any of P's business which he places with C. If A does not receive his commission he may wish to sue P, and he will do so under their contract of agency. That is a matter between P and A, and of no interest to C. It is governed by the rules for contracts of agency. These rules, just a specialized sub-set of the rules of contract generally, will not be further discussed here.

13.03 The second set of legal questions raised by an agency concerns how the relationship is created, whether and how it is that A's actions bind his principal, and whether A is ever left with any personal liability of his own. We begin by considering the first of these issues.

Creation of agency

13.04 There are three important ways in which an agency may be created.

1 By express appointment

This is, of course, the commonest way to create an agency. Generally no formalities are necessary: the appointment may be oral or in writing. To take an example, the employees of a trading company are frequently expressly appointed by their contract of employment to act as the agents of the company and to place and receive orders on its behalf.

2 By estoppel

If P by his words or conduct leads C to believe that A is his agent, and C deals with A on that basis, P cannot escape the contract by saying that, in fact, A was not his agent. In these circumstances P will be stopped, or 'estopped', from making that assertion.

3 By ratification

If A, not in fact being P's agent, purports to contract with C on P's behalf, and P then discovers the contract, likes the look of it and ratifies and adopts it, then at law A is deemed to be P's agent for the purposes of that contract. The precise working of the rules of ratification are rather involved.

Authorization

13.05 The effect of an agent's words or actions will depend crucially on whether or not he was authorized by his principal to say or do them. The agent's authority will usually be an actual authority, that is, an authority which he has expressly or impliedly been granted by his principal. But the scope of the agent's authority may, most importantly, be enlarged by the addition of his ostensible authority.

13.06 Ostensible authority is another manifestation of the operation of estoppel. If P represents to C that his agent A has an authority wider than, in fact, has been expressly or impliedly granted by P to A, and in reliance on that representation C contracts with P through A, then P will be stopped ('estopped') from denying that the scope of A's authority was wide enough to include the contract that has been made.

The liabilities of principal and agent

13.07 We now consider the liabilities of both principal and agent with the contracting third party C, and the discussion is divided into those cases in which the agent is authorized to enter into the transaction, and those in which he is not so authorized.

The agent acts within the scope of his authority

13.08 This division has three sub-divisions, depending on how much the contracting party C knows about the principal. The agent may tell C that P exists, and name him. Or he may tell C that he has a principal, but not name him. Or – still less communicative – he may not tell C that he has a principal at all, so that as far as C is concerned he is contracting with A direct.

1 Principal is named

This is in a sense the paradigm example of agency in action. A drops out of the picture altogether, the contract is between P and C and A can neither sue nor be sued on the P–C contract.

2 Existence of principal disclosed, but not his identity

The general rule is the same as in case 1.

3 Neither name nor existence of principal disclosed to C

This case is described as the case of the undisclosed principal. The rule here is somewhat counter-intuitive: both the agent and the principal may sue on the contract, and C may sue the agent, and, if and when he discovers his identity, the principal.

The agent acts outside the scope of his authority

13.09 The position as regards the principal is clear. The principal is not party to any contract, and can neither sue nor be sued upon it. This of course would have to be the case, for really in these circumstances there is no agency operating at all. But it is important to remember that ostensible authority may fix a principal with liability when the agent is acting outside his express or implied authority.

13.10 The position of the agent is more complex. We first consider the position of the agent as far as benefits under the contract are concerned – whether the agent can sue upon the contract. If the agent purported to contract as agent for a named principal, then the agent cannot sue on the contract. On the other hand, if the name of the principal is not disclosed the agent can sue upon the contract as if it were his own.

13.11 Turning now to the liability of an unauthorized agent to be sued by C, the position depends on what the agent thought was the true position between himself and P. If A knows all along that he does not have P's authority to enter into the contract, then C can sue A, although for the tort of deceit, rather than under the contract.

13.12 If, on the other hand, A genuinely thought that he was authorized by P to enter into the contract, he cannot be sued by P for deceit – after all, he has not been deceitful, merely mistaken. But C has an alternative means of enforcing his contract. A court will infer the existence of a collateral contract by A (as principal) with C, under which A warranted that he had P's authority to contract. This is a quite separate contract to the non-existent contract which C thought he was entering into with P, but from C's point of view it is just as good, for now C can sue A instead.

14 Limitation under the Limitation Act 1980

14.01 Armed with the information derived from this chapter a prospective claimant should have some idea of what his contract is, whether it has been breached, what he can do about it, and who he should sue. There is one more point to consider.

14.02 An action for breach of contract must generally be commenced within six years. Time begins to run – the six years starts – when the contract is breached. This may mean that the claimant can sue before any real physical damage has been experienced.

Suppose the defendant is an architect who has, in breach of contract, designed foundations for a building which are inadequate, and it is clear that in ten to twenty years' time the building will fall down if remedial works are not carried out. The claimant can sue straight away. Of course, although no physical damage has yet occurred there has been economic loss because the defendant has got out of the contract a building worth much less than what he paid for it, and it is obviously right that he should be able to sue straightaway.

14.03 The exception to this rule is that a claimant may sue on a contract contained in a deed up to twelve years after the contract was breached. It is for this reason that building contracts – which may take more than six years from inception to completion – are frequently made under deed.

14.04 The law on limitation periods is to be found in the Limitation Act 1980. The law on limitation periods for suing on a tort is different and more complicated, and is explained in Chapter 3.

3

The English law of tort

VINCENT MORAN

1 Introduction

1.01 The law of tort is concerned with conduct which causes harm to a party's personal, proprietary or financial interests. It is the law of wrongdoing. Its aim is to define obligations that should be imposed on members of society for the benefit of all. Its purpose is to compensate (or sometimes to prevent in the first place) interference with personal, proprietary, or, sometimes, non-physical interests (such as a person's reputation or financial position). The law of tort therefore provides a system of loss distribution and regulates behaviour within society.

1.02 A general definition is difficult because it is impossible to fit the various separate torts that have been recognised by the common law into a single system of classification. The best that one can say is that torts are legally wrongful acts or omissions. However, to be actionable it is not enough that an act or omission as a matter of fact harms another person's interests in some way. The wrong must also interfere with some legal right of the complaining party.

1.03 The various categories of tortious rights provide the basis for assessing when actionable interference has occurred and when a legal remedy is available. But the law does not go so far as to protect parties against all forms of morally reprehensible behaviour, as Lord Atkin described in *Donoghue v Stevenson* [1932] AC 562 at 580:

> 'Acts or omissions which any moral code would censure cannot in a practical world be treated so as to give a right to every person injured by them to demand relief. In this way rules of law arise which limit the range of complaints and the extent of their remedy.'

1.04 A factual situation may give rise to actions in a variety of overlapping torts. Further, the same circumstances may give rise to concurrent claims both in tort and contract (see generally Chapter 2). However, in contrast to the law of contract, which effectively seeks to enforce promises, the interests protected by tort are more diverse. Contractual duties are agreed by the parties themselves, whereas tortious duties are imposed automatically by the general law. Contractual duties are therefore said to be owed *in personam* (i.e. to the other contracting party only), whereas tortious duties may be owed *in rem* (to persons in general).

2 Negligence

2.01 The tort of negligence is concerned with the careless infliction of harm or damage. It has three essential elements, namely (a) the existence of a legal duty of care, (b) a breach of that duty, and (c) consequential damage.

The legal duty to take care

2.02 The concept of the duty of care defines those persons to which another may be liable for his negligent acts or omissions. The traditional approach to defining the situations that give rise to a duty of care was based upon a process of piecemeal extension by analogy with existing cases, rather than on the basis of a general principle. The first notable attempt to elicit a more principled approach occurred in the landmark case of *Donoghue v Stevenson* [1932] AC 562. There, the plaintiff, who was given a bottle of ginger beer by a friend, alleged that she had become ill after drinking it due to the presence of a decomposed snail in the bottle. As the plaintiff had no contractual relationship with the seller, since it was her friend who had purchased it from the shop, she attempted to sue the manufacturer in tort.

2.03 The House of Lords held that a manufacturer of bottled ginger beer (or other articles) did owe the ultimate purchaser or consumer a legal duty to take reasonable care to ensure that it was free from a defect likely to cause injury to health. Therefore in principle the plaintiff had a cause of action against the ginger beer's manufacturer. However, the main significance of the case is contained in Lord Atkin's description of the general concept of the duty of care:

> 'The rule that you are to love your neighbour becomes in law, you must not injure your neighbour: and the lawyer's question, who is my neighbour? receives a restricted reply. You must take reasonable care to avoid acts or omissions which you can reasonably foresee would be likely to injure your neighbour. Who, then, in law is my neighbour? The answer seems to be – persons who are so closely affected by my act that I ought reasonably to have them in contemplation as being so affected when I am directing my mind to the acts or omissions which are called in question.'

2.04 What became known as Lord Atkin's 'neighbour principle' was initially criticised as being too broad, but in time it became accepted and remains today the central concept to an understanding of the tort of negligence. In the 1970s there was a more ambitious development of a general principle of liability in negligence. This was based on a 'two-stage test' derived from the decisions of the House of Lords in *Dorset Yacht Co. Limited v Home Office* [1970] AC 1004 and *Anns v Merton London Borough Council* [1978] AC 728. The first stage involved a consideration of whether there was a reasonable foreseeability of harm to the plaintiff. If so, there would be liability unless, under the second stage, there was some public policy reason to negate it. The piecemeal approach to the recognition of duty of care relationships was now very much in decline.

2.05 The 'two-stage test' represented a very wide application of Lord Atkin's dicta and it was at first applied with enthusiasm. However, increasingly it appeared to many judicial eyes to herald an unwarranted potential extension of liability into situations previously not covered by the tort of negligence. As a result there followed a steady retreat from the acceptance of a general principle of liability back to the traditional emphasis on existing case analogy and the incremental approach to the extension of liability situations. This has manifested itself in the development of a 'three-stage test' involving a consideration of (a) foreseeability of damage, (b) the relationship of neighbourhood or proximity between the parties, and (c) an assessment of whether the situation is one which in all the circumstances the court considers it fair and reasonable for the imposition of a legal duty.

2.06 Thus, in *Caparo Industries v Dickman* [1990] 2 AC 605 Lord Bridge described the judicial rejection since Anns of the ability of a general single principle to provide a practical test as follows:

> '… the concepts of proximity and fairness … are not susceptible of any such precise definition as would be necessary to give them utility as practical tests, but amount in effect to little more than convenient labels to attach to the features of different specific situations which, on a detailed examination of all the circumstances, the law recognises pragmatically as giving rise to a duty of care of a given scope. Whilst recognising, of course, the importance of the underlying general principles common to the whole field of negligence, I think the law has now moved in the direction of attaching greater significance to the more traditional categorisation of distinct and recognisable situations as guides to the existence, the scope and the limits of the varied duties of care which the law imposes.'

2.07 The Anns 'two-stage test' was further undermined by Lord Keith in the important decision of the House of Lords in *Murphy v Brentwood District Council* [1991] AC 398. In relation to the consideration of the duty of care in novel situations Lord Keith commented at p. 461:

> 'As regards the ingredients necessary to establish such a duty in novel situations, I consider that an incremental approach … is to be preferred to the two-stage test.'

2.08 In *Henderson v Merrett Syndicates Ltd* [1995] 2 AC 145 the House of Lords emphasised the central importance of the concept of an 'assumption of responsibility' to the question of whether or not a duty of care in negligence is owed by one party to another. The relationship between this approach and the three stage test has yet to be fully explored by the courts, although at present it is probably best to view the assumption of responsibility approach as a parallel test, or as representing a refinement of the general three stage analysis (as Sir Brian Neil LJ stated in *Bank of Credit and Commerce International (Overseas) Ltd v Price Waterhouse* (No. 2) [1998] PNLR 564). The three stage test has been re-asserted by the House of Lords in *Phelps v Hillingdon LBC* [2001] 2 AC 619 per Lord Slynn at 653. Further in *South Australia Asset Management Corp v York Montague Ltd* [1997] AC 1 the House of Lords also emphasised the need to consider whether the scope of the duty of care (whether in contract or tort) is sufficient to embrace the kind of damage complained of in a particular case.

2.09 However, it should be noted that *Murphy v Brentwood* and most of the cases connected with this retreat from the recognition of a general principle of liability in negligence have been mainly concerned with the duty of care to avoid causing economic loss (for which see Section 2.20 below). In respect of non-economic loss situations, it is suggested that the Anns approach still provides a useful framework for the consideration of the existence of a legal duty of care. There should be little difficulty in considering whether such a duty exists where either damage to the person or property has been occasioned. Although at least conceptually the approach to testing the existence of a duty of care in a given situation is not affected by the kind of harm sustained on the facts of the case under consideration (as explained by the House of Lords in *Marc Rich & Co v Bishop Rock Marine Co. Ltd* [1996] AC 211).

Relationship to any duties existing in the law of contract

2.10 As well as emphasising the importance of the concept of an assumption of responsibility to defining the existence and scope of

any duty of care in the tort, *Henderson v Merrett* also decided that concurrent duties of care in the tort of negligence may be owed by one party to another even if a contract already existed between them. Thus even if an architect has a contract of retainer with his client, he will also owe the client a concurrent duty of care in the tort of negligence (but see the first instance decision in *Payne v John Setchell* – discussed below – which if correct would lead to a limitation in the extent of any concurrent tortuous duty owed by professionals to their clients).

2.11 Although generally the nature of any tortious duty to take reasonable care against causing damage to the other party is likely to be co-terminous with the implied contractual duty to take reasonable care in the provision of services under their contract (see, for example, *Storey v Charles Church Developments Ltd* [1996] 12 Const LJ 206), the contents of the parties' contract may create stricter contractual duties than are owed in the general law of negligence, or, alternatively, the circumstances of the parties relationship may, in extreme situations, lead to the creation of wider tortious duties than have been created by the contract of retainer (see in the context of a surveyor's negligence action *Holt v Payne Skillington* [1995] 77 BLR 51).

Breach of duty

2.12 In general a person acts in breach of a duty of care when behaving carelessly. As Alderson J stated in *Blyth v Birmingham Waterworks Company* [1856] 11 Ex 781:

> 'Negligence is the omission to do something which a reasonable man, guided upon those considerations which ordinarily regulate the conduct of human affairs, would do, or doing something which a prudent and reasonable man would not do.'

2.13 The standard of care required, then, is that of the reasonable and prudent man; the elusive 'man on the Clapham omnibus'. It is not a counsel of perfection and mere error does not necessarily amount to negligence. The standard applied is objective in that it does not take account of an individual's particular weaknesses. However, where a person holds himself out as having a special skill or being a professional (such as an architect), the standard of care expected of him is higher than one would expect of a layman. He is under a duty to exercise the standard of care in his activities which could reasonably be expected from a competent member of that trade or profession, whatever his actual level of experience or qualification. In the case of architects (as with other professionals) the test is whether there is a responsible body of architects that could have acted as the architect being criticised has (see *Nye Saunders v Bristow* [1987] 37 BLR 92 per Stephen Brown LJ at 103). In general the duty owed by construction professionals is unaffected by the relative experience or inexperience of their clients (see *Gloucestershire Health Authority v Torpy* [1997] CILL 1281). In contrast, however, there are also circumstances where the law accepts a lower standard of care from people, such as at times of emergency or dilemma (or, outside the field of professional negligence, generally in the level of care expected from children).

2.14 The value of the concept of 'reasonable care' lies in its flexibility. What will be considered by a court as 'reasonable' depends on the specific facts of a particular case and the attitude of the judge. Precedent is seldom cited or useful in this respect. However, in general the assessment of reasonableness involves a consideration of three main factors: (a) the degree of likelihood of harm, (b) the cost and practicability of measures to avoid it, and (c) the seriousness of the possible consequences. The application and balancing of these factors is best illustrated by reference to actual cases.

2.15 In *Brewer v Delo* [1967] 1 LIR 488, a case which involved a golfer hitting another player with a golf ball, it was held that the risk was so slight as to be unforeseeable and therefore the golfer had not acted negligently. Similarly in *Bolton v Stone* [1951] AC 850 the occupiers of a cricket ground were held not to be liable for a cricket ball that had left the pitch and struck the plaintiff because of the improbability of such an incident occurring. Finally, in

The Wagon Mound (No. 2) [1967] 1 AC 617, crude oil escaped from a ship onto the surface of the water in Sydney Harbour. It subsequently caught fire and caused substantial damage to a wharf and two ships. However, notwithstanding expert evidence that the risk of the oil catching fire had been very small, it was held that the defendants were negligent in not taking steps to abate what was nevertheless a real risk and one which, if it occurred, was very likely to cause substantial damage.

Damage must be caused by the breach

2.16 In order to establish liability in negligence it is necessary to prove that the careless conduct has caused actual damage. There are three requirements in this process. The first is that, on the balance of probabilities, there must as a matter of fact be a connection between the negligent conduct and the damage (causation in fact). The second is that the harm or damage caused is of a kind that was a foreseeable consequence of such conduct (causation in law). The third overarching requirement is that the breach of duty be the 'dominant and effective' cause of the loss. This latter test really represents the application of judicial common sense to cases which satisfy the first two requirements, but nevertheless involve losses which should not be recognised as caused as a matter of law by the relevant breach of duty under consideration.

2.17 Foreseeability of harm therefore plays a role in all three constituents of the tort of negligence: duty of care, breach and damage. In certain respects this makes a separate consideration of these factors artificial. However, foreseeability of damage has a slightly different application when considering the causation of actionable damage. In assessing the existence and breach of a duty of care, it is the reasonable foreseeability of a risk of some damage that is being considered. Foreseeability of the occurrence of a particular kind of damage does not affect the existence of this duty or the assessment of carelessness, but it does dictate whether the damage that has been caused is actionable in law.

2.18 If the kind of damage actually caused was not foreseeable, there is no liability in negligence. However, as long as the kind of damage is reasonably foreseeable there will be potential liability even if the factual manner in which it was caused was extremely unusual and unforeseeable in itself. In *Hughes v Lord Advocate* [1963] AC 837 workmen left a manhole overnight covered by a tent and surrounded by paraffin lamps, but otherwise unguarded. The eight-year-old plaintiff ventured into the tent, fell down the manhole, dragged some of the lamps down with him and thereby caused an explosion which caused him to be severely burned. The House of Lords held that although the manner of the explosion was highly unusual, the source of the danger and kind of damage that materialized (i.e. burns from the lit paraffin) were reasonably foreseeable and therefore the workmen were liable.

2.19 As noted above, however, it is sometimes simplistic to view the law of causation as simply a consideration of the first two requirements outlined in paragraph 2.14 above. The courts may apply a less precise test of judicial common sense to distinguish between the effective cause of a loss from conduct which merely provides the occasion for it (as applied by the Court of Appeal in *Galoo v Bright Grahame Murray* [1994] 1 WLR 1360). Ultimately this factor reflects the reality that judicial policy can play as important role in deciding where responsibility for losses should fall (on the professional, his client or a third party) as any easily definable rules or principles of law.

Economic loss

(a) Introduction

2.20 Economic loss is a category of non-physical damage. It consists of financial losses (such as lost profits), as opposed to personal injury or physical damage to property. Unfortunately, as well as being an area of the utmost practical importance for architects, the concept of a duty of care to prevent economic loss is also one of the more demanding aspects of the law of tort.

2.21 The tort of negligence originally developed in the late nineteenth and early twentieth centuries as a cause of action for a party who had been physically injured by the careless acts of another. It also quickly developed into a remedy for careless damage to property. However, the attempt from about the 1960s (associated with the developing concept of a general principle of liability in negligence described above) to extend its ambit to economic losses generally has been largely unsuccessful. Today, economic loss is not always irrecoverable, but it requires a claimant to prove the exceptional circumstances necessary in order to establish that a defendant owed him a duty not to cause such damage. This long-standing reluctance to recognise a duty of care to prevent economic loss has been largely based on what is referred to as the 'floodgates' argument – the concern that it would widen the potential scale of liability in tort to an indeterminable extent.

(b) Distinguishing consequential and pure economic loss

2.22 Although there is no general liability for economic loss which is disassociated from physical damage, economic loss consequential to damage to property is treated separately and is generally recoverable. The distinction between such 'consequential' economic loss and 'pure' economic loss is not always clear. Perhaps the best illustration is provided by the case of *Spartan Steel and Alloys Ltd v Martin & Co. (Contractors Ltd)* [1973] 1 QB 27. In this case the defendants negligently cut off an electricity cable which supplied the plaintiff's factory. As a result some of the plaintiff's molten metal that was being worked upon at the factory was damaged, causing the plaintiff to make a smaller profit on its eventual sale. Production was also delayed generally at the factory and the plaintiff lost the opportunity to make profits on this lost production. It was held that although the economic loss caused by the general delay in production was not recoverable (being pure economic loss), the lost profit from the molten metal actually in production at the time of the power cut was recoverable as it was immediately consequential to the physical damage to the molten metal itself. This was because, economic loss immediately consequential to damage to property is recoverable in negligence.

(c) Liability for negligent statements

2.23 The first exception to the general rule of there being no duty to avoid causing pure economic loss was provided in the area of negligent mis-statement and the line of authorities following *Hedley Byrne & Co. Ltd v Heller & Partners* [1963] AC 465. In this seminal case, the defendants gave a favourable financial reference to the plaintiff's bankers in respect of one of the plaintiff's clients. The plaintiff relied on this incorrect reference and as a result suffered financial losses when the client became insolvent. The House of Lords held that a defendant would be liable for such negligent mis-statements if: (a) there was a 'special relationship' based upon an assumption of responsibility between the parties, (b) the defendant knew or ought to have known that the plaintiff was likely to rely upon his statement, and (c) in all the circumstances it was reasonable for the plaintiff to so rely on the defendant's statement.

2.24 In accordance with the retreat from an acceptance of a general principle of liability in negligence and, in particular, its extension to economic loss generally, the circumstances where the courts will now recognise the required 'special relationship' may have narrowed since the 1970s. In *Caparo v Dickman* [1990] 2 AC 605 the House of Lords held that auditors of a company's financial reports did not owe a duty of care to prospective share purchasers to avoid negligent mis-statements because, unlike a company's existing shareholders, the parties were not in a relationship of sufficient proximity. Liability for economic loss caused by negligent mis-statement was to be restricted to situations where the statement was given to a known recipient for a specific purpose of which the maker of the statement was aware.

2.25 This represented a narrow interpretation of the *Hedley Byrne* principle consistent with the revival of the incremental approach to liability discussed in paragraph 2.06 above. Although there is now authority for the need to emphasise a more flexible concept of 'assumption of responsibility' as the basis for potential liability (see paragraph 2.33 below), it is submitted that these restrictive criteria will probably continue to be applied by the courts.

2.26 Liability for negligent mis-statement may be of relevance to architects when giving their clients advice, for example in relation to cost estimates or which builders to use. In *Nye Saunders v Bristow* [1987] 37 BLR 92 although there was no allegation of defective work, the architect was found to be in breach of a *Hedley Byrne* type duty by not advising his client as to the possible effect of inflation on his estimate for the cost of proposed works.

(d) Liability for negligent conduct

2.27 In contrast to the position with negligent statements, the attempt in a number of leading cases since the 1970s to extend liability for pure economic loss to negligent conduct has largely failed. The initial momentum for such an extension was provided by *Anns v Merton* which concerned structural damage in a building that had been caused by defective foundations. The House of Lords allowed the recovery in tort of the pure economic loss caused by the need to carry out repairs so that the property was no longer a threat to health and safety.

2.28 However, in its recent decisions in *Murphy v Brentwood District Council* [1991] 1AC 398 and *Department of the Environment v Thomas Bates & Sons Ltd* [1991] 1AC 499 the House of Lords has overruled *Anns v Merton*. The facts of *Murphy v Brentwood* also concerned a house which had been built on improper foundations allegedly due to the Council's negligence in passing the building plans. It was held that the Council did not owe a duty in tort to the owner or purchaser of property in respect of the costs of remedying such defects in the property. The repair costs were held to be pure economic loss and irrecoverable, whether or not the defects amounted to a threat to health or safety.

2.29 There were two main reasons for the decision in *Murphy v Brentwood*. First, it was considered established law that in tort the manufacturer of a chattel owed no duty in respect of defects that did not cause personal injury or damage to other property. Thus, in *Donoghue v Stevenson* (see paragraphs 2.02 and 2.03 above) the defendant was not liable for the diminution in value of the bottle of ginger beer by reason of the presence of a decomposed snail in it. Mrs Donoghue could only recover damages against the manufacturer in respect of the physical harm caused to her by drinking it. Therefore, the defective house in *Murphy v Brentwood* was effectively considered analogous to the bottle of ginger beer in *Donoghue v Stevenson*: their Lordships held that it would be anomalous in principle if someone involved in the construction of a building should be in any different position from the manufacturer of bottled ginger beer or any other chattel.

2.30 The second main justification was that innovation in the law of consumer protection against defects in the quality of products should be left to Parliament, especially in the light of the remedies provided by the Defective Premises Act 1972 in the case of residential dwellings (for which see Section 3 below).

2.31 This latter justification is not very convincing since most decisions in this field, including *Donoghue v Stevenson* itself, can be viewed as essentially judicially created consumer-protection law in any case. However, it does illustrate the influence of judicial policy in the court's approach to the recognition of a duty of care in novel situations. Further, although *Murphy v Brentwood* has certainly simplified the law in this area, there remain recognized exceptions to the general rule against the existence of a duty of care to prevent economic loss in negligence.

(e) Exceptions to Murphy v Brentwood

2.32 First, the position in respect of economic loss consequential to physical damage and negligent mis-statements remains unaffected by the decision (see paragraph 2.20 above).

2.33 In addition, in *Murphy v Brentwood* their Lordships recognised that damage to a building caused by defects in a discrete part of it could in certain circumstances be recoverable in tort. Under the pre-*Murphy v Brentwood* 'complex structure theory' the individual parts of a building (such as the foundations, walls or roof) could be treated as distinct items of property. Therefore liability for damage caused to, say, the roof by a defect in the foundations could be justified by treating the building as a complex structure and depicting the damaged roof as a separate piece of damaged property. This analysis was proposed as a means of reconciling the post-*Anns v Merton* recognition of liability in negligence for defective premises with the established principle that there is no tortious liability for defective products.

2.34 In *Murphy v Brentwood* their Lordships rejected the complex structure theory and viewed the damaged house as a single piece of property (i.e. not a complex structure). However, they have left open the possibility of liability in the normal way where the item within a building that causes the damage is a distinct one (perhaps a faulty electrical fuse box which causes a fire) and is built or installed by a separate party from the builder. If damage is caused by such a 'non-integral' part of the building, it may be considered as damage caused to separate property (which under normal principles would be actionable damage in negligence). Therefore, in place of the complex structure analysis, their Lordships appear to have left a more restrictive 'non-integral piece of property' theory as a possible basis for continuing liability in tort for defective premises (see also *Jacob v Morton* [1994] 72 BLR 92 and *Bellefield Computer Services Ltd v E Turner & Sons Limited* [2000] BLR 97 for an analysis of this exception).

2.35 This concept is illustrated by the case of *Nitrigin Eireann Teoranta v Inco Alloys* [1992] 1 All ER 854. The defendants had manufactured and supplied the plaintiff's factory with some alloy tubing in 1981 which had developed cracks by 1983. It was held that although the cracked tubing in 1983 constituted pure economic loss (because at this time there was no damage to other property), damage to the factory caused by an explosion in 1984 (itself caused by the continuing weakness in the tubing) did give rise to a cause of action in negligence. The structure of the factory surrounding the tubing was considered to be separate property and therefore this damage was not pure economic loss.

2.36 Two other bases for liability in negligence for defective premises have, in theory, survived the decision in *Murphy v Brentwood*, although their application in practice is extremely unlikely. First, Lord Bridge suggested that there may be a duty to prevent economic loss where the defective building is so close to its boundary that by reason of its defects the building might cause physical damage or injury to persons on neighbouring land or the highway. However, finding liability in these circumstances would appear to contradict the reasoning in the rest of their Lordships' judgments in *Murphy v Brentwood*. It is submitted that the better view is that the cost of repairing such defects would still be irrecoverable in negligence as it amounts to pure economic loss. However, until this point is clarified by future decisions it will remain a possible, if unlikely, basis for such liability.

2.37 Second, there is the anomalous case of *Junior Books v Veitchi & Co.* [1983] 1 AC 520 which the House of Lords could not bring itself to overrule in addition to *Anns v Merton*. In *Junior Books* the defendants were specialist floor sub-contractors who were engaged by main contractors to lay a floor in the factory of the plaintiff, with whom they had no formal contract. The floor subsequently cracked up and the plaintiff sued for the cost of relaying it. The House of Lords held that on the particular facts of the case, there was such a close relationship between the parties that the defendants' duty to take care to the plaintiff extended to preventing economic loss due to defects in their laying of the floor. This decision at first appears completely contradictory to the reasoning in *Murphy v Brentwood*, although some of their Lordships sought to explain it as a special application of the *Hedley Byrne* principle. One view is that *Junior Books* will continue to be considered as an anomalous case decided very much on its own facts, and not one that establishes as a matter of principle a further category of exceptions from the main decision in *Murphy v Brentwood*.

(f) The effect of Henderson v Merrett

2.38 However, an alternative interpretation is now possible in the light of Lord Goff's landmark judgment in the decision of the House of Lords in *Henderson v Merrett Syndicates Limited* [1994] 3 WLR 761. Here their Lordships unanimously held that a concurrent duty of care was owed in tort by managing agents to Lloyd's names notwithstanding the existence of a contractual relationship between them. The decision therefore established that concurrent duties in tort may exist between parties in a contractual relationship. However of more significance in the present context are Lord Goff's comments on the ambit of the duty of care in tort under the *Hedley Byrne* principle.

2.39 In addition to characterizing the basis of such liability as being the voluntary assumption of responsibility by one party to another, Lord Goff also interpreted the *Hedley Byrne* principle as applying to the provision of professional services generally, whether by words or actions. Thus at p. 776 of his judgment he concludes:

'... the concept provides its own explanation why there is no problem in cases of this kind about liability for pure economic loss: for if a person assumes responsibility to another in respect of certain services, there is no reason why he should not be liable in damages for that other in respect of economic loss which flows from the negligent performance of those services. It follows that, once the case is identified as falling within the *Hedley Byrne* principle, there should be no need to embark upon any further enquiry whether it is 'fair, just and reasonable' to impose liability for economic loss – a point which is, I consider, of some importance in the present case.'

2.40 This represents a major conceptual extension of the category of conduct in which the courts may recognise a duty to prevent causing economic loss. Although it is not as yet clear how the courts will apply Lord Goff's judgment in this respect (and in particular its relationship to the decision in *Murphy v Brentwood*), it is submitted that the courts will probably expressly recognise from now on liability for economic losses caused by the negligent actions of professionals if there is a *Hedley Byrne* type special relationship with/assumption of responsibility toward the party suffering damage. Invariably, of course, this will be the case where there is a contractual relationship between an architect and his client.

2.41 However the tension between the decisions in *Murphy v Brentwood* and *Henderson v Merrett* has become most clear in the case of liability in tort for defective building works. It is not easy to rationalise the apparent difference of approach in the authorities toward the builder who carries out as part of his services in constructing a wall a negligent design function (and who may well therefore be liable on *Hedley Byrne* principles) and a builder who does not carry out any design function (and who therefore would not normally be considered to be liable in tort for any defects in the wall itself on the basis of *Murphy v Brentwood*). In both situations the builder provides a service and could well be said to have assumed responsibility for the competency of his work in a *Henderson v Merrett* sense.

2.42 This apparent dichotomy between the law's approach to the liability of a simple builder compared to a design and building contractor or a construction professional has been grappled with at first instance in the decision in *Payne v John Setchell Ltd* [2002] BLR 48. Here it was held (rather surprisingly it is suggested) that both construction professionals (such as architects) and building contractors may only be under a duty of care in tort to take reasonable care against causing their contractual clients personal injury or damage to property *other than the building/item of work that is the subject matter of their services*. Thus, the dichotomy was resolved in this case by a finding that neither the contractor nor the construction

professional should owe a duty of care in the ordinary course of events in respect of defects in quality to the product of their work or services.

2.43 It is suggested that this approach is probably wrong as it appears to rest upon the assumption that *Murphy v Brentwood* is authority for the proposition that a building contractor can *never* owe his client a duty of care in tort in respect of the quality of his work. However, *Murphy v Brentwood* did not directly decide this point, rather it dealt with the responsibility in tort of a local authority in respect of such defects. The better position in the light of *Henderson v Merrett* would appear to be that if a building contractor can be taken on the facts of a particular case to have assumed responsibility toward his client for his work a tortious duty in respect of the quality of that work may arise (for support for this proposition see *Bellefield Computer Services Ltd v E Turner & Sons Ltd* [2000] BLR 96 per Schieman LJ at 102).

(g) Continuing evolution of the law

2.44 Finally, in the light of *Henderson v Merrett* it should be emphasised that *Murphy v Brentwood* does not shut off the possible recognition of new categories of relationships in which a non-contractual duty to avoid causing economic loss will be recognised. For example, in *Punjab National Bank v de Boinville* [1992] 1 WLR 1138 the Court of Appeal held that (a) the relationship between an insurance broker and his client was a recognised exceptional category of case where such a duty existed, and (b) it was, on the facts of the case, a justified extension of this category to hold that a broker owed a like duty to a non-client where the broker knew that the insurance policy was to be assigned to this person and that he had been involved in instructing the broker in the first place.

(h) Conclusion

2.45 In summary, as far as the particular position of professional architects is concerned the consequences of the landmark decisions in *Murphy v Brentwood* and *Henderson v Merrett* are probably as follows:

1. A duty of care in tort will be owed by an architect to his client in relation to economic losses of a similar nature and extent as that created by any contract between the parties.

2. Liability for economic loss claims by third parties (i.e. those not in a contractual relationship with the architect) for defective work (subject to the existence of a *Hedley Byrne* relationship or assumption of responsibility) has been eliminated.

3. However, potential *Donoghue v Stevenson* type liability for damage caused to other property or the person as a result of such work remains: for example, if a piece of roofing falls off a building due to an architect's negligent design and breaks a person's leg or dents their car (whether or not that person is the owner of the building or a client).

4. The principle at 3 above extends to make an architect potentially liable to subsequent owners of a building in respect of damage caused to other property or the person by latent defects in the building attributable to his negligence (see *Baxall Securities Ltd v Sheard Walshaw Partnership* [2002] BLR 100)

5. There will be a revival of interest in potential liability pursuant to the Defective Premises Act 1972 (see below).

6. Otherwise there will be a re-focusing of attention on possible *Hedley Byrne* relationships/assumption of responsibility as the only other effective basis for liability in tort for defective work to buildings.

7. It is submitted that in practice the existence of a sufficiently proximate relationship to attract such liability between an architect and a client will rarely occur outside contractual relationships.

8. Where there is a relationship of proximity between an architect and his client or third party, the architect will owe a duty of care to prevent causing purely economic losses as a result of careless statements (via negligent designs, certification or advice) and, probably, his conduct and provision of his services in general.

9 An architect may also in appropriate circumstances owe his client or a third party a personal duty of care – distinct from the responsibility assumed by the firm or company for which he works (in the light of *Merrett v Babb* [2001] 3 WLR 1 which was a case where a surveyor was found to have owed his client a personal duty of care in respect of a valuation report prepared for mortgage purposes).

3 The Defective Premises Act 1972

3.01 Section 1 of the Act provides:
'1   A person taking on work for the provision of a dwelling (whether the dwelling is provided by the erection or by the conversion or enlargement of a building) owes a duty –
(a) if the dwelling is provided to the order of any person, to that person; and
(b) without prejudice to paragraph (a) above, to every person who acquires an interest (whether legal or equitable) in the dwelling;
to see that the work which he takes on is done in a workmanlike or, as the case may be, professional manner, with proper materials and so that as regards that work the dwelling will be fit for habitation when completed.'

3.02 All building professionals, including architects, can be 'persons taking on work' pursuant to the Act if the work undertaken is concerned with a dwelling. The duty created by the Act is owed to the person for whom the dwelling is provided, although the main purpose for the act was to confer a right of action on subsequent owners of the dwelling which they would otherwise not have. Although not specified under the Act, the appropriate remedy for breach of its duty is damages. The duty cannot be avoided by exclusion clauses.

3.03 The person undertaking the work is liable not only for his own work, but also for the work of independent sub-contractors employed by him if they are engaged in the course of his business. The reference to a 'dwelling' implies that the Act is limited to property capable of being used as a residence. However, the Act does not apply to remedial work to an existing building. Further, liability under the Act is limited to a period of six years after the completion of the work concerned. This special limitation period provides a major restriction on the potential significance of the Act.

3.04 The Act appears to impose a dual statutory duty to ensure that (a) work is done in a workmanlike manner, and (b) as regards that work the dwelling will be fit for human habitation. It is unclear to what extent the latter requirement restricts liability under the Act for defective work. In *Thompson v Clive Alexander & Partners* [1993] 59 BLR 77 it was held that allegations of defective work alone on the part of an architect were not capable of amounting to a breach of the Act. It was held that the provision regarding fitness for habitation was the measure of the standard required in performance of the duty pursuant to section 1(1) and that trivial defects were not intended to be covered by the statute. There is authority to the contrary that suggests that the unfitness for habitation requirement adds nothing to the main one that the work is to be done properly. However, on its proper construction the Act probably does not cover every defective piece of work and something more than trivial defects are required to be in breach of it, although the precise ambit of the duty will have to await further litigation.

3.05 Notwithstanding these restrictions it is likely that liability under the Act will be of greater significance for architects and other building professionals in the future than it has been to date. There are two main reasons for this. First, although the decision in *Murphy v Brentwood* limited liability in negligence for pure economic loss caused to third parties by defective property, such pure economic loss is still recoverable under the Defective Premises Act 1972. Typically claims against architects involve a large proportion of purely economic losses, therefore attention is likely to concentrate in the future on potential liability under the Act.

3.06 Second, the exception to liability created by section 2 of the Act which excludes certain approved building schemes from its provisions is likely to be of less significance in the future. This is because the last NHBC Vendor–Purchaser Insurance scheme to be approved by the Secretary of State as an 'approved scheme' under section 2 was in 1979. However, some time before 1988 the NHBC and the Secretary of State agreed that due to changes in the 1979 approved scheme it was no longer effective. No further scheme has been approved. Thus, there is potentially a large amount of post-1979 building work that will no longer be caught by section 2 and will now be subject to the Act's duties.

4 Nuisance

4.01 The tort of nuisance is concerned with the unjustified interference with a party's use of land. Whether activity which may as a matter of fact be a considerable nuisance to an individual is actionable in law depends, as in the case of the tort of negligence, on a consideration of all the circumstances of the case and the proof of consequential actionable damage. Although most nuisances arise out of a continuing state of affairs, an isolated occurrence can be sufficient if physical damage is caused.

4.02 There are two varieties of actionable nuisance; public and private. A public nuisance is one that inflicts damage, annoyance or inconvenience on a class of persons or persons generally. It is a criminal offence and only actionable in tort if an individual member of the public has suffered some particular kind of foreseeable damage to a greater extent than the public at large, or where some private right has also been interfered with. Examples of public nuisances can include selling food unfit for human consumption, causing dangerous obstructions to the highway, and (by way of statutory nuisances) water and atmospheric pollution.

4.03 A private nuisance is an unlawful act which interferes with a party's use or enjoyment of land or of some right connected with it. Traditionally interference with enjoyment of land in which the claimant had some kind of proprietary interest was one of the defining characteristics of a private nuisance. However, in *Khorasandjian v Bush* [1993] QB 727 a majority of the Court of Appeal granted an injunction against the defendant to prevent him telephoning the plaintiff at her mother's home (in which she was staying as a mere licensee with no proprietary interest). This decision may in time be seen as the precursor of a wider concept of actionable nuisance amounting to a general tort of harassment, and possibly the beginning of a tort of invasion of privacy. At present, however, it is submitted that the decision is best seen as a narrow extension of the availability of an action in private nuisance to interference with the enjoyment of premises at which the plaintiff lives, whether or not pursuant to a proprietary interest in the property itself. It is possible however that the requirement for a claimant to have a legal interest in land before making a claim in nuisance may have been further eroded by Article 8 of the Human Rights Act 1998 (see *McKenna v British Aluminium Ltd*, The Times 25 April 2002 and *Marcic v Thams Water Utilities Ltd* [2002] 2 AllER 55).

4.04 A private nuisance consists of a party doing some act which is not limited to his own land but affects another party's occupation of land, by either: (a) causing an encroachment onto the neighbouring land (for example, when trees overhang it or tree roots grow into the neighbouring land), (b) causing physical damage to the land or buildings (such as when there is an emission of smoke or other fumes which damage his neighbour's crops or property), or (c) causing an unreasonable interference with a neighbour's enjoyment of his land (such as causing too much noise or obnoxious smells to pass over it).

4.05 The actual or prospective infliction of damage is a necessary ingredient of an actionable nuisance. In a nuisance of the kind at (a) damage is presumed once the encroachment is proved. In (b) there must be proof of actual or prospective physical damage. Therefore in both these cases the requirement of damage is an objective test which does not involve a further examination of the surrounding circumstances. In nuisances of the kind at (c), however, there is no objective standard applied by the courts. Whether the acts complained of amount to the unreasonable use of land is a question of degree. The nuisance needs to amount to a material interference with the use of other land that an average man (with no particular susceptibilities or special interests) would consider unreasonable in all the circumstances of the particular case. The essence of this kind of nuisance is something coming onto or encroaching onto the claimant's land (see *Hunter v Canary Wharf Limited* [1997] AC 655 and *Anglian Water Services v Crawshaw Robins & Co* [2001] BLR 173).

4.06 The duration and timing of the acts complained of is a relevant factor in this balancing of neighbours' interests. So too is the character of the locality. In *Sturges v Bridgman* [1879] 11 ChD 852 at 856 Thesiger LJ put it as follows:

'… whether anything is a nuisance or not is a question to be determined, not merely by an abstract consideration of the thing itself, but in reference to its circumstances: what would be a nuisance in Belgrave Square would not necessarily be so in Bermondsey; and where a locality is devoted to a particular trade or manufacture carried on by the traders or manufacturers in a particular and established manner not constituting a public nuisance, judges … would be justified in finding … that the trade or manufacture so carried on in that locality is not a private or actionable wrong.'

4.07 The conduct of the defendant may also be a relevant factor. In *Hollywood Silver Fox Farm Ltd v Emmett* [1936] 2 KB 468 the defendant maliciously encouraged his son to fire shotguns on his own land but as near as possible to the plaintiff's adjoining property in order to disrupt his business of breeding silver foxes. Although entitled to shoot on his own land, the Court held that the defendant was nevertheless creating a nuisance. The Court held that the defendant's intention to alarm the plaintiff's foxes was a relevant factor in reaching this conclusion and specifically limited the injunction granted against the defendant to prevent the making of loud noises so as to alarm the plaintiff's foxes. Similarly, it is a nuisance if a person deliberately uses his land in a manner which he knows will cause an unreasonable interference with another's, whether or not he believes that he is entitled to do the act or has taken all reasonable steps (short of not doing the act itself) to prevent it amounting to a nuisance.

4.08 Traditionally it was accepted that outside this kind of conduct nuisance had an uncertain overlap with the tort of negligence. There were some situations in which it involved negligent behaviour and others where this was not considered a requirement for liability. As Lord Reid rather confusingly put it in *The Wagon Mound* (No. 2):

'It is quite true that negligence is not an essential element in nuisance. Nuisance is a term used to cover a wide variety of tortious acts or omissions and in many negligence in the narrow sense is not essential … although negligence may not be necessary, fault of some kind is almost always necessary and fault generally involves foreseeability.'

4.09 Not surprisingly, a degree of confusion has been introduced by this distinction between negligence, on the one hand, and the requirement of some kind of fault, incorporating the concept of foreseeability, on the other. It is now established that liability in nuisance is not strict and that foreseeability of damage is a necessary ingredient (see *Leaky v National Trust* [1980] QB 485). However, the requirement of foreseeability of damage does not necessarily imply the need for negligent conduct, but may sometimes only be relevant to what kind of damage will be actionable. Further, the concept of 'fault' in nuisance is better viewed as unreasonable conduct (which is the essence of the tort) and may not always amount to negligent conduct (in the sense used in the tort of negligence). (see *Cambridge Water Co Ltd v Eastern Counties Leather Plc* [1994] 2 AC 264 and *Jan de Nul (UK) v NV Royal Belge* [2000] 2 Lloyd's Rep 700).

4.10 Although increasingly the distinction between negligence and nuisance has become blurred (and in practice they have to a large extent become assimilated) they are not synonymous in principle. The following points should be emphasised: (a) where the nuisance is the interference with a natural right incidental to land ownership (such as the right to obtain water from a well) then liability is strict, (b) the act complained of may constitute the required 'unreasonable user' of land to constitute a nuisance without necessarily amounting to 'negligent' behaviour, (c) economic loss is generally recoverable in nuisance, (d) some kinds of damage recognised and protected in nuisance (such as creating an unreasonable noise or smell, or harassment such as in *Khorasandjian v Bush* above) would not amount to actionable damage in the tort of negligence, and (e) the remedy of an injunction is available to prevent an anticipated or continuing nuisance, but not to prevent someone acting negligently.

5 The rule in *Rylands v Fletcher*

5.01 An example of strict liability in tort (which does not require the proof of negligence or intent on the part of the wrongdoer) is the rule as stated by Blackburn J in *Rylands v Fletcher* [1866] LR 1 Ex 265 at 279:

'We think that the true rule of law is, that the person who for his own purposes brings on his land and collects and keeps there anything likely to do mischief if it escapes must keep it in at his peril, and, if he does not do so, is prima facie answerable for all the damage which is the natural consequence of its escape.'

5.02 In the House of Lords the rule was limited to apply only to the 'non-natural user' of land. The courts have failed to clarify precisely what non-natural user of land consists of and in what particular circumstances the rule should apply. However, it has been applied to water, fire, explosives, poison, and, in *Hale v Jennings Brothers* [1938] 1 All ER 579, to a seat becoming detached from a high-speed fairground roundabout. In general, the rule is applicable where a person brings onto his land something that is 'dangerous', in the sense that if the thing escapes from the land it would be likely to cause either personal or physical damage.

5.03 There are various specific defences available to *Rylands v Fletcher* liability, namely (a) that the escape of the dangerous thing was caused by an Act of God, (b) that it was caused by the independent act of a stranger (though not an independent contractor), or the claimant himself, (c) that the claimant has consented to the dangerous thing being kept on the defendant's land, and (d) that the dangerous thing has been stored pursuant to some statutory duty (in which case negligence must be established on the part of the defendant).

5.04 The tendency of the courts to adopt a very restrictive interpretation of what was considered as non-natural use of land and therefore a limited application of *Rylands v Fletcher* was considered in *Cambridge Water Co. Ltd v Eastern Counties Leather Plc* [1994] 2 AC 264. In its first consideration of the rule for over half a century, the House of Lords took the view that the rule should be seen as no more than an extension of the law of nuisance to cases of isolated escapes from land.

5.05 Although the House of Lords considered that the concept of non-natural user had been unjustifiably extended by the courts, a restrictive interpretation of the rule was nevertheless confirmed as it found that foreseeability of harm of the relevant type was a prerequisite to liability under the rule (as in the case of nuisance). In an approach reminiscent of the House of Lords' attitude in *Murphy v Brentwood* to economic loss, the imposition of no-fault liability for all damage caused by operations of high risk was considered a more appropriate role for parliamentary, not judicial, intervention.

5.06 As in the case of nuisance it has been held that it is arguable that a claimant need not have a proprietary interest in the land affected

to bring a claim under the rule in *Rylands v Fletcher* (see *McKenna v British Aluminium Ltd*, The Times 25 April 2002). However, unlike the tort of nuisance, pure economic losses are irrecoverable under this rule (see *Anglian Water Services v Crawshaw Robins & Co* [2001] BLR 173 at para 149).

6 Trespass

6.01 Trespass to the person involves an interference, however slight, with a person's right to the security of his body. It can be of three varieties: (a) a 'battery' which is caused by unlawful physical contact, (b) an 'assault' which is where the innocent party is caused to fear the immediate infliction of such contact, and (c) 'false imprisonment' which involves the complete deprivation of liberty without proper cause for any period of time.

6.02 The tort of trespass to land involves any unjustifiable entry upon land in possession of another, however temporary or minor the intrusion. It is also a trespass to leave, place or throw anything onto another party's land, although if the material passes onto that party's land pursuant to the defendant exercising his own proprietary rights it is a nuisance. Unlike nuisance or negligence trespass is actionable without proof of damage, although if consequential harm or losses are thereby caused damages are recoverable. Ignorance of the law or the fact of trespass provides no defence for a trespasser.

6.03 As far as architects and building professionals are concerned, even the smallest infringements may be actionable. Thus setting foot without permission on land adjoining the property where work is being conducted will constitute a trespass, as will allowing equipment or other material to rest against, hang over, fall upon or be thrown over adjoining land. However, it should be emphasized that trespass is only a civil wrong which involves no automatic criminal liability in the absence of aggravating circumstances (such as criminal damage).

7 Breach of statutory duty

7.01 Breach of a duty imposed by statute may lead to civil liability in tort. There is a vast array of statutory duties covering a wide variety of activities. In any particular case, however, in order to establish civil liability for breach of the statutory duty the claimant must prove: (a) that he is part of the class of persons intended to be protected by the statute, (b) that the loss or damage he has suffered is of a kind intended to be prevented under the statute, (c) that there is no express provision in the statute that civil liability is not created by a breach of its provisions, (d) that on the balance of probabilities his injury, loss or damage was caused by the breach of statutory duty, and (e) that there has been a breach of the relevant statutory duty by the defendant.

7.02 Some statutory duties are akin to the duty of care in the tort of negligence and are based upon what is considered to be reasonable behaviour in all the circumstances of the case. Others, notably in the field of health and safety in the workplace, impose strict liability for damage caused in certain circumstances. The Consumer Protection Act 1987, in response to an EEC directive, even extended statutory strict liability in certain circumstances into the field of defective domestic consumer products (the very area which gave birth to Lord Atkin's 'neighbour principle' in *Donoghue v Stevenson*).

7.03 As far as architects are concerned, the most important statutory duties are those imposed by the Defective Premises Act 1972 (which has been discussed above) and the Occupier's Liability Acts of 1957 and 1984. These impose duties on the occupiers of land (which an architect could be considered as if supervising a building project) in respect of consensual and non-consensual visitors to the land not unlike those owed at common law in the tort of negligence. There is probably no civil liability, however, for breaches of the Building Act 1984 and its associated Building Regulations.

8 Inducing breach of contract/wrongful interference with contract

8.01 It is possible that in exercising a contract administration function (in certifying payments for example) an architect could be accused by a disappointed contractor (or conceivably an employer) of the tort of inducing a breach of contract or wrongful interference with contract.

8.02 In order to succeed in such an action a claimant would however have to establish more than just an error or a negligent error in the certification process – it would need to be established that the architect had deliberately misapplied the relevant provisions of the building contract with the intention of depriving the contractor/employer of a benefit that they would otherwise have been entitled to (see *Lubenham Fidelities & Investment Co Ltd v South Pembrokeshire District Council* [1986] 6 Con LR 85).

9 Limitation periods

9.01 To avoid against the risk of stale claims being litigated as a matter of public policy the law imposes time limits within which causes of action must be commenced if they are to remain actionable. The law aims to give claimants a reasonable opportunity to bring claims and defendants the assurance that the threat of liability will not be eternal and that any claim that they may have to face will not be so old as to prejudice the fairness of any proceedings. The two statutes that govern these time limits are The Limitation Act 1980 and The Latent Damage Act 1986.

9.02 Section 2 of the Limitation Act 1980 provides for tortious actions a prima facie limitation period of six years from the accrual of the cause of action. However, in personal injury cases the period is three years. Therefore when damage is an essential ingredient in liability (such as in negligence), time begins to run from the date that damage occurs. If further damage occurs subsequently, then in respect of the additional damage time will run from this later date. If there is a trespass, libel or other act which in itself amounts to an actionable tort, time begins to run from the date of the act itself. In the cases of continuing torts therefore (such as nuisance or trespass) the limitation period begins on each repetition of the wrong. In calculating whether the limitation period has expired, the date on which the cause of action accrues is normally excluded and the date on which the action is commenced is included.

9.03 However, these prima facie limitation periods may not be applicable in certain exceptional circumstances. In relation to personal injuries cases, section 33 of the Limitation Act 1980 provides the court with a general discretion to disapply the primary limitation period of three years if it considers it reasonable to do so. Further, section 32 provides that in a case where either: (a) there has been fraud by the defendant, or (b) any fact relevant to the

claimant's cause of action has been deliberately concealed from him by the defendant, or (c) the action is for relief from the consequences of mistake, the limitation period shall not begin to run until the claimant has discovered this fraud, concealment or mistake, or until he could with reasonable diligence have done so. In building cases section 32 may become relevant where a party deliberately conceals negligent design or construction work by building over and hiding defects.

9.04 The common law rule that the cause of action in negligence accrues when damage is caused creates serious difficulties in construction cases. Often damage which is caused in the process of building works is not discovered until some time after the building is completed. However, in *Pirelli General Cable Works v Oscar Faber* [1983] 2 AC 1 the House of Lords held that a cause of action for negligent advice by an engineer in connection with the design of a chimney accrued when damage, in the form of cracks in the chimney, first occurred. The fact that they may only become reasonably discoverable some time later was held not to be relevant. This approach left open the possibility of claimants becoming statute barred before they had a means of knowing that a cause of action actually existed.

9.05 The perceived injustice of this rule was addressed in the Latent Damage Act 1986. The Act modifies the limitation period for claims other than for personal injuries in the tort of negligence. The period should either be six years from the date that the cause of action accrued (on the basis of the *Pirelli* test for the time of damage), or, if this expires later, three years from the time the claimant knew certain material facts about the damage. This latter period is subject to a longstop provision expiring 15 years from the date of the negligent act or omission.

9.06 Regrettably, this has not entirely clarified matters. There remains the question of what constitutes damage in the first place. In *Pirelli* the House of Lords decided (save possibly in a case where a defect were so serious that the building was effectively predisposed to subsequent physical manifestation of damage) that there was actionable damage only when there were actual cracks in the chimney. The difficulty with this proposition is reconciling it with the House of Lords' decision in *Murphy v Brentwood*. As we have seen, there it was held that damage of the kind which occurred in *Pirelli* was really economic loss, not physical damage, and therefore no longer recoverable. However, their Lordships also rather confusingly approved the previous decision in *Pirelli* which suggests that if there is liability in negligence for defectively constructed buildings (which could now probably only be pursuant to a *Hedley Byrne* relationship or one where damage is caused by a non-integral item in the building) the time for the accrual of the cause of action for limitation purposes starts at the time physical damage first occurs.

9.07 In practice, in defective building cases the courts have tended to apply this 'manifestation of physical damage' test for deciding when a cause of action in tort accrues. However, it is submitted that the post-*Murphy v Brentwood* characterisation of defective building work as economic loss (which logically may be present before there is any physical manifestation of it) is irreconcilable with the *Pirelli* test. Either such economic loss is suffered at the date on which the negligent service which caused it was relied upon (which would probably be an earlier date than the date of its physical manifestation) or it occurs at the date that the 'market' is able objectively to recognise and measure the financial scale of the loss suffered (which would suggest a later date for the accrual of the cause of action, namely the date of discoverability of the physical manifestation of defects by the market). It is submitted that the earlier 'date of reliance' test will probably in due course be adopted as the most consistent position.

9.08 However in *Invercargill City Council v Hamlin* [1996] AC 624 the Privy Council, in declining to follow the approach in *Pirelli*, held that the cause of action in negligence associated with the defective construction of foundations (similar to the facts of

Murphy v Brentwood) accrued when the market value of the house fell as a result of the defects complained of, i.e. only once the market reflected the loss that had been suffered. In contrast, in an analogous case called *Bank of East Asia Limited v Tsien Wui Marble Factory Limited* the majority of the Hong Kong Court of Final Appeal endorsed the approach in *Pirelli*. In the result this important area of the law is still in an unsatisfactorily unclear state.

10   Remedies

10.01 The principal remedies in tort are the provision of damages and the granting of an injunction. The general aim of an award of damages is to compensate the claimant for the damage and losses sustained as a result of the tort. In principle, damages are intended to put the claimant into the same position as he would have been in if the tort had not occurred. This restitutionary principle is inappropriate where personal injury has been caused, and so in these cases the courts apply a more general principle of what is fair and reasonable in all the circumstances. However, damages are only recoverable in respect of losses actually sustained and the claimant is under a duty to mitigate his losses by taking all reasonable steps to limit them.

10.02 In addition a claimant may only recover damages in respect of losses that are reasonably foreseeable consequences of the defendant's tort (reasonable foreseeability has already been discussed in relation to the existence and breach of duty). Further, as also referred to above, the law does not always recognise a duty of care to prevent certain kinds of loss (such as pure economic loss or nervous shock or embarrassment caused by an invasion of privacy). Thus, for all of these reasons it is not unusual for a claimant's actual losses suffered as a result of a tort to be greater than those that are compensated in law.

10.03 The remedy by way of injunction is aimed at preventing loss and damage, rather than compensating for it. It operates to prevent an anticipated tort or restrain the continuance of one (such as in the case of continuing torts like nuisance or trespass). An injunction will be available where the threatened tort is such that the claimant could not be compensated adequately in damages for its occurrence. Injunctions are of two varieties: first, 'prohibitive injunctions' which order a party not to do certain things that would otherwise constitute a legal wrong; second, 'mandatory injunctions' in which the court directs a defendant positively to do certain things to prevent a tort being committed or continued.

11   Apportionment of liability

11.01 More than one person can be responsible for the same damage. The claimant is under a duty in tort to take reasonable care of his own safety. If the claimant is the only cause of the damage, then he will not succeed in a tortious action against another person. If the claimant and one or more other persons are at fault, then damages are apportioned pursuant to the Law Reform (Contributory Negligence) Act 1945 according to the court's assessment of the relative degree of fault of the parties.

11.02 In assessing this relative responsibility the court considers both the causative potency of the parties' actions (i.e. how important was each party's role as a matter of fact to the ensuing damage) and their relative moral blameworthiness (for example, if one party to a road traffic accident is drunk at the time, he is likely to be apportioned more of the blame). Contributory negligence applies to liability in negligence, nuisance, the rule in *Rylands v Fletcher*, trespass, under the Occupier's Liability Acts and other breaches of statutory duty.

11.03 Further, section 1 of the Civil Liability (Contribution) Act 1978 provides:

> 'Subject to the following provisions of this section, any person liable in respect of any damage suffered by another person may recover contribution from any other person liable in respect of the same damage (whether jointly with him or otherwise).'

11.04 Thus, between themselves, defendants are also able to apportion blame and restrict their relative contribution to the claimant's damages. This may take the form of an apportionment of blame at the trial of the matter or the commencement of separate proceedings (called part 20 proceedings) by a defendant against another party who is said to be jointly or wholly to blame. Of course if two or more persons are responsible for the claimant's damage, he may seek a remedy against either or both of them under the doctrine of joint and several liability.

12   Conclusion

The above has, no doubt, given some indication of the complex ever-changing nature of the law of tort and its relevance to the everyday activities of professional architects. Unfortunately, given the restrictions on space, this chapter is unavoidably limited in its scope and introductory by nature.

4

English land law

MARTIN DIXON*

1 Land law and conveyancing distinguished

1.01 This chapter is intended to give an impression of those aspects of land law that are relevant to architects, either in their professional capacity as designers of buildings for clients, as tenants of their offices or as prospective purchasers of land for redevelopment. At the outset, however, it is necessary to distinguish 'land law' as such from 'conveyancing'. Land law is concerned with the rights of a landowner in, or over, his own land and also with the rights that others may have over that land. The landowner's right of ownership of their land is often expressed by saying that they have an 'estate' in the land (i.e. a 'title' which may be either freehold or leasehold), while the rights of others in that land (or technically, in that 'estate') is often described by saying that they have a 'proprietary interest' (or just 'interest') in it. By way of contrast, the law of conveyancing is concerned with the mechanics of the creation and transfer of estates and interests in and over land, usually, but not necessarily, pursuant to a contract between a seller and purchaser. Typically, an owner of an estate in land (being either 'the owner' under a freehold or lease) will transfer that estate to a purchaser, with the sale/purchase being subject to existing interests in the land and, possibly, creating new ones. An architect need not concern himself with the procedures and mechanics of conveyancing, for in the normal course of events such matters will be entrusted to a property professional such as a solicitor or licensed conveyancer. Indeed, because of the new regime of electronic conveyancing that began to be introduced in to England and Wales on 13 October 2003, wherein much of the conveyancing process will be conducted electronically without paper, it would be imprudent to attempt a conveyancing transaction without professional advice. Nevertheless, a certain amount must be said about title to land in England and Wales (being estates) and the methods that exist to protect other persons' property interests in that land.

1.02 Many of the concepts that underlie English land law are ancient and this is reflected in the curious terminology that is associated with the subject. However, the law was greatly simplified and restructured in 1925 by a series of important statutes. These, and land later statutes building on them, form the foundation of modern law and, generally, were designed to facilitate the easy transfer of land so that it could be used to its full economic potential. As part of this continuing development, a major reforming statute came into force on 13 October 2003. The new Land Registration Act 2002 has replaced in full the Land Registration Act 1925. Although primarily designed to simply the conveyancing process, the Land Registration Act 2002 will introduce electronic, paper free, conveyancing to England and Wales and should, in time, speed up the conveyancing process and reduce costs. Necessarily, this reform of the conveyancing process has required some changes to the substantive principles of land law.

Title to land

1.03 Title to land in England and Wales is either 'unregistered' or 'registered', although the latter is by now the most common. Since 1 December 1990, all land (or more accurately, title to land) in England and Wales must be 'registered' consequent on a transfer of ownership (or other specified event) and, in time, unregistered conveyancing will disappear. The Land Registry estimate that virtually all transferable titles will be registered by 2010, but already all major urban areas consist substantially of 'registered title' and the Land Registration Act 2002 will greatly speed up the process. In particular, owners of substantial parcels of land – such as local authorities – are being encouraged to voluntarily register their land and many are taking advantage of lower fees and free assistance from the Land Registry. For the architect, as with others interested in the precise details of ownership and obligations affecting land, the achievement of widespread registration of title will greatly assist the development process.

1.04 For the moment, however, some land of unregistered title still exists. In unregistered conveyancing – being land where the title is *not* recorded on a register maintained by Her Majesty's Land Registry – the landowner will be either a freeholder or a leaseholder: i.e. have the equivalent of absolute ownership (freehold), or have such ownership for a precise amount of time under a lease from the freeholder (e.g. a 125-year residential lease of an apartment flat). On the sale of the freehold, or upon an assignment (sale or transfer) of a lease, the seller's proof of title is found in the title deeds to the property (which may be held by a lender if there is a mortgage) and the purchaser's solicitor will investigate these title deeds to satisfy himself on behalf of his client that the seller does indeed have title to the land. The purchaser's solicitor will investigate and verify all dealings with the land revealed by these deeds going back to the first valid conveyance of it more than 15 years old. That conveyance is known as 'the root of title' and is the proof of title required by the purchaser (Law of Property Act 1969, section 23). In addition, a physical inspection of the land may be desirable in order to discover any other person's interests in the land that might not be revealed by the title deeds: e.g. ancient rights of way, shared sewers, rights of light, etc. So, with unregistered land, the title of the vendor will be investigated (by documentary and physical inspection), a root of title produced and, following a successful completion of the sale, the purchaser's solicitor will apply for 'first registration' of title. Thereafter, the land becomes and remains registered land.

1.05 Other persons' rights in unregistered land (interests) are either 'legal' or 'equitable' in character. The distinction was once of great significance and although it is now unnecessary to explain in

---

* This chapter has been modelled on an earlier draft prepared by Charles Harpum, now of Falcon Chambers.

detail why some rights are legal and some equitable, its origins lay in the type of interest at issue and the manner in which the interest was first created. Fortunately, it will usually be readily apparent whether any given interest in the land is 'legal' or 'equitable'. The relevance of the distinction today lies in the effect that legal or equitable interests in unregistered land have when the title (the freehold or leasehold estate) to that land is transferred to another person, such as on sale. So, legal rights are 'binding on all the world', regardless of whether a purchaser of land (freehold or leasehold) knows of them or not. This means simply that a purchaser of the land (or any new owner) is bound to give effect to the interest. Most easements (such as a right of way or right to light) and most mortgages are legal rights and a purchaser of unregistered land cannot escape them by saying that he did not know of their existence, even if they were not discovered from the title deeds or inspection of the land. By contrast, equitable rights are binding on a purchaser only in certain circumstances, although they will always be binding on a person who received land by way of gift or under a will. The circumstances in which equitable interests over unregistered land will bind a purchaser are either:

1   Where the equitable interest over the land about to be purchased qualifies as a 'land charge' under the Land Charges Act 1972 *and* the interest is registered as a land charge in the appropriate manner. This system of registration is *entirely separate* from that pertaining to registered land. It means that if the equitable interest is a land charge (and this is defined in the Land Charges Act 1972) and is *not* registered, it cannot affect a purchaser of the land even if he knew about it, provided no fraud is involved.
2   Where the equitable interest over the land about to be purchased does not qualify as a land charge, the purchaser is bound only if he had 'notice' of the equitable interest. Such notice may be 'actual' (as where the purchaser is told or sees that an equitable interest exists), 'constructive' (as where a reasonable purchaser would have realized from the available facts that such an interest existed: e.g. a path is visible) or 'imputed' (as where the purchaser's agent (e.g. solicitor) has actual or constructive notice). In the absence of such notice, the purchaser cannot be affected by the equitable interest and may use the land without regard to it. Note, however, that the number of equitable interests that depend

on the 'doctrine of notice' for their validity against a purchaser is quite limited. Most equitable interests are land charges.

Land charges under the Land Charges Act 1972

1.06   As noted above, most equitable interests in unregistered land are registrable as land charges under the Land Charges Act 1972. This has nothing to do with registered land, although the registers are maintained by Her Majesty's Land Registry. Some of the most important of these registrable equitable interests from an architect's point of view are:

1   Estate contracts: i.e. contracts for the sale of land or of any interest in land, including contracts to grant leases, options to purchase land (i.e. a standing offer by a landowner to sell), and rights of pre-emption (i.e. rights of first refusal should a landowner decide to sell).
2   Restrictive covenants (being promises not to use the land for certain purposes, such as building or trade or business and see below paragraph 4.01), *except* those found in a lease (for which special rules exist) and those entered into before 1926 (to which the law of 'notice' applies).
3   Certain types of easement (such as rights of way or light), being those not originally created by a deed (a formal document) or those that endure only for the life of a given person.

Registration of these land charges ensures that the interest will be enforceable against all persons who come into possession or ownership of the unregistered land, regardless of any question of notice. If the interest is registrable but not actually registered, it will be void (i.e. unenforceable) against a purchaser of the land regardless of whether he knows of it. This will be so even if the sum paid by the purchaser is only a fraction of the true value of the property (*Midland Bank Trust Co. Ltd v Green* [1981] AC 513). Land charge registration suffers from a serious defect in that registration of the charge is not made against the land itself, but against the name of the landowner who created the charge, even if that was many years ago. Consequently, in order to search the Land Charges Register (to find any binding interests prior to a purchase), it is necessary to discover the names of all the persons who have owned the land. This is done by looking at the title deeds. However, it is only obligatory for the seller to provide the title deeds back to a good root of title: which may be only 15 years old. It is often impossible, therefore, to discover the names of all relevant landowners (i.e. going back to 1925 when land charge registration was introduced). Nevertheless, because registration of the land charge ensures that it is binding, a purchaser will still be bound by it, even though he could not have discovered it because he did not know the name against which to search! Under the Law of Property Act 1969, compensation is payable for any loss suffered in these cases. It is worth remembering that any person may search the Land Charges Register, and that an Official Certificate of Search is conclusive in favour of a purchaser, actual or intending and this will be useful in respect of potential development projects. There is, in addition, one clear advantage: a Certificate of Search is to be regarded as conclusive, thus if a Certificate of Search does not reveal a registered land charge, the purchaser will take free of it, provided that he searched against the correct name, even if the charge was actually registered. Note also, as mentioned above, that even an unregistered land charge (i.e. one that should have been registered but is not) is enforceable against someone who is not a purchaser. Thus, a person receiving the land by gift, or under a will, or even a squatter, is bound by all land charges – registered or not.

Registered land

1.07 Registered land is quite different from land of unregistered title and most titles are now of their type. In a relatively short time, registered land will be the only type of land that is commonly transferred. It has many advantages over unregistered land in terms of certainty about estates and interests in the land and in respect of ease of transactions. The system is now governed by the Land Registration Act 2002.

1   The actual title (the estate) to the land is itself registered, eliminating the need for title deeds. Details of most (but not all) interests affecting the land will also appear on the Register, and such 'encumbrances' are registered against the land itself (identified by a unique title number) and not against the name of the landowner at the time the encumbrance was created. Transfer of the land is effected by registering the purchaser as the new 'registered proprietor'. Freeholds and very many (but not yet all) leaseholds may be registered as titles. As long as the land is registered, and the postcode or address is known, it is now possible for any person to do an on-line search of the land register for a nominal sum (www.landregisteronline.gov.uk) which will reveal the name of the owners, the existence of any mortgage and some (but not all) other interests affecting the land and often the price paid by the current owners.
2   The Register of Title is conclusive as to the nature of the title to the land and the doctrine of notice and the idea of land charges have no application. If for any reason the Register is not a true reflection of the title, it may, in certain circumstances, be 'altered' on application to the Registrar or the Court, but the circumstances in which this is permitted are narrowly drawn. Any person suffering loss as a result of a qualifying alteration may be entitled to compensation out of public funds. Note also, that because it is the Register of Title itself that is conclusive, if an erroneous Search Certificate is issued that fails to disclose an entry on the Register, a purchaser will still be bound by the interest protected by the entry, but will be entitled to compensation.
3   An intending purchaser of registered land (including a person proposing to take a significant interest in the land, such as a bank lending on mortgage or a person paying for an option to purchase) will take the following steps:
    (a) Inspect the Register. The Land Register is a public document and may be inspected by any person on payment of the appropriate fee. This may be done informally on line as noted above, but an Official Search should be obtained before any offer to purchase or lend is made. Usually, the property professional employed by the purchaser will obtain the Official Search. Of course, architects may identify owners of land for themselves even if the land is not yet up for sale (e.g. as having development potential) by means of the on-line search process.
    (b) Inspect the land itself, because the Register is not conclusive on all matters. Certain rights – called 'interests that override' – may not appear on the Register but they are automatically binding on any transferee of the land (including a purchaser) by force of statute, irrespective of whether the purchaser knew about them. These include certain types of legal easements, legal leases of 7 years or less, local land charges (see below, paragraph 1.08), and the rights of persons (including squatters) in actual occupation of the land, (provided the actual occupation is discoverable on a reasonable inspection of the land or the interest of the occupier is known of by the transferee). This last category can be a trap for the unwary, but much less so than was previously the case now that the Land Registration Act 2002 is in force. It means that a person may gain protection (i.e. may enforce their interest against a transferee) for most property rights (e.g. leases, shares of ownership) by virtue of being in 'discoverable actual occupation' of the land over which the right exists: *Williams & Glyn's Bank Ltd v Boland* [1981] AC 487. Consequently, a proper inspection of the land is vital and questions should be asked of any person who is, or appears to be, in occupation of the land. If necessary, the written consent of such persons to the proposed transaction should be obtained and this should be a matter of priority for the property professional engaged to manage the transaction.

Local land charges

1.08 Irrespective of whether the land is registered or unregistered, there are certain rights that are registrable quite separately in a register kept by all local authorities (e.g. District Councils and Unitary Authorities). These are 'local land charges' and they are regulated by the Local Land Charges Act 1975, which came into force in 1977. These charges are registered by reference to the land which they affect and not against the name of the landowner and should not be confused with land charges under the Land Charges Act 1972. Registration of a local land charge constitutes actual notice of it to all persons for all purposes. A local land charge is, however, enforceable even if not registered, but a purchaser of land burdened by an unregistered local land charge will be entitled to compensation from the local authority. Local land charges are numerous and of considerable practical importance. A search of the local land charges register held by the relevant local authority is vital before proceeding to deal with the land, either by way of purchase or development. They include:

1   Preservation instructions as to ancient monuments
2   Lists of buildings of special architectural or historic interest
3   Planning restrictions
4   Drainage schemes
5   Charges under the Public Health and Highway Acts.

1.09 As a matter of general good practice, an architect will be well advised to find out from the client what adverse rights (if any) affect the client's property before undertaking any scheme of work. It is particularly important that he discovers the existence of any easements, restrictive covenants or local land charges because these may constrict the architect in his plans. For example, the existence of a neighbour's right to light or right of way, or ability to enforce a building restriction (a restrictive covenant) can affect radically any plans for development, as might any local land charges registered against the land.

2   The extent and meaning of 'land' and intrusions upon it

2.01 'Land' in English law includes not only the soil but also:

1   Any buildings, parts of buildings, or similar structures.
2   Anything permanently attached to the soil (so-called, 'fixtures', see paragraph 5.03, which may include garden plants, greenhouses, even garden statues).

3 Rights under the land. It has never been settled how far down the rights of a landowner extend, though it is commonly said that they extend to the centre of the earth. Certainly they go down as far as the limits of economic exploitation. A landowner is therefore entitled to the minerals under his land, though all gold, silver, coal and petroleum are vested in the Crown.

4 Rights above the land to such height as is necessary for the ordinary use and enjoyment of land and the structures upon it (*Baron Bernstein v Skyviews & General Ltd* [1978] QB 479, 488). Thus, the flight of building cranes over a neighbouring property may be a trespass and this should be remembered when considering developments requiring such machinery.

5 Intangible rights such as easements (e.g. such as rights of way or rights to light), profits (such as a right to fish on another's land) and restrictive covenants (rights to prevent activities on another's land).

Trespass

2.02 Any unjustifiable intrusion (i.e. without permission or without right) by one person upon land in the possession of another is a trespass – a 'tort'. It is likewise a trespass to place anything on or in the land in the possession of another (e.g. by driving a nail into his wall, or propping a ladder against his house). It is a popular misconception that to be actionable as a tort, the trespass must involve damage to the claimant's property. Even if no damage is done, the court may restrain the trespass by injunction, binding immediately. See, e.g. *Anchor Brewhouse Developments Ltd v Berkley House (Dockland Developments) Ltd* [1987] 2 EGLR 173, where the trespass arose out of building works on land adjacent to that of the claimant. Consequently, if construction work is likely to necessitate an incursion on to neighbouring land in some way – e.g. to erect scaffolding, or because a crane jib will swing over that land – then the client must come to an arrangement with the landowner, unless the client can prove some right to enter on the land (such as under the Access to Neighbouring Land Act). Such permission will usually take the form of a 'contractual licence', being a temporary permission, often granted in return for a payment or other consideration (paragraph 2.04). But if a permanent incursion is contemplated – e.g. by the overhanging eaves of a building, the footings of a garage or the line of a boundary wall – it may be better to negotiate an easement (see paragraph 3.01).

2.03 In the absence of any easements, restrictive covenants or other binding agreements (e.g. a contract between landowner and neighbour), a person is generally free as a matter of private law to build anywhere on his own land. Necessarily, of course, there may be planning issues and other related matters that restrict this in practice. Note, however, that in some circumstances, the process of development may give rise to a claim by a neighbour in 'nuisance', such as where there is an unjustifiable interference with a neighbouring landowner's use and enjoyment of his own land through excessive noise or dust (see *Hunter v Canary Wharf Ltd* [1997] AC 655).

Licences

2.04 As noted above, a neighbour may give another person permission to use his land by means of a 'contractual licence' and it is convenient at this point to discuss licences generally. A licence is permission to do something that would otherwise be a trespass. For example, in the absence of an easement of way, a contractual licence permitting the passage and re-passage of construction traffic over neighbouring land might be required for some developments. There are several types of licence, of which only two need be considered here. First, there is a bare licence, i.e. permission to enter land, given quite gratuitously without any counter-benefit for the landowner giving the permission. It is revocable at any time by the licensor/landowner (though such notice must be reasonable in the circumstances) and, on such revocation, the licensee becomes a trespasser, although he is entitled to a reasonable time to enable him to leave the land once notice of termination has expired. The second type of licence is the contractual licence mentioned above. This is a licence that is granted for some counter-benefit, usually a fee. Whether a contractual licence can be revoked depends upon the interpretation

and meaning of the contract under which it was given. If a licence is either expressly or by necessary implication irrevocable during its agreed duration (e.g. the erection of scaffolding on a neighbour's land for 6 months), the licensor will be unable to prevent the licensee from going on to the land for the purpose of the licence. Any attempted revocation of the licence can be prevented by the grant of an injunction or in appropriate circumstances, by a decree of specific performance, that is an order forcing the licensor to permit the licensee to enter (*Verrall v Great Yarmouth Borough Council* [1981] QB 202). If a licence is silent as to the duration or terms on which it can be revoked, a court may supply such terms as is reasonable having regard to the circumstances in which the licence was granted (*Parker, the 9th Earl of Macclesfield v Hon Jocelyn Parker*, 2003).

Easements

2.05 If a landowner has an easement over adjacent land – such as a right of way – any interference with it by the owner of the burdened land (the 'servient' land) will not constitute a trespass but will be a 'nuisance'. However, not every interference with an easement will amount to a nuisance. If the easement is a positive one, being one which allows the person entitled to the benefit of it to do something on the burdened land (e.g. a right of way by foot or vehicle), the interference will constitute a nuisance only if it prevents the practical and substantial enjoyment of the easement. If the easement is negative, being one which allows the person entitled to the benefit of it to prevent the use of the burdened land in a certain way (e.g. a right of light, being the prevention of building), the interference will be actionable only if it substantially interferes with the enjoyment of the right. (On positive and negative easements, see paragraph 3.03.)

Boundaries

2.06 A boundary has been defined as an imaginary line that marks the confines or line of division of two contiguous parcels of land (*Halsbury's Laws of England* (4th edn), vol. 4, paragraph 831). Boundaries are fixed in one of three ways: (a) by proven acts of the respective owners; (b) by statutes or by orders of authorities having jurisdiction; or (c) in the absence of either of these, by legal presumption. Note, however, that as Lord Hoffmann said in *Alan Wibberley Building Ltd v Insley* (April 1999), '[b]oundary disputes are a particularly painful form of litigation. Feelings run high and disproportionate amounts of money are spent'. While it is true, therefore, that the law on boundaries *should* be as clear as possible, the best approach is to agree matters such as the precise line of a boundary before development takes place and thus avoid resort to law.

1 Proved acts of the parties

(a) The parties may expressly agree on the boundaries. This is by far the best approach, particularly where new development is concerned. It is best to have the agreement formally drawn up by a solicitor or licensed conveyancer.

(b) The boundaries may be defined by the title deeds. These may in turn refer to a plan or to an Ordnance Survey map. As far as plans are concerned, the boundary lines are usually 'for the purposes of identification only' and, unless the context makes clear (as was the case in *Fisher v Winch* [1939] 1 KB 666), they do not purport to fix the exact boundary. Where the 'plan line' is for purposes of identification only, topographical features and other evidence may be used to find the exact line. Likewise, Ordnance Survey maps do not purport to fix private boundaries and it is the practice of the Survey to draw the boundary line down the middle of a boundary feature (e.g. down the middle of a ditch) regardless of where the boundary line actually runs in law. If the title deeds do refer to an Ordnance Survey map, then that map will be conclusive in so far as it defines the *general* boundary. Again, however, unless the context makes clear, this may simply indicate the general line, not its precise course. In the case of registered land, the plans used by the Land Registry are based on the Ordnance Survey maps, but once again the boundaries on them are regarded as general and are not intended to be fixed precisely by the plan. A little-used procedure – unlikely to gain popularity even under the new law – exists by which the boundary of registered land may be defined exactly, and where this has been done the plan on the Register is definitive and is noted as such.

(c) A boundary of unregistered land may be proved by showing 12 or more years' undisturbed possession. This may extend to possession of a boundary wall (*Prudential Assurance v Waterloo Real Estate* [1999]).

(d) A boundary of registered land may be proved by showing at least 10 years undisturbed possession, but such boundary is only conclusive when an application is made to the land registry and the register of title is amended accordingly. This may extend to possession of a boundary wall (*Prudential Assurance v Waterloo Real Estate* [1999]).

2 Orders of competent authorities

Establishment of boundaries by orders of authorities is now largely historical. Under the Enclosure Acts, the Tithe Acts, and certain Agricultural Acts, awards defining boundaries precisely could be made. These may still be relevant in some rural areas. Similarly, a boundary may be fixed by judicial decision, e.g. in an action for trespass or for the recovery of land.

3 Legal presumption

In the absence of clear definition by the above methods, certain rebuttable presumptions apply, being 'default' rules that will operate unless contrary evidence is available.

(a) Hedges and ditches. It is presumed that a person excavating a ditch will not dig into his neighbour's land, but that he will dig at the very edge of his own property, making a bank on his side of the ditch with the soil that he removes. On top of that bank a hedge is usually planted. He is, therefore, owner of both the hedge and the ditch. This presumption applies only where the ditch is known to be artificial, but it is readily applicable in cases of doubt, including cases where reference is made to a plan or Ordnance Survey map defining general boundaries (*Alan Wibberley Building Ltd v Insley* [1999]).

(b) Fences. It is said that there is a presumption that a wooden fence belongs to the owner of the land on whose side the posts are placed, on the basis that a landowner will use his land to the fullest extent (and display the better side of the fence to his neighbour!). Likewise, it is often said that nails are 'driven home'. These presumptions are, however, unsupported by authority and must be regarded as uncertain. Most modern plans mark the fence owned by the property in question by the indication of a 'T' on the plan.

(c) Highways. The boundary between lands separated by a highway or a private right of way is presumed to be the middle line of the highway or private right of way. There is no such presumption with railways. The bed of a railway will be the property of Network Rail, or its successors.

(d) The seashore. The boundary line between the seashore and the adjoining land is (unless usage to the contrary is proved) the line of the median high tide between the ordinary spring and neap tide (*Attorney General v Chambers* [1854] 4 De GM & G 206 at 218). *Prima facie* the seashore belongs to the Crown.

(e) Rivers and streams. If a river or stream is tidal, the soil of the bed of the river or stream belongs to the Crown, or the Duchies of Cornwall or Lancaster, where appropriate. As a general rule, the boundary between the bed of a tidal stream and adjoining land is the line of medium high water mark. If the river or stream is non-tidal, it is assumed that adjoining owners own land to the middle of the flowing water, known as the 'thalweg' (although this may not be the middle of the river itself).

(f) Walls. If the division between two properties is a wall and the exact line of the boundary is not known, in determining the ownership of the wall, certain presumptions apply. Party walls outside London and Bristol (for the situation in London and Bristol, see Chapter 26) are subject to rights at common law. The usual, but by no means necessary, presumption is that the party wall is divided longitudinally into two strips, one belonging to each of the neighbouring owners, but where each half is subject to a right (an easement) of support in favour of the other. If one owner removes his building, he is obliged to waterproof the exposed party wall. (See Chapter 26 for the complicated procedures necessary when changes to party walls are contemplated in London.) Extensions to existing buildings can bear only on the half of the wall belonging to the owner of the building being extended, unless the consent of the adjoining owner is obtained. Note also that a former party wall can come under the exclusive ownership of one of the neighbours consequent upon the relevant period of undisturbed adverse possession, plus registration in the case of registered title.

3 Easements

3.01 Easements are rights that one owner of land may acquire over the land of another. They should be distinguished from other similar rights such as (i) profits, i.e. rights to take something off another's land, e.g. to cut grass or peat, or to shoot or fish; (ii) natural rights, e.g. rights of support of land (but not of buildings, which is a true easement); (iii) public rights, e.g. rights of way over a highway or rights of common; (iv) restrictive covenants (paragraph 4.01); and licences (paragraph 2.04).

3.02 The essentials of an easement are:

1 There must be a dominant and a servient tenement, where a 'tenement' is a plot of land held by a freeholder or leaseholder. The dominant tenement is the land benefited by the easement, the servient land is the land burdened. Note, therefore, it is impossible for someone occupying land as only a mere licensee to either give or enjoy an easement.

2 The easement must 'benefit' the dominant tenement to which it will become attached. So, although the two plots need not be contiguous or adjacent, they must be sufficiently close for the dominant tenement to be benefited by the easement. A landowner at one end of the village is unlikely to enjoy an easement of way over land at the other.

3 The two tenements must not be owned *and* occupied by the same person. Hence, a tenant can have an easement over land occupied by his landlord, as both tenements are owned by the same person, but they are not also occupied by him.

4 The easement claimed must be 'capable of forming the subject matter of a grant', i.e. of being created by deed. This means that the right alleged to be an easement must be sufficiently well defined, certain and limited in scope to qualify as an easement. So, although there are well-established categories of easements – rights of way, rights to light, rights of support – the list is not closed. New rights can become recognized as being capable of being 'granted', hence of being easements. Modern examples include the right to use a letterbox, the right to park a car on adjoining land and cross it with shopping trolleys, the right to locate a television aerial (and hence a satellite dish) on a neighbour's land, the right to display signs, the right to moor boats and the right to use paths in a park for pleasure and not simply for getting from one place to another. Against this, certain rights cannot exist as easements: e.g. a right to a view; to privacy; to a general flow of air (as distinct to a flow through an air duct); to have a property protected from the weather and a general right to light (as opposed to a right through a defined aperture).

3.03 It is often said that easements may be either positive or negative, although there is no consequence in the distinction. A positive easement is one which enables the dominant owner to do some act upon the servient tenement, e.g. walk or drive along a right of way. A negative easement allows the dominant owner to prevent the servient owner from doing something on his land, e.g. a right to light, which restricts the servient owner's ability to build. Some easements do not readily fall into either category, e.g. a right of support for a building.

3.04 Easements may be acquired in a number of ways:

1 By express grant or reservation. A landowner may by deed (or written contract if the easement is to be equitable) expressly

grant an easement over his land in favour of a neighbouring landowner. Equally, if a landowner is selling off part of his land, he may expressly grant an easement in the purchaser's favour (burdening the land he retains), or expressly reserve to himself an easement (burdening the land sold), in the documents that carry out the sale. Both express grant and reservation are common when a plot is divided into sub-plots and sold to different purchasers, as with a green field housing development.

2 By implied reservation. This occurs when the parties to a transaction concerning land have not expressly mentioned easements in the documents carrying out the transaction. So, if a landowner sells off part of his land and retains the rest, he may fail to reserve expressly any easements burdening the part sold (for the benefit of the part he retains). However, in two situations, easements may be implied in his favour – meaning that they will be treated as if they were deliberately *reserved* for the benefit of the land retained. These are easements of necessity and easements necessary to give effect to the common intentions of the parties. An easement of necessity in this context means an easement without which the vendor's retained land cannot be used at all. For example, if he retains land to which there is no access (often called a land-locked close), an easement of necessity will be impliedly reserved over the land that he has sold for the benefit of the land he retains. An easement in the common intention of the parties means an easement which both parties accepted should exist as being required to put into effect a shared intention for the use of the land retained at the time of sale. Such an implied reservation can be difficult to prove, but a rare example is *Peckham v Ellison* (1999) concerning access via a rear pathway.

3 By implied grant. In similar fashion to the above, if a purchaser buys land from a seller (the seller again retaining certain land), and no easements are expressly *granted* to the purchaser for the benefit of the land sold, easements may be implied in favour of the land sold, burdening the land retained, in the following circumstances:

(a) Easements of necessity, which in this context mean easements without which the purchaser cannot enjoy the land.

(b) Easements necessary to give effect to the common intentions of the parties, as where the shared intention of seller and purchaser is that a dwelling shall be built on the land sold, but no easements permitting access by construction traffic are expressly granted (*Stafford v Lee*).

(c) Easements within the rule in *Wheeldon v Burrows* [1879] 12 ChD 31. This is best explained by an example. A landowner owns two adjacent plots, A and B. He does certain things on plot B for the benefit of A which would amount to an easement if A and B were separately owned: e.g. he walks over plot B, to get to plot A. This is called a 'quasi-easement'. When he sells off plot A, retaining plot B, the purchaser of plot A will acquire an easement to do those acts over plot B (walk across it) which the common owner had hitherto done, providing the quasi-easement was 'continuous and apparent', i.e. discernible on a careful inspection of the land; necessary for the reasonable enjoyment of plot A; and had been and was at the time of the grant used by the grantor for the benefit of plot A.

(d) Under the statutory 'general words' of section 62 of the Law of Property Act 1925. By virtue of this statutory provision, there will pass on every conveyance of land (meaning a transfer by deed only), unless a contrary intention is shown, all 'liberties, privileges, easements, rights and advantages whatsoever appertaining to or reputed to appertain to the land'. The somewhat unexpected and dramatic effect of this section is that it will convert merely permissive uses (i.e. licences) into full easements if a person sells land which, prior to the sale, was occupied by a person to whom he (the seller) gave some personal right over land he himself retained. Again, an example will make matters clearer. So, X, a freeholder, permits Y, a tenant of another part of X's land, to drive over that part of X's land that X himself occupies. X then sells and conveys to Y (or any other person) the land of which Y has hitherto been a leaseholder. On the conveyance, Y acquires a full easement to drive over X's land (*International Tea Stores Co. v Hobbs* [1903] 2 Ch 165).

Although section 62 has this effect only if the subsequent sale is by deed and only if different people were occupying the two plots of land involved (but see a contrary view in *Platt v Crouch*, 2003), it is imperative to appreciate the unexpected effect that the section may have. It is imperative, therefore, for a seller of land to exclude the effect of section 62 LPA 1925 in any conveyance to which he is party – just in case. The same might also be said of the rule in *Wheeldon v Burrows*, above.

4 By prescription. Long use by a claimant of a 'right' over the defendant's land ('*nec vi, nec clam, nec precario*' – without force, secrecy, or permission) can give rise to easements. An easement by prescription can only be claimed by one freehold owner against another and, with certain exceptions, 'user' must be shown to have been continuous over the relevant period. The rules concerning prescription are complicated (and unsatisfactory), but essentially there are three methods of acquiring easements by prescription: (a) at common law; (b) under the doctrine of 'lost modern grant'; and (c) under the Prescription Act 1832.

(a) At common law an easement can be acquired by prescription only if it can be proved to have been used from time immemorial (i.e. set in law at 1189!). In fact, use for 20 years before the claim is made would normally be accepted. However, a claim can always be defeated by showing that the alleged right could not have existed since 1189. For example, there can be no prescriptive right to light under this head for a building that was constructed 'only' in 1585. Hence, 'pure' common law claims are rare.

(b) The doctrine of lost modern grant was invented because of the ease with which it was possible to defeat a claim to prescription at common law. Where the origin of an alleged easement cannot otherwise be accounted for, then provided that there has been upwards of 20 years' use of the right, the court will presume that the right was lawfully granted and that the document making the grant has been lost. Of course, this is a complete fiction, but the presumption can be rebutted only by evidence that the existence of such a grant was impossible. The evidence necessary to persuade a court to infer a 'lost' modern grant must be stronger than that required to prove common law prescription and it can be invoked only if common law prescription is for some reason excluded.

(c) The Prescription Act 1832 laid down time periods for prescription in general and for rights of light in particular (the latter are discussed in paragraph 3.08). The Act provides that uninterrupted use for 20 years before some action by the dominant owner for confirmation of an easement or by the servient owner for a declaration that a right does not exist, means that the claim cannot be defeated merely by showing that the claimed easement cannot have existed since 1189. The Act further provides that user without interruption for 40 years prior to a court action gives an absolute and unchallengeable easement. In both cases, user must be of right, i.e. *nec vi, nec clam, nec precario*. 'Interruption' is important because if a person wishes to establish an easement by prescription, he must not acquiesce in the interruption of his right for one year by the owner of the property over which he wishes to establish the easement. Any period during which the owner of the land over which the easement is claimed could not give consent to establishing an easement (e.g. because he was an infant or a lunatic) must be added to the 20-year period. This is part of the fiction that such rights are 'granted' by somebody, so cannot exist if there was nobody to grant them!

Extinguishment of easements

3.05 Apart from an express release by deed (i.e. deliberate agreement between the owners of the dominant and servient land), the most important method of extinguishing an easement is when the dominant and servient tenements come into the same ownership *and* possession. For example, acquisition and occupation by an owner of his neighbour's land will extinguish all easements previously existing between them and thus any subsequent development that would otherwise require the existence of easements (e.g. rights to lay water pipes, cables, etc.) must also include the new, express grant of such rights.

Types of easement

3.06 As noted above, the 'list' of easements is not closed, and new types of easement will be required as the uses of land change and as construction methods develop. The following are examples of common types of easement:

1 Rights of way. A right of way, whether acquired expressly, impliedly, or by prescription, may be limited as to both frequency and type of use, e.g. a right obtained for passage by horse and cart in the nineteenth century will not extend to passage for many caravans if the dominant tenement has become a caravan park. It is a matter of construction of the easement (i.e. an interpretation of what it means) whether the easement gives a right to pass on foot or with vehicles or whether it includes the right to stop and park. A 'general' easement will usually encompass these rights on the basis that the grantor of the easement (he who first created it) cannot 'derogate from his grant' by claiming at a later date that some lesser use was intended. If that was intended, it should have been made clear at the time the easement was created.

2 Rights of support. Although the natural right of support for land by other land has been distinguished from an easement (paragraph 3.01), it is possible for one building to acquire an easement of support against another after a period of 20 years prescriptive use (i.e. in the absence of any express grant of right). The only way of preventing this would be for the owner of the alleged supporting building to seek a declaration during the 20 years that the supported building has no right to support. It should be noted that where two detached buildings adjoin on separate plots, an easement cannot be acquired requiring a person who removes his abutting wall to weatherproof the exposed flank wall of the remaining building (unless the wall is a party wall: paragraph 2.05).

3 Rights of light.
(a) To a considerable extent, the law relating to rights of light has been rendered of secondary importance by daylighting regulations under planning legislation and related planning controls (Chapter 14), but a knowledge of the law is still required. There is no easement of light generally, but only in respect of some definite opening, such as a window or skylight. The owner of the dominant tenement has a right only to such amount of light as is necessary for 'ordinary purposes'. Many years' enjoyment of an exceptionally large amount of light does not prevent an adjoining owner from building so as to reduce light; see the claim made by an architect, but denied by the court, that he had enjoyed and needed more light for his studio than for ordinary office purposes (*Ambler v Gordon* [1905] 1 KB 417). The decision about whether enough light is left for ordinary purposes after building depends on observation and light measurement. The so-called 45° rule from the centre of a window can do no more than help the judge make up his mind, although a reduction of more than 50% of previous light suggests that too much light has been denied. It should also be noted that if light could be obtained from an existing but blocked skylight, then this must be counted as an available alternative source in determining whether there is enough light for 'ordinary purposes'.
(b) Under the Prescription Act 1832, as amended by the Rights of Light Act 1959, it is provided that an absolute right of light can be obtained after 20 years' uninterrupted use (the 1959 Act provided a temporary extension of the period to 27 years' due to the then abundance of bomb-damaged sites and the slow pace of redevelopment). The 1959 Act provides that a local land charge may be registered (see paragraph 1.09), indicating the presence of a theoretical wall of stated dimensions in such a position as would prevent an adjoining owner from claiming a prescriptive right of light. This useful provision avoids a landowner having to erect screens and hoardings (subject to planning permission: Chapter 14) to prevent a right of light being acquired over his land! Instead, he can register a local land charge that has the same effect as if the light had been blocked by a wall or screen, so preventing the neighbour's 20-year use.

4 Restrictive covenants

4.01 A restrictive covenant is a binding obligation that restricts an owner of servient land (burdened land) in his use and enjoyment of that land. The covenant must be made for the benefit of dominant land (benefited land) belonging to the covenantee, being the person who may enforce the covenant. Typical examples are covenants not to build above a given height or in a given place, or covenants restricting the user of the land to given purposes: e.g. no trade or business. Although to some extent superseded by planning controls, restrictive covenants still have a valuable role to play, particularly in preserving the character of housing estates and other homogenous developments. The essentials of a restrictive covenant are:

1 That it is in substance negative: a covenant that requires the person burdened to spend money is *not* negative (e.g. a covenant to fence or repair is not negative).
2 That it is made between the covenantor (the person making the promise, whose land is burdened) and the covenantee (the person who can enforce the promise) for the benefit of the covenantee's land.
3 That the parties intend the burden of the covenant to run with the covenantor's land so as to bind not only the covenantor but also his successors in title. So, all subsequent owners of the burdened land can be prevented from carrying out the prohibited use.

4.02 A restrictive convenant is an equitable interest in land and therefore requires registration as a land charge in unregistered land (unless the covenant is contained in a lease, for which different rules apply). If the burdened land is registered, a restrictive covenant is protected by registering a Notice (usually an Agreed Notice) against the servient land on the Register of Title. These matters will usually be dealt with by the solicitor etc. at the time the covenant was first created. If a restrictive covenant complies with the requirements listed in paragraph 4.01 and is properly protected by registration, it will bind the covenantor's successors in title. The usual remedy for infringement of a restrictive covenant is an injunction to restrain further breaches, but the court may give damages either in addition to or in lieu of an injunction. The rules on the passing of the benefit of restrictive covenants are complex and need not be considered here, save to say that it is very probable that a successor in ownership to the land benefited will be able to enforce the covenant against the person now owning the land burdened. Hence, restrictive covenants affect both burdened and benefited land long after they were first created. There is in consequence a procedure for their removal (see below 4.04).

4.03 Architects should request that their clients obtain confirmation that there are no restrictive covenants applying to a site that could affect the proposed design and use of a building or indeed whether a building can be constructed at all. An architect must proceed with caution as, e.g. a simple covenant 'not to carry on any trade or business' on the land may effectively destroy a development. Although the point has never been tested in court, an architect who continued to act for a client in designing a building that was known by both of them to contravene a restrictive covenant could be liable jointly with his client for the tort of conspiracy, i.e. of agreeing to do an unlawful act.

Discharge of restrictive covenants

4.04 Many restrictive covenants imposed in former years are no longer of real benefit to the owners of adjoining lands and may indeed be anti-social or in conflict with reasonable redevelopment proposals. Consequently, power is given to the Lands Tribunal by section 84 of the Law of Property Act 1925, as amended by section 28 of the Law of Property Act 1969, for the discharge or modification of any covenant if the Tribunal is satisfied that, among other things, changes in the neighbourhood make the covenant obsolete or that the restriction does not now secure practical advantages of substantial value to the person entitled to its benefit or is contrary to public policy (i.e. planning policy). Compensation may be awarded in lieu of the covenant. However, it is not enough to secure the discharge of a covenant that development in violation of an existing covenant would add amenity to the land or to the neighbourhood. Some reason why the private law rights of others should be overridden must be found and this will become more acute as human rights legislation (protecting private property) takes full effect.

5   Landlord and tenant

Landlord and tenant covenants

5.01 The vast majority of leases with which architects are concerned on behalf of their clients, particularly of trade and business premises, are the subject of formal agreements defining precisely the respective rights and obligations of the parties. Whether the architect's client is a tenant who wishes to rebuild, alter, or repair premises, or a landlord who requires evidence to recover damages from a tenant who has failed to observe a promise (covenant) for repair, regard must be had first to the express terms of the lease and the client's solicitor should be asked to advise on the meaning and extent of the terms. The following general remarks, except where otherwise stated, introduce the law only in so far as the lease itself does not make any express provision.

The doctrine of waste and repairing obligations

5.02 'Waste' consists of an act or omission that causes or is likely to cause a lasting alteration to the nature of the land or premises. A tenant of land for more than one year is, apart from statute and any terms of the lease, liable for 'voluntary waste' (any positive act such as pulling down or altering the premises) and 'permissive waste' (any omission, such as allowing the premises to fall into disrepair). In practice, however, the great majority of leases will contain clear repairing covenants going beyond these obligations. Normally, the landlord is responsible for external repairs and the tenant for internal repairs. In any event, in respect of a lease of a dwelling house or flat for less than 7 years (excluding some leases granted to local authorities and other public sector bodies), the landlord is obliged to keep the exterior and general structure in repair and to keep in repair and working order all installations relating to heating and amenities: Housing Act 1985, section 11. Finally, there is a third type of waste: 'ameliorating waste', being some change that improves the value of the landlord's interest (his 'reversion'). The courts are very unlikely to restrain acts of ameliorating waste by the tenant precisely because they add value to the landlord's interest.

Fixtures

5.03 Prima facie, anything that is attached to the land becomes part of the land and therefore the property of the landowner. If, therefore, a tenant attaches something to land that has been leased to him, it will presumptively become the property of the landlord. However, two questions arise. First, is the addition to the land in truth a 'fixture' in the sense that it has become part of the land or does it remain a 'chattel' – the personal property of the tenant? Second, even if it is a fixture, is it of a kind that for special reasons a tenant may remove at the end of the lease?

1   Fixture or chattel? In deciding whether something attached to the land is a fixture or a chattel, two matters are considered:
    (a) How is the thing attached to the land? If it is attached so that it can be removed readily without damaging the fabric of the land or the buildings on it, it may be regarded as a chattel and therefore as the property of the tenant. This is the 'degree of annexation' test. For example, something resting on the land by its own weight is likely to be a chattel: a usual garden ornament and even a temporary housing structure (e.g. Portakabin) may fall into this category.
    (b) Why is the thing attached? This is the 'purpose of annexation' test and can override the 'degree' test. If the thing is attached to the land simply because it cannot otherwise be used or enjoyed as a chattel (e.g. a dentist's chair bolted to the floor or a tapestry fixed to a wall), then it remains a chattel. Conversely, if the thing is attached in order to improve the land permanently, then it is a fixture. So, a garden ornament forming part of an integrated garden design may well be a fixture as an object intended to form part of the land and which increases its value.

2   Tenant's fixtures. Even if the thing is a fixture, a tenant who has attached it may be able to remove it at the end of his lease under special rules. In the case of non-agricultural leases, the tenant may remove trade, domestic and ornamental fixtures before the expiry of the tenancy. He must make good any damage to the premises occasioned by the removal of the fixtures. If the lease is of agricultural land, the tenant can remove all fixtures that he has attached within 2 months of the lease expiring. The landlord has the option to purchase them if he wishes.

Alterations and improvements

5.04 In the absence of any term in the lease regulating the matter, the tenant should obtain the landlord's consent to do any alterations. This is because any alteration to the premises will constitute waste (voluntary or ameliorating) and may be a breach of the terms of the lease. It is common for a lease to contain an express condition that no alterations shall be made without the landlord's consent, although in most cases such consent may not be unreasonably withheld where the alteration constitutes an improvement, Landlord and Tenant Act 1927, section 19. Whether a proposed alteration is 'an improvement' is a question of fact to be considered from the tenant's point of view. It should be noted that it is the tenant's responsibility to prove that the landlord's consent is being unreasonably withheld, that the landlord may object on aesthetic, artistic, and even sentimental grounds, and that although the above Act forbids the taking of any payment as a condition of giving consent, the landlord may reasonably require the tenant to pay the landlord's legal and other expenses (including architect's and surveyor's fees) plus a reasonable amount for any diminution in the value not only of the leased premises but also of any adjoining premises of the landlord.

Repairing covenants generally

5.05 Architects are frequently asked to prepare a 'schedule of dilapidations' at the start, during, or at the end of a lease. This will be used as a basis of assessing the extent of the repairing obligations of the parties under the lease. The importance of initial schedules is that in the absence of any covenant to do works as a condition of the grant of the lease, any repairing covenant must be interpreted with reference to the original condition of the premises. Thus, the original condition as detailed in the schedule is crucial. The extent of repairing obligations turns on the words used in the lease. For example, often the tenant's obligation is to 'repair, keep in repair and deliver the premises in repair at the end of the term' which encompasses an on-going obligation throughout the lease and an obligation to leave the premises in much the same condition as they were found. The actual meaning of 'repair' – or rather, what is a 'disrepair' so as to trigger the repairing obligation – can vary according to the circumstances of each case, including the length of the lease, purpose of the lease and location of the property. So, 'repair' may include the replacement or renewal of parts of a building but not renewal of the whole or substantially the whole of the premises. A common repairing obligation placed on tenants and found in leases of houses or flats is to 'keep and deliver up premises in good and tenantable repair' and (in the absence of a countervailing obligation of the landlord: such as in premises of low rent) the covenant can include an obligation to put the premises into repair (even if they were in disrepair by the omissions of another) as well as to keep them in repair. The quality of such repair must be such 'as having regard to the age, character and locality of the premises would make it reasonably fit for occupation by another reasonably minded tenant of the same class' (*Proudfoot v Hart* [1890] 25 QBD 42, 55).

Exception to tenant's repairing obligations

5.06 The tenant is usually not liable for any damage that can be said to be a result of 'fair wear and tear' but it is the tenant's responsibility to prove that a bad state of repair is within the exception. In general terms, the phrase means that the tenant is not responsible for damage resulting from exposure to the natural elements or reasonable use of the property. However, although not liable for direct damage due to fair wear and tear (e.g. a slate blown off a roof), the tenant could be liable for any consequential damage that then occurs (e.g. water damage to the interior). It is often the case, therefore, that tenants will carry out minor repairs for which they are not technically liable in order to prevent wider disrepair for which they would be liable.

Dilapidations

5.07 If asked to prepare a schedule of dilapidations, an architect should first find out from his client's solicitor the terms of the lease so that he is clear which portions of the building come within the repairing covenant. These are the only portions he need examine. As some tenant's fixtures are removable by the tenant, only dilapidations to landlord's fixtures need usually be catalogued. (Note, however, because of the difficulties of assessing ownership of fixtures, it is often wise to examine dilapidations on anything that is at all doubtful.) Estimates of the cost of making good dilapidations are often required. Unless an architect has much experience of this kind of work, it is advisable to involve a quantity surveyor or similar professional. When landlord and tenant cannot agree about the extent of the damage or the extent of responsibility for making them good, their dispute may have to be resolved in the courts or by arbitration. In such cases, the schedule of dilapidations becomes evidence, and it is therefore important that it is very clearly drawn. Where the parties agree to appoint an architect or surveyor to prepare a schedule of dilapidations, then, by analogy with the cases on valuations, if no reasons for the schedule are given and it was made honestly and in good faith, it cannot be set aside by the courts, even though it turns out to be mistaken: *Campbell v Edwards* [1976] 1 WLR 403. If reasons are given for the schedule and they are fundamentally erroneous, it may be set aside: *Burgess v Purchase & Sons (Farms) Ltd* [1983] Ch 216. When making an inspection for a schedule the possibility that matters might come to court should be borne in mind.

Consents

5.08 It must be emphasized that what has been stated is always subject to the express wording of the lease and also to the many statutory provisions for the protection of tenants of certain types of premises, particularly houses. Architects should remember that a client's tenancy may come at the end of a long line of underleases, and the consent of superior landlords may be required for any work that the client has requested. The client's solicitor should be consulted to determine the existence of any superior landlords.

Enforcement of repairing covenants

5.09 Under the Leasehold Property (Repairs) Act 1938, as extended by the Landlord and Tenant Act 1954, a landlord cannot forfeit the lease (i.e. force its early termination) or even begin an action for damages in respect of a tenant's failure to observe a repairing covenant unless he has first served on the tenant a notice under section 146 of the Law of Property Act 1925 clearly specifying the alleged breach of covenant. If the tenant serves a counter-notice within 28 days, the landlord cannot take any action without the consent of the court. Architects are frequently asked to produce a schedule of defects to accompany a notice (see also paragraph 5.06).

6 Surveys of property to be purchased

6.01 Architects are often asked to inspect property for clients who intend to purchase it or take a lease. A physical inspection of the property is required, bearing in mind the proposed use and taking into account all defects and dilapidations. Useful guides to technical points to be noted in such a survey are given in *Architectural Practice and Procedure* and in *Guide to Domestic Building Surveys*.

6.02 It is important to note that if defects are not observed and noted, the architect may be held to be negligent. For example, where a surveyor failed to report that the timbers of a house were badly affected by death-watch beetle and worm, he was held liable in negligence to the purchaser of that property (*Phillips v Ward* [1956] 1 WLR 471). The measure of damages in such a case is the difference between the market value of the property with the defect and the purchase price paid by the client. It is *not* the difference between the market value with the defect and the value of the property as it would have been if it had been as described (*Perry v Sidney Phillips & Son* [1982] 1 WLR 1297).

Hidden defects

6.03 It is often wise, particularly when investigating old property, to open up and inspect hidden portions of the building. If this is not done, the limitations of the investigation should be clearly pointed out to the client, and he should be asked to take a decision as to whether the expense of opening up is worthwhile. He must, of course, be informed of the probability or otherwise of, e.g. rot. If rot is discovered and it was not mentioned in the survey and the architect did not recommend opening up to check, he is almost certainly negligent.

7 Mortgages

7.01 It is not proposed to discuss this subject in detail, but architects should remember that alteration to premises will alter the value of the mortgagee's (the lender's) security. For this reason, most mortgages contain covenants requiring the borrower to obtain the mortgagee's consent to any proposed works. As with leases, there may be several lenders who have advanced different amounts at different times and these will rank in order of their priority. The architect should ask the client whether the property is mortgaged and request him to obtain any necessary consents.

8 Business tenancies – architects' offices

8.01 This review of business tenancies can be in outline only, and it is written from the point of view of architects as tenants of office premises. Three preliminary matters of importance should be noted:

1 An architect should be careful if a lease includes an absolute right for the landlord to forfeit the lease (i.e. terminate it early) in the event of bankruptcy. It is difficult – if not impossible – to raise finance from institutional lenders on the security of such a lease because the value of the architect's interest in the land is precarious.

2 Care should be taken to check the wording of covenants concerning assignment (transfer of the lease to another) or subletting (creation of a sub-lease, with the architect becoming landlord of the occupier). The immediate lease offered to the architect and any superior lease (as where the architect's landlord is a tenant of the freeholder) should be inspected. Particularly, the architect should examine the circumstances in which the landlord can give or refuse his consent to assignment or underletting.

3 For leases granted on or after 1 January 1996, the Landlord and Tenant (Covenants) Act 1995 has introduced a new statutory code for the enforcement of leasehold covenants. This has a number of consequences and the architect should discuss this fully with his solicitor. In particular, the architect should note that if he takes an assignment of a lease from an existing tenant, he is likely to be taking on all the obligations of the original tenant. Secondly, if the architect assigns the lease, he is likely to be required to guarantee performance of the leasehold covenants by the person to whom he assigns. Thirdly, there are some circumstances where a landlord can make the giving of his consent to assignment dependent on the fulfilment of stringent conditions, even if these are not reasonable. For leases granted before 1 January 1996, different rules apply and enquires should again be made of the solicitor handling the matter.

Protection of business tenants

8.02 Part II of the Landlord and Tenant Act 1954, as amended by Part I of the Law of Property Act 1969, provides a substantial measure of protection to occupiers of business premises by providing in effect that the tenant may continue in occupancy indefinitely, unless the landlord satisfies the court that a new tenancy ought not to be granted for certain defined statutory reasons (paragraph 8.03). If the tenant receives not less than 6 nor more than 12 months' notice of a purported termination, expiring not earlier than the existing tenancy would otherwise have ended, the tenant may within 2 months of receipt serve a counter-notice on the landlord that he is unwilling to leave and then apply to the court for a new tenancy.

8.03 There are a number of reasons that might prevent the grant of a new tenancy to the tenant; i.e. different circumstances that the landlord can rely on to recover the premises at the end of the original lease. The first three, if proved, conclusively prevent the tenant gaining a new tenancy, the latter four giving the court a discretion to deny a tenancy.

1   If, on termination of the existing tenancy, the landlord intends to demolish or reconstruct the premises and could not reasonably do so without possession of the whole, a new tenancy will be denied and the tenant must quit. (Since the 1969 Act, this does not prevent a new tenancy of the whole or part of the premises if the landlord will be able to do the work without seriously 'interfering' with the tenant's business.)
2   If the landlord proves that he intends to occupy the premises for his own business or as a residence a new tenancy will be denied. (Since 1969 the landlord may successfully resist a new tenancy if he intends the premises to be occupied by a company in which he has a controlling interest.)
3   If the landlord proves the premises are part of a larger holding for which he could obtain a substantially larger rent than for the individual parts, a new tenancy of the part will be denied.
4   If the tenant fails to keep the premises in repair, the court may deny a new tenancy.
5   If there are persistent delays in paying rent, the court may deny a new tenancy.
6   If there are breaches of covenant, the court may deny a new tenancy.
7   If the landlord is willing to provide suitable alternative accommodation on reasonable terms, the court may deny a new tenancy.

It should be noted, however, that their area of the law is likely to be reformed in the near future and so it will be necessary for the architect – as with all tenants of business premises – to such specialist advice.

Compensation

8.04 If the court cannot grant a new tenancy for any of the first three reasons above, the tenant will be entitled to compensation at the rateable value or twice the rateable value where the tenant and his predecessors in the same business have occupied for 14 years or more.

New tenancy

8.05 If the landlord is unable to rely successfully on any of the above grounds, a new tenancy of the business premises can be granted. The court will fix the terms of the tenancy, including the rent and length, provided this does not exceed 14 years.

9 Estoppel

9.01 It will not usually be the case that the architect will have many dealings with his client's neighbours. Such matters will usually be dealt with by the client or his solicitor and this is by far the best option. However, circumstances may arise where the architect enters discussions about rights or interests affecting either his client's or the neighbour's land: e.g. discussions about the route of a new access way, the extent of overhanging eaves, drainage channels, etc. In such cases, the architect must take care not to make representations concerning his client's land that could later be held to be binding on his client: e.g. as to the route of the access. Although it is difficult to prove an 'estoppel' – i.e. that the architect has represented something about his client's land that the client is later held to – the architect should always make it clear that any agreement or offer with a neighbouring landowner is subject to written confirmation and should not be relied on by the neighbour until such confirmation is given. This is very important as the courts will enforce an estoppel against a person making such a representation and this can have serious consequences for the viability of the development.

5

Introduction to Scots law

PETER MCCORMACK

1 Law and Scotland

1.01 Scotland has always had a legal system separate and distinct from that of England. The two kingdoms were unified as the United Kingdom of Great Britain with effect from 1707 by the Treaty of Union and the two Acts of Union (one Scottish, one English), but the continuing separate identity of the Scots legal system was ensured by Articles 18 and 19 of the Treaty. In some areas of the law, there is little or no difference between Scotland and England, but in other areas the differences are such that the two jurisdictions might be in different states.

1.02 Until very recently the two jurisdictions have shared the same legislative body, the UK Parliament. Although many Acts of Parliament have applied only to Scotland, the UK majority of MPs has determined the nature and content of Scottish statute law. The restricted resource of UK Parliamentary time has also restricted the flow of Scottish legislation. From 1 July 1999 the position changed radically when the new Scottish Parliament went 'live'.

1.03 The Scotland Act 1998 created the devolved Scottish Parliament, the first elections which took place on 6 May 1999. The Scottish Parliament can pass laws (known as Acts of the Scottish Parliament) on any subject whatsoever, unless the Act stipulates otherwise. (This approach is in contrast to that of the ill-fated Scottish Assembly of the late 1970s, which could only legislate in areas explicitly specified under the Scotland Act 1978, had it come into force.) Under the 1998 Act, the UK Parliament retains the right to make laws for Scotland on any subject, including devolved areas, but political sensitivities will no doubt influence the extent to which it seeks to override the Scottish Parliament. Since July 1999 the flow of Scottish legislation affecting devolved matters has increased, and the legislation depends on voting majorities in the Scottish Parliament which are independent of and possibly different from UK Parliamentary majorities. In devolved matters, Scotland is governed by the Scottish Executive led by its First Minister. The form of proportional representation used for elections to the Scottish Parliament makes coalition or minority government more likely than in the UK Parliament. In fact after both Scottish general elections to date the Executive has been formed by a coalition of the Labour and Liberal Democrat Parties.

2 Sources

Parliamentary laws

2.01 Statutes (or Acts) of Parliament are one of the most important sources of law in Scotland. Some statutes of the old pre-1707 Scottish Parliament are still in force, written as they are in Scots rather than modern English! Acts of the UK Parliament, depending on their terms (usually found in the 'extent' section), can apply to all of the UK, including Scotland, or only to Scotland, or not to Scotland at all. Since July 1999 Acts of the Scottish Parliament apply to Scotland, and fewer UK Acts are likely so to apply.

2.02 Many important areas of the law remain outwith the legislative power of the Scottish Parliament, however. These include many aspects of business and commercial law. Architects should note that regulation of their profession is a matter outwith the competence of the Scottish Parliament, as is regulation of the sale and supply of goods and services to consumers.

2.03 Many Acts of Parliament include provisions allowing further detailed laws to be made by secondary legislation, known as Statutory Instruments. These pass through Parliament comparatively quickly and simply compared with Acts of Parliament. Some laws are made as orders by the government acting under the Royal Prerogative. In devolved areas, secondary laws may also be made by ministers of the Scottish Executive.

European laws

2.04 The UK has been a member of what is now the European Union since 1973. Many parts of the Treaty of Rome are directly applicable as law in Scotland. EU Regulations, made by the EU's Council of Ministers, are also directly applicable as law. EU Directives are not usually directly applicable as law, but require member states to implement them by way of domestic legislation. The Scottish Parliament requires to implement EU directives which affect devolved matters.

2.05 Until recently, although the UK as a member state of the Council of Europe has been a signatory to the Convention on Human Rights, the Convention was not in general directly enforceable before Scottish courts. This changed from October 2000 when the Human Rights Act 1998 came fully into force. The Act obliges Scottish courts to interpret legislation so far as possible to make it compatible with human rights under the Convention. The courts are also entitled to declare that an Act of the UK or Scottish Parliament is incompatible with such human rights.

Common law

2.06 Not every law can be found in or derived from an Act of Parliament. Many laws are simply part of the unwritten law of the land. For example, there is no statute in Scotland which provides that murder or theft are criminal offences. Such laws form what is known as the common law. The principles of Scottish common law are illustrated by reported decisions of the Scottish courts over the centuries. Such reported decisions may be described as 'precedents', but Scottish courts tend to be more concerned to discover the principle which justifies any particular law rather than to search, perhaps forlornly, for an example which sets a precedent. Rules of common

law may be changed by statute, and may be thought of as the legal background to statutory law.

2.07 Reporting of court decisions did not become properly systematic in Scotland until the early nineteenth century. There are certain historical textbooks, however, which pre-date that time and which are regarded as having authority broadly equivalent to court decisions as statements of the law. These books are known as 'institutional writings', and include Craig's *Jus Feudale* (1655), Stair's *Institutions of the Law of Scotland* (1681), Bankton's *Institute of the Laws of Scotland* (1751–53), Erskine's *Institute of the Law of Scotland* (1773) and Bell's *Commentaries on the Laws of Scotland* (1804) and *Principles of the Law of Scotland* (1829).

2.08 Decisions of Scottish courts are now widely available in the official series of reports called Session Cases (since 1821), as well as in the *Scots Law Times* (since 1893) and other more recent series of reports. Recent decisions of the Court of Session have been available since 1999 on the Internet at the website www.scotcourts.gov.uk.

Influence of Roman law

2.09 It is sometimes said that Scots law, unlike English law, is based on Roman law. While this is not immediately apparent today, some Scots common law is based on the system of Roman law which applied in the Eastern Roman Empire around the time of the Emperor Justinian in the sixth Century AD. There are two reasons for the influence of Roman law in Scotland. First, prior to the Reformation, much jurisdiction of private law was in the hands of ecclesiastical courts, which administered canon law with an ultimate appeal to the Papal Court at Rome; this formed the basis of matrimonial law and influenced other branches, such as the law of succession and the law of contract. Second, for many years Scotland was more in touch with other European countries than with England. Many Scots lawyers underwent part of their legal education abroad, particularly in Holland and, as a result, were influenced by the study of Roman law in Continental universities.

Equity in Scots law

2.10 The dichotomy in English law between common law and equity, which were administered by separate courts, was never a feature of Scots law. Scottish courts have long taken equitable principles into consideration, and equity is regarded as a principle which forms part of the law rather than as a force acting in opposition to it.

3 Courts and the legal profession

European Court

3.01 In civil matters (i.e. non-criminal matters) the Scottish legal system is subject ultimately to decisions of the European Court of Justice based in Luxembourg. The British judge in the European Court happens to be a Scottish lawyer, Judge David Edward QC. The European Court expects national courts to apply European law where that law is clear. Where difficult questions of European law arise, the European Court can interpret its proper application.

House of Lords

3.02 Subject to the European Court, the ultimate court of appeal in civil matters is the House of Lords, the judicial committee of which deals with appeals on points of law from the Inner House of the Court of Session. The House of Lords usually has a minimum of two Scottish judges to ensure that some Scottish experience is brought to bear in Scottish appeals. The Scottish judges on the judicial committee are presently Lord Hope of Craighead and Lord Rodger of Earlsferry.

Court of Session

3.03 The supreme court in Scotland is the Court of Session, which is based only in Edinburgh. There are presently about 30 judges, also known in their civil capacity as Senators of the College of Justice. When judges hear cases alone, they are said to be sitting as

'Outer House' judges, and when they hear appeals together in groups (usually of three) they are sitting as 'Inner House' judges. The most senior Scottish judge, presently Lord Cullen, is known as the 'Lord President' in his civil capacity. Inner House sittings chaired by the Lord President are known as the 'First Division'. The second most senior Scottish judge, presently Lord Gill, is known as the Lord Justice-Clerk, who chairs Inner House sittings known as the 'Second Division'. Inner House courts are sometimes chaired by other senior judges, when they are called 'Extra Divisions'. The Inner House primarily hears appeals from the Outer House or the Sheriff Court. The opinion of a Court of Session judge is formally equal in authority to that of any other judge, and so the unanimous decision of three judges (in any Division) can only by overruled by the House of Lords or by a larger Inner House Court (of five or seven or even more). Such larger Inner House sittings are referred to as Full Benches. The Outer House of the Court of Session can entertain almost any kind of action, save those where no more than £1500 is claimed, which must be raised in the lower, local courts – the Sheriff Courts.

Sheriff Courts

3.04 Scotland is divided into six Sheriffdoms, in which most large towns have a Sheriff Court. Most actions may be raised in the Sheriff Court: there is no maximum amount which may be sued for, but actions which seek to challenge the validity of documents (actions of reduction) must be raised in the Court of Session. If no more than £1500 is sued for then only the Sheriff Courts have jurisdiction. Sheriff Court judges are known as Sheriffs, and each Sheriffdom is presided over by a Sheriff Principal. Appeals may be made from decisions of Sheriffs either to the Sheriff Principal or directly to the Inner House of the Court of Session. Appeals may also be made from the decision of a Sheriff Principal to the Inner House.

Criminal courts

3.05 Crime (in increasing order of seriousness) is dealt with by District Courts (presided over by magistrates), Sheriff Courts and the High Court of Justiciary. The High Court comprises the same judges as the Court of Session, but sits in various major cities and towns around Scotland (permanently in Glasgow and Edinburgh). Appeals lie to the Court of Criminal Appeal in Edinburgh, presided over by the Lord Justice General (who is always the same person as the Lord President), the Lord Justice-Clerk or another senior judge. Unlike in civil matters, there is no appeal to the House of Lords. An exception to this rule is where an accused person claims that the prosecutor is acting in breach of his human rights. As such a breach would be forbidden as beyond the powers of the prosecutor under the Scotland Act 1998, the accused person may appeal to the judicial committee of the Privy Council. The criminal courts are subject to the European Court in matters of interpretation of European law which are occasionally relevant.

Legal profession

3.06 As in England, the legal profession in Scotland is divided into two branches, solicitors and advocates (equivalent to barristers in England). By far the more numerous are solicitors, who deal directly with clients and see to all their legal affairs. All solicitors are members of the Law Society of Scotland which is their statutory regulatory body. The Society has for the past few years operated an Accredited Specialists' Scheme whereby areas of specialization may be recognized. There are presently twelve such areas, including construction law and planning law. Actions concerning personal injuries commenced in the Court of Session since April 2003 also have their own 'fast-track' procedure.

3.07 The other branch of the profession consists of advocates divided into senior counsel (QCs) and junior counsel. They all belong to the Faculty of Advocates, a collegiate professional body which maintains the Advocates Library, a library with legal copyright which was founded in 1689 and the non-legal texts of which were donated to the Scottish nation to found the National Library of Scotland in

the 1920s. Advocates specialize in the presentation of cases before courts and other tribunals and in giving opinions on matters of law. In general they only receive instructions indirectly from clients through their solicitors, but members of certain organizations (including the Architects Registration Council of the UK, the Association of Consultant Architects, the Royal Incorporation of Architects in Scotland, the Royal Institute of Chartered Surveyors, and the Royal Town Planning Institute) may in many circumstances instruct counsel direct.

4 Branches of the law

4.01 Differences among branches of English and Scottish law of interest to architects will be mentioned when particular topics are discussed later in this book. At this stage, only some of the more important differences are mentioned.

Contract

4.02 In Scots law the element of consideration essential to the formation of a binding contract is unnecessary. A contract is an agreement between parties which is intended to have legal effect. It is therefore perfectly possible to have a gratuitous contract, i.e. one which all obligations rest on one side.

4.03 Sealed contracts have no place in Scots law but some contracts must be in writing to be properly constituted, the most important examples of these being contracts relating to heritable property, i.e. land and buildings, and leases. The Requirements of Writing (Scotland) Act 1995 introduced changes for executing legal documents under Scots law. For example, documents which used to require two witnesses now require only one. The provisions of the Act are complex and care needs to be taken to avoid becoming committed to a legally enforceable contract by informal documentation or actings. In case of any doubt legal advice should be sought.

Jus quaesitum tertio

4.04 In Scots law, parties to a contract may confer an enforceable right on a third party who takes no part in the formation of the contract. Provided appropriate circumstances obtain, a right known as a *jus quaesitum tertio* can be conferred on the third party, which enables the third party to enforce provisions in their favour agreed upon by the contracting parties. This is particularly important in relation to enforcement of building conditions. In the Scottish feudal system (see paragraph 4.08 below), where several feuars or vassals hold land from the same superior, building conditions imposed in the feu contract may, in appropriate circumstances, be enforceable by one feuar against another; for example, alterations or particular kinds may be prevented.

Partnership

4.05 In contrast to the English position, a Scottish partnership is not in law simply a collection of individuals. The firm has a legal personality – i.e. an existence of its own – separate from those persons who compose it, and it can, for example, sue for debts owed to it in its own name. The separate existence of the firm does not, however, prevent the personal liability of the partners from being unlimited. Partnership law is dealt with in detail in Chapter 29.

Delict

4.06 The law of delict is that part of the law which deals with righting of legal wrongs, in the civil, as opposed to the criminal, sense. Broadly it is the Scottish equivalent of the English law of tort. The background and details of the Scots law of delict and the English law of torts are different in too many respects to mention here. They broadly cover the same ground, with the Scottish law concentrating more on general principle and less on specific wrongs than the corresponding English law. Although the wrong complained of may arise out of deliberate conduct, most actions based in delict arise out of negligence.

Property

4.07 Property law is perhaps the field in which Scots and English law diverge most widely, particularly in relation to the law of land ownership. Differences are so great and so fundamental that detailed consideration of them is deferred to Chapter 6.

4.08 Brief mention may be made, however, of the feudal system of land ownership which has uniquely persisted in Scotland. All land is owned in theory ultimately by the Crown. Parcels of land may be held from the Crown by vassals, so that the Crown is the ultimate superior. The immediate vassals of the Crown may sell parcels of land not absolutely, but under 'feu dispositions', the effect of which is to create a sub-vassal of the vassal, who becomes the sub-vassal's superior. This process of feuing land may continue indefinitely in a downwards chain of superiors and vassals, so one ends up with a pyramid-like system with the Crown at the apex and the ultimate vassals at the bottom. It is the ultimate vassal who enjoys the usual rights of land ownership, but each feu contract in the chain of ownership may create obligations and restrictions which burden the full enjoyment of ownership. Abolition of the feudal system has been an early priority of the Scottish Parliament Legislation which abolishes the system, namely the Abolition of Feudal Tenure etc. (Scotland) Act 2000 and the Title Conditions (Scotland) Act 2003 has been enacted, and it is anticipated that it will largely come into force from about November 2004. The Acts make detailed provision for the continued effect of certain kinds of feudal conditions.

Limitation periods

4.09 Limitation periods also differ in some respects between Scots and English law. Legal advice should always be sought in any question of when proceedings should be commenced. In general terms actions for personal injuries require to be raised within three years of the date of the incident giving rise to the right of action (or from death arising if in a fatal accident case). Actions for enforcement of civil obligations, e.g. contracts or debt, must generally be raised within five years from when the right of action comes into existence. There are various other periods which should be considered, e.g. in relation to obligations relating to land. Legislation regarding statutory periods is principally to be found in the Prescription and Limitation (Scotland) Act 1973.

6

Scots land law

ANGUS STEWART QC

1 Introduction

1.01 It may be helpful to start with the fourfold classfication of property and its terminology:

- Heritage or heritable property, i.e. land and buildings
- Incorporeal heritable property, i.e. rights over land and buildings
- Movable property, i.e. money and goods
- Incorporeal movable property, e.g. shares, debts, copyright

The importance of the distinctions is that for the various kinds of property there are different mechanisms for constituting and transferring title, rights and obligations; and the classes of property receive different treatment for a variety of purposes, e.g. succession on death, taxation.

1.02 The categories are not hard and fast. Movable property can become heritable by incorporation or attachment or on the accessory principle. Building materials are movable: but when incorporated into a building they become part of the heritage. Articles installed in a building (e.g. light fittings, central heating systems, machinery) are also part of the heritage if sufficiently attached. The important point is generally the degree of physical connection – whether, for example, the thing in question can be removed without damage to itself or the heritage. Things may also be heritable because they are essential accessories of the heritage as, for example, the keys of a house, or unattached articles essential for the operation of fixed machinery.

1.03 Equally heritable property can become movable by severance. Examples are minerals mined or quarried from the land, or standing timber which is felled.

1.04 There can be significant financial consequences. The value of premises for rating or security purposes depends on what plant and machinery is counted in as part of the heritage. Buildings are generally sold 'complete with fixtures and fittings': but it would be unwise to assume that any particularly valuable item is included. Felled timber and harvested crops are not generally included in a sale of land.

Corporeal and incorporeal property

1.05 Heritable and movable property are both further classified as corporeal or incorporeal, the former being tangible, the latter consisting of intangible rights. Examples of incorporeal heritable property are servitude rights (paragraph 3.07), such as rights of wayleave for pipes, or security rights in heritage. Thus rights of a building society over property on the security of which it has given a loan are incorporeal heritable property. Examples of incorporeal movable property are money debts, shares in a partnership or limited company and intellectual property rights.

2 Title to heritage and title conditions

2.01 For centuries public recording of the deed of grant or contract has been essential to perfect the title to heritage in Scotland. Traditionally, deeds have been recorded in the Register of Sasines. If a deed recorded in the Register appears good and has been followed by possession for 10 years, the title is beyond challenge. Under the Land Registration (Scotland) Act 1979, the traditional system is being replaced, in one area after another, by a new, simplified system of registration of titles in the Land Register for Scotland. In general, an entry in the title sheet made up by the Keeper represents an unchallengeable entitlement to the registered interest, be it a right of ownership, security or wayleave. Entries in the title sheet are conclusive of the location and extent of the property and of all interests affecting it. The technical content of deeds is reduced and conveyancing simplified. Registered titles are backed by a State guarantee. In exceptional cases the Keeper can accept a title for registration under exclusion of guarantee. A non guaranteed title becomes unchallengeable if possession follows for ten years after registration. About half of the properties in Scotland are now (2004) entered in the Land Register

Divided ownership and shared ownership

2.02 Ownership may be divided and shared in a number of ways. The right of occupation and use, or life-rent, may belong to one owner and the reversionary interest, or fee, to another. Separate flats in a single tenement block can be held on distinct titles with the proprietors having shared rights in the underlying land, the stair, the roof, etc. and mutual rights in the floor/ceiling joists. Minerals in and under the land may be reserved to separate ownership. It is commonplace for two and sometimes more individuals to be recorded as *pro indiviso* co-owners of a single dwelling-house. The common law on allocation of responsibilities for co-owned property is well developed; and there are mechanisms for selling up and dividing the proceeds under court supervision in the event of deadlock.

2.03 Under the feudal system ownership of heritage was divided vertically between 'superiors' who retained the radical right or *dominium directum* and 'vassals' who enjoyed the *dominium utile*. The Crown was the paramount superior. The characteristic of feudal tenure was its perpetual quality; and the characteristic of feudal title conditions was that they continued to burden the vassal's heritage through all changes of ownership. The main use and value of the system, as developed over the centuries, lay in the framework it provided for imposing long-term control for communal benefit on the development and use of land.

Abolition of the feudal system

2.04 The Abolition of Feudal Tenure etc. (Scotland) Act 2000 (as amended) abolishes the feudal system with effect from 28

November 2004. From the appointed day all lingering monetary obligations, known as 'feu duties', are automatically abolished.

2.05 The Act abolishes all 'superiorities' and in every case consolidates outright ownership in the *dominium utile*.

2.06 The Act abolishes the superior's right to 'irritate the feu', i.e. to recover the property in the event of non-payment of feu duty or breach of a feudal title condition.

2.07 The Act abolishes feudal title conditions or 'real burdens' insofar as enforceable by former feudal superiors in that capacity. Feudal title conditions which are intended also to be enforceable by co-proprietors, for example where there is a common scheme of development, remain enforceable at the instance of co-proprietors (paragraph 2.16 below). Non-feudal title conditions, imposed by conveyances or agreements which do not purport to create or give effect to a feudal relationship of 'superior' and 'vassal', but which are capable of being constituted as real burdens, are unaffected by the Act. It has been estimated that at least one-half of title conditions are unaffected by the Act. The Act does not affect personal conditions included in titles to heritage. The Act has no effect on servitudes (paragraphs 3.07 and 3.10 below). The 2000 Act has to be read with the Title Conditions (Scotland) Act 2003, coming into force on the appointed day, which amends the 2000 Act, codifies the law on title conditions and introduces new ways of creating conditions and new types of condition.

2.08 An incidental effect of the abolition of feudal tenure is that business partnerships such as architects' firms can now own heritage in their own name. The traditional approach, whereby partnership property is held in the name of trustees on behalf of the partnership, may continue to be used.

Continuation of feudal title conditions

2.09 Though superiors' rights of enforcement as such are abolished by the 2000 Act, feudal title conditions not expressly abolished are or can generally be preserved for enforcement by owners of benefited properties, former superiors and official bodies as the case may be.

Facility, service, and amenity conditions

2.10 The bulk of title conditions have been usefully classified as 'facility conditions', 'service conditions', and 'amenity conditions'. Facility conditions are typically concerned with the management and maintenance of common facilities such as common parts of a tenement building, common recreational areas, private roads, private sewerage systems, and boundary walls. Service conditions bind the owner of the burdened property to permit services, such as water or electricity, to be supplied to the benefited property. Amenity conditions typically preserve the amenity of neighbouring properties by prohibiting specified development and use of the burdened property.

2.11 There is a difference in the mechanism for the perpetuation of feudal facility/service conditions and of amenity conditions respectively. Feudal facility and service conditions are preserved automatically and are enforceable by all benefited proprietors. Feudal amenity conditions are saved only if the superior 'reallots' the benefit to specified neighbouring properties by statutory notice and registration in the Land Register. The 2000 Act section 18 lays down stringent prerequisites for registration. For example, the benefited property must have a permanent building for 'human habitation or resort'; and the building must lie within 100 metres of the burdened property. In certain circumstances the Lands Tribunal for Scotland has power to waive compliance. The 100 metre rule does not apply to conditions giving rights to enter, to extract minerals from or to fish for salmon in the burdened property.

Conservation conditions

2.12 Feudal title conditions designed to preserve or protect the architectural or historical characteristics of land and buildings or to conserve special characteristics of the natural environment can be saved if the former feudal superior is the Scottish Executive or a recognized conservation body. Notice has to be given and the conditions have to be registered before the statutory deadline.

Maritime conditions

2.13 Feudal title conditions affecting the foreshore or sea bed in favour of the Crown are automatically converted on the appointed day into 'maritime conditions' and continue in force. No notice is required.

Pre-emption, redemption, and reversion

2.14 Feudal titles may contain conditions giving the superior the right to buy back the property. A pre-emption clause stipulates that if the burdened owner wishes to sell he or she must first offer the property to the superior, either at a fixed price or, more commonly, at the price which he or she has been offered on exposure for sale and for which he or she would sell in the event of no pre-emption. Such a right is now exercisable on the occasion of the first sale only and must be exercised within 21 days of the burdened owner's offer to the superior. A redemption clause allows buy-back at any time for a fixed period. Under clauses of reversion the property reverts to the superior with or without compensation on the occurrence of some specified event such as, typically, the cessation of use of the property for a charitable purpose. These clauses can be preserved by a notice and registration or can be converted into personal rights under the 2000 Act as amended by the Title Conditions (Scotland) Act 2003.

Development conditions: compensation

2.15 If the effect of a feudal title condition is to reserve the development value to the superior, compensation has to be paid to the former superior if relevant development takes place within 20 years, provided the condition is a qualifying condition and has been duly registered before the statutory deadline. Disputes about compensation may be referred to the Lands Tribunal for Scotland.

Ius quaesitum tertio

2.16 As indicated above feudal title conditions conceived for the benefit of the neighbourhood and inserted into all titles in a common scheme of development remain enforceable by any of the neighbours even if no longer by the superior. This right is called *ius quaesitum tertio*. If, for example, a superior has at some time feued out lots of land on which buildings are to be erected according to a uniform plan, one neighbour has the right to object to another departing from the plan or breaching other conditions. The breach must affect the complainer directly in some way, for instance by damaging the amenity of his or her property.

Creation of new title conditions

2.17 The Title Conditions (Scotland) Act 2003 codifies the common law with a number of innovations. From 28 November 2004 any deed can be used to create perpetual title conditions affecting land, i.e. 'real burdens'. For reciprocal conditions the benefited and burdened properties must be specified and the conditions must be registered against both properties.

2.18 The 2003 Act provides in a number of ways for the regulation of common interests in related properties. 'Manager burdens' may be inserted to constitute the owner of one property the manager of all related properties. 'Community burdens' may be constituted where four or more units have mutual rights and obligations. Part 6 of the Act introduces a model Development Management Scheme.

2.19 The Act creates a number of new types of burden or labels for burdens in respect of which there is no benefited property. 'Maritime burdens' may be reserved to the Crown for public benefit. 'Conservation burdens' may be created in favour of the Scottish Ministers or conservation bodies recognized by them. 'Economic development burdens' may be inserted in favour of the Scottish Ministers and local authorities with the object of promoting development. 'Rural housing burdens' may be inserted to give a right of pre-emption in favour of rural housing bodies. 'Health care burdens' in favour of NHS Trusts or the Scottish Ministers may be inserted for the purpose of promoting facilities for health care.

Enforceability

2.20 Proprietors of benefited properties may enforce facility, service, and amenity conditions. Maritime, conservation, economic development, rural housing, and health care conditions are enforceable by the relevant official bodies. Where the statutory provisions for preservation or conversion have been complied with, former superiors and their assignees can enforce rights of pre-emption, redemption and reversion, and can claim compensation where development value is reserved. Individual proprietors having the benefit of *ius quaesitum tertio* can enforce title conditions. The new 'community burdens' for managing developments of four or more units are enforceable by a majority. Where there is a 'manager burden' a two-thirds majority of owners can dismiss and appoint managers.

2.21 Conditions to be enforceable must be precise. The presumption is that the owners are free to do as they wish with their property. Any ambiguity will be construed in favour of the owner of the allegedly burdened property.

Altering and discharging title conditions

2.22 Title conditions can be altered and discharged by waiver or by agreement or by order of the Lands Tribunal. Under the Conveyancing and Feudal Reform (Scotland) Act 1970 (as amended) and the Title Conditions (Scotland) Act 2003 the Lands Tribunal has power to vary, discharge, renew and preserve title conditions, and 'land obligations' generally in accordance with specified statutory criteria. This includes powers formerly held by a sheriff (Chapter 5) under the Housing (Scotland) Act 1966 to allow the division of a single dwelling house into two or more dwellings contrary to the title conditions. The Lands Tribunal has power to order payment of compensation and to add or substitute different provisions. It is, of course, still open to parties to come to a private arrangement, and there may be situations in which such an arrangement is more convenient than an application to the Tribunal.

Extinction of title conditions

2.23 Non-feudal irritancies are extinguished by the 2003 Act. Under the Act other title conditions may be susceptible to extinction by prescription 5 years after the commencement of any unchallenged breach, or *pro tanto* by acquiescence in breaches. Some title conditions which have existed for 100 years may be extinguished by a notice of termination, if uncontested. There are complex rules for the extinction of manager burdens. After the appointed day it is no longer competent to create negative servitudes. Existing negative servitudes become real burdens and are extinguished unless registered within 10 years. Real burdens and servitudes are extinguished by compulsory purchase.

Leases

2.24 A proprietor may lease his property to another, the basis of the contract being that the tenant has the right to occupy and make use of the property in return for payment of rent. There are numerous statutory provisions regulating leases of various kinds, mainly by restricting rents or providing some degree of security of tenure for the tenant.

Business tenancies

2.25 The statutory provisions relating to security of tenure in business tenancies which apply in England (Chapter 4) do not extend to Scotland. The architect who rents office premises in Scotland relies on the contract with his landlord for the terms of his tenure, there being no corresponding Scottish legislation.

Surveys

2.26 The responsibilities of Scottish architects with regard to surveys are the same as for English architects (Chapter 32).

3   Other restrictions on heritable property

3.01 Numerous other restrictions, both statutory and otherwise, may affect the proprietor of heritable property. Houses let for multiple occupation by more than two unrelated persons have to be licensed by local authorities for compliance with fire, health, and safety precautions in terms of the Civic Government (Scotland) Act 1982 and orders made thereunder.

Statutory restrictions

3.02 It is not proposed to enter into the statutory restrictions in detail, but obvious examples of these are the Town and Country Planning Acts and the statutes and regulations governing compulsory purchase (Chapter 23). Various bodies have power to enter land or premises compulsorily (Chapter 20). A number of uses are not permitted except under licence (sale of alcohol, gaming, sex shops, etc.). The Public Health (Scotland) Acts prohibit the carrying on of a large number of activities, defined as statutory nuisances, on various kinds of property. A proprietor is also subject to building regulations administered by the appropriate local authority in respect of any building operations he may wish to carry out (Chapter 22). A statutory right to continue in occupation of the family home is given to the spouse of the owner or tenant by the Matrimonial Homes (Family Protection) Scotland Act 1981. The right can be enforced against third parties who should protect their interest by getting the protected spouse's consent to any transaction in accordance with the statutory formalities. Unless 'de-crofted', croft land and buildings continue subject to the statutory crofting regime even after purchase by the crofting tenant.

3.03 In addition the occupier of premises is obliged under the Occupiers' Liability (Scotland) Act 1960 to take reasonable care to see that persons entering the premises (which include land and other types of property) do not suffer injury owing to the state of the premises. Failure to take care results in liability for accidents.

Common structures

3.04 In his use of his property the proprietor may also have to take into account the interests of his neighbours in a variety of ways. Where there is a common gable or dividing wall between two properties, either proprietor may object to the other carrying out operations which may be injurious to it, since it is common property. Where the property is a flatted or tenement building in which each house is owned separately, each proprietor has a common interest in the property outwith his own, so far as necessary for his support and shelter. Thus although the external walls of each property belong to individual proprietors, they may not interfere with them in such a way as to endanger the other properties. Similarly each proprietor is sole owner of his floors and ceilings, to the mid-point of the joists, but must not interfere with them in such a way as to weaken his neighbour's floor or ceiling. The roof of a tenement property belongs to the owner of the top storey, but all proprietors in the building have a common interest in seeing that it is properly maintained, and they may compel the owner to keep it in repair and to refrain from damaging it. Common stairs and passages are the common property of all to whose premises they form an access, and all are obliged to maintain them. If alterations to common property or the roof are contemplated it is often (though not always) necessary to obtain the consent of all proprietors. Clients should be advised to consult their solicitors who can check the titles and, if necessary, attempt to obtain consents.

3.05 These rules apply to all tenement property in Scotland, unless, as frequently happens, there is express provision in the titles, in which case the provisions in the titles prevail over the common law rules. A check on the titles by the client's solicitor should reveal title conditions which may affect design.

3.06 It often happens that there are difficulties in getting all proprietors in a tenement building to agree to mutual repairs. There may be difficulty in deciding, without legal advice, whether a particular repair is a mutual responsibility or in agreeing how the cost of the repair should be allocated. There may be a property management or factoring arrangement. Local authorities have statutory powers to carry out repairs and charge the cost to all proprietors in proportion to the rateable value of their properties. The local authority should be applied to in the case of deadlock among the proprietors. Under the Civic Government (Scotland) Act 1982 councils have powers to light common stairs and passages and to require common areas to be kept clean and properly decorated. Fire authorities have power to deal with fire hazards in common areas.

Servitudes

3.07 Servitudes are roughly similar to easements in English law. A servitude is an obligation on one piece of heritage, the 'servient tenement', to provide some service for a neighbouring property, the 'dominant tenement'. Servitudes are founded on agreement and traditionally might be expressed or implied and either positive or negative. A positive servitude entitles the proprietor of the dominant tenement to act on or in relation to the servient tenement, for example by taking access across it. A negative servitude entitles the proprietor of the dominant tenement to require his neighbour to refrain from acting in certain ways, for example from building above a certain height, for the purpose of preserving the amenity of the dominant tenement. Property may be subject to many different kinds of servitude, including servitudes of support, stillicide (*cf.* eavesdrop) and light, affecting mainly urban property, and servitudes of way or access and drawing or conducting water, affecting land.

3.08 The Title Conditions (Scotland) Act 2003 provides that, subject to the existing rule about constitution by uninterrupted use for 20 years, new positive servitudes can be created only by registration against both the benefited and burdened properties. A new positive servitude need no longer be of a type already recognized by the law. It is expressly provided that the right to lead services over other land may be constituted as a positive servitude. Existing real burdens conferring a right of entry (other than for ancillary purposes) are automatically converted to positive servitudes.

3.09 Under the Act of 2003 it is no longer competent to create negative servitudes. Existing negative servitudes are automatically converted into real burdens. Converted servitudes will be extinguished in 10 years unless registered against the burdened property in accordance with the statutory provisions.

3.10 Many of the matters which are subjects of servitudes, including support and light, are within the provisions of the Scottish Building Regulations (Chapter 22).

Natural rights

3.11 A proprietor may also have to take account of natural rights of his neighbours or others. Natural rights arise independently of any separate contract or title, through ownership of the land. They include the right of support of land. Thus a proprietor may not quarry up to the boundary of his land if this would lead to subsidence of his neighbour's land. He is not entitled to interfere with a stream flowing through his land in such a way as to change its natural flow as it comes to his neighbour's land, since all the riparian proprietors have a common interest in the stream and may object if they are deprived of its natural flow. He may not carry on operations on his property which constitute a 'nuisance', i.e. which interfere with his neighbour's right to the comfortable enjoyment of his property. What is or is not a nuisance at common law depends on the nature of the neighbourhood, but it may consist of excessive noise or foul smells. If a nuisance has existed without challenge for a period of 20 years or more, however, it cannot be objected to.

Rights of way

3.12 Land may be subject to a public right of way, which is a right for members of the public to pass by a definite route over land from one public place to another. Such a right is almost invariably constituted by use for a period of 20 years, and lapses if not used for that period.

3.13 The Prescription and Limitation (Scotland) Act 1973 now gives in one statute the various periods of occupation or use required to set up rights over land, from ownership to rights of way, and conversely the periods of non-use which will defeat claims, for example of servitude.

Land Reform (Scotland) Act 2003

3.14 The Land Reform (Scotland) Act 2003, Part 1, gives the public the right to enter all land for recreational and educational purposes, etc., and to cross all land for the purpose of getting from one place to another, subject to limited exceptions. The exceptions include buildings and other structures, industrial plant, caravans, tents or other places used for privacy or shelter and contiguous land, private gardens, to which there is a right of common access, and land under cultivation. Building and engineering sites are expressly excepted from the right of public access.

3.15 Part 2 of the Act gives local communities a right to buy land with which the community has a connection when the land comes to be sold. Part 3 of the Act gives crofting communities a right to buy.

4 Sale of land and buildings

4.01 The law does not recognize word-of-mouth agreements for the sale of land or buildings. Agreements for the sale of heritage must be in writing, signed and witnessed. Agreements once completed in normal Scottish form are binding and cannot be withdrawn from unilaterally. But such agreements do not of themselves effect a transfer of the property. Property is transferred when the title is delivered and recorded. Purchasers should normally not alter or spend money on property until they have a title. Since the title supersedes the sale agreement, purchasers' legal advisers should ensure that all sale conditions which are meant to have continuing effect are either incorporated into the title or otherwise kept in force.

4.02 The contract of sale is concluded and is binding on the purchaser and the seller when a written offer to purchase has been accepted in writing. It is too late thereafter for the purchaser to complain about the structural state of the property or that it is less extensive than he believed or is subject to title conditions that prevent his using it in the way he intended.

4.03 Normally missives of sale are concluded by solicitors acting for the parties. Prospective purchasers would be well advised not to sign agreements prepared by house builders or developers without taking legal advice.

7

Introduction to Northern Ireland's legal system

JONATHAN L. DUNLOP AND BRIAN SHERRARD

1 Background

1.01 By virtue of its peculiar political history, Northern Ireland's legal development is intricate. Prior to the arrival of the Normans in Ireland in 1169, Brehon law governed Ireland. This was based upon traditional custom. As the Norman Conquest extended throughout Ireland post-1169, English common law gained increasing importance. The influence of English law ebbed and flowed until the early seventeenth century. After the Flight of the Earls and the Plantation of Ulster, however, English common law gained supremacy throughout Ireland and Brehon law ceased to apply – as established by the case of *Tanistry* (1607).

1.02 The legal system of Northern Ireland is one of 'common law' as are those of England and Wales, the Republic of Ireland, and numerous New World countries such as the USA, Canada and Australia to which it was exported. The reader is referred to the description of the common law given in the introductory section to this text for a more detailed explanation but the essential feature of the common law system is the doctrine of binding judicial precedent. This means that a decision on a point of law made by a court in the jurisdiction binds all lower courts in subsequent cases.

2 Northern Ireland's constitutional history

2.01 From the arrival of the Normans until 1495 both the Parliaments of Ireland and England claimed power to make laws for Ireland. In 1495 Poyning's Law settled the question of supremacy providing as it did that only legislation approved by the English Council could be passed by the Parliament in Ireland.

The Parliament in Ireland continued to exist until 1800 when it was abolished by the Act of Union. From then until 1921 the only Parliament passing laws for Ireland was the Parliament of the United Kingdom sitting at Westminster.

2.02 With partition came separate legal systems in the north and south. A devolved Northern Ireland Parliament was established in 1921 and it has sat at Stormont from 1932. This dealt with all matters transferred to it by the UK Parliament. There were certain matters, known as 'excepted matters' and 'reserved matters', in respect of which the Northern Ireland Parliament never had jurisdiction. 'Excepted matters' were those which were retained by the Parliament at Westminster and included foreign relations, the armed forces and external trade. 'Reserved matters' were those matters earmarked for the Council of Ireland and included all matters relating to the Supreme Court of Northern Ireland. The Northern Ireland Parliament had two chambers: a House of Commons and a Senate. In addition,

there were also elections of Northern Ireland representatives to the Westminster Parliament.

2.03 Devolution continued until March 1972 when it was suspended and direct rule commenced. This was always intended as a temporary measure and the laws in respect of the reclaimed transferred matters were made from 1972 onwards by way of Order-in-Council, a procedure whereby legislation does not journey fully through all stages of readings in both houses of the UK Parliament.

2.04 Since 1972 executive powers have been exercised by the Secretary of State for Northern Ireland with the activities of the various Stormont ministries being conducted by government departments e.g. the Department of Environment (NI) or the Department of Agriculture (NI). With the exception of a period in 1974, when the first Assembly briefly sat, this has continued to be the position until the implementation of a new Northern Ireland Assembly and Executive under the Northern Ireland Act of 1998.

3 The courts and the judiciary

3.01 The Government of Ireland Act 1920 created separate court structures in Ireland, north and south. A Supreme Court of Judicature was set up in Northern Ireland, which contains the High Court, the Crown Court and the Court of Appeal. The Crown Court deals with the more serious criminal matters. The High Court, which sits at the Royal Courts of Justice, Chichester Street, Belfast, consists of three divisions – the Family Division, the Queen's Bench Division and the Chancery Division. Cases are assigned to each division according to the nature of the subject matter. The Chancery Division will tend to deal with disputes about land and other property, inheritance and trusts and the construction of documents. Commercial matters and contractual disputes and other matters such as negligence suits will more usually be dealt with in the Queen's Bench Division.

3.02 Civil claims worth less than £15 000 will usually be dealt with by the County Court. Northern Ireland is divided geographically into seven County Court divisions and claims are brought either in the division in which the defendant resides or carries on business or in the division where the cause of action arose, such as where the negligent act took place or the breach of contract occurred.

3.03 The Magistrates' Courts are separated into 21 Petty Sessions districts and deal with less serious criminal matters, domestic matters such as the maintenance of dependants, and civil prosecutions such as street trading offences and some offences under the Companies (NI) Order 1986 such as penalizing directors for the late filing of company accounts. Northern Ireland has only legally trained Magistrates, being either solicitors or barristers of at least seven years' standing. This is unlike England and Wales where magistrates' courts are made up of a lay panel assisted by a legally trained clerk.

3.04 At the date of writing there are eleven High Court Judges all of whom are appointed by the Queen on the advice of the Lord Chancellor. The senior judicial figure in Northern Ireland is the Lord Chief Justice of Northern Ireland (at present Sir Robert Carswell). The Court of Appeal consists of the Lord Chief Justice and three other judges called Lord Justices of Appeal. The Court of Appeal deals with all appeals on a point of law from the High Court, the Crown Court and also the inferior courts. Appeal from the Court of Appeal may, in certain instances, be made to the House of Lords, where appeals will be decided according to Northern Ireland law.

3.05 County Court Judges sit throughout Northern Ireland. Given the volume of County Court business there is a considerable number of part-time Deputy County Court Judges who sit as and when required who are either practising barristers or practising solicitors. In addition, there are four District Judges (all of whom are Deputy County Court Judges).

3.06 The District Judge's Court has a monetary limit of £3000. The District Judges also sit as arbitrators in the Small Claims Court, which has a monetary jurisdiction of £1000. The Small Claims Court was established to provide a cost-effective way of dealing with less substantial claims. While barristers and solicitors may, and often do, appear in the Small Claims Court, the procedure is more relaxed with the laws of evidence not being strictly applied and applicants are encouraged to appear in person. There are excepted matters such as road traffic accidents, which cannot be dealt with by small claims procedure even where the value is less than £1000.

4 The legal profession

4.01 There are two branches of the legal profession in Northern Ireland: solicitors and barristers. Solicitors in private practice work individually or in partnerships, the size of which vary considerably throughout the jurisdiction. The work of a solicitor is manifold and includes conveyancing, the drafting of contracts and other legal documents, and preparing cases for court. While solicitors have rights of audience in the Magistrates' Courts, County Courts and Crown Courts and can thus speak on behalf of their clients, a barrister will often be engaged at this stage.

Barristers continue to have sole rights of audience in the High Court and Court of Appeal in Northern Ireland. They will, therefore, argue the case in court and help to prepare all the necessary proceedings. They may also be engaged in advising on or researching particular points of law. By reason of their professional rules, barristers are self-employed. Unlike in England and Wales, where barristers are part of sets of practices known as 'chambers', in Northern Ireland barristers work out of the Bar Library housed in the Royal Courts of Justice, Chichester Street, Belfast. Similar systems operate in Edinburgh and Dublin. Traditionally clients may not engage a barrister directly; the solicitor does this on the client's behalf. This particular rule has been relaxed in respect of certain categories of professional clients such as accountants and architects who may, in appropriate circumstances, take advantage of Direct Professional Access to barristers. As in other jurisdictions in the UK, barristers are either Junior Counsel or Senior Counsel. The latter are referred to as Queen's Counsel (QC).

5 Sources of law

5.01 Many common law countries such as the Republic of Ireland and the USA have written constitutions. These are superior laws against which the validity of other laws can be tested. The UK has no such superior body of law. Rather, there is an 'unwritten constitution'. This means that the UK constitution consists of the body of law on the statute book at any point of time, of the decisions of courts handed down in the past and of the traditions of the rule of law and parliamentary democracy recognized in the UK.

5.02 Because Northern Ireland is a common law system there is a considerable body of case law. This is to be found in a series of law reports such as the Northern Ireland Law Reports. Decisions from other common law jurisdictions, while not binding, are highly persuasive. Thus reports such as the Law Reports of England and Wales are heavily relied on in court. Increasingly, too, European legislation is impacting upon the UK domestic courts. This is especially so in the areas of competition law, corporate law and consumer protection and human rights.

Legislation

5.03 The legislation that applies to Northern Ireland consists of Acts of Parliament called 'statutes' (known as primary legislation) and also Rules and Regulations made under the authority of Acts of Parliament (known as secondary legislation). In Northern Ireland, as in any other part of the UK, courts cannot refuse to apply primary legislation on the ground that it is unconstitutional. Only later Parliaments can undo what an earlier Parliament has done – this is known as the doctrine of 'Parliamentary Sovereignty'. Secondary legislation may, however, be challenged on the grounds of being unlawful.

There are a number of different sources of primary legislation applicable to Northern Ireland:

- The Parliament of Ireland, 1310–1800
- The Parliament of England, 1226–1707
- The Parliament of Great Britain, 1707–1800
- The Parliament of the United Kingdom, 1800–present
- The Parliament of Northern Ireland, 1921–1972 (the date of its suspension)
- The Northern Ireland Assembly of 1974.

Branches of law

5.04 The basic divisions of law in Northern Ireland are consistent with those in England and Wales. There is a primary distinction between criminal law and civil law. The architect is, of course, more likely to be in contact with the civil law. This may be further divided, for example, into contract law, tort law, company law, employment law and planning law. As has been mentioned, there may be different pieces of legislation in force in Northern Ireland and specific differences will be identified in the relevant chapters.

6 Limitation periods

6.01 While limitation periods are essentially in keeping with those applicable to England and Wales it is vital that legal advice be sought in respect of when proceedings may be issued. Leaving the issue of proceedings too long may result in the claim becoming statute barred under the Limitation (NI) Order 1989, whatever the substantive merits of the case may be.

7 Contract law in Northern Ireland

7.01 The common and statute law of Northern Ireland in respect of contracts is the same as that of England and Wales for all practical purposes. The differences which exist are of form rather than substance due to Northern Ireland having its own legislative system. The following statutes referred to in the text, i.e.

Sale of Goods Act 1979
Supply of Goods and Services Act 1982
Unfair Contract Terms Act 1977
Unfair Terms in Consumer Contracts Regulations 1994

all apply to Northern Ireland and came into effect on the same dates as in England and Wales.

The Limitation Act 1980 does not apply in Northern Ireland and readers should refer to the Limitations (NI) Order 1989 (1989/1339). However, substantive law of limitations is the same in both jurisdictions.

7.02 An illustration of the desire to the courts of Northern Ireland to maintain parity with the law of England and Wales in commercial matters is to be found in *Beaufort Developments (NI) Ltd v Gilbert Ash (NI) Ltd and Anor* [1997] NI 142 (CA) where the Court of Appeal in Northern Ireland followed *Northern Regional Health Authority v Derek Crouch Constructions Co. Ltd* [1984] QB 664 (CA) even though it felt that decision was wrong (see op.cit. at p. 155 d–j) which decision along with *Crouch* was then overruled by the House of Lords on appeal (see [1998] 2 AllER 778 (HL)) so that the law of Northern Ireland and that of England and Wales remains the same in this respect.

8 Law of tort in Northern Ireland

8.01 The common law of Northern Ireland and England and Wales is the same in all material respects. There are some differences in the statute law which are noted below. In personal injury claims there are substantial differences in the levels of awards between the two jurisdictions. The Judicial Studies Board for Northern Ireland has issued its own *Guidelines for the Assessment of General Damages in Personal Injury Cases in Northern Ireland* dated February 1997.

Table of statutory equivalents

Defective Premises Act 1972	Defective Premises (NI) Order 1975
Occupier's Liability Act 1957	Occupier's Liability Act (NI) 1957
Occupier's Liability Act 1984	Occupier's Liability (NI) Order 1987
Building Act 1984	Building Regulations (NI) Order 1979 and the Planning and Building Regulations (Amendment) (NI) Order 1990
Limitation Act 1980	Limitation (NI) Order 1989
Latent Damage Act 1986	Originally Limitation (Amendment) (NI) Order 1987 but now the Limitation (NI) Order 1989
Law Reform (Contributory Negligence) Act 1945	Law Reform (Miscellaneous Provisions) Act (NI) 1948
Civil Liability (Contribution) Act 1978	Extends to Northern Ireland

9 Northern Ireland land law

Introduction

9.01 In England and Wales land law was greatly simplified by a series of statutes passed in 1925, chief among them being the Law of Property Act. This legislation was not extended to Northern Ireland, leaving the jurisdiction with statutes long since repealed in other parts of the UK e.g. the Settled Land Acts 1882–1890 and the Conveyancing Act 1881. Moreover, in some respects Northern Ireland has land law significantly different in detail from that which ever existed in England, e.g., the law of landlord and tenant, as still largely governed by the Landlord and Tenant Law Amendment, Ireland, Act 1860. The result is that Northern Ireland land law bears a substantial cosmetic similarity to that in England – the language and theory are largely the same – but has equally substantial differences of detail. Those dealing with this complicated area would be well advised to consult specialist texts and seek legal advice.

The extent of land

9.02 In broad terms, 'land' in Northern Ireland bears the same generally understood meaning as in England (i.e. buildings, fixtures, rights above and below ground and easements) and the reader is referred to paragraph 2.01 of Chapter 4. Similarly, as in England, an intrusion onto another's land is likely to be a trespass unless the intruder has a licence to be present (see paragraph 2.02 of Chapter 4). Boundaries are more often than not clear from the title deeds to the land. In registered land the description of the land in the register is not conclusive of the boundaries, although a procedure exists whereby adjoining owners may have their boundaries entered conclusively and in some circumstances the Registrar may enter boundaries as conclusive. In cases of dispute, a number of presumptions exist, for details of which readers should refer to specialist conveyancing texts. By way of example, in relation to party walls, a rebuttable presumption may arise of a tenancy in common. It should be noted that the Party Walls Act 1996 does not extend to Northern Ireland.

Title

9.03 A person buying land will invariably want to:

- substantiate the vendor's claim to ownership and
- clarify who else has interests in the land and the nature of those interests.

As in England and Wales, in Northern Ireland there are two distinct systems of registration – the registration of deeds system which is concerned with 'unregistered' land, and the registration of title system for 'registered' land. As a very general rule of thumb, much of the urban land in Northern Ireland is unregistered while title to agricultural land is generally registered. This is because when tenant farmers were given the opportunity to buy the fee simple estates in their land by means of land purchase annuities under the Land Purchase Acts of the late nineteenth century registration of those titles was made compulsory.

9.04 The Registration of Deeds Act (Northern Ireland) 1970, as amended by the Registration (Land and Deeds) (Northern Ireland) Order 1992, is the main legislation concerning unregistered land. The Act governs the Registry of Deeds, where memorials of conveyances and deeds relating to pieces of unregistered land are registered. Where a purchaser is buying unregistered land the vendor's proof of title is found in the title deeds, which are investigated by the purchaser's solicitor. The solicitor will search the Registry of Deeds to confirm the priority of the vendor's title and to discover other burdens affecting the land. As a general rule, the priority of interests in the land depends upon the date of registration of the interest rather than the date when it is created. The system does not guarantee the actual integrity of the interest itself, but merely priority between valid registered interests. Registration is not compulsory, although it is clearly advisable if the interest is to bind those coming later to the land. However, if a person has *actual* knowledge of a prior document which has not been registered, that unregistered document will enjoy priority over the registration of his subsequent document transferring to him an estate. The effectiveness of the system is also limited by the fact that registration is confined to interests that have been created by writing, with the result that interests otherwise created, e.g. an equitable mortgage by way of deposit of title deeds, remain unregisterable. The priority of such interests are determined by general principles of law including the equitable doctrine of notice.

9.05 The system of registration of title in Northern Ireland is similar to that in England in both theory and practice. The main legislation concerning this area is the Land Registration Act (Northern Ireland) 1970 as amended by the Registration (Land and Deeds) (Northern Ireland) Order 1992. While in the case of unregistered land, registration in the Registry of Deeds simply notes the existence of a deed and helps determine the priority of interests in the land, the system of registration of title provides an authorized record of the ownership of land and those burdens which affect it. A purchaser of unregistered land will have to examine the title deeds to establish good title, and search the Registry of Deeds to confirm the priority of interests in the land, while in theory a purchaser of registered land should find conclusive evidence of the title from the title register. If there are lingering doubts surrounding the antecedents of title prior to first registration, this may be reflected in the class of title registered. A purchaser of registered land takes it subject to the matters on the register affecting the land at the date of his registration. However, a major drawback of the system is that certain categories of interest (listed in Schedule 5 to the 1970 Act) may bind a registering purchaser even though they do not appear on the register. Perhaps the most troublesome of these is in paragraph 15 of Part 1 of Schedule 5 which protects the right of every person in actual occupation of the land. This had been used to give protection to those who claim to have an equitable interest in the land through, e.g., contributions to the purchase price, despite the fact that they do not appear on the register as having an interest. For this reason most purchasers will inquire of all occupants as to their rights in the property and inspect the land for signs of any other overriding interests, e.g. squatters or rights of way arising through long use. While the registration of title system is not without flaws, the 1970 Act makes provision for a policy of compulsory registration so that unregistered land will become a thing of the past. From 1 May 2003 all of Northern Ireland falls within a compulsory first registration area so where there is a sale of land the title must now be registered in the Land Registry.

9.06 In addition to registration of title and deeds there exists a Statutory Charges Register, established by the Statutory Charges Register Act (Northern Ireland) 1951 and now governed by the Land Registration Act (Northern Ireland) 1970. The Statutory Charges Register applied to both registered and unregistered land and is used to register the wide range of charges contained in Schedule 11 of the 1970 Act. The relevant charges are generally created by local authorities or government. Purchasers of registered and unregistered land will be bound by statutory charges registered in accordance with section 88 of the 1970 Act.

Easements

9.07 The basic components of any easement (i.e. dominant and servient tenement, benefit to the dominant tenement, separate ownership or at least occupation, and capacity to be the subject matter of a grant) are *substantially* the same in Northern Ireland as they are in England, as are the ways in which easements may be acquired. Readers are referred to section 3 of Chapter 4. However, there are a number of significant legislative and other differences that may be dealt with in passing. Section 62 of the Law of Property Act 1925 (referred to in paragraph 3.03 of Chapter 4 does not extend to Northern Ireland, although much of the same provision is applied by section 6 of the Conveyancing Act 1881. In relation to prescription (at paragraph 3.04 of Chapter 4) while English courts have restricted prescription between freeholders, the same approach has not been so vigorously adopted in Ireland where the prevalence of very long leases has diminished the meaningful distinction between freeholds and many leaseholds. The Rights of Light Act 1959 (as noted at paragraph 3.06 Chapter 4) does not apply in Northern Ireland where the Rights of Light Act (Northern Ireland) 1961 performs much the same function and theoretical wall obstruction notices are registered in the Statutory Charges Registry.

Freehold covenants

9.08 The law relating to freehold covenants is *substantially* the same in Northern Ireland as in England, and readers are referred to paragraph 3 of Chapter 4. It may, however, be more difficult in Northern Ireland to establish that the benefit of a covenant has run with the land as section 78 of the Law of Property Act does not apply. The most important point to bear in mind is that, as yet, the burden of a positive covenant (usually identified by the need to take action or spend money) will not usually run with the land so as to bind the covenantor's successors, but the burden of a negative covenant (i.e. a covenant not to do something) may run in certain circumstances. This has proved a controversial distinction, and readers should be aware that Article 34 of the Property (Northern Ireland) Order 1997 now provides for the burden of specified positive convenants contained in deeds made after the appointed day to run. (Article 34 was commenced on 10 January 2000 by the Property (1997 Order)

(Commencement No. 2) Order (Northern Ireland) 1999 (SR 1999/461).) Covenants are registerable burdens under Schedule 6 to the Land Registration Act (Northern Ireland) 1997 and should be registered if they are to bind subsequent purchasers of the land. Similarly, in relation to unregistered land, a deed creating a covenant should be registered in the Registry of Deeds.

Discharging burdens by way of the Property (Northern Ireland) Order 1978

9.09 The Property (Northern Ireland) Order 1978 provides a mechanism for identifying, modifying, and extinguishing certain impediments to the enjoyment of land. The impediments concerned include restrictive covenants and easements. The power to identify, modify, and extinguish is with the Lands Tribunal on the application of a person interested in the land. In relation to modification and extinguishment, for the Lands Tribunal to make such an order, it has to be satisfied that the impediment unreasonably impedes the enjoyment of the land, or if not modified or extinguished, would do so. However, without the permission of the Lands Tribunal, no application can be made to modify or extinguish an impediment arising under any provision contained in a lease until the expiration of 21 years from the beginning of the term. In determining whether an impediment affecting any land ought to be modified or extinguished the Lands Tribunal is obliged to take account of a number of factors including the purpose for which the impediment was created, any change in the character of the land or neighbourhood, whether the impediment secures any practical benefit to any person and any other material circumstance. Where the Lands Tribunal modifies or extinguishes an impediment it may add or substitute any new impediment as appears reasonable any may direct the applicant to pay compensation to the person entitled to the benefit of the impediment. Where the Lands Tribunal makes an order identifying, modifying, or extinguishing an impediment, it is registered in the Land Registry or Registry of Deeds as appropriate.

Leasehold covenants

9.10 The law of landlord and tenant in Northern Ireland is similar in language and theory to that in England, but is significantly different when examined in detail. The main legislative provision governing the relationship is the Landlord and Tenant Law Amendment Act, Ireland, 1860, commonly known as 'Deasy's Act'. A consequence of the Land Purchase Acts of the late 19th century was to render most of the agricultural land in Northern Ireland freehold. However, in urban areas much of land is held on long lease. Such leases are frequently for much greater terms than those encountered in England, with the effect that there is often not much practical difference between freeholders and long leaseholders. At least one advantage of conveyancing by way of long lease is the ability of the landlord and his successors in title to exercise control over what the tenant and his successors in title do with the land. This is achieved by covenants in the lease. Covenants can arise expressly from the lease or be implied by common law or statute. Both at common law and by statute the benefit and the burden of those covenants entered into by the landlord and tenant may be enforceable by and against their successors in title. Statutory provision to this effect may be found in section 10 and 11 of the Conveyancing Act 1881 and sections 12 and 13 of Deasy's Act. However, property transfer by way of long lease in Northern Ireland is probably coming to an end as regards dwellings. From 10 January 2000, the Property (Northern Ireland) Order 1997 has prohibited the creation of long leases. (Property (1997 Order) (Commencement No. 2) Order (Northern Ireland) 1999 (SR 1999/461).) Since 29 July 2002 the Ground Rents Act (Northern Ireland) 2001 has empowered payers of ground rents on residential properties to buy out their ground rents and acquire a freehold title. A compulsory dwelling ground rent redemption scheme, which has been legislated for since the Property (Northern Ireland) Order 1997, but which is now to be found in the Ground Rents Act (Northern Ireland) 2001, has yet to be brought into force, and will require redemption on conveyance.

9.11 As regards the doctrine of waste, the general rule, as gathered from section 26 of Deasy's Act, is that in the absence of an express agreement to the contrary tenants are liable for permissive and voluntary waste. Section 42 of Deasy's Act implies an agreement by the tenant to keep the premises in good and substantial repair and condition, although leases will generally include express repairing covenants. By section 17 of Deasy's Act, subject to the terms of the lease, a tenant is entitled to remove his fixtures where that can be done without substantial damage to the freehold, although they should be removed during the tenancy or in some circumstances within two months of determination of the tenancy. Neither section 19 of the Landlord and Tenant Act 1977 (as referred to in paragraph 5.04 of Chapter 4) nor the amended Leasehold Property (Repairs) Act 1938 (as referred to in paragraph 5.09 of Chapter 4) extend to Northern Ireland. The Defective Premises (Landlord's Liability) Act (NI) 2001, which came into force on 2 July 2002, imposes a duty of care and limits certain landlords' immunity from liability in a similar manner to the Defective Premises Act 1972.

Business tenancies

9.12 Business tenants in Northern Ireland have enjoyed special statutory protection since 1906. Indeed, it has been suggested that the Town Tenants (Ireland) Act of that year provided a precedent for the protection offered to English tenants by the Landlord and Tenant Act 1927. The modern Northern Ireland law is contained in the Business Tenancies (Northern Ireland) Order 1996 which is similar in principle, although not exact detail, to the present English legislation on the subject. The central policy of the 1996 Order is to provide that business tenancies continue indefinitely, unless brought to an end by mechanisms provided. A tenancy under the Order may be terminated by a notice to determine served by the landlord in accordance with Article 6, or where appropriate, a request for a new tenancy made by the tenant in accordance with Article 7. Article 12 provides grounds upon which the landlord may oppose a new tenancy. These include breaches by the tenant, e.g. failure to repair, persistent delay in paying rent, and requirements of the landlord, e.g. to develop the premises or to occupy for his own business. In the event of a dispute, the decision as to whether the tenant is entitled to a new tenancy is a matter for the Lands Tribunal. Where the Lands Tribunal makes an order for the grant of a new tenancy, in the absence of agreement between the parties as to the appropriate term, the Tribunal may fix a term not exceeding 15 years. Article 23 provides for disturbance compensation to be paid to a quitting tenant where the landlord has objected to a new tenancy on a no fault ground and in consequence the tenant does not make or alternatively withdraws an application, or a new tenancy is not granted.

Part Two
The law of building contracts

8

Introduction to building contracts

ANTHONY SPEAIGHT QC

1 The nature of building contracts

1.01 The general principles of the English law of contract were discussed in Chapter 2. A building contract is a particular type of contract governed by those general principles. Contracts for building work can vary greatly. Many such contracts are made every week by word of mouth between homeowners and self-employed sole builders: in such cases the only express terms will be a brief description of the work to be done and a price. Other building contracts are so complicated that the documents embodying the contract contain more words than the entire works of Shakespeare. However, most contracts for building work have certain characteristics in common. The contract will usually be one for the undertaking of labour and the supply of materials. The person who is engaging and paying the builder is normally referred to as 'the employer': in most cases this is the person who owns the site or the building at which the construction works are to be carried out. The builder is traditionally referred to as 'the contractor'. In many such contracts there is a certifying officer who plays a role in fixing the amounts of instalment payments and other matters of importance to the project, such as the date of completion, by the issue of certificates. The person who performs the certification function is very frequently an architect; and is sometimes referred to as 'the architect' even when he is not.

1.02 Assuming that the parties who are proposing to enter into a building contract have decided that they will record their agreement in writing, there is no reason in theory why they should not sit down and draft a written agreement for themselves in their own words. But in practice that rarely happens. Because building contracts have so many standard features, and because the complexity of the building process is such that a comprehensive contract is likely to be a lengthy document, it is usually best to use standard forms. An added benefit is that commercial and professional parties are likely to be familiar with the relevant forms, so that there should be a set of common expectations in regard to the parties' obligations. Typically such a form will be the subject of a few minor alterations, and certain additions, negotiated between the parties. If parties decide that they will use a standard form, they have complete freedom what form to choose. There is nothing to prevent an enterprising individual publishing his own form, and selling as many copies as he can to anybody whom he can convince of the merits of his draft. Indeed, in 1982 the Association of Consultant Architects (ACA) did just that: disliking the 1980 Joint Contracts Tribunal Form which had just been published, the ACA published their own standard form (see Chapter 10). More recently, Sir Michael Latham's report 'Constructing the Team' published by HMSO in 1994 proposed a new family of interlocking building contracts developed from the New Engineering Contract (see Chapter 10). However, for most practical purposes in the architectural profession the use of a standard form means the use of a form published by the body now known as The Joint Contracts Tribunal Limited (JCT).

2 History of the Joint Contracts Tribunal

2.01 By the end of the nineteenth century a standard form of building contract was in fairly common use. For many years it was known as 'the RIBA form of contract'. Indeed, that title achieved such currency that it continued to be used in some quarters long after the correct name of the form had become 'the JCT form'. The JCT was established in 1931. It consisted of the RIBA and what was then the NFBTE (National Federation of Building Trades Employers). Its object was to publish and where necessary amend a standard form of building contract. The JCT published important new editions of the form in 1939 and in 1963.

2.02 In 1964 an official report entitled 'The Placing and Management of Contracts for Building and Civil Engineering Work' was published (the Banwell Report). This report recommended that the conditions on which sub-contractors tender and enter into contracts should be standardised. Accordingly, in 1966 the JCT obtained authority from its constituent members to assume responsibility for the production of standard forms of sub-contract.

2.03 Over the years the JCT expanded to include various organizations in addition to its original constituent bodies. It now consists of the Association of Consulting Engineers, the British Property Federation, the Construction Confederation, the Local Government Association, the National Specialist Contractors Council, the Royal Institute of British Architects, the Royal Institution of Chartered Surveyors and the Scottish Building Contract Committee. The JCT is therefore now broad-based.

2.04 In 1980 the JCT published a new standard form. The 1980 standard form was much longer than the 1963 form, and many practitioners found it daunting and unmanageable. At first there was some doubt how widely it would be used, and for a number of years the 1963 form continued to be adopted on projects quite frequently. However, with time the 1980 form became established. For sub-contracts the JCT published not only a standard form of sub-contract, which interlocked with the standard form of main contract, but also a set of supplementary documents for the submission of tenders, making nominations and the like. The main contract was subject to many amendments and was republished in a 1998 edition. The commentary in Chapter 9 discusses the 1998 form.

3 The JCT family of forms

3.01 The number of versions and forms published by the JCT has grown. Amendments are made frequently. The main forms and associated documents at the time of writing are as set out below. It should be noted that the list below is not exhaustive and is subject to revision. The JCT web site at www.jctltd.co.uk provides an up to date list of forms.

Main contracts

1 The Standard Form of Building Contract (JCT 98) in the following variants:
   Local authorities edition with quantities
   Local authorities edition without quantities
   Local authorities edition with approximate quantities
   Private edition with quantities
   Private edition without quantities
   Private edition with approximate quantities
   There is also a Contractor's Designed Portion Supplement (CDPS)
   (There are also fluctuations supplements.)
2 Major Project Form (MPF 03)
3 Intermediate Form of Building Contract (IFC 98)
4 Standard Form of Building Contract With Contractor's Design (WCD 98)
5 Management Contract (MC 98).
6 Minor Works Agreement (MW 98)
7 Prime Cost Contract (PCC 98)
8 Measured Term Contract (MTC 98)
9 Jobbing Agreement (JA 90). This consists of the tender JA/T and the agreement conditions JA/C
10 Agreement for Housing Grant Works (HG(A))
11 Building Contract for Home Owner/Occupier (where the client deals directly with the builder) (HO/B)
12 Building Contract for Home Owner/Occupier (who has appointed a consultant) (HO/C)
13 Contract for Home Repairs and Maintenance (HO/RM)
14 Construction Management Documentation (CM 02)

Sub-contracts

15 Nominated sub-contractor documents for use with JCT 98:
   NSC/T Part 1: Invitation to Tender
   NSC/T Part 2: Tender
   NSC/T Part 3: Particular conditions
   NSC/W: Standard Form of Employer/Nominated Sub-contractor Agreement
   NSC/N: Standard Form of Nomination for Sub-contractor
   NSC/A: Standard Form of Articles of Nominated Sub-Contract Agreement between a Contractor and a Nominated Sub-contractor
   NSC/C: Standard Conditions of Nominated Sub-Contract (incorporated by reference into NSC/A)
16 Domestic Sub-Contract 2002 Edition
   DSC/A-Sub-Contract Agreement
   DSC/C-Sub-Contract Conditions
17 Named sub-contractor documentation for use with IFC 98:
   NAM/T 98 (Tender and Agreement)
   NAM/SC 98 (Sub-Contract Conditions)
18 Works contract documents for use with MC 98:
   WKS/1 Section 1: Invitation to Tender
   WKS/1 Section 2: Tender by Works Contractor
   WKS/1 Section 3: Agreement
   WKS/2 Conditions of Contract
   WKS/3 Employer/Works Contractor Agreement
19 Prime Cost Nominated Sub-Contract 1998 (under PCC 98)
   NSC/T(PCC): Part 1 – Invitation to Tender
   NSC/T(PCC): Part 2 – Tender by Sub-Contractor
   NSC/T(PCC): Part 3 – Particular Conditions
   NSC/A(PCC) – Articles of Agreement
   NSC/N(PCC) – Nomination Instruction
   NSC/W(PCC) – Agreement
   NSC/C(PCC) – Conditions

3.02 A prospective employer looking for a way through the maze of forms which now exist might find it useful to take the following approach, in order to decide which form will be best suited to his requirements in any particular situation.

First decision: who will design the works?

3.03 First, decide who is going to design the proposed building. The broad options are between the traditional approach of engaging an architect to design a building and then employing a building contractor to construct in accordance with the designs; and handing the entire package of the project over to a contractor who is engaged both to design and to build on the basis of a relatively brief statement of the employer's requirements. In the latter case, the appropriate form is the Standard Form of Building Contract With Contractor's Design (CD 98).

3.04 A variant on the design-and-build option sometimes arises when within a project being carried out with an architect's design it is desired that the contractor should himself design one portion. In that case the employer should be advised to use JCT 98 coupled with the Contractor's Designed Portion Supplement. Further brief commentary on CD 98 and CDPS 98 is contained in Chapter 10.

Second decision: will the works be designed before the start of the contract?

3.05 If the employer decides that the works are to be designed by an architect or some other professional consultant on his behalf, rather than the building contractor, the next question is whether the employer is content to wait for the works to be designed before he engages a building contractor to start work. In the traditional scheme of a building project the works are designed as the first stage, and thereafter the employer seeks tenders for executing the designs. That arrangement continues to offer a prospective employer many advantages, notably cost control. But in recent years different contractual arrangements have often been used by developers for whom speed of start and completion of a project have for sound commercial reasons been more important than the optimum control of the building costs component of expenditure. Particularly at times of high interest rates or a booming market, developers may judge speed of completion to be the paramount commercial consideration.

3.06 The pure option of a contract to suit the employer who wants to embark on a project before the design is formalised is the JCT Standard Form of Prime Cost Contract. Under this form of contract the building contractor is entitled to be paid whatever turns out to be the cost to him of doing the work ('the prime cost') plus a fixed fee. In practice this form is often thought of as appropriate when work is very urgently required, such as after fire damage, or when the scope of the work cannot be ascertained until the work has been commenced.

3.07 An alternative option for an employer who is able to have some limited design work carried out is a management contract, under which a building contractor undertakes to organise other contractors, known as 'works contractors' to carry out a building project. During the 1980s large contractors who were undertaking work in this way provided their own forms of contract, and the arrangement's popularity grew. In 1987 the JCT published a Standard Form of Management Contract, now available in a 1998 edition. The 'management contractor' is paid a fixed fee plus the prime cost of his own on-site management staff and of the works contractors. This arrangement has appealed to a number of developers in recent years. It enables a quick start to be made on a project, as the design need not be particularly detailed when the management contractor is engaged. It also tends to promote a speedy completion. The management contractor may be able to effect very good supervision and management of all the works on site, and the contract may contain incentives to him to secure a speedy completion. See Chapter 10 for further discussion of management contracting.

Third decision: how firm a price is required?

3.08 If the works are to be designed by an architect before a building contract is entered into, the next consideration is how firm a price the employer wants. If he wants certainty, then he should put out to tender a set of drawings and bills of quantities which specify the works in terms of quality and quantity. That process should lead to the making of a contract in the JCT 98 Standard Form With

Quantities, which may be regarded as the basic form of fixed price contract. The price will only alter pursuant to the operation of specific provisions of the contract – for example, where varied work is ordered.

3.09 A fixed price may also be obtained by using the Standard Form Without Quantities. Here the work is defined not in Bills of Quantities but in a Specification. Again, the price will only alter pursuant to the operation of specific provisions of the contract.

3.10 An employer who for the sake of a slightly earlier start is willing to embark on a project with only an indication of the likely price may, instead of either of the above versions of the contract, use a bill of approximate quantities. The difference from a normal bill of quantities is that it is prepared from less complete design information, and so can be drafted at a slightly earlier stage. The works are substantially designed but not completely detailed. The price ultimately to be paid is dependent upon measurement of the actual work done on the basis of the rates set out in the Bills of Approximate Quantities.

Fourth decision: how large is the project?

3.11 All the standard forms so far mentioned are far too complicated for small projects. In 1968 the JCT published an Agreement for Minor Works, which was replaced in 1980. The advice of the JCT was that the 1980 form be used on contracts up to the value of £70 000 (at 1992 prices). There is now a 1998 edition (MW 98). Perhaps the easiest way to state a lawyer's assessment of when this form is suitable is to identify when it is not suitable. It is not appropriate:

- When a project will go on so long that fluctuations are required
- When the employer wishes to nominate sub-contractors
- When the works have not yet been sufficiently designed to enable a fixed price to have been tendered, or when pricing against a detailed bill of quantities is required. (See further discussion in Chapter 10.)

3.12 If the client is a home owner undertaking works on his own dwelling then one should use a form in the new JCT Building Contract for Home Owner/Occupier family.

3.13 In 1984 the JCT published a form for medium-sized contracts, which required a contract more detailed than MW 80 but did not require the full complexities of the standard forms. This was called the Intermediate Form of Building Contract (IFC 84). There is now a 1998 edition (IFC 98). The JCT's advice in its Practice Note 20 was that this form would be suitable when the value was not more than £280 000 (at 1992 prices) and the contract period was not more than 12 months. Today the JCT prefers to focus on the length and complexity of a project, rather than price in order to determine suitability of contract form. It suggests the standard form for projects of more than 12 months duration, or for works involving a high degree of building services or other specialist works. Below that level of complexity, the JCT suggests IFC if detailed control procedures are required, or if a bill of quantities is to be used, or if the architect wishes to designate sub-contractors.

3.14 At the top end of size, the new JCT Major Works Form 2003 (MPF) may be appropriate. It has the advantages of clarity and relative brevity. It is suitable for well resourced contractors and employers able to undertake their own detailed risk management.

3.15 Where an employer has a regular flow of minor works, such as regular maintenance jobs, there is now an alternative to entering an entirely separate contract for each such job. The JCT in 1989 published a form intended to be suitable for an employer who wished to engage a contractor under a single contract to undertake all the small jobs which might arise in relation to a particular property or set of properties over a specific period. This is known as the Measured Term Contract. The current edition is MTC 98. It provides a framework under which orders for individual items of work may be placed. Further comment is made in Chapter 10.

3.16 An employer who wants to make a distinct contract for a small maintenance item may, as an alternative to MW 98, use the 1990 Jobbing Agreement (JA 90). This is suitable only for employers who are large organisations, such as local authorities, or who have experience in ordering small jobbing work and dealing with contractors' accounts. The terms of this contract provide for a single payment following checking by the employer of the contractor's account. The JCT recommends its use for work worth up to £10 000 (at 1990 prices) and of duration not exceeding one month. (See also Chapter 10.)

3.17 Because the standard forms take effect by agreement and not by statute, they can be amended in any way the parties choose, but care should be taken when attempting any amendment lest unintended ambiguities and inconsistencies are introduced.

3.18 Chapter 9 gives a full commentary on the 1998 main contract form as it currently stands. Chapter 10 discusses the sub-contract documentation published by the JCT and some other standard forms.

4 Building contracts in Scotland*

4.01 The standard forms of building contract issued by the Joint Contracts Tribunal Limited are drafted with the law of England and Wales in mind. As the commentator on the JCT 80 contract in *Keating on Building Contracts* points out, where the works in question are to be carried out in Scotland, those forms are unlikely to be appropriate, and recourse should be had to the standard forms of building contract which are issued by the Scottish Building Contracts Committee. These make allowance for the different legal background in Scotland in the context of which the contract made between the parties will have to operate.

4.02 In framing its standard form contracts, the SBCC tries to keep as much of the material which appears in any given JCT contract in its Scottish counterpart as possible. In consequence, not only are most of the provisions of the Scottish Building Contract of 1999 common to that document and the 1998 JCT Standard Form of Building Contract, but authority drawn from English law on the parallel provisions of the co-relative JCT form is frequently cited and founded on in cases arising out of SBCC ones. In this chapter, it is proposed only to call attention to some of those areas of concern to the architect where the law of Scotland as declared in its courts has produced either results different from those obtaining in England in similar circumstances or differences in emphasis on matters which end in a common result.

4.03 The principal method which the SBCC has used to bring about the large measure of congruence between its forms and those of the JCT is the inclusion in the formal contract document, which takes the place of the Articles of Agreement in the JCT regime, of a provision to the effect that the contract shall be governed by the terms of the chosen JCT form as those stand amended by such of the JCT Amendments as the parties may have selected and by the provisions of the Scottish supplement appended to the contract as Appendix I thereof. The Abstract of Conditions normally features as Appendix II of the contract. It is by way of the formal contract document and the Scottish Supplement that the changes to the original JCT drafting of the Form chosen by the parties are made to reflect the Scottish element of the works. Of course, there is no rule of law which prevents the parties from making amendments of their own to the terms of the SBCC contract, and that is frequently done. The architect who is contemplating such alternations, should, however, consider whether in the context of Scots law, those changes will have the effect which he may know from experience they would have in England and Wales.

4.04 It is normal for the Form of Agreement to contain only three specifically Scottish provisions, although as the portion of the contract which is executed, it is in relation to this part that regard must

* This section was written by Robert Howie.

be had to the requirements of Scots law regarding the execution of a formal self-proving contract. Those requirements vary depending on the status of the executing party, but will for the most part be found in the Requirements of Writing (Scotland) Act 1995. It is also in the Form of Agreement that there will be found the clause in which Scots law is chosen as the governing law of the contract, and the clause whereby disputes are referred to arbitration. The pre-printed SBCC Forms do not include any express choice of jurisdiction clause in relation to disputes which are litigated, presumably because the assumption is that disputes will be settled by arbitration; and that in those cases where arbitration is not provided for, the definition of 'Court' for the purposes of the contract as meaning 'the Court of Session' is thought to have the effect of prorogating the jurisdiction of that Court. It may be, however, that in cases where arbitration has been provided for but not utilized, Court proceedings can still be brought in the Sheriff Court, or, indeed, in any Court to the territorial jurisdiction of which the Defender is subject. There is, however, an implicit choice of jurisdiction in favour of the Court of Session in relation to disputes arising out of an arbitration relative to the contract, and, in light of the choice of Scots law as the governing law, there is an obvious practical convenience, not to say saving in cost, in suing, if needs be, on other matters in Scotland also.

4.05 The majority of the Scottish amendments are made in the Scottish Supplement which forms Appendix I. Some of these are merely matters of substitution of legal terminology (substituting 'assignation' for 'assignment', 'heritable' for 'real', etc.), but others are of more substantial import. The provisions regarding determination on insolvency are normally amended to reflect peculiarities of Scottish company and insolvency law, such as the ability to appoint a judicial factor on the estates of a Scottish registered limited liability Company, and the effects of the separate legal personality from its members which is accorded a Scottish Partnership. There are usually special provisions made about the purchase of off-site materials, which reflect differences between the common laws of property in England and Scotland and lengthy provisions about arbitration supplant those which are made for English arbitrations in the co-relative portions of the JCT forms.

4.06 It should not be assumed from this that all differences between English and Scottish law have been accounted for in the SBCC Forms: they have not. One major area of difficulty which arises in Scotland with the terms of a JCT form which are unamended by the counterpart SBCC Form concerns the trust fund sought to be created over the contractual retention monies by Clause 30.5 of the JCT 98 Contract. Whatever may be the position in England, these provisions are not in Scotland sufficient to create a trust over the retention monies in favour of the contractor on which he can rely in the event of the insolvency of the employer. The practical failure of these provisions from the point of view of the contractor was graphically illustrated by the decision in *Balfour Beatty-Ltd v Britannia Life Ltd* [1997] SLT 10, a case decided in the context of very similar provisions in the SBCC Management and Works Contracts. In that case, the contract's provisions were judicially stigmatized as being 'wholly ineffective to achieve what may have been the intended purpose of the draftsman', because they did not serve to create a trust or other property right in specific assets of the management contractor. At best for the contractor, he can only make use of the clause to sue the employer for specific implement of the obligation to set up a trust in the retention monies (see *Fairclough Scotland Ltd v Jamaica Street Ltd*, 30 April 1992, unreported) – and that remedy is apt to be stultified if the employer becomes insolvent in the interim, or, pleading dispute about his right to set off monies, insists on putting the matter to arbitration or adjudication.

4.07 There are also other areas (of perhaps more immediate concern to the architect than the trust obligations of the employer in relation to retention monies) in which the Scottish courts have taken a different approach from that followed south of the border. A significant example arises in relation to the hierarchy provisions of the JCT Standard Form Building Contract, whereby any provisions in the bills of quantities inconsistent with those of the JCT standard

form are subordinated to that form. Of late years, a practice appears to have grown up in Scotland whereby the formal contract is not executed, but the contract is allowed to rest on the bills of quantities and the form of tender referring thereto, duly accepted, which incorporates the terms of the JCT form including the hierarchy clause. The bills will frequently amend the Conditions heavily, and, with a view to circumventing the hierarchy clause, will preface those amendments with a term to the effect that 'Notwithstanding the provisions of [the hierarchy clause] of the said Conditions, the amendments and modifications detailed hereunder shall apply…'

The perils of adopting this practice were recently highlighted in *Barry D. Trentham Ltd v McNeil* 1996 SLT 202, where that term was implicitly held to be ineffective to prevent the hierarchy clause from operating to strike down any inconsistent clause in the Bills, albeit that it might be quite evident that all the special clauses of the contract drawn with the particular project in mind were to be found with bills. It is suggested that, in the light of the *Trentham* case, and the prior decision which it followed, it would be unwise for an architect who wished to amend the JCT or SBCC Forms to carry out that exercise in the contract bills: the better course would seem to be to secure the execution of a formal contract in amended terms, and to number among the amendments the necessary changes to the hierarchy clause itself.

4.08 Certification, too, is an area in which the Scottish courts have not always taken the same line as their English counterparts. As in England, the architect, when acting as certifier, is regarded as exercising a quasi-judicial office in which he should resist interference from his employer. He is expected to take care not to exceed his jurisdiction in that office, and to avoid issuing certificates which he has not been given competence by the parties' contract to issue. (cf. *Amec Mining Ltd v The Scottish Coal Company Ltd,* 6 August 2003, unreported). If he does issue such certificates, they will be invalid. But on the controversial matter of the extent of the conclusive effect to be afforded an Architect's Final Certificate under the JCT Standard Form Contracts, the current leading decision in the Court of Session (*Belcher Food Products Ltd v Messrs Miller & Black* 1999 SLT 142) would seem to have taken a more restrictive view of the ambit within which the Final Certificate is conclusive than have the English cases. It would appear from that decision that in, Scotland at least, the Certificate will not operate as conclusive evidence as to the adequacy of workmanship or materials unless the contractual standard for such workmanship or materials has been stated in the contract to be 'the reasonable satisfaction of the Architect'.

4.09 It also behoves the architect to pay close attention to the insurance provisions of the JCT contracts. In Clauses 22A, B and C of the 1998 Standard Form, provisions are made as to the allocation of responsibilities to insure the works and existing structures as between the employer and contractor. Over the past 10 years or so, the predecessors of these provisions have given rise to not a little litigation in Scotland, including two cases which reached the House of Lords. The net effect of that litigation is in certain circumstances to prevent the employer from suing the contractor or a sub-contractor for damage wrought by the latter either to the works themselves or to the building in which the works are taking place. In light of recent decisions in England concerning the liability of a project manager for failing to check that the appropriate insurances were in place, it is suggested that the employer's architect in Scotland who fails so to check is likely to be at risk of liability to his client if the application in the circumstances of the case in question of the above-mentioned House of Lords cases restricting the scope of the duty of care owed to the employer by the contractor or sub-contractor precludes that client from recovering his losses from the contractor or sub-contractor the fault of which had brought them about.

4.10 Time-bar is a further matter which is prone to give rise to difficulty, particularly when the client is English and used to dealing with a six-year limitation period. It should be recalled that in Scotland the operative doctrine in the building contract context will be prescription rather than limitation, and more importantly, that prescription strikes after five years in breach of contract and implement of contract cases, not six. Complexities can attend the ascertainment of the date when the period of prescription commenced running, particularly in cases where – as in most JCT Forms – there is provision for certification of practical completion and the making good of defects. On such matters, it may be thought appropriate to seek legal advice in light of the circumstances which obtain in the individual case in question, but it is always necessary to be alive to the risk that valuable legal rights may be lost through prescription. It should be remembered that the ways in which prescription may be stopped from running are very limited (acts amounting to a 'relevant claim' or 'relevant acknowledgement' within the meaning of the Prescription and Limitation (Scotland) Act 1973 are called for) and that in the case of arbitration, particular pitfalls await the person who seeks to interrupt prescription by means of preliminary notice to arbitrate. A reference to adjudication, it is thought, is not a 'relevant claim'. The safest course is usually simply to sue in court, if needs be by way of recourse to the declarator *ad ante* procedure, for, saving one rather unlikely case, an action served on the person against whom the claim is asserted is always a 'relevant claim'.

4.11 The longest section of separate provision for Scotland in the SBCC contract is that which is concerned with adjudication and arbitration. As will be seen in the following part of this chapter, the laws of England and Scotland on arbitration are very different, and accordingly, separate and detailed provisions have to be made for Scottish arbitrations.

5 Building Contracts in Northern Ireland

5.01 As stated earlier in this work, the substantive law of contract of Northern Ireland is the same as that of England and Wales. This applies to building contracts equally which are no different from other contracts. The comments and opinions expressed in the chapters of this part are of equal validity in Northern Ireland. Standard form contracts such as those published by the JCT and ICE, and the GC/Works form are all in everyday use in Northern Ireland. There are no separate issuing bodies within the jurisdiction as this is unnecessary.

The Royal Society of Ulster Architects has however published an Adaptation Schedule with the consent of the JCT containing the amendments necessary to effect the difference in the applicable law for use with their contracts in Northern Ireland.

9

The JCT Standard Form of Building Contract, 1998 edition

MUHAMMED HAQUE*

The text of the Standard Form discussed in this chapter is from the Private With Quantities 1998 edition, which was re-issued in July 2003 to incorporate Amendments 1 to 5.

The current edition broadly consolidates the clauses of the 1980 edition of contract, thus the commentary below will be relevant to the 1980 edition. Appropriate care should of course be taken to ensure that the context of the clause is identical when considering any case law applying to the 1980 edition.

1 Articles of Agreement

1.01 The part of the form that contains the Articles of Agreement has three elements: the front page, the recitals and the articles. Their purpose is to narrate the fundamental terms of the contract. The front page, when filled in, identifies the parties and the date upon which the contract is made. The recitals (the statements which commence with 'Whereas') record the nature of the intended works, identify the documents in which those works are described (the Bills of Quantities and Contract Drawings) and name the person who has prepared those documents. This person is usually, but not invariably, the architect named in Article 3. The articles state shortly the substance of the parties' agreement.

1.02 The 1998 contract introduced new contractual documentation to the JCT framework including the Activity Schedule (Clause 30.2) and the Information Release Schedule (Clause 5.4). More importantly the contract complies with the provisions of the Housing Grants, Construction and Regeneration Act 1996. The adjudication process introduced by this statute has dramatically altered the legal framework for claiming monies due under the contract. Broadly speaking when payments become ostensibly due during the performance of the contract (for example, by certification) employers are obliged to make these payments unless they serve a withholding notice. A rapid adjudication can then occur, the results of which are binding upon the parties. Readers are referred to the 'Adjudication' chapter for a fuller discussion.

1.03 Articles 1 and 2 define the basic contractual obligations of the parties. The contractor agrees to carry out and complete the works in compliance with the Contract Documents (defined in Clause 1.3 as the Contract Drawings, the Contract Bills, the Articles of Agreement, the Conditions and the Appendix). The employer, in consideration, agrees to pay the contractor the Contract Sum at the times and in the manner specified in the conditions. These articles provide the bedrock for the remainder of the contract: they identify the contract as a lump-sum contract, with the contractor's manner of payment being in accordance with the issue of Architect's Certificates (Clause 30).

1.04 Article 3 identifies the architect, and only applies where the person concerned is entitled to use the name 'architect' under and in accordance with the Architects Act 1997. Article 4 identifies the Quantity Surveyor, who may be the same person named as the architect.

1.05 The Court of Appeal held in *Croudace v London Borough of Lambeth* (1986) 33 BLR 20 that if the architect ceases to act, the employer comes under a duty to appoint another, and if he fails to do so he will be in breach of contract. The employer is required to nominate a replacement within a reasonable time and in any case not later than 21 days after cessation. The contractor has a right to object to the nominee within 7 days. If he chooses to do so the dispute will be referred to an adjudicator under Article 5.

1.06 Article 5 introduces adjudication provisions (pursuant to section 108(1) of the Housing Grants, Construction and Regeneration Act 1996). The contractor or employer has the right to refer any dispute or difference under the contract to adjudication. Article 7B allows the parties to omit the arbitration clause from the contract. Subject therefore to the operation of the adjudication provisions (Clause 41A), the parties may take any dispute directly to court

1.07 The Arbitration Agreement is contained in Article 7A, if the parties wish to apply it. The application of the arbitration procedure is subject to the operation of the adjudication procedure. If applied, disputes arising during the progress of the works or after the completion or abandonment of the works may be referred to arbitration in accordance with Clause 41B (subject to exceptions).

1.08 The main exception is that matters connected to the enforcement of decisions of the Adjudicator cannot be referred to Arbitration. Disputes under Clause 31 relating to the statutory tax deduction scheme (except to the extent provided in Clause 31.9), and under Clause 3 of the VAT agreement are also excluded from the arbitration provisions. The object of these exclusions is clear: statute provides alternative methods of resolving disputes relating to these matters.

1.09 If legal proceedings are brought against a party, that party may apply to stay those proceedings insofar as they are covered by a valid arbitration clause. It should do so before acknowledging those proceedings or taking any step to answer the substantive claim. The Court then *must* stay those proceedings – it has no discretion (section 9(4) of the Arbitration Act 1996).

1.10 The Articles conclude with a space for the appropriate attestation clause. If the contract is to be executed by an individual as a deed following the Law of Property (Miscellaneous Provisions) Act 1989 there is no longer any requirement that it be executed under seal (although the use of a seal will not invalidate it). The instrument must make it clear on its face that it is intended to be a deed and must be signed by the person in the presence of a witness who attests the signature (or if it is signed at the person's direction in his presence it must be attested by two witnesses). Further, the instrument must be

* In early editions this chapter was written by the late Donald Keating QC, who gave permission for his text to be used as the basis for the chapter in subsequent editions.

delivered as a deed by the person or by a person authorized to do so on his behalf. If the contract is to be executed by a company, the Companies Act 1989 provides that a document executed by a company which makes it clear on its face that it is intended to be a deed has effect, upon delivery, as a deed, and it is presumed to be delivered upon execution, unless a contrary intention is proved. A document may be executed by a company by affixing its seal but, irrespective of whether or not the company has a seal, a document signed by a director and the secretary of the company or by two directors and expressed to be executed by the company has the same effect as if executed under the common seal of the company.

1.11 In deciding whether the agreement should be made as a deed or not, the key factor is that if it is made as a deed, the limitation period for bringing actions is 12 years from the date of the breach of contract (section 8 of the Limitation Act 1980); otherwise it is 6 years (section 5 of the Limitation Act 1980).

Part 1 Conditions: General

2 Clause 1: Interpretation, definitions, etc.

2.01 The purpose of this clause is to provide a list of definitions of the main terms used in the contract, such definitions (save for

'person' and 'provisional sum') commencing with capital letters. Note that a 'person' may be an individual, firm (partnership) or body corporate. It is therefore possible for the architect, under Clause 8.6, to issue an instruction for the exclusion from the works of an entire firm of sub-contractors, for example.

2.02 The Guidance Note to Clause 1.5 states that:

(i) The architect is not, under the Standard Form, made responsible for the supervision of the works which the contractor is to carry out and complete; and
(ii) That nothing in the Conditions of the Standard Form makes the contractor other than responsible for carrying out and completing the Works as stated in Clause 2.1.

This means that it is no defence in proceedings between employer and contractor for a contractor to say that work or material was inspected by the architect. It is not, however, to suggest that an employer could not bring an action against the architect for failing to use reasonable skill and care to ensure conformity with the design, as opposed to ensuring detail.

2.03 Clause 1.7 specifies the manner of giving or service of any notice or document where that is not prescribed in the contract. This would apply, for example, to the issue of an Architect's Instruction (Clause 4.1.1): it would have to be served by 'any effective means'

Part 1: General

1   **Interpretation, definitions etc.**

1·1   Unless otherwise specifically stated a reference in the Articles of Agreement, the Conditions or the Appendix to any clause means that clause of the Conditions.

1·2   The Articles of Agreement, the Conditions and the Appendix are to be read as a whole and the effect or operation of any article or clause in the Conditions or item in or entry in the Appendix must therefore unless otherwise specifically stated be read subject to any relevant qualification or modification in any other article or any of the clauses in the Conditions or item in or entry in the Appendix.

1·3   Unless the context otherwise requires or the Articles or the Conditions or an item in or entry in the Appendix specifically otherwise provides, the following words and phrases in the Articles of Agreement, the Conditions and the Appendix shall have the meanings given below or as ascribed in the article, clause or Appendix item to which reference is made:

Word or phrase	Meaning
3·3A Quotation:	a Quotation by a Nominated Sub-Contractor pursuant to **clause 3·3A** of Conditions NSC/C *(Conditions of Nominated Sub-Contract).*
13A Quotation:	see **clause 13A·1·1.**
Activity Schedule:	the schedule of activities as attached to the Appendix with each activity priced and with the sum of those prices being the Contract Sum excluding provisional sums, prime cost sums and any Contractor's profit thereon and the value of work for which Approximate Quantities are included in the Contract Bills: see **clause 30·2·1.**
Adjudication Agreement:	see **clause 41A·2·1.**
Adjudicator:	any individual appointed pursuant to **clause 41A** as the Adjudicator.
All Risks Insurance.	see **clause 22·2.**
Analysis:	see **clause 42·13.**
Appendix:	the Appendix to the Conditions as completed by the parties.
Approximate Quantity:	a quantity in the Contract Bills identified therein as an approximate quantity. [n]
Arbitrator:	the person appointed under **clause 41B** to be the Arbitrator.
Architect:	the person entitled to the use of the name 'Architect' and named in **article 3** or any successor duly appointed under **article 3** or otherwise agreed as the person to be the Architect.
Articles or Articles of Agreement:	the Articles of Agreement to which the Conditions are annexed, and references to any recital are to the recitals set out before the Articles.
Base Date:	the date stated in the **Appendix**.

Word or phrase	Meaning
CDM Regulations:	the Construction (Design and Management) Regulations 1994 or any remaking thereof or any amendment to a regulation therein.
Certificate of Completion of Making Good Defects:	see **clause 17·4**.
Completion Date:	the Date for Completion as fixed and stated in the **Appendix** or any date fixed either under **clause 25** or in a confirmed acceptance of a 13A Quotation.
Conditions:	the clauses 1 to 37, either clause 38 or 39 or 40, clauses 41A, 41B, 41C and 42 and the Supplemental Provisions ('the VAT Agreement') annexed to the Articles of Agreement.
confirmed acceptance:	see **clause 13A·3·2**.
Contract Bills:	the Bills of Quantities referred to in the **First recital** which have been priced by the Contractor and signed by or on behalf of the Parties to this Contract.
Contract Documents:	the Contract Drawings, the Contract Bills, the Articles of Agreement, the Conditions and the Appendix.
Contract Drawings:	the Drawings referred to in the **First recital** which have been signed by or on behalf of the Parties to this Contract.
Contract Sum:	the sum named in **article 2** but subject to **clause 15·2**.
Contractor:	the person named as Contractor in the Articles of Agreement.
Contractor's Statement:	see **clause 42**.
Date for Completion:	the date fixed and stated in the **Appendix**.
Date of Possession:	the date stated in the **Appendix** under the reference to **clause 23·1**.
Defects Liability Period:	the period named in the **Appendix** under the reference to **clause 17·2**.
Domestic Sub-Contractor:	see **clause 19·2**.
Employer:	the person named as Employer in the Articles of Agreement.

Word or phrase	Meaning
Excepted Risks:	ionising radiations or contamination by radioactivity from any nuclear fuel or from any nuclear waste from the combustion of nuclear fuel, radioactive toxic explosive or other hazardous properties of any explosive nuclear assembly or nuclear component thereof, pressure waves caused by aircraft or other aerial devices travelling at sonic or supersonic speeds.
Final Certificate:	the certificate to which **clause 30·8** refers.
Health and Safety Plan:	where it is stated in the Appendix that all the CDM Regulations apply, the plan provided to the Principal Contractor and developed by him to comply with regulation 15(4) of the CDM Regulations and, for the purpose of regulation 10 of the CDM Regulations, received by the Employer before any construction work under this Contract has started; and any further development of that plan by the Principal Contractor during the progress of the Works.
Information Release Schedule:	the schedule referred to in the **Sixth recital** or as varied pursuant to **clause 5·4·1**.
Interim Certificate:	any one of the certificates to which **clauses 30·1** and **30·7** and the entry in the **Appendix** under the reference to **clause 30·1·3** refer.
Joint Fire Code:	the Joint Code of Practice on the Protection from Fire of Construction Sites and Buildings Undergoing Renovation which is published by the Building Employers Confederation (now Construction Confederation), the Loss Prevention Council and the National Contractors' Group with the support of the Association of British Insurers, the Chief and Assistant Chief Fire Officers Association and the London Fire Brigade which is current at the Base Date.
Joint Names Policy:	see **clause 22·2**.
Nominated Sub-Contract:	an Agreement NSC/A *(Articles of Nominated Sub-Contract Agreement)*, the Conditions NSC/C *(Conditions of Nominated Sub-Contract)* incorporated therein and the documents annexed thereto.
Nominated Sub-Contractor:	see **clause 35·1**.
Nominated Supplier:	see **clause 36·1·1**.
Numbered Documents:	the Numbered Documents annexed to Agreement NSC/A *(Articles of Nominated Sub-Contract Agreement)*.
Parties:	the Employer and the Contractor named as the Employer and the Contractor in the Articles of Agreement.
Party:	the Employer or the Contractor named as the Employer or the Contractor in the Articles of Agreement.
Performance Specified Work:	see **clause 42·1**.
Period of Interim Certificates:	the period named in the **Appendix** under the reference to **clause 30·1·3**.
person:	an individual, firm (partnership) or body corporate.
Planning Supervisor:	the Architect or the other person named in **article 6·1** or any successor duly appointed by the Employer as the Planning Supervisor pursuant to regulation 6(5) of the CDM Regulations.

Word or phrase	*Meaning*
Practical Completion:	see **clause 17·1**.
Price Statement:	see **clause 13·4·1·2 Alternative A**.
Principal Contractor:	the Contractor or any other contractor duly appointed by the Employer as the Principal Contractor pursuant to regulation 6(5) of the CDM Regulations.
provisional sum:	includes a sum provided for work whether or not identified as being for defined or undefined work* and a provisional sum for Performance Specified Work: see **clause 42·7**.
Public Holiday:	Christmas Day, Good Friday or a day which under the Banking and Financial Dealings Act 1971 is a bank holiday. [o]
Quantity Surveyor:	the person named in **article 4** or any successor duly appointed under **article 4** or otherwise agreed as the person to be the Quantity Surveyor.
Relevant Event:	any one of the events set out in **clause 25·4**.
Retention:	see **clause 30·2**.
Retention Percentage:	see **clause 30·4·1·1** and any entry in the **Appendix** under the reference to **clause 30·4·1·1**.
Site Materials:	all unfixed materials and goods delivered to, placed on or adjacent to the Works and intended for incorporation therein.
Specified Perils:	fire, lightning, explosion, storm, tempest, flood, bursting or overflowing of water tanks, apparatus or pipes, earthquake, aircraft and other aerial devices or articles dropped therefrom, riot and civil commotion, but excluding Excepted Risks.
Statutory Requirements:	see **clause 6·1·1**.
Valuation:	a valuation by the Quantity Surveyor pursuant to **clause 13·4·1·2 Alternative B** or the amount of any Price Statement or any part thereof accepted pursuant to **clause 13·4·1·2 paragraph A2** or amended Price Statement or any part thereof accepted pursuant to **clause 13·4·1·2 paragraph A4·2**.
Variation:	see **clause 13·1**.
VAT Agreement:	see **clause 15·1**.
Works:	the works briefly described in the **First recital** and shown upon, described by or referred to in the Contract Documents and including any changes made to these works in accordance with this Contract.

1·4   [Number not used]

Contractor's responsibility

1·5   Notwithstanding any obligation of the Architect to the Employer and whether or not the Employer appoints a clerk of works, the Contractor shall remain wholly responsible for carrying out and completing the Works in all respects in accordance with the Conditions, whether or not the Architect or the clerk of works, if appointed, at any time goes on to the Works or to any workshop or other place where work is being prepared to inspect the same or otherwise, or the Architect includes the value of any work, materials or goods in a certificate for payment or issues the certificate of Practical Completion or the Certificate of Completion of Making Good Defects.

1·6   If the Employer pursuant to article 6·1 or to article 6·2 by a further appointment replaces the Planning Supervisor referred to in, or appointed pursuant to, article 6·1 or replaces the Contractor or any other contractor appointed as the Principal Contractor, the Employer shall immediately upon such further appointment notify the Contractor in writing of the name and address of the new appointee.

1·7   Where the Contract does not specifically state the manner of giving or service of any notice or other document required or authorised in pursuance of this Contract such notice or other document shall be given or served by any effective means to any agreed address. If no address has been agreed then if given or served by being addressed, pre-paid and delivered by post to the addressee's last known principal business address or, where the addressee is a body corporate, to the body's registered or principal office it shall be treated as having been effectively given or served.

1·8   Where under this Contract an act is required to be done within a specified period of days after or from a specified date, the period shall begin immediately after that date. Where the period would include a day which is a Public Holiday that day shall be excluded.

1·9   The Employer may give written notice to the Contractor that from the date stated in the notice the individual identified in the notice will exercise all the functions ascribed to the Employer in the Conditions subject to any exceptions stated in the notice. [p]

1·10   Whatever the nationality, residence or domicile of the Employer, the Contractor or any sub-contractor or supplier and wherever the Works are situated the law of England shall be the law applicable to this Contract. [q]

1·11   Where the Appendix so states, the 'Supplemental Provisions for EDI' annexed to the Conditions shall apply.

to an 'agreed address'. If there is no agreed address then the document or notice can be served at the last known principal business address or registered office. This would constitute 'effective means', although any other 'effective means' are equally valid.

2.04 Clause 1.12 excludes the effect of the Contracts (Rights of Third Parties) Act 1999.

3 Clause 2: Contractor's obligations

3.01 In carrying and completing the contract works, the contractor is both entitled to the benefit of the conditions and subject to the obligations which they impose upon him.

The position of the architect

3.02 The architect is the employer's agent with authority to exercise those powers conferred on him by the contract. As such, he is both entitled and obliged to protect the employer's interests. Formerly the courts took the view that because of the grave disadvantages which would be suffered by the contractor if the architect failed to certify properly or otherwise exercise in a proper manner duties given to him by the contract, the architect was to some extent in an independent 'quasi-judicial' position, and immune from actions for negligence by either party when performing functions requiring the exercise of his independent professional judgement and the application of his mind fairly and impartially between the parties. However in *Sutcliffe v Thackrah* [1974] AC 727, it was held that an architect was liable to his employer for negligently over-certifying on interim certificates, and the House of Lords said that the architect enjoyed no such 'quasi-judicial' immunity.

3.03 In *Pacific Associates v Baxter* [1990] QB 993, the Court of Appeal held that an engineer (and by analogy an architect) could not be sued by the contractor for negligently issuing a certificate for the contractor's payment. The decision turned on the fact that the contractor could challenge the certificate (by going to arbitration). If there is no challenge mechanism (as there is in the JCT family of contracts) there might exist the possibility that an architect may be liable to a contractor for negligent under-certification.

Similarly it is likely that an employer will not be under a duty to ensure that the architect discharged his duties correctly. In *Hiap Hong & Co Pte Ltd v Hong Huat Development Co (Pte) Ltd* [2001] 17 Const LJ 530 the Singapore Court of Appeal held that the architect was under a duty to act independently. He was not subject to the instructions of either employer or contractor and had to reach his own decisions. He was not an agent of the owners. The control exercised over the architect by the owner was limited to acts that were performed by the architect on the owner's behalf, but this did not include the architect's certification duties.

3.04 The architect must at all times seek to perform as exactly as possible his duties under the contract. Thus, for example, it is wrong to permit a contractor to carry out work to a standard lower than that required by the contract because the architect discovers that the contractor has tendered low. It is also wrong to insist on a standard of work higher than the contract standard because the employer demands it. Architects are reminded that quite apart from what the courts have explained as their role under the Building Contract, the RIBA Code of Professional Conduct requires all members and students of the RIBA to act impartially in all matters of dispute between the building owner and the contractor and to interpret the conditions of the Building Contract with entire fairness as between the parties.

3.05 This duty to act fairly is often extremely difficult for a client to appreciate, but is essential to the correct functioning of the contract. The foregoing does not mean that the architect may not consult with the employer on matters within the sphere of his independent duty, but obliges the architect when he comes to make his decision to make up his own mind, doing his best to decide in accordance with the contract terms, interpreted against the background of the circumstances prevailing at the time of entering into the contract. He should then certify or give his decision accordingly whether or not he thinks it will please the employer. It is in this way that the architect must act in an independent manner.

Clause 2.1 provides that where and to the extent that approval of the quality of materials or of the standards of workmanship is a matter for the opinion of the architect, such policy and standards shall be to the reasonable satisfaction of the architect. Under Clause 30.9 the effect of the final certificate is conclusive evidence that the quality of materials or standard of workmanship are to the

2   Contractor's obligations

2·1   The Contractor shall upon and subject to the Conditions carry out and complete the Works in compliance with the Contract Documents, using materials and workmanship of the quality and standards therein specified, provided that where and to the extent that approval of the quality of materials or of the standards of workmanship is a matter for the opinion of the Architect such quality and standards shall be to the reasonable satisfaction of the Architect.

2·2   ·1   Nothing contained in the Contract Bills shall override or modify the application or interpretation of that which is contained in the Articles of Agreement, the Conditions or the Appendix.

2·2   ·2   Subject always to clause 2·2·1:

·2   ·1   the Contract Bills (or any addendum bill issued as part of the information referred to in clause 13A·1·1 for the purpose of obtaining a 13A Quotation), unless otherwise specifically stated therein in respect of any specified item or items, are to have been prepared in accordance with the Standard Method of Measurement of Building Works, 7th Edition, published by the Royal Institution of Chartered Surveyors and the Building Employers Confederation (now Construction Confederation);

·2   ·2   if in the Contract Bills (or in any addendum bill issued as part of the information referred to in clause 13A·1·1 for the purpose of obtaining a 13A Quotation which Quotation has been accepted by the Employer) there is any departure from the method of preparation referred to in clause 2·2·2·1 or any error in description or in quantity or omission of items (including any error in or omission of information in any item which is the subject of a provisional sum for defined work*) then such departure or error or omission shall not vitiate this Contract but the departure or error or omission shall be corrected; where the description of a provisional sum for defined work* does not provide the information required by General Rule 10.3 in the Standard Method of Measurement the correction shall be made by correcting the description so that it does provide such information; any such correction under this clause 2·2·2 shall be treated as if it were a Variation required by an instruction of the Architect under clause 13·2.

2·3   If the Contractor shall find any discrepancy in or divergence between any two or more of the following documents, including a divergence between parts of any one of them or between documents of the same description, namely:

2·3   ·1   the Contract Drawings,

2·3   ·2   the Contract Bills,

2·3   ·3   any instruction issued by the Architect under the Conditions (save insofar as any such instruction requires a Variation in accordance with the provisions of clause 13·2),

2·3   ·4   any drawings or documents issued by the Architect under clause 5·3·1·1, 5·4·1, 5·4·2 or 7, and

2·3   ·5   the Numbered Documents,

he shall immediately give to the Architect a written notice specifying the discrepancy or divergence, and the Architect shall issue instructions in regard thereto.

2·4   ·1   If the Contractor shall find any discrepancy or divergence between his Statement in respect of Performance Specified Work and any instruction of the Architect issued after receipt by the Architect of the Contractor's Statement, he shall immediately give to the Architect a written notice specifying the discrepancy or divergence, and the Architect shall issue instructions in regard thereto.

2·4   ·2   If the Contractor or the Architect shall find any discrepancy in the Contractor's Statement, the Contractor shall correct the Statement to remove the discrepancy and inform the Architect in writing of the correction made. Such correction shall be at no cost to the Employer.

reasonable satisfaction of the architect, where they are *expressly* required to be so (thus negating the effect of *Crown Estates v John Mowlem & Co. Limited* [1994] 10 Const LJ 311 (CA), which was decided on the previous wording: see paragraph 33.26 below).

3.06 It is not the architect's function to direct the contractor in the way he shall carry out the works, save where the conditions expressly give him this power (see Clause 13).

Liability for design

3.07 It is thought that provided the contractor carries out the work strictly in accordance with the contract documents, he is not responsible if the works prove to be unsuitable for the purpose which the employer or architect had in mind. In relation to performance-specified work, Clause 42.17.1.2 specifically provides that nothing in the contract is to operate as a guarantee of fitness for purpose of performance specified work. Further, Clause 6.1.5 provides that as long as the contractor complies with Clause 6.1.2 (which requires him to report any divergences he finds between the statutory requirements and the works as proposed), he will not be liable to the employer if the works do not comply with the statutory requirements. The contractor is required under Clause 2.3 to bring to the architect's attention any discrepancies which he finds between the various contract documents. It is probably also the contractor's implied duty to bring to the architect's attention any obvious errors in the architect's design of which the contractor has actual knowledge.

3.08 Clause 2.2.1 provides that nothing in the bills shall override or modify the interpretation of the articles, conditions or appendix. Thus if a provision in the bills conflicts with anything in these latter documents, the latter prevail as a matter of interpretation (see *Gleesons v Hillingdon* [1970] 215 EG 165, *English Industrial Estates v George Wimpey* [1973] 1 Lloyd's Reports 118 and *Henry Boot Construction Limited v Central Lancashire New Town Development Corporation* [1980] 15 BLR 1).

3.09 Under Clause 2.2.2.1 (unless otherwise expressly stated in respect of any specified item or items), the contract bills are to have been prepared in accordance with the principles of the Standard Method of Measurement, seventh edition (SMM). If they have not been so prepared, this constitutes an error which must be corrected. By virtue of Clause 2.2.2.2 the correction is to be treated as though it were a variation required by the architect. SMM expressly requires bills fully and accurately to describe the work. For example, if in carrying out work it becomes clear that excavation of rock is necessary and that the bills should have stated that excavation would be required, it seems that the contractor will become entitled to extra payment for all such excavation (see *Bryant & Son Limited v Birmingham Hospital Saturday Fund* [1938] 1 All ER 503).

4 Clause 3: Contract sum – additions or deductions – adjustment – interim certificates

4.01 This clause makes it clear that where adjustments are made in the contract sum, as soon as the adjustment has been quantified, whether in whole or in part, it is to be taken into account in computing the next interim certificate, not left until the final certificate.

5 Clause 4: Architect's/contract administrator's instructions

5.01 The contractor must comply with the architect's instructions. Failure to do so gives rise to the right under Clause 4.1.2 to have work carried out by others, and in some circumstances can result in the employer having the right to determine the contractor's employment (see Clause 27.2).

Power to issue instructions

5.02 The architect, by Clause 4.1, can only issue instructions where express power is given. In some instances the employer's consent is required. The most important powers for the issue of instructions relate to:

1. Clause 2.3 (discrepancies in documents).
2. Clause 2.4 (divergence between performance specified work and architect's instructions).
3. Clause 6.1.3 (divergence between statutory requirements and documents).
4. Clause 6.1.6 (divergence between statutory requirements and contractor's statement).
5. Clause 7 (levels).
6. Clause 8.3 (opening up and tests).
7. Clause 8.4 (removal of work, materials and goods).
8. Clause 8.4.4 (inspections and tests).
9. Clause 8.5 (failure to comply with Clause 8.1.3).
10. Clause 8.6 (exclusions of persons from the works).
11. Clause 12 (instructions to clerk of works).
12. Clause 13.2 (variations) – subject to right of reasonable objection in Clause 4.1.1.
12. Clause 13.3 (instructions on provisional sums).
13. Clause 17.2 (defects, shrinkages or other faults)
14. Clause 17.3 (rectification of defects).
15. Clause 23.2 (postponement of work).
16. Clause 34.2 (antiquities).
17. Clause 35.5 (removal of contractor's objection)
18. Clause 35.6 (nomination of sub-contractor).
19. Clause 35.18 (nomination of persons to undertake rectification works).
20. Clause 35.24.6.1 (notice specifying default of nominated sub-contractor).
21. Clause 36.2 (nominating a supplier).
22. Clause 42.11 (variations to performance specified work).
23. Clause 42.14 (instructions to integrate performance specified work with the design of the works).

5.03 The architect will not usually be able to vary the works simply to have them carried out by a different contractor (see *Commissioner for Main Roads v Reed & Stuart Pty* [1974] 12 BLR 55).

If the contractor does not comply with any instructions properly given by the architect, then the architect may give written notice to the contractor to comply. If compliance is achieved within 7 days, Clause 4.1.2 allows the employer to employ others to carry out and complete the works.

5.04 Under Clause 4.2 the contractor may request the architect to specify in writing the provision of the conditions which empower the issue of an instruction. If the architect specifies a provision and the contractor then obeys the instruction, the instruction is deemed

---

3   **Contract Sum – additions or deductions – adjustment – Interim Certificates**

Where in the Conditions it is provided that an amount is to be added to or deducted from the Contract Sum or dealt with by adjustment of the Contract Sum then as soon as such amount is ascertained in whole or in part such amount shall be taken into account in the computation of the next Interim Certificate following such whole or partial ascertainment.

4   Architect's instructions

4·1   ·1   The Contractor shall forthwith comply with all instructions issued to him by the Architect in regard to any matter in respect of which the Architect is expressly empowered by the Conditions to issue instructions; save that:

　　　·1   ·1   where such instruction is one requiring a Variation within the meaning of clause 13·1·2 the Contractor need not comply to the extent that he makes reasonable objection in writing to the Architect to such compliance;

　　　·1   ·2   where pursuant to clause 13·2·3 clause 13A applies to an instruction, the Variation to which that instruction refers shall not be carried out until

　　　　　–   the Architect has issued to the Contractor a confirmed acceptance of the 13A Quotation

　　　　　　or

　　　　　–   an instruction in respect of the Variation has been issued under clause 13A·4·1.

4·1   ·2   If within 7 days after receipt of a written notice from the Architect requiring compliance with an instruction the Contractor does not comply therewith, then the Employer may employ and pay other persons to execute any work whatsoever which may be necessary to give effect to such instruction; and all costs incurred in connection with such employment may be deducted by him from any monies due or to become due to the Contractor under this Contract or may be recoverable from the Contractor by the Employer as a debt.

4·2   Upon receipt of what purports to be an instruction issued to him by the Architect the Contractor may request the Architect to specify in writing the provision of the Conditions which empowers the issue of the said instruction. The Architect shall forthwith comply with any such request, and if the Contractor shall thereafter comply with the said instruction (neither Party before such compliance having invoked the procedures under this Contract relevant to the resolution of disputes or differences in order that it may be decided whether the provision specified by the Architect empowers the issue of the said instruction), then the issue of the same shall be deemed for all the purposes of this Contract to have been empowered by the provision of the Conditions specified by the Architect in answer to the Contractor's request.

4·3   ·1   All instructions issued by the Architect shall be issued in writing.

4·3   ·2   If the Architect purports to issue an instruction otherwise than in writing it shall be of no immediate effect, but shall be confirmed in writing by the Contractor to the Architect within 7 days, and if not dissented from in writing by the Architect to the Contractor within 7 days from receipt of the Contractor's confirmation shall take effect as from the expiration of the latter said 7 days. Provided always:

　　　·2   ·1   that if the Architect within 7 days of giving such an instruction otherwise than in writing shall himself confirm the same in writing, then the Contractor shall not be obliged to confirm as aforesaid, and the said instruction shall take effect as from the date of the Architect's confirmation; and

　　　·2   ·2   that if neither the Contractor nor the Architect shall confirm such an instruction in the manner and at the time aforesaid but the Contractor shall nevertheless comply with the same, then the Architect may confirm the same in writing at any time prior to the issue of the Final Certificate, and the said instruction shall thereupon be deemed to have taken effect on the date on which it was issued otherwise than in writing by the Architect.

to be empowered by the provision in the contract specified in the architect's answer. If the contractor is not satisfied with the architect's answer, the matter may be referred to adjudication or arbitration during the progress of the works.

Form of instructions

5.05 Under Clause 4.3.1, instructions are to be in writing, but note the elaborate provisions in Clause 4.3.2 for confirmation in writing if the architect purports to issue an oral instruction.

Site meeting minutes

5.06 Sometimes the architect and the contractor expressly agree that site meeting minutes are to operate as the confirmation of oral instructions contemplated by Clause 4.3. If there is no express agreement as to the status of the minute, in each case it must be decided whether in fact it was intended that the minutes should act as written confirmation of the instructions. Significant factors to take into account would be the authorship of the minutes and whether they are accepted by all parties as a true record of the meeting.

6 Clause 5: Contract documents – other documents – issue of certificates

6.01 This clause is concerned with matters of contract administration, namely the custody and issue of the contract and other documents. Clause 5.3.1.2 in particular should be noted: this requires the contractor to supply the architect with two copies of his master programme for the execution of the works and to update it to take account of extensions of time granted under Clause 25. This master programme does not, however, impose any obligation beyond those imposed by the contract documents (Clause 5.3.2). Clause 5.9 provides that the contractor is also required to supply as-built drawings for performance specified work before the date of practical completion (if specified or instructed).

6.02 By Clause 5.4.1, where, at the time of the contract, the employer has provided the contractor with an Information Release Schedule (see the 6th recital to the Articles of Agreement), the architect is required by Clause 5.4.1 to provide information to the contractor in accordance with the times in the schedule. There is a proviso that the employer and contractor may agree to vary those times. If all the information required by the contractor is not covered by the Information Release Schedule (or if there is no Information Release Schedule) then the architect is required, by Clause 5.4.2, to provide such information when it is reasonably necessary to do so.

6.03 All certificates which the conditions require to be issued by the architect are to be issued to the employer with a copy to the contractor (Clause 5.8).

7 Clause 6: Statutory obligations, notices, fees and charges

7.01 This clause imposes heavy obligations. The contractor has to comply with and give all relevant statutory notices and also comply with relevant statutory requirements, including the Building Regulations 1991.

7.02 By Clause 6.1.2, the contractor is required to give written notice to the architect of any divergence that he finds between the statutory requirements and the documents referred to in Clause 2.3 or any instruction requiring a variation issued in accordance with Clause 13.2. The architect is required to issue instructions in relation to the divergence, and this instruction will be treated as an instruction requiring a variation under Clause 13.2.

7.03 The contractor may be liable to the employer for breach of Clause 6.1.1, where he carries out work that does not comply with the Building Regulations. However, he is not liable if the reason for non-compliance is that he has followed the architect's design and instructions, provided that he has complied with his obligation under Clause 6.1.2.

7.04 By Clause 6.1.6, the contractor and the architect are required to give written notice to the other of any divergence they may find between the statutory requirements and the contractor's statement in respect of performance specified work. The contractor is required to inform the architect in writing of his proposed amendment and the architect then must issue instructions in relation to the divergence. In this case the compliance with the instructions will be at no cost to the employer unless the divergence has resulted from a change in the statutory requirements after the base date.

7.05 Work carried out by local authorities or statutory undertakers in pursuance of their statutory obligations is excluded by Clause 6.3 from the provisions of Clauses 19 and 35 which relate to domestic and nominated sub-contractors respectively. It is important to note that this applies only where the work is being carried out by the local authority or statutory undertaker 'solely in pursuance of its statutory obligations' and would not apply where, for example, an electricity board were carrying out works as sub-contractors in the normal way (see *Henry Boot Construction Limited v Central Lancashire New Town Development Corporation* [1980] 15 BLR 1).

8 Clause 6A: Provisions for use where the Appendix states that all the CDM Regulations apply

8.01 This clause outlines the obligations of the parties when they have agreed all the CDM Regulations should apply.

8.02 Article 6.1 of the contract states that the 'Planning Supervisor' shall mean the architect, unless the employer has appointed another person as such. Article 6.2 states that the 'Principal Contractor' shall mean the contractor, or any other contractor the employer appoints as such. Clause 6A.1 places an obligation upon the employer to ensure that the Planning Supervisor and Principal Contractor (where he is not the contractor under the JCT Contract) carry out their duties under the CDM regulations. Clause 6A.2 simply states where the contractor is the Principal Contractor he should comply with his duties set out in the CDM Regulations.

8.03 The contractor should ensure that any sub-contractor (through the contractor) provides the Planning Supervisor or Principal Contractor with the information required by the Planning Supervisor to enable him to prepare the Health and Safety File required by the CDM Regulations (Clause 6A.4). This should be done within the reasonable time required by the Planning Supervisor.

9 Clause 7: Levels and setting out of the works

9.01 The architect must determine the ground level information required to set out the works, and provide drawings containing that information to the contractor. Unless the architect with the employer's consent instructs that any errors arising from inaccurate setting out by the contractor are not to be amended, the contractor must amend them at his own cost. If the architect does instruct that the errors need not be amended, an appropriate deduction in respect of the errors is to be made from the contract sum.

10 Clause 8: Work, materials and goods

10.01 This clause defines the kind and standard of materials and workmanship required by the contract and gives the architect

5   Contract Documents – other documents – issue of certificates

5·1   The Contract Drawings and the Contract Bills shall remain in the custody of the Architect or the Quantity Surveyor so as to be available at all reasonable times for the inspection of the Employer and of the Contractor.

5·2   Immediately after the execution of this Contract the Architect without charge to the Contractor shall provide him (unless he shall have been previously so provided) with:

5·2   ·1   one copy certified on behalf of the Employer of the Contract Documents;

5·2   ·2   two further copies of the Contract Drawings; and

5·2   ·3   two copies of the unpriced Bills of Quantities.

5·3   ·1   So soon as is possible after the execution of this Contract:

·1   ·1   the Architect without charge to the Contractor shall provide him (unless he shall have been previously so provided) with 2 copies of any descriptive schedules or other like documents necessary for use in carrying out the Works; and

·1   ·2   the Contractor without charge to the Employer shall provide the Architect (unless he shall have been previously so provided) with 2 copies of his master programme for the execution of the Works and within 14 days of any decision by the Architect under clause 25·3·1 or of the date of issue of a confirmed acceptance of a 13A Quotation with 2 copies of any amendments and revisions to take account of that decision or of that confirmed acceptance. [r]

5·3   ·2   Nothing contained in the descriptive schedules or other like documents referred to in clause 5·3·1·1 (nor in the master programme for the execution of the Works or any amendment to that programme or revision therein referred to in clause 5·3·1·2) shall impose any obligation beyond those imposed by the Contract Documents. [s]

5·4   ·1   Except to the extent that the Architect is prevented by the act or default of the Contractor or of any person for whom the Contractor is responsible, the Architect shall ensure that 2 copies of the information referred to in the Information Release Schedule are released at the time stated in the Schedule provided that the Employer and Contractor may agree, which agreement shall not be unreasonably withheld or delayed, to vary any such time.

5·4   ·2   Except to the extent included in the Information Release Schedule the Architect as and when from time to time may be necessary without charge to the Contractor shall provide him with 2 copies of such further drawings or details which are reasonably necessary to explain and amplify the Contract Drawings and shall issue such instructions (including those for or in regard to the expenditure of provisional sums) to enable the Contractor to carry out and complete the Works in accordance with the Conditions. Such provision shall be made or instructions given at a time when, having regard to the progress of the Works, or, where in the opinion of the Architect Practical Completion of the Works is likely to be achieved before the Completion Date, having regard to such Completion Date, it was reasonably necessary for the Contractor to receive such further drawings or details or instructions. Where the Contractor is aware and has reasonable grounds for believing that the Architect is not so aware of the time when it is necessary for the Contractor to receive such further drawings or details or instructions the Contractor shall, if and to the extent that it is reasonably practicable to do so, advise the Architect of the time sufficiently in advance of when the Contractor needs such further drawings or details or instructions to enable the Architect to fulfill his obligations under clause 5·4·2.

5·5   The Contractor shall keep one copy of the Contract Drawings, one copy of the unpriced Bills of Quantities, one copy of the descriptive schedules or other like documents referred to in clause 5·3·1·1, one copy of the master programme referred to in clause 5·3·1·2 (unless clause 5·3·1·2 has been deleted) and one copy of the drawings and details referred to in clause 5·4·2 upon the site so as to be available to the Architect or his representative at all reasonable times.

5·6   Upon final payment under clause 30·8 the Contractor shall if so requested by the Architect forthwith return to him all drawings, details, descriptive schedules and other documents of a like nature which bear the name of the Architect.

5·7   None of the documents provided in accordance with the Information Release Schedule or mentioned in clause 5 shall be used by the Contractor for any purpose other than this Contract, and neither the Employer, the Architect nor the Quantity Surveyor shall divulge or use except for the purposes of this Contract any of the rates or prices in the Contract Bills.

5·8 Except where otherwise specifically so provided any certificate to be issued by the Architect under the Conditions shall be issued to the Employer, and immediately upon the issue of any such certificate the Architect shall send a duplicate copy thereof to the Contractor.

5·9 Before the date of Practical Completion the Contractor shall without further charge to the Employer supply to the Employer such drawings and information showing or describing any Performance Specified Work as built, and concerning the maintenance and operation of any Performance Specified Work including any installations forming a part thereof, as may be specified in the Contract Bills or in an instruction on the expenditure of the provisional sum for the Performance Specified Work.

6 Statutory obligations, notices, fees and charges

6·1 ·1 Subject to clause 6·1·5 the Contractor shall comply with, and give all notices required by, any Act of Parliament, any instrument, rule or order made under any Act of Parliament, or any regulation or byelaw of any local authority or of any statutory undertaker which has any jurisdiction with regard to the Works or with whose systems the same are or will be connected (all requirements to be so complied with being referred to in the Conditions as 'the Statutory Requirements').

6·1 ·2 If the Contractor shall find any divergence between the Statutory Requirements and all or any of the documents referred to in clause 2·3 or between the Statutory Requirements and any instruction of the Architect requiring a Variation issued in accordance with clause 13·2, he shall immediately give to the Architect a written notice specifying the divergence.

6·1 ·3 If the Contractor gives notice under clause 6·1·2 or if the Architect shall otherwise discover or receive notice of a divergence between the Statutory Requirements and all or any of the documents referred to in clause 2·3 or between the Statutory Requirements and any instruction requiring a Variation issued in accordance with clause 13·2, the Architect shall within 7 days of the discovery or receipt of a notice issue instructions in relation to the divergence. If and insofar as the instructions require the Works to be varied, they shall be treated as if they were Architect's Instructions requiring a Variation issued in accordance with clause 13·2.

6·1 ·4 ·1 If in any emergency compliance with clause 6·1·1 requires the Contractor to supply materials or execute work before receiving instructions under clause 6·1·3 the Contractor shall supply such limited materials and execute such limited work as are reasonably necessary to secure immediate compliance with the Statutory Requirements.

·4 ·2 The Contractor shall forthwith inform the Architect of the emergency and of the steps that he is taking under clause 6·1·4·1.

·4 ·3 Work executed and materials supplied by the Contractor under clause 6·1·4·1 shall be treated as if they had been executed and supplied pursuant to an Architect's instruction requiring a Variation issued in accordance with clause 13·2 provided that the emergency arose because of a divergence between the Statutory Requirements and all or any of the documents referred to in clause 2·3 or between the Statutory Requirements and any instruction requiring a Variation issued in accordance with clause 13·2, and the Contractor has complied with clause 6·1·4·2.

6·1 ·5 Provided that the Contractor complies with clause 6·1·2, the Contractor shall not be liable to the Employer under this Contract if the Works do not comply with the Statutory Requirements where and to the extent that such non-compliance of the Works results from the Contractor having carried out work in accordance with the documents referred to in clause 2·3 or with any instruction requiring a Variation issued by the Architect in accordance with clause 13·2.

6·1   ·6   If the Contractor or the Architect shall find any divergence between the Statutory Requirements and any Contractor's Statement he shall immediately give the other a written notice specifying the divergence. The Contractor shall inform the Architect in writing of his proposed amendment for removing the divergence; and the Architect shall issue instructions in regard thereto. The Contractor's compliance with such instructions shall be subject to clause 42·15 and at no cost to the Employer save as provided in clause 6·1·7.

6·1   ·7   If after the Base Date there is a change in the Statutory Requirements which necessitates some alteration or modification to any Performance Specified Work such alteration or modification shall be treated as if it were an instruction of the Architect under clause 13·2 requiring a Variation.

6·2   The Contractor shall pay and indemnify the Employer against liability in respect of any fees or charges (including any rates or taxes) legally demandable under any Act of Parliament, any instrument, rule or order made under any Act of Parliament, or any regulation or byelaw of any local authority or of any statutory undertaker in respect of the Works. The amount of any such fees or charges (including any rates or taxes other than value added tax) shall be added to the Contract Sum unless they:

6·2   ·1   arise in respect of work executed or materials or goods supplied by a local authority or statutory undertaker as a Nominated Sub-Contractor or as a Nominated Supplier; or

6·2   ·2   are priced in the Contract Bills; or

6·2   ·3   are stated by way of a provisional sum in the Contract Bills.

6·3   The provisions of clauses 19 and 35 shall not apply to the execution of part of the Works by a local authority or a statutory undertaker executing such work solely in pursuance of its statutory obligations and such bodies shall not be sub-contractors within the terms of this Contract.

6A   Provisions for use where the Appendix states that all the CDM Regulations apply

6A·1   The Employer shall ensure:

that the Planning Supervisor carries out all the duties of a planning supervisor under the CDM Regulations; and

where the Contractor is not the Principal Contractor, that the Principal Contractor carries out all the duties of a principal contractor under the CDM Regulations.

6A·2   Where the Contractor is and while he remains the Principal Contractor, the Contractor shall comply with all the duties of a principal contractor set out in the CDM Regulations; and in particular shall ensure that the Health and Safety Plan has the features required by regulation 15(4) of the CDM Regulations. Any amendment by the Contractor to the Health and Safety Plan shall be notified to the Employer, who shall where relevant thereupon notify the Planning Supervisor and the Architect.

6A·3   Clause 6A·3 applies from the time the Employer pursuant to article 6·2 appoints a successor to the Contractor as the Principal Contractor. The Contractor shall comply at no cost to the Employer with all the reasonable requirements of the Principal Contractor to the extent that such requirements are necessary for compliance with the CDM Regulations; and, notwithstanding clause 25, no extension of time shall be given in respect of such compliance.

6A·4   Within the time reasonably required in writing by the Planning Supervisor to the Contractor, the Contractor shall provide, and shall ensure that any sub-contractor, through the Contractor, provides, such information to the Planning Supervisor or, if the Contractor is not the Principal Contractor, to the Principal Contractor as the Planning Supervisor reasonably requires for the preparation, pursuant to regulations 14(d), 14(e) and 14(f) of the CDM Regulations, of the health and safety file required by the CDM Regulations.

---

7   Levels and setting out of the Works

The Architect shall determine any levels which may be required for the execution of the Works, and shall provide the Contractor by way of accurately dimensioned drawings with such information as shall enable the Contractor to set out the Works at ground level. The Contractor shall be responsible for and shall, at no cost to the Employer, amend any errors arising from his own inaccurate setting out. With the consent of the Employer the Architect may instruct that such errors shall not be amended and an appropriate deduction for such errors not required to be amended shall be made from the Contract Sum.

---

important powers. The contractor cannot be required to provide that which may have become unobtainable since the date of tender. He is not permitted to substitute an alternative for materials or goods described in a Contractor's Statement for Performance Specified Work without the architect's consent in writing, such consent not to be unreasonably withheld or delayed (Clause 8.1.4).

Express obligations

10.02 All work must be carried out to the reasonable satisfaction of the architect (to the extent that Clause 2.1 requires), and must be carried out to the standards in the contract bills (if therein specified), or otherwise to a standard appropriate to the works.

10.03 All work must be carried out in a proper and workmanlike manner (Clause 8.1.3). If there is any failure to comply with this obligation the architect has a power under Clause 8.5 to issue any instructions which are necessary as a result, including an instruction requiring a variation. No addition to the contract sum shall be made in respect of compliance with such an instruction and no extension of time will be given.

Implied obligations

10.04 In so far as the contract bills do not describe standards of materials or goods, the contractor must supply them in accordance with the standards implied by law: that is materials or goods which are reasonably fit for the purpose for which they will be used and are of satisfactory quality. However, these implied obligations may be excluded if the circumstances show that the parties did not intend them to apply. Thus:

1 There is no obligation as to fitness for a particular purpose if that purpose was not made known to the contractor at the time of making the contract.
2 There is no obligation as to fitness for purpose of materials where there was no reliance upon the skill and judgement of the contractor in the choice of those materials. Thus, for example, if an architect, without reliance on a contractor, specified for use on a roof 'Somerset 13' tiles, then the contractor is not liable if Somerset 13 tiles of good quality are not fit for use on that roof. The contractor is, however, liable if the tiles fail because, for example, they laminate owing to some latent defect of quality even though the defect could not have been detected by the exercise of proper care and skill on his part (see *Young and Marten v McManus Childs Limited* [1968] 2 All ER 1169; *Norta Wallpapers v John Sisk* [1976] 14 BLR 49 (an Irish case); and *Comyn Ching & Co. (London) Limited v Oriental Tube Co. Limited* [1979] 17 BLR 47).

10.05 There is no obligation as to latent defects of quality of materials where the circumstances show that the parties do not intend the contractor to accept such obligations. Thus it seems (though the point is not clear) that in the example just cited the contractor

would not have been liable for the latent defects in the tiles if the employer (or the architect on his behalf) had required the contractor to purchase them from a supplier who, to the knowledge of the parties, would only supply them upon terms which substantially limited the contractor's remedies against the supplier in respect of such defects (see *Young and Marten* (above)).

10.06 In the case of a nominated supplier whose sale contract restricts, limits or excludes liability to the contractor, where the architect specifically has approved such restriction, limitation or exclusion, the employer's rights against the contractor are restricted, limited or excluded to the same extent – see Clause 36.5.1.

10.07 By virtue of Clause 42.17.1.2, nothing in the contract is to operate as a guarantee of fitness for purpose of performance specified work.

Position of employer

10.08 If there is no breach of an express or implied term, the employer has no remedy against the contractor, sub-contractor or supplier under the terms of the contract. It is important that the employer has a remedy against *some* party should the material or works be deficient. If the contractor will not accept liability, one way of protecting the employer is to obtain a warranty direct from the supplier or sub-contractor concerned. The JCT issues a Standard Form of Employer/Nominated Sub-Contractor Agreement (NSC/W) and a Standard Form of Tender by Nominated Supplier (TNS/1) which contain such 'direct warranties'.

10.09 If the architect is involved in the early stages of the contract, he may wish to recommend to the employer the entering of direct warranties with sub-contractors and suppliers as a matter of course.

Effect of price on standards

10.10 The quality required by the contract is generally not dependent on whether the price for a piece of work is low or high, unless the parties have expressly or by implication agreed that prices should be considered. However, it seems that the architect can accept a lower standard than usual where the parties have agreed at the time of the contract the price is low and that the contractor is to 'build down to a price'. A suitable term should be included in the contract documents to make the intentions of the parties clear.

Effect of proposed use of works on standards

10.11 Where the use is known to the contractor at the time of contract it can, probably, be taken into account in considering the requisite standard where the bills are silent. But it is better to have express agreements for possible matters of dispute, for example as to tolerances and how far they are cumulative.

8   Work, materials and goods

8·1   ·1   All materials and goods shall, so far as procurable, be of the kinds and standards described in the Contract Bills, and also, in regard to any Performance Specified Work, in the Contractor's Statement, provided that materials and goods shall be to the reasonable satisfaction of the Architect where and to the extent that this is required in accordance with clause 2·1.

8·1   ·2   All workmanship shall be of the standards described in the Contract Bills, and also, in regard to any Performance Specified Work, in the Contractor's Statement, or, to the extent that no such standards are described in the Contract Bills, or, in regard to any Performance Specified Work, in the Contractor's Statement, shall be of a standard appropriate to the Works, provided that workmanship shall be to the reasonable satisfaction of the Architect where and to the extent that this is required in accordance with clause 2·1.

8·1   ·3   All work shall be carried out in a proper and workmanlike manner and in accordance with the Health and Safety Plan.

8·1   ·4   The Contractor shall not substitute any materials or goods described in any Contractor's Statement for Performance Specified Work without the Architect's consent in writing which consent shall not be unreasonably withheld or delayed. No such consent shall relieve the Contractor of any other obligation under this Contract.

8·2   ·1   The Contractor shall upon the request of the Architect provide him with vouchers to prove that the materials and goods comply with clause 8·1.

8·2   ·2   In respect of any materials, goods or workmanship, as comprised in executed work, which are to be to the reasonable satisfaction of the Architect in accordance with clause 2·1, the Architect shall express any dissatisfaction within a reasonable time from the execution of the unsatisfactory work.

8·3   The Architect may issue instructions requiring the Contractor to open up for inspection any work covered up or to arrange for or carry out any test of any materials or goods (whether or not already incorporated in the Works) or of any executed work, and the cost of such opening up or testing (together with the cost of making good in consequence thereof) shall be added to the Contract Sum unless provided for in the Contract Bills or unless the inspection or test shows that the materials, goods or work are not in accordance with this Contract.

8·4   If any work, materials or goods are not in accordance with this Contract the Architect, without prejudice to the generality of his powers, may:

8·4   ·1   notwithstanding the power of the Architect under clause 8·4·2, issue instructions in regard to the removal from the site of all or any of such work, materials or goods; and/or

8·4   ·2   after consultation with the Contractor (who shall immediately consult with any relevant Nominated Sub-Contractor) and with the agreement of the Employer, allow all or any of such work, materials or goods to remain and confirm this in writing to the Contractor (which shall not be construed as a Variation) and where so allowed and confirmed an appropriate deduction shall be made in the adjustment of the Contract Sum; and/or

8·4   ·3   after consultation with the Contractor (who shall immediately consult with any relevant Nominated Sub-Contractor) issue such instructions requiring a Variation as are reasonably necessary as a consequence of such an instruction under clause 8·4·1 or such confirmation under clause 8·4·2 and to the extent that such instructions are so necessary and notwithstanding clauses 13·4, 25 and 26 no addition to the Contract Sum shall be made and no extension of time shall be given; and/or

8·4   ·4   having had due regard to the Code of Practice appended to these Conditions *(following clause 42)*, issue such instructions under clause 8·3 to open up for inspection or to test as are reasonable in all the circumstances to establish to the reasonable satisfaction of the Architect the likelihood or extent, as appropriate to the circumstances, of any further similar non-compliance. To the extent that such instructions are so reasonable, whatever the results of the opening up for inspection or test, and notwithstanding clauses 8·3 and 26 no addition to the Contract Sum shall be made. Clause 25·4·5·2 shall apply unless as stated therein the inspection or test showed that the work, materials or goods were not in accordance with this Contract.

8·5 Where there is any failure to comply with clause 8·1·3 in regard to the carrying out of the work in a proper and workmanlike manner the Architect, without prejudice to the generality of his powers, may, after consultation with the Contractor (who shall immediately consult with any relevant Nominated Sub-Contractor), issue such instructions whether requiring a Variation or otherwise as are reasonably necessary as a consequence thereof. To the extent that such instructions are so necessary and notwithstanding clauses 13·4 and 25 and 26 no addition to the Contract Sum shall be made and no extension of time shall be given in respect of compliance by the Contractor with such instruction.

8·6 The Architect may (but not unreasonably or vexatiously) issue instructions requiring the exclusion from the site of any person employed thereon.

Clause 8.3: Testing

10.12 The architect is not bound to order tests under this clause before saying that he is not reasonably satisfied with any work. If he does order a test, and the work, materials or goods are found to be satisfactory, the contractor has a right to an extension of time (Clause 25.4.5.2), payment of loss and expense (Clause 26.2.2), and the cost of the tests. It is thought that where tests of part of a class of work, e.g. piling, show that the whole must be rejected, the contractor is not entitled to payment for tests in respect of those parts, e.g. individual piles, which pass the test or to the other rights set out above.

Clause 8.4: Removal

10.13 Clause 8.4.1 empowers the architect to order removal from site of defective work. A notice which merely condemns the work and does not require its removal is not a valid notice under Clause 8.4.1 (see *Holland Hannen & Cubitts (Northern) Limited v Welsh Health Technical Services Organisation* [1981] 18 BLR 80). There is no provision for re-execution, because upon the removal of the unsatisfactory work, materials or goods, the contractor's duty to complete remains and no further instruction is necessary. Clauses 8.4.2–4 contain additional powers for the architect. See Clauses 4.1.2 and 27.2 for the remedies for non-compliance. Defects which appear after practical completion are dealt with under Clause 17.

10.14 In 1988 a Code of Practice was introduced to help in the fair and reasonable operation of the provisions in Clause 8.4.4 for opening up. The architect is required to have due regard for this code, but its terms are not as such a mandatory part of the contract.

11 Clause 9: Royalties and patent rights

11.01 The contractor is by this clause obliged to indemnify the employer in respect of any infringement of patent rights. However, if the use of a patented article by the contractor was in compliance with an instruction of the architect, then the contractor has no such liability, and, indeed, is entitled to be repaid by the employer any liability which he has incurred. In practice, the erection of new buildings rarely involves an infringement of patent rights, which essentially protect the intellectual property in new inventions.

12 Clause 10: Person-in-charge

12.01 The person-in-charge on site is the contractor's agent to receive instructions. To avoid confusion he should be named.

13 Clause 11: Access for architect to the works

13.01 In the absence of express provision doubts might arise as to the architect's right of access to the site, since the contractor is entitled as against the employer to free and uninterrupted possession of the site during the progress of the works. Therefore Clause 11 reserves to the architect and his representative a right of access to the works. There is a similar right of access in relation to workshops and other places in the possession of the contractor or a sub-contractor where work is being prepared for incorporation in the works. This right is subject to such reasonable restrictions of the contractor and sub-contractor as are necessary to protect any proprietary right in the work for the contract. The provisions relating to sub-contractors do not, of course, directly affect the obligations of the sub-contractors, but the contractor would be liable in damages to the employer if the employer could establish damage flowing from failure by the contractor to ensure that the appropriate terms were included in the sub-contracts.

14 Clause 12: Clerk of works

14.01 The clerk of works is to act 'solely as inspector'. He is not the architect's agent to give instructions, and it will be a source of confusion and dispute if he purports to do so. If the clerk of works gives 'directions' they are to be of no effect unless converted into architect's instructions by the architect within two working days. Such directions can lead to uncertainty on the part of the contractor. It is suggested that the clerk of works be discouraged from giving directions in ordinary circumstances. However, if directions are to be given, the problems will be minimized if they are in writing and the architect immediately confirms, amends or rejects them.

14.02 In *Kensington and Chelsea and Westminster Area Health Authority v Wettern Composites* [1984] 1 Con LR 114 at 137–139 it was held that the employer was responsible for the contributory negligence of the clerk of works, because the clerk of works was his employee. Responsibility for his acts was not borne by the architect, even though he was acting under the direction and control of the architect.

Work done before confirmation of directions

14.03 The architect can, if the work done before confirmation of directions constitutes a variation, subsequently sanction it in writing under Clause 13.2. This may be particularly appropriate where the contractor has carried out extra work in an emergency upon the direction of the clerk of works.

Code of Practice: referred to in clause 8·4·4

This is the Code of Practice referred to in clause 8·4·4. The purpose of the Code is to help in the fair and reasonable operation of the requirements of clause 8·4·4.

The Architect and the Contractor should endeavour to agree the amount and method of opening up or testing but in any case in issuing his instructions pursuant to clause 8·4·4 the Architect is required to consider the following criteria:

·1   the need in the event of non-compliance to demonstrate at no cost to the Employer either that it is unique and not likely to occur in similar elements of the Works or alternatively the extent of any similar non-compliance in the Works already constructed or still to be constructed;

·2   the need to discover whether any non-compliance in a primary structural element is a failure of workmanship and/or materials such that rigorous testing of similar elements must take place; or where the non-compliance is in a less significant element whether it is such as is to be statistically expected and can be simply repaired; or whether the non-compliance indicates an inherent weakness such as can only be found by selective testing the extent of which must depend upon the importance of any detail concerned;

·3   the significance of the non-compliance having regard to the nature of the work in which it has occurred;

·4   the consequence of any similar non-compliance on the safety of the building, its effect on users, adjoining property, the public, and compliance with any Statutory Requirements;

·5   the level and standard of supervision and control of the Works by the Contractor;

·6   the relevant records of the Contractor and where relevant of any sub-contractor resulting from the supervision and control referred to in paragraph 2·5 above or otherwise;

·7   any Codes of Practice or similar advice issued by a responsible body which are applicable to the non-complying work, materials or goods;

·8   any failure by the Contractor to carry out, or to secure the carrying out of, any tests specified in the Contract Documents or in an instruction of the Architect;

·9   the reason for the non-compliance when this has been established;

·10   any technical advice that the Contractor has obtained in respect of the non-complying work, materials or goods;

·11   current recognised testing procedures;

·12   the practicability of progressive testing in establishing whether any similar non-compliance is reasonably likely;

·13   if alternative testing methods are available, the time required for and the consequential costs of such alternative testing methods;

·14   any proposals of the Contractor;

·15   any other relevant matters.

9 Royalties and patent rights

9·1 All royalties or other sums payable in respect of the supply and use in carrying out the Works as described by or referred to in the Contract Bills of any patented articles, processes or inventions shall be deemed to have been included in the Contract Sum, and the Contractor shall indemnify the Employer from and against all claims, proceedings, damage, costs and expense which may be brought or made against the Employer or to which he may be put by reason of the Contractor infringing or being held to have infringed any patent rights in relation to any such articles, processes or inventions.

9·2 Provided that where in compliance with Architect's instructions the Contractor shall supply and use in carrying out the Works any patented articles, processes or inventions, the Contractor shall not be liable in respect of any infringement or alleged infringement of any patent rights in relation to any such articles, processes or inventions and all royalties damages or other monies which the Contractor may be liable to pay to the persons entitled to such patent rights shall be added to the Contract Sum.

10 Person-in-charge

The Contractor shall constantly keep upon the site a competent person-in-charge and any instructions given to him by the Architect or directions given to him by the clerk of works in accordance with clause 12 shall be deemed to have been issued to the Contractor.

11 Access for Architect to the Works

The Architect and his representatives shall at all reasonable times have access to the Works and to the workshops or other places of the Contractor where work is being prepared for this Contract, and when work is to be so prepared in workshops or other places of a Domestic Sub-Contractor or a Nominated Sub-Contractor the Contractor shall by a term in the sub-contract so far as possible secure a similar right of access to those workshops or places for the Architect and his representatives and shall do all things reasonably necessary to make such right effective. Access in accordance with clause 11 may be subject to such reasonable restrictions of the Contractor or any Domestic Sub-Contractor or any Nominated Sub-Contractor as are necessary to protect any proprietary right of the Contractor or of any Domestic or Nominated Sub-Contractor in the work referred to in clause 11.

12 Clerk of works

The Employer shall be entitled to appoint a clerk of works whose duty shall be to act solely as inspector on behalf of the Employer under the directions of the Architect and the Contractor shall afford every reasonable facility for the performance of that duty. If any direction is given to the Contractor by the clerk of works the same shall be of no effect unless given in regard to a matter in respect of which the Architect is expressly empowered by the Conditions to issue instructions and unless confirmed in writing by the Architect within 2 working days of such direction being given. If any such direction is so given and confirmed then as from the date of issue of that confirmation it shall be deemed to be an Architect's instruction.

Resident architect

14.04 A person entitled 'resident architect' is sometimes appointed to the site of a large contract. His position should be sharply distinguished from that of the clerk of works and should be defined in a communication to the contractor stating clearly how far, if at all, he is not to have all the powers to issue architect's instructions given by the terms of the contract.

15 Clause 13: Variations and provisional sums

15.01 This clause is essentially concerned with three matters:

1   Defining what constitutes a variation.
2   Defining the method in which variations are to be ordered.
3   Laying down the rules for valuing variations.

Definition of variation

15.02 Clause 13.1 defines variation in wide terms. Not only does it include alterations in the work itself (Clause 13.1.1), but also, by Clause 13.1.2, the imposition of or alterations in obligations or restrictions in relation to such matters as site access, working space, working hours and work sequence. Clause 13.1.3 excludes from the definition of variation nomination of a sub-contractor to supply and fix materials or goods or to execute work for which the measured quantities have been set out and priced by the contractor in the contract bills for supply and fixing or execution by the contractor. Thus the employer is not entitled to vary the work by ordering the omission of work and nominating a sub-contractor to carry it out.

15.03 Disputes frequently arise between employer and contractor as to whether work constitutes a variation and such disputes were frequently referred to arbitration. The architect's decision as to what constitutes and does not constitute a variation will be subject to the adjudication process, if one party wishes to operate it.

Deemed variations

15.04 This term is frequently used to denote an occurrence which entitles (or is alleged to entitle) the contractor to extra payments even though the requirements of Clause 13 have not been complied with. There are two principal occurrences which often give rise to a deemed variation:

1   The bills of quantities are inaccurate and fail to record correctly the quantity of work actually required. In these circumstances, the contractor is entitled to extra payment under Clause 2.2.2.2, since the Standard Method of Measurement (SMM) referred to in Clause 2.2.2.1 requires bills of quantities to describe the work fully and accurately.
2   Misstatements or inaccuracies in the bills of quantities may constitute an actionable misrepresentation for which the contractor is entitled to damages under the Misrepresentation Act 1967.

Limits on the architect's powers

15.05 Despite the apparent breadth of the architect's powers to order variations, it is generally thought he cannot order variations of such extent or nature as to alter the nature of the works as originally contemplated. The architect's powers are limited to those given by the conditions, which he has no power to vary or waive. Thus he cannot without the contractor's agreement require work that is the subject matter of a prime cost sum (Clause 35) to be carried out by the contractor, and may not be able to omit work in order to have it carried out by another contractor or nominated sub-contractor (see *Commissioner for Main Roads v Reed & Stuart Pty* [1974] 12 BLR 55). He cannot, it is thought, order variations after practical completion. He is, however, entitled to vary work which is to be carried out by nominated sub-contractors.

Prime costs, provisional sums and approximate quantities

15.06 Where work can be described but the quantity of work required cannot be accurately determined, an estimate of the quantity is to be given. This is identified as an approximate quantity. A provisional sum represents a sum which is included to meet unforeseen contingencies (which may not arise). Prime cost sums are pre-estimates of expenditure which it is known will be incurred when the contract is entered into. More detailed definitions of these terms are set out in SMM. An instruction to expend a provisional sum is valued in the same way as a variation (Clause 13.3).

Procedure

15.07 Clause 13.2 lays down the procedure for requiring a variation. All variations require the issue of an architect's instruction. Varied work may be subsequently sanctioned by the architect, as well as in advance of its being undertaken. In principle, in the absence of an architect's instruction, the contractor is not entitled to extra payment for any increased costs due to variations (although the architect's decision not to give a certificate sanctioning the variation is subject to review). Merely permitting the contractor to alter the proposed method of construction at the contractor's request does not ordinarily amount to a variation, although the particular circumstances must always be considered (see *Simplex Concrete Piles v Borough of St Pancras* [1958] 14 BLR 80).

Valuation rules

15.08 Clause 13.5 lays down the rules for valuing work for which an approximate quantity has been included in the contract bills or additional or substituted work which is capable of measurement. The task of measurement is to be carried out by the quantity surveyor, who is to value the work in accordance with the rules laid down in Clauses 13.5.1 to 13.5.7, whichever are appropriate.

15.09 Under Clause 13.5.2 where work is omitted from the contract bills, the amount of the omission is to be determined by the rates and prices for such work in the contract bills. By Clause 13.5.3 measurement of variations is to be carried out in accordance with SMM, allowance is to be given for any percentage of lump sum adjustment, and preliminary items are also subject to adjustment. Preliminary items defined by SMM consist broadly of overhead items which the contractor will incur, such as plant, site establishment, etc. Where work is incapable of valuation by measurement, Clause 13.5.4 requires it to be valued at day work rates.

15.10 Clause 13.5.5 deals with what might be termed indirect variations, where a variation which directly affects one aspect of the work also has indirect effects on another aspect. For example, the architect may require work to be carried out in a different sequence from that envisaged, resulting in certain finishing trades being obliged to work in parts of the building which are not fully watertight. In such circumstances the contractor would be entitled to be paid as if the altered work were itself the subject of a variation by virtue of Clause 13.5.5.

15.11 Clause 13.5.7 provides a 'fall back' method of valuing a variation to produce a fair result where none of the other methods can be applied. The proviso to Clause 13.5.7 excludes additional payment for items which the contractor would be able to claim as loss and/or expense under any other provision of the contract. Thus the policy of the 1988 JCT Form is to divorce completely claims for variations from claims for loss and expense.

15.12 An alternative valuation method to the above rules is included in Clause 13.4.1.2. This allows the contractor to submit a 'Price Statement' to the employer, valuing a variation (for example). The Quantity Surveyor may then accept, or object, giving reason for those objections.

Sub-contract work

15.13 Under Clause 13.4.1.3 variations to Nominated Sub-Contract works are to be valued in accordance with the provisions of the relevant Nominated Sub-Contract, unless the contractor and sub-contract agree otherwise and the employer gives his approval. Where the contractor tenders for provisional work which has become the subject of a prime cost sum and that tender is accepted, any variation is to be valued in accordance with the contractor's tender for that work (Clause 13.4.2).

Disputes about valuations

15.14 The rule of valuation contained in Clause 13.5.1.3 (work not of similar character to work set out in the contract bills) is in practice probably the most difficult to apply. It is necessary to decide first, whether it applies and then, if it does, how to apply it. It seems that one must look at the position at the time of acceptance of the tender and consider the character of the work then priced and the conditions under which the parties must have contemplated it would be carried out. If the character of the various works or the conditions under which they were carried out differ, then this rule applies. The following, it is thought, may be examples of its application: material change in quantities; winter working instead of summer working; wet instead of dry; high instead of low; confined working space instead of ample working space. If it does apply, it is necessary to look at its effect, which must vary according to circumstances. In some cases a 'fair valuation' may result in no or very little change from bill rates. Indeed, the wording of this sub-clause is so wide that the payment of less than bill rates might be justified. Note, however, that a claim under Clause 13.5.1.3 must be sharply differentiated from a claim for loss and expense (see above).

Daywork

15.15 Subject to any special agreement, the quantity surveyor must carry out the valuation in accordance with the rules laid down in this clause, but the architect is not bound to follow the quantity surveyor's valuation. The responsibility for valuation rests ultimately with the architect, who may in a particular case take the view that the quantity surveyor has failed to apply the rules laid down correctly in principle. He may, for example, consider that varied work should have been valued at bill rates, whereas the quantity surveyor has valued it at 'fair' rates. In these circumstances the architect is entitled and bound to overrule the quantity surveyor (*R B Burden Limited v Swansea Corporation* [1957] 3 All ER 243). The quantity surveyor has no authority to vary the terms of the contract (see *John Laing Construction Limited v County and District Properties Limited* [1982] 23 BLR 1).

Errors in the bills

15.16 The contractor may have made errors in pricing his tender on the basis of the bills of quantities, either by totalling figures incorrectly or by inserting a rate for a particular item which is manifestly excessive or too low. The parties are precluded from disputing the total contract sum by the wording of Clause 14. Where a particular item is priced manifestly too low, contractors sometimes argue that if work the subject of the uneconomic rate becomes the subject of variation it should be valued at an economic rate and not at the bill rate. It is submitted that in the absence of any claim for rectification being sustainable an architect would be in breach of his duty to his employer were he to agree to this course without the employer's express agreement.

---

13 **Variations and provisional sums**

13·1 The term 'Variation' as used in the Conditions means:

13·1 ·1 the alteration or modification of the design, quality or quantity of the Works including

   ·1 ·1 the addition, omission or substitution of any work,

   ·1 ·2 the alteration of the kind or standard of any of the materials or goods to be used in the Works,

   ·1 ·3 the removal from the site of any work executed or materials or goods brought thereon by the Contractor for the purposes of the Works other than work materials or goods which are not in accordance with this Contract;

13·1 ·2 the imposition by the Employer of any obligations or restrictions in regard to the matters set out in clauses 13·1·2·1 to 13·1·2·4 or the addition to or alteration or omission of any such obligations or restrictions so imposed or imposed by the Employer in the Contract Bills in regard to:

   ·2 ·1 access to the site or use of any specific parts of the site;

   ·2 ·2 limitations of working space;

   ·2 ·3 limitations of working hours;

·2   ·4   the execution or completion of the work in any specific order;

but excludes

13·1   ·3   nomination of a sub-contractor to supply and fix materials or goods or to execute work of which the measured quantities have been set out and priced by the Contractor in the Contract Bills for supply and fixing or execution by the Contractor.

13·2   ·1   The Architect may issue instructions requiring a Variation.

13·2   ·2   Any instruction under clause 13·2·1 shall be subject to the Contractor's right of reasonable objection set out in clause 4·1·1.

13·2   ·3   The valuation of a Variation instructed under clause 13·2·1 shall be in accordance with clause 13·4·1·1 unless the instruction states that the treatment and valuation of the Variation are to be in accordance with clause 13A or unless the Variation is one to which clause 13A·8 applies. Where the instruction so states, clause 13A shall apply unless the Contractor within 7 days (or such other period as may be agreed) of receipt of the instruction states in writing that he disagrees with the application of clause 13A to such instruction. If the Contractor so disagrees, clause 13A shall not apply to such instruction and the Variation shall not be carried out unless and until the Architect instructs that the Variation is to be carried out and is to be valued pursuant to clause 13·4·1. [t]

13·2   ·4   The Architect may sanction in writing any Variation made by the Contractor otherwise than pursuant to an instruction of the Architect.

13·2   ·5   No Variation required by the Architect or subsequently sanctioned by him shall vitiate this Contract.

13·3   The Architect shall issue instructions in regard to:

13·3   ·1   the expenditure of provisional sums included in the Contract Bills; [u] and

13·3   ·2   the expenditure of provisional sums included in a Nominated Sub-Contract.

13·4   ·1   ·1   Subject to clause 13·4·1·3

–   all Variations required by an instruction of the Architect or subsequently sanctioned by him in writing, and

–   all work which under the Conditions is to be treated as if it were a Variation required by an instruction of the Architect under clause 13·2, and

–   all work executed by the Contractor in accordance with instructions by the Architect as to the expenditure of provisional sums which are included in the Contract Bills, and

–   all work executed by the Contractor for which an Approximate Quantity has been included in the Contract Bills

shall, unless otherwise agreed by the Employer and the Contractor, be valued (in the Conditions called 'the Valuation'), under Alternative A in clause 13·4·1·2 or, to the extent that Alternative A is not implemented by the Contractor or, if implemented, to the extent that the Price Statement or amended Price Statement is not accepted, under Alternative B in clause 13·4·1·2. Clause 13·4·1·1 shall not apply in respect of a Variation for which the Architect has issued a confirmed acceptance of a 13A Quotation or is a Variation to which clause 13A·8 applies.

13·4 **·1** **·2** ***Alternative A: Contractor's Price Statement***

Paragraph:

A1   Without prejudice to his obligation to comply with any instruction or to execute any work to which clause 13·4·1·1 refers, the Contractor may within 21 days from receipt of the instruction or from commencement of work for which an Approximate Quantity is included in the Contract documents or, if later, from receipt of sufficient information to enable the Contractor to prepare his Price Statement, submit to the Quantity Surveyor his price ('Price Statement') for such compliance or for such work.

      The Price Statement shall state the Contractor's price for the work which shall be based on the provisions of clause 13·5 *(valuation rules)* and may also separately attach the Contractor's requirements for:

    ·1   any amount to be paid in lieu of any ascertainment under clause 26·1 of direct loss and/or expense not included in any accepted 13A Quotation or in any previous ascertainment under clause 26;

    ·2   any adjustment to the time for the completion of the Works to the extent that such adjustment is not included in any revision of the Completion Date that has been made by the Architect under clause 25·3 or in his confirmed acceptance of any 13A Quotation. *(See paragraph A7)*

A2   Within 21 days of receipt of a Price Statement the Quantity Surveyor, after consultation with the Architect, shall notify the Contractor in writing

    either

    ·1   that the Price Statement is accepted

    or

    ·2   that the Price Statement, or a part thereof, is not accepted.

A3   Where the Price Statement or a part thereof has been accepted the price in that accepted Price Statement or in that part which has been accepted shall in accordance with clause 13·7 be added to or deducted from the Contract Sum.

A4   Where the Price Statement or a part thereof has not been accepted:

    ·1   the Quantity Surveyor shall include in his notification to the Contractor the reasons for not having accepted the Price Statement or a part thereof and set out those reasons in similar detail to that given by the Contractor in his Price Statement and supply an amended Price Statement which is acceptable to the Quantity Surveyor after consultation with the Architect;

    ·2   within 14 days from receipt of the amended Price Statement the Contractor shall state whether or not he accepts the amended Price Statement or part thereof and if accepted paragraph A3 shall apply to that amended Price Statement or part thereof; if no statement within the 14 day period is made the Contractor shall be deemed not to have accepted, in whole or in part, the amended Price Statement;

    ·3   to the extent that the amended Price Statement is not accepted by the Contractor, the Contractor's Price Statement and the amended Price Statement may be referred either by the Employer or by the Contractor as a dispute or difference to the Adjudicator in accordance with the provisions of clause 41A.

A5   Where no notification has been given pursuant to paragraph A2 the Price Statement is deemed not to have been accepted, and the Contractor may, on or after the expiry of the 21 day period to which paragraph A2 refers, refer his Price Statement as a dispute or difference to the Adjudicator in accordance with the provisions of clause 41A.

A6   Where a Price Statement is not accepted by the Quantity Surveyor after consultation with the Architect or an amended Price Statement has not been accepted by the Contractor and no reference to the Adjudicator under paragraph A4·3 or paragraph A5 has been made, Alternative B shall apply.

A7 ·1   Where the Contractor pursuant to paragraph A1 has attached his requirements to his Price Statement the Quantity Surveyor after consultation with the Architect shall within 21 days of receipt thereof notify the Contractor

·1 ·1   either that the requirement in paragraph A1·1 in respect of the amount to be paid in lieu of any ascertainment under clause 26·1 is accepted or that the requirement is not accepted and clause 26·1 shall apply in respect of the ascertainment of any direct loss and/or expense; and

·1 ·2   either that the requirement in paragraph A1·2 in respect of an adjustment to the time for the completion of the Works is accepted or that the requirement is not accepted and clause 25 shall apply in respect of any such adjustment.

A7 ·2   If the Quantity Surveyor has not notified the Contractor within the 21 days specified in paragraph A7·1, clause 25 and clause 26 shall apply as if no requirements had been attached to the Price Statement.

·1 ·2   ***Alternative B***

The Valuation shall be made by the Quantity Surveyor in accordance with the provisions of clauses 13·5·1 to 13·5·7.

·1 ·3   The valuation of Variations to the sub-contract works executed by a Nominated Sub-Contractor in accordance with instructions of the Architect and of all instructions issued under clause 13·3·2 and all work executed by a Nominated Sub-Contractor for which an Approximate Quantity is included in any bills of quantities included in the Numbered Documents shall (unless otherwise agreed by the Contractor and the Nominated Sub-Contractor concerned with the approval of the Employer) be made in accordance with the relevant provisions of Conditions NSC/C.

13·4 ·2   Where under the instruction of the Architect as to the expenditure of a provisional sum a prime cost sum arises and the Contractor under clause 35·2 tenders for the work covered by that prime cost sum and that tender is accepted by or on behalf of the Employer, that work shall be valued in accordance with the accepted tender of the Contractor and shall not be included in the Valuation of the instruction of the Architect in regard to the expenditure of the provisional sum.

13·5 ·1   To the extent that the Valuation relates to the execution of additional or substituted work which can properly be valued by measurement or to the execution of work for which an Approximate Quantity is included in the Contract Bills such work shall be measured and shall be valued in accordance with the following rules:

·1 ·1   where the additional or substituted work is of similar character to, is executed under similar conditions as, and does not significantly change the quantity of, work set out in the Contract Bills the rates and prices for the work so set out shall determine the Valuation;

·1 ·2   where the additional or substituted work is of similar character to work set out in the Contract Bills but is not executed under similar conditions thereto and/or significantly changes the quantity thereof, the rates and prices for the work so set out shall be the basis for determining the valuation and the valuation shall include a fair allowance for such difference in conditions and/or quantity;

·1 ·3   where the additional or substituted work is not of similar character to work set out in the Contract Bills the work shall be valued at fair rates and prices;

·1 ·4   where the Approximate Quantity is a reasonably accurate forecast of the quantity of work required the rate or price for the Approximate Quantity shall determine the Valuation;

·1 ·5 where the Approximate Quantity is not a reasonably accurate forecast of the quantity of work required the rate or price for that Approximate Quantity shall be the basis for determining the Valuation and the Valuation shall include a fair allowance for such difference in quantity.

Provided that clause 13·5·1·4 and clause 13·5·1·5 shall only apply to the extent that the work has not been altered or modified other than in quantity.

13·5 ·2 To the extent that the Valuation relates to the omission of work set out in the Contract Bills the rates and prices for such work therein set out shall determine the valuation of the work omitted.

13·5 ·3 In any valuation of work under clauses 13·5·1 and 13·5·2:

·3 ·1 measurement shall be in accordance with the same principles as those governing the preparation of the Contract Bills as referred to in clause 2·2·2·1;

·3 ·2 allowance shall be made for any percentage or lump sum adjustments in the Contract Bills; and

·3 ·3 allowance, where appropriate, shall be made for any addition to or reduction of preliminary items of the type referred to in the Standard Method of Measurement, 7th Edition, Section A (Preliminaries/General Conditions); provided that no such allowance shall be made in respect of compliance with an Architect's instruction for the expenditure of a provisional sum for defined work.*

13·5 ·4 To the extent that the Valuation relates to the execution of additional or substituted work which cannot properly be valued by measurement the Valuation shall comprise:

·4 ·1 the prime cost of such work (calculated in accordance with the 'Definition of Prime Cost of Daywork carried out under a Building Contract' issued by the Royal Institution of Chartered Surveyors and the Building Employers Confederation (now Construction Confederation) which was current at the Base Date) together with percentage additions to each section of the prime cost at the rates set out by the Contractor in the Contract Bills; or

·4 ·2 where the work is within the province of any specialist trade and the said Institution and the appropriate [v] body representing the employers in that trade have agreed and issued a definition of prime cost of daywork, the prime cost of such work calculated in accordance with that definition which was current at the Base Date together with percentage additions on the prime cost at the rates set out by the Contractor in the Contract Bills.

Provided that in any case vouchers specifying the time daily spent upon the work, the workmen's names, the plant and the materials employed shall be delivered for verification to the Architect or his authorised representative not later than the end of the week following that in which the work has been executed.

13·5 ·5 If

compliance with any instruction requiring a Variation or

compliance with any instruction as to the expenditure of a provisional sum for undefined work* or

compliance with any instruction as to the expenditure of a provisional sum for defined work* to the extent that the instruction for that work differs from the description given for such work in the Contract Bills or

the execution of work for which an Approximate Quantity is included in the Contract Bills to such extent as the quantity is more or less than the quantity ascribed to that work in the Contract Bills

substantially changes the conditions under which any other work is executed, then such other work shall be treated as if it had been the subject of an instruction of the Architect requiring a Variation under clause 13·2 which shall be valued in accordance with the provisions of clause 13.

13·5 ·6 ·1 The Valuation of Performance Specified Work shall include allowance for the addition or omission of any relevant work involved in the preparation and production of drawings, schedules or other documents;

·6 ·2 the Valuation of additional or substituted work related to Performance Specified Work shall be consistent with the rates and prices of work of a similar character set out in the Contract Bills or the Analysis making due allowance for any changes in the conditions under which the work is carried out and/or any significant change in the quantity of the work set out in the Contract Bills or in the Contractor's Statement. Where there is no work of a similar character set out in the Contract Bills or the Contractor's Statement a fair valuation shall be made;

·6 ·3 the Valuation of the omission of work relating to Performance Specified Work shall be in accordance with the rates and prices for such work set out in the Contract Bills or the Analysis;

·6 ·4 any valuation of work under clauses 13·5·6·2 and 13·5·6·3 shall include allowance for any necessary addition to or reduction of preliminary items of the type referred to in the Standard Method of Measurement, 7th Edition, Section A (Preliminaries/General Conditions);

·6 ·5 where an appropriate basis of a fair valuation of additional or substituted work relating to Performance Specified Work is daywork the Valuation shall be in accordance with clauses 13·5·4·1 or 13·5·4·2 and the proviso to clause 13·5·4 shall apply;

·6 ·6 if

compliance with any instruction under clause 42·11 requiring a Variation to Performance Specified Work or

compliance with any instruction as to the expenditure of a provisional sum for Performance Specified Work to the extent that the instruction for that Work differs from the information provided in the Contract Bills pursuant to clause 42·7·2 and/or 42·7·3 for such Performance Specified Work

substantially changes the conditions under which any other work is executed (including any other Performance Specified Work) then such other work (including any other Performance Specified Work) shall be treated as if it had been the subject of an instruction of the Architect requiring a Variation under clause 13·2 or, if relevant, under clause 42·11 which shall be valued in accordance with the provisions of clause 13·5.

13·5 ·7 To the extent that the Valuation does not relate to the execution of additional or substituted work or the omission of work or to the extent that the valuation of any work or liabilities directly associated with a Variation cannot reasonably be effected in the Valuation by the application of clauses 13·5·1 to ·6 a fair valuation thereof shall be made.

Provided that no allowance shall be made under clause 13·5 for any effect upon the regular progress of the Works or for any other direct loss and/or expense for which the Contractor would be reimbursed by payment under any other provision in the Conditions.

13·6 Where it is necessary to measure work for the purpose of the Valuation the Quantity Surveyor shall give to the Contractor an opportunity of being present at the time of such measurement and of taking such notes and measurements as the Contractor may require.

13·7 Effect shall be given to the Valuation under clause 13·4·1·1, to an agreement by the Employer and the Contractor to which clause 13·4·1·1 refers, to a 13A Quotation for which the Architect has issued a confirmed acceptance and to a valuation pursuant to clause 13A·8 by addition to or deduction from the Contract Sum.

16 Clause 13A: Variation instruction – contractor's quotation in compliance with the instruction

16.01 Clause 13A is an alternative to the traditional method of valuing in accordance with the valuation rules in Clause 13.5. It is for the architect in the first instance to decide whether he wishes Clause 13A to be used. If so he must specify this in his instruction. If he does the clause 13A method will apply, unless, within 7 days, the contractor states in writing that he disagrees with the application of Clause 13A to the instruction. If the contractor does that, then the valuation rules in Clauses 13.4 and 13.5 will apply.

16.02 At the heart of the Clause 13A method of valuing is what is called a '13A Quotation'. This is a quotation to be provided by the contractor. If the system is to work properly the architect's variation instruction must give the contractor sufficient information to provide a quotation; Clause 13A.1.1 specifically directs this. The JCT suggests that the information be in a similar format to that provided at tender stage, such as drawings, an addendum bill of quantities or a specification. If the contractor considers that the information provided is insufficient, then he has the right within 7 days to request further information. The contractor is allowed 21 days from receipt of the instruction to provide the information. But if there has been a request by him for further information, the 21-day period runs from the receipt of the further information.

16.03 The 13A Quotation must provide not merely a price for the variation. It must give the value of the entire adjustment to the contract sum including the effect on any other work. In addition it must give all the other matters listed in Clause 13A.2, including any adjustment to the time required for completion of the works, any sum by way of 'direct loss and expense' (see Clause 26) and a fee for preparing the 13A Quotation.

16.04 On receipt of the 13A Quotation the employer must choose to accept it or not to accept it. If the employer decides to accept it, he should notify the contractor directly. The architect should then confirm the acceptance by giving the contractor in writing the information specified in Clause 13A.3.2. It might be thought that the effect of such acceptance would be that the contractor's price became binding: that, after all, is the normal meaning in law of accepting a quotation. But that is not quite so. The price to be paid for the varied work is a valuation to be made in due course by the quantity surveyor on a fair and reasonable basis: however, the quantity surveyor is directed to make that assessment having regard to the content of the 13A Quotation and disregarding the normal valuation rules.

16.05 The alternative course for the employer is not to accept the 13A Quotation. That may happen for two different reasons. One is simply that the employer considers the contractor's price excessive. In that case the architect should instruct that the variation is to be carried out in any event and to be valued in accordance with the normal valuation rules. The other reason is that, having seen the cost or delay implications, the employer decides that he does not want to have the varied work after all. In that case the architect should instruct the contractor that the varied work is not to be carried out. Whatever the reason for the non-acceptance of a 13A Quotation, the contractor is entitled to be paid a fair and reasonable fee for preparing it.

16.06 If the variation affects work by a nominated sub-contractor, then the contractor may seek a similar quotation from the sub-contractor. A similar amendment has been made to the Conditions of Sub-Contract (NSC/C). The sub-contractor's quotation is called a 3.3A Quotation, which, of course, is a reference to the new clause number in NSC/C. The contractor will use the contents of the 3.3A Quotation when preparing his 13A Quotation.

16.07 Architects should not seek to employ the 13A Quotation procedure in the following situations, to which it is inappropriate:

- To a variation instruction which requires virtually immediate compliance
- To a variation which amounts to a minor amendment or correction to information in the contract documents.

17 Clause 14: Contract sum

17.01 Unless there is a case for rectification the parties are bound by any errors incorporated into the contract sum. Rectification is available either where the document fails to record the mutual intentions of the parties or where it fails to record accurately the intention of one party only, where the other with knowledge of the other party's error has nevertheless stood by and allowed the other to sign the agreement (see *Bates v Wyndhams* [1981] 1 All ER 1077).

18 Clause 15: Value added tax – supplemental provisions

18.01 When value added tax was introduced the Joint Contracts Tribunal decided that the contract sum, that is, the sum in Article 2, should be exclusive of VAT. A separate document was issued by the JCT originally entitled 'supplemental VAT Agreement'. The general intention was that the contractor should be entitled to recover from the employer, as an additional sum, such VAT as he might have to pay to HM Customs and Excise on his supply of goods and services to the employer. The agreement also provided machinery for dealing with difficulties which might arise. Today the equivalent document is entitled 'Supplemental Provisions (the VAT Agreement)'. It is normally to be found at the back of JCT contracts. The view is taken that Clause 15.1 sufficiently incorporates it, and that there is no need for parties separately to execute it.

18.02 In the early days of VAT a considerable amount of building work was outside the scope of VAT. The scheme then was the contractor would analyse each supply into that element which attracted VAT and that which was zero-rated. Progressively, more and more building work has come within the scope of VAT. Therefore, in 1989 a simpler alternative was introduced, contained in Clause 1A of the supplemental provisions. That provides a scheme for use when the contractor is aware at the outset that all supplies will be standard rated, or, in occasional cases, zero-rated. The Appendix now contains an entry for the parties to indicate whether or not the simpler Clause 1A scheme is to apply.

18.03 Tax is a complicated subject, and one wholly outside the scope of this chapter. On any point of difficulty architects should take advice from an accountant, or a solicitor or barrister specializing in tax matters.

19 Clause 16: Materials and goods unfixed or off-site

19.01 This clause should be read in conjunction with Clause 30.2. The position as to materials and goods intended for the works is as follows:

1 As soon as materials or goods are brought onto or adjacent to the works, they must not be removed without the architect's consent (Clause 16.1).
2 As soon as materials or goods are paid for, property passes to the employer (Clause 16.1).
3 As soon as materials or goods are incorporated into the works, property passes to the owner of the land by operation of law whether the goods are paid for or not.

13A   Variation instruction – Contractor's quotation in compliance with the instruction

13A   Clause 13A shall only apply to an instruction where pursuant to clause 13·2·3 the Contractor has not disagreed with the application of clause 13A to such instruction.

13A·1 ·1   The instruction to which clause 13A is to apply shall have provided sufficient information [w] to enable the Contractor to provide a quotation, which shall comprise the matters set out in clause 13A·2 (a '13A Quotation'), in compliance with the instruction; and in respect of any part of the Variation which relates to the work of any Nominated Sub-Contractor sufficient information to enable the Contractor to obtain a 3·3A Quotation from the Nominated Sub-Contractor in accordance with clause 3·3A·1·2 of the Conditions NSC/C. If the Contractor reasonably considers that the information provided is not sufficient, then, not later than 7 days from the receipt of the instruction, he shall request the Architect to supply sufficient further information.

13A·1 ·2   The Contractor shall submit to the Quantity Surveyor his 13A Quotation in compliance with the instruction and shall include therein 3·3A Quotations in respect of any parts of the Variation which relate to the work of Nominated Sub-Contractors not later than 21 days from

the date of receipt of the instruction

or   if applicable, the date of receipt by the Contractor of the sufficient further information to which clause 13A·1·1 refers

whichever date is the later and the 13A Quotation shall remain open for acceptance by the Employer for 7 days from its receipt by the Quantity Surveyor.

13A·1 ·3   The Variation for which the Contractor has submitted his 13A Quotation shall not be carried out by the Contractor or as relevant by any Nominated Sub-Contractor until receipt by the Contractor of the confirmed acceptance issued by the Architect pursuant to clause 13A·3·2.

13A·2   The 13A Quotation shall separately comprise:

13A·2 ·1   the value of the adjustment to the Contract Sum (other than any amount to which clause 13A·2·3 refers) including therein the effect of the instruction on any other work including that of Nominated Sub-Contractors supported by all necessary calculations by reference, where relevant, to the rates and prices in the Contract Bills and including, where appropriate, allowances for any adjustment of preliminary items;

13A·2 ·2   any adjustment to the time required for completion of the Works (including where relevant stating an earlier Completion Date than the Date for Completion given in the Appendix) to the extent that such adjustment is not included in any revision of the Completion Date that has been made by the Architect under clause 25·3 or in his confirmed acceptance of any other 13A Quotation;

13A·2 ·3   the amount to be paid in lieu of any ascertainment under clause 26·1 of direct loss and/or expense not included in any other accepted 13A Quotation or in any previous ascertainment under clause 26;

13A·2 ·4   a fair and reasonable amount in respect of the cost of preparing the 13A Quotation;

and, where specifically required by the instruction, shall provide indicative information in statements on

13A·2 ·5   the additional resources (if any) required to carry out the Variation; and

13A·2 ·6   the method of carrying out the Variation.

Each part of the 13A Quotation shall contain reasonably sufficient supporting information to enable that part to be evaluated by or on behalf of the Employer.

13A·3 ·1   If the Employer wishes to accept a 13A Quotation the Employer shall so notify the Contractor in writing not later than the last day of the period for acceptance stated in clause 13A·1·2.

13A·3 ·2 If the Employer accepts a 13A Quotation the Architect shall, immediately upon that acceptance, confirm such acceptance by stating in writing to the Contractor (in clause 13A and elsewhere in the Conditions called a 'confirmed acceptance'):

    ·2 ·1 that the Contractor is to carry out the Variation;

    ·2 ·2 the adjustment of the Contract Sum, including therein any amounts to which clause 13A·2·3 and clause 13A·2·4 refer, to be made for complying with the instruction requiring the Variation;

    ·2 ·3 any adjustment to the time required by the Contractor for completion of the Works and the revised Completion Date arising therefrom (which, where relevant, may be a date earlier than the Date for Completion given in the Appendix) and, where relevant, any revised period or periods for the completion of the Nominated Sub-Contract work of each Nominated Sub-Contractor; and

    ·2 ·4 that the Contractor, pursuant to clause 3·3A·3 of the Conditions NSC/C, shall accept any 3·3A Quotation included in the 13A Quotation for which the confirmed acceptance has been issued.

13A·4 If the Employer does not accept the 13A Quotation by the expiry of the period for acceptance stated in clause 13A·1·2, the Architect shall, on the expiry of that period,

either

13A·4 ·1 instruct that the Variation is to be carried out and is to be valued pursuant to clause 13·4·1;

or

13A·4 ·2 instruct that the Variation is not to be carried out.

13A·5 If a 13A Quotation is not accepted a fair and reasonable amount shall be added to the Contract Sum in respect of the cost of preparation of the 13A Quotation provided that the 13A Quotation has been prepared on a fair and reasonable basis. The non-acceptance by the Employer of a 13A Quotation shall not of itself be evidence that the Quotation was not prepared on a fair and reasonable basis.

13A·6 If the Architect has not, under clause 13A·3·2, issued a confirmed acceptance of a 13A Quotation neither the Employer nor the Contractor may use that 13A Quotation for any purpose whatsoever.

13A·7 The Employer and the Contractor may agree to increase or reduce the number of days stated in clause 13A·1·1 and/or in clause 13A·1·2 and any such agreement shall be confirmed in writing by the Employer to the Contractor. Where relevant the Contractor shall notify each Nominated Sub-Contractor of any agreed increase or reduction pursuant to this clause 13A·7.

13A·8 If the Architect issues an instruction requiring a Variation to work for which a 13A Quotation has been given and in respect of which the Architect has issued a confirmed acceptance to the Contractor such Variation shall not be valued under clause 13·5; but the Quantity Surveyor shall make a valuation of such Variation on a fair and reasonable basis having regard to the content of such 13A Quotation and shall include in that valuation the direct loss and/or expense, if any, incurred by the Contractor because the regular progress of the Works or any part thereof has been materially affected by compliance with the instruction requiring the Variation.

14   Contract Sum

14·1   The quality and quantity of the work included in the Contract Sum shall be deemed to be that which is set out in the Contract Bills.

14·2   The Contract Sum shall not be adjusted or altered in any way whatsoever otherwise than in accordance with the express provisions of the Conditions, and subject to clause 2·2·2·2 any error whether of arithmetic or not in the computation of the Contract Sum shall be deemed to have been accepted by the parties hereto.

15   Value added tax – supplemental provisions

15·1   In clause 15 and in the supplemental provisions pursuant hereto (hereinafter called the 'VAT Agreement') 'tax' means the value added tax introduced by the Finance Act 1972 which is under the care and management of the Commissioners of Customs and Excise (hereinafter and in the VAT Agreement called 'the Commissioners').

15·2   Any reference in the Conditions to 'Contract Sum' shall be regarded as such Sum exclusive of any tax and recovery by the Contractor from the Employer of tax properly chargeable by the Commissioners on the Contractor under or by virtue of the Finance Act 1972 or any amendment or re-enactment thereof on the supply of goods and services under this Contract shall be under the provisions of clause 15 and of the VAT Agreement. Clause 1A of the VAT Agreement shall only apply where so stated in the Appendix. [x]

15·3   To the extent that after the Base Date the supply of goods and services to the Employer becomes exempt from the tax there shall be paid to the Contractor an amount equal to the loss of credit (input tax) on the supply to the Contractor of goods and services which contribute exclusively to the Works.

16   Materials and goods unfixed or off-site

16·1   Unfixed materials and goods delivered to, placed on or adjacent to the Works and intended therefor shall not be removed except for use upon the Works unless the Architect has consented in writing to such removal which consent shall not be unreasonably delayed or withheld. Where the value of any such materials or goods has in accordance with clause 30·2 been included in any Interim Certificate under which the amount properly due to the Contractor has been paid by the Employer, such materials and goods shall become the property of the Employer, but, subject to clause 22B or 22C (if applicable), the Contractor shall remain responsible for loss or damage to the same.

16·2   Where the value of any 'listed items' has in accordance with clause 30·3 been included in any Interim Certificate under which the amount properly due to the Contractor has been paid by the Employer, such listed items shall become the property of the Employer and thereafter the Contractor shall not, except for use upon the Works, remove or cause or permit the same to be moved or removed from the premises where they are, but the Contractor shall nevertheless be responsible for any loss thereof or damage thereto and for the cost of storage, handling and insurance of the same until such time as they are delivered to and placed on or adjacent to the Works whereupon the provisions of clause 16·1 (except the words "Where the value" to the words "the property of the Employer, but,") shall apply thereto.

19.02 The architect has a discretion whether to certify for the value of goods and materials 'off-site' under Clause 30.3. If off-site materials are certified and paid for, the property passes to the employer (Clause 16.2). The employer does not usually have an interest in or right to retain the contractor's plant and equipment (but see Clause 27.6.1 and 27.6.3).

20 Clause 17: Practical completion and defects liability

20.01 This clause provides for the issue of a certificate of practical completion when, in the opinion of the architect, practical completion has been achieved (and if the contractor has complied with Clauses 6A.4 and 5.9 so far as applicable).

20.02 The Appendix requires a Defects Liability Period to be stated. In default, the contract specifies the period to be 6 months. If any defects, shrinkages or faults (due to materials or works not in accordance with the contract, or to frost occurring before practical completion) appear within this period, the architect should list these in a schedule of defects. This must be delivered to the contractor no later than 14 days after the end of the Defects Liability Period. The contractor must then, within a reasonable time, make good these defects at his own cost (Clause 17.2). An alternative procedure is to allow the defects to remain and make a deduction from the contract sum.

20.03 The architect also has power before issuing the comprehensive schedule of defects to issue instructions requiring the contractor to make good particular defects (Clause 17.3). In practice the architect may wish to leave the delivery of schedule of defects as late as possible, using the Clause 17.3 procedure until then. (See also paragraph 20.13 below.)

20.04 After all such defects, shrinkages or faults have been corrected, the architect should issue a Certificate of Completion of Making Good Defects.

Meaning of practical completion

20.05 The term 'practical completion' is not defined in the contract, but it has been said (by Lord Dilhorne in *Westminster City Council v Jarvis Limited* [1970] 1 All ER 943 at 948) that it does not mean the stage when the work 'was almost but not entirely finished', but 'the completion of all the construction work that has to be done'. Such completion is subject to defects which may thereafter appear and require action under Clause 17. In the same case in the Court of Appeal, Salmon LJ said: 'I take these words to mean completion for all practical purposes, i.e. for the purpose of allowing [the employer] to take possession of the works and use them as intended. If "completion" in Clause 21 [Clause 23 of the 1998 JCT Form] means completion down to the last detail, however trivial and unimportant, then Clause 22 [Clause 24 of the 1998 Form] would be a penalty clause and as such unenforceable'. Neither explanation is binding as to the meaning of the words for the purposes of considering whether the contractor has reached the stage of practical completion. However, it is suggested that the architect can issue his certificate despite very minor defects (applying the *de minimis* principle (*HW Nevill (Sunblest) Limited v Wm Press & Son Limited* [1981] 20 BLR 78)) if:

1 He is reasonably satisfied the works accord with the contract.
2 There is adequate retention.
3 The employer will not suffer loss due to disturbance or otherwise.
4 He obtains a written acknowledgement of the existence of the defect and an undertaking to put it right from the contractor. If the defects are other than trivial, the views of the employer should first be obtained.

It goes without saying that the architect must exercise the above discretion with extreme care.

Form of certificate

20.06 This is not prescribed by the contract, but it should be clear and definite. The RIBA issue suitable forms.

Effect of certificate of practical completion

20.07 The practical completion certificate has the following important effects:

1 It marks the date when the employer re-takes possession of the site (subject to Clauses 18 and 23.3).
2 It fixes the commencement of the defects liability period (as defined in the Appendix).
3 It fixes the period for the final adjustment of the contract sum (Clause 30.6.1.1).
4 It gives rise to the rights to the release of the first half of the retention percentage (Clause 30.4.1).
5 It marks the time for the release of the obligation to insure under Clause 22A.1 where this applies.
6 It marks the end of liability for liquidated damages under Clause 24.
7 It marks the end of liability for frost damage (Clause 17.2).

20.08 The employer's remedies for defective work are not limited to those contained in Clause 17 (i.e. requiring the contractor to make good defects and non-release of retention). He may additionally sue for damages for breach of contract (*HW Nevill (Sunblest) Limited v Wm Press & Son Limited* [1981] 20 BLR 78).

Meaning of defects

20.09 For the contractor's obligation as to standards of workmanship, materials, and goods, see Clauses 2 and 8, and the notes thereto. Defects are, generally, work, materials and goods which are not in conformity with the contract documents. They do not include a failure by the architect to design the works, for example.

20.10 The contractor is not obliged to remedy work left defective by a Nominated Sub-Contractor (Clause 19.5.2 and see *Fairclough v Rhuddlan Borough Council* [1985] 30 BLR 26).

20.11 It is, in general, no excuse for a contractor to say that the architect or the Clerk of Works ought to have observed bad work during site inspections.

Frost damage

20.12 The contractor is not responsible for frost damage after practical completion unless the architect certifies that the damage is due to injury which took place before practical completion.

Instructions under Clause 17.3 making good defects

20.13 This clause enables the architect to issue instructions before the delivery of the schedule of defects when he 'considers it necessary so to do'. One of the matters to be taken into account in considering whether it is necessary to issue such instructions is whether it is reasonable to leave the defect unremedied until after the issue of the schedule.

Architect's remedies

20.14 A notice under Clause 4.1.2 can be given for breach of an instruction to make good defects. If the notice is not complied with, others can be employed to do the necessary work and the cost deducted from the retention percentage. Further, until defects have been made good, the architect need not and should not issue his certificate of completion of making good defects. The second half of the retention percentage will not be released, and issue of the final certificate with the protection it usually affords to the contractor (see Clause 30) may be delayed. The power of determination under Clause 27 is not designed to be exercised after practical completion; however, the remedies set out above ought to be sufficient to make it unnecessary to attempt to rely on Clause 27.

Irremediable breach

20.15 The architect may require a defect to be remedied in an instruction or in the schedule, but then find on representation by the contractor that it cannot be remedied except at a cost which is unreasonable in comparison with the loss to the employer and the nature of the defect. If the employer consents, the architect may issue the Certificate of Making Good Defects under Clause 17.4, having made an 'appropriate' reduction from the Contract Sum by the amount certified for payment in respect of the works not properly carried out (Clause 17.2 and Clause 17.3). This deduction will usually be the amount by which the works are reduced in value by reason of the unremedied defect.

Defects appearing after the expiry of the defects liability period

20.16 If defects appear after the issue of the certificate under Clause 17.4, the architect can no longer issue instructions under Clause 17, but the appearance of the defect is the disclosure of a breach of contract by the contractor. The employer is entitled to damages, and the architect should adjust any further certificate to reflect the effect on the value of the works. In accordance with common law rules as to mitigation of damages, the contractor, if it is reasonable to do so, should be given the opportunity of rectifying the defects. A final certificate should not be issued if the defects are unremedied (see Clause 30.9).

Practical completion of part

20.17 Clause 18 makes provision for 'partial' practical completion where the employer takes possession of part of the work before completion of the work as a whole. Therefore, the procedure laid down under Clause 17 may be applied a number of times during the course of the contract.

21 Clause 18: Partial possession by employer

21.01 This clause provides for the situation where, before the works are completed, the employer, with the consent of the contractor, takes possession of part or parts of the works. It provides provisions as to practical completion, defects, insurance, and retention percentage for application to each part analogous to those which apply to the whole, and for proportionate reduction of any liquidated damages payable. The appropriate Appendix entry (referring to Clause 24.2) must be completed so as to allow the proper operation of Clause 18.1.4, otherwise liquidated damages will not be enforceable. In *Bramall & Ogden Limited v Sheffield City Council* [1983] 29 BLR 73 (a case on JCT 63), the Appendix was completed so as to allow a sum in damages for each uncompleted dwelling. This was held to be inconsistent with Clause 16(e) (equivalent to JCT 98 Clause 18.1.4). If possession is given in sections, the architect must apply Clause 18 and has no power without

---

17   Practical Completion and defects liability

17·1   When in the opinion of the Architect Practical Completion of the Works is achieved and the Contractor has complied sufficiently with clause 6A·4, and, if relevant, the Contractor has complied with clause 5·9 *(Supply of as-built drawings etc. – Performance Specified Work)*, he shall forthwith issue a certificate to that effect and Practical Completion of the Works shall be deemed for all the purposes of this Contract to have taken place on the day named in such certificate.

17·2   Any defects, shrinkages or other faults which shall appear within the Defects Liability Period and which are due to materials or workmanship not in accordance with this Contract or to frost occurring before Practical Completion of the Works, shall be specified by the Architect in a schedule of defects which he shall deliver to the Contractor as an instruction of the Architect not later than 14 days after the expiration of the said Defects Liability Period, and within a reasonable time after receipt of such schedule the defects, shrinkages and other faults therein specified shall be made good by the Contractor at no cost to the Employer unless the Architect with the consent of the Employer shall otherwise instruct; and if the Architect does so otherwise instruct then an appropriate deduction in respect of any such defects, shrinkages or other faults not made good shall be made from the Contract Sum.

17·3   Notwithstanding clause 17·2 the Architect may whenever he considers it necessary so to do issue instructions requiring any defect, shrinkage or other fault which shall appear within the Defects Liability Period and which is due to materials or workmanship not in accordance with this Contract or to frost occurring before Practical Completion of the Works, to be made good, and the Contractor shall within a reasonable time after receipt of such instructions comply with the same at no cost to the Employer unless the Architect with the consent of the Employer shall otherwise instruct; and if the Architect does so otherwise instruct then an appropriate deduction in respect of any such defects, shrinkages or other faults not made good shall be made from the Contract Sum. Provided that no such instructions shall be issued after delivery of a schedule of defects or after 14 days from the expiration of the Defects Liability Period.

17·4   When in the opinion of the Architect any defects, shrinkages or other faults which he may have required to be made good under clauses 17·2 and 17·3 shall have been made good he shall issue a certificate to that effect, and completion of making good defects shall be deemed for all the purposes of this Contract to have taken place on the day named in such certificate (the 'Certificate of Completion of Making Good Defects').

17·5   In no case shall the Contractor be required to make good at his own cost any damage by frost which may appear after Practical Completion, unless the Architect shall certify that such damage is due to injury which took place before Practical Completion.

18   Partial possession by Employer

18·1   If at any time or times before the date of issue by the Architect of the certificate of Practical Completion the Employer wishes to take possession of any part or parts of the Works and the consent of the Contractor (which consent shall not be unreasonably delayed or withheld) has been obtained, then, notwithstanding anything expressed or implied elsewhere in this Contract, the Employer may take possession thereof. The Architect shall thereupon issue to the Contractor on behalf of the Employer a written statement identifying the part or parts of the Works taken into possession and giving the date when the Employer took possession (in clauses 18, 20·3, 22·3·1 and 22C·1 referred to as 'the relevant part' and 'the relevant date' respectively).

18·1   ·1   For the purposes of clauses 17·2, 17·3, 17·5 and 30·4·1·2 Practical Completion of the relevant part shall be deemed to have occurred and the Defects Liability Period in respect of the relevant part shall be deemed to have commenced on the relevant date.

18·1   ·2   When in the opinion of the Architect any defects, shrinkages or other faults in the relevant part which he may have required to be made good under clause 17·2 or clause 17·3 shall have been made good he shall issue a certificate to that effect.

18·1   ·3   As from the relevant date the obligation of the Contractor under clause 22A or of the Employer under clause 22B·1 or clause 22C·2 whichever is applicable to insure shall terminate in respect of the relevant part but not further or otherwise; and where clause 22C applies the obligation of the Employer to insure under clause 22C·1 shall from the relevant date include the relevant part.

18·1   ·4   In lieu of any sum to be paid by the Contractor or withheld or deducted by the Employer under clause 24 in respect of any period during which the Works may remain incomplete occurring after the relevant date there shall be paid such sum as bears the same ratio to the sum which would be paid apart from the provisions of clause 18 as the Contract Sum less the amount contained therein in respect of the relevant part bears to the Contract Sum; or the Employer may give a notice pursuant to clause 30·1·1·4 that he will deduct such sum from the monies due to the Contractor.

the consent of the parties to issue a certificate of practical completion for an average date of completion.

Duty to complete in sections

21.02 This clause does not impose a duty to complete in sections. Equally, if the contractor is delayed and therefore subject to liquidated damages, he is not entitled to any contra-credit for having completed some of the work before the contractual completion date. If sectional completion is required, the JCT Sectional Completion Supplement should be employed.

22   Clause 19: Assignment and sub-contracts

22.01 At law, a party may assign the benefit of a contract on giving notice of the assignment to the other party, but may not assign the burden without the other party's consent. This clause prohibits either party making *any* assignment without the written consent of the other. The rationale behind this is to ensure that the original contracting parties are not brought into direct contractual relations with third parties with whom they may not wish to contract. The House of Lords held in *Linden Garden Trust Limited v Lenesta Sludge Disposals Limited* [1993] 3 All ER 417 that any purported assignment would be invalid under this clause, and therefore not effective to transfer any rights of action under the contract. This is emphasized by the fact that Clause 1.12 expressly excludes the effect of the Contracts (Rights of Third Parties) Act 1999.

22.02 Clauses 19.2, 19.3 and 19.4 make specific provision for 'domestic sub-contractors', i.e. sub-contractors to whom the contractor delegates part of the work but who are not nominated pursuant to Clause 35. Clause 19.2.2 imposes a general prohibition on subletting any portion of the works without the consent of the architect, whose consent shall not be unreasonably withheld. Any person other than a nominated sub-contractor to whom a portion of the work is sublet is called a domestic sub-contractor (19.2.1).

Lists of domestic sub-contractors

22.03 Clause 19.3 makes further provision for domestic sub-contractors. It applies whenever the bills provide in respect of any work that the work is to be carried out by a person selected from a list contained in or annexed to the contract bills at the sole discretion of the contractor. This recognizes a practice which has been adopted by some employers. Clause 19.3.2.1 provides that this list must comprise not less than three persons and is subject to amendment by either the employer or the contractor with the consent of the other so as to add further names to the list at any time prior to the execution of a binding sub-contract. If at any time prior to the sub-contract being entered into less than three persons on the list are prepared to carry out the work in question by virtue of Clause 19.3.2.2 either further names are to be added to the list or the work is to be carried out by the contractor who may, if he wishes, sublet to a domestic sub-contractor under Clause 19.2 (subject to the architect's approval).

22.04 This procedure is only available where the work is measured or described in the bills and priced by the contractor, therefore it can never apply where the work in question is the subject of a provisional or prime cost sum or where for some other reason the work is not included in the bills.

22.05 Clause 19.4.1 provides, perhaps unnecessarily, that any domestic sub-contract is subject to a condition that the domestic sub-contractor's employment shall determine if the contractor's employment under the main contract is determined. Since domestic sub-contractors will not, of course, be parties to this contract, any rights they may have in fact against the main contractor on such determination would not be affected by this clause.

19   Assignment and sub-contracts

19·1   ·1   Neither the Employer nor the Contractor shall, without the written consent of the other, assign this Contract.

may at any time after Practical Completion of the Works assign to any such transferee or lessee the right to bring proceedings in the name of the Employer (whether by arbitration or litigation) to enforce any of the terms of this Contract made for the benefit of the Employer hereunder. The assignee shall be estopped from disputing any enforceable agreements reached between the Employer and the Contractor and which arise out of and relate to this Contract (whether or not they are or appear to be a derogation from the right assigned) and made prior to the date of any assignment.

19·2   ·1   A person to whom the Contractor sub-lets any portion of the Works other than a Nominated Sub-Contractor is in this Contract referred to as a 'Domestic Sub-Contractor'.

19·2   ·2   The Contractor shall not without the written consent of the Architect (which consent shall not be unreasonably delayed or withheld) sub-let any portion of the Works. The Contractor shall remain wholly responsible for carrying out and completing the Works in all respects in accordance with clause 2·1 notwithstanding the sub-letting of any portion of the Works.

19·3   ·1   Where the Contract Bills provide that certain work measured or otherwise described in those Bills and priced by the Contractor must be carried out by persons named in a list in or annexed to the Contract Bills and selected therefrom by and at the sole discretion of the Contractor the provisions of clause 19·3 shall apply in respect of that list.

19·3   ·2   ·1   The list referred to in clause 19·3·1 must comprise not less than three persons. Either the Employer (or the Architect on his behalf) or the Contractor shall be entitled with the consent of the other, which consent shall not be unreasonably delayed or withheld, to add [y] additional persons to the list at any time prior to the execution of a binding sub-contract agreement.

           ·2   ·2   If at any time prior to the execution of a binding sub-contract agreement and for whatever reason less than three persons named in the list are able and willing to carry out the relevant work then

                       either the Employer and the Contractor shall by agreement (which agreement shall not be unreasonably delayed or withheld) add [y] the names of other persons so that the list comprises not less than three such persons

                       or the work shall be carried out by the Contractor who may sub-let to a Domestic Sub-Contractor in accordance with clause 19·2.

19·3   ·3   A person selected by the Contractor under clause 19·3 from the aforesaid list shall be a Domestic Sub-Contractor.

19·4   It shall be a condition in any sub-letting to which clause 19·2 or 19·3 refers that:

19·4   ·1   the employment of the Domestic Sub-Contractor under the sub-contract shall determine immediately upon the determination (for any reason) of the Contractor's employment under this Contract; and

19·4   ·2   the sub-contract shall provide that:

           ·2   ·1   subject to clause 16·1 of these Conditions (in clauses 19·4·2·2 to ·4 called 'the Main Contract Conditions'), unfixed materials and goods delivered to, placed on or adjacent to the Works by the sub-contractor and intended therefor shall not be removed except for use on the Works unless the Contractor has consented in writing to such removal, which consent shall not be unreasonably delayed or withheld;

           ·2   ·2   where, in accordance with clause 30·2 of the Main Contract Conditions, the value of any such materials or goods shall have been included in any Interim Certificate under which the amount properly due to the Contractor shall have been paid by the Employer to the Contractor, such materials or goods shall be and become the property of the Employer and the sub-contractor shall not deny that such materials or goods are and have become the property of the Employer;

·2 ·3 provided that if the Contractor shall pay the sub-contractor for any such materials or goods before the value therefor has, in accordance with clause 30·2 of the Main Contract Conditions, been included in any Interim Certificate under which the amount properly due to the Contractor has been paid by the Employer to the Contractor, such materials or goods shall upon such payment by the Contractor be and become the property of the Contractor;

·2 ·4 the operation of clauses 19·4·2·1 to ·3 hereof shall be without prejudice to any property in any materials or goods passing to the Contractor as provided in clause 30·3 of the Main Contract Conditions *(off-site materials or goods)*; and

19·4 ·3 the sub-contract shall provide that if the Contractor fails properly to pay the amount, or any part thereof, due to the sub-contractor by the final date for its payment stated in the sub-contract, the Contractor shall pay to the sub-contractor in addition to the amount not properly paid simple interest thereon for the period until such payment is made; that the payment of such simple interest shall be treated as a debt due to the sub-contractor by the Contractor; that the rate of interest payable shall be five per cent (5%) over the Base Rate of the Bank of England which is current at the date the payment by the Contractor became overdue; and that any payment of simple interest shall not in any circumstances be construed as a waiver by the sub-contractor of his right to proper payment of the principal amounts due from the Contractor to the sub-contractor in accordance with, and within the time stated in, the sub-contract or of any rights of the sub-contractor under the sub-contract in regard to suspension of the performance of his obligations to the Contractor under the sub-contract or determination of his employment for the failure by the Contractor properly to pay any amount due under the sub-contract to the sub-contractor.

19·5 ·1 The provisions of this Contract relating to Nominated Sub-Contractors are set out in Part 2 of the Conditions. Save as otherwise expressed in the Conditions the Contractor shall remain wholly responsible for carrying out and completing the Works in all respects in accordance with clause 2·1, notwithstanding the nomination of a sub-contractor to supply and fix materials or goods or to execute work.

19·5 ·2 Subject to clause 35·2 the Contractor is not himself required, unless otherwise agreed, to supply and fix materials or goods or to execute work which is to be carried out by a Nominated Sub-Contractor.

22.06 Clause 19.4.2 makes provision for the passing of property. These provisions are without prejudice to the provisions of Clause 30.3.5 as to the passing of property in materials which are included in an interim certificate when stored off-site.

22.07 Clause 19.5.1 provides that, subject to Part 2 (dealing with nominated sub-contractors) the contractor remains wholly responsible for the carrying out and completing of the works to the standards required by Clause 2.1, notwithstanding the nomination of a sub-contractor who will actually supply and fix materials or goods or to execute work. Clause 35.2.1 (in Part 2) however states that the contractor will not be responsible to the employer for:

1 The design of nominated sub-contract works insofar as they have been designed by a nominated sub-contractor
2 The selection of the kinds of materials and goods for nominated sub-contract works insofar as they have been selected by a nominated sub-contractor
3 The satisfaction of any performance specification insofar as it is included in the description of nominated sub-contract works
4 The provision of information required to be provided by the nominated sub-contractor (pursuant to Agreement NSC/W).

22.08 Clause 19.5.2 makes it clear that (apart from the provisions of Clause 35.2) unless agreed the contractor is not himself required to carry out work for which provision is made for execution by a nominated sub-contractor. This confirms the position as laid down in *North West Metropolitan Hospital Board v T A Bickerton & Son Limited* [1970] 1 WLR 607, where it was held that where a nominated sub-contractor failed to perform, it was the duty of the employer to renominate a further nominated sub-contractor.

23 Clause 20: Injury to persons and property and indemnity to employer

Contractor's liability under Clauses 20.1 and 20.2 in respect of personal injury and injury or damage to property

23.01 Clause 20.1 requires the contractor to indemnify the employer against liability, claims, losses and expenses, etc. arising from the death or personal injury to any person occasioned in the carrying out of the works. However the contractor is not liable for any act or neglect of the employer or those persons for whom the employer is responsible (including employees).

23.02 Clause 20.2 deals with damage to property other than the works themselves (see next paragraph). It requires the contractor to indemnify the employer against liability etc. arising from damage to property, real or personal, occasioned by the carrying out of the works. It differs from Clause 20.1 in that the onus is implicitly on the *employer* to show that the injury or damage was due to negligence, breach of statutory duty, omission or default on the part of the contractor or those for whom the contractor is responsible. The contractor will not be liable for any act or neglect of the employer or those persons for whom the employer is responsible, or any local authority or statutory undertaker.

23.03 In Clause 20.2 'property, real or personal' does not include the works, work executed or site materials before the issue of the Certificate of Practical Completion or the determination of the employment of the contractor (Clause 20.3).

23.04 If Clauses 22B or 22C apply, the contractor is liable to the employer under Clause 20 for claims by third parties whose property is damaged and for claims by the employer in respect of his own property. However Clause 20 is not concerned with the works themselves being defectively executed as a result of the contractor's negligence (see *City of Manchester v Fram Gerrard* [1964] 6 BLR 70).

23.05 If, however, Clause 22C.1 applies ('Insurance of existing structures'), then the indemnity excludes loss or damage to any property required to be insured under that clause which is caused by a Specified Peril. In *Ossory Road (Skelmersdale) Limited v Balfour Beatty Building Limited* [1993] CILL 882, it was stated that where the contractor negligently damaged an existing structure, and such damage was caused by a Specified Peril (fire), the contractor would not be liable to the employer for loss or damage suffered or for third party claims against the employer. This approach was affirmed by the Court of Appeal in *Scottish & Newcastle Plc v GD Construction (St Albans) Ltd* [2003] EWCA Civ 16, who held that the effect of requiring the employer to take out joint names insurance with the contractor, was that the parties allocated to the employer the risk of loss or damage by a fire caused by the negligence of a sub-contractor.

23.06 In addition to his liability under Clause 20.2, the contractor must as an incident of his duty to complete, make good damage to the works. This would apply, for example, to damage caused by vandalism or theft occurring before practical completion (provided it was not caused by the employer's negligence or default and was not within the risks accepted by the employer where Clauses 22B or 22C are used). The contractor's plant, equipment, and unfixed goods and materials are at his risk. Goods and materials when certified remain at his risk.

24 Clause 21: Insurance against injury to person or property

24.01 Clause 21.1.1.1 requires the contractor to take out and maintain insurance in respect of claims arising under Clauses 20.1 and 20.2 (see above).

24.02 Clause 21.2.1 obligates the contractor, if required by the architect, to take out insurance in the names of contractor and employer in respect of liability, loss, claims, etc. for damage to property caused by collapse, subsidence, heave, vibration, weakening or removal of support or lowering of ground water arising out of the actual execution of the works. This is subject to certain exceptions, which include damage caused by the contractor's own negligence, design errors, injury for which the employer should insure (under Clause 22C.1 if applicable) and inevitable damage which is a reasonably foreseeable consequence of undertaking the work.

24.03 The amount spent by the contractor in taking out or maintaining the 21.2.1 insurance is added to the contract sum (Clause 21.2.3).

---

20   **Injury to persons and property and indemnity to Employer**

20·1   The Contractor shall be liable for, and shall indemnify the Employer against, any expense, liability, loss, claim or proceedings whatsoever arising under any statute or at common law in respect of personal injury to or the death of any person whomsoever arising out of or in the course of or caused by the carrying out of the Works, except to the extent that the same is due to any act or neglect of the Employer or of any person for whom the Employer is responsible including the persons employed or otherwise engaged by the Employer to whom clause 29 refers.

20·2   The Contractor shall be liable for, and shall indemnify the Employer against, any expense, liability, loss, claim or proceedings in respect of any loss, injury or damage whatsoever to any property real or personal in so far as such loss, injury or damage arises out of or in the course of or by reason of the carrying out of the Works and to the extent that the same is due to any negligence, breach of statutory duty, omission or default of the Contractor, his servants or agents or of any person employed or engaged upon or in connection with the Works or any part thereof, his servants or agents or of any other person who may properly be on the site upon or in connection with the Works or any part thereof, his servants or agents, other than the Employer or any person employed, engaged or authorised by him or by any local authority or statutory undertaker executing work solely in pursuance of its statutory rights or obligations. This liability and indemnity is subject to clause 20·3 and, where clause 22C·1 is applicable, excludes loss or damage to any property required to be insured thereunder caused by a Specified Peril.

20·3   ·1   Subject to clause 20·3·2 the reference in clause 20·2 to 'property real or personal' does not include the Works, work executed and/or Site Materials up to and including the date of issue of the certificate of Practical Completion or up to and including the date of determination of the employment of the Contractor (whether or not the validity of that determination is disputed) under clause 27 or clause 28 or clause 28A or, where clause 22C applies, under clause 27 or clause 28 or clause 28A or clause 22C·4·3, whichever is the earlier.

20·3   ·2   If clause 18 has been operated then, in respect of the relevant part and as from the relevant date, such relevant part shall not be regarded as 'the Works' or 'work executed' for the purpose of clause 20·3·1.

21   Insurance against injury to persons or property

21·1   ·1   ·1   Without prejudice to his obligation to indemnify the Employer under clause 20 the Contractor shall take out and maintain insurance which shall comply with clause 21·1·1·2 in respect of claims arising out of his liability referred to in clauses 20·1 and 20·2.

·1   ·2   The insurance in respect of claims for personal injury to or the death of any person under a contract of service or apprenticeship with the Contractor, and arising out of and in the course of such person's employment, shall comply with all relevant legislation. For all other claims to which clause 21·1·1·1 applies the insurance cover [z]:

   –   shall indemnify the Employer in like manner to the Contractor but only to the extent that the Contractor may be liable to indemnify the Employer under the terms of this Contract; and

   –   shall be not less than the sum stated in the Appendix [aa] for any one occurrence or series of occurrences arising out of one event.

21·1   ·2   As and when he is reasonably required to do so by the Employer the Contractor shall send to the Architect for inspection by the Employer documentary evidence that the insurances required by clause 21·1·1·1 have been taken out and are being maintained, but at any time the Employer may (but not unreasonably or vexatiously) require to have sent to the Architect for inspection by the Employer the relevant policy or policies and the premium receipts therefor.

21·1   ·3   If the Contractor defaults in taking out or in maintaining insurance as provided in clause 21·1·1·1 the Employer may himself insure against any liability or expense which he may incur arising out of such default and a sum or sums equivalent to the amount paid or payable by him in respect of premiums therefor may be deducted by him from any monies due or to become due to the Contractor under this Contract or such amount may be recoverable by the Employer from the Contractor as a debt.

21·2   ·1   Where it is stated in the Appendix that the insurance to which clause 21·2·1 refers may be required by the Employer the Contractor shall, if so instructed by the Architect, take out a policy of insurance in the names of the Employer and the Contractor [bb] for such amount of indemnity as is stated in the Appendix in respect of any expense, liability, loss, claim or proceedings which the Employer may incur or sustain by reason of injury or damage to any property caused by collapse, subsidence, heave, vibration, weakening or removal of support or lowering of ground water arising out of or in the course of or by reason of the carrying out of the Works excepting injury or damage:

   ·1   ·1   for which the Contractor is liable under clause 20·2;

   ·1   ·2   attributable to errors or omissions in the designing of the Works;

   ·1   ·3   which can reasonably be foreseen to be inevitable having regard to the nature of the work to be executed and the manner of its execution;

   ·1   ·4   which it is the responsibility of the Employer to insure under clause 22C·1 (if applicable);

   ·1   ·5   to the Works and Site Materials brought on to the site of the Contract for the purpose of its execution except in so far as any part or parts thereof are the subject of a certificate of Practical Completion;

   ·1   ·6   arising from any consequence of war, invasion, act of foreign enemy, hostilities (whether war be declared or not), civil war, rebellion or revolution, insurrection or military or usurped power;

   ·1   ·7   directly or indirectly caused by or contributed to by or arising from the Excepted Risks;

   ·1   ·8   directly or indirectly caused by or arising out of pollution or contamination of buildings or other structure or of water or land or the atmosphere happening during the period of insurance; save that this exception shall not apply in respect of pollution or contamination caused by a sudden identifiable, unintended and unexpected incident which takes place in its entirety at a specific moment in time and place during the period of insurance provided that all pollution or contamination which arises out of one incident shall be considered for the purpose of this insurance to have occurred at the time such incident takes place;

·1   ·9   which results in any costs or expenses being incurred by the Employer or in any other sums being payable by the Employer in respect of damages for breach of contract except to the extent that such costs or expenses or damages would have attached in the absence of any contract.

21·2   ·2   Any such insurance as is referred to in clause 21·2·1 shall be placed with insurers to be approved by the Employer, and the Contractor shall send to the Architect for deposit with the Employer the policy or policies and the premium receipts therefor.

21·2   ·3   The amounts expended by the Contractor to take out and maintain the insurance referred to in clause 21·2·1 shall be added to the Contract Sum.

21·2   ·4   If the Contractor defaults in taking out or in maintaining the Joint Names Policy as provided in clause 21·2·1 the Employer may himself insure against any risk in respect of which the default shall have occurred.

21·3   Notwithstanding the provisions of clauses 20·1, 20·2 and 21·1·1, the Contractor shall not be liable either to indemnify the Employer or to insure against any personal injury to or the death of any person or any damage, loss or injury caused to the Works or Site Materials, work executed, the site, or any property, by the effect of an Excepted Risk.

25 Clauses 22 to 22FC: Insurance of the works

25.01 Clause 22 provides for all-risks insurance of the works. There are three alternatives, any one of which may be stated in the Appendix to apply. Two are to be used for new works: Clauses 22A or 22B. Clause 22A requires the contractor to take out the policy to cover Clause 22 perils; Clause 22B requires the employer to take out the policy. Clause 22C relates to works to existing buildings. It requires the employer to take out a joint names insurance covering the existing structures and the new works. In some circumstances sub-contractors are entitled to the benefit of the insurance (Clause 22.3).

25.02 Clause 22D allows the employer, should he so wish, to have effected on his behalf an insurance covering the loss or damage he will suffer as a result of late possession of the works in the event of an extension of time under Clause 25.3, resulting from damage to the works by a specified peril.

25.03 The parties may decide that the Joint Fire Code (the 'Joint Code of Practice on the Protection from Fire of Construction Sites and Buildings Undergoing Renovation') applies. If so, Clause 22FC places a duty upon the contractor and employer each to comply with the same, and to ensure the compliance of those for whom they are responsible. The employer and contractor mutually indemnify each other in the event that either breaches the code (Clause 22FC.4).

26 Clause 23: Date of possession, completion and postponement

26.01 This clause should be read in conjunction with Clause 24 (damages for non-completion) and Clause 25 (extension of time).

26.02 If 'possession of the site' cannot be given on the date for possession, the employer is in serious breach of contract and the contractor is entitled to claim damages. Giving 'possession' is a matter of fact. It was held in *Whittal Builders v Chester Le Street DC* [1987] 40 BLR 82 that giving possession in stages was a breach of this term. In addition the employer would be unable to deduct liquidated damages for non-completion on the due date. There is no contractual provision enabling the architect to award an extension of time in such circumstances (the provision enabling the architect to postpone the 'work' gives him no power to postpone possession of the site). The best that can be done is to reach an agreement between the contractor and the employer to alter the dates for possession and completion. These difficulties do not exist where Clause 23.1.2 applies (see below).

Use without possession

26.03 Once the contractor has possession of the site, he is deemed to retain it for the purpose of works insurance until Practical Completion. If the employer takes partial possession (pursuant to Clause 18) then Practical Completion is deemed to have occurred in respect of that part. The employer is not otherwise entitled to take possession of any part of the works.

26.04 The employer may however, with the consent of the contractor, use the site of the works before Practical Completion without taking possession (Clause 23.3.2) as long as he notifies the works insurers and receives confirmation that the insurance will not be prejudiced.

Postponement

26.05 If Clause 23.1.2 is stated in the Appendix to apply, the employer may defer giving possession for a period up to 6 weeks or such shorter period as is stated in the Appendix. If the employer does defer giving possession, the contractor has the right to an extension of time (Clause 25.4.13) and to consequently claim loss and expense (Clause 26.2.5).

27 Clause 24: Damages for non-completion

27.01 This clause gives the employer the right, if the architect certifies under this clause that the contractor has failed to achieve practical completion by the completion date, to deduct or claim liquidated and ascertained damages at the rate stated in the Appendix. The issue of a certificate under Clause 24.1 is a condition precedent to the employer's right to deduct liquidated damages (see *Ramac Construction v Lesser* [1975] 2 Lloyd's Reports 430).

22   Insurance of the Works [cc]

22·1   Clause 22A or clause 22B or clause 22C shall apply whichever clause is stated to apply in the Appendix.

All Risks Insurance: [dd]   insurance which provides cover against any physical loss or damage to work executed and Site Materials and against the reasonable cost of the removal and disposal of debris and of any shoring and propping of the Works which results from such physical loss or damage but excluding the cost necessary to repair, replace or rectify

1   property which is defective due to

·1   wear and tear,

·2   obsolescence,

·3   deterioration, rust or mildew;

[ee]   2   any work executed or any Site Materials lost or damaged as a result of its own defect in design, plan, specification, material or workmanship or any other work executed which is lost or damaged in consequence thereof where such work relied for its support or stability on such work which was defective;

3   loss or damage caused by or arising from

·1   any consequence of war, invasion, act of foreign enemy, hostilities (whether war be declared or not), civil war, rebellion, revolution, insurrection, military or usurped power, confiscation, commandeering, nationalisation or requisition or loss or destruction of or damage to any property by or under the order of any government *de jure* or *de facto* or public, municipal or local authority;

·2   disappearance or shortage if such disappearance or shortage is only revealed when an inventory is made or is not traceable to an identifiable event,

·3   an Excepted Risk (as defined in clause 1·3);

and if the Contract is carried out in Northern Ireland

·4   civil commotion;

·5   any unlawful, wanton or malicious act committed maliciously by a person or persons acting on behalf of or in connection with an unlawful association; 'unlawful association' shall mean any organisation which is engaged in terrorism and includes an organisation which at any relevant time is a proscribed organisation within the meaning of the Northern Ireland (Emergency Provisions) Act 1973; 'terrorism' means the use of violence for political ends and includes any use of violence for the purpose of putting the public or any section of the public in fear.

Joint Names Policy:　　　　　　　a policy of insurance which includes the Employer and the Contractor as the insured and under which the insurers have no right of recourse against any person named as an insured, or, pursuant to clause 22·3, recognised as an insured thereunder.

22·3 ·1 The Contractor where clause 22A applies, and the Employer where either clause 22B or clause 22C applies, shall ensure that the Joint Names Policy referred to in clause 22A·1 or clause 22A·3 or the Joint Names Policies referred to in clause 22B·1 or in clauses 22C·1 and 22C·2 shall

either provide for recognition of each sub-contractor nominated by the Architect as an insured under the relevant Joint Names Policy

or include a waiver by the relevant insurers of any right of subrogation which they may have against any such Nominated Sub-Contractor

in respect of loss or damage by the Specified Perils to the Works and Site Materials where clause 22A or clause 22B or clause 22C·2 applies and, where clause 22C·1 applies, in respect of loss or damage by the Specified Perils to the existing structures (which shall include from the relevant date any relevant part to which clause 18·1·3 refers) together with the contents thereof owned by the Employer or for which he is responsible; and that this recognition or waiver shall continue up to and including the date of issue of the certificate of practical completion of the sub-contract works (as referred to in clause 2·11 of Conditions NSC/C or the date of determination of the employment of the Contractor (whether or not the validity of that determination is contested) under clause 27 or clause 28 or clause 28A or, where clause 22C applies, under clause 27 or clause 28 or clause 28A or clause 22C·4·3, whichever is the earlier. The provisions of clause 22·3·1 shall apply also in respect of any Joint Names Policy taken out by the Employer under clause 22A·2 or by the Contractor under clause 22B·2 or under clause 22C·3 in respect of a default by the Employer under clause 22C·2.

22·3 ·2 Except in respect of the Joint Names Policy referred to in clause 22C·1 (or the Joint Names Policy referred to in clause 22C·3 in respect of a default by the Employer under clause 22C·1) the provisions of clause 22·3·1 in regard to recognition or waiver shall apply to Domestic Sub-Contractors. Such recognition or waiver for Domestic Sub-Contractors shall continue up to and including the date of issue of any certificate or other document which states that the domestic sub-contract works are practically complete or the date of determination of the employment of the Contractor as referred to in clause 22·3·1, whichever is the earlier.

22A Erection of new buildings – All Risks Insurance of the Works by the Contractor [cc]

22A·1 The Contractor shall take out and maintain a Joint Names Policy for All Risks Insurance for cover no less than that defined in clause 22·2 [dd] [ff] for the full reinstatement value of the Works (plus the percentage, if any, to cover professional fees stated in the Appendix) and shall (subject to clause 18·1·3) maintain such Joint Names Policy up to and including the date of issue of the certificate of Practical Completion or up to and including the date of determination of the employment of the Contractor under clause 27 or clause 28 or clause 28A (whether or not the validity of that determination is contested), whichever is the earlier.

Where the Employer's status for VAT purposes is exempt or partially exempt the full reinstatement value to which this clause refers shall be inclusive of any VAT on the supply of the work and materials referred to in clause 22A·4·3 for which the Contractor is chargeable by the Commissioners.

22A·2 The Joint Names Policy referred to in clause 22A·1 shall be taken out with insurers approved by the Employer, and the Contractor shall send to the Architect for deposit with the Employer that Policy and the premium receipt therefor and also any relevant endorsement or endorsements thereof as may be required to comply with the obligation to maintain that Policy set out in clause 22A·1 and the premium receipts therefor. If the Contractor defaults in taking out or in maintaining the Joint Names Policy as required by clauses 22A·1 and 22A·2 the Employer may himself take out and maintain a Joint Names Policy against any risk in respect of which the default shall have occurred and a sum or sums equivalent to the amount paid or payable by him in respect of premiums therefor may be deducted by him from any monies due or to become due to the Contractor under this Contract or such amount may be recoverable by the Employer from the Contractor as a debt.

22A·3 ·1 If the Contractor independently of his obligations under this Contract maintains a policy of insurance which provides (*inter alia*) All Risks Insurance for cover no less than that defined in clause 22·2 for the full reinstatement value of the Works (plus the percentage, if any, to cover professional fees stated in the Appendix) then the maintenance by the Contractor of such policy shall, if the policy is a Joint Names Policy in respect of the aforesaid Works, be a discharge of the Contractor's obligation to take out and maintain a Joint Names Policy under clause 22A·1. If and so long as the Contractor is able to send to the Architect for inspection by the Employer as and when he is reasonably required to do so by the Employer documentary evidence that such a policy is being maintained then the Contractor shall be discharged from his obligation under clause 22A·2 to deposit the policy and the premium receipt with the Employer but on any occasion the Employer may (but not unreasonably or vexatiously) require to have sent to the Architect for inspection by the Employer the policy to which clause 22A·3·1 refers and the premium receipts therefor. The annual renewal date, as supplied by the Contractor, of the insurance referred to in clause 22A·3·1 is stated in the Appendix.

22A·3 ·2 The provisions of clause 22A·2 shall apply in regard to any default in taking out or in maintaining insurance under clause 22A·3·1.

22A·4 ·1 If any loss or damage affecting work executed or any part thereof or any Site Materials is occasioned by any one or more of the risks covered by the Joint Names Policy referred to in clause 22A·1 or clause 22A·2 or clause 22A·3 then, upon discovering the said loss or damage, the Contractor shall forthwith give notice in writing both to the Architect and to the Employer of the extent, nature and location thereof.

22A·4 ·2 The occurrence of such loss or damage shall be disregarded in computing any amounts payable to the Contractor under or by virtue of this Contract.

22A·4 ·3 After any inspection required by the insurers in respect of a claim under the Joint Names Policy referred to in clause 22A·1 or clause 22A·2 or clause 22A·3 has been completed the Contractor with due diligence shall restore such work damaged, replace or repair any such Site Materials which have been lost or damaged, remove and dispose of any debris and proceed with the carrying out and completion of the Works.

22A·4 ·4 The Contractor, for himself and for all Nominated and Domestic Sub-Contractors who are, pursuant to clause 22·3, recognised as an insured under the Joint Names Policy referred to in clause 22A·1 or clause 22A·2 or clause 22A·3, shall authorise the insurers to pay all monies from such insurance in respect of the loss or damage referred to in clause 22A·4·1 to the Employer. The Employer shall pay all such monies (less only the amount properly incurred by the Employer in respect of professional fees but not exceeding the amount arrived at by applying the percentage to cover professional fees stated in the Appendix to the amount of the monies so paid excluding any amount included therein for professional fees) to the Contractor by instalments under certificates of the Architect issued at the Period of Interim Certificates.

22A·4 ·5 The Contractor shall not be entitled to any payment in respect of the restoration, replacement or repair of such loss or damage and (when required) the removal and disposal of debris other than the monies received under the aforesaid insurance.

22B   Erection of new buildings – All Risks Insurance of the Works by the Employer [cc]

22B·1   The Employer shall take out and maintain a Joint Names Policy for All Risks Insurance for cover no less than that defined in clause 22·2 [dd] [ff] for the full reinstatement value of the Works (plus the percentage, if any, to cover professional fees stated in the Appendix) and shall (subject to clause 18·1·3) maintain such Joint Names Policy up to and including the date of issue of the certificate of Practical Completion or up to and including the date of determination of the employment of the Contractor under clause 27 or clause 28 or clause 28A (whether or not the validity of that determination is contested), whichever is the earlier.

Where the Employer's status for VAT purposes is exempt or partially exempt the full reinstatement value to which this clause refers shall be inclusive of any VAT on the supply of the work and materials referred to in clause 22B·3·3 for which the Contractor is chargeable by the Commissioners.

22B·2   The Employer shall, as and when reasonably required to do so by the Contractor, produce documentary evidence and receipts showing that the Joint Names Policy required under clause 22B·1 has been taken out and is being maintained. If the Employer defaults in taking out or in maintaining the Joint Names Policy required under clause 22B·1 then the Contractor may himself take out and maintain a Joint Names Policy against any risk in respect of which a default shall have occurred and a sum or sums equivalent to the amount paid or payable by him in respect of the premiums therefor shall be added to the Contract Sum.

22B·3   ·1   If any loss or damage affecting work executed or any part thereof or any Site Materials is occasioned by any one or more of the risks covered by the Joint Names Policy referred to in clause 22B·1 or clause 22B·2 then, upon discovering the said loss or damage, the Contractor shall forthwith give notice in writing both to the Architect and to the Employer of the extent, nature and location thereof.

22B·3   ·2   The occurrence of such loss or damage shall be disregarded in computing any amounts payable to the Contractor under or by virtue of this Contract.

22B·3   ·3   After any inspection required by the insurers in respect of a claim under the Joint Names Policy referred to in clause 22B·1 or clause 22B·2 has been completed the Contractor with due diligence shall restore such work damaged, replace or repair any such Site Materials which have been lost or damaged, remove and dispose of any debris and proceed with the carrying out and completion of the Works.

22B·3   ·4   The Contractor, for himself and for all Nominated and Domestic Sub-Contractors who are, pursuant to clause 22·3, recognised as an insured under the Joint Names Policy referred to in clause 22B·1 or clause 22B·2, shall authorise the insurers to pay all monies from such insurance in respect of the loss or damage referred to in clause 22B·3·1 to the Employer.

22B·3   ·5   The restoration, replacement or repair of such loss or damage and (when required) the removal and disposal of debris shall be treated as if they were a Variation required by an instruction of the Architect under clause 13·2.

22C   Insurance of existing structures – insurance of Works in or extensions to existing structures [cc]

22C·1   The Employer shall take out and maintain a Joint Names Policy in respect of the existing structures (which shall include from the relevant date any relevant part to which clause 18·1·3 refers) together with the contents thereof owned by him or for which he is responsible, for the full cost of reinstatement, repair or replacement of loss or damage due to one or more of the Specified Perils [gg] up to and including the date of issue of the certificate of Practical Completion or up to and including the date of determination of the employment of the Contractor under clause 22C·4·3 or clause 27 or clause 28 or clause 28A (whether or not the validity of that determination is contested), whichever is the earlier. The Contractor, for himself and for all Nominated Sub-Contractors who are, pursuant to clause 22·3·1, recognised as an insured under the Joint Names Policy referred to in clause 22C·1 or clause 22C·3, shall authorise the insurers to pay all monies from such insurance in respect of loss or damage to the Employer. [hh]

Where the Employer's status for VAT purposes is exempt or partially exempt the full cost of reinstatement, repair or replacement of loss or damage to which this clause refers shall be inclusive of any VAT chargeable on the supply of such reinstatement, repair or replacement.

22C·2 The Employer shall take out and maintain a Joint Names Policy for All Risks Insurance for cover no less than that defined in clause 22·2 [dd] [gg] for the full reinstatement value of the Works (plus the percentage, if any, to cover professional fees stated in the Appendix) and shall (subject to clause 18·1·3) maintain such Joint Names Policy up to and including the date of issue of the certificate of Practical Completion or up to and including the date of determination of the employment of the Contractor under clause 22C·4·3 or clause 27 or clause 28 or clause 28A (whether or not the validity of that determination is contested), whichever is the earlier.

Where the Employer's status for VAT purposes is exempt or partially exempt the full reinstatement value to which this clause refers shall be inclusive of any VAT on the supply of the work and materials referred to in clause 22C·4·4·1 for which the Contractor is chargeable by the Commissioners.

22C·3 The Employer shall, as and when reasonably required to do so by the Contractor, produce documentary evidence and receipts showing that the Joint Names Policy required under clause 22C·1 or clause 22C·2 has been taken out and is being maintained. If the Employer defaults in taking out or in maintaining the Joint Names Policy required under clause 22C·1 the Contractor may himself take out and maintain a Joint Names Policy against any risk in respect of which the default shall have occurred and for that purpose shall have such right of entry and inspection as may be required to make a survey and inventory of the existing structures and the relevant contents. If the Employer defaults in taking out or in maintaining the Joint Names Policy required under clause 22C·2 the Contractor may take out and maintain a Joint Names Policy against any risk in respect of which the default shall have occurred. A sum or sums equivalent to the premiums paid or payable by the Contractor pursuant to clause 22C·3 shall be added to the Contract Sum.

22C·4 If any loss or damage affecting work executed or any part thereof or any Site Materials is occasioned by any one or more of the risks covered by the Joint Names Policy referred to in clause 22C·2 or clause 22C·3 then, upon discovering the said loss or damage, the Contractor shall forthwith give notice in writing both to the Architect and to the Employer of the extent, nature and location thereof and

22C·4 ·1 the occurrence of such loss or damage shall be disregarded in computing any amounts payable to the Contractor under or by virtue of this Contract;

22C·4 ·2 the Contractor, for himself and for all Nominated and Domestic Sub-Contractors who are, pursuant to clause 22·3, recognised as an insured under the Joint Names Policy referred to in clause 22C·2 or clause 22C·3, shall authorise the insurers to pay all monies from such insurance in respect of the loss or damage referred to in clause 22C·4 to the Employer;

22C·4 ·3 ·1 if it is just and equitable so to do the employment of the Contractor under this Contract may within 28 days of the occurrence of such loss or damage be determined at the option of either Party by notice by registered post or recorded delivery from either Party to the other. Within 7 days of receiving such a notice (but not thereafter) either Party may invoke the relevant procedures applicable under the Contract to the resolution of disputes or differences in order that it may be decided whether such determination is just and equitable;

·3 ·2 upon the giving or receiving by the Employer of a notice of determination, or where the relevant procedures referred to in clause 22C·4·3·1 have been invoked and the notice of determination has been upheld, the provisions of clauses 28A·4 and 28A·5 (except clause 28A·5·5) shall apply.

22C·4 ·4   If no notice of determination is served under clause 22C·4·3·1, or where the relevant procedures referred to in clause 22C·4·3·1 have been invoked and the notice of determination has not been upheld, then

  ·4   ·1   after any inspection required by the insurers in respect of a claim under the Joint Names Policy referred to in clause 22C·2 or clause 22C·3 has been completed, the Contractor with due diligence shall restore such work damaged, replace or repair any such Site Materials which have been lost or damaged, remove and dispose of any debris and proceed with the carrying out and completion of the Works; and

  ·4   ·2   the restoration, replacement or repair of such loss or damage and (when required) the removal and disposal of debris shall be treated as if they were a Variation required by an instruction of the Architect under clause 13·2.

22D   Insurance for Employer's loss of liquidated damages – clause 25·4·3

22D·1   Where it is stated in the Appendix that the insurance to which clause 22D refers may be required by the Employer then forthwith after the Contract has been entered into the Architect shall either inform the Contractor that no such insurance is required or instruct the Contractor to obtain a quotation for such insurance. This quotation shall be for an insurance on an agreed value basis [ii] to be taken out and maintained by the Contractor until the date of Practical Completion and which will provide for payment to the Employer of a sum calculated by reference to clause 22D·3 in the event of loss or damage to the Works, work executed, Site Materials, temporary buildings, plant and equipment for use in connection with and on or adjacent to the Works by any one or more of the Specified Perils and which loss or damage results in the Architect giving an extension of time under clause 25·3 in respect of the Relevant Event in clause 25·4·3. The Architect shall obtain from the Employer any information which the Contractor reasonably requires to obtain such quotation. The Contractor shall send to the Architect as soon as practicable the quotation which he has obtained and the Architect shall thereafter instruct the Contractor whether or not the Employer wishes the Contractor to accept that quotation and such instruction shall not be unreasonably withheld or delayed. If the Contractor is instructed to accept the quotation the Contractor shall forthwith take out and maintain the relevant policy and send it to the Architect for deposit with the Employer, together with the premium receipt therefor and also any relevant endorsement or endorsements thereof and the premium receipts therefor.

22D·2   The sum insured by the relevant policy shall be a sum calculated at the rate stated in the Appendix as liquidated and ascertained damages for the period of time stated in the Appendix.

22D·3   Payment in respect of this insurance shall be calculated at the rate referred to in clause 22D·2 (or any revised rate produced by the application of clause 18·1·4) for the period of any extension of time finally given by the Architect as referred to in clause 22D·1 or for the period of time stated in the Appendix, whichever is the less.

22D·4   The amounts expended by the Contractor to take out and maintain the insurance referred to in clause 22D·1 shall be added to the Contract Sum. If the Contractor defaults in taking out or in maintaining the insurance referred to in clause 22D·1 the Employer may himself insure against any risk in respect of which the default shall have occurred.

22FC   Joint Fire Code – compliance

22FC   ·1   Clause 22FC applies where it is stated in the Appendix that the Joint Fire Code applies.

22FC   ·2   ·1   The Employer shall comply with the Joint Fire Code and ensure such compliance by his servants or agents and by any person employed, engaged or authorised by him upon or in connection with the Works or any part thereof other than the Contractor and the persons for whom the Contractor is responsible pursuant to clause 22FC·2·2.

·2 ·2 The Contractor shall comply with the Joint Fire Code and ensure such compliance by his servants or agents or by any person employed or engaged by him upon or in connection with the Works or any part thereof their servants or agents or by any other person who may properly be on the site upon or in connection with the Works or any part thereof other than the Employer or any person employed, engaged or authorised by him or by any local authority or statutory undertaker executing work solely in pursuance of its statutory rights or obligations.

22FC ·3 ·1 If a breach of the Joint Fire Code occurs and the insurer under the Joint Names Policy in respect of the Works specifies by notice the remedial measures he requires ('the Remedial Measures') and the time by which such Remedial Measures are to be completed ('the Remedial Measures Completion Date') the Contractor shall ensure that the Remedial Measures are carried out, where relevant in accordance with the instructions of the Architect, by the Remedial Measures Completion Date.

·3 ·2 If the Contractor, within 7 days of receipt of a notice specifying the Remedial Measures, does not begin to carry out or thereafter fails without reasonable cause regularly and diligently to proceed with the Remedial Measures then the Employer may employ and pay other persons to carry out the Remedial Measures; and, subject to clause 22FC·4, all costs incurred in connection with such employment may be withheld and/or deducted by him from any monies due or to become due to the Contractor or may be recoverable from the Contractor by the Employer as a debt.

22FC ·4 The Contractor shall indemnify the Employer and the Employer shall indemnify the Contractor in respect of the consequences of a breach of the Joint Fire Code to the extent that these consequences result from a breach by the Contractor or by the Employer of their respective obligations under clause 22FC.

22FC ·5 If after the Base Date the Joint Fire Code is amended and the Joint Fire Code as amended is, under the Joint Names Policy, applicable to the Works, the net extra cost, if any, of compliance by the Contractor with the amended Joint Fire Code shall be added to the Contract Sum.

27.02 The certificate is, it seems, required in order to ensure that the architect has properly considered any notices of delay under Clause 25 and has granted all extensions of time to which the contractor is entitled. Under Clause 25 provision is made for reassessment of the need for extension of time throughout the contract period: Clause 24.2.2 makes provision for the situation where, after liquidated damages have been deducted, a later completion date is fixed under Clause 25.3.3 than that on the basis of which liquidated damages were deducted. In these circumstances, the employer would be obliged to pay or repay to the contractor amounts in respect of the period up to such later completion date. Clause 24.2.2 does not state whether the employer must pay interest on any damages repaid and it is unclear at present what the correct interpretation of the clause is.

27.03 Clause 24 provides 2 methods by which the employer may recover liquidated damages that are due: either as a debt (Clause 24.2.1.1) or by deduction from monies due to the contractor (Clause 24.2.1.2). The latter method now requires notice to be given to the contractor (under Clause 30.1.1.4 or Clause 30.8.3), to ensure compliance with section 111 of the Housing Grants, Construction and Regeneration Act 1996.

Procedure

27.04 The requisite Clause 30.1.1.4 or Clause 30.8.3 notice should set out the amount that is proposed to be withheld and the ground or grounds for withholding payment. Under the 1963 JCT Form it has been held that no certificate under Clause 22 of that form (the equivalent clause to Clause 24) could be issued after the issue of the final certificate (*Fairweather v Asden Securities* [1979] 12 BLR 40). It is thought the position is the same under the 1998 Form.

Advantage of liquidated damages

27.05 If there is no provision for liquidated damages, ascertainment of the damage suffered by reason of non-completion can involve the parties in long and costly proceedings. Where the parties have made and agreed upon a genuine pre-estimate of damages, such proceedings are avoided. The rate agreed, termed here 'liquidated and ascertained damages', will be given effect to by the courts without enquiring into the actual loss suffered.

Liquidated damages and penalties distinguished

27.06 In circumstances where the liquidated damages are construed as a penalty, the contractor can have the agreed rate of liquidated damages set aside and make the employer prove and be limited to his actual loss. It is therefore extremely important that liquidated damages should be stated in the Appendix in such a way that they cannot be construed as being a penalty. This is particularly likely to happen, as it did in *Bramall & Ogden Limited v Sheffield City Council* [1983] 29 BLR 73 where sectional is required, but the Sectional Completion Supplement was not used.

Delay partly employer's fault

27.07 At common law an employer who is partly responsible for delay could not rely on a liquidated damages clause. However, under Clause 25 extensions of time may be granted in respect of relevant events which include delay caused by the employer's fault, and, provided such extensions are properly granted, the right to liquidated damages is preserved.

27.08 Failure to grant proper extensions of time in respect of such relevant events as arise through the employer's fault will disentitle

23   Date of Possession, completion and postponement

23·1 ·1   On the Date of Possession possession of the site shall be given to the Contractor who shall thereupon begin the Works and regularly and diligently proceed with the same and shall complete the same on or before the Completion Date.

23·1 ·2   Where clause 23·1·2 is stated in the Appendix to apply the Employer may defer the giving of possession for a period not exceeding six weeks or such lesser period stated in the Appendix calculated from the Date of Possession.

23·2   The Architect may issue instructions in regard to the postponement of any work to be executed under the provisions of this Contract.

23·3 ·1   For the purposes of the Works insurances the Contractor shall retain possession of the site and the Works up to and including the date of issue of the certificate of Practical Completion, and, subject to clause 18, the Employer shall not be entitled to take possession of any part or parts of the Works until that date.

23·3 ·2   Notwithstanding the provisions of clause 23·3·1 the Employer may, with the consent in writing of the Contractor, use or occupy the site or the Works or part thereof whether for the purposes of storage of his goods or otherwise before the date of issue of the certificate of Practical Completion by the Architect. Before the Contractor shall give his consent to such use or occupation the Contractor or the Employer shall notify the insurers under clause 22A or clause 22B or clause 22C·2 to ·4 whichever may be applicable and obtain confirmation that such use or occupation will not prejudice the insurance. Subject to such confirmation the consent of the Contractor shall not be unreasonably delayed or withheld.

23·3 ·3   Where clause 22A·2 or clause 22A·3 applies and the insurers in giving the confirmation referred to in clause 23·3·2 have made it a condition of such confirmation that an additional premium is required the Contractor shall notify the Employer of the amount of the additional premium. If the Employer continues to require use or occupation under clause 23·3·2 the additional premium required shall be added to the Contract Sum and the Contractor shall provide the Employer, if so requested, with the additional premium receipt therefor.

him from claiming liquidated damages. In *Percy Bilton Limited v Greater London Council* [1982] 2 All ER 623 (HL), it was held that delay caused by the bankruptcy of a nominated sub-contractor (for which no provision for extension is made by Clause 25) did not arise through any fault of the employer, so as to disentitle him from claiming liquidated damages. Failure to give possession of the site on the due date where Clause 23.1.2 is not applicable, could result in the right to liquidated damages being lost, as this is not a ground for extension under Clause 25, but is a fault of the employer (see *Rapid Building Group Ltd v Ealing Family Housing Association Ltd* [1984] 29 BLR 5).

28   Clause 25: Extension of time

28.01   Clause 25 makes provisions for extensions of time through delay caused by 'relevant events' as defined in Clause 25.4. When it becomes reasonably apparent that the progress of the works is being or is likely to be delayed, the contractor is obliged to give written notice forthwith to the architect of the material circumstances identifying:

1   The cause or causes of the delay.
2   Any event which in his opinion is a 'relevant event'.

28.02   Clause 25.2.2 requires the contractor to give particulars of the expected effects of the cause of delay and an estimate of the extent of delay in completion of the works beyond the completion date, resulting from that particular delay (whether or not that delay will be concurrent with a delay resulting from any other relevant event). This information should be included in the notice where possible, alternatively it should be given in writing as soon as possible after the issue of the notice.

28.03   It is clear that the contractor is required to give full particulars and all details of the delay, even if the delay is the contractor's own fault. Obviously, more than one notice under Clause 25 may be served during the currency of the contract.

28.04   It was held in *Balfour Beatty Building Limited v Chestermount Properties Limited* [1993] 62 BLR 1 that where the works are delayed as a result of the contractor's fault, so that the original completion date has passed, the architect still has power on the happening of a relevant event to refix the completion date. The appropriate way to do this is to take the original completion date and add the number of days which the architect regards as fair and reasonable in all the circumstances, even if the effect of this is that the new completion date has already passed before the happening of the relevant event. It would be wrong in principle to refix the completion date by starting at the date of the relevant event and adding days to that date.

Position of sub-contractors

28.05   Where any notice by the contractor makes reference to a nominated sub-contractor, the contractor must serve a copy of the notice and the details given under Clause 25.2.2 on the nominated sub-contractor. The purpose of this provision is to protect the position of a nominated sub-contractor on whom the main contractor is seeking to cast blame for the delay.

24 Damages for non-completion

24·1 If the Contractor fails to complete the Works by the Completion Date then the Architect shall issue a certificate to that effect. In the event of a new Completion Date being fixed after the issue of such a certificate such fixing shall cancel that certificate and the Architect shall issue such further certificate under clause 24·1 as may be necessary.

24·2 **·1** Provided:
  – the Architect has issued a certificate under clause 24·1; and
  – the Employer has informed the Contractor in writing before the date of the Final Certificate that he may require payment of, or may withhold or deduct, liquidated and ascertained damages,
the Employer may, not later than 5 days before the final date for payment of the debt due under the Final Certificate:

either

  ·1 **·1** require in writing the Contractor to pay to the Employer liquidated and ascertained damages at the rate stated in the Appendix (or at such lesser rate as may be specified in writing by the Employer) for the period between the Completion Date and the date of Practical Completion and the Employer may recover the same as a debt;

  or

  ·1 **·2** give a notice pursuant to clause 30·1·1·4 or clause 30·8·3 to the Contractor that he will deduct from monies due to the Contractor liquidated and ascertained damages at the rate stated in the Appendix (or at such lesser rate as may be specified in the notice) for the period between the Completion Date and the date of Practical Completion.

24·2 **·2** If, under clause 25·3·3, the Architect fixes a later Completion Date or a later Completion Date is stated in a confirmed acceptance of a 13A Quotation, the Employer shall pay or repay to the Contractor any amounts recovered, allowed or paid under clause 24·2·1 for the period up to such later Completion Date.

24·2 **·3** Notwithstanding the issue of any further certificate of the Architect under clause 24·1 any requirement of the Employer which has been previously stated in writing in accordance with clause 24·2·1 shall remain effective unless withdrawn by the Employer.

Architect's action

28.06 On receipt of the contractor's notice, particulars, and estimate, the architect must first decide whether the contractor is entitled to an extension of time in principle (i.e. whether the delay is caused by a relevant event as defined by Clause 25.4) and second, whether the occurrence of the relevant event will, in fact, cause delay beyond the completion date. Having decided these two points, the architect grants an extension of time if he thinks that it is fair and reasonable to do so, by fixing a new completion date which is notified to the contractor in writing. His notice must state which of the relevant events he has taken into account and the extent, if any, to which he has had regard to any instruction issued under Clause 13.2 since the fixing of the previous completion date requiring as a variation the omission of any work (Clause 25.3.1.4).

28.07 The architect is not bound to allocate the extension period between the relevant events, e.g. by awarding so many weeks for adverse weather or for some variations, etc., but, if necessary for ascertainment of loss and expense under Clause 26.1, he should state what extension has been granted for relevant events covered by Clauses 25.4.5.1, 25.4.5.2, 25.4.5.6, 25.4.5.8 and 25.4.5.12 (Clause 26.3).

28.08 If reasonably practicable, he must either issue a new completion date or notify the contractor of his decision not to do so no later than 12 weeks from receipt of the contractor's notice, reasonably sufficient particulars and estimate or (where there are fewer than 12 weeks to completion) not later than the completion date.

28.09 Under Clause 25.3.2, if the architect has already exercised his power to grant an extension he may fix a completion date which is earlier than the previously extended completion date if he thinks it fair and reasonable, having regard to variations requiring the omission of work which have been issued after the last occasion on which an extension of time was granted. This is, however, subject to the proviso that (under Clause 25.3.6) no completion date can be fixed earlier than the date for completion stated in the Appendix. Thus the architect is entitled to reduce a previously granted extension of time if work is subsequently ordered to be omitted, thereby reducing the amount of the contractor's commitments and justifying an earlier completion date. RIBA Publications Ltd publish a form of 'Notification of Revision to Completion Date'.

Duties of architect after practical completion

28.10 When practical completion has occurred, provision is made for the architect finally to review the position as regards extensions of time. He must do this within 12 weeks after practical completion (Clause 25.3.3). He may fix a later completion date than that previously fixed and in so doing take into account all relevant events whether or not specifically notified by the contractor. It is also open to him to fix an earlier completion date, having regard to omissions which have occurred since the last occasion when an extension of time was granted. Alternatively, he may simply confirm the previously fixed completion date.

Relevant events

Clause 25.4.1

28.11 The meaning of the term 'force majeure' is difficult to state exactly, but very broadly the words extend to special circumstances quite outside the control of the contractor proceeding from a cause which is inevitable and unforeseeable. Such happenings will not by their very nature have been dealt with elsewhere in the contract. Interference by government and the effect of epidemics are examples of events which are probably within this clause. Financial difficulties experienced by the contractor are equally clearly not within this definition.

Clause 25.4.2

28.12 Exceptionally adverse weather conditions require quite unusual severity: it will frequently be necessary to establish this with the aid of weather charts covering a considerable period. Note that the definition includes exceptional extremes of heat and dryness, as well as the more normal British weather; such extremes of heat and dryness can, of course, have a serious effect on progress.

Clause 25.4.3

28.13 Loss from specified perils (defined in Clause 1.3): these contingencies are very wide, and in some instances may be due to an act of negligence on the part of the contractor, at any rate in their underlying causes.

Clause 25.4.6

28.14 This clause relates to delays arising from the architect's failure to release information (whether or not there is an Information Release Schedule). It was held in *Percy Bilton Limited v Greater London Council* [1982] 2 All ER 623 (HL) that delay by the employer in nominating a replacement for a nominated sub-contractor fell within the predecessor of this sub-clause. It should be noted that a default by the employer of the kind described in this sub-clause gives rise to a right in the contractor to determine his employment under Clause 28.2.2.

Clause 25.4.7

28.15 Where this sub-clause applies, neither the nominated sub-contractor, the nominated supplier nor the contractor has to pay liquidated damages. The extension must be granted whatever the cause of the delay, including the making good by a nominated sub-contractor of his own bad work before completion of the sub-contract work (see *Westminster City Council v Jarvis Limited* [1970] 1 All ER 943). But where defects are discovered in the sub-contract works after the nominated sub-contractor has purported to complete the works and the works have been accepted by the architect and the contractor, there is no right to an extension even where the work has been accepted with some suspicions (see *Westminster City Council* above). The employer's interests in respect of loss caused by delay on the part of nominated sub-contractors and nominated suppliers can be protected by obtaining warranties of timely completion from them.

Clause 25.4.8

28.16 In *Henry Boot Construction Limited v Central Lancashire New Town Development Corporation* [1980] 15 BLR 1, it was held that work carried out by statutory undertakers under contracts with the employer fell within this sub-clause rather than Clause 25.4.11, even though the work was referred to in the bills of quantities as work in respect of which direct payment would be made by the employer and the amounts deducted from the final account.

Clause 25.4.9

28.17 This clause will tend to reduce the scope of the 'force majeure' relevant event.

Clause 25.4.10

28.18 Although the wording of this sub-clause is, on the face of it, wide, it is thought that it is not of as great assistance to contractors as it may first appear: the requirement is the contractor's 'inability for reasons beyond his control' to procure the necessary labour or materials. A contractor could not bring himself within this sub-clause merely because performance had become more difficult (because, for example, labour rates had risen and it was therefore necessary for the contractor to pay uneconomically high prices for labour or materials having regard to his tender). It is also necessary that the contractor could not have reasonably foreseen the shortage of labour or material: if, upon enquiry, those shortages may well have been discernible then the contractor is not entitled to an extension.

---

25   Extension of time [jj]

25·1   In clause 25 any reference to delay, notice or extension of time includes further delay, further notice or further extension of time.

25·2   ·1   ·1   If and whenever it becomes reasonably apparent that the progress of the Works is being or is likely to be delayed the Contractor shall forthwith give written notice to the Architect of the material circumstances including the cause or causes of the delay and identify in such notice any event which in his opinion is a Relevant Event.

·1   ·2   Where the material circumstances of which written notice has been given under clause 25·2·1·1 include reference to a Nominated Sub-Contractor, the Contractor shall forthwith send a copy of such written notice to the Nominated Sub-Contractor concerned.

25·2 ·2 In respect of each and every Relevant Event identified in the notice given in accordance with clause 25·2·1·1 the Contractor shall, if practicable in such notice, or otherwise in writing as soon as possible after such notice:

·2 ·1 give particulars of the expected effects thereof; and

·2 ·2 estimate the extent, if any, of the expected delay in the completion of the Works beyond the Completion Date resulting therefrom whether or not concurrently with delay resulting from any other Relevant Event

and shall give such particulars and estimate to any Nominated Sub-Contractor to whom a copy of any written notice has been given under clause 25·2·1·2.

25·2 ·3 The Contractor shall give such further written notices to the Architect, and send a copy to any Nominated Sub-Contractor to whom a copy of any written notice has been given under clause 25·2·1·2, as may be reasonably necessary or as the Architect may reasonably require for keeping up to date the particulars and estimate referred to in clauses 25·2·2·1 and 25·2·2·2 including any material change in such particulars or estimate.

25·3 ·1 If, in the opinion of the Architect, upon receipt of any notice, particulars and estimate under clauses 25·2·1·1, 25·2·2 and 25·2·3.

·1 ·1 any of the events which are stated by the Contractor to be the cause of the delay is a Relevant Event and

·1 ·2 the completion of the Works is likely to be delayed thereby beyond the Completion Date

the Architect shall in writing to the Contractor give an extension of time by fixing such later date as the Completion Date as he then estimates to be fair and reasonable. The Architect shall, in fixing such new Completion Date, state:

·1 ·3 which of the Relevant Events he has taken into account and

·1 ·4 the extent, if any, to which he has had regard to any instructions issued under clause 13·2 which require as a Variation the omission of any work or obligation and/or under clause 13·3 in regard to the expenditure of a provisional sum for defined work or for Performance Specified Work which results in the omission of any such work,

and shall, if reasonably practicable having regard to the sufficiency of the aforesaid notice, particulars and estimate, fix such new Completion Date not later than 12 weeks from receipt of the notice and of reasonably sufficient particulars and estimate, or, where the period between receipt thereof and the Completion Date is less than 12 weeks, not later than the Completion Date.

If, in the opinion of the Architect, upon receipt of any such notice, particulars and estimate, it is not fair and reasonable to fix a later date as a new Completion Date, the Architect shall if reasonably practicable having regard to the sufficiency of the aforesaid notice, particulars and estimate so notify the Contractor in writing not later than 12 weeks from receipt of the notice, particulars and estimate, or, where the period between receipt thereof and the Completion Date is less than 12 weeks, not later than the Completion Date.

25·3 ·2 After the first exercise by the Architect of his duty under clause 25·3·1 or after any revision to the Completion Date stated by the Architect in a confirmed acceptance of a 13A Quotation in respect of a Variation the Architect may in writing fix a Completion Date earlier than that previously fixed under clause 25 or than that stated by the Architect in a confirmed acceptance of a 13A Quotation if in his opinion the fixing of such earlier Completion Date is fair and reasonable having regard to any instructions issued after the last occasion on which the Architect fixed a new Completion Date

— under clause 13·2 which require or sanction as a Variation the omission of any work or obligation; and/or

— under clause 13·3 in regard to the expenditure of a provisional sum for defined work or for Performance Specified Work which result in the omission of any such work.

Provided that no decision under clause 25·3·2 shall alter the length of any adjustment to the time required by the Contractor for the completion of the Works in respect of a Variation for which a 13A Quotation has been given and which has been stated in a confirmed acceptance of a 13A Quotation or in respect of a Variation or work for which an adjustment to the time for completion of the Works has been accepted pursuant to clause 13·4·1·2 paragraph A7.

25·3 ·3 After the Completion Date, if this occurs before the date of Practical Completion, the Architect may, and not later than the expiry of 12 weeks after the date of Practical Completion shall, in writing to the Contractor either

·3 ·1 fix a Completion Date later than that previously fixed if in his opinion the fixing of such later Completion Date is fair and reasonable having regard to any of the Relevant Events, whether upon reviewing a previous decision or otherwise and whether or not the Relevant Event has been specifically notified by the Contractor under clause 25·2·1·1; or

·3 ·2 fix a Completion Date earlier than that previously fixed under clause 25 or stated in a confirmed acceptance of a 13A Quotation if in his opinion the fixing of such earlier Completion Date is fair and reasonable having regard to any instructions issued after the last occasion on which the Architect fixed a new Completion Date

– under clause 13·2 which require or sanction as a Variation the omission of any work or obligation; and/or

– under clause 13·3 in regard to the expenditure of a provisional sum for defined work or for Performance Specified Work which result in the omission of any such work; or

·3 ·3 confirm to the Contractor the Completion Date previously fixed or stated in a confirmed acceptance of a 13A Quotation.

Provided that no decision under clause 25·3·3·1 or clause 25·3·3·2 shall alter the length of any adjustment to the time required by the Contractor for the completion of the Works in respect of a Variation for which a 13A Quotation has been given and which has been stated in a confirmed acceptance of a 13A Quotation.

25·3 ·4 Provided always that:

·4 ·1 the Contractor shall use constantly his best endeavours to prevent delay in the progress of the Works, howsoever caused, and to prevent the completion of the Works being delayed or further delayed beyond the Completion Date;

·4 ·2 the Contractor shall do all that may reasonably be required to the satisfaction of the Architect to proceed with the Works.

25·3 ·5 The Architect shall notify in writing to every Nominated Sub-Contractor each decision of the Architect under clause 25·3 fixing a Completion Date and each revised Completion Date stated in the confirmed acceptance of a 13A Quotation together with, where relevant, any revised period or periods for the completion of the work of each Nominated Sub-Contractor stated in such confirmed acceptance.

25·3 ·6 No decision of the Architect under clause 25·3·2 or clause 25·3·3·2 shall fix a Completion Date earlier than the Date for Completion stated in the Appendix.

25·4 The following are the Relevant Events referred to in clause 25:

25·4 ·1 force majeure;

25·4 ·2 exceptionally adverse weather conditions;

25·4 ·3 loss or damage occasioned by any one or more of the Specified Perils;

25·4 ·4 civil commotion, local combination of workmen, strike or lock-out affecting any of the trades employed upon the Works or any of the trades engaged in the preparation, manufacture or transportation of any of the goods or materials required for the Works;

25·4   ·5   compliance with the Architect's instructions

  ·5   ·1   under clauses 2·3, 2·4·1, 13·2 (except for a confirmed acceptance of a 13A Quotation), 13·3 (except compliance with an Architect's instruction for the expenditure of a provisional sum for defined work* or of a provisional sum for Performance Specified Work), 13A·4·1, 23·2, 34, 35 or 36; or

  ·5   ·2   in regard to the opening up for inspection of any work covered up or the testing of any of the work, materials or goods in accordance with clause 8·3 (including making good in consequence of such opening up or testing) unless the inspection or test showed that the work, materials or goods were not in accordance with this Contract;

25·4   ·6   ·1   where an Information Release Schedule has been provided, failure of the Architect to comply with clause 5·4·1;

  ·6   ·2   failure of the Architect to comply with clause 5·4·2;

25·4   ·7   delay on the part of Nominated Sub-Contractors or Nominated Suppliers which the Contractor has taken all practicable steps to avoid or reduce;

25·4   ·8   ·1   the execution of work not forming part of this Contract by the Employer himself or by persons employed or otherwise engaged by the Employer as referred to in clause 29 or the failure to execute such work;

  ·8   ·2   the supply by the Employer of materials and goods which the Employer has agreed to provide for the Works or the failure so to supply;

25·4   ·9   the exercise after the Base Date by the United Kingdom Government of any statutory power which directly affects the execution of the Works by restricting the availability or use of labour which is essential to the proper carrying out of the Works or preventing the Contractor from, or delaying the Contractor in, securing such goods or materials or such fuel or energy as are essential to the proper carrying out of the Works;

25·4   ·10   ·1   the Contractor's inability for reasons beyond his control and which he could not reasonably have foreseen at the Base Date to secure such labour as is essential to the proper carrying out of the Works; or

  ·10   ·2   the Contractor's inability for reasons beyond his control and which he could not reasonably have foreseen at the Base Date to secure such goods or materials as are essential to the proper carrying out of the Works;

25·4   ·11   the carrying out by a local authority or statutory undertaker of work in pursuance of its statutory obligations in relation to the Works, or the failure to carry out such work;

25·4   ·12   failure of the Employer to give in due time ingress to or egress from the site of the Works or any part thereof through or over any land, buildings, way or passage adjoining or connected with the site and in the possession and control of the Employer, in accordance with the Contract Bills and/or the Contract Drawings, after receipt by the Architect of such notice, if any, as the Contractor is required to give, or failure of the Employer to give such ingress or egress as otherwise agreed between the Architect and the Contractor;

25·4   ·13   where clause 23·1·2 is stated in the Appendix to apply, the deferment by the Employer of giving possession of the site under clause 23·1·2;

25·4   ·14   by reason of the execution of work for which an Approximate Quantity is included in the Contract Bills which is not a reasonably accurate forecast of the quantity of work required;

25·4   ·15   delay which the Contractor has taken all practicable steps to avoid or reduce consequent upon a change in the Statutory Requirements after the Base Date which necessitates some alteration or modification to any Performance Specified Work;

25·4   ·16   the use or threat of terrorism and/or the activity of the relevant authorities in dealing with such use or threat;

25·4   ·17   compliance or non-compliance by the Employer with clause 6A·1;

25·4   ·18   delay arising from a suspension by the Contractor of the performance of his obligations under the Contract to the Employer pursuant to clause 30·1·4.

Clause 25.4.11

28.19 This sub-clause covers delay caused by local authorities and statutory undertakers in performing their statutory obligations. Where the contractor has no choice but to employ these local authorities or statutory undertakers, it is thought unjust that he should be penalised for their delay. This sub-clause does not apply where such a body is carrying out work extending beyond its statutory obligations as sub-contractors (see *Henry Boot Construction Limited v Central Lancashire New Town Development Corporation* [1980] 15 BLR 1, paragraph 28.16 above).

Clause 25.4.12

28.20 This clause applies if the employer is in possession and control of land adjoining or connected with the site and fails to give access to the site in accordance with the contract bills and/or the contract drawings after any required notice given by the contractor. Alternatively, it would apply if the employer failed to give access as otherwise agreed between the architect, presumably acting with the consent of the employer, and the contractor. This latter situation may cover agreed wayleaves, etc.

Clause 25.4.18

28.21 This is a new 'relevant event' introduced by Amendment 18. The new Clause 30.1.4 allows the contractor to suspend performance of the Works if the employer fails to pay him (pursuant to contract). This suspension is not to be construed as a failure to proceed diligently with the Works, but entitles the contractor to an extension of time.

29   Clause 26: Loss and expense caused by matters materially affecting regular progress of the works

Nature of Clause 26

29.01 Clause 26 entitles the contractor to claim direct loss and/or expense arising as a result of the regular progress of the works (or part of them) being materially affected by any of the list of matters contained in Clause 26.2 or by deferment of possession under Clause 23.1.2. This is a carefully restricted list of circumstances under which the contractor may obtain payment. Note also that since Amendment 4:2002 the list includes a 'catch-all' clause to the effect that any impediment, prevention or default by the employer (or his agents) will entitle the contractor to claim under the clause, unless the contractor (or his agents) contributed to the default. By Clause 26.6 the provisions of Clause 26 are without prejudice to any other rights and remedies which the contractor may possess, and therefore the provisions of Clause 26 do not preclude any claim by the contractor for damages for breach of contract, negligence, misrepresentation, etc. The word 'direct' means damages which flow naturally from the breach (see *Saint Line Limited v Richardson* [1940] 2 KB 99) and excludes claims for consequential loss (see *Cawoods v Croudace* [1978] 2 Lloyd's Reports 55). It is thought that in general the computation of the amount of direct loss and/or expense is to follow the lines for computation for ordinary damages for breach of contract, although, of course, a claim under Clause 26 is not a claim for breach of contract as such. See *Wright Limited v PH & T (Holdings) Limited* [1980] 13 BLR 26. In *Minter v Welsh Health Technical Services Organization* [1980] 13 BLR 1, it was held that under the 1963 JCT Form Clause 24(1) that the contractor could claim as part of his direct loss and/or expense the amount of finance charges he incurred in respect of the amount of such loss and expense.

Notice

29.02 Clause 26.1 requires the contractor to make a written application to the architect stating that he has incurred or is likely to incur such loss and expense. Once a notice has been given, the loss and expense must be ascertained from time to time by the architect or quantity surveyor. Only one such notice need be given (reversing the position under the previous JCT Form) (see *Minter v Welsh Health Technical Services Organization* [1980] 13 BLR 1). Under Clause 26.1 the application must be made as soon as it has become or should reasonably have become apparent to the contractor that regular progress is being affected. The contractor must submit information in support of his application, and must on request supply a breakdown of the loss and/or expense (see Clause 26.1.3). It is thought that the requirement of a notice is a condition precedent to the contractor's rights under this clause.

29.03 All that is required under Clause 26 is that direct loss and/or expense arises because 'regular progress of the works' is 'materially affected' or because giving possession of the site has been deferred under Clause 23.1.2. There is no requirement that progress be delayed, or that the whole of the works be affected. It could apply, for example, where the contractor is obliged to bring extra operatives on site, or where there is a loss of productivity of a certain trade.

29.04 It should be noted that any possible overlap between the operation of Clause 26 and Clause 13 is precluded by the proviso contained in Clause 13.5.7.

Provisions relating to nominated sub-contractors

29.05 Clause 26.4 contains provisions to deal with the situation where a nominated sub-contractor claims loss and expense under Clause 4.38.1 of Sub-Contract Conditions NSC/C. The contractor is under an obligation to pass such application on to the architect, who then reaches a decision on it and instructs the quantity surveyor to ascertain the amount of loss and expense incurred (or he may carry out this exercise himself). To the extent that it is necessary for the ascertainment of such loss and expense, the architect must state in writing to the contractor (with a copy to the sub-contractor) the revised period for completion of the sub-contract works to which he gave consent in respect of each event set out in Clauses 2.6.5.1 (so far as that clause refers to Clauses 2.3, 13.2, 13.3 and 23.2 of the main contract conditions), 2.6.5.2, 2.6.6, 2.6.8, 2.6.12 and 2.6.15 of Conditions NSC/C. This applies to such matters as discrepancies in sub-contract documents, variations, expenditure of provisional sums, postponement, exceptionally adverse weather conditions, delayed instructions, delay caused by the employer carrying out work not forming part of the main contract, and delay in giving access, etc. to the sub-contractor.

29.06 The provisions of Clause 26 are without prejudice to any other rights and remedies which the contractor may possess. The contractor may pursue a claim for damages, even if a claim under Clause 26 fails (see *Fairclough v Vale of Belvoir Superstore* [1991] 56 BLR 74), or may even make a claim under Clause 26 in order to obtain prompt reimbursement and later claim damages for breach of contract taking into account the amount awarded under Clause 26 (*London Borough of Merton v Leach* [1985] 32 BLR 51).

Claims generally

29.07 The term 'claim' has no exact meaning, but for present purposes it may be considered any claim for payment by the contractor other than in respect of the original contract price. Any such claims fall under one of the following categories:

1   A right to payment arising under a clause of the contract
2   A claim for damages for breach of contract
3   A claim under neither 1 nor 2.

If a claim comes within (1), the architect follows whatever procedure the contract prescribes according to the clause relied on by the contractor. The architect need not consult the employer, although he may do so if he thinks it desirable. If the claim falls within (2), the architect has no formal role under the contract in relation to it. He should consult the employer and should not include in a certificate any sum in respect of such a claim without the employer's agreement, as the contract gives him no power to certify in respect of a contractual

26 **Loss and expense caused by matters materially affecting regular progress of the Works**

26·1 If the Contractor makes written application to the Architect stating that he has incurred or is likely to incur direct loss and/or expense (of which the Contractor may give his quantification) in the execution of this Contract for which he would not be reimbursed by a payment under any other provision in this Contract due to deferment of giving possession of the site under clause 23·1·2 where clause 23·1·2 is stated in the Appendix to be applicable or because the regular progress of the Works or of any part thereof has been or is likely to be materially affected by any one or more of the matters referred to in clause 26·2; and if and as soon as the Architect is of the opinion that the direct loss and/or expense has been incurred or is likely to be incurred due to any such deferment of giving possession or that the regular progress of the Works or of any part thereof has been or is likely to be so materially affected as set out in the application of the Contractor then the Architect from time to time thereafter shall ascertain, or shall instruct the Quantity Surveyor to ascertain, the amount of such loss and/or expense which has been or is being incurred by the Contractor; provided always that:

26·1 **·1** the Contractor's application shall be made as soon as it has become, or should reasonably have become, apparent to him that the regular progress of the Works or of any part thereof has been or was likely to be affected as aforesaid; and

·2 the Contractor shall in support of his application submit to the Architect upon request such information as should reasonably enable the Architect to form an opinion as aforesaid; and

·3 the Contractor shall submit to the Architect or to the Quantity Surveyor upon request such details of such loss and/or expense as are reasonably necessary for such ascertainment as aforesaid.

26·2 The following are the matters referred to in clause 26·1:

26·2 **·1** **·1** where an Information Release Schedule has been provided, failure of the Architect to comply with clause 5·4·1;

·1 **·2** failure of the Architect to comply with clause 5·4·2;

26·2 **·2** the opening up for inspection of any work covered up or the testing of any of the work, materials or goods in accordance with clause 8·3 (including making good in consequence of such opening up or testing), unless the inspection or test showed that the work, materials or goods were not in accordance with this Contract;

26·2 **·3** any discrepancy in or divergence between the Contract Drawings and/or the Contract Bills and/or the Numbered Documents;

26·2 **·4** **·1** the execution of work not forming part of this Contract by the Employer himself or by persons employed or otherwise engaged by the Employer as referred to in clause 29 or the failure to execute such work;

·4 **·2** the supply by the Employer of materials and goods which the Employer has agreed to provide for the Works or the failure so to supply;

26·2 **·5** Architect's instructions under clause 23·2 issued in regard to the postponement of any work to be executed under the provisions of this Contract;

26·2 **·6** failure of the Employer to give in due time ingress to or egress from the site of the Works or any part thereof through or over any land, buildings, way or passage adjoining or connected with the site and in the possession and control of the Employer, in accordance with the Contract Bills and/or the Contract Drawings, after receipt by the Architect of such notice, if any, as the Contractor is required to give, or failure of the Employer to give such ingress or egress as otherwise agreed between the Architect and the Contractor;

26·2 ·7   Architect's instructions issued

under clause 13·2 or clause 13A·4·1 requiring a Variation (except for a Variation for which the Architect has given a confirmed acceptance of a 13A Quotation or for a Variation thereto) or

under clause 13·3 in regard to the expenditure of provisional sums (other than instructions to which clause 13·4·2 refers or an instruction for the expenditure of a provisional sum for defined work* or of a provisional sum for Performance Specified Work);

26·2 ·8   the execution of work for which an Approximate Quantity is included in the Contract Bills which is not a reasonably accurate forecast of the quantity of work required;

26·2 ·9   compliance or non-compliance by the Employer with clause 6A·1;

26·2 ·10 suspension by the Contractor of the performance of his obligations under the Contract to the Employer pursuant to clause 30·1·4 provided the suspension was not frivolous or vexatious.

26·3   If and to the extent that it is necessary for ascertainment under clause 26·1 of loss and/or expense the Architect shall state in writing to the Contractor what extension of time, if any, has been made under clause 25 in respect of the Relevant Event or Events referred to in clause 25·4·5·1 (so far as that clause refers to clauses 2·3, 13·2, 13·3 and 23·2) and in clauses 25·4·5·2, 25·4·6, 25·4·8 and 25·4·12.

26·4 ·1   The Contractor upon receipt of a written application properly made by a Nominated Sub-Contractor under clause 4·38·1 of Conditions NSC/C shall pass to the Architect a copy of that written application. If and as soon as the Architect is of the opinion that the loss and/or expense to which the said clause 4·38·1 refers has been incurred or is likely to be incurred due to any deferment of the giving of possession where clause 23·1·2 is stated in the Appendix to apply or that the regular progress of the sub-contract works or of any part thereof has been or is likely to be materially affected as referred to in clause 4·38·1 of Conditions NSC/C and as set out in the application of the Nominated Sub-Contractor then the Architect shall himself ascertain, or shall instruct the Quantity Surveyor to ascertain, the amount of loss and/or expense to which the said clause 4·38·1 refers.

26·4 ·2   If and to the extent that it is necessary for the ascertainment of such loss and/or expense the Architect shall state in writing to the Contractor with a copy to the Nominated Sub-Contractor concerned what was the length of the revision of the period or periods for completion of the sub-contract works or of any part thereof to which he gave consent in respect of the Relevant Event or Events set out in clause 2·6·5·1 (so far as that clause refers to clauses 2·3, 13·2, 13·3 and 23·2 of the Main Contract Conditions), 2·6·5·2, 2·6·6, 2·6·8, 2·6·12 and 2·6·15 of Conditions NSC/C.

26·5   Any amount from time to time ascertained under clause 26 shall be added to the Contract Sum.

26·6   The provisions of clause 26 are without prejudice to any other rights and remedies which the Contractor may possess.

claim for damages. Other, non-contractual, claims may be made, such as a claim for damages in tort, a restitutionary claim, or a claim to an ex gratia payment. In relation to these the architect should only act as directed by the employer.

30 Clause 27: Determination by employer

30.01 This clause makes provision for the following matters:

1 Discretionary determination by the employer in event of certain defaults by the contractor
2 Automatic determination of the contractor's employment in the event of bankruptcy or liquidation (subject to an option to reinstate if the employer and contractor so agree)
3 The rights and duties of the parties following determination of the contractor's employment.

Determination on notice

30.02 The employer is entitled to determine the contractor's employment in the circumstances specified in Clause 27.2, subject to the giving of the notices to be issued by the architect required by the clause. Notices under Clauses 27.2.1 to .4 must, by virtue of Clause 27.1 be in writing and be given by actual delivery, by special delivery or by recorded delivery.

30.03 It was held in *West Faulkner Associates v London Borough of Newham* (1993) 8 Const. LJ 232, a case on JCT 63 Clause 25(1)(b), which is in identical terms to Clause 27.2.1.2 that

27 Determination by Employer

27·1 Any notice or further notice to which clauses 27·2·1, 27·2·2, 27·2·3 and 27·3·4 refer shall be in writing and given by actual delivery, or by special delivery or by recorded delivery. If sent by special delivery or recorded delivery the notice or further notice shall, subject to proof to the contrary, be deemed to have been received 48 hours after the date of posting (excluding Saturday and Sunday and Public Holidays).

27·2 ·1 If, before the date of Practical Completion, the Contractor shall make a default in any one or more of the following respects:

   ·1 ·1 without reasonable cause he wholly or substantially suspends the carrying out of the Works; or

   ·1 ·2 he fails to proceed regularly and diligently with the Works; or

   ·1 ·3 he refuses or neglects to comply with a written notice or instruction from the Architect requiring him to remove any work, materials or goods not in accordance with this Contract and by such refusal or neglect the Works are materially affected; or

   ·1 ·4 he fails to comply with the provisions of clause 19·1·1 or clause 19·2·2; or

   ·1 ·5 he fails pursuant to the Conditions to comply with the requirements of the CDM Regulations,

   the Architect may give to the Contractor a notice specifying the default or defaults (the 'specified default or defaults').

27·2 ·2 If the Contractor continues a specified default for 14 days from receipt of the notice under clause 27·2·1 then the Employer may on, or within 10 days from, the expiry of that 14 days by a further notice to the Contractor determine the employment of the Contractor under this Contract. Such determination shall take effect on the date of receipt of such further notice.

27·2 ·3 If

   the Contractor ends the specified default or defaults, or

   the Employer does not give the further notice referred to in clause 27·2·2

   and the Contractor repeats a specified default (whether previously repeated or not) then, upon or within a reasonable time after such repetition, the Employer may by notice to the Contractor determine the employment of the Contractor under this Contract. Such determination shall take effect on the date of receipt of such notice.

27·2 ·4 A notice of determination under clause 27·2·2 or clause 27·2·3 shall not be given unreasonably or vexatiously.

27·3 ·1 If the Contractor

   makes a composition or arrangement with his creditors, or becomes bankrupt, or,

   being a company,

   makes a proposal for a voluntary arrangement for a composition of debts or scheme of arrangement to be approved in accordance with the Companies Act 1985 or the Insolvency Act 1986 as the case may be or any amendment or re-enactment thereof, or

   has a provisional liquidator appointed, or

   has a winding-up order made, or

   passes a resolution for voluntary winding-up (except for the purposes of amalgamation or reconstruction), or

   under the Insolvency Act 1986 or any amendment or re-enactment thereof has an administrator or an administrative receiver appointed

   then:

27·3 ·2 the Contractor shall immediately inform the Employer in writing if he has made a composition or arrangement with his creditors, or, being a company, has made a proposal for a voluntary arrangement for a composition of debts or scheme of arrangement to be approved in accordance with the Companies Act 1985 or the Insolvency Act 1986 as the case may be or any amendment or re-enactment thereof;

27·3 **·3** where a provisional liquidator or trustee in bankruptcy is appointed or a winding-up order is made or the Contractor passes a resolution for voluntary winding-up (except for the purposes of amalgamation or reconstruction) the employment of the Contractor under this Contract shall be forthwith automatically determined but the said employment may be reinstated if the Employer and the Contractor [kk] shall so agree;

27·3 **·4** where clause 27·3·3 does not apply the Employer may at any time, unless an agreement to which clause 27·5·2·1 refers has been made, by notice to the Contractor determine the employment of the Contractor under this Contract and such determination shall take effect on the date of receipt of such notice.

27·4 The Employer shall be entitled to determine the employment of the Contractor, under this or any other contract, if the Contractor shall have offered or given or agreed to give to any person any gift or consideration of any kind as an inducement or reward for doing or forbearing to do or for having done or forborne to do any action in relation to the obtaining or execution of this or any other contract with the Employer, or for showing or forbearing to show favour or disfavour to any person in relation to this or any other contract with the Employer, or if the like acts shall have been done by any person employed by the Contractor or acting on his behalf (whether with or without the knowledge of the Contractor), or if in relation to this or any other contract with the Employer the Contractor or any person employed by him or acting on his behalf shall have committed an offence under the Prevention of Corruption Acts 1889 to 1916.

27·5 Clauses 27·5·1 to 27·5·4 are only applicable where clause 27·3·4 applies.

27·5 **·1** From the date when, under clause 27·3·4, the Employer could first give notice to determine the employment of the Contractor, the Employer, subject to clause 27·5·3, shall not be bound by any provisions of this Contract to make any further payment thereunder and the Contractor shall not be bound to continue to carry out and complete the Works in compliance with clause 2·1.

27·5 **·2** Clause 27·5·1 shall apply until

either

·2 **·1** the Employer makes an agreement (a '27·5·2·1 agreement') with the Contractor on the continuation or novation or conditional novation of this Contract, in which case this Contract shall be subject to the terms set out in the 27·5·2·1 agreement

or

·2 **·2** the Employer determines the employment of the Contractor under this Contract in accordance with clause 27·3·4, in which case the provisions of clause 27·6 or clause 27·7 shall apply.

27·5 **·3** Notwithstanding clause 27·5·1, in the period before either a 27·5·2·1 agreement is made or the Employer under clause 27·3·4 determines the employment of the Contractor, the Employer and the Contractor may make an interim arrangement for work to be carried out. Subject to clause 27·5·4 any right of set-off which the Employer may have shall not be exercisable in respect of any payment due from the Employer to the Contractor under such interim arrangement.

27·5 **·4** From the date when, under clause 27·3·4, the Employer may first determine the employment of the Contractor (but subject to any agreement made pursuant to clause 27·5·2·1 or arrangement made pursuant to clause 27·5·3) the Employer may take reasonable measures to ensure that Site Materials, the site and the Works are adequately protected and that Site Materials are retained in, on the site of or adjacent to the Works as the case may be. The Contractor shall allow and shall in no way hinder or delay the taking of the aforesaid measures. The Employer may deduct the reasonable cost of taking such measures from any monies due or to become due to the Contractor under this Contract (including any amount due under an agreement to which clause 27·5·2·1, or under an interim arrangement to which clause 27·5·3, refers) or may recover the same from the Contractor as a debt.

27·6   In the event of the determination of the employment of the Contractor under clause 27·2·2, 27·2·3, 27·3·3, 27·3·4 or 27·4 and so long as that employment has not been reinstated then:

27·6   ·1   the Employer may employ and pay other persons to carry out and complete the Works and to make good defects of the kind referred to in clause 17 and he or they may enter upon the site and the Works and use all temporary buildings, plant, tools, equipment and Site Materials, and may purchase all materials and goods necessary for the carrying out and completion of the Works and for the making good of defects as aforesaid; provided that where the aforesaid temporary buildings, plant, tools, equipment and Site Materials are not owned by the Contractor the consent of the owner thereof to such use is obtained by the Employer;

27·6   ·2   ·1   except where an insolvency event listed in clause 27·3·1 (other than the Contractor being a company making a proposal for a voluntary arrangement for a composition of debts or scheme of arrangement to be approved in accordance with the Companies Act 1985 or the insolvency Act 1986 as the case may be or any amendment or re-enactment) has occurred the Contractor shall, if so required by the Employer or by the Architect on behalf of the Employer within 14 days of the date of determination, assign to the Employer without payment the benefit of any agreement for the supply of materials or goods and/or for the execution of any work for the purposes of this Contract to the extent that the same is assignable;

   ·2   ·2   except where the Contractor has a trustee in bankruptcy appointed or being a company has a provisional liquidator appointed or has a petition alleging insolvency filed against it which is subsisting or passes a resolution for voluntary winding-up (other than for the purposes of amalgamation or reconstruction) which takes effect as a creditors' voluntary liquidation, the Employer may pay any supplier or sub-contractor for any materials or goods delivered or works executed for the purposes of this Contract before or after the date of determination in so far as the price thereof has not already been discharged by the Contractor. Payments made under clause 27·6·2·2 may be deducted from any sum due or to become due to the Contractor or may be recoverable from the Contractor by the Employer as a debt;

27·6   ·3   the Contractor shall, when required in writing by the Architect so to do (but not before), remove from the Works any temporary buildings, plant, tools, equipment, goods and materials belonging to him and the Contractor shall have removed by their owner any temporary buildings, plant, tools, equipment, goods and materials not owned by him. If within a reasonable time after such requirement has been made the Contractor has not complied therewith in respect of temporary buildings, plant, tools, equipment, goods and materials belonging to him, then the Employer may (but without being responsible for any loss or damage) remove and sell any such property of the Contractor, holding the proceeds less all costs incurred to the credit of the Contractor.

27·6   ·4   ·1   Subject to clauses 27·5·3 and 27·6·4·2 the provisions of this Contract which require any further payment or any release or further release of Retention to the Contractor shall not apply; provided that clause 27·6·4·1 shall not be construed so as to prevent the enforcement by the Contractor of any rights under this Contract in respect of amounts properly due to be discharged by the Employer to the Contractor which the Employer has unreasonably not discharged and which, where clause 27·3·4 applies, have accrued 28 days or more before the date when under clause 27·3·4 the Employer could first give notice to determine the employment of the Contractor or, where clause 27·3·4 does not apply, which have accrued 28 days or more before the date of determination of the employment of the Contractor.

   ·4   ·2   Upon the completion of the Works and the making good of defects as referred to in clause 27·6·1 (but subject, where relevant, to the exercise of the right under clause 17·2 and/or clause 17·3 of the Architect, with the consent of the Employer, not to require defects of the kind referred to in clause 17 to be made good) then within a reasonable time thereafter an account in respect of the matters referred to in clause 27·6·5 shall be set out either in a statement prepared by the Employer or in a certificate issued by the Architect.

27·6   ·5   ·1   The amount of expenses properly incurred by the Employer including those incurred pursuant to clause 27·6·1 and of any direct loss and/or damage caused to the Employer as a result of the determination;

   ·5   ·2   the amount of any payment made to the Contractor;

> **·5** **·3** the total amount which would have been payable for the Works in accordance with this Contract.
>
> **27·6** **·6** If the sum of the amounts stated under clauses 27·6·5·1 and 27·6·5·2 exceeds or is less than the amount stated under clause 27·6·5·3 the difference shall be a debt payable by the Contractor to the Employer or by the Employer to the Contractor as the case may be.
>
> **27·7** **·1** If the Employer decides after the determination of the employment of the Contractor not to have the Works carried out and completed, he shall so notify the Contractor in writing within 6 months from the date of such determination. Within a reasonable time from the date of such written notification the Employer shall send to the Contractor a statement of account setting out:
>
> **·1** **·1** the total value of work properly executed at the date of determination of the employment of the Contractor, such value to be ascertained in accordance with the Conditions as if the employment of the Contractor had not been determined, together with any amounts due to the Contractor under the Conditions not included in such total value;
>
> **·1** **·2** the amount of any expenses properly incurred by the Employer and of any direct loss and/or damage caused to the Employer as a result of the determination.
>
> After taking into account amounts previously paid to the Contractor under this Contract, if the amount stated under clause 27·7·1·2 exceeds or is less than the amount stated under clause 27·7·1·1 the difference shall be a debt payable by the Contractor to the Employer or by the Employer to the Contractor as the case may be.
>
> **27·7** **·2** If after the expiry of the 6 month period referred to in clause 27·7·1 the Employer has not begun to operate the provisions of clause 27·6·1 and has not given a written notification pursuant to clause 27·7·1 the Contractor may require by notice in writing to the Employer that he states whether clauses 27·6·1 to 27·6·6 are to apply and, if not to apply, require that a statement of account pursuant to clause 27·7·1 be prepared by the Employer for submission to the Contractor.
>
> **27·8** The provisions of clauses 27·2 to 27·7 are without prejudice to any other rights and remedies which the Employer may possess.

'regularly and diligently' meant that a contractor must perform his duties in such a way as to achieve his contractual obligations. This clause requires a contractor to plan work, to lead and manage his workforce, to provide sufficient and proper materials and to employ competent tradesmen so that the works are fully carried out to an acceptable standard and that all time, sequence and other provisions of the contract are fulfilled. The architect will be in breach of contract if he fails to serve a notice under the clause if an ordinarily competent architect would have done so in the same circumstances.

30.04 At common law a party is entitled to treat a contract as repudiated and therefore at an end if the other party so conducts himself as to show no intention to go on with the contract (see *Universal Cargo Carriers v Citati* [1957] 2 QB 401). The purpose of Clause 27 is to confer on the employer additional and alternative rights by which he may determine the contractor's employment, without having to prove that the contractor has repudiated the contract. However, having regard to the provision of Clause 27.2.4 (which requires that notice should not be given unreasonably or vexatiously), there is sometimes uncertainty as to whether the circumstances which exist justify determination of the contractor's employment. See *J M Hill & Sons Limited v London Borough of Camden* [1980] 18 BLR 31, CA; see also *John Jarvis Limited v Rockdale Housing Association Limited* (1986) 36 BLR 48, CA, on the corresponding provisions in Clause 28.

30.05 Under Clause 27.4 the employer is entitled to determine the contractor's employment on discovery of corrupt practices by the contractor, and in this case the requirements of Clause 27.2 do not have to be complied with.

Insolvency

30.06 If the contractor makes a composition or arrangement with his creditors or, if a company, has made a proposal for a voluntary arrangement for a composition of debts or scheme of arrangement for approval under the Insolvency Act 1986 or the Companies Act 1985, he must immediately inform the employer in writing. The employer then has a right under Clause 27.3.4 to determine the employment of the contractor by notice. If he chooses not to do so, then all rights and duties under the contract are effectively suspended pending the making of an agreement under Clause 27.5.2.1 or the determination of the employment by notice.

30.07 The employment of the contractor determines automatically if a provisional liquidator or trustee in bankruptcy is appointed or a winding up order is made, or the contractor passes a resolution for voluntary winding up (except for the purposes of amalgamation or reconstruction), subject to the option of reinstatement.

Rights of parties after determination

30.08 Clause 27.6 governs the rights of the parties after determination. Briefly, the position is that:

1 The employer is entitled to get the work completed by others and to take an assignment of contracts for supply of materials and sub-contracts (except where the determination occurs by reason of the contractor's insolvency).
2 The employer is entitled to make direct payment to suppliers or sub-contractors, again except where determination occurs by reason of the contractor's insolvency.

3   The contractor is obliged within a reasonable time of notice being given by the architect (but not before) to remove all temporary buildings, plant, tools, equipment, goods and materials belonging to him and to have removed by their owner all such items which do not belong to him.

30.09 Typically, the employer will obtain a new contractor to carry out and complete the work. Under Clause 27.6.4.1, the employer is not bound to make any further payments to the contractor whose employment has been determined. Upon completion of the works and making good defects an account will be taken by the architect (Clause 27.6.4.2). If the employer has in fact got the work completed for less than he would have had to pay the contractor, the contractor is in principle entitled to be paid the difference, but if (as is far more likely) the work has cost more than the contractor would have charged, the contractor is obliged to pay the difference to the employer. In addition the architect must certify the amount of direct loss and/or damage caused to the employer by the determination, and this will be taken into account (Clause 27.6.5).

31 Clause 28: Determination by contractor

31.01 This clause, which should be compared with Clause 27, entitles the contractor to determine his own employment in certain circumstances. Clause 28.2.1.1 provides for determination for non-payment of amounts due on a certificate; Clause 28.2.1.2 deals with obstruction of certificates; Clause 28.2.1.3 deals with failure to comply with Clause 19.1.1 (prohibition against assigning without consent). Clause 28.2.2 deals with suspension of the work. The procedure is in two stages: first, a notice of specified default or suspension event, then, if the default or event continues or is repeated, a notice of determination.

Clause 28.2.1.1: Non-payment of certificates

31.02 If the employer intends to withhold payment from the contractor he must give the requisite notice under Clause 30.1.1.4, otherwise he must pay the amount due under any certificate. This clause conforms with the requirements of the Housing Grants, Construction and Regeneration Act 1996. *Morgan Building Services (LLC) Ltd v Jervis* [2003] EWCA Civ 1563. Such a withholding notice would permit the contractor to commence an adjudication if so desired.

Clause 28.2.1.2: Obstruction of certificates

31.03 Interference with or obstruction of issue of certificates by the employer includes preventing the architect from performing his duties, directing the architect as to the amount for which he is to give his certificate or as to the decision he should arrive at on matters which are within the sphere of the architect's independent duty.

Clause 28.2.2: Suspension of work

31.04 Clause 28.2.2 relates to suspension of the works for a continuous period of the length stated in the Appendix. Care must be taken to ensure that the periods in the Appendix are reasonably sufficient. Clause 28.2.2 has been amended following the decision in *John Jarvis Ltd v Rockdale Housing Association Limited* (1986) 36 BLR 48 CA, in which it was held that the words 'unless caused by some negligence or default of the contractor' did not include nominated sub-contractors. This is now expressly spelt out by the sub-clause. Therefore the main contractor is entitled to determine his employment if the work is suspended by reason of the default of a nominated sub-contractor.

31.05 In the same case it was held that notice under the previous Clause 28.1.3 (now 28.2.3) was not given 'unreasonably or vexatiously' unless a reasonable contractor in the same circumstances would have thought it unreasonable or vexatious to give the notice.

Clause 28.3: Insolvency of employer

31.06 Clause 28.3 provides that the employer must inform the contractor immediately in writing if any of the following events happen:
Being an individual:

1   He makes a composition or arrangement with his creditors.
2   He becomes bankrupt.

Being a company:

1   It makes a proposal for a voluntary arrangement for a composition of debts or a scheme of arrangement for approval under the Insolvency Act 1986 or the Companies Act 1985.
2   It has a provisional liquidator appointed.

---

28   Determination by Contractor

28·1   Any notice or further notice to which clauses 28·2·1, 28·2·2, 28·2·3, 28·2·4 and 28·3 refer shall be in writing and given by actual delivery, or by special delivery or by recorded delivery. If sent by special delivery or recorded delivery the notice or further notice shall, subject to proof to the contrary, be deemed to have been received 48 hours after the date of posting (excluding Saturday and Sunday and Public Holidays).

28·2   **·1**   If the Employer shall make default in any one or more of the following respects:

   ·1   **·1**   he does not pay by the final date for payment the amount properly due to the Contractor in respect of any certificate and/or any VAT on that amount pursuant to the VAT Agreement; or

   ·1   **·2**   he interferes with or obstructs the issue of any certificate due under this Contract; or

   ·1   **·3**   he fails to comply with the provisions of clause 19·1·1; or

   ·1   **·4**   he fails pursuant to the Conditions to comply with the requirements of the CDM Regulations,

   the Contractor may give to the Employer a notice specifying the default or defaults (the 'specified default or defaults').

28·2   ·2   If, before the date of Practical Completion, the carrying out of the whole or substantially the whole of the uncompleted Works is suspended for the continuous period of the length stated in the Appendix by reason of one or more of the following events:

·1   ·1   where an Information Release Schedule has been provided, failure of the Architect to comply with clause 5·4·1, or

·1   ·2   failure of the Architect to comply with clause 5·4·2, or

·2   ·2   Architect's instructions issued under clause 2·3, 13·2 or 23·2 unless caused by reason of some negligence or default of the Contractor, his servants or agents or of any person employed or engaged upon or in connection with the Works or any part thereof, his servants or agents other than a Nominated Sub-Contractor, the Employer or any person employed or engaged by the Employer; or

·2   ·3   delay in the execution of work not forming part of this Contract by the Employer himself or by persons employed or otherwise engaged by the Employer as referred to in clause 29 or the failure to execute such work or delay in the supply by the Employer of materials and goods which the Employer has agreed to supply for the Works or the failure so to supply; or

·2   ·4   failure of the Employer to give in due time ingress to or egress from the site of the Works or any part thereof through or over any land, buildings, way or passage adjoining or connected with the site and in the possession and control of the Employer, in accordance with the relevant Contract Documents, after receipt by the Architect of such notice, if any, as the Contractor is required to give, or failure of the Employer to give such ingress or egress as otherwise agreed between the Architect and the Contractor,

the Contractor may give to the Employer a notice specifying the event or events ('the specified suspension event or events').

28·2   ·3   If

–   the Employer continues a specified default, or

–   a specified suspension event is continued

for 14 days from receipt of the notice under clause 28·2·1 or clause 28·2·2 then the Contractor may on, or within 10 days from, the expiry of that 14 days by a further notice to the Employer determine the employment of the Contractor under this Contract. Such determination shall take effect on the date of receipt of such further notice.

28·2   ·4   If

–   the Employer ends the specified default or defaults, or

–   the specified suspension event or events cease, or

–   the Contractor does not give the further notice referred to in clause 28·2·3

and

–   the Employer repeats (whether previously repeated or not) a specified default, or

–   a specified suspension event is repeated for whatever period (whether previously repeated or not), whereby the regular progress of the Works is or is likely to be materially affected

then, upon or within a reasonable time after such repetition, the Contractor may by notice to the Employer determine the employment of the Contractor under this Contract. Such determination shall take effect on the date of receipt of such notice.

28·2   ·5   A notice of determination under clause 28·2·3 or clause 28·2·4 shall not be given unreasonably or vexatiously.

28·3 ·1 If the Employer [II]

makes a composition or arrangement with his creditors, or becomes bankrupt, or,

being a company,

makes a proposal for a voluntary arrangement for a composition of debts or scheme of arrangement to be approved in accordance with the Companies Act 1985 or the Insolvency Act 1986 as the case may be or any amendment or re-enactment thereof, or

has a provisional liquidator appointed, or

has a winding-up order made, or

passes a resolution for voluntary winding-up (except for the purposes of amalgamation or reconstruction), or

under the Insolvency Act 1986 or any amendment or re-enactment thereof has an administrator or an administrative receiver appointed

then:

28·3 ·2 the Employer shall immediately inform the Contractor in writing if he has made a composition or arrangement with his creditors, or, being a company, has made a proposal for a voluntary arrangement for a composition of debts or scheme of arrangement to be approved in accordance with the Companies Act 1985 or the Insolvency Act 1986 or any amendment or re-enactment thereof as the case may be;

28·3 ·3 the Contractor may by notice to the Employer determine the employment of the Contractor under this Contract. Such determination shall take effect on the date of receipt of such notice. Provided that after the occurrence of any of the events set out in clause 28·3·1 and before the taking effect of any notice of determination of his employment issued by the Contractor pursuant to clause 28·3·3 the obligation of the Contractor to carry out and complete the Works in compliance with clause 2·1 shall be suspended.

28·4 In the event of the determination of the employment of the Contractor under clause 28·2·3, 28·2·4 or 28·3·3 and so long as that employment has not been reinstated the provisions of clauses 28·4·1, 28·4·2 and 28·4·3 shall apply; such application shall be without prejudice to the accrued rights or remedies of either party or to any liability of the classes mentioned in clause 20 which may accrue either before the Contractor or any sub-contractors, their servants or agents or others employed on or engaged upon or in connection with the Works or any part thereof other than the Employer or any person employed or engaged by the Employer shall have removed his or their temporary buildings, plant, tools, equipment, goods or materials (including Site Materials) or by reason of his or their so removing the same. Subject to clauses 28·4·2 and 28·4·3 the provisions of this Contract which require any payment or release or further release of Retention to the Contractor shall not apply.

28·4 ·1 The Contractor shall, with all reasonable dispatch and in such manner and with such precautions as will prevent injury, death or damage of the classes in respect of which before the date of determination he was liable to indemnify the Employer under clause 20, remove from the site all his temporary buildings, plant, tools, equipment, goods and materials (including Site Materials) and shall ensure that his sub-contractors do the same, but subject always to the provisions of clause 28·4·3·5.

28·4 ·2 Within 28 days of the determination of the employment of the Contractor the Employer shall pay to the Contractor the Retention deducted by the Employer prior to the determination of the employment of the Contractor but subject to any right of the Employer of deduction therefrom which has accrued before the date of determination of the Contractor's employment.

28·4 ·3 The Contractor shall with reasonable dispatch prepare an account setting out the sum of the amounts referred to in clauses 28·4·3·1 to 28·4·3·5 which shall include as relevant amounts in respect of all Nominated Sub-Contractors:

·3 ·1   the total value of work properly executed at the date of determination of the employment of the Contractor, such value to be ascertained in accordance with the Conditions as if the employment of the Contractor had not been determined, together with any amounts due to the Contractor under the Conditions not included in such total value; and

·3 ·2   any sum ascertained in respect of direct loss and/or expense under clauses 26 and 34·3 (whether ascertained before or after the date of determination); and

·3 ·3   the reasonable cost of removal pursuant to clause 28·4·1; and

·3 ·4   any direct loss and/or damage caused to the Contractor by the determination; and

·3 ·5   the cost of materials or goods (including Site Materials) properly ordered for the Works for which the Contractor shall have paid or for which the Contractor is legally bound to pay, and on such payment in full by the Employer such materials or goods shall become the property of the Employer.

After taking into account amounts previously paid to the Contractor under this Contract the Employer shall pay to the Contractor the amount properly due in respect of this account within 28 days of its submission by the Contractor to the Employer but without any deduction of Retention.

28·5   The provisions of clauses 28·2 to 28·4 are without prejudice to any other rights and remedies which the Contractor may possess.

3   It has a winding-up order made.
4   It passes a resolution for voluntary winding up (except for the purposes of amalgamation or reconstruction).
5   It has an administrator or administrative receiver appointed under the Insolvency Act 1986.

Unlike the provisions under Clause 27 in relation to the insolvency of the contractor, in none of these circumstances is the contract automatically brought to an end, but instead the contractor has a right to determine his employment by notice in the event of the insolvency of the employer.

Rights of parties after determination

31.07   Clause 28.4 governs the rights of the parties after determination. In summary:

1   The contractor is to remove his temporary buildings, plant, etc. from the site with all reasonable dispatch and ensure that his sub-contractors do the same.
2   Within 28 days of the determination the employer must pay to the contractor the retention held at the date of the determination, less any amounts which have accrued due to the employer.
3   The contractor is to prepare an account of sums due to him for the items set out in Clause 28.4.3.
4   The employer shall pay the amount properly due in respect of the items in Clause 28.4.3 within 28 days of the submission of the account.

32 Clause 28A: Determination by employer or contractor

32.01   Either party may determine the employment of the contractor where the works have been suspended for the relevant continuous period stated in the Appendix by reason of one of the events specified in 28A.1.1. Again, care should be taken to ensure that the periods provided in the Appendix are reasonably sufficient.

Rights of parties after determination

32.02   The rights and duties of the parties after determination may be summarized as follows:

1   The contractor is to remove his temporary buildings, plant, etc. from the site with all reasonable dispatch.
2   Within 28 days of the determination of the employment the employer is to pay one half of the retention monies held at the date of determination to the contractor, less any monies which have accrued to the employer.
3   The contractor is to provide the employer within 2 months after the determination with all documents necessary for the preparation of an account by the employer.
4   The employer shall pay the contractor within 28 days the amounts properly due in respect of the items listed in Clause 28A.5.

33 Clause 29: Works by employer or person employed or engaged by the employer

33.01   This clause governs the position where the employer wishes to carry out certain work himself (or via persons employed by him) while the contractor is engaged on the works. Where this work is described in the bills the contractor is obliged to permit the employer to carry the work out, but where it is not, the contractor is required to give his consent, which must not be unreasonably withheld. Clause 29.3 makes it clear that there is no relationship between the contractor and persons so employed. (For the meaning of 'work not forming part of this contract' see *Henry Boot Construction Limited v Central Lancashire New Town Development Corporation* (1980) 15 BLR 1).

34 Clause 30: Certificates and payments

34.01   This clause provides for:

1   Interim certificates and the contractor's right to suspension for non-payment (Clause 30.1)

2 Rules for ascertainment of amounts due in interim certificates (Clause 30.2)
3 Rules for valuing off-site materials or goods (Clause 30.3)
4 Rules for ascertainment of retention (Clause 30.4)
5 Rules on treatment of retention (Clause 30.5)
6 Final adjustment of contract sum (Clause 30.6)
7 Final adjustment of nominated sub-contract sums (Clause 30.7)
8 Issue and effect of final certificate (Clauses 30.8 and 30.9).

Interim certificates

34.02 The architect is under a duty to issue certificates at the periods specified in the Appendix showing the amount due to the contractor and (in accordance with section 110 of the Housing Grants, Construction and Regeneration Act 1996) stating to what the payment relates, the basis of the calculation and a final date for payment. If he certifies an excessive amount, he may be liable to the employer in damages (see *Sutcliffe v Thackrah* [1974] AC 727). There is a new version of Clause 30.1.3, where Amendment 2:2000 is used.

34.03 Certificates are payable within 14 days of issue. Interest is due in the event of late payment (Clause 30.1.1.1). Clause 30.1.1.3 requires the employer, within 5 days of the issue of an interim certificate, to give a payment-notice, that is, a notice to the contractor of the amount that he proposes to pay and the basis of such. This is a statutory requirement of HGCRA 1996 section 110(2). However, Clause 30.1.1.5 in effect allows him to simply pay the total amount due under the certificate without giving the payment-notice. This may avoid unnecessary administration where there is no objection to the total certified. If, however, the employer proposes to deduct or withhold any amount he must provide a payment-notice.

34.04 Under Clause 30.1.1.2, the employer is entitled in the exercise of a right under the contract to make a deduction from interim certificates, including retention money included in such certificates, subject to a restriction in relation to retention payable to a nominated sub-contractor (Clause 35.13.5.3.2). Clause 30.1.1.4 provides for the withholding-notice required by HGCRA 1996 section 111. This is mandatory: *Morgan Building Services (LLC) Ltd v Jervis* [2003] EWCA Civ 1563. The clause states that the employer *may*, within 5 days of final payment becoming due, give written notice to the contractor of any payment that he proposes to withhold, and the basis for such. If a payment-notice has been issued under Clause 30.1.1.3, covering the matters otherwise required by Clause 30.1.1.4 (i.e. reasons and amount of deductions), it can double as a withholding-notice and a separate notice under Clause 30.1.1.4 would be superfluous. Only if the payment-notice is insufficient, or if new matters have arisen, will a separate withholding-notice be required under Clause 30.1.1.4.

34.05 The contract does not cover the position if defects appear within the last 5 days (i.e. after the time for issue of a withholding-notice). It is not clear whether there could be a valid ground for holding up the payment or whether the architect would have to take the defects into account in the following certificate.

34.06 Clause 30.1.2.1 provides that valuations may be carried out by the quantity surveyor, although the architect should ensure that the quantity surveyor adopts the correct principles when making such valuations.

28A   Determination by Employer or Contractor

28A·1 ·1   If, before the date of Practical Completion, the carrying out of the whole or substantially the whole of the uncompleted Works is suspended for the relevant continuous period of the length stated in the Appendix by reason of one or more of the following events:

1   1   force majeure; or

·1   ·2   loss or damage to the Works occasioned by any one or more of the Specified Perils; or

·1   ·3   civil commotion; or

·1   ·4   Architect's instructions issued under clause 2·3, 13·2 or 23·2 which have been issued as a result of the negligence or default of any local authority or statutory undertaker executing work solely in pursuance of its statutory obligations; or

·1   ·5   hostilities involving the United Kingdom (whether war be declared or not); or

·1   ·6   terrorist activity

then the Employer or the Contractor may upon the expiry of the aforesaid relevant period of suspension give notice in writing to the other by actual delivery or by special delivery or recorded delivery that unless the suspension is terminated within 7 days after the date of receipt of that notice the employment of the Contractor under this Contract will determine 7 days after the date of receipt of the aforesaid notice; and the employment of the Contractor shall so determine 7 days after receipt of such notice. If sent by special delivery or recorded delivery the notice shall, subject to proof to the contrary, be deemed to have been received 48 hours after the date of posting (excluding Saturday and Sunday and Public Holidays).

28A·1 ·2   The Contractor shall not be entitled to give notice under clause 28A·1·1 in respect of the matter referred to in clause 28A·1·1·2 where the loss or damage to the Works occasioned by any one or more of the Specified Perils was caused by some negligence or default of the Contractor, his servants or agents or of any person employed or engaged upon or in connection with the Works or any part thereof, his servants or agents other than the Employer or any person employed or engaged by the Employer or by any local authority or statutory undertaker executing work solely in pursuance of its statutory obligations.

28A·1 **·3**   A notice of determination under clause 28A·1·1 shall not be given unreasonably or vexatiously.

28A·2   Upon determination of the employment of the Contractor under clause 28A·1·1 the provisions of this Contract which require any further payment or any release or further release of Retention to the Contractor shall not apply; and the provisions of clauses 28A·3 to 28A·6 shall apply.

28A·3   The Contractor shall, with all reasonable dispatch and in such manner and with such precautions as will prevent injury, death or damage of the classes in respect of which before the date of determination of his employment he was liable to indemnify the Employer under clause 20, remove from the site all his temporary buildings, plant, tools, equipment, goods and materials (including Site Materials) and shall ensure that his sub-contractors do the same, but subject always to the provisions of clause 28A·5·4.

28A·4   The Employer shall pay to the Contractor one half of the Retention deducted by the Employer prior to the determination of the employment of the Contractor within 28 days of the date of determination of the Contractor's employment and the other half as part of the account to which clause 28A·5 refers but subject to any right of deduction therefrom which has accrued before the date of such determination.

28A·5   The Contractor shall, not later than 2 months after the date of the determination of the Contractor's employment, provide the Employer with all documents (including those relating to Nominated Sub-Contractors and Nominated Suppliers) necessary for the preparation of the account to which this clause refers. Subject to due discharge by the Contractor of this obligation the Employer shall with reasonable dispatch prepare an account setting out the sum of the amounts referred to in clauses 28A·5·1 to 28A·5·4 and, if clause 28A·6 applies, clause 28A·5·5, which shall include as relevant amounts in respect of all Nominated Sub-Contractors:

28A·5 **·1**   the total value of work properly executed at the date of determination of the employment of the Contractor, such value to be ascertained in accordance with the Conditions as if the employment of the Contractor had not been determined, together with any amounts due to the Contractor under the Conditions not included in such total value; and

28A·5 **·2**   any sum ascertained in respect of direct loss and/or expense under clauses 26 and 34·3 (whether ascertained before or after the date of determination); and

28A·5 **·3**   the reasonable cost of removal under clause 28A·3; and

28A·5 **·4**   the cost of materials or goods (including Site Materials) properly ordered for the Works for which the Contractor shall have paid or for which the Contractor is legally bound to pay, and on such payment in full by the Employer such materials or goods shall become the property of the Employer; and

28A·5 **·5**   any direct loss and/or damage caused to the Contractor by the determination.

After taking into account amounts previously paid to the Contractor under this Contract the Employer shall pay to the Contractor the amount properly due in respect of this account within 28 days of its submission by the Employer to the Contractor but without deduction of any Retention.

28A·6   Where determination of the employment of the Contractor has occurred in respect of the matter referred to in clause 28A·1·1·2 and the loss or damage to the Works occasioned by any one or more of the Specified Perils was caused by some negligence or default of the Employer or of any person for whom the Employer is responsible, then upon such determination of the employment of the Contractor the account prepared under clause 28A·5 shall include the amount, if any, to which clause 28A·5·5 refers.

28A·7   The Employer shall inform the Contractor in writing which part or parts of the amounts paid or payable under clause 28A·5 is or are fairly and reasonably attributable to any Nominated Sub-Contractor and shall so inform each Nominated Sub-Contractor in writing.

29   Works by Employer or persons employed or engaged by Employer

29·1   Where the Contract Bills, in regard to any work not forming part of this Contract and which is to be carried out by the Employer himself or by persons employed or otherwise engaged by him, provide such information as is necessary to enable the Contractor to carry out and complete the Works in accordance with the Conditions, the Contractor shall permit the execution of such work.

29·2   Where the Contract Bills do not provide the information referred to in clause 29·1 and the Employer requires the execution of work not forming part of this Contract by the Employer himself or by persons employed or otherwise engaged by the Employer, then the Employer may, with the consent of the Contractor (which consent shall not be unreasonably delayed or withheld), arrange for the execution of such work.

29·3   Every person employed or otherwise engaged by the Employer as referred to in clauses 29·1 and 29·2 shall for the purpose of clause 20 be deemed to be a person for whom the Employer is responsible and not to be a sub-contractor.

30   Certificates and payments

30·1   ·1   ·1   The Architect shall from time to time as provided in clause 30 issue Interim Certificates stating the amount due to the Contractor from the Employer specifying to what the amount relates and the basis on which that amount was calculated; and the final date for payment pursuant to an Interim Certificate shall be 14 days from the date of issue of each Interim Certificate.

If the Employer fails properly to pay the amount, or any part thereof, due to the Contractor under the Conditions by the final date for its payment the Employer shall pay to the Contractor in addition to the amount not properly paid simple interest thereon for the period until such payment is made. Payment of such simple interest shall be treated as a debt due to the Contractor by the Employer. The rate of interest payable shall be five per cent (5%) over the Base Rate of the Bank of England which is current at the date the payment by the Employer became overdue. Any payment of simple interest under this clause 30·1·1·1 shall not in any circumstances be construed as a waiver by the Contractor of his right to proper payment of the principal amount due from the Employer to the Contractor in accordance with, and within the time stated in, the Conditions or of the rights of the Contractor in regard to suspension of the performance of his obligations under this Contract to the Employer pursuant to clause 30·1·4 or to determination of his employment pursuant to the default referred to in clause 28·2·1·1.

·1   ·2   Notwithstanding the fiduciary interest of the Employer in the Retention as stated in clause 30·5·1 the Employer is entitled to exercise any right under this Contract of withholding and/or deduction from monies due or to become due to the Contractor against any amount so due under an Interim Certificate whether or not any Retention is included in that Interim Certificate by the operation of clause 30·4. Such withholding and/or deduction is subject to the restriction in clause 35·13·5·3·2.

·1   ·3   Not later than 5 days after the date of issue of an Interim Certificate the Employer shall give a written notice to the Contractor which shall, in respect of the amount stated as due in that Interim Certificate, specify the amount of the payment proposed to be made, to what the amount of the payment relates and the basis on which that amount is calculated.

·1   ·4   Not later than 5 days before the final date for payment of the amount due pursuant to clause 30·1·1·1 the Employer may give a written notice to the Contractor which shall specify any amount proposed to be withheld and/or deducted from that due amount, the ground or grounds for such withholding and/or deduction and the amount of withholding and/or deduction attributable to each ground.

·1   ·5   Where the Employer does not give any written notice pursuant to clause 30·1·1·3 and/or to clause 30·1·1·4 the Employer shall pay the Contractor the amount due pursuant to clause 30·1·1·1.

30·1   ·1   ·6   Where it is stated in the Appendix that clause 30·1·1·6 applies, the advance payment identified in the Appendix shall be paid to the Contractor on the date stated in the Appendix and such advance payment shall be reimbursed to the Employer by the Contractor on the terms stated in the Appendix. Provided that where the Appendix states that an advance payment bond is required such payment shall only be made if the Contractor has provided to the Employer such bond from a surety approved by the Employer on the terms agreed between the British Bankers' Association and the JCT and annexed to the Appendix unless pursuant to the Seventh Recital a bond on other terms is required by the Employer.

30·1   ·2   ·1   Interim valuations shall be made by the Quantity Surveyor whenever the Architect considers them to be necessary for the purpose of ascertaining the amount to be stated as due in an Interim Certificate. [mm]

             ·2   ·2   Without prejudice to the obligation of the Architect to issue Interim Certificates as stated in clause 30·1·1·1, the Contractor, not later than 7 days before the date of an Interim Certificate, may submit to the Quantity Surveyor an application which sets out what the Contractor considers to be the amount of the gross valuation pursuant to clause 30·2. The Contractor shall include with his application any application made to the Contractor by a Nominated Sub-Contractor which sets out what the Nominated Sub-Contractor considers to be the amount of the gross valuation pursuant to clause 4·17 of Conditions NSC/C. If the Contractor submits such an application the Quantity Surveyor shall make an interim valuation. To the extent that the Quantity Surveyor disagrees with the gross valuation in the Contractor's application and/or in a Nominated Sub-Contractor's application the Quantity Surveyor at the same time as making the valuation shall submit to the Contractor a statement, which shall be in similar detail to that given in the application, which identifies such disagreement.

30·1   ·3   Interim Certificates shall be issued at the Period of Interim Certificates specified in the Appendix up to and including the end of the period during which the certificate of Practical Completion is issued. Thereafter Interim Certificates shall be issued as and when further amounts are ascertained as payable to the Contractor from the Employer and after the expiration of the Defects Liability Period named in the Appendix or upon the issue of the Certificate of Completion of Making Good Defects (whichever is the later) provided always that the Architect shall not be required to issue an Interim Certificate within one calendar month of having issued a previous Interim Certificate.

30·1   ·4   Without prejudice to any other rights and remedies which the Contractor may possess, if the Employer shall, subject to any notice issued pursuant to clause 30·1·1·4, fail to pay the Contractor in full (including any VAT due pursuant to the VAT Agreement) by the final date for payment as required by the Conditions and such failure shall continue for 7 days after the Contractor has given to the Employer, with a copy to the Architect, written notice of his intention to suspend the performance of his obligations under this Contract to the Employer and the ground or grounds on which it is intended to suspend performance then the Contractor may suspend such performance of his obligations under this Contract to the Employer until payment in full occurs. Such suspension shall not be treated as a suspension to which clause 27·2·1·1 refers or a failure to proceed regularly and diligently with the Works to which clause 27·2·1·2 refers.

30·2   The amount stated as due in an Interim Certificate, subject to any agreement between the parties as to stage payments, shall be the gross valuation as referred to in clause 30·2 less

            any amount which may be deducted and retained by the Employer as provided in clause 30·4 (in the Conditions called 'the Retention') and

            the amount of any advance payment or part thereof due for reimbursement to the Employer in accordance with the terms for such reimbursement stated in the Appendix pursuant to clause 30·1·1·6 and

            the total amount stated as due in Interim Certificates previously issued under the Conditions.

            The gross valuation shall be the total of the amounts referred to in clauses 30·2·1 and 30·2·2 less the total of the amounts referred to in clause 30·2·3 and applied up to and including a date not more than 7 days before the date of the Interim Certificate.

30·2 ·1   There shall be included the following which are subject to Retention:

  ·1 ·1   the total value of the work properly executed by the Contractor including any work so executed to which Alternative B in clause 13·4·1·2 applies or to which a Price Statement or any part thereof accepted pursuant to clause 13·4·1·2 paragraph A2 or amended Price Statement or any part thereof accepted pursuant to clause 13·4·1·2 paragraph A4·2 applies but excluding any restoration, replacement or repair of loss or damage and removal and disposal of debris which in clauses 22B·3·5 and 22C·4·4·2 are treated as if they were a Variation, together with, where applicable, any adjustment of that value under clause 40. Where it is stated in the Appendix that a priced Activity Schedule is attached thereto the value of the work to which the Activity Schedule relates shall be the total of the various sums which result from the application of the proportion of the work in an activity listed in the Activity Schedule properly executed to the price for that work as stated in the Activity Schedule;

  ·1 ·2   the total value of the materials and goods delivered to or adjacent to the Works for incorporation therein by the Contractor but not so incorporated, provided that the value of such materials and goods shall only be included as and from such times as they are reasonably, properly and not prematurely so delivered and are adequately protected against weather and other casualties;

  ·1 ·3   the total value of any materials or goods or items pre-fabricated which are 'listed items' the value of which is required pursuant to clause 30·3 to be included in the amount stated as due in the Interim Certificate;

  ·1 ·4   the amounts referred to in clause 4·17·1 of Conditions NSC/C in respect of each Nominated Sub-Contractor;

  ·1 ·5   the profit of the Contractor upon the total of the amounts referred to in clauses 30·2·1·4 and 30·2·2·5 less the total of the amount referred to in clause 30·2·3·2 at the rates included in the Contract Bills, or, in the case where the nomination arises from an instruction as to the expenditure of a provisional sum, at rates related thereto, or, if none, at reasonable rates.

30·2 ·2   There shall be included the following which are not subject to Retention:

  ·2 ·1   any amounts to be included in Interim Certificates in accordance with clause 3 as a result of payments made or costs incurred by the Contractor under clauses 6·2, 8·3, 9·2, 21·2·3, 22B·2 and 22C·3;

  ·2 ·2   any amounts ascertained under clause 26·1 or 34·3 or in respect of any restoration, replacement or repair of loss or damage and removal and disposal of debris which in clauses 22B·3·5 and 22C·4·4·2 are treated as if they were a Variation;

  ·2 ·3   any amount to which clause 35·17 refers;

  ·2 ·4   any amount payable to the Contractor under clause 38 or 39, if applicable;

  ·2 ·5   the amounts referred to in clause 4·17·2 of Conditions NSC/C in respect of each Nominated Sub-Contractor.

30·2 ·3   There shall be deducted the following which are not subject to Retention:

  ·3 ·1   any amount deductible under clause 7 or 8·4·2 or 17·2 or 17·3 or any amount allowable by the Contractor to the Employer under clause 38 or 39, if applicable;

  ·3 ·2   any amount referred to in clause 4·17·3 of Conditions NSC/C in respect of each Nominated Sub-Contractor.

30·3   The materials or goods or items pre-fabricated for inclusion in the Works to which this clause refers ('the listed items') shall have been listed by the Employer in a list supplied to the Contractor and annexed to the Contract Bills. The amount stated as due in an Interim Certificate shall include the value of any listed items before delivery thereof to or adjacent to the Works provided that the following conditions have been fulfilled:

30·3 ·1   the Contractor has provided the Architect with reasonable proof that the property in uniquely identified listed items is vested in the Contractor so that, pursuant to clause 16·2, after the amount in respect thereof included in an Interim Certificate as properly due to the Contractor has been paid by the Employer, the uniquely identified listed items shall become the property of the Employer; and, if so stated in the Appendix, has also provided from a surety approved by the Employer a bond in favour of the Employer on the terms agreed between the JCT and the British Bankers' Association and annexed to the Appendix unless pursuant to the Seventh recital a bond on other terms is required by the Employer;

30·3   ·2   the Contractor in respect of listed items which are not uniquely identified has provided the Architect

with reasonable proof that the property in such listed items is vested in the Contractor so that, pursuant to clause 16·2, after the amount in respect thereof included in an Interim Certificate as properly due to the Contractor has been paid by the Employer, such listed items shall become the property of the Employer; and

the Contractor has provided from a surety approved by the Employer a bond in favour of the Employer on the terms agreed between the JCT and the British Bankers' Association and annexed to the Appendix unless pursuant to the Seventh recital a bond on other terms is required by the Employer;

30·3   ·3   the listed items are in accordance with the Contract;

30·3   ·4   the listed items at the premises where they have been manufactured or assembled or stored

either

are set apart

or

have been clearly and visibly marked individually or in sets by letters or figures or by reference to a pre-determined code

and identify

·4   ·1   the Employer and to whose order they are held; and

·4   ·2   their destination as the Works;

30·3   ·5   the Contractor has provided the Employer with reasonable proof that the listed items are insured against loss or damage for their full value under a policy of insurance protecting the interests of the Employer and the Contractor in respect of the Specified Perils, during the period commencing with the transfer of property in the listed items to the Contractor until they are delivered to, or adjacent to, the Works.

30·4   ·1   The Retention which the Employer may deduct and retain as referred to in clause 30·2 shall be such percentage of the total amount included under clause 30·2·1 in any Interim Certificate as arises from the operation of the following rules:

·1   ·1   the percentage (in the Conditions and Appendix called 'the Retention Percentage') deductible under clause 30·4·1·2 shall be 5 per cent (unless a lower rate shall have been agreed between the parties and specified in the Appendix as the Retention Percentage); and the percentage deductible under clause 30·4·1·3 shall be one half of the Retention Percentage; [nn]

·1   ·2   [oo] the Retention Percentage may be deducted from so much of the said total amount as relates to:

work which has not reached Practical Completion (as referred to in clauses 17·1, 18·1·1 or 35·16); and amounts in respect of the value of materials and goods included under clauses 30·2·1·2, 30·2·1·3 and 30·2·1·4 (so far as that clause relates to materials and goods as referred to in clause 4·17·1 of Conditions NSC/C);

·1 ·3 [oo] half the Retention Percentage may be deducted from so much of the said total amount as relates to work which has reached Practical Completion (as referred to in clauses 17·1, 18·1·1 or 35·16) but in respect of which a Certificate of Completion of Making Good Defects under clause 17·4 or a certificate under clause 18·1·2 or an Interim Certificate under clause 35·17 has not been issued.

30·4 ·2 The Retention deducted from the value of work executed by the Contractor or any Nominated Sub-Contractor, and from the value of materials and goods intended for incorporation in the Works but not so incorporated, and specified in the statements issued under clause 30·5·2·1, is hereinafter referred to as the 'Contractor's retention' and the 'Nominated Sub-Contract retention' respectively.

30·5 The Retention shall be subject to the following rules:

30·5 ·1 the Employer's interest in the Retention is fiduciary as trustee for the Contractor and for any Nominated Sub-Contractor (but without obligation to invest);

30·5 ·2 ·1 at the date of each Interim Certificate the Architect shall prepare, or instruct the Quantity Surveyor to prepare, a statement specifying the Contractor's retention and the Nominated Sub-Contract retention for each Nominated Sub-Contractor deducted in arriving at the amount stated as due in such Interim Certificate;

·2 ·2 such statement shall be issued by the Architect to the Employer, to the Contractor and to each Nominated Sub-Contractor whose work is referred to in the statement.

30·5 ·3 The Employer shall, to the extent that the Employer exercises his right under clause 30·4, if the Contractor or any Nominated Sub-Contractor so requests, at the date of payment under each Interim Certificate place the Retention in a separate banking account (so designated as to identify the amount as the Retention held by the Employer on trust as provided in clause 30·5·1) and certify to the Architect with a copy to the Contractor that such amount has been so placed. The Employer shall be entitled to the full beneficial interest in any interest accruing in the separate banking account and shall be under no duty to account for any such interest to the Contractor or any sub-contractor.

30·5 ·4 Where the Employer exercises the right to withhold and/or deduct referred to in clause 30·1·1·2 against any Retention he shall inform the Contractor of the amount of that withholding and/or deduction from either the Contractor's retention or the Nominated Sub-Contract retention of any Nominated Sub-Contractor by reference to the latest statement issued under clause 30·5·2·1.

30·6 ·1 ·1 Not later than 6 months after Practical Completion of the Works the Contractor shall provide the Architect, or, if so instructed by the Architect, the Quantity Surveyor, with all documents necessary for the purposes of the adjustment of the Contract Sum including all documents relating to the accounts of Nominated Sub-Contractors and Nominated Suppliers.

·1 ·2 Not later than 3 months after receipt by the Architect or by the Quantity Surveyor of the documents referred to in clause 30·6·1·1

·2 ·1 the Architect, or, if the Architect has so instructed, the Quantity Surveyor, shall ascertain (unless previously ascertained) any loss and/or expense under clauses 26·1, 26·4·1 and 34·3, and

·2 ·2 the Quantity Surveyor shall prepare a statement of all adjustments to be made to the Contract Sum as referred to in clause 30·6·2 other than any to which clause 30·6·1·2·1 applies

and the Architect shall forthwith send a copy of any ascertainment to which clause 30·6·1·2·1 refers and of the statement prepared in compliance with clause 30·6·1·2·2 to the Contractor and the relevant extract therefrom to each Nominated Sub-Contractor.

30·6   ·2   The Contract Sum shall be adjusted by:

–   the amount of any Valuations agreed by the Employer and the Contractor to which clause 13·4·1·1 refers, and

–   the amounts stated in any 13A Quotations for which the Architect has issued to the Contractor a confirmed acceptance pursuant to clause 13A·3·2 and for the amount of any Variations thereto as valued pursuant to clause 13A·8, and

–   the amount of any Price Statement or any part thereof accepted pursuant to clause 13·4·1·2 paragraph A2 or amended Price Statement or any part thereof accepted pursuant to clause 13·4·1·2 paragraph A4·2

and as follows:

there shall be deducted:

·2   ·1   all prime cost sums, all amounts in respect of sub-contractors named as referred to in clause 35·1, the certified value of any work by a Nominated Sub-Contractor, whose employment has been determined in accordance with clause 35·24, which was not in accordance with the relevant Sub-Contract but which has been paid or otherwise discharged by the Employer, and any Contractor's profit thereon included in the Contract Bills;

·2   ·2   all provisional sums and the value of all work for which an Approximate Quantity is included in the Contract Bills;

·2   ·3   the amount of the valuation under clause 13·5·2 of items omitted in accordance with a Variation required by the Architect under clause 13·2, or subsequently sanctioned by him in writing, together with the amount included in the Contract Bills for any other work as referred to in clause 13·5·5 which is to be valued under clause 13·5;

·2   ·4   any amount deducted or deductible under clause 7 or 8·4·2 or 17·2 or 17·3 or any amount allowed or allowable to the Employer under clause 38, 39 or 40, whichever is applicable;

·2   ·5   any other amount which is required by this Contract to be deducted from the Contract Sum;

there shall be added:

·2   ·6   the amounts of the nominated sub-contract sums or tender sums for all Nominated Sub-Contractors as finally adjusted or ascertained under all relevant provisions of Conditions NSC/C;

·2   ·7   the tender sum (or such other sum as is appropriate in accordance with the terms of the tender as accepted by or on behalf of the Employer) for any work for which a tender made under clause 35·2 has been accepted;

·2   ·8   any amounts properly chargeable to the Employer in accordance with the nomination instruction of the Architect in respect of materials or goods supplied by Nominated Suppliers; such amounts shall include the discount for cash of 5 per cent referred to in clause 36 but shall exclude any value added tax which is treated, or is capable of being treated, as input tax (as referred to in the Finance Act 1972) by the Contractor;

·2   ·9   the profit of the Contractor upon the amounts referred to in clauses 30·6·2·6, 30·6·2·7 and 30·6·2·8 at the rates included in the Contract Bills or in the cases where the nomination arises from an instruction as to the expenditure of a provisional sum at rates related thereto or if none at reasonable rates;

·2   ·10   any amounts paid or payable by the Employer to the Contractor as a result of payments made or costs incurred by the Contractor under clauses 6·2, 8·3, 9·2 and 21·2·3;

·2   ·11   the amount of the Valuation under clause 13·5 of any Variation, including the valuation of other work as referred to in clause 13·5·5, other than the amount of the valuation of any omission under clause 13·5·2;

·2 ·12 the amount of the Valuation of work executed by, or the amount of any disbursements by, the Contractor in accordance with instructions of the Architect as to the expenditure of provisional sums included in the Contract Bills and of all work for which an Approximate Quantity is included in the Contract Bills;

·2 ·13 any amount ascertained under clause 26·1 or 34·3;

·2 ·14 any amount paid by the Contractor under clause 22B or clause 22C which the Contractor is entitled to have added to the Contract Sum;

·2 ·15 any amount paid or payable to the Contractor under clause 38, 39 or 40, whichever is applicable;

·2 ·16 any other amount which is required by this Contract to be added to the Contract Sum;

·2 ·17 any amount to be paid in lieu of any ascertainment under clause 26·1 accepted pursuant to clause 13·4·1·2 paragraph A7.

30·7 So soon as is practicable but not less than 28 days before the date of issue of the Final Certificate referred to in clause 30·8 and notwithstanding that a period of one month may not have elapsed since the issue of the previous Interim Certificate, the Architect shall issue an Interim Certificate the gross valuation for which shall include the amounts of the sub-contract sums for all Nominated Sub-Contracts as finally adjusted or ascertained under all relevant provisions of Conditions NSC/C.

30·8 ·1 The Architect shall issue the Final Certificate (and inform each Nominated Sub-Contractor of the date of its issue) not later than 2 months after whichever of the following occurs last:

the end of the Defects Liability Period;

the date of issue of the Certificate of Completion of Making Good Defects under clause 17·4;

the date on which the Architect sent a copy to the Contractor of any ascertainment to which clause 30·6·1·2·1 refers and of the statement prepared in compliance with clause 30·6·1·2·2.

The Final Certificate shall state:

·1 ·1 the sum of the amounts already stated as due in Interim Certificates plus the amount of any advance payment paid pursuant to clause 30·1·1·6, and

·1 ·2 the Contract Sum adjusted as necessary in accordance with clause 30·6·2, and

·1 ·3 to what the amount relates and the basis on which the statement in the Final Certificate has been calculated

and the difference (if any) between the two sums shall (without prejudice to the rights of the Contractor in respect of any Interim Certificates which have subject to any notice issued pursuant to clause 30·1·1·4 not been paid in full by the Employer by the final date for payment of such Certificate) be expressed in the said Certificate as a balance due to the Contractor from the Employer or to the Employer from the Contractor as the case may be.

30·8 ·2 Not later than 5 days after the date of issue of the Final Certificate the Employer shall give a written notice to the Contractor which shall, in respect of any balance stated as due to the Contractor from the Employer in the Final Certificate, specify the amount of the payment proposed to be made, to what the amount of the payment relates and the basis on which that amount is calculated.

30·8 ·3   The final date for payment of the said balance payable by the Employer to the Contractor or by the Contractor to the Employer as the case may be shall be 28 days from the date of issue of the said Certificate. Not later than 5 days before the final date for payment of the balance the Employer may give a written notice to the Contractor which shall specify any amount proposed to be withheld and/or deducted from any balance due to the Contractor, the ground or grounds for such withholding and/or deduction and the amount of withholding and/or deduction attributable to each ground.

30·8 ·4   Where the Employer does not give a written notice pursuant to clause 30·8·2 and/or clause 30·8·3 the Employer shall pay the Contractor the balance stated as due to the Contractor in the Final Certificate.

30·8 ·5   If the Employer or the Contractor fails properly to pay the said balance, or any part thereof, by the final date for its payment the Employer or the Contractor as the case may be shall pay to the other, in addition to the balance not properly paid, simple interest thereon for the period until such payment is made. The rate of interest payable shall be five per cent (5%) over the Base Rate of the Bank of England which is current at the date the payment by the Employer or by the Contractor as the case may be became overdue. Any payment of simple interest under this clause 30·8 shall not in any circumstances be construed as a waiver by the Contractor or by the Employer as the case may be of his right to proper payment of the aforesaid balance due from the Employer to the Contractor or from the Contractor to the Employer in accordance with this clause 30·8.

30·8 ·6   Liability for payment of the balance pursuant to clause 30·8·3 and of any interest pursuant to clause 30·8·5 shall be treated as a debt due to the Contractor by the Employer or to the Employer by the Contractor as the case may be.

30·9 ·1   Except as provided in clauses 30·9·2 and 30·9·3 (and save in respect of fraud), the Final Certificate shall have effect in any proceedings under or arising out of or in connection with this Contract (whether by adjudication under article 5 or by arbitration under article 7A or by legal proceedings under article 7B) as

    ·1   ·1   conclusive evidence that where and to the extent that any of the particular qualities of any materials or goods or any particular standard of an item of workmanship was described expressly in the Contract Drawings or the Contract Bills, or in any of the Numbered Documents, or in any instruction issued by the Architect under the Conditions, or in any drawings or documents issued by the Architect under clause 5·3·1·1 or 5·4 or 7, to be for the approval of the Architect, the particular quality or standard was to the reasonable satisfaction of the Architect, but such Certificate shall not be conclusive evidence that such or any other materials or goods or workmanship comply or complies with any other requirement or term of this Contract, and

    ·1   ·2   conclusive evidence that any necessary effect has been given to all the terms of this Contract which require that an amount is to be added to or deducted from the Contract Sum or an adjustment is to be made of the Contract Sum save where there has been any accidental inclusion or exclusion of any work, materials, goods or figure in any computation or any arithmetical error in any computation, in which event the Final Certificate shall have effect as conclusive evidence as to all other computations, and

    ·1   ·3   conclusive evidence that all and only such extensions of time, if any, as are due under clause 25 have been given, and

    ·1   ·4   conclusive evidence that the reimbursement of direct loss and/or expense, if any, to the Contractor pursuant to clause 26·1 is in final settlement of all and any claims which the Contractor has or may have arising out of the occurrence of any of the matters referred to in clause 26·2 whether such claim be for breach of contract, duty of care, statutory duty or otherwise.

30·9 ·2   If any adjudication, arbitration or other proceedings have been commenced by either Party before the Final Certificate has been issued the Final Certificate shall have effect as conclusive evidence as provided in clause 30·9·1 after either

    ·2   ·1   such proceedings have been concluded, whereupon the Final Certificate shall be subject to the terms of any decision, award or judgment in or settlement of such proceedings, or

·2 ·2 a period of 12 months after the issue of the Final Certificate during which neither Party has taken any further step in such proceedings, whereupon the Final Certificate shall be subject to any terms agreed in partial settlement,

whichever shall be the earlier.

30·9 ·3 If any adjudication, arbitration or other proceedings have been commenced by either Party within 28 days after the Final Certificate has been issued, the Final Certificate shall have effect as conclusive evidence as provided in clause 30·9·1 save only in respect of all matters to which those proceedings relate.

30·9 ·4 Where pursuant to clause 41A·7·1 either Party wishes to have a dispute or difference on which an Adjudicator has given his decision on a date which is after the date of issue of the Final Certificate finally determined by arbitration or legal proceedings, either Party may commence arbitration or legal proceedings within 28 days of the date on which the Adjudicator gave his decision.

30·10 Save as aforesaid no certificate of the Architect shall of itself be conclusive evidence that

30·10 ·1 any works, materials or goods

or

30·10 ·2 any Performance Specified Work

to which it relates are in accordance with this Contract.

34.07 The contractor is permitted to submit an application to the Quantity Surveyor stating what he considers to be the gross valuation of the works (Clause 30.1.2.2). It should be noted that the architect must issue interim certificates irrespective of whether there has been any such application.

34.08 Under Clause 30.1.4 the contractor is entitled to suspend the performance of *all* his obligations under the contract for non-payment by the employer (and not just the obligation to perform the works). Thus, for example, the contractor may suspend his insurance cover. The implications of doing so should be brought to the employer's notice.

Amounts due in interim certificates

34.09 The amount to be included in interim certificates is defined by Clauses 30.2.1 and 30.2.2, which deal with matters which are and are not subject to retention respectively. The principal item in Clause 30.2.1 is the total value of work properly executed by the contractor (Clause 30.2.1.1). This means that the amounts certified should take into account adjustments for variation, price fluctuations, and defects. RIBA Publications Ltd publish forms of interim certificate and direction, and a statement of retention. Clause 30.2.1.1 now includes provisions for where a Price Statement is accepted, and further that the prices to be used in the valuation should be ascertained from a priced Activity Schedule (if one is used).

34.10 Clause 30.2.2 deals with matters which are not subject to retention. Broadly, retention is to be deducted where the contractor has some responsibility for the matters in question so that the employer's interests have to be protected by making the deduction. There will be no retention in instances where the employer's interests do not require such protection: thus, for example, amounts of direct loss and/or expense payable to the contractor and included in interim certificates are not subject to retention (see Clause 30.2.2.1).

Valuation of off-site materials

34.11 Clause 30.3 deals with certification in respect of prefabricated goods and materials not on site. If goods and materials are not on the site, the employer has less protection in the event of the contractor's insolvency and certain other circumstances than if they are on the site.

34.12 The JCT98 introduces a substantially revised procedure for certifying off-site goods. In essence, if the employer wishes to pay for goods before their delivery to site, he must list those goods and attach the list to the Contract Bills ('the listed items'). The contractor must then fulfil certain conditions if he desires to be paid for those goods in interim valuations:

1 If the goods are 'uniquely identified listed items' (e.g. a boiler from a specified supplier) then the contractor must provide reasonable proof to the architect that the property has vested in him, and (if so stated in the Appendix) provide a bond from a surety.
2 If the goods are 'listed items which are not uniquely identified' (e.g. a quantity of bricks) then the contractor must provide reasonable proof to the architect that the property has vested in him, and further *must* provide a bond from a surety. The listed items must be in accordance with the contract.

34.13 The contract also requires that the items, if off-site, should be set apart or visibly individually marked (Clause 30.3.4), should identify the employer (Clause 30.3.4.1) and the destination (as the works) (Clause 30.3.4.2).

34.14 The contractor should supply reasonable proof that the listed items are insured against Specified Perils for the period from the transfer of property to the contractor to their delivery to the works.

34.15 As to what constitutes 'reasonable proof':

1 Where the listed items are purchased from a supplier by the contractor, the contractor should provide the architect with

(i) a copy of the contract of sale; (ii) a statement from the supplier that all pre-conditions in the contract relating to the passing of title to the contractor have been fulfilled; and (iii) a statement from the supplier that the supplier's property in the listed items is not subject to any charge or encumbrance which would prevent the passing of property unconditionally to the contractor.

2   Where the listed items are purchased from a supplier by a sub-contractor, the contractor should provide the architect with (i) a copy of the sub-contract with the sub-contractor stating the conditions required to be fulfilled before the property passes from the sub-contractor to the contractor; and (ii) a written statement from the sub-contractor that those conditions have been fulfilled.

3   Where the listed items are manufactured or assembled by a sub-contractor, the contractor should provide the architect with (i) a copy of the sub-contract with the sub-contractor stating the conditions required to be fulfilled before the property passes from the sub-contractor to the contractor; and (ii) a written statement from the sub-contractor that those conditions have been fulfilled.

Set-off

34.16 If the employer proposes to make a deduction he must follow the statutory notice procedure: see paragraph 34.04 above.

Retention

34.17 The purpose of retention is to provide the employer with security for the contractor's due performance of his obligations in relation to the quality of the work. The percentage of retention is 5% unless the parties have agreed a lesser rate for work which has not reached practical completion (Clause 30.4.1.1), and half of that on work which has reached practical completion. When the certificate of making good defects is issued, it has the effect of releasing the retention in respect of the works or that part of them to which that certificate relates.

Rules on treatment of retention

34.18 Under Clause 30.5.1, the employer holds the retention monies on trust for the contractor and any nominated sub-contractor. In *Wates Construction Limited v Franthom Property Limited* [1991] 53 BLR 23, CA, it was held that Clause 30.5.1 had the effect of requiring the employer to place the retention monies in a separate bank account if so required. The intention is that the retention money should, in effect, be set aside as a separate fund to be used only for the purpose of providing the employer with security against the making good of defects, and the purpose of making the employer a trustee is to protect the retention money against his liquidation. If no actual separate fund is set up, in the event of the employer's liquidation there will be no effective trust, and therefore the contractor will have to prove for his retention monies along with the general creditors (see *MacJordan Construction Limited v Brookmount Erostin Limited* [1992] BCLC 350, CA) so it is important to ensure that the exercise of setting up a separate fund is carried out. If the employer fails to do this the court will grant a mandatory injunction enforcing the obligation before liquidation, but the Court of Appeal considered that it would be unlikely to do so after liquidation, as to do so might constitute a preference under the Insolvency Act 1986. If the case involved a solvent employer but an insolvent contractor, and the employer had failed in his contractual obligation to set the retention monies aside, the court would treat the fund as having been set aside to prevent the employer relying on his breach of contract. However, the court will not grant an injunction compelling the employer to set aside the retention money in a separate fund where the employer has a claim against the contractor for a greater amount (see *Henry Boot Building Ltd v The Croydon Hotel and Leisure Co Ltd* [1985] 36 BLR 41).

34.19 In *Re Arthur Sanders Limited* [1981] 17 BLR 125, it was held that where the contractor had gone into liquidation, its liquidator was entitled to recover from the employer a sum representing the amount of retention due to a nominated sub-contractor notwithstanding that the liquidator conceded that the employer was entitled to withhold that part of the retention which related to the value of the contractor's own work. The reason given in that case by the employer for withholding the retention was that the contractor owed the employer money in respect of damages sustained by the employer as a result of the contractor's default on another contract. It is, however, doubtful that the employer is entitled to withhold retention money due to a contractor on the grounds that the employer has a claim against the contractor in relation to some other contract, since the employer's right to retention monies is restricted to claims arising out of the failure by the contractor to execute correctly the work covered by the contract in question (see *National Westminster Bank v Halesowen Pressworks and Assemblies Limited* [1972] AC 785).

Final adjustment of contract sum

34.20 Clause 30.6 provides a detailed guide as to how the final account is to be prepared. Subject to the architect's decision on matters of principle, this will be prepared by the quantity surveyor.

Final adjustment of sub-contract sum

34.21 Clause 30.7 relates to the final adjustment or ascertainment of all nominated sub-contract sums. This must be carried out not less than 28 days before the date of issue of the final certificate.

Final certificate

34.22 The responsibility for issuing this certificate is a heavy one, and the architect should not issue it unless he is satisfied that the contract has been fully complied with. It must be issued within 2 months of the latest of the following events:

1   The end of the defects liability period
2   The issue of the Certificate of Completion of making good defects under Clause 17.4
3   The date upon which the architect sent a copy of any ascertainment to which Clause 30.6.1.2.1 refers and of the statement prepared in compliance with Clause 30.6.1.2.2.

The form of the final certificate is governed by Clauses 30.8.1.1, 30.8.1.2 and 30.8.1.3. Note that the final certificate may show a balance in favour of the employer if monies have been overpaid in earlier certificates. It is not necessary to hold back payment from earlier certificates merely to keep something in reserve for the purposes of the final certificate, although it is often considered prudent. RIBA Publications Ltd publish a form of Final Certificate.

34.23 Again various notice provisions are required to be followed by the employer if he wishes to withhold any sums (Clauses 30.8.2 and 30.8.3). There is a right to interest in the event of late payment (Clause 30.8.5).

Effect of final certificate

34.24 The final certificate is not merely the last certificate; it is, if properly issued in accordance with the contract, a document of considerable legal importance. Subject to certain qualifications, it is conclusive evidence of the following matters:

1   Where the quality of materials or the standards of workmanship are to be to the reasonable satisfaction of the architect, they are to his reasonable satisfaction, but it is not conclusive evidence

that the materials or goods or workmanship comply with any other contractual requirement (Clause 30.9.1.1).

2 All the terms of the contract which require an adjustment to be made of the contract sum have been complied with (Clause 30.9.1.2).

3 All and only such extensions of time as are due under Clause 25 have been given (Clause 30.9.1.3).

4 The reimbursement of direct loss and/or expense, if any, to the contractor pursuant to Clause 26.1 is in final settlement of all claims arising out of the matters referred to in Clause 26.2 (Clause 30.9.1.4).

34.25 In summary the qualifications are:

1 Where proceedings have been commenced by either party before the issue of the final certificate, the conclusiveness of the certificate becomes limited as set out in Clause 30.9.2.

2 Where proceedings have been commenced by either party within 28 days after its issue, the final certificate is then conclusive save only in respect of all matters to which the proceedings relate (see Clause 30.9.3).

3 Fraud (Clause 30.9.1).

4 Accidental inclusion or exclusion of items or arithmetical error (Clause 30.9.1.2).

34.26 In JCT 98 Clause 30.9.1.1 limits those matters upon which the architect's opinion of reasonable satisfaction is conclusive evidence to *only* those items which are *expressly* stated to be to the architect's reasonable satisfaction.

34.27 Clause 30.9.3 provides that if any arbitration, adjudication or other proceedings have been commenced within 28 days of the issue of the Final Certificate, then the Final Certificate has effect in respect of all matters save for those which are subject to the proceedings. Clause 30.9.4 provides that where the parties received an adjudicator's decision after the issue of the Final Certificate, and now wish the subject matter of the decision to be litigated or arbitrated, then either party may commence proceedings within 28 days of that decision. It does not mention the evidential effect of the Final Certificate. It is probably intended to mean that the Final Certificate (as confirmed or amended by the adjudicator's decision) does not have conclusive effect provided that legal or arbitration proceedings are commenced within 28 days after the adjudicator's decision.

35 Clause 31: ICTA 1988 – statutory tax deduction

35.01 The provisions of Clause 31 are of more relevance to accountants than to architects, and do not justify commentary in this chapter.

35.02 There is no Clause 32 or 33 in this contract.

---

31 **Statutory tax deduction scheme**

31·1 In this Condition 'the Act' means the Income and Corporation Taxes Act 1988; 'the Regulations' means the Income Tax (Sub-Contractors in the Construction Industry) Regulations 1993 S.I. No. 743; "'contractor'" means a person who is a contractor for the purposes of the Act and the Regulations; 'evidence' means such evidence as is required by the Regulations to be produced to a 'contractor' for the verification of a 'sub-contractor's' tax certificate; 'statutory deduction' means the deduction referred to in S.559(4) of the Act or such other deduction as may be in force at the relevant time; "'sub-contractor'" means a person who is a sub-contractor for the purposes of the Act and the Regulations; 'tax certificate' is a certificate issuable under S.561 of the Act.

31·2 ·1 Clauses 31·3 to ·9 shall not apply if, in the Appendix, the Employer is stated not to be a 'contractor'.

31·2 ·2 If in the Appendix the words "is a 'contractor'" are deleted, nevertheless if, at any time up to the issue and payment of the Final Certificate, the Employer becomes such a 'contractor', the Employer shall so inform the Contractor and the provisions of clause 31 shall immediately thereupon become operative.

31·3 ·1 Not later than 21 days before the first payment under this Contract is due to the Contractor or after clause 31·2·2 has become operative the Contractor shall:

either

·1 ·1 provide the Employer with the evidence that the Contractor is entitled to be paid without the statutory deduction;

or

·1 ·2 inform the Employer in writing, and send a duplicate copy to the Architect, that he is not entitled to be paid without the statutory deduction.

31·3 ·2 If the Employer is not satisfied with the validity of the evidence submitted in accordance with clause 31·3·1·1, he shall within 14 days of the Contractor submitting such evidence notify the Contractor in writing that he intends to make the statutory deduction from payments due under this Contract to the Contractor who is a 'sub-contractor' and give his reasons for that decision. The Employer shall at the same time comply with clause 31·6·1.

31·4   ·1   Where clause 31·3·1·2 applies, the Contractor shall immediately inform the Employer if he obtains a tax certificate and thereupon clause 31·3·1·1 shall apply.

31·4   ·2   If the period for which the tax certificate has been issued to the Contractor expires before the final payment is made to the Contractor under this Contract the Contractor shall not later than 28 days before the date of expiry:

either

·2   ·1   provide the Employer with evidence that the Contractor from the said date of expiry is entitled to be paid for a further period without the statutory deduction in which case the provisions of clause 31·3·2 shall apply if the Employer is not satisfied with the evidence;

or

·2   ·2   inform the Employer in writing that he will not be entitled to be paid without the statutory deduction after the said date of expiry.

31·4   ·3   The Contractor shall immediately inform the Employer in writing if his current tax certificate is cancelled and give the date of such cancellation.

31·5   The Employer shall, as a 'contractor' in accordance with the Regulations, send promptly to the Inland Revenue any voucher which, in compliance with the Contractor's obligations as a 'sub-contractor' under the Regulations, the Contractor gives to the Employer.

31·6   ·1   If at any time the Employer is of the opinion (whether because of the information given under clause 31·3·1·2 or of the expiry or cancellation of the Contractor's tax certificate or otherwise) that he will be required by the Act to make a statutory deduction from any payment due to be made the Employer shall immediately so notify the Contractor in writing and require the Contractor to state not later than 7 days before each future payment becomes due (or within 10 days of such notification if that is later) the amount to be included in such payment which represents the direct cost to the Contractor and any other person of materials used or to be used in carrying out the Works.

31·6   ·2   Where the Contractor complies with clause 31·6·1 he shall indemnify the Employer against loss or expense caused to the Employer by any incorrect statement of the amount of direct cost referred to in clause 31·6·1.

31·6   ·3   Where the Contractor does not comply with clause 31·6·1 the Employer shall be entitled to make a fair estimate of the amount of direct cost referred to in clause 31·6·1.

31·7   Where any error or omission has occurred in calculating or making the statutory deduction the Employer shall correct that error or omission by repayment to, or by deduction from payments to, the Contractor as the case may be subject only to any statutory obligation on the Employer not to make such correction.

31·8   If compliance with clause 31 involves the Employer or the Contractor in not complying with any other of the Conditions, then the provisions of clause 31 shall prevail.

31·9   The relevant procedures applicable under the Contract to the resolution of disputes or differences shall apply to any dispute or difference between the Employer and the Contractor as to the operation of clause 31 except where the Act or the Regulations or any other Act of Parliament or statutory instrument, rule or order made under an Act of Parliament provide for some other method of resolving such dispute or difference.

32   [Number not used]

33   [Number not used]

---

34 Antiquities

34·1 All fossils, antiquities and other objects of interest or value which may be found on the site or in excavating the same during the progress of the Works shall become the property of the Employer and upon discovery of such an object the Contractor shall forthwith:

34·1 ·1 use his best endeavours not to disturb the object and shall cease work if and insofar as the continuance of work would endanger the object or prevent or impede its excavation or its removal;

34·1 ·2 take all steps which may be necessary to preserve the object in the exact position and condition in which it was found; and

34·1 ·3 inform the Architect or the clerk of works of the discovery and precise location of the object.

34·2 The Architect shall issue instructions in regard to what is to be done concerning an object reported by the Contractor under clause 34·1, and (without prejudice to the generality of his power) such instructions may require the Contractor to permit the examination, excavation or removal of the object by a third party. Any such third party shall for the purposes of clause 20 be deemed to be a person for whom the Employer is responsible and not to be a sub-contractor.

34·3 ·1 If in the opinion of the Architect compliance with the provisions of clause 34·1 or with an instruction issued under clause 34·2 has involved the Contractor in direct loss and/or expense for which he would not be reimbursed by a payment made under any other provision of this Contract then the Architect himself shall ascertain or shall instruct the Quantity Surveyor to ascertain the amount of such loss and/or expense.

34·3 ·2 If and to the extent that it is necessary for the ascertainment of such loss and/or expense the Architect shall state in writing to the Contractor what extension of time, if any, has been made under clause 25 in respect of the Relevant Event referred to in clause 25·4·5·1 so far as that clause refers to clause 34.

34·3 ·3 Any amount from time to time so ascertained shall be added to the Contract Sum.

---

36 Clause 34: Antiquities

36.01 The contractor has an obligation to preserve antiquities etc. This may give rise to claimable loss and expense. The words 'direct loss and expense' bear the same meaning as in Clause 26, as to which see the discussion in the notes to that clause.

Part 2 Conditions: Nominated sub-contractors and nominated suppliers

37 Clause 35: Nominated sub-contractors

General introduction

37.01 This clause, which is for use when the architect has reserved to himself the final selection of sub-contractors to supply and fix goods or execute work, is one of the most elaborate in the whole contract. This reflects the importance of nominated sub-contractors in the building industry: frequently work carried out by nominated sub-contractors forms a high proportion of the value of the contract as a whole. They play an especially large role in areas of specialist work in foundation construction and mechanical and electrical services.

37.02 The clause is primarily concerned with the following areas:

1 Ways of nomination
2 Procedure for nomination
3 Payment of nominated sub-contractor
4 Extensions of time
5 Failure to complete nominated sub-contract works and the consequences thereof
6 Practical completion of nominated sub-contract works
7 Final payment to nominated sub-contractor
8 Renomination
9 Determination of employment of nominated sub-contractor.

Ways of nomination

37.03 There are eight ways in which a sub-contractor can be nominated (see Clauses 35.1 and 42.18):

1 By the use of a prime cost sum in the contract bills
2 By naming a sub-contractor in the contract bills
3 By the use of a prime cost sum in any instruction in relation to the expenditure of a provisional sum (except a provisional sum relating to performance specified work) included in the contract bills
4 By naming a sub-contractor in a similar instruction
5 By the use of a prime cost sum in any instruction requiring a variation to be effected (provided that the work is both additional to that in the contract drawings and bills and is of a similar kind to that which the contract bills stated would be supplied and fixed or executed by a nominated sub-contractor)
6 By naming a sub-contractor in a similar instruction
7 By the use of a prime cost sum by agreement with the contractor
8 By naming a sub-contractor by agreement with the contractor.

37.04 Under Clause 35.2 the architect has a discretion to allow the contractor to tender for work which it is proposed should be carried out by a nominated Sub-contractor if 'in the ordinary course of his business' he 'directly carries out works' of the type in question.

Procedure

37.05 There is only been one procedure for nomination of a sub-contractor, which is as follows:

1 The architect sends to all sub-contractors whom he wishes to invite to tender a completed form NSC/T Part 1 (Invitation to Tender), the numbered tender documents, a copy of the Appendix to the main contract as completed and a Form NSC/W (Employer/Nominated Sub-contractor Agreement).
2 The sub-contractor submits a tender on Form NSC/T Part 2 and returns the executed NSC/W.
3 The architect decides which of the tenderers he proposes to nominate and the employer executes the relevant NSC/W and signs as approved the relevant NSC/T Part 2. The architect then issues an instruction to the contractor on NSC/N, the nomination instruction, enclosing with it copies of NSC/T Parts 1 and 2, the numbered tender documents and NSC/W. The architect must also send a copy of NSC/N to the successful tenderer, together with a copy of the completed Appendix for the main contract.

Contractor's right of objection

37.06 The contractor then has a right of 'reasonable objection' to any proposed nominated sub-contractor under Clause 35.5.1. The contractor should not be allowed to use this right so as to endeavour to place himself in a better position for tendering for the work himself under Clause 35.2.

Completion of Agreement

37.07 If the contractor does not object, the contractor must complete in agreement with the Nominated Sub-contractor NSC/T Part 3, and must execute NSC/A with the sub-contractor and send a copy of each to the architect (Clause 35.7).

37.08 If the contractor is unable to comply with the requirements of Clause 35.7 within 10 working days he should notify the architect of either when he expects to have complied (Clause 35.8.1), or that the non-compliance is for other reasons. These may include a discrepancy in documents or any reasons the sub-contractor gives, and should be identified in the Contractor's notice (Clause 35.8.2).

37.09 If Clause 35.8.1 applies then the architect should consult with the contractor to fix a date when the contractor should have complied with Clause 35.7 (Clause 35.9.1). If Clause 35.8.2 applies, the architect should reply to the contractor stating that he does not consider that the matters in the contractor's notice justify non-compliance (in which case the contractor should comply), or that they do, whence the architect should issue further instructions to ensure compliance.

Payment of nominated sub-contractor

37.10 Under Clause 35.13.3, the contractor is obliged to provide the architect with reasonable proof that sums previously certified to the nominated sub-contractor have been paid to him before the issue of the next interim certificate; failure to provide such proof entitles the employer to make direct payment to the sub-contractor of an amount which the contractor has failed to pass on to the nominated sub-contractor. Before the employer does this, however, the architect is obliged to issue a certificate under Clause 35.13.5.1 stating the amount in respect of which the contractor has failed to provide proof of payment to the nominated sub-contractor. This amount is then deducted from money which would otherwise be due to the contractor and paid direct to the nominated sub-contractor (Clause 35.13.5.2). Various limitations on the operation of Clause 35.13.5.2 are set out in Clause 35.13.5.3.

37.11 Architects should ensure that:

1 Nominated sub-contractors are informed of the amount shown as due to them in interim certificates issued to the contractor.
2 Proof is required from the contractor that nominated sub-contractors have been paid sums previously shown as due to them in interim certificates before issuing a new certificate.
3 If necessary, Clause 35.13.5.2 is operated and direct payment made to the nominated sub-contractors concerned.

37.12 Under Clause 35.13.4, the contractor is relieved from the obligation to furnish reasonable proof of payment if this is due to some failure or omission of the nominated sub-contractor.

37.13 Under Clause 35.13.5.3.4, the right to make direct payments ceases on the insolvency of the contractor.

Extensions of time

37.14 Extensions of time for the sub-contract works can only be granted with the consent of the architect under the relevant terms of NSC/C. Clause 35.14.1 makes it clear that the contractor cannot give an extension of time to the sub-contractor on his own without the architect's consent. Under Clause 35.14.2, the architect is obliged to operate the relevant provisions of NSC/C upon receipt of any notice, particulars, estimate and request for extension of time from the contractor or sub-contractor.

Failure to complete nominated sub-contract works

37.15 If the nominated sub-contractor fails to complete the sub-contract works within the sub-contract period or any extended time granted by the contractor with the architect's consent and the architect is satisfied that Clause 35.14 has been properly applied, then the architect must certify this to the contractor (see Clause 35.15.1). This certificate is important since under NSC/C, the contractor will be entitled to damages equivalent to any loss or damage suffered by him as a result of the sub-contractor's failure to complete. It is a condition precedent to the right under NSC/C that a certificate is issued under this clause of the main contract (see *Brightside Kilpatrick Engineering v Mitchell Construction [1973] Limited* [1975] 2 Lloyd's Reports 493).

Practical completion of nominated sub-contract works

37.16 Each nominated sub-contract is the subject of a separate certificate of practical completion under Clause 35.16.

Final payment of nominated sub-contractors

37.17 Where a certificate of practical completion of nominated sub-contract works has been issued, the architect may (and must within 12 months) issue an interim certificate including the amount of the relevant sub-contract sum or ascertained final sub-contract sum as finally adjusted under the relevant provisions of the nominated sub-contract, provided that the sub-contractor has made good defects and provided all documents necessary for the final adjustment of the sub-contract sum to take place (see Clause 35.17).

37.18 This procedure is conditional on Clause 5 of Agreement NSC/W (Employer/Nominated Sub-contractor Agreement) remaining in force unamended. This clause imposes on the nominated sub-contractor an obligation to indemnify the employer against any failure by the nominated sub-contractor to remedy defects which occur between the final payment to the nominated sub-contractor and the issue of the final certificate relating to the work as a whole, and thus protects the employer's rights in the event of the nominated sub-contractor failing to remedy such defects.

37.19 By Clause 35.18 if the nominated sub-contractor fails to remedy such defects, the architect must issue an instruction nominating

Part 2: Nominated Sub-Contractors and Nominated Suppliers

Nominated Sub-Contractors

35 **GENERAL**

35·1 Where

35·1 ·1 in the Contract Bills; or

35·1 ·2 in any instruction of the Architect under clause 13·3 on the expenditure of a provisional sum included in the Contract Bills; or

35·1 ·3 in any instruction of the Architect under clause 13·2 requiring a Variation to the extent, but not further or otherwise,

   ·3 ·1 that it consists of work additional to that shown upon the Contract Drawings and described by or referred to in the Contract Bills and

   ·3 ·2 that any supply and fixing of materials or goods or any execution of work by a Nominated Sub-Contractor in connection with such additional work is of a similar kind to any supply and fixing of materials or the execution of work for which the Contract Bills provided that the Architect would nominate a sub-contractor; or

35·1 ·4 by agreement (which agreement shall not be unreasonably delayed or withheld) between the Contractor and the Architect on behalf of the Employer

the Architect has, whether by the use of a prime cost sum or by naming a sub-contractor, reserved to himself the final selection and approval of the sub-contractor to the Contractor who shall supply and fix any materials or goods or execute work, the sub-contractor so named or to be selected and approved shall be nominated in accordance with the provisions of clause 35 and a sub-contractor so nominated shall be a Nominated Sub-Contractor for all the purposes of this Contract. The provisions of clause 35·1 shall apply notwithstanding the requirement in rule A51 of the Standard Method of Measurement, 7th Edition, for a PC sum to be included in the Bills of Quantities in respect of Nominated Sub-Contractors; where however such sum is included in the Contract Bills the provisions of the aforesaid rule A51 shall apply in respect thereof.

35·2 ·1 Where the Contractor in the ordinary course of his business directly carries out works included in the Contract Bills and to which clause 35 applies, and where items of such works are set out in the Appendix and the Architect is prepared to receive tenders from the Contractor for such items, then the Contractor shall be permitted to tender for the same or any of them but without prejudice to the Employer's right to reject the lowest or any tender. If the Contractor's tender is accepted, he shall not sub-let the work to a Domestic Sub-Contractor without the consent of the Architect. Provided that where an item for which the Architect intends to nominate a sub-contractor is included in Architect's instructions issued under clause 13·3 it shall be deemed for the purposes of clause 35·2·1 to have been included in the Contract Bills and the item of work to which it relates shall likewise be deemed to have been set out in the Appendix.

35·2 ·2 It shall be a condition of any tender accepted under clause 35·2 that clause 13 shall apply in respect of the items of work included in the tender as if for the reference therein to the Contract Drawings and the Contract Bills there were references to the equivalent documents included in or referred to in the tender submitted under clause 35·2.

35·2 ·3 None of the provisions of clause 35 other than clause 35·2 shall apply to works for which a tender of the Contractor is accepted under clause 35·2.

PROCEDURE FOR NOMINATION OF A SUB-CONTRACTOR

35·3 The nomination of a sub-contractor to which clause 35·1 applies shall be effected in accordance with clauses 35·4 to 35·9 inclusive.

35·4   The following documents relating to Nominated Sub-Contractors are issued by the JCT and are referred to in the Conditions and in those documents by the use either of the name or of the identification term:

Name of document	*Identification term*
The Standard Form of Nominated Sub-Contract Tender 1998 Edition which comprises:	NSC/T
Part 1: The Employer's Invitation to Tender to a Sub-Contractor	– Part 1
Part 2: Tender by a Sub-Contractor	– Part 2
Part 3: Particular Conditions (to be agreed by a Contractor and a Sub-Contractor nominated under clause 35·6)	– Part 3
The Standard Form of Articles of Nominated Sub-Contract Agreement between a Contractor and a Nominated Sub-Contractor, 1998 Edition	Agreement NSC/A
The Standard Conditions of Nominated Sub-Contract, 1998 Edition, incorporated by reference into Agreement NSC/A	Conditions NSC/C
The Standard Form of Employer/Nominated Sub-Contractor Agreement, 1998 Edition	Agreement NSC/W
The Standard Form of Nomination Instruction for a Sub-Contractor	Nomination NSC/N

35·5   ·1   No person against whom the Contractor makes a reasonable objection shall be a Nominated Sub-Contractor. The Contractor shall make such reasonable objection in writing at the earliest practicable moment but in any case not later than 7 working days from receipt of the instruction of the Architect under clause 35·6 nominating the sub-contractor.

35·5   ·2   Where such reasonable objection is made the Architect may either issue further instructions to remove the objection so that the Contractor can then comply with clause 35·7 in respect of such nomination instruction or cancel such nomination instruction and issue an instruction either under clause 13·2 omitting the work which was the subject of that nomination instruction or under clause 35·6 nominating another sub-contractor therefor. A copy of any instruction issued under clause 35·5·2 shall be sent by the Architect to the sub-contractor.

35·6   The Architect shall issue an instruction to the Contractor on Nomination NSC/N nominating the sub-contractor which shall be accompanied by:

35·6   ·1   NSC/T Part 1 completed by the Architect and NSC/T Part 2 completed and signed by the sub-contractor and signed by or on behalf of the Employer as 'approved' together with a copy of the numbered tender documents listed in and enclosed with NSC/T Part 1 together with any additional documents and/or amendments thereto as have been approved by the Architect;

35·6   ·2   a copy of the completed Agreement NSC/W entered into between the Employer and the sub-contractor;

35·6   ·3   confirmation of any alterations to the information given in NSC/T Part 1

item 7: obligations or restrictions imposed by the Employer
item 8: order of Works: Employer's requirements
item 9: type and location of access; and

35·6   ·4   a copy of the Principal Contractor's Health and Safety Plan.

A copy of the instruction shall be sent by the Architect to the sub-contractor together with a copy of the completed Appendix for the Main Contract.

35·7   The Contractor shall forthwith upon receipt of such instruction:

35·7   ·1   complete in agreement with the sub-contractor NSC/T Part 3 and have that completed NSC/T Part 3 signed by or on behalf of the Contractor and by or on behalf of the sub-contractor; and

35·7   ·2   execute Agreement NSC/A with the sub-contractor

and thereupon shall send a copy of the completed Agreement NSC/A and of the agreed and signed NSC/T Part 3 (but **not** the other Annexures to Agreement NSC/A) to the Architect.

35·8   If the Contractor, having used his best endeavours, has not, within 10 working days from receipt of such instruction, complied with clause 35·7, the Contractor shall thereupon by a notice in writing inform the Architect

either

35·8   ·1   of the date by which he expects to have complied with clause 35·7

or

35·8   ·2   that the non-compliance is due to other matters identified in the Contractor's notice. [pp]

35·9   Within a reasonable time after receipt of a notice under clause 35·8 the Architect shall:

35·9   ·1   where **clause 35·8·1 applies**, after consultation with the Contractor and so far as he considers it reasonable, fix a later date by which the Contractor shall have complied with clause 35·7;

35·9   2   where **clause 35·8·2 applies**, inform the Contractor in writing

either   that he does not consider that the matters identified in the notice justify non-compliance by the Contractor with such nomination instruction, in which case the Contractor shall comply with clause 35·7 in respect of such nomination instruction

or   that he does consider that the matters identified in the notice justify non-compliance by the Contractor with such nomination instruction, in which case the Architect shall either issue further instructions so that the Contractor can then comply with clause 35·7 in respect of such nomination instruction or cancel such nomination instruction and issue an instruction either under clause 13·2 omitting the work which was the subject of the nomination instruction or under clause 35·6 nominating another sub-contractor therefor. A copy of any instruction issued under clause 35·9·2 shall be sent by the Architect to the sub-contractor.

35·10   [Number not used]

35·11   [Number not used]

35·12   [Number not used]

PAYMENT OF NOMINATED SUB-CONTRACTOR

35·13 ·1   The Architect shall on the issue of each Interim Certificate:

·1 ·1   direct the Contractor as to the amount of each interim or final payment to Nominated Sub-Contractors which is included in the amount stated as due in Interim Certificates and the amount of such interim or final payment shall be computed by the Architect in accordance with the relevant provisions of Conditions NSC/C; and

·1 ·2   forthwith inform each Nominated Sub-Contractor of the amount of any interim or final payment directed in accordance with clause 35·13·1·1.

35·13 ·2   Each payment directed under clause 35·13·1·1 shall be paid by the Contractor by the final date for its payment in accordance with Conditions NSC/C.

35·13 ·3   Before the issue of each Interim Certificate (other than the first Interim Certificate) and of the Final Certificate the Contractor shall provide the Architect with reasonable proof of payment by the Contractor pursuant to clause 35·13·2.

35·13 ·4   If the Contractor is unable to provide the reasonable proof referred to in clause 35·13·3 because of some failure or omission of the Nominated Sub-Contractor to provide any document or other evidence to the Contractor which the Contractor may reasonably require and the Architect is reasonably satisfied that this is the sole reason why reasonable proof is not furnished by the Contractor, the provisions of clause 35·13·5 shall not apply and the provisions of clause 35·13·3 shall be regarded as having been satisfied.

35·13 ·5 ·1   If the Contractor fails to provide reasonable proof under clause 35·13·3, the Architect shall issue a certificate to that effect stating the amount in respect of which the Contractor has failed to provide such proof, and the Architect shall issue a copy of the certificate to the Nominated Sub-Contractor concerned.

·5 ·2   Provided that the Architect has issued the certificate under clause 35·13·5·1, and subject to clause 35·13·5·3, the amount of any future payment otherwise due to the Contractor under this Contract (after deducting any amounts due to the Employer from the Contractor under this Contract) shall be reduced by any amounts due to Nominated Sub-Contractors which the Contractor has failed to discharge (together with the amount of any value added tax which would have been due to the Nominated Sub-Contractors) and the Employer shall himself pay the same to the Nominated Sub-Contractors concerned. Provided that the Employer shall in no circumstances be obliged to pay amounts to Nominated Sub-Contractors in excess of amounts available for reduction as aforesaid.

·5 ·3   The operation of clause 35·13·5·2 shall be subject to the following:

·3 ·1   where the Contractor would otherwise be entitled to payment of an amount stated as due in an Interim Certificate under clause 30, the reduction and payment to the Nominated Sub-Contractors referred to in clause 35·13·5·2 shall be made at the same time as the Employer pays the Contractor any balance due under clause 30 or, if there is no such balance, not later than the expiry of the period of 14 days within which the Contractor would otherwise be entitled to payment;

·3 ·2   where the sum due to the Contractor is the Retention or any part thereof, the reduction and payment to the Nominated Sub-Contractors referred to in clause 35·13·5·2 shall not exceed any part of the Contractor's retention (as defined in clause 30·4·2) which would otherwise be due for payment to the Contractor;

·3 ·3   where the Employer has to pay 2 or more Nominated Sub-Contractors but the amount due or to become due to the Contractor is insufficient to enable the Employer to pay the Nominated Sub-Contractors in full, the Employer shall apply the amount available pro rata to the amounts from time to time remaining undischarged by the Contractor or adopt such other method of apportionment as may appear to the Employer to be fair and reasonable having regard to all the relevant circumstances;

·3 ·4 clause 35·13·5·2 shall cease to have effect absolutely if at the date when the reduction and payment to the Nominated Sub-Contractors referred to in clause 35·13·5·2 would otherwise be made there is in existence

either a Petition which has been presented to the Court for the winding up of the Contractor

or a resolution properly passed for the winding up of the Contractor other than for the purposes of amalgamation or reconstruction

whichever shall have first occurred. [qq]

35·13 ·6 Where, in accordance with clause 2·2 of Agreement NSC/W, the Employer, before the date of the issue of an instruction nominating a sub-contractor, has paid to him an amount in respect of design work and/or materials or goods and/or fabrication which is/ are included in the subject of the sub-contract sum or tender sum:

·6 ·1 the Employer shall send to the Contractor the written statement of the Nominated Sub-Contractor of the amount to be credited to the Contractor, and

·6 ·2 the Employer may make withholdings or deductions up to the amount of such credit from the amounts stated as due to the Contractor in any of the Interim Certificates which include amounts of interim or final payment to the Nominated Sub-Contractor; provided that the amount so withheld or deducted from that stated as due in any one Interim Certificate shall not exceed the amount of payment to the Nominated Sub-Contractor included therein as directed by the Architect.

EXTENSION OF PERIOD OR PERIODS FOR COMPLETION OF NOMINATED SUB-CONTRACT WORKS

35·14 ·1 The Contractor shall not grant to any Nominated Sub-Contractor any extension of the period or periods within which the sub-contract works (or where the sub-contract works are to be completed in parts any part thereof) are to be completed except in accordance with the relevant provisions of Conditions NSC/C which require the written consent of the Architect to any such grant.

35·14 ·2 The Architect shall operate the relevant provisions of Conditions NSC/C upon receiving any notice, particulars and estimate and a request from the Contractor and any Nominated Sub-Contractor for his written consent to an extension of the period or periods for the completion of the sub-contract works or any part thereof as referred to in clause 2·3 of Conditions NSC/C.

FAILURE TO COMPLETE NOMINATED SUB-CONTRACT WORKS

35·15 ·1 If any Nominated Sub-Contractor fails to complete the sub-contract works (or where the sub-contract works are to be completed in parts any part thereof) within the period specified in the Nominated Sub-Contract or within any extended time granted by the Contractor with the written consent of the Architect, and the Contractor so notifies the Architect with a copy to the Nominated Sub-Contractor, then, provided that the Architect is satisfied that clause 35·14 has been properly applied, the Architect shall so certify in writing to the Contractor. Immediately upon the issue of such a certificate the Architect shall send a duplicate thereof to the Nominated Sub-Contractor.

35·15 ·2 The certificate of the Architect under clause 35·15·1 shall be issued not later than 2 months from the date of notification to the Architect that the Nominated Sub-Contractor has failed to complete the sub-contract works or any part thereof.

PRACTICAL COMPLETION OF NOMINATED SUB-CONTRACT WORKS

35·16   When in the opinion of the Architect practical completion of the works executed by a Nominated Sub-Contractor is achieved and the Sub-Contractor has complied sufficiently with clause 5E·5 of Conditions NSC/C he shall forthwith issue a certificate to that effect and practical completion of such works shall be deemed to have taken place on the day named in such certificate, a duplicate copy of which shall be sent by the Architect to the Nominated Sub-Contractor; where clause 18 applies practical completion of works executed by a Nominated Sub-Contractor in a relevant part shall be deemed to have occurred on the relevant date to which clause 18·1 refers and the Architect shall send to the Nominated Sub-Contractor a copy of the written statement which he has issued pursuant to clause 18·1.

EARLY FINAL PAYMENT OF NOMINATED SUB-CONTRACTORS

35·17   Provided clause 5 of Agreement NSC/W remains in force unamended, then at any time after the day named in the certificate issued under clause 35·16 the Architect may, and on the expiry of 12 months from the aforesaid day shall, issue an Interim Certificate the gross valuation for which shall include the amount of the relevant sub-contract sum or ascertained final sub-contract sum as finally adjusted or ascertained under the relevant provisions of Conditions NSC/C; provided always that the Nominated Sub-Contractor:

35·17   ·1   has in the opinion of the Architect and the Contractor remedied any defects, shrinkages or other faults which have appeared and which the Nominated Sub-Contractor is bound to remedy under the Nominated Sub-Contract; and

35·17   ·2   has sent through the Contractor to the Architect or the Quantity Surveyor all documents necessary for the final adjustment of the sub-contract sum or the computation of the ascertained final sub-contract sum referred to in clause 35·17.

35·18   Upon payment by the Contractor by the final date for payment to the Nominated Sub-Contractor ('the original sub-contractor') of the amount certified under clause 35·17 then:

35·18   ·1   ·1   if the original sub-contractor fails to rectify any defect, shrinkage or other fault in the sub-contract works which he is bound to remedy under the Nominated Sub-Contract and which appears before the issue of the Final Certificate under clause 30·8 the Architect shall issue an instruction nominating a person ('the substituted sub-contractor') to carry out such rectification work and all the provisions relating to Nominated Sub-Contractors in clause 35 shall apply to such further nomination;

            ·1   ·2   the Employer shall take such steps as may be reasonable to recover, under the Agreement NSC/W, from the original sub-contractor a sum equal to the sub-contract price of the substituted sub-contractor. The Contractor shall pay or allow to the Employer any difference between the amount so recovered by the Employer and the sub-contract price of the substituted sub-contractor provided that, before the further nomination has been made, the Contractor has agreed (which agreement shall not be unreasonably delayed or withheld) to the sub-contract price to be charged by the substituted sub-contractor.

35·18   ·2   Nothing in clause 35·18 shall override or modify the provisions of clause 35·21.

35·19   Notwithstanding any final payment to a Nominated Sub-Contractor under the provisions of clause 35:

35·19   ·1   until the date of Practical Completion of the Works or the date when the Employer takes possession of the Works, whichever first occurs, the Contractor shall be responsible for loss or damage to the sub-contract works for which a payment to which clause 35·17 refers has been made to the same extent but not further or otherwise than he is responsible for that part of the Works for which a payment as aforesaid has not been made;

35·19   ·2   the provisions of clause 22A or 22B or 22C whichever is applicable shall remain in full force and effect.

POSITION OF EMPLOYER IN RELATION TO NOMINATED SUB-CONTRACTOR

35·20 Neither the existence nor the exercise of the powers in clause 35 nor anything else contained in the Conditions shall render the Employer in any way liable to any Nominated Sub-Contractor except by way and in the terms of the Agreement NSC/W.

CLAUSE 2·1 OF AGREEMENT NSC/W – POSITION OF CONTRACTOR

35·21 The Contractor shall not be responsible to the Employer for:

  ·1 the design of any nominated sub-contract works insofar as such nominated sub-contract works have been designed by a Nominated Sub-Contractor;

  ·2 the selection of the kinds of materials and goods for any nominated sub-contract works insofar as such kinds of materials and goods have been selected by a Nominated Sub-Contractor;

  ·3 the satisfaction of any performance specification or requirement insofar as such performance specification or requirement is included or referred to in the description of any nominated sub-contract works included in or annexed to the numbered tender documents enclosed with any NSC/T Part 1;

  ·4 the provision of any information required to be provided pursuant to Agreement NSC/W in reasonable time so that the Architect can comply with the provisions of clauses 5·4·1 and 5·4·2 in respect thereof.

  Nothing in this clause 35·21 shall affect the obligations of the Contractor under this Contract in regard to the supply of workmanship, materials and goods by a Nominated Sub-Contractor.

RESTRICTIONS IN CONTRACTS OF SALE ETC. – LIMITATION OF LIABILITY OF NOMINATED SUB-CONTRACTORS

35·22 Where any liability of the Nominated Sub-Contractor to the Contractor is limited under the provisions of clause 1·7 of Conditions NSC/C, the liability of the Contractor to the Employer shall be limited to the same extent.

35·23 [Number not used]

CIRCUMSTANCES WHERE RE-NOMINATION NECESSARY

35·24 If in respect of any Nominated Sub-Contract:

35·24 ·1 the Contractor informs the Architect that in the opinion of the Contractor the Nominated Sub-Contractor has made default in respect of any one or more of the matters referred to in clauses 7·1·1·1 to 7·1·1·4 of Conditions NSC/C; and the Contractor has passed to the Architect any observations of the Nominated Sub-Contractor in regard to the matters on which the Contractor considers the Nominated Sub-Contractor is in default; and the Architect is reasonably of the opinion that the Nominated Sub-Contractor has made default; or

35·24 ·2 the Contractor informs the Architect that one of the insolvency events referred to in clause 7·2·1 of Conditions NSC/C *(Insolvency of Nominated Sub-Contractor)* has occurred and **either** that under clause 7·2·3 of the aforesaid Conditions the employment of the Nominated Sub-Contractor has been automatically determined **or** that under clause 7·2·4 of those Conditions the Contractor has an option, with the written consent of the Architect, to determine the employment of the Nominated Sub-Contractor; or

35·24 ·3 the Nominated Sub-Contractor determines his employment under clause 7·7 of Conditions NSC/C; or

35·24   ·4   the Contractor has been required by the Employer to determine the employment of the Nominated Sub-Contractor under clause 7·3 of Conditions NSC/C and has so determined that employment; or

35·24   ·5   work properly executed or materials or goods properly fixed or supplied by the Nominated Sub-Contractor have to be taken down and/or re-executed or re-fixed or re-supplied ('work to be re-executed') as a result of compliance by the Contractor or by any other Nominated Sub-Contractor with any instruction or other exercise of a power of the Architect under clauses 7 or 8·4 or 17·2 or 17·3 and the Nominated Sub-Contractor cannot be required under the Nominated Sub-Contract and does not agree to carry out the work to be re-executed;

then:

35·24   ·6   Where **clause 35·24·1 applies:**

·6   ·1   the Architect shall issue an instruction to the Contractor to give to the Nominated Sub-Contractor the notice specifying the default or defaults to which clause 7·1·1 of Conditions NSC/C refers; and may in that instruction state that the Contractor must obtain a further instruction of the Architect before determining the employment of the Nominated Sub-Contractor under clause 7·1·2 or 7·1·3 of Conditions NSC/C; and

·6   ·2   the Contractor shall inform the Architect whether, following the giving of that notice for which the Architect has issued an instruction under clause 35·24·6·1, the employment of the Nominated Sub-Contractor has been determined by the Contractor under clause 7·1·2 or 7·1·3 of Conditions NSC/C; or where the further instruction referred to in clause 35·24·6·1 has been given by the Architect the Contractor shall confirm that the employment of the Nominated Sub-Contractor has been determined; then

·6   ·3   if the Contractor informs or confirms to the Architect that the employment of the Nominated Sub-Contractor has been so determined the Architect shall make such further nomination of a sub-contractor in accordance with clause 35 as may be necessary to supply and fix the materials or goods or to execute the work and to make good or re-supply or re-execute as necessary any work executed by or any materials or goods supplied by the Nominated Sub-Contractor whose employment has been determined which were not in accordance with the relevant Nominated Sub-Contract.

35·24   ·7   ·1   Where **clause 35·24·2 applies** and the Contractor has an option under clause 7·2·4 of Conditions NSC/C *(Insolvency of Nominated Sub-Contractor)* to determine the employment of the Nominated Sub-Contractor, clause 35·24·7·2 shall apply in respect of the written consent of the Architect to any determination of the employment of the Nominated Sub-Contractor.

·7   ·2   Where

–   the administrator or the administrative receiver of the Nominated Sub-Contractor, or

–   the Nominated Sub-Contractor after making a composition or arrangement with his creditors or, being a company, after making a voluntary arrangement for a composition of debts or a scheme of arrangement approved in accordance with the Companies Act 1985 or the Insolvency Act 1986 or any amendment or re-enactment thereof as the case may be

is, to the reasonable satisfaction of the Contractor and the Architect, prepared and able to continue to carry out the relevant Nominated Sub-Contract and to meet the liabilities thereunder, the Architect may withhold his consent. Where continuation on such terms does not apply the Architect shall give his consent to a determination by the Contractor of the employment of the Nominated Sub-Contractor unless the Employer and the Contractor otherwise agree.

·7   ·3   Where the written consent of the Architect to the determination of the employment of the Nominated Sub-Contractor has been given and the Contractor has determined that employment or where, under clause 7·2·3 of the Conditions NSC/C, the employment of the Nominated Sub-Contractor has been automatically determined the following shall apply. The Architect shall make such further nomination of a sub-contractor in accordance with clause 35 as may be necessary to supply and fix the materials or goods or to execute the work and to make good or re-supply or re-execute as necessary any work executed by or any materials or goods supplied by the Nominated Sub-Contractor whose employment has been determined which were not in accordance with the relevant Nominated Sub-Contract.

·7 ·4 Where **clause 35·24·4 applies** the Architect shall make such further nomination of a sub-contractor in accordance with clause 35 as may be necessary to supply and fix the materials or goods or to execute the work and to make good or re-supply or re-execute as necessary any work executed by or any materials or goods supplied by the Nominated Sub-Contractor whose employment has been determined which were not in accordance with the relevant Nominated Sub-Contract.

35·24 ·8 ·1 Where **clause 35·24·3 applies** the Architect shall make such further nomination of a sub-contractor in accordance with clause 35 as may be necessary to supply and fix the materials or goods or to execute the work and to make good or re-supply or re-execute as necessary any work executed by or any materials or goods supplied by the Nominated Sub-Contractor who has determined his employment which were not in accordance with the relevant Nominated Sub-Contract.

·8 ·2 Where **clause 35·24·5 applies** the Architect shall make such further nomination of a sub-contractor in accordance with clause 35 as may be necessary to carry out the work to be re-executed referred to in clause 35·24·5.

35·24 ·9 The amount properly payable to the Nominated Sub-Contractor under the Nominated Sub-Contract resulting from such further nomination under clause 35·24·6·3 or 35·24·7·3 or 35·24·7·4 shall be included in the amount stated as due in Interim Certificates and added to the Contract Sum. Where clauses 35·24·3 and 35·24·8·1 apply any extra amount, payable by the Employer in respect of the sub-contractor nominated under the further nomination over the price of the Nominated Sub-Contractor who has validly determined his employment under his Nominated Sub-Contract, and where clauses 35·24·5 and 35·24·8·2 apply the amount payable by the Employer, resulting from such further nomination may at the time or any time after such amount is certified in respect of the sub-contractor nominated under the further nomination be deducted by the Employer from monies due or to become due to the Contractor under this Contract or may be recoverable from the Contractor by the Employer as a debt.

35·24 ·10 The Architect shall make the further nomination of a sub-contractor as referred to in clauses 35·24·6·3, 35·24·7, 35·24·8·1 and 35·24·8·2 within a reasonable time, having regard to all the circumstances, after the obligation to make such further nomination has arisen.

DETERMINATION OR DETERMINATION OF EMPLOYMENT OF NOMINATED SUB-CONTRACTOR – ARCHITECT'S INSTRUCTIONS

35·25 The Contractor shall not determine any Nominated Sub-Contract by virtue of any right to which he may be or may become entitled without an instruction from the Architect so to do.

35·26 ·1 Where the employment of the Nominated Sub-Contractor is determined under clauses 7·1 to 7·5 of Conditions NSC/C, the Architect shall provide the Contractor with the information and with the direction in an Interim Certificate to enable the Contractor to comply with clause 7·5·2 of Conditions NSC/C: namely the amount of expenses properly incurred by the Employer and the amount of direct loss and/or damage caused to the Employer by the determination of the employment of the Nominated Sub-Contractor; and shall, pursuant to clause 35·13·1, issue an Interim Certificate which certifies the value of any work executed or goods and materials supplied by the Nominated Sub-Contractor to the extent that such value has not been included in previous Interim Certificates.

35·26 ·2 Where the employment of the Nominated Sub-Contractor is determined under clause 7·7 of Conditions NSC/C and clause 7·8 of those Conditions applies, the Architect shall, pursuant to clause 35·13·1, issue an Interim Certificate which certifies the value of any work executed or goods and materials supplied by the Nominated Sub-Contractor to the extent that such value has not been included in previous Interim Certificates.

a substituted sub-contractor to make them good. This substituted sub-contractor is to be regarded as a nominated sub-contractor.

37.20 The primary liability for defective work, including defective work carried out by nominated sub-contractors, rests with the contractor, but the effect of Clause 35.18 is that the employer agrees with the contractor first to seek to pursue his remedies against the nominated sub-contractor under NSC/W in respect of the failure to make good the defects. Thereafter, the employer is entitled to look to the contractor for reimbursement, provided the contractor has agreed (which agreement is not to be unreasonably withheld) to the sub-contract prices charged by the substituted sub-contractor.

37.21 Under Clause 35.19, notwithstanding any final payment to a nominated sub-contractor, the contractor remains responsible for loss or damage to the sub-contract works until practical completion to the same extent as he was responsible before the payment was made.

Renomination

37.22 Under Clause 27 of the 1963 JCT Form it was held that where a nominated sub-contractor failed to complete his work the employer was under a duty to nominate a new nominated sub-contractor (see *North West Metropolitan Hospital Board v T A Bickerton & Son Limited* [1970] 1 WLR 607). Another case under JCT 63 (*Fairclough Building Limited v Rhuddlan Borough Council* [1985] 30 BLR 26, CA), established that the duty extended to a duty to nominate a new nominated sub-contractor to carry out any necessary remedial work to the sub-contract works. The contractor is entitled to an extension of time if the renomination does not match the original programme. This remains the position under the 1998 JCT Form. Renomination must be made within a reasonable time (Clause 35.24.10).

37.23 The duty to renominate may arise in five circumstances:

1 Where the architect is reasonably of the opinion that the sub-contractor has made default, following the contractor informing him that in the contractor's opinion the nominated sub-contractor has made default in respect of any one or more of the matters referred to in Clauses 7.1.1.1–4 of NSC/C and passing on to the architect any observations of the sub-contractor in regard to the matters in question (Clause 35.24.1).
2 Where one of the insolvency events in Clause 7.2.1 of NSC/C has happened to the nominated sub-contractor (see Clause 35.24.2).
3 Where the nominated sub-contractor has determined his employment under Clause 7.7 of NSC/C (Clause 35.24.3).
4 Where the contractor has been required by the employer to determine the employment of the sub-contractor under Clause 7.3 of NSC/C and has done so (Clause 35.24.4).
5 Where work, etc. properly executed has to be re-executed as a result of compliance with an instruction by the architect under Clauses 7, 8.4, 17.2 or 17.3 and the nominated sub-contractor cannot be required to carry out the work under the sub-contract and does not agree to do so (Clause 35.24.5).

37.24 Where (1) above applies, prior to determination, provision is made by Clause 35.24.6 for the following procedure to be adopted: the architect first instructs the contractor to give a notice to the sub-contractor specifying the default. The architect may instruct the contractor to include in that notice a statement that the contractor requires a further instruction of the architect before determining the sub-contractor's employment. Then the contractor informs the architect whether he has determined the sub-contractor's employment; where the further instruction from the architect is required and has been given, the contractor is to confirm that the employment of the sub-contractor has been determined. Thereafter, the architect is obliged to nominate a new sub-contractor. Where the sub-contractor's employment has been determined for failure to

remove defective work or to remedy defects, the contractor is to be given the opportunity to agree a price to be charged by the substituted sub-contractor.

37.25 The contractor is not entitled to determine a nominated sub-contractor's employment under Clause 35.24.1 for default without an architect's instruction, and the procedure for determining a nominated sub-contractor's employment is as laid down in Clause 35.24. Architects must be careful to ensure that where it is sought to determine the sub-contractor's employment under Clause 35.24.1, they fully investigate the circumstances before issuing an instruction to determine the sub-contractor's employment. In particular, they must ensure that they receive all representations which the sub-contractor wishes to make as to his alleged default. Where the sub-contractor's employment is determined, the architect must make clear to the contractor which amounts included in the amount stated as due in an interim certificate are due in respect of the value of work executed or materials or goods supplied by the nominated sub-contractor.

37.26 Clause 7.5.2 of NSC/C entitles the architect to certify in respect of the amount of expenses properly incurred by the employer and the amount of direct loss and/or damage caused to the employer by the determination of the sub-contract. When the sub-contractor's employment is determined, the employer is entitled to deduct from sums otherwise payable to the sub-contractor the amount of any damage suffered by him. The contractor is obliged by this provision to give effect to this deduction.

37.27 Where (2) above applies and there has not been an automatic termination of the sub-contractor's employment, the architect is obliged to nominate a new sub-contractor only if he consents to the determination of the employment of the insolvent nominated sub-contractor. Clause 35.24.7 provides for circumstances in which the architect's consent may be withheld and the option to determine the contract consequently not exercised. This clearly may be advantageous in some circumstances.

37.28 Where (3) above applies, the architect is to nominate a new sub-contractor, but the extra cost of employing the new sub-contractor is to be deducted from money otherwise payable to the contractor.

38 Clause 36: Nominated suppliers

38.01 There are four ways in which a supplier may be nominated, as set out in Clauses 36.1.1.1–4. The first three (Clauses 36.1.1.1–3) all have as their hallmark the inclusion of a prime cost or provisional sum in the bills. The fourth, contained in Clause 36.1.1.4, deals with the situation where a variation occurs and the architect specifies materials or goods for which there is a sole supplier, in which case those goods are to be made the subject of a prime cost sum, and the sole supplier is deemed to have been nominated as a nominated supplier by the architect. Clause 36.1.2 makes it clear that apart from this situation, no nominated supplier situation arises unless goods are the subject of a prime cost sum, even though there is a 'sole supplier' as defined by Clause 36.1.1.3.

Clause 36.1.1.3: Sole supplier

38.02 The meaning of these words is unclear: In the case of proprietary goods produced by a single manufacturer the matter is straightforward. In other cases there may be more difficulty. How far afield must the contractor look for supplies? England? The European Union? Where there is more than one supplier, it would presumably be a question of fact and degree as to whether the contractor could obtain the material in question from only one of those suppliers. The number of suppliers, their physical proximity to the work, and the lead time for delivery would be factors in deciding whether there is a sole supplier for the purposes of this clause.

Nominated Suppliers

36·1 ·1 In the Conditions 'Nominated Supplier' means a supplier to the Contractor who is nominated by the Architect in one of the following ways to supply materials or goods which are to be fixed by the Contractor:

·1 ·1 where a prime cost sum is included in the Contract Bills in respect of those materials or goods and the supplier is either named in the Contract Bills or subsequently named by the Architect in an instruction issued under clause 36·2;

·1 ·2 where a provisional sum is included in the Contract Bills and in any instruction by the Architect in regard to the expenditure of such sum the supply of materials or goods is made the subject of a prime cost sum and the supplier is named by the Architect in that instruction or in an instruction issued under clause 36·2;

·1 ·3 where a provisional sum is included in the Contract Bills and in any instruction by the Architect in regard to the expenditure of such a sum materials or goods are specified for which there is a sole source of supply in that there is only one supplier from whom the Contractor can obtain them, in which case the supply of materials or goods shall be made the subject of a prime cost sum in the instructions issued by the Architect in regard to the expenditure of the provisional sum and the sole supplier shall be deemed to have been nominated by the Architect;

·1 ·4 where the Architect requires under clause 13·2, or subsequently sanctions, a Variation and specifies materials or goods for which there is a sole supplier as referred to in clause 36·1·1·3, in which case the supply of the materials or goods shall be made the subject of a prime cost sum in the instruction or written sanction issued by the Architect under clause 13·2 and the sole supplier shall be deemed to have been nominated by the Architect.

36·1 ·2 In the Conditions the expression 'Nominated Supplier' shall not apply to a supplier of materials or goods which are specified in the Contract Bills to be fixed by the Contractor unless such materials or goods are the subject of a prime cost sum in the Contract Bills, notwithstanding that the supplier has been named in the Contract Bills or that there is a sole supplier of such materials or goods as defined in clause 36·1·1·3.

36·2 The Architect shall issue instructions for the purpose of nominating a supplier for any materials or goods in respect of which a prime cost sum is included in the Contract Bills or arises under clause 36·1.

36·3 ·1 For the purposes of clause 30·6·2·8 the amounts 'properly chargeable to the Employer in accordance with the nomination instruction of the Architect' shall include the total amount paid or payable in respect of the materials or goods less any discount other than the discount referred to in clause 36·4·4, properly so chargeable to the Employer and shall include where applicable:

·1 ·1 any tax (other than any value added tax which is treated, or is capable of being treated, as input tax (as referred to in the Finance Act 1972) by the Contractor) or duty not otherwise recoverable under this Contract by whomsoever payable which is payable under or by virtue of any Act of Parliament on the import, purchase, sale, appropriation, processing, alteration, adapting for sale or use of the materials or goods to be supplied; and

·1 ·2 the net cost of appropriate packing, carriage and delivery after allowing for any credit for return of any packing to the supplier; and

·1 ·3 the amount of any price adjustment properly paid or payable to, or allowed or allowable by, the supplier less any discount other than a cash discount for payment in full within 30 days of the end of the month during which delivery is made.

36·3 ·2 Where in the opinion of the Architect the Contractor properly incurs expense, which would not be reimbursed under clause 36·3·1 or otherwise under this Contract, in obtaining the materials or goods from the Nominated Supplier such expense shall be added to the Contract Sum.

36·4   Save where the Architect and the Contractor shall otherwise agree, the Architect shall only nominate as a supplier a person who will enter into a contract of sale with the Contractor which provides, inter alia:

36·4   ·1   that the materials or goods to be supplied shall be of the quality and standard specified provided that where and to the extent that approval of the quality of materials or of the standards of workmanship is a matter for the opinion of the Architect such quality and standards shall be to the reasonable satisfaction of the Architect;

36·4   ·2   that the Nominated Supplier shall make good by replacement or otherwise any defects in the materials or goods supplied which appear up to and including the last day of the Defects Liability Period under this Contract and shall bear any expenses reasonably incurred by the Contractor as a direct consequence of such defects provided that:

   ·2   ·1   where the materials or goods have been used or fixed such defects are not such that reasonable examination by the Contractor ought to have revealed them before using or fixing;

   ·2   ·2   such defects are due solely to defective workmanship or material in the materials or goods supplied and shall not have been caused by improper storage by the Contractor or by misuse or by any act or neglect of either the Contractor, the Architect or the Employer or by any person or persons for whom they may be responsible or by any other person for whom the Nominated Supplier is not responsible;

36·4   ·3   that delivery of the materials or goods supplied shall be commenced, carried out and completed in accordance with a delivery programme to be agreed between the Contractor and the Nominated Supplier including, to the extent agreed, the following grounds on which that programme may be varied:

   force majeure; or

   civil commotion, local combination of workmen, strike or lock-out; or

   any instruction of the Architect under clause 13·2 *(Variations)* or clause 13·3 *(provisional sums)*; or

   failure of the Architect to supply to the Nominated Supplier within due time any necessary information for which he has specifically applied in writing on a date which was neither unreasonably distant from nor unreasonably close to the date on which it was necessary for him to receive the same; or

   exceptionally adverse weather conditions

   or, if no such programme is agreed, delivery shall be commenced, carried out and completed in accordance with the reasonable directions of the Contractor;

36·4   ·4   that the Nominated Supplier shall allow the Contractor a discount for cash of 5 per cent on all payments if the Contractor makes payment in full within 30 days of the end of the month during which delivery is made;

36·4   ·5   that the Nominated Supplier shall not be obliged to make any delivery of materials or goods (except any which may have been paid for in full less only any discount for cash) after the determination (for any reason) of the Contractor's employment under this Contract;

36·4   ·6   that full discharge by the Contractor in respect of payments for materials or goods supplied by the Nominated Supplier shall be effected within 30 days of the end of the month during which delivery is made less only a discount for cash of 5 per cent if so paid;

36·4   ·7   that the ownership of materials or goods shall pass to the Contractor upon delivery by the Nominated Supplier to or to the order of the Contractor, whether or not payment has been made in full;

36·4   ·8   that if any dispute or difference between the Contractor and the Nominated Supplier is referred to arbitration the provisions of clause 41B shall apply;

36·4 ·9 that no provision in the contract of sale shall override, modify or affect in any way whatsoever the provisions in the contract of sale which are included therein to give effect to clauses 36·4·1 to 36·4·9 inclusive.

36·5 ·1 Subject to clauses 36·5·2 and 36·5·3, where the said contract of sale between the Contractor and the Nominated Supplier in any way restricts, limits or excludes the liability of the Nominated Supplier to the Contractor in respect of materials or goods supplied or to be supplied, and the Architect has specifically approved in writing the said restrictions, limitations or exclusions, the liability of the Contractor to the Employer in respect of the said materials or goods shall be restricted, limited or excluded to the same extent.

36·5 ·2 The Contractor shall not be obliged to enter into a contract with the Nominated Supplier until the Architect has specifically approved in writing the said restrictions, limitations or exclusions.

36·5 ·3 Nothing in clause 36·5 shall be construed as enabling the Architect to nominate a supplier otherwise than in accordance with the provisions stated in clause 36·4.

38.03 Clause 36.3 lays down rules for ascertaining the amount to be set against prime cost sums in respect of nominated suppliers' materials. In addition, under Clause 36.3.2, the contractor is entitled to recover expenses properly incurred and which he would not have incurred had he not obtained the materials or goods from the nominated supplier. This would include, for example, extra travelling costs in the case where a supplier is nominated whose distance from the works was more than an alternative source of supply of the same or similar materials.

Terms of nominated supplier's contracts

38.04 Under Clause 36.4, the architect is not (save by agreement with the contractor) to nominate a supplier whose terms of sale do not conform to certain criteria. These cover such matters as standard of materials, replacement of defective materials, delivery times, discount, passing of property on delivery, and submission to the arbitration provisions in Clause 41B of the contract.

Contractor's liability for goods supplied by nominated supplier

38.05 Nomination itself ordinarily shows that there has been no reliance on the contractor's skill and judgement so that the contractor is not liable if the goods of the nominated supplier of good quality are unfit for their intended purpose. In addition, Clause 36.5.1 expressly exempts the contractor from liability to the employer in respect of defects in goods supplied by a nominated supplier to the extent that the contract between the contractor and the nominated supplier contains similar exemptions, provided that the exemptions have been specifically approved by the architect. Even without such a provision it is unlikely that the contractor would be held responsible to the employer if the goods supplied by the nominated supplier failed to answer to their purpose (see *Young and Marten v McManus Childs* [1968] 2 All ER 1181). The employer's interests vis-à-vis the nominated supplier are to be protected by the direct warranty Tender TNS/1. It is therefore of the utmost importance that the architect should ensure that this form of direct warranty is entered into in all cases where nominated suppliers are involved.

Part 3 Conditions: Fluctuations

39 Clauses 37 to 40

39.01 Clause 37.1 identifies three different bases, namely those set out in Clauses 38, 39, and 40, by reference to which fluctuations are to be calculated. Clause 37.2 provides that Clause 38 shall apply where neither Clause 39 nor 40 is identified in the Appendix.

39.02 Clause 38 allows fluctuations in prices arising from changes in the matters specified in Clause 38.1.1, namely rates of contribution, levy, or tax payable by the contractor. These cover such matters as national insurance contributions. VAT is dealt with specifically by the VAT agreement and is not within Clause 38. Apart from changes in tax rates, no other price changes are taken into account where the parties contract on the basis that fluctuations are to be governed by Clause 38.

39.03 Clause 39 and Clause 40 both provide for what are known as 'full' fluctuations entitling the contractor to recover extra costs of labour and materials as from a date specified in the contract. The system under Clause 39 is as follows:

39.04 In respect of labour costs, extra costs as a result of awards by the National Joint Council for the Building Industry are recoverable – this also applies to reimbursement of travelling charges (see Clause 39.1.5).

39.05 Tax increases are recoverable under Clause 38. JCT Practice Note 17 gives guidance on the choice of fluctuations provisions. NJCC Procedure Note 7 contains information about Clauses 38.7 and 39.8.

39.06 Material increases are recoverable based on the increases over a price list to be submitted by the contractor and attached to the contract bills current at the date of tender. This forms a list of basic prices, and if an increase above the basic prices occurs, the contractor is entitled to reimbursement.

39.07 Under Clause 40, adjustment of prices takes place in accordance with the formula rules issued by the JCT, using those current at the date of tender. Monthly bulletins are issued by the JCT giving details of price changes, and the contract sum falls to be adjusted in accordance with these.

Fluctuations where contractor is guilty of delay

39.08 In principle, the contractor is not entitled to price increases under the fluctuations clauses where these price increases arise during a period after the contractual completion date: this provides an added incentive to the contractor to meet the completion date. This is subject, however, to no amendments having been made to Clause 25, and to the architect having, in respect of every written notification by the contractor under Clause 25, fixed or confirmed in writing a completion date in accordance with that clause (see Clause 38.4.8, Clause 39.5.8, and Clause 40.7.2). It is therefore incumbent on the architect to ensure that Clause 25 is properly administered, and that no amendments have been made to Clause 25, or alternatively that the appropriate parts of the fluctuations clauses are amended so as to delete the provision removing the 'freeze' on fluctuations if Clause 25 is amended.

Part 4 Conditions: Settlement of disputes – adjudication – arbitration – litigation

40   Clauses 41A, 41B, 41C

40.01 There has been a change in direction of both the attitude and practicality of litigating the JCT contract.

40.02 The key development is the mandatory imposition of the Housing Grants, Construction and Regeneration Act 1996 into almost all construction contracts. This introduced a third forum for disputes: that of adjudication. The intention of the Act was to enable disputes arising during the course of the contract to be temporarily determined by an adjudicator, pending final review by the courts or in arbitration. This has broadly succeeded.

The overruling of *Northern Regional Health Authority v Derek Crouch Construction Co Ltd* [1984] QB 644 by the House of Lords in *Beaufort Developments Limited v Gilbert-Ash (Northern Ireland) Limited* [1998] 88 BLR 1 has allowed parties to challenge decisions and interim certificates of the architect in other than in arbitral proceedings. The parties now have a tactical choice to litigate or arbitrate.

40.03 The full scope of the adjudication, arbitration and litigation processes are dealt with elsewhere in this book. The below is really an overview of these complementary and developing areas.

Clause 41A: Adjudication

40.04 Clause 41A provides the procedural rules governing a dispute referred to adjudication under Article 5. Unless the parties agree to extend the period or the referring party consents to allowing the adjudicator an extra 14 days, the adjudicator has 28 days from the date that the dispute is referred to him to provide a decision to the parties. The adjudicator's decision is not final although, in practice, the decision of the adjudicator is difficult to challenge. In *Macob Civil Engineering v Morrison Construction* [1999] 3 BLR 93 it was held that even if there is a challenge to the validity or correctness of an adjudicator's decision, in general the decision is binding and enforceable by summary judgement. The judgement must be complied with, even though the substance of the dispute will only be finally resolved in arbitration or other litigation. In *Bouygues UK Ltd v Dahl-Jensen* [2000] BLR 49 it was held that a court will seek to enforce an adjudication even in the event of an obvious flaw in the reasoning of the adjudicator. The position is otherwise if a real doubt is shown concerning whether the adjudicator's decision was within his jurisdiction. In this event summary enforcement of the adjudicator's decision will not be granted: *Project Consultancy Group v Trustees of the Gray Trust* [1999] 65 Con LR 146.

By starting court proceedings a party does not waive the right to an adjudication. However, although a court will generally grant summary judgement to enforce an adjudication, it may stay the execution if the substantive issues are close to being finally determined in litigation, and there is doubt over the receiving parties ability to repay: *Herschel Engineering Ltd v Breen Property Ltd* [2000] BLR 272. Once there has been a compromise settling any disputes, no further dispute exists that could be referred to adjudication under the Housing Grants, Construction and Regeneration Act

---

Part 3: Fluctuations

37   **·1**   Fluctuations shall be dealt with in accordance with whichever of the following alternatives
clause 38; or
clause 39 [rr]; or
clause 40 [ss]
is identified in the Appendix. The provisions so identified shall be [tt] deemed to be incorporated with the Conditions as executed by the parties hereto.

37   **·2**   Clause 38 shall apply where neither clause 39 nor clause 40 is identified in the Appendix.

37   **·3**   Neither clause 38 nor clause 39 nor clause 40 shall apply in respect of the work for which the Architect has issued to the Contractor a confirmed acceptance of a 13A Quotation or in respect of a Variation to such work.

Clause 38: Contribution, levy and tax fluctuations
Clause 39: Labour and materials cost and tax fluctuations
Clause 40: Use of price adjustment formulae

These clauses are published separately in 'Fluctuations: Fluctuation clauses for use with the Private versions'.

1996 s.108: *Shepherd Construction Ltd v Mecright Ltd* [2000] BLR 489.

Clause 41B: Arbitration

40.05 The parties have a choice whether or not to include the arbitration provisions as part of the agreement between them. Where the employer or the contractor requires a dispute to be referred to arbitration he is to give written notice to the other.

40.06 The award of the arbitrator is final and binding on the parties (Clause 41B.3) subject to rights of appeal on questions of law (Clause 41B.4.2) and applications for determination of questions of law (Clause 41B.4.1) under sections 45(2)(a) and 69(2)(a) of the Arbitration Act 1996.

40.07 Clause 41B.2 sets out the powers of the arbitrator:

1 To rectify the contract
2 To direct measurements and valuations that he thinks desirable in order to determine the rights of the parties
3 To ascertain and award any sum that he thinks should have been included in any certificate
4 To open up, review and revise any certificate, decision, opinion, requirement or notice
5 To determine all matters in dispute submitted to him.

40.08 It should be noted that the above powers of the arbitrator are subject to the provisions concerning the effect of the final certificate.

Clause 41C: Litigation

40.09 The parties have an unfettered choice under the contract to dispense with arbitration altogether, and apply straight to the Courts. This is a tactical decision to be made by the parties at a very early stage in the contractual process. Litigation has certain advantages over arbitration:

1 Cases are heard by judges with considerable experience of construction litigation, usually in the Technology and Construction Court.
2 Judges have a full range of preliminary remedies available to them, e.g. the power to grant injunctions.
3 Questions of law and fact may be appealed directly to the Court of Appeal.
4 Apart from standard Court fees no further fees are payable. 5 Co-defendants and third parties may be joined in the same action.

40.10 Against this arbitration offers flexibility in the way that the matters are to be decided and (unless there is an appeal to the Court) privacy. However, architects should be slow to advise their clients to litigation before exploring other avenues of dispute resolution. In *Paul Thomas Construction Ltd v Hyland* [2002] 18 Const LJ 345 the Claimant started proceedings after refusing to participate in adjudication and generally not co-operating. Indemnity costs were awarded against the Claimant.

Part 5 Conditions: Performance specified work

41 Clause 42

41.01 Performance specified work must be identified as such in the Appendix, and will normally comprise materials and components or assemblies of a kind or standard to satisfy design requirements given in the tender documents for the contract, for example trussed rafters or pre-cast concrete floor units. The provisions for

performance specified work should not be used for items which will materially affect the appearance of the building or which may result in changes in the design of other work (except at the point of interface with the performance specified work), or which will affect the use of the finished building, so that it would be essential to examine and accept the contractor's proposals for the work before acceptance of the tender. Performance specified work may not be provided by a nominated sub-contractor or by a nominated supplier.

41.02 The architect will prepare or direct the preparation of documents showing or describing the requirements for the components or assemblies comprised in the performance specified work, and these documents, which should include enough information for the tenderer to include or allow for the price or rates for the item if required to do so, will be included in the tender documents for the main contract. The contractor may then tender for the performance specified work. There may be either a firm price or a provisional sum (Clause 42.1.4).

Contractor's statement

41.03 The contractor will be required to provide the architect with a statement at the time stated in the contract bills, including information in drawn, diagrammatic or scheduled form and with calculations as required, more particularly showing or describing the performance specified work as the contractor intends to carry it out (Clause 42.2). The architect may require this statement to be amended by written notice if it is in his opinion deficient in form or detail, or if it contains a deficiency which would adversely affect the performance required by the employer from that work.

41.04 The architect must issue instructions necessary for the integration of the performance specified work within the works under Clause 42.14 within a reasonable time before the contractor intends to carry out the work.

41.05 The contractor's price for the work will be adjustable in the event of variation of the work by the architect (see Clause 13.5.6), a correction under Clause 2.2.2.2, a change in statutory requirements or the application to the work of the fluctuations provisions or Clause 26.

Part 4: Settlement of disputes – adjudication – arbitration – legal proceedings [uu]

41A   Adjudication

41A·1   Clause 41A applies where, pursuant to article 5, either Party refers any dispute or difference arising under this Contract to adjudication.

41A·2   The Adjudicator to decide the dispute or difference shall be either an individual agreed by the Parties or, on the application of either Party, an individual to be nominated as the Adjudicator by the person named in the Appendix ('the nominator'). Provided that [vv]

41A·2 ·1   no Adjudicator shall be agreed or nominated under clause 41A·2 or clause 41A·3 who will not execute the Standard Agreement for the appointment of an Adjudicator issued by the JCT (the 'JCT Adjudication Agreement' [ww]) with the Parties, [vv] and

41A·2 ·2   where either Party has given notice of his intention to refer a dispute or difference to adjudication then

– any agreement by the Parties on the appointment of an adjudicator must be reached with the object of securing the appointment of, and the referral of the dispute or difference to, the Adjudicator within 7 days of the date of the notice of intention to refer *(see clause 41A·4·1)*;

– any application to the nominator must be made with the object of securing the appointment of, and the referral of the dispute or difference to, the Adjudicator within 7 days of the date of the notice of intention to refer.

Upon agreement by the Parties on the appointment of the Adjudicator or upon receipt by the Parties from the nominator of the name of the nominated Adjudicator the Parties shall thereupon execute with the Adjudicator the JCT Adjudication Agreement.

41A·3   If the Adjudicator dies or becomes ill or is unavailable for some other cause and is thus unable to adjudicate on a dispute or difference referred to him, the Parties may either agree upon an individual to replace the Adjudicator or either Party may apply to the nominator for the nomination of an adjudicator to adjudicate that dispute or difference; and the Parties shall execute the JCT Adjudication Agreement with the agreed or nominated Adjudicator.

41A·4 ·1   When pursuant to article 5 a Party requires a dispute or difference to be referred to adjudication then that Party shall give notice to the other Party of his intention to refer the dispute or difference, briefly identified in the notice, to adjudication. If an Adjudicator is agreed or appointed within 7 days of the notice then the Party giving the notice shall refer the dispute or difference to the Adjudicator ('the referral') within 7 days of the notice. If an Adjudicator is not agreed or appointed within 7 days of the notice the referral shall be made immediately on such agreement or appointment. The said Party shall include with that referral particulars of the dispute or difference together with a summary of the contentions on which he relies, a statement of the relief or remedy which is sought and any material he wishes the Adjudicator to consider. The referral and its accompanying documentation shall be copied simultaneously to the other Party.

41A·4 ·2 The referral by a Party with its accompanying documentation to the Adjudicator and the copies thereof to be provided to the other Party shall be given by actual delivery or by FAX or by special delivery or recorded delivery. If given by FAX then, for record purposes, the referral and its accompanying documentation must forthwith be sent by first class post or given by actual delivery. If sent by special delivery or recorded delivery the referral and its accompanying documentation shall, subject to proof to the contrary, be deemed to have been received 48 hours after the date of posting subject to the exclusion of Sundays and any Public Holiday.

41A·5 ·1 The Adjudicator shall immediately upon receipt of the referral and its accompanying documentation confirm the date of that receipt to the Parties.

41A·5 ·2 The Party not making the referral may, by the same means stated in clause 41A·4·2, send to the Adjudicator within 7 days of the date of the referral, with a copy to the other Party, a written statement of the contentions on which he relies and any material he wishes the Adjudicator to consider.

41A·5 ·3 The Adjudicator shall within 28 days of the referral under clause 41A·4·1 and acting as an Adjudicator for the purposes of S.108 of the Housing Grants, Construction and Regeneration Act 1996 and not as an expert or an arbitrator reach his decision and forthwith send that decision in writing to the Parties. Provided that the Party who has made the referral may consent to allowing the Adjudicator to extend the period of 28 days by up to 14 days; and that by agreement between the Parties after the referral has been made a longer period than 28 days may be notified jointly by the Parties to the Adjudicator within which to reach his decision.

41A·5 ·4 The Adjudicator shall not be obliged to give reasons for his decision.

41A·5 ·5 In reaching his decision the Adjudicator shall act impartially and set his own procedure; and at his absolute discretion may take the initiative in ascertaining the facts and the law as he considers necessary in respect of the referral which may include the following:

·5 ·1 using his own knowledge and/or experience;

·5 ·2 opening up, reviewing and revising any certificate, opinion, decision, requirement or notice issued, given or made under the Contract as if no such certificate, opinion, decision, requirement or notice had been issued, given or made;

·5 ·3 requiring from the Parties further information than that contained in the notice of referral and its accompanying documentation or in any written statement provided by the Parties including the results of any tests that have been made or of any opening up;

·5 ·4 requiring the Parties to carry out tests or additional tests or to open up work or further open up work;

·5 ·5 visiting the site of the Works or any workshop where work is being or has been prepared for the Contract;

·5 ·6 obtaining such information as he considers necessary from any employee or representative of the Parties provided that before obtaining information from an employee of a Party he has given prior notice to that Party;

·5 ·7 obtaining from others such information and advice as he considers necessary on technical and on legal matters subject to giving prior notice to the Parties together with a statement or estimate of the cost involved;

·5 ·8 having regard to any term of the Contract relating to the payment of interest, deciding the circumstances in which or the period for which a simple rate of interest shall be paid.

41A·5 ·6 Any failure by either Party to enter into the JCT Adjudication Agreement or to comply with any requirement of the Adjudicator under clause 41A·5·5 or with any provision in or requirement under clause 41A shall not invalidate the decision of the Adjudicator.

41A·5 ·7 The Parties shall meet their own costs of the adjudication except that the Adjudicator may direct as to who should pay the cost of any test or opening up if required pursuant to clause 41A·5·5·4.

41A·6 ·1   The Adjudicator in his decision shall state how payment of his fee and reasonable expenses is to be apportioned as between the Parties. In default of such statement the Parties shall bear the cost of the Adjudicator's fee and reasonable expenses in equal proportions.

41A·6 ·2   The Parties shall be jointly and severally liable to the Adjudicator for his fee and for all expenses reasonably incurred by the Adjudicator pursuant to the adjudication.

41A·7 ·1   The decision of the Adjudicator shall be binding on the Parties until the dispute or difference is finally determined by arbitration or by legal proceedings [xx] or by an agreement in writing between the Parties made after the decision of the Adjudicator has been given.

41A·7 ·2   The Parties shall, without prejudice to their other rights under the Contract, comply with the decision of the Adjudicator; and the Employer and the Contractor shall ensure that the decision of the Adjudicator is given effect.

41A·7 ·3   If either Party does not comply with the decision of the Adjudicator the other Party shall be entitled to take legal proceedings to secure such compliance pending any final determination of the referred dispute or difference pursuant to clause 41A·7·1.

41A·8   The Adjudicator shall not be liable for anything done or omitted in the discharge or purported discharge of his functions as Adjudicator unless the act or omission is in bad faith and this protection from liability shall similarly extend to any employee or agent of the Adjudicator.

41B   Arbitration

A reference in clause 41B to a Rule or Rules is a reference to the JCT 1998 edition of the Construction Industry Model Arbitration Rules (CIMAR) current at the Base Date.

41B·1 ·1   Where pursuant to article 7A either Party requires a dispute or difference to be referred to arbitration then that Party shall serve on the other Party a notice of arbitration to such effect in accordance with Rule 2.1 which states:

> "Arbitral proceedings are begun in respect of a dispute when one party serves on the other a written notice of arbitration identifying the dispute and requiring him to agree to the appointment of an arbitrator";

and an arbitrator shall be an individual agreed by the Parties or appointed by the person named in the Appendix in accordance with Rule 2.3 which states:

> "If the parties fail to agree on the name of an arbitrator within 14 days (or any agreed extension) after:
> (i)   the notice of arbitration is served, or
> (ii)   a previously appointed arbitrator ceases to hold office for any reason,
> either party may apply for the appointment of an arbitrator to the person so empowered."

By Rule 2.5:

> "the arbitrator's appointment takes effect upon his agreement to act or his appointment under Rule 2.3, whether or not his terms have been accepted."

41B·1 ·2   Where two or more related arbitral proceedings in respect of the Works fall under separate arbitration agreements, Rules 2.6, 2.7 and 2.8 shall apply thereto.

41B·1 ·3   After an arbitrator has been appointed either Party may give a further notice of arbitration to the other Party and to the Arbitrator referring any other dispute which falls under article 7A to be decided in the arbitral proceedings and Rule 3.3 shall apply thereto.

41B·2 Subject to the provisions of article 7A and clause 30·9 the Arbitrator shall, without prejudice to the generality of his powers, have power to rectify this Contract so that it accurately reflects the true agreement made by the Parties, to direct such measurements and/or valuations as may in his opinion be desirable in order to determine the rights of the Parties and to ascertain and award any sum which ought to have been the subject of or included in any certificate and to open up, review and revise any certificate, opinion, decision, requirement or notice and to determine all matters in dispute which shall be submitted to him in the same manner as if no such certificate, opinion, decision, requirement or notice had been given.

41B·3 Subject to clause 41B·4 the award of such Arbitrator shall be final and binding on the Parties.

41B·4 The Parties hereby agree pursuant to S. 45(2)(a) and S. 69(2)(a) of the Arbitration Act 1996 that either Party may (upon notice to the other Party and to the Arbitrator):

41B·4 ·1 apply to the courts to determine any question of law arising in the course of the reference; and

41B·4 ·2 appeal to the courts on any question of law arising out of an award made in an arbitration under this Arbitration Agreement.

41B·5 The provisions of the Arbitration Act 1996 or any amendment thereof shall apply to any arbitration under this Contract wherever the same, or any part of it, shall be conducted. [yy]

41B·6 The arbitration shall be conducted in accordance with the JCT 1998 edition of the Construction Industry Model Arbitration Rules (CIMAR) current at the Base Date. Provided that if any amendments to the Rules so current have been issued by the JCT after the Base Date the Parties may, by a joint notice in writing to the Arbitrator, state that they wish the arbitration to be conducted in accordance with the Rules as so amended.

41C **Legal proceedings**

41C·1 Where article 7B applies any dispute or difference shall be determined by legal proceedings pursuant to article 7B.

Part 5: Performance Specified Work [zz]

42·1   The term 'Performance Specified Work' means work:

42·1   ·1   identified in the Appendix, and

42·1   ·2   which is to be provided by the Contractor, and

42·1   ·3   for which certain requirements have been predetermined and are shown on the Contract Drawings, and

42·1   ·4   in respect of which the performance which the Employer requires from such work and which the Contractor, by this Contract and subject to the Conditions, is required to achieve has been stated in the Contract Bills and these Bills have included

either   information relating thereto sufficient to have enabled the Contractor to price such Performance Specified Work
or   a provisional sum in respect of the Performance Specified Work together with the information relating thereto as referred to in clause 42·7.

42·2   Before carrying out any Performance Specified Work, the Contractor shall provide the Architect with a document or set of documents, referred to in these Conditions as the 'Contractor's Statement'. Before so providing the Contractor shall have referred the draft of such Statement to the Planning Supervisor and shall have made such amendments, if any, as may have been necessary to take account of the comments of the Planning Supervisor. Subject to the Conditions the Contractor shall carry out the Performance Specified Work in accordance with that Statement.

42·3   The Contractor's Statement shall be sufficient in form and detail adequately to explain the Contractor's proposals for the execution of the Performance Specified Work. It shall include any information which is required to be included therein by the Contract Bills or, where there is a provisional sum for the Performance Specified Work, by the instruction of the Architect on the expenditure of that sum; and may include information in drawn or scheduled form and a statement of calculations; and, if applicable, shall be provided in reasonable time so that the Architect can provide the information, drawings and details as he is required to provide pursuant to clauses 5·4·1 and 5·4·2.

42·4   The Contractor's Statement shall be provided to the Architect:
   – by any date for its provision given in the Contract Bills or
   – by any reasonable date for its provision given in the instruction by the Architect on the expenditure of a provisional sum for Performance Specified Work.
   If no such date is given it shall be provided at a reasonable time before the Contractor intends to carry out the Performance Specified Work.

42·5   Within 14 days after receipt of the Contractor's Statement the Architect may, if he is of the opinion that such Statement is deficient in form and/or detail adequately to explain the Contractor's proposals for the execution of the Performance Specified Work, by notice in writing require the Contractor to amend such Statement so that it is in the opinion of the Architect not deficient. A copy of the Statement as so amended shall be provided to the Architect. Whether or not an amendment is required by the Architect, the Contractor is responsible in accordance with the Conditions for any deficiency in such Statement and for the Performance Specified Work to which such Statement refers.

42·6   If the Architect shall find anything in the Contractor's Statement which appears to the Architect to be a deficiency which would adversely affect the performance required by the Employer from the relevant Performance Specified Work, he shall immediately give notice to the Contractor specifying the deficiency. Whether or not a notice is given by the Architect, the Contractor is responsible in accordance with the Conditions for the Performance Specified Work.

42·7   A provisional sum for Performance Specified Work means a sum provided in the Contract Bills for Performance Specified Work where the following information has been provided in the Contract Bills:

42·7 ·1 the performance which the Employer requires from such work;

42·7 ·2 the location of such Performance Specified Work in the building;

42·7 ·3 information relating thereto sufficient to have enabled the Contractor to have made due allowance in programming for the execution of such Performance Specified Work and for pricing all preliminary items relevant to such Performance Specified Work.

42·8 No instruction of the Architect pursuant to clause 13·3·1 on the expenditure of provisional sums included in the Contract Bills shall require Performance Specified Work except an instruction on the expenditure of a provisional sum included in the Contract Bills for Performance Specified Work.

42·9 The inclusion of Performance Specified Work in the Contract Bills shall not be regarded as a departure from the method of preparation of these Bills referred to in clause 2·2·2·1.

42·10 If in the Contract Bills there is any error or omission in the information which, pursuant to clause 42·7·2 and/or 42·7·3, is to be included in the Contract Bills in respect of a provisional sum for Performance Specified Work such error or omission shall be corrected so that it does provide such information; and any such correction shall be treated as if it were a Variation required by an instruction of the Architect under clause 13·2.

42·11 Subject to clause 42·12 the Architect may issue instructions under clause 13·2 requiring a Variation to Performance Specified Work.

42·12 No instruction of the Architect under clause 13·2 may require as a Variation the provision by the Contractor of Performance Specified Work additional to that which has been identified in the Appendix unless the Employer and the Contractor otherwise agree.

42·13 Where the Contract Bills do not provide an analysis of the portion of the Contract Sum which relates to any Performance Specified Work the Contractor shall provide such an analysis ('the Analysis') within 14 days of being required to do so by the Architect.

42·14 The Architect shall, within a reasonable time before the Contractor intends to carry out the Performance Specified Work, give any instructions necessary for the integration of such Performance Specified Work with the design of the Works. The Contractor shall, subject to clause 42·15, comply with any such instruction.

42·15 If the Contractor is of the opinion that compliance with any instruction of the Architect injuriously affects the efficacy of the Performance Specified Work, he shall within 7 days of receipt of the relevant instruction specify by notice in writing to the Architect such injurious affection. Except where the Architect amends the instruction to remove such injurious affection, the instruction shall not have effect without the written consent of the Contractor which consent shall not be unreasonably withheld or delayed.

42·16 Except for any extension of time in respect of the Relevant Event stated in clause 25·4·15 an extension of time shall not be given under clause 25·3 and clauses 26·1 and 28·2·2 shall not have effect where and to the extent that the cause of the progress of the Works having been delayed, affected or suspended is that the Architect has not received the Contractor's Statement by the time referred to in clause 42·4 or any amendment to the Contractor's Statement pursuant to clause 42·5.

42·17 ·1 The Contractor shall exercise reasonable skill and care in the provision of Performance Specified Work provided that:

·1 ·1 clause 42·17 shall not be construed so as to affect the obligations of the Contractor under this Contract in regard to the supply of workmanship, materials and goods; and

·1 ·2 nothing in this Contract shall operate as a guarantee of fitness for purpose of the Performance Specified Work.

42·17 ·2 The Contractor's obligation under clause 42·17·1 shall in no way be modified by any service in respect of any Performance Specified Work which he has obtained from others and, in particular, the Contractor shall be responsible for any such service as if such services had been undertaken by the Contractor himself.

42·18 Performance Specified Work pursuant to clause 42 shall not be provided by a Nominated Sub-Contractor under a Nominated Sub-Contract or by a Nominated Supplier under a contract of sale to which clause 36 refers.

42 Appendix

42.01 Architects should ensure that the Appendix is completed. It is not unknown for this to be overlooked. Care should be taken to follow the format and instructions. In *Temloc v Errill Properties* [1987] 39 BLR 30 an entry of the word 'nil' was made in respect of the liquidated and ascertained damages. Did this mean that there were to be no damages for delay payable at all, no matter how late completion? Or did it mean that damages for delay were not to be at a pre-agreed rate, but were left to be assessed, if they arose, on normal common law principles, namely to compensate for any actual loss which could be proved? The Court of Appeal held that it meant there were to be no damages for delay at all. Obviously, parties should try to avoid creating uncertainties of that character.

Appendix

Subject	
Statutory tax deduction scheme	Employer at Base Date *is a 'contractor'/is not a 'contractor' for the purposes of the Act and the Regulations
CDM Regulations	*All the CDM Regulations apply/ Regulations 7 and 13 only of the CDM Regulations apply
Dispute or difference – settlement of disputes	*Clause 41B applies *Delete if disputes are to be decided by legal proceedings and article 7B is thus to apply *See the Guidance Note to JCT 80 Amendment 18 on factors to be taken into account by the Parties considering whether disputes are to be decided by arbitration or by legal proceedings*
Base Date	_____
Date for Completion	_____
Electronic data interchange	The JCT Supplemental Provisions for EDI *apply/do not apply If applicable: the EDI Agreement to which the Supplemental Provisions refer is: *the EDI Association Standard EDI Agreement *the European Model EDI Agreement
VAT Agreement	Clause 1A of the VAT Agreement *applies/does not apply [x]
Defects Liability Period (if none other stated is 6 months from the day named in the certificate of Practical Completion of the Works)	_____
Assignment by Employer of benefits after Practical Completion	Clause 19·1·2 *applies/does not apply
Insurance cover for any one occurrence or series of occurrences arising out of one event	£ _____

Clause etc.	Subject	
21·2·1	Insurance – liability of Employer	Insurance *may be required/is not required Amount of indemnity for any one occurrence or series of occurrences arising out of one event £ _____ [aaa]
22·1	Insurance of the Works – alternative clauses	*Clause 22A/Clause 22B/Clause 22C applies (See footnote [cc] to clause 22)
*22A, 22B·1, 22C·2	Percentage to cover professional fees	_____
22A·3·1	Annual renewal date of insurance as supplied by Contractor	_____
22D	Insurance for Employer's loss of liquidated damages – clause 25·4·3	Insurance *may be required/is not required
22D·2	Period of time	_____
22FC·1	Joint Fire Code	The Joint Fire Code *applies/does not apply If the Joint Fire Code is applicable, state whether the insurer under clause 22A or clause 22B or clause 22C·2 has specified that the Works are a 'Large Project': *YES/NO (where clause 22A applies these entries are made on information supplied by the Contractor)
23·1·1	Date of Possession	_____
23·1·2, 25·4·13, 26·1	Deferment of the Date of Possession	Clause 23·1·2 *applies/does not apply Period of deferment if it is to be less than 6 weeks is _____
24·2	Liquidated and ascertained damages	at the rate of £ _____ per _____
28·2·2	Period of suspension (if none stated is 1 month)	_____
28A·1·1·1 to 28A·1·1·3	Period of suspension (if none stated is 3 months)	_____
28A·1·1·4 to 28A·1·1·6	Period of suspension (if none stated is 1 month)	_____

Clause etc.	*Subject*	
30·1·1·6	Advance payment	Clause 30·1·1·6 *applies/does not apply If applicable: the advance payment will be **£ _____ / _____ % of the Contract Sum and will be paid to the Contractor on _____ and will be reimbursed to the Employer in the following amount(s) and at the following time(s) _____ _____ _____ An advance payment bond *is/is not required _____
30·1·3	Period of Interim Certificates (if none stated is 1 month)	
30·2·1·1	Gross valuation	A priced Activity Schedule *is/is not attached to this Appendix
30·3·1	Listed items – uniquely identified	*For uniquely identified listed items a bond as referred to in clause 30·3·1 in respect of payment for such items is required for £ _____ *Delete if no bond is required
30·3·2	Listed items – not uniquely identified	*For listed items that are not uniquely identified a bond as referred to in clause 30·3·2 in respect of payment for such items is required for £ _____ *Delete if clause 30·3·2 does not apply
30·4·1·1	Retention Percentage (if less than 5 per cent) [bbb]	_____
35·2	Work reserved for Nominated Sub-Contractors for which the Contractor desires to tender	_____
37	Fluctuations: (if alternative required is not shown clause 38 shall apply)	clause 38 [ccc] clause 39 clause 40

SPECIMEN COPY

Clause etc.	Subject	
38·7 or 39·8	Percentage addition	————————————————————
40·1·1·1	Formula Rules	rule 3: Base Month
		———————————————— 19 ————
		rules 10 and 30 (i): Part I/Part II [ddd] of Section 2 of the Formula Rules is to apply
41A·2	Adjudication – nominator of Adjudicator (if no nominator is selected the nominator shall be the President or a Vice-President of the Royal Institute of British Architects)	President or a Vice-President or Chairman or a Vice-Chairman: *Royal Institute of British Architects *Royal Institution of Chartered Surveyors *Construction Confederation *National Specialist Contractors Council *Delete all but one
41B·1	Arbitration – appointor of Arbitrator (if no appointor is selected the appointor shall be the President or a Vice-President of the Royal Institute of British Architects)	President or a Vice-President: *Royal Institute of British Architects *Royal Institution of Chartered Surveyors *Chartered Institute of Arbitrators *Delete all but one
42·1·1	Performance Specified Work	Identify below or on a separate sheet each item of Performance Specified Work to be provided by the Contractor and insert the relevant reference in the Contract Bills [zz]

10

Other standard forms of building contract

ALEXANDER HICKEY

1 Introduction

1.01 This chapter discusses standard forms of building contract other than the Joint Contracts Tribunal (JCT) 98 Standard Form of Contract (reproduced with a commentary in Chapter 9). The extensive family of JCT standard Form Contracts has already been introduced in Chapter 8, each of which is suited to a slightly different situation. As well as the JCT family of forms, there are a number of standard forms issued by other bodies such as the Association of Consultant Architects (ACA) and the Institution of Civil Engineers (ICE). All of these forms are regularly amended, sometimes several times a year: it is sometimes difficult for ordinary practitioners involved in the construction industry to keep up with the issue of the various supplementary amendments. Fortunately there was a general overhaul of most of the standard forms to incorporate all the existing updates when they were reissued in 1998, brought about by the need to incorporate the adjudication and payment provisions required by the Housing Grants, Construction and Regeneration Act 1996. Since then, however, the amendments have continued to flow. There have been five general amendments since then which affect the JCT suite of forms, including the following forms WCD 98, IFC 98, MC 98 and NSC 98 and MW 98 which are discussed below. The general amendments are

- Amendment 1: Construction Industry Scheme (CIS) (June 1999)
- Amendment 2: Sundry Amendments (January 2000)
- Amendment 3: Terrorism cover/Joint Fire Cost/CIS (January 2001)
- Amendment 4: Extension of time/Loss and expense/Advance payment (January 2002)
- Amendment 5: Construction Skills Certification Scheme (July 2003)

although there are some minor differences between the forms as to the scope of Amendment 4: for example, MC 98 only amends the extension of time provisions, whereas MW 98 makes various amendments to dispute resolution, defects liability progress payments and deduction notices as well as attestation. None of these amendments merits any particular discussion in this chapter. However, Amendment 2 is notable because it excludes the operation of the Contract (Right of Third Parties) Act 1999. In addition some interesting new forms have been introduced.

1.02 It is beyond the scope of this book to provide a commentary on every standard form or to set out the various amendments that have been made. Instead this chapter give a brief summary of the more important forms in use in the marketplace and to introduce some new forms, namely JCT Domestic Subcontract, 2002, JCT Building Contract for a Homeowner/Occupier 1999 and the radical new JCT Major Projects Form 2003. It is possible that the last of these forms marks the start of a trend for future standard forms.

Will the JCT follow suit in future editions of the other forms in order to reduce the length, complexity and technicality of the contract forms? This 'less is more' approach will certainly require a change in habits and a leap of faith by those in the industry used to the traditional type of standard form contract that JCT 98 exemplifies.

1.03 This chapter begins with an examination of nominated sub-contracting because it is so closely connected with JCT 98 that an understanding of the main contract without a serious assessment of nominated sub-contracting would be thoroughly incomplete. Furthermore, an understanding of this most important scheme of employer-controlled sub-contracting, provides a useful grounding when confronted with sub-contracts issued for use under other forms of contract.

2 JCT documents for entering into nominated sub-contracts

2.01 For many years the standard form of sub-contract was a document published by the NFBTE and FASS known as 'the green form'. It was intended for use when the Main Contract was in the JCT 1963 standard form. In 1980 the JCT for the first time published its own documents for nominated sub-contracts. This comprised documents labelled NSC/1, NSC/2 and 2a, NSC/3 and NSC/4. They provided two alternative procedures known as 'the basic method' and 'the alternative method'. Many users found these documents exceedingly complicated. In 1991 the JCT reviewed the nominated sub-contracts documents with a view to their simplification. As a result JCT published a new set of documents: the two previous procedures were replaced by a single method known as 'the 1991 method'. See the discussion at section 37 of Chapter 9.

2.02 For the purpose of this family of JCT documents a nominated sub-contractor has a definition, which is contained in Clause 35.1 of the main contract. Where the architect has by the use of a prime cost sum or by naming a sub-contractor reserved to himself the final selection and approval of a sub-contractor, that sub-contractor is a 'nominated sub-contractor'.

2.03 A book entitled *Procedure for Nomination of a Sub-Contractor 1998 edition – NSC Specimen Documents* has been published by RIBA Publications for the JCT. This book provides the texts of the NSC documents, other than the Conditions known as NSC/C which are published separately. With the exception of the Conditions, the NSC documents are otherwise available only in the form of multi-copy pads.

The Invitation to Tender NSC/T: Part 1

2.04 The normal first step in the nomination procedure is for the architect to complete the Invitation to Tender form, which is labelled

NSC/T: Part 1, and to send it to the prospective sub-contractors from whom he would be pleased to receive a tender. The architect has to fill in a certain number of details on the form before issuing it. The principal matters are:

- Description and location of the main contract works
- The identity of the main contractor, design team and employer
- Form of main contract, any changes from the printed form
- Earliest and latest starting dates for the sub-contract works
- Certain proposed details of the sub-contract, including attendance items, fluctuations.

The form requests the tendering of a VAT-exclusive price.

2.05 It is intended that the architect should issue information such as drawings, specification, bill of quantities and/or a schedule of rates with this form in order to describe the sub-contract works in sufficient detail to permit a tender to be prepared. He should also issue the Planning Supervisor's health and safety plan, and the Principal Contractor's health and safety plan if it is available (see Chapter 21 on the Construction (Design and Management) Regulations). It is also intended that the architect should send out a copy of the Appendix to the main contract as it has been, or is intended to be, completed. The form anticipates that the sub-contractor will be required to enter into a direct warranty agreement, called the Employer/Nominated Sub-Contractor Agreement which is known as NSC/W (see below).

Tender by a Sub-Contractor NSC/T: Part 2

2.06 This document is provided for the sub-contractor to complete with details of his tender. The form provides for the submission of the following:

- A VAT-exclusive sum
- A schedule of rates
- Daywork percentages, or alternatively a schedule of daywork prices
- Fluctuations basis
- Requirements for general attendance by the main contractor if outside the scope of general attendance
- Earliest and latest starting dates
- Periods required for submission for approval of all necessary sub-contractor drawings
- Period required for the execution of the sub-contract works off- and on-site
- Any special conditions or arrangements required.

2.07 If the sub-contractor does not know the identity of the main contractor when he submits the tender, he is allowed seven days after he discovers the identity of the main contractor in which he may withdraw his tender.

2.08 When the architect and the employer have considered the tenders received from prospective sub-contractors, and have reached a decision on which one to appoint, the architect should arrange for the employer to sign the tender of the chosen sub-contractor as having been approved. The form provides a space for such approval at the very end. Alternatively, the architect may be authorized to sign on behalf of the employer.

2.09 Rather than immediately make the formal nomination, the architect has the alternative option of ordering design work or the fabrication of components from the proposed sub-contractor, provided both sub-contractor and employer have completed the Employer/Nominated Sub-Contractor Agreement NSC/W. That possibility arises because Clause 2.2.1 of NSC/W permits direct employment of the sub-contractor by the employer prior to the issue of the Nomination Instruction.

Nomination Instruction NSC/N

2.10 When it has been decided which sub-contractor to appoint, the architect should prepare this nomination form. It is perfectly possible for all the steps in the NSC procedure up to this point to have been carried out prior to the engagement of a main contractor. But the Nomination Instruction cannot, by its nature, be issued until there is a main contractor to receive it. The form is to be sent to the main contractor together with the completed NSC/T: Part 1, identifying any alterations to it, and NSC/T: Part 2 signed as 'approved', and NSC/W in respect of that sub-contractor. Also enclosed should be the sub-contract tender drawings, specification and bill of quantities together with the Principal Contractor's health and safety plan if it has not already been provided. This form and its enclosures should also be sent directly to the sub-contractor together with a completed copy of the Appendix to the main contract.

2.11 The purpose of NSC/N is to constitute the notice of nomination stipulated by Clause 35.6 of JCT 98. The text to be filled in on NSC/N by the architect amounts to no more than simple details which have already been given on NSC/T Part 1. The main contractor is then required by his own contractual obligations in Clause 35.7 of the JCT 98 main contract, and reminded by the text of NSC/N, to take the following steps:

1 To complete in agreement with the sub-contractor the document known as NSC/T: Part 3, and have the completed document executed by both main contractor and sub-contractor and
2 To execute the Standard Form of Articles of Nominated Sub-Contract Agreement between a contractor and a nominated sub-contractor, known as NSC/A.

The architect should ensure that the main contractor sends him a copy of the completed NSC/T: Part 3 and NSC/A.

2.12 The main contractor is allowed the opportunity to register an objection to the identity of the proposed nominated sub-contractor named on the Nomination Instruction. But it must be a 'reasonable objection', it must be made in writing, and in any event it must be within seven working days of receipt of the Nomination Instruction (Clause 35.5.1 of JCT 98).

Particular Conditions to be Agreed between a Contractor and a Sub-Contractor NSC/T: Part 3

2.13 The procedure places the obligation on the main contractor and the sub-contractor to attempt to agree between themselves on certain matters of some importance which the NSC documents call the 'Particular Conditions'. These matters are the following:

1 Programme details. Once specified, the dates on this document will assume contractual effect. Clause 2.1 of NSC/C states that the sub-contractor shall carry out and complete the works in accordance with these programme details. The components of the programme details are:
    (i) Earliest and latest starting date on site. This is the third occasion that such dates will have been given under the procedure. But on the previous two occasions, that is by the architect on NSC/T Part 1 and by the sub-contractor on NSC/T Part 2, they were indicative only: they had no contractual effect. On this third occasion the dates will have contractual effect.
    (ii) Periods required for submission of all necessary sub-contractor drawings, etc., and for the execution of off-site and on-site works. It is envisaged that a notice will be given to the sub-contractor to commence on-site works, and that the length of this notice period will also be a 'Particular Condition'.
    (iii) Other details and arrangements. If the main contractor and sub-contractor can agree a programme for the sub-contract works, it may be attached.
2 Amount of insurance cover for any one occurrence or series of occurrences arising from one event.
3 VAT regime. There are a number of variants.
4 Any other matters, including special conditions or agreements on employment of labour, limitation of working hours, safety or site security.

5 Changes to information given in NSC/T: Part 1. The employer or architect may have changed their minds since the Invitation to Tender (NSC/T Part 1) about the obligations, the order of the works, the employer's requirements or the type and location of access. Any such alteration should have been specified on an enclosure with the Nomination Instruction NSC/N.

6 Arbitration provisions are to be deleted if final disputes are to be decided by litigation. Appointer of the adjudicator, and if appropriate, the arbitrator, are named. If nobody is named, the default appointer in both cases will be the President of the RICS.

2.14 If the main contractor has not been able to agree the Particular Conditions within 10 days of receipt of the Nomination Instruction, he should report in writing to the architect giving reasons for his non-compliance (Clause 35.8 of the JCT 98). Unless the contractor's notice is merely by way of an application for extension of time, the architect will then have to decide, within a reasonable time, how to break the impasse (JCT 98 Clause 35.9). His options are in effect to decree that the point in question does not matter, or to decree that it does matter and to issue a further instruction to deal with it, or, in a more extreme case, to order omission of the item of work or to nominate another sub-contractor. If he is minded to issue an instruction, he should bear in mind that he has no power to order a proposed subcontractor to do things until that person has signed a contract with either the employer (NSC/W 2.2.1) or the main contractor.

Articles of Nominated Sub-Contract Agreement NSC/A

2.15 This is the formal sub-contract between the contractor and sub-contractor. Its function largely is to identify the other sub-contract documents. It will state, if correctly completed, whether the sectional completion supplement or self-vouchering applies. It will state that the standard Conditions NSC/C are to apply unamended, or, if amended, what the amendments are. The numbered tender documents will be annexures, as will NSC/T: Part 3. It is also prescribed that NSC/T: Parts 1 and 2 will be annexures, but that does not mean that in all cases the proposals in them will have been adopted or will be terms of the contract.

3 The Nominated Sub-Contract Conditions (NSC/C 1998 edition)

3.01 The JCT first published a form of Nominated Sub-Contract conditions in 1980 called NSC/4. There was a variant for use when the nominated sub-contractor had not been nominated by NSC/1, which was labelled NSC/4a. Between 1983 and 1990 there were nine amendments to NSC/4 and NSC/4a. In 1991 the JCT published a revised edition of Nominated Sub-Contract Conditions labelled NSC/C. Whereas NSC/4 had some 38 clauses and was found to be a form of massive complexity, NSC/C, although still lengthy, had the material rearranged into 8 sections. This format has been retained in the current 1998 edition. However, there is an unnecessary confusion through the use of both the term 'Section' and the term 'Clause' in respect of the divisions. Each part of the form is called a 'Section', within which the text is broken down by decimal markings into 1.1, 1.2, etc. Those divisions are called Clause 1.1, Clause 1.2, etc.

Section 1: Intentions of the Parties

3.02 This section begins with definitions. Most are straightforward. An exception, and worthy of mention, are 'Sub-Contract Sum' and 'Tender Sum', which are the two alternative ways of expressing the price in tender documents and the Articles. The reader is referred to Articles in NSC/A, which baldly use the terms without explanation. The difference is as follows. A 'Sub-Contract Sum' is a lump sum price where the price tendered and agreed will be the sum paid, subject to changes by variations. A 'Tender Sum', on the other hand, is the expression used where the contract is on a remeasurement basis: the contractor will be paid according to the work actually done, as ascertained by remeasurement.

3.03 Section 1 attempts two things which any good contract ought to achieve – namely, to identify the sub-contract documents, and to express an order of priority between them, that is to say which is to prevail in the case of inconsistency. By Clause 1.5 the sub-contract documents are listed as NSC/C, NSC/A and the documents annexed to NSC/A. The last-mentioned category includes NSC/T: Parts 1 and 2, which contain proposals which may well be different from the terms on which the parties ultimately settled. Therefore, it is important that the instructions given in the JCT scheme be followed in respect of deleting and altering the text of NSC/T: Part 2 before annexing it to NSC/A. The main contract is given top place in the priority by Clause 1.6, but since this will presumably be JCT 98, there ought not to be any conflict between it and the sub-contract documents. No priority is expressed between drawings and specifications. In the event of conflict between the Sub-Contract Conditions and other subcontract documents, the former prevail.

3.04 Clause 1.9 contains the fundamental obligation of the sub-contractor.

Execution of the Sub-Contract Works – Sub-Contractor's obligations

1.9 ·1 The Sub-Contractor shall carry out and complete the Sub-Contract Works in compliance with the Sub-Contract Documents and in conformity with all reasonable directions and requirements of the Contractor (so far as they may apply) regulating for the time being the due carrying out of the Works.

·2 All materials and goods shall, so far as procurable, be of the kinds and standards described in the Sub-Contract Documents provided that where and to the extent that approval of the quality and standards of materials and goods is a matter for the opinion of the Architect such quality and standards shall be to the reasonable satisfaction of the Architect.

·3 All workmanship shall be of the standards described in the Sub-Contract Documents, or, to the extent that no such standards are described in the Sub-Contract Documents, shall be of a standard appropriate to the Sub-Contract Works provided that where and to the extent that approval of workmanship is a matter for the opinion of the Architect such workmanship shall be to the reasonable satisfaction of the Architect.

·4 All work shall be carried out in a proper and workmanlike manner and in accordance with the Health and Safety Plan.

3.05 Clause 1.13 is one of a number of provisions aimed at overcoming problems which the sub-contractor may face by reason of not having a direct contractual nexus with the employer (except on the limited matters covered by the direct Employer/Nominated Sub-Contractor Agreement NSC/W).

Benefits under Main Contract

1.13 ·1 The Contractor will so far as he lawfully can at the request of the Sub-Contractor obtain for him any rights or benefits of the provisions of the Main Contract so far as the same are applicable to the Sub-Contract Works and not inconsistent with the express terms of the Sub-Contract but not further or otherwise. Any action taken by the Contractor in compliance with any aforesaid request shall be at the cost of the Sub-Contractor and may include the provision by the Sub-Contractor of such indemnity and security as the Contractor may reasonably require.

In *Gordon Durham v Haden Young* [1990] 52 BLR 61 H H Judge Thayne Forbes held that one of the rights under the main contract to which a similarly worded clause in the 'green form' could apply was the power of an arbitrator to open up, review and revise certificates.

Section 2: Commencement and completion

3.06 By Clause 2.1 the sub-contractor's fundamental obligation is to carry out and complete the sub-contract works 'in accordance with the agreed programme details in NSC/T: Part 3 item 1, and reasonably in accordance with the progress of the works'. Often there will be a programme document; and, if there is, it ought to have been referred to in item 1 of NSC/T: Part 3 among the Particular Conditions. But such a programme is not obligatory. If there is no such programme document, the 'programme details' must mean the statement in NSC/T: Part 3 of the period required for on-site works. If there is a programme document, then Clause 2.1 would seem to require the sub-contractor not merely to finish on time, but also to proceed towards completion at the speed and in the manner indicated on the programme. On the other hand, if there is no programme document, the bare obligation in NSC/T: Part 3 is to finish within a stated number of weeks. However, this must be read in the light of Clause 7.1 which gives the Contractor a right to determine the employment of the Sub-Contractor for failure to proceed regularly and diligently. Clause 2.1 specifically refers to the notice to start which is mentioned on the standard form of NSC/T: Part 3 (see above).

3.07 The remainder of this section is concerned with extensions of time. The procedure seems cumbersome, but it has not been easy to think of a simpler one which would meet all the conflicting interests of different parties when works have become delayed. The steps are as follows:

1 The sub-contractor gives written notice to the main contractor of material circumstances including the cause of delay. He must as soon as possible give full particulars of the expected effects and estimate the extent of delay (Clause 2.2).
2 The main contractor must inform the architect of the notice and send on the particulars and estimate (Clause 2.2).
3 The architect forms an opinion whether delay has been caused by either a 'relevant event' or by the default of the main contractor. If he decides that it has, he gives written consent to the contractor to give an extension of time, mentioning the amount of extension he considers fair and reasonable (Clause 2.3). The relevant events are set out in Clause 2.6 (see box).
4 The main contractor is then required to grant an extension of time (Clause 2.3).

The main contractor is prohibited by the terms of the main contract JCT 98 from granting an extension of time to a sub-contractor other than with the written consent of the architect (see Chapter 9, paragraph 37.14). However, in practice it is more likely that the main contractor will try to prevent the sub-contractor obtaining an extension of time, rather than that he will be over-enthusiastic about allowing an extension. For often, when a delay has occurred, the main contractor and sub-contractor will be blaming each other as responsible for it.

2.6 The following are the Relevant Events referred to in clause 2.3.1:

·1 force majeure;

·2 exceptionally adverse weather conditions;

·3 loss or damage occasioned by any one or more of the Specified Perils;

·4 civil commotion, local combination of workmen, strike or lock-out affecting any of the trades employed upon the Works or any of the trades engaged in the preparation, manufacture or transportation of any of the goods or materials required for the Works;

·5 compliance by the Contractor and/or the Sub-Contractor with the Architect's instructions:

·1 under clauses 2.3, 13.2 (except for a confirmed acceptance of a 13A Quotation), 13.3 (except, where bills of quantities are included in the Numbered Documents, compliance with an Architect's instruction for the expenditure of a provisional sum for defined work), 13A.4.1, 23.2, 34, 35, or 36 of the Main Contract Conditions, or

·2 in regard to the opening up for inspection of any work covered up or the testing of any of the work, materials or goods in accordance with clause 8.3 of the Main Contract Conditions (including making good in consequence of such opening up or testing) unless the inspection or test showed that the work, materials or goods were not in accordance with the Main Contract or the Sub-Contract as the case may be;

·6 ·1 where an Information Release schedule has been provided, failure of the Architect to comply with Clause 5.4.1 of the Main Contract Conditions.

·2 failure of the Architect to comply with Clause 5.4.2 of the Main Contract Conditions.

except to the extent that the failure referred to in Clause 2.6.6.1 or Clause 2.6.6.2 results from a breach by the Sub-Contractor of his obligations to the Employer under Clause 3.2 of Agreement NSC/W;

·7 delay on the part of nominated Sub-Contractors (other than the Sub-Contractor) or of nominated suppliers in respect of the Works which the Contractor has taken all practicable steps to avoid or reduce;

·8 ·1 the execution of work not forming part of the Main Contract by the Employer himself or by persons employed or otherwise engaged by the Employer as referred to in Clause 29 of the Main Contract Conditions or the failure to execute such work;

·2 the supply by the Employer of materials and goods which the Employer has agreed to provide for the Works or the failure so to supply;

·9 the exercise after the Base Date by the United Kingdom Government of any statutory power which directly affects the execution of the Works by restricting the availability or use of labour which is essential to the proper carrying out of the Works, or preventing the Contractor or the Sub-Contractor from, or delaying the Contractor or the Sub-Contractor in, securing such goods or materials or such fuel or energy as are essential to the proper carrying out of the Works;

·10 ·1 the Contractor's or the Sub-Contractor's inability for reasons beyond his control and which he could not reasonably have foreseen at the Base Date for the purposes of the Main Contract or the Sub-Contract as the case may be to secure such labour as is essential to the proper carrying out of the Works; or

·2 the Contractor's or the Sub-Contractor's inability for reasons beyond his control and which he could not reasonably have foreseen at the Base Date for the purposes of the Main Contract or the Sub-Contract as the case may be to secure such goods or materials as are essential to the proper carrying out of the Works;

·11 the carrying out by a local authority or statutory undertaker of work in pursuance of its statutory obligations in relation to the Works, or the failure to carry out such work;

·12 failure of the Employer to give in due time ingress to or egress from the site of the Works or any part thereof through or over any land, buildings, way or passage adjoining or connected with the site and in the possession and control of the Employer, in accordance with the Contract Bills and/or the Contract Drawings, after receipt by the Architect of such notice, if any, as the Contractor is required to give, or failure of the Employer to give such ingress or egress as otherwise agreed between the Architect and the Contractor;

·13 delay arising from

·1 a suspension by the Contractor of the performance of his obligations under the Main Contract to the Employer pursuant to Clause 30.1.4 of the Main Contract Conditions; and/or

·2 the valid exercise by the Sub-Contractor of the right pursuant to Clause 4.21.1 to suspend the performance of his obligations under the Sub-Contract to the Contractor;

·14 Where it is stated in the completed Appendix of the Main Contract Conditions (attached to NSC/T Part 1 or, if different, in the completed Appendix of the Main Contract Conditions enclosed with the copy of Nomination NSC/N sent to the Sub-Contractor by the Architect) that clause 23.1.2 of the Main Contract Conditions applies to the Main Contract, any deferment by the Employer in giving possession of the site of the Works to the Contractor;

·15 where bills of quantities are included in the Numbered Documents, by reason of the execution of work for which an Approximate Quantity is included in those bills which is not a reasonably accurate forecast of the quantity of work required;

·16 the use or threat of terrorism and/or the activity of the relevant authorities in dealing with such use or threat;

·17 compliance or non-compliance by the Employer with clause 6A.1 of the Main Contract Conditions. (*Employer's obligation – Planning Supervisor – Principal Contractor where not the Contractor*)

3.08 What can the sub-contractor do if he is dissatisfied with the architect's decision on his application for an extension of time? If a main contractor feels aggrieved by an architect's decision he may start one of the dispute resolution procedures against the employer, in which the tribunal will have power to open up, review and revise the certificate, opinion or decision in question. But the sub-contractor has no direct contractual relationship with the employer (except in respect of the limited matters covered by the direct NSC/W agreement), and, therefore, there could be some difficulty in the sub-contractor commencing any proceedings directly against the employer. The JCT family of forms' solution to this situation is to permit the sub-contractor to 'borrow' the main contractor's name, and, in his name, to start dispute resolution proceedings against the employer. There are other situations in which it has been found satisfactory for the law to permit one person to step into the shoes of another for the purposes of litigation: an obvious example is when an insurance company, which has paid out to an insured, seeks to recover its outlay from a third party responsible for the loss using the insured's name. But the arrangement for a sub-contractor to use a main contractor's name against an employer seems far less happy. Sir John Donaldson said in *Northern Regional Health Authority v Derek Crouch Construction* [1984] 1 QB 644 that every conceivable complication would arise if a main contractor disagreed with the case which a sub-contractor wished to submit in its name. Be that as it may, name-borrowing is the regime which exists (Clause 2.7). If a sub-contractor wishes to challenge the architect's decision on an extension of time, he uses the main contractor's name to do so. It has been held that there is an implied term of this subcontract that, if the sub-contractor exercises his right to commence a name-borrowing arbitration, the main contractor will render to the sub-contractor such assistance and co-operation as may be necessary in order to enable the sub-contractor properly to conduct the arbitration (*Lorne Stewart v William Sindall* (1986) 35 BLR 109).

3.09 If the sub-contractor fails to complete on time, he becomes liable to pay to the main contractor 'a sum equivalent to any loss and/or damage suffered or incurred by the Contractor and caused by the failure of the Sub-Contractor as aforesaid' (Clause 2.9). The main contractor's right to such payment is subject to the architect having certified, under Clause 35.15 of JCT 98, the sub-contractor's failure to complete in accordance with Clause 2.8–9. This certificate is indispensable: in legal parlance it is a 'condition precedent' to the right (see *Brightside Kilpatrick v Mitchell Construction* [1975] 2 Lloyd's Reports 493). A bald statement by the architect that the sub-contractor is in delay is probably insufficient. The certificate should state that the sub-contract works ought to have been completed within the period for completion stated in the programme details in NSC/T: Part 3 item 1 or any revised or extended period.

3.10 Practical completion of the works of a nominated sub-contractor is certified by the architect (Clause 2.11, Clause 35.16 of JCT 98).

3.11 A Supplement is provided listing modifications to the text of NSC/C if there is to be sectional completion (Clause 2.15).

Section 3: Control of the works

3.12 The architect acting under JCT 98 can give 'instructions' to the main contractor. If the architect wishes to give an instruction related to sub-contract work, he must do so via the main contractor. When the main contractor receives an instruction from the architect which relates to the work of a nominated sub-contractor, he is entitled – indeed, he is required – to pass the instruction on to the nominated sub-contractor (Clause 3.3.1), who is required to comply with it (Clause 3.3.2). Thereby, the architect has as much control over the work of the nominated sub-contractor as he has over the work of the main contractor, notwithstanding that the sub-contractor is not (except for the limited matters covered by NSC/W) in direct contractual relations with the employer, whose agent the architect is.

3.13 The main contractor is entitled to give a further type of order to a nominated sub-contractor called a 'reasonable direction'

(Clause 3.3.1). It is believed that this provision is intended to cover such matters as the general organization of the site.

3.14 If the architect issues an instruction in respect of 'non-complying work' under Clauses 8.4 or 8.5 of the Main Contract JCT 98, and the work in question was work of a sub-contractor, then the sub-contractor must comply with the architect's instruction (Clauses 3.4–3.9).

3.15 The sub-contractor is given the right to request, via the main contractor, that the architect specify in writing the provision under which any instruction has been issued. He is also given the right to invoke the dispute resolution procedures under the main contract in the name of the main contractor to have the question determined 'whether the provision specified by the architect empowers the issue of the said instruction' (Clause 3.11). It would seem that the tribunal is thereby given jurisdiction not merely to decide whether the architect has specified the right clause in answer to the challenge, but also whether on the facts of the case the giving of the instruction was justified.

3.16 The sub-contractor requires the written consent of both architect and main contractor to sub-let any portion of the work, but such consent shall not be unreasonably withheld (Clause 3.14).

Section 4: Payment

3.17 As already mentioned, there are two different ways in which the contract price can be expressed:

1 'Sub-Contract Sum'. This is a fixed lump-sum price. The final payment will vary from it only to the extent that the contract works were varied or that there were provisional sums.
2 'Tender Sum'. This is the method of payment where the price ultimately to be paid will be determined by remeasurement at the conclusion of the works. In this case the price actually payable is called the 'Ascertained Final Sub-Contract Sum'.

A choice between these two options is made by the architect at the outset when he completes NSC/T: Part 1. There is lengthy text in NSC/C explaining how both options are to be carried out. Depending on which of these two options has been chosen, one or other of these chunks of text will be deemed to be deleted: happily there is no need for the parties actually to strike a line through any parts of the text.

3.18 In the case of a lump-sum contract, a valuation function is carried out by the quantity surveyor who was named in NSC/T: Part 1 as the quantity surveyor named in the main contract. He values variations, expenditure of provisional sums, and work for which an approximate quantity was indicated in bills of quantities which were a numbered document annexed to NSC/A.

3.19 In the case of a remeasurement contract, it is again the same quantity surveyor who is responsible for determining the ascertained final Sub-Contract Sum. If the sub-contractor has attached a schedule of rates to NSC/T: Part 2, this will be used in determining the valuation (Clause 4.12). The fact that it is a remeasurement sub-contract does not affect the sub-contractor's obligation to complete the work (*Ibmac v Marshall* [1968] EGD 218, 611).

3.20 The main contract JCT 98 requires the architect to include in interim certificates the amounts due to a nominated sub-contractor without application (Clause 30.2 of JCT 98). The main contractor must inform the sub-contractor of sums included in an interim certificate in respect of that sub-contractor, which are described as 'Amount A' in NSC/C, not later than five days after the issue of that interim certificate. At the same time, the main contractor must state any other sums owed by him to the sub-contractor arising from, for example, a loss and expense claim made by the sub-contractor. These sums are described as 'Amount B' (Clause 4.16.1.1).

3.21 The main contractor's payment obligation is to pay Amounts A and B to the sub-contractor within seventeen days from the date of issue of the relevant interim certificate (Clause 4.16.1.1). There is a right for the sub-contractor to suspend work if he is not paid, provided he first gives seven days' notice in writing of his intention to suspend (Clause 4.21). In most cases the main contractor's obligation will be met by actually making payment. But can a good discharge be effected by the main contractor 'setting-off' a sum due from the sub-contractor to him, that is deducting a cross-claim? If the cross-claim is as certain as the debt certified then there would be obvious injustice in denying the right to set-off. At the other end of the spectrum, it is equally clearly unjust to allow a specious complaint to stand as an excuse for not paying a certified sum. But in the face of the complexity of most building projects how is a court to know whether an alleged cross-claim is specious without embarking on a full investigation of the merits? And the time involved in doing that will provide to the person putting up a specious cross-claim the very delay in payment which is his aim. In the early 1970s the courts' policy was that such delay in payment of a certified sum was to be avoided by giving summary judgment on any certified sum, irrespective of any alleged cross-claim (*Dawnays v Minter* [1971] 1 WLR 1205). In 1974 the House of Lords reversed that policy and refused summary judgement where a party wished to advance a cross-claim (*Modern Engineering (Bristol) v Gilbert-Ash* [1974] AC 689), but it is uncertain how far that decision depends on express wording in a contract. The new solution to this practical dilemma is found in the sub-contractor's right to refer questions of non-payment to adjudication for a quick decision. In Clause 4.16.1.2, NSC/C has not sought to limit matters in respect of which sums can be set-off. It requires the main contractor, not later than five days before payment is due, to give written notice to the sub-contractor of sums which are to be withheld and the basis for doing so. In the event that the sub-contractor disputes the main contractor's right to set-off these sums, he can refer the matter to adjudication (Section 9A).

3.22 The right to recover direct loss and expense between contractor and sub-contractor is mutual. If either the main contractor or the sub-contractor is responsible for adversely affecting the progress of the works, the other, by following prescribed procedures, can make financial recovery (Clauses 4.38–4.41).

3.23 There is a provision for the Final Certificate issued in respect of the main contract under Clause 30.8 of JCT 98 to have effect as conclusive evidence that the sub-contract works have been carried out to the reasonable satisfaction of the architect in certain respects (Clause 4.25). This applies where the relevant contractual document expressly describes an item as being for the approval of the architect. It does not extend any further. The wording reflects the effect of the term relating to the Final Certificate in the main contract, which was changed following the surprising Court of Appeal decision in *Crown Estates v John Mowlem & Co Ltd* [1994] 70 BLR 1. It reduces the extent to which the Final Certificate creates a bar on a claim made by the employer in respect of defective work.

3.24 Specific provision is made by NSC/C in regard to the passing of property. The general law is that if a builder incorporates a building material into a property, ownership of that material passes to the owner of the property, whether he has been paid for his work or not. But there have been cases where there was a conflict between that principle and another fundamental principle of the law: that nobody can give something which does not belong to him. A related difficulty was illustrated by *Dawber Williamson v Humberside County Council* (1979) 14 BLR 70. A roofing sub-contractor delivered materials to the site. Prior to their fixing, their value was certified and paid by the employer to the main contractor, but the main contractor went into liquidation without paying for the materials. So the question arose who owned the materials. The court accepted the sub-contractor's argument that he still owned them. Happy result as that was for the sub-contractor, who would otherwise have lost any realistic prospect of payment, it meant that the employer had to pay out for them a second time. The JCT decided that their policy towards the problem of which innocent party should lose out when a main contractor becomes insolvent was that it should be the sub-contractor rather than the employer. As soon as the employer has

paid the main contractor for a material, even if not yet fixed, and even if the material belongs to a sub-contractor, 'property' in it, i.e. ownership, should pass to the employer. The implementation of that policy requires provisions in both the main and sub contracts (Clause 16.1 of JCT 98; NSC/C Clause 4.15.4).

3.25 There is a further name-borrowing provision whereby a sub-contractor can use the main contractor's name in dispute proceedings against the employer if he feels aggrieved by any decision as to the amount certified by the architect (Clause 4.20).

Sections 4A, 4B, 4C: Fluctuations

3.26 There are three different regimes offered for dealing with fluctuations. NSC/T Parts 1 and 2 should specify which is to apply. They are known as:

1 Contribution, levy and tax fluctuations (Clause 4A)
2 Labour and materials cost and tax fluctuations (Clause 4B)
3 Formula adjustment (Clause 4C).

Section 5: Statutory obligations

3.27 NSC/C makes provision for:

1 Value added tax – standard arrangements (Clause 5A)
2 Value added tax – special arrangements (Clause 5B)
3 Income and Corporation Taxes Act 1988 – tax deduction scheme (Clauses 5C and 5D).

This book does not deal with tax law, which is a highly specialist subject.

Section 6: Injury, damage and insurance

3.28 The sub-contractor undertakes to indemnify the main contractor against personal injury or death caused by the carrying out of the sub-contract works unless these occurred as result of the fault of the main contractor or employer. In other words the sub-contractor is liable unless he can prove that it was the fault of one of the other parties to the contracts (Clause 6.2). The sub-contractor undertakes to indemnify the main contractor in respect of damage to property provided that this is due to the negligence, omission or default of the sub-contractor. In other words, the sub-contractor is liable only if somebody else can prove that it was the sub-contractor's fault (Clause 6.3).

3.29 The sub-contractor undertakes to insure in respect of his liability for personal injury, death and damage to property (Clause 6.5). Depending on which of the insurance options in the main contract has been selected, that is Clauses 22A, 22B and 22C (see Chapter 9, Section 25), there is an appropriate passage of text in NSC/C.

Section 7: Determination

3.30 There is a scheme for a sub-contractor to be sacked from a project where his work is unsatisfactory. The grounds for such dismissal are:

1 Wholly or substantially suspending work
2 Failing to proceed regularly and diligently
3 Refusing or neglecting after notice in writing from the main contractor to remove defective work or materials
4 Assigning the sub-contract or sub-letting part without consent
5 Failing to comply with the requirements of the Construction (Design and Management) Regulations ('CDM Regulations').

For such a dismissal to be carried out, both architect and main contractor must be involved. The main contractor must inform the architect that the sub-contractor is in default in one of these respects. If the matter is to go any further, the architect must then instruct the main contractor to proceed; if the architect does so, the main contractor serves a formal notice on the sub-contractor. When the matter is referred to him, the architect must decide whether the main contractor should be allowed to determine the sub-contractor's contract without more ado upon default after the formal notice, or whether the main contractor must obtain the architect's sanction before proceeding to that step. If the power to determine is exercised by the main contractor for no good reason, the main contractor is likely to be liable to the sub-contractor in damages. However, this may not be so if the main contractor genuinely, but wrongly, believes he is entitled to determine (*Woodar v Wimpey* [1980] 1 All ER 571).

3.31 Insolvency and corruption are also grounds on which a sub-contractor's employment can be ended.

3.32 The sub-contractor has his own right to end his employment. Grounds for doing so are that the main contractor has wholly or substantially suspended work or has unreasonably failed to proceed, or that the main contractor has failed to comply with the requirements of the CDM Regulations.

3.33 If the main contractor's employment under the main contract is ended, then the sub-contract automatically ends (Clause 7.10).

Section 9: Settlement of disputes – adjudication and arbitration

3.34 Provisions for adjudication in Section 9A reflect the requirements in the Housing Grants, Construction and Regeneration Act 1996. These provisions are in similar terms to those in JCT 98. A dispute or difference can be referred to adjudication at any time for a quick decision which binds the parties unless or until the dispute is finally determined by arbitration, litigation, or agreement.

3.35 It is open to the parties to agree to litigate or arbitrate. Since the decision of the House of Lords in *Beaufort Developments Ltd v Gilbert Ash NI Ltd* (1998) 88 BLR 1, a decision to litigate does not necessarily preclude the tribunal from reviewing or revising decisions made by the architect. There is an arbitration clause in Section 9B similar to that in the main contract JCT 98. Arbitration will be subject to the Construction Industry Model Arbitration Rules (CIMAR) which include provisions to encourage two arbitrations to be dealt with by the same arbitrator if the disputes are connected. This can arise if there is a connected dispute being submitted to arbitration between the employer and the main contractor, or between the main contractor and another nominated sub-contractor, or between the sub-contractor and the employer under NSC/W.

3.36 There are provisions throughout the NSC/C which entitle the sub-contractor to borrow the name of the main contractor to pursue matters against the employer or to challenge decisions of the architect. Such proceedings are taken by the main contractor under the provisions of the main contract. These provisions extend to adjudication (referring as they do to 'any dispute proceedings').

3.37 The table below summarizes the role of each of the NSC documents:

NSC/T: Part 1	Employer invites tender from sub-contractor
NSC/T: Part 2	Sub-contractor returns tender to employer
NSC/W	Warranty between employer and sub-contractor, if required
NSC/N	Employer's instruction nominating sub-contractor to main contractor
NSC/T: Part 3	Completed by main contractor and sub-contractor; particular conditions superseding those in earlier NSC/T documents
NSC/A	Articles of agreement between main contractor and sub-contractor
NSC/C	Conditions of agreement between main contractor and sub-contractor.

4 JCT Standard Form of Domestic Sub-Contract 2002 (DSC)

4.01 For many years the JCT did not have a domestic sub-contract form. Instead, there was widespread use of a sub-contract form

drafted by the Construction Federation, called DOM 1 which was effectively adopted by the industry as a sub-contract form to fit with the JCT main contract. The fit was not perfect, but did the job. In 2002 a new blue form from the JCT arrived which is intended to fit with JCT 98 and replace DOM 1. It is called the JCT Standard Form of Domestic Sub-Contract 2002 ('DSC'). Perhaps because the industry is used to DOM 1 and old habits die hard, the JCT has really tinkered around the edges rather than try to reinvent the wheel. The JCT also plans to provide a domestic design and build sub-contract to replace the DOM 2 in the near future. Although generally similar in content to DOM 1 the DSC has a different structure, preferring to group clauses together into themes, not dissimilar to the Nominated Sub-Contract form, but there are some useful developments in the right direction. The form comprises a Sub-Contract Agreement (known as DSC/A) and Sub-Contract Conditions (known as DSC/C) and comes with optional Fluctuations clauses and a Guide book. The DSC/A contains the Articles of agreement which the parties must be careful to complete. The DSC/C are incorporated in the DSC/A expressly by reference so that they can remain 'on the shelf'. However, the DSC/C often contain options in a number of clauses so it is vital that the DSC/A sets out which options are chosen by the parties.

4.02 The DSC/A begins by naming the parties, identifying the Sub-Contract Works and the Main Contract Works, sets out a number of recitals followed by the terms set out in Articles 1 to 5B which are to be completed/deleted as appropriate.

4.03 Article 1 sets out what the Sub-Contract consists of, namely, the Articles, the Particular Conditions, the Schedule of Information attached to the DSC/A, the Numbered Documents, any other documents annexed to the Agreement and the DSC/C together with Codes of Practice A and B and the optional fluctuations clauses. Article 1 needs to be completed and appropriate options chosen. If any revisions to the DSC/C are negotiated they should be referred to in this Article and the schedule of modifications should be annexed to the Agreement.

4.04 Article 2 provides that the Sub-Contractor will upon and subject to the Sub-Contract carry out and complete the Sub-Contract Works. Article 3 provides for payment, details of which have to be filled in. There is a choice of either a fixed sum known as the Sub-Contract Sum or a Tender Sum, which will be subject to remeasurement and valuation.

4.05 Article 4 provides for adjudication in accordance with Clause 9A of the DSC/C. Article 5A provides for arbitration of disputes or differences or 5B for court proceedings, depending upon which package is chosen in the Particular Conditions item 13.

4.06 Then follows the Particular Conditions which the parties have to agree and fill in on the DSC/A, namely:

1　Programme details, including procurement times for materials and fabrication, the required notice period for commencement of works on site, the period of time needed to carry out the Sub-Contract Works and any further details that may clarify or qualify the programme periods.
2　Incorporation of the various elements Sub-Contract Works into the Main Contract Works before practical completion of the Sub-Contract Works.
3　Attendances to be provided by the Sub-Contractor free of charge.
4　The appropriate retention percentage.
5　A Sub-Contractors bond in lieu of retention (this is an optional alternative to 4 – see Clause 4.19 of DSC/C – which was not previously available under DOM 1).
6　Payment Dates for the first, interim and final payments (see DSC/C Clause 4 – discussed below – which differ from the DOM 1 regime).
7　Payments for listed items of goods and materials before work on site.
8　Specifying the insurance cover for any one occurrence or series of occurrences arising out of one event.

9 Sub-Contract Base Date.

10 Dayworks formula unless a dayworks schedule forms part of the Numbered Documents.

11 Fluctuations.

12 Numbered Documents which should be listed out.

13 Dispute resolution package to be selected (from a choice of arbitration or litigation as well as the right to adjudicate and the necessary appointing bodies).

4.07 Next in the DSC/A there is a Schedule of Information which the Contractor should complete with the necessary details of the Main Contract. The Appendix to the Main Contract and any special amendments must be annexed to this Schedule. Importantly, the Schedule should also list out the information relating to the Main Contract which the Sub-Contractor has had either a reasonable opportunity to inspect or has had a copy. Included within the Schedule should be the relevant parts, and details, of the Health and Safety plan (which should be annexed) and programme information giving the earliest start and end dates for the Sub-Contract Works and any dates when the site is closed for holidays.

4.08 The Numbered Documents should contain the particulars of the Sub-Contract Works in the form of drawings, specifications, bills of quantities, schedule of rates and the like, as well as day-works schedule, modifications to the DSC/C, and any other documents listed in Particular Conditions item 12.

4.09 So far as the conditions are concerned, the DSC/C is generally in line with the sub-contract provisions in the Nominated Sub-Contract form (discussed above in section 3 of this chapter) with some notable difference to reflect the fact that the Main Contract rather than the Architect is in charge of overseeing and administering the Sub-Contractor's Works and to reflect the fact that the Sub-Contractor is not nominated by the Employer (so name-borrowing provisions do not apply). Accordingly, for example, under DSC/C Clause 2, the Main Contractor assesses whether or not to grant an extension of time to the Sub-Contractor (rather than being directed by the Architect as under NSC Clause 2). In practice, it is unlikely that the Main Contractor will grant such an extension of time, unless he himself is able to obtain one from the Architect. Similarly under Clause 2 it is the Main Contractor, rather than the Architect, who decides when the Sub-Contract Works have reached practical completion. In Clause 3, the Main Contractor has the control over the Sub-Contract Works and issues instructions to the Sub-Contractor, but any instruction issued by the Architect affecting the Sub-Contract Works which is then issued to the Sub-Contractor by the Main Contractor is deemed to be the Main Contractor's instruction. It is the Main Contractor who values the Sub-Contractor's Works.

4.10 One notable new feature of the DSC (which differs from DOM 1) is the Sub-Contractor's right in Clauses 4.4.2 and 4.9.2 to have the opportunity to be present at any measurement of the valuations and to take such notes and measurements as he shall require. This provision is part of the general approach to ensure a level of transparency and openness between Main Contractors and Sub-Contractors that did not exist with DOM 1. There are other clauses which demonstrate this approach, such as Clauses 1.15.1 and 1.15.2 which oblige the parties to provide further drawings and information to each other and Clause 1.20 which imposes an obligation on the Main Contractor upon request to inform the Sub-Contractor of all Certificates issued under the Main Contract and the content of them and any notice of suspension of the Main Contract Works. Clearly, it is up to Sub-Contractors to take the initiative to be kept informed, but it means that the bad old days of Main Contractors not keeping the Sub-Contractors fully 'in the loop' about the Main Contract Works are over.

4.11 Further differences from DOM 1 can be found in the payment regime in clause 4 which are tied to the payment provisions under the Main Contract in a way that DOM 1 was not. Under DOM 1 interim payments under the Sub-Contract fell due a month after commencement of the works irrespective of the dates for payment of the Main Contractor under the Main Contract. This caused administrative – not to mention cash-flow – problems if the payment regimes started out of kilter. The DSC provides at Clause 4.15 that the Sub-Contractor's first payment falls due on the first Interim Certificate date under the Main Contract after commencement of the Sub-Contract Works on site. In practice this should mean that the Sub-Contractor's first payment will be made earlier than used to be the case. However, under DOM 1 the Sub-Contractor had to wait 17 days between the due date for an interim payment and the final date for the interim payment whereas under the DSC that period has been stretched to 21 days. The rationale is to help give the Main Contractor some breathing space. However, it is unlikely to be popular with Sub-Contractors.

4.12 The Sub-Contractor must notify the Contractor when in his opinion his Works have reached practical completion (as had been the position under DOM 1). Unlike DOM 1, if the Contractor disagrees not only must he state his reasons but he must also say when in his view practical completion has been reached. The final tranche of retention monies which, under DOM 1, became due when the Certificate of Making Good Defects has been issued is now dealt with by Clause 4.18 of the DSC/C, where the parties are to agree when defects have been made good: a failure to agree on this could result in adjudication.

4.13 The DSC is clearer and a neater fit with JCT 98 than DOM 1 and goes a long way to promoting transparency and co-operation between Main Contractors and Sub-Contractors.

5 JCT Intermediate Form of Building Contract (IFC 98)

5.01 The JCT Intermediate form was published in 1984 and was known as IFC 84. Between 1986 and 1998 there were 12 amendments. The form has now been published as IFC 98, incorporating all the previous amendments and restructuring the articles. The genesis of the form owes something to the disenchantment of the construction industry with JCT 80 on its publication. Many people found JCT 80 so daunting and complicated that they went on using JCT 1963. For such persons IFC 84 was offered as a form of contract which in terms of length and complexity resembled JCT 1963, but which essentially had the benefit of up-to-date drafting. In most significant respects the characteristics of IFC 98 correspond to JCT 98. One major difference from JCT 98 is in respect of the nomination of sub-contractors.

5.02 Sub-contracting under IFC 84 is thus its one distinctive characteristic. A new concept has been created, 'the named sub-contractor'. The lengthy discussion on earlier pages of this chapter will have shown just how complicated nominating sub-contracting under JCT 98 has become. One can applaud the initiative to provide a simpler alternative. However, there are those who consider that unnecessary confusion has been created by the introduction of yet another species of sub-contractor, whose distinction from the recognized categories of nominated and domestic sub-contractors is imperfectly drawn. A separate family of sub-contract documents is intended for use with IFC 98, namely:

NAM/T: Tender and Agreement for named sub-contractor

NAM/SC: Sub-Contract Conditions for named sub-contractor

NAM/FR: Formula Rules for named sub-contractor

ESA/1:   Employer/Specialist Agreement to provide a direct warranty where a portion of the design is provided by a named sub-contractor.

IFC also has its own Fluctuations Supplement and Sectional Completion Supplement.

5.03 Other differences from JCT 98 are:

1 Certification procedures are simpler; 95% of the value of work executed and materials on site is included in interim certificates, 97.5% at practical completion.

2 There is no provision for nominated suppliers.

3 There is no provision for performance specified work.

Advantages

5.04 It is less complex than JCT 98 but still covers most of the same ground. IFC 98 is also significantly shorter at 63 pages than JCT 98 at 104 pages. IFC 98 is a well-drafted form in the sense that it should ensure smooth administration, and in that it has been well thought out.

Disadvantages

5.05 Although not quite so complex as JCT 98, it is still a very complicated contract. By reason of its central importance in the JCT family, most people working in construction will have some familiarity with JCT 98, and they may find the differences between JCT 98 and IFC 98 simply a distraction. However, in its 1998 version the intermediate form has moved closer to the main form: for example IFC 98, unlike its predecessor IFC 84, includes provisions for partial possession. The 'named sub-contractor' arrangements remain a potential source of complication.

6 JCT Minor Works Agreement 1998 (MW 98)

6.01 The first form intended for minor works was published in 1968. The present 1998 edition of the minor works form (MW 98) is based upon the 1980 edition and incorporates the eleven amendments made to the 1980 form between 1980 and 1998. Practice Note M2 which applies to MW 98 states that the Form is generally suitable for contracts up to the value of £70 000, based on 1992 prices. The Minor Works form has proved to be very popular.

6.02 It is a fixed price lump-sum contract. It is not envisaged that there will be bills of quantities, but that the works will be sufficiently clearly defined by drawings and/or specifications and/or schedules to permit accurate tendering. Practice Note M2 does, however, suggest that bills may be required where the Works are complex. The contract is to be administered by an architect who will issue certificates, but the scale of contract administration is much less than under JCT 98. For example, there is no provision for the architect to certify that works have not been completed by the completion date. The general theme of the contract is simplicity.

6.03 MW 98 is different from IFC 98, generally in the direction of greater simplification, in the following respects:

1 Extension of time. There is no list of circumstances justifying an extension. Instead the contractor is entitled to an extension if the delay is for 'reasons beyond the control of the Contractor'. However, the clause continues: 'Reasons within the control of the Contractor include default of the Contractor or of others employed or engaged by or under him for or in connection with the Works and of any supplier of goods or materials for the Works.'

2 There is no scope for the employer to direct the use of a particular sub-contractor and no standard form of sub-contract which would apply to such sub-contractors. Practice Note M2 suggests that the Employer could control the selection of a specialist sub-contractor by entering into a direct contract with them. In the absence of amendments to MW 98, such an arrangement would leave the Employer carrying the risk of the default of the specialist.

3 Retentions are not treated as trust moneys.

4 Interim valuation is given a much broader treatment, reflecting the anticipated absence of bills: 'The certificate shall state to what the progress payment relates and the basis on which the amount of the progress payment was calculated.'

5 Loss and expense. There is no separate provision for the contractor to claim for loss and expense. The onus falls upon the Architect to value variations on a fair and reasonable basis.

'Variations' specifically includes a change to the period within which the Works are to be carried out, and the valuation of such variations is said to include any direct loss and/or expense incurred by the Contractor. The method of assessment is much more rough and ready, being 'on a fair and reasonable basis using where relevant prices in the priced Specification/schedules/schedules of rates'.

6 No provision for partial possession or sectional completion.

7 No provisions for opening up and testing.

8 Ownership of unfixed materials. There is no provision requiring the contractor to include a clause in sub-contracts that ownership of unfixed materials will pass to the employer as soon as paid for.

9 No provisions for fluctuations of work and materials, which reflects the anticipated short period of works carried out under this form. Changes in contributions, levies and taxes are allowed.

Advantages

6.04 Simplicity and ease of administration.

Disadvantages

6.05 Many matters are left sketchily defined.

7 JCT Building Contract for a Homeowner/Occupier 2002

7.01 This is a contract for use by householders who deal directly with a builder for home improvements, extensions or repairs and is aimed at works where the assistance of professional consultants is not needed. Often householders have works carried out at their properties without any formal contract at all, usually just a builder's estimate. This can frequently end in tears, usually because there has been a lack of effective communication about the parties' respective expectations at the outset and, on the part of householders, lack of unawareness of the vicissitudes of the building industry. By using this new contract, it is hoped that such problems will not arise. The contract is easily understandable, avoids technical or legal jargon – it won a crystal mark for clarity by the Plain English Campaign – and contains helpful guidance notes which give practical advice to ensure that householders get a fair deal. The form is in two parts the first of which comprises a pro-forma contract which the parties use to fill in all the necessary details and the second part of which comprises 11 general conditions. The builder is known as the 'contractor' and the householder is known as the 'customer' which perhaps emphasizes that this, unlike other contracts, is a consumer contract.

Pro-forma contract

7.02 The pro-forma contract is made up of sections A to K and at various places makes references to the conditions in part 2. At the beginning of the pro-forma the address where the work is to be carried out and the parties' details are set out. This includes details of whether the contractor is registered for VAT. At the end of the pro-forma the parties sign and date the document.

7.03 In Section A the parties give a short description of the work to be done, together with tick boxes for the customer to complete to identify the applicable contract documents such as the quotation, drawings and specification. Section B sets out that the contractor will obtain the necessary local authority permissions for planning and building regulations and party wall consents unless the customer agrees to obtain some or all of them by ticking the appropriate boxes. The customer is also informed that the contractor cannot start work until planning permission has been granted but that he can start work without building regulations provided that 48 hours notice has been given to the local authority. By ticking boxes in Section C the customer agrees to allow the contractor the use of electricity/water/toilet or telephone facilities free of charge.

7.04 Section D sets out what the VAT inclusive price for the work is and gives some general rules on what the price includes. Most important of these are the rule that the price includes the contractor's cost of dealing with any unexpected problems which he could have discovered by carrying out a careful inspection before the price is agreed and the rule that if the customer changes the work details the price will increase or decrease depending upon the changes. Section E provides that the customer will pay 95% of the price by the time that the work is completed and includes tick boxes for choosing a single payment when the work is finished or payment by instalments at agreed stages. The remaining 5% is not payable for a further 3 months after the work has been completed.

7.05 Section F sets out the working period. The customer can choose from two options: either the work should start not later than a certain date and be finished by a certain date, or specifying a number of weeks for the work to be finished from a start date to be agreed. The work is finished when the contractor has properly done everything shown in the work details or any changes made to them. The work period can be extended in certain circumstances.

7.06 Section G provides that the contractor will give the customer any guarantees issued by the manufacturer of the products installed in the work. Section H provides that before the work starts the customer will inform his household insurers that the work is about to start and the contractor will have an 'all risks' insurance policy to cover the full costs of any damage to the works and unfixed materials and an up-to-date public liability policy for death or injury to people and damage to property.

7.07 Section I provides a space for filling in the normal working hours per day, Monday to Friday unless the parties agree otherwise. Section J provides whether or not the premises will be lived in during the works and that the contractor will take common sense precautions to deter intruders if the premises are unoccupied at any time while the works are being carried out.

7.08 Section K provides the dispute resolution package. This is perhaps the most controversial of the terms because, as well as providing for the court to resolve disputes, it also makes provision for either party to refer disputes to adjudication '*as well as the right to go to court*'. The appointment of an adjudicator is to be made either by the RICS or the RIBA under a scheme run by those bodies, but the decision is to be given within 21 days. Clearly the adjudication is not an adjudication under the HCGRA 1996 because that Act specifically excludes contracts for works done for a residential occupier. The adjudication is thus entirely contractual but it is probably intended that it should be run along the same lines as an adjudication under the Act. However, it is far from clear what status an adjudication decision will have: i.e. whether an adjudication decision is intended to be binding unless and until a court decides otherwise or whether it is finally binding as an alternative to litigation in court. Nor is it entirely clear what the costs position will be in adjudicated disputes. Usually in HCGRA 1996 adjudications each party bears his own costs of the adjudication unless there is some other agreement. Under this contract, however, the costs of going to adjudication and the rules and procedures are said to become part of the contract but whether this means that the parties bear their own costs, or whether they get added to the price in any event is not at all clear. This provision is not satisfactory as it currently stands and parties would be well advised to delete the adjudication provision.

Conditions

7.09 By Clause 1 of the conditions the contractor's responsibilities are set out. They include the type of things that customers would normally expect, such as the contractor turning up to do the work at regular hours to complete the work within the agreed period, to carry out – competently and carefully – the agreed work as set out in the work details, to use suitable materials which should be new (unless otherwise agreed), to tidy up tools, to take away builders rubbish and to be responsible for any damage caused by him during the works. Clause 2 of the conditions sets out the customer's responsibilities which are to allow access to the contractor during the agreed working hours during the working period, to keep the premises clear from obstructions during the works and to allow the contractor to carry out the work in the order that the contractor feels necessary to finish the work on time. Clause 3 provides for compliance with health and safety issues.

7.10 Clause 4 of the conditions provides that only the customer can make changes to the work details. If a change increases the amount of work and the contractor agrees to the changes he will quote a price for the extra work and time involved and the customer can then decide whether or not to go ahead with the change. If the change involves a decrease in the amount of work the contractor will make an appropriate reduction in the price. If the change alters the cost of any items in the work details without increasing or reducing the amount of work involved an appropriate adjustment will be made.

7.11 Clause 5 of the conditions provides that if the contractor has to spend extra time on the work because of changes or if the work cannot be finished on time because of reasons beyond the contractor's control including delay caused by the customer, the customer will extend the working period by a fair and reasonable amount. The contractor can claim any reasonable costs arising from any extended period because of any delay caused by the customer, but not otherwise.

7.12 Clause 6 of the conditions provides for payment as described generally already in section E of the pro-forma. The contractor has to issue an itemised invoice showing the rate of VAT charged for each item. The customer has to pay the 95% of the invoice within 14 days. The remaining 5% is retained until the end of 3 months after the work has been finished. The customer has to pay that remaining 5% no later than 14 days after the contractor has put right all faults which the customer has promptly reported to him at any time between the start of the work and 3 months after the work was finished.

7.13 Clause 7 provides that the contractor continues to be responsible for any faults in the work (other than fair wear and tear) that occur within 6 years after carrying out the work. This, of course, is simply a statement of the position under the Limitation Act 1980.

7.14 Clause 8 provides for the parties to terminate the contract. If the contractor does not turn up regularly to carry out the work or is incompetent or careless so that the work is not of an acceptable standard or he is not meeting his health and safety and environmental responsibilities the customer can give him a 7-day written warning requiring him to correct matters. If the contractor does not correct matters, the customer can then give him written notice of termination which takes effect immediately. The contractor can terminate – using the same notification process – if the customer does not pay an amount due without good reasons or prevents or obstructs the contractor from carrying out his work. If the customer terminates the contract he does not have to pay the contractor any money due until the work has been completed by another contractor. If the contractor terminates the contract, the customer has to pay him within 14 days for work carried out and unfixed materials. Clause 9 provides that if either party becomes insolvent the contract will come to an end unless an insolvency practitioner makes suitable arrangements to allow the contract to continue.

7.15 Clause 10 provides that the parties can claim from each other the costs and expenses for breaches of contract and does not rule out any other legal remedies they may have. Clause 11 provides that the law of the contract is the law of England and Wales.

7.16 The JCT has also introduced some variations on the same theme with two further forms which are similar in style and content to the Homeowner Contract. The first variation covers those projects where homeowners require professional assistance with designs, drawings, specifications, applications for permissions for planning and building regulations approval or party wall consents as well as to inspect the building work and/or act and as the homeowner's representative when dealing with the contractor. The JCT has published a separate Consultancy Agreement which sets out the terms of the professional consultant's appointment. The modified Homeowner Contract (with Consultant) not only sets out the obligations of builder and customer in relation to the work/payment but also includes provisions that cover the consultant's role in dealing with the builder. There is also a further short contract designed for customers carrying out repairs and maintenance to their homes.

Advantages

7.17 These are sensible additions to the JCT family which are specially tailored for construction contracts with consumers and will, if used extensively, seek to improve their lot. A potential problem is lack of awareness by consumers (and builders who deal with consumers) that these contract forms exist. Any builder who is not prepared to sign up to such a contract is probably best avoided in the first place.

Disadvantages

7.18 The adjudication provisions have not been properly thought out and are best avoided altogether.

8 JCT Conditions of Contract for Building Works of a Jobbing Character (JA/C 90)

8.01 In simple terms this may be said to be a contract for even smaller jobs than MW 98. It is intended to be used by organizations such as local authorities, who regularly employ building contractors to carry out small works, for example, maintenance jobs on a stock of houses. Unlike MW 98, there is no architect or other professional contract administrator. The JCT suggest its use for jobs up to £10 000 in value (at 1990 prices) with a duration of up to one month and where only one payment is envisaged.

8.02 JA/C 90, which contains the contract conditions, can be used with either the employer's own works order or with a JCT four-page document entitled Standard Form of Tender and Agreement for Building Works of a Jobbing Character (JA/T 90). With an economy not found in most other JCT documentation this document is designed to serve three separate purposes at three successive stages: as an invitation to tender, a returned tender and an executed agreement.

8.03 Among differences from MW 98 are the following:

1 Extension of time. In the absence of a certifier, the employer decides in the first instance whether an extension of time is justified. That decision is subject to review in dispute proceedings.
2 There are no interim payments. The contractor is to submit one invoice after completion of the works. (The statutory right to interim payments under the Housing Grants, Construction and Regeneration Act 1996 does not apply where the duration of the work is agreed to be less than 45 days.)
3 Valuation. If the parties cannot agree, the employer values in the first instance, subject to dispute proceedings.
4 There is no certificate of practical completion.
5 There is no retention.
6 There are no express grounds for termination, other than corruption.

9 JCT Standard Form of Measured Term Contract 1998

9.01 This form is intended for use by the same kind of employers as JA/C 90, that is, large organizations who are accustomed to employing building contractors on small jobs. Typical would be the owner of a housing stock on which there are regular maintenance jobs. This form is for use if such an employer wishes to enter an umbrella contract with a building contractor to cover a series of such small jobs, rather than enter a separate JA/C 90 contract for each individual job. Measured term contracts have for some years been in use by housing authorities and other commercial organizations with regular maintenance programmes.

9.02 This contract is quite unlike any other in that it does not involve an obligation by the employer to order any item of work at all. Rather it creates a framework for subsequent orders. Unlike JA/C 90, this contract does involve a contract administrator: he, rather than the employer, places the order which initiates each job, and he values the work in accordance with an agreed schedule of rates. The contractor is obliged to carry out any order which is given. The 'contract area' is the district, estate or whatever, which is identified in the recitals as the geographical territory of the contract.

9.03 The Appendix to this form of contract is unusually important. It identifies a list of properties which may be the location of works ordered under the contract. It states the period over which work may be ordered under the contract, normally at least one year. It gives an indication, though not a guarantee, of the value of work which will be ordered. It mentions the type of work which may be ordered under the contract.

10 JCT Standard Form of Building Contract with Contractor's Design 1998 (CD 98)

10.01 There emerged in the 1970s the concept of a contract under which a package deal of both design and build would be provided. The notion was supported by a NEDO report 'Construction for Industrial Recovery'. Originally it was envisaged that it would be used by local authorities for public housing projects. In fact, it has been more used for commercial light industrial building and by developers for offices and shops. In 1981 the JCT published its design and build form which was known as CD 81. There were twelve subsequent amendments all of which have been incorporated, together with some corrections, into the 1998 form (CD 98).

10.02 The basic problem of a fixed-price package deal contract for a new building is that, unless the building is to some extent defined in the contract, the employer has no certainty what he will be provided with for his money. On the other hand, if the building is described in detail in the contract, then one has not moved far from the traditional procurement method of design before contract. CD 98 tackles this problem by the concept of a statement of 'Employer's Requirements'. This statement can, at the employer's choice, be anything from a three-line performance specification to a completely developed scheme design, with outline specifications and drawings. It must be stated clearly whether employer or contractor is responsible for obtaining approvals.

10.03 It would have been perfectly feasible to leave the contractor to implement the Employer's Requirements as he saw fit. But CD 98 carries the pre-contractual definition of the project a stage further by a second concept, the 'Contractor's Proposals'. These are drafted by the prospective contractor in response to the Employer's Requirements and supplied together with a tender figure. The employer must examine these proposals: indeed, a recital in the articles declares that the employer has done so. Obviously the proposals should respond to, and be compatible with, the employer's requirements. But what if there is some divergence? The contract provides that the proposals prevail. Therefore, in his own interests the employer must consider the proposals very carefully before entering into a CD 98 contract.

10.04 The contract is a fixed price contract, payable in stages or periodically. It is not envisaged that there will be a bill of quantities or schedule of rates. There is no architect, contract administrator or other certifier.

10.05 The contractor assumes a liability, wholly alien to a contractor's obligation under a traditional contract, for the design. Design work may have been carried out for the employer in putting together the Employer's Requirements. In that case the designer of that initial work often becomes linked contractually to the main contractor, making the main contractor the single point of responsibility for the design of the entire project. Under Clause 2.5, the contractor's liability for design is said to be the same as that which would apply to an architect acting independently under a separate contract with the employer. An architect acting under such circumstances normally has a duty to carry out work with reasonable professional skill and care. This clause may not, however, conclusively limit his responsibility in law for design work. For example, in the case of housing work, he will have assumed a responsibility under the Defective Premises Act 1972, which probably involves a strict obligation that work has been done so as to make the dwelling reasonably fit for human habitation.

10.06 Provision is made for the employer to intervene while works are ongoing. There are powers given to the employer to name subcontractors, to comment on the contractor's drawings while works are ongoing and to issue instructions to vary the works, called 'change orders'. Such powers are, however, contrary to the idea of a fixed price package deal based upon the Employer's Requirements. Consequently the contractor has a right of reasonable objection to change orders. Changes to the Employer's Requirements at a late stage will result in increased costs.

Advantages

10.07 The employer can look to one person as responsible for all aspects of the project. If defects later come to light, he does not have to work out whether it has been caused by bad design or bad workmanship before he knows to whom to complain. The employer also benefits from certainty of cost, provided he does not change the Employer's Requirements once the contractor has been employed.

Disadvantages

10.08 The employer does not know quite what the building presented at the end of the project will be like, unless he has spelled out his employer's requirements in a very detailed manner. But if he has done that, part of the point of a design-and-build contract may be thought to be lost. Similarly, the employer has limited control over what happens during the course of the project: he can issue change orders but the contractor can object to them. The employer does not have somebody looking after his interests when design decisions are taken, and endeavouring to satisfy his requirements, in the same way as he would if his own architect were running the contract.

11 JCT 98 – Contractor's Designed Portion Supplement 1998 (CDPS 98)

11.01 This supplement is intended to be used with JCT 98 where the contractor is required to design one element in a contract, the remainder of which will be procured under the usual JCT 98 terms. An example would be the erection of a building with a standard steel structural frame, where the main contractor was a specialist in such frames and took on the responsibility for the design of that element.

11.02 CDPS 98 is a fifteen-page document to be used in conjunction with the main JCT Standard Form. There are two versions, one to accompany JCT 98 forms with quantities, and one for the JCT 98 forms without quantities. The supplement modifies JCT 98 to make the contractor responsible for the design of the identified portion. The integration of this design into the works as a whole is the responsibility of the architect. There are 'Employer's Requirements' and 'Contractor's Proposals' in relation to this portion, reminiscent of the statements which form the foundation of CD 98.

12 JCT Major Project Form 2003 (MPF)

12.01 The JCT Major Project Form 2003 edition (MPF) is a radical departure from the usual forms produced by the JCT. It is a design and build form which has moved away from the traditional JCT 98 With Contractor's Design form (WCD 98). MPF is aimed at employers and contractors undertaking very large commercial projects who are experienced and have their own in-house procedures for detailed risk management. It may be supposed that the form is named 'Major Project' for good reason – in order to dissuade parties from using it as a substitute for JCT 98 With Contractor's Design. However, despite the serious health warning it comes with, it remains to be seen whether parties will be irresistibly drawn to using it – in preference to the traditional forms – in a much wider range of projects because of its straightforward approach. Already the JCT plans to bring out a sub-contract form to fit alongside MPF. Some predict that future traditional procurement forms will follow its format.

12.02 The main attraction of MPF is that instead of wading through 85,000 words of WCD 98 the new MPF is a model of conciseness at only 14,500 words long. The form is well-set out and uses uncomplicated language. The contract documentation and procedures are simplified. The traditional Articles of Agreement have been dispensed with and instead the parties execute the Contract Conditions as a Deed incorporating by reference all of the other necessary documents. These are:

- The Appendix. This sets out all of the project-specific information referred to in the Contract Conditions, the Requirements, the Proposals, the Pricing Document and the Third Party Schedule. In effect this document contains the information that under other forms is usually to be found in the Articles of Agreement. Where possible, the Appendix contains 'default options' to make the Contract workable in the event that the parties fail to complete the Appendix.
- The Requirements. This document sets out what the employer requires the contractor to provide and the manner in which it is to be provided. The Requirements should contain all of the criteria that the employer considers to be important but allowing sufficient flexibility for the contractor to be innovative. It is here that the employer sets out important matters such as the requirements for the design programme and production of design documentation for review, the performance specifications and standards which are to be achieved by the contractor, stipulations about what is required to achieve practical completion and details of restrictions on access to the site and other trades that will be working on the site during the project.
- The Proposals. This is the contractor's document setting out what the contractor will provide to meet the Requirements.
- The Pricing Document. This document contains the contract sum analysis and payment regime. So far as the contract sum analysis is concerned this is likely to include the usual schedule of rates, labour rates, preliminaries and the like. As to the payment regime there are three prescribed options but the parties are free to agree their own bespoke payment basis. The three prescribed options are (1) interim monthly valuations for the work executed to date (2) stage payments per month of a proportion of the Contract Sum referable to completion of a stage and (3) progress payments by reference to a schedule of monthly payments.
- The Third Party Schedule. This document sets out all those third parties who are interested in the benefit of the contract and who are to have rights to enforce the terms of the contract which are for their benefit. These third parties are funders, insurers, tenants and purchasers. Others may be specially added if the parties wish although no framework exists for that as yet.

12.03 A product of MPF's conciseness of drafting means that the allocation of risk between the parties is more sharply focused so the parties clearly know where they stand. Most of the risk and responsibility is placed on the Contractor. In return, the Contractor is given much more flexibility commensurate with his increased risk and responsibility. Additionally, he is given some incentives. The intention of the contract is that once the Employer has defined the requirements and given the Contractor access to the site – rather than exclusive 'possession' – the Contractor is pretty much left to get on with the project.

12.04 The most significant area of risk is that the Contractor is completely responsible for design and construction beyond that which is set out in the Employer's Requirements. If the Employer's Requirements are not adequate the Contractor has to make a decision on how to proceed in order to meet the Employer's expectations. If there are discrepancies within the Employer's Requirements or between the Requirements and the Proposals the Contractor chooses which he will follow. Conversely, if there are discrepancies within the Contractor's Proposals the Employer can decide which the contractor should follow. Instead of asking the Employer about design and construction detailing, the Contractor has to decide. However, none of these decisions will amount to a 'Change' or variation entitling the Contractor to an adjustment to the contract sum or an extension of time. However, the Contractor is not given an entirely a free hand. The MPF has introduced a procedure for submission and approval of the Contractor's design after the contract has been made. The parties will be expected to have agreed a design programme. The Contractor will submit his Design Documents for the Employer's approval or comment in sufficient time before procurement and construction. The Employer has a short period of time – unless the parties have agreed otherwise, the period is 14 days – to give his approval and/or comments by marking the design according to the following system:

'A Action' which means that the Contractor must complete the project strictly in accordance with the Design Documents;
'B Action' which means that the Contractor should complete the project in accordance with the Design Documents incorporating the Employer's comments; or
'C Action' which vetoes the design and requires the Contractor to resubmit a design which conforms to the Contract.

The Employer can only mark the design 'B Action' or 'C Action' if he considers that the Design Document is not in accordance with the Contract, not because the Employer does not like that particular design or would prefer some alternative. If the Contractor disagrees with the comment he has 7 days to notify the Employer with reasons why the comments give rise to a 'Change' and the Employer then has 7 days to confirm or withdraw his comment. If the Contractor does not give notification within the 7 days, he will not be allowed to argue later on that there was a Change. The design submittal procedure does not alter the Contractor's responsibility for the Design (including any work necessary as a result of comments by the Employer).

12.05 Compared to other JCT forms, the MPF has shifted most of the risk onto the Contractor in other ways. Closely associated with the design risk of the Contractor, the MPF provides an option for the Employer's contracts with 'pre-appointed' consultants to be 'novated' to the Contractor, i.e. substituting the Contractor as party to the contract with the consultants instead of the Employer. That in itself is nothing new. However, whereas traditional design and build contracts provide for novation in respect of consultants' services in areas where the Contractor has assumed design liability, the MPF novation suggests that the Contractor will assume responsibility for the full range of services provided by the consultants both before and after novation (other than preparation of the Requirements). Contractors should be careful to investigate thoroughly precisely what services have been provided before agreeing to this option. The JCT envisages that a standard form for novation agreement will eventually accompany the MPF but it is proving difficult to get consensus on the appropriate terms. In the meantime, the novation option should be approached very cautiously by anyone using MPF because the indemnities and warranties are extremely complicated and can leave the Contractor unprotected.

12.06 Similarly, the Employer can name or nominate specialist consultants and contractors within the Requirements, which the Contractor is obliged to use in performing the contract. However,

unlike nomination and named procedures in traditional JCT forms, the Contractor will take full responsibility for the performance of these named specialists.

12.07 The Contractor now has to bear the risk of ground conditions and man-made obstructions (unless the parties agree to an optional clause providing otherwise). The Contractor also bears the risk of industrial disputes, exceptionally adverse weather, delay to supply chains of labour or materials and delays by statutory undertakers. None of these matters will entitle the Contractor to claim an extension of time or loss and expense.

12.08 Generally, the Contractor has to perform the contract in accordance with the standard normally expected in traditional design and build contract, namely by using reasonable skill and care, although there is an optional 'fitness for purpose' clause. However, the MPF specifically obliges the Contractor to comply strictly with any relevant statutory requirements, fitness for purpose of materials and any performance specification or performance testing requirements.

12.09 Claims for loss and expense will only be due where the Employer interferes with the Contractor's regular progress, or for breaches or acts of prevention by the Employer, or as a result of the Contractor suspending his works in accordance with section 112 of the HGCRA 1996. The intention of this clause is to prevent claims for loss and expense being made as a result of Changes. Instead, Changes are (generally) to be valued separately in accordance with the machinery in Clause 20.

12.10 So what are the incentives for Contractors? Probably most significant is that there are no retention provisions: this will provide the Contractor with increased cash flow throughout the project. Secondly, there are bonuses for acceleration and early completion at levels to be set out in the Appendix. Thirdly, the Contractor is encouraged to suggest value engineering amendments to the Requirements or Proposals which, if instructed as a Change, will result in financial benefits to be shared between the Employer and Contractor in the proportions identified in the Appendix. Fourthly, where there are concurrent delays, one of which is the fault of the Contractor, the other the Employer's fault there will be an adjustment to the Completion date.

12.11 There are a number of other important departures from traditional standard forms. Beyond a basic requirement for the Contractor to maintain professional indemnity insurance MPF does not provide a requirement for insurance or for joint names insurance, although it provides a framework for allowing insurance policies to be identified in the Appendix. The reason for this is probably because major projects require bespoke insurance packages.

12.12 In a further break from tradition, arbitration has been abandoned as a method of dispute resolution. Instead, the MPF permits mediation, adjudication or litigation in Court.

12.13 In a ground-breaking development, the MPF is the first to embrace the Contracts (Rights of Third Parties) Act 1999. Instead of the myriad collateral warranties usually found in large projects, there is a Third Parties Rights Schedules where the parties can identify the third parties who may enforce terms in the contract for their benefit. This will include funders, purchasers and tenants. However, at this stage the available rights appear similar to the traditional collateral warranties, which may not have been wise but at least provides users with some fairly familiar territory to start with. Funders receive the benefit of a warranty from the Contractor that it will comply with the Contract and 'step in' rights in the event that the funder terminates its agreement to finance the Contractor or the Contractor seeks to terminate the Contract. The first purchasers or tenants also receive the benefit of a warranty from the Contractor that it has completed the project in accordance with the Contract. No warranties are called for from sub-contractors and consultants and it is up to the Contractor to ensure that it has secured the appropriate obligations from them. The warranties can only be assigned twice.

Advantages

12.14 MPF is a simpler, clearer form than the traditional standard forms. It is expected that other forms will follow suit. The contractor has more flexibility but more responsibility.

Disadvantages

12.15 It is not suitable unless the parties have excellent internal risk management procedures. The contractor takes considerable more risk.

13 JCT Standard Form of Management Contract 1998 edition (MC 98)

13.01 At much the same time as 'design-and-build' was emerging, another new procurement method was starting to appear, known as 'management contracting'. Under this arrangement a large firm of building contractors would assume responsibility to an employer for the erection of a building. But rather than carrying out construction work themselves, they would sub-contract the entire works to others, known as 'works contractors', reserving to themselves a role as managers and for the provision of basic site services. This form of arrangement was attractive to developers for whom speed of commencement and completion was of paramount importance. The arrangement was also potentially attractive to an employer who was undertaking a particularly complex project on which strong management would be advantageous. During the 1970s and 1980s the large companies carrying out management contracting developed their own forms of contract.

13.02 Initially there was no standard form, nor one negotiated between representatives of different interests. Then in 1987 the JCT published its Standard Form of Management Contract. Only peripheral amendments were made over time to the form. The contract has now been published in a 1998 edition which incorporates those minor amendments, and also takes account of the requirements of the Housing Grants, Construction and Regeneration Act 1996. There is a family of documents for use in connection with the works contractors' contracts:

Works Contract /1
    Section 1:   Invitation to tender
    Section 2:   Tender by works contractor
    Section 3:   Articles of agreement
Works Contract /2:   Works contract conditions
Works Contract /3:   Employer/works contractor agreement
Works Contract phased completion supplement.

It will be seen that in a general way they follow the scheme of the JCT 98 nominated sub-contractor documents.

13.03 This is a 'cost-plus' type of contract. The management contractor is entitled to be reimbursed whatever he has to pay to the works contractors. In addition he is entitled to be reimbursed his own costs for providing site services and to be paid a fee. The contract envisages the appointment of an architect and other design professionals by the employer: the management contractor will work in liaison with them. Since the paramount concern of employers using this form of contract tends to be speed, the management contractor is often appointed at much the same time as the architect. The contract envisages that the management contractor will perform services in the pre-construction, as well as the construction, period.

13.04 In practical terms the dominant obligation of the management contractor is usually to get the project completed by the contractual completion date. There are provisions for extension of time and liquidated damages. There are also provisions for the recovery of loss and expense upon the regular progress of the works being disrupted, but, since it is the works contractors who are doing the

construction work, it is they, rather than the management contractor, who will in the first instance make such applications. Consistent with the general theme of reimbursement to the management contractor of his outlay, he will be entitled to recover from the employer payments of this character which he has to make to works contractors, unless caused by his own default.

13.05 The management contractor also has an obligation under the contract to achieve as cheap an outcome as possible. He undertakes to ensure that the project is carried through in an economical and expeditious manner. A 'Contract Cost Plan', prepared by the employer in conjunction with the management contractor, is annexed to the contract. The management contractor is under an obligation to identify areas of potential increases or savings in the Contract Cost Plan.

13.06 Most unusually for a standard form contract, but again consistent with the priority attached to speed, a jurisdiction is conferred on the architect to require an acceleration of the works or change the sequence of them. This includes a power of making the completion date earlier. The management contractor is given a right of reasonable objection to such changes.

Advantages

13.07 Management contracting is an attractive choice for a property developer for whom interest charges are a major commercial consideration, since this is the method of procurement which tends to allow the quickest start to the works. It has been found by many developers to offer the best prospect of a speedy completion. It provides stronger management of the works than any other: since the management contractor has no responsibility for any hands-on construction he has nothing to distract him from using his experience of running construction projects to drive the project to an efficient and fast completion. The arrangement is attractive to management contractors because they assume virtually no financial risk.

Disadvantages

13.08 The employer does not have any certainty as to the cost of the project. The employer cannot look to one person for the assumption of design as well as construction responsibility.

14 GC/Works/1 (1998 edition)

14.01 The government works or GC family of forms of contract are published by HMSO. The forms have been progressively developed from terms originally drafted to procure defence works before the Second World War. In 1973 the government issued GC/Works/1 which was a lump sum with quantities contract. The present 1998 edition comprises three sets of standard conditions drafted by the Property Advisors to the Civil Estate (PACE). Changes have been incorporated to meet the recommendations of the Latham report and to accommodate the requirements of the Housing Grants, Construction and Regeneration Act 1996. In addition, the 1998 edition has responded to pressure placed upon those responsible for the form to adopt successful aspects of the private sector version of the form, PSA/1, which was published in 1994. The form is intended for use both on building and engineering work. There is another government form for minor works, namely GC/Works/2. Historically there has been a little consultation, but no negotiation, in the drafting of the GC forms. The 1998 GC/Works/1 form acknowledges input from external users of the form in drafting the latest amendments.

14.02 The GC/Works/1 1998 family of forms comprises four documents, those being the three sets of standard conditions and a fourth document which contains forms and commentary to be used with the other three:

1 With Quantities General Conditions
2 Without Quantities General Conditions
3 Single Stage Design and Build General Conditions
4 Model Forms and Commentary.

15 ACA Form of Building Agreement 1982 (third edition 1998)

15.01 Many members of the Association of Consultant Architects (ACA) were deeply dissatisfied with JCT 80 by reason of its complexity. At the same time they recognized that with the passage of time it would become increasingly unwise to continue to use JCT 63. In 1982 ACA published its own form of contract. In 1984 ACA published a second edition. The third edition followed in 1998 and was reprinted in 2003.

15.02 The contract is basically a lump sum 'with quantities' type of contract. But the contractor does not take the risk of errors in the bills of quantities: if there is an error the architect shall determine a fair adjustment. There is an option to cater for a portion of contractor design. A simple fluctuations clause is available.

15.03 The ACA took the view, in earlier editions of the form, that arbitration was not necessarily the most desirable form of dispute resolution. Previous forms required the parties to choose between three options of dispute resolution: litigation, straight arbitration, or adjudication with arbitration to follow. The 1998 edition has had to take account of the statutory requirement for adjudication. In so doing the ACA have adopted provisions which seek to minimize recourse to arbitration or litigation. The parties have to choose at the time of contracting between arbitration and litigation as the final dispute resolution method. Where there is an adjudication, the contract provides that the adjudicator's decision is final and binding unless notice is given by either side, within 20 days of that decision, that legal proceedings have been commenced or that the dispute has been referred to arbitration. When a notice of arbitration is given, the contract provides a conciliation method which the parties can at that stage agree to try before proceeding with the arbitration.

15.04 There is also an ACA Form of Sub-Contract. The current issue is dated 1998.

Advantages

15.05 The ACA form has many of the good points of the New Engineering Contract (NEC) (see below) without the bad points. It has the merits of brevity, simplicity and clarity, but not to such a striking degree as to be likely to create problems. It is a contract of similar length, and degree of detail, to IFC 98, but its drafting is regarded by many as easier to understand. There is far less detail to be entered by the parties than required by the NEC's Contract Data. Despite many years of use, there is no known occasion on which the meaning of any part of the contract has had to be litigated – but that may merely reflect the relatively limited number of contracts made upon this form.

Disadvantages

15.06 The ACA contract is not the product of negotiation, and some commentators regard that as a criticism. It is said that the ACA form is more favourable to the employer than the JCT form. For example, there is no restriction on assignment by the employer after completion of the works. There is also provision for the employer to name sub-contractors and suppliers, but in the event that those named default, the contractor takes full responsibility for them.

16 The NEC Engineering and Construction Contract

16.01 In 1993 the Institution of Civil Engineers published a contract which had 'New' in its title and was new in its nature. Despite its genesis, the form can be used on building contracts as well as on engineering contracts. Unlike the JCT contracts which have all evolved from the old RIBA forms, it acknowledged no ancestry among previous forms. The New Engineering Contract (NEC) consciously turned its back on all previous forms. Its authors believed that the existing forms promoted a confrontational culture in the construction industry. Strong encouragement to use it in building projects was given by the report of Sir Michael Latham, 'Constructing the Team' (1994). A second edition was published in 1995, and a 1998 addendum addressed the requirements of the Housing Grants, Construction and Regeneration Act 1996. The form, although still generally known as 'the NEC', is strictly called the 'NEC Engineering and Construction Contract', the reason being that the Institution of Civil Engineers intended to publish other forms prefix 'NEC'. Since 1993 the other available NEC contracts are the Sub-Contract, the Short Sub-Contract, Professional Services Contract and the Adjudicator's Contract. They follow the general style and content of the NEC Engineering and Construction Contract but are not discussed here. Among construction lawyers there are currently two schools of thought about the NEC Engineering and Construction Contract: there are some great enthusiasts, and a large number of sceptics.

16.02 For architects who have become familiar with any of the JCT contracts, the NEC Engineering and Construction Contract involves a massive leap into uncharted territory. Apart from the fact that the parties are still called 'the Employer' and 'the Contractor', almost every other expression is different. Instead of an 'architect' or 'engineer', there are two different actors called respectively, 'the Supervisor' and 'the Project Manager', both employed by the employer. Some of the new expressions are just new labels for recognized concepts, while others connote novel concepts.

16.03 The drafting of the clauses is also novel. Instead of indicating a contractual undertaking by an expression connoting obligation such as, 'X shall perform Y', the NEC Engineering and Construction Contract says 'X performs Y'. This may generate confusion, since any contract contains text which does not connote obligations, such as statements of what parties may do, but are not obliged to do. The numbering of clauses is to be applauded for avoiding the multiple decimal points of recent JCT contracts, although strangely the first clause is number 10. Ease of use is also promoted by the comprehensive index.

16.04 There is no formal agreement as such. That is, there is no form to fulfil the role of 'Articles of Agreement' in a JCT contract, where the parties enter their signatures or affix their seals to bring the contract into being. Appendix 3 of the Guidance Notes provides a sample form of agreement which includes a space for the parties to identify which documents form part of the agreement. Those who use the NEC have to exercise care to either adopt this form or to otherwise record if and when they are committing themselves to a contract, and which options they are selecting.

16.05 There is an eleven-page section entitled 'Contract Data', which is reminiscent of the Appendix to a JCT contract. Part is completed by the employer, part by the contractor. The information to be inserted is detailed and needs careful consideration. For example, in relation to 'Compensation events' (read: 'relevant event' in JCT-speak), there must be an entry for 'the number of days with snow lying at … hours GMT'. Space is also left for additional compensation events to be identified, and the example indicated in the Guidance Notes includes 'working hours with windspeeds exceeding 60 km/hr'.

16.06 The drafting of the arbitration clause is skimpy, and the mode of appointment of an arbitrator, and other provisions concerning arbitration, left for the parties to specify. The contract had its own adjudication provisions which pre-dated the Housing Grants, Construction and Regeneration Act 1996. The adjudication requirements of the Act have been incorporated by an optional section, Y(UK)2. This is intended to be used for UK contracts. It amends the original adjudication provisions, although these remain intact for non-UK contracts. The UK adjudication provisions provide for a two-stage process. Although any dispute can be referred to adjudication, a dispute is deemed not to arise until four weeks after a notice of dissatisfaction has been served by one party on the other. (This provision is probably ineffective, as contravening the requirements of the 1996 Act.) Meanwhile, within two weeks of the notice of dissatisfaction being served, the parties must meet and seek to resolve the matter.

16.07 The NEC can be regarded as comprising three elements:

1   Nine 'core clauses'. These numbered clauses will be used in every contract.
2   Six 'main options', identified by letter 'A' to 'F'. These are payment mechanisms and only one of them must be chosen.
3   'Secondary options'. identified by letters 'G' to 'Z'. These may be regarded as optional add-ons. Save that a few cannot be used with some of the main options, the parties can pick as many or as few of these as they want.

16.08 The six main options, of which one must be chosen, are:

Option A Priced contract with activity schedule
Option B Priced contract with bill of quantities
Option C Target contract with activity schedule
Option D Target contract with bill of quantities
Option E Cost reimbursable contract
Option F Management contract

Broadly speaking, these options allow the choice between a fixed-price contract, a remeasurement contract, a cost plus contract or a management contract.

16.09 Through the use of the secondary options the parties can add matters such as sectional completion, retention and damages for delay. The UK adjudication option, Y(UK)2, is one of these secondary options. The NEC Engineering and Construction Contract takes a contractor's designed portion in its stride by simply stating 'The Contractor designs the parts of the works which the Works Information states he is to design' (Clause 21.1).

Advantages

16.10 The two great virtues of the NEC Engineering and Construction Contract are, first, its simplicity and clarity of expression, and, second, its policy of promoting a cooperative, as opposed to a confrontational, approach.

Disadvantages

16.11 The meaning of some clauses is vague by reason of the brief, generalized, or novel way in which they are expressed. Some lawyers predict that there will have to be litigation to resolve uncertainties of meaning. Those who embark on a contract under the NEC Engineering and Construction Contract have to learn a new contractual language and new contractual roles.

11

Contractor and sub-contractor collateral warranties

ANN MINOGUE

1 Architects and collateral warranties

1.01 Architects are likely to encounter collateral warranties in two circumstances. First, and most importantly, they themselves may be asked to provide collateral warranties, and second they may be expected to advise their clients – the employer under the building contract – on collateral warranties to be given by contractors and sub-contractors either to the employer or to third parties such as funders, purchasers or tenants. Although in most cases employers will take direct legal advice on the provision of collateral warranties to third parties, architects should still be aware of the nature of these collateral warranties in case advice is required. In the case of collateral warranties required under standard documents, such as JCT forms, in favour of the employer, architects should satisfy themselves that the appropriate collateral warranties are obtained from contractors or sub-contractors in favour of the employer. The detailed terms of architects' collateral warranties are dealt with elsewhere in this book. This chapter will look at collateral warranties generally, but will then concentrate on contractor/sub-contractor collateral warranties.

2 What is a collateral warranty?

2.01 A collateral warranty is a form of contract which runs alongside, and is usually supplemental to, another contract. Usually a collateral warranty creates a contractual relationship between two parties where none would otherwise exist. It takes the form of a contract between the party to the underlying contract who is providing services or carrying out work and a third party who has an interest in the proper performance of that contract. In this text, the person giving the collateral warranty will be called 'the warrantor' and the person to whom it is given 'the beneficiary'.

3 Why have collateral warranties become so important?

3.01 The legal doctrine of privity of contract means that remedies for the improper performance of obligations under a contract are – subject to Contracts (Rights of Third parties) Act 1999 (see below) – limited to the parties to that contract. For example, under the JCT 1998 Standard Form of Building Contract, if no collateral warranty is obtained and a sub-contractor is in breach of his sub-contract, the employer will not be able to sue him for breach of contract as the employer is not a party to the sub-contract. The employer would have to make his claim against the main contractor with whom he would have a contract and the main contractor would, in turn, claim against the defaulting sub-contractor. A particular problem arises where the sub-contractor's default does not place the main contractor in breach of the main contract: the clearest example is where

a nominated sub-contractor provides late or incorrect design information for work which does not constitute 'Performance Specified Work' or part of 'the Contractor's Designed Portion'. Even where this problem does not arise, if the contractor is insolvent, the employer will find himself unable to recover any of his losses from the insolvent main contractor and, without a collateral warranty, he cannot sue the sub-contractor for any breach of contract by him prior to the insolvency.

3.02 It was a desire to circumvent the legal problems that stem from the law of privity of contract that led to the development of the tort of negligence as set out in the famous case of *Donoghue v Stevenson* [1932] AC 562. That case established the 'neighbour' principle which obliges a party to take care to avoid acts which it can reasonably foresee are likely to injure its neighbour. 'Neighbours' were defined as being those so closely affected by a party's act that that party ought to have had them in contemplation when carrying out the act in question. 'Injury' initially meant physical harm but the courts came to extend it to financial loss. A duty of care in negligence is owed only to neighbours but there is no need for neighbours to be contractually linked to create a liability.

3.03 For many years the tort of negligence applied to cases of defective buildings, the leading case being *Anns v Merton London Borough Council* [1978] AC 728. Builders, architects and others involved in the construction process were held to owe fairly wide duties of care to all those who might reasonably be expected to be affected by their negligent actions. This duty of care protected tenants and purchasers of developments. Therefore, parties who needed to be protected from negligent and defective building design or work were advised that they had some legal protection under the tort of negligence without needing any direct contractual link with the builders and designers.

3.04 The cases of *D & F Estates Limited and Others v The Church Commissioners of England and Others* [1988] 49 BLR 1 and *Murphy v Brentwood District Council* [1991] 1 AC 398 dramatically altered the established legal position relating to defective buildings and negligence so that a builder would not be liable in tort to successive owners of a building (i.e. those with no contractual link to him) for any defects in the building itself. It was held that the cost of rectifying defects was economic loss and that this type of loss was not ordinarily recoverable in the tort of negligence. The builder would only be liable in tort if any defect caused personal injury or damage to other property (i.e. something other than the building). The principles governing liabilities in tort are discussed in more detail in Chapter 3.

3.05 The decisions in *D & F Estates* and *Murphy* left third parties legally exposed. As a result, collateral warranties became increasingly important as the only means of protection for third parties who were prevented from recovering losses suffered due to defective building work. It has now become common practice for employers, purchasers, tenants, funders, freeholders and others to require contractors, sub-contractors, and professional consultants with whom they do not have a contractual link to provide collateral warranties to enable them to recover directly for any defects and other losses arising from their work.

3.06 Although recent decisions of the House of Lords *(St Martins Property Corporation Ltd v Sir Robert McAlpine Ltd* [1994] AC 85) and of the Court of Appeal *(Darlington Borough Council v Wiltshier Northern Limited* [1995] 1 WLR 68 and *Sir Alfred McAlpine Limited v Panatown Limited* [1998] 88 BLR 67) may enable contractual claims to be pursued on behalf of subsequent purchasers of a defective building, even though the purchaser has no contractual link with the contractor, the extent of the comfort afforded by these decisions is so imprecise that employers are usually still advised to ask for collateral warranties on behalf of purchasers, tenants and funders.

3.07 In addition, the courts have tried to avoid the draconian effects of the decisions in *D&F Estates* and *Murphy* by further developing the law of negligent misstatement under which professionals who give negligent advice can still be held liable for pure economic loss even to persons with whom they have no contract. The leading authority is *Hedley Byrne & Co v Heller and Partners* [1964] AC 465 and the doctrine has recently been extended in cases such as *Henderson v Merrett Syndicates Limited* [1995] 2 AC 145. The precise ambit though of this exception too is uncertain and has not caused the torrent of demands for collateral warranties to ebb.

3.08 One final general point on collateral warranties – the Contracts (Rights of Third Parties) Act, 1999 which came fully into force in May 2000, radically affects the law in this area and particularly it will change the position as stated in paragraph 3.01 above. The Act confers on a third party 'a right to enforce a term of the contract' where *either* the contract contains an express term to that effect *or* where the contract purports to confer a benefit on that third party. In both cases, the third party must be expressly identified in the contract by name, class or description, but need not be in existence at the time of the contract. The third party must, however, be capable of being ascertained with certainty. Accordingly, a general reference to 'purchasers of the building when completed' would be enforceable.

A 'right to enforce a term of the contract' in these circumstances means both the right to all of the remedies which would have been available to a third party through the courts if it had been a party to the contract but subject to the terms of the contract including any relevant exclusions of liability or restrictions in the contract. In other words, contractual damages are recoverable but the parties can agree that recovery is excluded or capped.

More problematically, the Act also states that where a third party has a right to enforce a term of a contract, the parties may not without his consent 'rescind the contract, or vary it in such a way as to extinguish or alter his entitlement under that right' in certain circumstances. This can be excluded by agreement or by the courts or the arbitrator in defined circumstances.

The third party's rights will be subject to all defences and setoffs that would have been available to the contracting party had the third party been a party to the original contract unless the parties provide otherwise in the contract.

The effects of this legislation in relation to the collateral warranties will be very far reaching indeed. In future, there will be no need for separate collateral warranties in favour of funders, purchasers and tenants. The relevant rights can be granted by a clause included in the original consultancy agreement or building contract. Those rights can be subject to exclusions and restrictions. In other words, the contractual damages which would otherwise be recoverable by the third party potentially include losses other than the cost of repair, but these can be subject to agreements that recovery is excluded or capped, that it is subject to 'net contribution clauses' and so on. Sub-contracts, too, can include a clause enabling the employer to pursue the sub-contractor directly, e.g. for

design errors where the main contractor has no responsibility for design as mentioned above, for any losses under JCT Management Contract 1998 where the management contractor's liability is limited to what he recovers and so on. There will in future be no need for NSC/W or Works Contract/3 Employer/Works Contractor Agreements provided of course that the appropriate rights are conferred by the underlying contract.

The initial reaction of most of the contract producing bodies to the Act was to exclude any third party rights whole-sale. This sweeping approach has more recently been superseded by a more careful and reflective use of the benefits that the Act has to offer. JCT Major Project Form published in 2003 is a case in point: while it excludes any third party rights generally, it sets out in a Third Party Rights Schedule specific rights to be vested in a funder or purchasers/tenants. The rights are triggered by a notice served by the employer on the contractor identifying the relevant party and the nature of its interest in the project. After triggering of the rights, the person identified in the employer's notice can pursue the contractor directly for breach of the provisions set out in the Third Party Rights Schedule. The rights themselves are not dissimilar from those set out in MCWa/F and MCWa/P&T and are discussed in more detail below. At the time of writing, the JCT drafting subcommittee is working on the possibility of extending the use of Contracts (Rights of Third Parties) Act 1999 as a mechanism for granting rights previously conferred by collateral warranties in other areas but, for the moment at least, collateral warranties remain a feature of JCT documentation.

4 Who needs the benefit of collateral warranties?

Employers

4.01 As noted in paragraph 3.01 above, employers require collateral warranties from the contracting industry in their favour in two different circumstances, either:

- To supplement and reinforce their direct contractual rights. So, for example, the employer may seek collateral warranties from key sub-contractors and suppliers in respect of materials and workmanship supplied or carried out by them even though he also has contractual rights against the main contractor. The main advantage to the employer of obtaining collateral warranties in such circumstances is that if such workmanship or materials were to prove defective, proceedings could be brought directly against the party responsible in addition to the contractor. This will be particularly useful if the main contractor has gone into liquidation. It is suggested that this doubling-up of contractual protection should be discouraged except in exceptional cases. It results in an over-proliferation of paperwork and interferes with proper management of the work.
- Where, but for the collateral warranty, the employer may have no enforceable contractual right for the design and construction work. This is most commonly the case where nominated or specialist sub-contractors carry out design work in connection with the development, but the main contractor has no responsibility for such design (as is the case if JCT 98 is used *without* Contractor's Designed Portion Supplement or Performance Specified Work). Equally, an employer would also require collateral warranties if he uses management contracting to procure his development. Otherwise, he may find himself without any remedy since the management contractor's liability for works contractors' shortcomings is limited by the terms of the management contract.

As noted above, in the first case, it is really for the employer to decide whether he feels he needs this supplemental protection. In the second case, though, there is a much greater obligation on the architect to ensure that the correct collateral warranties are in place since, if they are not, the employer may well be left without any contractual remedy at all in respect of parts of the design of the development where the architect has agreed that such design will be carried out by the sub-contractor. SFA/99 excludes the architect's responsibility for such design and, in these circumstances, there must be a good argument that the architect has failed in his duties to the employer if he does not advise him that collateral warranties should be obtained.

Purchasers

4.02 Purchasers cannot generally sue vendors for defects in the development in the absence of express contractual undertakings from the vendor. A purchaser from an original employer would have no direct contractual link with those involved in the construction process unless the benefits of the construction contracts and the various consultancy agreements were assigned to him. Usually this will not be possible without the prior consent of the contractor or consultants. Sometimes, the building contract may be amended so that the contractor is obliged to consent to the assignment in advance of it. Purchasers from original developers were specifically mentioned in *D & F Estates* and *Murphy* as having no rights in negligence against contractors for any defects arising in any building purchased. As a result, purchasers will often require collateral warranties to ensure that they are protected.

Tenants

4.03 A prospective tenant of a new development may require collateral warranties if the lease is to be granted on a full repairing basis, so that the landlord accepts no liability for defects in the building and the tenant becomes liable to carry out repairs at his own cost. With full repairing leases it is desirable that the tenant obtains collateral warranties from those involved in the construction process in order that he can recover, via a direct contractual link, repair costs from those responsible. Even where the landlord does accept some liability for defects in the building, tenants will usually also want a collateral warranty from the design and construction team in order to protect themselves against insolvency of the landlord developers.

Funders

4.04 Where a bank or institution provides finance for a development and takes a legal charge over the property to be developed, the funder will be concerned that on completion it is free of defects and is of a sufficient quality and value to provide adequate security for the loan. Without a collateral warranty, a funder will have no direct contractual relationship with any of those involved in the design and construction of the development. A funder will usually want any collateral warranty to contain 'step-in' rights so that, should the employer/borrower default under the funding agreement, or act in such a way that would enable the contractor to terminate the building contract, the funder could 'step-in' and take over the completion of the development. It should be noted that although funders commonly require collateral warranties from sub-contractors including 'step-in' rights, it is hard to see that a funder could ever step into a sub-contract. His rights of 'step in' should be restricted to the contracts specifically entered into by the employer/borrower.

Other third parties

4.05 Collateral warranties may be required in a number of other circumstances. For instance, where development work is dependent on the consent of a neighbouring landowner, that neighbouring landowner may require a collateral warranty from those involved in the construction process to ensure that, should any damage occur to his property or should his business be disrupted as a result of the works, he would be able to recover from those responsible any costs incurred in repairing the damage and any loss of profit. Collateral warranties may also be required where a developer lets a development to a tenant who carries out fitting-out works. In such circumstances the developer may require a collateral warranty from the tenant's designer and fit-out contractor to ensure such works are performed correctly.

5 Who should provide collateral warranties?

5.01 Exactly which contractor or sub-contractor should provide warranties depends upon the form of contractual procurement used.

JCT 98 (and traditional forms of contracting)

5.02 Under traditional forms of contract – discussed comprehensively in Chapter 9 – the main contractor is fully responsible for his own and his sub-contractors, or suppliers, standard of workmanship and for the quality of all materials used but not for any sub-contractor's or supplier's design. The main contractor can, moreover, claim loss and expense for delay or errors in the design of nominated sub-contractors. JCT warranty forms NSC/W (for nominated sub-contractors) and TNS/2 (for nominated suppliers) were specifically drafted to give the employer redress in such circumstances.

NSC/W and TNS/2 provide a direct contractual link between a nominated sub-contractor or supplier and the employer. As both forms of warranty are broadly similar, this section will concentrate on NSC/W (last re-printed in 2000). Under Clause 2.1 of NSC/W, the nominated sub-contractor warrants that he has exercised reasonable skill and care in the design of the sub-contract works, in the selection of the goods and materials to be used in the sub-contract works and in the satisfaction of any performance specification set out in the sub-contract. It is important to note that the warranty provided only extends to reasonable skill and care. It does not extend to suitability for required purpose which would, if the design formed part of a contract for the supply of goods and services and if the employer was relying on the skill and knowledge of the sub-contractor, be implied by the Supply of Goods and Services Act 1982. Accordingly, an employer seeking to rely on NSC/W would have to prove that the sub-contractor was negligent in designing the sub-contract works, selecting materials, etc., rather than merely having to show that the design or the goods and materials selected were unsuitable. In addition, the wording of Clause 5.3 ensures that NSC/W provides protection to the employer in respect of latent defects in workmanship after the final certificate has been issued under the main contract.

Under Clauses 25.3 and 26.4 of JCT 1998, the main contractor will be able to claim an extension of time and loss and expense from the employer due to delay for the late issue of design information to the contractor caused in turn by delays by the nominated sub-contractor. To provide the employer with some redress, Clauses 3.2 and 3.3 of NSC/W make the nominated sub-contractors liable to the employer for any delay in issuing sub-contract design information to the architect; any delay which may result in the determination of the sub-contract under Clause 35.24 of the JCT 98 main contract; and any delay that may otherwise allow the main contractor to claim an extension of time under the main contract.

Clause 11A of NSC/W provides that all disputes may be referred to adjudication. Clause 11B and 11C then provide the options of arbitration or litigation as the procedure for disputes resolution. A major disadvantage of arbitration is that, as the Arbitration Act 1996 makes no provision for proceedings between more than two parties, arbitration is not well suited to dealing with multi-party proceedings of the type which are common in complicated construction disputes where it is often unclear as to who is responsible for any particular defect. To overcome these problems the JCT have adopted the Construction Industry Model Arbitration Rules (CIMAR) and have attempted to draft Clause 11B of NSC/W to allow for multi-party arbitrations. However, the relevant provisions are highly complicated and it is very unclear as to whether or not they would work in practice. If multi-party proceedings are envisaged it would be easier to refer such disputes to the courts.

Third parties may require warranties from the various design sub-contractors as noted in Section 4 above.

JCT 98 with Contractor's Design (and other design-and-build contracts)

5.03 Under design-and-build contracts, the contractor usually has the main responsibility for both the design and construction of the works. It is common for contractors, however, to sub-let the design of the works to independent firms of consultants. Employers and third parties may seek a warranty from the design consultants or indeed from sub-contractors in case, at a future date, defects arise in the works due to the design which cause losses that can not be recovered due to the contractor's liquidation, due to the inadequacy of the contractor's insurance cover, or due to a contractual cap on the contractor's liability. For the reasons outlined above, the proliferation of this doubling up of contractual protection by use of collateral warranties should be discouraged.

JCT Management Contract 1998 (and other forms of management contract)

5.04 In the JCT Management Contract, and in most other similar forms, the management contractor is liable for all the work carried out by the works contractors, including any design work. It provides, however, that the employer will have to pay the management contractor to remedy any default of the works contractors. This rule applies where the management contractor is unable to recover from a defaulting works contractor. This can obviously present problems to the employer should the management contractor be unable to recover or if the management contractor becomes insolvent. To deal with this problem a form of direct warranty agreement known as Works Contract/3 (the Employer/ Works Contractor Agreement) has been prepared for use with JCT Management Contract. This form is in many ways similar to NSC/W and TNS/2 and imposes on the works contractors a duty to use all reasonable skill and care in the design of any part of the works he designs and in the selection of any materials or goods he may select. Form WC/3 also obliges the works contractor to provide any design information to the management contractor on time. It does not, however, extend to delay by matters other than design so that the employer would have no direct claim against a works contractor in respect of simple delay in the carrying out of the work on site. It would be prudent to amend Form WC/3 to protect the employer against *any* breach by the works contractor of his obligations. In addition, inevitably it will be usual for any third party with an interest in the development to seek collateral warranties from all the principal works contractors as well.

Construction management

5.05 In construction management contracts the employer engages a construction manager and also directly engages the contractors, usually known as trade contractors, who are actually to undertake the on-site works. As the construction manager will not ordinarily be liable for breaches of the trade contracts, the employer bears the risk of trade contractor insolvency and has no main contractor to sue for such breaches. It will therefore be usual for any third party with an interest in a development to seek collateral warranties from all the principal trade contractors as well as the construction manager.

6 Standard forms of collateral warranty

6.01 Initially collateral warranties in favour of third parties such as funders, purchasers and tenants tended to be tailor-made, usually to suit the requirements of particular employers. As they reallocate risk amongst the parties, they are often the subject of extensive negotiation. Non-standard warranties can vary greatly in scope and complexity with some drafted to be more favourable to beneficiaries and some to warrantors. They can also be known by a variety of names such as 'Duty of Care Agreement', or simply 'Warranty Agreement' and can be drafted as deeds or simple contract letter form agreements. As tailor-made warranties can be very diverse and negotiating them can lead to extensive argument before a development is begun, a number of standard forms have been drafted and are often used at least as a basis for these documents. The main standard form contractor and sub-contractor warranties are set out below.

Contractor's warranties

6.02 The JCT have produced warranties to be given by contractors to funders and purchasers/tenants. These warranties, MCWa/F and MCWa/P&T can be used with the Standard Form of Building Contract JCT 1998, the Design and Build Contract JCT 1998 and the Intermediate Form of Building Contract IFC 98. The warranties were first published in 1993 but are now in their second edition, 2001. They were intended to be compatible with the standard form of Consultants' warranties but the relevant JCT working party was not able to reach agreement on the terms of these collateral warranties from consultants – see Chapter 31.

Sub-contractor's warranties

6.03 NSC/W and TNS/2 for use with JCT 1998 have already been mentioned as has the Employer/Works Contractor Agreement WC/3 for use with JCT Management Contract 1998.

7 Key clauses of the JCT Standard Forms of Main Contractor Warranty

7.01 This section will comment on the Standard Forms of Main Contractor Warranty, MCWa/P&T and MCWa/F, although comparative reference will also be made to consultants' warranties which are examined in more detail in Chapter 31. Because the terms of the contractors' warranties and the consultants' warranties do elide in a number of respects, much of what is said in relation to consultants' warranties is relevant to this Section too. Cross-reference should be made to Part 4, Chapter 31.

The warranty itself

7.02 Most forms of warranty start by imposing a contractual obligation on the warrantor in favour of the beneficiary. Such a warranty in a contractor collateral warranty usually refers to the terms of the main contract. Clause 1 of MCWa/P&T states:

> 'The Contractor warrants that it has carried out the Works in accordance with the Building Contract.'

This wording reflects the fact that such warranties are intended to be given *after* practical completion. Under this wording the contractor's liability under the warranty to the third party will be the same as its obligations under the main contract to the employer. The contractor's obligations under JCT 98, JCT With Contractor's Design 98 and IFC 98 are similar in that the contractor has an absolute duty to complete the contract works in accordance with the contract and specification. This position contrasts with a consultant's obligations under consultancy appointments and warranties which are usually limited to a duty to exercise reasonable skill and care in the performance of his duties.

Economic and consequential loss

7.03 Under the law of negligence, losses which are deemed to be purely economic are generally not recoverable as noted in Section 3 above. Under contract law, however, such 'economic' loss can be recoverable. Therefore, if an employer suffers a loss of profit, a loss of rent revenue, or a diminution in value in his property due to a breach of contract by a contractor, he can claim such loss from the contractor in contract. Contractors have resisted the imposition of such all-embracing liability in collateral warranties. As a result of this, Clause 1(a) of MCWa/P&T (but not MCWa/F) contains three possible alternative drafting options which require amendment or deletion from the text of the printed form in order to select the option which is to apply. The options are as follows:

- To restrict the contractor's liability to reasonable costs of repair only and to exclude *all* other losses suffered or incurred by the beneficiary as a result of the contractor's breach of Clause 1. If this is to be adopted, then the words '*AND*' should be deleted as should both alternative Clauses 1(a)(i). Clause 1(b) then provides that the contractor is not liable for any losses incurred other than repair costs as referred to in Clause 1(a).

- To make the contractor liable for the costs of repair incurred by the beneficiary, and in addition, to cap his other liability for damages which would otherwise be recoverable by the beneficiary in accordance with common law principles including loss of profit, loss of rent revenue, etc., as outlined above to a maximum amount in respect of *each* breach of Clause 1. If this option is to be adopted, then the second alternative Clause 1(a)(i) should be deleted.
- To make the contractor responsible for costs of repair and in addition to impose on him further liability for damages for breach of contract as outlined above, but capped at a maximum amount in aggregate under the collateral warranty. If this option is to be adopted, then the first alternative Clause 1(a)(i) should be deleted.

A final option not contemplated by the drafting of MCWa/P&T but which will undoubtedly be used in practice is to leave the contractor's liability for other losses unlimited so that it is assessed in accordance with the normal principles governing recovery of damages at common law. If this option is required, then Clause 1(b) should be deleted in the third line of Clause 1(a) as should both alternative Clauses 1(a)(i) and Clause 1(b) itself.

Plainly, at this point, the Architect might be well advised to suggest to his client that he needs independent legal advice before attempting to complete MCWa/P&T.

Joint liability and contribution clauses

7.04 A further limitation on the beneficiary's right to claim damages from a contractor applies in the case where the contractor is not the only person responsible for the defect. MCWa/P&T contains a net contribution clause which limits the liability of the warrantor to the proportion of the costs incurred by the beneficiary which it would be fair for him to pay having regard to his own and the other parties share of the blame. The relevant clause is Clause 1(c) which states:

'The contractor's liability to the purchaser/tenant under this agreement shall be limited to the proportion of the purchaser's/tenant's losses which it would be just and equitable to require the contractor to pay having regard to the extent of the contractor's responsibility for the same, on the following assumptions, namely that:

(i) [[●] 'the consultant[s]'] engaged by the employer has/have provided contractual undertakings to the purchaser/tenant as regards the performance of his/their services in connection with the works in accordance with the terms of his/their respective consultancy agreements and that there are no limitations on liability as between the consultant and the employer in the consultancy agreement[s];

(ii) [[●] 'the sub-contractor[s]'] has/have provided a warranty to the purchaser/tenant in respect of design of the sub-contract works that it/they has/have carried out and for which there is no liability of the contractor to the employer under the building contract;

(iii) that the consultants and the sub-contractors have paid to the purchaser/tenant such proportion of the purchaser's/tenant's losses which it would be just and equitable for them to pay having regard to the extent of their responsibility for the purchaser's/tenant's loses.'

This clause operates by 'assuming' that the consultants have a legal liability to the beneficiary, even if in fact the beneficiary has not obtained collateral warranties from those other parties. The purpose of the clause is to entitle the court to calculate what percentage of the blame should be apportioned to those other parties. This is a calculation which the court is used to making under the Civil Liability (Contribution) Act 1978 where, for instance, two drivers negligently contribute to causing the same crash. Clause 1(c) is simply intended to cap the damages for which the contractor is liable, and it is a significant limitation on the value to a beneficiary of the MCWa warranties.

Deleterious material clauses

7.05 Most forms of collateral warranty to funders, purchasers and tenants contain provisions related to excluded materials. Clause 2 of the MCWa warranties contains such provisions whereby the contractor warrants absolutely that materials will not be used except in accordance with good practice guidelines:

'... it has not and will not use materials in the works other than in accordance with the guidelines contained in the edition of the publication 'Good Practice in Selection of Construction Materials' (Ove Arup & Partners) current at the date of the building contract.'

The situation is different with consultants' collateral warranties as consultants only warrant in their appointments that they have exercised reasonable skill and care in the performance of their services and they therefore cannot offer an absolute warranty as to the use of materials. This approach is to be preferred to the previous practice of using extensive and out-dated lists of materials compiled by lawyers on a random and ill-informed basis.

Step-in rights

7.06 Where a warranty is to be provided to a funder or funding institution it is common for the warranty to contain step-in rights. Clauses 5 to 7 of MCWa/F enable the funder to step into the employer's shoes should the employer behave in such a way as would enable the contractor to terminate the contract. This is most likely to occur if the employer encounters financial difficulties and is unable to pay the contractor. Step-in provisions such as these permit the fund actually to take on the duties, rights and responsibilities of the employer. Again, the effect of these provisions is elaborated in Part 4.

Insurance clauses

7.07 Contractors' warranties will not usually contain insurance clauses unless the contractor is to be responsible for some elements of the design of the works. Where such design obligations exist, they are often required to be backed by professional indemnity insurance. The relevant clause of the MCWa warranties is Clause 5 in MCWa/P&T and Clause 9 in MCWa/F.

It is important to ensure that the insurance will be available up to the limit stated in the clause for any one claim rather than up to that limit for all claims unless the clause has been amended to accommodate an aggregate limit. The insurance clauses contain provisions requiring the contractor to maintain the insurance for a certain period. This time limit should be at least as long as the contractor's liability under the warranty, if the warranty contains an expiry date. The clauses state that insurance shall be maintained so long as it is available at commercially reasonable rates. This allows contractors to cease maintaining insurance if insurance premiums rise to an exorbitant level or if restrictions on level are imposed by insurers as has happened since 9/11. However, the warranty also requires the contractor to notify the beneficiary if such insurance is no longer available.

Limitation

7.08 Most standard forms of warranty allow for the execution of a warranty as either a simple contract or as a deed. Where a warranty is signed as a simple contract consideration is required (see for example the consideration recital immediately before Clause 1 of the MCWa warranties), and the limitation period for the warranty will run for six years from the date of any breach of the warranty. Where a warranty is executed as a deed, no consideration is required and the limitation period will run for 12 years from any breach. For this reason, beneficiaries tend to favour the execution of warranties as deeds, although the method of execution of the warranty should reflect that of the underlying contract to ensure that the warrantor's liability under the warranty lasts for a similar period as his liability under the contract. In addition to this cut-off period provided by the law on limitation, it is common to see clauses in warranties which limit the liability of the warrantor to a specific period of time, often calculated as a certain number of years following practical completion. For example, Clause 8 in MCWa/P&T states that:

> 'No action or proceedings for any breach of this Agreement shall be commenced against the Contractor after the expiry of [ ] years from the date of Practical Completion of the Works …'

The advantage to a contractor of such a clause is that it provides a fixed period under which the contractor will be liable and the contractor knows exactly when his liability under the warranty will end. As drafted, however, it does not affect his tortious liability. The inclusion of such a clause can significantly reduce the potential liability of the contractor to the beneficiary if a short period is included.

Delay

7.09 If a contractor is in delay in completing the works under the building contract, the employer's remedy lies in liquidated and ascertained damage which may be deducted from monies due to the contractor in accordance with the provisions of the building contract. Plainly, the contractor does not want to create an alternative remedy for delay which might otherwise by-pass the provisions for liquidated and ascertained damages contained in the building contract by giving a collateral warranty which, under the terms of Clause 1, would give funders, purchasers and tenants a claim for unlimited damages for failure to complete the works in accordance with the building contract. For this reason, a new Clause 14 has appeared in MCWa/F (Clause 9 in MCWa/P&T) which states that:

> '… the contractor shall have no liability under this agreement for delay under the building contract unless and until the funder serves notice pursuant to Clause 5 or Clause 6 (the 'step-in' provisions). For the avoidance of doubt the contractor shall not be required to pay liquidated and ascertained damage in respect of the period of delay where the same has been paid to or deducted by the employer.'

This provision is acceptable to most funders, purchasers and tenants if properly advised.

Assignment

7.10 When developments are sold, or some other change of ownership takes place, it is common for the potential purchaser to request that any existing warranties are assigned to him. Under common law, the benefits of a contract can be assigned unless there is an express prohibition against assignment in the contract. Sometimes, the warrantor may require that assignments be permissible only with his consent, which shall not be unreasonably withheld. Alternatively the warrantor may only allow the assignment of the warranty a limited number of times, for example twice, or to purchasers or tenants of a specified part of the development. The standard form contemplates assignment without consent, but only on a limited number of occasions. The client should be advised that, without some ability to assign the warranty at least once or twice,

the marketability of a development may be adversely affected as potential future purchasers may be put off if they are unable to obtain the comfort of the relevant collateral warranties.

8 Key clauses of Third Party Rights schedule in JCT Major Project Form 2003 edition

8.01 As noted above, JCT Major Project Form for the first time in the JCT Suite of Documentation adopts Contracts (Rights of Third Parties) Act 1999 as the mechanism for conferring rights on funders, purchasers and tenants. The rights themselves are set out in the Third Party Rights Schedule and follow very closely the key clauses of MCWa/F and MCWa/P&T. Certain key differences are noted below.

Joint liability and contribution clauses

8.02 The Major Projects Form is a design and build form of contract under which the contractor completes any further design required for the execution of the works. Accordingly, he has responsibility for *all* design going forward whether it be carried out by sub-consultants or sub-contractors to him. In these circumstances, a net contribution clause of the type discussed above is inappropriate and does not appear in the Third Party Rights Schedule.

Economic and consequential loss

8.03 As noted above, in respect of CoWa/F there is no restriction on recoverable loss. However, the third party rights in favour of a purchaser or tenant contains the options noted above in respect of exclusions and caps on liability in addition to the costs of repair. The options are addressed in the Appendix to the Major Project Form. It is vital that the Appendix is properly completed since the fallback is a complete exclusion of losses other than the cost of repair.

Step-In under Third Party Rights

8.04 Contracts (Rights of Third Parties) Act 1999 can only be used to confer on a third party '*a right*'. As noted in paragraph 3.08, it cannot be used to impose an obligation on a party who is not a party to the contract. Since the essence of the '*step-in*' rights contained in collateral warranties is to impose on the funder the obligation to pay the contractor amounts due under the building contract after '*step-in*', it has been suggested that third party rights cannot be used as the mechanism for creating enforceable '*step-in*' provisions for funders. The Major Project Form overcomes this dilemma by making the grant of the rights by the contractor to the funder conditional upon the funder accepting liability for payment and performance of the employer's obligations in his notice. Unless the notice contains this assumption of responsibility, it is invalid and the funder is not able to exercise his step-in rights. A leading QC's opinion obtained by the JCT is clear that this mechanism is valid.

12

Payment rules

MATTHEW NEEDHAM-LAING

'The Housing Grants Construction and Regeneration Act 1996 (and the Statutory Instrument made under it) constitutes a remarkable (and possibly unique) intervention in very carefully selected parts of the construction industry whereby the ordinary freedom of contract between commercial parties (without regard to bargaining power) to regulate their relationships has been overridden in a number of areas ...' (His Honour Judge Humphrey Lloyd QC in *Outwing Construction Ltd v H Randell & Son Ltd* [1999] 15 Const LJ Vol. 3.)

1 Introduction

1.01 In this chapter we look at the provisions of the Housing Grants Construction and Regeneration Act 1996 Part II, referred to throughout this chapter as 'the Act', together with the subordinate legislation that Parliament has passed pursuant to the Act, in particular the Scheme for Construction Contracts (England and Wales) Regulations 1998, referred to throughout this chapter as 'the Scheme'. Part I of the Scheme deals with adjudication while Part II of the Scheme is concerned with payment. It is Part II of the Scheme which is dealt with in this chapter.

1.02 Architects need to be aware of the practical effects of this legislation on contracts in the construction industry and take this into consideration when:

1 Negotiating their own terms of appointment with their clients.
2 Advising clients on the forms of building contract which may be used to employ the Contractor.
3 Acting as Contract Administrator during the course of the building works.

1.03 Architects need to appreciate the circumstances when the Scheme applies and be able to explain its impact to clients who may not be aware of the legislation. This is particularly so with professional appointments which can have a tendency to be less formal in their formation; for instance, the architects appointment can be an exchange of letters which may refer to the conditions of engagement, rather than the more formal contract documentation which is used by the client to employ the Contractor.

1.04 The respective drafting bodies involved in the standard forms of building contracts and standard forms of the appointment have published new editions of their terms and conditions, which are compliant with the provisions of the Act. The RIBA's Standard Form of Agreement for the appointment of an Architect (SFA/99) and Small Works appointment (SW/99) have been updated and comply with this legislation. Most of the standard forms of contract which the architect will deal with in the course of practice will comply with the Act. They will probably differ from the Scheme, in matters such as when payments become due, the period of time

between the date when a payment becomes due and the final date for payment and the time period within which the notice of intention to withhold payment must be served. The architect as contract administrator will be expected to be familiar with these provisions and advise the client accordingly. The Architect therefore needs to be aware of the differences between the standard forms of contract and the Scheme, particularly if referring to case law as many of the cases are concerned with contracts which incorporate the Scheme, or the decision is dependent on the particular payment terms contained in the contract which was the subject of the dispute.

In the event that the client intends to use a bespoke form of contract, then the architect should compare the payment terms in the client's proposed contract with the payment provisions in the Act. If the proposed contract is not compliant with the Act then it will be necessary to consider which payment provisions in the Scheme will be incorporated into the client's contract and advise the client of the effect the Scheme will have on the proposed contract. Even if the client is not prepared to alter its contract the architect must be aware of the effect the Act and the Scheme will have on the manner in which the contract is administered.

2 Background to the legislation

2.01 In July 1994 Sir Michael Latham published his report titled 'Constructing the Team', which contained the results of his investigation into the construction industry and made a number of proposals for future contracts to remedy some of the abuses which Sir Michael had discovered were prevalent within it. Sir Michael felt that all parties should be encouraged to use standard forms of contract without amendment and that when any of the standard forms were used the following matters in relation to payment should be regarded as unfair and invalid:

1 Any attempt to amend or delete the sections relating to terms and conditions of payment, including the right of interest on late payments.
2 The exercise of any right of set-off, contra-charge or abatement without:
  (a) Giving notice in advance.
  (b) Specifying the exact reason for the deduction.
3 To seek set-off in respect of any contract other than the one in progress.
4 'Pay when paid' conditions should be explicitly declared unfair and invalid.

2.02 Sir Michael made a number of other recommendations in his report, particularly in relation to adjudication, which are outside the scope of this chapter. He believed that in order to instil confidence within the construction industry, these central provisions should be underpinned by legislation. As a result, the Conservative government passed the Act, which imposes some of the recommendations made by Sir Michael in the form of rights which one party is free to exercise if he so wishes. The Act achieves this by requiring the parties to expressly include within their contract, clauses which reflect the relevant recommendations, failing which the relevant regulations contained in the Scheme are automatically implied into the contract.

2.03 The Act grants three important rights insofar as the parties' entitlement to payment is concerned:

1 The right to payment by instalments for contracts lasting 45 days or more.
2 The ability of a party to suspend performance if it has not been paid within a specified period.
3 The outlawing of pay when paid clause, except in specific circumstances.

2.04 The Act confers these rights upon the parties by permitting the parties to a construction contract to include them voluntarily in the contract together with such other additions or refinements as they wish, provided those additions or refinements do not offend against the basic rights themselves. If the construction contract does not contain these rights then the payment regulations within the Scheme come into effect by being implied into the contract. The Scheme's regulations are therefore default provisions; it is always necessary to consider whether the construction contract complies with the Act in order to determine whether the regulations contained in the Scheme are to be incorporated into it. The payment regulations in this respect differ from the regulations in the Scheme relating to adjudication. If a construction contract does not comply with any one of the adjudication provisions in the Act, then the Scheme's regulations are incorporated into the construction contract in total. On the other hand, if a construction contract does not comply with any of the rights relating to payment, then it is only the non-compliant provisions within the construction contract which are replaced by the relevant payment regulation within the Scheme, and not the Scheme's payment regulations in total.

2.05 It is also worth bearing in mind that even if the contract is not a construction contract, the parties are still free to agree payment terms, which comply with the Act or incorporate the payment regulations of the Scheme. The fact that some or all of the terms and conditions of a contract comply with the Act does not necessarily mean that the contract falls within the definition of a 'construction contract'. In situations where there is a dispute as to payment it is important to consider if the contract in question is one to which the Act applies and if it does are the terms relating to payment compliant with the Act.

3 To which contracts does the Act apply?

3.01 Sections 104–107 of the Act identify the requirements with which a 'construction contract' must comply before the payment provisions apply.

3.02 Section 104(1) essentially defines a 'construction contract' as a contract to carry out 'construction operations' which in turn are defined in section 105(1). The two sections therefore need to be read together and in doing so it will be clear that it is only in exceptional circumstances that a contract for building or construction work will not fall within the ambit of the Act. Section 104(2) extends the definition of a construction contract to include:

1 Architectural, design or surveying work in relation to construction operations; or
2 The provision of advice on building, engineering, interior or exterior decoration or on the laying out of landscape in relation to construction operations.

3.03 It is clearly the intention of the Act to grant the members of the design, or professional, team the same rights to payments as those granted to contractors or sub-contractors by section 104(1).

The legislation, however, may not have been drafted sufficiently widely to cover all members of the professional team. For example, it could be argued that the planning supervisor provides advice on health and safety matters, which is not advice on building or engineering and, consequently, his appointment does not fall within the definition of a construction contract. Future case law should eventually clarify this potential anomaly.

3.04 If the architect is appointed as lead consultant and the client requires all the other professionals to be appointed by the architect so that there is one point of responsibility for the professional team, then the architect must ensure that the sub-consultant's terms of appointment comply with the Act. The architect must, when making payment to the sub-consultants, comply with all the relevant notice provisions, which the Act imposes in relation to payment. To maintain cash flow, the architect will need to ensure that the payment terms of its appointment with the client operate in advance of those of its sub-consultants so if any deductions are made to its fees, these can be passed on to the appropriate sub-consultant without breaching the notice periods.

3.05 There are occasions where architects are initially appointed to provide design services in relation to construction operations and subsequently the client extends the scope of architect's services to advise on matters such as the design of soft furnishings, letterheads, corporate logo, etc. which, do not fall within the definition of 'construction operations'. If the client increases the architect's scope of services by way of a variation to the existing appointment then the Act will continue to apply. If however the client employs the architect under a second separate appointment to carry out the additional services, the Act will not apply to the second appointment, if it does not relate to 'construction operations'. It is obviously unsatisfactory, from the viewpoint of the client and the architect, for two different sets of payment provisions to be operating. This problem can be avoided if both appointments are on the RIBA standard forms of appointment, so that payment provisions, which comply with the Act, are contractually agreed between the client and architect. Unfortunately communications between client and architect are frequently less formal, with the client instructing the architect orally in meetings or over the telephone. The difficulties that can arise in these circumstances are discussed in paragraph 3.16 below.

3.06 The Act only applies to contracts, which have been entered into after 1 May 1998 (the date of commencement of the Act) and then only where the 'construction operations' are carried out in the United Kingdom.

3.07 It is the location of the 'construction operations' which is important, and, consequently, the Act would not apply to an appointment, which states that the law of the contract is English but the construction work is outside the United Kingdom. The provisions of the Act would, however, apply to a construction contract, where the work was to be carried out inside the United Kingdom but the law of the contract is of a foreign country, a not-uncommon situation with construction work at docks or harbours.

3.08 This situation arose in the case of *Comsite Projects Ltd v Andritz AG* [2003] EWHC (TCC) which concerned the installation of building services including lighting, emergency power small power distribution, alarm systems, heating, ventilation and building management systems to a building which housed water treatment plant and in particular plant which dried and baked sludge pellets. The building was located on the Isle of White, but the contract contained a provision where in the event of a dispute the courts of Austria had jurisdiction to determine the dispute in accordance with Austrian law. Comsite Projects Ltd applied to the United Kingdom courts for declarations that their work under the contract fell within the definition of 'construction operations' as defined in section 104 of the Act and consequently they were entitled to refer disputes to adjudication. Andritz AG (an Austrian registered company) argued that the contract works fell within the exceptions to the definition of 'construction operations', contained in section 105 of the Act, and in any event the Austrian Courts, not the United Kingdom courts had jurisdiction to determine the disputes. The Judge decided that the contract works did not fall within those construction operations which were exempt from the operation of the Act by virtue of section 105 and consequently the Act applied. While the parties were particularly concerned with whether adjudication was available to them to resolve disputes, judicial comments in the Court of Appeal (Lord Justice Ward in *RJT Consulting Engineers Ltd v DM Engineering (Northern Ireland)* Ltd [2002] BLR 217) have made it clear that once a contract falls within the definition of 'construction contract' then all of the Act applies including the payment provisions.

3.09 The final and probably the most important requirement is that the contract must be in writing (section 107(1)) if the Act is to apply. This is probably one of the more likely reasons why a contract does not comply with the Act and it is in the Architect's interest to have a written record of its appointment. The definition of a contract in writing is similar to that contained in the 1996 Arbitration Act and extends beyond what most commercial persons would regard as an agreement in writing. The definition includes contracts made by exchange of letters or faxes (section 107(2)(b)) or where an oral agreement is evidenced in writing by one of the parties or by a third party (section 107(4)). One can foresee circumstances arising at an initial meeting between the client and his potential architect, the terms of an agreement are discussed and the discussion is recorded in the minutes of the meeting, either by the client or the architect, or perhaps by a third party; under the Act, this would be an agreement in writing.

3.10 It is worth noting that section 107(6) states that references in the Act to anything being 'written' or 'in writing' include it being recorded by any means, indicating that tape recordings and e-mails fall within the definition.

3.11 The extent to which the agreement must be recorded in writing, before the Act applies has been the subject of judicial clarification by the Court of Appeal in *RJT Consulting Engineers Ltd v DM Engineering (Northern Ireland) Ltd* [2002] BLR 217. The case decided what was meant by the words 'evidenced in writing' in the Act and whether the contract in dispute was sufficiently evidenced in writing so that statutory adjudication, (an adjudication under the Scheme rather than adjudication provisions agreed in the contract) was available to resolve disputes. The case is not directly related to the payment provisions, however, Lord Justice Ward made it clear in his judgement that what was meant by the words 'evidenced in writing' was equally applicable to determine whether the payment provisions in the Act were applicable to the contract.

3.12 The Adjudicator and the Judge at first instance considered that for the purposes of Section 107(1) it was sufficient if there was evidence of the existence of a contract in the form of fee notes from RJT to DM, a number of invoices which set out the nature of the work, the names of the client and the identity of the place of the work. There were minutes taken during meetings when the work was carried out which clearly identified the parties and the nature of the work, which needed to be done. There was also correspondence around the dispute, which identified the parties and the nature of the work. The Court of Appeal decided that this evidence supported the conclusion that there was a contract in existence between the parties, but it did not evidence the terms of the contract. It did not amount to a contract 'evidenced in writing'. The terms and conditions of the agreement were oral and not evidenced in writing.

3.13 The question then arose as to whether or not the whole agreement had to be in writing or merely the part, which was relevant to the dispute. The Court of Appeal was divided on the issue but by a majority of two to one decided that the whole agreement had to be evidenced in writing. The dissenting judgement Lord Justice Auld considered that it was sufficient if the terms of the agreement, which were material to the dispute were recorded in writing. It is not possible to reconcile the dissenting judgement of LJ Auld with the

decisions of LJ Ward and LJ Robert Walker, who both considered that the entire agreement between the parties had to be evidenced in writing. In relation to adjudication the judgement of LJ Auld may be preferable, but in relation to the payment provisions, in the writers opinion, the preferred interpretation of section 107(1) is that of LJ Ward and LJ Robert Walker; the entire agreement should be in writing otherwise a situation may arise, if parts of the agreement relating to payment are agreed orally where it could become impossible to determine whether they comply with the Act and if not which parts of the Scheme should be incorporated into the agreement between the parties.

3.14 Section 107(5) of the Act states that an exchange of submissions in adjudication proceedings, arbitral or legal proceedings which allege there was an agreement, but that it was not in writing and that allegation is not denied, then submissions constitute an agreement in writing. This section is not consistent with the majority view in *RJT Consulting Engineers Ltd v DM Engineering (Northern Ireland) Ltd*, as section 107(5) apparently makes it permissible for only part of the agreement to be evidenced in writing, not the whole agreement. The majority of the Court of Appeal considered section 107(5) as a specific and possible exceptional provision. The Court of Appeal considered an exchange of written submissions in adjudication proceedings had to do more than evidence the existence of a 'construction contract'. The submissions had to evidence the terms of the 'construction contract', which may be material to the dispute, which was being referred to adjudication. Lord Justice Auld, who gave the (minority decision) disagreed and was of the opinion that section 107(5) was not an exceptional provision, but an illustration of the intention behind the Act not to exclude contracts from the ambit of the Act simply because the written record of the agreement was in some immaterial way incomplete.

3.15 Section 107(5) reproduces the words of section 5, sub-section (5) of the Arbitration Act 1996, which refers to the requirement that an arbitration clause must be in writing. The effect of the provision in the Arbitration Act is that if the parties make an oral agreement to arbitrate and the existence of the arbitration agreement is then subsequently contained in one party's submissions in arbitral or legal proceedings and not denied by the other party this satisfies the requirement that the arbitration agreement is evidenced in writing. In the writers opinion the wholesale rewriting of section 5 of the Arbitration Act into section 7 of the Act is not illustrative of the intention of the Act not to exclude contracts where the written record of the agreement was in some material way incomplete.

3.16 The dangers of agreeing oral variations to contracts which are in writing and which would otherwise fall within the ambit of the Act were exposed in *Carillion Construction Ltd v Devonport Royal Dockyard* [2003] BLR 79. The contract between the parties was contained within two documents, which apparently would have complied with the provisions of Section 107, however during the course of the works, discussions took place to revise the payment provisions. It was alleged by Carillion that the parties agreed to change the basis of payment from that contained in the contract to a 'cost reimbursable' basis of payment. Devonport denied that there was an agreement to change the basis of payment and even if there had been an agreement to that effect it was not evidenced in writing. His Honour Judge Bowsher QC did not list all the documents to which he was referred during the course of the hearing (the impression from the law report is that there were a considerable number) however while those documents did evidence the fact there were discussions about changing the basis of payment under the contract, they did not evidence the existence of an oral agreement that the payment terms should become 'cost reimbursable'.

3.17 Carillion in advancing their arguments as to the existence of the agreement to vary the payment terms had also sought to rely upon section 107(3):

> 'Where parties agree otherwise than in writing by reference to terms which are in writing they make an agreement in writing'

This sub-section of the Act reproduces the words of section 5, sub-section (3) of the Arbitration Act 1996, which refers to the requirement that an arbitration clause must be in writing. The effect of the provision in the Arbitration Act is that if the parties make an oral agreement, which referred to terms and conditions contained in a Standard Form of Contract, then an arbitration clause contained in those standard terms will satisfy the requirement, that an agreement to arbitrate has to be in writing.

3.18 The Judge pointed out that the standard terms of any construction agreement would not include vital terms like the description of the work to be done, the price to be paid or the time in which the work was to be completed. He was not sure when section 107(3) would be applicable but suggested that it might be applicable in rare situations where, for example, an employer approached an architect with a draft written agreement containing all the vital terms required by law to form a contract (the services to be performed and the fee to be paid), the architect read it and then shook hands with the employer on it as an agreed deal. His Honour Judge Bowsher was clear, however, that section 107(3) used the words *by reference to terms that are in writing* and not *by reference to a previous agreement in writing* the section was therefore not intended to cover a situation where there had previously been a contract in writing but the parties had orally and without a written record agreed a fundamental change in the terms of the written contract.

3.19 Judge Bowsher's comments are particularly relevant to architects who are in the habit of using the Conditions of the Engagement (CE/99). Either the letter of appointment must contain the relevant information concerning scope of the services and the fee to be charged in respect of them, or the Schedules in CE/99 must be completed and sent to the client with the letter of appointment. It will not be sufficient to merely refer in the letter of appointment to the CE/99 and either be silent on such matters as the fee or fail to complete the Schedules, as there is a real risk that the courts may not regard the appointment as being evidenced in writing.

4 Contracts excluded from the payment provisions

4.01 Contracts specifically excluded from the ambit of the Act are:

1 Contracts of employment (section 104(3))
2 Matters identified in section 105(2)
3 Contracts with a residential occupier (section 106(1))
4 Any other contract excluded by order of the Secretary of State.

4.02 Contracts of employment are contracts of service or apprenticeship between an employer and an individual employee. This would appear to be relatively straightforward, however, difficulties arise where self-employed technicians are working in the architect's office; are they an employee or are they a sub-consultant? A detailed discussion as to the various tests the courts apply to determine the type of contract that exists between the employer and a self-employed person is unfortunately beyond the scope of this chapter.

4.03 Section 105 of the Act lists the matters specifically excluded from the definition of 'construction operations'. These primarily concern construction operations relating to drilling and mining of minerals, oil or natural gas, the nuclear processing, power generation or water supply and treatment industries, or the chemical, pharmaceuticals, oil, gas, steel or food and drink industries. There have been a number of cases in which the parties have argued whether a particular type of work falls within the list of excluded matters, for example *Homer Burgess Ltd v Chirex (Annan) Ltd* [2000] BLR 124. Pipe work linking pieces of equipment used for processing pharmaceuticals clearly part of the plant as the plant would not operate without it. *ABB Zantingh Ltd v Zedal Building Services Ltd* [2001] BLR 66. Cable, cable trays and the like became plant when it was worked into the plant or if it joined two pieces of plant. The decisions in each case are fact specific, however the courts appear to approach the question on the basis of whether the work in question is necessary (rather than required by legislation for health and safety purposes) for the operation of the equipment or plant which is excluded from the definition of 'construction operations' (*Comsite Projects Ltd v Andritz AG* [2003] EWHC 958(TCC)). Of more relevance to the architect, the section also excludes contracts for the manufacture or delivery to site of various building materials, plant and machinery or components for heating, ventilation, power supply, drainage, sanitation, water supply or fire protection or for security or communication systems where the contract does not include for those components to be installed in the building as well. In addition, the section also excludes works which are of a wholly artistic nature.

4.04 A residential occupier is a person who is having construction works carried out on their house or flat which they occupy or intend to occupy. The definition does not extend to the construction work being carried out on two properties for residential occupiers where one of the properties is for their occupation and the other is for sale to realise a profit (*Samual Thomas Construction Ltd v Bick and Bick [aka J&B Developments [2000]* unreported). Similarly, a contract for work on an entire block of flats one of which is owned by the contracting party is not a contract with a residential occupier. A contract with an individual flat owner who is having work done to their flat which they intended to occupy once the building work is completed would be a contract with a residential occupier. The fact that one of the parties to the contract is a residential occupier does not prevent the parties from agreeing payment provisions, which are in compliance with the Act. For example *Lovell Projects Ltd v Legg and Carver* [2003] Cill 2019 where the defendant argued that they were not bound by the adjudication provisions contained in the JCT Minor Works Contract as they were a residential occupier and by reason of the Unfair Terms in Consumer Contract Regulations 1999. The Court found that the defendant had insisted that the contract terms were to be the JCT Minor Works and as such they were bound by the terms and conditions including the terms concerning adjudication. It is clear that the same principle is applicable to the payment provisions.

4.05 The list of construction contracts that have been excluded by the Secretary of State is extensive and reference should be made to the relevant statutory instruments (the Construction Contracts (England and Wales) Exclusion Order 1998 No. 648). However, it is worth noting that the following have been excluded:

1 The power of highway authorities to adopt by agreement roads under section 38 of the Highways Act. (SI 1998/648, art 3(a))
2 The power of highway authorities, to enter into agreements for the execution of work, under section 278 of the Highways Act 1980. (SI 1998/648, art 3(a))
3 Planning agreements under section 106, which is an agreement imposing planning obligations on the land owner, and section 106a, which is a modificational discharge of planning obligations, or section 299a, relating to Crown planning obligations, of the Town and Country Planning Act 1990. (SI 1998/648, art 3(b))
4 Agreements to adopt sewer, drainage or sewage disposal work under section 104 of the Water Industry Act 1991. (SI 1998/648, art 3(c))
5 Externally financed development agreements under the National Health Service (Private Finance) Act 1997 (SI 1998/648, art 3(d))
6 Construction contracts entered into under the Private Finance Initiative, provided it fulfils a number of conditions which are set out in the relevant statutory instrument (SI 1998/648, art 4(1))
7 Finance agreements such as contracts for insurance, contract where the principal obligations include the lending of money, guarantees bonds including advance payment, retention and performance bonds, etc. (SI 1998/648, art 5(1))
8 Development agreements where the agreement includes a provision for the grant or disposal of a parcel of land upon which the principal construction operations are to take place. (SI 1998/648, art 6(1))

5 The payment provisions in detail

5.01 Sections 109–113 of the Act deal with the parties' right to payment in connection with a construction contract.

5.02 In summary these rights are:

1 The right for a party to be paid by stage payments throughout the duration of the contract where this is agreed between the parties or where the contract is estimated to be 45 days or more in duration.
2 The right to be informed of the amount to be paid in any stage payment, and when that money is due for payment.
3 The right to be given notice if it is intended that any payment be withheld.
4 The right to suspend performance if payment is not made within the specified time.
5 Making 'pay when paid' clauses ineffective except where a third party or any other person payment by whom is a condition of payment is insolvent.

The majority of standard forms of construction contract have been amended to include these rights within them but it is necessary to consider these provisions if:

1 The contract has been further amended; or
2 The contract has been specially drafted for the project concerned; or
3 An informal agreement has been reached between the client and the contractor for example, an exchange of letters or reference to terms and conditions of contract within various written documents.

In these circumstances, it will be necessary to ascertain whether the terms and conditions of the contract comply with the provisions of the Act and, if they do not, which regulations within the Scheme apply.

Payments by Instalments

5.03 A party to a construction contract is entitled to payment by instalments unless the contract specifies that the duration of the work is to be 45 days or less or if it has been agreed by the parties, or if it is estimated, that the work will be of a duration of less than 45 days. When calculating the duration of the work, Christmas Day, Good Friday or other bank holidays should not be included but weekends are included within the 45-day period. The same method of calculation should be adopted when determining notice periods under the Scheme.

5.04 Section 109(2) of the Act states that the parties are free to agree the amounts of each instalment and the intervals at which or the mechanism by which 'payments become due'. It is therefore perfectly possible for instalments of the contract price to be made on completion of stages of the work, rather than at regular periodic intervals. If the intervals for determining when periodic payments are to be made is not agreed, then the Scheme imposes a period of 28 days, referred to in the Scheme as the 'relevant period'.

5.05 If the parties to the contract for construction work, which are expected to exceed 45 days, have not agreed the mechanism by which 'payments become due' under the contract, then regulations 4, 5 and 7 of the Scheme will be implied into the contract.

In relation to instalments (interim payments), regulation 4 stipulates that the date a payment becomes due, is the latter of either:

(a) the expiry of 7 days following the 'relevant period' of 28 days; or
(b) the making of a claim in writing, which must specify the amount of any payment considered due and the basis on which the sum is calculated.

In relation to final payment, regulation 5 stipulates that the date a payment becomes due, is the latter of either:

(a) 30 days following completion of the work; or
(b) the making of a claim in writing which must specify the amount of any payment considered to be due and the basis on which the sum is calculated.

Regulation 7 is concerned with payments other than interim or final payments, though it is not clear what these other payments might be. These other payments become due on which ever is the latter of either:

(a) 7 days following completion of the work; or
(b) the making of a claim in writing, which must specify the amount of any payment considered to be due and the basis on which the sum is calculated.

5.06 Where the contract specifies, or the parties agree that the duration of the construction work is estimated to be less than 45 days, then regulation 6 applies and payments become due on the latter of either:

(a) expiry of 30 days following completion of the work; or
(b) the making of a claim in writing which must specify the amount, if any payment considered to be due and the basis on which the sum is calculated.

It would appear that regulation 7 also applies to contracts where the duration of the construction work is expected to be less than 45 days, but again it is not clear in what circumstances the other payments may arise.

5.07 Where the parties to a construction contract fail to agree that amount of any stage or periodic payments, which become due under the contract, then regulations 2 to 4 of the Scheme apply.

5.08 Regulation 2 of the Scheme provides a method of calculating the amount to be paid for each relevant period, as follows:

(a) the value of work carried out from the commencement of the contract up to the end of the relevant period and, essentially this consists of the value of work performed in accordance with the contract plus (if the contract so stipulates) payment for materials delivered to site for the purpose of the works plus (if the contract so stipulates) any other payments payable from the commencement of the contract to the end of the relevant period; *less*
(b) the aggregate of any sums previously paid or are due for payment.

Architects will be familiar with this method of calculating the amount due to the contractor, as it is the method adopted in the JCT family of contracts.

5.09 Regulation 2 of the Scheme must be read in conjunction with regulation 12, which defines the 'value of work' as *an amount determined in accordance with the construction contract under which the work is performed or, where the contract contains no such provisions, the cost of any work performed in accordance with that contract together with an amount equal to an overhead or profit included in the contract price.* This enables a valuation to take place where there are no rates and prices in the contract or where the work has been varied.

5.10 The Scheme imposes, in regulation 2(4), a maximum on the total amounts to be paid in any relevant period by stipulating the amount *shall not exceed the difference between the contract price and the aggregate of the instalments or stage periodic payments which have become due.* The 'contract price' is defined in regulation 12 of the Scheme as being the *entire sum payable under the construction contract in respect of the work.*

Dates for payment

5.11 The Act identifies two dates of importance, the date when a payment becomes 'due' and also 'the final date' by which payment must be made. The date a 'payment becomes due' starts the clock running on the timetable by which the paying party must serve their Section 110 Notice.

5.12 Having calculated the sum due for a particular instalment, regulation 9 of the Scheme requires that the paying party must issue a notice to the party whom payment is due, not later than 5 days after the date the payment becomes due under the contract. The Act leaves it open to the parties to agree the mechanism for determining when payments become due under the contract, however, if there is no adequate mechanism then Regulations 3 to 7 of the Scheme shall be implied into the contract. Regulation 9 of the Scheme corresponds with and repeats section 110(2) of the Act, and these notices are commonly referred to as 'Section 110 Notices'. A Section 110 Notice must specify the amount (if any) of the payment made or the paying party proposes to pay, and the basis upon which that amount is calculated. For the purposes of the Act and the Scheme the Section 110 Notice will be compliant if it contains the information referred to in paragraph 5.08 above, namely the aggregate value of work which has been carried out in accordance with the contract together with any other payments due under the contract less the aggregate value of sums which have previously been paid or are due for payment, to leave a balance which is payable for the relevant period in question. There is no sanction on the paying party if they fail to issue a Section 110 Notice. (*SL Timber Systems Ltd v Carillion Constructions Ltd.*)

5.13 The date when a 'payment becomes due' also sets the clock running on the timetable for service by the paying party of a notice pursuant to Section 111 of the Act identifying any amounts it intends to withhold from the sum due and the grounds for doing so, commonly referred to as the 'Withholding Notice'.

5.14 The date when a 'payment becomes due' also sets the clock running for the 'final date for payment' which is the date when payment must be made. If payment has not been made by the 'final date for payment', the party to whom the money is owed is entitled to charge interest and if it wishes serve a notice of intention to suspend performance of the contract pursuant to section 112 of the Act. The paying party may pay the instalment of the contract price at any time between the date payment becomes 'due for payment' and the 'final date for payment'.

5.15 The parties are entitled to agree the length of the time between the date a 'payment becomes due' and the 'final date for payment' arises. The parties are also entitled to agree the timetable for service of the Withholding Notices. They are not entitled to alter the period of time after date a 'payment becomes due' by which the Section 110 Notice, which must be served. This notice must always be served not later than five days after the date on which a payment became due, though there is no sanction under the Act of the Scheme if the paying party fails to serve this notice.

5.16 If the construction contract does not identify a 'final date for payment', then Regulation 8 of the Scheme provides that the 'final date for payment' is 17 days after the date the 'payment becomes due'.

Notice to withhold payment, the 'Withholding Notice'

5.17 The right to withhold payment from a party at common law arises by set-off or abatement. Set-off allows a paying party to deduct monies owed from sums due to the receiving party. The monies or debt to be deducted from the sums that are due need not relate to the same contract but could relate to different contracts between the same parties. The test as to whether it is permissible to set off a debt under one contract against a sum due under another contract is whether the debt to be set off is sufficiently closely connected with the sum to be paid, that it would be unjust to allow the payment without taking into account the debt to be set off.

5.18 Abatement, on the other hand, is the withholding of money as a result of a breach of contract by a party which reduces the value of the work done by that party. The amount of money withheld must equate to the reduction of the value of the work done by that party on that contract. The most common form of abatement is for defective work.

5.19 The Section 111(1) of the Act purports to limit the paying party's right to withhold or reduce a payment, which is due under the contract by virtue of the common law rights of set off or abatement.

5.20 Section 111 prevents the paying party from exercising its right to set off or abate the sums due for payment to the receiving party unless and until it has given a notice, (commonly called the 'Withholding Notice') to the receiving party specifying the amount proposed to be withheld and the grounds for withholding payment. If there is more than one ground for deducting sums, then that notice must specify each ground. This notice must be given prior to the date for final payment; otherwise, the paying party may not withhold that payment after the final date. The parties are free to agree the prescribed period within which the notice may be given and the Act anticipates that the notice 'to withhold payment may be combined with the Section 110 Notice.

5.21 If no agreement is reach between the parties as to the period when the Withholding Notice may be given, then regulation 10 of the Scheme applies. This stipulates that a notice shall be given not later than seven days before the final date, for payment in the contract or, if there is no final date, regulation 8 of the Scheme imposes a final date as 17 days from the date a payment becomes due.

5.22 Section 111 has been the subject of a considerable amount of litigation with courts interpreting the section in essentially two ways. These can be termed as the 'wide' or the 'narrow' interpretations of the section. The wide interpretation mainly favoured by contractors is that once it is shown that there is sum identified as due for payment in a Section 110 Notice and no Withholding Notice has been issued in respect of it then the sum due for payment must be paid. (*Whiteways Contractors v Impresa Castelli* [2000] 16 Const LJ 453 and *KNS Industrial Services v Sindall* [2001] 75 Con LR 71.) The narrow interpretation favoured by clients is to the effect that if work has not been done or not done in accordance with the requirements of the contract then there can be no sum due under the contract and accordingly section 111 does not apply as it is only relevant to sums which are due under the contract. (*Woods v Hardwicke* [2001] BLR 23 *SL Timber Systems Limited v Carillion Construction Limited* [2001] BLR 516.)

5.23 Fortunately the court of appeal decision in *Rupert Morgan Building Services (LLC) Ltd v David Jervis and Harriet Jervis* [2003] EWCA Civ 1563 has resolved the differences of opinion. Section 111 is a provision about cash flow aimed at addressing the problem of main contractors abusing their position to wrongfully withhold payment from sub-contractors. The section equally covers the situation of a client wrongfully withholding payment from a main contractor. In the absence of a Withholding Notice the client or the main contractor (as the case maybe) is prevented from withholding the sum due. The party entitled to payment is entitled to receive the sum due by the final date for payment without deduction. The disadvantage for the paying party is that if it has made an error in the amount due and over paid, it is at risk of losing the over payment in the event that the receiving party becomes insolvent. The paying party may however correct the situation by adjusting the next payment to the receiving party, either by correctly calculating the amount due for payment in the Section 110 Notice (which can double as a Withholding Notice if it contains the appropriate information) or by issuing a Withholding Notice within the time allowed, to account for the error in the earlier payment. The Withholding Notice does *not* create an irrebuttable presumption that the sum due for payment was in the final analysis properly payable, and consequently a paying party who has not issued a Withholding Notice may still raise matters which would justify the reduction of a payment in adjudication, arbitration or legal proceedings.

5.24 It is important in considering this judgement to study the contract to ascertain how a payment becomes due under the contract. In *Rupert Morgan Building Services (LLC) Ltd v David Jervis and Harriet Jervis* the contract in question was standard form published by the Architecture and Surveying Institute. A sum became due under that contract, on being certified by the architect. Contrast this with the situation in *SL Timber Systems v Carillion Construction* [2001] BLR 516 where the sum claimed was not contractually due under the contract, i.e. the date the 'payment become due' had not occurred in respect of the sum claimed, consequently the failure to serve a Withholding Notice was irrelevant. In the SFA/99 the date a 'payment becomes due' is the date the architect issues his or her account. Under the JCT 98 Standard Form, Intermediate Form and Minor Works Form, the date a 'payment becomes due' is the date of an interim or final certificate. In each case once those payments are contractually due, failure by the client to serve a Withholding Notice will entitle either the architect to payment of the sum stated in the account, or the contractor to the sum certified in the certificate.

5.25 The *Rupert Morgan Building Services (LLC) Ltd v David Jervis and Harriet Jervis* case is of further relevance to architects because of comments by Lord Justice Jacob, which, while not forming part of the decision that is binding on the lower courts certainly indicate views on the architect's duties to its client. Lord Justice Jacob while referring to the client's risk of losing money as a result of making an over payment to a contractor who subsequently became insolvent stated:

> 'But the risk is one which he can avoid by checking the certificate and giving a timeous withholding notice. No doubt a good architect would inform a lay client about the possibility of serving such a notice – indeed the architect may (I express no opinion) have a duty to do so. Moreover the client may (again I express no opinion) have a remedy against the architect if the latter negligently issues a certificate for to much.'

The writer believes the Court's message is clear, architects at least in relation to lay clients and possibly more experienced clients, have a duty to advise the client of the effect of the payment provisions in the building contract and in particular the notice provisions in section 110 and section 111.

6 The right to suspend performance for non-payment

6.01 This must be regarded as one of the most powerful sanctions given by statute to a party attempting to recover money. Prior to the Act, any suspension of performance by a party carried with it the potential risk of being regarded as repudiation of the contract, for which the suspending party could be liable for damages. The Act now sets out in Section 112 a series of clear steps for notices, which must be given to each of the parties to the contract before the right to suspend arises.

6.02 If a party has not received a sum due under the contract, in full, by the final date for payment, and no effective notice of withholding payment has been given, then that party has the right to suspend the performance of its obligations under the contract until payment has been made. The Act stipulates that the right to suspend performance may not be exercised without first giving the party in default at least seven days' written notice of the intention to suspend performance of the contract by the party owed the money. The notice must state the ground or grounds upon which it is intended to suspend performance. The right to suspend performances ceases when the party in default makes payment in full of the amount due.

6.03 The Act anticipates that the suspension of performance by one party will naturally affect the period within which, or the date by which, the contract should have been completed. The Act therefore provides that when calculating the time period within which the contract should have been completed, or the date by which completion should be achieved, a period of suspension of performance should be disregarded in computing the time for performance under the contract.

6.04 In relation to architects, this right to extend the contractual time period by the equivalent period of suspension does not really

protect the architect from the consequences of suspending work. If an architect suspends work for a week at a critical stage during the course of the building contract then the knock-on consequences of that suspension may extend the period over which the architect must carry out the services, for example, because the building contract has been delayed for a longer period than the period of suspension. The Act, however, only permits the period of suspension to be taken into account when calculating the time for performance of the architect's obligations under the architect's appointment and not the consequential delay that flows from the suspension. The SFA/99 and SW/99 merely follow the Act in disregarding the period of suspension when computing any contractual date for completion of the services.

6.05 A building contractor faces a similar dilemma when considering whether to suspend work for non-payment. The JCT have addressed this problem by incorporating a clause into the standard form of contract to the effect that the time for performance of the building contract will be extended for any delay that arises out of the suspension of performance of the contract. Architects may wish to include a similar express provisions within their own terms of appointment.

7 'Pay when paid' clauses

7.01 The Act renders ineffective any clause in a construction contract which makes receiving payment conditional upon the payer receiving payment from a third party. The exception to this is where the third party becomes insolvent and then a 'pay when paid' clause in a contract would be effective. The Act defines insolvency, but any architect experiencing the insolvency of their client should contact a solicitor who is a specialist in insolvency law.

7.02 The 'pay when paid' clause may have been rendered ineffective by the Act but the author is aware of attempts in contracts to circumvent its effect by means of a 'pay when certified' clause. This type of clause leaves the party to whom money is owed in no better position than it would have been under a 'pay when paid' clause and architects need to be vigilant for 'pay when certified' clauses being introduced into their terms of appointment, particularly if they are working for a contractor on a design and build appointment.

Interest on late payment of debts

7.03 The final matter to consider in relation to payment is the architect's entitlement to interest if payment is not made by the final date for payment. Interest can be claimed on late payment if there is an express term in the contract, or under the Late Payment of Debts (Interest) Act 1988. SFA/99 and SW/99 both contain a clause that stipulates interest is to be paid at 8% over the bank of England base rate, in the event of a bill not being paid within 30 days.

7.04 If the appointment contains no express entitlement to interest on late payment of debts, then the architect will have to rely on the statutory provisions, which entitle him to claim simple interest on the outstanding debt from the day after the final date for payment, either agreed by the parties or as determined under the Scheme. The rate of interest is set by the Secretary of State. (SI 2002/1675 art 4.) The rate of interest as at November 2003 was 8% over the rate of interest set by the Bank of England Monetary Policy Committee as at the 30th June (in respect of interest which starts to run between 1st July and 31st December) or 31st December (in respect of interest which starts to run between 1st January and 30th June).

Part Three

Dispute resolution

13

Litigation

ANTHONY SPEAIGHT QC*

1   Methods of dispute resolution

1.01 It is in the nature of human life that from time to time there are disagreements. Sometimes such disputes can be sorted out by agreement. But if they cannot, the parties have to resort to some outside agency. In earlier times and in more primitive societies, that agency tended to be the ruler – a feudal lord, a tribal chief, or possibly the king. In all modern societies the outside agency provided for dispute resolution takes the form of a court system.

1.02 Litigation is the process of dispute resolution before a court. In many spheres of activity litigation is almost the invariable mode of dispute resolution. But in the construction world today it is not the only, nor even the most common, process. Most construction contracts contain an arbitration clause, by which the parties agree to be bound by the decision of a private dispute resolution mechanism: for many years arbitration was the most common mode of determining construction disputes. Arbitration differs from litigation in that it takes place in private, and that the decision-maker, often an architect, is appointed by agreement of the parties. On the other hand, the actual nature of the proceedings is similar to litigation: the hearing is preceded by formal pleadings, and exchange of documents, and witnesses give evidence on oath. Arbitration is discussed in Chapter 14. Today arbitration has been overtaken in popularity by adjudication, which is discussed in Chapter 15. Adjudication is similar to arbitration in that the decision-maker may well be an architect, but the procedures are far more summary and the decision is binding for only a temporary period. By legislation in 1996 a right to adjudication is now compulsory in almost all construction contracts. Such is the attraction of a quick decision that not only is adjudication today being used with great frequency, but hardly ever are adjudicator's decisions being challenged in subsequent litigation or arbitration. Of growing popularity, too, is mediation, which refers to consensual meetings by parties with a neutral facilitator: the success rate in achieving a settlement at mediations is very high. Mediation is described in Chapter 16 evertheless, litigation remains the fallback method of dispute resolution. The existence of litigation underpins the efficacy of the other modes.

2   Litigation in England and Wales

2.01 Construction litigation in England and Wales usually takes place in the Technology and Construction Court (the TCC). The TCC is a specialist division of the High Court. There are seven permanent TCC judges who sit in London. In addition there are some 20 Circuit Judges based in other major cities who sit as TCC judges when the need arises in their area. The modern TCC was

created in 1998. Previously there had been a similar arrangement under which a number of judges had the less than meaningful designation of 'Official Referees'. The TCC is presided over by a High Court judge, who hears some cases himself. The first appointee to this position was Mr Justice Dyson, who had been a distinguished construction practitioner at the Bar, and who has subsequently been promoted to even greater judicial distinction. He has been succeeded at the TCC by Mr Justice Forbes, who had also been a construction specialist at the Bar.

2.02 All citizens have the right to conduct their own cases in court. But construction disputes are normally matters of such complexity that litigants in person are almost always at a real disadvantage to parties who are legally presented. In practice almost all litigants in the TCC are represented. Unless a party is acting in person, the administrative aspects of litigation, such as issuing the claim form, must be undertaken by a member of a profession which has been approved to act as a 'litigator'. Only one profession has such approval – solicitors, that is members of the Law Society of England and Wales. The solicitor almost invariably instructs a barrister to act as advocate in the TCC. There is a corps of about 200 barristers who have specialist experience of construction work. They are members of the Technology and Construction Bar Association. In addition to their advocacy work, they often undertake advisory work. Architects today can instruct a barrister directly, and over the last decade many have done so, both for advice on contractual issues and for advocacy in planning inquiries.

2.03 An alternative venue for civil disputes is the County Court. There are County Courts in all towns of any size. An architect would be likely to use a County Court if obliged to sue a client for unpaid fees. In such proceedings an architect might choose to act in person. The court office will provide factual information as to the procedures. If, however, the response to the fees claim should be, as is sometimes the case, an allegation of professional negligence, then, of course, insurers should be notified, and a full legal team will certainly be required.

2.04 Civil procedure has recently undergone major changes. The Civil Procedure Rules, which came into force in April 1999, implement ideas proposed by Lord Woolf, who is now Lord Chief Justice. These Rules apply to both High Court and County Court. A significant feature of the new regime is encouragement of settlement. There are likely to be penalties in the payment of higher costs to be paid to the other side if parties unreasonably refuse to mediate, or decline to accept an offer in settlement, or fail to disclose sufficient information at an early stage. In fact, considerable exchange of information is expected to take place even before proceedings are commenced. The Pre-Action Protocol for Construction and Engineering Disputes requires not only the supply in correspondence of details of what parties will be saying but also an off-the-record meeting.

* The section on litigation in Scotland has been contributed by Peter McCormack, and that on litigation in Northern Ireland by Jonathan L. Dunlop.

3   Litigation in Scotland

3.01 The court system in Scotland has been described in paragraphs 3.01–3.05 of Chapter 5.

Architects are more likely to be involved as parties or witnesses in civil actions in the Court of Session or the Sheriff Court. A party commencing an action (the 'pursuer') does so by serving a writ setting out his case (a 'summons' in the Court of Session or an 'initial writ' in the Sheriff Court) on the party being sued (the 'defender'). The parties have fixed times in which the defender lodges his answers ('defences') and they adjust their written cases in response to each other. A document called the 'closed record' (the latter word unusually having its emphasis on the second syllable!) is then printed which contains the final version of each party's written case. There may then be a legal debate between the parties as to the legal soundness of their cases assuming that they are factually true, or as to the sufficiency of detail specified. Cases which can only be resolved by hearing evidence as to the facts come before a single judge or sheriff for a hearing known as a proof when evidence is given by witnesses and speeches are then made on behalf of each party. At the end of a proof, the judge or sheriff usually does not give an immediate decision, but gives a later written decision. In the Court of Session only, some cases mainly being simple personal injury actions may be heard by a judge and jury of twelve (a 'jury trial') instead of by a judge alone. Since 1994 in the Court of Session there has been a special 'fast-track' procedure for Commercial Actions available to parties with business-related disputes. (Actions concerning personal injury, commenced in the Court of Session since April 2003 also have their own 'fast-track' procedure.)

4   Litigation in Northern Ireland

The court system in Northern Ireland has been described in paragraphs 3.01–3.07 of Chapter 7.

4.01 An architect may come into contact with the courts either as a party to proceedings or as an expert witness. In civil claims the plaintiff will bring his claim against the other party, known as the defendant. In the High Court this will be by way of writ or other originating process and in the County Court by way of a civil bill. The reform of civil procedure introduced into England and Wales following the Woolf Report has not been adopted in Northern Ireland. A review of civil justice in Northern Ireland is currently underway under the chairmanship of Lord Justice Campbell but when its work is completed it is expected that significant procedural differences will remain.

4.02 Generally, the successful party will have his costs paid by the losing side. This will not usually be the case, however, if the losing party is legally assisted under the Legal Aid, Advice and Assistance (NI) Order 1981. In practice, costs will not be ordered against an unsuccessful party in the Small Claims Court.

14

Arbitration

ANDREW FOYLE AND MELANIE WILLEMS

1 What is arbitration?

1.01 Arbitration is a process whereby parties agree to refer an existing or future dispute to the determination of one or more independent persons (the arbitrator or the tribunal) in a judicial manner. The decision of the arbitrator is expressed in an award, which (subject to satisfying certain legal requirements relating to the manner in which the decision is made) will be binding on the parties and enforceable in law. The law recognizes and supports the arbitral process by providing a statutory and common law framework for arbitrations.

1.02 Arbitration is a consensual process; unless the parties have agreed to refer their dispute to arbitration, there can be no arbitration. To explain this by an example, if a creditor claims that a debtor owes him money, unless the parties have agreed to resolve their disputes in a different way, the creditor can commence a court action (litigation) to recover the debt and the debtor cannot prevent him from commencing the proceedings. However, the creditor could not unilaterally refer the dispute to arbitration. Parties resolve their disputes by arbitration because that is what they have agreed to do.

2 The relevance of arbitration law to architects

2.01 Architects are almost bound to come across arbitration at some point during their professional careers for two principal reasons. First, the standard forms of agreements used in the construction industry (including the standard terms of engagement for architects) provide that disputes will be determined by arbitration and not by the courts. Second, the construction industry is a fertile source of disputes.

2.02 Also, an architect may be required to give factual evidence during an arbitration arising out of a project in which he or she has been involved. Architects commonly act as experts in arbitration proceedings. An architect may be appointed as an arbitrator.

3 The purpose of this chapter

3.01 The purpose of this chapter is to provide architects with a summary of the legal framework for arbitrations and of the arbitral process. The chapter is not intended to be a manual on how to conduct an arbitration, nor is it a comprehensive reference work on the topic. There are many substantial books which fulfil these roles and interested readers should refer to the bibliography at the end of this book for more information.

3.02 This chapter mentions the growing importance of methods such as adjudication and mediation which have evolved as alternatives to litigation and arbitration.

3.03 It was once said that arbitration was the alternative to dispute resolution by litigation in the courts, but, as arbitration became more cumbersome and expensive, mimicking many of the procedures which have made litigation expensive, pressure grew for alternatives to both litigation and arbitration. It has, of course, always been possible for parties to resolve their disputes by negotiation and agreement. However, negotiating a settlement to a dispute is often difficult, and so a number of techniques have evolved which are designed to help the parties to achieve a negotiated settlement of their disputes. These techniques have become known by the collective name of 'alternative dispute resolution' or ADR. ADR is now widely recognized as a successful method of resolving disputes cheaply *and* quickly. A number of construction industry standard forms incorporate ADR into their dispute resolution clauses. ADR is likely to continue to be used increasingly in the construction industry, so it is important that architects are aware of the main ADR techniques.

3.04 Reference will be made to a number of standard forms and other documents, using the following abbreviations:

1 JCT 1998: the Joint Contracts Tribunal Standard Form of Building Contract, 1998 edition
2 CE/99: the Conditions of Engagement for the appointment of an Architect
3 NSC/C 1998: the Standard Form of Nominated Subcontract issued by the JCT
4 CIMAR: the Construction Industry Model Arbitration Rules.

4 The Arbitration Act 1996

4.01 The most recent major development in the law of arbitration is coming into effect on 31 January 1997 of the Arbitration Act 1996 (the Act). The Act applies to all arbitration proceedings commenced on or after that date, whether or not the arbitration agreement was made prior to that date. The Act replaces the 1950, 1975 and 1979 Arbitration Acts and the Consumer Arbitration Agreements Act 1988.

4.02 The preamble to the Act states that its purpose is to 'restate and improve the law relating to arbitration ...'. Although the effect of some case law has been incorporated into the Act there has been no attempt to codify the entire common law, which will continue to apply to the extent that it has not been varied by the Act.

4.03 Much of the Act reflects three principles which are set out in section 1:

1 The object of arbitration is to obtain the fair resolution of disputes by an impartial tribunal without unnecessary delay or expense
2 The parties should be free to agree how their disputes are resolved, subject only to such safeguards as are necessary in the public interest

3   The court should not intervene in arbitrations save as expressly provided in the Act.

4.04   The Act specifies the duty of the Tribunal. Section 33 provides that the Tribunal shall:

'(a)   Act fairly and impartially as between the parties, giving each party a reasonable opportunity of putting his case and dealing with that of his opponent; and

(b)   Adopt procedures suitable to the circumstances of the particular case, avoiding unnecessary delay or expense, so as to provide a fair means for the resolution of the matters falling to be determined.'

The Tribunal is required to comply with this general duty in conducting the arbitral proceedings, in its decisions on matters of procedure and evidence and in the exercise of all other powers conferred on it. Arbitrators should have their obligations under this clause at the forefront of their minds throughout an arbitration.

4.05   The Act has generally been welcomed as a substantial improvement to the law of arbitration. It sets out the law in a simple and logical manner which should make the law intelligible to the layman.

4.06   The Act only applies to arbitration agreements which are made or evidenced in writing (see later for comments on this requirement). The Act defines an 'arbitration agreement' as follows:

'… an agreement to submit to arbitration present or future disputes (whether they are contractual or not).' (sub-section 6(1))

4.07   Oral arbitration agreements will be very rare and so this chapter refers only to arbitrations to which the Act applies.

5 The importance of deciding whether a process is or is not 'arbitration'

5.01   The most important reason for distinguishing 'arbitration' from other decision-making or dispute-resolution processes is that if the process is arbitration, and in particular, if it is governed by the Act, the parties will be afforded a number of legal rights and remedies in respect of the process, and the parties may seek to use the powers of the courts to enforce those rights or to obtain the remedies.

5.02   There are a number of situations where a third party may be called on to resolve a dispute between others. If the agreement expressly describes the process as 'arbitration' then it will be clear that the third party must act as an arbitrator and that, if he does, his decision or award will be enforceable in law. But even if the agreement does not expressly refer to arbitration, the courts might consider the process to be an arbitration so that the third party must comply with the legal requirements of arbitration.

5.03   Arbitration has the following characteristics which can be contrasted from other methods of resolving disputes:

1   There must be a valid agreement to arbitrate. An arbitration agreement itself must either form part of a valid, binding contract between the parties or it must amount to such a contract. In other words, the parties must have the relevant capacity to make a contract, the terms of the contract must be sufficiently clear for it to be enforceable and there must be consideration, etc. All these issues are dealt with in respect of contracts generally elsewhere in this book. Arbitration agreements are considered in more detail later.

2   The decision made by the process will be a final and binding determination of the parties' legal rights, enforceable in law. This is to be contrasted with, for example, an agreement to engage in mediation (a form of ADR) where it is of the essence of the process that any view about the dispute expressed by the mediator will not be binding on the parties.

Arbitration should be contrasted with 'adjudication' which, by virtue of the Housing Grants Construction and Regeneration Act 1996, is now compulsory for most written construction contracts. The decision of the Adjudicator is an interim binding decision, which is binding on the parties until the dispute is finally determined by legal proceedings (commonly arbitration) or by agreement of the parties.

3 The arbitrator is obliged to act impartially. He should be independent of the parties, even though he may be the nominee of one of them on a tribunal of three arbitrators.

4 The arbitrator is obliged to carry out his functions in a judicial manner in accordance with the rules of natural justice. This feature distinguishes the arbitration process from various other dispute resolution processes which are to be found in commercial contracts, such as determination by an expert, who is expressly required to 'act as an expert and not as an arbitrator'. An expert can resolve a dispute by making his own enquiries or by using his own knowledge of the subject matter of the dispute. Apart from exceptional cases (commonly found in shipping and commodities arbitrations) an arbitrator cannot do this.

Architects are often said to be acting in an arbitral or 'quasi arbitral' manner when considering and certifying applications for extensions of time and other claims under the building contracts, but that description is wrong. An architect who carries out such valuation and certification functions is not acting as an arbitrator. The architect in this context has a duty to act fairly but he does not have a duty to act judicially.

5 The arbitration tribunal must be appointed by the parties, or by a method to which they have consented. This emphasizes the consensual nature of the process.

6 The parties to the arbitration process must be the same as the parties whose rights are being determined, and who will be bound by the arbitration award. In most construction industry arbitrations there will be little doubt that this requirement has been met.

6 The advantages and disadvantages of arbitration compared to litigation in court

6.01 Because arbitration is a consensual process, it follows that at some point, either when they are negotiating a contract, or later, after a dispute has arisen, the parties have a choice. They must decide whether to choose arbitration as the process by which their disputes will be determined. This choice is explicitly provided in the JCT 1998 Standard Form of Building Contract, 1998 edition, which requires the parties to choose between arbitration and litigation. If parties do not choose arbitration, disputes which cannot be resolved amicably must be determined by the courts.

Advantages

6.02 Arbitration has a number of potential advantages over court proceedings:

1 The technical expertise of the arbitrator: The parties may feel that they would prefer technical disputes to be decided by an arbitrator with the relevant technical expertise. This is, of course, a point of particular relevance in the construction industry where disputes about the construction process may often involve technical, architectural, engineering or quantity surveying/valuation issues. It should be noted that, notwithstanding any technical expertise the arbitrator may have, he should only decide the dispute in accordance with the evidence presented to him by the parties.

2 Privacy: Arbitration proceedings are private and confidential as between the parties. Proceedings in court are (in general) open to the public. The fact that a claim form has been issued by one party against another is a matter of public record. It is often important to parties that their 'dirty washing' should not be aired in the public forum of the courts and it is for this reason that arbitration clauses are often found in partnership agreements (including architectural partnerships) where it is felt that public knowledge of a dispute between partners could be very damaging for the partnership business.

3 Flexibility: The parties can have a great deal of control over the procedure, for example, by choosing their own arbitrator, fixing the venue for the hearing and setting the timetable for the dispute to be dealt with. It is an underlying principle of the Act

that, subject to certain mandatory requirements, the parties are free to choose their own procedures for the resolution of their disputes. In litigation, the rules are determined by the court, in accordance with the Civil Procedure Rules. Disclosure of documents (which is explained later in this chapter) is an example of the difference. In litigation, standard disclosure of documents is nearly always required. In arbitration, disclosure is subject to the discretion of the tribunal.

4 The ability to exclude appeals: Parties are sometimes keen that, whatever the decision on a particular dispute may be, it should be final and binding in the sense that it is not subject to an appeal. It is not possible to agree to exclude rights of appeal from a decision of the courts but such agreements are possible with respect to arbitrations (see below).

5 The duty of tribunal to adopt procedures which are suitable to the circumstances of the case, avoiding unnecessary delay and expense, should mean that arbitration proceedings are quicker and more economical than equivalent proceedings in court.

6 The tribunal may be granted powers by the parties, or by the Act, which a judge does not have. For example, the Act gives an arbitrator a wider power to award interest on a compound basis, than is available to the court.

7 In cases involving foreign parties it can sometimes be easier to enforce the arbitration award in the foreign country. Many countries are parties to the New York Convention on the Recognition and Enforcement of Foreign Arbitral Awards (1958) and have agreed to recognize and enforce foreign arbitration awards. While the judgment of the English courts will often be recognized and enforced in many countries, there are many who recognize English arbitration awards but not English judgments.

6.03 In general it is true that arbitration proceedings can and should offer many of these advantages. However, prior to the Act, there was increasing concern that arbitration had failed to fulfil its potential as an efficient and effective means of resolving disputes. This was particularly so in the case of complex construction industry disputes. In those cases the arbitration process bore a very close resemblance to equivalent proceedings in court. It was increasingly like 'litigation without the wigs'. With this type of case, arbitration was rarely faster than litigation and was, often more, not less expensive. One reason for the greater expense is that parties to an arbitration must pay the fees of the tribunal (which could be up to three arbitrators) and pay for the hire of the room or rooms used for the hearing. By contrast, the fees for issuing proceedings in court and for obtaining a hearing date are almost nominal, with no charge for the services of the judge or for the use of the court room.

Comparison with court process

6.04 On 26 April 1999 new Civil Procedure Rules and Practice Directions came into force, governing the handling of all civil cases in the High Court and the County Courts. These rules introduce a number of radical features including the concept of a proactive judge whose task will be to manage the conduct of the case. The Rules include an 'Overriding Objective' which requires the parties and the courts to ensure that cases are handled justly. Parties are to be on an equal footing and expense is saved by dealing with the case in a manner which is proportionate to the amount of money involved, the importance of the case, the complexity of the issues and the parties' financial position. The Overriding Objective which applies to court proceedings is, perhaps, analogous to the general duty imposed on an Arbitral Tribunal by section 33 of the Act.

6.05 In the case of arbitration, savings in delay and expense depend on the qualities of the chosen Arbitral Tribunal. Even before the Act, an Arbitral Tribunal could properly have adopted 'procedures suitable to the circumstances of the particular case, avoiding unnecessary delay or expense' (section 33(1)(b) of the Act). All Arbitral Tribunals are now to adopt such procedures.

6.06 Construction industry disputes of any reasonable size are generally referred to a specialist court of the High Court now called the Technology and Construction Court (TCC) (previously the Official Referees Court). In the major provincial centres, TCC business tends to be dealt with by designated judges, although there is no separate TCC in those centres. Judges in the TCC are experienced in dealing with construction industry disputes. They are well aware of the terms of most of the standard forms of contract used by the industry and can quickly grasp the technical issues which arise. The TCC court has been at the forefront of adopting innovative procedures to reduce the delay and expense of litigation, even before the introduction of the reforms to the Civil Procedure Rules.

Disadvantages

6.07 One disadvantage of arbitration proceedings is the lack of an effective means to deal with disputes involving more than two parties. This is important in the construction industry where disputes may arise between the employer, architect, contractor and subcontractor which relate to the same subject matter. For example, the employer wishes to recover damages arising from a defect which is partly caused by the architect's design and partly by the contractor's poor workmanship. Unless special provision is made in all of the arbitration agreements whereby the parties agree that the separate disputes can be determined by the same arbitral tribunal, the disputes cannot be heard together. Even where such special provision is made, careful drafting is required to ensure that the arbitrations can be heard together. Unless there are effective provisions written into the arbitration agreements, even if the same arbitrator is appointed to deal with the various disputes between the different parties, he does not have power to order the various arbitrations to be heard at the same time unless all the parties consent (section 35 of the Act).

6.08 Where no provision is made for multiparty disputes (or where provision is made but it does not cover the circumstances which have arisen) then the party who is 'common' to both disputes may consider that he may be prejudiced by the risk of inconsistent decisions between the various arbitration tribunals.

6.09 Examples of agreements which provided for multiparty disputes are the JCT forms of main contract and sub-contracts which provide for multiparty arbitration in certain circumstances.

They seek to do this by reference to CIMAR, which both forms of contract adopt as the applicable rules for arbitrations arising out of those contracts. CIMAR provides detailed rules relating to the joinder of two arbitrations and the appointment of the tribunal. It is beyond the scope of this chapter to summarize the relevant rules.

6.10 Another possible disadvantage with arbitration is that it is less effective than litigation at dealing with the reluctant defendant. Defendants often raise a number of weak defences or counterclaims simply as a means of delaying the day when they have to pay their creditors. The courts provide procedures for dealing with those defences which are obviously weak, in addition to providing a range of sanctions which can be used to prevent one of the parties from 'dragging its feet' during the litigation process. The equivalent arbitration procedures and sanctions are less effective, mainly because a failure to meet key deadlines is not (as in the case of some litigation deadlines) an event of default which automatically enables the claimant to a default judgment. Also, there is a view that means of enforcing an arbitral award are not as fast as the means of enforcing a court judgment.

6.11 Notwithstanding some of the drawbacks of arbitration, there is no doubt that arbitration can be used to great advantage, and in cases where the tribunal makes sensible use of the procedures which are appropriate to the particular circumstances of the case, some of which are explicitly provided in the established rules of arbitration (such as the short hearing procedure and documents only procedure which is permitted by CIMAR), the process can offer an efficient and economical way of resolving a dispute. Whatever the relative merits of arbitration when compared to litigation, it is clear that arbitration clauses will continue to be incorporated into construction industry standard forms.

7 The arbitration agreement

7.01 The Act only applies where the arbitration agreement is in writing. Section 5(2) of the Act provides that there is an agreement in writing:

1 If the agreement is made in writing (whether or not it is signed by the parties)
2 If the agreement is made by exchange of communications in writing or
3 If the agreement is evidenced in writing.

Also (by sub-section (3), where parties agree otherwise than in writing by reference to terms which are in writing, they make an agreement in writing.

7.02 So, for example, an agreement between an architect and employer, which adopted the standard CE/99, would satisfy the 'in writing' requirement of the Act, because the CE/99 are written and contain an arbitration clause.

7.03 Because arbitration is a consensual process, the arbitration agreement is the very foundation of the process and can (or should) fulfil a number of important functions:

1 The agreement establishes and delimits the scope of the jurisdiction of the arbitration tribunal by defining the categories of dispute which can be referred to arbitration. For example, the model letter of appointment referred to in CE/99 provides that 'a dispute or difference arising under this Agreement shall be referred by either party to arbitration'.
2 The agreement establishes the composition of the arbitration tribunal or the method by which the tribunal will be appointed. For example CE/99 provides that the dispute shall be referred to a person to be agreed between the parties or, failing agreement within 14 days a person nominated by the President of the RIBA. The agreement should therefore state the number of arbitrators, their qualifications and how they will be appointed. If the agreement fails to deal with any of these matters, the Act provides default provisions to fill the gaps.
3 The agreement may prescribe the procedure or rules which the tribunal should follow. This may be done by setting out the procedure extensively (or specific procedural points) or, more usually, by reference to some other document which contains the procedure. For example, JCT 1998 incorporates CIMAR.
4 They may make other provisions in relation to the rules of law which the arbitration tribunal will apply. In English arbitration agreements which do not involve foreign parties, this provision is not usually necessary.

Each of these matters is considered below.

8 The jurisdiction of the arbitration tribunal

8.01 An award made by a tribunal which does not have jurisdiction to determine the dispute is not enforceable and can be set aside as a nullity. If there is no arbitration agreement then the tribunal does not have jurisdiction to determine anything at all. In para 8.02, where there is an arbitration agreement, the particular dispute must fall within the scope of disputes covered by that agreement, otherwise the tribunal will not have jurisdiction to determine that dispute. In para 8.03, the tribunal can only determine disputes which are actually referred to it by the notice of arbitration or which the parties later agree (either expressly or by their conduct) should be determined by the tribunal.

8.02 It may be easy to determine whether there is actually an arbitration agreement, but what if the agreement which contains the arbitration clause never came into effect (for example, the parties work to a letter of intent which is never converted to binding contract), or the contract is set aside because it is void or voidable, or is terminated as a result of one party's breach? It might be thought that in any of these circumstances there would be no arbitration agreement because the substantive agreement which contains the arbitration clause does not exist or is terminated. However, it is now established (and confirmed in section 7 of the Act) that ... 'unless otherwise agreed by the parties, an arbitration agreement which forms or was intended to form part of another agreement (whether or not in writing) shall not be regarded as invalid, non existent or ineffective because that other agreement is invalid, or did not come into existence or has become ineffective and it shall for that purpose be treated as a distinct agreement'. The arbitration agreement is therefore separate from the substantive agreement in which it may be incorporated.

8.03 The second aspect is whether the dispute in question falls within the scope of the disputes covered by the arbitration agreement. In most construction contracts which adopt one of the standard forms there will be little doubt about this issue. The arbitration agreement in Article 7A of the JCT 1998 applies to 'any dispute or difference as to any matter or thing of whatsoever nature arising under this Contract or in connection therewith except for ...' certain specified exceptions. It is hard to imagine any dispute between the employer and the contractor relating to the particular contract which might fall outside the scope of this arbitration clause, other than matters which fall within the specified exceptions.

8.04 While a dispute may fall within the scope of the arbitration clause, it is also necessary to consider whether there is any preliminary step to be completed before the dispute is capable of being referred to arbitration. For example, in the ICE contract conditions, a dispute must first be referred to the Engineer for his decision before it can be referred to arbitration.

8.05 Most arbitration clauses contain agreements to refer future disputes to arbitration (as opposed to agreements to refer a particular dispute to arbitration which must be made after the dispute has arisen). In such cases, the tribunal is only seised of jurisdiction if the particular dispute has been referred to arbitration. The disputes referred to arbitration are usually defined in the claimant's notice requesting arbitration. Other disputes can be determined by the tribunal by agreement or by the service of further notices of arbitration, although in the latter case, the dispute will not necessarily be determined by the same arbitral tribunal, unless the rules permit (CIMAR give the tribunal a discretion to allow additional disputes to be referred to the same tribunal). The notice of arbitration must describe all of the disputes to be referred to arbitration adequately.

8.06 This is especially important where the claim may shortly become time barred by reason of the Limitation Act 1980. A new claim, which is outside the scope of the original notice, introduced by a party after the limitation period has expired, could be defeated by a Limitation Act defence.

8.07 The arbitration clause or the substantive contract may also include time limits by which claims must be notified or referred to arbitration. Failure to comply with these time limits can provide a complete defence to the claim. However, section 12 of the Act gives the court power to extend time in certain circumstances. This power is described in more detail below.

9 Who decides if the tribunal has jurisdiction?

9.01 Who should decide if a party contends that the tribunal has no jurisdiction to determine the dispute, for example because there is no arbitration agreement? Logic might suggest that the tribunal cannot decide that question because, if there is no arbitration agreement, there is no validly appointed tribunal. However, section 30 of the Act provides that, unless otherwise agreed by the parties, the arbitral tribunal may rule on its own substantive jurisdiction, which will include whether there is a valid arbitration agreement, whether the tribunal is properly constituted and what matters have been submitted to arbitration in accordance with the agreement. Any such ruling may be challenged by proceedings in court. A party who wishes to object to the substantive jurisdiction of the tribunal must raise the objection not later than the time he takes the first step in the proceedings to contest the merits.

9.02 An objection during the course of the arbitral proceedings that the tribunal is exceeding its substantive jurisdiction must be made as soon as possible after the matter alleged to be beyond its jurisdiction is raised. Under section 32 of the Act, the court may, on the application of a party, determine any question as to the substantive jurisdiction of the tribunal. Applications to the court may only be made with the agreement of all other parties to the proceedings or with the permission of the tribunal. Even then the court must be satisfied that the determination of a question is likely to produce a substantial saving in costs and that the application has been made without delay and there is good reason why the matter should be decided by the court.

10 The composition of the arbitration tribunal

10.01 The second function of the arbitration agreement is to deal with the number of arbitrators and how they are to be appointed. It may also deal with other matters relating to the tribunal, such as the qualifications and (in international agreements) nationality of the arbitrators. Although highly desirable, it is not essential that the arbitration agreement deals with these matters. If it does not, the Act will provide the missing essential ingredients. In the absence of agreement between the parties:

1 Section 15 of the Act provides that the reference to arbitration shall be deemed to be a reference to a sole arbitrator.
2 Section 16 of the Act sets out the procedure for appointing the arbitrator or arbitrators. If the tribunal is to consist of a sole arbitrator, the parties are jointly to appoint the arbitrator. If the tribunal is to consist of two arbitrators, each party is to appoint one arbitrator. If the tribunal is to consist of three arbitrators, each party is to appoint one arbitrator and those two arbitrators are to appoint a third arbitrator as the Chairman of the tribunal.
3 Section 17 of the Act provides that where each of two parties is to appoint an arbitrator and one party refuses or fails to do so, the other party, after giving notice to the party in default, may appoint his arbitrator as sole arbitrator. In the event of a failure of the procedure for the appointment of the arbitral tribunal and in the absence of agreement between the parties, any party may apply to the court to exercise its powers under Section 18 of the Act. These include the power of the court to make any necessary appointments itself.

11 The number of arbitrators

11.01 It is theoretically possible for an arbitration agreement to specify that the arbitration tribunal should be composed of any number of arbitrators. However, it is very rare for there to be more than three. This is sensible for the practical reasons of cost and avoiding the difficulties of co-ordinating a large number of arbitrators to attend preliminary meetings and the hearing itself. Under section 15(2) of the Act, unless otherwise agreed by the parties, an agreement that the number of arbitrators shall be two or any other even number shall be understood as requiring the appointment of an additional arbitrator as Chairman of the tribunal.

11.02 When three arbitrators are appointed, unless a contrary intention is expressed, the award of the majority of them will be binding.

11.03 Although in some cases an arbitrator may have been appointed by only one of the parties, it is not that arbitrator's function to act as a 'champion' of the party who appointed him. He must be independent of both parties and act impartially at all times. He must hear the evidence, listen to the argument, and then make his decision in the proper way. There is a limited exception to this rule in the case of some shipping and commodities arbitrations where, if two arbitrators fail to agree, they then become 'advocates' of their appointing parties to argue the case before the umpire.

11.04 There is a procedure, which is rarely if ever used in construction disputes, but which historically has been used in shipping arbitrations, whereby the parties agree that the tribunal should be made up of only two arbitrators, one appointed by each party. The two arbitrators hear the dispute. If they agree on an award then their award is binding. If they do not agree then the dispute is referred to a third person called an 'umpire'. The umpire may have attended the proceedings or he may at this stage hear the dispute (in the case of some arbitrations he may do this by reviewing the papers referred to the two arbitrators, and not by a full rehearing of the arbitration). In order to ascertain whether the umpire is under an obligation to agree with one of the arbitrators or whether he may make an independent decision it is necessary to look at the arbitration agreement itself. Should this not specify the position, section 21 of the Act makes it clear that where two arbitrators are at deadlock, they must give notice to the parties and the umpire. He will effectively take up the reference as if he were a sole arbitrator, and the powers of the original two arbitrators will fall away. It will be clear from this rather basic description of the umpire procedure, why the construction industry has not been attracted by the use of two man tribunals assisted by a mediator.

11.05 Although some construction industry disputes (particularly international disputes) are dealt with by an arbitration tribunal of three arbitrators, it is most common to provide that disputes be resolved by a sole arbitrator. This is the provision which is found in CE/99 and also in the various JCT 1998 forms of contract.

12 The qualifications of arbitrators

12.01 It is not necessary for an arbitrator to have any particular qualification, but it is desirable that the arbitrator should be familiar with arbitration and preferably have some experience of acting as an arbitrator.

12.02 Where the appointing body is one which maintains a list of arbitrators (such as the Chartered Institute of Arbitrators, or the RIBA or the RICS) it is likely that the appointed arbitrator will have such experience and, in the case of the Chartered Institute, the person nominated will almost certainly be a fellow of the Chartered Institute and have undertaken further practical training as an arbitrator.

12.03 In this context the term 'qualification' may cover not only academic or other qualifications to act as an arbitrator, but also any other particular quality that the arbitration agreement specifies that the arbitrator should have.

13 Appointment of the tribunal in multi-party disputes

13.01 Multiparty disputes are a common feature of construction projects and efforts have been made in the standard forms of contracts to provide a mechanism for these disputes to be determined by the same tribunal. Where there is a multiparty arbitration, the arbitration agreement should make particular provision for the appointment of the tribunal. For example, the JCT 1998 forms of contract and the associated subcontract forms adopt the CIMAR provisions relating to the appointment of the tribunal.

14 Prescribing the arbitration procedure

14.01 'Party autonomy' is one of the underlying principles of the Act. This means that, subject to certain mandatory provisions, the parties are free to choose their own procedure. Typically, the

procedure is specified in the arbitration agreement, often by adopting established rules of arbitration. If no procedure is referred to in the arbitration agreement or agreed separately by the parties, then the arbitration tribunal is said to be master of its own procedure. This is reflected in sub-section 34(1) of the Act which provides that 'it shall be for the tribunal to decide all procedural and evidential matters, subject to the right of the parties to agree any matter'. The arbitration clause in CE/99 is silent as to the procedure which the arbitrator must follow.

14.02 Theoretically, leaving the procedure to be worked out by an experienced arbitrator should introduce the flexibility for the arbitrator to 'tailor' the procedure to deal with the particular dispute before him. Under the Act, the tribunal has a positive duty to adopt appropriate procedures for the circumstances of the case (see section 33). Most of the standard form agreements used in the construction industry specify the rules which will apply. For example, the various JCT forms of contract now provide that disputes shall be dealt with in accordance with CIMAR and the various forms of contract published by the ICE provide for the dispute to be dealt with in accordance with the ICE Arbitration Procedure 1997. These procedures present a range of options for the parties and for the tribunal, giving the parties the advantage of some certainty, and the tribunal the comfort that if it adopts an option envisaged by the prescribed rules then it less likely that its decision will be attacked on the grounds of serious irregularity under section 68 of the Act. Arbitration procedure is dealt with in a little more detail later in this chapter.

15 Other provisions which may be found in arbitration agreements

15.01 A number of other provisions may be included in arbitration agreements. For example, the arbitration clause is often part of a longer dispute-resolution provision, which may require the parties to exhaust other means of resolving their disputes before referring the dispute to arbitration. The agreement may specify the manner in which the arbitration is to be commenced, for example how and where the arbitration notice is to be served. Also, whether the arbitration tribunal is obliged to apply the law strictly or entitled to decide the dispute *ex aqueo et bono* (meaning according to equity and good conscience). The agreement may also specify when the proceedings are deemed to have been commenced for the purposes of the Limitation Act. In arbitrations involving foreign parties, the agreement should refer to the language of the arbitration, the place of arbitration and the applicable law.

16 How to commence arbitration proceedings

16.01 It is important to know how to commence arbitration proceedings because a mistake may mean that a claim becomes time barred as a result of the expiration of a limitation period. If the arbitration agreement does not specify how and when proceedings are deemed to be commenced then the provisions of section 14 of the Act will apply. The precise mechanism will depend on whether the arbitration agreement names a designated arbitrator or requires the parties to appoint the arbitrator or a third party to do so. The underlying principle is that arbitral proceedings are commenced in respect of a matter when one party serves on the other party a notice in writing requiring him or them to submit that matter to the persons named or designated or to be appointed as arbitrator.

16.02 The form of notice need not be long or complex but it is important that it should identify the matters to be referred to arbitration in broad terms and comply with the requirements of the arbitration agreement or section 14, if the agreement is silent. The arbitration notice should be served in accordance with the provisions of the arbitration agreement or, if there are no provisions, the method of service is set out in section 76 of the Act. The notice may be served by any effective means. If a notice is served, addressed, prepaid and delivered by post to the addressee's last known principal residence or principal business address or, if a body corporate, to the registered or principal office, it shall be treated as effectively served.

17 Arbitration procedure or rules

17.01 Once commenced, the arbitration will be conducted in accordance with the procedure or rules agreed between the parties, or failing agreement, as determined by the tribunal. In either case the tribunal must comply with the general duty specified in section 33 to act fairly and impartially between parties, giving each party a reasonable opportunity to put his case and to deal with that of his opponent and adopting procedures which are appropriate for the circumstances of the case. The objectives of the procedures can be summarized as follows:

1 First, to define the issues in the arbitration with sufficient precision so that each side can prepare the evidence and argument which it will rely upon to prove its case and disprove the other party's case and (which is, in effect, the correlative of this point) so that neither side can be said to be taken by surprise by evidence or argument presented by its opponent.
2 Second, to make provision for the exchange of information and evidence relating to the matters in dispute.
3 Third, to make provision for the way in which the hearing itself will be conducted (if, indeed, a hearing is held).

17.02 Usually the specified rules, will deal with these matters, while allowing the tribunal some discretion as to how they are applied. In most cases of any size, there will be a meeting with the tribunal at an early stage in the proceedings when the tribunal will make an 'order for directions'. In substantial cases, these directions, and the need for further directions, are reviewed at a 'pre-trial review' or a 'hearing for directions' which is held by the arbitration tribunal much nearer to the trial date.

18 The general duty of the parties

18.01 Section 40 of the Act imposes a general duty on the parties to 'do all things necessary for the proper and expeditious conduct of the arbitral proceedings'. This includes complying without delay with the tribunal's directions and orders and also any step to obtain a decision of the court on a preliminary question of jurisdiction or law.

19 Definition of the issues

19.01 In most cases, the parties will be required to serve on each other a 'statement of case'. As the name suggests, this document sets out the nature of each side's case. The amount of information included in the statement of case will depend on the circumstances of the case. Sometimes, the statement will include full submissions of fact and law, supported by the copies of the documents on which the party relies. The normal requirement is that the statements of case should set out, as concisely as possible, the material facts on which the party relies in support of its case.

19.02 In large construction disputes, which can involve complex issues of fact and substantial quantities of documents, it may be necessary for the parties to serve schedules providing details of the factual matters which are in dispute. These large disputes call for all of the skills of the tribunal to devise procedures which will be appropriate and enable the arbitration to proceed to a speedy conclusion.

20 The exchange of information and evidence

Disclosure of documents

20.01 In litigation, after the parties have exchanged their statements of case, each is required to disclose to the other documents in its possession, custody or control which relate to the matters in issue.

20.02 Disclosure of documents has never been mandatory in arbitration proceedings but there was a tendency for arbitrators to copy the litigation procedures to the extent of requiring the parties to make a full disclosure of their documents. However, the more modern approach in arbitration is not to require the parties to produce more than the documents on which it relies plus specific categories of documents which may be requested by the other party. Even then, the tribunal may decline to order a party to produce documents requested by the other party.

20.03 The modern approach is reflected in section 34(2)(d) of the Act which leaves it to the tribunal to decide 'whether any and if so which documents or classes of documents should be disclosed between and produced by the parties and at what stage'.

20.04 The manner in which documents are disclosed is also important. In litigation, parties are required to list all of the documents produced. Arbitrators could impose a similar requirement but the more modern approach is to require the parties to identify the documents by more general categories, such as by file.

20.05 Certain categories of documents, referred to as 'privileged documents' need not be disclosed. For most practical circumstances which architects are likely to come across, the only relevant categories of privilege are legal professional privilege and communications between the parties on a 'without prejudice' basis.

20.06 Documents covered by legal professional privilege are communications between clients and their qualified lawyers which come into existence for the purpose of providing the client with legal advice. Documents produced by the lawyers, or at their request in order to collect or prepare evidence for the arbitration are also privileged. It should be noted, however, that legal professional privilege only applies to communications between clients and their qualified lawyers and to documents prepared by or at the request of qualified lawyers. There are a great number of construction industry arbitrations where lawyers are not involved but other consultants are engaged. Communications with such consultants and documents prepared by them will not be covered by legal professional privilege (see *New Victoria Hospital v Ryan* (Court of Appeal) 4 December 1992).

20.07 Without prejudice communications are communications between the parties or their advisers, whether or not marked 'without prejudice', which comprise negotiations to settle the dispute or part of the dispute and which are intended to be made on a 'without prejudice basis' (in other words on the basis that they should not be referred to in the arbitration).

21 Evidence of fact and expert evidence

21.01 One of the main tasks of the tribunal is to establish the facts of the case. The way in which facts are proved will depend on the procedure adopted by the tribunal. Subject to any agreement between the parties, section 34(2) of the Act confers on the tribunal wide powers and discretion to decide how the facts will be proved. For example, the tribunal can decide whether to apply the strict rules of evidence as to the admissibility, relevance or weight of any material (oral, written or other) sought to be tendered on any matters of fact or opinion. The tribunal can also decide whether it should take the initiative in ascertaining the facts by making its own enquiries. The tribunal can decide whether and to what extent there should be oral or written evidence or submissions. Under section 37, the tribunal has the power to appoint experts or legal advisers to report to it and to the parties and to appoint assessors to assist it on technical matters.

21.02 In litigation, facts are proved by the evidence of witnesses which is normally given partly in writing (in the form of a witness statement) and partly through oral examination, usually cross examination. In arbitration proceedings, the tribunal has the discretion to establish the facts on the basis of documents alone,

possibly supplemented by written witness statements or by oral examination of all or some of the witnesses.

21.03 Because the tribunal is not bound by the strict rules of evidence which apply in court it can admit hearsay evidence and decide how much weight should be given to that evidence.

21.04 Construction disputes frequently raise important issues which turn on opinion evidence and not just evidence of fact. For example, if the tribunal has to decide whether an architect failed to use reasonable care and skill in designing a building it must first establish as a matter of fact how the building was actually designed. Whether that design was negligent is a matter of opinion. For that reason, most arbitration rules provide for the possibility of expert evidence being given on matters of opinion.

21.05 The collection and service of expert evidence is usually an expensive part of the arbitral process, with each party having its own expert and the tribunal having to assess and weigh the evidence of both experts to decide the dispute. For this reason, the tribunal is given the power to appoint experts to report to it and to the parties (section 37 of the Act). In those circumstances, the parties are given a reasonable opportunity to comment on any information, opinion or advice offered by any such expert.

21.06 Where the tribunal permits the parties to use their own experts, it is usually directed that the two experts meet with a view to narrowing and defining the issues in dispute. The duties of the expert are described below in the section referring to the architect as expert.

22 The arbitration hearing

22.01 A party may be represented in arbitration proceedings by a lawyer or any other person chosen by him.

22.02 The arbitration hearing is an expensive stage in the arbitration. In large arbitrations, the practice developed of following the court procedure for the conduct of the hearings. This would involve the claimant's representative opening the arbitration by explaining the whole of the case to the arbitrator and then taking the arbitrator through all of the relevant documents and correspondence. The claimant would then call his witnesses of fact and expert witnesses. Each witness would give their evidence in chief orally. The witness would then be cross-examined by the respondent's representative and might then be re-examined by the claimant's representative. The respondent's representative would present his case in a similar manner.

22.03 Today this 'traditional' approach is very rare. While the tribunal has a duty to allow each party a reasonable opportunity of putting his case and dealing with that of his opponent, it is quite consistent with that obligation to adopt procedures which curtail substantially the amount of oral presentation and argument at the hearing. Nowadays, tribunals increasingly require the parties to put in written submissions of law and take steps to reduce the length of the oral hearing.

22.04 In cases where there are significant factual disputes, it is more than likely that the tribunal will require the oral examination of witnesses, even though the witnesses will have served written witness statements. The sequence in which witnesses are called by the parties is a matter for them and the tribunal. Most commonly the claimant calls all of his witnesses of fact and expert witnesses and then the respondent calls all of his witnesses. However, sometimes it is the case that the claimant will call all of his witnesses dealing with a particular topic (whether a factual topic or an issue of expert evidence) and the respondent will then call his witnesses dealing with that particular topic. The most appropriate procedure varies from case to case.

22.05 After the arbitrator has heard the evidence, the representatives of the parties will make their closing submissions. Again, it is common for these submissions to be put in writing and in more complex cases the arbitrator may order a short adjournment to give the parties the chance to prepare their submissions in the light of all the evidence which has been given and ask for those submissions to be delivered to him in writing. The arbitrator may then ask for a further short hearing to deal with any questions which he has on the written submissions.

23 The award

23.01 Having heard the evidence and submissions, the tribunal renders its decision in the form of an award. The parties are free to agree that the tribunal may make provisional awards. This is often necessary where the tribunal wishes to make a provisional order for the payment of money or the disposal of property. The tribunal only has the power to make provisional awards if the parties agree.

23.02 The parties are also free to agree the form of the final award but if there is no agreement the Act provides that the award should be in writing signed by all the arbitrators or those who assent to the award and shall contain the tribunal's reasons unless it is an agreed award or the parties have agreed to dispense with reasons. The award is also required to state the seat (location) of the arbitration and the date when it is made.

23.03 Unless otherwise agreed by the parties, the tribunal may make more than one award at different times on different aspects of the matters to be determined. Typically this is done where the tribunal deals with issues of liability before considering the quantum of the claim.

23.04 The tribunal also has power to award simple or compound interest from such dates and at such rates and on such amounts as it considers just. The ability of the tribunal to award compound interest is wider than the equivalent power of the court.

23.05 The requirement to provide reasons as part of the award is to allow the court to consider any appeal. Accordingly, the arbitrator must state all his findings of fact (although he need not recite all the evidence which leads to the findings) and briefly state his reasoning on the issues of law.

23.06 All awards, whether including reasons or not, should be certain (in the sense of being sufficiently clear and unambiguous), and final (unless clearly intended to be an interim award). If the reference to arbitration calls for an award in money terms, then the award should be in an appropriate form to allow it to be enforced as if it were a judgment of the High Court, i.e. it should specify precisely the sum of money found to be due, and which of the parties is to make the payment.

24 Costs

24.01 The costs of an arbitration will include the arbitrator's fees and expenses, the fees and expenses of any arbitral institution involved and the legal or other costs of the parties. The tribunal will deal with the allocation of costs in its award. Unless the parties have otherwise agreed, the general principle is that costs should follow the event unless it appears to the tribunal that in the circumstances this is not appropriate in relation to the whole or part of the cost. For example, the tribunal might take account that the claimant declined an offer to settle the claim for more than the amount of the eventual award. Or that the claimant, while the overall winner, lost on a number of issues which took up substantial time at the hearing.

24.02 While the parties are free to make their own agreement relating to the award of costs, they cannot agree *before* a dispute has arisen that one party is to pay the whole or part of the costs of the arbitration in any event.

24.03 The parties can agree what costs will be recoverable and what fees will be paid to the arbitrator for his services. If the parties do not agree any of these matters then the provisions of the Act will apply.

24.04 The Act also gives the tribunal the power (unless otherwise agreed by the parties) to direct that the recoverable costs of the arbitration, or of any part of the arbitral proceedings, shall be limited to a specified amount. This is a potentially important provision since it provides the tribunal with the means to ensure that the parties use the most economic and efficient procedures to bring their dispute to a point of determination.

25 The power of the tribunal in the case of a party's default

25.01 One advantage of litigation over arbitration is that the court is better able to deal with a party in default. This is not to suggest, however, that an arbitration tribunal is powerless to deal with a party's default. The parties have an explicit duty to comply without delay with the orders of the tribunal (see above) and can agree on the powers of the tribunal in case of a party's default. If there is no agreed provision then section 41 of the Act gives the tribunal power to dismiss a claim if there has been inordinate and inexcusable delay on the part of a claimant to pursue his claim (subject to the tribunal being satisfied on certain conditions). The Act also gives the tribunal power to continue the proceedings in the absence of a party in default and may make an award on the basis of the evidence before it. This is to deal with a defendant who fails to comply with the tribunal's directions or to participate in the proceedings. The tribunal's power to make peremptory orders is supplemented by the power of the court to enforce such orders (see later).

26 Arbitration procedures found in construction industry cases

26.01 There are two sets of rules commonly used in construction industry disputes because they are adopted in the standard building and civil engineering contract forms. CIMAR are adopted by the JCT contracts and the ICE Arbitration Procedure (England & Wales), 1997 edition (the ICE Procedure) by the ICE contract. Both sets of rules were issued after the Act was enacted and take advantage of its provisions. Both deal expressly with many of the powers expressly or impliedly given to arbitrators and/or the courts by the Act. CIMAR actually sets out applicable sections of the Act in its rules.

26.02 Some features of CIMAR which are worth noting are:

1 The provisions relating to the joinder of separate arbitrations
2 The arbitrator is required to consider the form of procedure which is most appropriate for the dispute as soon as he is appointed. The rules offer three options
 (i) A short hearing procedure
 (ii) A documents only procedure
 (iii) A full procedure with a hearing.
3 If there is no joint decision by the parties as to which procedure shall apply then the arbitrator shall direct which procedure is to be followed. The rules give guidance on this. They state that a short hearing is appropriate where the matters in dispute are to be determined principally by the arbitrator inspecting work, materials, machinery, etc. A documents only procedure is appropriate where the issues do not require oral evidence or because the sums in dispute do not warrant the cost of a hearing. Where neither of the previous two procedures is appropriate, the full procedure should be adopted 'subject to such modification as is appropriate to the particular matters in issue'.
4 The provisions relating to the award of costs, which flesh out the circumstances the arbitrator can take into account when making that decision.

26.03 In general the ICE Procedure allows the arbitrator the flexibility to handle the case in the manner he considers to be appropriate. The arbitrator may order the parties to define their cases by delivering pleadings, or statements of case or whatever other means the arbitrator considers to be appropriate. Express provision is made for the arbitrator to determine which documents or classes of documents should be disclosed between the parties and at what stage.

26.04 The ICE Procedure also includes two optional procedures which may be adopted when the parties so agree (the arbitrator may invite the parties to agree to these procedures but he cannot order them to do so):

1 There is provision for a 'short procedure': according to this procedure each side delivers to each other and to the arbitrator a file containing a statement as to orders or awards sought, reasons relied upon by the parties and copies of any documents relied upon. The arbitrator may view the site or the works and may in his sole discretion permit the parties to submit further information or documents. Within 30 days of completing these steps the arbitrator then fixes a date for the hearing of oral submissions and for putting questions to witnesses, the parties and their representatives. However, the short procedure can be 'disapplied' on the insistence of any party, merely by serving notice before the arbitrator has made his award, without the need to give reasons.
2 There is a 'special procedure for experts': according to this procedure, parties submit a file containing a statement of factual findings sought, a report or statement from an expert and any other document relied upon by the parties. There is then a hearing for experts to express their views and be examined by the arbitrator. The rules provide that no costs of legal representation are allowed if this procedure is followed.

27 The role of the courts in arbitration proceedings

27.01 There is a limit to what can be achieved by a tribunal if a party refuses to comply with the arbitration agreement or with the tribunal's directions or award. Ultimately, resort must be made to the courts to enforce the process. The Act provides the necessary 'legal infrastructure' for arbitration by giving the court powers to support the process not only by enforcing decisions and awards of arbitral tribunals but also by providing a remedy if the arbitral tribunal ignores the fundamental requirements of arbitration. The powers of the court can loosely be divided into the following categories, being powers to:

1 Enforce the arbitration agreement
2 Support of the arbitration process

3 Supervise the arbitration process
4 Decide points of law
5 Consider appeals and applications to set aside the award; and
6 Enforce the award.

27.02 The general policy of the Act, and therefore that of the courts, is that if the parties have agreed that their disputes should be resolved by arbitration then that agreement should be upheld. The objective of the court's powers is to ensure that the arbitration process runs smoothly and fairly. Even if the court intervenes in the arbitration process it is the arbitration tribunal, not the court, which resolves the substantive dispute.

28 Powers to enforce the arbitration agreement – 'staying' of court proceedings in favour of arbitration

28.01 If a party to an arbitration agreement commences proceedings in court in respect of a matter covered by the arbitration agreement then the Act gives the courts the power to hold that party to his agreement to arbitrate by ordering a 'stay' (which means a suspension) of the court proceedings. The effect of the stay will be that if the party who brought the court action still wishes to pursue his claim, he will only be able to do so by arbitration.

28.02 An application to stay court proceedings must be made before the applicant has taken any step in the proceedings to answer the substantive claim. If he does take such a step he will waive his right to a stay.

28.03 Subject to that, section 9(4) of the Act provides that 'the court *shall* grant a stay unless satisfied that the arbitration agreement is null and void, inoperative or incapable of being performed' [emphasis added].

29 The court's powers exercisable in support of the arbitration process

29.01 A number of powers exercisable by the court have already been mentioned in this chapter, for example, in relation to the appointment of arbitrators. This power also extends to cases where an appointed arbitrator refuses to act, is incapable of acting, or dies; where an arbitration agreement provides for the appointment of an arbitrator by some third party and he refuses to make the appointment or does not make it within a reasonable time; and where two arbitrators are required or are at liberty to appoint an umpire or third party and do not appoint him.

29.02 The court may also extend time limits for commencing arbitration proceedings under section 12 of the Act, where the terms of an arbitration agreement provide that any claim shall be barred or extinguished unless the claimant takes some step to commence the proceedings within a time fixed by the agreement. It should be emphasized that the circumstances in which the court will extend time are limited and it would be unwise to assume that an extension will be granted. The applicant should first exhaust any available arbitral process for obtaining an extension of time. The court must then be satisfied that the circumstances are such as were outside the reasonable contemplation of the parties when they agreed the provision in question, and that it would be just to extend the time, or that the conduct of one party makes it just to hold the other party to the strict terms of the provision in question.

29.03 The powers of the court in relation to arbitral proceedings are set out in sections 42–45 of the Act. Section 42 deals with the enforcement of peremptory orders of the tribunal, section 43 with securing the attendance of witnesses, section 44 with various powers exercisable in support of the arbitral proceedings and section 45 with determination of preliminary points of law. There are a number of common themes. First, with the exception of section 43, the court's powers are subject to any contrary agreement between the parties. That contrary agreement might be expressed in the rules which apply to the proceedings. Second, the powers of the court are in support of the arbitral proceedings, so generally the court will not exercise the power unless the applicant has exhausted any available arbitral process or the application is made with the consent of the tribunal.

29.04 The range of powers included in section 44 includes the taking and preservation of evidence, making orders relating to property which is the subject of the proceedings, the sale of any goods the subject of the proceedings and the granting of an interim injunction for the appointment of a receiver. The underlying rationale of the powers exercisable under section 44 is the recognition that a party may need to take prompt action to preserve its rights (for example by applying for an interim injunction) and it may be unable to secure those rights through arbitration for the simple reason that the arbitral tribunal has not been constituted.

29.05 The power of the court to determine a preliminary point of law under section 45 of the Act is to be distinguished from an appeal against the arbitrator's award (see later). Section 45 provides a means for the parties or the tribunal to obtain a ruling from the court on a point of law which substantially affects the rights of one or more of the parties. An application can only be made with the consent of all the parties or with the permission of the tribunal. Even then the court must be satisfied that the determination of the question is likely to produce substantial savings in costs and that the application was made without delay.

30 Enforcement of arbitration awards

30.01 Arbitration awards may, with leave of the court, be enforced in the same manner as a judgment of the High Court (section 66 of the Act). Obtaining leave is almost always a pure formality unless the respondent can say that there was some severe defect in the arbitration process, such as problems with the arbitration tribunal's jurisdiction.

31 The court's powers to supervise the arbitration process

31.01 Although the underlying principle of the Act is to allow the arbitration process to take its own course, with the minimum or interference from the court, nonetheless the court is concerned to ensure that the arbitration is conducted in accordance with the basic standards of fairness and natural justice. The principal means by which the court exercises this supervisory role are through the power to remove an arbitrator or the power to set aside an award if there is a procedural irregularity.

31.02 Under section 23 of the Act, the court has power to remove an arbitrator on any of the following grounds:

'(a) that circumstances exist that give rise to justifiable doubts as to his impartiality,
(b) that he does not possess the qualifications required by the arbitration agreement;
(c) that he is physically or mentally incapable of conducting the proceedings or there are justifiable doubts as to his capacity to do so;
(d) that he has refused or failed –
  (i) properly to conduct the proceedings; or
  (ii) to use all reasonable despatch in conducting the proceedings or making an award,
    and that sub-stantial injustice has been or will be caused to the applicant.'

31.03 The court has also power to set aside or vary an arbitration award on the application of one of the parties challenging an award

of the tribunal on the ground that the tribunal lacked substantive jurisdiction (section 67).

31.04 The court can also set aside, vary or remit an award back to the tribunal on the ground of 'serious irregularity' affecting the tribunal, the proceedings or the award (section 68). A serious irregularity means an irregularity of one or more of the following kinds which the court considers has caused or will cause substantial injustice to the applicant –

'(a) failure by the [arbitral] tribunal to comply with section 33 [under which it is obliged to act fairly and impartially and adopt procedures suitable to the circumstances of the particular case] ...
(b) the tribunal exceeding its powers ...
(c) failure by the tribunal to conduct the proceedings in accordance with the procedure agreed by the parties;
(d) failure by the tribunal to deal with all the issues that were put to it;
(e) any arbitral or other institution or person vested by the parties with powers in relation to the proceedings or the award exceeding its powers;
(f) uncertainty or ambiguity as to the effect of the award;
(g) the award being obtained by fraud or the award or the way in which it was procured being contrary to public policy;
(h) failure to comply with the requirements as to the form of the award; or
(i) any irregularity in the conduct of the proceedings or in the award which is admitted by the tribunal or by any arbitral or other institution or person vested by the parties with powers in relation to the proceedings or the award.'

31.05 The court's powers under sections 67 and 68 are subject to certain conditions, such as a time limit and the need to exhaust remedies available under the arbitral process. The right to make such a challenge can be lost (see section 73) by, for example, failing to make a timely and effective objection to the exercise of jurisdiction by the tribunal or to the offending conduct or action.

32 Appeals on points of law

32.01 A party's right to apply to set aside an award on the grounds of a serious irregularity cannot be excluded by agreement (although the right can be lost by conduct) but if the tribunal, having conducted the arbitration proceedings properly, reaches the wrong conclusion, it can be very difficult to challenge the award. The right to appeal to the courts can be excluded by agreement and is restricted to appeals on points of law. An appeal can only be made with the leave of the court, which will only be granted if the court is satisfied:

'(a) that the determination of the question will substantially affect the rights of one or more of the parties,
(b) that the question is one which the tribunal was asked to determine,
(c) that, on the basis of the findings of fact in the award –
  (i) the decision of the tribunal on the question is obviously wrong, or
  (ii) the question is one of general public importance and the decision of the tribunal is at least open to serious doubt, and
(d) that, despite the agreement of the parties to resolve the matter by arbitration, it is just and proper in all the circumstances for the court to determine the question.'

(See section 69(3) of the Act.)

32.02 In practice, in a 'one-off' dispute (that is, a dispute which does not relate to a standard provision in a construction agreement), leave to appeal will usually only be granted in respect of a question of law if it is apparent to the judge that the arbitrator's award is obviously wrong. Even then, if the judge considers that it is possible that argument could persuade him that the arbitrator might be right, he will often not grant leave. In cases concerning the meaning of standard terms in contracts, the judge will take a less strict approach, but leave should not be given even in those cases, unless the judge considers that a strong prima facie case has been made out that the arbitrator was wrong in his construction of the contract. When the events to which the standard clause were applied in the particular arbitration were themselves 'one-off' events, the stricter criteria would, nevertheless, be applied.

32.03 Appeals from arbitration awards will therefore be infrequent. If an appeal is allowed, the court may confirm, vary, set aside, or remit the award for the reconsideration of the arbitrator, together with the court's opinion on the question of law which was the subject of the appeal.

33 The architect as arbitrator

33.01 As can be seen from the relatively brief description of the law of arbitration set out in this chapter, the acceptance of the position of arbitrator is not something to be undertaken lightly. An architect who undertakes arbitrations should have a good working knowledge of the law and practice of arbitrations in addition to the law and practice of the construction industry. Furthermore, acting as an arbitrator can be time-consuming if the arbitration goes to a full hearing. After the hearing, the arbitrator must set aside sufficient time to write the award. This will involve reviewing all of the evidence and the submissions put to him during the proceedings.

33.02 When an arbitrator undertakes his appointment he is entitled to 'such reasonable fees as are appropriate in the circumstances' (section 64(1) of the Act) to be paid by the parties. If nothing is agreed between the arbitrator and the parties when he accepts his appointment then the arbitrator usually assesses what he considers to be a reasonable sum for his services and makes that sum, and the identity of the person who is liable to pay that sum, part of his award. The actual recovery of his fees is usually dealt with by notifying the parties that the arbitration award is available to be collected on payment of his fees. This is usually a sufficient incentive for the claimant to pay the arbitrator's fees (whether or not he is made liable for them by the award) so that he may obtain the award and (if he has been successful) proceed to enforce it.

33.03 However, statistically most arbitrations settle before the final award. In these circumstances the law probably is that the arbitrator is entitled to reasonable remuneration from the parties in respect of the work which he has carried out but that he is not entitled to payment (either as 'remuneration' or as 'damages' for lost opportunity) in respect of the fees which he would have earned had there been a hearing and final award.

33.04 If there is a dispute between the arbitrator and the parties with regard to the level of his remuneration then there are various ways for that to be determined by the court, depending on the circumstances of the case.

33.05 For these reasons, experienced arbitrators do not accept their appointment until the parties have accepted the arbitrator's terms of engagement. These terms usually provide that both parties are jointly and severally liable for the arbitrator's fees. It is common for arbitrators and parties to agree that there should be hourly remuneration rates for preparatory reading and interlocutory hearings and daily rates of remuneration for the hearing of the arbitration itself. It is also common for 'cancellation charges' to be stipulated by arbitrators to protect them from loss of revenue in the event that the arbitration is settled before the award is made. Arbitrators often also stipulate that they require some security on account of likely fees.

33.06 An arbitrator is generally not liable for his actions as arbitrator. Section 29(1) of the Act (which applies notwithstanding any contrary agreement between the parties) provides that an arbitrator is not liable for anything done or omitted to be done in the discharge or purported discharge of his functions as arbitrator unless the act or omission can be shown to have been in bad faith. The

arbitrator's position is therefore different from that of judges who, when acting in their judicial capacity, are immune even where they have acted maliciously. The burden of proving bad faith on the part of an arbitrator lies on the person alleging it. In one case it was held that bad faith covered malice in the sense of personal spite or desire to injure for improper reasons.

33.07 Section 24(4) of the Act provides that 'Where the court removes an arbitrator, it may make such order as it thinks fit with respect to his entitlement (if any) to fees or expenses, or the repayment of any fees or expenses already paid'. The Act does not deal explicitly with the position where an award has been set aside on the grounds of 'serious irregularity' caused by the arbitrator's failure to conduct the proceedings properly. Logic would suggest that the court would order an arbitrator to refund his fees if the circumstances were sufficiently serious.

33.08 Perhaps the best advice for an architect contemplating accepting an appointment as an arbitrator (in addition to the advice in paragraph 6.01 above) is to ensure that he is covered by appropriate professional indemnity insurance.

33.09 Architects who act as arbitrators may wish to have their own legal advice, if the dispute raises difficult issues of law. Section 37(1) of the Act provides that unless the parties agree otherwise, the arbitrator may appoint experts/legal advisers to report to him and to the parties and to attend the proceedings. However, the parties must be given a reasonable opportunity to comment on any information, opinion or advice offered.

33.10 It must, however, be the arbitrator, and not the legal adviser, who makes decisions and is seen to make decisions, even on points of law. He must not merely adopt the views put forward by the legal adviser without considering the matter himself.

33.11 The fees of the legal assessor are part of the fees of the arbitration and are recoverable by the arbitrator from the parties (see section 37(2) of the Act).

34 The architect as expert witness

34.01 Experienced architects may be requested to provide expert evidence in arbitration proceedings. The function of an expert witness is to state his professional opinion on the relevant issues in the arbitration. The opinion should be stated clearly, first in a written report, which is served prior to the hearing, itself and then orally at the hearing. Usually the expert will meet his opposite number before the hearing to identify common ground and define the issues on which they disagree.

34.02 An architect needs no special training to be an expert, since it is his expertise as an architect which is being called on. However, it is important to understand the nature of the role of the expert in the proceedings, since experts commonly believe that it is their task to advocate their party's case, to the extent of compromising their own opinion. Guidelines for expert witnesses in litigation and arbitration were given by the court in *National Justice Compania Naviera SA v The Prudential Assurance Company Limited (the Ikarian Reefer)* [1993] 2 Lloyd's Reports 68 (QBD). The court advised that:

1 Expert evidence should be and should be seen to be independently produced by the expert witness, albeit that the expert is giving evidence on behalf of one of the parties and he should co-operate with the party's legal team in identifying the issues which he is to address and on the overall structure for his report.
2 The expert witness should present an objective unbiased opinion regarding matters which fall within his expertise.
3 An expert witness should never assume the role of advocate.
4 Any facts or assumptions upon which the expert witness's opinion is founded must be stated together with any material facts which could detract from his concluded opinion.
5 Any photographs, survey reports, plans and any other document upon which the expert witness has relied in his evidence must

be provided to the other parties in the legal proceedings/arbitration at the same time as expert reports are exchanged.

6 If the expert witness does not have sufficient data available to him to form a properly researched conclusion, this fact must be revealed to the court/arbitrator together with an indication that the opinion is no more than provisional.

7 If any of the subject matter of the dispute falls outside the area of the expert witness's expertise, he is under a duty to inform the court/arbitrator in his report. Likewise, he should make it clear if, when under cross-examination, he is asked questions which are not within the area of his expertise.

8 Where the expert witness is unable to swear on oath that his report contains the truth, the whole truth, and nothing but the truth, this qualification must be stated in the report.

9 If an expert witness changes his mind with respect to a material issue of his evidence after reports have been exchanged, this change of view should immediately be communicated through the parties' representatives to the other side, and where appropriate to the court/arbitrator.

34.03 The Civil Procedure Rules governing court proceedings state that:

'(a) It is the duty of an expert to help the court on the matters within his expertise.

(b) This duty overrides any obligation to the person from whom he has received instructions or by whom he is paid.'

(See rule 35.3.)

34.04 The Civil Procedure Rules also require an expert to state the substance of all material instructions on the basis of which his report was written. This is a major change as previously communications between a party's lawyer and his expert were legally privileged. It is likely that arbitrators may follow the lead given by the courts by making it clear to experts appointed by the parties that they have a duty to the tribunal. They could also require the expert to summarize his instructions in his report.

15

Adjudication*

ANDREW BARTLETT QC AND KIM FRANKLIN

1 The nature of adjudication

1.01 Adjudication cannot be defined with precision because the details of an adjudicator's functions depend upon the particular terms upon which the adjudicator is appointed. Broadly, it may be stated that adjudication is a summary process by which disputes between the parties to a contract are decided by a third party adjudicator. The adjudicator's decision is binding on the parties until the dispute is finally determined by legal proceedings, arbitration or agreement. The decision thus has 'an ephemeral and subordinate character'. In the construction industry adjudication is used to obtain a quick neutral decision on disputes arising from a project. Adjudication should be distinguished from other forms of dispute resolution such as mediation, expert determination and arbitration.

1.02 An adjudicator is appointed to decide whether in the circumstances of a dispute a particular right exists and should be enforced. Unless the parties specifically agree, an adjudicator is not appointed to adapt the terms of the contract or to vary, add to, or take away from the terms of the contract. Like a contract administrator, an adjudicator must apply the terms of the contract, but decisions of an adjudicator are more immediately enforceable pending the result of litigation or arbitration.

1.03 The Latham Report (Constructing the Team, HMSO 1994) was concerned with establishing best practice in project strategy, risk assessment and effective procurement.

The intention of Parliament in enacting the Housing Grants Construction Regeneration Act 1996 was to introduce a speedy mechanism for settling disputes in construction contracts on a provisional interim basis, and requiring the decisions of adjudicators to be enforced pending the final determination of disputes by arbitration, litigation or agreement.

1.04 The statutory right to adjudication therefore provides an interim remedy. However, it should be noted that there is no time limit on the right to go to adjudication, and there is a trend towards the use of adjudication after (sometimes long after) projects have finished.

It is inherent in the system of speedy adjudication that injustices will occur, because from time to time, adjudicators will make mistakes.

1.05 Sometimes those mistakes will be glaringly obvious and disastrous in their consequences for the losing party. The victims

of mistakes will usually be able to recoup their losses by subsequent arbitration or litigation, and possibly even by a subsequent adjudication. Sometimes, they will not be able to do so, where, for example, there is an unforeseen intervening insolvency, either of the victim or of the fortunate beneficiary of the mistake.

A party to a construction contract has the right to refer a dispute arising under the contract to an adjudicator by virtue of HGCRA 1996.

2 Construction contract

2.01 What amounts to a 'construction contract' for the purpose of the right to adjudication is defined in great detail in the Act and by statutory instrument.

It should be noted that the term 'construction contract' includes engagements of professionals providing design or advice in relation to construction operations.

3 Compliance with section 108

3.01 The contract must provide for an adjudication complying in all respects with HGCRA 1996, s 108. Parties cannot contract out of the right of adjudication.

If the contract does not provide for adjudication, or the adjudication for which it provides falls short of the requirements of HGCRA 1996, s 108 in any respect, the adjudication provisions of the Scheme for Construction Contracts apply. Even if the contractual provisions fall short in only one respect, i.e. sufficient to bring into effect as implied terms of the contract the whole of the Scheme provisions for adjudication.

4 Existence of dispute

4.01 A dispute must exist before it can be referred to adjudication. 'Dispute' includes any difference. Sometimes it suits one party to contend that no dispute exists, in order to resist the adjudication process. In *Halki Shipping Corp v Sopex Oils Ltd* ([1998] 2 All ER 23), in the context of Arbitration Act 1996, s 9 the Court of Appeal held that, if a claim is not admitted and paid, there is a 'dispute', even if the claim is indisputable. In the context of adjudication a range of views has been expressed about what is needed to bring a dispute into existence. Some judges have insisted on the strict *Halki Shipping* approach. Others have taken a more pragmatic and flexible approach, holding that a 'dispute' can only arise once the subject-matter of the claim, issue or other matter has been brought to the attention of the opposing party and that party has had an opportunity of considering and admitting, modifying or rejecting the claim or assertion. (*Fastrack Contractors Ltd v Morrison Construction Ltd* [2000]

* The text of this chapter is a shortened version of Emden's Construction Law, Part V Dispute Resolution, Chapter 1, Adjudication, written and edited by Andrew Bartlett QC. The reader is referred to this regularly updated loose leaf work for a fuller and more detailed discussion of this complex and rapidly developing area of construction law.

BLR 168, HHJ Thornton QC. See also Hitec Power Protection BV v MCI Worldcom Ltd [2002] EWHC 1953, TCC, HHJ Seymour QC; Carillion Construction Ltd v Devonport Royal Dockyard Ltd (unreported, 27 November 2002), TCC, HHJ Bowsher QC.)

5 Notice of adjudication

5.01 The contract must enable a party to give notice at any time of his intention to refer a dispute to adjudication. (HGCRA 1996 s 108(2)(a)). The primary purpose of this right is to enable disputes to be referred during the progress of the works, in contrast to the situation under some forms of arbitration clause, where the arbitration cannot be proceeded with until after practical completion or abandonment of the work. But the right is not limited to the duration of the works. The notice of adjudication may be given at any time. It could be given while arbitration or litigation is proceeding, in the hope of producing a quick decision acceptable to both sides in order to short-circuit long and expensive proceedings.

5.02 The notice of adjudication defines what it is that the adjudicator is required to decide. The referral notice and subsequent documents do not define the scope of the dispute, unless they amount to an agreement to alter the scope defined by the notice of adjudication. A party who identifies the dispute in simple or general terms has to accept that any ground that exists which might justify the non-payment or termination complained of is comprehended within the dispute for which adjudication is sought.

6 Adjudicator's powers and duties

6.01 The contract must impose on the adjudicator a duty to act impartially and to reach a decision in the time allowed. (HGCRA 1996 s 108(2)(e)). The contract cannot impose these duties directly, since the adjudicator is not a party to the contract. In practice, therefore, they must be expressly or impliedly incorporated in the terms of the adjudicator's appointment. While the adjudicator must act impartially, there is no requirement here that he be independent of the parties. The architect or engineer under a construction contract could in theory be nominated as the adjudicator, although this is unlikely to occur in practice, since one of the reasons for introducing a system of adjudication was dissatisfaction with the traditional conflicting roles of the architect or engineer as simultaneously both impartial certifier and agent of the employer, and there would be a risk of challenge for bias. The contract must also give the adjudicator the power to take the initiative in ascertaining the facts and the law. The adjudicator is entitled to be proactive and adopt an inquisitorial role, seeking out the evidence and other material which he considers appropriate for enabling him to decide the dispute referred to him. The adjudicator may make site visits, interview relevant personnel, and obtain legal or expert advice. Within the constraints of the applicable adjudication rules, the adjudicator should tailor the procedure to the nature and size of the dispute. Unless prohibited by the applicable rules, the adjudicator may conduct a formal oral hearing if he thinks fit, but this is likely to be a relatively rare occurrence. An informal meeting with the parties is more common. Some cases are suitable to be disposed of on written submissions alone.

6.02 It has been suggested that, if the courts were to hold that adjudication procedures are required to conform to the Human Rights Act, an adjudicator could decline to act, on the ground that the 28 day time limit makes a fair hearing impossible to conduct. In the case of a complex dispute where the strict 28 day time limit prejudices the respondent, it is difficult to see how the limit could be justified under the Act as being in the interests of the wider community, particularly given the unfairness of the provision that an extension may only be granted if the claimant agrees. However, it would seem that he ought to proceed in reliance on the Human Rights Act 1998, s 6(2) on the ground that primary legislation (that is, HGCRA 1996, s 108(2)) gives him no choice as to the time limit. (*Austin Hall Building Ltd v Buckland Securities Ltd* [2001] BLR 272, HHJ Bowsher QC.)

7 Adjudicator's immunity

7.01 The contract must provide that the adjudicator is not liable for anything done or omitted in the discharge or purported discharge of his functions as adjudicator unless the act or omission is in bad faith, and that any employee or agent of the adjudicator is similarly protected from liability. If the adjudicator has any connection with a party or any personal interest in the subject-matter of the dispute, he would be wise to disclose it at the time of appointment; otherwise, such non-disclosure may give credence to subsequent allegations of bad faith.

8 Effect of adjudicator's decision

8.01 The contract must provide that the decision of the adjudicator is binding until the dispute is finally determined by legal proceedings, by arbitration (if the contract provides for arbitration or the parties otherwise agree to arbitration) or by agreement. The parties are free to agree, if they wish, to accept the decision of the adjudicator as finally determining the dispute.

9 Adjudication under the Scheme for Construction Contracts

9.01 Where the construction contract does not fulfil the whole of the requirements of HGCRA 1996, s 108(1)–(4), the adjudication provisions in the Scheme for Construction Contracts (The Scheme is contained in the Scheme for Construction Contracts (England and Wales) Regulations 1998, SI 1998/649. The Scottish version, which is almost identical, is in the Scheme for Construction Contracts (Scotland) Regulations 1998, SI 1998/687.) have effect as implied terms of the contract. Parties may, if they wish, expressly incorporate the Scheme provisions into their contract. Adjudication under the Scheme applies only to disputes 'arising under the contract'.

9.02 To get the adjudication started there are three steps that the referring party must take:

(a) Give notice of adjudication.
(b) Either directly or via a nominating body, request an adjudicator to act.
(c) Give a referral notice.

9.03 The first step after giving notice of adjudication is that the referring party must make a request for an adjudicator to act. The adjudicator may be named in the construction contract, or may be specially agreed by the parties, or the contract may specify a nominating body whose function is to select a person to act. If none of these applies, the referring party may direct the request for an adjudicator to any nominating body. The request must be accompanied by a copy of the notice of adjudication. The Scheme does not expressly state a time within which the request must be made, but in practice it should be made at the same time as the giving of the notice of adjudication.

10 Referral notice

10.01 Once the Scheme adjudicator has been selected, the referring party must give notice referring the dispute to the adjudicator. This must be done within 7 days from the date of the notice of adjudication. It must be accompanied by copies of, or relevant extracts from, the construction contract and such other documents as the referring party intends to rely upon. At the same time copies of the referral notice and enclosures must be sent to every other party to the dispute. Only an existing dispute may validly be referred to the adjudicator. The referring party may include further details, clarification or correction of claims already in dispute, or may confine the reference to something less than the totality of the matters then in dispute, but is not entitled (unless the other party agrees) to raise other matters which have not been disputed.

11 Adjudicator's powers and duties

11.01 The Scheme repeats the requirement of the HGCRA 1996 that the adjudicator must act impartially. He must carry out his duties in accordance with any relevant terms of the contract and must reach his decision in accordance with the law applicable in relation to the contract. He is also under a duty to avoid incurring unnecessary expense.

11.02 The Scheme gives the adjudicator wide procedural powers: see Scheme Pt I para 13. There is a clear onus on the adjudicator to decide the appropriate procedure for the particular dispute, and there appears to be an expectation that he will take the initiative in obtaining the evidence or other material that he needs in order to reach a decision. Given the tight timetable for reaching a decision, his power to limit the quantity of material submitted to him is of great practical importance. Delaying tactics should not be allowed, and recalcitrant parties are liable to find that adverse inferences are drawn.

11.03 The even-handed judicial element in the adjudicator's function is illustrated by the terms of the Scheme. He may meet and question a party to the contract and that party's representatives. But, having done so, he must make available to the other party the information obtained, if he is going to take account of it. (This provision is an indication that the rules of natural justice are intended to apply to adjudication under the Scheme.) This must be for the purpose of enabling the other party to respond to it.

11.04 The Scheme adjudicator should reach his decision within 28 days after the date of the referral notice. The referring party can allow him an extra 14 days. The parties may agree to a longer period than the 28 days, but such an agreement is only valid if it is made after the giving of the referral notice. If the adjudicator fails to reach his decision in time, the parties are entitled to start again with a new adjudicator.

11.05 The Scheme adjudicator must decide the matters in dispute. He has no jurisdiction to decide any other matters. However, he may take into account any other matters (1) which the parties to the dispute agree should be within the scope of the adjudication or (2) which are matters under the contract which he considers are necessarily connected with the dispute. (Scheme Pt I para 20. Contrast the practical effect given to a supervening cross-claim in *KNS Industrial Services (Birmingham) Ltd v Sindall Ltd* [2000] CILL 1652, HHJ Humphrey LLoyd QC. But the authority of the latter case is doubtful in the light of Ferson Contractors Ltd v Levolux AT Ltd [2003] EWCA Civ 11.)

11.06 In *Northern Developments (Cumbria) Ltd v J & J Nichol* [2000] BLR 158, HHJ Bowsher QC, the main contractor argued that its set-off against the sub-contractor for damages for repudiation was necessarily connected with the sub-contractor's claim for payment for work done. The Judge ruled that, since the repudiation damages had not been notified in the withholding-notice relating to the payment claimed by the sub-contractor, it followed from HGCRA 1996, s 111(1) that the adjudicator had no jurisdiction to take them into account. This seems a harsh decision, since the alleged repudiation occurred after, and as a response to, the withholding-notice. It was therefore impossible to mention it in the notice. Within these limits, he may open up, revise and review any decision taken or any certificate given by any person referred to in the contract unless the contract states that the decision or certificate is final and conclusive.

11.07 A Scheme adjudicator has a duty to provide reasons for his decision, if requested by one of the parties to the dispute. Any such request should be made in advance.

12 Effect of adjudicator's decision

12.01 The Scheme follows and slightly extends the provisions of HGCRA 1996, s 108(3) in stating that the decision shall be binding on the parties, and they shall comply with it until the dispute is finally determined by legal proceedings, by arbitration (if the contract provides for arbitration or the parties otherwise agree to arbitration) or by agreement between the parties.

13 Costs and fees

13.01 The general rule is that the adjudicator is entitled to the payment of such reasonable amount as he may determine by way of fees and expenses reasonably incurred by him. The parties are jointly and severally liable to pay the fees and expenses. Further provisions of the Scheme deal with various situations where an adjudicator resigns or otherwise ceases to act. The adjudicator may determine in what proportions the parties, as between each other, should bear his fees and expenses.

13.02 There is no express or implied provision in the Scheme enabling the adjudicator to order one party to pay the costs incurred by the other party. Such a term is not necessary for the purpose of making the adjudication procedure efficacious, and therefore cannot be implied. The result is that, in a Scheme adjudication, costs may not be awarded as between the parties, unless the parties enlarge the adjudicator's jurisdiction by agreeing that he may award such costs. Such an agreement was held to have been made by implication in a case where both parties asked the adjudicator to award party costs. (*Northern Developments (Cumbria) Ltd v J & J Nichol* [2000] BLR 158, HHJ Bowsher QC.)

14 Enforcement of adjudicator's decisions

14.01 The process of adjudication will be practically effective where the losing party is willing to comply temporarily with the decision or, even more so, where the parties are willing to treat the adjudicator's decision as a final resolution of the dispute. Where the losing party is not willing to comply, the effectiveness of the adjudicator's decision depends on whether it can be enforced. The key to enforcement lies in the contractually binding nature of the decision. It is inherent in contractual provisions for adjudication that the parties are under obligation to do all things necessary for the proper conduct of the adjudication. Similarly, once the adjudicator's decision has been given, each party, having contractually agreed to adjudication, is under a contractual obligation to comply with the decision unless and until it is altered by litigation, arbitration or agreement. The enforcement of the decision therefore depends primarily upon the availability of remedies for the enforcement of contractual obligations.

15 Summary judgment

15.01 In the ordinary case of an adjudicator's decision requiring the payment of a sum of money by one party to the other, the most appropriate means of enforcement is an application for summary judgment under Part 24 of the Civil Procedure Rules. The fact that the adjudicator's decision is only of temporary effect is not an obstacle. The grant of summary judgment does not pre-empt any later decision that an arbitrator or court dealing with the substance of the dispute may make. (*Macob Civil Engineering Ltd v Morrison Construction Ltd* (1999) 64 ConLR 1.)

15.02 There are limited circumstances in which a losing party, faced with the adjudicator's decision that he must pay the claimant, will be able successfully to contest an application for summary judgment. The losing party will not be able to rely in defence upon some mere error by the adjudicator: the losing party needs to contend that the decision is not contractually binding on him because the adjudicator did not have jurisdiction to decide as he did.

15.03 In general, once an adjudicator has decided that a sum should be paid, the court will require that actual payment be effected. It will not revisit the merits of the adjudicator's decision, nor will it usually permit legal procedures to be used so as to freeze or delay the making of the payment. (*A & D Maintenance and Construction Ltd v Pagehurst Construction Services Ltd* [1999] CILL 1518.)

16 Challenging the adjudicator's decision or jurisdiction

16.01 The ordinary method of challenging the decision is the indirect method of taking the subject matter of the dispute to arbitration or litigation. A challenge to the merits of the decision has no effect on the temporary enforcement of the adjudicator's decision pending final determination of the dispute. Temporary enforcement is, however, vulnerable to challenges of a jurisdictional nature.

16.02 In principle it is open to the losing party to take both courses, i.e. to take the merits of the dispute to arbitration or litigation, and at the same time to resist enforcement of the adjudicator's decision on jurisdictional grounds. A reference of the underlying dispute to arbitration does not of itself involve adopting any position as to the validity of the adjudicator's decision.

17 Effect of defences and cross-claims not considered by adjudicator

17.01 A question that frequently arises is whether a party who is required to make a payment ordered by the adjudicator may avoid doing so by relying on defences or cross-claims. Where the adjudicator has already, in the course of the adjudication, considered the substance of the particular defence or cross-claim, it follows that his decision must be honoured and the losing party cannot seek to set up the same defence or cross-claim as a reason for not paying the sum ordered by the adjudicator. The parties must accept on a temporarily binding basis both the decision itself and any assumptions upon which the decision must have been based.

18 Where adjudicator's decision final

18.01 The parties may agree to accept the adjudicator's decision as final. They may do this directly by an express agreement, or indirectly through the operation of contractual terms. Under the ICE Conditions the adjudication decision becomes final unless the dispute is referred to arbitration within 3 months of the giving of the decision. Once the decision is accepted as final, the result is that the parties have arrived at a contractually binding resolution of their dispute. This may be enforced by the same methods as any other contract or contractually binding settlement. An application may be made to the court for summary judgment. The decision still cannot be enforced as an arbitration award, since there was never any submission to arbitration and there is no arbitral award within the meaning of the Arbitration Act 1996. It is likely that, in order to lend support to the process of adjudication, the court may be willing to enforce a final decision of an adjudicator (other than for the payment of money by one party to the other) by means of a final mandatory injunction.

19 Practical importance of jurisdictional issues

19.01 A losing party may be faced with an adverse decision in which the adjudicator has clearly made a mistake. If the adjudicator decided the dispute that was referred to him, but his decision was merely mistaken, then it stands as a valid and binding decision, even if the mistake was of fundamental importance. (*Bouygues UK Ltd v Dahl-Jensen UK Ltd* [2000] BLR 522, CA. The adjudicator's decision was wrong because his calculations had the effect of mistakenly releasing retention. That was an error within his jurisdiction. Cf *Shimizu Europe Ltd v Automajor Ltd* [2002] BLR 113, TCC, HHJ Seymour QC.) To avoid enforcement the losing party will normally need to convince the court that the decision has no legal effect because the mistake is such that he went outside his jurisdiction.

19.02 The HGCRA 1996 gives no explicit guidance concerning the scope of legitimate jurisdictional challenge. It seems clear that for policy reasons the court will lean towards upholding the adjudicator's decision where it properly can. For this reason it has been said that, for example in deciding whether the adjudicator has decided the wrong question rather than given a wrong answer to the right question, the court will bear in mind that the speedy nature of the adjudication process means that mistakes will inevitably occur, and will guard against characterising a mistaken answer to an issue that lies within the scope of the reference as an excess of jurisdiction. Furthermore, the court will give a fair, natural and sensible interpretation to the decision in the light of the disputes that are the subject of the reference. What constitutes a jurisdictional error is currently a matter of controversy and the law is in a state of development. An authoritative solution to the controversy will depend upon careful definition of the nature and extent of the jurisdiction conferred upon the adjudicator by the contract (including the applicable adjudication rules), read against the background of the general law and of the provisions of HGCRA 1996, s 108.

20 Initial jurisdiction: the 10 conditions

20.01 To constitute a valid adjudication under HGCRA 1996, Part II, 10 initial conditions must be fulfilled. There must be (1) an existing dispute (2) between parties to the contract, (3) arising under the contract. The contract must be (4) a construction contract (5) made in writing (6) on or after 1 May 1998, (7) relating to construction operations within the territorial application of the statutory provisions and (8) not excluded by HGCRA 1996, s 106. The dispute must be (9) validly referred under the contractual provisions to (10) a properly appointed adjudicator.

21 Straying from the confines of the dispute

21.01 The dispute which the adjudicator must decide is defined by the notice of adjudication. The adjudicator's jurisdiction is limited to the issues validly put before him by the parties. If the adjudicator confines himself to a determination of the issues that were put before him by the parties, then the parties are bound by his determination, notwithstanding that he may have fallen into error. Thus if the adjudicator has answered the right question in the wrong way, his decision will be binding. But if he has answered the wrong question, his decision will be a nullity. In one case the adjudicator would not have had jurisdiction to consider an extension of time claim if it had stood alone, because at the time of the notice of adjudication a dispute on it had not crystallised (the contract administrator had received additional information on the previous day and needed time to consider it). However, there was a clear dispute over whether the employer was entitled to terminate the contract for failure to proceed regularly and diligently, and for that purpose the adjudicator had to consider to what extension the contractor was entitled. The adjudicator therefore had jurisdiction. By contrast, where the contractor, after terminating the sub-contract, claimed recovery of cross-claims, but the parties agreed that the sub-contractor's final account was excluded from the ambit of the adjudication, the adjudicator exceeded his jurisdiction in ordering payment to the contractor, since there was no firm starting point from which to calculate what was due.

22 Errors of law

22.01 The adjudicator may make an error of law which results in his assuming jurisdiction when one of the initial conditions has not been met. Such an error cannot give him a jurisdiction that he does not in truth possess. More controversial jurisdictional issues arise where the error of law does not go to one of the initial conditions, but is an error made in the course of deciding a matter that is within the adjudicator's jurisdiction.

23 Procedural irregularities

23.01 A tribunal with limited jurisdiction goes outside its jurisdiction if it fails to act fairly towards the person who will be adversely affected by the decision by not observing either one or other of the two fundamental rights accorded to him by the rules of natural justice or fairness, i.e., (1) to have afforded to him a reasonable opportunity of learning what is alleged against him and of putting forward his own case in answer to it, and (2) the absence of personal bias against him on the part of the person making the decision. Dyson J has stated that an adjudicator's decision is not invalidated by procedural breach or some failure to observe natural justice (*Macob Civil Engineering Ltd v Morrison Construction Ltd* (1999) 64 ConLR 1; *Project Consultancy Group v Trustees of the Gray Trust* (1999) 65 ConLR 146. See also *Sherwood & Casson Ltd v Mackenzie* [2000] CILL 1577, HHJ Thornton QC.), but the courts have subsequently refused to enforce adjudication decisions by summary judgment in several cases where there were or appeared to have been breaches of the rules of natural justice. (E.g. *Discain Project Services Ltd v Opecprime Development Ltd* [2000] BLR 402, HHJ Bowsher QC; *Woods Hardwick Ltd v Chiltern Air Conditioning* [2000] CILL 1698, HHJ Thornton QC; *Glencot Development & Design Co Ltd v Ben Barrett & Son (Contractors) Ltd* [2001] BLR 207, HHJ Humphrey LLoyd QC.) The view that seems to prevail at present is that an adjudicator must conduct the adjudication in accordance with the rules of natural justice or as fairly as the limitations imposed by Parliament permit; and, if there is a relevant and substantial breach, the court will not enforce the adjudicator's decision. In considering whether there is a relevant breach of natural justice it has to be remembered that the adjudicator is charged with ascertaining the facts and the law, and the adjudication process envisaged by the Act is a process far removed from the traditional adversarial format adopted in the courts. The statutory time constraints must also be taken into account.

23.02 The first rule of natural justice is broken if the adjudicator rests his decision on matters which the aggrieved party was given no reasonable opportunity to deal with. As in *Discain Project Services Ltd v Opecprime Development Ltd* ([2000] BLR 402, HHJ Bowsher QC; *Discain Project Services Ltd v Opecprime Development Ltd (No 2)* [2001] BLR 285, HHJ Bowsher QC.) where there were private conversations between the adjudicator and the representative of one party; *Woods Hardwick Ltd v Chiltern Air Conditioning* ([2000] CILL 1698, HHJ Thornton QC.) where the Scheme adjudicator obtained additional information from applicant and witnesses but did not inform respondent or give opportunity to comment; *Balfour Beatty Construction Ltd v London Borough of Lambeth* ([2002] BLR 288, HHJ Humphrey LLoyd QC.) where the adjudicator made good the defects in the claimant's case without giving the respondent the opportunity to comment on either his methodology or its results.

23.03 The second rule of natural justice is broken if the adjudicator is guilty of bias, or if the circumstances are such as would lead a fair-minded and informed observer to conclude that there was a real possibility that the adjudicator was biased. (*Magill v Porter* [2001] UKHL 67 at para 103.) Examples in adjudication cases include: *Discain Project Services Ltd v Opecprime Development Ltd*; *Woods Hardwick Ltd v Chiltern Air Conditioning*, *Glencot Development & Design Co Ltd v Ben Barrett & Son (Contractors) Ltd* ([2001] BLR 207, HHJ Humphrey LLoyd QC.) where the adjudicator had private discussions with each party in role of mediator and *R G Carter Ltd v Edmund Nuttall Ltd* ((unreported, 18 April 2002), TCC, HHJ Bowsher QC) where bias was not established in the case of an adjudicator who had made an earlier adjudication decision between same parties in excess of his jurisdiction.

24 Unreasonableness or bad faith

24.01 An adjudication decision cannot be challenged on jurisdictional grounds merely because the decision is unreasonable in the ordinary sense. However, it is possible that a decision might be open to challenge on the ground of what is known as unreasonableness in the *Wednesbury* sense. A decision unreasonable in the *Wednesbury* sense is one that is so unreasonable that no reasonable tribunal could have made it. (*Associated Provincial Picture Houses Ltd v Wednesbury Corporation* [1947] 2 All ER 680, CA.) On the same reasoning a decision would be invalid if it were motivated by bad faith or irrelevant considerations.

16

Mediation

CHRISTOPHER MIERS

'Mediation is not in law compulsory... but alternative dispute resolution is at the heart of today's civil justice system...' (Mr Justice Lightman in his judgment in *Hurst v Leeming [2002] EWHC 1051 (Ch).*)

1 Background

1.01 Whilst mediation is said to have been founded in China and the Far East, modern mediation has its roots in the USA. Mediation in the USA developed from the early 20th century, and by the 1970s its potential for reducing court case loads was well recognised. In the UK, the use of mediation in the resolution of family disputes was developed from the late 1970s and early 1980s. By the early 1990s, court-annexed family mediations were well established.*

1.02 Prior to the late 1990s, proposing mediation was frequently mistaken for a sign of weakness in a party's case, and the opportunity to mediate was therefore overlooked. Following the Civil Justice Reforms initiated by Lord Woolf in England and Wales, which came into force in 1998, parties in dispute are now far more willing to mediate, including within the construction industry. In most construction disputes a genuine attempt to settle a dispute by mediation is now accepted as a sensible and necessary step, and is invariably encouraged by the Courts.

1.03 The increase in popularity of mediation has been matched by an increase in the number of trained mediators, and in the number of independent bodies who train and accredit mediators.

2 The principles

2.01 Mediation in the UK construction industry is a process of structured negotiation aided by a neutral third party mediator. A mediator does not decide the dispute. Unlike in litigation, arbitration or adjudication, the resolution is a matter for the parties' own agreement.

2.02 The process is voluntary and consensual, although the mediation process may be incorporated into the dispute resolution procedures in a contract. A mediation can be undertaken at any time, including during the course of another dispute resolution process, such as litigation or arbitration, and where the dispute involves more than two parties. The parties enter into the mediation accepting that, however strong they believe their position to be in respect of the matters in dispute, they will benefit from being able to reach an agreed settlement on acceptable terms, without further prolongation of the dispute.

* Mediation: Principles, process, practice, by L. Boulle and M. Nesic.

2.03 There are two main forms of mediation: facilitative and evaluative. In facilitative mediation, the mediator assists the parties to reach agreement through a structured process without providing his own opinion on the merits of any party's case. In evaluative mediation, by contrast, the mediator may express a view on the merits of an element of the dispute. In each case the objective is to reach a binding agreement which settles either all or some of the matters in dispute. Most mediations in the UK are facilitative, and frequently the terms of the Mediation Agreement prevent the mediator from providing any opinion on the merits of the issues in dispute unless otherwise agreed beforehand by the parties.

3 Typical mediation process in construction disputes

Reaching agreement to mediate

3.01 The first step in the mediation process is reaching agreement between the disputing parties to attempt to settle the dispute by mediation. This in itself can take time and require persuasive negotiation, in particular where there are several parties to the dispute. The parties frequently have different views on the merits of mediation, and also on the optimum stage of the dispute for conducting a mediation.

3.02 Mediation is frequently included in standard forms of contract, such as in the SFA/99 Standard Form of Agreement (Clause 9.1 of SFA/99 refers to the RIBA Mediation Service, and in the JCT Major Project Form 2003, as an optional first stage in attempting to resolve a dispute. JCT also publish Practice Note 28 referring to mediation on a building contractor or sub-contractor dispute.

3.03 If the dispute is in litigation, the Court is likely to apply cost penalties to a party which does not participate or attempt to participate in some form of alternative dispute resolution (For example, *Dunnett v Railtrack plc (CA)* and *Leicester Circuits Ltd v Coates Brothers plc.*) (ADR). This does not necessarily have to be mediation (*Corenso (UK) Ltd v The Burnden Group plc.*). Where a case is very unlikely to be settled by ADR, the Court may consider it reasonable for a party to decline mediation or other form of alternative dispute resolution (*Hurst v Leeming*, as above.). The potential of mediation to bring about settlement is well described by Mr Justice Lightman:

'... the mediation process itself can and does often bring about a more sensible and more conciliatory attitude on the part of the parties than might otherwise be expected to prevail before the mediation, and may produce a recognition of the strengths and weaknesses by each party of this own case and that of his opponent, and a willingness to accept the give and take essential to a successful mediation. What appears to be incapable of mediation before the mediation process begins often proves capable of satisfactory resolution later'. (Mr Justice Lightman in his judgment in *Hurst v Leeming* as above.)

Selecting a mediator

3.04 Occasionally where there is a mediation clause within a contract, a mediator may be named in advance. It is more common however to select a mediator at the time of the dispute and this gives the parties greater flexibility to determine any appropriate expertise which may be desirable in the mediator, depending on the nature of the dispute.

3.05 There are several professional and independent bodies with lists of experienced mediators, which can provide names of mediators on enquiry. These include: RIBA (The RIBA also provides a conciliation service which in most respects is similar to mediation.), CEDR (One of the earliest independent bodies to promote the use of mediation in the UK was the Centre for Dispute Resolution (CEDR), now named the Centre for Effective Dispute Resolution.), CIArb, RICS, CIOB and others. One of these bodies may provide a selection of alternative names of mediators for the parties subsequently to agree if possible, or it may nominate a single mediator, depending on the parties' request. In some mediations a second, assistant- or co-mediator, may also be requested.

3.06 Once selected, the mediator will normally require the parties to sign up to a Mediation Agreement. CEDR provides a Model Mediation Agreement which is available from its web site (www.cedr.co.uk). There is also a brief example Mediation Agreement attached to JCT Practice Note 28. In every case, the parties should enquire of the mediator whether there is a particular Code of Conduct or Mediation Procedure under which the mediator will be operating.

3.07 It is normal practice for the Mediation Agreement to require the parties to pay the mediator's fees in equal proportions.

Preparation for the mediation

3.08 Once appointed, the mediator will set out the procedure to be adopted, generally in discussion with the parties. This will normally include for each party to prepare and submit a Case Summary and a core of relevant documents, each to be provided to the mediator and to the other party before the mediation. The mediator will also set a date for the mediation itself, and the duration of the mediation taking into account the size and complexity of the dispute, by discussion with the parties. Typically a mediation in respect of a small and/or straightforward dispute might be set down for 1/2–1 day, whereas a more complex and more substantial dispute may be set down for longer (As much as 5 days in the more extreme cases.).

3.09 In addition to the documents provided to the mediator and to the other parties, a party may wish to prepare and take to the mediation additional documents which it intends to show only to the mediator in confidence.

3.10 Dependent on the size and nature of the dispute, the parties will need to consider whether there is a need for legal representation, and expert evidence. It is not unusual to be represented.

The mediation

3.11 Mediations tend to follow typical structures, although each mediation can be managed by the mediator in any manner to suit the particular nature of the dispute and the positions of the parties.

3.12 The mediation will normally take place in a neutral venue, although sometimes for reasons of costs one party will agree that the mediation can take place at the premises of the other party. For a two-party dispute, three rooms will normally be required: the main room for a round-table meeting of the parties and the mediator together; and a separate break-out room for each party.

3.13 For each party, the mediation will normally be attended by: a senior member of staff from the party itself; a legal representative if appropriate such as a solicitor or barrister or both; and where appropriate one or more expert witnesses. In some cases on substantial claims, a member of the insurers and of the underwriters may also attend. It is important that each party attending has the authority to come to an agreement.

3.14 The mediator will normally structure the mediation to meet with the parties together and separately. In a typical mediation, the mediation will commence with all parties gathered together, with each party invited to make a brief opening statement highlighting what they consider to be the principal issues. The benefit of this opening statement is not only to assist the other parties in understanding their position, but also to listen to the position of the other parties, and thereby gain a greater understanding of the obstacles to settlement. Depending upon the nature of the issues in dispute, and the potential for genuine dialogue in the wider group, the mediator may thereafter elect to speak to the parties separately, each in their own break-out room. In a multiparty case, typically the mediator at this stage may choose to speak with all of the defendants together, without the claimant being present.

3.15 Through this next stage of the process, the mediator will work with the parties to establish the critical issues, to identify the obstacles to settlement, to assist each party in taking a realistic look at its own position, and to consider creatively the possible solutions to the dispute. The mediator will facilitate progressive negotiations between the parties.

3.16 During the course of separate meetings with the mediator, a party will frequently wish to disclose matters to the mediator which are confidential and not for repeating to the other parties. This is a normal part of the process, and the mediator will only divulge to another party details which he has been expressly authorised to divulge. Where the mediator considers it to be appropriate, he may call the parties back together into a group meeting, from time to time.

3.17 Mediators will not normally give advice to any party, nor will they comment on the likely outcome of the dispute if it were allowed to run to litigation or arbitration, unless the parties have agreed in advance that he should do so. An experienced mediator should, however, push each party to recognise weaknesses in their case, and to consider the strong points in the case of the other parties.

3.18 In considering and exploring offers for settlement, the mediator will assist a party in considering the alternatives to not achieving settlement, in terms of the escalating costs of continuing the dispute, the investment of time required by the party itself, the relatively long delay in otherwise achieving resolution of the dispute, and the lack of control of an outcome which is achieved other than by negotiation. In considering the acceptability of a sum being offered to settle the dispute, the mediator will also encourage a party to take account of the risk of proceeding, losing and paying the other parties' costs. All these factors need to be taken into account, when weighing up the acceptability of the best offer to settle which can be achieved through the mediation.

Agreement

3.19 If agreement is reached, parties can decide whether to set out the agreement in a written signed document with the intention of it becoming a binding contractual agreement. This is a preferred option, in order to secure the agreement achieved before the parties leave the mediation. In certain cases parties wish to reflect on the agreement before finally signing up to a binding settlement, and it is not uncommon for parties to leave the mediation and thereafter to conclude a settlement agreement in the next few days. However, reaching a binding agreement at the end of the mediation is preferable, in order to avoid subsequent change in a party's position.

4   Mediation in practice

Advantages and disadvantages

4.01 In every dispute the opportunities for settling the dispute by ADR should be considered. The occasions when ADR may not be suitable will be the minority of instances.

The principal advantages of mediation are:

1. the opportunity for immediate settlement of the dispute;
2. a quick and relatively cheap way of settling the dispute;
3. the terms of any agreement remain within your control;
4. hidden agenda items can be taken into account;
5. gaining an early understanding of your opponent's case;
6. the mediation is confidential, unless the parties agree otherwise;
7. the mediation negotiations will focus only on the big issue items.

Typical disadvantages of mediation are:

1. achieving settlement generally requires compromise;
2. the parties must achieve a signed settlement agreement before the agreement will be enforceable;
3. a party may feel forced into a settlement which is below its reasonable expectation of the outcome of the case;
4. if the agreement is unsuccessful, some costs will have been wasted.

The importance of preparation

4.02 Good preparation is vital to enhance the likelihood of an outcome which you consider acceptable. Be on top of all of the facts, and consider beforehand the various arguments that are likely to be raised. Undertake a realistic review of the weaknesses of your arguments and the areas of risk.

4.03 Settlement through mediation invariable involves a degree of compromise. A party going into a mediation needs to consider in detail beforehand, and to agree with other colleagues whose decision will be needed, on their worst acceptable settlement beyond which settlement will not be possible. Matters of costs already incurred and interest should be calculated in advance, to be considered in addition to the main sum in dispute, since a mediation settlement will normally be a single figure to sweep up all parts of a claim.

Selecting the right moment for mediation

4.04 The timing of the mediation relative to the progress of any ancillary formal dispute resolution process such as litigation or arbitration, is likely to be relevant to the chances of the success of the mediation. Parties may naturally wish to mediate at the earliest possible date to reduce costs. However, generally a certain amount of initial investigation needs to be carried out by each party, to ascertain the facts surrounding the issues in dispute, and possibly to obtain an initial expert opinion, before each party will be in a position to form a view as to the merits of their case. In the absence of a realistic view in particular in respect of the weaknesses of a party's own position, settlement of the dispute will be unlikely. An over optimistic claimant is unlikely to be in a position to accept a settlement at a realistic level, and the claimant will therefore need to have time to follow through its own enquiry processes in the hands of its advisors and, where appropriate, experts, before being able to arrive at a realistic settlement proposition.

4.05 In construction disputes, for the purpose of initiating an action in Court, each party is obliged by the Civil Procedure Rules to adhere to the Pre-Action Protocol for the Construction and Engineering Disputes (This can be found on the Court Services web site: www.lcd.gov.uk). Adhering to the Pre-Action Protocol requires each party to conduct a substantial amount of work up-front, in order to set out the details of the claim, and to consider in reasonable detail a response to the claim, following which the parties are required to attend a Pre-Action Meeting. The aim of the meeting is, amongst other matters, for the parties to consider whether, and if so how, the dispute might be resolved without recourse to litigation. In respect of each agreed issue or the dispute as a whole, the parties are obliged to consider whether some form of alternative dispute resolution procedure (Pre-Action Protocol for the Construction and Engineering Disputes, paragraph 5.4.) would be more suitable than litigation. The parties are therefore required to consider at the earliest reasonable stage the possibility of settling the dispute by means other than litigation.

17

Building dispute resolution in Scotland

ROBERT HOWIE

1 Arbitration in Scotland

1.01 It is common to find in building contracts in Scotland provisions for the arbitration of disputes which arise thereunder or in connection therewith. Indeed, an arbitration clause appears in the Scottish supplement to the JCT Standard Form Contract which is published by the Scottish Building Contract Committee. It is important to bear in mind that arbitration in Scotland proceeds upon a quite different basis from arbitration in England, and in consequence, there is usually little reliance placed on English authority when questions of Scottish arbitration law come before the courts. Whereas arbitration law in England is largely based on statute, as matters presently stand, the basis of domestic arbitration is almost exclusively the common law, statutory intervention being limited to the Arbitration (Scotland) Act 1894, the Articles of Regulation, 1695 and the third Section of the Administration of Justice (Scotland) Act 1972. The English Arbitration Act 1996, like its statutory predecessors in 1950 and 1979, does not apply to domestic arbitration in Scotland.

1.02 However, in one important area, parliament has intervened. Unlike the rest of the United Kingdom, Scotland has adopted the UNCITRAL model law for arbitration: it did so by the Law Reform (Miscellaneous Provisions) (Scotland) Act 1990, section 66. One might expect the practical importance of that adoption to be very limited in the context of Scottish construction contracts, for the UNCITRAL law applies only to 'international' commercial arbitrations, and in Scotland those may be expected to be uncommon. However, the definition accorded the word 'international' is a special one, the result of which is likely to render a dispute between a Scottish registered company and one registered in any other part of the United Kingdom, 'international', and thus subject to the provisions of the UNCITRAL model laws. But although this result is likely, it is not inevitable, and unfortunately satellite litigation can break out in the course of the arbitration as to whether or not the dispute is truly subject to the UNCITRAL model law. In the 'Fennica' 6 July 2000, unreported, the Court of Session ordered an arbiter to hear a proof on contested averments of fact regarding the applicability of the model law to the arbitration in question after the arbiter had purported to decide that matter without hearing evidence. The proof lasted a week, and the satellite dispute delayed the main arbitration by 18 months! The architect, in considering whether or not to advise a client that he should seek to include in his contract an arbitration clause, ought therefore to give consideration to the question whether or not any dispute which may arise in relation to that contract will be 'international' within the meaning of the Law Reform (Miscellaneous Provisions) (Scotland) Act 1990, by which the UNCITRAL law is introduced. If any such dispute will be 'international', it is thought that it will be subject to the restrictions of the UNCITRAL model law, most notably those which restrict the ability of either party to seek a Stated Case for the Opinion of Court of Session on a point of law arising in the arbitration. Those restrictions, and therefore arbitration in a potential UNCITRAL case, may not always be thought to be of advantage: the case may throw up a dispute in which the client's rights may depend on legal issues, and the arbiter may not be legally qualified. At the outset, when it will not be known whether or not disputes will arise, still less what the issues in them may be, it may well be quite impossible to tell whether arbitration is likely to be advantageous to the architect's client. In such circumstances, the prudent course may be to exclude the arbitration clause from the parties' contract, leaving it to them to agree to arbitration themselves (if so desired) on individual disputes as those arise, and to tailor the selection of arbiter and his powers on a case-by-case basis as may be thought requisite to secure the resolution of the particular question or questions which have given rise to the dispute in hand.

1.03 It is not necessary for a building contract to contain an arbitration clause in order to allow the parties to adopt that mode of dispute resolution in relation to a given dispute if they both wish to do that. The existence or otherwise of an arbitration clause in a contract assumes importance when, at the time when a dispute arises the parties are not in agreement as to whether or not that dispute should be remitted to arbitration. If there is no arbitration clause incorporated into the contract, then because the basis of all jurisdiction in arbitration is consensual, the party opposed to arbitration can refuse to assent to it, and may effectively force his contradictor to litigate in order to secure a resolution of the dispute. But if, on the other hand, such a clause has been incorporated, the party insisting on arbitration can force his opponent to arbitrate as he had contracted to do, and, assuming that the obligation to arbitrate has not been waived, will be entitled to the sist (anglicé stay) of any Court proceedings about the dispute raised against him by the other party until the arbitration is completed or for some reason breaks down. This, of course, assumes that there exists a dispute between the parties, and that it falls within the ambit of the arbitration clause as properly construed. For it is a precondition of any arbitration that there is a dispute between the parties which may be arbitrated. It has been the practice of the court to decline to sist actions for arbitration (particularly where the demand for a sist is made in answer to a motion for summary decree in a court action designed to enforce one party's claims against the other) where the court is not persuaded that there exists a *bona fide* dispute between the parties, as opposed to a mere refusal by A to meet a claim made upon him by B. It is also necessary if is a sist is to be secured, that the dispute in question should fall within the purview of the arbitration clause properly construed. Whether, in any given case, that requirement is met is a strictly legal question on which advice should be taken, but in the context of Clause 41 of the SBCC Agreement, it should rarely cause much difficulty, since that clause remits to arbitration any dispute arising under or in connection with the contract. Other clauses, however, particularly in bespoke contracts, may give rise to much greater difficulty.

1.04 Even where an arbitration clause appears in the contract, however, it is impossible to insist that a given dispute be arbitrated where either of the parties seeking so to insist has waived the right to do so or has become personally barred from so insisting, or the right so to insist has itself prescribed. The architect, if he should find himself involved with the initial stages of a dispute as agent for the employer, should therefore be alert to the danger of so acting – or failing to act – as to set up a plea of waiver or personal bar against his employer, a plea which may serve to prevent that employer from insisting that the dispute be arbitrated rather than publicly canvassed in court. Since both waiver and personal bar involve questions of fact, it is not possible to indicate in advance what conduct by the Architect may be found to raise such a plea. It is a matter in which the architect concerned about the problem should take advice in light of the circumstances of the case which faces him. Prescription of the right to arbitrate through the elapse of five years since the right came into existence without that right being exercised or being the subject of a relevant claim or acknowledgement for the purposes of the Prescription and Limitation (Scotland) Act 1973 is unlikely to be a matter which will arise as an issue of immediate practical importance for the architect, but it has been known to happen, and should not be overlooked. Moreover, extreme delays in proceeding with either arbitration or court action may allow the court to prevent the case from proceeding at all, if to do otherwise would entail a breach of the Defender's human rights (see *Newman Shop-fitters Ltd v MJ Gleeson plc*, 2003 SLT (Sh.Ct.) 83). Again, this is a matter on which the architect should take advice.

1.05 An issue which the architect is more likely to encounter, particularly in the context of the SBCC Standard Form Contracts, is the obverse of the prescription question: the prematurity of arbitration. It will be recalled that the Standard Form Building Contract contains provisions which preclude recourse to arbitration until the date of practical completion or alleged practical completion of the works. In the event that an arbitration has begun prior to that date, the party instigating it runs the risk of seeing his claim dismissed with an award of expenses being made against him unless his case has been brought in connection with one of the matters (the proper issue of certificates, etc.) excluded by the JCT Clause from the ambit of the general embargo on arbitration prior to practical completion. It should be borne in mind, however, that even if the right to arbitrate may be not lost through the passage of time, the underlying contractual rights about which the parties are in dispute may be being lost or rendered unprovable by that mechanism. It will be recalled that in varying regards conclusive effect is accorded the Final Certificate if proceedings in relation to those matters have not been begun before a date 28 days after the issue of the certificate in question. The architect should thus bear in mind that, even if the right to arbitration is not in danger of being prescribed, it may be that recourse to arbitration or court proceedings is required promptly if underlying rights are not to be destroyed by prescription or by conclusive evidence provisions in the contract.

1.06 Given that, as noticed above, the jurisdiction of an arbiter in Scotland derives from the contract of the parties, both the identity of the arbitral tribunal and the powers that are to be exercised by it are a matter for the consent of the parties. To combat the obvious problem that, once they are at odds over some dispute, the parties may fail to agree upon the identity of their arbiter, the SBCC Arbitration Clause follows the common practice of providing that, failing agreement between the parties on the matter within a specified time, either party may apply to a nominating body to appoint an arbiter. In practice, not many arbiters in construction disputes in Scotland are appointed in that way; at length, agreement, howsoever reluctant, usually prevails. The clause provides for different possible appointing bodies. When the terms of the clause are being considered at the outset, before the building contract is entered into, it may be appropriate to consider which appointing body would be most likely to appoint an arbiter skilled in the resolution of the kind of dispute which is apt to arise in connection with that contract. In that regard, it should not be overlooked that although a dispute may at first sight appear to relate to one discipline, a more detailed consideration of it

may disclose that the decisive issues will enter another discipline, and that in consequence a choice between competing areas of expertise of potential arbiters has to be made in deciding what category of person would make the best potential arbiter. The clause also gives rise to a practical problem to which the architect may wish to direct his client's attention at the contracting stage. Many arbiters appoint clerks to assist them, and usually both arbiter and clerk charge fees for their services. A number of arbiters proceed upon the footing of terms and conditions of appointment as arbiters, governing matters such as joint and several liability for fees and expenses and the size of those fees. Theoretically, fee scales in such terms and conditions form the terms of a separate ancillary contract between the arbiter and parties to which all consent. But in reality, where the arbiter is imposed on parties by the appointing authority and that arbiter presents terms which are unacceptable to a party (e.g. as regards the daily rate of remuneration), it would seem to be open to some doubt what that party can do to reject those terms if the arbiter is minded to insist on them. That result appears to follow from the unqualified and unconditional nature of the agreement embodied in the SBCC form to accept as arbiter such person as the appointing authority may specify. To avoid it, therefore, it may be desired to amend the standard form clause so as to render the agreement to accept the arbiter subject to prior agreement having been reached on the terms and conditions upon which he will act as such. The danger in such amendment is that, unless carefully drafted, it opens up the opportunity to frustrate – or at least gravely delay – the arbitration process through dispute about ancillary questions such as the arbiter's fees.

1.07 There is in Scots law no objection in principle to the appointment of the architect himself as the arbiter, but although that practice was not uncommon in the nineteenth century, it is now viewed with some disfavour. Where the architect himself is appointed, he should be particularly scrupulous not to prejudge the issues which may be put to him for his decision (although he will not be assumed so to prejudge matters merely on account of his previous involvement in the case), and to apply the rules of natural justice in disposing of the dispute.

1.08 The powers available to the arbiter are also a matter to which some consideration should be given by an architect faced with the need to advise a client about either an arbitration clause in a contract or an executory Deed of Submission whereby an arbitration clause may be sought to be put into effect after a dispute has arisen. The latter instrument may be sought to be used by the opposing party to narrow down or alternatively to widen the powers accorded the arbiter in the original clause, and the architect should be on guard against any such amendment which might prejudice his client's interest. At the stage of framing the initial clause, similar care ought to be taken. At the outset, it will be impossible to tell what powers it might be tactically advantageous to the client for the arbiter to have, so the course of prudence – assuming that an arbitration clause is to be incorporated at all – is probably to seek to keep those powers wider, rather than narrower. The critical consideration is that, in the absence of special power accorded him by the parties in their contract of arbitration, an arbiter in Scotland has no power to assess or award damages, or to entertain a plea of compensation (anglicé, set off). Given the frequency with which demands for damages are made in building contract cases, or claims made are met with assertions of the right to compensate under the Act of 1592 in respect of some cross-claim, the omission from the arbiter's arsenal of these powers is likely to prove improvident. In addition to these well-known problem areas, other potential difficulties may merit attention: the ability of the arbiter to award interest on damages from a date prior to decree, the general unavailability of caution for expenses, and the doubts which attend the ability to hear quasi-contractual claims or claims for rectification of the underlying building contract. The SBCC arbitration clause is drawn in broad terms so far as powers are concerned, but even in that case, certain powers are not accorded the arbiter, most notably the power to rectify the building contract in which the arbitration clause appears. The SBCC provisions on arbitration refer onto the Scottish Arbitration Code. This purports to give power to the architect to rectify the contract, 'to the extent permitted by law', but since the statute introducing rectification into Scots law allowed it to be undertaken only by 'the Court', it may well be that this provision of the Code has in fact no content. It is thought that where an unforeseen rectification problem arises in the course of an arbitration where special power anent rectification has not been given to the arbiter, the proper course is for the parties to take that question to the court for resolution, procedure in the arbitration being sisted pending that resolution. (cf. *Bovis Construction (Scotland) Ltd v Glantre Engineering Ltd*, 27 July 1997, unreported).

1.09 The circumstances in which an arbiter's decision, actual or prospective, may be brought before the court are matters with which the architect is unlikely to be concerned, unless he himself is arbiter. In purely domestic arbitrations, it is open to a party to an arbitration to invite the arbiter, prior to issuing his decision on matter which involves questions of law, to state a case for the Opinion of the Court of Session on such questions. In domestic arbitrations, that right has a statutory origin in section 3 of the Administration of Justice (Scotland) Act 1972. Prior to the coming into force of that section, the stated case procedure was available only in certain statutory arbitrations; in other cases, the arbiter's decision on the points of law was final. If the parties so desire, that finality may be maintained even today by the inclusion in their arbitration contract of a provision excluding for that arbitration the operation of section 3. It should be noted, however, that any such exclusion must appear in the original 'agreement to refer' and not merely in a later implementing Deed of Submission. If a case is to be stated, it must be stated before the arbiter issues his award on the matter in question. It is for this reason usual, where Stated Case procedure is available, to require the arbiter to issue his proposed findings in draft form prior to his issuing his award, so that, if it be thought appropriate, a Stated Case may be presented to the court within the period allowed by the third section. The detailed rules for the procedure to be followed in the Stated Case procedure are set out in part 2 of Chapter 41 of the Rules of the Court of Session, 1994, to which reference should be made. Whether or not to state a case is a matter for the arbiter's discretion, although where he refuses to state a case on a given question, he may be ordained by the Inner House of the Court of Session to do so under the procedure set out in Rule of Court 41.8. Where the application for a Stated Case is made before the facts of the dispute have been determined, the arbiter is empowered to defer consideration of the application until after that determination, and his exercise of that discretion will not be interfered with by the Court of Session under Rule of Court 41.8. As in other cases, however, that exercise is ultimately subject to judicial review in the Court of Session. Once a case has been presented to the Court, it is unlikely that the arbiter will have any further concern with it until the Court delivers its Opinion. For the purposes of the arbitration in which it is given, that Opinion is determinative of the legal issues with which it deals. No appeal from an Opinion of the Court of Session under this procedure lies to the House of Lords and it is misconduct on the part of the arbiter for him not to follow it. In UNCITRAL cases, it is thought that the Court can intervene only in the circumstances set out in the Schedule to the 1990 Act.

1.10 Once the arbiter has pronounced his final Interlocutor, he is *functus officio* and has no further jurisdiction over the parties. (cf. *Mowlem (Scotland) Ltd v Inverclyde Council*, 1 October 2003, unreported). His award is *res iudicata* between them, but only as regards those matters which were in fact submitted to him and adjudicated upon. Matters not so submitted may be the subject of litigation, even if they might originally have been submitted to the arbiter. The arbiter's final interlocutor, however, like his other actings in the arbitration, is ultimately subject to the supervisory jurisdiction of the Court of Session by way of judicial review. Thus, his award may be challenged and, indeed, reduced, where the arbiter has exceeded the jurisdiction confided to him by the parties, failed to exhaust his jurisdiction, acted in breach of natural justice, breached the provisions of the 25th article of the Articles of Regulation 1695 (which are concerned with bribery, corruption and falsehood), been biased, or generally acted in a manner which

is 'unreasonable' in the special sense in which that term is used in administrative law. His award is not subject to review, however, merely because a decision arrived at is wrong in law or based on erroneous findings in fact.

2 Adjudication in Scotland

2.01 The Housing Grants, Construction and Regeneration Act 1996 was passed by Parliament as an Act having application across the whole of the United Kingdom. Unsurprisingly, therefore, adjudication in Scotland shares much in common with adjudication in England and Wales: English cases are frequently cited in Scottish decisions on adjudication – indeed, there is scarcely a single Scottish case in which English authority is not cited – and occasionally, Scottish cases are relied upon in the English Courts *Homer Burgess Limited v Chirex (Annan) Ltd* 2000 SLT 277 is probably the most frequently cited Scottish case, but *SL Timber Systems Ltd v Carillion Construction Ltd* 2002 SLT 997 and *Ballast plc v The Burrell Company (Construction Management) Ltd* 2001 SLT 1039 have also made appearances in the English cases. But although the Court has sometimes sought to avoid differences arising between the Scots and English laws regarding adjudication (*Gillies Ramsay Diamond, Petitioner* 2003 SLT 162), particularly in the fields of enforcement and challenge of adjudicator's awards, there are some significant differences between the law concerning adjudication which obtains in Scotland and the English law with which many readers of this work will be more familiar. Though it may be tempting to him to pass over these as Scottish peculiarities with which he will have no concern, given the ease with which cases can acquire a cross-border dimension, some knowledge of the Scottish position may yet be of use to the English reader.

2.02 From the point of view of the architect, not the least of the significant features about adjudications in Scotland is their use as a mechanism for the recovery of professional fees, and the prosecution by that route of claims by employers for damages for breach of contract on the part of members of the professional team. It is understood that adjudications against members of the professional team are relatively more common in Scotland than they are in England, and where English professionals undertake work on Scottish building projects, this risk must be borne in mind. A contract whereunder an architect agrees to act as a contract administrator under a building contract has been held to be a 'construction contract' for the purposes of the 1996 Act (*Gillies Ramsay Diamond, Petitioner* 2003 SLT 162 upheld on appeal, 24th December 2003, unreported), and it is thought that the same would hold true of a contract to act as a project manager for the construction or refurbishment of a building.

2.03 For an employer wishing to pursue a claim against his architect, there are decided tactical attractions in proceeding by way of adjudication. Not infrequently, losses sustained by the employer have been contributed to through the actions of different members of the professional team as well as the contractor. Determination of the loss which is attributable to each may be far from easy. Where Court proceedings to recoup these losses are raised, the ensuing action can become costly and time-consuming for the pursuing employer, given the likelihood that third party notices will be served by the Defenders in order to bring the contractors and other professionals into the action either in order to prosecute claims for indemnity or relief against them or to contend that those others alone are liable to the Pursuer for his losses (See Chapter 26 of the Act of Sederunt (Rules of the Court of Session, 1994) 1994, SI 1994/1443). Matters may become yet more complicated for the Pursuer, for he may have to adopt such contentions for his own protection, and may face from some of those thus added to his action, defences alleging matters such as limitation of liability, the protection of a final certificate or the benefit of a 'net contribution' clause. All these problems the employer can avoid by adjudicating, since all the other claims among the other parties do not involve a dispute 'under the contract' between the employer and his architect, and so cannot fall within the jurisdiction of the adjudicator (S108, 1996

Act; cf. *Barr Ltd v LAW Mining Ltd* 2003 SLT 488). He can recover all his losses from the architect (assuming the latter has no 'net contribution' clause in his contract) relying on the doctrine of joint and several liability (*Clydesdale Bank plc v Messrs MacLay Collier & Partners* [1998] SLT 1102, though an engineering case, is a typical example of this being done), and leave it to the architect – or his underwriters – to sue the other parties in an effort to recoup the architect's losses. Lastly, in the event of his success in obtaining damages (particularly if he achieves a level of damages which, if not what he sought, he is prepared to rest content with), it is thought that the employer can effectively place upon the architect in any subsequent court action pursuant to Subsection 108(3) of the 1996 Act, the burden of proving that he did not breach his contract with the employer in order to recover the monies paid out as damages in obedience to the adjudicator's award. Although the matter is not uncontroversial, it is thought that the Lord Ordinary's remark at first instance in *City Inn Ltd v Shepherd Construction Ltd* to the effect that an adjudicator's decision does not alter the burden of proof in a Section 108(3) action applies only to the class of case (of which *City Inn* was an example) where the claimant in the adjudication seeks as pursuer in the court action to recover more than he obtained at the hands of the adjudicator. (*City Inn Ltd v Shepherd Construction Ltd* 2002 SLT 781 at paragraph 59. This point was not challenged in the subsequent reclaiming motion (*Anglicè* appeal). See 2003 SLT 885).

2.04 The law governing the actual operation of an adjudication is not dissimilar to that in England. It has been suggested that adjudication is a species of arbitration in Scotland (*Deko Scotland Ltd v Edinburgh Royal Joint Venture* 2003 SLT 727), but in contrast to the position of an arbiter, an adjudicator in Scotland has been held to be able to award damages for breach of contract even though he has not been expressly empowered so to do (*Gillies Ramsay Diamond, Petitioner, supra.*) It is thought that, by parity of reasoning, an adjudicator ought to be able to entertain a plea of compensation under the Compensation Act 1592, even though an arbiter needs special power to do so. The entertaining of such a plea by the adjudicator in *Allied London & Scottish Properties plc v Riverbrae Construction Ltd* 2000 SLT 981 was not criticized in the subsequent litigation. It is thought, however, that he could not entertain a claim for rectification of the contract or its inducement by misrepresentation. Nor, in cases where damages are awarded, can he award interest from prior to the date of his decree in the absence of a special power so to do The Interest on Damages (Scotland) Acts 1958 and 1971 which introduced the ability to award interest from before the date of decree in damages cases have not been extended to arbitrations or adjudications. In the normal case, he can allocate as between the parties responsibility for payment of his own fees and outlays, but without special power to that effect, he cannot award the parties their legal expenses. In those cases where such power is given and exercised, however, those expenses awarded are subject to taxation by the Auditor of Court in exactly the same way as expenses awarded by the Court and it is only a taxed amount of expenses that the Court will be willing to enforce in the context of an action to obtain payment of the sums awarded by the adjudicator (*Deko Scotland Ltd, supra*). In Scotland, as well as in England, adjudicators are required to follow the rules of natural justice (*Ballast plc supra*; *Karl Construction (Scotland) Ltd v Sweeney Civil Engineering (Scotland) Ltd* [2002] SCLR 766), and they must decide the dispute according to the parties' legal entitlements rather than *ex aequo et bono*. The leading case on natural justice in adjudication in Scotland is now *Costain Ltd v Strathclyde Builders Ltd* 2004 SLT 102, a case which has given rise to some disquiet amongst adjudicators. The case contains an extended discussion of the place of natural justice in adjudications. In *Costain Ltd*, which was concerned with the failure of the adjudicator to disclose to the parties, and invite their comments on, legal advice received by him, the Court held that as well as keeping free of bias, the adjudicator had a separate and additional overriding duty not, perhaps, always recognised in the English cases to hear both parties to the case on all material (including legal advice, received by the adjudicator) which might be relevant to the case in hand. In a case where that had not been done, it would be enough to justify the reduction of the adjudicator's decision that

there was a possibility of injustice arising as a result of the breach: it was not necessary that actual prejudice be shown to have resulted. The adjudicator must also adhere to the statutory time limits for the reaching of his decision (which means issuing it to the parties), although it has been held that his failure to do so, while a serious matter, does not entail a vitiation of the award made by him (*St Andrews Bay Development Ltd v HBG Management Ltd* 2003 SLT 740). With respect to the Lord Ordinary who so decided, it is submitted that it is not self-evidently correct that, at least in cases under the statutory scheme, a failure to promulgate the decision within the time limit does not avoid that decision if it be later promulgated. The safe course for any architect sitting as an adjudicator is to obviate that kind of argument at the outset by issuing his decision to the parties within that number of days which they have conferred upon him for the delivery of his decision.

2.05 By contrast with those matters, however, the question of retention and the compensation of competing cross-claims is an area where Scots law is apt to part company from its southern neighbour. An exclusion in a Scottish contract of rights of 'set off' has been held not to prevent the taking of a plea of retention in Scottish proceedings (*A v B* 2003 SLT 242), and the view has been expressed that, notwithstanding the *prima facie* restriction of the adjudicator's jurisdiction to single disputes, an arbiter to whom is referred a question such as 'to payment of what sum is the Claimant entitled?' must entertain such a plea of retention raised in defence of the claim, and all the disputed issues, such as late completion and damages (liquidated or otherwise) which may underpin it. (*Construction Centre Group Ltd v Highland Council* 2002 SLT 1274). The same logic would seem to apply to pleas of compensation under the 1592 Act, though in that case, the pre-existing liquidation of the debts said to extinguish the sum claimed or part thereof is at least likely to make the entertaining of that plea a less daunting task for the adjudicator faced with the statutory time limit on the making of his decision.

2.06 The ability of the unsuccessful party in an adjudication to resist enforcement of the award on the grounds of retention or compensation of cross-claims has also given rise to some difficulty. A plea of retention cannot, it seems, be raised to suspend enforcement of an award – at least if it could have been pleaded before the adjudicator and was not (*A v B, supra*) – and it appears that the position in relation to compensation is similar (*Construction Centre Group Ltd v Highland Council 2003 SLT 623*). The position in relation to the compensation of debts, or rights to withhold which could not competently have been put before the adjudicator, because, for example, they arose in the period after the award was made, is unclear.

2.07 Probably the most important areas of difference between the laws in England and Scotland in relation to adjudication concern the questions of enforcement or challenge of awards. Such are the differences in this area that it can become an important question for the adviser of a client who has received a decision from an adjudicator whether he should seek to challenge or enforce that decision in England or in Scotland. Provided that the Defender is subject to the jurisdiction of the Scottish Courts (as many main contractors and employers will be) there is no necessary objection to the enforcement there of awards made by English adjudicators in respect of English building contracts (See *Comsite Projects Ltd v Andritz AG* [2003] EWHC 958). A clause prorogating the jurisdiction of an English Court in relation to disputes under the contract may not in itself preclude enforcement in Scotland of the adjudicator's award meantime (See *Comsite Projects Ltd v Andritz AG* [2003] EWHC 958). Such enforcement actions have already been brought in Scotland, and, indeed, the oft-cited *Homer Burgess Ltd* is an early example *Vaughan Engineering Ltd v Hinkins & Frewin Ltd* 2003 SLT 428 is a more recent one. The main reason for seeking to enforce an English award in Scotland, it is thought, would be to allow a successful, but financially seriously straitened party faced with the prospect of cross-claims or a cross-action under Subsection 108(3) of the 1996 Act at the instance of his opponent, to seek a court decree for the monies awarded him by the adjudicator which he could then enforce by diligence. Whereas in England the court has held that it will stay execution of the decree in circumstances of that class (See, for example, *Baldwin's Industrial Services plc v Barr Limited* [2003] BLR 176; *Rainford House Ltd v Cadogan Ltd* [2001] BLR 416), it has been held in Outer House of the Court of Session that in Scotland there is no power so to do, and that the insolvency of the successful party is no ground for withholding an immediately enforceable decree for the sum awarded by the adjudicator (*SL Timber Systems Ltd, supra*). By seeking to enforce his adjudicator's award in Scotland, therefore, the financially stricken subcontractor – or perhaps its bankers – can secure the benefit of a perhaps fortunate adjudicator's award, and avoid those protections afforded by the English courts on which his opponent may hope, and expect, to be able to rely in avoiding the need to pay out *ad interim* to one likely to be unable to repay in the event of the payer's success in the cross-action.

2.08 By way of contrast, the second major difference between English and Scots law in this area relates to the challenge of awards made by adjudicators. In Scotland, it is not necessary for a party dissatisfied with an adjudicator's decision to wait for his opponent to attempt to enforce it and then defend the enforcement proceedings on whatever grounds may cause him to be so dissatisfied. For in Scotland, unlike England, the adjudicator's decisions are subject to judicial review, and that method of challenge is not infrequently resorted to (*Allied London & Scottish Properties plc, supra, Watson Building Services Ltd v Harrison* 2001 SLT 846 and *Gillies Ramsay Diamond, Petitioner, supra* are all judicial reviews). There is no time limit for the raising of such petitions, albeit that a degree of promptitude in raising any proposed review is expected. The availability of judicial review in Scotland as a mode of reviewing adjudication decisions has tended to cause a greater resort to administrative law cases as a source of precedent on review than has perhaps been the case in England. Thus, it has been stated that the decision of an adjudicator is subject to reduction in the event that it is 'Wednesbury unreasonable' (See *Ballast plc, supra*.), and it has been argued that reduction is similarly available if other elements of the classical Scottish touchstone of administrative law grounds of reduction set out in *Wordie Property Ltd v Secretary of State for Scotland* 1984 SLT 345 are not complied with. Likewise, the argument has been

advanced that inadequacy of reasoning on the part of an adjudicator in his Decision and Note of Reasons is in itself an error of law such as entitles the Court of Session to reduce his decision. In the recalaiming motion in *Gillies Ramsay Diamond, Petitioner*, the argument was advanced that, on the basis of House of Lords cases such as *O'Reilly v Mackman* [1983] 2 AC 287, there is no distinction between *intra vires* and *ultra vires* errors of law in adjudication, so that the award should be reduced as would, say, a planning authority's decision letter be, if it were disfigured by errors of law about the merits of the case, even if it displayed none about jurisdictional matters. A decision to that effect would have to run counter to those made by the Court of Appeal *in Bouygues Offshore (UK) Ltd v Dahl-Jensen (UK) Ltd* [2002] BLR 522 and *C & B Scene Concept Design Ltd v Isobars Ltd* [2002] 82 Con. L.R. 154, as well as the Scottish rule about the review of arbiters' decisions noted in paragraph 1.10 above. The argument, however, was rejected, since *O'Reilly* and similar cases were concerned with English public law notions rather than contractually based jurisdictions such as adjudications, and for cases of the latter class, the Scottish rule in arbitration cases was the better guide, as well as the one more consonant with the policy of the adjudication provisions of the 1996 Act. Parliament had provided a mechanism for undoing the effects of adjudicators' errors in the shape of the s.108(3) action, and it was unnecessary to call into existence another (*Gilles Ramsay Diamond, Petitioner*, 24th December, 2003, unreported). Whilst in England, the argument from *O'Reilly* may still be open, as it was advanced in neither *Bouygues Offshore (UK) Ltd* nor *C & B Scene Concept Design, Ltd*, and features in the pages of 'Emden's Construction Law', in Scotland, it is now firmly excluded.

2.09 The private international law implications of such actions have not, it is fair to say, been fully worked out. The jurisdictional question has not really been canvassed, although decisions in relation to other classes of judicial review and private law matters may point the way forward (For example, *Bank of Scotland v Investment Management Regulatory Organization Ltd* 1989 SC 107), and the plea of *forum non conveniens* originally laid in *Homer Burgess Ltd* was departed from. The architect who conceives that he, or his client, may find themselves in the cross-border 'debateable land' should therefore seek advice.

18

Building dispute resolution in Northern Ireland

BRIAN SPEERS AND FERGUSON BELL

1 Adjudication

1.01 The adjudication provisions and payment rules contained in the Housing Grants, Construction and Regeneration Act 1996 as supplemented by the Scheme for Construction Contracts (England and Wales) Regulations 1998 and the Construction Contracts (England and Wales) Exclusion order 1998 are correspondingly enacted in Northern Ireland in the Construction Contracts (Northern Ireland) Order 1997 as supplemented by the Scheme for Construction Contracts in Northern Ireland Regulations (Northern Ireland) 1999 and the Construction Contracts Exclusion Order (Northern Ireland) 1999, which came into force in Northern Ireland on 1 June 1999.

Article 7 of the Order gives any party to a construction contract in Northern Ireland a right to refer disputes to a quick, impartial and investigative adjudication procedure and if no adequate procedure is agreed in the contract the procedure set out in the Scheme will apply.

The Order also – (a) gives a contractor a statutory right to insist on payment by instalments where the work is to last 45 days or more (*Article 8*), (b) requires construction contracts to provide a mechanism for determining the amount of payments and set a final date for payment of sums due (*Article 9*), (c) obliges a payer to give a contractor notice with reasons, before the final date of payment, if he intends to withhold payment (*Article 10*) and (d) makes unenforceable contract provisions which have the effect of making payment dependent upon receipt of payment from a third party, unless payment is delayed because a third party has become insolvent (*Article 12*).

1.02 Some adjudicators in Northern Ireland have reported facing the occasional jurisdictional challenge, primarily on the ground that they lack the authority to deal with the issues raised, and allegations of bias or procedural unfairness sometimes resulting in a refusal to co-operate with the adjudicator or to comply with the decision, leading in such instances to a challenge to any legal proceedings brought to enforce it.

Enforcement proceedings are normally brought by way of application for Summary Judgment pursuant to Order 14 of the Rules of the Supreme Court for the sum due on foot of the adjudicator's decision.

The Courts in Northern Ireland have readily given support to the adjudication process by abridging time as appropriate and granting Summary judgment except in cases where it would obviously lead to a substantial injustice.

2 Arbitration

2.01 The law of arbitration in Northern Ireland is now identical to that to England and Wales as the Arbitration Act 1996 applies to Northern Ireland and came into force on 31 January 1997.

As the Civil Procedure Rules do not apply in Northern Ireland, applications to the Court in relation to arbitration are made under Order 73 of the Rules of the Supreme Court (the White Book) which also came into force on 31 January 1997.

Recent cases in the High Court of Justice in Northern Ireland concerning arbitration decisions and arbitration procedure have included applications to extend the time within which a reference to arbitration can be made; a consideration of 'serious irregularity' as described in Section 68 of the Arbitration Act 1996; and various applications to stay proceedings on the basis that a valid arbitration agreement subsists between the parties.

3 Other forms of dispute resolution

3.01 The High Court of Justice in Northern Ireland, Queen's Bench (Commercial list) Practice Direction No 1/2000 amended 7 October 2002 states in paragraph 8 that:

> 'the Commercial List Judge may draw the attention of the parties to commercial litigation to the existence of alternative means by which a case or a specific issue/issues therein may be resolved including, in particular, a suitable form of alternative dispute resolution. In appropriate cases the Commercial List Judge may require the parties to justify a decision not to resort to an appropriate form of dispute resolution.'

Encouragement to use mediation is an increasing trend in the Commercial Court which deals with most construction disputes in Northern Ireland.

Part Four

Statutory framework and regulation

19

Statutory authorities in England and Wales

ROBERT WHITE*

1 Local government

Introduction: relevant local government authorities

1.01 Local government in England and Wales, outside London, was completely reorganized on 1 April 1974, when the Local Government Act 1972 came into force. The pattern of local authorities is now simpler than it was before 1974, but Greater London (reorganized in 1965 by the London Government Act 1963) is administered differently, and there are also less important differences between England and Wales. These three parts of the country should therefore now be considered separately.

Local government in England and Wales consists of the administration by locally elected bodies of powers conferred and duties imposed by the Parliament.

Local Authorities are subject to the direction, control and supervision of the government, to the extent that Parliament has legislated for that direction, control and supervision in statute or in other legislation.

The Labour government elected in 1997 proposed a package of measures for the reform and modernization of local government in England and Wales.

In particular the Local Government Act 2000 gave local authorities general powers to promote the well-being of their community; established executive and scrutiny arrangements within local government; modernized the laws relating to the conduct of members; and changed some of the local government election procedures. The Government of Wales Act 1998 devolved certain powers from Westminster to Wales. The Regional Development Agencies Act 1998 has created nine regional development agencies in England to promote sustainable economic development, and social and physical regeneration.

1.02 In London, the Local Government Act 1985 abolished the Greater London Council and redistributed its functions between the 32 London boroughs, the City of London and new specialized representative bodies (e.g. the London Fire and Civil Defence Authority). Housing is the responsibility of the boroughs and the City. The Greater London Authority (GLA) Act 1999 established the GLA, which is comprised of the London Assembly and the Mayor of London. The London Borough Councils and the Common Council of the City of London remain in place, although some of their responsibilities and functions have been affected by the creation of the GLA.

1.03 In England outside the London area, the country is divided between six metropolitan areas (West Midlands, Merseyside, Greater Manchester, West Yorkshire, South Yorkshire, and Tyne and

Wear) and the 'ordinary' counties. Between 1974 and 1985 in the metropolitan areas there was a metropolitan county for each area, and a varying number of metropolitan districts, each with a council, within each county. Since 1985 the metropolitan counties have been abolished and their functions redistributed to the metropolitan districts and specialized representative bodies.

1.04 Outside the metropolitan areas the structure until recently comprised 38 counties (each with a county council) and approximately 390 districts (each again with a council). However, following the recommendations of the Local Government Commission, several of the former county councils have been abolished in favour of new unitary authorities, which combine the functions of county and district councils. In the remaining non-metropolitan counties, two tiers of government have been retained, although in some cases large cities have been given unitary status with the county and district councils retaining their responsibilities for the remaining parts of the area.

1.05 In addition, rural parishes which existed before 1974 have been allowed to continue. Further, some of the pre-1974 district councils have been re-formed with parish council status. As an additional complication, district councils have been allowed to apply for a charter giving themselves the status of a borough, although this is solely a ceremonial matter. Some parishes have been allowed to call themselves 'towns' and have appointed 'town mayors', again with no real legal significance. The parishes ('communities' in Wales) have very few substantial functions, but may provide and maintain recreation grounds, bus shelters, and roadside seats.

1.06 In Wales there are no metropolitan areas. The former structure of 8 counties divided into 37 districts, with councils at each level, was abolished on 1 April 1996, since when all local administration has been undertaken by 22 new unitary authorities (11 counties and 11 county boroughs). The Government of Wales Act 1998 provided for the devolution of certain powers from ministers to the National Assembly for Wales. In effect the newly created Welsh Assembly has taken over the responsibilities that the Secretary of State for Wales previously exercised in Wales.

General characteristics of local authorities

1.07 The essential characteristics of every local authority under this complicated system is that it is governed by a council elected on a wide franchise at four-year intervals. In districts, one-third of the councillors retire on three out of four years every year: but a non-metropolitan district may resolve that all their members shall retire together. In counties all members retire together every fourth year. Some changes were made to the system of election of councillors by the Local Government Act 2000.

The term of office for an elected Mayor is 4 years.

---

* This chapter draws heavily on the chapter written for the first edition by Professor J. F. Garner.

237

1.08 Local authorities are legal persons, capable of suing and being sued in the courts, entrusted by Parliament with a range of functions over a precisely limited geographical area. Each local authority is subject to the doctrine of *ultra vires*; i.e. it can perform only those functions conferred on it by Parliament, and only in such a manner as Parliament may have laid down. On the other hand, within the powers defined by Parliament, each local authority is its own master. In the two- or three-tier system there is no question of an appeal from the lower-rank authorities (the district or the parish) to the higher rank (the county council) or from the parish to the district. If the individual authority has acted within its statutory powers, its decision is final, except in cases precisely laid down by Parliament, where (as in many planning situations) there may be a right of appeal to a minister of the central government (Chapter 23). If, however, a local authority has overstepped the limits of its legal powers, a private citizen who has been aggrieved in consequence may apply to the courts for an order requiring the errant local authority to keep within its powers. Thus, a ratepayer at Fulham successfully obtained an order against the borough council, requiring the council to stop spending ratepayers' money on the provision of a service for washing clothes for members of the public, when the council had statutory powers to provide a service for washing only the bodies of members of the public (*Attorney General v Fulham BC* [1921] 1 Ch 440).

Human Rights

1.09 The enactment of the Human Rights Act 1998 has added a significant new dimension to the statutory duties of local authorities. The basic purpose of the Act is 'to give further effect to rights and freedoms guaranteed under the European Convention of Human Rights'. Of particular relevance to local authorities, the Act provides that it is unlawful for a public authority to act in a way which is incompatible with any Convention right.

Officers

1.10 All local authorities are alike in that they employ officers and other staff to carry out their instructions, while the elected members assembled in council make decisions as to what is to be done. Officers of the authority – chief executive, solicitor, treasurer, surveyor, architect, planning officer, and many others – play a large part in the decision-making process: they advise the council on the courses of action open to them, and also on the consequences of taking such actions. When a decision has been taken, it is then the duty of appropriate officers of the council to implement it: to notify persons concerned and to take any executive decisions or other action necessary to give effect to the main decision. It is sometimes said that the officers give advice and take action, while the council decides all matters of policy; although basically true (for statutes almost invariably confer the power to exercise discretion on the authority itself) this does not clarify what happens in practice. 'Policy' is incapable of precise definition, for what is policy to some local authorities and in some circumstances may be regarded as routine administration by other authorities or in different circumstances. For example, some local authorities like to settle the details of each renovation grant approved under the Local Government and Housing Act 1989, though most authorities would be content to leave details of such matters to their officers, trusting them to bring before the council (or a committee) particulars of any difficult case.

Committees

1.11 In practice, all local authorities conduct their affairs by the committee system. Committees, consisting of named councillors, are usually considerably smaller in membership than the council as a whole and are entrusted with specified functions of the council. (There are no general rules, but a council of, say, 48 members may place about 12 councillors on each of its committees. Recently there has been a tendency to streamline committee organization, leaving more routine matters to the discretion of officers.) Thus, every county council has a planning committee and a finance committee,

and most district councils will have a parks committee and a housing committee, although details vary from authority to authority. Since 1974, committees have tended to be wider in scope, and policy or 'general resources' committees are common. Every matter requiring a council decision within the terms of reference of a particular committee is first brought before the committee. The committee then considers the matter and either recommends a certain decision to the council or may itself make the decision. Whether the committee decides on behalf of the council depends on whether the council has delegated to the committee power to take the decision on its behalf, either in that particular matter, or in matters of that kind or falling within a particular class.

1.12 Section 101 of the Local Government Act 1972 confers on all local authorities power to arrange for any of its functions (except levying a charge or raising a loan) to be discharged by a committee, a sub-committee, or an officer. However, this does not authorize the delegation of any function to a committee comprising only one member: *R v Secretary of State for the Environment ex p. London Borough of Hillingdon* [1986] 2 All ER 273.

The Local Government Act 2000 requires each local authority in England and Wales to adopt 'executive arrangements' in one of a number of specified forms. 'Executive arrangements' are arrangements made by the authority for, and in connection with the creation and operation of an executive for the authority under which certain of the authority's functions are the responsibility of the executive. Local authorities are required to put in place scrutiny and overview committees. A division has been created within each local authority between the making of decisions and the granting of those decisions. The purpose of the reforms is 'to deliver greater efficiency, transparency and accountability of local authorities', ensuring that decisions are taken more quickly and efficiently than under the previous system and that bodies responsible for decisions can be more readily identified by the public and held to account in public by overview and scrutiny committees.

The executive must take one of the three specified forms. The three forms are:

1 a directly elected mayor and cabinet executive;
2 a leader of the council and cabinet executive;
3 a directly elected mayor and council manager executive.

The Act sets out the functions that are and are not to be the responsibility of the executive of the council. In particular the functions of town and country planning; licensing and registration are expressly stated not to be executive responsibilities.

1.13 Proceedings in committee are normally held in public and tend to be informal. Officers attend, and volunteer advice and often take part in the discussion, although any decision is taken on the vote or assent of the councillors present. Council meetings and meetings of specified committees such as the education committee are more formal; the press and members of the public are entitled to be present unless they have been excluded by special resolution of the council passed because of the intention to discuss exempted information, such as facts regarding individual council employees (Local Government (Access to Information) Act 1985), and proceedings are conducted in accordance with the council's standing orders. Officers do not speak at a council meeting unless their advice is expressly requested, and as much business consists of receipt of reports from committees, discussion tends to be confined to more controversial topics.

1.14 Because of the presence of the press and public, party politics tend to be more obvious at council meetings; often in committee, members from opposing political parties will agree, and members of a single party may disagree with one another. In recent years, however, there has been a tendency for authorities to be more closely organized on party political lines. When this occurs, 'group' meetings may be held preceding the committee meetings. Thus on important matters, decisions at committee meetings tend to be 'rubber stamps' of decisions already taken at the group meeting of the political party in power on the council. It has been held that it is legitimate, when deciding how to vote, for a councillor to have regard to party loyalty and party policy, provided they do not 'dominate so as to exclude other considerations or deprive the councillor of real choice: *R v Waltham Forest London Borough Council ex p. Baxter* [1988] 1 QB 419. However, the Local Ombudsman's finding of maladministration where members of a planning committee were heavily influenced by party political loyalty, which was not material to the planning application before them, has been upheld: *R v Local Commissioner for Administration in the North and North East England, ex p. Liverpool City Council* (2000) 2 LGLR 603.

The law relating to the conduct of members was radically overhauled by the Local Government Act 2000. The Secretary of State has directed that all local authorities must develop their own codes of conduct. Each member is under a duty to comply with the authority's code.

1.15 The law requires that councils must meet at least four times a year. Most councils arrange committee meetings in a cycle, monthly or perhaps every six weeks, so that each committee will normally meet at least once between council meetings. The system whereby committees are given delegated powers (as is now customary) provides for a reasonably expeditious dispatch of business, but there may be long delays where the council meets less often than once a month, and there is no adequate provision for delegation to committees and/or to officers.

Officers' powers

1.16 All discretionary powers are in the first instance conferred on a local authority, but under section 101 of the Local Government Act 1972, every local authority has wide powers to delegate any of its discretionary decisions to any of its officers; a power which is often used, especially in planning. But there must in every instance be a clear delegation before an officer can decide on behalf of his authority. Therefore, when an officer of a council who was asked for information as to the planning position in respect of a particular piece of land carelessly gave the wrong information, saying that planning permission was not required, it was held by the courts that the council were not bound by this statement. It could not be taken as the decision of the council, as the officer had in that case no power to act on their behalf: *Southend-on-Sea Corporation v Hodgson (Wickford) Ltd* [1961] 2 All ER 46. This decision is still good law in circumstances where powers have not been expressly delegated to the officer concerned (see *Western Fish Products Ltd v Penwith DC* [1979] 77 LGR 185).

1.17 There is a very limited exception to this principle where the planning officer concerned has 'ostensible' authority to make a decision. In *Camden London Borough Council v Secretary of State for the Environment* [1993] 67 P&CR 59 the High Court held that the Council was precluded from taking enforcement action in circumstances where its planning officer had written to the developer, stating that variations to an approved plan were 'minor and would not constitute development requiring planning permission'. However, there will need to be some evidence to justify the assumption that the officer's actions will bind the authority, and the type and scale of the development will be a relevant factor. The larger the development, the less reasonable it will be to assume that the planning officer is authorized to make a decision upon it.

1.18 Local authorities do not stand outside the common law in respect of acts of negligence by their officers and employees. However, the House of Lords has held that a local authority is not generally liable in negligence to owners/occupiers of buildings for failings in the authority's enforcement of the Building Regulations concerning the defective construction of those buildings: *Murphy v Brentwood District Council* [1990] 2 All ER 908. Local planning authorities are also not liable for negligence in the grant of planning permission: see *Strable v Dartford Borough Council* [1984] JPL 329; *Lam v Brennan* [1997] 3 PLR 22.

1.19 An alternative non-judicial method by which an aggrieved individual may seek redress against a local authority's actions or inaction is to make a complaint to the Local Ombudsman under the Local Government Act 1974 (as amended). If the Local Ombudsman finds that a complainant has suffered injustice as a consequence of maladministration by the local authority he may publish such a finding and recommend a suitable remedy (which can include financial compensation). The local authority are obliged to have regard to the report, but they cannot be compelled in law to implement the Local Ombudsman's recommendations to alleviate the injustice. In recent years approximately 40% of complaints to the Local Ombudsman have been about housing matters and a further 25% have concerned planning functions. The Commission for Local Administration in England can be contacted directly at 21 Queen Anne's Gate, London SW1H 9BU (Tel. 0207 915 3210). There is a separate Commission for Local Administration in Wales. In addition to investigating maladministration, the Welsh Commission also has functions relating to the conduct of members of authorities in Wales.

Finding the right officer

1.20 Architects in the course of their professional business are obliged to have dealings with numerous local authority officials. Table 19.1 shows the purposes for which a permission, licence, or certificate may have to be obtained from the local authority, giving the officers initially responsible (see Chapters 21 and 23). First, however, it is essential to ascertain the authority in whose area the site lies.

Local government: distribution of planning functions

1.21 Within Greater London, the London Borough Council (or, as the case may be, the City of London) is both the local planning

Table 19.1 Responsibilities of local authority officers

Subject matter	Officer	Local authority
Planning	Planning officer or surveyor	DC
Building regulations	Building inspector or surveyor	DC
Development in a private street	Surveyor	CC
Surface water sewerage	Engineer	SU
Sewer connections	Engineer	SU
Blocked sewers	Engineer	SU
Housing grants; housing generally	Environmental health officer or (sometimes) surveyor	DC
Height of chimneys or other clean air matters	Environmental health officer	DC
Petroleum licensing; most other licensing	Petroleum inspector (often environmental health officer or surveyor)	CC or DC
Music and dancing licences	Licensing officer*	
Liquor licences	Licensing officer*	

Key: CC, county council; DC, district council; SU, sewerage undertaker

Notes

A company operating under the Water Act 1989, whose functions may be exercised by the district council under an arrangement with the sewerage undertaker.

London In Greater London, in all cases (except for liquor licences) the responsible authority is the London borough council or the Common Council of the City.

Planning In planning the authority given above should be contacted in the first instance, although the county council may ultimately make the decision.

Roads In the counties highway functions are commonly administered by district or divisional surveyors, responsible to the county surveyor but stationed locally often at district council offices.

In the case of trunk and special roads (motorways) the highway authority is the Secretary of State for Transport, but the local county surveyor acts as his agent at local level. Maintenance of urban roads may be claimed by the DC.

Under the Local Government (Miscellaneous Provisions) Act 1982, several activities are made subject to licensing (e.g. acupuncture, tattooing, take-away food shops, etc.). These provisions are administered by the district council.

* Under Licensing Act 2003.

authority and the mineral planning authority. The London Mayor must prepare and publish a 'spatial development strategy' (SDS). He is empowered to direct the local planning authority of a London Borough to refuse an application for planning permission of a prescribed description in any particular. He must monitor the implementation of the SDS and monitor the UDP of each London Borough Council so that it is in accordance with the SDS. Similarly, within the metropolitan areas outside London, the metropolitan district councils fulfil both local planning and mineral planning functions. Within London and in the metropolitan areas outside London, the relevant authorities are responsible under Part II, Town and Country Planning Act 1990 for the production of 'unitary development plans', which are effectively a combination of the former structure plans and local plans.

1.22 For non-metropolitan areas where there is a unitary authority, those authorities are the local planning authority for all purposes within its area, and (with two exceptions) are responsible for preparing and maintaining both a structure plan and a local plan. The Secretary of State has the power to extend the requirement to prepare a unitary development plan to all unitary authorities, but to date has only done so for the Isle of Wight and Herefordshire.

1.23 For non-metropolitan areas where there is a two-tier local government structure, the vast majority of development control functions are vested in the districts, which are responsible for the preparation of district-wide local plans. County Councils are responsible for the preparation of structure plans, minerals local plans (section 37, Town and Country Planning Act 1990) and (except in Wales) waste local plans (section 38, Town and Country Planning Act 1990). However, the jurisdiction of the county council in matters of development control is limited to 'county matters', namely those associated with mineral planning and waste disposal.

1.24 In Wales, the local planning authority is the county council or the county borough council. All local planning authorities and the National Parks Authority within Wales are required to prepare and maintain unitary development plans for their areas.

1.25 Within the national parks, the functions formerly vested in the Planning Board in the Peak District and Lake District Parks, and elsewhere in the county planning authority, now vest in the National Parks authority for that area (section 4A, Town and Country Planning Act 1990). In relation to tree preservation and replacement (sections 198 to 201 and 206 to 209, 211 to 214) and the powers under section 215 (power to require proper maintenance of land) the district planning authority whose area includes that part of the Park has concurrent jurisdiction (section 4(2)).

1.26 Within the Norfolk and Suffolk Broads, the Broads Authority is the sole district planning authority for non-county matters (section 5, Town and Country Planning Act 1990).

1.27 Overlooking this general structure, the Secretary of State for the Department of Transport, Environment and the Regions has wide-ranging supervisory powers. There is a right of appeal to him from all adverse development control decisions and enforcement notices, although not from a breach of condition notice. He may remove jurisdiction from the local planning authority in particular cases by calling a planning application in for his own determination (section 77, Town and Country Planning Act 1990). His approval is required for structure plans, and he may call in unitary development plans and local plans for approval (although the latter power is rarely exercised).

Local government: other functions

1.28 Outside London, county councils are responsible for fire services, main and district highways, refuse disposal, and a few other functions. Outside the metropolitan areas county councils are also responsible for education and welfare services, which in the metropolitan areas are the responsibility of the district councils.

1.29 All district councils are responsible for housing, refuse collection, drainage, clean air and public health generally (but not sewerage and water supply), development control, parks and open spaces, and building controls, etc. A district council may also (by arrangement with the county council) undertake the maintenance of urban roads (other than trunk roads), bridleways, and footpaths within its district. Part 1 of the Local Government Act 1988 now states that if local authorities wish to provide certain designated services themselves (notably the collection of refuse) they must first subject the service to tender from private contractors.

1.30 From 1974 to 1989 the provision and maintenance of sewers and sewerage disposal, together with water supply and distribution and the prevention of river pollution, was the responsibility of special authorities, the ten regional water authorities (nine in England, one in Wales). Under the Water Act 1989 the water industry was privatized and as a consequence the sewerage functions of the former water authorities have passed to successor companies, which are in most instances also responsible for water supply, except in those areas where this was formerly the responsibility of statutory water companies which remain in existence. Water and sewerage undertakers are forbidden from causing river pollution, the prevention of which is now the responsibility of the Environment Agency. The successor companies are constituted under the regime of the Companies Acts and are appointed by the Secretary of State to act as water and/or sewerage undertakers. Customers can make complaints to a specially constituted Customer Services Committee who must investigate the matter and may make representations to the Director General, who in turn may issue an order, or suggest that the Secretary of State do so, requiring appropriate action to be taken by the relevant undertaker (sections 28 and 30, Water Industry Act 1991).

2 Other statutory bodies

English heritage

2.01 The Historic Buildings and Monuments Commission for England, more commonly known as 'English Heritage', was established under the National Heritage Act 1983. It is a body corporate whose members are appointed by the Secretary of State, and who serve for a maximum of five years. Its functions include making grants in relation to historic buildings and conservation areas, acquiring historic buildings, acquiring or becoming the guardian of ancient monuments, and undertaking archaeological investigation and publishing the results. Within Greater London, it has the power, concurrently with the London Boroughs, to take enforcement action against breaches of listed building control (section 45, Planning (Listed Buildings and Conservation Areas) Act 1990).

2.02 Its duties are, so far as practicable in exercising its functions, to secure the preservation of ancient monuments and historic buildings in England; to promote the preservation and enhancement of the character and appearance of conservation areas situated in England; and to promote the public's enjoyment and advance their knowledge of ancient monuments and historic buildings situated in England (section 33).

2.03 English Heritage plays an important role in the listing of buildings: although ultimate responsibility for deciding which buildings should (and should not) be listed rests with the Secretary of State for National Heritage, English Heritage may compile lists of buildings of special architectural or historic interest for the Secretary of State's approval, and must be consulted by him before he compiles, approves, adds to or modifies any such list (section 1, Planning (Listed Buildings and Conservation Areas) Act 1990).

2.04 English Heritage must be consulted by the planning authority on a range of applications, including the demolition in whole or part or the material alteration of a listed building; development likely to affect the site of a scheduled monument, development likely to affect any Grade I or Grade II registered garden or park of special historic interest: Article 10, General Development Procedure Order 1995.

2.05 English Heritage publishes a wide range of advice on the care of historic buildings, such as *The Repair of Historic Buildings: Advice on Principles and Methods*, and its guidance on *The Conversion of Historic Farm Buildings*. Early consultation with the Commission will often be useful.

English Nature and the Countryside Council for Wales

2.06 In 1991, the nature conservation functions previously exercisable in respect of England and Wales by the Nature Conservancy Council were transferred to the Nature Conservancy Council for England (more commonly known as 'English Nature') and the Countryside Council for Wales (Environmental Protection Act 1990).

2.07 The two bodies are responsible for the establishment, maintenance and management of nature reserves, the notification and protection of SSSIs, the provision of advice for the Secretary of State on the development and implementation of policies for or affecting nature conservation in their areas, the provision of advice and the dissemination of knowledge about nature conservation in their areas, and the commissioning or support of research which is relevant to their functions. They also advise the Secretary of State of any endangered animal or plant which should be added to or removed from the lists of protected species.

2.08 English Nature and CCW must be consulted by planning authorities before permission is granted for development of land in a SSSI, in any consultation area around a SSSI, or for development which is likely to affect a SSSI: Article 10, General Development Procedure Order 1995. Consultation areas are defined by English Nature and may extend up to a maximum of 2 kilometres from the boundary of the SSSI.

The Environment Agency

2.09 The Environment Agency was established under the Environment Act 1995 as a body corporate, and has inherited functions previously carried out by the National Rivers Authority; the Waste Regulation Authorities; HM Inspectorate of Pollution; and certain functions of the Secretary of State in relation to radioactive substances, 'special category effluent' and sludge. The Agency has functions with respect to pollution control, water resources, environmental duties with respect to sites of special interest and flood defence.

2.10 Its principal aim in discharging its functions, as set out in section 4, is 'so to protect or enhance the environment, taken as a whole, as to make the contribution towards attaining the objective of achieving sustainable development', in which regard the Agency receives guidance from ministers on the extent of the contribution the Agency is expected to make.

2.11 The Agency must be consulted by the planning authority on any application for development involving mining operations; the carrying out of works or operations in the bed of or on the banks of a riverbed or stream; the refining or storage of mineral oils or derivatives; the deposit of refuse or waste; use of land as a cemetery; fish farming, and (with certain minor exceptions) the retention, treatment or disposal of sewage, trade waste, slurry or sludge: Article 10, General Development Procedure Order 1995.

2.12 The functions carried out by the Environment Agency are, in Scotland, largely mirrored by the Scottish Environment Protection Agency.

3 Statutory undertakers: connections to services

3.01 When starting to design a building for a client, any architect is obliged at an early stage to consider the availability of mains services and the rights of his client as landowner regarding the various

statutory undertakers: sewer and highway authorities, water, gas, and electricity supply undertakings, and possibly the water undertaker if it is proposed to use a water course as a means of disposing of effluent from the building. The legal provisions regulating these matters are discussed below.

Sewers

3.02 Sewers are conduits (artificial or natural) used for conveying effluent (i.e. waste liquids – clear water, surface water from covered surfaces, land or buildings, foul water, or trade effluent) from two or more buildings not within the same curtilage. (Curtilage: in non-technical terms, the natural boundaries of a particular building; thus the curtilage of an ordinary dwelling house would include the garage, the garden and its appurtenances, and any outbuildings.) A conduit which takes effluent from one building only or from a number of buildings all within the same curtilage is in law a 'drain'. This distinction is important, as a landowner never has any legal right to let his effluent flow into a drain belonging to another person (even if that other person is a local authority) unless he has acquired such a right by at least 20 years' use or as the result of an agreement with the other person (Chapter 2). The same rule applies to a private sewer; but if the conduit to which he proposes to drain his effluent is a public sewer, he will have certain valuable rights to use it.

3.03 All public sewers are vested in (owned by) the sewerage undertakers, and a sewer is a public sewer if it existed as a sewer (regardless of who constructed it) before 1 October 1937, if it was constructed by a local authority after 1 October 1937 and before 1 April 1974, or by a water authority before 1 November 1989, or by a sewerage undertaker after 1 November 1989 and was not designed to serve only property belonging to a local authority (e.g. a council housing estate), or if it has been adopted as a public sewer since 1 October 1937.

Rights to connection

3.04 By section 106 of the Water Industry Act 1991, the owner or occupier of any premises in the area of a sewerage undertaker has a right to cause his own drains or private sewer to communicate with the public sewers of that undertaker and to discharge foul and surface water from his premises to it. Connecting sewers or drains from the premises to the public sewer must be constructed at the expense of the landowner concerned. Sometimes – but not often – the sewerage undertaker may itself construct 'laterals', or connecting drains leading from the main sewer to the boundary of the street to which house drains may be connected.

3.05 There are a few exceptions to this general rule:

1 No substance likely to injure the sewer or to interfere with the free flow of its contents, no chemical refuse or waste steam, or any petroleum spirit or calcium carbide, may be caused to flow into a public sewer (section 111, Water Industry Act 1991).
2 The general rule does not apply to trade effluents (section 106(2)(a)).
3 The general rule does not permit a communication directly with a storm-water overflow sewer (section 106(2)(c)).
4 Where separate public sewers are provided for foul and for surface water, foul water may not be discharged into a sewer provided for surface water, and surface water may not, without the consent of the sewerage undertaker, be discharged into a sewer provided for foul water (section 106(2)(b) of the Act). It is particularly important that an architect should know whether the undertaker's sewerage network is designed on the separate system, as he may in turn have to provide a separate drainage for the building he is designing.

Procedure

3.06 A person wishing to connect his sewer or drain to a public sewer must give the sewerage undertaker written notice of his proposal, and the undertaker may within 21 days of notice refuse to permit him to make the communication if the mode of construction or condition of the drain or sewer is such that the making of the communication would be prejudicial to their sewerage system (section 106(4) of the Act), but they may not so refuse for any other reason. Any dispute with the undertaker under these provisions may be settled by way of an application to the local magistrates, or in some cases by a reference to arbitration.

3.07 Alternatively, where proposals have been served on the undertaker, the undertaker may within 14 days of service give notice that it intends to make the communication to the public sewer itself (section 107 of the Act). The private landowner is then obliged to permit the undertaker to do the work of making the house drains or sewer connect with the public sewer, and he has to bear the sewerage undertaker's reasonable expenses so incurred. The undertaker is not obliged to make the communication until his reasonable estimate of the cost has been paid, or security for such payment has been given.

3.08 When making the communication, the undertaker (or the private owner if he is allowed to do the work himself) has power as necessary to break open any street (section 107(6) of the Act).

Approval of drainage

3.09 The arrangements proposed to be made for the 'satisfactory provision' for drainage of a building must be approved by the district council or London Borough Council at the time when the building plans are considered under the Building Regulations (section 21, Building Act 1984 and Chapter 21). Disposal of the effluent may be to a public sewer, or to a cesspool or private septic tank, and in the case of surface water to a highway drain or a watercourse or to the sea. In this instance note that the powers remain with the district council and have not been transferred to the sewerage undertaker.

3.10 If there is no existing main sewer into which the property could be drained, the owner or occupier (usually with the owners, etc., of other premises) may requisition the sewerage undertaker to provide a public sewer, under section 98 of the Water Industry Act 1991. They must then satisfy conditions specified by the undertaker the most important of which is likely to be that those requisitioning the sewer shall undertake to meet any 'relevant deficit' of the undertaker in consequence of constructing the sewer. This section applies only to sewers to be used for domestic purposes.

Highway drains

3.11 A landowner has no legal right to cause his drains (or sewers) to be connected with a highway drain, and this applies equally to surface water drains taking effluent from roads and paved surfaces on a private housing estate. Such drains may, in accordance with the statutory provisions outlined above, be connected with a public sewer, but if it is desired to connect with a drain or sewer provided for the drainage of a highway and vested in the highway authority, the consent of the highway authority must first be obtained. The highway authority will normally be the county council.

3.12 A public sewer may be used to take surface water from a highway, but that does not affect its status as a public sewer, nor does the fact that house drains may in the past have been connected (probably unlawfully) with a highway drain convert such highway drain into a public sewer (*Rickarby v New Forest RDC* [1910] 26 TLR 586). It is only to public sewers that drains or sewers may be connected as of right.

Rivers

3.13 If it is desired to discharge effluent into a watercourse the consent of the Environment Agency must be obtained for making of a new or altered discharge of trade or sewage effluent under section 88(2) of the Water Resources Act 1991. Consents may be granted subject to conditions. The Secretary of State may direct particular applications for consent to be transmitted to him, and may cause an inquiry to be held into the application (Water Resources Act 1991,

Schedule 10, as amended by Schedule 22 of the Environment Act 1995).

3.14 If a person causes or knowingly permits the discharge of effluent into a watercourse without the permission of the Environment Agency he commits an offence under section 85 of the Water Resources Act 1991.

The sea

3.15 A private landowner has at common law no legal right to discharge his sewage or other polluting matter to the sea; indeed, as the Crown originally owned the foreshore between high and low tides, he might not have any legal right to take his drain or sewer as far as the water. However, even if such a right can be acquired (and at the present day the Crown's rights have in many cases been sold or leased to local authorities or private landowners) it seems that the discharge of sewage by means of a pipe into the sea is subject to the same control of the Environment Agency (Water Resources Act 1991: see definition of 'controlled waters' in section 104, which includes coastal waters and territorial waters).

3.16 There must also be no nuisance caused as a consequence, and no breach of a local by-law made by a sea fisheries committee prohibiting the discharge of matter detrimental to sea fish or sea fishing (section 5, Sea Fisheries Regulations Act 1966). If effluent discharging into the sea does cause a nuisance, any person harmed thereby can take proceedings for an injunction and/or damages, as in *Foster v Warblington UDC* [1906] 1 KB 648, where guests at a banquet were poisoned from oysters taken from a bed which had been affected by sewage.

Trade effluents

3.17 In the case of a proposed discharge of 'trade effluent', the special controls of the Water Industry Act 1991, Chapter III, apply. 'Trade effluent' is defined in the Act of 1991 as meaning 'any liquid, either with or without particles of matter in suspension therein, which is wholly or in part produced by the course of any trade or industry carried on at trade premises, and, in relation to any trade premises, means any such liquid as aforesaid which is so produced in the course of any trade or industry carried on at those premises, but does not include domestic sewage' (section 141(1) 1991 Act). 'Trade premises' are defined as 'any premises used or intended to be used for carrying on any trade or industry' (including agriculture, horticulture, fish farming and scientific research) (sections 141(1) and 141(2) of the Water Industry Act 1991).

3.18 Where it is intended to discharge trade effluent as defined above into a public sewer, consent has first to be obtained from the sewerage undertaker. This is done by the owner or occupier of the premises serving on the undertaker a 'trade effluent notice'. This must specify (in writing) the nature or composition of the proposed effluent, the maximum quantity to be discharged in any one day, and the highest proposed rate of discharge of the effluent. This notice (for which there is no standard form) is then treated by the undertaker as an application for their consent to the proposed discharge. No effluent may then be discharged for a period of two months (or such less time as may be agreed by the undertaker).

3.19 A decision, when given by the undertaker, may be a refusal to permit the discharge or a consent thereto, and in the latter case a consent may be given subject to conditions as to a number of matters 'including a payment by the occupier of the trade premises of charges for the reception and disposal of the effluent', as specified in section 121 of the Water Industry Act 1991. These conditions may be varied (not more frequently than once every two years) by direction given by the sewerage undertaker (section 124). The owner or occupier of trade premises has a right of appeal to the Director General of Water Services against a refusal of consent to a discharge, against the conditions imposed in such a consent, or against a direction subsequently given varying the conditions (sections 122 and 126, Water Industry Act 1991). On appeal, the Director General may review all the conditions, whether or not they have been appealed against, and substitute for them any other set of conditions or annul any of the conditions (section 122(3)).

3.20 In practice, however, it is frequently desirable for an industrialist's professional advisers to discuss disposal of trade effluent with the officers of the sewerage undertaker, with a view to an agreement being entered into between the owner of the premises and the undertaker under section 129 of the Water Industry Act 1991. This will avoid the need to serve a trade effluent notice, and better terms can often be obtained by negotiation than by the more formal procedure of the trade effluent notice. The contents of any such agreement becomes public property, as a copy has to be kept at the sewerage undertaker's offices and made available for inspection and copying by any person (section 196, Water Industry Act 1991).

Water supply

3.21 The water supply authority will be the local water undertaker (a company appointed for a designated area of England and Wales by the Secretary of State (section 6, Water Industry Act 1991), but where before 1989 supply was made by a statutory water company this may remain in existence. The statutory water companies may have their own private Acts of Parliament regulating their affairs. Readers dealing in practice with a particular water undertaking should ascertain whether there are any local statutory variations.

Rights to connection: domestic premises

3.22 If the owner or occupier of premises within the area served by a water undertaker wishes to have a supply for domestic purposes, he may serve a notice requiring the undertaker to connect a service pipe to those premises to provide a supply of water for domestic purposes (section 45, Water Industry Act 1991).

3.23 Note that the obligation is to provide a *connection*. The undertaker is only required to lay that part of the service pipe serving the premises which leads from the main to the boundary of the street in which the main is laid or to the stopcock; the laying of the remainder is the responsibility of the owner or occupier. If the supply pipe passes through any property belonging to another owner, his consent must be obtained in the form of an express easement or a licence (Chapter 2). Any breaking up of streets must be effected by the undertakers and not by the owner requiring the supply.

3.24 Where a notice has been served under section 45, the undertaker is under a duty to make the connection. This must generally be done within 21 days of the service of the connection notice or, where it is necessary for the person serving the notice to lay any part of the service pipe himself, within 21 days of the date on which he gives notice stating that the pipe has been laid. Work carried out by the undertaker will be done at the expense of the person requesting the connection, and the undertaker may make it a condition of installation that a meter is installed, and may insist that the plumbing of the premises is compatible with such a meter (section 47).

3.25 Once a connection has been made, the undertaker is under a duty to provide a supply of water. The undertaker will have an excuse for not providing a supply if such failure is due to the carrying out of 'necessary works' (section 60, Water Industry Act 1991).

3.26 This assumes, of course, that the water main in the nearest street is within a reasonable distance from the house or other premises to be served. Where the main is not readily available, the owner of the premises may serve a requisition on the undertaker requiring them to extend their mains (section 41, Water Industry Act 1991). Where such a notice is served the water undertaker may require the owner to undertake to pay an annual sum not exceeding the amount (if any) by which the water charges payable for the use during that year of that main are exceeded by the annual borrowing costs of a loan of the amount required for the provision of that main. Such payments may be levied for a maximum of 12 years following the provision of

the main (section 42, 1991 Act). Provided those conditions have been satisfied, the water undertaker must extend their main within a period of three months (section 44, 1991 Act).

Right to connection: non-domestic premises

3.27 Owners or occupiers of premises requiring a supply of water for industrial or other (non-domestic) purposes must come to terms for a supply with the undertakers or, failing agreement, according to terms determined by the Director General of Water Services (sections 55 and 56, Water Industry Act 1991).

Gas supply

3.28 Following the privatization of the gas industry in 1986, the privileges previously conferred on the British Gas Corporation have been abolished, and gas is now supplied by a number of different companies. Under the Gas Act 1995, the Director General of Gas Supply may grant licences (1) to public gas transporters, authorizing them to carry gas through pipes to any premises in their authorized area and to convey gas to any pipeline system operated by another transporter; and (2) to gas suppliers, authorizing them to supply gas to specified premises. A person may not hold licences for both the public transport and the supply of gas (sections 5–7).

3.29 If the owner or occupier of premises requires a supply of gas for any purpose (not necessarily domestic), he may serve a notice on the public gas transporter for the area specifying the premises, and the day on which it is desired the service shall begin – and a reasonable time must be given (section 10, Gas Act 1986, as amended by the Gas Act 1995). The transporter must comply with such a request, but only if the premises are within 23 metres of any of their mains not being a main used for a separate supply for industrial purposes or for conveying gas in bulk, or could be connected to any such main by a pipe supplied and laid by the owner or occupier of the premises.

Electricity supply

3.30 The Electricity Act 1989 provided for the privatizing of the generation and supply of electricity. The Secretary of State is authorized to license persons to generate, transmit and supply electricity in designated areas (section 6, 1989 Act).

3.31 Under section 16 of the 1989 Act, the licensed public electricity supplier for an area is under a duty to give a supply to premises where requested by the owner or occupier (who must serve a notice specifying the premises, the date supply should commence, the maximum power which may be required and the minimum period for which the supply is required). Where such a request necessitates the provision of electrical lines or plant by the public electricity supplier they may require any expenses reasonably incurred in providing the supply to be paid by the consumer requesting the supply (section 19, 1989 Act). Any dispute arising out of the above obligations may be referred by either the consumer or supplier to the Director General of Electricity Supply for resolution (section 23, 1989 Act).

Telephones

3.32 The Telecommunications Act 1984 provided for the privatization of British Telecommunications. Today consumers can obtain telecommunication services from British Telecommunications plc or other licensed operators (e.g. Mercury Communications) (section 7, Telecommunications Act 1984). The terms for the provision of telecommunications services depends upon (1) the licence conditions regulating the particular telecommunications company approved by the Secretary of State for Trade and Industry under the Telecommunications Act 1984 and (2) the standard contracts offered by the specific company supplying the service. For example, condition 1 of the licence issued to British Telecommunications plc obliges the company 'to provide every person who requests the provision of such services at any time in the Licensed Area

(a) voice telephony services; and (b) other telecommunications services consisting in the conveyance of Messages'.

Construction of mains

3.33 All the utility undertakings have inherent powers to negotiate on terms with private landowners for the grant of easements or 'wayleaves' (Chapter 2) to enable them to place mains, cables, wires, apparatus, and so on over or under privately owned land. They also have powers to break open public streets for the purpose of constructing mains. Water and sewerage undertakers (Water Industry Act 1991, Schedule 6), gas transporters (Gas Act 1986, Schedule 3), electricity suppliers (Electricity Act 1989, Schedule 16) and licensed telecommunications operators (Telecommunications Act 1984, Schedule 2) all have statutory powers enabling them to place such mains and apparatus in private land, without the consent of the landowner or occupier concerned, on payment of proper compensation. Private persons have no such compulsory rights, although rights may be compulsorily acquired for an oil or other pipeline under the Pipelines Act 1962.

3.34 All the utility undertakers can also be authorized, without the consent of the landowner, to place their mains, apparatus, etc., on 'controlled land' (land forming part of a street or highway maintainable or prospectively maintainable at public expense – paragraphs 3.01 ff) or in land between the boundary of such a highway and any improvement line prescribed for the street (New Roads and Street Works Act 1991, Part III).

4 Private streets

4.01 It is not within the scope of this chapter to describe the whole law governing the making up of a private street by county councils at the expense of the frontagers to such a street, but the special rules that regulate the construction of a building in a 'private street' can be outlined.

Definition

4.02 A private street may or may not be a highway (i.e. any way, footpath, bridlepath, or carriageway over which members of the public have rights to pass and repass), but the word 'private' means not that it is necessarily closed to the public (although it may be), but that the street has not been adopted by a highway authority, and therefore it is not maintainable by them on behalf of the public. It must also be a 'street', an expression which has not been precisely defined, but which includes a cul-de-sac, lane, or passage (section 331(1), Highways Act 1980). This does not mean, however, that every country road is a street; in a leading case, it was said by Pollock, Master of the Rolls, that

> 'it appears to me that what one has to find before one can determine that the highway in question is a street, is that the highway has become a street in the ordinary acceptation of that word, because by reason of the number of houses, their continuity and their proximity to one another, what would be a road or highway has been converted into a street'. (*Attorney General v Laird* [1925] 1 Ch 318 at p. 329)

Advance payments code

4.03 As a general principle, before a new building may be erected in a new street as explained above, the developer must either pay to the local authority or secure to their satisfaction (by means of a bond or mortgage, etc.) a sum equivalent to the estimated cost, apportioned to the extent of the frontage of the proposed building to the private street, of carrying out street works to such an extent that the street would be adopted by the highway authority (the advance payments code – section 219, Highways Act 1980). 'Street works' means sewering, levelling, paving, metalling, flagging, channelling, making good, and lighting. The standards required are not specified in the legislation, but clearly they must not be unreasonably stringent.

In general, the standard prevailing for similar streets in the authority's district is required.

Section 38 of Highways Act 1980

4.04 However, the necessity to pay or give security in advance of the building work being started can be avoided if an agreement has been entered into with the local authority under section 38 of the Highways Act 1980, pursuant to an exception from the general principle contained in section 219(4)(d) of the Act.

4.05 Under section 38, the local authority may enter into an agreement with the developer of land on either side or both sides of a private street; the authority can agree to adopt the street as a highway maintainable at public expense when all the street works have been carried out to their satisfaction, and the developer agrees to carry them out within a stated time. If the works are not so carried out, the local authority can still use their statutory powers to carry out the works (or to complete them), at the expense of the frontagers; it is therefore customary for the developer to enter into a bond for his performance with a bank or an insurance company.

4.06 Such an agreement takes the street, or the part of the street to which the agreement relates, outside the operation of the above general principle. The developer can then sell building plots or completed houses 'free of road charges' to purchasers. Though the street may not have been made up at the time of purchase, the purchaser is protected, as the developer has agreed to make up the street; if he fails to carry out his promise, the local authority will be able to sue on the bond and recover sufficient to pay for street works expenses without having to charge them to the frontagers. If the authority should proceed against the frontagers, they in turn normally have a remedy against the developer and on the bond, but this may depend on the terms of their purchase.

4.07 The architect is not necessarily professionally concerned in such matters, but it is suggested that it is his duty to be aware of the potential expense to his client of building in an unmade private street, and he should advise his client to consult his solicitor in any difficult case, or where the exact legal position is not clear.

5 Grants

5.01 Below are considered circumstances in which a building owner is able to obtain a grant from the local authority (in this case, the district council) for some alteration or extension of his dwelling. All statutory provisions considered here concern dwelling-houses (or flats and so on), but it may be possible in development areas and enterprise zones (Local Government, Planning and Land Act 1980) to obtain grants for industrial development.

5.02 Up until July 2003 grants were available pursuant to the Housing Grants, Construction and Regeneration Act 1996. From 18 July 2003 that Act was repealed and replaced by the Regulatory Reform (Housing Assistance) (England and Wales) Order 2002. The Government has published a guidance document entitled Housing Renewal Guidance (Consultative Document) 2002 which should be read by all architects when seeking to obtain grant money on behalf of their clients in connection with alteration or extension of dwellings.

Under the Order, for the purpose of improving living conditions in their area, local authorities may provide direct or indirect assistance to a person for the purposes of enabling him:

(a) to acquire living accommodation;
(b) to adapt or improve living accommodation;
(c) to repair living accommodation;
(d) to demolish buildings comprising or including living accommodation;
(e) where buildings comprising or including living accommodation have been demolished, and to construct buildings that comprise or include replacement living accommodation.

Assistance may be provided in any form and may be subject to conditions, including as to repayment or making a contribution towards the assisted work. Examples of possible conditions, e.g. as to eligibility and payment are given in the guidance. Before imposing a condition as to repayment or contribution the authority must have regard to the ability of the person to make the repayment or contribution. The primary methods of assistance, will be grants or loans, although other form of assistance, e.g. discounted materials, access to a tool hire scheme may also be provided.

A mandatory grant remains available for the provision of facilities for a disabled person in a dwelling. Applicants must be 18 years old and are means tested. There is a maximum level of grant. For further information, see the terms of the above Order.

Agriculture

5.03 Under the Hill Farming and Livestock Rearing Acts 1946 and 1959, a grant may be obtained from the Minister of Agriculture, Fisheries and Food towards the cost of improving a dwelling as part of a scheme prepared with 'a view to the rehabilitation of livestock rearing land'.

Conversion of closets

5.04 A grant not exceeding half the cost may be claimed towards the expenditure incurred by the owners of a dwelling in converting an earth or pail closet to a WC, either pursuant to a notice served by the authority, or where it is proposed to undertake the work voluntarily. In the latter case the grant is payable at the local authority's discretion (section 66, Building Act 1984).

Clean air

5.05 Where a private dwelling (an expression which includes part of a house) is situated within a smoke control area, a grant may be claimed from the local authority amounting to 70% of the expenditure reasonably incurred in adapting any fireplace or fireplaces in the dwelling to enable them to burn only 'authorized fuels' such as gas, electricity, coke, or specially prepared solid fuels (Clean Air Act 1993, section 25 and Schedule 2). A similar grant may be obtainable for certain religious buildings (section 26).

Historic buildings

5.06 In the case of a building of historic or architectural interest, whether or not it is 'listed' as such (under section 1 of the Planning (Listed Buildings and Conservation Areas) Act 1990), a grant towards the cost of repair or maintenance may be obtained from the local authority under section 57 of the 1990 Act, but such grants are entirely discretionary and no amounts are specified in the legislation. Grants and loans are also available from English Heritage for the maintenance and repair of buildings of outstanding historical or architectural interest. The power to make such payments is found in section 3A of the Historic Buildings and Ancient Monuments Act 1953. Normally, the Commission only make payments for the maintenance and repair (excluding routine work) of outstanding Grade I or II buildings. The Commission do not normally make payments towards repair schemes costing less than £10 000. Where grants are given they are generally at the rate of 40% of approved expenditure. A similar scheme is administered in Wales by the Secretary of State for the Principality.

Airport noise

5.07 Under the Civil Aviation Act 1982, section 79, a grant may be obtained from the manager of the aerodrome (a subsidiary company of BAA plc) for a building 'near' an aerodrome towards the cost of insulating it, or any part of it, against noise attributable to the use of the aerodrome. The details of such grants are specified in schemes approved by the Secretary of State for Transport, and further particulars are obtainable from the Secretary of State or BAA plc (130 Wilton Road, London SW1V 1LQ).

Water supply

5.08 The local authority has a discretionary power to make a grant towards all or any part of the expenses incurred in the provision of a separate service pipe for the supply of water for any house which has a piped supply from a main, but which does not have a separate service pipe (section 523, Housing Act 1985).

6 Housing associations and societies

6.01 A housing association may be formed on a charitable basis for provision of houses for those in need, or for special groups of persons, such as elderly or handicapped, in a specified area. Such an association may also be constituted by an industrial firm for housing its employees, or by a group of persons proposing to build its own homes by voluntary (or part voluntary) and co-operative labour. Frequently such associations are strictly housing societies having acquired corporate personality by registration with the Registrar of Friendly Societies. However, a housing association (which may be incorporated as a company under the Companies Acts, or by other means) which complies with the provisions of the Housing Acts (see definition in section 1 of the Housing Associations Act 1985) and, in particular, does not trade for profit, is entitled to be considered for certain benefits under the Housing Acts. Tenants of a housing association who have occupied their homes for at least five years will have a right to purchase the dwelling under Part V of the Housing Act 1985.

Benefits

6.02 First, the association may be able to obtain 'assistance' from the local housing authority in whose area they propose to build. This may mean making arrangements so that the association can improve existing council-owned houses, or acquisition of land by the local authority, which can then be sold or leased to the association for building houses; or, with the consent of the Secretary of State for the Environment, the authority may make grants or loans on mortgage (at favourable rates of interest – usually 0.25% above the ruling rate charged to local authorities by the Public Works Loan Board) to the association to enable them to build houses. They may be able to obtain a grant from the Housing Corporation (or in Wales a separate organization called Housing for Wales, Part II of the Housing Act 1988) towards the expenses of forming and running the association (section 50, Housing Act 1988). Registered housing associations may also be able to obtain grants from the Secretary of State where the associations' activities have incurred a liability for income or corporation tax (section 54, Housing Act 1988).

Housing Corporation loans

6.03 These provisions depend on the goodwill of the local authority; a housing association cannot insist on being given assistance. As an alternative, an association may be able to get help by ways of loans for obtaining land and general advice from the Housing Corporation, a public body set up under the Housing Act 1964.

Setting up a housing association

6.04 In practice people proposing to form a housing society would be well advised to obtain advice from the Housing Corporation (Maple House, 149 Tottenham Court Rd, London W1P 0BN), and those proposing to set up an association should get in touch with the National Federation of Housing Associations (175 Gray's Inn Road, London WC1X 8UP).

7 Special premises

7.01 If an architect is designing any kind of building, he must take into account the controls exercised under town and country planning legislation (Chapter 23) and under the Building Regulations (Chapter 21); and he must consider the question of sewerage and mains services and the other matters discussed in this chapter. But if his building is of a specialized kind, or is to be used for some specialized purpose, additional controls may have to be considered; the more usual types of special control are outlined below.

Factories

7.02 The Factories Act 1961 imposes an *a posteriori* control over certain constructional matters in a factory (as defined in Factories Act 1961, section 175); there is no special control over plans (other than normal controls of the planning legislation and the Building Regulations), but if the requirements of the Act are not met in a particular factory, the occupier or (in a tenement factory) the owner will be liable to be prosecuted for an offence. Many of these requirements relate to the use and fencing of machinery, keeping walls and floors clean, and so on, and as such they are not of direct concern to the architect.

7.03 A fire certificate will have to be obtained if more than 20 persons are employed or more than 10 persons are employed above (or below) the ground floor (Fire Precautions (Factories, Offices, Shops and Railway Premises) Order 1989, SI 1989/76). If a certificate is not required, certain less stringent fire precautions must be observed, including a general duty to provide adequate means of escape in cases of fire (section 9A of the Fire Precautions Act 1971).

7.04 The effluent from a factory's sewers or drains may well be 'trade effluent' and will then be subject to the special control of the Water Industry Act 1991, Chapter III.

7.05 Under the Clean Air Act 1993 factories are subject to several constructional controls operating quite independently of the Building Regulations, but administered by the same local authorities (district councils). Thus any furnace installed in a building which will be used to burn pulverized fuel, or to burn any other solid matter at a rate of 45.4 kg per hour or more, or any liquid or gaseous matter at a rate of 366.4 kW or more, must be provided with plant for arresting emissions of grit and dust which has been approved by the local authority or has been installed with plans and specifications submitted to and approved by the local authority (section 6, Clean Air Act 1993).

7.06 Limits are set by regulations for the rates of emission of grit and dust, and there are certain exemptions from the provisions of section 5 (see the Clean Air (Emissions of Grit and Dust from Furnaces) Regulations 1971). In addition, a furnace of a type to which the section applies (section 14, see 1993 Act), may not be used in a building unless the height of the chimney serving the furnace has been approved by the local authority (section 15, 1993 Act).

Public houses and restaurants

7.07 A public house or other premises used for the sale of intoxicating liquor either on or off the premises must be licensed by the local magistrates under the Licensing Act 1953. A new 'onlicence' may not be granted unless the premises are in the opinion of the magistrates 'structurally' adapted to the class of licence required (section 4(2), Licensing Act 1964). The magistrates themselves are the final judges of what is or is not structurally adapted. In the case of a licence for a restaurant or guest house or the like, an application may be refused by the magistrates on the grounds that the premises are not 'suitable or convenient' for the use contemplated (section 98). A restaurant licence may be granted only for premises structurally adapted and bona fide used or intended to be used for the provision of 'the customary main meal for the accommodation of persons frequenting the premises' (section 94). Other alterations to licensed premises, e.g. where there will be increased facilities for drinking, must be the subject of a formal consent obtained from the magistrates (section 20).

7.08 These controls are operated at the discretion of the magistrates. In practice they will normally not approve an application until they have received a report on the premises (or the proposed premises) from suitably qualified persons, such as an officer of the local fire brigade, an environmental health officer, and often a senior police officer. But such requirements are at their discretion, and details vary among different benches.

7.09 Under section 20 of the Local Government (Miscellaneous Provisions) Act 1976, as amended by section 4 of the Disabled

Persons Act 1981, the local authority may by notice require the owner or occupier of any premises used for public entertainment or exhibitions or as a betting office to provide and maintain in suitable positions a specified reasonable number of sanitary appliances for the use of persons frequenting the premises. When complying with such a notice, provision must be made, as far as is practicable and reasonable in the circumstances, for the needs of disabled people (section 6, Chronically Sick and Disabled Persons Act 1970). If a 'refreshment house' is to be kept open late at night, a special licence will be required from the district council under the Refreshment Houses Acts 1860 to 1967.

7.10 The Licensing Act 2003 has radically overhauled the licensing laws. It is not expected to come into effect until 2005. Under the Act an application for a licence for the sale of retail by alcohol, supply of alcohol by a club, the provision of regulated entertainment (such as music and dancing), or a late night refreshment venue must be made to the local authority within which the premises are located. Each council is required under the Act to produce a statement of licensing policy. An appeal lies against an adverse decision of the licensing authority to the Magistrate's Court. For more information please refer to the provisions of the Act.

Hotels

7.11 A fire certificate under the Fire Precautions Act 1971 is required for hotels. An application for a certificate must be made to the fire authority in respect of any new or existing hotel, and this application must be made on the prescribed form (copies of which will be obtainable from the fire authority, i.e. the county council). The authority may ask for plans of the building in support of the application, and they will carry out an inspection. They may then require steps to be taken as to the provision and availability of means of escape in case of fire and as to the means for fighting fire and giving warning in case of fire. If and when they are satisfied as to these matters, a fire certificate will be issued, which may itself impose requirements as to these and related matters. A right of appeal to the local magistrates lies against requirements so imposed by the fire authority.

7.12 It is a criminal offence under the Act to put premises to a 'designated use' (this includes a hotel) unless there is a valid fire certificate in force or an application is pending, and it is similarly an offence to fail to comply with any requirement imposed by a certificate. Hotels will, of course, also have to comply with the legal provisions about intoxicating liquor (paragraph 7.07), and possibly in relation to music and dancing (paragraph 7.10).

Petroleum

7.13 Any premises used for keeping petroleum spirit must be licensed by the county council; otherwise the occupier is guilty of an offence (section 1, Petroleum Consolidation Act 1928). The only exception is when the spirit is kept in separate vessels containing not more than 1 pint (0.57 litre), with the total quantity not exceeding 3 gallons (13.64 litres). Detailed conditions are usually imposed when such a licence is granted, and these normally follow the model conditions recommended by the Home Office. Petroleum licences are usually renewable each year at a fee (section 2).

Theatres and cinemas

7.14 Theatres are subject to control under the Theatres Act 1968. No premises may be used for the public performance of a play except in accordance with the terms of a licence granted by the local authority and in granting such a licence, conditions may be imposed as to structure, exits, safety curtains, and so on, but not so as to impose any censorship on the plays given in the theatre. (Theatres Act 1968, section 12 and Schedule 1. The local authorities responsible for administering these provisions are the county councils and in London the city/borough councils (see section 18).)

7.15 Similarly, showing cinematograph films at an exhibition of moving pictures (section 21, Cinemas Act 1985) must be licensed by the local authority, and structural matters will normally be provided for in the licence (section 1, Cinemas Act 1985). The local authority is the district council.

Shops and offices

7.16 Shops, offices, and railway premises where persons other than close relatives of the employer are employed to work are subject to control by the district council, under the Offices, Shops and Railway Premises Act 1963, provided the time worked at the premises exceeds 21 hours a week (sections 1–3). This Act provides for such matters as cleanliness, temperature within rooms, ventilation, lighting, and the provision of WCs (if necessary for both sexes), washing accommodation, and so on. The standards specified are detailed, and the Act and regulations made thereunder should be referred to by architects designing such a building. See the Workplace (Health, Safety and Welfare) Regulations 1992, SI 1992/3004. A fire certificate or special fire precautions are required for shops, offices, railway premises, and factories (paragraph 6.03).

Food premises

7.17 In addition, if any part of the premises is used for a business involving food, the more stringent provisions of the Food Safety (General Food Hygiene) Regulations 1995, SI 1995/1763 made under the Food Safety Act 1990 must be observed. Premises used as a slaughterhouse or a knacker's yard for the slaughter of animals need to be licensed under the Slaughterhouses Act 1974.

Miscellaneous

7.18 Licences from the district council are also required for the storage or manufacture of rag flock (Rag Flock and Other Filling Materials Act 1951), for the use of premises as a shop for the sale of pet animals (Pet Animals Act 1951), for storage or sale of scrap metal (Scrap Metal Dealers Act 1964), for boarding cats and dogs (Animal Boarding Establishments Act 1963) or for guard dog kennels (Guard Dogs Act 1975), and for keeping a riding establishment (Riding Establishment Acts 1964 and 1970). Nursing homes must now be registered by the Secretary of State (Registered Homes Act 1984, Part II). In all these cases the suitability or otherwise of the premises for the particular purpose may be an issue in the grant or refusal of the licence.

7.19 Caravan sites used for human habitation also need a licence in addition to planning permission (Caravan Sites and Control of Development Act 1960, Part 1), and detailed conditions as to hygiene and sanitary requirements are customarily imposed. In many districts it will also be necessary to obtain a licence from the council if premises are to be used as a sex shop or for the practice of tattooing or acupuncture or electrolysis or ear-piercing (Local Government (Miscellaneous Provisions) Act 1982). Closing orders may be made restricting the hours for the opening of take-away food shops and late night refreshment houses (sections 4 and 7, 1982 Act).

20

Statutory authorities in Scotland

ANGUS STEWART QC

1 Introduction: government in Scotland

1.01 The Scotland Act 1998 devolves many central government functions to the Scottish Executive. Law-making for these functions is devolved to the Scottish Parliament. Regulation of the architectural profession is reserved to Westminster. Devolved matters relevant to architectural practice in Scotland include:

Local government
Housing
Land-use, planning and building control
Inland waterways
Liquor licensing
Environmental protection
Built heritage
Natural heritage
Road transport

The substantive law in devolved areas continues as before until altered by the Scottish Parliament. Functions previously exercised by the Secretary of State for Scotland in relation to matters now devolved, for example in relation to planning, are exercised by the Scottish Ministers.

Local authorities

1.02 The Local Government etc. (Scotland) Act 1994 created 32 single-tier, all-purpose, local government authorities in Scotland. Rockall is part of the Western Isles authority area. In general the new authorities inherit and exercise for their area all functions previously confided to regional, district and islands councils. Sewerage and water, however, have been reorganized and removed from local authority control (without, as yet, being privatized). At the same time as the 1994 Act abolished the strategically sized regional councils, it recognized in a variety of ways the need for inter-local authority cooperation: structure plans may extend to the district of more than one local authority; local authorities have power to make cooperative arrangements for education; there are only eight police authorities, six of which are joint boards comprising up to twelve local authorities; there are, similarly, eight fire brigades; there is a Strathclyde Passenger Transport Authority; and the Act generally encourages the formation of joint boards involving two or more councils for the more efficient discharge of other functions. Representative community councils with no statutory functions continue as previously.

1.03 Acts and proceedings of the Scottish Executive, the Scottish Parliament, local authorities, water and sewerage authorities and joint boards and other statutory authorities are subject to judicial review. This means, among other things, that there may be a remedy even where the specific legislation does not provide a right of appeal.

Local government officers and committees

1.04 Local councils are elected every three years. Councils have to choose a convener and may also choose a deputy convener. Councils appoint officials and staff to enable them to carry out their statutory functions. A chief social work officer and certain other officials have to be appointed. Otherwise councils have wide discretion in the matter of their internal organization. The top official, responsible for coordinating the various branches of the authority's activity, tends to be styled 'Chief Executive'. Departmental chiefs may be called 'directors', 'managers', 'heads', etc. From the architect's point of view the key officials will be in the departments, which go by many different names, responsible for planning and building control. Certain officials, such as the assessor/council tax registration officer and electoral registration officer, have specific statutory duties which they must perform regardless of any instructions from the authority.

1.05 Much of the work of local councils is delegated to committees. There is likely to be a committee for each service department, such as development, education or housing, with sub-committees for each departmental section. Policy may be left to the appropriate service committee in the area of its responsibility. In addition to standing committees such as these, the authority may also set up special committees from time to time to deal with particular problems as they arise.

1.06 In general, committees are composed of council members only. Employed officials are present at committee meetings to give advice when required, but without the right to vote.

Lawyers going the Circuit

Scottish Water

1.07 The Water Industry (Scotland) Act 2002 provides for the establishment of a nationwide authority Scottish Water as successor to the three regional authorities which previously exercised water and sewerage functions under the 1994 Act. The property and functions of the existing authorities have now transferred to Scottish Water.

National Parks

1.08 Special considerations may apply to development within national parks designated in terms of orders made under the National Parks (Scotland) Act 2000. Various regulatory functions, including planning functions, may be devolved upon or transferred to national parks' authorities. Two national parks have been designated: Loch Lomond & the Trossachs and Grampians.

2 Connection to services

2.01 The 2002 Act is primarily concerned with organization and does not re-enact or spell out in detail the powers and functions which have been transferred from the old to the new authorities. The main local authority functions for present purposes are to be found in the Building (Scotland) Acts, the Sewerage (Scotland) Act 1968, the Town and Country Planning (Scotland) Acts, the Water (Scotland) Act 1980, the Civic Government (Scotland) Act 1982 and the Roads (Scotland) Act 1984. Under the Act of 1982 the Sheriff can authorize connections to services through other parts of a building in multiple ownership. The Water Environment and Water Services (Scotland) Act 2003 amends the 1968 and 1980 Acts to qualify the authority's duties to make provision by reference to ministerial directions as to 'reasonable cost' in specific cases. The Act changes the system for funding new connections and adds sustainable urban drainage (SUD) systems to Scottish Water's core functions as provider of sewerage services.

Sewers

2.02 The Sewerage (Scotland) Act 1968 as amended by the Local Government etc. (Scotland) Act 1994 and now by the 2000 and 2003 Acts details the powers and functions of sewerage authorities. The 1968 Act consolidated and simplified all previous legislation and introduced a statutory definition of 'drains' and 'sewers': drains are pipes within the curtilage of premises used for draining buildings and yards within the same curtilage; sewers are all pipes, except drains as defined, used for draining buildings and yards.

2.03 Public sewers are vested in sewerage authorities, as are various new sewers. Junctions to public sewers are also vested in sewerage authorities. If a private drain is connected to a public sewer, it is the sewerage authority's responsibility to maintain the junction. The 1994 Act makes new provision for the construction and maintenance of private sewers not connecting to the public system.

2.04 Sewerage authorities are obliged to provide public sewers as may be necessary for draining their area of domestic sewage, surface water and trade effluent. The authority has to take public sewers to such point as will enable owners of premises to connect their drains at reasonable cost. This is subject to the important proviso that the authority need itself do nothing which is not practicable at a reasonable cost. Nevertheless, the responsibility for providing sewers is clearly that of the sewerage authority, while the responsibility for installing drains in indvidual premises is that of the proprietor.

2.05 Sewerage authorities have powers to construct, close or alter sewers or sewage treatment works. Where they are not under an obligation to provide public sewers (i.e. where it is not practicable for them to do so at reasonable cost), they may enter into an agreement on construction and taking over of sewers and treatment works with any person they are satisfied is about to construct premises in their area. Where sewerage authorities come under the obligation to provide sewers, they may not enter into such agreements. The 1994 Act introduces more flexible arrangements for the construction of private sewers (including sewers to be connected to the public system) and gives sewerage authorities power, subject to the same safeguards which apply in relation to construction of public sewers, to authorize construction of private sewers on third parties' property. The 1994 Act also makes it easier to get the sewerage authority to empty a septic tank, with a right of appeal to the Sheriff in the event of refusal.

2.06 Where a new development is proposed with appropriate permissions the responsibility for providing sewers rests with the sewerage authority, although this does not apply in the case of an individual house where all that is necessary is a drain or private sewer to connect with the public system. The situation may arise where a delay by the authority holds up development. If a developer chooses to install sewers at his own expense, he will be able to recover from the authority only if, from the start, he adopts the correct procedure (*Lawrence Building Co. v Lanarkshire County Council* [1978] SC 30). In terms of amendments introduced by the Water Environment and Water Services (Scotland) Act 2003 Part 2, the vesting of private sewers, SUD systems and treatment works is dependent on compliance with such standards as may be laid down by statutory regulations.

Drains

2.07 Any owner of premises is entitled to connect his drains or private sewer to a public sewer and to allow his drains to empty into a public sewer on giving the sewerage authority 28 days' notice. However, the authority may refuse permission or grant it subject to conditions. A proprietor may connect his drains to a sewer in a different sewerage area, but he must first serve notice on both authorities. The Minister has powers to require the authority in whose area the premises are situated to pay for the service which the other authority is providing.

2.08 Where a notice regarding connection of a drain or sewer to a public sewer is served on a sewerage authority, the authority has powers to direct the manner in which the junction is to be constructed and to supervise construction. The authority has the same powers in relation to any new drain or private sewer if it appears likely that the drain or sewer will be wanted by it to form part of the public system. Authorities are bound to meet the extra cost arising from implementation of their instructions. To allow supervision, three days' notice of the start of work must be given to the authority.

2.09 A sewerage authority can also require defects in private drains and sewers to be remedied and may itself carry out the work if the proprietor fails to do so. Where the defect represents a health hazard, the authority is empowered to carry out emergency repairs on 48-hour notice. The cost of repairs carried out by the authority can be reovered from proprietors.

2.10 Sewage discharged into a public sewer must not be of such a nature as to cause damage to the sewer or, through mixture with other sewage, to cause a nuisance.

Trade effluent

2.11 The discharge of trade effluent into public sewers and other disposal and treatment of trade effluent is regulated by Part II of the 1968 Act as amended. New discharges can be made only with the consent of the sewerage authority. Application for consent is made by serving a trade effluent notice on the authority which must specify the nature of the effluent, the maximum daily quantity and the maximum hourly rate of discharge. The application has to be determined within three months. Consent may be granted subject to conditions. There is a right to appeal to the Minister. Sewerage authorities have power to treat and dispose of trade effluent by agreement with the occupiers of trade premises.

Scottish Environment Protection Agency (SEPA)

2.12 The Scottish Environment Protection Agency (SEPA) constituted by the Environment Act 1995 has assumed the functions of the River Purification Boards, HM Industrial Pollution Inspectorate and the waste and air pollution powers of local councils. SEPA has functions in relation to approving discharges of sewage and other effluent, the provision of septic tanks, etc. The Environment and Water Services (Scotland) Act 2003 implements the Community framework directive for action in the field of water policy 2000/60/EC. The Act sets out the duties of the Scottish Ministers and SEPA in relation to protection of the water environment.

Water supply

2.13 Substantive legislation on water supply is consolidated in the Water (Scotland) Act 1980 as amended by the Local Government etc. (Scotland) Act 1994 and now by the 2000 and 2003 Acts. In terms of the 1980 Act persons erecting new buildings of any type are obliged to make adequate provison to the satisfaction of the water authority for a supply of clean water for the domestic purposes of persons occupying or using the building. Water authorities may also require house owners to provide water supplies in, or if that be impracticable, immediately outside their houses.

2.14 Water authorities are under an obligation to provide supplies of wholesome water to every part of their areas where a supply is required for domestic purposes and can be provided at reasonable cost. They are obliged to lay main water pipes so that buildings where domestic supplies are required can be connected at a reasonable cost. When a question arises as to whether water can be supplied in this manner to any area at a reasonable cost, the Scottish Executive must decide, if requested to do so by ten or more local electors.

2.15 In terms of amendments introduced by the Water Environment and Water Services (Scotland) Act 2003 Part 2, the duty to lay supply pipes does not apply where there is an agreement with a third party to lay pipes; and third parties may be authorized by Scottish Water to lay mains and communication pipes under roads and on any land to connect to public mains. As a rule vesting takes place when a third party system connects with a public main but Scottish Water may determine that there shall be no vesting and that the duty of maintenance remains with the third party. Compliance with such standards as may be laid down by statutory regulations is a prerequisite of vesting. Vesting may be subject to conditions about costs on either side. Advance agreement is recommended.

2.16 Water authorities are also obliged to supply water on reasonable terms for non-domestic purposes, provided that to do so would not prejudice their ability to supply water for domestic purposes.

2.17 The procedure for obtaining a water supply for domestic purposes is regulated by the third schedule to the Water (Scotland) Act 1980 as amended. Broadly, the supply pipe is laid by the customer and then attached to the communication pipe by the water authority. The customer has to give 14 days' notice to the water authority and has to meet the expense of laying the supply pipe and obtain the appropriate consents but must not break open the street. The authority has to lay the communication pipe and connect it with the supply pipe and must also lay any part of the supply pipe which has to be laid in a street. The latter cost is recoverable from the customer.

2.18 The water authority may require a separate service pipe for each house supplied by them with water. The authority may serve notice on exisiting customers requiring provision of a separate service pipe. If the customer fails to comply the authority may execute the work and recover the cost.

Gas, electricity and telephones

2.19 On these topics reference should be made to Chapter 19, paragraph 3.28 to 3.32 as what is said there applies also in Scotland. The Gas Act 1986 applies with minor modifications in Scotland as in England. Likewise the Electricity Act 1989 applies with small modifications. Storage of liquid and gaseous fuel in tanks, cylinders for domestic use, etc. is regulated by the Scottish Building Regulations.

Construction of mains

2.20 Again the remarks on this topic in Chapter 19 (paragraphs 3.33 to 3.34) should be referred to. The authority for water and-sewerage authorities to lay mains is contained in the Water (Scotland) Act 1980 as amended.

3 Private streets and footpaths

3.01 The law on roads, streets and footpaths is consolidated in the Roads (Scotland) Act 1984 as amended by the Local Government etc. (Scotland) Act 1994, etc.

3.02 The 1984 Act defines roads as ways over which there is a public right of passage by any means, i.e. roads includes footpaths subject to a public right of passage. Public roads are roads entered by local councils in their 'list of public roads' and are roads which those authorities are bound to maintain. Private roads are roads which the authorities are not bound to maintain. The authorities can require frontagers to make up and maintain a private road. When a road has been properly made up, the council is bound to take it over and add it to the list of public roads if application is made by the requisite number of frontagers.

Footpaths

3.03 The above provisions apply to footpaths as well as vehicular routes. The authorities are also empowered to take over footpaths in new developments.

4 Grants

4.01 Local councils have power in terms Part XIII of the Housing (Scotland) Act 1987, as amended, to make payment of grants for improvement and repair of dwelling houses. Improvement grants are mandatory for provision of 'standard amenities'. Standard amenities include a water supply for washing and cooking, facilities for washing and bathing and a WC. The amenities must be for the exclusive use of the occupants of a dwelling house. Discretionary improvement grants are available for alteration and enlargement of dwellings and to make dwellings suitable for disabled occupation. The Housing (Scotland) Act 2001 amends the 1987 Act and extends eligibility for improvement grants to works including the provision of heating systems and insulation, replacement of unsafe electrical wiring, installation of mains powered smoke detectors and (in tenement properties) phone entry systems and fire-retardant entry doors for each house. The maximum approved expense for grant is £20,000.

Works such as lead piping replacement and installation of smoke alarms for the deaf may attract grant aid under this head. Repair grants are mandatory for dwelling houses within Housing Action Areas and where repairs notices have been served. Discretionary repair grants are subject to property value limits and needs assessments. Generally grant conditions have to be recorded or registered in the title or land registers.

4.02 In terms of section 233 of the 1987 Act assistance may be available to install separate service pipes to houses sharing the same water supply. Thermal insulation grants for roof space insulation, draught-proofing and insulation of water tanks and cylinders previously available from local councils in terms of Part XIII of the Housing (Scotland) Act 1987 are now administered by the Energy Action Grants Agency (EAGA) Scotland in terms of the Social Security Act 1990, section 15 and regulations made thereunder. From July 1999 grant aid in Scotland extends to wall insulation and heating systems controls. Comprehensive energy advice is available from the network of Energy Efficiency Advice Centres. Grants for means of escape from fire from houses in multiple occupation may be available in terms of section 249 of the 1987 Act. Environmental improvement grants for communal spaces are payable under section 251 of the 1987 Act as amended.

4.03 Various grants are available for improvement or rebuilding of agricultural workers' cottages. It is not proposed to examine these in detail. It should also be noted that special grants may be available in the Highlands, the Islands and in crofting areas for the erection, improvement or re-building of dwelling houses and other buildings under the Crofting Acts and regulations from 1955 onwards. Improvement and repair grants made in respect of croft houses are subject to special conditions in terms of section 256 of the Housing (Scotland) Act 1987.

4.04 Other grants are payable by various authorities. The Clean Air Acts and the Airport Authority Act apply in Scotland, and grants may be obtained where appropriate (Chapter 19, paragraphs 5.19 and 5.21).

5 Housing associations

5.01 The Scottish housing association scene was dominated from 1988 to 2001 by Scottish Homes, a body constituted by the Housing (Scotland) Act 1988. Under the Housing (Scotland) Act 2001 the functions of Scottish Homes have been transferred to the Scottish Ministers and the stock has either been transferred to local associations or to Scottish Ministers. Transferred functions include the duty to maintain a register of housing associations, promoting the formation of associations and exercising supervision and control over registered associatins. Housing associations with registered offices in England are subject to regulation under English law.

5.02 Housing associations as defined by the Housing Act 1985 as amended and satisfying the criteria for registration established from time to time may register. Registration brings associations under the supervision and control of the Scottish Ministers and confers the benefit of eligibility for the capital grants.

5.03 By virtue of sections 59 and 60 of the Housing Act 1988 as amended, local councils, with ministerial consent, are empowered to promote the formation and extension of housing associations and to give them assistance.

6 Special considerations

6.01 Special controls and regulatory regimes apply to a variety of premises, sites and structures. Some examples may be given.

Premises licensed for sale and consumption of alcohol

6.02 In terms of the Licensing (Scotland) Act 1976 as amended by the Local Government etc. (Scotland) Act 1994 liquor licensing is the function of licensing boards constituted by local councils. The suitability of premises is explicitly a matter for licensing boards in a number of important respects. Licenses may be refused on grounds related to the suitability of the premises, their location, character and condition. No reconstruction, extension or alteration of licensed premises which affects the public is permitted without licensing board approval. On any application for renewal the licensing board may require structural alterations to be made. Where a new licence is applied for, statutory certificates in relation to planning, building control and food hygiene must be presented. The board is also bound to consult with the fire authority.

Other licensed premises

6.03 In terms of the Betting, Gaming and Lotteries Act 1963, only premises licensed for that purpose may be used as betting offices.

In terms of the Gaming Act 1968 as amended, the licensing board may refuse a licence on the ground that the premises are unsuitable by reason of their lay-out, character, condition or location. Premises used for gaming, including bingo, have to be licensed. There is regulation of premises where gaming machines are placed by licensing and registration. In terms of the Theatres Act 1968 as amended, no premises may be used for the public performance of plays unless licensed by the local council. In terms of the Cinemas Act 1985 as amended, no premises may be used for showing films unless licensed by the local council. The Cinematograph (Safety) (Scotland) Regulations 1955 make detailed provision for the design and construction of cinemas. Premises may be licensed by local councils for public entertainment, indoor sports entertainment and late hours catering in terms of the Civic Government (Scotland) Act 1982 as amended. There is a licensing scheme for sex shops in terms of section 45 and Schedule 2 of the 1982 Act.

Sports grounds

6.04 Following the tragedy at Glasgow Rangers' Ibrox stadium in 1971 in which 66 people were killed and 140 were injured, the Safety of Sports Grounds Act 1975 was enacted. Local councils are responsible for issuing safety certificates for large sports stadia designated by the Minister in terms of the Act. The Fire Safety and Safety of Places of Sport Act 1987 extended regulation to all stands with covered accommodation for more than 500 spectators.

Nursing homes and residential establishments

6.05 Nursing homes have to be registered with the area health board in terms of the Nursing Homes Registration (Scotland) Act 1938 as amended. The board may refuse registration for reasons connected with situation, construction, state of repair of the premises, etc. Part IV of the Social Work (Scotland) Act 1968 as amended makes provision for registration of a variety of residential establishments including residential homes for the elderly and independent schools. The local council is the responsible authority. The council may refuse registration for reasons connected with situation, construction, state of repair of the premises, etc.

Workplaces

6.06 Health and safety legislation raises many design issues in relation to workplaces of all kinds. The traditional regime has been substantially replaced by regulation under the Health and Safety at Work Act 1974, much of it Europe-inspired and of wider application. A theme of the new regime is the emphasis on risk assessment. Having regard to the terms of the Workplace (Health, Safety and Welfare) Regulations 1992, although there is no duty laid directly on the designer, consideration should to be given to such things as ventilation, temperature, lighting, room dimensions, layout of workstations, design and materials of all surfaces, floors, window and doors, provision of washing and sanitary facilities. Where appropriate there has to be accommodation for storing clothing and changing. There have to be rest facilities for pregnant women and nursing mothers. Sections 42 and 43 of the Offices, Shops and Railways Premises Act 1963 continue in force in relation to the suitability of common parts of buildings in multiple occupation.

6.07 Particular health and safety regulations raise design issues in relation to particular kinds of premises, substances, operations or equipment. For example, the Manual Handling Operations Regulations 1992 direct attention to risk factors arising from the working environment; and the Health and Safety (Display Screen Equipment) Regulations 1992 set out minimum qualitative requirements for work stations in relation to space, lighting, reflections and glare, etc. The Health and Safety Commission should be able to advise of applicable regulations.

Building sites

6.08 Architects and engineers have to be aware of the raft of regulations designed to procure health and safety in relation to building and engineering sites and operations. Involvement in the design of permanent, temporary and protective works, the scheduling of works, the organization of working practices, etc. involves the potential for causing accidents and for liability, direct and indirect. Reference should be made to Chapter 28.

Fire precautions

6.09 All premises except private dwellings are, unless specifically exempted, subject to a process of fire certification by the local fire service in terms of the Fire Precautions Act 1971 as amended by the Fire Safety and Safety of Places of Sport Act 1987. Where there is excessive risk, use of premises may be prohibited or restricted by an order of the Sheriff made at the instance of the fire service. The Fire Precautions (Workplace) Regulations 1997 make provision for exit routes, emergency doors and signs. See Chapter 22.

Houses in multiple occupation

6.10 Houses let for multiple occupation by more than two unrelated persons have to be licensed by local authorities for compliance with fire, health and safety precautions in terms of the Civic Government (Scotland) Act 1982 and orders made thereunder.

21

Construction legislation in England and Wales

OLIVER PALMER

1 Building Acts and Regulations

1.01 Planning legislation is largely concerned with policy and, in relation to the external appearance of a building, with safeguarding of amenity (Chapter 23). But obtaining planning permission is only the first legal hurdle. The architect is then faced with controls over the construction and design of buildings.

In England and Wales the basic framework of control is found in the Building Act 1984 and in the Regulations made under it. An important feature of the present system of building control is that there are two alternative means of control – one by local authorities operating under the Building Regulations 2000, and the other by a system of private certification which relies on 'approved inspectors' operating under the Building (Approved Inspectors, etc.) Regulations 1985 (as amended).

In practice, most building work will be subject to control by the local authority but there has been an increase in the number of approved inspectors, both individuals and corporate bodies who have been given licence to operate (see paragraph 3.03).

1.02 The Building Act 1984 applies in England and Wales (for Northern Ireland see section 9 of this chapter; for Scotland see Chapter 22). The Building Regulations 2000 (section 2) are made under this Act which also contains provisions linked to the deposit of plans for building regulations purposes and provisions relating to existing buildings. Some sections of the Act have not been brought into force and others repealed (Checklist 21.1) or amended (Checklist 21.2).

There may also be additional provisions in local Acts and the local authority must say, if asked, whether a local Act applies in its area.

Checklist 21.1: The Building Act 1984

Provisions not yet in force

Section	Content
	Part I
	Type approval of building matter
12	Power of Secretary of State to approve type of building matter
13	Delegation of power to approve
	Passing of plans
(section 18 was repealed by the *Building (Amendment) Regulations 2001*)	
20	Use of materials unsuitable for permanent building
(sections 26–29 were repealed by the Building Regulations 1985)	
(section 30 was repealed by the Building Act 1984 (Appointed Day and Repeal Order) 1985)	
	Proposed departure from plans
31	Proposed departure from plans
	Tests for conformity with Building Regulations
33	Tests for conformity with building regulations
	Breach of Building Regulations
38	Civil liability
	Appeals in certain cases
42	Appeal and statement of case to High Court in certain cases
43	Procedure on appeal to Secretary of State on certain matters
	Application of Building Regulations to Crown, etc.
44	Application to Crown
45	Application to United Kingdom Atomic Energy Authority

Checklist 21.2: Amendments to the Building Act and the principal regulations 2000 (SI 2000 No. 2531)

The Building (Amendment) Regulations 2001 (SI 2001 No. 3335) coming into force: 1 April 2002

Regulation	Amendment
Changes to the Building Act	
3(1)	Repeal section 18; in section 21 repeal subsections (1) and (2)
3(2)	In subsection 21(3) substitution
3(3)	In subsection 21(4) substitution
3(4)	In section 59 (drainage of building) omission in subsection (1)(a); after subsection (4) insert new subsection (5) (later renumbered subsection (6))
Changes to the Building Regulations	
2(2)	In regulation 2 (interpretation) substitution
2(3)	In regulation 3(1) (meaning of building work) insertion
2(4)	After regulation 3(1) insert new paragraph 3(1A)
2(5)	In regulation 6 (requirements relating to material change of use) paragraph (1)(a) substitutions and insertions
2(6)	In regulation 8 (limitation on requirements) insertion
2(7)	In regulation 12 (giving a building notice or deposit of plans) after paragraph (4) insert new paragraph (4A)
2(8)	In regulation 13 (particulars and plans where a building notice is given) omit sub-paragraph (2)(c)(ii)
2(9)	In regulation 14 (full plans) after paragraph (3)(a) insert sub-paragraph (aa)
2(10)	After regulation 14 add new regulation 14A (consultation with sewerage undertaker)
2(11)	For regualtion 18 (testing of drains and private sewers) substitute new regulation 18 (testing of building work)
2(12)	For Parts H, J and L of Schedule 1 substitute new Parts
Transitional provisions	
4(1)–(6)	

Checklist 21.2: continued

The Building (Amendment) Regulations 2002 (SI 2002 No. 440) coming into force: 1 April 2002

Regulation	*Amendment*
Changes to the Building Act	
4	In section 59 (drainage of building) subsection (5), inserted by 2001 amendment regulations, renumbered (6)
Changes to the Building Regulations	
2(2)	In regulation 12 (giving a building notice or deposit of plans) substitute new paragraph (5)
2(3)	In regulation 15 (notice of commencement and completion of certain stages of work) in paras (1) to (4) substitution; after paragraph (7) add new paragraph (8)
2(4)	After regulation 16 add new regulation 16A (provisions applicable to replacement windows, rooflights, roof windows and doors)
2(5)	In regulation 20 (supervision of building work other than by local authorities) after '16' insert new '16A'
2(6)	After Schedule 2 insert new Schedule 2A
Transitional provisions	
3	Application of new regulation 16A subject to conditions

The Building (Amendment) (No. 2) Regulations 2002 (SI 2002 No. 2871) coming into force: 1 July 2003 except regulation 2(8) 1 March 2003 and regulation 2(7) (testing in relation to the erection of houses or buildings containing flats) 1 January 2004

Regulation	*Amendment*
Changes to the Building Act	
	None
Changes to the Building Regulations	
2(2)	In regulation 2 (interpretation) insertion in paragraph (2)
2(3)	In regulation 5 (meaning of material change of use) omission in paragraph (f); insert new paragraph (h)
2(4)	In regulation 6 (requirements relating to material change of use) in paragraph (1)(d) omission; after paragraph (1)(e) insert new paragraph (1)(e)
2(5)	For regulation 8 (limitation on requirements) substitute new regulation 8
2(6)	In regulation 20(1) (supervision of building work other than by local authorities) substitution
2(7)	After regulation 20 insert new regulation 20A (sound insulation testing)
2(8)	For Part B of Schedule 1 (fire safety) substitute new Part B (the substitution is limited to some insertions in requirements B1 and B2)
2(9)	For Part E of Schedule 1 (resistance to the passage of sound) substitute new Part E (set out in Schedule 2 in amending regulations)
Transitional provisions	
3(1)–(5) and 4(1) and (2)	

The Building (Amendment) Regulations 2003 (SI 2003 No. 2692) coming into force: 1 May 2004 except regulations 2(1), 2(8) and 3(5) 1 December 2003

Regulation	*Amendment*
Changes to the Building Act	
	None
Changes to The Building Regulations	
2(2)	in regulation 2 (interpretation) insertion in paragraph (1)
2(3)	in regulation 3 (meaning of building work) substitution in paragraph (3)
2(4)	in regulation 5 (meaning of material cange of use) insertion of new paragraph (j)

Checklist 21.2: continued

2(5)	in regulation 6 (requirements relating to material change of use) insertion of new paragraphs (1)(g) and 2(d)
2(6)	in Schedule 1 substitution of new paragraphs (a) and (b) in requirement H3 (rainwater drainage)
2(7)	for Part M substitution of new Part
2(8)	in Schedule 2A omissions in columns 1 and 2
Transitional provisions	
3(1) to (5)	

For the additional provisions in Inner London, where some sections of the *London Building Acts 1939 to 1982* are still in force and may still apply, see section 6. For additional provisions in local Acts outside London see section 7. Finally there may be relevant provisions in national Acts (see section 8).

2 The Building Regulations 2000

2.01 The Building Regulations 2000 (as amended) contain the detailed technical and procedural rules and governing building control by local authorities. The Building (Approved Inspectors, etc.) Regulations 2000 (as amended) set out the procedures to be adopted by an approved inspector (see section 3 of this chapter).

Technical requirements

2.02 The Building Regulations require that all 'building work' must be carried out in accordance with the requirements of Schedule 1 but there are important limitations on the requirements. Regulation 8 states that nothing need be done other than the works necessary to secure reasonable standards of health and safety for persons in and about buildings, or matters connected with buildings. This limitation does not apply to requirement H2 in Part H (drainage and waste disposal) and J6 in Part J (combustion appliances and fuel storage systems), or to any of the requirements in Parts L (conservation of fuel and power) and M (access to and use of buildings).

2.03 Checklist 21.3 sets out the requirements of Schedule to the regulations and, subject to certain exemptions (see section 4 of this chapter), all 'building work' must be carried out so that the relevant requirements are met.

There is an Approved Document (AD) for each Part of the schedule giving guidance to meeting the requirements. There are also two ADs giving guidance to meeting all the requirements relevant to *Timber intermediate floors for dwellings* and *Basements for dwellings*.

Checklist 21.3: Technical requirements in Schedule 1 of the Building Regulations 2000 (as amended by the Building (Amendments) Regulations 2001, 2002, 2002 (No. 2) and 2003

SCHEDULE 1 – REQUIREMENTS	Regulations 4 and 6
Requirement	Limits on application
PART A: STRUCTURE	

Loading

A1 (1) The building shall be constructed so that the combined dead, imposed and wind loads are sustained and transmitted by it to the ground –
(a) safely; and
(b) without causing such deflection or deformation of any part of the building, or such movement of the ground, as will impair the stability of any part of another building.

Checklist 21.3: continued

(2) In assessing whether a building complies with sub-paragraph (1) regard shall be had to the imposed and wind loads to which it is likely to be subjected in the ordinary course of its use for the purpose for which it is intended.

Ground movement

A2 The building shall be constructed so that movements caused by –

(a) swelling, shrinkage or freezing of the subsoil; or

(b) land slip or subsidence (other than subsidence arising from shrinkage), in so far as the risk can be reasonably foreseen, will not impair the stability of any part of the building.

Disproportionate collapse

A3 The building shall be constructed so that in the event of an accident, the structure will not suffer collapse to an extent disproportionate to the cause of the damage.

This requirement applies only to a building having five or more storeys (each basement level being counted as one storey), excluding a storey with a roof space where the slope of the roof does not exceed 70° to the horizontal.

PART B: FIRE SAFETY

Means of warning and escape

B1 The building shall be designed and constructed so that there are appropriate provisions for the early warning of fire, and appropriate means of escape in case of fire from the building to a place of safety outside the building capable of being safely and effectively used at all material times.

Requirement B1 does not apply to any prison provided under section 33 of the Prisons Act 1952 (power to provide prisons, etc.).

Internal fire spread (linings)

B2 (1) To inhibit the spread of fire within the building the internal linings shall –

(a) resist the spread of flame over their surfaces; and

(b) have, if ignited, either a rate of heat release or a rate of fire growth which is reasonable in the circumstances.

(2) In this paragraph, 'internal linings' means the materials or products used in lining any partition, wall, ceiling or other internal structure.

Internal fire spread (structure)

B3 (1) The building shall be designed and constructed so that in the event of fire, its stability will be maintained for a reasonable period.

(2) A wall common to two or more buildings shall be designed and constructed so that it resists the spread of fire between those buildings. For the purposes of this sub-paragraph a house in a terrace and a semi detached house are each to be treated as a separate building.

(3) To inhibit the spread of fire within the building, it shall be sub-divided

Requirement B3 (3) does not apply to material alterations to any prison

with fire-resisting construction to an extent appropriate to the size and intended use of the building.

(4) The building shall be designed and constructed so that the unseen spread of fire and smoke within concealed spaces in its structure and fabric is inhibited.

External fire spread

B4 (1) The external walls of the building shall resist the spread of fire over the walls and from one building to another, having regard to the height, use and position of the building.

(2) The roof of the building shall resist the spread of fire over the roof and from one building to another, having regard to the use and position of the building.

Access and facilities for the fire service

B5 (1) The building shall be designed and constructed so as to provide facilities to assist fire-fighters in the protection of life.

(2) Provision shall be made within the site of the building to enable fire appliances to gain access to the building.

PART C: SITE PREPARATION AND RESISTANCE TO MOISTURE

Preparation of site

C1 The ground to be covered by the building shall be reasonably free from vegetable matter

Dangerous and offensive substances

C2 Precautions shall be taken to avoid danger to health and safety caused by substances found on or in the ground to be covered by the building.

Subsoil drainage

C3 Subsoil drainage shall be provided if it is needed to avoid –

(a) the passage of ground moisture to the interior of the building; and

(b) damage to the fabric of the building.

Resistance to weather and ground moisture

C4 The walls, floors and roof of the building shall resist the passage of moisture to the inside of the building.

PART D: TOXIC SUBSTANCES

Cavity insulation

D1 If insulating material is inserted into a cavity in a cavity wall reasonable precautions shall be taken to prevent the subsequent permeation of any toxic fumes from that material into any part of the building occupied by people.

provided under section 33 of the Prisons Act 1952.

Checklist 21.3: continued

Protection against sound from other parts of the building and adjoining buildings

E1 Dwelling-houses, flats and rooms for residential purposes shall be designed and constructed in such a way that they provide reasonable resistance to sound from other parts of the same building and from adjoining buildings.

Protection against sound within a dwelling-house, etc.

E2 Dwelling-houses, flats and rooms for residential purposes shall be designed and constructed in such a way that –

(a) internal walls between a bedroom or a room containing a water closet, and other rooms; and

(b) internal floors provide reasonable resistance to sound.

Reverberation in common internal parts of buildings containing flats or rooms for residential purposes

E3 The common internal parts of buildings which contain flats or rooms for residential purposes shall be designed and constructed in such a way as to prevent more reverberation around the common parts than is reasonable.

Acoustic conditions in schools

E4 (1) Each room or other space in a school building shall be designed and constructed in such a way that it has the acoustic conditions and the insulation against disturbance by noise appropriate to its intended use.

(2) For the purposes of this part – 'school' has the same meaning as in section 4 of the Education Act 1966 and 'school building' means any building forming a school or part of a school.

Means of ventilation

F1 There shall be adequate means of ventilation provided for people in the building.

Requirement F1 does not apply to a building or space within a building –

(a) into which people do not normally go; or

(b) which is used solely for storage; or

(c) which is a garage used solely in connection with a single dwelling.

Condensation

F2 Adequate provision shall be made to prevent excessive condensation.

(a) in a roof; or

(b) in a roof void above an insulated ceiling.

Checklist 21.3: continued

Sanitary conveniences and washing facilities

G1 (1) Adequate sanitary conveniences shall be provided in rooms provided for that purpose, or in bathrooms. Any such room or bathroom shall be separated from places where food is prepared.

(2) Adequate washbasins shall be provided in –

(a) rooms containing water closets; or

(b) rooms or spaces adjacent to rooms containing water closets. Any such room or space shall be separated from places where food is prepared.

(3) There shall be a suitable installation for the provision of hot and cold water to washbasins provided in accordance with paragraph (2).

(4) Sanitary conveniences and washbasins to which this paragraph applies shall be designed and installed so as to allow effective cleaning.

Bathrooms

G2 A bathroom shall be provided containing either a fixed bath or shower bath, and there shall be a suitable installation for the provision of hot and cold water to the bath or shower bath.

Requirement G2 applies only to dwellings.

Hot water storage

G3 A hot water storage system that has a hot water storage vessel which does not incorporate a vent pipe to the atmosphere shall be installed by a person competent to do so, and there shall be precautions –

(a) to prevent the temperature of stored water at any time exceeding 100°C; and

(b) to ensure that the hot water discharged from safety devices is safely conveyed to where it is visible but will not cause danger to persons in or about the building.

Foul water drainage

H1 (1) An adequate system of drainage shall be provided to carry foul water from appliances within the building to one of the following, listed in order of priority –

(a) a public sewer; or, where that is not reasonably practicable,

(b) a private sewer communicating with a public sewer; or, where that is not reasonably practicable,

(c) either a septic tank which has an appropriate form of secondary treatment or another wastewater treatment system; or, where that is not reasonably practicable,

(d) a cesspool.

Requirement H1 does not apply to the diversion of water which has been used for personal washing or for the washing of clothes, linen, or other articles to collection systems for reuse.

Checklist 21.3: continued

(2) In this part 'foul water' means wastewater which comprises or includes –

(a) waste water from a sanitary convenience, bidet or appliance used for washing receptacles for foul waste; or

(b) water which has been used for food preparation, cooking or washing.

Wastewater treatment systems and cesspools

H2 (1) Any septic tank and its form of secondary treatment, other wastewater treatment system or cesspool, shall be so sited and constructed that –

(a) it is not prejudicial to the health of any person;

(b) it will not contaminate any watercourse, underground water or water supply;

(c) there are adequate means for emptying and maintenance; and

(d) where relevant, it will function to a sufficient standard for the protection of health in the event of a power failure.

(2) Any septic tank, holding tank which is part of a wastewater treatment system or cesspool shall be –

(a) of adequate capacity;

(b) so constructed that it is impermeable to liquids; and

(c) adequately ventilated.

(3) Where a foul water drainage system from a building discharges to a septic tank, wastewater treatment system or cesspool, a durable notice shall be affixed in a suitable place in the building containing information on any continuing maintenance required to avoid risks to health.

Rainwater drainage

H3 (1) Adequate provision shall be made for rainwater to be carried from the roof of the building.

(2) Paved areas around the building shall be so constructed as to be adequately drained.

Requirement H3 (2) applies only to paved areas –

(a) which provide access to the building pursuant to paragraph M2 of Schedule 1 (access to and use of buildings);

(b) which provide access to or from a place of storage pursuant to paragraph H6 (2) of Schedule 1 (solid waste storage); or

(c) in any passage giving access to the building, where this is intended to be used in common by the occupiers of one or more other buildings.

(3) Rainwater from a system provided pursuant to sub-paragraphs (1) or (2) shall discharge to one of the following, listed in order of priority –

(a) an adequate soakaway or some other adequate system of infiltration system; or, where that is not reasonably practicable,

Checklist 21.3: continued

(b) a watercourse; or, where that is not reasonably practicable,

(c) a sewer.

Building over sewers

H4 (1) The erection of extension of a building or work involving the underpinning of a building shall be carried out in a way that is not detrimental to the building or building extension or to the continued maintenance of the drain, sewer or disposal main.

(2) In this paragraph 'disposal main' means any pipe, tunnel or conduit used for the conveyance of effluent to or from a sewage disposal works, which is not a public sewer.

(3) In this paragraph and paragraph H5 'map of sewers' means any records kept by a sewerage undertaker under section 199 of the Water Industry Act 1991.

Requirement H4 only applies to work carried out –

(a) over a drain, sewer, or disposal main which is shown on any map of sewers; or

(b) on any site or in such a manner as may result in interference with the use of, or obstruction of the access of any person to, any drain, sewer or disposal main which is shown on any map of sewers.

Separate systems of drainage

H5 Any system for discharging water to a sewer which is provided pursuant to paragraph H3 shall be separate from that provided for the conveyance of foul water from the building.

Requirement H5 applies only to a system provided in connection with the erection or extension of a building where it is reasonably practicable for the system to discharge directly or indirectly to a sewer for the separate conveyance of surface water which is –

(a) shown on a map of sewers; or

(b) under construction either by the sewerage undertaker or by some other person (where the sewer is subject of an agreement to make a declaration of vesting pursuant to section 104 of the Water Industry Act 1991).

Solid waste storage

H6 (1) Adequate provision shall be made for storage of solid waste.

(2) Adequate means of access shall be provided –

(a) for people in the building to the place of storage; and

(b) from the place of storage to a collection point (where one has been specified by the waste collection authority under section 46 (household waste) or section 47 (commercial waste) of the Environmental Protection Act 1990, or to a street (where no collection point has been specified).

Air supply

J1 Combustion appliances shall be so installed that there is an adequate supply of air to them for combustion, to prevent overheating and for the efficient working of any flue.

Requirements J1, J2, and J3 apply only to fixed combustion appliances (including incinerators).

Checklist 21.3: continued

Discharge of products of combustion

J2 Combustion appliances shall have adequate provision for the discharge of products of combustion to the outside air.

Protection of the building

J3 Combustion appliances and flue-pipes shall be so installed, and fireplaces and chimneys shall be so constructed and installed, as to reduce to a reasonable level the risk of people suffering burns or the building catching fire in consequence of their use.

Provision of information

J4 Where a hearth, fireplace, flue or chimney is provided or extended, a durable notice containing information on the performance capabilities of the hearth, fireplace or chimney shall be affixed in a suitable place in the building for the purpose of enabling combustion appliances to be safely installed.

Protection of liquid fuel storage systems

J5 Liquid fuel storage systems and the pipes connecting them to combustion appliances shall be so constructed and separated from buildings and the boundary of the premises as to reduce to a reasonable level the risk of the fuel igniting in the event of fire in adjacent buildings or premises.

Requirement J5 applies only to –
(a) fixed oil storage tanks with capacities greater than 90 litres and connecting pipes; and
(b) fixed liquid petroleum gas storage installations with capacities greater than 150 litres and connecting pipes, which are located outside the building and which serve fixed combustion appliances (including incinerators) in the building.

Protection against pollution

J6 Oil storage tanks and the pipes connecting them to combustion appliances shall –
(a) be so constructed and protected as to reduce to a reasonable level the risk of the oil escaping and causing pollution; and
(b) have affixed in a prominent position a durable notice containing information on how to respond to an oil escape so as to reduce to a reasonable level the risk of pollution.

Requirement J6 applies only to fixed oil storage tanks with capacities of 3500 litres or less, and connecting pipes which are –
(a) located outside the building; and
(b) serve fixed combustion appliances (including incinerators) in a building used wholly or mainly as a private dwelling, but does not apply to buried systems.

PART K: PROTECTION FROM FALLING COLLISION AND IMPACT

Stairs, ladders, and ramps

K1 Stairs, ladders and ramps shall be so designed, constructed and installed as to be safe for people moving between different levels in or about the building.

Requirement K1 applies only to stairs, ladders and ramps which form part of the building.

Protection from falling

K2 (a) Any stairs, ramps, floors and balconies, and any roof to which people have access; and
(b) any light well, basement area or similar sunken area connected to a building, shall be provided with barriers where they are necessary to

Requirement K2 (a) applies only to stairs and ramps which form part of the building.

Checklist 21.3: continued

protect people in or about the building from falling.

Vehicle barriers and loading bays

K3 (1) Vehicle ramps and any levels in a building to which vehicles have access, shall be provided with barriers where it is necessary to protect in or about the building.
(2) Vehicle loading bays shall be constructed in such a way, or be provided with such features as may be necessary to protect people in them from collision with vehicles.

Protection from collision with open windows, etc.

K4 Provision shall be made to prevent people moving in or about the building from collision with open windows, skylights or ventilators.

Requirement K4 does not apply to dwellings.

Protection against impact from and trapping by doors

K5 (1) Provision shall be made to prevent any door or gate –
(a) which slides or opens upwards, from falling onto any person; and
(b) which is powered, from trapping any person.
(2) Provision shall be made for powered doors and gates to be opened in the event of a power failure.
Provision shall be made to ensure a clear view of the space on either side of a swing door or gate.

Requirement K5 does not apply to –
(a) dwellings; or
(b) any door or gate which is part of a lift.

PART L: CONSERVATION OF FUEL AND POWER

Dwellings

L1 Reasonable provision shall be made for the conservation of fuel and power in dwellings by –
(a) limiting the heat loss:
(i) through the fabric of the building;
(ii) from hot water pipes and hot air ducts used for space heating; and
(iii) from hot water vessels
(b) providing space heating and hot water systems which are energy-efficient.
(c) providing lighting systems with appropriate lamps and sufficient controls so that the energy can be used efficiently.
(d) providing sufficient information with the heating and hot water services so that building occupiers can operate and maintain the services in such a manner as to use no more energy than is reasonable in the circumstances.

The requirement for sufficient controls in paragraph (1)(c) applies only to external lighting systems fixed to the building.

Buildings other than dwellings

L2 Reasonable provision shall be made for the conservation of fuel and power in buildings other than dwellings by –
(a) limiting the heat losses and gains through the fabric of the building;

Checklist 21.3: continued

(b) limiting the heat loss –
(i) from hot water pipes and hot air ducts used for space heating; and
(ii) from hot water vessels and hot water service pipes;
(c) providing space heating and hot water systems which are energy efficient;
(d) limiting exposure to solar heating;
(e) making provision where air conditioning and mechanical ventilation systems are installed, so that no more energy needs to be used than is reasonable in the circumstances;

Requirements L2 (e) and (f) apply only in buildings and parts of buildings where more than 200 square metres of floor area is to be served by air conditioning or mechanical ventilation systems.

(f) limiting the heating gains by chilled water and refrigerent vessels and pipes and air ducts that serve air conditioning systems;

(g) providing lighting systems that are energy-efficient; and

Requirement L2 (g) applies only in buildings and parts of buildings where more than 100 square metres of floor area is to be served by artificial lighting.

(h) providing sufficient information with the relevant services so that the building can be operated and maintained in such a manner as to use no more energy than is reasonable in the circumstances.

PART M: ACCESS TO AND USE OF BUILDINGS

Access and use
M1 Reasonable provision shall be made for people to
(a) gain access to; and

(b) use the building and its facilities

The requirements of this Part do not apply to –
(a) an extension of or material alteration of a dwelling; or
(b) any part of a building which is used solely to enable the building or any service or fitting in the building to be inspected, repaired or maintained.

Access to extensions to buildings other than dwellings
M2 Suitable independant access shall be provided to the extension where reasonably practicable

Requirement M2 does not apply where suitable access to the extension is provided through the building that is extended

Sanitary conveniences in extension to buildings other than dwellings
M3 If sanitary conveniences are provided in any building that is to be extended, reasonable provision shall be made within the extension for sanitary conveniences.

Requirement M3 does not apply where there is reasonable provision for sanitary conveniences elsewhere in the bilding, such that people occupied in, or otherwise having occasion to enter the extension, can gain access to and use those sanitary conveniences

Sanitary conveniences in dwellings
M4 – (1) Reasonable provision shall be made in the entrance storey for sanitary conveniences, or where the entrance storey contains no habitable rooms, reasonable provision shall be made in either the entrance storey or principle storey
(2) In this paragraph 'entrance storey' means the storey which

Checklist 21.3: continued

contains the principle entrance and 'principal storey' means the storey nearest to the entrance storey which contains a habitable room, or if there are two such storeys equally near, either such storey.

PART N: GLAZING – SAFETY IN RELATION TO IMPACT, OPENING AND CLEANING

Protection against impact
N1 Glazing, with which people are likely to come into contact while in passage in or about the building, shall –
(a) if broken on impact, break in a way which is unlikely to cause injury; or
(b) resist impact without breaking; or
(c) be shielded or protected from impact.

Manifestation of glazing
N2 Transparent glazing, with which people are likely to collide with in passage in or about the building, shall incorporate features which make it apparent.

Requirement N2 does not apply to dwellings.

Safe opening and closing of windows, etc.
N3 Windows, skylights and ventilators which can be opened by people in or about the building shall be so constructed or equipped that they may be opened, closed or adjusted safely.

Requirement N3 does not apply to dwellings.

Safe access for cleaning windows etc.
N4 Provision shall be made for any windows, skylights or any transparent or translucent walls, ceilings or roofs to be safely accessible for cleaning.

Requirement N4 does not apply to –
(a) dwellings; or
(b) any transparent or translucent elements whose surface are not intended to be cleaned.

Finally, there is an AD supporting regulation 7 which now implements the Construction Products Directive. Products bearing the CE mark may not be rejected if they are being used for their intended purpose and are not damaged (see also Constructions Products Regulations 1991 as amended, Chapter 28). Note that the CE mark only underwrites the capability of a product to enable the works to meet the essential requirements of the Directive, reflecting the requirements of the building regulations, if the building is properly designed and built and its scope is therefore more limited than a European product standard. However, the mark does, in most cases, assert that the product is, subject to normal maintenance, capable of satisfying the essential requirements for an economically reasonable working life.

Approved documents

2.04 The Building Regulations 2000 contain no technical detail but are supported by a series of 14 approved documents. The status and use of these documents is laid down in sections 6 and 7 of the Building Act 1984. The purpose of the documents is to give practical guidance with respect to the requirements of any provision of the building regulations. The documents may be approved by the Secretary of State or by some other body designated by him.

The current approved documents all refer to other non-statutory material, including British Standards and certificates issued by the British Board of Agrément. The documents are intended to give designers a considerable amount of flexibility. The details within the documents do not have to be followed if the requirements can be met in some other way.

2.05 Section 7 of the 1984 Act specifies the legal effect of the documents. Failure to comply with their recommendations does not involve civil or criminal liability, but they can be relied on by either party to any proceedings for alleged contravention of the regulation requirements. Thus if an architect proves that he has complied with the requirements of an approved document in any proceedings which are brought against him, he can rely on this as 'tending to negative liability'. Conversely, his failure to so comply may be relied on by the local authority as 'tending to establish liability', and the onus will be on the architect to establish that he has met the functional requirement in some other way.

In *Rickards v Kerrier District Council* [1987] CILL 345, in enforcement proceedings under section 36 of the 1984 Act, the High Court had to consider the application of section 6. The judge held that the burden of proving non-compliance with the Regulations was on the local authority, but if they established that the works did not comply with an approved document, then the burden shifted.

2.06 Space does not permit a detailed analysis of the technical content of the approved documents and readers should refer to the Manual to the Building Regulations 1999, a definitive treatment of the subject.

Procedural rules

2.07 Subject to a number of exemptions (see section 4) the requirements of Part II of the regulations must be met where a person intends to carry out 'building work' or make a 'material change of use' which is subject to the control of the local authority, the procedural requirements of Part V (see sections 2.16–2.18) must be met, and the work must comply with the relevant technical requirements of Schedule 1 of the regulations.

Building work is defined in regulation 3 and the related requirements are set out in regulation 4.

A material change of use is defined in regulation 5 and the related requirements are set out in regulation 6. A local authority is defined in section 126 of the Act as a district council, a London Borough, the Inner and Middle Temples, the City of London and the Isles of Scilly.

The building work or the material change of use may be controlled by the local authority (see section 2.16) or other than by the local authority e.g. by an Approved Inspector (see section 3).

2.08 The Building Regulations 2000 as amended are not a self-sufficient code and other legislation (and non-statutory documents) must be referred to (see sections 5–8).

Nature of approval

2.09 Before considering the procedural requirements in detail several important matters must be emphasized: discretion of local authorities, breach of building regulations, enforcement and dispensation and relaxation of requirements (see paragraphs 2.10 to 2.15).

Discretion of local authority

2.10 Section 16 of the Act provides that the local authority must pass the plans of any proposed work unless they are defective or show that the work would contravene any of the regulations or unless some other provision of the Act requires or authorizes it to reject the plans. 'Plans' include drawings, specifications and information in any form (section 126 of the Act).

When considering whether the work does show a contravention it should be borne in mind that the regulations require only compliance with the Requirements in Schedule 1, not the guidance in the relevant Approved Document (see paragraph 2.05).

Where the building notice procedure is followed (see paragraph 2.17) the local authority may specify in writing such plans as it requires to discharge its functions (regulation 13(5)). Note that these plans will not be treated as having been deposited and they will not be passed or rejected.

Where the full plans procedure is followed (see paragraph 2.18) some local authorities may decline to 'register', i.e. accept, plans on the ground that they are defective (which here probably means incomplete) citing regulation 14(3)(b) which requires the plans to show that the work would comply with the regulations. In practice, it is unlikely that plans can be sufficiently full for that purpose but the local authority may be interpreting its function as requiring it to approve proposed work.

When Parliament introduced the procedure for depositing full plans, it stated that its purpose was to enable the depositor (and particularly builders before they started the work) to know whether what was being proposed showed a contravention; it follows that what the plans do not show will not elicit that information. It should be noted that the time limit for passing or rejecting the plans begins to run from the date they are deposited (not the date they are 'registered'), that if the plans are defective they can be passed subject to conditions (enabling the plans to be passed in stages) and that the work can be started within two days of the deposit.

The local authority, under its duty to enforce the regulations, also has discretion to decide whether or not to inspect building work in progress and they must give proper consideration to the question. 'It is for the local authority, a public and elected body, to decide upon the scale of resources which it can make available to carry out its functions ... – how many inspectors, with what expert qualifications, it should recruit, how often inspections are to be made, what tests it should carry out – must be for its decision' (per Lord Wilberforce in *Anns v London Borough of Merton* [1978] AC 728). This is without prejudice to the need for the person carrying out the work to give the notices required by regulation 15.

Breach of building regulations

2.11 Section 35 of the Building Act provides that a contravention of the regulations is an offence. The position appears to be that the local authority can take enforcement action where an event to which a procedural regulation attaches a requirement has occurred, for example, if building work has started without a building notice being given or full plans deposited, or if a notice required by regulation 15 has not been given.

However, where the building work contravenes a technical requirement the question arises whether an offence can be said to have been committed before the building work is complete.

On the one hand the person carrying out the work will say that the offending work will be remedied before the building work, or perhaps the relevant stage of the work, is completed. On the other hand the regulations require the 'building work' to comply and regulation 15 requires notices to be given of the commencement and completion of certain stages of the work, at completion of the building work, and of completion before occupation if the building is to be occupied before completion. In some cases it also provides for notices to be given for remedial work to be carried out and requires notice of its completion to be given within a reasonable time. If the local authority intends to institute proceedings they are likely to be decided summarily, i.e. by the magistrates court, when the authority must give notice of its intention within six months of the date of the alleged offence (but see also section 2.13).

2.12 A related matter is whether a breach of any duty imposed by the building regulations could give rise to a liability in damages. Section 38 of the Act (civil liability) provides that a 'breach of duty imposed by building regulations, so far as it causes damage, is actionable' where 'damage' is defined as including death or injury (including any disease and any impairment of a person's physical or mental condition). However, the section has not been brought into force and meanwhile, unless and until it is, the position appears to be that as the duty on a local authority to enforce the building regulations is not absolute a breach of the regulations does not, of itself, give rise to liability for damages. For example, a failure to reject plans is not actionable in the absence of negligence.

Enforcement

2.13 Section 36 of the Building Act provides that, without prejudice to its right to take proceedings under section 35, the local authority can by notice (a 'section 36 notice') require the offending work to be removed or corrected but it has only 12 months from the date it was completed in which to do so and cannot do so at all if the work is in accordance with plans which were passed or not rejected within the time limit. However, this does not prevent an application for an injunction (with the consent and in the name of the Attorney General) to remove or correct the work but the court can order the local authority to pay the owner of the work such compensation as it thinks just.

2.14 The person on whom a section 36 notice is served has a right of appeal to the magistrates' court and an important procedure is provided by section 37 of the 1984 Act. Under section 37, the recipient of a section 36 notice may notify the local authority of his intention to obtain from a 'suitably qualified person' a written report about the matter to which the section 36 notice relates. The expert's report is then submitted to the local authority and in light of that report the authority may withdraw the notice and pay the expenses reasonably incurred in obtaining the report which will relate to technical matters. If the local authority rejects the report, it can then be used as evidence in any appeal under section 40 of the Act, and if the appeal is successful the appellant would normally recover the costs of obtaining the report as well as his other costs: 1984 Act, section 40(6).

Dispensations and relaxations

2.15 Section 8 of the Building Act conferred on the Secretary of State the power to dispense with or relax any regulation requirement 'if he considers that the operation of (that) requirement would be unreasonable in relation to the particular case'. Sections 9 and 10 of the 1984 Act laid down the procedure for application. It applies whether the *building notice* or *full plans* procedure has been followed. The power has since been delegated to local authorities (see regulation 11).

If the local authority refuses the application; the applicant has a right to appeal to the Secretary of State within one month. If the local authority fails to give a decision within two months section 39 provides that the application is deemed to be refused and the applicant may appeal forthwith (for more detailed information see *A Guide to Determinations and Appeals 2001* published by DTLR, now the Office of the Deputy Prime Minister).

However, nearly all the technical requirements of the regulations are now in functional form to require that the level of provision is 'adequate', 'satisfactory' or 'reasonable' and it would not normally be acceptable to dispense with the whole requirement. The question which then arises is whether the proposal meets the requirement (in a few cases a 'nil' provision may do so) when an application for a determination is the proper course of action (see section 2.19 of this chapter).

Control of building work by the local authorities

2.16 Unless the developer wishes to employ an approved inspector (see section 3) the general rule is that anyone intending to carry out 'building work' or make a 'material change of use' must give a building notice (see regulations 12 and 13 and paragraph 2.17) or submit full plans (see regulations 12 and 14 and paragraph 2.18). However, full plans must be deposited (see regulation 12) if the building is to be put to a 'relevant use', or the building to be erected will front onto a private street, or building work is to be carried out in relation to which Requirement H4 (building over sewers) of Schedule 1 imposes a requirement.

Whichever procedure is adopted the work may be inspected by the local authority's building control officer who may test any building work to establish whether it complies with regulation 7 or any applicable Requirements of Schedule 1 (regulation 18 (testing of building work), no longer limited to Part H (drains and sewers)) and who may also take such samples of materials to be used in the work as may be necessary to establish whether they comply with the provisions of the regulations (regulation 19).

Building work is defined in regulation 3 to mean the erection or extension of a building, the provision or extension of a controlled service, the 'material alteration' of a building or controlled service, work required by regulation 6 if a 'material change of use' occurs, the insertion of insulating material into a cavity wall and work involving underpinning. A *material change of use* is defined in regulation 5 to mean one which would result in a relevant change of occupancy or remove exemption under Schedule 2.

A *material alteration* is defined in regulation 3(2) as one which would result in an existing building not meeting the requirements of Schedule 1 relating to structure, fire safety (except B2), and access and facilities for disabled persons either:

1 where previously it had; or
2 making it more unsatisfactory than it was before in respect of those particular requirements.

A *relevant use* is defined in regulation 12(1) to mean a workplace to which Part II of the Fire Precautions (Workplace) Regulations apply or a use designated under the Fire Precautions Act 1971 (see section 8).

The charges which may be made can vary between local authority districts but only subject to the *Building (Local Authority Charges) Regulations 1998*.

Building notice procedure

2.17 The procedure is governed by section 16 of the Building Act and regulations 12 and 13. It is not available if the building is (or is intended) to be put to a 'relevant' use, or is to be erected and will front a private street, or includes building work for which Requirement H4 of Schedule 1 imposes a requirement (regulations 12(1), (4) and (4A)).

There is no prescribed form but the notice must be signed by or on behalf of the person intending to carry out the work and it must contain or be accompanied by the information listed in regulation 13. The local authority is not required to accept or reject the notice and has no power to do so. However, the authority may ask for any plans and information it needs to enable it to discharge its building control functions and may specify a time limit for their provision (these plans will not be treated as having been deposited and the local authority has no power to pass or reject them). Information may also be required in connection with the linked powers under the Act (see paragraph 5 of this chapter). Once the notice has been given with the required charge the work can start provided the authority is given at least two days notice (regulation 15(1)(a)).

A building notice ceases to have effect after three years if, within that period, the local authority gives formal notice to that effect and the work has not started (regulation 13(7)).

Deposit of plans procedure

2.18 The advantage of this procedure, if the developer wishes to adopt it (or the building notice procedure is not available, see paragraph 2.17), is that the local authority cannot take any action under section 36 of the Building Act if the work is carried out in conformity with the plans as passed.

The procedure is governed by section 16 of the Building Act and regulations 12 (giving of a building notice or deposit of plans) and 14 (full plans). Again there is no prescribed form but the deposited plans must be signed by or on behalf of the person intending to carry out the work and they must contain or be accompanied by the information listed in regulation 14. Once the plans have been deposited (whether or not they have been passed or rejected) with the required charge the work can start provided the authority is given at least two days notice (regulation 15(1)(a)). The charge which may be made is governed by the *Building (Local Authority Charges) Regulations 1998*.

The local authority must pass or reject the deposited plans within five weeks unless the period is extended, subject to the written agreement of the depositor and the local authority during the five week period, to take it to two months. Both times run from the date when the plans are deposited, again with the appropriate charge. Where (for any reason) the authority has not given notice of passing or rejecting the plans within the time limit it must refund any plan charge paid.

If the local authority does reject the plans it must give its reasons and, ideally, it will do so in sufficient detail (and in sufficient time) for the depositor to make the necessary changes.

The deposit of the plans is of no effect after three years if, within that period, the local authority gives formal notice to that effect and the work has not started (section 32 of the Building Act).

Plans will usually be deposited with the local authority in whose area the intended work will be carried out. However, the individual local authorities co-ordinate their services regionally and nationally through the Local Authority Building Control (LABC). This runs a Partner Authority scheme which enables plans to be deposited with the local authority of your choice to be handled by LABC together with the local authority in the area in which the intended work is to be carried out. It also runs the LANTAC Type Approval scheme which enables standard designs to be approved for nationwide use. Details of these schemes are available on the LABC website.

Applications for determination

2.19 If there is a dispute between a local authority and the person proposing to carry out the work as to whether the plans comply with the requirements of the regulations, section 16(10) of the Act provides for that person to apply to the Secretary of State for a determination. A fee of half the plans fee up to a maximum of £500 is payable for this service.

However, the application can only be made where *full plans* procedure has been followed, after the plans have been deposited and before the work to which the application relates has been started (for more detailed information see *A Guide to Determinations and Appeals 2001* published by DTLR, now the Office of the Deputy Prime Minister).

Completion certificates

2.20 Local authorities will issue completion certificates (see regulation 17) where one is requested at the time of application or it is notified that the building is to be put to a relevant use as defined in regulation 12(1).

Unauthorized building work

2.21 Where building work has been carried out without approval and notice was not given, the owner may apply for a regularization certificate (regulation 21). A certificate will be issued if the work complies.

Energy rating

2.22 Where a new dwelling is created by 'building work' or by a 'material change of use' in connection with which 'building work' is carried out the energy rating of the dwelling must be calculated by a procedure approved by the Secretary of State and notified to the local authority (see regulation 16). The approved procedure is the Standard Assessment Procedure (SAP) available from the Building Research Establishment.

3 Control of building work other than by the local authority

3.01 Part II of the Building Act enables the person intending to carry out the work to appoint an approved inspector to take over from the local authority the responsibility for ensuring compliance with The Building Regulations.

It also enables approved public bodies to supervise their own work but none have yet been approved.

Approved inspectors

3.02 The procedures for ensuring compliance with the building regulations are governed by Part II of the Building Act and the *Building (Approved Inspectors) Regulations 2000*. Section 49 of the Building Act defines an approved inspector, authorized under the Building Act to carry out building control work in England and Wales, as a corporate body approved by the Secretary of State (or by a body designated by him for that purpose) or as an individual (not a firm) approved by a designated body.

The Secretary of State has designated the Construction Industry Council (CIC) as the body to receive all applications from corporate bodies and individuals for approved inspector status and for deciding on the applications. With one exception approved inspectors are authorized to deal with all types of building other than new-build housing for sale. The exception is Building Control Services Ltd, a subsidiary of the National House Building Council (NHBC), which is authorized to deal with all types of building.

3.03 The CIC maintains the registers of all corporate and individual inspectors and the Association of Corporate Approved Inspectors holds a list of corporate approved inspectors. These lists are available on the respective websites. The approved inspector's charges are negotiable on a case-by-case basis.

4 Exemptions from control

4.01 There is a definition of a 'building' in section 121 (interpretation) of the Building Act and section 4(1) exempts certain types of buildings; the exemption for school buildings has been withdrawn in favour of the building regulations though there are limited additional requirements in the *Education (School Premises) Regulations 1999*.

4.02 There is a narrower interpretation of a building in regulation 2(1) and there are further exemptions in regulation 9 (exempt buildings and work) and Schedule 2 of the building regulations. Even when the building or work is not exempt there are Limits on the application of some of the requirements in Schedule 1 (requirements).

4.03 In addition to the exemptions from the technical requirements there are two exemptions from the procedural requirements. A person approved under regulation 3 of the *Gas Safety (Installation and Use) Regulations 1998* who intends to carry out building work consisting only of the installation of a heat producing gas appliance is exempted by Regulation 12(5) from giving a building notice or depositing full plans. Where a person who is registered under the Fenestration Self-Assessment Scheme by Fensa Ltd who intends to carry out work which consists only of the replacement of a door, window, rooflight, roof window or door regulation 16A authorizes the local authority to accept a certificate from the person carrying out the work that it meets the requirements of regulation 4 (requirements relating to building work), regulation 7 (materials and workmanship) and Schedule 1 (requirements).

5 Other controls under the Building Act

5.01 Local authorities exercise a number of statutory public health functions in conjunction with the process of building control. These provisions are commonly called 'the linked powers' because their operation is linked with the authority's building control functions, both in checking deposited plans or considering a building notice, and under the private certification scheme. The most important of these linked powers are described below.

Building over sewers and drains

5.02 Section 99 of the Water Industry Act 1991 states that sewerage undertakers must keep a map showing the location of all public sewers and supply a copy to local authorities for public inspection. The map distinguishes among public sewers, those with respect to which a vesting declaration has been made but which has not yet taken effect, and those subject to an agreement as to future declaration. Where separate sewers are reserved for foul and surface water, this must be clearly shown. These four groups of sewers and drains are shown on the map.

5.03 Following the repeal of section 18 of the Building Act this section is no longer a linked power. Instead Requirement H4 (building over sewers) of Schedule 1 of the building regulations now applies and regulation 14(3)(aa) requires that, where full plans have been deposited, particulars must be given of the precautions to be taken in building over a drain, sewer or disposal main shown on the map of sewers and regulation 14A requires the local authority to consult the sewerage undertaker and 'to have regard to its views' (but not more).

New buildings and drains

5.04 Following the repeal of subsections 21(1) and (2) of the Building Act this section is no longer a linked power. Instead Part H (drainage and waste disposal) of Schedule 1 of the building regulations now applies.

In *Chesterton RDC v Ralph Thompson, Ltd* [1947] KB 300, the High Court held that the local authority is not entitled to reject plans on the ground that the sewerage system, into which the drains lead, is unsatisfactory. What the local authority must consider is the drainage of the particular building only.

5.05 Under section 21(3)(ff) of the Act the local authority can determine the method of disposal from a drain – a connection to a sewer or discharge to a cesspool or some other place – provided that, in the case of a sewer, it satisfies certain conditions. A drain is defined as being used for the drainage of one or more buildings within the same curtilage and a sewer (which may be private or public) as being used for the drainage of buildings within two or more curtilages.

Under section 22 the local authority can determine whether a building shall be drained separately into a sewer or 'in combination' with two or more other buildings by means of a private sewer discharging to the sewer if it appears to the authority the buildings may be drained more economically or advantageously in this way. However, it can only do this when the relevant drains are first laid, not in respect of any building for whose drainage plans have previously been passed by it unless the owners agree.

Water supply

5.06 The effect of section 25 of the 1984 Act is that drawings of a house deposited with the local authority are to be rejected, unless 'there is put before (the local authority) a proposal which appears to it to be satisfactory for providing the occupants with a supply of wholesome water sufficient for their domestic purposes', and if possible the water is to be from a piped supply.

Fire safety

5.07 Section 24, a linked power, required the local authority to reject plans if the entrances and exits of buildings where large numbers of the public were to be admitted were unsatisfactory but it has been of no effect since 1992 when building regulations were made. Section 71, not a linked power, applies to the same buildings but is limited to existing buildings, the means of escape from which are normally controlled under other legislation.

Height of chimneys

5.08 Section 74 of the Building Act enables the local authority, when a building ('the taller building') is being erected or raised to a height greater than an adjoining building, to require any chimney of the adjoining building within six feet of the taller building to be raised to the height of the taller building.

Section 16 of the *Clean Air Act 1993*, a linked power, requires the local authority to reject plans unless it is satisfied that the height of any chimney will be sufficient to prevent, as far as practicable, the smoke, grit, dust or gases from becoming prejudicial to health or a nuisance (see also section 8.09(ff) of this chapter).

Continuing requirements

5.09 Section 2 of the Building Act provides for building regulations to be made imposing continuing requirements on owners and occupiers of buildings but none have been made.

6 Local legislation in Inner London

6.01 Inner London consists of the City of London and the twelve London Boroughs of Camden, Greenwich, Hackney, Hammersmith, Islington, Kensington and Chelsea, Lambeth, Lewisham, Southwark, Tower Hamlets, Wandsworth, and Westminister: London Government Act 1963, section 43.

6.02 Until 1986 the London Building Acts and Bye-laws formed a code of control which governed the design, construction and use of buildings in the area and differed from that which operated elsewhere. On 6 January 1986 the *Building (Inner London) Regulations 1985* came into effect, repealed the Bye-laws, applied most of the national regulations and amended the London Building Acts. On 1 June 1987 the *Building (Inner London) Regulations 1987* came into effect and applied the remaining national regulations.

The local authority, acting as the building control body and headed by the Chief Building Control Officer, is responsible for enforcing the building regulations. The sections of the London Building Acts which are still in force are usually administered by the local building control in the person of the chief officer acting as a District Surveyor. The more important of the remaining sections of the Act are summarized below (see paragraphs 6.03 to 6.05) but space does not permit a detailed examination of all the remaining sections which include special and temporary structures (sections 29 and 30) and dangerous and neglected structures (sections 60–70). For a full treatment see the *Guide to Building Control in Inner London 1987* by P. H. Pitt.

Fire safety – precautions against fire

6.03 Section 20 of the London Building Act applies to –

(a) buildings of excess height – over 30 metres or over 25 metres if the area of the building exceeds 930 square metres; and
(b) buildings in excess cube – over 7100 cubic metres if used for trade (including warehouses and department stores) or manufacture.

Except in the case of a trade building which is properly sub-divided into divisions of less than 7100 cubic metres section 20 buildings require the consent of the local authority (a copy of the plans will be sent for comment to the London Fire and Civil Defence Authority). The consent will be subject to a schedule of requirements which may include higher standards of fire resistance and the provision of automatic sprinklers, hose reels, dry risers, firemens' lifts, emergency lighting and escape routes. Full details will be required and approval must be obtained of all electrical installations, heating and ventilating systems, sprinkler installations, etc. Additional precautions can be required for 'special fire risk areas' (defined in section 20(2D)) such as any storey of a garage located in a basement or not properly ventilated.

Fire safety – uniting of buildings

6.04 Section 21 applies to buildings to which, if united, would not meet the continuing requirements of the Act.

The section requires the consent of the local authority to forming openings for access from one building to another without passing into the external air. The section also imposes limitations on forming openings in walls separating divisions of buildings of the warehouse class or used for trade purposes.

Fire safety – means of escape

6.05 Part V/section 34 applies, with exceptions, to –
  Public buildings
  Places of worship or assembly.
  Every other new building which –
  (a) if single storey exceeds 600 square feet in area.
  (b) if more than one storey exceeds 1000 square feet in area (excluding basements used only for storage).

The exceptions are places of entertainment dealt with under the licensing procedure, private houses in single-family occupation which do not have a floor at a height of more than 20 feet, and houses or flats of three or more storeys.

The section requires approval to the means of escape. Notice must be given and plans deposited before or at the same time as any other notice is given or plans are deposited in respect of the building. The local authority has two months from the deposit (or such longer period as may be agreed in writing) in which to approve or refuse the proposed means of escape. Approval may be subject to conditions.

Notice of Objection

6.06 Where a notice is given or plans deposited in respect of a building affected by the provisions of the Acts, and it discloses a contravention of the provisions, the district surveyor must serve Notice of Objection on the builder or owner or other person causing or directing the work. In effect this provides a *locus poenitentiae* (an opportunity for repentence).

However, an appeal may be made to the magistrates' court within 14 days after service of the notice: 1939 Act, section 39.

Notice of irregularity

6.07 The district surveyor also has power to serve a Notice of Irregularity under section 88 of the 1939 Act. This can be served after the builder has completed the work. It was decided in *Coggin v Duff* [1907] 96 LT 670, that failure to give Notice of Objection is not a bar to proceedings under Notice of Irregularity. This notice will be served where work has been done and it is found that some contravention exists or that the work is so far advanced that the district surveyor cannot ascertain whether anything has been done in contravention. Its effect is to require the builder within 48 hours to amend any contravention or to open up as much of the work as may be necessary for the district surveyor to ascertain whether or not a contravention exists. The opening-up and rectification is done at the builder's or owner's expense. The notice cannot be served on the builder when he has completed the building, but there is power to serve notice on the owner, occupier, or other person directing the work.

6.08 The sanction behind a Notice of Irregularity is a fine. However, the district surveyor may apply to the magistrates' court for an order requiring the builder to comply within a stated time. Failure to obey an order of the court renders the builder liable to a daily fine: 1939 Act, section 148.

Powers of entry

6.09 The district surveyor and other authorized officers have wide powers of entry, inspection and examination to enable them to carry out their functions: e.g. section 142 of the London Building Acts (Amendment) Act 1939.

Appeals tribunals

6.10 Provision exists in the London Building Acts for special Tribunals of Appeal (one for each of the building control authorities) which hear appeals referred to them under the London Building Acts: 1939 Act, section 109. The Tribunals have power to award costs and wide powers to order the production of documents, plans, specifications, and so on. A further appeal lies, by way of case stated, to the High Court: 1939 Act, section 116.

Dwelling houses on low-lying land

6.11 Part XII of the London Building Act 1930 prohibits the erection or rebuilding of dwelling houses on low-lying land without the consent of the appropriate Inner London Borough council.

Party structures

6.12 Part VI of the 1939 Act has been repealed, subject to transitional provisions, by the Party Wall etc. Act 1996 which is applicable throughout England and Wales (see section 8.21).

7 Local legislation outside Inner London

7.01 Although the Building Act 1984 and Regulations made under it were intended to provide a national code of building control, there are many provisions in local Acts which impose additional controls on the construction of buildings.

7.02 Section 90 of the Building Act provides that where (outside Inner London) a local Act imposes obligations or restrictions on the construction, nature or situation of buildings the local authority shall keep a copy of those provisions at its offices for inspection by the public at all reasonable times free of charge.

The provisions of local Acts may include fire safety requirements relating to high buildings (over six storeys), large storage buildings (exceeding 7000 cubic metres), underground and multi-storey parking places, access for the fire service and means of escape. They may also include requirements relating to the separation of foul and rainwater drainage systems and the external storage of flammable materials. The authorities concerned are of the opinion that their local Act requirements are an essential part of the machinery of control and this list is not exhaustive. For a full treatment see the *Guide to Building Control by Local Acts 1987* by P. H. Pitt.

7.03 Where an Approved Inspector is responsible for compliance with the building regulations the *Building (Approved Inspectors) Regulations 2000* require him to consult the Fire Authority where a local Act requires and the Building Act provides that local authority can reject the Approved Inspector's initial notice where the proposed work would 'contravene any local enactment which authorizes it to reject plans submitted in accordance with the building regulations'. However, the local authority is responsible for ensuring that the work complies with the local Act.

8 Other national legislation

8.01 Many general statutes contain further provisions affecting the construction of buildings, although this is not apparent from the titles of the Acts concerned. There are also numerous statutory instruments made under powers conferred by many of these Acts. In this section some statutory rules which affect the bulk of building developments will be considered. This list does not claim to be exhaustive, nor does it cover all the relevant sections. (Some provisions of statutes not discussed here are covered in Chapter 19.)

8.02 Certain requirements are dealt with automatically on the deposit of drawings under the Building Regulations or, in some cases, at the same time as the application for planning permission. The following are some of the more important provisions which are relevant at that stage.

The responsibility for the enforcement of the various Acts will fall on a variety of different bodies. Some are departments of the local authority but others are not when the building control body may be required to consult them. For the rest architect has no option but to negotiate.

The Fire Precautions Act 1971

8.03 The Act was enacted to meet the criticism that the legislation was not providing sufficient protection for the occupants of certain non-domestic buildings in the event of a fire. The Building Regulations would continue to deal with the design of all buildings and the Act would designate certain non-dometsic uses and deal with their safety in use through a system of inspection and fire-certificates. Section 13 of the Act (the statutory bar) would stop the fier authority from requiring alterations to a building insofar as it met the Regulations.

In practice the inter-action between the building regulations and the Act has not always been without its uncertainties and the work of inspection and certification has placed a heavy workload on the fire authorities.

8.04 A system of risk assessments for all non-domestic buildings, for which the employer will have continuing responsibility, is replacing the certification of designated buildings (see paragraph 8.07). In addition safety, including fire safety, during the construction phase is now subject to regulation (see paragraph 8.06).

Clearly these changes have implications for architects including at the design stage, when a building is in use (if they are instructed to carry out a risk assessment) and when they are employers in their own right.

8.05 The design of all types of domestic and non-domestic buildings (if they are not exempt) will continue to be governed by Part B of the Building Regulations, supported by the guidance in Approved Document B and its European Supplement.

The relevant building control body is responsible for enforcing these regulations but must consult the fire authority if the building is to be put a 'relevant use', defined (regulation 12(1)) as a workplace to which Part II of the *Fire Precautions (Workplace) Regulations 1997* applies, or a to use designated under section 1 of the Act. These uses are –

1 Hotels and boarding houses where sleeping accommodation is provided for six or more guests or staff on the ground floor (or for any number elsewhere).
2 Factories, offices, shops and railway premises where more than 20 people are employed on the ground floor (or more than 10 elsewhere) or (in factories only) explosives or highly flammable materials are stored or used on the premises.

8.06 Construction sites are subject to the *Construction (Health, Safety and Welfare) Regulations 1996* (which for this purpose replace the *Fire Precautions (Workplace) Regulations 1997*). The Health and Safety Executive (HSE) is responsible for enforcing these regulations (see also paragraph 8.20).

8.07 The use of non-domestic premises will be subject to a risk assessment to be carried out by the employer under the *Management of Health and Safety at Work Regulations 1999* and *Fire Precautions (Workplace) Regulations 1997* (see section 8.06 the above). The employer is responsible for making the assessments and acting on them and the fire authority is expected to be made responsible for enforcing the regulations.

8.08 Certain special fire risks are also required to have a certificate from the HSE under the *Fire Certificates (Special Premises) Regulations 1976*. The HSE is responsible for enforcing these regulations.

Sports grounds may be subject to certification under the *Fire Safety and Safety of Places of Sports Act 1987* (if not certificated under the Act they are subject to the *Fire Precautions (Workplace) Regulations 1997*). Environmental health officers are responsible for enforcing these regulations.

In addition, bodies responsible for enforcing legislation to which other special classes of buildings and building uses are subject may call on the fire authority to provide advice (see paras 8.25 and 8.26).

The Clean Air Act 1993

8.09 Among other things, this Act controls the height of chimneys on industrial premises, types of installation, and the treatment of offensive fumes from appliances.

8.10 Sections 14 and 15 of the 1993 Act require the approval of the local authority for the height of a chimney serving a furnace, and approval may be granted subject to conditions as to the rate and/or quality of emissions from the chimney. There is a right of appeal to the Secretary of State.

8.11 Similarly, section 16 of the Act provides that in other cases the local authority must reject plans of buildings other than residences, shops, or offices unless the height of the chimney as shown on the drawings will so far on practicable, be sufficient to prevent fumes from being a nuisance or a health hazard. The factors to be considered are the purpose of the chimney, the position and description of nearby buildings, level of neighbouring ground, and other relevant matters. These provisions represent an important negative control (see Chapter 19, paragraph 4.15).

Highways Act 1980

8.12 The Act contains several provisions of interest to architects. They include the construction of a new street (sections 186–196 of the Act), improvement lines (section 73), building lines (section 74), means of access (sections 124 and 184), building over highways (section 177) and precautions against accidents (sections 139, 140 and 168). Some may be enforced by the highway authority, others implemented by conditions attached to planning consents (see Chapter 23).

For provisions relating to a private street (one not adopted by the highway authority) and the procedures which enable a private street to be adopted under section 38 of the Act as a highway maintainable at the public expense (see Chapter 19, section 4).

8.13 Section 73 requires the highway authority's consent, where an improvement line has been prescribed, to the erection of a building and the making of any permanent excavation in front of the improvement line. This may be granted with conditions. There is a right of appeal against a refusal of consent or its granting subject to conditions.

8.14 Section 74 requires the highway authority's consent to the erection of a new building (but not a boundary wall) in front of the building linc. This may be granted with conditions or for a limited time.

8.15 Section 124 enables the Secretary of State, by order, to authorize the highway authority to stop up a private access to the highway if he considers that the access is likely to cause danger to, or interfere unnecessarily, with traffic on the highway. However, the order can only be made where no access to the premises from the highway is reasonably required or where another reasonably convenient means of access is available or will be provided. There is an objection procedure and compensation may be payable.

8.16 Sections 139 and 140 require precautions to be taken where a person is carrying out works in the street such as the planking and strutting of drainage works and shoring up any building adjoining a street. Stringent safety precautions must be observed in relation to builder's skips. They must not be placed on the highway without the authority's consent. This may be granted subject to conditions.

Section 168 provides that if, in the course of carrying out building work in or near the highway an accident gives rise to the risk of serious bodily injury to a person in the street, the owner of the land is guilty of an offence. Hoardings and scaffolding in or adjoining the highway require a licence from the highway authority.

8.17 Section 177 requires a license from the highway authority for the construction and subsequent alteration of buildings or parts of buildings over highways maintained at public expense. This may be granted subject to conditions and is registerable as a local land charge (see Chapter 4, section 1.05).

8.18 Section 184 enables a building owner to initiate proposals to create a new means of access to his property to be constructed at his own expense for, for example, a carriage crossing to a garage. In certain circumstance the authority may, on its initiative, construct the crossing at the owner's expense.

8.19 Sections 186–196 provide that when a new street is to be established an order will be made and, where Bye-laws are in force, they will prescribe the centre line and lines defining the minimum width. Any plans showing a contravention of the Bye-laws must be rejected.

Health and Safety at Work etc. Act 1974

8.20 The Act and the regulations made under it contain provisions relating to health and safety during the construction process and in the workplace and the design and specification should take account of these requirements (see also Chapter 28).

The Construction (Design and Management) Regulations 1994 made under the Act require the architect to identify the risks which could arise during the construction due to the design and specification, eliminate them where possible, reduce them where they cannot be eliminated and notify any significant risks which remain. The architect must also advise the client of the need to appoint a planning supervisor. The HSE publishes a code of practice *Managing Health and Safety in Construction 2002*.

The Workplace (Health Safety and Welfare) Regulations 1992 require employers to ensure, as far as is reasonably practicable, the health, safety and welfare of their employers at work. The regulations, which expand on these duties, include requirements for ventilation, lighting, sanitary conveniences, washing facilities, drinking water, etc. (see Chapter 28).

Much asbestos had been introduced in buildings before its use was restricted. Now the *Control of Asbestos at Work Regulations 2002*, which come into force on 21 May 2004 and apply to non-domestic premises, also to the common parts of residential rented premises. They require employers to manage the risk (removal is seen as the last resort) and clean their premises. This has implications, not least at the survey stage, for architects concerned with work which could damage or disturb asbestos already in a building.

Party Wall etc. Act 1996

8.21 The Act which came into force on 1 July 1996. It drew on the sections of the London Building Act dealing with party walls which it replaced and it applies to the whole of England and Wales (except the four Temples) to provide a national framework for preventing and resolving disputes between neighbouring owners in respect of party walls and similar matters. It deals with three main issues: construction of new walls on boundaries between adjoining owners' land (section 1), repair, etc. of party wall and rights of owner (section 2) and excavation near to neighbouring buildings (section 6) (see chapter 26 for procedures).

Environment Acts 1995/1999

8.22 The Act is administered by the Environment Agency. Matters of concern to the Agency include contaminated land, flooding and the disposal of effluents.

Contaminated land may, on the advice of the Agency, be subject to planning conditions. It is also subject to Requirement C2 (dangerous and offensive substances) of Schedule 1 of the building regulations and such substances if 'found on or in the ground to be covered by the building', should be notified to the local authority's environmental officer who will advise. Radon may be a particular concern in specified areas.

Flooding may also, on the advice of the Agency, be subject to planning conditions to limit possible obstructions to flows (which

may be contaminated by sewage). Flooding as such is not a matter for the building regulations but Requirement C3 (subsoil drainage), requiring either drainage to be provided or measures to be taken (such as tanking) to prevent ground moisture entering the building or damaging its fabric, may be relevant.

Effluent disposal is unlikely to be subject to planning conditions (except perhaps in the case of major projects) but the consent of the Agency to outfalls is required (except for infiltration systems) and may be subject to conditions. Requirement H1(1)(c) (foul water drainage), H2(1)(b) (wastewater systems) and H3(3)(b) (rainwater drainage) of the building regulations may be relevant.

Disability Discrimination Act 1995

8.23 Part 3 of the Act comes into force on 1 October 2004 and enables a person who considers that, by reason of 'a physical or mental impairment which has a substantial and long-term adverse effect on (their) ability to carry out normal day-to-day activities', they suffer discrimination due to a physical feature of a building to take a provider of goods or services to court. The provider has three options – to remove the feature, alter the feature or avoid the feature – by providing a 'reasonable' means of avoiding the feature i.e. an alternative service.

The *Disability Discrimination (Providers of Services) (Adjustment of Premises) Regulations 2001* made under the Act provide that it is not reasonable for a provider to have to remove or alter a physical feature which satisfies a 'relevant design standard'. The Schedule to the regulations provides that *Approved Document M* (access and facilities for disabled people) is, subject to conditions, a relevant standard.

The scope of the Act, which is overseen by the Disability Rights Commission, is wider than the scope of the building regulations and advice can be sought from the local authority's Access Officer or through the National Register of Access Consultants if an access audit is sought.

Housing Act 1985

8.24 The Act contains provisions relating to the fitness of dwellings, including houses in multiple occupation, and some environmental health authorities use their wide-ranging powers to seek to impose requirements which the building regulations have dropped (such as minimum ceiling heights and ventilated WC lobbies) or have chosen not to introduce (such as integrated smoke detection and alarm systems in blocks of purpose-built self-contained flats). The Act is enforced by environmental health officers and negotiation seems to be the best policy.

Special classes of building

8.25 The legislation dealt with so far is, in one sense, of general application. The architect dealing with the design and construction of specialized types of building may find that special controls apply. All these specialized provisions are extremely complex, and space does not permit any detailed examination of them.

8.26 They range from premises (such as nursing homes and schools) to special risks (such as cinemas and the keeping of radioactive substances). In some cases the inspection of the premises will be delegated to the fire authority (see also Chapter 19).

22

Construction regulations in Scotland

PETER FRANKLIN

1 Introduction

1.01 Building control in Scotland is based on Building Acts. To understand Scottish practice, a knowledge of the Acts is required, as well as of the Regulations made under them. The Building Standards (Scotland) Regulations 1990 are only one part of the whole scene, although admittedly a very important part. Anyone trying to compare Scottish and English building control must bear the above in mind, so that there is a comparison of like with like wherever possible.

1.02 This study is intended to describe the main provisions of the Act and procedures laid down under it, as well as the various Statutory Instruments associated with it. In regard to the Building Standards Regulations themselves, it is obviously impossible to go into minute detail regarding interpretations, etc. The object of each part of the Regulations has, therefore, been stated and reference made to the more important provisions and, where thought applicable, to individual regulations.

Historical background

1.03 Building control is not new, and records of building law go back to the pre-Christian era. The first known are those found in the Mosaic Law of King Hammurabi of Persia c.2000 BC. Fire precautions which have always formed a major part of building codes were an accepted factor of Roman law and of English law from the twelfth century.

Dean of Guild Courts

1.04 In Scotland building control in royal burghs was exercised by Dean of Guild Courts where these existed. Originally, the Dean of Guild was the president of the merchants' guild, which was composed of traders who had acquired the freedom of a royal burgh. The post is an ancient one, e.g. in 1403 one Simon de Schele was appointed Dean of Guild and Keeper of the Kirk Work by Edinburgh Town Council. The Dean of Guild Court's original mercantile jurisdiction fell gradually into disuse to be replaced by a jurisdiction over such areas as markets, streets, and buildings. 'Questions of neighbourhood' were dealt with by Edinburgh Dean of Guild as early as 1584. Gradually the scope and nature of the powers of the Dean of Guild Courts became more precise until during the last 150 years they were subjected to a process of statutory modification.

1.05 Not all burghs had Dean of Guild Courts, and it was not until 1947 that the Local Government (Scotland) Act required burghs without Dean of Guild Courts to appoint one. In other burghs, the functions of the Dean of Guild Courts were either carried out by magistrates or the town council itself. In counties, plans were usually approved by a sub-committee of the public health committee. There was no warrant procedure as in burghs.

By-laws

1.06 During the last 150 years, statutory requirements laid the foundation of specific and more widely applicable standards. The Burgh Police Act 1833 empowered burghs to adopt powers of paving, lighting, cleansing, watching, and supplying water. However, the building legislation content of the nineteenth-century Acts was not large and was related mainly to ruinous property and drainage, attention to the latter being attracted by the large-scale outbreaks of cholera at that time. In 1892 the Burgh Police Act introduced a detailed set of building rules which were repealed by the 1903 Burgh Police Act. This Act gave powers to burghs to make by-laws in respect of building and public health matters. Meanwhile in the counties, the Public Health (Scotland) Act 1897 had already given them the power to make similar by-laws.

1.07 By-laws made under these Acts, although limited in scope, remained the main form of building control until 1932 when the Department of Health for Scotland published model building by-laws for both burghs and countries. Local authorities could, if they wished, adopt these by-laws for application in their own area. However, many did not. The model by-laws were revised in 1934 and 1937, but, apart from a widening of scope, later editions did not differ much from the original 1932 version. A much more comprehensive review was carried out in 1954. Although many local authorities adopted the 1954 model by-laws, adoption was at the discretion of the local authority and many did not. (By 1957, 26 of the 33 counties, 127 of the 173 small burghs, 13 of the 20 large burghs, and none of the cities had adopted the model by-laws.) However, Edinburgh, Aberdeen, and Glasgow had local Acts which combined many of the requirements of old statutes and by-laws with local features.

1.08 The then existing legislation fell short of the requirements of a modern building code able to cope with the rapidly expanding building of post-war Scotland where new techniques and materials were rapidly being introduced. It was decided that the whole concept of building control should be reviewed, and to this end a committee under the chairmanship of C. W. G. Guest QC, later Lord Guest, was appointed by the Secretary of State.

1.09 The committee's terms of reference required that it examine the existing law pertaining to building and jurisdiction of the Dean of Guild Courts and make recommendations on the future form of a building control system for counties and burghs, which was to be flexible enough to take account of new techniques and materials.

1.10 The committee published its report in October 1957. Its main recommendation was that legislation was essential to enable a comprehensive building code to be set up in the form of national regulations to achieve uniformity throughout the country. The basic purpose of building control should be the protection of the public interest as regards health and safety. The law must ensure that occupants, neighbours, and passers-by are protected by preventing the erection of buildings that are liable to collapse or lead to unhealthy or insanitary conditions. It must also prevent individual and collective fire hazards.

1.11 The recommendations were accepted and led to the existing form of control now established in Scotland.

Review of the building control system

1.12 During the period from its introduction until the late 1970s the building control system was kept under constant review. Some of the principles in the original legislation were expanded, and amendments, additions and deletions were made, where necessary to the regulations. This is a continuous process necessary to keep abreast of developments in building practice, technology and materials.

1.13 It is a principle of good management, however, that every so often a detailed analysis and examination be carried out on any system and building control is no exception. It was with this view in mind, together with government's determination to remove unnecessary restrictions on individual freedoms and minimize the involvement of central government, that the Secretary of State decided in 1980 that the Scottish Development Department should undertake a comprehensive review of building control.

1.14 In July 1980, in order to gauge the climate of opinion, a wide field of Scottish Interests were invited to give views on the following:

1 The structure and operation of the present system in Scotland with relevance to any major deficiencies and areas of difficulty;
2 Changes which might be introduced to make the system more efficient without undermining the protection of public health and safety.

1.15 These consultations revealed that there was wide agreement that the basic framework of building control works satisfactorily, but with scope for improvement. The first priority was seen as rationalizing over-complex building standards regulations. Other areas of concern involved inconsistent interpretation of regulations by enforcing authorities, differences of technical detail within the UK, the effect of liability for latent danger and the scope for private sector involvement. The Secretary of State announced in May 1981 that as a result of the comments received and the parallel review being undertaken in England and Wales proposals for change would be further developed.

Consultative Paper – The Future of Building Control in Scotland

1.16 In 1983, the Scottish Development Department issued for comment a Consultative Paper – The Future of Building Control in Scotland – and invited comment from interested bodies.

The paper was the outcome of the Secretary of State's statement of May 1981 (paragraph 1.15) and the object of the review was stated as:

1 Upholding the prime purposes of building control as laid down in the Building Acts
2 Securing simplicity in operation
3 Promoting consistency in interpretation and enforcement
4 Minimizing central government involvement
5 Providing for increased participation by the private sector within a system of control which continued to be based on enforcement by *local authorities*
6 Making the system self-financing.

1.17 The paper was divided into various headings under which proposals were described in general terms. These headings were as follows:

Simplification of the Building Standards Regulations
Liaison and Co-operation between Building Control Authorities
Certification and Type Approvals

Appeals
Liability for Latent Damage
Relaxation of Building Standards Regulations
Exempted Works
Fees for Building Warrants
Other Procedural Refinements.

The paper concluded that earlier consultations endorsed the views that the Scottish building control system was founded on sound principles, but was in need of alterations and improvements rather than demolition and replacement. Many of the proposals could be implemented under existing powers given in the Building Acts with priority being given to the preparation of a more compact and rational set of Building Standards Regulations.

1.18 As a result of the Consultative Paper, a large number of those consulted submitted many and varied comments to the Department. After these comments had been given serious consideration, a statement of intent was issued by the Secretary of State on 29 November 1985. The statement sums up the results of the consultations and the actions to be followed as a result of the exercise.

Statement of Intent by Secretary of State, 29 November 1985

1.19 The statement by the Secretary of State put forward a series of proposals based on the headings in paragraph 1.17. These can be summarized as follows:

1 *Building Standards Regulations* Particular attention would be focused upon matters of health, safety and conservation of energy while taking account of welfare and convenience. The revised Regulations would take the form of a functional statement coupled with a qualifying standard and backed up by supporting technical documents. The standards will be prescribed by Statutory Instrument. A revision of the technical content would be carried out at the same time.
2 *Certification* Powers would be legislated for to give local authorities, within clearly defined limits, the right to accept at their discretion certificates from suitably qualified persons responsible for designing a building.
3 *Liaison/co-ordination between building control authorities* After listening to various views put forward, the Government proposed to build on its previous liaison meetings with the Scottish Association of Chief Building Control Offices. It will set up a committee chaired and serviced by the Scottish Development Department which will meet at regular intervals. (See paragraph 1.21)
4 *Appeals* The present system of appeals to the Sheriff would be retained.
5 *Relaxation of the regulations* Delegation of the power to relax regulations for all buildings would be delegated in stages to local authorities. The Secretary of State would retain the responsibility for all Class Relaxations and in respect of buildings owned by the local authority in its own area.
6 *Exempted works* There would be much wider exemption from the Regulations in respect of small buildings including additions to existing buildings. Limited requirements would be retained in certain cases in respect of drainage and structure.
7 *Other procedural matters* Fees would be kept under constant review.

Progress arising from the Statement of Intent

Simplification of the building standards regulations

1.20 As a result of further consultation a new set of regulations was drafted and came into force on 1st April 1991.

Liaison on harmonizing technical content within the UK has formed an important part of the exercise and joint meetings with DoE and NI form a regular feature of the consultation.

The class warrant will be binding on all local authority building control departments. Powers have been taken to extend the scope of exemption in the regulations to parts of a building.

Relaxations

1.23 (See paragraph 2.46).

Consultative paper 2001

1.24 Following the principles described in Para 1.13 above the new Scottish Executive issued a new consultation paper seeking views on the future of the building control system in the light of advances in the building processes, enforcement and legislation. As a result a new Building (Scotland) Act was passed by the Scottish parliament and a completely new set of regulations was issued for consultation with an implementation date of spring 2005.

2 Building (Scotland) Acts 1959 and 1970

2.01 As a direct result of the deliberations of the Guest Committee, the Building (Scotland) Act 1959 was passed. The aim of the Act was to introduce a system which while utilizing some of the then current practice in a more modern form, produced new procedures and standards which were flexible enough to meet rapidly changing building processes. The Act itself was unique in UK legislation and gave Scotland the lead in the field of national building control.

2.02 Certain sections of the Act came into effect on the day the Act was passed, 30 April 1959, but the main provisions did not come into effect until 15 June 1964, a day appointed by the Secretary of State.

2.03 In common with much of our legislation, the Building Acts have in their short history been subject to amendment because of changes in other spheres of Government and in particular the effect of the Local Government (Scotland) Acts 1973 and 1994, the Health and Safety at Work etc. Act 1974 and the Housing (Scotland) Act 1986. While the basic philosophy of the original Building Act and that of 1970 has not changed, details in the enforcement of the requirements and indeed the scope of the Act have been altered. These have been incorporated in the text.

The Act is laid out in four parts, and a brief summary of the content of each is given below.

Local authorities

2.04 The requirement in the 1959 Act for local authorities to appoint building authorities was amended by the Local Government (Scotland) Act 1973. This identified those local authorities in which building control was vested. The Act empowered the authorities to set up their own means of control and this gave rise to a wide diversity of different solutions. These varied from large departments with considerable devolved powers given to officials, to all applications having to be put before committees. While the principle of the Local Government Act was to give autonomy to authorities, the lack of central Government guidance or suggested model for a building control department led in turn to anomalies which were not so apparent under the specific legislation of the 1959 Act. From 1 April 1996, the existing local authorities were replaced by new unitary authorities under the Local Government etc. Scotland Act 1994. While procedures will remain basically the same, the new authorities may well differ in the placing and management of building control departments within the new administrative frameworks.

Building Standards

2.05 Part II of the Building (Scotland) Act 1959, as amended by section 75 and Schedule 7 of the Health and Safety at Work Act 1974, deals with building standards and building operations. Section 3 of the Act gives the Secretary of State power to prescribe Building Standards Regulations and details the necessary procedure to be

Liaison with local authorities

1.21 A Building Control Forum as envisaged in the Statement of Intent was set up and met for the first time on 12 September 1985. Its terms of reference were those set out in the Secretary of State's statement and to fulfil these terms the Forum were required to:

1 Identify inconsistencies of interpretation and administration of the regulations
2 Ensure authoritative consideration of ways to eliminate such difficulties
3 Ensure effective communication of the Forum's advice and recommendations to all parties involved with building control (these would include existing professional bodies, trade interests, developers, etc.) and allow them to raise problems, subject to suitable arrangements being worked out, with the Forum.

It should be stressed, however, that the Forum is *not* an alternative to the courts and will not consider the content of the Regulations. The latter is the province of the Building Standards Advisory Committee (BSAC).

New powers

1.22 New powers were taken in the Housing (Scotland) Act 1986 with regard to certification and class warrants. These powers when they are introduced into the system will considerably speed up the process of work starting on site once designs are completed.

The Department will seek an independent assessment from designated bodies as to the building or part of the building's compliance with regulations – thus involving the private sector in the decision-making process.

carried out before making regulations (described below in paragraph 2.15). The basis of the Building Standards Regulations is stated as follows: 'they shall be such as in the opinion of the Secretary of State can reasonably be expected to be attained in buildings of the classes to which they relate, having regard to the need for securing the health, safety, welfare and convenience of the persons who inhabit or frequent such buildings and the safety of the public generally and for furthering the conservation of fuel and power'. The standards may make reference to any document published by the Secretary of State or other persons. This means in practice that the Secretary of State can 'deem to satisfy' any document he thinks fit. It is worth noting the fact that the power to make regulations contains two qualifying phrases, i.e. 'in the opinion of' and 'can reasonably', and may well explain the compromise situations which sometimes affect a final regulation as compared with original proposals and indeed technical advice. Certain buildings are exempted from regulations, e.g. Crown buildings and some Atomic Energy Authority Buildings (but see paragraph 1.19 above). The Secretary of State was also given the power to repeal or modify any enactment in force before or passed in the same session as the Health and Safety at Work Act etc. 1974 if he considers it inconsistent with or unnecessary or requires alteration in consequence of any provision of the Building Standards Regulations.

2.06 The Secretary of State may also make regulations for the conduct of building operations as he thinks necessary to secure the safety of the general public.

2.07 Only the Secretary of State is given power to relax Building Standards Regulations. However, Section 2 of the 1970 Act gives the Secretary of State power to make regulations delegating the power to give relaxation to the local authority.

Class warrants (formerly known as type approvals)

2.08 Under the Health and Safety at Work etc. Act 1974 powers were taken to issue type approvals. The system of type approvals required a designating order to bring it into place. The designating order was never made. When new powers were being taken under the Housing (Scotland) Act 1986 it was decided to redefine the type approval system at the same time. This was done and the term 'type approval' was changed to 'class warrant'.

The basis of a class warrant system is that the Secretary of State would have the power to issue such warrants in respect of buildings which are of a repetitive nature which comply with the relevant building standards. For example, a standard house plan which is built in various areas all over the country might be given a class warrant in respect of its design above damp proof course. The class warrant which is binding on all local authority building control authorities will alleviate the need for separate sets of plans to be prepared for each authority and avoid differences of interpretation. It will speed up the process of commencement of building once plans are completed.

The Scottish Development Department will seek an independent assessment from designated bodies as to the building's compliance with building standards before making a decision on an application for class warrant. This involves the private sector in the decision-making process.

It might also be useful to compare the term 'class warrant' with the term 'class relaxation' in order to avoid confusion. The former would apply where a building, component, etc., met the regulations. The latter would apply where building, etc., does not meet the regulations but is given a waiver of a regulation or regulations either conditionally or unconditionally.

Warrants for construction and demolition

2.09 A warrant for construction is issued subject to the conditions that the building is built in accordance with the description in the warrant, drawings, and specification. The building must also conform to the Building Standards Regulations and any direction from

the Secretary of State relaxing any of the Regulations. The local authority cannot impose any other constructional conditions. The warrant is not subject to any requirements for planning permission. The attention of local authorities, regarding the issue of warrants and attempts to impose conditions, was drawn to the relevant statutory instruments by a Building Note 6/77 issued by the Scottish Development Department in December 1977.

Local authorities have the power, however, to grant warrant for work to be carried out in stages. This is a discretionary power. Warrant for the demolition of a building must state the length of time the works will take and must include a method statement showing how the applicant intends to demolish the building.

2.10 Section 6(8) as amended by the 1970 Act gives provisions where it would be competent for a buildings authority to refuse warrant. This important section is worthy of careful study, as incorrect interpretation could cause inconvenience and delay. Local authorities can refuse warrant if:

1 The application has not been made in the prescribed manner.
2 The authority considers that application for alterations or extensions to a building would result in either of the following:
   (a) where a building conforms to the Regulations at the time of application, but would fail to conform as a direct result of the proposed works or;
   (b) where a building fails to conform to the Regulations at the time of application and would fail to conform to an even greater degree as a direct result of the proposed works.

2.11 The phrase 'as a direct result' is the important point. The following examples may help to elucidate it:

1 An existing cottage, built pre-Regulation, has a roof which is nearer its boundary than would be permitted by current Regulations. Should an extension to the cottage be built, the roof of which meets the current Regulations, then the existing roof is still acceptable. In other words the new works are not affecting the existing roof and making it fail the Regulations to any greater degree.
2 An extension to a factory resulted in the travel distance within the building as a whole being made worse; therefore the travel distance of the whole building, new and existing, was subject to the building standards for a new building.

Travel distance in relation to means of escape from fire is measured from a point on a storey to a protected doorway in accordance with rules laid down in the Regulations.

In regard to the term 'change of use', which plays an important part in determining this area of building control law, particular attention must be paid to the definition of 'change of use'. The meaning is different to that used in England and Wales and failure to appreciate that fact in its context could involve unnecessary extra work. Change of use applies to a component or element of structure as much as to the whole building.

2.12 Section 8 of the Act which allowed the local authority power to issue permission to occupy portions of roads for the deposit of materials was amended by the Road Traffic Act 1984 which transfers the power to the highway authority.

Certificates of completion

2.13 Section 9 relates to the issue of completion certificates by the buildings authority. Where electrical installations are concerned, another certificate is required from the installer certifying that the installations meet the necessary requirements of the Building Standards Regulations. No person may occupy a building erected under warrant unless a certificate of completion has been issued. However, temporary certificates may be issued at the discretion of the buildings authority. The Secretary of State has powers to extend the provision for certification to other than electrical installations, e.g. gas installations.

It should be noted that under an amendment introduced by the Health and Safety at Work Act etc. 1974 and activated by

'Get on with it. ... I've got my warrant.'

Commencement Order No. 2 under that Act, the wording of section 9 in respect of completion certificates was modified. The granting of the certificate is now qualified in respect of the building authority's inspection of the building by the words 'so far as they are able to ascertain after taking all reasonable steps in that behalf'.

This phrase recognizes that it is impossible for a building control officer to be continually on site inspecting the construction of a building at all times – indeed, that is not his job. Local authorities were worried that the previous phrasing of the certificate, with its blanket statement that 'the building met both regulations and plans completely', placed an unacceptable and unreasonable liability on their shoulders and represented for the rewording of the certificate in the new terms.

2.14 Powers are given in section 9 to deal with buildings erected without warrant or in contravention of warrant, and procedures are described. Section 11 of the 1959 Act empowers the authority to enforce certain provisions of the Building Standards Regulations on existing buildings.

Self-certification of design

2.15 Following upon the Secretary of State's statement of Intent of November 1984, powers were taken in the Housing (Scotland) Act 1986, section 19 to introduce a new section to the Building (Scotland) Act 1959 in respect of self certification of design only. The local authority retains final control over the assessment of compliance of a building through its powers to grant or refuse a certificate of Completion Under Section 9 of the 1959 Act.

Benefits of self-certification of design are:

1   The speeding up of the processing of applications for warrants by allowing local authorities to accept without further checking certificates of compliance for certain requirements of regulations.
2   The promoting of a degree of self-regulation by the private sector within the framework of local authority building control.
3   The reduction of the workload of local authority building control departments.
4   Recognizing existing good practice by the acceptance of design certificates from, for example, qualified structural and civil engineers.

The introduction of the powers will be by designating order. The parts of the Regulations and who will be entitled to certify have yet to be specified. (See paragraph 2.17 below.)

New Regulations

2.16 Section 12 requires the Secretary of State to appoint a Building Standards Advisory Committee, the main purposes of which are to advise him on the making of Building Standards Regulations and keeping the operation of the Regulations under review. The members of the committee are selected as individuals and not as representatives of particular interests. It should be noted, however, that various professional, commercial, research bodies, etc., do nominate representatives for consideration as members. The committee is usually reconstituted at three-year intervals. The present committee includes representatives from building control, architecture, engineering, law, fire services, building, material producers and local government administration.

2.17 The procedure for making regulations is as follows: the Secretary of State consults the Building Standards Advisory Committee and other such bodies which are representative of the interests concerned. In practice, over 200 bodies are asked for their comments regarding proposed amendments to the Building Regulations. The first of these, the Building (Self Certification of Structural Design) (Scotland) Building Regulations 1992 (1992 No. 1911 (S194)) was made on 28 July 1992. This allows certificates to be submitted in respect of structural requirements of Building Standard Regulation 11. The certificate must be issued by chartered, civil or structural engineers meeting the conditions laid down. Consequential amendments to the Procedure Regulations and Forms Regulations are included in this SI.

Dangerous buildings

2.18 Part III deals with dangerous buildings and goes into detail regarding action to be taken to make them safe, the powers of local authorities with regard to purchasing buildings where owners cannot be found, and the selling of materials from buildings demolished by the local authority.

Civil liability

2.19 The new section 19A lays down breaches of regulations which may be actionable so far as damage is concerned. Damage includes death or injury of persons.

This section has not yet been brought into operation.

Crown rights

2.20 The Secretary of State has made it clear that Crown buildings should conform to the Building Standards Regulations regarding new buildings and extensions and alterations to other buildings. While Crown buildings do not have to follow the warrant application procedure to local authorities some Crown Bodies, e.g. The Scottish Prison Service, have a full building control system.

Enforcement officers

2.21 Section 21 of the 1959 Act, which laid down a requirement for the appointment of masters of works, was repealed by the Local Government (Scotland) Act 1973 and the enforcement of building control left in the hands of local authorities. There are at present, therefore, no specific qualifications laid down for building control officers.

Schedules

2.22 These relate to matters in regard of which regulations may be made, recovery of expenses, evacuation of dangerous buildings, minor and consequential amendments of enactments.

Commencement Orders

2.23 It should be noted that the extra powers contained in the Health and Safety at Work Act and the Housing (Scotland) Act 1986 have to be activated by Commencement Order, and the first of these was issued as Commencement No. 2 Order 1975 and came into force on 27 March 1975. A further order – Commencement No. 6 Order 1980 – came into force on 17 March 1980 and deals with increased penalties for contravention under certain provisions of the Building (Scotland) Act 1959.

Other provisions

2.24 Part IV is concerned with supplementary provisions and deals with appeals, references to other enactments such as Ancient Monuments Acts, building preservation orders and so on, inspection and tests, penalties, fees, transitional provisions, and general interpretation.

Building (Scotland) Act 1970

2.25 The main purpose of the Building (Scotland) Act 1970 was to amend the 1959 Act as regards making Building Standards Regulations, depositing building materials on roads, and application for warrants. These points have already been mentioned.

2.26 The following additional powers were granted under the Act. Section 2 gives the Secretary of State powers to delegate to local authorities the power of relaxation, and a new form of relaxation power in respect of certain classes of buildings. This power, which might be described as an 'omnibus relaxation', permits him to direct that a building which may not meet the exact requirements of the Regulations can nevertheless be accepted by local authorities when warrant applications are made. It should be remembered that the term 'building' is defined in both the Act and Standards Regulations and covers both a whole building and its constituent parts. Class relaxations have been issued, e.g. for air supported structures, framed structures, various components in chimney and fire protection. These are situations where individual relaxations would be required in each case.

Section 4 permits the Secretary of State to call in any application for warrant received by a local authority and enables him to determine whether the building concerned will conform to the Building Standards Regulations, to give relaxations, and to impose, after consulting the Building Standards Advisory Committee, requirements additional to or more onerous than those in the Building Standards Regulations. This power is most useful in very large and complex developments where, for instance, the traditional means of protection from fire have to be supplemented by automatic detection systems and sophisticated ventilation schemes.

Building (Procedure) (Scotland) Regulations and subsequent amendments

2.27 The Procedure Regulations were laid before Parliament on 9 November 1981 and came into force on 30 November 1981. These regulations are still in force, but have seen subject to a series of amendments since that time. Many of these merely reflect changes in references to other legislation or to the regular upgrading of fee charges.

Several important changes have, however, been introduced by a series of subsequent amendments. These include.

1 In 1987 the waiving of fees for building operations consisting of the alteration or extension of a building to provide facilities for disabled persons who frequent the building or in the case of a dwelling inhabit the building.
2 In 1991 a new definition of 'disabled person', deletion of the definitions of 'affected proprietor' and 'road authority', revised instructions on the keeping of records and requirements in respect of warrant applications for demolition.
3 In 1997 requiring the submission of energy ratings for dwellings created by construction or change of use (this amendment made under the Building (Scotland) Amendment Regulations 1997).

Interpretation

2.28 Part I of the Regulations deals with interpretation, citation and revocation, definitions, powers of local authorities to charge fees, to issue warrants for the construction of a building in specified stages, and details of certificates of completion. Attention is drawn specifically to the following points:

1 Duration of warrant. A warrant is valid for three years only. This does not mean that a building must be completed within three years of the issue of warrant; it means that construction must be commenced within three years. A warrant is only a permission to construct and is required before the commencement of work to ensure that the building will comply with the Regulations. (See also Section 6 of the 1959 Act.) The interpretation of this section has led to some confusion in the past and draft regulations include a proposal to include both a starting and completion date to clarify the position.
2 Local authorities must either grant or refuse an application for a completion certificate within 14 days from the date on which the local authority receives the application, and in the event of a refusal must notify the applicant as to that refusal.
3 The description of the prescribed stages of construction, where work is permitted, under a warrant issued by stages.

Applications for warrant

2.29 Part II of the Regulations deals with applications for warrant. The 1981 Regulations considerably simplify the previous process, particularly in the light of neighbour notification requirements introduced in August 1981 under planning procedures. The following is a précis of the new arrangements. The applicant must lodge his application with the local authority in writing on the appropriate forms. It can be signed by the applicant or by his agent. The application should be accompanied by the principal plan and a duly certified copy. If a direction relaxing any regulation has already been given by the Secretary of State, this should accompany the application. The local authority may ask for additional plans and information and, if necessary, up to two extra copies of the application and plans lodged with it. The form and scale of the plans required are described in Schedule 1, Section H of the Regulations.

2.30 When the application is received, the local authority shall 'forthwith' – the regulation term – consider and determine the application. The local authority shall not refuse an application without giving the applicant notification of the proposed grounds of refusal and an opportunity of being heard and making written representations. Any such oral or written representations must be taken account of in finally determining the application.

Calling in warrants

2.31 Part III deals with the procedure to be followed where the Secretary of State 'calls in' an application for warrant to deal with it partly or wholly by himself. Where the Secretary of State calls in an application for warrant, the local authority must send him the plans, confirmation that the application has been properly made, copies of any previous warrants dealing with temporary buildings and which relate to the application under consideration, and any comments the local authority may wish to make. If on consideration the Secretary of State decides to impose more onerous requirements additional to or more serious than those in the Building Regulations at present, he must consult the applicant, the local authority, the Building Standards Advisory Committee, and any other person he thinks might have an interest. If the Secretary of State thinks fit, he may convene a hearing for the interested parties. It should be stressed that this procedure may also apply only in respect of individual parts of Regulations and in such a case the Secretary of State would then return the application, along with his requirements, for the local authority to process in the normal way. It is for the local authority to notify the applicant of the Secretary of State's decisions and his reasons for those decisions.

Local authority relaxation

2.32 Part IV gives the procedures to be followed by local authorities when dealing with applications for relaxation. These have been considerably simplified from the previous Regulations and give the local authority discretion in relation to who is to be notified as an affected proprietor.

2.33 Part V gives the procedure for appealing to the Secretary of State against the refusal of a local authority to grant relaxation or against a condition of relaxation.

Relaxation by Secretary of State

2.34 Part VI gives the procedure for application to the Secretary of State for a relaxation. The new procedures in Part IV are, in effect, now very closely allied to those which have applied under this part for some years. The applicant must lodge a copy of his plans and application with the local authority when he makes his application to the Secretary of State. The Secretary of State may consult by means of a draft direction with the applicant and other persons he considers to have an interest, and in his final determination shall take into consideration any comments made. The Secretary of State can, however, issue final direction without consultation, and this has, in fact, been done in certain cases.

Class relaxations

2.35 These are the province of the Secretary of State and relate to a general relaxation, binding on all local authorities, in respect of either a building type or a component of a building. Class relaxations usually refer to individual regulations and parts of the Regulations and may be conditional.

The Secretary of State must consult the Building Standards Advisory Committee and such other bodies as he deems have an interest before making his determination of an application. The relaxations are only granted after a detailed investigation including results of research and testing. It must be stressed that a class relaxation must *not* be confused with a class warrant. The form of the 1990 regulations should dispense with the need for this power to be used as frequently as in the past although there may be a special case to be considered.

This has been borne out by the fact that in October 2003 only four class relaxations are current. These relate to an Air house, a ventilation unit and two in respect of the conservation of fuel and power. Full details can be obtain on the following website http//www.scotland.gov.uk/about/DD/BSD/00018201/ClassRelaxations.aspx

Orders made by local authorities

2.36 Part IX deals with orders relating to buildings constructed without or in contravention of warrant and in respect of dangerous buildings. The part goes into detail regarding notices, appeals, and, where necessary, the convening of hearings.

General

2.37 Part X deals with procedure to be followed at hearings, appointment of assessors (if deemed necessary), maintenance of records, and inspection of records and applications (which must be available for inspection by the public at all reasonable hours). Decisions of the local authority must follow laid-down rules and must be made in writing. Where an application is refused or, for example, where a relaxation is given despite objections, the local authority must state the reasons for their decision.

2.38 Persons carrying out building operations under warrant must give notice to the local authority:

1 Of the date on which work commenced within seven days of that date
2 When a drain has been laid and is ready for inspection and test
3 When a drain has been infilled and is ready for the second inspection or test
4 Of the date on which operations are completed.

Items (1) and (4) shall be in writing, except in the case of (4) where an application for a certificate of completion has been made in the prescribed form.

Plans to be submitted

2.39 Schedule 1 goes into detail of the particulars of plans required and the minimum scales to which they have to be drawn. The Schedule is divided into sections relating to whether the application for warrant deals with erection, alteration, extension, change of use, or demolition of a building. In the case of demolition the 1991 amendments require details of the construction of the building to be demolished and the method of demolition.

2.40 Schedule 2 gives the table of fees applicable for a warrant. The fee scale is based on the estimated cost of the operations and ranges from £5 for small works to figures in excess of £1000. The fees are a once-only charge – there are no extra fees for inspection, etc. The figures are regularly upgraded to take account of inflation.

Building Operations (Scotland) Regulations 1975

2.41 The Secretary of State had powers conferred on him by Section 5 of the Building (Scotland) Act 1959 to make regulations for the conduct of operations for the construction, repair, maintenance, or demolition of buildings, as he thinks expedient for securing the safety of the public while building operations are in progress.

2.42 The Building Operations (Scotland) Regulations 1975, which came into operation on 16 May 1975, revoke the previous Regulations made in 1963. They lay down requirements for the safety of passersby and deal with such matters as the erection of hoardings, barricades and fences, footpaths with safe platforms, handrails, steps or ramps, overhead coverings, and so on. In addition, protective works are to be properly lit to the satisfaction of the local authority.

2.43 There are also provisions for clearing footpaths and the securing of partly constructed or demolished buildings. A special regulation deals with additional requirements for demolition operations.

These Regulations are administered by the local authority. At the time of writing these are being revised.

Building (Forms) (Scotland) Regulation 1991

2.44 Section 24 of the Building (Scotland) Act 1959 gave the Secretary of State power to make Regulations prescribing the type of form to be used in the various procedures under the Act.

2.45 The Regulations were completely revised and issued in 1991 coming into force on 1 April 1991. A minor amendment was made in the Building (Self Certification of Structural Design) (Scotland) Regulations 1992. The Regulations prescribe the forms in which applications for warrants, notices, orders, and other documents should be made under the Act. The Regulations are the latest in a series which have been updated in the light of changes to principal legislation and to related regulations. The Regulations provide a common system of forms applicable throughout Scotland for building control purposes. The Building (Scotland) Amendment Regulations 1997 require the application for a certificate of completion to include a statement of the energy rating calculation for a completed dwelling.

Building Standards (Relaxation by Local Authorities), (Scotland) Regulations 1997

2.46 These regulations supersede all previous legislation in this field. They delegate powers to local authorities to relax or dispense with the requirements of the building standards regulations in relation to all buildings including change of use. The Secretary of State retains powers in respect of warrants subject to 'call-in' procedures and appeals by aggrieved parties against local authority decisions.

2.47 The delegation is in respect of individual buildings and must not be confused with class relaxations (paragraph 2.34).

The procedure to be followed both in applying for relaxation and in appealing against a decision of a local authority, should this be sought, is detailed under the Building (Procedure) (Scotland) Regulations 1981 and the Building (Forms) (Scotland) Regulations 1991.

Building (Scotland) Act 2003

2.48 This Act, introduced by the Scottish Parliament will, when fully implemented, replace the Building Scotland Acts 1959 and 1970 as amended over the years.

It consolidates the main features of that Act and extends and introduces new powers.

The Act is of considerable length and complexity and space means that only a brief outline is given here. The document can be downloaded from the Scottish Executive website. http://www.hmso.gov.uk/legislation/scotland/acts2003/20030008.htm

The Act is in six parts, these include powers to make and relax building regulations, issue guidance documents, approve construction works etc. It also covers compliance and enforcement, dangerous and defective buildings, general matters such as BSAC, fees, verifiers etc. together with schedules and repeals of associated legislation.

2.49   Comments
1   The original powers to make building regulations have been extended to include 'furthering the achievement of sustainable development'.
2   The Act contains the important change in that while at present the Technical Standards are mandatory the proposed new edition will provided much greater flexibility in interpretation.
3   The Act also introduces Clauses regarding the powers of verifiers (a new term), approved certifiers of design and of construction. These would allow for powers being given to non-local authority persons or bodies.
4   The introduction of continuing powers.
5   The process of warrant approvals etc. are spelt out in detail.
6   The powers of BSAC are continued with a wider remit. *Note*. These may be further extended by proposals to form a *Building Standards Agency* which will enable direct involvement in the interpretation of the regulations. This will require a separate Statutory Instrument.

2.50 **Note** the powers of the Secretary of State in respect of Health and Safety were among others transferred to the new Scottish Parliament (see also paragraph 4.15).

3 Building Standards (Scotland) Regulations 1990 and subsequent amendments 1993–2002

3.01 A completely new and revised set of Regulations in a different format were laid before Parliament on 19 November 1990 coming into force on 1 April 1991. The Regulations take the form of a short statutory instrument which gives the requirements in a functional form under each of the familiar rubrics of the older style regulations. As the Scottish Regulations are standards regulations as required under the primary legislation, the statutory instrument requires to be supported by technical standards which have legal status. Published along with the statutory instrument, therefore, was a large and comprehensive set of technical standards in a separate loose-leaf document of A4 size, compliance with which meets the Regulations. The 1990 regulations and the Technical Standards have been the subject of a series of amendments. The latest in 1999 resulted in the issue of a completely new consolidated and amended set of Technical Standards. (Building Standards and Procedure (Scotland) Regulations 1999 SSI 99 No. 173). The opportunity was taken to revise the style and presentation of the document. These and subsequent amendments are available in a loose-leaf format.

3.02 While the statutory instrument gives the requirements in functional form, the Technical Standards document is the actual working document. It is laid out in 19 separate sections, 16 of which relate to the relevant clause in the statutory instrument, plus an introductory section, an appendix listing publications used in the Technical Standards and an index.

Each part has basically two sections. The first repeats the regulation and then gives the required standard and the second section gives deemed to satisfy provisions for certain standards. The 'deemed to satisfy' may relate to a code of practice, a detailed specification, etc.

The introduction to the Technical Standards makes it clear that full acceptance is accorded to national standards and technical specifications recognized in other Member States of the European Community which provide equivalent standards of protection or performance, e.g. in Part B: Fitness of Materials.

3.03 It is essential when using the Technical Standards to remember that all definitions are in Part A, and that when a defined term appears in the standard it is printed in italics. When an asterisk appears against a standard it indicates that there is a deemed to satisfy provision in the Part.

3.04 The interpretation of the Regulations is the province of the local authorities that have building control functions. If any dispute arises regarding interpretation, the final decision rests with the Sheriff Court.

The following paragraphs give a brief description of the requirements of the separate parts of the regulations and the appropriate Technical Standard.

Part 1 of the Regulations and Part A of the Technical Standards

3.05 Part 1 gives the general requirements including citation and interpretation. The latter gives the definitions required for the Regulations. These are repeated in Part A of the Standards together with additional definitions for terms used only in the Technical Standards. It is important to check the definitions in the latest amended Regulations and Technical Standards against earlier editions. Some have been amended in the Technical Standards e.g. conservatories and several new ones have been added, e.g. 'notified body'.

Regulations 3 and 4 are important at the outset of a project as they describe types of buildings which are exempt from the regulations or do not require a warrant. A designer should check the schedules to these Regulations carefully. Both exempted classes and fixtures not requiring a warrant have been subject to amendment.

Regulation 5 describes limited-life buildings as those 'erected for a period of up to 5 years'. Again it is important to check this requirement at the outset of a design as special provisions for such buildings can be found in the Regulations, e.g. in respect of site preparations. Regulation 6 is extremely important as it classifies buildings by purpose group (in Schedule 3). The classification affects all areas of the Regulations when applied to building types, particularly in respect of fire safety, ventilation and sanitary requirements.

Regulation 7 as read with Schedule 4 refers to occupant capacity (i.e. the number of persons a room or storey is deemed to accommodate for Regulations purposes). This capacity determines the required standards within the purposes group and is vitally important in respect of means of escape from fire, ventilation and sanitary accommodation. Note that where a room or space is likely to have more than one use the greatest occupant capacity applies. New occupant load factors in respect of shopping centres malls and food courts have been added to Schedule 4.

Regulation 5 as read with Schedule 5 gives the rules of measurement for regulation purposes.

Part A must be carefully applied at the outset of any design as failure to correctly identify its application to the building could cause problems later in the project's life and be expensive and difficult to remedy.

Part 2 of the Regulations and Technical Standards

3.06 This part is the meat of the Regulations and within it are found all the requirements. These are given as functional requirements, with the standards detailed in the Technical Standards; Regulation 9 states that compliance with the Regulations can only be met by the relevant standards. Conformity with the Technical Standards shall be deemed to satisfy compliance.

Fitness of materials (Regulation 10)

3.07 The requirements are given in functional terms and amplified in Part B of the Technical Standards. The use of national codes, Agrément Certificates or equivalent standards recognized by any Member State of the European Community is deemed to satisfy. In addition reference is made to a European technical approval in accordance with Council Directive 89/106/EEC to test evidence from the National Measurement Accreditation Service or similar.

Part B allows material whose suitability depends on suitable maintenance or periodic renewal, provided that replacement is reasonably practicable.

Structure (Regulation 11)

3.08 This regulation requires that every building shall be constructed so that all loads on a building are sustained by the building and safely transmitted to the ground while retaining the stability of the structure. Part C of the Technical Standards give methods of calculations and also lists the relevant criteria to be followed in all cases. In addition rules relating to buildings of five storeys or more (including every basement storey) are given for dealing with disproportionate collapse. This owes its existence to the aftermath of Ronan Point and is intended to give safeguards against progressive collapse. An amendment in 1994 redrafted the regulation to refer to 'damage' causing collapse rather than 'failure'. The position in regard to a storey in the roof space when calculating the number of storeys for the purpose of disproportionate collapse has been clarified. See also the Small Buildings Guide (second edition) published with the Technical Standards and which is deemed to satisfy the regulations.

Structural fire precautions (Regulation 12)

3.09 The theory of fire resistance embodied in the old by-laws, which national regulations replaced, was intended to ensure that each individual building would contain its own fire as far as possible and would be protected from outside. This applied as much to buildings on a plot of land in one occupation as to buildings on separate plots. Two changes were made by Regulations in 1963 and continued in subsequent revisions. These were that it was considered unnecessary that buildings should resist fire from outside if they were capable of containing any fire starting within them and that control should be restricted to safeguarding public interest by preventing general conflagration.

3.10 The Regulation requires that in the event of fire, the building, for a reasonable period, will maintain its stability and inhibit the spread of fire and smoke both within the building and to and from the building.

3.11 Part D of the Technical Standards attempts to achieve its purposes of laying down requirements for fire resistance of the structure. It controls the type of materials used, specifying non-combustibility where necessary as well as surface classification of lining materials. Fire resistance criteria are based on those found in BS fire tests notably BS 476 and its various parts. Roofs do not require fire resistance, not being classified as an element of structure, but they are given a classification in the 'deemed to satisfy' provisions based on the roof's ability to resist penetration by burning brands and the resistance of the surface to spread of flame.

3.12 Large buildings are required to be divided into compartments by means of compartment walls and separating floors and similarly buildings in different occupation have to be separated by such floors and walls. The concept of sub-compartmentation in hospitals has been recognised in the latest edition of the Technical Standards. Concessions for certain buildings in respect of non-combustibility requirements are given where there is a low fire load and risk. Technical Standards now include separate requirements for shared residential accommodation such as nurses' homes, certain single-storey commercial buildings and enclosed shopping centres with malls.

There are also strong criteria to prevent the passage of fire via pipes and ducts which penetrate compartments and separating floors and walls. Additionally cavity barriers and fire stops are required to prevent rapid spread of fire along cavities such as certain suspended ceilings and roof voids, etc.

There is, however, an acceptance of the principle that if a building is far enough from its boundary it will not spread fire to buildings on adjoining land in different occupation.

3.13 Technical Standards include references to certain small buildings attached to, or within the curtilage of dwellings in Purpose Group 1 and not exempted by Schedule 1. These are in the nature of a relaxation of certain requirements applied to buildings of a higher fire risk.

Means of escape from fire; Facilities of firefighting; Means of warning of fire in dwellings (Regulation 13)

3.14 The regulation requires that a building be required to be provided with adequate means of escape in the event of fire, adequate firefighting facilities and means of warning the occupants of dwellings of the outbreak of fire. This Part also now contains requirements for the disabled previously contained in the deleted Part T.

3.15 In meeting the requirements of the Regulations, the Technical Standards, Part E, go into considerable detail, backed up by explanatory diagrams, tables and 'deemed to satisfy' clauses, the latter giving detailed specifications on meeting the regulations (See also paragraph 5.04 for further information on the use of fire engineering techniques).

The intention is that a person should be able to reach a place of safety or a protected zone within 2½ minutes of becoming aware of fire. Exit widths are calculated using a unit width of 530 mm per person and a discharge rate of 40 persons per minute. (This is a fairly slow rate and is based on a heavily loaded occupancy.) The travel distance from any point to the place of safety or protected zone varies with the purpose group and differential travel distances are given in tabular form.

Every escape route (as defined in Part A) must lead to a place of safety directly or by way of a protected zone. This in turn means the protected zones have to meet specific requirements in the standards, e.g. enclosure of stairs and ramps.

Where, because of the purpose group classification, there is an additional perceived risk, requirements as to the layout of the building within the area between a point and a protected door are specified – for example in high blocks of flats. There is also a requirement in certain residential buildings with only one escape route to make provision for emergency escape windows which have a specified size and location. There is now a requirement for smoke alarms and/or fire detection systems in dwellings based on size and Purpose Group.

The part also has detailed requirements for assembly buildings, hospitals, shopping centres with malls, certain residential buildings and specified parts of buildings such as stages, mechanical ventilation systems, places of special fire risk, accommodation stairs and escalators, fire doors, fixed seating, emergency lighting.

3.16 The part includes requirements to assist firefighters. These range from the provision of fire mains and hydrants to access for firefighting vehicles. The latter are differentiated depending on the size and height of a building or whether or not wet or dry fire mains are fitted. In respect of hydrant provision the standards recognize the difficulties faced by buildings in remote areas and accept for firefighting purposes, water other than through water mains, for example rivers, lochs, static water tanks, always provided access for a pumping appliance is available.

Combustion Appliance Installations (Regulation 14) and Storage of Liquid and Gaseous Fuels (Regulation 15)

3.17 The requirements of Regulation 14 apply to any appliance designed to burn solid fuel (including wood and peat) or gaseous or liquid fuel. The Regulation requires the appliances to operate safely so that their operation does not cause damage to the building, the products of combustion are not a hazard to health and sufficient air

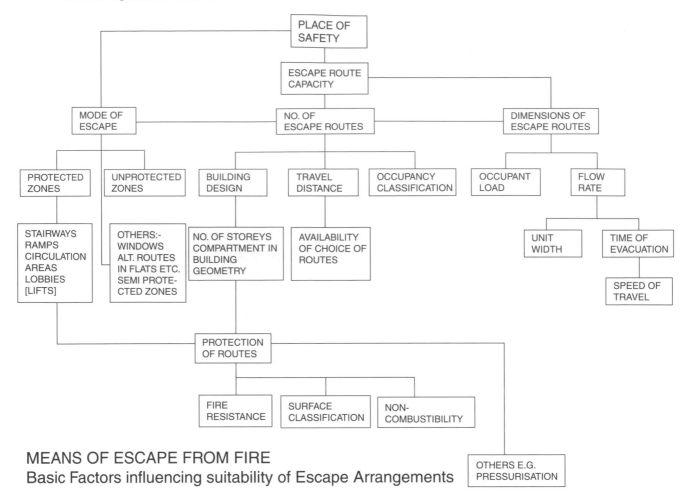

PLACE OF SAFETY

ESCAPE ROUTE CAPACITY

MODE OF ESCAPE

NO. OF ESCAPE ROUTES

DIMENSIONS OF ESCAPE ROUTES

PROTECTED ZONES

UNPROTECTED ZONES

BUILDING DESIGN

TRAVEL DISTANCE

OCCUPANCY CLASSIFICATION

OCCUPANT LOAD

FLOW RATE

STAIRWAYS RAMPS CIRCULATION AREAS LOBBIES [LIFTS]

OTHERS:- WINDOWS ALT. ROUTES IN FLATS ETC. SEMI PROTE-CTED ZONES

NO. OF STOREYS COMPARTMENT IN BUILDING GEOMETRY

AVAILABILITY OF CHOICE OF ROUTES

UNIT WIDTH

TIME OF EVACUATION

SPEED OF TRAVEL

PROTECTION OF ROUTES

FIRE RESISTANCE

SURFACE CLASSIFICATION

NON-COMBUSTIBILITY

OTHERS E.G. PRESSURISATION

MEANS OF ESCAPE FROM FIRE
Basic Factors influencing suitability of Escape Arrangements

"THE ESCAPE ROUTE WIDTH MUST HAVE A MAXIMUM HEIGHT OF 2 METRES"

"(SUITABLE) ACCESS REQUIRED FOR FIREFIGHTERS"

for combustion is provided. The storage of fuel oil or liquid petroleum gas supplying appliances providing space and water heating and cooking facilities are covered by Regulation 15 subject to limitations. In the case of oil storage tanks the regulation only applies to tanks of over 90 litres capacity and in the case of LPG over 150 litres (water equivalent). Attention must be paid to the application of the scope of the regulation as other storage facilities may be subject to different legislation, e.g. Health and Safety legislation. Part F has undergone a complete revision in the 1999 amendments.

3.18 Part F of the Technical Standards gives full details of the requirements and deemed to satisfy provisions. It is divided into seven main sub-sections. These cover Large combustion appliances, general standards for small combustion appliance installations, specific requirements for solid fuel, gas and oil installations, and storage of liquid and gaseous fuels. There are deemed to satisfy provisions for all sections.

3.19 The 1999 amendments raised the rating of small appliance installations to 50 kW output rating for solid fuel and a net input rating of 70 kW for oil and gas. Above these figures an appliance comes into the category of a large appliance installation.

The requirements for large installations are given in functional terms, but those for smaller installations are given in detail with references to codes of practice as acceptable 'deemed to satisfy' provisions.

3.20 The object of Part F is to prevent the ignition of any part of a building or damage to persons from the use of an appliance and its associated flues or chimneys. It also recognizes the need for suitable supplies of combustion air to enable appliances to operate safely. The part, therefore, goes into detail regarding construction, installation and operation of all matters relating to the primary object of safety of persons.

3.21 The requirements for safe fuel storage recognize the considerable increase in the use of such fuels as LPG and the risks associated with improper storage. In the case of oil storage attention is drawn both to the requirements for catchpits and the concession given to very small storage tanks.

Preparation of sites and resistance to moisture (Regulations 16, 17 and 18)

3.22 These Regulations are drafted in functional terms as are the standards in Part G of the Technical Standards. They are, however, backed up by a comprehensive 'deemed to satisfy' set of provisions together with illustrated details.

3.23 Part G contains requirements in respect of site and ground immediately adjoining a site. These must be prepared and treated to protect the building *and its users* from harmful effects caused by harmful and dangerous substances, matter in the surface soil and vegetable matter. Harmful and dangerous substances are defined in Regulation 16 and have a very wide application. A site must also be safeguarded from any harmful effects of ground and flood water and existing drains as far as reasonably practicable. The deemed to satisfy provisions contain recommendations regarding measures against the ingress of radon gas. *Note*: there are disapplications for certain temporary buildings.

3.24 A building must be so constructed to protect the building and its occupants from the harmful effects of rising damp and the effects of precipitation, e.g. rain and snow. In addition buildings of Purpose Group 1 shall be constructed to protect the building and users, as far as reasonably practicable from the effects of condensation, both surface and interstitial.

Attached to this part is an Appendix which is not part of the standards or deemed to satisfy provisions, but gives useful guidance on sites where harmful or dangerous substances are suspected to be present or where serious or coastal flooding has occurred and is at further risk.

Resistance to the transmission of sound (Regulations 19–20)

3.25 The Regulations relate only to dwellings other than wholly detached dwellings and the walls and floors between dwellings and other parts of a building, e.g. the floor of a flat over an office or shop. The requirements apply to both airborne and impact sound.

3.26 Part H of the Technical Standards, in its 'deemed to satisfy' provisions goes into great detail in describing methods of meeting the standards and gives examples and illustrations of acceptable constructions. The part draws attention to the fact that the standards required should be achieved by common, economically viable forms of construction which must be allied to good standards of workmanship.

Conservation of fuel and power (Regulation 22)

3.27 The scope of the requirements for conservation of fuel and power were considerably widened when the original plans to make regulations under the Building (Scotland) Act 1959 were changed to include conservation of energy (Health and Safety at Work etc. Act 1974, Chapter 37, Clause 75, Schedule 7). The regulation applies to all buildings other than those exempted in Regulation 22(2) (as amended). These include unheated buildings or those with a limited space heating system for frost protection or unheated parts of a building in purpose Group 1A which do not form part of a dwelling.

3.28 Part J of the Technical Standards, as amended, gives the requirements under six main headings. These are:

1 Application
2 Buildings in Purpose Group 1
3 Buidlings in Purpose Groups 2–7
4 Limiting Infiltration
5 The Conservation of Fuel and Power: the building services, heating and hot water
6 The Conservation of Fuel and Power: the building services, artificial lighting

3.29 The standards give very detailed methods of meeting the requirements. These use one of the following methods:

1 The elemental approach
2 Calculated Standards
3 Energy use

For dwellings the chosen method for producing an energy rating is the Standard Assessment Method (SAP) (the government's Standard Assessment Procedure for energy rating of dwellings, 1998 edition (SAP 1998), published by BRE).

3.30 The standards for building services include controls for heating systems, hot water storage vessels and insulation of hot water storage vessels and pipes and ducts. The standards for insulation are backed up by 'deemed to satisfy' provisions. A comprehensive series of appendices is attached to the part giving illustrative details explaining methods of calculations etc.

Ventilation of buildings (Regulation 23)

3.31 The requirements for ventilation are to ensure an adequate supply of air is available for human occupation and can be provided either by natural, mechanical or joint natural/mechanical means. *Note*: the air for combustion appliances is extra and subject to Part F of the Technical Standards. The original regulations have been considerably slimmed down and, with the exception of the requirements for dwellings and the location of ventilation openings, are largely dependent on the use of 'deemed to satisfy' provisions. Part K does not apply to buildings to which certain other legislation applies, e.g. the Factories Act 1961 (1961 C34). It should be noted that the standards now require a trickle ventilator in addition to an opening area of ventilation when natural ventilation is provided in dwellings, rooms in other buildings as well as mechanical extraction for bath and shower rooms.

Drainage and sanitary facilities (Regulations 24, 25 and 25A)

3.32 The Regulations require adequate drainage and sanitary facilities to a building including specific requirements for disabled persons. Part M of the Technical Handbook, in its standards for both drainage and pipework give functional requirements which are backed up with extensive use of codes and specifications in the 'deemed to satisfy' provisions. Every building is required to have a drainage system connected to a public sewer or a private sewage works. The latter may be septic tanks in rural areas, but it should be noted that the wording ensures that cesspools are not acceptable. A septic tank is considered to be a private sewage treatment works and its installation and disposal of its effluent should be in accordance with BS 6297. Regard has to be paid to any case where the Scottish Environmental Protection Agency (SEPA) has issued a Prohibition Notice on the control of discharges. The requirements are very flexible so as to permit a wide variety of different materials both above and below ground.

3.33 The standards for sanitary facilities provision now include a requirement for sanitary facilities for the disabled in buildings other than dwellings and accessible sanitary facilities in dwellings. The latter is a new concept and when read with Technical Standard Q2.11 could have a marked effect on the design of dwellings. While the term 'adequate' will mean that sanitary appliances will require a suitable water supply, public water supplies are the responsibility of the regional councils (from 1996 the new Regional Water Authorities) and designers should liaise with them at an early stage. There are areas of the country which are not served by a public supply and recourse has to be made to a private supply. Such supplies should be tested for adequacy and potency including chemical and bacteriological testing.

Electrical installations (Regulations 26 and 26A)

3.34 Both the Regulation and standards are written in functional terms, with exceptions for certain buildings, e.g. buildings to which the Mines and Quarries Act 1954 and the Factories Act 1961 apply. The 1999 amendments have included the requirement (previously in the deleted Part T) for the provision of a hearing aid system for certain auditoria and conference halls and situations where a glazed screen separates the public from a vendor or service provider. The requirements will be met when the installation meets the relevant requirements of BS 7671: 1992.

Miscellaneous hazards (Regulations 27 and 28)

3.35 These Regulations bring together a miscellany of safety requirements to prevent accidents. Part P of the Technical Handbook gives standards relating to collision with projections and glazing, cleaning of windows, safety on escalators and passenger conveyers, and discharge of steam pipes. There is also a standard relating to the danger of malfunction of an unvented hot water storage system. The standard is met by the requirements of a detailed specification in the 'deemed to satisfy' provisions. By the 1994 Regulations, additional requirements are imposed in relation to the positioning of manual controls for the operation of windows and rooflights for means of access to roofs in building other than housing.

Facilities for dwellings (Regulation 29)

3.36 Until 1986, the Building Regulations gave standards in great detail in relation to housing. Since that date the requirements have been reduced to a minimum even to removing minimum ceiling heights. Part Q gives standards in relation to adequate sleeping, kitchen, window space, heating, access between storeys and access from a suitable road. Where available an electricity supply is required.

Storage of waste (Regulations 30 and 31)

3.37 The requirements for solid waste storage apply to dwellings and require that adequate facilities be provided to facilitate access for storage and removal, minimize health risks and prevent contamination of water supplies and watercourses. Similarly dungsteads and farm effluent tanks must be so constructed, positioned and protected to minimize danger to health and safety and contamination of water supplies and watercourses. Part R of the Technical Standards gives detailed standards backed up by references to relevant British Standards in the 'deemed to satisfy' provisions.

Access to and movement within buildings, and protective barriers (Regulation 32)

3.38 This part has been completely revised and now includes several requirements previously contained in the deleted Part T. The Regulations require that stairs and ramps must provide a safe means of passage for users of a building. Protective barriers are required as necessary to stairs, ramps, raised floors, balconies, etc. Part S of the Technical Standards gives very detailed standards for the construction of stairs, landings and protective barriers. Certain areas which have limited access, e.g. in industrial and agricultural buildings, may have stairs and fixed ladders complying with the appropriate 'deemed to satisfy' provision. The requirements for access for the disabled are extensive and include the provision of suitable car parking spaces and access from them to the principal entrance of a building, access within a building and throughout storeys of the building (subject to certain exemptions), and adequate and suitable wheelchair spaces in auditoria and spectator fixed seating areas. Part Q now contains requirements for access for the disabled to and within buildings.

Appendix to the Technical Standards

3.39 This includes reference to all British Standards and Codes of Practice and to other publications such as BRE reports referred to in the main text.

3.40 The Regulations are subject to regular scrutiny and, where necessary, alteration in order to take cognizance of new building materials and processes and to take account of new Codes of Practice, etc. The form and presentation of the Regulations is now such that amendments will in the main be made to the Technical Standards handbook rather than to the statutory instruments.

Proposed new Building Regulations

3.41 The Scottish Executive issued a consultative document on the future of the building control system in 2001 and a follow-up document after consideration of the comments on the original document in 2002. They subsequently issued a draft set of building regulations for consultation. These aim is to lay new building regulations (which incorporate the operations regulations – see para 2.41), new procedure regulations and separate fees regulations in the autumn of 2004 to come into force in 2005. These Regulations and the accompanying guidance documents will contain separate documents for domestic and non-domestic buildings and will have a status more akin to the Approved Documents in England. The new regulations will allow alternative methods to be accepted to meet their requirements and be more flexible than at present including the greater use of the wide range of specialist documents available and compliance with the Construction Products Directive. This approach will require a greater basic knowledge of fundamental building theory and principles and it should help to avoid the sometimes dogmatic 'book only' interpretational disputes which occasionally plague the building processes.

The draft runs to 1000 pages and the Scottish Executive have issued the draft in various forms including CD. The draft can also be viewed on their website.

4 Other national legislation affecting building

4.01 The following list of legislation (although not completely exhaustive) applies in Scotland, and the comments under each heading may give guidance regarding the Scottish scene. *NOTE*: the new

Building (Scotland) Act 2003 will amend many of the relevant references to building control when fully implemented.

Offices, Shops and Railway Premises Act 1963

4.02 Precise standards for ventilation, means of escape from fire, and occupant load factors are laid down in the Building Standards Regulations. The requirements in the Offices, Shops and Railway Premises Act 1963 are in general framed so that standards of the Building Regulations are *usually* taken by the enforcing authority to meet the requirements of the Act. However, the Building Standards Regulations accept the Sanitary Convenience Regulations 1964 (Regulation D25(2)(C) of the Building Regulations gives exceptions to the provision of sanitary accommodation).

Section 29 of the Offices, Shops and Railway Premises Act previously covered fire and certification, but has been repealed and responsibility passed to the Fire Precautions Act from 1 January 1977. Check also the amendments contained in the Health and Safety at Work etc. Act 1974.

Clean Air Acts 1993

4.03 Sections 14 and 15 of this Act provide a new control for the heights of chimneys serving furnaces. The situation, therefore, is that special application must be made to the local authority for chimney height approval for furnace chimneys. The height of non-furnace chimneys is dealt with under the Building Regulations without need for special application. Constructional details of all chimneys are of course subject to local authority approval. See Chapter 19, paragraphs 7.05 and 7.06 and Chapter 19, paragraphs 8.09–8.11.

Factories Act 1961

4.04 Provisions of Part K (ventilation) do not apply to premises subject to the Factories Act 1961, and it is advised that particular ventilation requirements should be discussed with the factory inspectorate at an early stage. However, means of escape for fire requirements are subject to Part E of the Building Standards Regulations. Fire certification previously under this Act is now the responsibility of the Fire Precautions Act as from 1 January 1977 – see the Fire Precautions (Factories, Offices, Shops and Railway Premises) Order 1976. In Scotland, fire authorities are area authorities, eight in number, with their boundaries roughly equivalent to the local authority regional boundaries, but with one brigade covering the Lothian and Borders area. Check carefully the implications of amendment contained in Health and Safety at Work etc. Act 1974.

Fire Precautions Act 1971

4.05 Under this Act, certain premises must obtain a fire certificate from the fire authority as to the suitability of their means of escape. The premises are designated by order, and on 31 January 1972 the Secretary of State designated hotels and boarding houses above a certain size as the first class of premises requiring certificates. The order came into force on 1 June 1972. As the Building Standards Regulations contain requirements for the provision of means of escape, certain sections of the Fire Precautions Act are disapplied to Scotland and certain others apply only to Scotland. Section 14 contains a statutory bar in that where the means of escape meet the Building Regulations requirements, then they must be accepted for fire certificate purposes. This does not mean that all existing premises necessarily have to meet Building Regulations standards for new buildings, and many will have reasonable means of escape at present (although not quite up to new building standards). The fire officer has scope to use his judgment in existing premises as far as the statutory bar allows. Attention is also drawn to the definition of 'owner' which differs from that in England. See Chapter 19, paragraph 6.03 ff.

Fire Certificates (Special Premises) Regulations 1976

4.06 These provide that a certificate issued by the Health and Safety Executive shall be required for premises of a kind specified in Schedule 1 of these Regulations and lay down the conditions which may be imposed. The statutory bar for building regulations does not apply to these buildings, but they are of such a specialized nature that close consultation would take place with the relevant authorities at an early stage of design. The Regulations came into force on 1 January 1977.

Sewerage (Scotland) Act 1968

4.07 This Act, which came into force on 1 May 1973, has a bearing on the requirements of the drainage section (Part M) of the Building Standards Regulations. The main effect is to limit the range of the Building Standards Regulations, as many parts of what were termed common drainage will in future become sewers-public or private and vested in Scottish Water the successors to previous local authorities and water authorities. The term 'drain' is defined as 'that within the cartilage of a building and for its own use'.

The Act under section 12 and subject to the conditions of that section gives an owner a right to connect to a Scottish Water sewer or sewage treatment works. The owner of any premises who proposes to connect his drains or sewers to a public sewer or works of a Scottish Water, or who is altering his drain or sewer in such a way as to interfere with those of a Scottish Water, must, however, give 28 days' notice to the Scottish Water, who may or may not give permission for the work to proceed. The authority can give conditional approval, and the owner has right of appeal against any decision.

Powers are given in the Act to require defects in drains or sewage treatment works to be remedied. Scottish Water have the powers to take over private sewage treatment works, including septic tanks. Other powers include rights to discharge trade effluents into public sewers, emptying of septic tanks, provision of temporary sanitary conveniences, etc.

Health and Safety at Work etc. Act 1974

4.08 The most important effect of this Act is contained in section 75 as read with Schedule 10. These clauses introduce amendments to the principal Building Acts and extend and alter the powers contained in them. It should be noted that in Part III of the Act only section 75 is applicable to Scotland. The powers under this section come into force only when the Secretary of State issues a designating order. To date, two such orders have been made: the Health and Safety at Work etc. Act 1974 (Commencement No. 2) Order 1975, and the Health and Safety at Work etc. Act 1974 (Commencement No. 6) Order 1980.

The Act also includes important changes in transferring fire certification carried out under other legislation, e.g. Offices, Shops and Railway Premises Act and Factories Act to the Fire Precautions Act.

Safety of Sports Ground Act 1975

4.09 This Act contains references to buildings authorities in sections 3(3), 4(7), 5(5), 10(5), and 11. Work carried out which requires structural attention is subject to Building Regulations and Procedures. It should also be noted that the only public enquiry in the UK under this Act took place in 1979 in Dundee, with the Secretary of State's decision being issued in 1980.

Fire Safety and Safety of Places of Sport Act 1987

4.10 As well as introducing a number of new requirements, the above Act contains amendments to the Factories Act, and the Offices, Shops and Railway Premises Act 1963. In addition it changes the term stadium in the Safety of Sports Ground Act 1975 to 'sports ground' which has a wider meaning.

In terms of Scots law, attention is drawn to section 7. Note that the references to building regulations in section 7(3), (4) and (5) relate to England and Wales only and that section 48 amends the Civic Government (Scotland) Act 1982, Section 98. This section at the moment gives the Secretary of State powers to make regulations for the safe operation of electrical luminous signs exceeding 650 volts. The reference to a limiting size has been replaced by a more functional description.

Licensing (Scotland) Act 1976

4.11 The Act contains references to building control in Section 23(3). Again, structural alterations and change of use are subject to building regulations and procedures.

Civic Government (Scotland) Act 1982

4.12 This Act covers a wide range of activities and functions controlled by local authorities. It gives power to make and enforce by-laws. Mention should be made of the powers to license various forms of businesses or functions: e.g. places of public entertainment.

Special attention is drawn to Part VIII, Buildings etc. This covers various requirements as to maintenance and repair of buildings, installation of lighting, fire precautions in common stairs. Of particular interest is Section 88 regarding the installation of pipes through a neighbouring property and the procedure to be followed where consent of the neighbouring owner has been withheld or refused.

Local Government etc. Scotland Act 1994

4.13 The act which changes the face of Scottish local authorities to unitary authorities from 1 April 1994 also amends many pieces of legislation including the definition of local authority in the 1959 Building Act. Water and sewerage services passed to three new regional water and sewerage authorities (these have now been amalgamated into one body – Scottish Water) and may have important implications for designers and builders.

The Fire Precautions (Workplace Regulations) 1997

4.14 These regulations may require works to be carried out in connection with means of escape from fire. Any construction works will in most cases be subject to the Building Standards Regulations.

The Scotland Act 1998

4.15 This major piece of constitutional legislation granted the go-ahead for a devolved Scottish parliament within the UK. The Parliament came into being in May 1999. Health and safety are included among the devolved powers to the new Parliament. Building control in general has been determined to be a devolved power. It should also be noted that with Building Control no longer having to fight for a place in a crowded Westminster legislation queue the opportunity to amend or consolidate Scottish legislation may well be speeded up as well as being closely scrutinized by MSPs. (See Paragraph 1.25 refereing to Building (Scotland) Act 2003)

5 General

5.01 The following points may be useful to persons wishing to design and build in Scotland for the first time:

1 Scots law differs from that of the rest of the UK (see Scottish articles in this handbook).
2 Building control is exercised by local authorities.
3 Warrant must be obtained from the local authority before any building (including alterations and extensions) can begin, and it is separate from planning permission. A fee related to the total cost of the job is usually payable in accordance with the scale laid down in the table of fees (Schedule 2 of the Procedure Regulations).
4 Ensure that the latest amendments to the Building Standards Regulations are available as well as a copy of the Regulations themselves, the Procedure Regulations, and the correct forms.
5 Relaxation of the Regulations in respect of referred warrants and appeals is the responsibility of the Secretary of State for Scotland.
6 If problems occur, consult the building control officer of the appropriate authority, but remember that although he will normally give advice, he is not there to design or redesign, draw or redraw plans.
7 Check carefully the requirements of the sewerage authority where appropriate.
8 Check carefully whether a class relaxation has been issued in respect of a new building product.

EEC

5.02 Legislation produced by the EEC is already having an effect on Building Regulations. The Construction Products Directive of 12/12/88 lays down requirements for all member countries and is very wide in its scope.

Directive 78/170/EEC covers the performance of heat generators and production of hot water in new industrial buildings and insulation of its distribution in new industrial building.

New Health and Safety directives being prepared will also affect Building Regulations. See Chapters 27 and Chapter 28.

Building Notes

5.03 The Scottish Executive issues a series of Building Notes giving guidance to local authorities and those having an interest in Building control matters. These are intended to clarify points that have been brought to the attention of the Executive or to give advice in respect of procedural and similar matters. There are some 17 Building notes still current and these vary from advice regarding building warrants to European matters on the one hand and technical matters such as unventilated hot water storage systems, locks on exit doors and Fitness of materials, fittings and components; and workmanship.

The current list can be accessed at the following website. http//www.scotland.gov.uk/about/DD/BSD/00018201/Regulation Notes.aspx

5.04 As an example Note 2/98 provides guidance and advice on fire engineering. It describes it as involving the analysis of fire safety from first principles and includes:

Initiation and development of fire within the enclosure of origin
Spread of smoke and toxic gases within and beyond the enclosure of origin
Spread of fire beyond the enclosure of origin
Detection of fire and activation of fire protection systems
Fire service intervention
Evacuation.

The note recommends the BS Draft for Development 240 'Fire Safety Engineering in Buildings' 1997 to local authorities when considering applications where fire matters are based on fire engineering principles.

BUILDING CONTROL IN SCOTLAND: CURRENT LEGISLATION

Building (Scotland) Act 1959 [Amended by much later legislation – no clean updated copy is available – last official revised copy is dated 1st October 1977]

The Building (Scotland) Act 1959 (Appointed Day) Order 1963: SI 1963 No 1896 (S.101)

Building (Scotland) Act 1970 [Used to amend the 1959 Act]

The Building (Scotland) Act 1970 (commencement) Order 1971: SI 1971 No 744 (S.102)

The Building Standards Advisory Committee (Scotland) Regulations 1959: SI 1959 No 1364 (S.84)

The Building Operations (Scotland) Regulations 1975: SI 1975 No 549 (S.74) [Out of date, requires amendment]

The Building (Procedure) (Scotland) Regulations 1981: SI 1981 No 1499 (S.152) [Amended as below plus by SI 1528 1991, SI 1911 1992, SI 2157 1997, SSI 174 1999]

The Building (Procedure) (Scotland) Amendment Regulations 1987: SI 1987 No 1232 (S.90)

The Building (Procedure) (Scotland) Amendment Regulations 1991: SI 1991 No 159 (S.14)

The Building (Procedure) (Scotland) Amendment Regulations 1995: SI 1995 No 1572 (S.112)

The Building Standards (Scotland) Regulations 1990: SI 1990 No 2179 (S.187) (and the associated Technical Standards for compliance with the regulations) [Amended as below]

The Building Standards (Scotland) Amendment Regulations 1993: SI 1993 No 1457 (S.191) (and associated Technical Standards amendments)

The Building Standards (Scotland) Amendment Regulations 1994: SI 1994 No 1266 (S.65) (and associated Technical Standards amendments)

The Building Standards (Scotland) Amendment Regulations 1996: SI 1996 No 2251 (S.183) (and associated Technical Standards amendments)

The Building (Scotland) Amendment Regulations 1997: SI 1997 No 2157 (S.150) (and associated Technical Standards amendments)

The Building Standards and Procedure Amendment (Scotland) Regulations 1999: SSI 1999 No 173 (and associated Technical Standards amendments)

The Building Standards (Scotland) Amendment Regulations 2001: SSI 2001 No 320 (and associated Technical Standards amendments)

The Building Standards (Scotland) Amendment Regulations 2001 Amendment Regulations 2002: SSI 2002 No 40 (brief amendment to deal with transition for conservatories)

The Building (Forms) (Scotland) Regulations 1991: SI 1991 No 160 (S.15) [Amended by SI 1911 1992 and SI 2157 1997]

The Building (Self Certification of Structural Design) (Scotland) Regulations 1992: SI 1992 No 1911 (S.194)

The Building Standards (Relaxation by Local Authorities) (Scotland) Regulations 1997: SI 1997 No 1872 (S.138)

Act of Sederunt (Summary Applications, Statutory Applications and Appeals etc Rules) 1999: SI 1999 No 929 (S.65) [Amended? by SI 1386 (S106)?]

(this replaced our specific Act of Sederunt (Building Appeals) 1964: SI 1964 No 817 (S.53)

23

Planning law in England and Wales

ANDREW FRASER-URQUHART*

Note

Throughout this chapter the following abbreviations are used:
TP = The Town and Country Planning Act 1990;
The 1990 Act = The Town and Country Planning Act 1990, except in
Section 5 of this chapter where it means the Planning (Listed
Buildings and Conservation Areas) Act 1990.

1 Introduction

1.01 Town and country planning control over the development of all
land (including buildings) in England and Wales is an administrative
process deriving from the Town and Country Planning Act 1947. See
Section 9 for the position in Scotland and Section 10 for the position
in Northern Ireland. It has operated since 1 July 1948 and was brought
about (to mention no other matter) for the simple reason that in
England and Wales there is a limited amount of land for an increasing
number of people who wish to live and work upon it and who, increasingly, call for more space both for working and for leisure. Thus the
pressure on a limited acreage of land is great and is getting greater.

1.02 Today the principal Act on the subject is the Town and
Country Planning Act 1990. It contains 337 sections and 17 schedules
and came into operation on 24 August 1990. Associated with the
principal Act are three further Acts related to planning, namely, the
Planning (Listed Buildings and Conservation Areas) Act 1990,
the Planning (Hazardous Substances) Act 1990 and the Planning
(Consequential Provisions) Act 1990. These four Acts are defined
(TP's. 336(1)) as 'the Planning Acts'.

1.03 No sooner were 'the Planning Acts' on the Statute Book than
the government had further thoughts about the control of land development. This led to the Planning and Compensation Act 1991 which
has rewritten (with important alterations) many of the provisions of
the Town and Country Planning Acts of 1990. But the Town and
Country Planning Act 1990 itself still remains the principal Act on the
subject. It is emphasized that any references in this chapter to sections
in, or to the contents of, the 1990 Acts are references to those sections
and to those contents as amended by the 1991 Act. Accordingly the
reader is warned that if he is buying Queen's Printers' copies of Town
and Country Planning Acts from The Stationery Office, (various
branches in major cities), or copies of subordinate rules, regulations
and codes (statutory instruments) made under such Acts, he must
remember that what he is buying is *not* an updated, current version of
how the document he is buying *must* be read today.

All the materials referred to in this chapter are amended with
remarkable frequency; readers are well advised to consult either a

---

* In previous editions this chapter was contributed by the late Sir Desmond Heap.
This is the second edition in which the chapter has been updated by Andrew
Fraser-Urquhart.

fully updated loose-leaf planning encyclopedia or an appropriate
Internet or other electronic resource.

1.04 Planning control over land development is rooted in central
government policy. Accordingly, attention is drawn to the various
Planning Policy Guidance Notes (PPG) first issued in 1988. These
are issued by the Department of the Environment from time to
time. The following notes have been issued so far:

1997/PPG1	General Policy and Principles (superseding General Policy and Principles, 1992)
1995/PPG2	Green Belts (superseding Green Belts, 1988)
2000/PPG3	Housing (superseding Land for Housing, 1992)
1992/PPG4	Industrial and Commercial Development and Small Firms (revised)
1992/PPG5	Simplified Planning Zones (revised)
1996/PPG6	Town Centres and Retail Developments (supersed-ing Town Centres and Retail Developments, 1988)
1997/PPG7	The Countryside: Environmental Quality and Economic and Social Development (superseding The Countryside and the Rural Economy, 1992)
2001/PPG8	Telecommunications (revised)
1994/PPG9	Nature Conservation
1999/PPG10	Planning and Waste Management
2000/PPG11	Regional Planning
1999/PPG12	Development Plans and Regional Planning Guidance (superseding Local Plans, 1988)
2001/PPG13	Transport
1990/PPG14	Development on Unstable Land
1994/PPG15	Planning and the Historic Environment
1990/PPG16	Archaeology and Planning
2002/PPG17	Planning for Open Space, Sport and Recreation
1991/PPG18	Enforcing Planning Control
1992/PPG19	Outdoor Advertisement Control
1992/PPG20	Coastal Planning
1992/PPG21	Tourism
1993/PPG22	Renewable Energy
1994/PPG23	Planning and Pollution Control
1994/PPG24	Planning and Noise

More detailed guidance and advice to local planning authorities is
contained in a series of Department of the Environment Circulars
and, increasingly, by Parliamentary Statements by Ministers. There
also exist a series of Regional Planning Guidance Notes, which, as
their name suggests, provide guidance on a regional basis. It is no
exaggeration to say that there is a morass of guidance, much of
which can be seen as in a state of flux, due to an ongoing process of
revision as central government policy evolves.

In Wales, central government advice is provided by a series of
Technical Advice Notes (Wales) which are broadly equivalent to
the PPGs.

Planning control process

1.05 The planning control process is a two-part process involving, on the one hand, the making of development plans (that is, blueprints for the future) that seek to show what the state of affairs will be when all foreseeable development (or non-development) in the area covered by the plan has been achieved. The other prong of the process is the day-to-day control over the carrying out of development through the medium of a grant or a refusal of planning permission for development. All this is a highly simplified, not to say over-simplified, statement of the entire complicated and sophisticated process of town planning control as it functions today.

1.06 In the ultimate analysis, all this control is done by the minister for town and country planning by whatever name he may be known. At the moment he is known as the First Secretary of State or Deputy Prime Minister, but this does not alter the fact that, one minister of the Crown is, by law, rendered responsible ultimately for the way in which all town planning control is carried out in England and Wales. For his actions he is answerable to Parliament. Thus the control is exercised, in the ultimate analysis, in accordance with the town and country planning policies of the central government for the time being in power at Westminster.

1.07 In this chapter no attention is given to the first prong of the process, namely, the making, approving, and bringing into operation of development plans comprising 'structure plans', 'local plans and 'unitary development plans'. Suffice it to say that the content of the relevant development plans is of extreme importance in any decision as to the grant or refusal of planning permissions, and development plans are adopted only after a lengthy process

involving public consultation and (in most cases) examination of draft development plans by a public inquiry.

It is assumed for the purpose of this chapter that all the requisite development plans are in operation. Accordingly, attention in succeeding paragraphs is given to the day-to-day process of development control through the medium of grants or refusals of planning permission for development.

1.08 Moreover, it should be made clear at the start that this chapter is written primarily for the guidance of architects; it is deliberately slanted in the direction of architects. An effort has been made to pick out from the surging cauldron of town planning controls some of the more important controls and particularly those that would affect an architect seeking to organize development on behalf of a client. Thus the chapter does not purport to deal with control over advertisements, caravans, mineral workings or hazardous substances.

1.09 Accordingly, there will be found in succeeding paragraphs a brief statement on local planning authorities (paragraph 2.09) and what they can do when faced with an application for planning permission for development (paragraph 4.11). Development itself is treated in some detail (paragraph 3.01) though, maybe, not in all the detail into which the expression breaks up once it is investigated. The method of making planning applications is dealt with, as are the consequences of a refusal or a grant of permission subject to conditions (paragraph 4.04). Special reference is made to buildings of special architectural or historic interest (paragraph 5.01) because these are matters which, although standing outside the main stream of town planning control, are nevertheless highly important matters to a developer and to any architect advising him.

There is a brief reference (paragraph 6.01) to the three new concepts in the planning field of urban development areas and corporations, of enterprise zones, and of simplified planning zones. There is reference to the enforcement of planning control over the development of land (paragraph 7.01) or, in other words, there is a statement on what happens, or does not happen, if a person does indeed carry out development without getting the appropriate planning permission in advance.

1.10 The length of this chapter has been limited. This means that it has not been possible in every instance to put in all the qualifications, exceptions, reservations, and so forth which, in a more categorical statement, would necessarily be appended to the general statements set out in the paragraphs which follow.

Accordingly, it is emphasized that this chapter is in the nature of a guide – a guide for architects. It is hoped that it will be helpful to them, but in the limited space available it cannot be an exhaustive statement on everything on which the chapter touches. Further information can be obtained from Sir Desmond Heap's *An Outline of Planning Law* (11th edition, Sweet & Maxwell, London).

2 Local planning authorities; or who is to deal with planning applications?

2.01 The first thing an architect seeking to carry out development must do is to inspect the site of the proposed development. It is most important nowadays to discover:

1 Whether it is a cleared site; or
2 Whether it contains a building and, if it does, whether that building is a building of special architectural or historic interest (see paragraph 5.01).

2.02 Second, the architect must consider carefully the definition of 'development' in the 1990 Act (section 55) and the possible effect of the Town and Country Planning (Use Classes) Order 1987. Many building operations and changes of use do not constitute development by virtue of the definitions and provisions of this section and the 1987 Order. If they do not, then nothing in the town planning Acts applies to them. 'Development' is defined in paragraph 3.01. Copies of the Town and Country Planning (Use Classes) Order 1987 (SI 1987 No. 764) and its two amending orders of 1992 (SI 1992 Nos 610 and 657) are available from The Stationery Office.

2.03 Third, the architect must examine closely the type of development which is sought to be carried out. Is it development which can be dealt with in the normal run of planning control, or will it be subject to some additional control over and above the normal run? It certainly will be if it happens to be development of land occupied by a building of special architectural or historic interest (paragraph 5.01) which has been listed by the Secretary of State.

2.04 Fourth, the architect must investigate generally the Town and Country Planning (General Permitted Development) Order 1995 (SI. 1995 No. 418). It will be necessary to do this sort of investigation in order to ascertain whether the development is 'permitted development' under the Order because, if it is, it gets automatic planning permission and there is no need to make any application to a local planning authority (see paragraph 4.02).

2.05 When considering the T & CP (General Permitted Development) Order 1995, the architect must satisfy himself whether the site for the development does, or does not:

1 Comprise so-called 'Article 1(4) land' (as defined in Article 1(4) of the T & CP (General Permitted Development) Order 1995
2 Comprise 'Article 1(5) land' (as defined in Article 1(5) of the Town and Country Planning (General Permitted Development) Order 1995), which land includes land within:
    (a) A national park declared under the National Parks and Access to the Countryside Act 1949
    (b) An area of outstanding natural beauty (AONB) declared under the same Act of 1949

(c) An area designated as a conservation area under section 69 of the Planning (Listed Buildings in Conservation Areas) Act 1990
    (d) An area specified for the purposes of the Wildlife and Countryside Act 1981, section 41(3) and
    (e) The Broads as defined in the Norfolk and Suffolk Broads Act 1988.
3 Comprise 'Article 1(6) land' (as defined in Article 1(6) of the Order which land includes:
    (a) Land in a National Park
    (b) In the Norfolk and Suffolk Broads (as defined above) and
    (c) In land outside a national park but within an area (specified in Article 1(6)) as set out in schedule 1, Part 3, of the aforesaid 1995 Order.

If the development site is on 'Article 1(4) land' or on 'Article 1(5) land' or on 'Article 1(6) land' then the amount of 'permitted development' (see paragraph 2.06) allowed on the site is constricted by the said 1995 Order. Copies of the Town and Country Planning (General Permitted Development) Order 1995 are obtainable from The Stationery Office (see paragraph 2.02). Any such land falls within what are nowadays called 'sensitive areas' and the relaxation of development control brought about by the General Development (Amendment) Order 1981 was denied to them – and is still denied to them by the Town and Country Planning (General Permitted Development) Order 1995.

2.06 Fifth, the architect must ascertain whether the development site is in an Urban Development Area (see paragraph 6.02); in an Enterprise Zone (see paragraph 6.10); or in a Simplified Planning Zone (see paragraph 6.14). If the site is in any one of these areas or zones, then the normal constraints of development control (e.g. the need to obtain, from a local planning authority, planning permission for development (see paragraph 2.10)) are relaxed (see paragraphs 6.01, 6.11 and 6.14).

2.07 All these are preliminary matters about which the architect should become fully informed at the outset. In this chapter it will be assumed, for the moment, that the architect is dealing with a cleared site (or, at least, a site not containing anything in the nature of a special building), and that the development he wishes to carry out is development that can be dealt with under the general run of town planning control and does not attract any additional, i.e. special, control. (The special control over development which is going to occupy the site of an existing building of architectural or historic interest is dealt with later.) For the moment it is assumed that the development which the architect is considering is straightforward building development not subject to any special form of control, but only to general town planning control under the Town and Country Planning Act 1990.

Which authority?

2.08 This being the case, the next thing which the architect must consider is the local government authority to whom the application for planning permission is to be made. It must be made to the local planning authority.

2.09 The local government system in England and Wales was completely reorganized as from 1 April 1974 under the provision of the Local Government Act 1972. It was further reorganized as from 1 April 1986 by the Local Government Act 1985 which abolished the Greater London Council and the six metropolitan county councils (but not the metropolitan counties themselves) of Greater Manchester, Merseyside, South Yorkshire, Tyne and Wear, West Midlands, and West Yorkshire respectively. The most recent change was the introduction in the mid-1990s of a series of 'unitary' authorities which took the functions of both district and county council in their areas.

2.10 After all the foregoing reorganizations the system (outside Greater London) provided for local government to be discharged either at three separate tiers, namely:

1 By 34 non-metropolitan county councils popularly called 'shire' county councils;

2 By 261 district councils (36 metropolitan district councils if they happen to be in a metropolitan county and 235 'shire' district councils if they happen to be in a 'shire' county) some of which have borough status; and

3 By parish councils;

or by one of the 45 Unitary Authorities.

2.11 In Greater London local government is carried out by each of the 32 London borough councils plus the Corporation of the City of London. The new Greater London Authority does not have any direct planning powers although its functions will have an effect on many planning-related matters.

2.12 The county councils and the district councils and the unitary councils are all local planning authorities and thus current nomenclature speaks of the 'county planning authority', the 'district planning authority' and the 'unitary planning authority'. A purchaser or a developer of land must, at the very start, ascertain which is the local planning authority for the purpose of whatever he wishes to do.

2.13 All applications for planning permission will go to the district planning authority or the unitary planning authority except (in the area of a shire district council) when the application relates to a 'County matter' (see TP, Schedule 1, paragraph 1) in which event the application is to be made to the shire county council (see paragraph 2.14). When an application is made to the district council, it is to be remembered that there are seven specified categories of development in which the interests of the county council receive special protection and in which consultation by the district council with the county council must take place. These refer to:

1 Development, the carrying out of which would 'materially conflict with or prejudice the implementation':
   (a) Of any policy or general proposal in a structure plan (whether approved or merely proposed)
   (b) Of any proposal to include in a structure plan any matter publicized by the county council
   (c) Of any 'fundamental provision' in an approved development plan
   (d) Of any proposal in a local plan prepared by the county council (whether or not it has yet been adopted)
   (e) Of any publicized proposal by the county council for inclusion in a local plan being prepared by them
   (f) Of any publicized proposal by the county council for alterations to a local plan
2 Any development which by reason of its scale, nature, or location would be of 'major importance' for the implementation of an approved structure plan
3 Any development likely to affect, or be affected by, mineral workings 'other than coal'
4 Any development of land the county council wishes to develop themselves
5 Any development which would prejudice development proposed by the county council
6 Any development of land in England which is land the county council propose shall be used for waste disposal
7 Any development which would prejudice a proposed use of land for waste disposal.

In each of the foregoing cases (the details of which are to be found in paragraph 7 of Schedule 1 to the Town and Country Planning Act 1990), where special protection is given to the interests of the county council, the district council must consult with the county council and take into account any representations made by the county council before they (the district council) determine the planning application. How long must these complicated consultations continue? That period has been fixed by the Town and Country Planning (General Development Procedure) Order 1995, article 11, as 14 days after notification to the county council. It must be noted that the General Development Procedure Order is a different order from the General Permitted Development Order; the former deals with the detailed procedure for handling planning applications and related matters whilst the latter sets out various types of development which are deemed to have planning permission.

2.14 The instances of 'county matters' when, in a shire county, the application for planning permission goes in the first place not to the district planning authority but to the county planning authority, are (TP, Schedule 1, paragraph 1):

1 Applications relating to mineral mining, working, and development (including the construction of cement works) (TP, Schedule 1, paragraph 1(1) (a)–(h) inclusive)
2 Applications relating to development straddling the boundary of a national park (TP Schedule 1, paragraph 1(1) (i)) and
3 Applications in England relating to waste disposal matters (TP, Schedule 1, paragraph 1(1) (j)) and Town and Country Planning (Prescription of County Matters) Regulations 1980 (SI 1980 No. 2010) which does not apply to Greater London.

2.15 Parish councils are not local planning authorities but, even so, have the right (if they have claimed it) to be consulted by the district council about planning applications for development falling within the area of the parish council (TP, Schedule 1, paragraph 8).

2.16 In Greater London the 32 London boroughs (each for its own borough) with the Common Council (for the City of London) are all local planning authorities (1990 Act, section 1(2)).

3 The meaning of development

3.01 The question as to whether that which the architect seeks to carry out is or is not development is a potentially difficult one. The meaning of 'development' is defined in the Town and Country Planning Act 1990, section 55, and it is a question of taking the relevant provisions of this Act, working carefully through them, and then applying the appropriate parts of these provisions to the matter in hand to ascertain if that which it is sought to do is, in law as well as in fact, development.

3.02 Putting the matter quite briefly, development consists of:

1 The carrying out of operations (that is to say, building, mining, engineering or other operations), or
2 The making of any material change in the use of land (including buildings on land).

It will be seen that the big cleavage in the definition is between the carrying out of operations, on the one hand, and the making of a material change of use, on the other.

What is an operation?

3.03 If the definitions of what constitutes development is important, it may be said that the definition of what does not constitute development is equally important. Section 55 of the 1990 Act contains quite a list of operations and uses which do not amount to development. If that which the architect seeks to do falls within this particular list, then he need worry no more about the 1990 Act or any part of it. In particular, purely internal works or works which do not materially affect the external appearance of a building are not development. (Remembering of course that this exception most definitely does not apply to Listed Buildings!).

What is a change of use?

3.04 This list of exceptions in section 55 of the 1990 Act must be read with the Town and Country Planning (Use Classes) Order 1987, which contains 11 classes of use. If that which the architect seeks to do is, in fact, a material change of use, then if the existing use is any one of those specified in the 1987 Order, and if the change of use will still leave the use within the same use-class, the proposed change of use will not, in law, constitute development. In short, a use may switch around without planning permission, provided its total manoeuvring does not take it out of its use-class as set out in the 1987 Order.

3.05 However, since the case of *City of London Corporation v Secretary of State for the Environment and Watling Street Properties Ltd* (1971) 23 P and CR 169, it is clear that, on granting planning permission, a local planning authority may impose such conditions as would prevent any future change of use, notwithstanding that any such change would not constitute development of land by virtue of the provisions of the Use Classes Order 1987 and section 55 (2) (f) of the 1990 Act. In effect, the local planning authority may remove from a developer the right to make a change of use even if that change of use would not normally (because of the Use Classes Order) need planning permission.

3.06 For the purpose of removing all doubt, section 55(3) of the 1990 Act specifically states that merely using a single dwelling house as two or more separate dwelling houses does involve making a material change of use and it is 'development' needing planning permission before it can take place. Thus the architect may carry out, at ground level or above, internal building operations (not affecting the exterior elevations) on a single house in order to adapt it for use as two houses. Such building operations will not need planning permission. However, when it comes to inaugurating the use of the former single house as two houses, this change of use will call for planning permission which may or may not be granted.

3.07 If the architect has any doubts as to whether that which he seeks to do is or is not 'development', he can apply (1990 Act, section 192) to the local planning authority for a certificate of lawfulness relating to any proposed use or development of land. Such a certificate relating to any existing use or development can be made under section 191 of the 1990 Act. In either case there is a right of appeal to the Secretary of State for the Environment (hereinafter referred to as 'the Secretary of State') against the decision of the authority (TP, section 195).

4 Control of development in general

4.01 Once the architect is satisfied that that which he seeks to do is indeed development, but is not an Enterprise Zone (see paragraphs 6.09 to 6.11 of this chapter) nor a Simplified Planning Zone (see paragraphs 6.12 to 6.15 of this chapter), he must next ascertain whether it falls within the privileged category of 'permitted development'. For this he will have to investigate the Town and Country Planning (General Permitted Development) Order 1995.

Permitted development

4.02 The 1995 Order carries no less than 84 separate classes of development which are categorized as permitted development, that is, they comprise development for which a grant of planning permission is automatically given by virtue of the General Permitted Development Order 1995 itself (TP, sections 58, 59, 60). If development falls within any one of these 84 classes of permitted development there is no need to make any application to any local planning authority for planning permission for the development. If the development is not permitted development, then a formal application must be made (TP, sections 58, 62).

4.03 It is to be stressed that the General Permitted Development Order of 1995 is a most important document. The 84 classes of permitted development are spread across 33 Parts – Part 1 to Part 33 respectively – as set out in Schedule 2 to the Order as follows:

Permitted Development Order 1995

Part	Class	Permitted development
1	A	Development within the curtilage of a dwelling-house. The enlargement, improvement or other alteration of a dwellinghouse
1	B	The enlargement of a dwellinghouse consisting of an addition or alteration to its roof
1	C	Any other addition to the roof of a dwellinghouse
1	D	The erection or construction of a porch outside any external door of a dwellinghouse
1	E	The provision within the curtilage of a dwellinghouse, of any building or enclosure,

		swimming or other pool required for a purpose incidental to the enjoyment of the dwellinghouse, or the maintenance, improvement or other alteration of such a building or enclosure
1	F	The provision within the curtilage of a dwellinghouse of a hard surface for any purpose incidental to the enjoyment of the dwellinghouse
1	G	The erection or provision within the curtilage of a dwellinghouse of a container for the storage of oil for domestic heating
1	H	The installation, alteration or replacement of a satellite antenna on a dwellinghouse or within the curtilage of a dwellinghouse
2	A to C	Minor operations
3	A to G	Changes of use
4	A to B	Temporary buildings and uses
5	A to B	Caravan sites
6	A to C	Agricultural buildings and operations
7	A	Forestry buildings and operations
8	A to D	Industrial and warehouse development
9	A	Repairs to unadopted streets and private ways
10	A	Repairs to services
11	A	Development under local or private Acts or Orders
12	A to B	Development by local authorities
13	A	Development by local highway authorities
14	A	Development by drainage bodies
15	A	Development by the National Rivers Authority
16	A	Development by or on behalf of sewerage undertakers
17	A to J	Development by statutory undertakers
18	A to I	Aviation development
19	A to C	Development ancillary to mining operations
20	A to E	Coal mining development by the Coal Authority Licensed Operators
21	A to B	Waste tipping at a mine
22	A to B	Mineral exploration
23	A to B	Removal of material from mineral-working deposits
24	A	Development by telecommunications code system operators
25	A to B	Other telecommunications development
26	A	Development by the Historic Buildings and Monuments Commission for England
27	A	Use by members of certain recreational organizations
28	A	Development at amusement parks
29	A	Driver information systems
30	A	Toll road facilities
31	A to B	Demolition of buildings
32	A	Schools, Colleges, Universities and Hospitals
33	A	Closed circuit television cameras

Other than permitted development – the planning application

4.04 If the proposed development does not fall within any of the 84 classes of 'permitted development' above mentioned, then a formal application for planning permission will need to be made (TP, section 57). Sections 58 and 62 of the Town and Country Planning Act 1990 require an application for planning permission for development to be made in accordance with provisions 'prescribed by regulations' which means the Town and Country Planning (Applications) Regulations 1988 (SI 1988 No. 1812) and the Town and Country Planning (General Development Procedure) Order 1995 to each of which reference must be made. The requisite form on which the application is lodged can be obtained from the local planning authority.

4.05 When making an application for planning permission for development reference must further be made to the Town and Country Planning (Environmental Impact Assessment) Regulations 1999. These regulations provide in broad terms that if a development is likely to have significant environmental impacts (a term which includes such matters as the effect on the landscape, or on air quality or on ecology) the planning application cannot be decided until the local planning authority has received and assessed so-called 'Environmental Information'. This must include an Environmental Statement, prepared by the developer which sets out the nature of the development, the effect it is likely to have and the measures which are proposed to deal with such effects.

A failure to comply with these regulations (which are detailed and complex) will render any planning permission liable to be quashed by the High Court on an application for judicial review. Such a legal challenge is an obvious tactic for person opposed to a development. While the regulations are most likely to be 'in play' in a large development when the architect may well be part of a team advising the developer, even a smaller scale development with particular effects may trigger the application of the regulations.

4.06 Although the application for planning permission will formally be made to a local planning authority it will often be the case that a good deal of 'negotiation' relating to the application will take place between the applicant's architect and officers of the local planning authority.

4.07 Recent caselaw from the House of Lords (see *R v East Sussex County Council exp. Reprotech (Pebsham) Ltd* [2002] UKLR 8) makes plain, however, that it is almost impossible for the discussions with a planning authority during such negotiations to be binding on the local planning authority when the formal decision comes to be made. Nevertheless, such discussions are sensible, if not essential, part of the process and can save a good deal of time and money.

4.08 Once that process has been undertaken, a formal application for planning permission can be made, on a form provided by the local planning authority. It is thoroughly advisable to accompany the formal application with a 'Design Statement' setting out the basis on which the architect has formed his views as to the type of design appropriate to the area and the nature of the design proposed. Fees are payable since 1 April 1981 to local planning authorities in respect of applications for planning permission, applications for approval of matters reserved in an outline planning permission, or applications for consent to display advertisements. The amount of the fees is set out in Schedule 1, Part II and Schedule 2 to the Town and Country Planning (Fees for Applications and Deemed Applications) Regulations 1989 (SI 1989 No. 193) as amended several times. Each of the amendments has led to a progressive increase in the fees, the latest rates operating as from 1 April 2002 (SI 2002 No. 768)

4.09 A reduced planning fee is payable, in certain circumstances, where more than one application for planning permission is made for the same development or for approval of the same reserved matters provided all the applications are made by the same applicant within a period of 28 days.

4.10 Certain applications are exempt from liability to a fee. These are:

1   Certain applications on behalf of a disabled person
2   Applications to renew a temporary permission
3   Certain revised applications and
4   Applications relating to 'permitted development' prevented by a direction under Article 4 of the (General Permitted Development) Order 1995.

There are no exemptions in respect of applications to display advertisements.

Deciding the planning application

4.11 As to what should be the attitude of a local planning authority when faced with an application for planning permission, attention should be paid to Planning Policy Guidance Note 1 (PPG1) dated 1997, entitled, 'General Policy and Principles' issued by the Department of the Environment. This is a most important document, both for the developer (and those advising him) as well as for the local planning authority.

4.12 PPG1 states the general principles underlying the entire system of control over land development and deals in particular with the important section 54A of the 1990 Act (inserted by the Planning and Compensation Act 1991) which is in the following terms: 'Where in making any determination under the Planning Acts, regard is to be had to the development plan, the determination shall be made in accordance with the plan unless material considerations indicate otherwise.'

4.13 Put simply, section 54A means that if the proposed development is in accordance with the development plan (generally the Local Plan and Structure Plan read together or the Unitary Development Plan) a presumption in favour of granting planning permission would exist. If it was not in accordance with the development plan, then good reasons would need to be shown as to why the development should be permitted. Thus, if a developer sought to put houses on a site allocated in the development plan for housing, there would need to be significant reasons as to why permission should not be granted. If, on the other land, the site for this proposed housing was allocated in the development plan for employment uses, then there would need to be good countervailing reasons as to why it should be permitted. These good reasons are described in the statutory language as 'material considerations'.

4.14 Material considerations might, for example, include the fact that a particular development, while contrary to the development plan, would generate considerable employment opportunities or would cause the removal of what was previously an 'eyesore'. Further, while the development plan for the purposes of section 54A is only the plan which has been formally adopted, if a later, revised, plan is at an advanced stage of the statutory consultation process, the provisions of that forthcoming development plan would be a material consideration. The provisions of PPGs and Department of Environment Circulars are also material.

4.15 Mention must in particular be made of the effect of PPG3. This Planning Policy Guidance Note on Housing brought about a fundamental shift in policy away from the development of large, spacious houses on Greenfield sites. Instead, housing is to be directed towards higher density development on land, primarily in urban areas, which has previously had development on it ('brownfield land'). PPG3 also sought to force developers to provide a much greater element of so-called 'affordable housing'. PPG3 is relatively recent (2000) and, importantly, in many areas post dates the adoption of the Local Plan. It often occurs, therefore, that a proposal for housing which is in accordance with a Local Plan is not in accordance with the new policy in PPG3. In those circumstances, the non-compliance with PPG3 is a compelling material consideration which invariably leads to a refusal of planning permission.

4.16 If the application for planning permission is refused, or is granted subject to conditions unacceptable to the applicant for planning permission, there is a right of appeal to the Secretary of State within 6 months of the authority's decision (TP, sections 78 and 79). Before deciding the appeal the Secretary of State must, if either the applicant for planning permission or the local planning authority so requests, afford each of them an opportunity of being heard by a person appointed by the Secretary of State – an inspector. Neither party can demand a public local inquiry although the Secretary of State (it is entirely a matter for him) frequently decides to hold such an inquiry. Procedure at such an inquiry is dealt with in the Town and Country Planning (Inquiries Procedure) Rules 2000 (SI 2000 No 1624). The decision of the Secretary of State is final (subject to appeal to the courts within six weeks on matters of law only), the procedure being regarded by the law as an administrative and not a justiciable procedure.

4.17 Under section 79 and Schedule 6 of the 1990 Act, it is open to the Secretary of State to empower his inspector holding a local enquiry not only to hold the inquiry but to determine the appeal. The Secretary of State has exercised this power by making the Town and Country Planning (Determination of Appeals by Appointed Persons) (Prescribed Classes) Regulations 1997 (SI 1997 No. 420), whereby all planning appeals and all enforcement appeals (except when affecting a statutory undertaker) are now heard and determined by an inspector appointed by the Secretary of State. The procedure at such appeals is found in the Town and Country Planning Appeals (Determination by Inspectors) (Inquiries Procedure) Rules 2000 (SI 2000 No. 1625)

4.18 In addition to appeals to the Secretary of State by private hearing or by public local inquiry (as above described), there is a third method of appeal by what is known as the 'Written Representation Process'. This is dealt with in the Town and Country Planning (Appeals) (Written Representations Procedure) Regulations 2000 (SI 2000 No. 1628).

4.19 In any planning appeal the Secretary of State may (if he can be persuaded) award costs to the appellant against the local planning authority (see DoE Circular 8/93) or vice versa. Costs can only be awarded where there has been 'unreasonable' behaviour by a party.

4.20 As an alternative to the consideration of planning applications by the local planning authority, the Secretary of State has power under TP, section 77 to 'call-in' the application, with the result that the Secretary of State himself makes the decision. This power is generally only used for the most major developments which would have effects outside the area of the local planning authority where the development would take place. Where a decision is 'called in' a public inquiry is held, so the Secretary of State when deciding has the benefit of advice from his Inspector. The Heathrow Terminal 5 Inquiry gives an indication of the scale and length which such Inquiries can reach.

Outline permission

4.21 If the architect knows exactly what he wants to do by way of building operations he will be able to put in a complete detailed application for planning permission. But it may be that he wants in the first place to 'test the temperature of the water', that is, to see what are his chances of getting planning permission at all for, say, a block of offices 20 storeys high. If he wishes to do this, then he can save time, trouble, and expense by putting in an application (TP, section 92) for outline planning permission so that the principle of having a block of offices 20 storeys high may be tested. If it is approved, then it will be necessary for the architect later on, within the period (if any) specified in the grant of outline planning permission and before he begins any development, to put in detailed plans and specifications for the approval of the local planning authority, these being what are called 'reserved matters', that is, matters reserved, at the stage when the local authority is granting the planning application in outline, for later and further consideration.

4.22 An outline application should make it clear that it is an application in outline and nothing more. Thus any plans and drawings which accompany it should be clearly marked as being by way of illustration only. At the stage of applying for outline permission, the architect should not fetter himself as to the styling of development. All he wants at the outline stage is to know whether or not he can, under any circumstances at all, have planning permission to do the sort of thing he wishes to do. If he gets that permission, then he must return, in due course, to the local planning authority with detailed plans and specifications so that the authority may consider these detailed matters.

4.23 If the outline application for planning permission is refused, there is a right of appeal against that refusal to the Secretary of State within 6 months. Similarly, if the outline application is granted but, later on, the local authority refuses to approve reserved matters, that is, refuses approval of detailed plans and specifications, then

again there is an appeal against such refusal to the Secretary of State (see paragraph 4.16).

4.24 It will be seen that for an applicant who does not own land and who wonders how much he ought to pay for it, the making of an outline application to test the position *vis-à-vis* the local planning authority is a useful arrangement. It is not necessary for the applicant to go into details and incur the expense thereby involved. All he wants to know before he makes his bid for the land is whether, if he is able to buy the land, he will then be able to develop it in anything like the manner he has in mind. To get to know this, all that he need do is make an outline planning application.

4.25 Sadly, this effective and convenient procedure is increasingly constricted, particularly in larger schemes, by the operation of the Environmental Assessment Regulations considered at paragraph ... above. The difficulty lies in the fact that if an application is too 'outline' the environmental impact may be impossible to properly assess. How, for example, can the impact on the landscape of a development be properly assessed when that development has not been designed? In the case of *R v Rochdale MBC ex p. Tew* [1999] 3 PLR 74, an outline application for a proposed business park, where the submitted plan was 'illustrative only' and did not even define which areas would be business premises and which would be housing, was granted outline permission. The level of the detail on the plan was thought to be quite sufficient for an outline application. The planning permission was, however, quashed on an application for judicial review because the plan was insufficiently detailed to be a proper foundation for the Environmental Assessment.

4.26 The common solution to this problem is the 'Masterplan'; a plan is drawn up which, while leaving some flexibility in matters of detailed design, shows definitely the location of internal roads, the location and density of different types of development and the main design features. The developer can then offer to submit himself to a condition on his outline planning permission that the development will be in accordance with the Masterplan. The Environmental impact of the scheme set out in the Masterplan can then be properly assessed and a lawful outline permission can be granted.

Notices re planning applications

4.27 Notice of the making of any application for planning permission to develop land must be given to the owner of the land and to any tenant of an agricultural holding any part of which is comprised in the land (TP, section 65; T and CP (General Development Procedure) Order 1995, Articles 6, 8 and Schedule 2, Parts 1 and 2). Any application for planning permission must be accompanied by a certificate indicating the giving of notice to owners and agricultural tenants. If the appropriate certificate is not included with the planning application, then the local planning authority 'shall not entertain' the application (TP, section 65 (5)).

General publicity

4.28 In addition to the foregoing personal or private publicity deriving from the notices referred to in the previous paragraph, there must be what can be called general publicity by newspaper advertisement for all planning applications (TP, section 65; T and CP (General Development Procedure) Order 1995, Article 8). Thus the owners and occupiers of neighbouring land will be informed, provided they keep a sharp eye open for newspaper planning advertisements, of any application to carry out development so that they may give their views and opinions to the local planning authority before a decision is arrived at. Such views and opinions must be considered by the local planning authority (TP, section 71).

Site notices

4.29 Moreover, a site notice, exhibited on the site where the development is to take place, may have to be given (T and CP (General Development Procedure) Order 1995, Article 8). Those instances in which a site notice may have to be posted are referred to in the 1990

Act, section 65 and Article 8 of the (General Development Procedure) Order 1995 and (so far as listed buildings and conservation areas are concerned) in the Planning (Listed Buildings and Conservation Areas) Act 1990, sections 67 and 73 and the Planning (Listed Buildings and Conservation Areas) Regulations 1990 (SI 1990 No. 1519).

Local authority procedure

4.30 On receipt of an application for planning permission, the local planning authority must consider the matter and, generally speaking, give a decision within eight weeks unless an extension of time is agreed (T & CP (General Development Procedure) Order 1995, Articles 20 and 21). The authority will probably need to consult the appropriate county council (*ibid.*, Article 11) and may also have to consult any parish council within whose area the proposed development is going to take place (*ibid.*, Article 13).

The authority may grant the application, may refuse it, or may grant it subject to conditions (TP, 1990 section 70). If the answer is a refusal or conditions are attached to the grant, the reasons for such action must be given (Development Procedure Order 1995, Article 22). This is to enable the applicant to challenge the decision of the local planning authority if the applicant decides to appeal to the Secretary of State, as he may do within a period of 6 months (TP, section 78; Development Procedure Order 1995 articles 22 and 23). If no decision is given within the appropriate period, the applicant may appeal (again, within 6 months) to the Secretary of State as if he had been faced with a refusal (TP, section 78; Development Procedure Order 1995, Article 23).

Conservation areas

4.31 If the site of the development is within a conservation area designated under the Planning (Listed Buildings and Conservation Areas) Act 1990, sections 69 and 70, then the local planning authority, in considering the application, will have to pay attention to sections 71, 72, 74 and 75 of that Act and to any directions given to them by the Secretary of State as to the manner in which they should consider applications for development within areas of special architectural or historic interest. Development in a conservation area must 'preserve or enhance' the appearance of the Conservation Area and detailed design will invariably be expected from the architect to demonstrate that this condition is complied with.

Conditions

4.32 The local planning authority in granting planning permission may attach such conditions as it thinks fit (TP 1990, section 70); but this does not mean that it can attach any conditions it likes; not at all. The conditions must be fit, that is to say, fit, meet, and proper from a town planning point of view, because the legislation under which all this control functions is town planning legislation.

4.33 A local planning authority in attaching conditions must ensure that the conditions fairly and reasonably relate to the development. The authority is not at liberty to use its powers for an ulterior object, however desirable that object may seem to be in the public interest. If it mistakes or misuses its power, however bona fide, the court can interfere by declaration of an injunction – per Lord Denning in *Pyx Granite Co. Ltd v Ministry of Housing and Local Government* [1958] 1 QB 554, CA.

4.34 Suppose one of the conditions attached to a grant is improper and thereby unlawful; does this invalidate the entire planning permission or can the unlawful condition be severed from the rest, leaving the planning permission intact but shorn of the improper condition? There have been several cases on this particularly difficult point, and the most authoritative guidance was offered in *Kent County Council v Kingsway Investments (Kent) Ltd* [1971] AC 72. It would appear from the decisions of the courts that the question of whether or not a planning permission is to be held wholly bad

and of no effect, by reason of the invalidity of some condition attached to it, is a matter which should be decided on the basis of common sense and with particular inquiry as to whether the valid condition is fundamental or trivial.

4.35 The views of the Secretary of State on attaching conditions to a grant of planning permission are set out at length in the interesting and instructive DoE Circular 1/85 to which reference can be made with advantage (see the Bibliography at the end of the book).

4.36 Local planning authorities seem to be increasingly intent on attaching to a grant of planning permission conditions which seek to recover for the authority something in the nature of a planning gain or benefit which the carrying out of the proposed development itself will bring to the authority in the nature, for example, of increased taxable value for the area of the authority.

4.37 The Annex to DoE Circular 1/85 (above mentioned) refers to this matter of the imposition of planning conditions the object of which is to secure some sort of a planning gain for the local planning authority (see paragraphs 20–21 and 63 of the Annex). The Annex sets out six tests to ascertain whether a planning condition is (as it should be) 'fair, reasonable and practical'. The six tests are (paragraph 11):

1 Necessity of the condition
2 Relevance of the condition to planning
3 Relevance of the condition to the development to be permitted
4 Enforceability of the condition
5 Precision of the condition and
6 Reasonableness of the condition in all other respects.

The Annex puts each of these six tests to close scrutiny which should certainly be read in full in the Annex itself. To take but one example (relating to test (1) about the necessity for a planning condition being imposed at all), the Annex, paragraph 12, declares:

'Test of need'

'12. In considering whether a particular condition is necessary, authorities should ask themselves whether planning permission would have to be refused if that condition were not to be imposed. If it would not, then the condition needs special and precise justification. The argument that a condition will do no harm is no justification for its imposition: as a matter of policy, a condition ought not to be imposed unless there is a definite need for it.'

Section 106 agreements

4.38 TP, section 106 provides that a developer may enter into either a unilateral undertaking or an agreement with the local planning authority (both referred to as a 'planning obligation') so as to offer some planning benefit as part of a package involving the grant of a planning permission. Most unusually in English Law, a section 106 undertaking or agreement binds both the current *and any future* owner of the land. A typical example of a section 106 agreement is that a developer might offer, as part of a package which led to grant of planning permission for a supermarket, to pay for the upgrading of the road junction giving access to the site of the new supermarket.

4.39 The Secretary of State has offered guidance as to the proper use of section 106 agreements (see Department of the Environment Circular 1/97).

Other Controls

4.40 It should be remembered that obtaining planning permission for development may not necessarily be the end of the matter. Certain specialized forms of development, e.g. development relating to the display of advertisements (TP, 1990 sections 220–225 and the T and CP Control of Advertisement Regulations 1992 – SI 1992 No. 666) or to the creation of caravan sites (Caravan Sites and the Control of Development Act 1960, Part I), are subject to additional control over and above the general run of town planning control.

4.41 Moreover, the architect must never forget that town planning control is a control which functions entirely without prejudice to the long-established control of building operations through the medium of building by-laws created under a code of law relating to public health and dating back to the Public Health Act 1875 and even before. Irrespective of town planning control, such detailed matters as the thickness of walls, the opening of exit doors in public places in an outward and not an inward direction, the provision of means of escape in case of fire – all these are matters which are entirely separate from the sort of control over development which is discussed in this chapter. (For such matters see Chapter 21.)

Duration of permission

4.42 Nowadays, any developer obtaining planning permission must remember that, unless the permission itself specifies otherwise, permission will last for only 5 years. This is to prevent, among other things, an accumulation in the records of local planning authorities of quantities of planning permissions granted from time to time over a long period of years and never acted upon. This had been going on for a long time, but was brought to an end by provisions in the Town and Country Planning Act 1968, now sections 91 to 96 of the 1990 Act.

4.43 Anybody in possession of a planning permission granted before 1 April 1969 must remember that if he did not begin his development before the beginning of 1968, then he must have begun it not later than five years from 1 April 1969, that is, not later than 1 April 1974, after which date the planning permission dissolves.

4.44 In the case of a planning permission granted on or since 1 April 1969, or granted in the future, the limitation is again five years from the date of the grant unless the grant otherwise provides.

4.45 If that which is obtained is an outline planning permission (as discussed in paragraph 4.18) granted on or since 1 April 1969, then it must be remembered that the submission of detailed plans and specifications under the aegis of that outline planning permission must be done not later than three years from the grant, while the development itself must be begun within five years of the grant or within two years of the final approval of any reserved matter, whichever of these two periods happens to be the longer. In the case of an outline planning permission granted before 1 April 1969, then the aforementioned periods of three and five years respectively run from 1 April 1969.

Starting development

4.46 When is a project of development to be regarded as having been begun? This is an important question. The 1990 Act provides the complete answer in section 56 by providing that a project of development is begun on the earliest date on which a material operation in connection with the development is started. A 'material operation' will include, among other things, the digging of a trench which is to contain the foundations of a building. Thus, only a trivial amount of labour needs to be spent in order to ensure that development has been begun and that a town planning permission has been embarked upon.

Abandoning development

4.47 A ticklish question has always been: can a planning permission be lost through non-use? Can it be abandoned? In *Pioneer Aggregates (UK) Ltd v Secretary of State for the Environment* [1985] AC 132, a decision of the House of Lords, it was held that there was no legal principle that a planning permission could be abandoned by the act of a party entitled to the benefit of the permission.

Completion notices

4.48 Having begun his development, a developer must remember not to rest unduly upon his oars. If he is dilatory it is open to the local planning authority to serve him with 'a completion notice' requiring the completion of his development within a certain period (TP, sections 94 and 96). A completion notice will declare that the relevant planning permission will cease to have effect on such date as may be specified in the notice but this date may not be earlier than 12 months from the date of the notice. A completion notice will not take effect unless and until it is confirmed by the Secretary of State, who may substitute a longer period for completion. Any person served with a completion notice may demand to be given an opportunity of being heard by an inspector appointed by the Secretary of State. Of course, a local planning authority, having served a completion notice, may for good and sufficient reason be prevailed upon to withdraw it; the law authorizes such withdrawal.

Revoking or modifying planning permission

4.49 It should be remembered that a planning permission once given ensures a right to develop for the benefit of all persons for the time being interested in the land, subject to any limitation of time contained in the grant of planning permission itself or imported into the matter by the 1990 Act, as mentioned in paragraph 4.34. This, however, is subject to the right of a local planning authority to revoke or modify a planning permission by means of an order made by the authority and confirmed by the Secretary of State (TP, sections 97–100, 102–104). Before confirming the order the Secretary of State must afford the owner and the occupier of the land affected by the order an opportunity of being heard by the Secretary of State's inspector. There are certain revoking or modifying orders which, being unopposed and unlikely to give rise to claims for compensation, can be made by the local planning authority without need for confirmation by the Secretary of State.

4.50 If the local planning authority wish to make a revocation or modifying order they must remember to do so before buildings authorized by the planning permission in question have been started. If they fail to do so, the revocation or modification may not affect so much of the building operations as have already been carried out. Compensation may become payable on the revocation or modification of a previously granted planning permission (TP, sections 115, 117, 118).

5 Buildings of special architectural or historical interest – listed buildings

5.01 The British public has tardily come to realize that the quality of life in the UK is still worth preserving, but if it is not exceptionally careful, the ambience of the physical environment in which it lives is going to slip away before its very eyes. There is an outcry against pollution of all kinds. We are reminded of our heritage and of the things that interest visitors when they come to the UK, and, for sure, they are far more interested in the Cotswolds than nuclear power stations, helpful on a dark night though the latter may be.

5.02 Buildings of special architectural or historic interest are great tourist attractions and, at the moment, tourism is one of the UK's biggest growth industries. Accordingly, the Planning (Listed Buildings and Conservation Areas) Act 1990 (hereafter in this section referred to as 'the 1990 Act') sets out to give further, better, and more decisive protection to buildings of the sort which are here called 'special buildings'.

Listing

5.03 Lists of special buildings are compiled under section 1 of the 1990 Act by the Secretary of State or the Historic Buildings and Monuments Commission for England (established under the National Heritage Act 1983). Once a building is listed it is no longer possible for a local authority to make (as hitherto) a building preservation order for it; in lieu the 1990 Act provides a different kind of protection (see further, paragraphs 5.09 and 5.10).

5.04 The owner of such a special building need not be consulted before it is listed; he is merely told what has occurred. However, the statutory list of special buildings must be kept open by the Secretary of State for free public inspection. Similarly, a local authority must also keep open for free public inspection any portion of the list which relates to their area.

5.05 To damage a listed building is to commit a criminal offence punishable with a fine up to level 3 on the Standard Scale (currently £1000) and a daily penalty of up to one-tenth of that scale (1990 Act, section 59) (see further, paragraph 5.13).

5.06 A local authority may carry out works urgently necessary for the preservation of an unoccupied listed building after giving the owner seven days' notice (the 1990 Act, sections 54, 55, 60, 76). A local authority may make a loan or a grant towards preserving buildings of special historic interest (whether listed or not) under section 59 of the 1990 Act.

5.07 In deciding whether to list a building or not, the Secretary of State may now take into account not only the building itself, but also its relationship to other buildings and the desirability of preserving features associated with the building but not actually forming part of the building. Thus, it is not solely the building which is to be considered but the entire setting of the building (the 1990 Act, section 1).

5.08 When speaking of a building it must be remembered that the law is so framed as to give protection to any object or structure fixed to a building or forming part of the land on which the building stands and comprised within the curtilage of the building (1990 Act, section 1 and see *Watts v the Secretary of State for the Environment* [1991], 'JPL'. 718).

Listed building consent

5.09 There is no provision for the owner of a special building to appeal against the listing of his building. Once the building is listed, the whole of the protective provisions of Part I of the 1990 Act automatically swing into operation. The consequence of this is that while (as already explained in paragraph 4.04) it is necessary to get planning permission for any kind of development, if the site of the development happens to be occupied in whole or in part by a listed building, then the development simply cannot take place unless an additional form of consent, known as 'listed building consent', is first obtained (the 1990 Act, sections 16, 17, 19).

5.10 Listed building consent must be obtained in order to demolish, alter, or extend a listed building (the 1990 Act, sections 7, 8, 9). It may be granted (like a planning permission) with or without conditions. The application for listed building consent is made to the local planning authority, and the procedure is given in sections 10–16 of the 1990 Act and in the Planning (Listed Buildings and Conservation Areas) Regulations 1990 (SI 1990 No. 1519). A grant of listed building consent will last for only five years. If planning permission for development has been granted, or if an application for planning permission has been duly made, and if there is a building (unlisted) on the site, the developer may, since 13 November 1980, apply to the Secretary of State for the Environment for a certificate that the Secretary will not list any such building for at least five years (the 1990 Act, section 6 and see *Amalgamated Investment and Property Co. Ltd v John Walker and Sons Ltd* [1976] 3 all ER 509 SA). This is a most useful provision when the architect feels that a building standing on the development site is potentially a 'listable' building.

5.11 In deciding whether or not to grant listed building consent with respect to a special building, the local planning authority must pay 'special regard' to the desirability of preserving the building or its setting and of preserving any features of special architectural or historic interest which the building possesses (the 1990 Act, sections 16, 72). Notwithstanding this, the authors take the view that the grant of planning permission is one thing and the grant of listed building consent is another. Merely because planning permission is granted for development, it does not follow that listed building consent will be given to remove some obstructive listed building to

allow such development to go forward. The planning permission, once granted, will (as explained in paragraph 4.42) last, generally speaking, for five years. During that time views and opinions about a listed building may change; views and opinions about architecture do tend to fluctuate. During the first years of the planning permission it may be impossible to get the requisite listed building consent to demolish some obstructive listed building. Later on different opinions about preservation may prevail or pressure to carry out development may become stronger. Thus, different considerations in the view of the authors apply when a local planning authority is considering whether it should grant planning permission for development and when it is considering whether it should grant listed building consent for the demolition of a listed building in order to allow planned development to go forward.

5.12 If listed building consent is refused, there is a right of appeal to the Secretary of State after the style of the appeal against refusal of planning permission (the 1990 Act, sections 20, 21 and the Planning (Listed Buildings and Conservation Areas) Regulations 1990 – SI 1990 No. 1519).

5.13 It is an offence to demolish, alter, or extend a listed building so as to affect its character as a building of special architectural or historic interest, without first getting listed building consent (the 1990 Act, sections 7–9; see also *Britain's Heritage v the Secretary of State and Others* (the *Peter Palumbo* case) [1991] 1WLR 153). It is also an offence to fail to comply with any conditions attached to such consent. The penalty for each of these offences is (on summary conviction) a fine of £20 000 or imprisonment for 6 months or both, and on conviction on indictment, a fine of unlimited amount or imprisonment for two years or both. It is, however, a defence to prove that any works carried out on a listed building were urgently necessary in the interests of safety or health, or for the preservation of the building and that notice in writing of the need for the works was given to the district planning authority as soon as was reasonably practicable (the 1990 Act, section 9).

5.14 If the owner is faced with a refusal of listed building consent and can demonstrate that in its present state his listed building has become incapable of reasonable beneficial use, then he may serve a listed building purchase notice on the local planning authority requiring the authority to purchase the building (the 1990 Act, sections 32–36 and the Planning (Listed Buildings and Conservation Areas) Regulations 1990 – SI 1990 No. 1519).

Listed building enforcement notice

5.15 If unauthorized works to a listed building are carried out, then the local planning authority, in addition to taking proceeding for the commission of a criminal offence, may serve a 'listed building enforcement notice' upon the owner, requiring full reinstatement of the listed building (the 1990 Act, section 38). There is a right of appeal against the notice to the Secretary of State (the 1990 Act, sections 39–41, 64, 65 and T and CP (Enforcement Notices and Appeals) Regulations 1990 – SI 1991 No. 2804). Penalties are provided in the case of non-compliance with the terms of the listed building enforcement notice. The guilty person is liable to a fine of £20 000 on summary conviction and of unlimited amount on conviction on indictment (the 1990 Act, section 43). These penalties are recoverable from the owner of the land who is in breach of the notice and this may include a subsequent owner. So the purchaser of a listed building must be careful to ascertain before he buys whether there are any listed building enforcement notices outstanding in respect of the building.

5.16 A local authority is authorized to acquire compulsorily any listed building which is not properly preserved (the 1990 Act, sections 49–50). This power may not be exercised until at least 2 months after the service on the owner of the building of a repairs notice specifying the work considered necessary for the proper preservation of the building. An owner faced with the possibility of having his listed building compulsorily acquired from him cannot appeal to the

Secretary of State, but curiously enough, he can, within 28 days, appeal to the local magistrates' court to stay the proceedings under the compulsory purchase order. If the court is satisfied that reasonable steps have been taken for properly preserving the building then the court may order accordingly. Against the order of the magistrates there is a further appeal to the Crown Court.

5.17 If a listed building is compulsorily acquired, then the compensation to be paid to the owner will, in general, disregard the depressive effect of the fact that the building has been listed. On the other hand, if it is established that the building has been allowed deliberately to fall into disrepair for the purpose of justifying the redevelopment of the site, then the 1990 Act provides for the payment of what is called 'minimum compensation'. This means that the compensation will be assessed at a price which disregards any profit which might have accrued to the owner from the redevelopment of the site. Against any direction in a compulsory purchase order providing for the payment of this minimum compensation there is a right of appeal and, again, this is to the local magistrates' court, with a further appeal to the Crown Court (the 1990 Act, section 50).

Building preservation notices

5.18 Are there any means today of protecting a building which is not a listed building, but which appears to the local planning authority to be of special architectural or historic interest? The answer is yes. Although the district planning authority can no longer make a building preservation order, it can serve on the owner of the building a building preservation notice which gives temporary protection for 6 months, during which time the building is protected just as if it were listed (the 1990 Act, section 3). The object of this is to give time for consideration by the local planning authority and the Secretary of State, or indeed by anybody else, as to whether the building should in fact be listed. If, at the end of 6 months, the Secretary of State will not make any such listing, then the building preservation notice automatically ceases, and the local planning authority may not serve a further building preservation notice within the next 12 months. Moreover, compensation may become payable to the owner of the building for loss or damage caused by the service of the building preservation notice which failed to be followed by the listing of the building.

5.19 Certain buildings of undoubted architectural and historic interest do not come within the protection of listing at all. These are:

1 Ecclesiastical buildings in use for church purposes (but not the parsonage house, which is capable of being listed)
2 A building included in the Schedule of monuments compiled and maintained by the Secretary of State under ancient monuments legislation.

Buildings in conservation areas

5.20 In addition to the special protection given to listed buildings as described above, the 1990 Act, section 74 gives protection to all buildings if they happen to be in a conservation area designated under section 69 of the 1990 Act.

6 Urban Development Corporations; enterprise zones; simplified planning zones

Urban development areas and corporations

6.01 The Local Government, Planning and Land Act 1980, Part XVI and Part XVIII (as amended by the Housing and Planning Act 1986, section 49 and the Leasehold Reform, Housing and Urban Development Act 1993, section 179) breaks new ground in the sphere of land development and planning control over such development by providing, respectively, for the establishment of Urban Development Corporations and Enterprise Zones, each of these is briefly dealt with in the following paragraphs.

6.02 The Secretary of State is now empowered to designate an area of land as an 'urban development area' and to establish an Urban Development Corporation to regenerate the area. All this is done by means of an order made by the Secretary of State and approved by affirmative resolution of each House of Parliament. On 14 November 1980 the then Minister for Local Government and Environmental Services, Mr Tom King, MP, declared: 'We shall shortly be bringing forward Orders under powers in the [Local Government, Planning and Land] Act to set up Urban Development Corporations as single-minded agencies to spearhead the regeneration of the London and Merseyside docklands and to introduce the bold new experiment of enterprise zones, where business can be freed from such detailed planning control'.

The requisite orders for the London and Merseyside docklands were made in 1981. Further areas have since been made (in 1987) establishing Urban Development Corporations for:

1 Trafford (Manchester)
2 The Black Country
3 Teesside
4 Tyne and Wear
5 Cardiff Bay

and (in 1988) for:

6 Leeds
7 Bristol
8 Sheffield
9 Wolverhampton.

6.03 An Urban Development Corporation (like a New Town Development Corporation) is not an elected body. It is appointed by the Secretary of State and comprises a chairman, a deputy chairman, together with not less than five, nor more than eleven, other members as the Secretary of State may see fit to appoint. In making these appointments the Secretary of State must consult such local government authorities as appear to him to be concerned with the regeneration of the urban development area, and he must have regard to the desirability of appointing persons having special knowledge of the locality where the area is situated.

6.04 The Urban Development Corporations will have the duty of regenerating their respective areas by:

1 Bringing land and buildings into effective use
2 Encouraging development of industry and commerce
3 Generating an attractive environment and
4 Ensuring that housing and social facilities are available.

The Urban Development Corporations will have powers similar to those of the New Town Development Corporations. They will be empowered to deal with matters of land assembly and disposal, planning, housing, and industrial promotion. They will be able to submit for approval by the Secretary of State their own proposals for the regeneration of their urban development areas. Before approving these proposals, the Secretary of State will need to consult any local planning authority within whose area the urban development area (or any part of it) falls.

6.05 An Urban Development Corporation may by order made by the Secretary of State (and subject to annulment by either House of Parliament) become the local planning authority for its own area (TP, section 7), thereby taking over all the planning control duties of any local government planning authority functioning within the urban development area. If this occurs, a developer of land within an urban development area will find himself more in contact with the appropriate urban development corporation than with the district planning authority when it comes to the matter of obtaining planning permission for development.

6.06 An Urban Development Corporation, once established, must prepare within 12 months a code of practice as to consultation with the relevant local government authorities relating to the manner in which the Corporation proposes to exercise its regeneration powers. This code of practice must be prepared (and may be revised from time to time) by the Urban Development Corporation acting in consultation with the relevant local government authorities.

6.07 An Urban Development Corporation may, by agreement approved by the Secretary of State with the concurrence of the Treasury, transfer the whole or any part of its undertaking to a local government authority. When all the property and undertakings of an Urban Development Corporation have been transferred, the Corporation may be dissolved by order made by the Secretary of State after consultation with each local authority in whose area all or part of the urban development area is situated.

6.08 It will be observed that, each time an Urban Development Corporation is established, there is bound to be a consequential diminution of the planning control powers of any local government planning authority functioning within the urban development area over whose regeneration it is the responsibility of the Urban Development Corporation to preside. Accordingly, it will not be surprising to find that the establishment of any Urban Development Corporation, and the demarcation of the boundaries of any urban development area, are matters which will be eyed critically by any local government authority out of whose area the urban development area is to be carved. On this it may be mentioned that the London borough of Southwark petitioned the House of Lords to have the boundaries of the London Dockland Development Corporation redrawn. The petition failed.

6.09 The trend to delegate planning powers to Urban Development Corporations seems to be on the wane; in recent years Corporations in, for example, Sheffield and Leeds have had the transfer of planning powers to them revoked.

Enterprise Zones

6.10 Part XVIII of, and Schedule 32 to, the Local Government, Planning and Land Act 1980 deals with the designation of Enterprise Zones within which special provisions relating to planning and rating (i.e. local council tax) will apply.

6.11 The following bodies may be invited by the Secretary of State to prepare a scheme with a view to the designation as an Enterprise Zone of the particular area of land for which the scheme was prepared. Such a scheme may be prepared by a district council, the council of a Welsh county or county borough, a London borough council, a New Town Corporation, or an Urban Development Corporation. If any such scheme is formally adopted by the scheme-making body, then the Secretary of State, if he thinks it expedient to do so, may designate the area to which the scheme relates as an Enterprise Zone. The important point about all this is that any order designating an Enterprise Zone is of itself to have the effect of granting planning permission for such development as may be specified in the scheme.

6.12 In the words of the Minister of Local Government and Environment Services (quoted above – paragraph 6.02), 'the bold new experiment of Enterprise Zones will so arrange things that business can be freed from detailed planning control'.

6.13 Between 1981 and 1996 almost 50 Enterprise Zones were set up and there is some limited empirical evidence to suggest that they have been successful in stimulating job-creation.

Simplified Planning Zones (SPZs)

6.14 In the White Paper (Cmnd 9571) dated July 1985 and entitled 'Lifting the Burden' – the Burden being that of various forms of government control (including planning and development control) over enterprise in all its manifestations – the government declared (paragraph 3.5): 'There is therefore always a presumption in favour of development, unless that development would cause demonstrable harm to interests of acknowledged importance.' (This statement must be carefully read in light of the statutory provisions of section 54A of the Town and Country Planning Act 1990; see paragraphs

4.06 and 4.08 of this chapter.) The White Paper went on (paragraph 3.6) to declare that:

> 'In line with this approach to the control of development, and in support of the general aim of deregulation, a number of other measures are being taken to simplify the planning system and reduce the burden of control:
>
> (i) It is proposed to introduce new legislation to permit the setting up of Simplified Planning Zones (SPZ) which will extend to other areas the type of planning regime already established in Enterprise Zones. This will enable the local planning authority to specify the types of development allowed in an area, so that developers can then carry out development that conforms to the scheme without the need for a planning application and the related fee. Planning permission for other types of development can be applied for in the normal way. This type of planning scheme has proved to be effective and successful in Enterprise Zones and can provide a real stimulus to the redevelopment of derelict or unused land and buildings in areas that are badly in need of regeneration. In addition to providing local planning authorities with powers to introduce SPZs, they will also require to consider proposals for the establishment of SPZs initiated by private developers. The Secretaries of State would have reserve powers to direct the preparation of proposals for an SPZ, similar to those that they already have to direct the preparation of alterations to development plans.'

6.15 The government fulfilled the foregoing promise by the enactment of the Housing and Planning Act 1986, Part II of which related to Simplified Planning Zones. Simplified Planning Zones are now dealt with in the Town and Country Planning Act 1990, sections 82–87, 94 and Schedule 1, paragraph 9 and Schedule 7, and in the Town and Country Planning (Simplified Planning Zones) Regulations 1992 (SI 1992 No. 2414). Simplified Planning Zones will be established by local planning authorities by means of a new system of Simplified Planning Zone Schemes (it is the word 'Scheme' which is the really important part of this expression) each of which will specify types of development permitted in a zone. A developer will be able to carry out such development without making an application for planning permission and paying the requisite fee.

6.16 The following land may not be included in a Simplified Planning Zone:

1 Land in a national park
2 Land in a conservation area
3 Land within the Norfolk and Suffolk Broads
4 Land in an area of outstanding natural beauty
5 Land in a greenbelt identified in a development plan and
6 Land notified under the Wildlife and Countryside Act 1981, sections 28 or 29, as an area of special scientific interest.

If, however, land in a Simplified Planning Zone becomes land in any one of the above descriptions, it does not thereby become excluded from the zone.

The Secretary of State may by order provide that no simplified planning zone scheme shall grant automatic planning permission for development:

1 In any area or areas specified in the order or
2 Of any development specified in the order.

But development already begun when the order of the Secretary of State comes into force is not affected.

6.17 Clearly the making of a Simplified Planning Zone Scheme is going to be no simple matter and is going to take time – months rather than weeks (or is it years rather than months?). The local planning authority will need to consider very closely the details of their proposals because the wider or more liberal the development automatically granted by the Scheme, the less will the authority, on an *ad hoc*, individual basis, be able to exercise their own policies relating to development control. Control by planning authorities of details about development permitted by the Scheme (e.g. the siting of buildings, the materials to be used in their construction, and the dimensions, design and external appearance of buildings) will be beyond control by the local planning authority unless they have been spelt out deliberately and in detail in the scheme itself. Yet if too much detail is put into a Scheme there is a chance that more objections to it will be lodged and, accordingly, the more protracted will be any public local inquiry relating to such objections.

On the other hand, a developer will wish to know (by his reading and examination of the scheme) with some certainty whether he may safely go ahead with his development without making any formal application for planning permission and paying the fees currently applicable in such a case, relying on the provisions of the scheme to support his action. After all, if he goes beyond the scope of the Scheme (including its conditions, limitations and exceptions) he is in danger of being faced with an enforcement notice on the basis that he has carried out development without planning permission. The developer may decide to take this risk or (if he has time on his hands) he may apply under section 192 of the 1990 Act for a determination by the local planning authority as to whether or not his development falls within the scope of the Scheme.

In short, the drafting of a Simplified Planning Zone Scheme may well be as big a headache to the local planning authority as the construing of the meaning and scope of the Scheme will be to a developer eager to press on with development which happens to be of an expensive and substantial nature. In such a case, and in order to be absolutely sure of his ground, will the developer seek an *ad hoc* grant of planning permission from the local planning authority? Will he think it better to be slow but sure rather than rapid and wrong? But if he does apply to the local planning authority for an *ad hoc* grant of planning permission, will the authority accept his application and deal with it in the ordinary way or will they refer the developer to the contents of their Simplified Planning Zone Scheme? We shall see.

7 Enforcement of planning control

7.01 The enforcement of planning control is dealt with in sections 171A to 196C of the Town and Country Planning Act 1990. Important new enforcement powers were added to the original 1990 Act by the Planning and Compensation Act 1991.

Time limits

7.02 If development consisting of building or other operations is carried out without planning permission and if the authorities allow four years to elapse without doing anything about the matter (i.e. without taking action by issuing an enforcement notice, as to which see paragraphs 7.06–7.08 below), then such development becomes validated automatically for town planning purposes and no enforcement action can be taken thereafter. It may be said at once that nothing in the 1990 Act interferes with this state of affairs so far as building development is concerned.

7.03 However, so far as development involving only a change of use of land is concerned, the equivalent time limit is 10 years from the date at which the change of use occurred. In order to take advantage of this time limit a developer must be able to demonstrate that the unlawful use has gone on continuously for over 10 years before the date of issue of any enforcement notice.

Certificates of lawful use

7.04 Until the Planning and Compensation Act 1991 development in respect of which the time limit for enforcement had expired was regarded as being 'established' but was not regarded as lawful. This bizarre situation led to great difficulty in assessing the lawfulness of development on land where there had previously been an 'established' but not 'lawful' use and was swept away by TP 1990, section 191 (as inserted into the 1990 Act by the 1991 Act). Henceforth, all development in respect of which the time limit for enforcement has expired is lawful.

7.05 A developer may now apply under TP, section 1991 for a 'certificate of lawful use or development'. This is obtained from the local planning authority, and there is a right of appeal to the Secretary of State if one is refused. The certificate makes it clear that the use in question, though originally instituted without planning permission, is now lawful and immune from enforcement action.

Enforcement notices

7.06 Enforcement action is by way of enforcement notice served by the local planning authority upon the owner and occupier of the land to which it relates (TP 1990, Part VII T and CP (Enforcement) (Inquiries Procedure) Rules 2000 (SI 2000 No 2686). Briefly, the notice must state exactly what the alleged breach of planning control is and the steps required to remedy the breach. There is an appeal to the Secretary of State against the notice, and the appeal must now state not only the grounds of the appeal but the facts on which it is based. The penalty for non-compliance with an enforcement notice is, on summary conviction, a fine of £20 000 or on conviction on indictment, a fine of unlimited amount (TP, section 179).

7.07 Architects should note that a local planning authority is never obliged to serve an enforcement notice whenever there has been a breach of planning control. The authority always has a discretion which it must be expected to exercise reasonably, as must any public authority holding discretionary powers. What the authority have to consider is whether, notwithstanding the breach of planning control, it is expedient to take enforcement action, and on this the authority must have regard not only to the provisions of the relevant development plan but also to 'any other material considerations'.

7.08 Without doubt, enforcement notices are very tricky things indeed, and the law reports are full of decisions of the courts in which the validity of such notices has been challenged successfully on the ground of some legal flaw in the drafting or the service of the notice. However, all these things are problems for the local authority rather than for the developer and his architect.

Stop notices

7.09 The legal pitfalls associated with an enforcement notice have, in the past, sometimes led a developer to spin out the appeal procedure while getting on in the meantime with his building development. There is an appeal to the High Court on a point of law from the Secretary of State's decision in an enforcement notice appeal, and there are further appeals (on points of law) to the Court of Appeal and to the House of Lords. This is still the position, but the 1990 Act prevents a building developer from continuing his building operations while the protracted appeals procedure is working itself out. There is no longer the possibility of (quite lawfully) finishing the building before the appeal to, and in, the House of Lords is concluded. The stop notice procedure prevents this from happening (TP, section 187).

7.10 Once an enforcement notice has been served, the local authority may follow it with a stop notice which brings all building operations or changes of use to a halt under a penalty, for breach of the notice, of £20 000 on summary conviction or of a fine of unlimited amount on conviction on indictment (TP, section 187).

7.11 A stop notice may also be served following an enforcement notice which relates, not to building or other operations, but to any material change in the use of land (TP 1990, section 183). If a stop notice is so served, it must be served within 12 months of the change of use occurring. But a stop notice on a change of use can never be served when the change of use is change of use of a building into use as a dwelling house (TP, section 183(4)).

7.12 There is no appeal against a stop notice. Such a notice is dependent entirely on the enforcement notice with which it is associated. If, on appeal, the enforcement notice fails, so does the stop notice. In this instance, compensation is payable under the 1990 Act in certain (but not all) cases for loss or damage arising from the stop notice (TP, section 186). Thus a local authority will be inclined to think twice before serving a stop notice.

Injunctions

7.13 TP, section 187B enables local planning authorities to seek injunctions in respect of actual or apprehended breaches of planning control. The use of injunctions by local planning authorities is on the increase and developers tempted by the apparent slowness of the statutory enforcement proceedings to step outside the law should beware. It is for the local planning authority, not the court, to determine whether it is necessary or expedient to restrain an actual or apprehended breach of planning control. An injunction can be sought irrespective of whether the local planning authority has exercised any of its other enforcement powers and irrespective of whether there are, for example, pending applications for planning permission. The court's consideration will simply be limited to an assessment of whether the circumstances of the case are such that only an injunction will actually be effective to stop the breach of planning control taking place.

Guidance

7.14 Department of the Environment Circular 10/97 and its nine Annexes give much useful guidance on the subject of enforcement notices, stop notices and injunctions to enforce planning control over land development.

24

Planning law in Scotland

STEVEN L. STUART

1 Introduction

1.01 The principal Act in respect of town and country planning in Scotland is the Town and Country Planning (Scotland) Act 1997. The other Act of significance is the Planning (Listed Buildings and Conservation Areas) (Scotland) Act 1997. There are a considerable number of statutory instruments dealing with planning matters. These are regulations or Orders made by the Secretary of State under powers granted by provisions in the principal Act or other Acts. These cover a wide variety of matters including procedure for making applications, for dealing with planning applications, fees for applications, permitted development (i.e. development granted planning permission by the terms of the order and not requiring an application for planning permission), development by planning authorities, appeals and inquiries procedure, tree preservation orders, specification of classes of use not involving development and enforcement of planning control.

1.02 Following the advent of the Scottish Parliament town and country planning is an area within the legislative competence of the Scottish Parliament and Orders and Regulations will be made by the relevant Scottish Minister. References in existing legislation to Ministers of the Crown, such as the Secretary of State shall be read so as to include Scottish Ministers. These are the First Minister and other Ministers such as one having departmental responsibility for town and country planning matters. Hereinafter reference shall be made to the Scottish Ministers rather than the Secretary of State as in the original enactment, order etc.

1.03 Government policy on various planning issues is found in various National Planning Policy Guidelines (NPPG) (which are being replaced by Scottish Planning Policies (SPP)). At the time of writing fifteen have been published. Perhaps the most significant in practical terms are (SPP1), The Planning System; (SPP2), Business and Industry; (SPP3), Land for Housing; NPPG8, Retailing; NPPG9, Provision of Roadside Facilities on Motorways and other Roads and NPPG15, Rural Development.

1.04 The Scottish Office advise in the form of official circulars and Planning Advice Notes (PANS) are regularly published. Useful ones are No. 36, Siting and Design of Houses in the Countryside; No. 40, Development Control (with 1997 addendum) and No. 48 on Planning Application Forms.

1.05 It is proposed to follow the general section headings in Chapter 21 drawing attention to the particular Scottish provisions and specific points worthy of note in relation to the Scottish system. More detailed information and treatment in respect of Scottish planning law is found in Scottish Planning Law and Procedure (W. Green, 2001) and a more concise text entitled *Planning* by Neil Collar (W. Green, 2nd edition, 1999). The principal statutes, statu-tory instruments, Scottish Office circulars, NPPGs and PANS together with articles on selected planning topics are published in loose-leaf format in the *Scottish Planning Encyclopaedia* (4 volumes, regularly updated, W. Green & Son, Edinburgh). Similar material although less extensive in terms of statutory coverage and exclud-ing articles is found in the *Scottish Planning Sourcebook* (3 volumes, regularly updated, Hillside Publishing, Dundee).

2 General

2.01 It is necessary to determine whether a proposed development is such as to require a grant of planning permission before it can be carried out. That depends on the definition of 'development' in section 26 of the principal Act (see section 4 of this chapter). It is development as there defined which requires planning permission. However, certain changes of use do not constitute development by virtue of the provisions of the Town and Country Planning (Use Classes) Order 1997 (SI 1997 No. 3061) as amended. Certain classes of development are permitted development in that permission is granted by the terms of the General Permitted Development (Scotland) Order 1992 (SI 1992 No. 223) as amended. It is to be noted that the Scottish Ministers or the planning authority may direct that development of any of the classes in the Order, with the exception of certain mineral operations should not be carried out without planning permission. There are certain other exceptions and quali-fications (see article 4 of the Order).

2.02 In relation to buildings which are listed as being of special architectural or historical interest special provisions apply under the Planning (Listed Buildings and Conservation Areas) (Scotland) Act 1997. In addition, under the same Act special provisions apply to proposals for development of buildings or land within a conserva-tion area designated as such by the local planning authority or the Scottish Ministers. For demolition of a building in such an area a consent known as conservation area consent is required.

2.03 If the site of the proposed development is within what is known as a Simplified Planning Zone then the relevant Simplified Planning Zone scheme provides planning permission within the area covered by the scheme for development in accord with it without the need for application.

3 The planning authority

3.01 A system of unitary (all functions) local authorities has been in place in Scotland since April 1996. Applications for planning permission are made to the local authority who are the planning authority.

3.02 It is possible for the Scottish Ministers to designate what is termed an enterprise zone and the relevant Order may provide that the enterprise zone authority shall be the planning authority for the zone for such purposes of the Planning Acts and in relation to such kinds of development as may be specified.

3.03 The Scottish Ministers retain power to give directions requiring applications to be referred to him for determination instead of by the planning authority. This is the power to 'call in' an application (section 46 of the Principal Act).

3.04 While informal negotiation frequently takes place between the applicant's architect and planning officers with a view to arriving at details for a proposal which the officers would find acceptable and recommend for approval to the planning committee, any comments or opinions voiced by the officer do not bind the planning authority. A planning authority is not ordinarily fettered in the exercise of its statutory functions by anything that has previously been said by any of its officers unless the officer was exercising delegated powers or, perhaps, that the statement was within the officers ostensible authority, that is, that the authority held the officer out as having the power to bind them in respect of a particular matter.

3.05 Fees payable in respect of various applications are found in the Town and Country Planning (Fees for Applications and Deemed Applications) (Scotland) Regulations 1997 (S1 1997 No. 10). Regulations 3, 10, 12, 13 and 14 and the Schedule are provided for therein (regulations 4 to 9) and refunds in respect of deemed application (regulation 11).

4 Development

4.01 The definition of 'development' is found in section 26(1) of the Principal Act and means the carrying out of building engineering mining or the operations in and over or under land or the making of any material change in the use of any buildings or land.

4.02 Building operations include demolition rebuilding and structural alteration and additions (section 26(4)). Section 26(2) sets out operations which do not involve development. These include works affecting only the interior of the building and which do not materi-

202

ally affect the exterior and the use of buildings or land within the curtilage of a dwelling house for a purpose incidental to the enjoyment of the dwelling house. The use as two or more separate dwelling houses of a building previously used as a single dwelling house involves a material change in the use of the building and each part of it (section 26(3)).

4.03 In relation to change in use the provisions of the Town and Country Planning (Use Classes) (Scotland) Order 1987 (SI 1997 No. 3061) should be noted. The Order specifies 11 classes of use. These include shops, financial, professional and other services, food and drink, business, general, industrial, storage and distributions and houses. Where a building or land is used for a purpose in any class the use of the building or land for any other purpose in the same class does not involve development. So, for example, a building may switch from use for the retail sale of goods other than food to use as a travel agency without involving development requiring planning permission or both are within class 1 shops. Incidental uses do not require planning permission merely because they fall within a different Use Class.

4.04 In cases of doubt it is possible to apply for a certificate of lawfulness of an existing or proposed use or development (sections 150 and 151 of the Principal Act) and there is provision for an appeal to the Scottish Ministers against a refusal or failure to give a decision.

5 Control of development

5.01 Where it is considered that the proposal involves 'development' it is necessary to determine whether the proposal is permitted development, that is, development which is granted permission by virtue of the Town and Country Planning (General Permitted Development (Scotland)) Order 1992 (SI 1992 No. 223) as amended (see section 31 of the Principal Act), there are 71 classes of development covered by 24 Parts in Schedule 1 to the Order. The Parts indicate general descriptions of groups of classes. Part 1, for example, covers development with the curtilage of a dwelling house, Part 2 minor operations, Part 3 changes of use, Part 6 agricultural buildings and operations, Part 8 industrial and warehouse operations and so on. A full explanation of 'permitted development' is found in Article 3. It is to be noted that the Order does not authorize development contrary to a condition imposed by a planning permission granted otherwise than by the Order. Directions restricting permitted development may be issued (Article 4).

Where a proposed development does not fall within the classes of permitted development an application for planning permission requires to be made (sections 32 and 33 of Principal Act). Detailed procedure is set out in the Procedure Order referred to earlier.

5.02 In relation to **determination** of a planning application the planning authority must have regard to the provisions of the Development Plan and to any other material considerations (section 37(2)). Section 25 provides that a determination shall be made in accordance with the development plan unless material considerations indicate otherwise. There is, thus, a presumption that the development plan is to govern the decision. The development plan is the approved Structure Plan and the adopted Local Plan wherein planning policies and proposals for the Structure Plan and Local Plan area are found. Material considerations are considerations relating to the use and development of land. These will depend on the nature of the particular proposal and its circumstances. SPP1 at paragraph 51 gives a non-exhaustive list of considerations which are generally regarded as material considerations. These include government policy and guidance, such as found in NPPGs, public representations (where relevant) consultation responses, impact on the locality and impact on the natural and built environment including layout siting design and external appearance. A replacement local plan particularly at an advanced stage of preparation which has not yet been adopted would also be a material consideration.

It should be noted that when determining whether to grant planning permission in respect to any buildings or land in a conservation area special attention shall be paid to the desirability of preserving or enhancing the character or appearance of that area (section 64 of the Town and Country Planning (Listed Buildings and Conservation Areas) (Scotland) Act 1997).

5.03 Refusal of an application is subject to a right of **appeal** to the Scottish Ministers within 6 months of the decision (section 47(1) of the Principal Act). Appeal may also be taken against what is termed a deemed refusal that is an application which has not been determined within 2 months of the date of receipt (section 47(2)).

The Scottish Ministers' obligation to determine appeals is ordinarily delegated to appointed officials known as Reporters although they may recall for their own determination particular cases. Appeals by statutory undertakers are reserved for determination by the Scottish Ministers. Appeals may be dealt with by the holding of a public local inquiry or, in the vast majority of cases, by way of written submissions. Procedural rules have been enacted in respect of appeals determined by public inquiry and written submissions.

5.04 While an application for planning permission may be detailed where full details of the building or other operation, e.g. erection of dwelling houses are set out in the plans submitted it is possible for application to be made only for what is termed **outline planning permission**. Such an application is one where the applicant seeks permission for the principle of development, e.g. residential or retail but with reservation for subsequent approval by the planning authority of matters particularized in the application 'reserved matters' (section 59(1)) of the Principal Act. 'Reserved matters' are defined in the Procedure Order as any matters in respect of which details have not been given in the application which concern the siting design or external appearance of the relevant building or the means of access to the building or the landscaping of the site (Article 2). Other matters not falling within the definition of reserved matters may still by way of condition be reserved for subsequent approval of the planning authority (*Inverclyde District Council v Inverkip Building Co. Ltd* [1983] SLT 563). Since it is the principle of development for which approval is sought it is important that any drawings and illustrations submitted with the application are marked as being indicative only. The right of appeal referred to above extends not only in respect of the refusal of outline planning permission but also any subsequent refusal of reserved matters.

5.05 There are detailed procedural provisions in respect of applications in the Town and Country Planning (General Development Procedure) (Scotland) Order 1992 (SI 1992 No. 224) as amended ('the Procedure Order'). This Order in furtherance of provisions in the Principal Act (sections 34 and 35) contains provision requiring notification of applications to owners, owner of neighbouring land and agricultural tenants (paragraphs 8 and 9). Generally neighbouring land is land which is conterminous with or within 4 metres of the boundary of the land to be developed but only if any part of the land is within 90 metres of any part of the development.

The applicant or his architect must also submit with the application form a certificate that he has given the requisite notice with details thereof or that he has been unable to do. In cases where the applicant is unable to notify neighbours or in cases of 'bad neighbour' development (Schedule 7 to the Order) then the planning authority must publish a newspaper advertisement of the application (cost to be paid for by applicant) (Article 12).

5.06 An application must be made on a form issued by and obtainable from the planning authority. It must describe the development (Articles 3 and 4 of the Procedure Order). In the case of an outline application there must be a plan sufficient to identify the relevant land. In relation to any other application there must also be submitted such other plans and drawings as may be necessary to describe the development. It is essential that the description of the proposed development in the application be accurate in terms of describing properly the development for which planning permission is sought. If it is not then even although the nature of the application is clear from the plans any grant of planning permission may be challenged by, e.g. an owner of neighbouring land to whom erroneous notification was given (*Cumming v Secretary of State for Scotland* [1993] SLT 228).

The Procedure Order also contains provisions (in article 15) in respect of bodies to be consulted before any grant of planning permission. This depends on the nature of the development and whether there are implications for the body concerned. The list includes the roads authority, the Scottish Ministers, the water and sewerage authority, Scottish Natural Heritage, the Scottish Environmental Protection Agency and the Health and Safety Executive. The Scottish Ministers may issue directions as to authorities, etc. to be consulted.

5.07 An application may be granted refused or granted subject to such conditions as the planning authority thinks fit (section 37(1) of Principal Act). In the case of refusal or conditional grant the reasons for the decision must be given (article 22(1)(a) of the Procedure Order). As noted earlier, a refusal may be appealed but so also may a conditional grant if the applicant is unhappy with any or all of the conditions imposed.

5.08 The power to impose **conditions** is found not only in section 37(1) referred to above but also in section 41(1) which is stated to be without prejudice to the former provision and empowers the imposition of conditions for regulating the development or use of any land under the control of the applicant (whether or not it is part of the application site) or requiring the carrying out of works on such land so far as appears to the authority to be expedient for the purposes of or in connection with the authorized development. Conditions may also authorize the removal of buildings or works authorized by the permission. Conditions may be imposed which depend on the actions of a third party. The applicant cannot lawfully be required to secure that such action is taken but the matter may be dealt with by a negative or suspensive condition to the effect that no development shall proceed until the specified action has been taken.

It is ultimately for the courts to determine whether a particular condition is lawful. However, certain tests have evolved. Essentially a planning condition must have a planning purpose, fairly and reasonably relate to the permitted development and not be so unreasonable that no planning authority could have imposed it. Detailed guidance is found in the Scottish Office Circular on the Use of Planning Conditions (4) 1998. It is stated therein that a condition should only be imposed where it is necessary, relevant to planning, relevant to the proposed development, enforceable, precise and reasonable in all other respects. In addition a condition should not derogate from a permission such as to result in a permission substantially different in character from that applied for. A condition requiring any consideration for the grant of planning permission cannot be imposed without statutory authority.

Careful consideration should be given in respect of appeals against conditions. The condition may be deleted or modified. A more onerous condition may be imposed by the Reporter or he may refuse permission. It is competent to do this even although the appeal is only against a condition (section 47(1)). It should also be noted that in the event of a Reporter's decision being appealed to the Court of Session, the Court has held that it has no power to sever an invalid condition from the rest of the permission so that the entire permission falls if a condition is held to be invalid (see *BAA v Secretary of State for Scotland* [1979] SC 200).

5.09 Section 75 of the Principal Act provides that a planning authority may enter into an **agreement** with any person interested in land in their area for the purpose of restricting or regulating the development or use of the land. Such an agreement may include incidental provisions including financial ones as appear to be necessary or expedient for the purposes of the agreement. On this basis the applicant may require to make payment in respect of the cost of providing, say, sewers and road access required by the development. Guidance on the scope of section 75 agreements is found in the Scottish Offices Circular 12/1996 (Planning Agreements). It is to be noted that the provision only relates to agreements. Unlike England and Wales it does not permit the developer to enter a unilateral undertaking to do something.

While a grant of planning permission authorizes the particular development to be carried out it will frequently be necessary separately to apply for building warrant from the local authority in respect of particular building operations.

5.10 A permission has a **duration** of 5 years unless the grant specifies a shorter or longer period. That means that development must be begun not later than the expiration of 5 years or the appropriate period beginning with the date of the permission (section 58). Section 27 sets out detailed provisions for the purpose of determining when development is taken to be initiated. For the purpose of section 58 development is taken to have begun on the earliest date on which any material operation comprised in the development begins to be carried out. That includes any construction work in the course of erection of a building, any demolition work and commonly the digging of a trench for the foundations of the buildings. Any one of the specified operations will have the effect that the development is begun (*City of Glasgow DC v Secretary of State for Scotland* [1993] SLT 268).

5.11 In relation to an outline planning permission application for approval of reserved matters must be made before the expiration of 3 years from the date of the outline permission (subject to certain qualifications) and the development itself must be begun (as explained above) within 5 years of the permission or within 2 years of the final approval of reserved matters or the final approval of the last reserved matter (section 59).

Although there is no legal principle that a planning permission could be abandoned by the actings of a party entitled to the benefit of the permission implementation of a permission may be physically impossible where another development under another permission has been implemented instead.

5.12 Where a planning permission is subject to a condition that the development must be begun before the expiry of a particular period and the development has been begun but not completed within that period the planning authority may serve a completion notice where they are of the opinion that it will not be begun within a reasonable period (section 61). The notice states that the permission will cease to have effect at the end of the period set out in the notice. There is a 12-month minimum period. The authority may withdraw a notice. The notice must be confirmed by the Scottish Minister before it takes effect. If it takes effect then at the end of the period the permission becomes invalid (section 62).

5.13 Section 65 of the Principal Act empowers a planning authority to revoke or modify a permission if it appears to them that it is expedient to do so. The authority must have regard to the development plan and other material considerations. The power may be exercised before the operations have been completed or the change of use has taken place as the case may be. In relation to operations the revocation does not affect such operations as have previously been carried out. Procedure is dealt with in sections 66 and 67. The planning authority may also make an order requiring discontinuance of use or alteration or removal of buildings or works (section 71). In relation to both sections 65 and 71 orders compensation may be payable (sections 76 and 83).

6 Listed buildings

6.01 The statutory provisions in respect of buildings of special architectural and historical interest are found in the Town and Country Planning (Listed Buildings and Conservation Area) (Scotland) Act 1997 (the 'Listed Buildings Act'). Lists of such buildings are compiled by the Scottish Ministers. It is to be noted that any object or structure fixed to a listed building and any object or structure within the curtilage of the building which though unfixed to it forms part of the land and has done so since before 1 July 1948 is treated as part of the building. Indeed the desirability of preserving such objects or structures on the ground of architectural or historical interest may be taken into account in considering whether to list a building. Similarly, in deciding whether to list a building the Scottish Ministers may have regard not only to the building itself but also any respect in which its exterior contributes to the architectural or historic interest of any group of buildings of which it forms part. There is no right of appeal against listing although the owner lessee and occupier must be advised.

6.02 No works for the demolition of a listed building or for its alteration or extension in any manner which would affect its character as a building of special architectural or historic interest unless the works are authorized (section 6). Such works are authorized if a written consent has been granted for their execution and the works are executed in accordance with the consent and any attached conditions (section 7). In relation to demolition this cannot take place until 3 months have elapsed following notice of the proposal being given to the Royal Commission in the Ancient and Historical Monuments of Scotland after the grant of listed building consent (section 7(2)). A listed building consent is required in addition to any planning permission which is required for the development irrespective of the listing of the building. Applications for listed building consent are made to the local planning authority (section 9). Procedure is set out in sections 9 to 16 of the Listed Buildings Act and the Town and Country Planning (Listed Buildings and Buildings in Conservation Areas) (Scotland) Regulations 1987 (SI 1987 No. 1529). There is a power of call in which may be exercised by the Minister. A listed building consent is granted subject to a condition that works permitted by it shall be commenced within the period specified in the consent. If none is specified there is a deemed condition that the works will be commenced within 5 years of the date of the grant of consent (section 16). There is no equivalent provision to section 6 of the English Act in Scotland. Listed building consent may be granted subject to conditions. These may include conditions relating to preservation of particular features of the building, the making good of damage caused to the building by the works, and re-construction following execution of the works using, where practicable, original materials with interior alterations as specified (sections 14(1) and 15(1)). They may also be reservation of specified details for subsequent approval (section 15(2)).

6.03 In reaching a decision on an application for listed building consent the planning authority or the Scottish Ministers shall have special regard to the desirability of preserving the building or its setting or any features of special architectural or historic interest which it possesses (section 14(2)). Accordingly, these are considerations which should be addressed by architect and client at the time of formulating the development proposals. These are, of course, different considerations from those which apply to an application for planning permission although, in considering whether to grant planning permission for development which affects a listed building or its setting, the same requirement, that is, to have special regard to the desirability of preserving the building or its setting etc. applies (section 59).

6.04 There is a right of appeal against a refusal of listed building consent or a grant subject to conditions. Where a listed building consent is refused then if the owner can establish that the building and land is incapable of reasonably beneficial use in its existing state he may serve a listed building purchase notice on the planning authority requiring them to purchase it (section 28). It is a criminal offence to execute or cause to be executed any works for the demolition of a listed building or for its alteration or execution in a manner which would affect its character as a building of special architectural or historic interest unless the works are authorized by which is meant that there is a listed building consent for the works concerned (section 8). Failure to comply with a condition under such a consent is also an offence punishable by fine and/or imprisonment.

Defensive provisions are found in section 8(3). These relate to establishing that the works were urgently necessary in the interests of health and safety or for preservation of the building although there are other specific related matters which require to be established.

6.05 The planning authority may serve a listed building enforcement notice where it appears to them that works have been or are being executed to a listed building in contravention of section 8 (see section 34). It is an offence not to comply with such a notice (section 39). It is to be noted that where after the period for compliance specified has elapsed with any required step not having been taken, the person who is 'for the time being owner of the land' is in breach of duty and guilty of an offence. There are defences available including not having been served with the notice or being aware of its existence (section 39(4)). There is a right of appeal against a notice (section 35).

Compulsory acquisition by the planning authority of a listed building in need of repair may be authorized after service of a repairs notice (section 42). There is a right of application to the sheriff for an order prohibiting further proceedings on the order. Compensation provisions are found in sections 44 and 45.

6.06 There are provisions enabling the planning authority to protect a building which is not listed but which appears to them to be of special architectural or historic interest and to be in danger of demolition or alteration in such a way as to affect its character as a building of such interest. In such a case they may serve a building preservation notice on the owner (section 3). It comes into force on being so served and remains in force for 6 months. The effect of the notice during that period is that the building is protected as if it were listed. During that period the Scottish Ministers can consider whether to list the building. If at the end of the period they do not do so the notice ceases and no further notice can be served within the next 12 months.

7 Enterprise zones and simplified planning zones

7.01 The Scottish Ministers may by order under Schedule 32 to the Local Government Planning and Land Act 1980 designate an enterprise zone. This has the effect of granting permission for development specified in the scheme for development of any class so specified (section 55 of the Principal Act). Planning permission so granted will be subject to the conditions, if any specified in the scheme or if there are none it will be unconditional. The enterprise zone authority may direct that any such permission shall not apply to a specified development or to specified classes of development either generally or within a specified area.

Similarly where a simplified planning zone scheme is in force the adoption or approval of such a scheme has the effect of granting planning permission for development specified in the scheme or for development of any class so specified. Such a permission may be unconditional or subject to conditions specified in the scheme (section 49 of the Principal Act). The planning authority has the power to make or alter such schemes. The types of conditions which may be specified are set out in section 51. Such a scheme has effect for a period of 10 years. A planning authority shall not include in a scheme development which require environmental assessment or is likely to affect a European site (regulation 20 of the Town and Country Planning (Simplified Planning Zones) (Scotland) Regulations 1995 (SI 1995 No. 2043)). Certain specified descriptions of land may not be included in such a zone.

8 Enforcement of planning control

8.01 The relevant provisions are found in Part VI of the Principal Act (sections 123 to 158). Where there has been a breach of planning control, i.e. development without planning permission or failing to comply with a condition, then, if the development consists of building or other operations, no enforcement action may be taken after the end of 4 years beginning with the date on which the operations were substantially completed. In the case of a change of use the period is 10 years, beginning with the date of the breach. It is possible, as noted earlier, to apply for a certificate of lawfulness of an existing or proposed use or development (sections 150 and 151).

8.02 Before taking enforcement action a planning authority, where it appears to them that there may have been a breach of planning control, may serve on the owner or occupier or any person using the land or carrying out operations on it a **planning contravention notice** requiring the giving of information about operations on and use of the land (section 125). Non-compliance with such a notice is a criminal offence (section 126).

8.03 Where it appears to the planning authority that there has been a breach of planning control they may serve an **enforcement notice** on the owner or occupier of the land (section 126). The notice must specify the matters considered to be a breach of planning control and the step required to remedy the breach or any injury to amenity caused by the breach. It should also specify a period for compliance with its terms (section 128). There is provision for appeal against such a notice (sections 130 to 133).

8.04 Where the planning authority consider it expedient that any activity specified in an enforcement notice as one which they require to cease should do so before the expiry of the period for compliance they may when they serve the enforcement notice or afterwards serve a **stop notice** prohibiting the activity (section 140) such a notice may not be served where the enforcement notice has taken effect (that date will be specified in the enforcement notice). A stop notice shall not prohibit the use of any building as a dwelling house and shall not prohibit any activity which has been carried out for a period of more than 4 years ending with the service of the notice. There is no right of appeal against a stop notice. It stands or falls with the relative enforcement notice.

8.05 A planning authority may, where a condition attaching to a planning permission has not been complied with, serve a **breach of condition notice** on any person carrying out the development or on any person having control of the land (section 145). The notice requires that the conditions specified be complied with. The notice should specify the steps to be taken or the activities which should cease to secure compliance. The period for compliance must be not less than 28 days.

8.06 Finally a planning authority may seek to restrain or prevent a breach of planning control by application for an **interdict** to the Sheriff Court or Court of Session (section 146).

8.07 Official guidance on enforcement matters is found in Scottish Office Circular 4/1999 on Planning Enforcement and in PAN 54 on the same topic.

25

Planning law in Northern Ireland

WILLIAM ORBINSON

Note:

Throughout this chapter the following abbreviations are used:
2003 Order = the Planning (Amendment) (Northern Ireland) Order 2003;
1991 Order = the Planning (Northern Ireland) Order 1991;
GDO = the Planning (General Development) Order (Northern Ireland) Order 1993, as amended;
UCO = the Planning (Use Classes) Order (Northern Ireland) 1989, as amended by the Planning (Use Classes) (Amendment) Orders (Northern Ireland) of 1993 and 1996.
Department = the Department of the Environment for Northern Ireland, Planning Service.

1 Introduction

1.01 With a few notable exceptions, the planning law of Northern Ireland is drawn from and broadly reflects the principles of English planning law.

1.02 There are three main differences between the two systems. First, for historical reasons planning functions in Northern Ireland lie with the Department of the Environment for Northern Ireland Planning Service, rather than with local councils. This does not greatly affect development planning and control on a substantive level, but it does have procedural implications which will be examined in the text. The second main difference is that, whereas in England development plans are given primacy and will be followed in determining an application for planning permission except where material considerations indicate otherwise, in Northern Ireland the Department has to have regard to all material considerations, including the relevant development plan so far as it is material to the application: Article 25(1) of the 1991 Order. This means that in Northern Ireland the Department must consider the relevant development plan, but need not slavishly adhere to it. Once in force, Article 30 of the 2003 Order will introduce a plan led system for Northern Ireland, though there is some debate as to whether the wording of the Article will necessarily have the effect of replicating the English position, or whether it contemplates more flexibility. In any event, it is not anticipated that Article 30 will come into force for some years until an updated suite of development plans is in place. The third main difference between the two systems is that appellate and inquiry functions in Northern Ireland are undertaken by the Planning Appeals Commission (PAC), an independent body created by statute, whereas in England the Inspectorate which deals with these matters is the creature of the Secretary of State for the Environment. For guidance on the role of the PAC, see *PAC: Principles of Decision-Taking* by William Orbinson, published by SLS Legal Publications (NI) 1999, and *NI Planning Policy* by William Orbinson, published by SLS Legal Publications (NI) 2003.

1.03 As in England, development control in Northern Ireland is shaped by central government policy, which is continually in a state of flux. The local equivalent to the English Planning Policy Guidance Notes (PPGs) are Planning Policy Statements (PPSs), which have been issued on the following topics: General Principles (PPS 1); Planning and Nature Conservation (PPS 2); Development Control: Roads Considerations (PPS 3); Industrial Development (PPS 4); Retailing and Town Centres (PPS 5); Planning, Archaeology and the Built Heritage (PPS 6); Quality Residential Environments (PPS 7); Enforcement of Planning Control (PPS 9); Telecommunications (PPS 10) and Planning and Waste Management (PPS 11). In addition, the Department has issued 15 Development Control Advice Notes. These apply throughout the region, and are supplemented at a local level by planning guidance issued by the Department's Divisional Planning Offices. Rural development is subject to the Planning Strategy for Rural Northern Ireland. This imposed policy constraints on development in the countryside, which are felt by many to be unduly restrictive in an area of the UK where much of the population lives and works in rural areas.

The Strategic Planning (NI) Order 1999 required the Department of Regional Development to formulate, in consultation with other Northern Ireland government departments, a strategy for the long-term development of the region. After a very long consultation process, Shaping our Future: Regional Development Strategy (RDS) for Northern Ireland 2025 was published in September 2001. It addresses:

- the forces driving change;
- the strategy's vision and guiding principles;
- spatial development strategy for the region;
- the Belfast Metropolitan Area;
- Londonderry/Derry: Regional City for the North West;
- rural Northern Ireland;
- meeting housing needs;
- supporting economic development;
- development of a regional transportation system;
- caring for the environment;
- implementation.

Generally, in exercising any functions in relation to development in Northern Ireland all Northern Ireland and UK government departments must have regard to the RDS. Department of the Environment policy documents and development plans, apart from three excepted plans, must be in general conformity with the RDS, as must any development scheme adopted or amended by the Department for Social Development under Article 86 of the 1991 Order. The RDS is a material consideration both at development plan and development control levels, and for both the Department of the Environment as planning authority, and the Planning Appeals Commission in relation to its functions. It is perhaps the best thought of by English practitioners as something similar to a Structure Plan.

Clearly, the range of planning policy in Northern Ireland remains by no means as comprehensive as the range in England, and it is accepted that when local policy is silent on an issue dealt with by English policy then English policy can be taken into account to the extent that it is relevant and can be applied to local circumstances. For further guidance on Northern Irish planning policy, see the author's *Northern Ireland Planning Policy and Index to Northern Ireland Planning Policy* published by SLS Legal Publications (NI) 2003.

1.04 Given the similarities between Northern Irish and English planning law, perhaps the best approach to writing his chapter is to work through the section headings in Chapter 23 on English planning law, identifying equivalent legislation and drawing out any distinctions between English and Northern Irish planning systems.

1.05 Paragraph 1.05 of Chapter 23 broadly applies in Northern Ireland. In Northern Ireland, both limbs of the planning process are carried out by the Department of the Environment for Northern Ireland, Planning Service, and therefore paragraph 1.06 of Chapter 23 is inapplicable. The approach followed in this chapter reflects that set out in paragraphs 1.07–1.10 of Chapter 23.

2 Who is to deal with planning applications?

2.01 The steps which should be followed by an architect seeking to carry out development in Northern Ireland mirror those set out in paragraphs 2.01–2.07 of Chapter 23.

2.02 Paragraph 2.02 of Chapter 23 examines the definition of development. In Northern Ireland, essentially the same definition of development applies. This can be found in Articles 11(1), 11(2) and 11(3) of the 1991 Order, which should be read in conjunction with the Planning (Use Classes) Order (Northern Ireland) 1989, as amended, which allows for changes of use to take place from one use to another within the same class without an application for planning permission being required. If in any doubt as to whether what is proposed would be lawful, an application can be made to the Department for a Certificate of lawfulness of proposed use or development under Article 83B of the 1991 Order, as inserted by Article 12 of the 2003 Order.

2.03 Paragraphs 2.05 and 2.06 of Chapter 23 examine the concept of permitted development in England. Broadly the same principles apply in Northern Ireland, but there are differences in the detailed provisions of the local legislation, which deserves scrutiny. Permitted development rights in Northern Ireland are set out in Article 3 of and Schedule 1 to the Planning (General Development) Order (Northern Ireland) 1993, as amended.

Schedule 1 sets out the classes of permitted development recognized by the GDO, and as appropriate under each class states any exclusions, conditions or provisions as to interpretation applicable to that class. Article 3(4) makes clear that permitted development rights do not override conditions imposed on any planning permission granted or deemed to be granted otherwise than by the General Development Order (GDO) itself, while paragraphs (5), (6) and (7) deal with the relationship between permitted development rights under the GDO and, respectively, certain roads projects, developments requiring any consent or approval, and pipelines for hazardous substances. It is possible under Article 4 of the GDO for the Department to issue a direction removing or restricting certain permitted development rights. Article 6 provides for directions removing or restricting permitted development rights under Part 16 of Schedule 1, which deals with mineral exploration. As in England, it is important to satisfy yourself that the proposal falls within the scope of permitted development rights before attempting to rely on those rights and you should be wary of the various limitations inherent in those rights and the various means of excluding or restricting those rights.

2.04 Paragraph 2.06 of Chapter 23 examines area and zone designations which relax planning controls. Urban Development Areas do not exist in Northern Ireland, but Enterprise Zones and Simplified Planning Zones do, and have the same effect as in England.

2.05 Paragraphs 2.08–2.16 of Chapter 23 discuss the rather complex allocation of planning functions between the diverse layers of local government in England and Wales. These paragraphs are not relevant to Northern Ireland, where all planning functions are performed by the Department through its Divisional Planning Offices spread throughout the region. Although there are hints that with increasing political stability planning functions may eventually be returned to Northern Ireland's district councils, the formal involvement of district councils in the development control process is at present limited to a statutory entitlement to be consulted on applications – Article 20(1) of the 1991 Order, Article 15(a), GDO – and indeed on most aspects of the planning system.

2.06 As in England, negotiation between the architect and the Department's planning officers can play an important role in expediting planning applications. The recent caselaw from the House of Lords (see *R v East Sussex County Council exp. Reprotech (Pebsham) Ltd* [2002] UKLR 8), which makes plain that it is almost impossible for what is said during such negotiations to be binding on the planning authority, is of highly persuasive effect in Northern Ireland, and is likely to be followed in our Courts. *Reprotech* has already been treated as effectively binding by the Planning Appeals Commission.

It should be stressed that extended negotiations can prejudice the client's interests, as the right to appeal on the basis of non-determination will be lost 6 months after the statutory period for determination expires, and also the policy context can markedly change while the negotiations are ongoing. Both these points have been vividly illustrated by the publication of the RDS. Many architects found that, having engaged in extended but positive negotiations with the Department on a housing proposal, they were then confronted with a *volte-face*, with the Department adopting the stance that the proposal would probably be unacceptable given the objectives of the RDS. Often, the architects then found that the time period for bringing a non-determination appeal had lapsed.

2.07 Paragraphs 2.26–2.28 of Chapter 23 deal with fees payable on planning and related applications in England, and the fees payable in Northern Ireland are levied and assessed on more or less the same basis, with the governing legislation being the Planning (Fees) Regulations (Northern Ireland) 1992, as amended.

As for exemptions, no fee is payable on applications where the Department is satisfied that the application is solely in relation to certain operations directed towards facilitating disabled access to buildings, or where a planning condition requires an application to be made for permission to effect a change of use from one use to another use lying within the same class of the UCO. Note that Article 11(3)(c) of the GDO provides that the period of time allowed for determination of planning applications begins to run only when the appropriate fee is paid.

3 The meaning of development

3.01 Paragraphs 3.01–3.06 of Chapter 23 examine the meaning of development, and again the principles followed in Northern Ireland largely mirror those applying in England. In Northern Ireland, the basic definition of development requiring planning permission discussed at paragraphs 3.01 and 3.02 of Chapter 23 appear in Article 11(1) and (1A) of the 1991 Order, as amended by Article 18 of the 2003 Order. Article 11(1A) provides that the term 'building operations' now includes demolition of buildings, rebuilding, structural alteration of or addition to buildings, and other operations normally undertaken by a person carrying on business as a builder. Article 11(3) of the 1991 Order provides that subdivision of a dwelling house, deposit of waste on land and display of advertisements on an external part of a building will amount to a material change in use, and therefore development requiring planning permission. Article 11(2) of the 1991 Order stipulates that the following do not amount to development: certain works of interior maintenance; maintenance of services by district councils or statutory undertakers; uses incidental to the enjoyment of a dwelling house conducted within its curtilage; the use of land for agriculture and forestry and the use for those purposes of any building occupied together with such land; changes of use from one use to another use within the same class of use set out in the Planning (Use Classes) Order (Northern Ireland) 1989, as amended. Paragraph 3.04 of Chapter 23, which focuses on the operation of the English Use Classes Order, applies just as well to the Northern Irish equivalent. The principle of *City of London Corporation v Secretary of State for the Environment and Watling Street Properties Ltd* discussed at paragraph 3.05 of Chapter 23 also applies in Northern Ireland.

3.02 Paragraph 3.07 of Chapter 23 addresses the very useful English procedure of applying for a certificate of lawfulness. Article 12 of the 2003 Order inserts Articles 83A and 83B into the 1991 Order, respectively, providing for certificates in relation to existing use or development and for certificates in relation to proposed use or development. Article 83E of the 1991 Order, as inserted by Article 12 of the 2003 Order, provides for appeals to the Planning Appeals Commission against refusal of a certificate or failure to give a decision on an application for a certificate.

4 Control of development in general

4.01 We looked in paragraph 2.03 above, at permitted development rights. Paragraphs 4.01–4.03 of Chapter 23 set out in detail the classes of permitted development provided for by the English GDO. The classes of permitted development applicable under the Northern Ireland GDO are set out in Schedule 1 to that Order, and the classes are broadly similar to those set out in paragraph 4.03 of Chapter 23. Before treating a proposal as falling within any of these classes of permitted development, it is essential to examine closely the terms of each category to ensure that what is proposed will come within the scope of permitted development. If it does not, then it will be necessary to make a formal application for planning permission.

An application for planning permission must be made in accordance with the procedures laid down in the GDO. The requisite forms can be obtained from the local Divisional Planning Office.

4.02 Paragraph 4.05 of Chapter 23 refers to the English provisions governing environmental impact assessment. This process stems from European legislation, and provides essential protection for the environment in relation to proposals apt to have significant environmental impacts. In Northern Ireland, it operates under the Planning (Environmental Impact Assessment) Regulations (Northern Ireland) 1999. The advice given to architects in paragraph 4.05 of Chapter 23 applies equally in Northern Ireland. If in any doubt as to the requirements of environmental impact assessment, the architect should seek specialist legal advice.

4.03 Paragraph 4.06 of Chapter 23 points out that PPG 1 sets out the general principles underlying development control. In Northern Ireland, these principles are set out in Planning Policy Statement I: General Principles. Section 54A of the 1990 English Act has as yet no equivalent provision in force in Northern Ireland, where the development plan remains just one of the material considerations which have to be taken into account in determining planning applications, and has no special status over and above the other material considerations. The test of whether a matter is a material consideration is whether it serves a planning purpose, and a planning purpose is a purpose which relates to the character and use of land.

4.04 Paragraphs 4.08–4.19 of Chapter 23 deal with appeals against refusal of planning permission and against grant of planning permission subject to conditions. In Northern Ireland, the right of appeal is granted by Article 32 of the 1991 Order, and an important difference from the English situation is that appeals are made to the PAC, whose decisions are final. The Commission is independent from the Department, and this independence no doubt partly explains the very high rate of successful appeals in the region.

Appeals must be brought within 6 months of the decision, or within such longer period as the PAC may allow. They may be made by notice in writing to the Commission, but the Commission has printed forms for this purpose, and it is the best to use these. All appeals in Northern Ireland are by way of oral hearing, unless unusually the Department, the Appellant and the Commission agree that determination by written representations is appropriate. Procedure at appeals has not been laid down by statute, but is subject to the rules of natural justice and administrative fairness and the requirements of Article 6 of the European Convention on Human Rights – For guidance, see the Commission's procedural guidance and the author's PAC: Principles of Decision-Taking. There is no right of further appeal against the Commission's appeal decisions, though the presence of legal flaws will ground a Judicial Review. In Northern Ireland, there is no power to award costs in any planning appeal, inquiry or hearing, regardless of how unreasonable or vexatious the behaviour of the parties.

4.05 Paragraph 4.14 of Chapter 23 explains the English 'call-in' procedure. There is no direct equivalent to this procedure in Northern Ireland, but arguably the Article 31 procedure covers more or less the same ground. Article 31 only relates to certain applications, broadly those of strategic planning significance. In such instances, the Department may apply Article 31 to the application. If the Department goes down this route, then it has a choice of two possible courses of action. First, it can issue a Notice of Opinion indicating the decision it proposes to make on the application, in which case the applicant may request a hearing into the matter by the PAC. Secondly, it can request that the Commission hold a public inquiry on the application. In either case, the Department must take into account the report of the Commission before deciding the application, but is under no obligation to accept the Commission's view and sometimes departs from it. While lawyers, particularly specialist planning barristers, are involved in planning appeals more often than not, it is virtually unheard of for specialist planning barristers not to be involved in Article 31 inquiries and hearings.

Naturally, the presence of specialist barristers means that there is a rigorous examination of the issues and arguments, and those used to English planning practice are often surprised, or dismayed, by the aggressive cross-examination seen in the Northern Irish planning system. While no Northern Irish inquiry has so far stretched out as long as the monumental Heathrow Terminal 5 inquiry, inquiries in Northern Ireland to tend to run for weeks or months.

Outline permission

4.06 Paragraphs 4.15–4.18 of Chapter 23 point out the benefits and mechanics of bringing an outline application, and the rights of appeal. Outline applications in Northern Ireland are made under Article 8(1) of the GDO, and the same principles apply as in England, except that appeals are brought to the PAC rather than the Secretary of State. It is important to note that an application for approval of reserved Matters can generally only be made within 3 years of the grant of outline planning permission: Article 35(2)(a), 1991 Order. Furthermore, outline applications can only be brought in relation to the erection of a building, and other forms of operational development must be the subject of an application for full planning permission. The tendency in Northern Ireland is for architects to opt for full applications. This often proves problematic, in that full applications lack the inherent flexibility of outline applications, so that detailed design difficulties can be hard to remedy and provide a potent source of material for objectors. It is strongly advised that outline applications be used in contentious cases.

Notices of planning applications

4.07 Under Article 7(4) of the GDO, the Department requires applicants to submit with their applications the addresses of those occupying neighbouring land. On receipt of this information, the Department notifies the residents of that land, so that they can make representations on the proposal. By Article 22(1) of the 1991 Order, the Department may not entertain an application for planning permission unless it is accompanied by a certificate under that

Article. In very broad terms, this certificate either indicates the nature of the applicant's interest in the site or deals with the giving of notice of the application to others interested in the site.

As in England, the submission of an Article 22 certificate is a condition precedent to the Department processing the application, though in Northern Ireland the courts have tended to overlook errors in certificates where those errors have not prejudiced anyone's interests.

General publicity

4.08 The English requirement for planning applications to be advertised is replicated by Article 21 of the 1991 Order, which stipulates that the Department must publish notice of each application in at least one newspaper circulating in the locality in which the land in question is situated. There is no requirement in Northern Ireland for notices to be displayed on site.

The Department's procedure for determining applications

4.09 Paragraph 4.22 of Chapter 23 sets out the time within which a planning application must be determined as eight weeks, unless a longer period is agreed. The same time limit applies in Northern Ireland: Article 11, GDO. Note that where an environmental statement is required under the environmental impact assessment procedure the period is extended to sixteen weeks: Regulation 10, Planning (Environmental Impact Assessment) Regulations (Northern Ireland) 1999. By the same token, the period for applying Article 31 is extended in cases where an environmental statement is required from 2 months to sixteen weeks, this period again running from receipt of the environmental statement: Regulation 11 of the 1999 Regulations. In Northern Ireland, there is an obligation on the Department to consult the local district council on the application: Article 15(a), GDO. In addition, the Department must consult the Department of Economic Development where the proposed development is within or adjacent to an area where highly explosive, inflammable or toxic substances are present: Article 15(b), GDO. As a matter of practice, the Department also consults the local environmental health department, its own Roads Service and Water Service, and any other body it feels can have a useful input into the process. This form of consultation is conducted on a non-statutory basis.

4.10 As in England, the Department may grant the application, refuse it, or grant it subject to conditions: Article 25(1), 1991 Order. Again the reasons for a refusal or grant subject to conditions must be stated – Article 13, GDO – and an appeal may be brought to the PAC within 6 months, or such longer period as the Commission may accept: Article 32, 1991 Order. Non-determination within the relevant statutory period entitles the applicant to appeal as if the application had 'been' refused: Article 33, 1991 Order. Importantly, there is no right of appeal in any circumstances for objectors or other third parties, and it has been held by the Northern Ireland High Court that such a right is not necessary to secure compliance with the European Convention on Human Rights. There is, though, considerable political pressure for the introduction of third party appeals, which are a long-established feature of the planning system in the Republic of Ireland.

Article 20 of the 2003 Order inserted Article 25A into the 1991 Order. Article 25A empowers the Department to decline to determine an application if within the period of 2 years ending with the date on which the application is received the Department has refused a similar application under Article 31 or the PAC has dismissed an appeal against the refusal of a similar application, and if there has been no significant change in material considerations in the meantime. There is no appeal against a decision to decline to determine, but that decision is potentially subject to judicial review.

Conservation areas

4.11 Paragraph 4.23 of Chapter 23 deals with development control in conservation areas. Much the same approach obtains in Northern Ireland, with designation taking place under Article 50(1) and (6) of the 1991 Order, and Article 50(5) requires the Department in the exercise of its powers under the 1991 Order to pay special regard to the desirability of preserving or enhancing the character or appearance of the area.

Conditions

4.12 Conditions are applied in Northern Ireland by virtue of Article 25(1) of the 1991 Order, and the tests for validity discussed at paragraphs 4.24–4.25 of Chapter 23 are the same as in England. The same approach is also taken to the impact of a flawed condition on the permission as a whole. Planning Policy Statement 1 sets out at paragraphs 56–58 the Department's approach to the imposition of planning conditions, but the English DoE Circular 1/85 discussed in paragraph 4.29 provides more detailed guidance on the tests for validity and reference may usefully be made to it.

Article 40 agreements

4.13 In broad terms, the Northern Ireland equivalent to the section 106 agreement examined at paragraphs 4.32–4.33 of Chapter 23 is a planning agreement reached under Article 40 of the 1991 Order. Paragraphs 62–66 of Planning Policy Statement 1 set out the Department's approach to Article 40 agreements, and further guidance in the roads context can be found in Planning Policy Statement 3. It should be noted that Article 23 of the 2003 Order substitutes a new Article 40 for the original Article 40 in the 1991 Order, and inserts Article 40A on the modification and discharge of planning agreements and Article 40B on appeals related to planning agreements.

Other controls

4.14 As in England, consents and approvals over and above planning permission may be necessary before the project can proceed. The most obvious example is building control approval, which is generally the responsibility of the local district council.

Duration of permission

4.15 The Northern Ireland equivalents to sections 91–96 of the 1990 English Act referred to at paragraph 4.54 of Chapter 23 are Articles 34 and 35 of the 1991 Order. By Article 34, each planning permission applied for is deemed to have been granted subject to a condition that the development permitted by a permission must be commenced not later than 5 years from the grant, or within such other period as the Department feels appropriate. In an outline application, work must begin not later than 5 years from the grant or within two years from final approval of reserved matters, whichever period is longer: Article 35 of the 1991 Order.

As in England, application for approval of reserved matters in outline cases must be made not later than 3 years from the grant. In change of use cases, the change must take place by the end of the period allowed.

Starting development

4.16 In Northern Ireland, development is taken to begin on the earliest date on which any of the operations set out in Article 36 of the 1991 Order begins. In essence, the relevant date in relation to building and mining operations is when any of the operations involved begins, whereas in change of use cases the relevant date is when the change of use occurs: Article 36(1) of the 1991 Order.

Abandonment?

4.17 The abandonment issue is dealt with in the same way in Northern Ireland as in England.

Completion orders

4.18 The Northern Ireland equivalent of the Completion Notice procedure discussed at paragraph 4.40 of Chapter 23 is the

Completion Order mechanism provided: for by Article 37 of the 1991 Order.

Revoking or modifying planning permission

4.19 Paragraphs 4.41–4.42 of Chapter 23 explain the English provisions regarding revocation and modification of planning permission. The position is much the same in Northern Ireland, with the power to revoke or modify being contained in Article 38 of the 1991 Order. The right to compensation in Northern Ireland arises under section 26 of the Land Development Values (Compensation) Act 1965. Article 39 of the 1991 Order allows for a discontinuance order to be made. The effect of a discontinuance order may be to compel discontinuance of a use of land, to impose conditions on that use, or to require the alteration or removal of buildings or works on the land. Application of a discontinuance order may entitle those affected to compensation under Article 65A of the Planning (Northern Ireland) Order 1972.

5 Listed buildings

5.01 Paragraphs 5.01–5.19 of Chapter 23 set out the English measures designed to protect listed buildings. More or less the same principles apply in Northern Ireland. Listing is done under Article 42 of the 1991 Order. Article 42(2) provides that the Department in compiling lists can take into account the extent to which the exterior of a building contributes to the architectural or historic interest of any group of buildings of which it forms part and also the desirability of preserving features of the building and features associated with the building which lie within its curtilage. The criteria applied by the Department in listing buildings are set out in its Memorandum No. 163 Criteria and standards for listing of July 1991. It should be noted that before listing a building the Department must consult the local district council and the Historic Buildings Council: Article 42(3). Note also the exclusions from the listing process provided for by Article 44(8) – essentially ecclesiastical buildings and certain historic monuments.

5.02 Article 44 provides for criminal liability in cases where damaging work or demolition is carried out, and as amended by Article 14 of the 2003 Order now sets onerous maximum penalties. Article 80 provides for urgent works of preservation, and Article 106 empowers the Department to make loans or grants for preservation purposes. Listed building consent is granted under Article 44, with the mechanics of that procedure being stipulated in Schedule 1 to the 1991 Order and by the Planning (Listed Buildings) Regulations (Northern Ireland) 1992. The local equivalent to the English procedure for obtaining a certificate that a building is not intended to be listed is Article 43 of the 1991 Order. The right of appeal against a refusal of consent lies under Schedule 1 to the 1991 Order, and criminal liability for conducting works affecting the character of a listed building without consent or for breaching conditions imposed on a consent arises under Article 44 of that Order. The 'urgent necessity' defence examined at paragraph 5.13 of Chapter 23 is provided for by Article 44(7) of the 1991 Order. It is possible under Article 48 to apply to the Department for a determination as to whether listed building consent is required for proposed works to a listed building.

5.03 The purchase notice procedure discussed at paragraph 5.14 of Chapter 23 operates in Northern Ireland under Article 94 of the 1991 Order, and the enforcement notice procedure and related right of appeal to the Planning Appeals Commission under, respectively, Articles 77 and 78, as amended by Article 14 of the 2003 Order. The compulsory purchase power is granted under Article 109, and Articles 87–93 of the Order make detailed provision for the implementation of the Article 109 power. Note that the right of appeal against compulsory acquisition lies to the PAC, and in this regard the time allowed for filing an appeal is the same as in England. Subject to the possibility of Judicial Review, the decision of the Commission will be final. For the provisions governing compensation for compulsory acquisition, see Schedule 6 to the Planning (Northern Ireland) Order 1972 and Article 88 of the 1991 Order.

Building preservation notices and temporary listing in urgent cases

5.04 Paragraph 5.18 of Chapter 23 discusses the use of building preservation notices in England. Article 42A of the 1991 Order, as inserted by Article 25 of the 2003 Order, introduced into Northern Ireland temporary listing by service of a building preservation notice. Article 42B of the 1991 Order, as inserted by Article 25 of the 2003 Order, provides for temporary listing in urgent cases by simply affixing the building preservation notice conspicuously to some object on the building in question. Article 42C of the 1991 Order, as inserted by Article 25 of the 2003 Order, provides for lapse of building preservation notices.

Building in conservation areas

5.05 The protection extended to buildings in an area designated under Article 50 of the 1991 Order as a conservation area arises under Article 51 of that Order.

6 Urban Development Corporations; Enterprise Zones; Simplified Planning Zones

6.01 There is no provision in Northern Ireland for Urban Development Corporations.

6.02 Enterprise Zone schemes are made under the Enterprise Zones (Northern Ireland) Order 1981, and the procedure for making schemes is reminiscent of the procedure for making development plans. Once in place, a scheme has rating implications and, by Article 19 of the 1991 Order, has the effect of granting planning permission for development of the type or class specified in the scheme.

6.03 Simplified Planning Zones are made under Article 14 of the 1991 Order, and it should be noted that certain types of land may not be zoned: conservation area land; land in a national park; land in an area of outstanding natural beauty or special scientific interest; land in a national nature reserve; green belt land; other land prescribed for this purpose by regulations. Again, the making of a Simplified Planning Zone resembles that for making a development plan, and once adopted a Zone is valid for 10 years. The adoption of a zone grants planning permission within that zone for the development specified in the scheme, other than development to which the Planning (Environmental Impact Assessment) Regulations (Northern Ireland) 1999, unless the development is Schedule 2 Development and the Department has determined that it is not Environmental Impact Assessment (EIA) Development.

7 Enforcement

7.01 Northern Ireland, enforcement of planning controls is provided for by Articles 68–76 of the 1991 Order, as amended by Articles 3–17 of the 2003 Order.

7.02 The time limits for immunity applicable in Northern Ireland are now essentially the same as in England.

7.03 As indicated above, Article 12 of the 2003 Order inserts certificate of lawful use or development procedures into the 1991 Order.

Enforcement notices

7.04 In essence, the content of paragraphs 7.06–7.08, of Chapter 23 apply equally to Northern Ireland. Notices are issued under Article 68 of the 1991 Order, as substituted by Article 7 of the 2003 Order, and the right of appeal is to the PAC under Article 69, as partly substituted by Article 8 of the 2003 Order. Crucially, any appeal must be received by the Commission before the date specified in the notice as the date upon which it takes effect. The decision of the Commission on an appeal is final, subject to the possibility of Judicial Review where some legal flaw is present in that decision. Failure to comply with a notice within the stated period is an offence contrary to Article 72 of the 1991 Order, as substituted by Article 9 of the 2003 Order.

7.05　The author would endorse the comment in paragraph 7.08 of Chapter 23 that enforcement notices are very 'tricky things indeed'. Generally speaking, the technical nature of the procedure is problematic for the Department, but by the same token this provides a rich source of challenges which the developer can exploit. Effective challenge to enforcement notices supposes an in-depth knowledge of enforcement law, and the author would strongly recommend that an architect confronted with an enforcement notice immediately take specialist legal advice.

7.06　In discussing enforcement notices, it is essential to bear in mind the effect of Article 69(9) of the 1991 Order. This provision states that if the recipient of an enforcement notice wishes to challenge it on any of the grounds upon which an appeal may be brought to the PAC he or she must do so by way of that appeal process, and cannot challenge the notice in any other venue. The danger here is that not pursuing appeal rights may dispense for ever with the possibility of challenge on many, perhaps most, of the conceivable grounds for attack. Experience suggests that once enforcement has reached the prosecution stage it can be extremely difficult to mount a defence which does not fall foul of Article 69(9), and the defendant may be reduced to testing the prosecution's evidence that the breach has continued after service of the notice.

Stop notices

7.07　The nature of the enforcement notice procedure is such that some considerable time may elapse before the notice comes into force, and in the meantime the breach of planning control persists. Article 73 of the 1991 Order, as partly substituted by Article 11 of the 2003 Order, therefore allows the Department to serve a stop notice. This prohibits the carrying out of relevant activities on the land affected immediately the notice comes into effect. A precondition for service of a stop notice is service of an enforcement notice.

7.08　A stop notice may not prohibit anyone from using a structure as his or her permanent residence: Article 73(3A) of the 1991 Order, as substituted by Article 11 of the 2003 Order.

7.09　There is no appeal against a stop notice, but if the recipient can show that the decision to issue it was legally flawed a Judicial Review may be mounted. Breach of the notice once the necessary site notice is displayed or the stop notice is served on the party in

breach is a criminal offence attracting onerous maximum penalties: Articles 73(7), 73(7C) and 73(7D) of the 1991 Order, as substituted by Article 11 of the 2003 Order. It is, though, a defence to prove that the defendant was not served with the notice and did not know and could not reasonably have been expected to know of the existence of the notice: Article 73(8) of the 1991 Order.

7.10　Article 67 of the Planning (Northern Ireland) Order 1972, as partly substituted by Article 11 of the 2003 Order, provides for compensation to be paid in certain circumstances where loss and damage arises from service of a stop notice.

Planning Contravention notices

7.11　Article 67C of the 1991 Order, as inserted by Article 3 of the 2003 Order, provides for the service of a planning contravention notice requiring the recipient to provide information relevant to possible breaches of planning control. Article 67D, as inserted by Article 3 of the 2003 Order, makes non-compliance with a notice and provision of misleading information criminal offences.

Breach of Condition notices

7.12　Article 76A of the 1991 Order, as inserted by Article 4 of the 2003 Order, provides for the service of a breach of condition notice compelling compliance with planning conditions, with breach of the notice being a criminal offence.

Injunctions

7.13　Article 76B of the 1991 Order, as inserted by Article 5 of the 2003 Order, enables the Department to seek injunctions to restrain actual or apprehended breaches of planning control, whether or not it has exercised or is proposing to exercise any of its other enforcement powers. It should be stressed that the grant of an injunction lies within the discretion of the Court, and in the first instance of the Department using this power the High Court declined to grant an injunction given the availability of other suitable enforcement powers: *57 Developments Ltd v DOENI*, unreported, 9th February 2004, Weatherup J.

Enforcement Policy

7.14　Paragraphs 67–70 of Planning Policy Statement 1 provide a summary of existing enforcement powers, but give little insight into the considerations at play when the Department initiates enforcement action. However, Planning Policy Statement 9: The Enforcement of Planning Control sets out the principles which guide enforcement action.

26

Party walls

GRAHAM NORTH

1 The Party Wall etc. Act 1996

1.01 The Party Wall etc. Act 1996 came into force in 1997 and extended the party wall legislation previously applying to London and set out in Part VI of the London Building Acts (Amendment) Act 1939 to the rest of England and Wales.

1.02 The Act sets out a procedure for serving Notices that must be followed if one is carrying out the following works:

Section 1 Building along the line of junction of the boundary which is not currently built on other than to the extent of a boundary wall (not being the wall of a building).

Section 2 Carrying out works to a party structure/party wall/party floor/party fence wall, such as underpinning, demolishing and rebuilding, raising, removing chimney breasts, cutting into install beams, injecting a damp-proof course, columns, etc.

Section 6 (a) Excavating or excavating to construct new foundations within 3 metres of an adjoining building and to a greater depth than the foundations of that adjoining building or structure (Figure 26.1).

(b) If one is excavating or excavating to construct foundations within 6 metres of an adjoining building or structure and to a depth which would intersect a 45° line drawn downwards from next door's footings (Figure 26.2).

1.03 Before the Act was passed, a party wall outside of London was defined as being severed vertically through its centre. One could carry out works to one's own half of the wall but not to the neighbour's side unless consent was given. In some cases, this provided difficulties if the party wall required underpinning or had to be raised for its full thickness.

2 Definitions

2.01 The Party Wall etc. Act now gives two definitions for a party wall:

1 *Section 20(a)* A wall which forms part of a building and stands on lands of different owners to a greater extent than the projection of any artificially formed support on which the wall rests.

2 *Section 20(b)* So much of a wall not being a wall referred to in Section 20(a) above as separate buildings belonging to different owners.

Figures 26.3 and 26.4 illustrate these definitions.

2.02 A **party structure** can be a party wall, party floor, partition or other structure separating buildings or parts of buildings approached solely by separate staircases or separate entrances. A **party fence wall** is a wall which does not form part of a building but stands astride the boundary.

3 Notices

3.01 The Act sets out the steps which must be followed if one is intending to carry out any of the works referred to above. This involves the service of notice, commonly known as a Party Structure Notice, Line of Junction Notice or a Foundation Notice and the notice must state:

- The name and address of the building owner.
- The nature and particulars of the proposed works.
- The date on which the proposed works will begin.

In respect of a Foundation Notice, it must also be accompanied by plans and sections showing:

- The site and depth of any excavation the building owner proposes to make.
- If he proposes to erect a building or structure, its site.

A Line of Junction Notice must describe the intended wall.

3.02 A Party Structure Notice must be served at least 2 months before the works are due to start, and in respect of a Foundation and Line of Junction Notice, 1 month before. Works to which these notices relate cannot start even after these periods if an award is yet to be agreed and published to the owners. Notices must be re-served after 12 months if an award has not been agreed within this time.

A notice is served on any owner who has an interest in their property of greater than 12 months. A building owner must be someone who has an interest in the land and is 'desirous of exercising rights' under the Act. A building owner can also be someone who has contracted to purchase an interest in the land or signed an agreement for a lease as long as this is for greater than 12 months.

It is vitally important that any notice served contains the correct information. Failure to include these details on the notice will render the notice invalid. Thereafter, any matter or award agreed by the surveyors following the service of a defective notice will also be invalid.

3.03 An adjoining owner has 14 days in which to dissent or consent to the works described in the notice otherwise he will be deemed to have dissented by default. Thereafter, a *dispute* arises and surveyors must be appointed to settle the matter by an award.

The parties can agree to the appointment of one surveyor, known as the 'agreed surveyor', a role which the surveyor can fulfil because of his statutory responsibility to act impartially. Alternatively, the adjoining owner can appoint their own surveyor. If there is no agreed surveyor but a surveyor appointed for each of the building and adjoining owners, then their first duty is to select

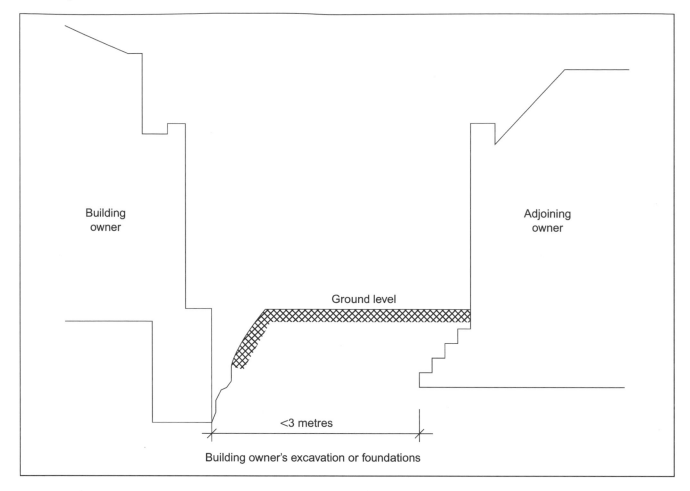

Figure 26.1 For a 3-metre notice.

a third surveyor who will adjudicate on any matter in dispute between the surveyors and in some instances between the owners.

3.04 If an adjoining owner fails to respond to a notice, then a written request must be made to him, either by the building owner or his surveyor if he has due authority, to appoint a surveyor within 10 days. If the adjoining owner ignores this request, then the building owner is in a position to appoint a surveyor for the adjoining owner.

4 The surveyors

4.01 The surveyor can be any person who is not a party to the matter. No specific qualifications are required but it is important to ensure that if such an appointment is accepted, that one has the knowledge and experience required. The appointment is personal to the individual.

4.02 It is the surveyors' duty in their award to determine the right for the works to be carried out, the time and manner of executing this work and any other matter arising out of or incidental to the dispute, including the costs of making the award.

4.03 If the surveyors are unable to agree, then an approach can be made to the third surveyor who will make his decision in the form of an award. Submissions to the third surveyor are normally in writing once the third surveyor has confirmed he is able to accept the appointment.

Information sent to the third surveyor should include copies of each surveyor's letter of appointment from the owner, copies of the notices and evidence that the third surveyor has been selected. An outline of the matters in dispute should be given along with supporting arguments.

4.04 One of the most important aspects of the award will be the Schedule of Condition taken of the adjoining property or land. This is normally in a written form and can be supplemented with photographs.

If the adjoining owner's surveyor fails to respond within 10 days to a written request from the building owner's surveyor or does not act *effectively* then the building owner's surveyor can proceed *ex parte* and this will be as effectual as if he had been the agreed surveyor.

5 The award

5.01 Once the award is agreed, it is published to the owners who have 14 days in which to appeal against the award in the County Court if they feel it has been made improperly or incorrectly.

The Act does not say that once the award is published to the owners that the building owner must wait 14 days before his works can start, although some awards will make that a condition. If an adjoining owner wishes to appeal against an award and in the meantime the building owner's works commence, then the adjoining owner must lodge an appeal and also obtain an injunction to prevent the works from proceeding further. Legal advice must be sought at this stage.

The surveyors decide who pays the fees for agreeing the award and any other costs arising from it. In the majority of cases, it is the building owner who will bear the fees for the surveyors appointed because the works will be for his benefit.

If there are works which are necessary to a party wall on account of defect or want of repair, then the costs of such works will be defrayed by the building owner and the adjoining owner with regard to the use which each of the owners make of the structure or wall concerned and the cause of the defect.

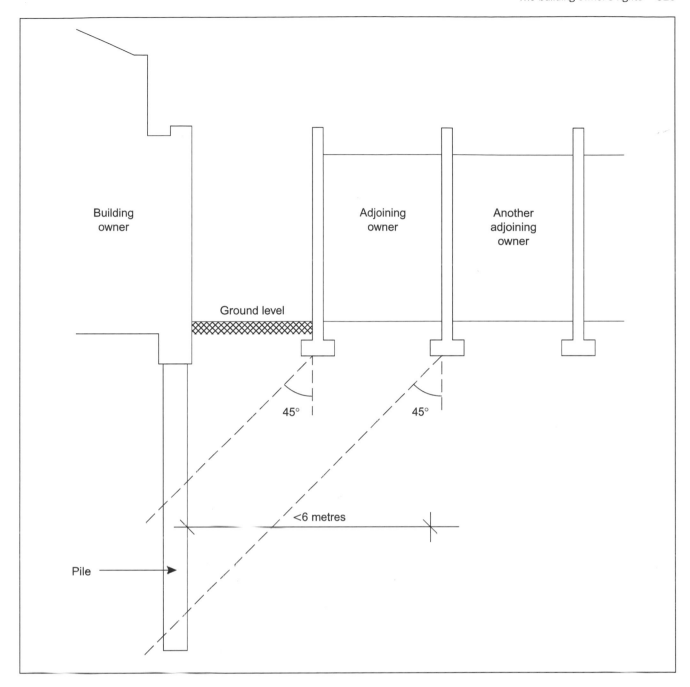

Figure 26.2 For a 6-metre notice.

6 The building owner's rights

6.01 Section 8 grants a building owner, his servants, agents and workmen, the right to enter the land of an adjoining owner for the purpose of executing any works under this Act. This could include the erection of scaffolding over the adjoining owner's land and buildings although details of the access will be agreed by the surveyors beforehand.

If an adjoining owner fails to give such access to the building owner, or to the surveyors if they need to carry out an inspection, to take a Schedule of Condition for example, then that owner would be guilty of an offence and liable on summary conviction to a fine imposed by the courts.

6.02 The Act does not permit a building owner to install *special foundations* on an adjoining owner's land unless the adjoining owner's consent is obtained. Special foundations are defined as foundations *in which an assemblage of beams or rods is employed for the purpose of distributing any load*.

If a building owner proposes to reduce the height of a party wall or party fence wall to no less than 2 metres in height, an adjoining owner can serve a counter-notice and insist that the wall is left at a greater height but the adjoining owner must bear the costs of the work necessary to achieve this. A building owner upon whom a counter-notice has been served must comply with the requirements of the counter-notice unless the works required would be injurious to him, cause him unnecessary inconvenience or delay in the execution of the works pursuant to the notice which he had served.

The Act also permits a building owner to chase into an adjoining owner's wall to install a flashing or other weatherproofing of a wall erected against the adjoining owner's wall (Section 2(2)(j)).

6.03 In the event of damage being caused to the adjoining owner's land or property, an adjoining owner can either insist that the building owner makes good that damage or he can request payment in lieu. The amount of any money to be paid to the adjoining owner in this situation is to be determined by the surveyors.

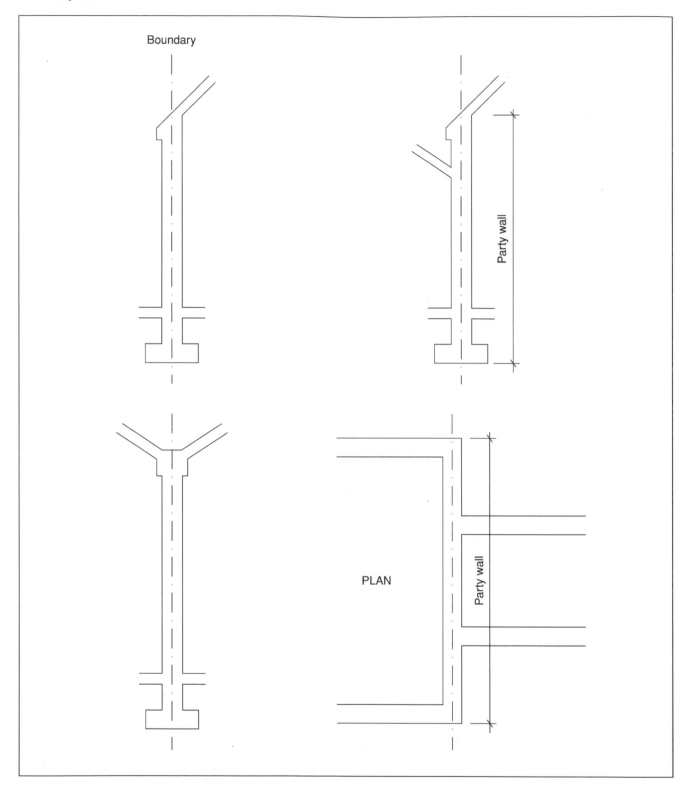

Figure 26.3 Party wall as defined by Section 20(a).

As far as the award is concerned, it is the building owner who is responsible for making good or paying for the damage, not the contractor. It is for the surveyors to determine what damage has been caused and the extent of remedial work necessary.

A building owner is not permitted to exercise any rights conferred upon him *in such a manner or at such time as to cause unnecessary inconvenience* to any adjoining owner or occupier (Section 7(1)). It is incumbent upon a building owner to ensure that he takes all reasonable measures to minimize any inconvenience to an adjoining owner.

6.04 It is vitally important that the procedures are followed. Failure to do so can lead to legal action from adjoining owner and subsequent delays to the works. The case of *Louis v Sadiq* (1997) is an example where works to a party wall started without the procedures being followed (this case was under the 1939 Act) and the court took a dim view of the building owner's failure to observe the legislation.

6.05 Where an adjoining owner may be vulnerable if the building owner does not honour his obligations, for example, if a party wall is to be demolished and rebuilt but the building owner disappears prior to reconstruction, the adjoining owner can request security for expenses. The request for such security must be in writing and made before the works commence. The amount of security will vary depending upon the extent of the works which may be necessary

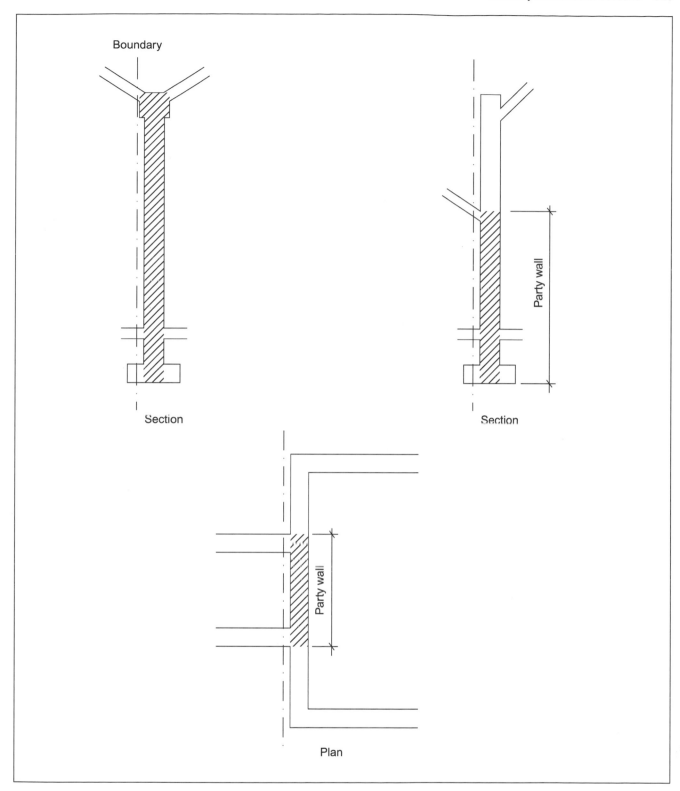

Figure 26.4 Party wall as defined by section 20(b)

if the adjoining owner has to complete them. However, the security requested should not be so much that to provide the money a building owner would be prohibited from commencing the works.

Security for expenses is usually provided as a financial deposit in an account from which the money can only be released upon the signatures of two of the three surveyors appointed. If there is no requirement to use the security then the money is released to the building owner with any interest which may have accrued.

6.06 The standard forms for notices, awards, letters of appointment, etc. are in various publications including the *RICS Guidance*

Note, the *RIBA Guidance Note* and the *Party Wall Act Explained*, published by the Pyramus and Thisbe Club.

7 Boundary structures in Scotland *

7.01 'Party wall' is not a term of art in Scotland. The Party Wall legislation does not extend to Scotland. North of the border, the

---

* This section was written by Angus Stewart Q.C.

common law, property titles and local by-laws regulate mutual boundary wall questions and other questions about 'joint ownership', 'common ownership' and 'common interest'. The common law has developed an elaborate doctrine of 'common interest', notably in relation to flats in different ownership within the same tenement building. Even where there is no co-ownership, proprietors may have a right based on common interest to object to operations on a mutual boundary structure, whether a wall, partition or floor/ceiling, or to require repairs to be carried out. The common interest extends to parts of the tenement building remote from the particular flat. Where it is proposed to carry out works on or adjacent to boundary structures or adjoining property and, in the case of buildings in multiple ownership, where it is proposed to carry out operations which may affect the stability of the building or interfere with services, legal advice should be taken. Where there is a question about maintenance or repairs to the common parts of a building or a development of several buildings, legal advice should be taken.

27

European Union law affecting architects

HIS HONOUR JUDGE ANDREW GEDDES AND CLARE POTTER*

1 The European Union and its institutions

Introduction

1.01 The opening up of the Single European Market has had and continues to have a profound effect on every sector of the UK construction industry. Building material producers have easier access to some 380 million people living in the European Union (EU) (a market which is a third larger than the USA, and double the Japanese). Building products and practices are being standardized, building contractors have greater opportunities to tender for public sector projects throughout the EU and architects, surveyors and other professionals are able to practise with greater ease in the EU. In addition, the growing tendency of the EU to insist on higher standards of protection for the consumer and for the environment is placing greater burdens on those working in the building industry who are affected by these matters.

1.02 The Single European Market provides an opportunity for the UK construction industry but it also poses a threat. UK suppliers, contractors and professionals are being exposed to increased competition in the UK from their competitors in the rest of the EU and it is anticipated that this threat will be at its most formidable in respect of the largest and most profitable contracts where economies of scale justify the effort involved in competing away from the home market.

1.03 If the UK construction industry is to compete successfully in this new environment it must have an understanding of those EU measures which affect it and ensure that its interests are taken into account when legislation is being drafted and standards are being agreed. A basic knowledge of the EU institutions and how they work is essential if this is to be achieved.

2 The founding treaties

2.01 The fifteen (and from 1 May 2004 twenty five) European countries which form the EU act and cooperate together within a complex legal framework. This comprises the European Communities (ECs), legal and institutional arrangements under which the EU member states accept the sovereignty of the Community institutions, notably in all aspects of economic activity including agriculture and transport, environmental issues and increasingly also in social matters, and arrangements for inter-governmental cooperation and development of policies in wider spheres, including foreign policy, defence and criminal justice. The ECs are founded on three treaties. The European Coal and Steel Community (ECSC) was set up by the treaty of Paris in 1951 and has now expired.

The two other ECs were established by the Treaties of Rome signed on 25 March 1952. The first of these established the European Atomic Energy Community (Euratom), and the second, and by far the most important, is the founding treaty of the EC, formerly the European Economic Community.

2.02 The initial objectives of the EC were the establishment of a customs union with free movement of goods between member states, the dismantling of quotas and barriers to trade of all kinds and the free movement of people, services and capital. The original EC Treaty also provided for the adoption of common policies on agriculture, transport and competition. It looked forward to the harmonization of laws and technical standards to facilitate its fundamental objectives and to the creation of a social fund and an Investment Bank.

The Single European Act (SEA) and the amending Treaties

2.03 By 1982 it was recognized that the progress towards the completion of a European Market without physical technical or fiscal barriers had been unacceptably slow and the European Council in that year pledged itself to the completion of this internal market as a high priority. In 1985 the Commission published its White Paper entitled 'Completing the Internal Market' in which it set out proposals for some 300 legislative measures which it considered would have to be adopted in order to achieve this aim. At the same time the member states agreed to amend parts of the Treaty of Rome so as to extend their scope and to facilitate the implementation of the legislative programme. The result was the Single European Act which came into force on 1 July 1987. The principal objective of the SEA was the removal by 31 December 1992 of all the remaining barriers within the EC to the free movement of goods, services, persons and capital. It introduced for the first time a system of qualified majority voting in the Council so that proposed legislation cannot so easily be blocked. The Act also provides for further technological development, the strengthening of economic and social ties and the improvement of the environment and working conditions throughout the Community.

The EC Treaty was further amended on 1 November 1993 when the Treaty on European Union (the Maastricht Treaty) was ratified. That Treaty marked a further step in the process of European integration and for the first time established that the new Community is both an economic and political entity in which its citizens are the possessors of enforceable Community rights. The Maastricht Treaty also laid the foundation for European Monetary Union and the adoption of a single European currency by the majority of the EU member states (currently excluding the UK). The Treaty of Amsterdam, which entered into force in May 1999, made further amendments to the EC Treaty and the Treaty on EU, notably in relation to external policy, the fundamental rights of Community citizens and

* Judge Geddes contributed this chapter in previous editions. It has been updated for this edition by Clare Potter.

cooperation in the areas of justice and home affairs. It also rationalized the texts of the Treaty of Rome and the Maastricht Treaty with the result that virtually every provision has been renumbered. Finally, the Treaty of Nice, which entered into force on 1 February 2003, made further amendments to the EC Treaty and the Treaty on EU, notably extending the use of qualified majority voting and making changes to the institutions to accommodate enlargement.

A new European constitution is currently in course of preparation. This will adapt the legal and institutional framework which has evolved over the course of more than 50 years to the requirements of the enlarged and wider reaching EU, creating stronger, partially elected, central institutions as well as increasing the role of the elected Parliament.

The member states

2.04 The founding member states were Belgium, France, (West) Germany, Italy, Luxembourg and the Netherlands. Denmark, Ireland and the UK became members in 1973. Greece entered the Community in 1981 and Portugal and Spain in 1986. Sweden, Finland and Austria joined in January 1995. Ten new member states are due to join the EU on 1 May 2004. They are: Cyprus, the Czech Republic, Estonia, Hungary, Latvia, Lithuania, Malta, Poland, the Slovak Republic and Slovenia. Bulgaria and Romania are scheduled to join in 2007.

The Community institutions and legislation

2.05 Each of the founding Treaties provided that the tasks entrusted to the ECSC, EC and Euratom should be carried out by four institutions: the Council, the Commission, the European Parliament and the Court of Justice. The Parliament and the Court of Justice were from the start common to all three communities and from 1967 this was also true of the Council and the Commission. The Treaty on EC confirmed the roles of the institutions in all areas of EU activity. The Council is assisted by a Committee of Permanent Representatives (COREPER) made up of representatives of the various member states and for EC and Euratom matters the Council and the Commission are assisted by an Economic and Social Committee acting in an advisory capacity.

The Commission

2.06 The Commission, whose headquarters is in Brussels, is currently composed of at least one representative from each member state and at November 2003 consisted of 20 members. Members of the Commission are appointed for 5 years. Following enlargement they will be appointed by the Commission President (who is appointed by the member states) in conjunction with the member states and the Parliament.

The Commission is supported by a staff of some 24,000 officials, a quarter of whom are involved in translation made necessary by the use of eleven official languages (There will be 20 languages from 1 May 2004.). The staff are mainly divided between a number of directorates-general, each with a separate share of responsibility. Commission decisions, however, are made on a corporate basis. The Commission is the official guardian of the Treaties and ensures that the EC rules and principles they contain are respected. It is responsible for proposing to the Council measures likely to advance the development of EC policies. Once a measure has been adopted it is the Commission's task to ensure that it is implemented throughout the Community. It has wide investigative powers which it may initiate itself or which it may set into motion as a result of a complaint by a third party. It can impose fines on individuals or companies found to be in breach of EC Rules and these frequently run into millions of pounds. An appeal against a Commission decision lies to the European Court of Justice. In addition the Commission can take a member state before the Court if they fail to respect their obligations.

The members of the Commission act only in the interest of the EC. During their term of office they must remain independent of the governments of the member states and of the Council. They are subject to the supervision of the European Parliament which is the only body that can force them to resign collectively.

The Council

2.07 The Council is made up of representatives of the governments of the member states. Each government normally sends one of its ministers. Its membership thus varies with the subjects proposed for discussion. The Foreign Minister is regarded as his country's

main representative in the Council but the other ministers meet frequently for more specialized Council meetings. The Presidency of the Council is held for a term of six months by each member in turn. The Council is, with the Parliament, the EC's principal legislative body and makes all the main policy decisions.

For some issues (such as taxation, and certain social and environmental matters) the Council must act unanimously if it wishes to alter the text of a proposal from the Commission. But the Council may now act in a wide range of matters by qualified or absolute majority. Under the qualified majority system the member states are allocated a block of votes according to their size, economic significance and the arrangements negotiated on their accession to the Treaties. The current rules require a minimum of 62 out of the total of 87 votes for a qualified majority. Following enlargement both an absolute minimum number of votes and the approval of the specified proportion of member states (a simple majority or two-thirds depending on the type of measure) will be needed. The groundwork for the Council's response to Commission proposals is carried out by officials of the member states, coordinated by COREPER.

EC legislation

2.08 Measures adopted by Council and by the Commission where it has decision-making powers have the force of law, which take precedence over the national laws of the member states. In some cases these measures have direct effect throughout the EC. In others the member states must first implement them by way of national legislation.

These measures may be:

1 Regulations, in which case they apply directly.
2 Directives which lay down compulsory objectives to be achieved by a certain date but leave to member states how they are to be implemented into national law. In certain defined circumstances when a member state has failed to implement a directive in due time a citizen can rely directly on the directive as against the state.
3 Decisions, which are binding only on the member states, companies or individuals to whom they are addressed.

The Council also from time to time adopts resolutions which are declarations of intent and do not have legal force.

Where a national measure implements a directive or even where that measure merely covers the same legislative field as a directive (e.g. because the national measure preceded the coming into force of the directive) the national measure must be construed in so far as possible to give effect to the purpose of the underlying directive as established in the light of the directive's preamble and any relevant decision of the European Court of Justice. In such cases therefore it is almost always necessary to look at both the directive and the relevant national measure before the true legal position can be established.

The European Court of Justice

2.09 The Court, which sits in Luxembourg, consists of fifteen judges assisted by eight advocates-general. Following enlargement there will be twenty five judges, one per member state. They are appointed for a period of six years by mutual consent of the member states and are entirely independent. The Court is entrusted with the interpretation of the Treaties and can quash any measures adopted by the Council or the Commission or declare incompatible acts of national governments which are incompatible with them. An application for this purpose may be made by an EC institution government or individual. The Court also gives judgment when requested to do so by a national court on any question of EC law.

Judgments of the Court in the field of EC law are binding on all national courts.

As from September 1989, a Court of First Instance has sat to hear cases principally relating to competition matters. An appeal on a point of law only lies from that court to the court.

The European Parliament

2.10 The Parliament which meets in plenary session in Strasbourg currently consists of 624 members elected from the member states broadly in proportion to their size. Elections take place every five years. The Parliament has an important part to play in three areas:

1 *It adopts and controls the EC budget.*
2 *It shares responsibility with the Council for the adoption of EC legislation.*
3 *It supervises activities of the EC institutions.* It has the power to question and criticize the Commission's proposals and activities in debate. It can exert influence through its budgetary power and has the power to dismiss the Commission by a two-thirds majority.

2.11 Following the Treaty of Nice, the maximum possible number of members of the Parliament will be 732, with 91 fewer seats for the current member states from 1 January 2004 to allow for members to be elected in the new member states. The members of Parliament sit in Europe-wide political groupings rather than national blocks and the Council is empowered to lay down rules and procedures to provide development of political parties at a European level.

3 Public procurement

Introduction

3.01 The opening up of procurement by government bodies and by utilities to EC-wide competition has been recognized by the member states as a key component in the creation of the internal European market. This huge sector of the economy has been estimated by the Commission to represent in excess of £720 billion. Although there are a number of directly effective Treaty provisions which must be taken into account in the award of public authority contracts these are insufficient to ensure that such contracts are opened up to Community-wide tendering. The EC has consequently adopted a number of specific measures whose purpose is to supplement the Treaty provisions by applying detailed rules to the award of contracts over a certain value by public bodies and utilities.

Equivalent objectives have been pursued at an international level under the auspices of the World Trade Organisation through the 1994 Agreement on Government Procurement (the 'GPA'). There are currently 12 signatories to the GPA including the USA and the EC. EC rules have been amended to take full account of these international obligations and to extend appropriate rights to contractors from GPA signatory countries.

The principal specific measures currently in force in the EC (as at December 2003) are:

- the Public Works Directive 93/37/EC, incorporated into UK law by the Public Works Contracts Regulations (as amended) SI 1991/2680, which applies to the award of construction and civil engineering contracts by public bodies;
- the Public Supplies Directive 93/36/EC, incorporated into UK law by the Public Supply Contracts Regulations (as amended) SI 1995/201, which applies to the procurement of goods by public bodies;
- the Public Services Directive 92/50/EC, implemented in the UK by the Public Services Contracts Regulations SI 1993/3228, which applies to the award of contracts for services by public bodies;
- the Utilities Directive 93/38/EC, which has been implemented in the UK by the Utilities Contracts Regulations SI 1995/2911, which covers contracts for works, supplies and services awarded by certain entities operating in the water, energy, transport and telecommunications sectors regardless of whether those entities are governed by public or private law;
- the Compliance Directive 89/665/EEC: this was originally introduced to address the low level of compliance by member states with the Public Works and Public Supplies Directives and the inadequacy or absence of remedies available to potential contractors or suppliers for breach of the Directives. The Compliance Directive (as amended) sets out the remedies which must be made available to those injured by a breach of the Works, Supplies or Services Directives.
- the Remedies Directive 92/13/EEC: this introduced equivalent remedies for breach of the Utilities Directive. Both the

Compliance Directive and the Remedies Directive have been implemented in the UK through amendment of the relevant UK implementing regulations referred to above.

On 2 February 2004 the Council adopted two new Directives of the European Parliament and of the Council to replace in their entirety the various measures outlined above. The first of these (a Directive on the coordination of procedures for the award of public works contracts, public supply contracts and public service contracts (the 'Public Sector Directive')) is intended to simplify and modernize, increase flexibility and in some respects standardize the procedural rules applicable to all kinds of public contracts. It also contains measures to ensure compliance and provide remedies to injured contractors. The second Directive (coordinating the procurement procedures of entities operating in the water, energy, transport and postal services sectors (the 'Excluded Sectors Directive')) updates the rules applying to award of works, supplies and service contracts by public and private entities operating in the defined sectors (the telecommunications sector has now been recognized as fully competitive). Many of the key provisions remain substantially unchanged in the new Directives. The member states have 21 months from publication to give effect to the new Directives in national law. This means that the new UK legislation to replace the various Regulations described above will need to be adopted before the end of 2005. In the following sections the current UK law (as at February 2004) is described and any significant differences in the new legislation are outlined.

The Works Directive and the Public Works Contracts Regulations 1991

3.02 The Directive and therefore the Regulations have three principal aims in respect of the contracts to which they apply:

1   EC-wide advertising of contracts above a certain value threshold so that contractors in every member state have an equal opportunity of expressing their interest in tendering and/or in tendering for them.
2   The prohibition of technical specifications in the contract documents which favour particular contractors.
3   The application of objective criteria in procedures leading to the award, and in the award itself.

In addition, the Regulations make available through the Courts certain remedies (including damages) to contractors who suffer or risk suffering loss as a result of a breach of the Regulations or any related Community obligation.

These aims are retained under the new Public Sector Directive. However, as part of the objective of modernizing the procurement rules there is an added objective of promoting and facilitating electronic purchasing systems and the use of electronic communications in procurement.

Contracts to which the Regulations apply

3.03 The Regulations apply whenever a 'contracting authority' whether by itself or through an agent seeks offers in relation to a proposed 'public works contract' other than a public works contract expressly excluded from the operation of the Regulations, regardless of whether a contract is awarded or not. Special rules apply under the Regulations where the public works contract is also a 'public works concession contract', which is defined as 'a public works contract under which the consideration given by the contracting authority consists of or includes the grant of a right to exploit the work or works to be carried out under the contract'.

Under the Public Sector Directive the procedural rules will apply to all public contracts other than those expressly excluded. Special rules for subsidized public housing schemes and public works concessions have been retained.

Meaning of 'contracting authority'

3.04 Contracting authorities under the Regulations include the state and state-controlled bodies, local authorities and certain bodies governed by public law. A list of 'contracting authorities' is set out in Regulation 3(1). The list is not definitive but is 'as exhaustive as possible'.

The Public Sector Directive permits reliance on 'central purchasing bodies', that is contracting authorities which acquire goods or services, or award contracts or framework agreements on behalf of contracting authorities. This recognizes a practice widely used in the EC of centralized purchasing via a specialized agency.

Meaning of 'public works contract'

3.05 A 'public works contract' is a contract in writing for money or monies worth for the construction or the design and construction of a 'work' or 'works' by a contracting authority, or a contract under which the contracting authority engages a person to carry out for the contracting authority a 'work' corresponding to specified requirements.

The 'works' referred to are any of the activities listed in a schedule to the Regulations. The schedule sets out a variety of building and civil engineering activities (e.g. 'construction of flats, office blocks, hospitals and other buildings both residential and non-residential') broken down into tasks (e.g. 'erection of and dismantling of scaffolding') carried out in the course of those activities. A 'work' is a larger concept and is defined as the outcome of any works which is sufficient of itself to fulfil an economic and technical function. Thus a 'work' would include the construction of an airport; it would also include the construction of its runways or of a terminal as both these are capable of fulfilling an economic and technical function but it would not include the associated drainage or electrical work as these are merely ancillary and cannot of themselves fulfil an economic and technical function. In some cases a contract may be for both works and services and/or for supplies of goods. There is no specific provision in the Regulations or the underlying Directive dealing with this situation. In *Gestion Hotelera v Communidad Autonoma de Canarias* (Case 331/92, 1994 ECR) the Court of Justice held that where works are incidental to the main object of the award (in this case, refurbishment of a hotel and casino as an adjunct to a casino concession) the award should not be characterized as a public works contract. In *R v Rhondda Cynon Taff Borough Council ex parte Kathro* (judgment of High Court Queen's Bench Division 6 July 2001) the judge indicated that the use of both a relative value and a principal purpose test might be legitimate. This case concerned a project being taken forward under the private finance initiative (PFI). PFI projects can raise particularly difficult classification issues since they frequently involve both major infrastructure works and provisions of services over a long period. It follows that, for example, a property management contract which incidentally includes a requirement from time to time to carry out some works is a services and not a works contract. A contract specifically for building maintenance or repair is on the other hand a works contract and the higher threshold will apply (see below).

These provisions of the Works Regulations defining what is meant by a public works contract are complemented by similar provisions in the Supply Regulations and the Services Regulations ensuring that each set of Regulations is mutually exclusive as regards the contracts to which they apply. In every case therefore it will be important to establish at the outset whether a public contract is a 'works', 'supply' or 'services' contract.

Under the new Public Sector Directive the distinction between works, supply and service contracts is maintained although all three are defined as sub-categories of public contracts.

The public works contracts excluded from the operation of the Regulations

Contracts related to certain utilities

3.06 The Works Regulations do not apply to the seeking of offers in relation to a proposed public works contract by a contracting authority for the purpose of carrying out certain activities in the water, transport, energy or telecommunications sectors. Such contracts will fall to be dealt with, if at all, under the Utilities Contracts Regulations. The activities concerned broadly comprise the operation or provision of public networks or facilities in the sectors referred to and the supply to such networks, together with certain mining activities in relation to gas, oil, coal, and other solid fuels.

Under the new rules, contracting authorities awarding contracts in the exercise of activities in the specified excluded sectors will be covered by the Excluded Sectors Directive. The excluded sectors are initially the operation of networks and associated activities relating to provision of water, energy, inland transport and reserved postal services. Public contracts awarded by bodies providing telecommunications networks or services are now excluded from the rules altogether when they are for the principal purpose of a telecommunications activity.

Secret contracts, contracts involving state security and contracts carried out pursuant to international agreement

3.07 In addition the Regulations do not apply to a public works contract which is classified by the Government as secret or where the carrying out of the work or works under it must be accompanied by special security measures approved by law or when the protection of the basic interests of the security of the UK require it. Certain contracts carried out pursuant to international agreements are also exempt.

Contracts below certain value thresholds

3.08 Most importantly of all, the Regulations do not apply to the seeking of offers in relation to a proposed public works contract where the estimated value of the contract (net of VAT) at the relevant time does not exceed specified thresholds:

- for public works contracts the euro equivalent of 5 000 000 special drawing rights (SDRs – a monetary unit used in international trade) for which the current sterling value (2004–2006) is £3 834 411
- for public works concessions €5 000 000 for which the sterling value (2004–2006) is £3 236 542.

Under the Public Sector Directive the relevant threshold (for contracts and concessions) is initially set at €6 242 000. This will be reviewed every two years to ensure that it continues to reflect the euro equivalent of the GPA threshold, which is expressed in SDRs. For as long as the UK remains outside the European monetary system a sterling equivalent of the euro threshold will also be fixed every two years.

The 'relevant time' is the date on which the contract notice would be sent to the *Official Journal* if the requirement to send such a notice applied to the contract in accordance with the Regulations (i.e. generally when the contracting authority forms the intention to seek offers in relation to the contract).

The 'estimated value' is the sum which the contracting authority expects to pay under the contract. However, where the public works contract is one of a number of contracts entered into or to be entered into for the carrying out of a 'work' the 'estimated value' is normally the aggregate of the sums which the contracting authority has paid or expects to pay under all the contracts for the carrying out of the work. Exceptionally, where one or more of the contracts is for less than €1 million (£647 308) such contracts need not be aggregated so long as in total they represent less than 20% of the total cost of the work. Thus for example where a contracting authority seeks offers in relation to site clearance at an estimated cost of €1 million for the purpose of constructing a hospital at an estimated cost of €20 million, the Regulations will apply both to the site clearance contract and the construction contract. If the cost of the site clearance was only €900 000 (and there were no other contracts which together with that one aggregated to €4 million or more) the contracting authority would not be required to comply with the Regulations in respect of that contract.

Where a contracting authority intends to provide any goods to the person awarded a public works contract for the purpose of carrying out that contract, the value of these must be taken into account when calculating the estimated value of the contract.

In relation to public works concession contracts the 'estimated value' is the payment which the contracting authority would expect to make for the carrying out of the work (taking into account any goods supplied by them) if it did not propose to grant a concession.

A contracting authority must not enter into separate contracts with the intention of avoiding the application of the Regulations to those contracts.

Rules governing technical specifications

3.09 Detailed rules as to the technical specifications which are permitted in public works contracts are set out in the Regulations. The purpose behind these rules is to avoid any discrimination against contractors who might be at a disadvantage if technical specifications were required which could only be met, or met more easily by a national contractor.

Technical specifications (which are defined in the Regulations) whether relating to the works themselves or to the goods to be used in them must be specified in the contract documents and subject to certain exceptions must always be defined by reference to any 'European specifications' which are relevant. 'European specification' means a common technical specification (i.e. one agreed by the member states), a British Standard implementing a European standard or European technical approval. The Commission have issued policy guidelines on what is meant by this obligation to refer to European standards.

Exceptionally technical specifications may be used which are defined other than by reference to a European standard.

The Public Sector Directive makes important changes to the rules relating to technical specifications but retains the aim of giving equal access to all tenderers and avoiding unjustified obstacles to open competition. Under the Directive greater emphasis will be placed on the use of performance or functional requirements (including, where justified, environmental characteristics) rather than European standards. Where reference to specific European, international or national standards is included a tender cannot be rejected on the grounds that it does not comply with that standard if the tenderer proves that its solution satisfies in an equivalent manner the technical requirements defined by the specification in question. Similarly tenderers will be able to rely on appropriate national or European standards to show that they satisfy performance or functional requirements.

Rules governing the procedures leading to the award of a public works contract

3.10 The principal requirement of the Regulations is that in seeking offers in relation to a public works contract from contractors or potential contractors who are nationals of and established in a member state, a contracting authority must use one of the following procedures:

- **The open procedure** whereby any person who is interested may submit a tender;
- **The restricted procedure** whereby only those persons selected by the contracting authority may submit tenders; and
- **The negotiated procedure** whereby the contracting authority negotiates the terms of the contract with one or more persons selected by it.

The Regulations lay down provisions for making the choice of procedure. The negotiated procedure may only be used in certain limited circumstances. Special rules apply in relation to a public housing scheme works contract and public works concessions.

The Public Sector Directive introduces a new competitive dialogue procedure which combines elements of the restricted and negotiated procedures using a dialogue with selected tenderers to define a specification which the tenderers will tender against. This procedure will be able to be used in a slightly wider range of situations than the negotiated procedure.

Advertising the intention to seek offers by means of a prior information notice

3.11 The contracting authority must publicize its intention to seek offers in relation to a public works contract in the *Official Journal* as soon as the decision approving the planning of works is taken (the 'prior information notice'). It must do this again at the start of the procedure leading to the award once this has been selected (the 'contract notice'), although the latter requirement is dispensed with in certain circumstances when the negotiated procedure is used. The form of the advertisement and the information which it must contain in relation to the proposed contract is specified in a schedule to the Regulations. If the notice is also to be published in the UK press it must be limited to the information published in the *Official Journal*.

Under the new Public Sector Directive contracting authorities will have the option of publishing prior information notices themselves on an electronic 'buyer profile' accessible via the internet.

Selection of contract award procedure

3.12 Normally a contracting authority must either use the open procedure or the restricted procedure, at its choice. The negotiated procedure may only be used in the exceptional circumstances specified in the Regulations. These are as follows:

1 Where the use of the open or restricted procedure was discontinued because of 'irregular' tenders or following an evaluation of offers made in accordance with the regulations relating to open or restricted procedures. However, the negotiated procedure may only then be used if the proposed terms of the contract are substantially unaltered from the proposed terms of the contract in relation to which offers were sought using the open or restricted procedure.

   A tender will be 'irregular' if for example the contractor fails to meet the requirements of, or the tender offers variation on, the requirements specified in the contract documents which are not permitted under the terms of the invitation to tender or the work, works, materials or goods do not meet the technical specifications of the contracting authority.

   The Regulations (and the directive) do not make clear in what circumstances a contracting authority would be entitled to discontinue the open or restricted procedure in the circumstances defined above. The correct approach is probably that they would be entitled to do so where after excluding irregular tenders and other tenders on grounds permitted by the Regulations (see below) there remained *insufficient* valid tenders for there to be any real competition. It will be noted at (4) below that absence of tenders is a separate ground for justifying use of the negotiated procedure.

2 When the work or works are to be carried out under the contract purely for the purpose of research experiment or development, but this exception will not apply if the works are to be carried out to establish their commercial viability or to recover their research and development costs.

   Once the experiment or trial has proved successful, this exception will cease to apply and if the contracting authority then decides to go ahead with further works it must comply with the Regulations if the contract is one which falls within their provisions.

3 Exceptionally, when the nature of the work or works to be carried out under the contract is such, or the risks attaching thereto are such, as not to permit overall pricing.

4 In the absence of tenders or of appropriate tenders in response to an invitation to tender by the contracting authority using the open or restricted procedure. However, again this exception may not be relied upon unless the proposed terms of the contract are substantially unaltered from the proposed terms of the contract in relation to which offers were sought using the open or restricted procedure.

5 When for technical or artistic reasons, or for reasons connected with the protection of exclusive rights, the work or works to be carried out under the contract may only be carried out by a particular person.

It might be argued by a disappointed contractor who had been excluded for technical reasons that given enough time he could have acquired the expertise and/or machinery to qualify technically but the exception can probably be relied upon where for technical reasons only one contractor can carry out the works within the time required by the contracting authority for their completion so long as this is reasonable. However, the European Court in Case 57/94, *Commission v Italian Republic*, stressed that the derogation must be interpreted strictly and that a contracting authority relying on technical reasons must show that the technical reasons make it absolutely essential that the contract is awarded to a particular person.

6 When (but only if it is strictly necessary) for reasons of extreme urgency brought about by events unforeseeable by and not attributable to the contracting authority, the time limits specified in the Regulations relating to the various contract award procedures cannot be met.

7 When a contracting authority wants a person who has entered into a public works contract with the contracting authority to carry out additional works which through unforeseen circumstances were not included in the project initially considered or in the original public works contract and,

   (a) such works cannot for technical or economic reasons be carried out separately from the works carried out under the original public works contract without great inconvenience to the contracting authority, or

   (b) such works can be carried out separately from the works carried out under the original public works contract but are strictly necessary to the later stages of the contract. However, this exception may not be relied upon where the aggregate value of the consideration to be given under contracts for the additional works exceeds 50% of the value of the consideration payable under the original contract.

   The value of the consideration must be taken to include the estimated value of any goods which the contracting authority provided to the person awarded the contract for the purposes of carrying out the contract.

8 When a contracting authority wishes a person who has entered into a public works contract with that contracting authority to carry out new works which are a repetition of works carried out under the original contract and which are in accordance with the project for the purpose of which the first contract was entered into. However, that exception may only be relied upon if the contract notice relating to the original contract stated that a public works contract for new works which would be a repetition of the works carried out under the original contract may be awarded using the negotiated procedure and unless the procedure for the award of the new contract is commenced within three years of the original contract being entered into.

In accordance with principles of Community law each of the above exceptions must be interpreted strictly.

The new competitive dialogue procedure introduced by the Public Sector Directive will be available where a contracting authority considers that use of the open or restricted procedures will not allow the award of the contract because it is not objectively able to define the technical specifications capable of satisfying its needs or objectives with sufficient precision to conduct an open or restricted procedure and/or because it is not able to specify the legal and/or financial make-up of a project. The new procedure is intended for use particularly for complex projects (for example where Public/Private Partnerships are involved) and it is not possible at the outset to determine how the project should be structured or what solution will best meet the contracting authority's objective. It is likely that the Commission will expect contracting authorities to look to the competitive dialogue procedure to provide flexibility in circumstances in which they might previously have sought to use the negotiated procedure.

The open procedure

3.13 As has already been noted the contracting authority must publicize its intention to seek offers in relation to the public works contract by sending to the *Official Journal* a notice (the 'contract notice') inviting tenders and containing specified information in relation to the contract.

Standard forms of notice have been produced by the Commission. These are incorporated by reference in the various UK implementing Regulations. Use of the standard forms is now mandatory. There are strict minimum time limits laid down for the receipt of tenders. These have been relaxed slightly to reflect the GPA obligation to allow a period sufficiently long for responsive tendering, although minimum periods still apply.

The contracting authority may only exclude a tender from the evaluation of offers if the contractor may be treated as ineligible on grounds specified in the Regulations or if a contractor fails to satisfy minimum standards of economic and financial standing and technical capacity required of contractors by the contracting authority when assessed according to the requirements of the Regulations.

Under the new Public Sector Directive it will be compulsory to exclude tenderers convicted of fraud, money laundering and certain related offences.

The restricted procedure

Selecting those invited to tender

3.14 When using the restricted procedure the contracting authority must, as with the open procedure, publish a contract notice as soon as possible after forming the intention to seek offers. The contract notice must be in the form prescribed by the Regulations which incorporate by reference the Commission's standard form inviting requests to be selected to tender. There are strict minimum time limits for receipt of requests to be selected to tender.

The contracting authority may exclude a contractor from those persons from whom it will make the selection of persons to be invited to tender only if the contractor may be treated as ineligible on a ground permitted by the Regulations or if the contractor fails to satisfy the minimum standards of economic and financial standing and technical capacity required of contractors by the contracting authority as assessed according to the requirements of the Regulations.

Having excluded any contractors as above, the contracting authority must select the contractors they intend to invite to tender solely on the basis of the information obtained regarding the contractor's past record, his economic standing and his technical capacity as permitted by the Regulations and in making the selection and in issuing invitations the contracting authority must not discriminate between contractors on the grounds of their nationality or the member state in which they are established. The contracting authority may prescribe the range within which the number of undertakings which they intend to invite will fall. The number invited must be not less than five nor more than twenty. If a range is to be specified it must be specified in the contract notice and in any event the number must be sufficient to ensure genuine competition.

The Public Sector Directive imposes requirements for greater transparency in relation to selection of those invited to tender in a restricted procedure. Thus, contracting authorities will be required to indicate in the contract notice the objective and non-discriminatory criteria they intend to use to select those to be invited to tender and the minimum (at least five) and, if applicable, maximum number of candidates they intend to invite.

The invitation to tender

3.15 The invitation to tender must be sent in writing simultaneously to each contractor selected to tender, and must be accompanied by the contract documents or contain the address from which they may be requested. The invitation to tender must include the specified information. As before, the Regulations lay down strict minimum time limits for the receipt of tenders. The new Public Sector Directors will allow use of shorter periods where electronic means are used to transmit information.

The negotiated procedure

3.16 In most cases where the negotiated procedure is used contracting authorities are not required to follow any procedural rules other than those relating to the exclusion of contractors on the ground of ineligibility and relating to their selection to negotiate. However, where a contracting authority uses the negotiated procedure:

1 Because it has discontinued the open or restricted procedures in the circumstances discussed above, or
2 Where the work or works are to be carried out for the purposes of research, experiment or development, or
3 Where the nature of the works does not permit overall pricing,

then unless in relation to (1) above, it has invited to negotiate every contractor who submitted a tender (not being an 'excluded' tender), the following rules apply in addition:

1 The contracting authority must publicize its intention to seek offers in relation to the public works contract by publishing a contract notice in the *Official Journal* in the form prescribed inviting requests to be selected to negotiate and containing the information specified.
2 The date fixed as the last date for the receipt of requests to be selected to negotiate must be specified in the contract notice and must be not less than 37 days (15 days in cases of urgency) from the date of dispatch of the notice.
3 Where there is a sufficient number of persons who are suitable to be selected to negotiate the contract, the number must be not less than three.

The Public Sector Directive makes specific provision for the procedure to take place in stages, with the number of tenders to be negotiated being reduced by application of the award criteria along the way. This reflects what is already a standard practice in the UK but which has no current legal basis in the Regulations.

The competitive dialogue procedure

Under the new competitive dialogue procedure, as under the restricted procedure, the contracting authority must publish a contract notice setting out their needs and requirements (which are to be defined either in the notice or in a descriptive document). The notice will identify the objective and non-discriminatory criteria to be applied to select candidates to participate in the dialogue and tendering process. A minimum of three candidates must be invited to participate.

The dialogue phase of the procedure will be opened with selected candidates on the basis of the requirements set out in the contract notice or descriptive document. The aim of the dialogue will be to identify and define the means best suited to satisfying the contracting authority's needs. All aspects of the contract can be discussed with chosen candidates during the dialogue phase. The contracting authority must ensure equality of treatment among tenderers, particularly in the way in which information is provided to tenderers.

When a solution which is capable of meeting the authority's need has been identified the authority will declare that the dialogue is concluded and invite tenderers to submit final tenders on the basis of the solution or solutions which have emerged from the dialogue.

Under the competitive dialogue procedure it will be permitted to conduct a series of stages with tenderers, or solutions, being eliminated along the way through application of the award criteria. This can only occur if it has been identified as a possibility in the contract notice or descriptive document.

Selection of contractors

Criteria for rejection of contractors

3.17 Detailed rules are laid down in the Regulations as to the only criteria on which applicants to tender and tenderers may be excluded as ineligible from the tendering process. These relate to the contractor's financial solvency and business and fiscal probity. In addition a contractor may be excluded as ineligible where he is not registered on the professional or trade register of the member state in which he is established. Special provisions apply in relation to contractors established in the UK, Ireland and Greece (where such registers do not exist) to enable them to satisfy this condition.

The contracting authority may require a contractor to provide such information as it considers it needs to satisfy itself that none of the exclusionary criteria apply, but it must accept as conclusive that the contractor does not fall within any of the grounds relating to financial solvency or fiscal probity, an extract from a judicial record or a certificate issued by a competent authority (whichever is appropriate) to this effect. In member states such as the UK where such documentary evidence is not available, provision is made for the evidence to be provided by binding declaration. Special rules apply to contractors registered on official lists.

Under the Public Sector Directive it will be mandatory to disqualify tenderers convicted of some offences. The other permitted grounds for exclusion remain.

Information as to economic and financial standing

3.18 Subject to a similar provision relating to the situation where the contractor is registered on an official list of recognized contractors, under the Regulations the contracting authority, in assessing whether a contractor meets any minimum standards of economic and financial standing, may apparently 'only' take into account any of the certain specified information and it may require a contractor to provide such of that information as it considers it needs to make the assessment or selection.

Where the information specified is not appropriate in a particular case, a contracting authority may require a contractor to provide other information to demonstrate the contractor's economic and financial standing. Where a contractor is unable for a valid reason to provide the information which the contracting authority has required, the contracting authority must accept such other information provided by the contractor as the contracting authority considers appropriate. The information required must be specified in the contract notice.

Information as to technical capacity

3.19 Again subject to a similar provision relating to the situation where the contractor is registered on an official list of recognized contractors, the contracting authority, in assessing whether a contractor meets any minimum standards of technical capacity, may under the Regulations 'only' take into account certain specified information and it may require a contractor to provide such of that information as it considers it needs to make the assessment or selection.

Limits on the information which may be required or taken into account

3.20 The mandatory nature of the Regulations as regards information which may be required and/or taken into account by a contracting authority when assessing a contractor's economic and financial standing and technical capacity is not reflected in the directive. The European Court has held in respect of the provision concerning economic and financial standing that 'it can be seen from the very wording of that Article and in particular the second paragraph thereof that the list of references mentioned therein is not exhaustive' and that consequently a contracting authority is entitled to require a contractor to furnish a statement of the total value of the works he has in hand as a reference within the meaning of that article. The list of references which may be required to establish technical capacity on the other hand is exhaustive and a contracting authority may not *require* a contractor to furnish further information on that topic. However there would appear to be nothing to prevent a contracting authority from *taking into account* other information relevant to technical capacity which the contracting authority has acquired by other means. That appears to have been the view taken by the English High Court in *GBM v Greenwich BC* [1993] 92LG R21 where in relation to a public works contract, it was held that a contracting authority was entitled to take into account when assessing a contractor's technical capacity, any independent knowledge it might have regarding a contractor's compliance with health and safety legislation when carrying out other contracts. Indeed it would seem remarkable if a contracting authority

were to be prohibited from taking into account for example, the technical performance of a contractor experienced by it during other dealings with that contractor. A contracting authority may require a contractor to provide information supplementing the information supplied in accordance with the Regulations or to clarify that information, provided that the information required is in respect of matters permitted by the Regulations.

A contracting authority must comply with such requirements as to the confidentiality of information provided to it by a supplier as the supplier may reasonably request.

The award of the public works contract

The basis for the award

3.21 The contracting authority must award the public works contract on the basis either of the tender (including in-house bids) which offers the lowest price or the one which is the most 'economically advantageous' (i.e. best value for money). In *R. v Portsmouth City Council* [1997] the Court of Appeal, applying a European Court decision, confirmed that where no criteria had been specified a contract must be awarded on the basis of lowest price.

The criteria which a contracting authority may use to determine that an offer is the most economically advantageous include price, period for completion, running costs, profitability and technical merit. The list is not exhaustive, but it is clear from the examples given that only objective criteria may be used which are relevant to the particular project, and uniformly applicable to all bidders.

All the criteria the contracting authority intends to apply in determining the most economically advantageous offer must be stated in the contract notice or contract documents preferably in descending order of importance. No criteria not mentioned in the notice or the contract documents may be used. Under the Public Sector Directive it will be necessary (unless demonstrably not possible) not only to identify all contract award criteria relevant to the best value assessment but also to indicate the relative weighting to be attached to each criterion. The new Directive recognizes that the objective and transparent criteria relevant to assessing the most economically advantageous tender may include environmental and social criteria, but only where these are directly related to the subject matter of the contract.

Contract performance conditions

3.22 A distinction, however, must be made between a contractual condition requiring the successful contractor to co-operate with some policy objective of the contracting authority and the criteria for the selection of contractors or for the award of the contract. Thus a condition attached to the award of a public works contract, under which the contractor is required to engage a given member of long-term unemployed, is compatible with the directive and therefore the Regulations. It is not relevant to the assessment of the contractor's economic, financial or technical capacity to carry out the work, nor does it form part of the criteria applied by the contracting authority to decide to whom to award the contract. Such conditions must, however, be compatible with the Treaty, particularly with those provisions on freedom to provide services, freedom of establishment and nondiscrimination on the grounds of nationality. They must also be mentioned in the contract notice. Thus it would be a breach of the Treaty if it appeared on the facts that the condition could only be fulfilled by national firms or it would be more difficult for tenderers coming from other member states to fulfil that condition. Even a request for information from tenderers (as opposed to the insertion of a contractual term) can in certain circumstances be in breach of the rules if such request would reasonably lead the tenderer to believe that discrimination on local or national grounds is likely to occur. In this context the UK Department of the Environment, basing itself on Treasury guidance, has published a circular to assist local authorities in complying with the rules governing public procurement. The circular clarifies the Commission's view that requiring the tenderer to give information on whether local labour and local experience will be used may imply that a tenderer using local labour would be more likely to win the contract. Local authorities are advised therefore not to put such requirements into contract notices.

When a contracting authority awards a public works contract on the basis of the offer which is most economically advantageous it may take account of offers which offer variations on the requirements specified in the contract documents if the offer meets the minimum requirements of the contracting authority and it has indicated in the contract notice that offers offering variations will be considered, and has stated in the contract documents the minimum requirements which the offer must meet and any specific requirements for the presentation of an offer offering variations.

Post-tender negotiations

3.23 It should also be stressed that in open and restricted procedures all negotiations with candidates or tenderers on fundamental aspects of the contract and in particular on prices are not permitted, although discussion with candidates or tenderers may be held for the purposes of clarifying or supplementing the content of their tenders or the requirements of the contracting authority, provided this does not involve unfairness to their competitors.

Under the new dialogue procedure discussion ("dialogue") may be held to establish a specification and project structure but, once the dialogue is concluded, tenderers must bid their firm, final price and no discussion on other fundamental terms will be permitted.

Abnormally low tenders

3.24 If an offer for a public works contract is or appears to be abnormally low the contracting authority may reject that offer but only if it has requested in writing an explanation of the offer or of those parts which it considers contribute to the offer being abnormally low and has:

1 if awarding the contract on the basis of lowest price, examined the details of all the offers made taking into account any explanation given to it of the abnormally low tender, before awarding the contract, or

2 if awarding the contract on the basis of the offer which is the most economically advantageous, taken any such explanation into account in assessing which is the most economically advantageous offer.

Thus a contracting authority may not automatically reject a tender because it fails to satisfy some predetermined mathematical criterion adopted in relation to the public works contract concerned. In every case, the contractor must be given an opportunity for explanation and thereafter the examination procedure specified must be followed.

If a contracting authority which rejects an abnormally low tender is awarding the contract on the basis of the offer which offers the lowest price, it must send a report justifying the rejection to the UK Government for onward transmission to the Commission.

Under the new Public Sector Directives it is recognized that abnormally low tenders may be facilitated by state aid granted to the tenderer. If a tenderer cannot prove that aid was granted legally a tender may be rejected on grounds that the tenderer has received unlawful state aid.

The contracting authority's obligations once the contract has been awarded

3.25 It may be a matter of considerable importance to disappointed tenderers to know the outcome of a contract award procedure, not least to establish whether there may be grounds on which to challenge the award. The Regulations impose upon contracting authorities the following obligations in this respect:

1 The authority must not later than 48 days after the award, send to the *Official Journal* a notice in the prescribed standard. The information required may be omitted in a particular case where to publish such information would impede law enforcement, would otherwise be contrary to the public interest, would prejudice the legitimate commercial interests of any person or might prejudice fair competition between contractors.

2 The authority must within 15 days of the date on which it receives a request from any unsuccessful contractor inform that contractor why he was unsuccessful and if the contractor was unsuccessful as a result of the evaluation of offers it must also tell him the name of the person awarded the contract. The Regulations also impose a requirement to tell any tenderer who submitted an admissible tender the characteristics and advantages of the successful tender, subject to the same considerations of confidentiality as apply to publication of a notice.

A contracting authority must in addition prepare a record in respect of each public works contract awarded containing specified information which must be available for transmission to the Commission if requested. Where a contracting authority decides not to award a public works contract which has been advertised nor to seek offers in relation to another public works contract for the same purpose it must inform the *Official Journal* of that decision and must, if so requested by any contractor who submitted an offer or who applied to be included amongst the persons to be selected to tender for or negotiate the contract, give the reasons for its decision. The Regulations impose a general requirement promptly to inform candidates of the decisions taken on contract awards.

Subsidized works contracts

3.26 Where a contracting authority undertakes to contribute more than half of the cost of certain specified public works contracts which will be or have been entered into by another body (other than another contracting authority), the contracting authority must make it a condition of making such contribution that that other body complies with the Regulations in relation to the contract as if it were a contracting authority, and must ensure that that body does so comply, or recover the contribution. The contracts to which this provision applies are those which are for carrying out any of the activities specified in Group 502 of Schedule 1 (civil engineering, construction of roads, bridges, railways, etc.) or for the carrying out of building works for hospitals, facilities intended for sports recreation and leisure, school and university buildings or buildings for administrative purposes.

Public housing scheme works contracts

3.27 A public housing scheme works contract is defined as 'a public works contract relating to the design and construction of a public housing scheme'. For the purpose of seeking offers in relation to a public housing scheme works contract where the size and complexity of the scheme and the estimated duration of the works involved require that the planning of the scheme be based from the outset on a close collaboration of a team comprising representatives of the contracting authority, experts and the contractor, the contracting authority may, subject as below, depart from the provisions of the Regulations in so far as it is necessary to do so to select the contractor who is most suitable for integration into the team. The contracting authority must in any event comply with the provisions relating to the restricted procedure up to the selection of contractors to be invited to tender. The contracting authority must in addition include in the contract notice a job description which is as accurate as possible so as to enable contractors to form a valid idea of the scheme and of the minimum standards relating to the business or professional status, the economic and financial standing and the technical capacity which the person awarded the contract will be expected to fill.

Public works concession contracts

3.28 The Regulations lay down special rules which apply to public works concession contracts. A public works concession contract is defined in the Regulations as 'a public works contract under which the consideration given by the contracting authority consists of or includes the grant of a right to exploit the work or works to be carried out under the contract'.

Obligations relating to employment protection and working conditions

3.29 A contracting authority which includes in the contract documents relating to a public work, information as to where a contractor may obtain information about obligations relating to employment protection and working conditions which will apply to the works to be carried out under the contract, must ask contractors to indicate that they have taken account of those obligations in preparing their tender, or in negotiating the contract.

The Supplies Directive and the Public Supply Contracts Regulations 1995

3.30 The Supply Regulations apply similar rules to those contained in the Works Regulations to public supply contracts. A public supply contract is defined as a contract in writing for money or monies worth for the purchase of goods (and their siting and installation if any) by a contracting authority or for the hire of goods by a contracting authority irrespective of whether or not the contracting authority becomes the owner of the goods at the end of the period of hire.

As public supply contracts are likely to be of marginal interest to architects it is not proposed to deal with the provisions of the Regulations in detail. The following points should however be noted:

- The value threshold for supply contracts (below which the Regulations do not apply) is set at the euro equivalent of 130 000 SDRs (£99 695 for 2004–2006) for GATT list bodies (effectively central Government bodies) and the euro equivalent of 20 000 SDRs (£153 376 for 2004–2006) for local authorities.
- When calculating the value of a contract for the purposes of the threshold the value of other contracts of a similar nature may have to be aggregated.
- The circumstances in which the negotiated procedure may be used are more limited than those set out in the Works Regulations.

The new Public Sector Directive introduces slightly more flexibility to use the negotiated procedure and the new competitive dialogue procedure for the award of supply contracts. The new electronic purchasing mechanisms – dynamic purchasing systems and electronic auctions – are expected to be of most relevance for purchase of goods and the provisions relating to framework agreements will allow contracting authorities to put in place call-off arrangements.

The Services Directive and the Public Services Contracts Regulations

3.31 As with the Works and Supply Regulations, the Services Regulations apply whenever a contracting authority whether by itself or through an agent, seeks offers in relation to a proposed 'public services contract' other than a public services contract which is excluded under the Regulations. However, unlike the Works and Supply Regulations, the extent of the application of the Services Regulations depends on the type of services contract concerned. The Regulations adopt a two-tier approach. Certain services listed in Part A of Schedule 1 to the Regulations are subject to the Regulations in full, while others listed in Part B of Schedule 1 are subject at present only to the regulations relating to technical specifications in contract documents (Regulation 8), contract award information (Regulation 22), certain reporting responsibilities (Regulations 27(2) and 28), and publication of notices (Regulation 29). Both Part A and Part B services are subject to Part 1 (General) and Part VII (applications to the court) of the Regulations. Part A comprises fourteen separate categories of service of which (j) 'architectural and related services' and (l) 'property management services' are of particular relevance to architects. Other services fall into Part B.

Contracts for both Part A services and Part B services are deemed to be for Part B services only if the value of the Part B services is equal to or greater than the value of the Part A services. Parts A and B of Schedule 1 contain references to the UN Central Products Classification (CPC). In order to establish which services fall into which Part of Schedule 1 it will usually be necessary to check the full CPC reference rather than rely on the abbreviated lists set out in the schedule. For example 'legal services' appear under Category 21 of Part B, but where legal services take the form of 'research and experimental development services on law' they will fall into Category 8 of Part A (research and development services) as provided for in CPC Reference 85203.

The Regulations only apply when a contracting authority 'seeks offers in relation to a proposed public services contract'. They impose obligations only in relation to service providers who are nationals of and established in a member state, or in certain other Relevant states including GPA signatory states but they do not require any preference to be given to offers from them. They do, however, prohibit treating non-EC service providers more favourably than EC service providers. The Regulations only apply when a contracting authority seeks offers from service providers which are not part of the same legal entity as itself, but they do not require a contracting authority to seek outside offers unless it chooses to do so. If it does do so it must treat any in-house offer on the same basis as the outside offers for the purpose of evaluating the bids. If the outside bid is successful the fact that the contract award procedure has been conducted does not mean that a contract has to be awarded. The contracting authority can choose not to accept the outside offer. There could be problems under domestic law however, if the contracting authority does not make it clear from the outset that it reserves the right not to award the contract.

Meaning of 'contracting authority'

3.32 The Regulations apply to the same bodies (contracting authorities) as the Works Directive. These include government, and government controlled bodies, local authorities and certain bodies governed by public law. A list of contracting authorities is set out at Regulation 3(1). Where a contracting authority joins with another person (e.g. a property developer) for the purpose of purchasing services, and both are parties to the contract, the Regulations will apply. The amount of the contracting authority's contribution is not relevant to the application of the threshold: the normal valuation rules apply to the contract as a whole.

Meaning of 'public services contract'

3.33 A public services contract is defined in the Regulations as 'a contract in writing for consideration (whatever the nature of the consideration) under which a contracting authority engages a person to provide services, excluding certain specified contracts for services (e.g. employment contracts and contracts with concessionaires).

In addition certain services contracts although 'public services contracts' for the purpose of the Regulations are excluded from its provisions (see Regulation 6).

Borderline cases

3.34 Where a contract is for both goods and services it will only fall within the scope of the Services Regulations if the consideration attributable to the services is greater than that attributable to the goods or to the works. Otherwise it will fall within the Supply Regulations. For example where a contracting authority seeks offers in relation to a contract for the provision of computer hardware and bespoke software, the contract will only be a services contract if the cost attributable to the development of the software exceeds the cost of the hardware.

Where a contract is for both services and works there is (as noted above) some doubt whether a value test or main object test is applicable.

The public services contracts excluded from the operation of the Regulations

3.35 The Services Regulations do not apply to the seeking of offers in relation to certain specified types of contract.

Contracts below certain value thresholds

3.36 Most importantly the Regulations do not apply to the seeking of offers in relation to a proposed public services contract where the 'estimated value' (net of VAT) at the 'relevant time' is less than the equivalent in € of 200 000 SDR (£53 376 for 2004–2006) or the equivalent in € of 130 000 SDR (£99 695) where the contracting authority is a GATT authority (a threshold of €200 000 (£129 462) applies to limited categories of services not covered by the GPA). The 'estimated value' is normally the sum which the contracting authority expects to pay under the contract and assuming that it exercises any options. Where appropriate these will be the insurance premiums payable in respect of insurance services, the fees, commissions or other remuneration payable for banking and financial services, and the fees or commissions payable for design services.

Aggregation provisions

3.37 Exceptionally the estimated value is to be calculated according to provisions in the Regulations relating to the aggregation of sums paid under a series of similar contracts. These are similar to, but not identical with, the parallel provisions contained in the Supply Regulations.

Rules governing technical specifications

3.38 The rules governing technical specifications are similar to those in the Works and Supply Regulations.

Rules governing the procedures leading to the award of a public services contract

Prior information notices

3.39 One of the fundamental aims of the EC procurement regime is to ensure that information about prospective contracts should be published throughout the European Community so as to enable potential contractors from all member states to compete on an equal footing.

As soon after the start of each financial year as possible, contracting authorities must publish a prior information notice in the *Official Journal* in the prescribed form setting out contracts for Part A services which it expects to enter into during that financial year and which are above the threshold either individually or because the aggregation provisions apply, and which are expected to total more than €750 000 (£485 481) for any one of the categories of services in Part A.

Selection of contract award procedure

3.40 As with the Works and Supply Regulations the contracting authority when seeking offers in relation to a proposed public services contract must use the open procedure, the restricted procedure, or the negotiated procedure. The Regulations lay down rules for making the choice of procedure.

Negotiated procedure

3.41 The negotiated procedure may only be used in the limited circumstances specified in the Regulations. There is slightly more flexibility to use the negotiated procedure for seeking offers for services contracts. In particular, the procedure can be used where the nature of the services is such that a specification cannot be drawn up to permit the award of a contract using open or restricted procedure. In circumstances other than those expressly permitted the contracting authority must use the open or restricted procedure. Where the negotiated procedure may be used prior publication of a contract notice in the *Official Journal* (and hence no open competition) is not always required.

A contracting authority may only exclude a services provider from those persons from whom it will make the selection of persons to be invited to negotiate the contract if the services provider may be treated as ineligible on a ground specified in the Regulations or if the services provider fails to satisfy the minimum standards of economic and financial standing, ability and technical capacity, required of services providers by the contracting authority as evaluated in accordance with the Regulations.

Once any services providers have been excluded in the manner described above, the contracting authority must make its selection of the services providers to be invited to negotiate in accordance with the rules laid down in the Regulations.

The open and restricted procedures

3.42 These are similar to those contained in the Works and Supplies Regulations, although it should be noted that under the Services Regulations the *ability* of the services provider is introduced as an additional criterion on which a contracting authority may make its selection of tenderers or those invited to tender.

The award of a public services contract

The basis for the award

3.43 As with the Works and Supply Regulations the contracting authority must award a public services contract on the basis of either the tender (including in-house bids) which offers the lowest price or the one which is 'the most economically advantageous to the contracting authority' (i.e. best value for money).

The criteria which a contracting authority may use to determine that an offer is the most economically advantageous include period of completion or delivery, quality, aesthetic and functional characteristics, technical merit, after-sales service, technical assistance and price. Other economic criteria would include security of supply, avoidance of monopoly and the risk of non-delivery because an offer is known to be based on an unapproved state aid that might have to be repaid. All the criteria which a contracting authority intends to apply in determining the most economically advantageous offer must be stated in the contract notice or contract documents, preferably in descending order of importance. A distinction must however be made between on the one hand a contractual condition requiring the successful services provider to cooperate with some policy objective of the contracting authority (e.g. ensuring that a proportion of its workforce is drawn from the ranks of the unemployed) and the criteria for the selection of services providers or the award of the public services contract on the other.

Where a contracting authority awards a public services contract on the basis of the offer which is most economically advantageous it may take account of offers which offer variations on the requirements specified in the contract documents if:

1 The offer meets the minimum requirements of the contracting authority, and
2 It has stated those minimum requirements and any specific requirements for the presentation of an offer offering variations in the contract documents. If a contracting authority will not accept variations it must state that fact in the contract notice. A contracting authority must not reject an offer offering variations on the contract specification on the ground that it would lead to the award of a public supply contract, nor may it reject an offer on the ground that reference has been made to European specifications or to national specifications which are permitted by the Regulations.

Abnormally low tenders

3.44 The rules relating to abnormally low tenders are similar to those contained in the Works and Supply Regulations.

Post-tender negotiations

3.45 It should be stressed that in open and restricted procedures all negotiations with candidates or tenderers on fundamental aspects of the contract and in particular on prices, are not permitted, although discussions with candidates or tenderers may be held for the purposes of clarifying or supplementing the content of their tenders or the requirements of the contracting authority provided this does not involve unfairness to their competitors.

Contracting authority's obligations once contract has been awarded

3.46 The Regulations impose certain reporting obligations on contracting authorities once the contract has been awarded.

Design contests

3.47 In addition the Regulations lay down rules which must be followed for the holding of certain design contests which may or may not be part of the procedure leading to the award of a public services contract.

A design contest will be caught by the Regulations:

1 If it is organized as part of a procedure leading to the award of a public services contract and the estimated value of the contract (after applying the aggregation provisions) is not less than the euro equivalent of 130 000 SDR (£99 695) or of €200 000 SDR (£153 376) according to whether or not the contracting authority is a GATT authority (again the threshold is €200 000 (£129 462) for limited categories of services not covered by the GPA), or

2 Whether or not it is organized as part of a procedure leading to the award of such a contract, if the aggregate of the value of the prizes or payments for the contest is not less than the applicable threshold (as in (1) this depends on whether the contracting authority is a GATT authority. This regulation only applies to Part A contracts.

Where a design contest is caught by the Regulations the following provisions apply:

● The contracting authority must publicize its intention to hold a contest by sending to the *Official Journal* a notice in a form substantially corresponding to that set out in Part F of Schedule 2 and containing the information there specified.
● The rules of the contest must be made available to all services providers who wish to participate.
● The number of services providers invited to participate may be restricted but the contracting authority must make the selection on the basis of clear and non-discriminatory criteria. The number participating must be sufficient to ensure that there is adequate competition.
● The participants' proposals must be submitted anonymously to a jury who must be individuals who are independent of the participants. Where the participants are required to possess a qualification at least one third of its jury must possess that qualification or its equivalent.
● The jury must make its decision independently and solely on the basis of the criteria set out in the published notice.
● Not later than 48 days after the jury has made its selection the contracting authority must publicize the result in the *Official Journal*.

Subsidized public services contracts

3.48 Regulation 25 imposes an obligation on a contracting authority which undertakes to contribute more than half of the cost of certain public services contracts entered into by a party other than a contracting authority to ensure that that party complies with the Regulations as if it were a contracting authority.

The public services contracts to which this provision applies are contracts which would qualify as public services contracts if the subsidized body were a contracting authority and which are contracts for services in connection with the carrying out of civil engineering projects such as the construction of roads, bridges and railways, etc. (Schedule 1 of the Works Regulations, Group 502), or for the carrying out of building work for hospitals, facilities intended for sports, recreation and leisure, school and university buildings, or buildings for administrative purposes.

Public Sector Directive

3.49 The new Public Sector Directive will make similar changes to the regime applying to the award of services contracts as to the rules for works contracts. In particular, it will introduce the new competitive dialogue, as an alternative to the open and restricted procedures for complex procurements and permit the use of framework agreements and purchasing via a central purchasing agency. It will require criteria for selection of tenderers invited to participate in restricted, negotiated and competitive dialogue procedures to be published in the contract notice and the relative weight given to evaluation criteria to be disclosed.

The Utilities Directive and the Utilities Contracts Regulations 1995

3.50 The Utilities Regulations apply similar rules to those contained in the Works and Supply Regulations to certain contracts for works, supplies or services entered into by entities operating in the water, energy, transport and (although now to a much lesser extent) telecommunications sectors. The entities affected are specified in Schedule 1 and in the Regulations are called utilities.

Certain contracts are excluded from the application of the Regulations principally where the contract is not for the purpose of carrying out an activity specified in the part of Schedule 1 in which the utility concerned is specified but also where the contract is for the purpose of carrying out an activity outside the territory of the Communities, contracts for resale, secret contracts, contracts connected with international agreements, certain contracts awarded by utilities operating in the telecommunications sector and those contracts whose value is beneath the threshold for coverage (the same thresholds apply as in the Works Supplies and Services Regulations). Certain contracts awarded by utilities operating in the energy sector may be exempt from the detailed rules of the Regulations in which case the utility must comply with the principles of non-discrimination and competitive procurement in seeking offers in relation to them.

Like the public procurement Regulations, the principal requirement of the Utilities Regulations is that in seeking offers in relation to a works, supply or services contract, a utility must use either the open procedure, the restricted procedure or the negotiated procedure. However, the Utilities Regulations in accordance with the Utilities Directive has adopted a more flexible approach to the choice of procedure than is contained in the earlier Regulations; so long as the utility makes a 'call for competition' as defined in the Regulations any of the three procedures may be used and in certain specified circumstances no call for competition need be made.

As with the public procurement Regulations, a utility is required to publicize the contracts which it expects to award in the *Official Journal* at least once a year and again when it starts the procedure leading to the award although the latter requirement is dispensed with in certain cases.

Unlike the earlier Regulations, the Utilities Regulations permit the operation of a system of qualification of providers, from which a utility may select suppliers or contractors to tender for or to negotiate a contract without advertisement at the start of the award procedure. In this case the existence of the qualification system must be advertised.

Similar to the public procurement Regulations, the Utilities Regulations lay down minimum time limits in relation to responses by potential providers to invitations to tender, to be selected to tender for or to negotiate the contract, and for obtaining the relevant documents. The Regulations also indicate the matters to which the utility may have regard in excluding tenders from providers who are regarded as ineligible or in selecting providers to tender for or to negotiate the contract, and as before they require that the utility award a contract on the basis either of the offer (including in-house bids) which offers the lowest price or the one which is the most economically advantageous. In addition the Regulations lay down similar rules in relation to technical specifications to publicizing their awards and to the keeping of records and to reporting.

The Regulations and the underlying Directive introduced a number of innovations into the Community procurement regime. A utility is permitted to advertise an arrangement which establishes the terms under which providers will enter contracts with it over a period of time (called in the Regulations 'framework arrangements') in which case it need not advertise the supply and works contracts made under it. Secondly a utility may, and in other limited circumstances must, reject an offer for a supply contract if more than 50% of the value of the goods are goods which originate in states with which the Communities have not concluded an agreement ensuring comparable and effective access to markets for undertakings in member states. The Utilities Directive and the Utilities Regulations have been amended to take account of the GPA. In particular, new thresholds have been introduced and minor changes made to procedures.

The new Excluded Sectors Directive replaces the Utilities Directive and updates the rules applicable to entities in the water, energy and transport sectors to reflect case law of the Court of Justice. Entities providing postal services on the basis of special or exclusive rights will be subject to the more flexible excluded sector regime.

Remedies for breach of the Community rules governing procurement

3.51 The Works, Supply, Utilities, and Services, Regulations provide a 'contractor', 'supplier' or 'services provider' (i.e. one who is a national of and established in a member state) and who suffers or risks suffering loss or damage as a result of a breach of the relevant Regulations or the breach of any Community obligation in respect of a contract to which the Regulations apply, with a right to obtain redress by way of court action. A 'services provider' includes one who provides architectural or related services (see paragraph 3.31 above). The remedies available and the procedure by which they may be obtained are very similar in respect of each of the Regulations. In this way the Regulations implement the 'Remedies' Directive and the 'Compliance' Directive already referred to.

The obligation on contracting authorities and utilities to comply with the provisions of the Regulations (other than certain provisions relating to reporting and the supply of information) and with enforceable Community obligations in respect of contracts falling within the Regulations, is conceived under the Regulations as a duty owed to providers the breach whereof gives rise to an action for breach of statutory duty.

A similar duty is placed upon a public works concessionaire to comply with the obligations placed upon it by regulation 26(3) of the Works Regulations and where such a duty is imposed the term 'contractor' includes any person who sought or who seeks or who would have wished to be the person to whom a contract to which Regulation 26(3) applies is awarded and who is a national of and established in a member state.

A breach of the duty referred to is not a criminal offence but is actionable by any provider who in consequence 'suffers or risks suffering loss or damage'. Proceedings brought in England and Wales and in Northern Ireland must be brought in the High Court, and in Scotland, before the Court of Session. However, proceedings under the Regulations may not be brought unless:

1 The provider bringing the proceedings has informed the contracting authority (including a concessionaire), or utility of the breach or apprehended breach of the duty referred to and of his intention to bring proceedings under the Regulations in respect of it; and
2 They are brought promptly, and in any event within three months from the date when grounds for the bringing of the proceedings first arose unless the court considers that there is good reason for extending the period within which proceedings may be brought.

In proceedings brought under each of the Regulations the court may, without prejudice to any other powers it may have:

1 by interim order (whether or not the defendant is the Crown) suspend the procedure leading to the award of the relevant contract, or suspend the implementation of any decision or action taken by the contracting authority or utility in the course of following such a procedure; and
2 if satisfied that a decision or action taken by a contracting authority or utility was in breach of the duty referred to,
   (a) order the setting aside of that decision or action or order the contracting authority or utility to amend any document,

(b) award damages to a contractor or supplier who has suffered loss or damage as a consequence of the breach, or
(c) do both of those things.

However, in proceedings brought under each of the Regulations, the court can only award damages if the contract in relation to which the breach occurred has been entered into. The court cannot therefore set aside a contract which has been entered into in breach of the Regulations. It is uncertain however whether such a contract in English law is unenforceable as between the parties to it on the grounds of public policy. It is submitted that where both parties are aware of the breach at the time of entering the contract (e.g. where the proposed contract was not advertised) public policy requires that the contract should be unenforceable by both parties. Where only one party is in breach without the other party's knowledge (e.g. where a contracting authority without justification selects a contractor who has not submitted the lowest tender) then the contract should only be unenforceable by the party in breach.

In the English courts any interim order under (1) above will be by way of interlocutory injunction which it is anticipated will be granted or refused on the familiar principles laid down by the House of Lords in *American Cyanamid Co. v Ethicon Ltd* [1975] AC 396. These principles may be summarized as follows:

1 The plaintiff must establish that he has a good arguable claim to the right he seeks to protect;
2 The court must not attempt to decide the claim on the affidavits; it is enough if the plaintiff shows that there is a serious question to be tried;
3 If the plaintiff satisfies these tests the grant or refusal of an injunction is a matter for the court's discretion on the balance of convenience including that of the public where this is affected.

Although the factors relevant to the exercise of the discretion are many and varied (of which the question whether damages would be a sufficient remedy is arguably the most important) in public procurement cases the question of the public interest is often likely to be decisive against the grant of the injunction. This fact is expressly recognized by both Remedies directives which provide that:

'The Member States may provide that when considering whether to order interim measures the body responsible may take into account the probable consequences of the measures for all interests likely to be harmed, as well as the public interest, and may decide not to grant such measures where their negative consequences could exceed their benefits. A decision not to grant interim measures shall not prejudice any other claim of the person seeking these measures.' (Article 2(4) of both directives.)

No such provision appears in the Regulations no doubt because it was considered that the practice of the courts when granting or refusing interlocutory injunctions was entirely consistent with the discretion given by the Remedies directive in this respect.

Even where the public interest element is not decisive the usual requirement that the plaintiff undertake to pay the defendant's damages caused by the injunction should it prove to have been wrongly granted will often dissuade a plaintiff from pursuing this remedy in public procurement cases where such damages are likely to be heavy. It has been suggested that because there is an obligation under EU law for member states to provide an effective remedy for breach of rights arising under Community law the strict conditions which usually apply to injunctions, including the requirement for an undertaking to pay the defendant's damages, should not apply. However, this approach has not to date been applied in the English Courts.

A provider may wish to have set aside a decision to reject his bid made on the basis of criteria not permitted by the Regulations, or a decision to exclude his bid as abnormally low where he has not been given an opportunity to give an explanation. Equally a provider may require that a contract document be amended so as to exclude a specification not permitted by the Regulations.

It will be noted that each of the Regulations while providing providers with a remedy in damages do not specify how those damages are to be assessed. In Community law it is left to national laws to provide the remedies required in order to ensure that

Community rights are protected, and until the first cases go through the courts it is uncertain how such damages will be assessed.

In the case of the Utilities Regulations alone the task of recovering certain damage is eased by Regulation 32(7) which provides that:

'Where in proceedings under this regulation the Court is satisfied that a provider would have had a real chance of being awarded a contract if that chance had not been adversely affected by a breach of the duty owed to him by the utility pursuant to [the Regulations] the provider shall be entitled to damages amounting to his costs in preparing his tender and in participating in the procedure leading to the award of the contract.'

Regulation 32(8) makes it clear that that remedy is without prejudice to a claim by a provider that he has suffered other loss or damage or that he is entitled to relief other than damages and further that subsection 7 is without prejudice to the matters on which a provider may be required to satisfy the court in respect of any other such claim.

To what standard the plaintiff will have to prove that he had a 'real chance' (identical words are used in Article 2(3) of the directive) of being awarded the contract is as yet unclear but it is submitted that this will be something less than on the balance of probabilities.

The role of the architect in relation to the procurement regulations

3.52 It is to be noted that the obligations imposed by the procurement Regulations are placed on the 'contracting authority' or utility concerned. However an architect employed by such a body may be under a contractual duty to carry out those obligations as its agent and liable to indemnify it where a breach of that duty results in loss. This could occur, for example where the contract award is delayed or where the authority or utility is compelled to pay damages as the result of an infringement.

On the other hand architects who wish to tender for public authority (and utility) contracts for architectural services will be able to take advantage of the provisions of the Services directive to ensure equal treatment with other EC architects. It should be borne in mind that the Services directive applies throughout the Community and that therefore a UK architect can as much take advantage of its provisions in another member state as architects from other member states can take advantage of it in the UK.

Public works contracts and article 28 EC

3.53 Even where a public procurement contract falls outside the provisions of the relevant directive, architects will still have to take care that they do not specify in such a manner as will render any public authority employer in breach of Article 28 EC.

Article 28 provides that:

'Quantitative restrictions on imports and all measures having equivalent effect shall, without prejudice to the following provisions be prohibited between Member States.'

In Case 45/87 *Commission v Ireland*, the Dundalk Urban District Council (a public body for whose acts the Irish Government are responsible), permitted the inclusion in the contract specification for a drinking water supply scheme of a clause providing that certain pipes should be certified as complying with an Irish standard and consequently refusing to consider without adequate justification a tender providing for such pipes manufactured to an alternative standard providing equivalent guarantees of safety, performance and reliability. The contract fell outside the provisions of the Works directive because it concerned the distribution of drinking water. Nevertheless, the Court held that Ireland had acted in breach of Article 28. Only one undertaking was capable of producing pipes to the required standard and that undertaking was situated in Ireland. Consequently, the inclusion of that specification had the effect of restricting the supply of the pipes needed to Irish manufacturers alone and was a quantitive restriction on imports or a measure having equivalent effect. The breach of Article 28 could

have been avoided if the specifier had added the words 'or equivalent' after the specification concerned.

4 Technical harmonization and standards

The Construction Products Directive 89/106 EEC

4.01 A major barrier to the free movement of construction products within the Community has been the differing national requirements relating to such matters as building safety, health, durability, energy economy and protection of the environment, which in turn directly influence national product standards, technical approvals and other technical specifications and provisions.

In order to overcome this problem, the Community has adopted the Construction Products directive whose aim is to provide for the free movement, sale and use of construction products which are fit for their intended use and have such characteristics that structures in which they are incorporated meet certain essential requirements. Products, in so far as these essential requirements relate to them, which do not meet the appropriate standard may not be placed on the market (Article 2).

4.02 These essential requirements are similar in style to the functional requirements of the Building Regulations in force in England and Wales, but rather wider in scope. They relate to mechanical resistance and stability, safety in case of fire, hygiene, health and the environment, safety in use, protection against noise, and energy economy and heat retention. These requirements must, subject to normal maintenance, be satisfied for an economically reasonable working life and generally provide protection against events which are foreseeable.

The performance levels of products complying with these essential requirements may, however, vary according to geographical or climatic conditions or in ways of life, as well as different levels of protection that may prevail at national regional or local level and member states may decide which class of performance level they require to be observed within their territory.

4.03 Products will be presumed to be fit for their intended use if they bear the CE conformity mark as provided (or in as provided for in Directive 93/68/EEC) showing that they comply with a European standard or a European technical approval or (when documents of this sort do not exist) relevant national standards or agreements recognized at Community level as meeting the essential requirements. If a manufacturer chooses to make a product which is not in conformity with these specifications, he has to prove that his product conforms to the essential requirements before he will be permitted to put it on the market. Conformity may be verified by third party certification.

4.04 European standards which will ensure that the essential requirements are met will be drawn up by a European standards body usually CEN or CENELEC. These will be published in the UK as identically worded British standards. European technical approvals will be issued by approved bodies designated for this purpose by the member states in accordance with guidelines prepared by the European body comprising the approved bodies from all the member states.

4.05 Member states are prohibited from interfering with the free movement of goods which satisfy the provisions of the directive and are to ensure that the use of such products is not impeded by any national rule or condition imposed by a public body, or private bodies acting as a public undertaking or acting as a public body on the basis of a monopoly position (Article 6). This would appear to include such bodies as the NHBC in their standard setting role.

4.06 The directive has been implemented in the UK by the Construction Products Regulations 1991 (SI 1991/1620) as amended by SI 1994/3051.

The implementation of the directive throughout the Community should greatly ease the task of the architect who is designing buildings in more than one member state as it means that he can now be sure that the products he specifies, so long as they comply with the directive, will comply with the regulations and requirements of every member state without his having to carry out a detailed check for that purpose.

5 Right of establishment and freedom to provide services – the Architects Directive 85/384 EEC

The background

5.01 Three of the fundamental principles underlying the Treaty of Rome are the free movement of workers, the freedom to set up business in any member state and the freedom to provide services in a member state, other than that in which the provider of these services is based. In order to ensure that those principles are met so far as architects are concerned the Community has adopted directive 85/384 EEC which has been implemented into UK law by the Architects' Qualifications (EEC Recognition) Order 1987 (SI 1987, No. 1824 as amended by SI1988/2241 and 2002/2842).

Mutual recognition of architectural qualifications

5.02 The directive allows architects with appropriate UK qualifications to practise anywhere in the EC and architects from other member states to have the equivalent right to practise in this country. The directive sets out in detail what are the minimum qualifications required for such mutual recognition and how these are to be proved.

Right of establishment and freedom to provide services

5.03 The directive similarly lays down rules for the mutual recognition of an architect's rights to set up in practice in a host member state or to provide architectural services in another member state.

The fundamental principle contained in the directive is that there must be no discrimination against other EC nationals which would make it more difficult for them to establish themselves or provide services in the host state than it would be for nationals of that state.

5.04 Similar provision has been made for the mutual recognition within the Community of those employed in the construction industry by the following measures:

1 **The Certificates of Experience Directive 64/77/EC** This directive aims to ensure that experience of doing a particular job in one member state is recognized in other member states. Certificates are issued by the competent authority in the state where the experience is gained so that a registration body in any other member state can recognize the holder as a suitably experienced person. In some European countries a period of experience and/or training is required before a person can set up as an independent plumber or electrician.

2 **First General Directive on Professional Qualifications 89/48/EC** This directive which has been implemented in the UK by the European Communities (Recognition of Professional Qualifications) Regulations 1991 (SI 1991 No. 824) deals with the general system for recognizing professional education and training in regulated professions for which university courses lasting at least three years are required. Courses for engineers, surveyors and other construction industry professionals lasting three years or more are covered by this directive.

3 **Second General Directive on Professional Qualifications 92/51/EC** This directive complements directive 89/48/EC by extending the regime provided by that directive to qualifications obtained on completion of such education and training over a shorter period, whether at secondary level (possibly complemented by professional training and experience), postsecondary level, or even merely through professional experience. It has

been implemented in the UK by the European Ccommissions (Recognition of professional qualifications) (Second General System) Regulations 1996 (SI 2374/1996).

It applies to any national of a member state who wishes to pursue a 'regulated' profession in a host member state, whether in a self-employed capacity or as an employed person, other than a profession covered by a specific directive establishing arrangements for mutual recognition of professional qualifications (e.g. the Architects directive), or an activity covered by certain specific directives principally concerned with introducing mutual recognition of technical skills based on experience in another member state and listed in an annex to the directive. The directive will only apply in cases where directive 89/48/EEC is inapplicable, i.e. where the training required in the host state is less than three years' higher education at university level.

6 The Product Liability Directive 85/374 IEEC and the Consumer Protection Act 1987

6.01 The Product Liability directive 85/374 which was adopted on 25 July 1985 was required to be implemented throughout the EC by 30 July 1988. It has been implemented into UK law by the Consumer Protection Act 1987, Part I.

6.02 The directive introduces into every member state a system of strict liability (i.e. without the need to prove negligence) for death, personal injury and damage to private property resulting from defective products put into circulation after the date when the national law came into force (in the UK this is 1 March 1988). A 'product' is very widely defined under the Act (section 1(2)) as:

'any goods or electricity and ... includes a product which is comprised in another product, whether by virtue of being a component part or raw material or otherwise'.

Goods are defined (section 45) as:

'substances, growing crops and things comprised in land by virtue of being attached to it ...'

It is clear therefore, that building products are covered by the Act and at first sight it might appear that buildings themselves and/or parts of buildings such as roofs or foundations are also covered.

6.03 However, by section 46(3) of the Act it is provided that:

'subject to subsection (4) below the performance of any contract by the erection of any building or structure on any land or by carrying out of any other building works shall be treated for the purpose of the Act as a supply of goods in so far as it involves the provision of any goods to any person by means of their incorporation into the building, structure or works'.

6.04 Subsection 4 provides in so far as is relevant:

'References in this Act to supplying goods shall not include references to supplying goods comprised in land where the supply is affected by the creation or disposal of an interest in land.'

In the case, therefore, of a builder building under a contract and who does not own the land on which he builds he may be liable as 'supplier' or 'producer' (see below) in respect of defective products supplied or produced by him and incorporated into the building whether by way of construction, alteration or repair and will not be liable as producer of the defective building itself or of its immovable parts such as foundations.

In the case of a speculative builder however, who builds on his own land and then effects the supply of that building by the creation or disposal of an interest in land (e.g. by sale of the freehold or lease) the Act appears to leave him liable as *producer* of the defective building while exempting him from any liability as supplier of any defective product comprised within the building. It is submitted that that is not the case.

6.05 By section 1(1) of the Act it is provided that the Act must be construed to give effect to the directive.

It is clear from the Recitals and from Article 2 that the directive does not apply to 'immovables' and that buildings and probably parts of buildings fall within that term. It is submitted therefore that when the Act is properly construed to give effect to the directive it must follow that a speculative builder cannot be liable under it as producer of a defective house.

Similarly, neither in Article 3(6) (which renders a supplier of a defective product liable if he fails to identify its producer within a reasonable time) nor anywhere else in the directive is any exemption from liability accorded *to the supplier* where the supply is effected by the creation or disposal of an interest in land. It is submitted therefore that no distinction should be made between the liability of a speculative builder and a contract builder under the Act and indeed it is difficult to see in logic why there should be any.

6.06 The Act places primary liability on the 'producer' of the product who will normally be the manufacturer but may also be the product's importer into the EC where it has been manufactured outside the EC. Secondary liability is placed on the supplier of the goods in question where that supplier fails to identify within a reasonable time the person who sold the goods to him.

It may be a matter of importance therefore to know who in a given case is the 'producer' or 'supplier' of a building product for the purpose of the Act. There is as yet no authority on the matter but the following is put forward as a tentative answer:

1 **Where the building is erected by a speculative builder** The builder alone will be the 'supplier' in the first instance of the products incorporated into the building and may therefore be liable as such under the Act (i.e. where he fails to identify his supplier within a reasonable time). He may also be liable as 'producer' of a product where he has given that product its 'essential characteristics' (see section 1(2)), an example of such a product would be concrete where this is mixed by the contractor, or where he has imported that product into the EC.

2 **When the building is erected under a contract with the building owner** The contract builder's liability as 'producer' and 'supplier' of the building products he incorporates into the building he erects will normally be no different from that of the speculative builder. However, circumstances may arise, whether by express agreement or otherwise, where the contractor acts as agent for the building owner or his architect in the 'production' or 'supply' of the product in question. In that case the building owner or the architect would be liable as 'producer' or 'supplier' under the Act in the same way as the contractor would have been. Such cases outside express contract are, however, likely to be rare. In *Young & Marten Ltd v McManuschilds* [1986] AC 454, HL, it was held that even where a product was specified that could only be purchased from one source, the contractor purchasing it was liable to the building owner for breach of implied warranty of merchantable quality where the product proved to be defective. It was implicit in that decision that the contractor was not acting as the building owner's agent in making the purchase.

6.07 Even where the builder is not acting as the building owner's agent, he may well wish in future to seek an indemnity from the building owner in respect of any liability he may incur under the Act, particularly in respect of any latent defects in products specified by the architect. Similarly, the building owner will no doubt seek an indemnity in respect of such liability from his architect.

6.08 Where the builder has no choice in the product he purchases and where the exercise of reasonable skill and care on his part in the selection of that product is ineffective in ensuring that the product is of merchantable quality (as might well be the case where there is a design defect) it would seem reasonable that ultimate liability under the Act (when this cannot be passed on to the others) should fall on the architect who has chosen the product and who has had the best chance of assessing that product's quality. Such indemnity provisions may well become a common feature of building and architectural service contracts in the future.

7 Safety and health at work

7.01 EC legislation on health and safety affects the construction industry's operation on site, in the design of buildings and civil engineering works and in the use of plant. In the UK existing legislation such as the Health and Safety at Work etc. Act 1974 already meets many of the requirements of the European directives. Additional regulations under the 1974 Act have or will be issued to cover the remaining requirements as they come into force.

7.02 The fundamental directive is the Safety and Health of Workers at Work Directive 89/391/EC which has been implemented in the UK by the Management of Health and Safety at Work Regulations 1992 (SI 1992 No. 2051). The directive sets out the responsibilities of employers and employees for safety and health at work and provides for further directives covering specific areas. Directives made under that framework directive which are of particular relevance to the construction industry are:

1 **Safety and Health for the Workplace Directive 89/654/EC** The directive lays down minimum safety and health requirements relating to the design structure and maintenance of buildings.
2 **Use of Work Equipment Directive 89/655/EC** The directive which has been implemented in the UK by the Provision and Use of Work Equipment Regulations 1992 (SI 1992 No. 2932) requires employers to provide for the safe use and maintenance of 'work equipment' (defined as any machine, apparatus, tool or installation at work) and sets out minimum safety and health requirements relating to training and safe operating procedures.
3 **Use of Personal Protective Equipment Directive 89/656/EC and 89/686/EC** These directives have been implemented in the UK by the Personal Protective Equipment at Work Regulations 1992 (SI 1992 No. 2966) and the Personal Protective Equipment (EC Directive) Regulations 1992 (SI 1992 No. 3139). They set out minimum health and safety requirements for the use by workers of PPE in the workplace and set minimum standards designed to ensure the health and safety of users of PPE.
4 **Mobile Machinery and Lifting Equipment Directive 91/368/EC** The directive which was required to be in force by 1 January 1993 extends the scope of the Machinery Directive 89/392/EC laying down essential safety requirements for mobile machinery and lifting equipment such as dumpers and cranes used on construction sites. Both directives have been implemented in the UK by SI 1992 No. 2932 referred to above.
5 **The Construction Sites Directive 92/57/EC** The directive lays down minimum safety and health requirements for temporary or mobile construction sites (defined as any construction site at which building or civil engineering works are carried out). It places particular responsibilities on 'project supervisors' who are 'any person responsible for the design and/or execution and/or supervision of the execution of a project acting on behalf of a client' (Article 2(d)) and would therefore include architects. Those responsibilities include:
   (a) Appointing one or more safety coordinators for safety and health matters for any construction site on which more than one contractor is present (Article 3(1)). The proper carrying out of the coordinators' duties is the responsibility of the project supervisor.
   (b) Ensuring that prior to the setting up of a construction site a 'safety and health plan' is drawn up in accordance with requirements set out in the directive (Article 3(2)).
   (c) In the case of construction sites on which work is scheduled to last longer than 30 working days and on which more than 20 workers are occupied simultaneously or on which the volume of work is scheduled to exceed 500 person days, communicating a 'prior notice' drawn up in accordance with the directive, to the competent authority (Article 3(3)).

(d) Taking account of the general principles of prevention concerning safety and health contained in directive 89/391/EC (above) during the various stages of designing and preparing the project, in particular:

(i) When architectural technical and/or organizational aspects are being decided, in order to plan the various items or stages of work which are to take place simultaneously or in succession.

(ii) When estimating the period required for completing such work or work stages. Account must also be taken each time this appears necessary of all safety and health plans drawn up or adjusted in accordance with requirements of the directive (Article 4).

The directive has been implemented in the UK by the Construction (Design and Management) Regulations 1994 (SI 1994 No. 3140).

The practical ramifications for architects of these directives are discussed in Chapter 28.

28

Health and safety law affecting architects

RICHARD DYTON

1 Introduction

1.01 Health and Safety is a major matter of debate between architects, employers and contractors. The most significant health and safety legislation ever to affect the construction industry was implemented by the Construction Design and Management (CDM) Regulations 1994, and came into effect on the 1 January 1996 (amended with effect from 2 October 2000). The legislation is complex and gives rise to additional costs in compliance.

The introduction of the CDM legislation saw a string of prosecutions by the Health and Safety Executive (which is the enforcement arm of the Health and Safety Commission) together with the publication of formal amendments to the standard forms of contract by the Joint Contracts Tribunal (JCT) and the Institution of Civil Engineers (ICE). This gave meat to the bones of the regulations by showing the type of incident that would be prosecuted and the effect of health and safety issues on the normal contractual relationship. In terms of the prosecutions, the Health and Safety Executive followed the spirit of the legislation and focused upon the 'client' as target, but at the same time held the designer responsible, in some cases, for failing to warn the client adequately of his responsibilities. The case law is considered later in the chapter and it highlights the increasing importance of architects being familiar with and adhering to health and safety legislation. In terms of the amendments to the standard forms of contract, these have increased the grounds for extensions of time and loss and expense for the contractor arising from the performance of the office-holders for health and safety purposes: the planning supervisor and the principal contractor.

Also of significance are the new Control of Asbestos at Work (CAW) Regulations (2002). The majority of the provisions in these Regulations were implemented in 2002 and the remaining provisions will have been implemented by the end of 2004. One of the, as yet unimplemented, provisions is considered to be so significant that an Approved Code of Practice (ACoP) has already been published about it. This provision imposes obligations on those who are in control of 'non-domestic premises'.

The scope of this chapter is to consider the structure of the existing legislation and, more importantly, to provide a practical guide to the obligations of the architect under the CDM Regulations in the context of the various stages within the project plan. The architect's existing and future obligations under the new CAW Regulations will also be explained. This should enable architects to advise clients how to minimize their exposure and so avoid prosecution.

2 Existing health and safety position

The Health and Safety at Work Act 1974

2.01 The Health and Safety at Work Act 1974 (HSW Act) enacted a system to replace progressively the older law which had grown up

piecemeal and which addressed only certain types of workplaces or processes (such as under the Factories Act 1961 and the Offices, Shops and Railway Premises Act 1963). The old system had left other workplaces uncovered by the legislation and the HSW Act provided the framework for a system of regulations applying generally to all workplaces, employers and employees. It also extended to many self-employed persons and to others such as manufacturers, designers and importers of articles to be used at work. Examples of the regulations which were brought in under the new policy were regulations covering the protection of eyes (Protection of Eyes Regulations 1974), noise (Noise at Work Regulations 1989), the use of lead (Control of Lead at Work Regulations 1980), the use of asbestos (Control of Asbestos at Work Regulations 1987), the control of industrial major hazards (Control of Industrial Major Accident Hazard Regulations 1984), and the control of substances hazardous to health (Control of Substances Hazardous to Health Regulations 1988). Many of these original regulations have now either been revoked or amended and other regulations exist in their place. The existing regulations are considered in more detail below.

Structure of the Act

2.02 The structure of the HSW Act is that sections 2–4 and 6 place general duties on employers, the self-employed, persons otherwise in control of premises and designers, manufacturers, importers or suppliers of articles for use at work. The duties are normally qualified by the phrase 'reasonably practicable'. Section 6 refers to the duties of designers together with those who manufacture and import or supply an article for use at work. The general obligation is:

> 'To ensure, so far as is reasonably practicable, that the article is so designed and constructed that it will be safe and without risks to health at all times when it is being set, used, cleaned or maintained by person at work'.

The structure of the HSW Act is, therefore, divided into general obligations under the Act itself and more specific obligations under the existing body of regulations.

Buildings and construction sites

2.03 The Health and Safety Executive (HSE) has, in a number of case applied the general obligation in relation to buildings and construction sites. Prosecutions of high-profile clients since the introduction of the CDM Regulations has completed the principle together with the imprisonment of one demolition contractor for flagrantly disregarding the asbestos regulations.

Liability under the Act and Regulations

2.04 Breaches of the Act or of the Regulations give rise to criminal liabilities which may lead to sentences of unlimited fines and/or a maximum term of imprisonment not exceeding two years. The policy of the Health and Safety Executive in enforcing the Regulations has been to prosecute and fine an organization rather than an individual, although there is nothing in law to prevent an individual being prosecuted and, ultimately, imprisoned. Codes of practice are regularly issued with the relevant Regulations, and these are used to flesh out the Regulations concerned. Breach of the codes is not, in itself, breach of the Regulations but the codes are admissible in criminal and, indeed, in civil proceedings to determine whether or not there has been a breach of the Regulations. Compliance with the relevant code raises the (rebuttable) presumption that the Regulations themselves have been complied with.

In the context of civil liability, there are two potential limbs: first, the tort of breach of statutory duty which is a 'strict' liability in the sense that it is not qualified by what is reasonable in the context of the profession at large (although the statutory duties in the Regulations themselves are usually qualified by statements such as 'so far as is reasonably practicable') and, second, the tort of negligence which arises from common standards becoming established in the profession of which the reasonable architect is deemed to have knowledge and breach of which thereby renders the architect liable.

Breach of the provisions of the Act does not itself give rise to a civil action for breach of statutory duty. However, if there is a breach of the Regulations this may enable a claimant to cite the breach as a basis for a civil claim depending upon whether the specific Regulations allow such a claim and whether the plain-tiff's interest is intended to be protected by the Regulations. Under the CDM Regulations, for example, breach of Regulation 10 which provides that the construction phase of any project cannot commence until a health and safety plan has been prepared, gives rise to civil liability without the need to prove negligence or breach of contract. From 27 October 2003, breach of the Management of Health and Safety at Work Regulations 1999 may also give rise to civil liability.

Inevitably, the influence of the Regulations will affect the law of negligence in setting specific legal standards in the context of health and safety. A failure to meet those standards may represent a breach of duty in negligence, even if the matter in question is not specifically covered by the Regulations. Therefore, liability is not restricted merely to claims based upon breach of statutory duty but also, indirectly, in the tort of negligence. In addition, the requirement for employers to carry out risk assessments is likely to be of significance when considering questions of foreseeability at common law.

Relevant Regulations

2.05 There are a large number of health and safety Regulations in addition to the CDM and CAW Regulations which, while not necessarily specific to the construction industry, affect the work of architects. Many of these Regulations apply to the duties of employers in the workplace. As such, the architect must have a general knowledge of these when designing such workplaces in order to avoid risks to the health of employees and generally to allow them to be safe. These Regulations are, briefly, as follows.

The Asbestos Prohibitions Regulations 1992 (implemented 1 January 1993)

2.06 These regulations prohibit the importation into the UK and the spraying of amphobole asbestos. They prohibit the supply and use of chrysotile asbestos. The regulations also prohibit the supply and use of products to which amphibole asbestos has intentionally been added. It is presumed that amphobole asbestos has been 'intentionally added' where the substance occurs in a product and is not a naturally occurring impurity. (See also paragraph 2.16 below).

The Workplace (Health, Safety and Welfare) Regulations 1992

2.07 These Regulations extend the duties of employers into areas not previously the subject of specific statutory provisions such as hospitals, schools, universities, hotels and court houses. The Regulations require that the workplace, equipment, devices and system shall be maintained in an efficient state, in efficient working order and in good repair. Specifically, the Regulations specify suitable provision for the ventilation, temperature, lighting, cleanliness and removal of waste materials, sufficient working area and suitable work station provision. There are a number of provisions relating to the condition of floors, windows, skylights, doors, gates, escalators, sanitary conveniences and washing facilities. Where the workplace is a building, the regulations now require the workplace to be appropriately stable & solid for the use it is to be put to. See Chapter 21. In the 2001 Court of Appeal case, *Parker v PFC Flooring Supplies Ltd*, the employer was held to have breached regulation 13(4) of these Regulations which gave rise to strict liability. Regulation 13(4) requires an employer to clearly indicate any area where there is a risk of a person falling any distance likely to cause personal injury. In this case the employee had fallen through a skylight in a roof and suffered spinal injuries leading to paralysis. The employer had not given an appropriate warning to his employee that he should not pursue access to the roof where it was reasonable and necessary to have given such a warning. This case highlights how thorough an employer must be in complying with Health and Safety Regulations. The duty to warn clearly extends to what most people would consider to be, entirely obvious risks.

The Personal Protective Equipment at Work Regulations 1992

2.08 The employer's obligations relate to the suitability of protective clothing to be worn by employees. In June 2003 in the case of *Fytche v Wincanton Logistics PLC*, the court held that regulation 7(1) of these Regulations imposed an absolute duty on employers to make sure protective equipment is kept in good condition. However, that duty only applied to risks against which the equipment was supposed to protect the employee. In this case, steel toe-capped boots were provided to the employee to protect his feet from falling objects. A tiny hole in the boots caused the employee to sustain frostbite but the employer was not liable for this injury as the boots were not intended to protect the employee from that type of harm.

The Manual Handling Operations Regulations 1992

2.09 This imposes obligations on an employer to avoid a manual handling operation where there is a risk of injury from that manual handling operation. The employer's duty is to take steps to reduce the risk of injury to the lowest level reasonably practicable. Regulation 4(1)(b) imposes the requirement to reduce the risk of injury to the lowest level practicable. It also requires an employer to make an assessment of the manual handling to be carried out and provide information to the employee as to the type of load to be lifted. A recent case held that these three requirements should not be read conjunctively so that breach of any of them could be enough to make the employer liable (*Swain v Denso Marston* [2000]). A further case stated that, in assessing whether a task involved a risk of injury and in assessing whether it was 'reasonably practicable' for an employer to avoid his employees being subjected to that risk, it was necessary to look at the particular activity in context (*Koonjul v Thameslink Healthcare Services NHS Trust*).

In determining whether the manual handling operations involve a risk of injury and in determining appropriate steps to reduce the risk, regard must be had to such things as the employee's suitability to the tasks he is carrying out, the employee's clothing, the results of any risk assessment that has been carried out under the

Management of Health and Safety at Work Regulations 1999 and the employee's knowledge and training.

The importance of an employer giving careful consideration to the type of tasks it will be asking its employees to carry out is clear. It is not enough to consider the tasks in their own right. The employer will have to address the individual employee's suitability to a task which is an onerous burden for the employer.

The Health and Safety (Display Screen Equipment) Regulations 1992

2.10 The employer must ensure that all display screen equipment which may be used for the purposes of the employer business meets the requirements set out in the Regulations. The employer is under an obligation to make an assessment of the relevant risks to health and safety from the operation and reduce the risks to the 'lowest extent reasonably practicable'. It requires employers to plan the activities of their 'users' so that there are periodic interruptions in their work on the display screen equipment. There must be appropriate eye and eyesight tests for the employees.

The Construction (Health, Safety and Welfare) Regulations 1996

2.11 The Regulations primarily affect contractors, as employers of the workforce. There are provisions relating to rail guards to protect the edges of falls of 2 m and the courts have shown that they are willing to enforce this provision. In the recent case of *Anthony Peter Nixon v Chanceoption Developments Ltd* [2002] the employer was held to be liable for injuries caused to an employee where there was evidence that the employer had breached these regulations. In this case an employee had fallen from scaffolding which did not have a guard rail despite there being a drop of more than seven feet.

In the case of *Gillespie v McFadden McManus Construction Ltd* [2003] the court held that it was not up to the employee to tell his employers that they were not complying with their duty under the regulations (and so were putting the employee in a dangerous position). Thus, there was no contributory negligence and the employee was awarded a large sum in damages. There are also important provisions that relate to transport and fire:

- Transport – every construction site should be organized so that pedestrians and vehicles can move safely without risk to health.
- Fire – provisions operate to prevent injury from fire, explosion, flood or substances likely to cause asphyxiation. Emergency exits must be provided to allow evacuation and these must be kept clear.

These regulations are currently under review by the HSE.

The Provision and Use of Work Equipment Regulations 1998

2.12 Work equipment is defined broadly to include anything from a pair of scissors to a steel rolling mill. There is an obligation on the employer and (with the revised Regulations) on others having 'control' of work equipment to ensure that work equipment is used only for the operations for which and under conditions for which it is suitable. If the equipment has a health risk, the employer (or relevant person) must restrict its use and maintenance to specific persons.

The Lifting Operations and Lifting Equipment Regulations 1998

2.13 The Regulations impose duties on employers, self employed persons and certain people having control of lifting equipment to ensure that the equipment is strong, stable, positioned and installed correctly, examined, inspected, marked and organized and in respect of which records are held.

2.14 The client, who may also be an employer, will rely upon the architect to advise him whether and what assessments are required

and the hazards which must be identified in the workplace. He will also rely upon the architect to advise him how to avoid any such hazards and thereby to avoid any potential liability under the Regulations. If the client is a developer who has only a short-term interest in the building, then collateral warranties may be granted to a purchaser or tenant who is to occupy the building or a unit of the building. If the purchaser or tenant is an employer and is found subsequently to be in breach of the regulations it is arguable that unless the architect has, at least, advised on compliance with the regulations and how best to design in order to ensure compliance, then an indemnity and/or damages could be sought. Such an indemnity could be in respect of the defence costs associated with a criminal prosecution or in respect of compensation paid out to employees.

The Management of Health and Safety at Work Regulations 1999

2.15 The basic obligation under these regulations requires employers to carry out a 'suitable and sufficient' assessment of the risks to the health and safety of his employees which they are exposed to whilst at work. The assessment must also consider the risks to the health and safety of other people not in his employment but arising out of his business. The purpose of the assessment is to identify measures the employer needs to take to comply with law. From 27 October 2003 these regulations will also enable employees to bring civil claims against their employers where they are in breach of duties imposed by these regulations. It will remain the case that it is not possible for non-employees to bring such civil claims. This right to bring civil claims will mean that a breach of the regulations by architects, as employers, can give rise to civil liability without the need to prove negligence or even a breach of contract.

The Control of Asbestos at Work Regulations 2002 (implemented 21 November 2002 – NB see exceptions to this below)

2.16 These regulations impose requirements on employers for the protection of their employees who might be exposed to asbestos at work and other people who might be affected by such work. The employer and the architect must be fully aware of the obligations these regulations impose. Even if the employer is aware of his responsibilities he may turn to the architect for advice on the practical implications of the regulations and how they can be complied with.

The regulations have been implemented with the exception of the regulation that imposes a duty to manage asbestos in non-domestic premises and the regulation which relates to the criteria for analysing materials that may contain asbestos. The former is implemented on 21 May 2004 and the latter on 21 November 2004.

The duty to manage asbestos in non-domestic premises will be of considerable significance in construction and building maintenance. It goes further than the duty imposed by the CDM Regulations (which requires the provision of information to the planning supervisor during the course of a project so that the presence of asbestos can be taken into account). The new regulation will require those people having control of non-domestic premises ('the dutyholders') to make an assessment as to whether asbestos is likely to be present. The circumstances in which an architect will fall within the definition of dutyholder is not clear. An architect will have 'control of non-domestic premises' in far more limited circumstances than, for example, the employer. An architect will be a dutyholder in respect of the premises he operates from if there is, 'by virtue of a contract or tenancy, an obligation of any extent in relation to the maintenance or repair' of the premises. It is advisable for an architect to expressly avoid this role where possible.

The dutyholder must work from the presumption that there is asbestos present, unless there is strong evidence to suggest the contrary. He must assess the risk and put together a plan to manage the risk that sets out the condition of the asbestos and how it is to be maintained. Anyone potentially at risk must be given access to the information on the condition and location of the asbestos. A written record of the location and condition of the asbestos must also be made and kept up to date. This will clearly impact upon an architect (if he has been deemed to be a dutyholder) at the initial stages of planning a project as well as throughout the construction phase.

An ACoP called 'The Management of Asbestos in Non-Domestic Premises' has already been published which will come into effect on 21 May 2004 (the same date that the regulation is implemented). The code has been published in advance to enable those who will have obligations under the new regulation to familiarize themselves with the obligations it will impose and begin putting measures in place that ensure they are complying with the regulation when it comes into effect. The ACoP provides practical guidance on the effect of the regulation and how to comply with it. As with other ACoPs, it will not be legally binding but, compliance with it raises the (rebuttable) presumption that the regulations have been complied with.

The Health and Safety Executive (HSE) has published other guidance documents that relate to the regulations (e. g. a regulatory impact assessment) and they can be obtained directly from the HSE.

Of particular relevance to architects are the regulations that are already in effect. These impose general obligations on employers in relation to asbestos. Before an employer can carry out work which may expose his employees to asbestos he must take a number of steps. The type of asbestos present must be identified; a detailed risk assessment must be carried out, and regularly reviewed, which records the risk to the health of his employees that exposure to asbestos will entail; a written plan of any work to be undertaken and how it is to be undertaken must be prepared. The relevant authority must be notified of the proposed works including brief details of it; and, any employees who are likely to be exposed to asbestos or who will supervise such employees must receive training.

In general, an employer must attempt to prevent the exposure of his employees to asbestos and, if that is not possible, employ protective methods such as the use of control measures and protective clothing so that exposure is minimized. An employer must have arrangements in place to deal with accidents, incidents and emergencies. There are other ongoing requirements that relate to matters such as maintaining the cleanliness of the premises, preventing the spread of asbestos, monitoring the asbestos fibres in the air and keeping health records for every employee.

3 Construction (Design and Management) Regulations (CDM)

Background

3.01 The impetus for the CDM Regulations was the increasing high level of fatal and non-fatal injuries to those working in the construction industry. Between 1 April 2001 and 31 March 2002 there were 85 fatal injuries in the U.K. In 1989 and 1990 the European Council of Ministers agreed to a Framework Directive on health and safety together with five other directives. These are described in Section 7 of Chapter 27. The Temporary or Mobile Construction Sites Directive is a further directive under the Framework Directive and its aim is to limit accidents and injuries to construction workers. Construction sites were specifically excluded from the scope of the Workplace Directive and, hence, this separate measure covers a wide range of construction activities and requires separate implementing legislation in the UK.

Effect of the Regulations

3.02 The implementing legislation takes the form of the CDM Regulations, which became effective on 31 March 1995 (amended with effect from 2 October 2000). The CDM Regulations were made under the authority of the Health and Safety at Work Act 1974. Subject to very few exceptions, the regulations relate to all aspects of construction and affect all those concerned in the construction process. Projects excluded from the regulations for Planning Supervisors (not designers) are:

1 Projects which are not expected to employ more than 5 persons on site at any one time;

2 Projects which will be no longer than 30 days or will involve no more than 500 person days of construction work, and
3 Minor works in premises normally inspected by a local authority.

The CDM Regulations dramatically changed the previous allocations of responsibility for health and safety between contractors, clients and consultants. No longer is the contractor solely responsible for health and safety on site. The Regulations create two new roles within construction projects, namely the planning supervisor and the principal contractor. They also impose specific obligations on designers to consider matters of safety in the execution of their designs and in the subsequent maintenance of the completed structure in subsequent years. The Amended Regulations have widened the duties imposed on designers. The term 'designer' has been considered in the courts and has been refined by the revised regulations. Consequently, it is now more important than ever for architects to know and understand the regulations and what compliance entails. The regulations provide for notification of construction projects to the Health and Safety Executive together with a detailed consideration of all variations and financial considerations on safety throughout the duration of the project.

The regulations contain transitional provisions all of which have now passed. For example, if the construction phase of a project started before April 1995, there was no requirement for the client to appoint a planning supervisor or principal contractor until 1 January 1996. Supplementing the amended regulations is a Revised Approved Code of Practice called 'Managing Health and Safety in Construction'. The revised ACoP is published by the HSE and it gives practical examples of how the regulations are intended to bite. Parts of the ACoP (the parts in bold type) have special legal status. If an architect is prosecuted for breaching health and safety law and it is proved that he has not complied with the parts of the ACoP with the special status, then he will be held to be at fault unless he can show compliance with the law in some other way. Compliance with the ACoP effectively gives rise to a presumption of compliance with the law.

In order to assess the effect of the revised regulations and ACoP upon architects, it is simpler to consider the impact they have at the various stages in a normal project plan.

Feasibility/outline proposals

3.03 At the feasibility stage the client has an obligation to appoint a planning supervisor who has responsibility for the health and safety aspects of the planning phase. The planning supervisor must prepare a health and safety plan setting out the overall arrangements for the safe operation of the project, monitor the health and safety aspects of the design, advise the client on the adequacy of resource provision for the project, verify that changes to the proposals contained in the tender by the principal contractor take account of health and safety matters and prepare a health and safety file (basically a maintenance manual with health and safety matters specifically noted). It is expected that the lead designer would normally be appointed by the client as the planning supervisor in the majority of projects. He must notify the Health and Safety Executive immediately following his appointment. The effect on the architect at the feasibility stage is therefore twofold: to advise the client of his health and safety responsibilities (and specifically his obligation to appoint a planning supervisor) and to assess and report to the client on the additional costs which the health and safety obligations will involve.

Scheme and Detailed Design

3.04 The CDM Regulations have two broad effects on the architect at this stage: the imposition of specific design obligations in relation to the safety of those who will be building, maintaining or repairing the structure; and the responsibility (if appointed) of the role of planning supervisor for a range of health and safety functions.

Designer

3.05 The definition of 'designer' has been considered by the courts and consequently refined by the amended regulations. In the case of *R v Wurth* [2000] it was determined that the regulation which imposes requirements on designers only applied to the actual preparation of designs. To own, arrange to have prepared, or to approve a design did not amount to having 'prepared a design'. As a result of this case the regulations were amended to ensure that in future 'designer' will include a designer's employee or other person who prepares a design for him. The definition will not, however, extend to an employer who supplies his employee to a designer. The amendment means that an architect needs to carefully monitor and supervise those people in his employ who are carrying out design work as he will be held responsible for their errors.

The revised ACoP contains twice as many pages of guidance on the regulation which relates to designers. It clarifies the roles and responsibilities of designers and emphasizes the importance of managing health and safety for the life of the project and beyond. It also includes key areas of the Management of Health and Safety at Work Regulations 1999 for ease of reference. Architects must also bear in mind that if they sub-contract design work they also have a duty under regulations 8 and 9 as to the competence of such sub-contractors. Architects should keep a copy of the ACoP close at hand because, as well as general guidance, it includes specific practical examples which will be of considerable assistance.

The designer's obligation is basically to design in such a way as to prevent construction workers being exposed to risks to their health and safety. What this means in practice is not entirely clear, since construction is inherently risky with hazards arising from a large number of potential sources, including feature of design, sequencing, co-ordination, methods of work, weather and lack of operative discipline or training. However, it is clear that designers will be under a duty to design in such a way as to reduce hazards by adhering to good practice (especially that described in the Codes of Practice) taking into account the normal health and safety considerations in relation to hazards identified in current trade literature, and identifying hazards that are exceptional in the circumstances of the particular project and sequencing operations.

Risk analyses and hazard management are already conducted by those responsible for problematic designs (particularly in civil engineering projects) such as large atria, deep excavations or box girder bridges. However, since there are now a large number of construction activities which will be covered ranging from renovations and repair to demolition, and from excavation to maintenance, decoration and cleaning work, the impact on the UK architect is substantial.

Since the designer must integrate his designs with those of specialist sub-contractors, he must give much greater thought to ways of eliminating, reducing or at least controlling hazards, not just in the original design but also if and when variations are instructed during the contract. Specific examples are how heavy loads can be installed (e.g. beams in section) so as to avoid manual handling by construction workers of excessive loads. Other examples which raise obvious problems relate to the duty to design to avoid health and safety problems for those who maintain or clean the structure. Thus, the cleaning of windows or glass atria must be considered at the design stage, as must also the re-pointing of brickwork and the replacement of roof linings in years to come.

Planning supervisor

3.06 Whether or not the architect is appointed as the planning supervisor, he must be aware of this role and, if he is not so appointed, must work closely with the planning supervisor to enable him to carry out his various duties. The first prosecution under the CDM Regulations (in 1996) was of an architectural practice, Taylor Young, who were convicted for failing to advise the client that a planning supervisor needed to be appointed. Briefly, the duties of a planning supervisor at this stage are as follows:

1   Ensuring that designers have complied with their design obligations in relation to health and safety issues. This means a prompting and coordinating duty to ensure that the designs of the entire professional team have considered all the health and safety angles.
2   Preparing a health and safety plan to be included in the tender documentation. The Health and Safety Executive have stated their intention to publish a model plan for this purpose and this should enable the contractor to price the procedures to deal with the identified hazards. The plan should specify the approach to the management of health and safety which the contractors should adopt, identify any potential hazards, and require the work to be carried out to recognized standards.
3   Compiling a health and safety file similar to but in much greater detail than the Maintenance Manual, and focusing particularly on health and safety aspects of materials used together with design implications that will affect those who will be maintaining and cleaning the structure.

Production information and tender action

3.07 The revised ACoP has widened the designer's duty to advise the employer of his health and safety obligations. The designer must alert the employer to the first three sections of the ACoP and to the HSE leaflet called 'Having Construction Work Done? Duties of Clients under the Construction (Design and Management) Regulations 1994'.

The architect will have a duty to check that the health and safety plan is included in the tender documentation. In the event that the architect is also appointed as the planning supervisor for the project, then these duties will be multiplied. Initially the planning supervisor prepares a health and safety plan and makes it available for inclusion in the tender documents. On return of the tender documents the planning supervisor checks that the contract period allows sufficient time for compliance with the health and safety measures. Thereafter, in this role (if he is so appointed), the architect has a duty to assess differences between tenders in relation to the health and safety plan, advise the client on the adequacy of time and money allocated to health and safety aspects, advise the client to appoint a principal contractor, prepare a health and safety file for each structure, and give notice of the project prior to construction to the Health and Safety Executive.

In any tender action, even if not appointed as the planning supervisor, the architect will have a duty to consider a contractor's health and safety record and advise the client accordingly. The architect will be involved in contractor pre-selection with one criterion being health and safety competence. Contractors will be requested to explain and justify their responses to health and safety requirements. A case on this particular area has highlighted the potential impact of the regulations. *General Building & Maintenance v Greenwich Borough Council* The Times 9 March 1993. This case concerns public sector work where Greenwich Borough Council invited tenders for repair and maintenance work on a stock of 34 000 dwellings. The estimated annual value of the contract was £12 million. The EC Public Procurement Regime therefore applied and when the local housing authority considered the 104 applications from contractors, it took into account their health and safety records as one of the factors used to shortlist those to be invited to tender. One of the contractors who was rejected, General Building and Maintenance, alleged that the housing authority was in breach of the Public Procurement Rules in excluding them since there was no specific wording which allowed the authority to consider and exclude a contractor on the basis of its health and safety record. The judge, however, applied a purposive interpretation to the Rules and held that since the Treaty of Rome expressly stated the need to promote improved working conditions and prevent occupational accidents and diseases, it would be 'incomprehensible' to conclude that consideration of health and safety issues was forbidden by the Rules.

In the light of this case, UK architects should be aware of the high priority given to health and safety issues by public sector clients and, so it appears, by the courts as well.

It is the duty of the client to appoint a *competent* principal contractor. The client will rely largely upon his professional adviser in this respect, and if no enquiries are made as to the health and safety record, it may constitute breach of the Regulations. In addition, the client must ensure that there are adequate resources in terms of time and financial provision to give effect to health and safety measures. Architects must carefully consider these points when assessing tender documents before recommending merely the lowest tender bid. The specific duties of the principal contractor are to prepare the initial execution stage of the health and safety plan and to draw in and coordinate the Health and Safety Plans of sub-contractors. It is also responsible for the execution of the project, controlling access and verifying the compliance of sub-contractors.

Operations on site and completion

3.08 If the roles of planning supervisor and architect are to be performed by the same person or firm (as is likely in the majority of cases) it is not difficult to conclude that the level of supervision required of the architect will be affected by his knowledge of the level of experience of the contractor and the risks and hazards identified in the health and safety plan. Thus, for instance, even if an experienced contractor is engaged it could be argued that the architect must be present on site to supervise at times of identified hazard. Failure to supervise at these times may constitute breach of appointment or, worse, may bring criminal sanctions following prosecution by the Health and Safety Executive. The Regulations do not, however, require the architect to dictate construction methods or to exercise a health and safety supervisory function over contractors as they carry out construction work. This is a common misconception and is an unfortunate result of the use of the title 'planning supervisor'. Thus, it is not intended that designers, for instance, should be required to prepare method statements or otherwise intrude into the contractor's domain.

Nevertheless, given that the nature of the architect's normal inspection duty and duty to warn of health and safety problems is dependent upon the circumstances of each project, the laying down of specific obligations by the Regulations is bound to have an effect upon that duty.

If a variation is requested, the architect's duty again is affected since, in relation to health and safety, the architect's role as designer means that he must consider the implications of variations and inform the planning supervisor of any impact on health and safety. If the architect is appointed as the planning supervisor for the project then he must discuss with the principal contractor as to how the variation could affect the health and safety plan and he must also advise the client on the adequacy of revised sums and time allowed to give effect to health and safety measures.

4 Summary and practical considerations

4.01 As has already been indicated, there are three principal areas of potential liability for the architect in failing to comply with obligations relating to health and safety:

1 Criminal prosecution with unlimited fines and/or a maximum of two years' imprisonment
2 Civil action based on breach of statutory duty (in limited circumstances) or based upon the tort of negligence by injured workers and
3 Contractual claims where Regulations are incorporated into the appointment or referred to in a collateral warranty.

The following procedures should be considered by architects in order to take into account the potential liabilities in the following ways:

1 Seek to acquire the necessary information and training by way of professional courses and by absorbing the limited literature on the subject. In this respect the Health and Safety Executive have issued a number of publications, for example, *Designing for Health and Safety in Construction* written from the designer's standpoint particularly for this purpose. This was published prior to the amendment of the CDM Regulations, and so, it is necessary to bear in mind that, although still useful, the document is not fully up-to-date. The revised ACoP is likely to be the most useful and up-to-date guidance document available to architects. Regular guidance notes are also published.
2 Review design management procedures. At the end of concept and scheme design, during detailed design and immediately before tender documents are prepared, architects are specifically building in 'breaks' to review formally and systematically whether health and safety matters have been considered as part of the design to reduce or control hazards. Those firms who are quality assured have less difficulty in introducing these reviews, since they would normally be part of QA system which would allow them to trace records to confirm that the review has been carried out.
3 Liaise with professional indemnity insurers. Liability both as a designer and planning supervisor (if this role were to be accepted) will be affected by the Regulations and so architects have found it necessary to check with their insurers whether their new potential liability would be covered. Generally, (although every policy is subject to its own terms and conditions) insurers have confirmed that the liability would be insured provided the architect does not accept any general duty above that of reasonable skill and care and diligence. It seems unlikely that any criminal penalty received by an architect would be covered by insurance, although the defence costs of the architect may be covered in some cases, either in the general wording, or by way of specific endorsement.
4 If the role of planning supervisor is to be adopted by the architect (and it appears that many firms have already conceded this principle since it will bring additional fee income) it is essential that the role be limited to one of *coordinating* all the relevant designers' designs rather than *ensuring* that each design will not expose workers to risks to their health and safety.
5 Architects should avoid incorporating, without qualification, the Regulations or the Codes of Practice into their appointment. The consequence of this would be that any breach of the Regulations or Code would incur contractual claims for damages with the breach forming the ground for the action. If incorporation becomes unavoidable then any duty to comply with the Regulations or Code should be qualified by 'reasonable skill and care'. This is particularly important if collateral warranties are to be issued to funds, tenants or purchasers who may seek to claim an indemnity from the architect if held liable for damages in respect of personal injury to workers. These types of claims may well be limited by the extent to which such damage could have been reasonably foreseeable at the time of entering into the warranty.
6 If architects are to provide indicative designs for temporary works, where they foresee problems, then those designs should only comprise ideas to be adopted, if appropriate, by a contractor who is then responsible for their sufficiency and implementation. In addition, if site visits result in an architect noting serious infringements of the Regulations or Code then any report to the principal contractor or ultimately the Health and Safety Executive must be qualified to the extent that such professional inspections do not attract liability which is properly the responsibility of others. This should be recorded in correspondence at the time.
7 It should be borne in mind that the CDM and the Construction (Health, Safety & Welfare) Regulations 1996 are currently under review by the HSE.
8 The Government and Health and Safety Commission's (HSC) has set national targets for improving health and safety performance generally over the next eight years. Of relevance to architects and the construction industry in general will be its targets relating to the reduction of falls from height. Specifically in relation to the construction industry, the HSC has set targets

relating to the reduction of fatal and major injuries and work-related ill health. It recognizes the need to 'radically' improve the health and safety performance in the industry.

9 Careful consideration should also be given to the Control of Asbestos at Work Regulations 2002 and its ACoP. Despite the fact that regulation 4 of these regulations is not due to be implemented until May 2004, preparatory steps need to be taken and review of current operating procedures should be undertaken now to ensure compliance is possible by May.

5 Health and safety law in Scotland*

5.01 The Health and Safety at Work Act 1974, and the aforementioned regulations are all applicable to Scotland. Part III of the Health and Safety at Work Act 1974 amends the Building Scotland Act 1959. Although there is provision in very rare circumstances for private prosecution, with these exceptions all prosecutions in Scotland are undertaken by the Crown. In health and safety prosecutions the Crown is advised by the Health and Safety Executive. The distinction between the Crown and the Health and Safety Executive in Scotland was emphasized in the recent case of *HM Advocate v Shell UK Limited* [2003] *SLT p1296*. The Health and Safety Executive had carried out investigations in January 2001 and on 19th December informed the Respondents by letter that a report had been sent to the Procurator Fiscal. The Respondents were not notified that they were to be prosecuted until the indictment containing the allegation was served on 6th March 2003. The question before the High Court of Justiciary was whether there had been unreasonable delay in commencing proceedings and whether the Respondents' rights in terms of Article 6(1) of the European Convention on Human Rights had been breached thereby. The Respondents argued that the appropriate starting point of the period which falls to be considered was the serving of the Executive's letter. By way of obiter dicta the Court stated that, 'the Executive of Session and for the moment to the House of Lords'. As a result of the separate appellate structure occasionally the interpretation of substantive law can be different until matters are finally resolved by the supreme appellate forum.

On occasions if spoken to be an authoritative expert witness the High Court will be prepared to accept as evidence codes of practice not approved in terms of Section 16 of the Health and Safety at Work Act 1974. In February 1996, the High Court on Appeal held that a sheriff was right to give effect to the British Standard Code of Practice of the Safe Use of Cranes after it had been spoken to by an inspector in the context of a criminal prosecution following the death of an employee at work.

5.02 In the context of civil liability many Regulations create statutory delicts and also assist in raising standards in industry; even regulations which do not create such statutory delicts by raising standards help create a common law delict if said standards are not reached. Scottish Courts have been happy to consider the corresponding European Directive but have been cautious about giving weight to guidance issued by the Health and Safety Executive.

* This section was written by Peter Grant Hutchinson.

6 Health and safety law in Northern Ireland

6.01 The substance of the law in Northern Ireland is the same as that in the rest of the United Kingdom but the relevant legislation is different. A table of the principal equivalents is set out below:

The Health and Safety at Work Act 1974	The Health and Safety at Work (NI) Order 1978 SI 1978/1039
Construction (Design and Management) Regulations 1994	Construction (Design and Management) Regulations (NI) 1995 (1995/209) Into operation: 26 June 1995. Amended with effect from 3 May 2001
Management and Health and Safety at Work Regulations 1999	Management of Health and Safety at Work Regulations (NI) 2000 (2000/3) Into operation: 1 February 2001
Workplace (Health, Safety and Welfare) Regulations 1992	Workplace (Health, Safety and Welfare) Regulations (NI) 1993 (1993/37) Into operation: 8 March 1993 but postponed until 1 January 1996 for existing workplaces
Provision and Use of Work Equipment Regulations 1998	Provision and Use of Work Equipment Regulation (NI) 1999 Into operation: 20 September 1999
Personal Protective Equipment at Work Regulations 1992	Provision and Use of Work Equipment Regulation (NI) 1993 Into operation: 22 February 1993
Manual Handling Operations Regulations 1992	Manual Handling Operations Regulations (NI) 1992 Into operation: 8 January 1993
Health and Safety (Display Screen Equipment) Regulations 1992	Health and Safety (Display Screen Equipment) Regulations (NI) 1992 Into operation: 1 January 1993
Construction (Health, Safety and Welfare Regulations 1996	Construction (Health, Safety and Welfare) Regulations (NI) 1996 Into operation: 6 January 1997
The Lifting operations and Lifting Equipment Regulations 1998	Lifting operations and Lifting Equipment Regulations (NI) 1999 Into operation: 20 September 1999
Control of Asbestos at work Regulations 2002	Control of Asbestos at work Regulations (NI) 2003 Into operation: 28 February 2003 except for regulation 4 on 21 May 2004 and regulation 20 on 21 November 2004

Part Five

The architect in practice

29

Legal organization of architects' offices

GRAHAM BROWN

1 Managing an architectural business

1.01 Management is a creative activity, the exercise of which is about making and maintaining dynamic cultures within and by which the objectives of people as individuals, teams and organizations are achieved.

The manager of an architectural business is concerned with three types of relationship: between the owners of the business and their clients, between employer and employee, and between the owners of the business themselves. Other chapters deal with the first and second of these. This chapter deals with the third.

Successful management of an architectural business is an essential pre-requisite for the successful management of architectural projects and, as such, is part of an architect's duty of care.

Critical to the success of any business is its legal form and structure. The choice, therefore, of the form of legal organisation is an important part of an architect's duty.

1.02 There are no formal restrictions in the professional codes to the structures under which architects carry on their business. The Architects Act 1997 permits registered persons to practise as partnerships or companies, limited or unlimited, provided that the work of their practice, insofar as it relates to architecture, is under the control and management of a registered person. The RIBA Code of Professional Conduct states in its preface that 'A member is at liberty to engage in any activity, whether as proprietor, director, principal, partner, manager, superintendent, controller or salaried employee of/or consultant to, any body corporate or unincorporate, or in any other capacity provided that his conduct complies with the Principles of this Code and the Rules applying to his circumstances'.

1.03 While architects may choose to practise as sole traders, to form companies or to create larger amalgamations as group practices or consortia, many architects still practise in partnership. The main choice for architects setting up in business is normally between partnerships and companies. A partnership provides the breadth of expertise a sole trader cannot provide without the formality of incorporating a registered company. The advantages and disadvantages of each will be discussed later. (See Checklist 29.3 for an outline of the principal differences between partnerships and companies.)

2 Partnership

2.01 The law of partnership is governed by the Partnership Act 1890. (Section numbers in the text which follows are from the 1890 Act.) Unless specified in a partnership agreement, the provisions of the Partnership Act will apply. Partnership is defined in section 1 as 'the relation which subsists between persons carrying on a business in common with a view to profit'. 'Business' includes the practice of architecture. A single act, such as designing a house, may make a

business and, if there is a series of such acts, a business will certainly be held to exist. 'A view to profit' requires only the intention to make a profit even if the architects fail to do so. The requirement of acting in common is important. It may be contrasted with barristers, who are in business with a view to profit but do not act in common: they merely share facilities. Unlike a company, a partnership has no legal personality. It is nothing more than the sum total of the individuals comprising it.

Formation of partnership

2.02 A partnership is a form of contract. Although many architects set up partnerships quite casually it is prudent to create the business formally and expressly by a deed of partnership executed under seal or written articles of partnership. The existence of a partnership can sometimes be inferred in law, however, from the behaviour of the individuals involved, even if no deed of partnership exists, and may exist even despite vigorous statements to the contrary.

Importance of clarity

2.03 Considerable importance may be attached to the existence of a partnership. For example, if two architects work together occasionally over several years and a case of negligence arises, both may be liable if a partnership exists even if only one of them has been negligent. If there is no partnership, however, one of them, if not personally involved in any negligence, will be safe from any claim. It can be vital to a client or supplier of a practice to establish whether he is dealing with a partnership or one person. Architects are recommended on all occasions to clarify their relationship with each other, particularly when working as group practices and consortia.

Sharing facilities and profits

2.04 If two or more architects do not intend to practise in partnership, but merely to share facilities, they must take great care to avoid the possibility of leading others into the assumption that they practise together as partners. Shared ownership of property, even if accompanied by sharing of net profits, is not normally on its own evidence of the existence of a partnership. Profit-sharing is, however, prima facie evidence of a partnership, but if it is just one piece of evidence among others it will be weighed with the other evidence. This is particularly important to architectural practices, since profit-sharing in the form of profit-related bonus payments is a common means of remunerating staff. Nevertheless, payment by profit-sharing will not of itself make an employee a partner in the business, nor will sharing in gross returns alone necessarily create a partnership. It is important to draft any contract of employment including any profit-sharing provision very carefully indeed. The relationship between the business and the outside world is important. Individuals can be 'held out' to the world as partners and the outside world will be entitled to treat them as partners. This can be done, for instance, by listing them as partners on the firm's notepaper.

Deed of partnership

2.05 Even though there are ways of determining whether a partnership exists, and the 1890 Act sets out terms which apply if partners have nothing written down, it is most important, if intending partners agree they are going into a business together, to set out the terms of their relationship in a deed of partnership since the terms expressed and implied by the Partnership Act can be draconian and unfair. The deed should cover the points outlined in Checklist 29.1.

Checklist 29.1 Items to be considered when drawing up a deed of partnership

---

Note: The terms of a partnership agreement, like any other contract, may be widely varied by mutual consent of the parties. Where no provision is made, those of the Partnership Act 1890 will apply. Figures in brackets refer to relevant clauses in that Act.

1 Name of firm

2 Place of business

3 Commencement date

4 Duration

5 Provision of capital:
   (a) Amount
   (b) Proportion to be contributed by each partner
   (c) Distinctions between what is not partnership capital (a premium) and capital which is partnership property (contribution to working capital)
   (d) Capital should be expressed in money terms
   (e) Any special agreement for interest on capital (24(3), (4))
   (f) Valuation and repayments on death, etc. (42 and 43)
   (g) Rules for settlement for accounts after dissolution (44)

6 Property:
   (a) What partners bring to the firm including contracts (20, 22, 24)
   (b) What belongs to firm as a whole (21)
   (c) What is co-owned but not partnership property
   (d) What is individually owned but used in the business (24)

7 Mutual rights and duties. If these are to be differentiated then they should be specified as holiday times, sabbaticals, work brought into the firm, etc.

8 Miscellaneous earnings. Whether or not income from lecturing, journalism, honoraria, etc. is to be paid into the firm.

9 Profits and losses. Basis for division among partners: if not equally then specified (24(1)). Any reservations such as about guaranteed minimum share of profits in any individual case.

10 Banking and accountants. Arrangements for signing cheques, presentation of audited accounts, etc.

11 Employment of *locum tenens*. Authority for, circumstances, and terms.

12 Constitution of firm. Provisions for changes (36).

13 Retirement at will. Age, fixed term or partnership for life, notice of retirement, etc. Arrangements for consultants and for payment during retirement. Repayment of capital and current accounts on death or retirement.

14 Dissolution. Any special circumstances (see Checklist 29.3).

15 Restrictions on practice. Any covenant restraining competition must be reasonable to interests of parties and public. Areas of operation.

16 Insurances. Various, including liability of surviving partners for dead partners' share in firm.

17 Arbitration. Method, number of arbitrators, etc.

Name of practice

2.06 In naming a firm, there are a number of considerations. Use of the words 'architect' or 'architects' is restricted by the Architects Act 1997. Only those persons who are on the Register of Architects maintained by the Architects Registration Board (ARB) are permitted to practise or carry on business under the name, style or title of 'architect', with the exception of 'landscape architects', 'naval architects' and 'golf course architects' who are outside the scope of the Act. It is important that any person wishing to use the words 'architect' or 'architects' in their practice name checks their acceptability first with ARB.

The provisions of the Business Names Act 1985 must be complied with if a partnership does not consist of the named partners. Certain names which are set out in statutory regulations or give the impression that the business is connected with HM Government or a local authority must gain the approval of the Secretary of State. The use in the firm's name of a retired, former or deceased partner may be permissible provided there is no intent to mislead; but caution is necessary to avoid the implication that such a person is still involved in the practice. The 1985 Act requires businesses to disclose certain information. The names and addresses of each partner must be prominently displayed at the business premises where the public have access. It is important to comply with the provisions of this Act. Failure to do so is a criminal offence or may render void contracts entered into by the practice. The Business Names Act requires that business documentation must contain the names of each partner. If there are more than 20 partners, however, the names of all partners can be omitted from business documents if they state the address of the principal place of business and also state that a full list of partners' names and relevant addresses may be inspected there.

Size of practice

2.07 There are still restrictions on the size of some partnerships. In the case of architects these have been removed by the Partnerships (Unrestricted Size) No. 4 Regulations 1970 so long as not less than three-quarters are registered under the Architects Act 1997.

Types of partner

2.08 The law is not concerned with distinctions between senior and junior partners. It is up to the partners to decide how to share profits, but they will be shared equally unless special provision is made. RIBA Practice Note (May 1974) strongly recommended that all persons who are held out to be partners shall be described as such without further distinction. In particular the term 'salaried partner' must be avoided. The purpose of this is to ensure that all persons described as partners share in the decision-making of the business and have access to appropriate information. They are also fully responsible for the professional conduct of the practice and for keeping themselves and their partners properly informed of partnership matters.

Associates

2.09 It is a common practice to recognize the status and contribution of senior staff by describing them as 'associates'. The title 'associate' is not referred to in the Partnership Act and it has no meaning in law. If it is not intended that associates be partners and share in the liabilities of the partnership, it is unwise to use the term 'associate partner', and its use can also contravene professional codes. If people are misled into thinking associates are partners, associates will find themselves liable as if they were partners, having all the obligations but without any of the rights or benefits.

Rights and liabilities of partners

2.10 Every partner has the following rights unless there is an agreement to the contrary:

1 To take full part in management of the business (Section 24(5)).
2 To have an equal share in profits and capital of the business (Section 24(1)).

3 To inspect the partnership books. These must be kept at the principal place of business of each firm (Section 24(9)).

4 To dissolve the partnership at any time by giving notice to the other partners (Section 26(1)).

5 By Section 24(2) a firm must indemnify every partner in respect of payments made and personal liabilities incurred by them in acting as necessary or in the ordinary and proper conduct of the business of the firm.

6 Not to have new partners added without their consent (Section 24(7)).

7 Not to have the fundamental nature of the partnership business altered without their consent. The consent of a majority of partners will suffice for changes in all other ordinary matters connected with the business.

8 Not to be expelled without express agreement (Section 25).

Rights to which partners are not entitled

2.11 By section 24(4) there is no right to interest on capital subscribed by a partner although by Section 24(3) there is a right to interest on capital subscribed beyond that which was agreed to be subscribed.

2.12 There is no right to remuneration for acting in the partnership business by Section 24(6).

Liabilities

2.13 Under English law a partnership is a collection of individuals and not a corporate body. In addition to all their normal individual liabilities, each partner has added responsibilities as a member of a partnership.

2.14 Legal action may be taken against a partner jointly, or jointly and severally. By Sections 9 and 10 of the Partnership Act every partner is personally liable jointly with all other partners for all debts and obligations incurred by the firm while he is a partner as well as jointly and severally for wrongs done by other partners acting in the ordinary course of the business of the firm or for wrongs done with the authority of co-partners. If a partnership is sued jointly, one or more partners may be sued at the same time. If an action is brought against a partnership jointly and severally, the partners may be sued singly or together. When judgment is given against one, further action may be brought against the others one by one or together until the full amount is paid. If only some of the partners are sued, they may apply to the courts to have their other partners enjoined as co-defendants.

2.15 The provisions of the Limitation Act 1980 and the Latent Damage Act 1986 apply to breaches of contract or of duty of care in tort.

2.16 Partners are not liable for the criminal actions of other partners unless they contributed to them or have knowledge of them. Architects may be liable, however, for breaches of their codes of professional conduct by fellow partners.

2.17 A partnership may indemnify one or more of its partners against the consequences of their liability. This device enables members of staff to share the management of a practice without outlaying capital to join the equity partnership.

2.18 A new partner entering a firm does not normally become liable for debts, obligations, or wrongs incurred or committed before their entry (Section 17(1)). If a partner retires he will still liable for debts or obligations incurred before his retirement (Section 17(2)). If he dies his estate will be liable for such debts or obligations. Moreover, a partner will continue to be treated as a member of the firm, attracting the usual liability, until notice of a change in the constitution of the partnership is advertised (Section 36).

2.19 Every partner is an agent of the practice. Any action undertaken by any partner in carrying out the business of the practice will bind the practice unless it is outside their authority to act for the practice in that particular matter, and the person with whom they are dealing knows that they have no authority or does not believe them to be a partner (Section 5).

2.20 Partners must render true accounts and full information on anything affecting the partnership or the partners (Section 28).

2.21 Partners are accountable to the partnership for any private profits they receive from any partnership transaction or from using partnership property, names, or connections (Section 29(1)).

2.22 If a partner, while still a partner, competes with the practice without the consent of the other partners he must pay all profits made in consequence to the practice (Section 30).

Relationship of partners to one another

2.23 A practice of any size may not discriminate against women partners with regard to the provision of benefits, facilities or services or by expelling her or subjecting her to detriment under the Sex Discrimination Act 1975 as amended by the Sex Discrimination Act 1986. Practices larger than six members may not discriminate in such matters on racial grounds under the Race Relations Act 1976.

Dissolution of partnerships

2.24 A partnership comes to an end:

1 At the end of a fixed term if it has been so set up.
2 At the end of a single specific commission, if it was set up for that commission alone.
3 On the death or bankruptcy of any partner unless the partnership agreement makes provision for continuity of the partnership.
4 If any partner gives notice.
5 By mutual consent.
6 By dissolution by the Court.

2.25 Prior to the Finance Act 1985 there were tax benefits in cessation and re-formation of a partnership, but these have now been ended.

2.26 If a partner wishes to end the firm but is prevented by his fellow partners, application may be made to the court for dissolution on one of the grounds shown in Checklist 29.2.

3 Limited liability partnerships

3.01 On 6 April 2001 Companies House introduced a new corporate identity known as the limited liability partnership (LLP). It is intended to give the benefits of limited liability and, at the same time, retain other characteristics of the traditional partnership. An LLP will be taxed in the same way as existing partnerships and the internal structure is similar to a partnership. Unlike a limited company, an LLP has no Memorandum and Articles of Association but it can be organised by a partnership agreement, designed to suit its members. An LLP is a separate legal entity. It is responsible for its assets and liabilities and the liability of its members are limited. But, as with companies, actions may be taken against individual members found to be negligent or fraudulent in their dealings.

3.02 Any firm of two or more members engaged in a profit making venture may form itself as an LLP. Many of the rules which apply to limited companies apply also to LLPs. These include registration of names and filing of annual accounts and returns at Companies House. The legislation used to create LLPs draws heavily upon the Companies Act in many significant respects.

Checklist 29.2: Grounds for dissolution of partnership

Note: Figures in brackets refer to relevant clauses in the Partnership Act 1890.

1   By agreement of parties:
  (a) Agreement per deed. End of fixed term or of single project.
  (b) By expiration, or notice (32). If for undefined time, any partner giving notice of intention (32(c)).
  (c) Illness. Special provisions in deed (to avoid need to apply to courts (35)).

Note: Expulsion. A majority of partners cannot expel unless express agreement in deed (25). There can be no implied consent to expel. Clarification required of arrangements in case partners fall out with each other.

2   By operation of law and courts:
  (a) Subject to express agreement, partnership is dissolved as regards all by death or bankruptcy of any partner (33).
  (b) Any event making it unlawful to carry on the business of the practice such as if a partner is insane, incapable of carrying on their part of agreement, guilty of conduct prejudicial to the interests of the firm, wilfully and persistently breaches the partnership agreement or if their conduct is such that the other partners can no longer carry on business with them.
  (c) If the firm can only carry on at a loss.
  (d) If, in the opinion of the courts, it is just and equitable that the firm should be dissolved.

---

4 Companies

View of the professional organizations

4.01 Under the RIBA Code of Professional Conduct the Institute may hold a member acting through a body corporate or unincorporate responsible for the acts of that body. This means that for the purposes of suspension or expulsion from the RIBA an architect who is a director of a company may be held personally liable for the acts of the company. This does not mean, however, that he or she will be held by the courts as personally liable in law for the acts of the company.

A separate legal persona

4.02 The most fundamental principle of company law is that a company is a distinct and separate entity in law from its members or directors. As a separate legal person a company can own and alienate property, sue and be sued, and enter into contracts in its own right. Although the company is owned by its members, or shareholders, and governed by its directors, or managing director, under the supervision of its shareholders, it is distinct in law from all of these. In relation to third parties it is the company only which is normally liable, not the shareholders or directors. This is so, however large the percentage of shares or debentures held by one shareholder. A company may be liable in contract, tort, crime and for matters of property. Only in rare cases can the directors or shareholders be held liable for debts and obligations of the company, for example, if they have been fraudulent or if directors allow the company to trade while it is insolvent.

Types of company

4.03 A company may be limited (by shares or guarantee) or unlimited. A company limited by shares is one in which the share-holders' liability to contribute to the company's assets is limited to the amount unpaid on their shares. A company limited by guarantee is one where the shareholders are liable as guarantors for an amount set out in the Memorandum (see paragraph 4.04) in the event of the company being wound up. An unlimited company is subject to the same rules as a limited company except that its shareholders are personally liable for all its debts and obligations in the event of the company being wound up. The normal vehicle used is a limited company limited by shares.

Formation of companies

4.04 Companies are normally formed by registration under the Companies Act 1985. Any two people can register a company. The following must be sent to the Company Registrar:

1 A Memorandum of Association setting out the objects of the company. A company may only pursue the objects conferred expressly or impliedly by the Memorandum. All other activity is *ultra vires* and void. For example, a company is not able to borrow money unless provision for this is set out in the Articles. Thus the drafting of a Memorandum of Association requires special care; it must also comply with the relevant ethical codes. The Memorandum should always contain provision for alteration as it can only be changed in certain circumstances as laid down by the Companies Act 1985.
2 Articles of Association containing the regulations of the company (subject to the Memorandum). Companies limited by shares need not register Articles but these will then be in the form of Table A in the Companies (Tables A–F) Regulations 1985 (SI 1985/805). The Articles may be altered by special resolution of a majority of at least three-quarters of its voting members.
3 A statement of initial nominal capital.
4 Particulars of the director(s) and secretary. There must be at least one director and one secretary. Any change in the directors or secretary must be notified to the Registrar of Companies. The Articles may require directors to have qualification shares. Anyone, even a corporation, may be a company director unless they are an undischarged bankrupt (though the court may give them leave to act) or are disqualified by the court under the Company Directors Disqualification Act 1986 or the Articles. The company may remove a director by ordinary resolution before the end of his term. Directors normally retire in rotation (one-third each year) but may resign by giving such notice as is required in the Articles. Directors are entitled only to such remuneration as is stated in the Articles. Companies may not loan to directors or connected persons except as provided under the 1985 Act.
5 Intended location of the registered office of the company.
6 The prescribed fee.

4.05 The Registrar of Companies will issue a Certificate of Incorporation as evidence that the company is legally registered, and give the company a registered number. Without a Certificate of Incorporation a company does not exist in law and cannot do business.

Public and private companies

4.06 Companies, whether limited or unlimited, may be either public or private. A public company is the only sort of company permitted to offer its shares to the public. Only companies with a nominal share capital of £50 000 may be public limited companies. The Memorandum of Association must state that the company is a public company. An architect's practice will normally incorporate as a private company. The individuals (who would otherwise be partners) are likely to be directors and shareholders.

Profits

4.07 Profits are distributed among shareholders in accordance with the rights attached to their shares. Although there is a presumption that all shares confer equal rights and equal liabilities, that can be rebutted by a power in the company's articles to issue different classes of shares. An example of a class of share is a preference share. Holders of preference shares will be entitled to dividends before ordinary shareholders. If there are insufficient funds, preference shareholders will be the only shareholders to receive dividends. Shares are also classed according to whether they have voting rights or not. In most architectural companies profits and dividends are small because directors are remunerated by salary under their service contracts with the company.

Name of company

4.08 Like partnerships, the name of a company is restricted by the Architects Act 1997 and the Business Names Act 1985. Limited companies must use the word 'limited' after their name. It is an offence for public companies to choose names giving the impression that they are private companies, and vice versa. The use of a name similar to that of another company with the same type of business may constitute an actionable tort.

4.09 A company must state its corporate name on all business documents and on its seal. It must display this name legibly on the outside of its business premises. Other particulars including the place of registration, the registered number and the address of the registered office must be on company business documents.

Size of company

4.10 A company may have an unlimited number of shareholders.

Rights and liabilities of shareholders

Rights

4.11 Shareholders holding shares with voting rights have the right to supervise the management of the company by voting in the annual general meeting, which meetings must be held each year at no greater than a 15 month interval, or in such extraordinary general meetings as may be called.

4.12 Shareholders are paid dividends out of the profits of the company, in accordance with the rights belonging to their shares.

Liabilities

4.13 A partnership is bound by contracts made by one of its partners and is liable in tort for the acts or omissions of each partner. In contrast, shareholders cannot make contracts binding on a company, nor are they liable personally for debts or obligations of other shareholders. Shareholders are liable, however, for torts and obligations of a limited company to the amount unpaid on the nominal value of their shares. Frequently this is academic. Many small limited companies only have £100 worth of share capital split into smaller proportions still. If the company is unlimited, shareholders will be liable for the debts and obligations of the company in the event of its winding-up.

4.14 When a company is dissolved by winding-up, both present members and those who have been members in the 12 months preceding the winding-up are required to contribute towards the liability of the company but, for the reasons given above, this contribution is normally nominal and therefore irrelevant. Only in the case of a substantial unpaid up shareholding could it assume any significance and this is likely to be most unusual. The liabilities of past company members are not so wide-reaching as those of partners.

Rights and liabilities of directors

4.15 Under the Articles, directors are normally given the power to manage the company under the ultimate supervision of shareholders. They may delegate the management to a managing director.

4.16 Directors are not servants or agents of a company and can only bind it if some organ of the company has conferred appropriate authority upon them. Authority for this depends on the Articles or by special resolution of the shareholders. A director may be held to have had usual authority or to have been held out as having authority and this will bind the company. The third party need not be familiar with the Articles in either case. A managing director can normally be expected to have authority to bind the company.

4.17 The Companies Act 1985 and 1989 and the Insolvency Act 1986 prescribe a large number of duties for directors. The main duties are:

1 Directors must prepare and disclose company accounts in a specified form stating the financial position of the company. They must keep the books at the registered office of the company available for inspection by company officers at any time.
2 Directors must prepare an annual report reviewing the business of the company and recommending the amount of dividends to be paid.
3 The company must be audited annually if its turnover exceeds a specified amount or if at least 10% of its shareholders request an audit.
4 The report and accounts must be filed with the Registrar of Companies at specified times to be available for inspection by the public.
5 The company may need to hold an annual general meeting of shareholders in each calendar year at no greater interval than once every 15 months but this may be dispensed with by elective resolution of the shareholders. Two persons can constitute a quorum. Extraordinary general meetings may be convened if there is some business the directors consider to be of special importance.
6 The company must keep a register of directors at its registered office disclosing certain information about directors and their interest in the shares or debentures of the company. These particulars must be notified to the Registrar, who must be informed of any changes. A register of members containing similar information must also be kept by the company.
7 Directors have no right to remuneration except that specified in the Articles. Remuneration of directors is normally voted on by the shareholders at their general meetings.
8 Directors owe the company a fiduciary duty of loyalty and good faith. They are considered trustees of company assets under their control. They must account to the company for any profits they make by virtue of their position as directors and cannot use their powers as directors except to benefit the company. They must always devote themselves to promoting the company's interests and act in its best interest. Their duty of loyalty means they cannot enter into engagements where their personal interests might conflict with the company's interest and they must disclose their personal interests in such engagements to the shareholders. This duty can continue even after a director leaves the company.
9 Directors owe a duty to the company to exercise reasonable care in the conduct of the business. Such duties are not unduly onerous. Courts are reluctant to intervene in areas involving business judgement. In some circumstances directors will be expected to seek specialist advice and will be liable if they do not. Directors will not be liable for anything they have been authorized to do by shareholders. This duty is not owed to shareholders, contractors or creditors (although a director may be liable to the creditor for fraudulent or wrongful trading). Since the duty is owed to the company, the company itself can sue directors who have been negligent or in breach of their fiduciary duties.

Dissolution

4.18 A company may be dissolved in two ways:

1 By winding-up under the Insolvency Act 1986. This may be voluntary or compulsory. Once a company has been wound up no judgment may be enforced against it.
2 By being struck off the Register under the Companies Act 1985. This happens, for instance if the company fails to file its annual accounts or returns. Companies may seek this form of dissolution themselves. They may do this to save the costs of a formal liquidation.

Companies versus partnerships

4.19 A list of the differences is set out in Checklist 29.3. The relative advantages and disadvantages will differ for individual businesses.

Managers need to assess the business priorities when making a decision to form a company or a partnership. The size of the business may be relevant to the decision. Smaller businesses may find the paperwork and administration required for a company too arduous. Taxation is another factor in the decision. This is beyond the scope of this chapter. Managers should seek professional advice from an accountant or from a local tax office.

Service companies

4.20 Service companies are formed to provide services to a partnership. The company may employ staff and hold the premises. It will also normally provide things such as office equipment, stationery, cars and accountancy services to the practice. The advantages of a service company are related to the balance between income and corporation tax.

Group practices and consortia

4.21 Architects' businesses may come together to work in several forms of association, whether for a single project or on a more permanent basis. This chapter is not concerned with the operational and management factors for and behind the choice of form, but only with the legal issues. Further guidance is given in the RIBA Architect's Handbook of Practice Management. The creation of any association should be checked carefully with the professional indemnity insurers of each party.

Loose groups

4.22 These are associations in which practices or individuals pool their knowledge and experience. Such a group does not need to be registered, but some short constitution is desirable which clearly distinguishes it from a partnership. In company law a more formal 'Memorandum and Articles of Association' is necessary and is of far greater significance. It must set out the most important provisions of the company's constitution, including the activities which the company may carry out.

Group practices

4.23 Practices may group together for their mutual benefit and to give better service while each retains some independence:

1 Association. The degree of association may vary considerably from simply sharing office accommodation, facilities and expense, to a fully comprehensive system of mutual help. Beyond agreeing to a division of overhead expenses each practice retains their profits and their normal responsibility to their respective clients.
2 Co-ordinated groups. For large development projects it is not unusual for the work to be undertaken by two or more architectural practices with one of them appointed to co-ordinate the activities of the others. Practices are liable to the co-ordinating practice for torts committed in their areas of activity. The arrangement may be constructed under head and sub-consultancy agreements.

Single project partnerships and group partnerships may be entered into on terms which are entirely a matter for individual agreements between the parties and are similar in law to any ordinary partnership.

Consortia

4.24 Consortia are little different in law from group practices. The term normally implies the association of practices with different professional skills acting as one in carrying out projects jointly yet retaining their separate identities and each with their own responsibility to the building owner. A consortium may be formed for the duration of a single project or on a more regular and permanent basis.

Difficulties

4.25 Any association of practices, whether permanent or temporary, must be very carefully planned. If practices are to merge completely,

Checklist 29.3: Differences between companies and partnerships Partnerships

Partnerships	Companies
1 No separate legal personality (except in Scotland).	1 Separate legal personality from its shareholders.
2 Partners have unlimited liability.	2 Shareholders are liable only to the amount unpaid on their shares but may be liable on personal guarantees for some liabilities.
3 Partners' interests may be difficult to transfer subject to valuation agreement.	3 Interest of shareholders are their shares which can be easier to transfer subject to restrictions in Articles (which they normally are) and to valuation agreement. Shares may be difficult to value.
4 May be difficult for a young architect to join a partnership since sufficient capital will need to have been accumulated to buy a share in the partnership or take over a retiring partner's interest.	4 It is easier to join a company as it does not necessarily involve buying in.
5 Only promotion is to become a partner, so career prospects may be limited.	5 More kinds of promotion possible including to directorship through employment structure. In small companies this is a more theoretical than practical advantage.
6 Difficult for partners to resign and subject to agreement.	6 Easy for directors to resign but liability remains for up to 12 months.
7 Management through meetings of partners.	7 Management through Board of Directors supervised by shareholders, meeting annually.
8 Partners share profits equally unless there is an agreement to the contrary.	8 Company profits are divided according to rights attached to the shares. Employees are remunerated by salary, shareholders by dividends. These can be mixed and matched.
9 Can be formed informally by just starting up business with another person.	9 Must be registered to come into existence but company formation can be quick and cost less than £100.
10 No restrictions on powers of partners subject to agreement.	10 A company only has the powers in the objects clause of its Memorandum but normally sweeping powers are incorporated as standard. Other powers are *ultra vires* and void.
11 Each partner can bind the partnership.	11 No shareholder can bind the company but directors can.
12 Partnership details cannot be inspected by the public.	12 Matters filed with the Registrar of Companies are open to public inspection including Memorandum, Articles, details of directors, secretary, and registered office.
13 Accounts need not be publicized.	13 Accounts must be filed annually with the Registrar of Companies.
14 No audit required.	14 Annual audit may be required.
15 Partnership must make annual tax returns but partners are liable individually for declaring and paying their own tax.	15 Company liable for all declarations and payments of tax.
16 Less administration required.	16 More administration required.
17 Money can be borrowed in the names of the partners but partnership debtors cannot be used as security for loans.	17 Can raise money if allowed by Memorandum by debentures for example, or by fixed and floating charges over assets.
18 Death or departure of a partner can cause dissolution of the partnership unless otherwise agreed.	18 Transfer of shares will not end a company's existence.
19 Many ways to dissolve a partnership including instantly by agreement.	19 A company is dissolved only by liquidation in accordance with the Companies Acts 1985 and 1989 and the Insolvency Act 1986 or by winding-up.

assets should be carefully assessed (including work in progress). Specific agreement is necessary on debts, including liabilities relating to previous contracts. These could be significant if a pre-merger project became the subject of a professional negligence claim.

Agreements

4.26 If practices are to preserve their own identities and to continue to practise in their own right as well as together on common projects, the form of agreement becomes more critical and more complex. A new group or consortium, partnership or company should be created to contract with clients for common projects. Its agreement must resolve how far the assets of member practices are brought in, the extent of liabilities of the group, and the degree of independence retained by each member practice to carry on its own activities. A solicitor should always be consulted.

5 Premises and persons

5.01 Employers are obliged under the general duty of care to protect employees against personal injury in the course of their employment. They are obliged by statute to provide employees with healthy, safe and decent working conditions. For office workers these were originally set out in the Offices, Shops and Railway Premises Act 1963, but this is now subordinate to the Health and Safety at Work Act 1974 (HASAW) together with regulations made under the two Acts. The

Health and Safety at Work Act 1974 shifted the focus from premises to people. This chapter is concerned with its impact on an architect as employer, employee, or occupier of premises.

Accidents

5.02 Employers are required to notify the enforcing authority of accidents on the premises, subject to the requirements of the Reporting of Injuries, Diseases, and Dangerous Occurrences Regulations (RIDDOR), which cause the death, or the disablement for more than three days, of a person employed to work on the premises. A record must be kept of all accidents as they occur. In any case this is useful as a check against the possibility of persons making claims for accidents which did not happen on office premises.

Employees' right to information

5.03 Because the HASAW Act is primarily for the benefit of employees, and because some employers are forgetful of their duties, the occupier is obliged to give employees information about the Act either by posting up an abstract in a sufficiently prominent place or by giving them an explanatory booklet.

Division of responsibility

5.04 One of the potentially confusing aspects of the Act is the division of responsibility between owner and occupier, particularly in multi-occupied buildings. The employer, if not the occupier, is responsible for notifying the occupier of accidents to his employees and for notifying his own employees of the provisions of the Act.

Single occupation

5.05 An employer who occupies a whole building is responsible for ensuring that all provisions of the HASAW Act are met.

Multi-occupation

5.06 When a building is in multi-occupation responsibility is divided. The owner is responsible for the fire certificate, fire alarms and signposting, and keeping free from obstruction all exits and means of escape in the building as a whole, cleaning, lighting and safety of the common parts, washing and sanitary facilities. Occupiers are responsible for all other provisions of the HASAW Act within the parts of the building they occupy.

Occupiers' Liability Acts 1957 and 1984

5.07 Occupiers owe a duty of care to all entrants on their premises. If the entrants are lawful visitors, reasonably practicable steps must be taken to make the premises safe for them and to protect them against all hazards, or give sufficient notice of them. Visiting workpeople such as window cleaners are responsible for their own safe working methods but if there are particular hazards in the area in which they will be working, then the employer, owner, or occupier has a common law duty to advise each visitor of those hazards. If it is foreseeable that persons unable to read warnings such as children or blind persons may be likely to get into hazardous areas, then protection must be adequate to keep them out. A duty of care is even owed to trespassers, although this duty is to take such care as is reasonable in all the circumstances of the case to see that they do not suffer injury on the premises by reason of the danger concerned. Sufficient warnings or discouragements will normally discharge the duty.

5.08 Responsibility for injury or damage arising from improper construction or maintenance, is not avoided by the transfer of the premises to another owner (Defective Premises Act 1972).

5.09 If a landlord has a repairing obligation to tenants, then the landlord has a responsibility to anyone who could be affected by the landlord's failure to keep the premises properly maintained.

Health and Safety at Work Act 1974

5.10 The Health and Safety of Work Act 1974 is directed at people who work, whether employer, employee, or self-employed persons, and their responsibilities to each other and to third parties who may be affected by the work process or its results. Under the Act employers must maintain safe systems of work and keep plant and premises in safe condition. Adequate instruction, training, and supervision must be given for the purposes of safety. This may extend to guidance or instruction to employees visiting buildings or construction sites in the course of their employment particularly at times when the premises or site may be otherwise unoccupied. RIBA Practice Note (May 1989) provides detailed guidance on safety procedures with particular reference to safety on site. Unless fewer than five people are employed, an employer must prepare a written statement of the business's safety policies, organization and arrangements and make this known and understood by all employees. Even if a written policy is not required, an employer is not entitled to disregard the Act.

5.11 Safety policy should deal with the safety responsibilities of all managers, inspection procedures, supervision, training, research and consultative arrangements regarding safety, fire drill procedure, reminders on keeping stairways and corridors free of obstructions, the marking and guarding of temporary hazards, use of machinery, accidents and first aid. Advice is obtainable from the Health and Safety Executive. However, employers should ensure that their safety policies are tailored specifically to meet the individual needs of their businesses. Anyone in a supervisory or managerial role will have specific health and safety responsibilities. While managers may delegate, they retain responsibility.

5.12 The employee in his turn has a duty to exercise reasonable care to himself and his fellow employees, to co-operate with his employer in carrying out statutory requirements and not to interfere with safety provisions. It is important for managers to remember that they are also employees.

5.13 A number of regulations are important to office environment and organization. Central to these are the Management of Health and Safety at Work Regulations 1992 containing the requirement, among other matters, that employers and the self-employed make and maintain a sufficient and suitable risk assessment for the purposes of identifying the measures required to be taken to comply with health and safety law. Equally important are the Workplace (Health, Safety and Welfare) Regulations 1992. More specific requirements are laid down in the Provision and Use of Work Equipment Regulations 1992, the Health and Safety (Display Screen Equipment) Regulations 1992, the Manual Handling Operations Regulations 1992 and the Personal Protective Equipment at Work Regulations 1992. The Health and Safety (First Aid) Regulations 1981 impose a duty upon employers to provide first aid equipment and facilities, to provide suitable persons with training in first aid, and to inform employees of the arrangements they have made. The British Safety Council Approved Code of Practice, Health and Safety (First Aid) Regulations 1981 is approved by the Health and Safety Commission to provide practical guidance in respect of the regulations. Although failure to comply with the Code's guidance is not in itself an offence, it is prudent to follow it. The Control of Substances Hazardous to Health Regulations 1994 (COSHH) impose a duty upon employers to ensure levels of hazardous substances do not harm employees or others who may be in contact with them. Hazardous substances used in the office include ammonia, solvents (for example correction fluid), adhesives, photocopy and laser printer toner, copier emissions, cleaning agents and dusts. The Electricity at Work Regulations 1989 require that electrical systems and equipment be maintained so far as is reasonably practical to prevent danger. Recommendations are provided on the frequency of formal inspection and electrical testing. The Health and Safety Executive publishes guidance enabling the obligations imposed by these, and other relevant regulations, to be met.

Enforcement

5.14 To ensure that the law on health and safety is respected, inspectors appointed by the enforcing authority have the power to enter premises to which the Act applies. They may inspect the premises, question anyone, or ask to see relevant certificates or notices. It is good practice to obtain evidence of their identity and authority before taking anyone round.

5.15 Inspectors have the power to make 'improvement' notices under which the offending practice must cease or the deficiency must be remedied within a certain period. They also have the power to issue a 'prohibition' notice under which the practice must cease or the premises must not be used until their requirements have been met. An appeal against a notice may be made to an industrial tribunal. Offences under the Health and Safety at Work Act are criminal offences, although breaches of the regulations made thereunder can also result in civil liability. It is an offence to contravene requirements imposed by a notice. The offender may be liable to a fine even though damage has not been suffered. Although insurance may be taken out against the possibility of damages being awarded, insurance may not be used to protect against the results of criminal acts, such as fines.

Fire certificate

5.16 Relevant legislation is the Fire Precautions (Factories, Offices, Shops and Railway Premises) Order 1989, and the Fire Precautions (Workplace) Regulations 1997 although the regulatory structure is poised for further development. Fire risk assessments are an important part of an employer's statutory duty of care.

5.17 A fire certificate is compulsory in the case of use as a place of work and a use for teaching, training or research, or use for any purpose involving access to the premises by members of the public unless no more than 20 people work in the relevant building at any one time with no more than 10 above the ground floor. A fire certificate must be obtained from the enforcing authority. For private practices this is normally the local fire authority. However, the fire authority may exempt premises from the need to have a fire certificate if it thinks fit or in certain specified cases. Even if exemption is granted, premises must still be provided with fire-fighting equipment and means of escape. If this duty is contravened, the fire authority will serve an improvement notice, non-compliance with which constitutes an offence. If the fire authority believes that the use of the premises involves a serious fire risk it may serve a notice prohibiting or restricting the use of the premises until the risk is removed.

5.18 For a certificate to be granted, requirements on means of escape, fire-fighting equipment, fire alarm systems and arrangements for fire drills must be satisfied. Failure to have a fire certificate, if not exempted, amounts to an offence.

5.19 Fire alarms must be tested at intervals and occupiers are required to take effective steps to ensure that all occupants are familiar with the means of escape and with the action to be taken in case of fire. Fire drills are the most effective way of doing this.

5.20 If, after a certificate has been issued or an exemption has been made, alterations are made to the premises which significantly affect the requirements of that certificate or exemption, the issuing authority must be advised. The authority has continuing powers of inspection to ensure the premises are kept to the original standard and whether changes have been made which render that standard inadequate.

6 Insurance

6.01 A practice protects itself by insurance against financial risks. Some of these are ordinary risks such as fire, some are eventualities which a practice is not obliged to cover but which, as a good employer, it may wish to provide for, such as prolonged sickness of a member of staff. There are cases, however, when a practice is obliged by law to cover damage caused to other persons. Varieties of insurance which cover all these risks are:

Public liability

6.02 An owner or a lessee of premises, or someone carrying on a business in premises, may be legally liable for personal injury or damage to property of third parties caused by their negligence or that of their staff.

6.03 Since several people may be involved in a single incident and the level of damages may be very high, it is important for cover to be:

1 Appropriate to status whether owner, lessee, or occupier.
2 Extended to cover the actions of employers and employees, not just on the premises, but anywhere while on business.
3 Extended to cover overseas if employers or employees are likely to be overseas on business.

Employers' liability

6.04 An employer is liable for personal injury caused to an employee in the course of employment by the employer's negligence or that of another member of staff, his agent or servant. It is important to arrange insurance to cover for injuries sustained:

1 During employment whether on or off the employer's premises.
2 Overseas if employees are likely to be overseas on business.

Employer's Liability (Compulsory Insurance) Act 1969

6.05 Employers are required by statute to take out specific insurance to meet their obligations. The Employer's Liability (Compulsory Insurance) Act 1969 and General Regulations 1971 as amended require that every employer who carries on business in Great Britain shall maintain insurance under approved policies with authorized insurers (that is persons lawfully carrying on a class of insurance business in Great Britain under Part II of the Companies Act 1967, as amended by the Insurance Companies Act 1974) against liability for bodily injury or disease sustained by employees and arising out of, and in the course of, their employment in that business. Cover must extend to an amount of £2 million for any one occurrence. Employers' liability policies are contracts of indemnity. The premium is often based on the amount of wages paid by the insured to employees during the year of insurance. The size of the business is immaterial. The Act also provides for employees not ordinarily resident but who may be temporarily in Great Britain in the course of employment for a continuous period of not less than 14 days. Copies of the insurance certificate must be displayed at the place or places of business for the information of employees.

Motor vehicles

6.06 Third party insurance cover is a legal requirement under the Road Traffic Act 1972 in respect of death or personal injury to third parties or damage to a third party's property. Cover may be invalidated if a car is used for purposes not covered by the policy. Cars owned and operated by a practice must therefore be covered for business use and cars owned by employees and used by them in their duties must be covered for occasional business use.

If staff use their own cars on practice business their cover must be adequate, particularly in respect of fellow employees. Their policies should be checked to ensure that they include a third party indemnity in favour of the employer, otherwise if a claim results from an incidents while the car is used on practice business, insurers may repudiate liability.

Professional indemnity

6.07 This is the insurance necessary to cover professional people for negligence. Such policies will normally only cover liabilities to third parties, not loss caused to a person's own business by reason of their negligence. Nor will they cover fraud.

6.08 Every architect in every form of practice is required by the Architects Registration Board to be covered by professional indemnity insurance. The scope of the policy, amount of the premium and other details are matters which must be worked out on an individual basis by the architect and an experienced insurance broker taking ARB's requirements into account.

6.09 In view of its importance, professional indemnity insurance is dealt with in a separate chapter. Incorporated practices also require professional indemnity insurance.

30

Architects' contracts with clients

SARAH LUPTON

1 The appointment

1.01 An architect has many factors to take into account when considering an offer of an appointment and it is important that their implications are thoroughly understood before entering into a legal commitment to undertake the commission.

He must be satisfied that the client has the authority and resources to commission the work; he must appreciate the background to the proposal and understand its scope, at least in outline, and he must be aware of any other consultants who have been, or are likely to be, associated with the project.

The architect must be satisfied that he has the experience and competence to undertake the work; that the office has the necessary finance, staff, and other resources; and that the proposal will not conflict with any relevant codes of professional conduct, other commissions and commitments in the office, and the policy of the practice.

The preliminary negotiations between the parties often involve the exchange of business references, especially where the architect and the potential client are previously unknown to each other. On occasions, extensive enquiries about the client and the client's business may be necessary.

It is not unusual for architects to be invited to enter into collateral agreements with funding bodies or other third parties as a condition of the appointment; the possible implications of these agreements need to be considered by the architect and in particular it is important to ensure that any liabilities incurred are covered by the architect's professional indemnity insurance cover. Occasionally clients ask the architect to enter into collateral agreements after the fees and terms of the appointment have been agreed but if this happens it is essential that the architect considers their conditions carefully, comparing them with those of the original appointment. If the proposed collateral agreements extend the services required or increase the architect's liabilities beyond those originally envisaged the terms of the appointment should be renegotiated.

1.02 Any appointment offered to an architect must be considered in relation to the requirements of the Architects Registration Board (ARB) Code of Conduct (Chapter 38), and also the codes of conduct of any other professional institutions of which the architect may be a member. The architect must be able to demonstrate that he has acted properly in obtaining the commission and is able to carry out the work in a suitable manner and in accordance with the appropriate codes and standards. An employer may not always be conscious of the constraints on the profession; the onus is on the architect to ensure that the employer is made aware of all the relevant matters.

The architect must consider his position in relation to any other architects who may have been involved in the same scheme. An employer is free to offer the commission to whomever he wishes, to obtain alternative schemes from different architects, and to make whatever arrangements for professional services he considers to be necessary. However, the architect is bound by the codes of professional conduct and must ensure that he has acted and continues to act properly and fairly in his dealings with other architects. In particular he must be able to show that he has not attempted to supplant another architect.

An architect who is approached by a potential client in connection with a project with which another architect has already been concerned has a duty to inform the first architect although the first architect has no power to prevent the second architect from proceeding with the work, provided that there is no breach of copyright. Apart from the professional obligation to advise the first architect it is commercially prudent to do so.

1.03 The need to consider the position of other architects is particularly important in large, complex projects involving various consultant architects providing different but related services, especially when the arrangements for professional services change during the project. The scope of services and the relationships between consultant architects and executive architects can on occasion be the cause of misunderstanding and even difficulties in evolving and changing circumstances. The onus is on the project leader to ensure that the roles, relationships and responsibilities of everyone involved are clearly understood but it is particularly important that the architects are fully aware of the extent of their individual duties and liabilities.

1.04 Increasingly clients appear to be seeking single all-in service appointments for the whole range of consultancy services required. The all-in services can be commissioned from an existing multi-discipline practice or from a single-discipline consultant who engages others as sub-consultants for any other specialist services that may be needed. Multi-disciplinary practices usually have their own well-established forms of agreement but in the case of the single-discipline consultant offering an all-in service care is needed in the drafting an agreed form of appointment. The standard conditions of services and remunerations of the various institutions still vary in detail although they are moving towards greater consistency and standardization. The consultants concerned have to agree upon a unified approach to services, payment, conditions and liabilities before an offer can be made to a potential client. It is particularly important that the extent of the liabilities which may be incurred are considered in relation to the current professional indemnity insurance of the consultants concerned and any changes that may be needed in the extent of the cover. It is essential that the lead consultant offering the all-in service and therefore being totally liable to the client confirms his position with his own professional indemnity insurers before making the offer.

The architect often acts as the lead-consultant in making an all-in service offer but occasionally the architect may act as a sub-consultant to a consultant from another discipline. Where the architect is required to act as a sub-consultant consideration should be given to the use of the sub-consultant agreement discussed below (5.02).

2 Agreement of appointment

2.01 Although in law a verbal agreement may be accepted as the basis of a contract of engagement between architect and employer, such an arrangement would not comply with the ARB and RIBA codes of conduct, and a formal procedure of appointment should always be adopted. Such a procedure creates a clearly identifiable legal basis for the commission and establishes a sound business approach to the relationship between the architect and the employer. The appointment may be made by either an exchange of letters or an exchange of a formal memorandum of agreement, in each case supported by appropriate supplementary material such as conditions of engagement.

An informal exchange of letters is frequently used but it is not recommended practice. Informal letters of appointment are liable to misinterpretation and misunderstanding and are often the source of difficulties and disagreements between the parties. In particular, they frequently neglect to cover matters required under the RIBA and ARB codes of conduct, for example the provisions for termination.

2.02 Various institutions publish standard forms of agreement and their use is strongly recommended. The format and content of these standard forms varies widely. The forms are generally self-explanatory but it is important that they are carefully read and fully understood by both the architect and the client before signing. With 'consumer' clients it is particularly important to discuss and agree all the terms of the standard form, as otherwise some of its terms may become void by operation of the Unfair Terms in Consumer Contracts Regulations 1994.

2.03 Where a standard form of agreement is not used, it is suggested that the following matters should be clearly identified in any exchange of letters between the parties:

1 The date of the agreement.
2 The name and address of the employer.
3 The name and address of the architect.
4 The title and address of the project.
5 The formal agreement to the appointment of the architect.
6 The basis of remuneration for the architect and the arrangements for payment.
7 The form and scope of services to be provided by the architect.
8 The allocation of responsibilities and any limitation of responsibilities.
9 The appointment procedure for a quantity surveyor, other consultants, and the clerk of works as appropriate.
10 The procedure to be followed in the event of the architect's incapacity.
11 The procedure for the termination of the agreement.
12 The procedure for resolving disputes between parties.
13 The name of an agreed adjudicator or the agreed nominator of an adjudicator.
14 The architects are subject to the disciplinary sanction of the ARB in relation to complaints of unacceptable professional conduct or serious professional incompetence.

The basis of remuneration and the scope of services may be further defined in other documents to which reference should be made in the agreement.

When, as occasionally happens, employers wish to use their own forms of agreement, attention should be drawn to the merits of using one of the standard forms; they are more likely to be comprehensive; they represent the interests of the parties in an equitable manner, and are widely recognized in the industry. Where the client insists on the use of a non-standard form its terms and conditions should be compared with those of the nearest equivalent standard form; in the case of differences the form should be sent to the architect's professional indemnity insurers and impartial advice should be sought before entering into an agreement. It is particularly important that forms of agreement are compatible with the requirements of the Housing Grants, Construction and Regeneration Act 1996 and Standard 11 of the ARB Code.

2.04 The authority of the architect is strictly limited to the terms of his appointment, that is, as shown in any form of agreement and conditions of engagement. It is in the interests of the employer, the architect, the quantity surveyor, and other independent consultants that these terms should be fully and clearly understood by everyone involved. It is not unusual for the form of services to be varied with changing circumstances during the work but it is essential that these changes are formally confirmed in amendments to the form of agreement.

2.05 Where a commission arises out of a recognized competition, the competition conditions usually form the conditions of the appointment. Difficulties develop occasionally when the subsequent building is substantially different from that originally envisaged and where there has been a material change in the conditions. The subsequent appointment of consultants other than the original competition winners can be the cause of serious difficulties.

2.06 The form of appointment agreement should be signed by both parties, witnessed and dated, each keeping a copy. The onus is on the architect to explain the professional obligation to enter into a formal agreement before work commences; beginning work without a clear agreement of services and charges is not only commercially unwise it is also a breach of the codes which could result in disciplinary action. Failure to agree and confirm the services to be given and the charges to be made is also the most common source of dispute between architects and clients. The absence of clear and precise terms of appointment make it hard for a conciliator, an adjudicator, an arbitrator or the courts to resolve disputes in an equitable manner.

2.07 The architect's contract of engagement is usually personal to himself or the partnership. He cannot delegate his duties completely, but he is under no obligation to carry out all the works personally or to go into every detail himself. The extent to which he may be prepared to delegate his duties to an assistant is a matter of competence, confidence, reliability, and experience of both the principal and the assistant. The architect is becoming increasingly dependent on the skill and labour of others within his office and elsewhere, but he remains responsible to his client within the terms of his appointment, and continues to be responsible for the acts and defaults of his subordinates. The subordinates in turn are responsible to their principal and could be held liable to their employers for results of their acts.

Where the business is conducted as an unlimited or a limited company, the relationships will depend upon the form of contract involved but the ethical responsibilities between the parties remain, and liability in tort continues regardless of the form of organization.

3 Termination

3.01 The contract of engagement between the architect and his employer may be terminated by either party at reasonable notice. Reasons for the termination need not be stated, but in the event of dispute over outstanding fees or payments, the cause of the termination would be of importance to an adjudicator, an arbitrator or a court in determining a decision or an award.

In the event of the termination of the contract, any outstanding fees for work properly carried out become due to the architect, but it is unlikely that the employer could be held responsible for any loss of anticipated profits on work not yet carried out.

3.02 Difficulties sometimes arise in connection with the use of material prepared before the termination of the engagement took place. The standard forms of appointment usually define the rights of the parties in such circumstances. In the absence of any statement concerning the use of material following the termination of an engagement, it is generally assumed that if the work was substantially advanced at the time of termination it would be unreasonable for the employer not to be entitled to complete the project. It is usually accepted that the employer is entitled to a licence to use the drawings to complete the work effectively. The copyright, of course, remains with the architect unless some other agreement is made.

3.03 In the event of the death or the incapacity of the architect, it is usually held that the employer is entitled to the use of the drawings and other documents to complete the work, provided that payment has been made. Provision for the procedure to be adopted in such circumstances should be included in the standard form of agreement. The death of either party to a personal contract generally dissolves the contract, but it is usually possible, with agreement, for a third party to assume responsibility for the completion of the contract.

Agreements of appointments between companies and partnerships, rather than between individuals, avoid the occasional embarrassing technical difficulties and delays that occur in the transfer of responsibility to others in the event of the death or incapacity of an individual.

3.04 In the event of termination on the grounds of the bankruptcy or liquidation, the contract can be continued if both parties wish to do so and the receiver agrees, and provided that assurances about the payment of any fees and monies which may become due can be secured. The bankruptcy of the architect can pose problems of professional indemnity insurance and other matters and it is rare for arrangements to be made for an insolvent practitioner to continue in business other than under a voluntary administration arrangement.

3.05 The Scheme for Construction Contracts and the standard forms of appointment make provision for the suspension of work in the event of non-payment of fees. Non-payment of fees may be the architect's reason for wishing to terminate an appointment but before doing so it would be prudent for the architect to give formal notice of the intention to suspend work unless payment is made within a stated period and only then if payment is still not forthcoming to proceed with the termination.

4 Ownership

4.01 Ownership of drawings and other documents is often cause for concern. Correspondence and other documents exchanged between the architect and others in connection with the approval of plans, the running of the project, or the administration of the contract by the architect in his role as an agent technically belong to the employer provided that payment has been made, although in practice it is most unusual for all these documents to be automatically transferred to the employer. Other material, especially design material, prepared in the architect's professional capacity belongs to the architect, and this accounts for the greater part of the documentation prepared in the course of a project.

5 Standard Forms of Agreement for the Appointment of an Architect

5.01 The RIBA Standard Forms of Agreement for the Appointment of an Architect are the most widely used forms of appointment and are likely to remain so although others are available. The New Engineering Contract (NEC) published by the Institution of Civil Engineers in 1993 and strongly advocated by Sir Michael Latham's 1994 report *Constructing the Team* included a Professional Services Contract (PSC) for use in any consultancy appointment including that of an architect. The Joint Contracts Tribunal publish a version of its HomeOwner/Occupier Contract which includes a form for appointment of a consultant.

The RIBA Standard Forms of Agreement for the Appointment of an Architect have a long history in the course of which they have on occasion been subject to litigation and official comment. The use of the forms is not and cannot be mandatory and the parties to the contract of appointment are free to use whatever version or form of appointment they wish and to amend the forms to suit their particular requirements. However, as the forms reflect the experience of consultants operating in all fields of activity and are consistent with current legislation an architect would have to have very good reasons not to recommend their use or to make significant amendments to them.

5.02 The Forms of Agreement introduced in 1999 provide a series of related appointment documents for use in various situations. The forms update and extend the previous documents, i.e. the Standard Form of Agreement for the Appointment of an Architect SFA/92, the Conditions of Engagement for the Appointment of an Architect CE/95, Small Works Conditions SW/96, and the Form of Appointment as Planning Supervisor PS/95. They took into account the Unfair Terms in Consumer Contracts Regulations 1994, the Arbitration Act 1996, and the Housing Grants, Construction and Regeneration Act 1996. The family of standard appointment documents comprises:

1 Standard Form of Agreement for the Appointment of an Architect (SFA/99)
2 Conditions of Engagement for the Appointment of an Architect (CE/99)
3 Employer's Requirements Supplement (Design and Build) for use with SFA/99 or CE/99 (DB1/99)
4 Contractor's Proposals Supplement (Design and Build) for use with SFA/99 (DB2/99)
5 Form of Appointment as Planning Supervisor (PS/99)
6 Form of Appointment as Sub-consultant (SC/99)
7 Form of Appointment as Project Manager (PM/99) and
8 Small Works Conditions (SW/99).

The Standard Form of Agreement for the Appointment of an Architect (SFA/99) is the key document. It is suitable for use where the architect provides services for a fully designed building project of any size or complexity; it can also be used where other professional services are provided. Its documentation comprises the Articles of Agreement, the Schedules, the Services Supplement, and the Conditions.

The Conditions of Engagement for the Appointment of an Architect (CE/99) and the Small Works Conditions (SW/99) are devised for use with letters of appointment for projects which are not regarded as being large enough to justify the full documentation of SFA/99.

The design and build forms i.e. the Employer's Requirements Supplement (Design and Build) (DB1/99) and the Contractor's Proposals Supplement (Design and Build) (DB2/99) are devised for use with either form SFA/99 or (in the case of DB1/99 only) form CE/99. Both forms, DB1/99 and DB2/99, include replacement Services Supplements for use where the 'consultant switch', i.e. the architect's transfer from the employer to the contractor is envisaged. DB1/99 can also be used where there is a change to design and build during the work. Both are appropriate for use where the Standard Form of Building Contract With Contractor's Design (WCD/99) is in use.

The Form of Appointment as Planning Supervisor (PS/99) under the Construction (Design and Management) Regulations 1994 reflects the layout and content of SFA/99. It is intended that it should be used with Articles of Agreement but guidance is offered for its use with a Letter of Appointment. Where the architect is commissioned as both architect and planning supervisor it is strongly recommended that the two appointments should be clearly separate and that both SFA/99 and PS/99 should be used. As a 'designer' under the regulations the architect is required to brief the 'client' on the requirements of the regulations, especially in relation to the 'client's duties'; role and duties of the 'planning supervisor', the 'principal contractor', and 'other contractors'; and the 'health and safety plan' and the 'health and safety file'. It is at the stage that the client's attention should be drawn to the Form of Appointment as Planning Supervisor (PS/99).

The Form of Appointment as Sub-consultant (SC/99) is devised for situations in which a consultant wishes, or is required by the client, to sub-contract part of his responsibility to another consultant who becomes a sub-consultant. It is not appropriate for use where the client wishes to make direct appointments with consultants. The client's consent to sub-contracting is required. The form can be used as printed regardless of the form of agreement between the client and the main consultant.

The need for a form of appointment for a project manager that is compatible with the architect's form of appointment has been apparent for some time. The Form of Appointment as Project

Manager (PM/99) complements but does not conflict with the architect's services under other RIBA standard forms of appointment.

The terminology, format and conditions of the documents are consistent but it is important that the architect should be sufficiently familiar with the differences in application and content of the forms in order to be able to advise clients on the selection of the form most appropriate to any given situation. It is particularly important that the architect is familiar with the conditions and is able to explain their meaning and application to a lay client.

All of the forms are available at RIBA bookshops and at www.ribabookshop.com

Plan of Work

5.03 As part of the development of SFA/99 and its associated documents revised versions of the Plan of Work were produced with the intention of forming a closer relationship between the schedules of service and the Plan of Work. This is published in two formats, as an Outline Plan of Work which was approved by RIBA Council in 1998, and as an expanded version entitled The Architects Plan of Work for the Procurement of Feasibility Studies, a Fully Designed Project, Employer's Requirements and Contractors Proposals, published in 2000. The revised versions make more effective provisions for appraisal and briefing, full design, Employer's Requirements and Contractor's Proposals.

Plan of Work Stages

A   Appraisal
B   Strategic Briefing

C   Outline Proposals
D   Detailed Proposals
F   Final Proposals

F   Production Information
F1
F2
G   Tender documentation
H   Tender Action

J   Mobilization
K   Construction to Practical Completion
L   After Practical Completion

Standard Form of Agreement for the Appointment of an Architect

5.04 The Standard Form of Agreement for the Appointment of an Architect (SFA/99, updated April 2000) comprises

Articles of Agreement
Schedule 1: Project Description
Schedule 2: Services
  Revised Plan of Work Stages
  Other activities
Schedule 3: Fees and expenses
Schedule 4: Other Appointments
Services Supplement: Design and Management
  Architect's design services
  Architect's management services
Conditions of Engagement

The Recitals make provision for the date of the agreement, details of the client and the architect, the title or description of the project and its address; it makes reference to Schedule 7; Project Description.

The seven articles of Agreement make reference to the Articles, the Conditions, the Appendix, Schedules 2, 3 and 4, Settlement of disputes and the Date. The Appendix to the Conditions requires insertion of the applicable law of the contract, and the name and/or nominator of the adjudicator, and makes optional ... optional provisions for the limitation of the time during which action or proceedings may be opened and for the limitation of the amount of liability

and the amount of professional indemnity insurance cover. The client's agreement or otherwise to the limitation of his rights is a matter of negotiation and agreement.

Potential clients may wish to impose their own particular conditions; the implications of any non-standard conditions need to be carefully assessed. If a substantial extension to the liability or duties of the architect is likely to be incurred appropriate additional reimbursement should be negotiated. Extensions of liability outside those of an existing professional indemnity policy should be discussed with the architect's broker or insurers before acceptance. In the case of public bodies and others requiring the architect to undertake to maintain professional indemnity insurance for six years following completion of the works: the architect must insist that the undertaking is subject to the reasonable availability of insurance cover.

The four schedules and the services supplement have an important role in SFA/99; care is needed in their completion. The extent to which it is possible to complete Schedule 1: Project Description depends upon the nature of the project and its circumstances but an attempt must be made in order that the basis of the architect's services and fees can be demonstrated. It is likely that on many occasions only a brief statement can be made at the outset and further descriptions will have to be added as the nature of the work becomes clearer. The intention of the project description in Schedule 1 to ensure that there can be no misunderstanding about the nature of the work. In addition to as precise a description of the project as possible it could refer to such matters phasing or sectional completion, special submissions and negotiations; site information on ownership, boundaries, easements, covenants, planning consents, surveys and investigations, Health and Safety matters provided by the client; organizational and operational matters; accommodation, space and use requirements, cost limits, key dates and programme requirements. Where an initial brief already exists it should be attached to the agreement and an appropriate reference made in the schedule.

Schedule 2: Services offers four options which have to be selected by deleting which of the following services are not required;

1   Perform the services as designer, design leader, lead consultant, during pre-construction and construction Work Stages OR
2   Perform the services for the Work Stages indicated below (i.e. Plan of Work Stages A, B, C, D, E, F, G, H, J, K, and L)
3   Make visits to the works at the anticipated frequency indicated below
4   Perform any other services identified below.

For Schedule 2 to be effective it is necessary for the architect to brief the client clearly on the architect's possible roles, the plan of work stages, site inspection procedures, and other services that might be undertaken by the architect. A limited checklist of some of the possible services that could be offered by an architect is included in the schedule. If for any reason the required services have to be varied during the work it is essential that Schedule 2 is revised and where appropriate changes are made in Schedule 3. An architect's failure to draw attention to changes in the nature or range of service required and the basis of payment can have embarrassing consequences for both the client and the architect.

For Schedule 3 parties have to agree on the method for calculating fees for normal services in relation to the services described in Schedule 2 and the percentages or lump sums involved. Provision is made in the conditions for the annual review of certain lump-sum figures and time charges; additional fees; and a fixed interest rate on late payments: Schedule 3 also covers expenses and disbursements; mileage rates; hourly rates or other bases for different categories of staff or individuals; and instalment payments.

Prospective clients frequently require an estimate of the anticipated total fees likely to be involved in projects. This is understandable but care is needed; difficulties often arise where fees have been forecast on the basis of a premature estimate of the likely total cost of the building work. If an estimate is made it is essential that the clients is properly briefed on the nature of the estimate and its limitations. Similarly, difficulties can arise when a forecast of the likely duration of work is offered in the case of work to be charged on a time basis.

The client should be reminded that the architect's fees and charges and those of other consultants are nett and do not include Value Added Tax (VAT) which is chargeable at the current rate regardless of the VAT status of the building work. Clients who are taxable persons under the Finance Act 1972 are able to recover such input tax from the Customs and Excise Department.

Architects carrying out work overseas in situations where the RIBA conditions of appointment do not apply are advised to follow any customary local scales of charges but where there are no local models it is suggested that the RIBA forms might be adapted to local circumstances.

Schedule 4: Other Appointments provides for the names and addresses of other consultants to be given. If these are not known at the time of the agreement it is suggested that the expression 'to be agreed' should be inserted or where the need for their use is not thought to be necessary the expression 'not applicable' should be entered although these expressions have no contractual significance.

The Services Supplement to SFA/99 is of considerable importance and merits careful study. It is in two parts, dividing the services into the Architect's Design Services and the Architect's Management Services.

The Architect's Design Services use the Plan of Work to detail the possible services of the architect in relation to each of the stages offering options for Alternative A where the architect provides cost advice and Alternative B where the architect provides information to enable the Quantity Surveyor to provide cost advice. The implications of these alternatives must be stressed; in both cases the onus on the architect to provide information is significant. In Alternative A the architect is required to provide cost estimates and cost advice during Plan of Work Stages A, C, D, E, F, and G and in Alternative B to provide the information for the quantity surveyor to do so.

The Architect's Management Services usefully groups and details the services under three headings which can be offered singly or in combination to suit the particular procurement arrangements preferred. The architect may be appointed;

As design leader AND/OR
As lead consultant (pre-construction) AND/OR
As lead consultant and contract administrator.

Not only does the division of the Architect's Management Services in this way offers a flexible model for use in different situations, it also can assist the architect in explaining the extent of the architect's possible duties to a lay client.

Other related forms of agreement

5.05 The forms are devised as a series of consistent and inter-related documents which have to be read in conjunction. The Conditions of Engagement for the Appointment of an Architect (CE/99) are similar to the Conditions of the Standard Form of Agreement for the Appointment of an Architect (SFA/99). The Small Works Conditions (SW/99) cover the same principles in a simplified version.

The Employer's Requirements Supplement (Design and Build) (DB1/99) form and the Contractor's Proposals Supplement (Design and Build) (DB2/99) form are adapted versions of the standard services statements. The supplements have to be attached as appropriate and SFA/99 or CE/99 have to be amended as indicated.

6 Speculative work and tendering for architects' services

6.01 The emergence of speculative work and competitive fee tendering over the last two decades has had a profound effect on the procedures of architects' negotiations with their clients and to some extent their relationships with clients. Speculative work in which the architect undertakes work at risk on the basis that payment will only be made in the event of the work proceeding is now widespread, especially in commercial and development work. Competitive fee tendering has also become commonplace with official and quasi-official bodies being obliged to obtain competitive tenders for substantial projects, and with private clients becoming more aware of the possibilities of competitive fee-tendering.

6.02 The extent to which an architect is prepared to undertake speculative work must depend upon many factors such as the policy of the practice, the architect's knowledge of the potential client, the nature of the proposed project, the likelihood of its success, the architect's existing commitments, the capacity of the office now and in the foreseeable future, the possible income and profit from the commission if it proceeds, the extent of competition for the work and so on. But regardless of these conditions and the fact that the architect may not be paid initially, it is important that there should be a formal agreement between the architect and the client defining the extent of the service to be provided by the architect and the commitment of the client to the architect in the event of the project proceeding. In the event of the project proceeding it is usual for the architect to be reimbursed for the initial work undertaken at risk.

The cost of speculative work undertaken at risk by an architect may be substantial and it is important that the practice should budget for non-fee-earning speculative work, as part of its overheads, fixing a limit to the amount it does, and maintaining strict record of time and costs. Where teams of design and other consultants are involved in joint submissions on a speculative basis it is becoming usual for the costs to be shared.

6.03 Architects should be particularly wary of invitations to prepare design solutions in conjunction with competitive fee tenders often on the basis of scant information – only rarely would such an invitation be acceptable. Architects should also endeavour to discover details of others invited to submit fee tenders and refuse to participate in competitive fee bidding in which the number of tenderers or the form of competition is unreasonable.

As the range of possible sources of design and procurement routes widens it is understandable that clients should increasingly make detailed enquiries about services and charges before making formal appointments. The basis of comparison is often inadequate; architects should endeavour to ensure that clients fully appreciate the nature of the service being offered and do not make appointments on the basis of fee alone. Potential clients are often unaware of fundamental differences between, say, conventional design services and design by a contractor's organization; more subtle differences in design services are certain to elude them unless they are carefully explained by the architect. The fee is determined by the service required and the cost of providing that service; unless this is known a fee quotation can be little more than a guess.

6.04 Dissatisfaction with the approach of some large commercial organizations seeking competitive fee bids led to the preparation and publication of the guidance note Guidance for Clients to Quality Based Section as part of the series *Engaging an Architect*, published by RIBA Enterprises.

7 Appointments required by statute

7.01 On occasion the architect may be engaged to carry out duties required by statute; these duties may be specified in detail as part of the schedule of services or reference may be made to the relevant statute. It has to be recognized by both the client and the architect that statutory duties are non-negotiable; if for any reason the architect cannot or is not allowed to comply with the requirements of the legislation the architect must withdraw, advising the client of the reasons for the termination of the appointment.

An appointment as a Construction (Design and Management) Regulations 1994 Planning Supervisor under the Health and Safety at Work etc. Act 1974 is probably the statutory appointment most frequently encountered. The duties are specified in detail in the regulations but payment arrangements and other matters have to be agreed between the parties. This appointment can be dealt with using the RIBA Standard Form (PS/99).

An appointment as a Surveyor under the Party Wall etc. Act 1996 is concerned with the carrying out of duties as specified in a disinterested and impartial manner regardless of the concerns of the parties. Again the duties are specified in detail in the Act but payment arrangements and other matters have to be agreed between the consultant and the parties involved; if the parties cannot agree on the appointment the local authority will make the appointment, unless the local authority is a party in the dispute in which case the Secretary of State will make the appointment. There is no RIBA standard form to cover such appointments, which should not be dealt with under, for example SFA/99, but should form a separate written agreement.

The most recent statutory duty is that of the adjudicator under Part 11 of the Housing Grants, Construction and Regeneration Act 1996 acting in the resolution of differences or disputes between the parties to a construction contract. The adjudicator is allowed considerable flexibility within the time scales of the Act in the carrying out of duties but generally adjudicator appointment agreements are tending to follow those of conventional appointments for arbitrators. Payment is usually on a time basis and it is now usual for the parties to agree an appropriate rate at the time of appointment. Various institutions publish standard terms of agreement for appointment of an adjudicator, for example the JCT and the CIC.

8 Scottish appointments*

8.01 The Architects Registration Board Code of Conduct (1999) paragraph 11.1 stipulates that architects should not undertake professional work unless the terms of the contract have been recorded in writing. This is sound practice as it reduces the scope for later disputes about the terms of the appointment. It is proper practice for appointments involving clients based in Scotland and services supplied or works located in Scotland to be in Scottish form. There are differences in substantive law, procedure, regulation and terminology which make this appropriate. While a simple exchange of letters is sufficient to form a written appointment in Scotland, the standard forms are to be preferred. It is desirable that contracts and appointments be formally executed in terms of the Requirements for Writing (Scotland)

* This section was written by Angus Stewart QC.

Act 1995. A clear decision should be taken at an early stage to proceed in this way, especially where one or more of the parties is or are accustomed to operating under non-Scottish conditions. The Royal Incorporation of Architects in Scotland (RIAS) publishes standard forms of appointment suitable for use in Scotland. These are in three versions: SCA/2000 which is applicable to the 'classic' architect to 'employer' client relationship where the architect goes on to be contract administrator; DBE/2000 which is suitable for the architect to 'employer' relationship in the early stages of design build; and DBC/2000 which is suitable for the architect to 'contractor' relationship in the later stages of design build. (The RIAS does not favour use of the 'novation' process in design and build, but prefers 'consultant switch' with two separate appointments, the first with the 'employer', in JCT parlance, and the second and subsequent appointment with the 'contractor'.) The RIAS does not currently publish a sub-consultant appointment though this is under consideration. As an alternative, the RIBA forms SFA/99 Standard Form, SC/99 Sub-consultant and PM/99 Project Manager as adapted for use in Scotland may be used. Guidance Notes are available. The following RIBA forms have *not* been adapted for use in Scotland and should *not* be used: CE/99 Conditions of Engagement; PS/99 Planning Supervisor; SW/99 Small Works; SFA/99 Design and Build Amendments; DB1/99 Employer Requirements; and DB2/99 Contractor's Proposals. Forms of Appointment and advice are available from the RIAS Bookshops at 15 Rutland Square, Edinburgh EH1 2BE; Tel: 0131 229 7545, Fax: 0131 229 228 2188, e-mail: bookshops@rias.org.uk and at Mackintosh School of Architecture, Scott Street, Glasgow G3 6NU; Tel: 0141 332 9414, Fax: 0141 332 9252, e-mail:rias@ riasglasgow. fsnet.co.uk

8.02 Statutory appointments as Planning Supervisor under the Construction (Design and Management) Regulations 1994 and as Adjudicator under Part 11 of the Housing Grants, Construction and Regeneration Act 1996 will also be encountered in Scotland, but the Party Wall Act 1996 does not extend to Scotland (see paragraph 7.01 above).

31

Architects' collateral warranties

ANN MINOGUE

1 Architects and collateral warranties

1.01 Architects are likely to encounter collateral warranties in two circumstances. First, and most importantly, they themselves may be asked to provide collateral warranties and, second, they may be expected to advise their clients – the employer under the building contract – on collateral warranties to be given by contractors and sub-contractors either to the employer or to funders, purchasers or tenants.

1.02 This chapter is concerned with the first of these circumstances and looks in more detail at the forms of collateral warranties which an architect is likely to encounter. This chapter cannot review all the permutations which have been dreamt up by solicitors to funders, purchasers and tenants, on the one hand, and solicitors to consultants, on the other, over the last two decades. What it aims to do is to discuss the basic obligation to provide collateral warranties and then to look at the provisions of CoWa/P&T in detail followed by the 'step-in' rights conferred by CoWa/F. These two documents are the standard forms of collateral warranty published by the British Property Federation but agreed with The Association of Consulting Engineers, The Royal Incorporation of Architects in Scotland, The Royal Institute of British Architects and The Royal Institution of Chartered Surveyors. The JCT in 1992/1993 established a Working Party to look at both consultants' and contractors' collateral warranties was not able to reach agreement on revisions which might be made to the existing standard forms of consultants' collateral warranties.

Inevitably, therefore, the parties to the original agreed BPF Standard Forms of Collateral Warranty have now divided into two camps: the Construction Industry Council has recently published new forms of collateral warranty – CIC/ConsWa/F and CIC/ConsWa/P&T – under its logo. The British Property Federation has drafted a new form of Consultancy Agreement which, at the time of publication of this book is shortly to be published which adopts the provisions for Third Party Rights used in JCT Major Project Form 2003 – see Chapter 11 but amended to reflect the different role of a consultant. At the same time, it is intended to produce new standard forms of collateral warranty – BPF CoWa/F and BPF CoWa/P&T as before – amended to correspond with the changes included in its Consultancy Agreement. Inevitably, this proliferation of different forms of collateral warranty will do nothing to help increase standardization in the construction industry. It seems inevitable that, instead, the property market, which had reached a degree of consensus on the appropriate provisions to include in collateral warranties, will now polarize and the length of this chapter in subsequent editions of this book will steadily increase.

For the purposes of this chapter, CIC/ConsWa/F and CIC/ConsWa/P&T will be used as a basis for explaining the usual terms of collateral warranties but reference will be made to those areas where the BPF Third Party Rights Schedule and the revised BPF collateral warranties are likely to differ from them.

2 The obligation to provide collateral warranties

2.01 There is obviously no general legal duty on anyone to agree the terms of or to enter into a collateral warranty in favour of a third party. If collateral warranties are required, then the employer is well advised to ensure that there is a binding obligation imposed by the terms of his consultancy agreement with the architect to grant collateral warranties.

2.02 The first standard set of conditions of engagement to acknowledge the existence of collateral warranties was the Standard Form of Agreement for the Appointment of an Architect (SFA/92) produced by the Royal Institute of British Architects. The provisions included in SFA/92 were very antagonistic to collateral warranties. They have been substantially revised in SFA/99 (update 2000). This defines a 'Third Party Agreement' as:

> 'An agreement between the Architect and a third party existing in parallel with the agreement between the Architect and the Client.'

SFA/99 contains two relevant clauses:

- Clause 5.6 states that if the architect is involved in extra work or incurs extra expense he is entitled to additional fees calculated on a time basis. Reasons for such entitlement include:

> 'The Architect consents to enter into any third party agreement the form or beneficiary of which had not been agreed by the Architect at the date of the Agreement.'

It is not clear at all how, in these circumstances, the architect is involved in 'extra work or incurs extra expense'. At one end of the spectrum, it is possible to see that he may be involved in legal fees in agreeing the form but, at the other, is it intended that any liability which he might incur under the third party agreement itself constitutes 'extra expense' for which he is entitled to be reimbursed? The drafting and rationale for this provision is very uncertain.

- Clause 7.5 states that:
> 'Where the Client has notified, prior to the signing of this Agreement, that he will require the Architect to enter into an agreement with third party or third parties, and, the terms of which and the names or categories of other parties who will sign similar agreements are set out in annex to this Agreement, then the Architects shall enter into such agreement or agreements...'

Accordingly, the client now has a binding commitment from the architect to enter into a collateral agreement with a third party stated.

2.03 As an aside, the defensive approach adopted by SFA/99 to the new Contracts (Rights of Third Parties) Act 1999 should also be noted here. Clause 7.6 of SFA/99 provides as follows:

'For the avoidance of doubt nothing in this Agreement shall confer or purport to confer on any third party any benefit or the right to enforce any term of this Agreement.'

In other words, all rights are excluded. It is to be hoped that in subsequent editions, the RIBA may feel able to be more receptive to the opportunities created by the Act.

2.04 Of course, in practice, architects will often be faced with tailor-made consultancy agreements and these will endeavour to protect the client by imposing specific obligations on the architect in relation to the provision of collateral warranties or third party rights.

What the client needs to include where he anticipates that he may need to call for collateral warranties is a clause requiring the architect to give collateral warranties to parties precisely defined in accordance with a stipulated form of collateral warranty which should be attached to the consultancy agreement. If no form is stipulated and attached, the obligation is merely to enter into a form as agreed, and, again, the clause simply amounts to an 'agreement to agree' and is unenforceable by the client if the architect simply refuses to agree a draft.

2.05 The relevant provision must define the persons to whom collateral warranties are to be given. This is where the first difficulties in negotiation usually arise. In order to maintain maximum flexibility, the client will want collateral warranties in favour of:

- Any person providing finance
- Any future purchaser of the project, or, where the project is capable of being divided into separate investment units, of any part of the project
- Any tenant of the project or of any part of the project
- If the nature of the profit-sharing or other arrangements for the project require, freeholders or borough councils or other third parties who may have a loss if the project is negligently designed or constructed.

Architects should not accept these open-ended provisions which raise the prospect of their being required to enter into collateral warranties with, say, 60 shop tenants on a shopping centre or tenants of kiosks in the lobby of a major office development. It behoves both parties to look sensibly at the nature of the project and to arrive at an equitable solution – perhaps, to give collateral warranties to tenants of the anchor stores only in a shopping centre, or tenants who take more than a certain amount of lettable area in the case of a multi-tenanted office development.

2.06 Finally, there is much debate about the enforceability of a simple obligation to enter into a collateral warranty. Will the courts order specific performance of an obligation to enter into an agreement by making the architect sign it or will they suggest that damages for breach of the contractual obligation undertaken by the architect is an adequate remedy for the client so that the client must show that he has suffered a loss (presumably his loss of a funder, purchaser or tenant) because the architect has failed to comply with his contract? The latter is most widely held but opinions differ. In any event, applying to the courts, with all the costs and delays that entails, is not a satisfactory position for a client who has a tenant waiting to sign a lease with him provided a collateral warranty is forthcoming from the architect. It is for this reason that powers of attorney are frequently inserted by clients in tailor-made consultancy agreements in addition to the basic obligation to provide the collateral warranty. The power of attorney authorizes the client to execute the collateral warranty on behalf of the architect if the architect, in breach of his contractual obligations, fails to execute it himself. Architects usually and perhaps understandably object to these provisions and yet they do no more than give the client rights to enforce an obligation in circumstances where the architect himself is in breach of contract.

2.07 The use of Contracts (Rights of Third Parties) Act 1999 to obviate the need to sign a multitude of separate collateral warranty

documents is discussed in detail in Chapter 11. The Act will not, of course, prevent debates about the potential beneficiaries of Third Party Rights and the issues discussed in paragraph 2.05 will continue. Nor will the Act obviate the need for debate about the terms of the Third Party Rights to be granted and the issues discussed below will still arise. The Act does, however, provide a much simpler mechanism for delivery of the Third Party Rights reducing the paper chase which exists at the moment. It is intended that the BPF Form of Consultancy Agreement – when published – will use a Third Party Rights Schedule similar to that adopted by JCT Major Project Form and described in Chapter 11 and its provisions can therefore be used as a model for incorporating the necessary mechanisms.

3 The terms of collateral warranties: CIC/ConsWa/P&T

Clause 1: The Warranty

'The Consultant warrants to the Purchaser/Tenant that it has exercised [and will continue to exercise] reasonable skill care and diligence in the performance of its services to the Client under the Appointment.'

3.01 Consultants generally warrant that they will exercise reasonable skill and care in the performance of their duties. Part II of the Supply of Goods and Services Act 1982 reflects this basic implied term. All the standard terms of engagement published by the relevant professional bodies provide for this or something similar. Consultants do not 'guarantee' results – they do not warrant that the results of their labours will be a building which is 'suitable' or which will comply with any particular performance specification or requirement. Hence, this basic warranty of, reasonable skill care and diligence.

3.02 Arguably, if under the terms of the consultancy agreement, the architect has assumed a higher duty of care – 'the skill, care and diligence reasonably to be expected of a properly qualified and competent consultant experienced in the provision of like services for projects of a similar size, scope and complexity to the Project' – then this duty of care might be reflected in the collateral warranty.

3.03 It should also be noted that the warranty relates to the 'Services' under the consultancy agreement. If, for example, the architect has been engaged to provide design services only and not inspection services, this formulation will relate the collateral warranty to the design services only. It is imperative, therefore, that any beneficiary of a collateral warranty also checks precisely the definition of services under the consultancy agreement.

Clause 2(a): The Exclusion of Economic and Consequential Loss

'… the Consultant shall be liable for the reasonable costs of repair, renewal and/or reinstatement of any part or parts of the Development to the extent that – the Purchaser/Tenant incurs such costs and/or – the Purchaser/the Tenant is or becomes liable either directly or by way of financial contribution for such costs. The Consultant shall not be liable for other losses incurred by the Purchaser/the Tenant.'

3.04 If this limitation on the basic warranty did *not* appear, then the architect would be liable to the purchaser/the tenant for damages for breach of contract assessed in accordance with the normal rules – broadly, contractual damages cover losses which are reasonably foreseeable at the date the contract was entered into as likely to arise as a result of the breach of it. In the case of the collateral warranty to a tenant, these would probably include cost of repair of defects caused by the consultant's negligence, additional professional fees, loss of profit, potentially business interruption and so on.

3.05 It is argued by the CIC that this is just too broad and the risks are unquantifiable. Accordingly, they accept that they must pick up the cost of repair as provided in Clause 1(a) but that all other losses should be excluded as the final sentence states. However, this is a position which architects may find difficult to sustain in practice under pressure from their clients. Clients, purchasers and tenants argue that designers and builders can anticipate the sort of business losses likely to be suffered by purchasers and tenants of the building and they would be liable for such losses if they had contracted with the owner/occupier in the usual way. Why should the architect escape this liability simply because he is working for a developer who is unlikely ever to go into occupation of the building? Accordingly, purchasers and tenants in particular would put a line through the whole of Clause 2(a). This leaves architects completely exposed to potential open-ended liability under the collateral warranty.

3.06 The British Property Federation argues that the drafting of Standard Collateral Warranties should anticipate the inevitable requirements of certain purchasers and tenants and, as with MCWa/P&T should reflect various alternative provisions in relation to losses other than the cost of repair. It is likely that the Third Party Rights Schedule in the BPF Consultancy Agreement and the revised BPF Forms of Collateral Warranty CoWa/P&T will omit the final sentence of the drafting of Clause 2(a) in CIC/ConsWa/P&T and substitute for it drafting which previously appeared in the BPF Guidance Notes as follows:

'The Consultant shall in addition be liable for other losses incurred by the Purchaser/the Tenant provided that the Purchaser/the Tenant has properly mitigated such losses and such additional liability of the Consultant shall not exceed [£•] in respect of each breach of the Consultant's warranty...'

This would seem to be a fair compromise and one which appears to be accepted, by a growing number of clients and, reluctantly, usually, but not always by purchasers and tenants. The architect should note that he must have regard when fixing the limit to the fact that he also has unlimited liability for repair costs so the cap may be less than the actual amount of his professional indemnity cover. He should also check whether his professional indemnity cover contained any aggregate caps on liability for specified risks (e.g. pollution and contamination) which might cause him to revisit this cap.

Clause 2(b): 'The Contribution Clause'

'Without prejudice to any other exclusion or limitation of liability, damages, loss, expense or costs the Consultant's liability for such costs of the repair, renewal and/or reinstatement in question shall be further limited to that proportion thereof as it would be just and equitable to require the Consultant to pay having regard to the extent of the Consultant's responsibility for the same and on the assumptions that:

(i) all other consultants and advisers, contractors and sub-contractors involved in and the Development have provided contractual undertakings on terms no less onerous than those set out in Clause 1 to the Purchaser/Tenant in respect of the carrying out of their obligations in connection with the Development;

(ii) there are no exclusions of or limitations of liability nor joint insurance or co- insurance provisions between the Purchaser/Tenant and any other party referred to in this Clause 2 and any such other party who is responsible to any extent for such costs is contractually liable to the Purchaser/Tenant for the same;

(iii) all the parties referred to in this Clause 2 have paid to the Purchaser/Tenant such proportion of such costs which it would be just and equitable for them to pay having regard to the extent of their responsibility for the same.'

This revised drafting by the CIC is very wide indeed in relation to the potential parties from whom contribution can be assessed – '*all other consultants and advisors, contractor and sub-contractors*'. Of course, not all of these parties will also give collateral warranties to any purchaser or tenant who will feel very exposed by agreeing to

such wording. The BPF in its Third Party Rights Schedule is likely to restrict the relevant third parties to other Consultants and the Building Contractor, these being the key players and the other parties from whom collateral warranties are likely to be sought by Purchasers and Tenants. It seems likely that this will be a future area of contention on collateral warranty wording though it has not been the case in the past.

3.07 The Civil Liability (Contribution) Act 1978 deals with contribution between people liable in respect of any damage in tort, for breach of contract or otherwise. Under the provisions of the Act, where two or more people have contributed to the same loss as a result of separately being in breach of contract, if one of them is sued for that loss, he can claim contribution from the others. Obviously this right of contribution will be much more difficult if, say, the architect has given a collateral warranty but the contractor, who may have contributed to the loss, has not. Equally, if both the architect and the contractor have given collateral warranties, but the contractor is insolvent so that there is no recovery from him, then the architect is left with the full extent of the liability.

The effect of Clause 1(b) is to try to ensure that, if there is a latent defect in the building and the purchaser/the tenant wishes to sue, his recovery against, say, the architect is assessed on the assumption that the architect is only liable for his 'share' of the contribution to the loss even if the purchaser/the tenant is unable to recover from the contractor who may have also contributed to the loss either because the contractor has not given a collateral warranty at all or, having done so, is insolvent so cannot meet his share.

3.08 Such clauses when they first appeared were resisted by purchasers and tenants who find it difficult to accept that they may be able to recover only 10% of their loss because of the contribution clause notwithstanding negligence by, say, the architect and breach of contract by the contractor. There is now an acceptance that in the context of the voluntary assumption of contractual responsibility inherent in the giving of a collateral warranty the principles of 'joint and several liability' under English law can operate unfairly, particularly in circumstances where one party's contribution to the loss is significantly more than another party's contribution but the first party cannot meet its share of responsibility. This is true in the case of, say, defective workmanship where the contractor may be held to be 80% or 90% culpable while the architect, who has also been negligent in failing to detect the defective workmanship in the course of his inspection duties, would normally bear only 20% to 10% of the share of the loss. If the contractor is not around, then obviously the architect must bear 100%. It is to be hoped that the consensus is not now de-railed.

3.09 There are, though, doubts as to the enforceability of 'the contribution clause'. In particular, there are elements of uncertainty in terms of the assumed nature and extent of the contractual undertakings which have been given by the other parties. In addition, there may be public policy issues involved in asking the courts to determine the potential liability by way of contribution of a party who is not involved in the proceedings, is not represented and does not have an opportunity to defend himself.

Clause 2(c): 'Defences of Liability'

'The Consultant shall be entitled in any action or proceedings by the Purchaser/the Tenant to rely on any limitation or exclusion in the Appointment and to raise the equivalent rights in defence of liability as it would have had against the Client under the Appointment.'

3.11 The purpose of this provision is to ensure that if, for example, the consultancy agreement contains a limitation on the architect's liability for negligence, that limitation is also imported into the collateral warranty and, hence, into the architect's relationship with the purchaser/the tenant. If it were not included, then there would be a strong argument that the purchaser/the tenant could sue the architect for an unlimited amount and, potentially, more than could be recovered from him by his client. It also allows the architect to argue, for example, that limitation periods for breach of the consultancy agreement have expired and, therefore, there is no claim against him by the purchaser/the tenant under the collateral warranty. The provision reinforces, should reinforcement be needed, the imperative that purchasers and tenants consider the terms of the consultancy agreement in order to determine the full extent of their rights under the collateral warranty.

3.12 But the provision is wider than this – if, for example, the architect's client requires him to produce a design detail in a certain way, perhaps against the advice of the architect, the architect will have a defence to any claim against him by the client. That defence will also be available, because of Clause 2(c), to the architect in any claim made against him by the purchaser/the tenant. Other 'rights in defence of liability' could arise through waivers, estoppels and so on.

3.13 In order to close the loop, the well-advised purchaser/tenant would ensure that he had included in his agreement with the client provisions prohibiting the client waiving, releasing or otherwise interfering with the architect in the performance of his duties so as to give rise to a 'defence of liability'. Although not watertight (since the circumstances in which the purchaser/the tenant is likely to sue the architect are circumstances where the developer is insolvent or cannot meet the liability in which case a claim for breach of contract against him is not much comfort), this does at least provide some protection to the purchaser or tenant who, hopefully, will not then find that his rights under the collateral warranty, when he comes to enforce them, are not worth anything.

Purchasers and tenants' solicitors sometimes try to include these prohibitions in the collateral warranty itself. It seems to be wrong in principle and it remains to be seen whether this approach will be adopted by the BPF. The relationship between the client and his architect is covered by the consultancy agreement and the collateral warranty should not interfere with that relationship. If the purchaser/tenant wish to interfere in that relationship, they should do so in the agreement between themselves and the client.

Clause 2(d): 'Independent Enquiry'

'The obligations of the Consultant under or pursuant to this Agreement shall not be released or diminished by the appointment of any person by the Purchaser/the Tenant to carry out any independent enquiry into any relevant matter.'

3.14 This provision is designed to prevent a contribution claim by the architect arising from the involvement of an independent surveyor or even an in-house surveyor by the purchaser/the tenant in the development. In other words, as between the architect and the purchaser/the tenant, the architect cannot argue that he is liable for less than the full amount of the damage suffered by the purchaser/the tenant (although he is not precluded from recovering a contribution from the purchaser/the tenant's independent surveyor if the latter too has been negligent).

Clause 3: 'Deleterious Materials'

3.15 Thankfully, the CIC has followed the approach adopted by the JCT in the MCWa Forms and the Consultant now warrants that he has exercised reasonable skill and care to see that materials are specified in accordance with the Guidelines contained in the addition of the publication *Good Practice in Selection of Construction Materials* (Ove Arup & Partners) current at the date of specification. This provision replaces the lengthy lists of materials which used to characterize Consultancy Agreements and collateral warranties, the death knell for which was sounded by the much publicized attack by the Kirkforthan Brick Company Limited (the only manufacturer of calcium silicate bricks in Scotland) on West Lothian District Council for '*reckless disparagement*' of their product. The only difficulty is that such lists were often used not just to forbid the use of specific products such as high alumina cement in structural elements but also to encourage environmentally friendly development by excluding also, for example, tropical

hardwoods from non-renewable sources. Accordingly, these provisions may be expanded by more sophisticated clients to include reference to their standard environmental policies.

3.16 It is anticipated that the Third Party Rights Schedule and the BPF Consultancy Agreement will follow this approach as well. It is likely, however, to require the Consultant to exercise reasonable skill, care and diligence to see that materials used in construction of those parts of the project to which the services relate will be in accordance with the *Good Practice Guide*. This is a point frequently raised by solicitors acting for purchasers and tenants.

Clause 4: Payment

'The Consultant acknowledges that the Client has paid all fees and expenses properly due and owing to the Consultant under the Appointment up to the date of this Agreement.'

3.17 The presence of this provision in the collateral warranty is, frankly, inexplicable. Given that a properly drafted consultancy agreement would oblige the architect to enter into the collateral warranty when requested, it can only work against the architect who will also be obliged to give this acknowledgement even in circumstances where the basic statement is untrue. The truth is that the relationship between the client and architect is governed by the consultancy agreement and not by the collateral warranty which should not interfere in these issues. The CIC has marked the provision – 'delete if not appropriate.' The BPF is likely to delete it.

Clause 5: 'Copyright'

3.18 This provision obliges the architect to give the purchaser/the tenant a wide-ranging licence to copy and use those documents prepared by or on behalf of the architect for any purpose related to the premises – that is those parts of the development which the purchaser/the tenant has bought or leased but not the whole. The licence extends to the copying and use of documents for an extension but not a right to reproduce the design for an extension. It should also be noted that, this provision refers to the licence being conditional upon:

'The Consultant having received payment of any fees properly due and owing as at the date of exercise by the licence.'

In other words, the architect can argue, in circumstances where entitlement is disputed under the consultancy agreement, that no copyright licence arises. This reflects the position of the architect under SFA/99. It will not be acceptable to funders, purchasers and tenants and is unlikely to appear in BPF warranties.

Clause 6: 'Professional Indemnity Insurance'

3.19 While the architect should check that his professional indemnity insurance corresponds with the obligation set out in the collateral warranty at the date it is executed, this obligation is, after that, largely of academic interest because:

- The obligation is probably too uncertain to be enforceable since it is qualified by the following proviso: 'Provided always that such insurance is available at commercially reasonable rates.'
- There is no effective sanction for a breach by the architect of his obligation to maintain professional indemnity insurance.

Clause 7: 'Assignment'

3.20 Here, the CIC collateral warranty provides for two assignments to person taking an assignment of the purchaser/tenant's interest. Ownership of premises does not change frequently nor are leases often assigned so this should meet most requirements of the purchasers or tenants.

It should be remembered that an assignment does not create new rights. It extinguishes the assignor's rights and, from the date of the assignment, gives the assignee the rights which the assignor would otherwise have had. It does not mean that the assignee's limitation period starts again following an assignment of the collateral warranty.

Similarly, it does not mean that the assignee can recover damages which would not have been recoverable by the assignor.

Equally, from the purchaser/tenant's point of view, if the architect has agreed to give him a collateral warranty in the first place because it is thought that the size of the interest which he is taking in the development warrants this degree of protection, and if that purchaser/tenant parts with his interest after occupying the building for, say, two years, then the new purchaser or tenant will still have losses if there are latent defects in the building caused by the architect's negligence. If he does not have the benefit of the collateral warranty, then he may have no redress whatsoever in respect of those losses.

Clause 8: 'Limitation'

'No action or proceedings for any breach of this Agreement shall be commenced against the Consultant after the expiry of —— years from the date of practical completion under the building contract.'

3.21 The CIC's guidance notes – assuming English law! – suggest that periods not exceeding six years should be inserted for consultancy agreements under hand and twelve years if the consultancy agreement is executed as a deed.

Even if such periods are included, there is a risk that Clause 8 will prevent claims being made against the architect by purchasers/tenants in circumstances where the client still has a valid claim against the architect for breach of the consultancy agreement and relevant limitation periods under the consultancy agreement have not expired. For example:-

- If an act of negligence is committed by the architect during the defects liability period or, indeed, if negligent advice is given by the architect in relation to a defect which appears after the defects liability period has expired, Clause 8 may bar a claim even though limitation periods are still open under the consultancy agreement.
- If indemnities are included in the consultancy agreement, those can have the effect of extending limitation periods.
- If there is evidence of deliberate concealment on the part of the architect.

CIC/ConsWa/F

3.22 This contains, at Clauses 5, 6 and 7, provisions conferring on the funders 'step-in rights' entitling the funder to 'take over' the appointment and to receive prior notice of termination of the appointment by the architect. They have limited application and they should only be included where such rights are properly covered under agreements between developers and their funders. The clauses warrant careful analysis.

- *Clause 5* This entitles the funder to serve notice on the architect upon termination of the finance agreement. In order to avoid an

argument by the developer that the architect is in breach of his obligations under the appointment, it is important in such circumstances to ensure that the developer acknowledges that the architect is entitled to rely on notice given by the funder and, hence, the fact that the developer is a party to CIC/ConsWa/F even though he derives no benefit under it.

- *Clause 6* This requires the architect to give notice to the funder before terminating the appointment for breach by the developer. Again, it entitles the funder to serve notice on the architect requiring the architect to act for the funder in such circumstances. The developer should ensure in these circumstances that he has proper protection under the terms of his agreement with the funder against improper service of notice by the funder.
- *Clause 7* Finally, this requires the funder to accept liability for fees payable to the architect including fees outstanding at the date of service of any notice. This clause sometimes causes difficulties with funders but, of course, if a funder does not agree to meet outstanding fees, the architect will simply serve further notice on the funder in respect of breach of payment obligations under the appointment. Clause 7 also provides that, if the funder nominates someone else to take over the appointment – perhaps, for example, another developer – it, the funder, will act as guarantor for the fees; in other words, the architect will not find himself in contract with a man of straw.

Another comment about these 'step-in rights' is that they can only appear as drafted in one collateral warranty on each project. If they are given to two or more different parties, the architect may be in an impossible position and may receive notices from two or more parties requiring him to contract with them. If step-in rights are to be given to more than one party, priority clauses must be included.

For comments on 'Step In' and Third Party Rights – see Chapter 11.

4 Practical advice

4.01 An architect being asked to sign a consultancy agreement which contains an obligation to provide collateral warranties in a stipulated form or indeed being asked to sign the collateral warranty itself *must* clarify with his insurers their precise policy in relation to the issue of these documents. Most professional indemnity insurance policies will contain a specific endorsement about collateral warranties stipulating the numbers which may be given and the terms which are insured. If there is no special endorsement insurers must be questioned carefully about their position to ensure that, by entering into express contractual commitments with third parties, the architect is not allowing insurers to avoid liability or is not activating one of the policy exclusions.

It is prudent to have all warranties which contain any departure from forms accepted by insurers agreed with insurers.

32

Architects' liability

KIM FRANKLIN AND RACHEL TOULSON

1 Introduction

1.01 This chapter is about liability to pay damages when things go wrong. 'Damages' are sums of money payable to compensate for harm done. The person seeking compensation may take the architect to court, or, if he has a contract with the architect, may set off his claim for damages against the architect's fees.

Different sources of liability

1.02 An architect may be liable to his client for breach of contract, through the tort of negligence or under statute. He may also be liable to those with whom he has no contract, 'third parties', through the tort of negligence or under statute. This chapter examines the basic principles of each of these types of liability.

An architect should have adequate skill and knowledge to enable him to originate, design and plan buildings or other works which require skilled design and arrange for and monitor their construction. Unlike the work carried out by a builder, success in the various tasks undertaken by an architect cannot, as a rule, be guaranteed. That is reflected in the standard usually applied when testing an architect's liability.

The question of professional liability can be approached under five broad headings, the first four of which are outlined in the remainder of this section:

1 A minimum standard of reasonable care is to be exercised in the discharge of professional duties carried out under a contract.
2 A higher duty to achieve particular results, comparable with the duty generally placed upon a builder, may be contracted for.
3 Duties under the law of tort to third parties. Such a duty may also be owed to a client concurrent with a contractual duty.
4 A more specialist duty may be owed in tort when giving advice, either to a client or to a third party.
5 Additional duties may be imposed by statutes. These are discussed in Section 5 of this chapter.

Contractual duty of care

1.03 A contractual duty of care is owed to the other party to the contract. For an architect, this is usually his client. An architect has a duty to use reasonable care and skill in the course of his engagement. If not expressly agreed, this duty is implied into contracts which an architect makes by section 13 of the Supply of Goods and Services Act 1982. The extent of this duty was described by McNair J in *Bolam v Friern Hospital Management Committee* [1957] 1 WLR 582, at p. 586.

'Where you get a situation which involves the use of some special skill or competence, then the test as to whether there has been negligence or not is not the test of the man on the top of a Clapham omnibus, because he has not got this special skill. The

test is the standard of the ordinary skilled man exercising and professing to have that special skill. A man need not possess the highest expert skill; it is well established law that it is sufficient if he exercises the ordinary skill of an ordinary competent man exercising that particular art.'

In summary, an architect will be tested against the conduct of other architects.

The degree of skill required to discharge the duty was considered by Denning LJ in *Greaves & Co. v Baynham Meikle* [1975] 1 WLR 1095. He stated:

'The law does not usually imply a warranty that [the professional man] will achieve the desired result, but only a term that he will use reasonable care and skill. The surgeon does not warrant that he will cure the patient. Nor does the solicitor warrant that he will win the case.'

So the courts recognize that failure is not conclusive evidence of breach of duty. An architect can defend himself and avoid liability by showing that he used reasonable skill and care. In this respect the architect differs from the builder and does not, as a rule, guarantee that he will achieve the desired end result.

Contractual duty of result

1.04 An architect can, however, under the express terms of his contract take on the responsibility to ensure that the end product will perform as required. This duty is much more onerous than that to take reasonable care and it may be difficult to obtain professional indemnity insurance for. In much of the relevant case law the court has had to decide, on the basis of the evidence, whether such a duty was in fact contracted for. The designers involved have often asserted that it was not.

Within the field of construction, such a duty is most likely to arise in design-and-build contracts. Where the architect is employed by the contractor, who as a rule has a duty to achieve a certain end result, it is easy to see how the architect runs the risk of having that onerous duty passed onto him. For example in *Greaves v Baynham Meikle* the contractors undertook to build a factory complex and warehouse, supplying all necessary labour, materials and expertise to produce the finished product. The contractors engaged the defendants, consultant structural engineers, to design the warehouse. The building was to be constructed according to a newly introduced method of composite construction and was to be used for storing and moving oil drums loaded onto stacker trucks. Within a few months of completion the first floor began to crack: the floors were not designed with sufficient strength to withstand the vibration which was produced by the stacker trucks. The contractors claimed an indemnity from the engineers on the grounds that the engineers had warranted that their design would produce a building fit for its purpose. The Court of Appeal explained that the professional man is not usually under a duty to achieve a specified result. But they went on to compare the situation with that when a dentist agrees to make a set of false teeth for a patient. In that case there is an implied warranty that they will fit his gums (*Samuels v Davies* [1943] KB 526). Denning LJ said:

'What then is the position when an architect or an engineer is employed to design a house or a bridge? Is he under an implied warranty that, if the work is carried out to his design, it will be reasonably fit for the purpose? Or is he only under a duty to use reasonable care and skill? In the present case . . . the evidence shows that both parties were of one mind on the matter. Their common intention was that the engineer should design a ware-house which would be fit for the purpose for which it was required. That common intention gives rise to a term implied in fact.'

He concluded:

'In the light of that evidence it seems to me that there was implied in fact a term that if the work was completed in accord-ance with the design it would be reasonably fit for the use of loaded stacker trucks. The engineers failed to make such a design and are therefore liable.'

Ordinarily the professional designer does not warrant the ultimate success of his design. As stated by Judge Lloyd QC in *Pyne v John Setchell Ltd* [2002] PNLR 7, "A professional person . . . does not normally undertake obligations of an absolute nature but only undertakes to exercise reasonable professional skill and care in the performance of the relevant service or in the production of the product." If, however, his involvement is either as part of a package deal to design, supply and erect an end product, or to design some-thing to comply with stated performance criteria then he may be obliged to ensure that the finished article is fit for its purpose. The extent of the duty owed will depend upon the nature of the contract.

Concurrent duties in tort and contract

1.05 The two levels of duty described above relate to contract. Different criteria apply to duties owed in tort. While tortious duties are generally relevant to third parties, it is clear following the House of Lords' decision in *Henderson v Merrett Syndicates Limited* [1994] 3 WLR 761 that tort can also be relied on by those in a contractual relationship. One reason a contracting party might choose to rely on tort is that it may extend the time within which legal action has to be started. This is much more fully discussed in Chapter 3 and in section 7 of this chapter.

Duties in tort to clients and third parties

1.06 An architect's duties to his client are defined by the contract between them. Third parties, such as builders or subsequent pur-chasers, may not have a contract with the architect.

If there is no contract between them and the architect, any rem-edy they may have against the architect will be in tort, or in some cases, statute. A common law duty in the tort of negligence can be summarized as being a duty to take care not to cause injury or loss to those whom it is foreseeable might be affected by the acts caus-ing such damage. This is discussed in more detail in Chapter 3.

The House of Lords revolutionized the law of tort in *Murphy v Brentwood District Council* [1990] 3 WLR 414 . This case severely limited the remedies available to third parties by restricting the losses which can be recovered in tort. Recoverable losses are now limited to personal injury and physical damage to property. Pure economic loss cannot be recovered, and that includes reduction in the value of property as a result of physical damage. Consequently there is usually no duty owed in tort to protect building owners or occupiers from the cost of repairing defects in their buildings or financial losses incurred by reason of remedial works.

Architects may, however, be vulnerable to claims relating to building defects brought under one of the exceptions to this rule. A building might have defects that threaten injury to passers-by and adjacent property. In that case, its owner may be able to claim, in tort, against those involved in its construction, the cost of repairing or demolishing the building so as to make it safe. This exception was relied upon in the case of *Morse v Barratt (Leeds) Limited*

[1992] 9 Constr LJ 158 but was rejected by Judge Hicks QC in *George Fischer Holding Ltd v Multi-Design Consultants Ltd* [1998] 61 Constr LR 85 at 109–111. Another exception is if damage to the building causes damage to other property of the claimant. Damages can be recovered in respect of that other property.

As a result of the restrictions placed upon recovery in tort, sub-sequent owners have sought to rely upon secondary contractual remedies, such as those given by collateral warranties. They may also be assisted by the Contracts (Rights of Third Parties) Act 1999. This Act enables a person who is not a party to a contract to enforce a term of that contract if this was the intention of the contracting parties. The third party must be identified by name, class or description in the contract. He will be entitled to the same remedies for breach of contract as if he had been a party to the contract. The Act applies to contracts made on or after 11 May 2000 (unless it is incorporated into contracts made earlier).

Duty in tort to clients and third parties when giving advice – *Hedley Byrne* duty

1.07 In the case of the professional man there is a further very important exception to the rule that damages cannot be recovered for pure economic loss. As a result of the decision of the House of Lords in *Hedley Byrne & Co. Ltd v Heller & Partners Ltd* [1964] AC 465 the professional man may owe a duty when giving advice to avoid causing economic loss to third parties who rely upon that advice. To decide whether the exception applies, the court will look for various indicators. These include a relationship equivalent to con-tract although there is in fact no contract, that it is reasonably fore-seeable that the advice may be relied upon by a known third party and that the person relying may thereby suffer loss. The facts of *Hedley Byrne* illustrate the type of relationship which the court will look for. The claimants asked the defendants, who were bankers, for a credit reference for a third party. There was no contract between the claimants and defendants. The claimants relied upon the reference, which was misleading. When the third party became insolvent, the claimants suffered a loss. They sought to recover that loss from the defendants, saying that it had been caused by their negligent advice in the credit reference.

The architect's position may be unclear. Depending upon the par-ticular circumstances, he could simply be seen to be providing a ser-vice, in which case he would be liable only for personal injury or damage to other property as defined in *Murphy v Brentwood*. Or he could be seen to be giving professional advice as in *Hedley Byrne v Heller*, in which case he might owe a duty to keep those whom he knows might rely on that advice safe from economic loss as well. The outcome in each case will depend upon the facts. In *Machin v Adams* [1997] 84 BLR 79 the Court of Appeal overturned the decision of the court below which had held that a certifier, Mr Bannister, owed a duty of a *Hedley Byrne*-type. Mr Bannister wrote a letter to a build-ing owner saying that works to a building were almost complete and were satisfactory. The building owner showed the letter to a prospec-tive purchaser who subsequently bought the building. The purchaser alleged that the works were defective and that she had thereby suf-fered an economic loss. The Court of Appeal said that on the facts Mr Bannister did not owe a duty of care in tort to the purchaser as he did not know that his letter would be used for that purpose. However, under certain circumstances it seems that such a 'letter of comfort' could give rise to a duty. Where the person trying to claim is a third party, Goff LJ in *Henderson v Merrett* said that the existence of a con-tractual chain may be inconsistent with a *Hedley Byrne*-type liability which seeks to short-circuit the contractual structure.

2 Liability for breach of contract

Contractual obligations

2.01 The meaning of 'contract' generally has been explained in Chapter 2. Specific features of contracts between architects and their clients have been discussed in Chapter 30. The contract between an architect and his client, which is the main focus of this part of the chapter, is an arrangement under which an architect makes various binding promises to his client in return for the client's promise to pay his fees. The architect's promises are both express and implied. His express promises will be to do a number of things that vary from job to job. The duties contracted for might include surveying the site and the subsoil, producing drawings, advising on building regulations and planning, selecting a contractor to do the works, recommending a form of contract for the engagement of the builder, inspecting the works, exercising powers under the client's contract with the builder, and so on. The express terms will often be incorporated by the use of a standard form of appointment such as that published by the RIBA. However, express terms can also be made orally in the course of a telephone call or other conversation, or in correspondence. Standard terms may be incorporated simply by reference to a standard form in correspondence.

2.02 In addition to these express terms, statute deems the architect to make various implied promises. Important terms are implied by the Supply of Goods and Services Act 1982 to use reasonable care and, in the absence of express terms as to time, to carry out work within a reasonable time. Because of these terms, the architect undertakes to carry out a *careful* survey, to draw up *competent* plans within a *reasonable* time, to take *care* in his selection of a builder, and so on. However, where an architect has undertaken an obligation to achieve a certain end result, the implied term as to skill and care will not protect him if he fails. The court can also imply terms into a contract if they are necessary to make it work and were contemplated by the parties at the time they made the contract. Unlike the terms implied by statute which are clear from the outset, this second category of implied terms will usually only be formulated after a dispute has arisen.

Breach of contract

2.03 A leading textbook on contract law defines a breach of contract as follows: 'A breach of contract is committed when a party without lawful excuse fails or refuses to perform what is due from him under the contract, performs defectively or incapacitates himself from performing' (Treitel, *The Law of Contract*, 9th edition, 1995). So if an architect does not do what he undertook to do, in the absence of any defence, he will have committed a breach of contract which makes him liable to the person who engaged him if he has suffered loss as a result. The duty to use skill and care can be thought of as a defence: the architect may be able to show that despite having failed, he was careful.

Liability will be measured in damages as a sum of money. That sum may wipe out the architect's claim for fees, but it is not limited to the amount of those fees. It may be substantially more. The extent to which the architect is liable may, however, be limited by an express term; a limitation clause. Care needs to be taken in writing such limitation clauses. They will be ineffective if they fall foul of the Unfair Contract Terms Act 1977 and of the Unfair Terms in Consumer Contracts Regulations 1999.

Liability for breach of contract includes liability for consequential loss, in so far as those losses are of a reasonably foreseeable type. Damages for breach can include the losses incurred by the client in meeting the contractor's claim for additional or abortive works caused by design faults. This is discussed further in paragraph 6.03 below.

The scope of the duty of care owed to the client in contract

2.04 Architects carry out an increasingly wide range of tasks. It is a question of law rather than of fact what aspects of an architect's work are capable of giving rise to liability if he carries them out without reasonable skill and care. Can he be liable for negligent legal advice? Can he be liable for negligently certifying work which has not been properly done? The answer in general is 'yes'. There are few, if any, aspects of an architect's work for which he cannot in principle be held liable to his client if he fails to take reasonable care. All the examples below relate to contractual liabilities to clients.

Site investigation

2.05 An architect can be held liable for failing to make an adequate examination of the site for a building, both in terms of measurement and as to what is underground. In *Eames London Estates Ltd v North Hertfordshire DC* [1981] 259 EG 491, the foundations of an industrial building built on made up ground which included tipped rubbish proved to be inadequate. The architect was found to be negligent. He had failed to satisfy himself as to the adequacy of the bearing capacity and had also disregarded a sub-contractor's query as to whether he should dig through the made up ground to the sub-soil. If the job of ascertaining the nature of the site is beyond the architect then he should advise the client to engage a specialist to make the necessary investigations.

The architect must take account of other things which may affect the building, such as the effect of planting or felling trees, the rights of neighbours, and of planning restrictions. Three cases illustrate that a wide range of matters should be considered. In *Balcombe v Wards Construction (Medway) Limited* [1981] 259 EG 765 an engineer was found to be negligent for failing to enquire whether a site which had been cleared for development had previously had trees on it. In *Re St Thomas à Becket, Framfield* [1989] 1 WLR 689, architects were blamed for supervising works to a church without ascertaining whether there was ecclesiastical authority for the execution of those works before they were begun. In *Armitage v Palmer* [1960] 175 EG 315 the court said that an architect could be liable to his client for siting a building so as to infringe the right to light of a neighbour.

Design

2.06 An architect may be liable to his client if errors or omissions are made in the plans, drawings or specifications. Liability cannot be escaped on the grounds that the design was delegated to someone else unless the contract permits delegation and exclude or limits the architect's liability for the delegated design.

In the event that the design is outside the expertise of the architect he should inform the client. In *Richard Roberts Holdings v Douglas Smith Stimpson Partnership* [1988] 46 BLR 50, architects were employed to design alterations to a dyeworks. They undertook to get quotations for the lining of a tank, although they had no specialist knowledge of the chemicals which were to be used in the tank. The lining failed. The architects were found to have been negligent. The court said that if the architects had felt that they could not form a reliable view as to what lining was required, they should have advised their client to take other advice.

Design includes the choice of materials for the building and ensuring that the building is functional. Two further tests are the design's 'buildability' and its 'supervisability'. In *Department of National Heritage v Steensen Varming Mulcahy* [1998] CILL 1422 the judge said that whether a design was buildable and supervisable related to the skill of the tradesmen who could reasonably be expected to be employed in building it.

Clients who sue their architects may rely upon failure to comply with Codes of Practice, Building Research Establishment recommendations and British Standards. Failure to follow such guidance is unlikely of itself to establish liability, but may persuade the court there has been negligence. In a New Zealand case, *Bevan Investments Ltd v Blackhall and Struthers (no. 2)* [1973] 2 NZLR 45 the judge said, 'Bearing in mind the function of codes, a design which departs substantially from them is prima facie a faulty design, unless it can be demonstrated that it conforms to accepted engineering practice by rational analysis'. On the other hand, the courts have emphasized that rigid adherence to codes and similar guidance will not necessarily save designers. Goff LJ in *Holland Hannen and Cubitts (Northern) Ltd v Welsh Health Technical Services Organisation* [1985] 35 BLR 1 said, 'It is plain from the evidence that the code of practice is no more than a guide for use by professional men, who have to exercise their own expertise'.

Inspection of the works and certification

2.07 Strictly speaking, the extent of the architect's duty to inspect the works is defined by his contract with his client. Successive revisions of the standard forms of appointment have tried to restrict the scope of this particular duty, retreating from supervision to inspection. However, difficulties arise when considering the architect's duty to inspect under his contract with his client together with any power which he has to issue certificates under the contract between his client and the contractor. Certification may of itself need detailed and frequent site visits. It is difficult to regard inspection and certification as wholly separate functions.

Inspection

2.08 In both inspecting and supervising the works and in certifying, the architect is ascertaining whether the works have been carried out to the required standard. Particular attention may therefore be required at certain stages, for example if part of the works is to be covered over. A pragmatic approach was advocated by the court in *Corfield v Grant* [1992] 29 Con LR 58, where the judge said that adequate supervision was tested not by counting the number of hours spent doing it, but by asking whether what was done was enough. At some stages exclusive attention is needed, while at others attention from time to time will be sufficient.

Certification

2.09 An architect may be empowered under the client's contract with the contractor to certify a range of matters which include payment, practical completion, making good of defects and final completion. Certificates may have far-reaching effects, for example binding a client to pay a certain sum to the contractor. Where the architect has these powers they cannot be delegated. Even where other construction professionals are involved, the final responsibility for certification rests with the certifier.

2.10 When an architect certifies that payments are due under a building contract, he often has to judge between the claims of the builder and the complaints of the client. Because of this, it was formerly held that when issuing certificates the architect was in the same position as an arbitrator or a judge, that is immune from all liability for negligence on grounds of public policy. This view was overturned by the House of Lords in *Sutcliffe v Thackrah* [1974] AC 727. In that case it was held that the client can sue the architect if he negligently overcertifies and thereby exposes his client to paying too much. Where a contract provides for certificates to value the work which has been properly executed, the architect should satisfy himself as to the quality of the work before issuing the certificate.

A further example of an architect being found liable for failure in certifying is found in *West Faulkner Associates v London Borough of Newham* [1992] 9 Constr LJ 232. The contractors performed very badly and the original programme fell behind. The client could not determine its contract with the contractors unless the architects issued a certificate under Clause 25 of the building contract stating that the contractors had failed to proceed 'regularly and diligently' with the works. The architects refused to issue a Clause 25 certificate. The judge held that the contractors' progress had not been regular and diligent, and therefore that the architects were in breach.

In *London Borough of Merton v Lowe* [1981] 18 BLR 130 architects were found to have been negligent in issuing a final certificate. By issuing it they had deprived their client of any right to proceed against the contractor. Such a situation potentially leaves the client looking to the architect in respect of all problems for which the

contractor would otherwise have been responsible. Following *Crown Estate Commissioners v John Mowlem* [1994] 70 BLR 1, in which the Court of Appeal held that the issuing of the JCT final certificate meant that all work and materials were to the satisfaction of the architect and therefore in accordance with the contract, amendments were introduced to standard building contracts to change the effect of final certificates to avoid this particular problem. However, this remains a helpful illustration of the need to understand the effects of certification.

Financial advice

2.11 An architect can be liable if he causes his client damage by negligent advice on likely building costs. In *Nye Saunders & Partners v Bristow* [1987] BLR 92 CA the architects were asked to estimate the cost of renovating a house within a budget of £250 000. In February 1974 the architects gave an estimate of £238 000. In August the estimate was revised and a new figure of £440 000 given. The client said that he had been misled. He terminated the architects' engagement and refused to pay fees totalling £15 000. The architects were found to have been negligent for failing to point out that the estimate was based on prices current in February during a time of very high inflation.

In *Partridge v Morris* [1995] CILL 1095 an architect was held to have been negligent in failing to advise properly as to the financial acceptability of a contractor. The judge said that she should have done one or more of the following; obtained a bank reference, obtained a trade credit reference, made enquires of other architects, carried out a company search or asked the contractor for a copy of their audited accounts. Furthermore, simply obtaining this information would not have sufficed. Proper consideration would have had to be given to it. In *Pozzolanic Lytag Ltd v Brian Hobson Associates* [1999] 15 Const LJ 135 the judge said that a project manager who obtained information about a sub-contractor's insurance could not simply act as a post box and pass it on. If the project manager did not have the expertise to advise on the adequacy of the insurance arrangements, he should either have got expert advice himself, or advised his client that expert advice was required.

Legal advice

2.12 Architects are expected to have some knowledge of the law as it affects their business. They can be liable for the consequences to their client if they do not. For example, a surveyor was engaged by a client whose land was the subject of a compulsory purchase by the local authority. The surveyor's task was to negotiate a claim for compensation from the local authority. A well-publicized contemporaneous Court of Appeal decision had condemned the basis upon which compensation had previously been calculated. The court had substituted a new basis which would have been more favourable to the client. In ignorance of that decision the surveyor negotiated a low figure calculated according to the old rules. He was found to be liable (*Weedon v Hindwood Clarke and Esplin* [1974] 234 EG 121).

The Court have commented on the need for architects to take legal advice, for example in *West Faulkner Associates v London Borough of Newham*, the facts of which are outlined in paragraph 2.10 above. In finding the architects negligent, the judge looked at the legal advice which they had and had not chosen to obtain in interpreting the meaning of 'regularly and diligently'. For further discussion of this topic, see Chapter 37.

There are, however, limits to the extent of legal knowledge which an architect is expected to have. This is illustrated by *B. L. Holdings Ltd v Robert J. Wood & Partners* [1979] 12 BLR 3, a case which also points out that it may be prudent to take legal advice if in doubt. An architect was told by the local planning department that an Office Development Permit was needed only if the floor area of the office part of the proposed development exceeded the specified size, and that the floor area of ancillary buildings could be disregarded. He followed this advice, but this view of the law was condemned as incorrect in the law suit which followed. The first court which heard the matter found that the architect had been negligent: he should have warned his client of any doubts about the planner's approach, and should also have suggested that legal advice be obtained.

The Court of Appeal reversed the decision. They found that the architect had not been negligent as the question as to what areas should be included in the calculation was a difficult one.

Continuing duty

2.13 In the absence of an express provision to the contrary, an architect is under a duty to review his design as necessary until the works are complete. In *Brickfield Properties Ltd v Newton* [1971] 1 WLR 859, Sachs LJ said: 'The architect is under a continuing duty to check that his design will work in practice and to correct any errors which may emerge. It savours of the ridiculous for the architect to be able to say ... "true my design was faulty, but of course, I saw to it that the contractors followed it faithfully"...'

The courts have tended to hold that this duty requires reactive rather than proactive conduct on the part of the architect. For a discussion of the authorities on this point, see the judgment of Dyson J in *New Ishington Health Authority v Pollard Thomas & Edwards* [2001] PNLR 515.

In *University of Glasgow v William Whitfield* [1988] 42 BLR 66 the Court held that an architect's duty to design extended beyond practical completion until final completion. The architects carried out work at the Hunterian Art Gallery, and no final certificate was ever issued. In 1981 they were called back to look at water ingress three years after practical completion. The judge found that the architects were liable in respect of the advice that they gave in 1981.

3 Liability for the tort of negligence

3.01 This section first considers the tort of negligence in relation to personal injury and physical damage. It then addresses possible duties under the more onerous *Hedley Byrne*-type liability for advice given, which extends recoverable losses to purely economic ones. These duties may be owed to parties with whom an architect has contracted and to third parties.

Personal injuries

3.02 There is no doubt that an architect may be liable for negligence which causes personal injury to a foreseeable victim. This was established in *Clay v A. J. Crump & Sons Ltd* [1964] 1 QB 533. An architect supervising demolition and rebuilding instructed the demolition contractor to leave a wall standing as a temporary measure which closed off one boundary to the site. He accepted the demolition contractor's word that the wall was safe, and, although he visited the site, he did not check for himself. Had he looked, he would have seen that the wall was tottering above a 6-foot trench cut under its foundations. The architect, together with the demolition contractor and the builder, was found liable when the wall collapsed and injured one of the builder's men.

It should be remembered when considering whether an architect was negligent that his main function is to see that his client gets value for money. The safety of the builder's employees is mainly a matter for the builder himself. Thus an architect is not negligent if, unlike the architect in *Clay v Crump*, he orders something to be done which involves danger only if it is done the wrong way. An architect was not negligent when he ordered a chase to be cut in a wall, and as a result of the builder choosing to do it without shoring the wall up, it fell and injured a workman (*Clayton v Woodman & Son Ltd* [1962] 1 WLR 585).

Liability to subsequent purchasers for defects in the building

3.03 An architect may owe a duty of care to subsequent purchasers and tenants of a building constructed to his design or under his supervision. Following the House of Lords' decision in *Murphy v Brentwood*, severe restrictions have been placed on losses which can be recovered, see above at paragraph 1.06. These limitations rendered such a duty of so little protection to third parties that the use of collateral or direct warranties developed which give the building user a contractual relationship with its designer. The general view now

is that, save in exceptional circumstances, an architect will not owe subsequent purchasers a duty of care in tort to prevent economic loss. Defects which do not cause personal injury or damage to property other than that which is defective are categorized as pure economic loss. The defective work itself is regarded as pure economic loss as it causes a reduction in the value of the building.

An example of when an engineer was found liable to subsequent purchasers is to be found in the case of *Payne v John Setchell* [2002] BLR 48. The defendant engineer had certified that the foundations of 4 cottages were satisfactory. They were defective. Judge Lloyd QC held that in issuing the certificates, the defendant had assumed a responsibility towards subsequent purchasers of the cottages. These purchasers had relied on the certificates and could therefore sue the defendant for damages for the dimination of the value of the cottages.

Liability to the builder for economic loss

3.04 Often there is no contract between the architect and contractor. However, under the terms of most building contracts the acts or omissions of the architect can affect the contractor, for example in condemning work or certifying payment. The question arises as to whether the architect can be liable to the contractor in respect of negligently exercising his powers under the building contract. The losses which the contractor might suffer arising from such negligence will almost certainly be economic. In order to succeed in any claim, therefore, the contractor would have to show that the architect owed him a *Hedley Byrne*-type duty of care. In each case it is necessary to examine the relevant facts, the relationship between the parties and their responsibilities in order to consider whether such a duty arises.

Execution of the works

3.05 In *Oldschool v Gleeson (Construction) Ltd* [1976] 4 BLR 103, Judge Stabb QC held that an architect did not owe a duty to tell the contractor how to carry out the work. He said:

'Not only has (the architect) no duty to instruct the builder how to do the work or what safety precautions to take but he has no right to do so, nor is he under any duty to the builder to detect faults during the progress of the work. The architect, in that respect, may be in breach of his duty to his client, but this does not excuse the builder. I take the view that the duty of care which an architect or a consulting engineer owes to a third party is limited by the assumption that the contractor who creates the work acts at all material times as a competent contractor.'

So an architect is generally under no duty to instruct the contractor in the manner of performance of his work. There may, however, be a duty to warn. It was suggested in *Victoria University of Manchester v Hugh Wilson* [1984] 2 Constr LR 43 that if an architect knew that the contractors were making a major mistake which would involve them in expense the architect would probably owe a duty to the contractors to warn them. The judge said, 'In those circumstances the architect would not be instructing the contractors in how to do their work but merely warning them of the probable consequences of persistence in the particular method which they had adopted.'

Worthy of note is the decision of Judge Hicks QC in *Plant Construction PLC v Clive Adams Associates* (No. 2) 58 Con LR 1. The claiment contracted with FMC to construct two pits. The second defendants were engaged as sub-contractors. FMC gave directions to the second defendants as to roof supports. These directions were followed. The roof collapsed. The second defendant had recognized the inadequacy of the methods directed by FMC and had warned the claiment. Judge Hicks QC held that this was not enough to discharge the second defendants' duty of care, but found the claimant 80% contributorily negligent.

Certification

3.06 In *Arenson v Arenson* [1977] AC 405 the House of Lords opened the way for contractors to bring a claim against architects for loss resulting from under-certification. Subsequently however there has been no reported case where a contractor has succeeded in such a claim. In *Pacific Associates v Baxter and Halcrow* [1988]

44 BLR 33 the Court of Appeal held that engineers who had rejected a contractor's claim for additional expenses were not liable for the loss they thereby suffered. There was a contractual structure in place by which matters could have been resolved and it was therefore inappropriate to impose a duty of care on the engineers. The decision is not as clear as it might be as it is heavily dependent upon its particular facts. However, it now seems unlikely that a claim by a contractor against a certifier would succeed.

Liability to other third parties for economic loss

3.07 An architect may find himself in the position of owing a duty of care to avoid economic loss to third parties other than the contractor. In *Smith v Eric Bush* [1990] 1 AC 831 the House of Lords found that a surveyor who had been employed by a lender to value a house might have a duty of care to the borrower to avoid economic loss. The duty would arise if he knew that the borrower would probably buy the house in reliance on his valuation. A similar result could arise if an architect gave advice to a third party knowing that they might rely upon it.

4 Liability in contract and in tort compared and contrasted

4.01 Liability in contract is narrower than liability in tort in one very important respect: it exists only towards the other party to the contract. English law recognizes the doctrine of privity of contract, which means that the rights and duties arising under a contract are limited to the contracting parties. Thus where an architect is engaged by a client, only the client can sue the architect for breach of contract. Third parties who are 'strangers to the contract' must base their claim in tort.

As mentioned above at paragraph 1.06, the doctrine of privity of contract has been modified by the Contracts (Rights of Third Parties) Act 1999. In addition, it is sometimes possible for the benefit of a contract to be assigned. That is, various legal formalities are performed by which someone other than the original contracting party is substituted as the party who is entitled to receive the benefits of the contract. The Court of Appeal in *Trendtex Trading Corporation v Crèdit Suisse* [1980] 3 All ER 721 said that where property is sold, a right to claim damages in respect of that property may be assigned with it.

There are limits on assignment. There can be no valid assignment of a right to personal services. This means that the client may not require the architect to carry on supervising the site for some other client, unless the architect consents.

4.02 In contract, unlike in tort, the parties have been able to negotiate their respective obligations in advance. Consequently contractual liability, although narrower than tortious liability in that it lies in favour of fewer persons, is usually more stringent. As we have seen, an architect sometimes by contract assumes a duty higher than a duty to take reasonable care. Firstly, he may sometimes guarantee his solution to a problem. Secondly, in contract he not only undertakes to take reasonable care himself, but also guarantees reasonable care by those to whom he delegates performance of parts of the work. That includes independent consultants to whom he sub-contracts. An employer is also vicariously liable in tort, but for the negligent acts of a narrower range of people. In tort, he is liable only for the acts of those whom the law quaintly terms his 'servants'; that means, by and large, his salaried employees.

Contractual liability is also more stringent in that economic loss can be recovered in claims in contract. In tort, economic loss can only be recovered where there is a special duty of care, described above as a *Hedley Byrne*-type duty.

There is, however, one respect in which contractual liability is less stringent than liability in tort. The rules about the time within which an action must be brought work more favourably to protect the defendant in contract claims.

From what has been said, it is clear that a claim in contract normally has, from the claimant's point of view, a number of advantages

over a claim in tort. However if there has been a significant lapse of time, a claimant may only be able to proceed in tort.

5 Statutory liability

5.01 In addition to the duties which arise under the common law in contract and in tort which have been described above, an architect may also owe duties which arise from statute.

The Defective Premises Act 1972, section 1

5.02 This provides that:

> 'A person taking on work for or in connection with the provision of a dwelling (whether the dwelling is provided by the erection or by the conversion or enlargement of a building) owes a duty
> (a) If the dwelling is provided to the order of any person, to that person; and
> (b) without prejudice to paragraph (a) above, to every person who acquires an interest (whether legal or equitable) in the dwelling:
> to see that the work which he takes on is done in a workmanlike or, as the case may be, professional manner, with proper materials and so that as regards that work the dwelling will be fit for habitation when completed.'

The scope of the duty

5.03 Architects undoubtedly count as persons 'taking on work for or in connection with the provision of a dwelling', although builders and their sub-contractors are the persons whom Parliament mainly had in mind. Under this statute, an architect owes a duty not merely to take reasonable care, but also to see that the work which he takes on is done in a careful manner. The level of his duty is like that of his duty in contract: he must take care himself, and he also must ensure that care is taken by those to whom he delegates parts of his work.

The elements of the duty for an architect are carrying out tasks undertaken in a professional manner, using proper materials and seeing that the dwelling is fit for habitation. In *Thompson v Clive Alexander & Partners* [1992] 28 Con LR 49 the judge found that these duties should be read together. It was not enough for a claimant to prove that defects arose because of the architects' failure to carry out their work in a professional manner or to use proper materials. He held that the duty imposed by section 1(1) of the Act was limited to the kind of defect in the work done and the materials used which made the dwelling unfit for habitation upon completion. However, the breach occurs as soon as there is work which is in breach of the Act. It was held in *Andrews v Schooling* [1991] 1 WLR 783 that it would be a breach simply to omit a damp-proof course, without having to wait for the building to become damp and thereby unfit for habitation as a result.

The duty under the Act is owed to the person to whose order the dwelling is provided, and to every other person 'who acquires an interest (whether legal or equitable) in the dwelling'. This means that the duty passes with the land in favour of subsequent owners, landlords, tenants, and mortgagees. There is no requirement for the person owing the duty to have received any payment for carrying out the works. The duty will therefore be owed to subsequent owners of a house which an architect has designed for himself.

Limitations on the duty

5.04 In a number of ways, the duty imposed by the Defective Premises Act 1972, section 1 is narrow. It applies only to dwellings. There is no liability under these provisions for defective work on other building types. The duties it creates are owed solely to those to whom the statute says they are owed. The Act applies to new buildings, conversions of existing buildings into dwellings and enlarging existing buildings. It has been held not to apply to remedial works carried out to an existing dwelling.

Section 2 excludes actions for breach of the duty created by section 1 in respect of houses covered by an 'approved scheme'.

The scheme principally envisaged by this section was the 10-year protection scheme of the National House Building Council. The idea behind the exemption was that houses covered by the NHBC scheme did not also require statutory protection. However, the last NHBC scheme to be approved was their 1979 scheme. Consequently owners of houses covered by NHBC schemes other than those of 1973, 1975, 1977 and 1979 can claim against builders and construction professionals under Section 1.

The Act in use

5.05 The Defective Premises Act was not widely used until after the courts restricted the losses which could be recovered through tort. Since those changes, the Act has regained prominence and is now regularly used by third parties against construction professionals. Claimants can almost certainly claim under the Act for pure economic loss.

The Building Regulations

5.06 Section 38 of the Building Act 1984 says that a breach of duty imposed by the Building Regulations, shall so far as it causes damage, be actionable except where the Regulations say otherwise. This section has not been brought into force, and it now seems unlikely that it ever will be.

In the absence of section 38, case law suggests that breach of the Building Regulations does not of itself give rise to liability in damages for breach of statutory duty. Notably this view was endorsed by the Court of Appeal in *Taylor Woodrow Construction v Charcon Structures Ltd* [1981] 30 BLR 76. In that case Waller LJ said that such a Regulation would be difficult to construe as imposing an absolute duty in an action for damages.

It seems therefore that unless or until section 38 of the 1984 Act is brought into force, a breach of the Building Regulations will not give rise to a claim for damages in the absence of negligence. However, it is possible that the court will look at breaches of Building Regulations, like breaches of Codes of Practice, as persuasive evidence of negligence.

The Construction (Design and Management) Regulations (CDM)

5.07 The CDM Regulations place a duty on architects to design in such a way as to reduce hazards. A full discussion can be found in Chapter 28. As with the Building Regulations, breach of these Regulations is not of itself actionable by claimants in the civil courts. However, breach may well help to persuade a judge that there has been negligence.

The Supply of Goods and Services Act 1982

5.08 Part II of the Act relates to contracts for the supply of services and this includes services provided by an architect for client. Section 13 says that in such a contract there is an implied term that the architect will carry out the service with reasonable skill and care. Section 14 says that if no time has been fixed by the contract in which the service is to be carried out, there is an implied term that the architect will carry it out in a reasonable time. These terms are implied into contracts, rather than the statutory duties outlined in paragraphs 5.02 to 5.07 which may be thought of as additional to other duties in tort and in contract.

6 Measure of damages

6.01 Once breach has been established, an architect who has been found liable will be ordered to pay damages to the claimant.

Principles of calculation

6.02 The basis of calculating damages is theoretically different in contract and in tort. The fundamental principle governing the measure of damages is that the claimant must be put (so far as money can do it) in the position he would have been in if the architect had properly discharged his duty. For breach of contract, damages are supposed to put the claimant in the position he would have been in if the defendant had kept his promise: the court looks forward to see where the claimant would have been. In tort, damages are supposed to put the claimant in the position he would have been in if the tortious act had never taken place: the court looks back to see where the claimant was before.

For some time these different principles made little difference to the damages awarded in the usual sort of case against architects, that is in which someone complains that because of the architect's breach his building is defective. Whether the claim was brought in contract or tort the damages recovered were the cost of rectifying the defects in the building.

The changes in the law of tort to restrict recoverable losses emphasized the difference between the two types of claim. If a client brings a claim against an architect for breach of contract he is entitled to claim the cost of remedying any defects and to recover losses incurred as a result of the works being carried out. Since *Murphy v Brentwood* it is unlikely that any remedy is available through the tort of negligence to those who do not have a contract with the architect unless the special *Hedley Byrne*-type duty when giving professional advice arises. If that applies, the adviser would be liable not only for the cost of repairing any physical damage caused by the advice but also for any financial losses caused.

A claimant who can sue a defendant in both contract and tort can get only one set of damages. Limited damages can also be recovered for inconvenience, distress and annoyance, if for example, the claimant has been kept out of his house while building works take much longer than they should have, or while extensive remedial works are executed.

Limitations on recoverable losses

6.03 Two important limitations on the extent of damages should be noted. Firstly, the claimant is under a duty to mitigate his loss. This means that he must behave reasonably to keep the damage as small as possible, and if he fails to do this, he cannot recover for the loss he could have avoided. Thus someone who complains of a defective roof on his house must get it mended as soon as possible. He is not allowed to let the rain wreck his ceilings and his furniture while he sues the architect or builder, and then add the cost of those things to the claim.

Secondly, a defendant is not liable to pay for damage of a kind which is not a reasonably foreseeable consequence of his negligence. For example, assume an architect specifies inappropriate windows for a jeweller's shop, and the owner of the shop later has to spend money on both replacing the windows and altering the structural openings to make them compatible with the new, more suitable windows. The cost of replacing the windows flows directly from the breach. Similarly, the costs of altering the openings will almost certainly also be recoverable. The value of sales lost as a result of the work having to be carried out, for example if the shop has to close for a day, will also have been foreseeable and therefore recoverable. However if the owner missed out on selling his entire stock of diamonds to a buyer who happened to visit the shop on the day it was closed, that loss is unlikely to be recoverable from the architect as it was not reasonably foreseeable.

If the type of damage is foreseeable, the defendant is liable even if the extent of the damage is not. In *Acrecrest Ltd v W. S. Hattrell & Partners* [1979] 252 EG 1107 an architect negligently failed to take account of the effect of the removal of some fruit trees on the behaviour of the clay subsoil when he calculated the depth of the foundations of a block of flats. Some slight damage from 'heave' was a foreseeable result. Unforeseeably, a row of mature elms was felled nearby as well, and the damage from heave – nearly all of which would have been prevented by adequate foundations – was far worse than could have been anticipated. The architect was held liable for the full extent of the damage.

The date of assessment

6.04 Formerly, the claimant was awarded the cost of reinstatement at the time when the damage occurred. In times of inflation and rising building costs, this rule was very good for defendant builders and architects: the longer they could avoid payment, the less in real terms they had to pay. In *Dodd Properties (Kent) Ltd v Canterbury City Council* [1980] 1 All ER 928, this rule was reversed. The defendant damaged the claimant's property in 1970 and was eventually found to be liable in 1978. The Court of Appeal held the claimant was entitled to the cost of repairs at the time when he could first reasonably have been expected to do them, which was when the defendant was made to pay for them.

Apportionment

6.05 Large building projects involve many different participants with different roles. Defects in a building may be the result of breaches of duty by more than one participant. Similarly, several parties may be responsible for the same defects but to a different extent. For example, the contractor may be in breach of contract for bad workmanship and the architect liable for failing to notice the contractor's breach when inspecting the works. In such cases the court can apportion responsibility between the various defendants. For example, in *Equitable Debenture Assets Corpn v Moss* [1984] 2 Con LR 1 the claimant's claim related to defective design of curtain walling and bad workmanship to the parapet walling. The specialist design sub-contractors were held 75% liable for the curtain walling and the architects 25%. The apportionment in respect of the parapet walling was 80% to the sub-contractors, 15% to the main contractors and 5% to the architects.

7 When liability is barred by lapse of time

7.01 Statute has imposed time limits for bringing legal action. If proceedings are started outside the time limits, the claim will be time barred.

Limitation Act 1980

7.02 Section 2 of this Act provides that certain types of action, of which claims against architects and builders for negligence are one, shall not be brought 'after the expiration of six years from the date on which the cause of action accrued'. The vital question is: When does a cause of action 'accrue'? In general, a cause of action accrues when facts *f* exist upon which the claimant has the right to sue. When this is depends on whether the claim is based on a breach of contract or on tort.

Contract

7.03 A person can first sue for a breach of contract when the breach of contract occurs; he does not have to wait until he suffers damage as a result. In the case of an architect who is sued for a negligent breach of contract, he can be sued from when he acts negligently. If he fails adequately to supervise the laying of drains or foundations, he can be sued there and then. So six years from that date, the cause of action against him in contract expires. It matters not that, during those six years, his client was unaware of the negligence because no flooding or cracking had yet occurred. If the flooding or cracking occurs after the six years from the negligent supervision, as far as the law of contract is concerned, that is just the client's bad luck. An exception to this rule arises if the architect deliberately concealed his negligence.

The six-year time period under contract can be extended to twelve years if the contract has been entered into as a deed. This was previously referred to as being a contract under seal.

Tort

7.04 In tort no one can be sued until damage is suffered, which means that the cause of action does not accrue until then. Thus in tort, time starts to run in the case of a defective building when the damage to it occurs. In *Pirelli General Cable Works v Oscar Faber* [1983] 2 AC 1 the House of Lords considered cracking which had occurred to the top of a chimney which was 160 feet high. Their Lordships ruled that the limitation period ran from the date when the damage occurred, not from when it could have been reasonably discovered which was not until some 2 years later.

The Latent Damage Act 1986

7.05 The time limits within which actions in the tort of negligence for defective buildings can be brought have been modified by the Latent Damage Act 1986. Under that Act such negligence claims become barred either six years from the date when damage occurred, or three years from the date when the claimant discovered the damage, whichever is the later. Actions in either case are subject to a 'long stop' of 15 years from the date of the negligence complained of.

It has been held that the Latent Damage Act applies to negligent advice as well as negligent acts (see, for example, *Campbell v Meacocks* [1993] CILL p. 886).

The Defective Premises Act 1972

7.06 By section 1(5) of the Defective Premises Act 1972 claims under the Act can only be brought within 6 years of the date on which the dwelling was completed. However, if remedial works are carried out, the 6 year period will start to run again from the date of those works.

7.07 The law of limitation in contract is more fully discussed in Chapter 2 and the law of limitation in tort in Chapter 3.

8 Liability in Scots law*

8.01 In substance Scots law in relation to the liability of an architect to pay damages in compensation is much the same as the law of England and Wales. Liability may arise from breach of contract at common law, from delict (fault and negligence) at common law and from breach of statutory duty. The *Bolam* test for professional negligence (paragraph 1.03 above) is drawn from the opinion of the Lord President in the Scottish case *Hunter v Hanley* [1955] SC 200. The rules for assessing damages are similar.

8.02 A possible area of difference from English law is in the question of third-party rights of recovery in delict at common law, for example when a subsequent purchaser who had nothing to do with the original commission sues the architect for design faults. While *Murphy v Brentwood District Council* has clearly limited rights of recovery in England (paragraph 1.06 above), an alternative approach, suggested by certain Commonwealth decisions, might be seen as persuasive in Scotland. The Contracts (Rights of Third Parties) Bill does not extend to Scotland. The common law of Scotland already recognizes that contracts may confer enforceable contractual rights on third parties, although the doctrine has yet to be exploited in the construction context (cf. *Strathford East Kilbride Ltd v HLM Design Limited* [1997] SCLR 877). As in England contractual warranties are in use. Another area of possible difference relates to the effect of final certificates. In *Belcher Food Products Ltd v Miller and Black and Other* [1999] SLT 142, Lord Gill reserved his opinion as to whether a JCT final certificate excluded the client's right of action against the contractor for faulty work and materials (see paragraph 2.10 above).

8.03 Scotland has its own scheme of time limits for suing (limitation) and extinction of claims by lapse of time (prescription). Most of the law on this subject likely to be encountered in practice is contained in the Prescription and Limitation (Scotland) Act 1973 (as amended). Subject to a number of qualifications and to the dispensing power of the court in appropriate cases, actions for, or which include a claim for compensation for personal injuries have to be brought within three years of the injury. Other claims for compensation have to be brought within five years of the damage and the court has no dispensing power. In the case of concealed damage, time starts to run only when the damage is discovered or becomes discoverable (cf. paragraphs 7.01 to 7.04 above). The Defective Premises Act 1972 does not extend to Scotland. Architects have to keep in mind time limits for legal claims when advising clients on the action to be taken in relation to building defects, or they will risk exposing themselves to liability. Remember, five years for building defects!

---

* This section was written by Angus Stewart QC.

33

Architects' professional indemnity insurance

JAMES LEABEATER

1 Why be insured?

In case of claims

1.01 If architects make mistakes they can cause their clients to suffer financial loss which is many times larger than the fees the architects received for the particular project. On larger projects, architects can be liable for millions of pounds in damages. If an architect practises in a limited company, a large claim can cause the company to become insolvent, thereby leaving the client without full compensation. If architects are practising as a partnership, the partners will each be personally liable for the full amount of the claim, which could potentially lead to partners being made bankrupt. Suitable professional indemnity insurance will, subject to the limits of cover, protect the company or partnership against the financial impact of the claim.

Professional rules

1.02 Standard 8 of the Architects' Code of Conduct (see Chapter 38) provides that architects should not undertake professional work without adequate and appropriate professional indemnity insurance cover. It lays down the minimum cover required, by reference to the gross fee income of the particular practice.

Required by clients

1.03 Since architects can cause substantial losses, clients will often require architects to provide proof of adequate insurance cover. Standard form agreements often require cover for the same reason: for example, Clause 7.4 of the SFA/99 (see Chapter 30) requires the architect to maintain insurance in the amount stated in the appendix to the agreement, which will be the subject of negotiation between the architect and client.

For these and other reasons architects need professional indemnity insurance, and they need to know the basic principles of how it works.

2 Some basic insurance principles

2.01 The subject matter of an insurance policy may be the property owned by the insured, which he wishes to insure (e.g. the contract works), or it may be liability on the part of a person or company to third parties (e.g. the liability of the architect to the client). In this chapter, we are concerned with the latter.

The broker

2.02 The insured arranges insurance through a broker. The broker is usually the agent of the insured, not the insurer, although he will have connections with different insurers.

The proposal

2.03 The insured will have to complete a proposal form. On the basis of that proposal form (and what the broker tells him) the insurer will offer to write the risk for a certain premium, subject to the terms of the proposed policy. There may be a process of negotiation about the terms of cover. The architect may then choose to accept the insurer's offer and there will come into existence a binding contract of insurance.

The insured will generally have to warrant that the facts stated on the proposal form are true. If they are not, the insurer may have the right to avoid liability. This is discussed further below.

Disclosure of material facts

2.04 As a matter of law, the parties to an insurance contract owe each other a duty of good faith. This is specific to insurance contracts, and arises principally because the insurer has to rely upon the insured and the broker for information about the risk. As part of the duty of good faith, the insured must disclose to the insurer every fact which is material before the risk is written. A fact is material if it would influence the judgment of a prudent insurer in fixing the premium or other terms, or determining whether he will take the risk.

If the insured fails to disclose a material fact, and if the non-disclosure of the material fact induced the insurer to enter into the contract on the relevant terms, then the insurer will be entitled to treat the insurance contract as avoided, so that he is not bound to indemnify under the contract, and (unless the failure to disclose was fraudulent) the insured recovers the premium he has paid. The insurer is allowed to avoid the contract even though the non-disclosure was innocent.

Only if there has been a significant loss do insurers usually carry out investigations into the insured whereby they discover grounds for avoidance. In such cases the remedy of the avoidance can be ruinous for the insured. It is therefore very important for the insured to make sure that he has disclosed all material facts accurately. If necessary, he should take advice from the broker on what to disclose.

The policy may contain a term that insurer agrees not to avoid the policy if the insured can establish that the failure to disclose was innocent.

2.05 The proposal form will set out a number of questions which must be answered accurately and fully. However, the insured must disclose all material facts even if they are not covered by any matters in the proposal form. In particular, he must disclose any claims made against him, and any negligent work carried out. More generally, he must disclose:

1 Facts indicating that the subject matter of the insurance is exposed to more than the ordinary degree of risk or that the liability of the insurer is greater than he would have expected it to be.
2 Facts indicating that the insured has some special motive: for example, that he has greatly over insured.
3 Facts showing that there is a moral hazard, suggesting that the insured is not a fit person to be insured: for example, that he has been convicted or suspected of fraud.
4 Facts which are to the insured's knowledge material or regarded by insurers as material.

2.06 The insured in general need not disclose:

1 Facts which are already known to the insurer or which it might reasonably be presumed to know.
2 Facts which the insurer could have discovered by making some enquiries.
3 Facts where the insurer has waived further information.
4 Facts tending to lessen the risk.

Terms of insurance policies

2.07 A further idiosyncrasy of insurance contracts is that the terms are classified differently. In other contracts, breach of a condition will give the innocent party the right to treat the contract as being at an end, whilst breach of a warranty will only give rise to a claim for damages. Under insurance contracts, the position is different.

1 A warranty must be exactly complied with, and if it is not so complied with, the insurer is discharged from all liability from the date of breach of the warranty.
2 Other terms may be 'conditions precedent'. Unless the insured complies with the condition precedent, insurers will (depending upon the particular clause) have no liability under the policy, or have no liability for a particular claim.
3 Otherwise, breach of a condition may give rise to a right on the part of insurer to reject a claim or (possibly) to avoid the policy; or may only give rise to a right to damages caused by the breach.

3 Professional indemnity insurance policies

3.01 There is no one standard architects' professional indemnity policy. Careful reference must be made to the actual terms of the particular policy to see what it covers and what it does not cover. Insurance contracts are interpreted by giving effect to the normal meaning of the language used. In the case of ambiguity, the court will favour the interpretation which is against the person who drafted it: almost always the insurer.

3.02 The purpose of a professional indemnity policy is to indemnify the insured in respect of claims made against or notified to him within the period of the policy for breach of professional duty. The policy will generally indemnify the insured against sums which he becomes legally liable to pay by way of compensation for breach of professional duty (in tort or contract) as a result of a Court Order, arbitration award or settlement. Architects would be well advised to ensure that the particular policy responds to sums which are awarded by adjudicators (see Chapter 15).

Limits of indemnity

3.03 The insured will be liable for a certain sum by way of excess or deductible in respect of each and every claim, although there may be a clause which allows related claims to be treated as one claim for the purposes of the deductible.

3.04 The insured must be careful to select an appropriate level of cover, depending on the value of the projects on which he works. It may, for example, be a limit of £5 m each and every claim including the claimant's legal costs. Other ways of limiting cover are to provide that there is an aggregate limit of (say) £5 m in respect of all claims made in the year, or in respect of a series of claims which are linked in a defined way (e.g. they arise out of the same originating cause).

3.05 The policy is likely to cover the insured's own legal costs in addition to sums payable to the third party. Whether such costs are included within the limit of indemnity or not depends upon the wording of the particular policy. If payment to the third party is greater than insurers' limit of indemnity, then insurers' liability to pay costs may be scaled down by the proportion which the level of indemnity bears to the total amount payable to the third party.

Claims made

3.06 Professional indemnity policies are usually 'claims made' policies: they respond to claims made against or notified to the

insured within the period of the policy, not claims arising out of a breach of duty within the policy period. Partners should ensure that the firm's policies continue to cover them against claims in retirement, and sole practitioners should obtain 'run off' cover to protect them through retirement.

3.07 The policy will require the insured to inform insurers of claims made as soon as possible. It will probably require the insured to inform insurers of any circumstance or event which is likely to result in a claim. Failure to do so may mean that insurers do not have to pay. The importance of timely notification of claims to insurers cannot be overstated.

3.08 An insurer will not generally be liable for claims which the insured knew about before the policy was agreed. They should be covered by the previous year's policy. The insured should therefore ensure that all claims or circumstances likely to give rise to a claim have been notified to insurers before the end of each policy year.

3.09 If the insured makes a fraudulent claim on the policy, then the insured is not permitted to recover at all in respect of that claim, even if the claim or part of it could have been made honestly. This rule arises from the duty of good faith. It may be reinforced by a term in the policy.

Control of the claim and subrogation

3.10 The insurer will be entitled to take control of the claim once it has been notified to it. The insured may not admit liability for any breach of duty or compensation without the insurer's consent. The insured will have to give all such assistance to insurer as is necessary for it to handle any claim. However, in the event of a dispute between the insured and insurer, the policy will probably provide that the insured need not contest any legal proceedings unless an independent lawyer (often a Queen's Counsel) has advised that such proceedings may be contested with the probability of success.

3.11 If the claim against the insured is successful, and the insurer indemnifies the insured for the loss, the insurer will be subrogated to the insured's position in respect of any possible claims against third parties (e.g. the building contractor) in respect of the loss. The insured may be required to allow the insurer to use his name to bring proceedings against such third parties. The policy will however generally provide that the insurer will not exercise rights of subrogation against employees of the insured, unless there was dishonest, criminal or malicious conduct on the part of the particular employee.

Exclusions

3.12 The insured should read the exclusions to cover with care. The following are common exclusions:

1 An excess or deductible (see paragraph 3.03 above).
2 Claims arising out of participation in a consortium or joint venture.
3 Claims arising out of any circumstance or event which has or should have been disclosed by the insured on the proposal form or renewal form (see paragraph 3.08 above).
4 Claims caused by a dishonest, fraudulent, criminal or malicious act or omission on the part of any partner, director or principal of the insured. Such conduct on the part of employees, on the other hand, if it leads to liability to third parties, will generally be covered by the policy.
5 Claims made out of performance warranties, collateral warranties, penalty clauses or liquidated damages clauses unless the liability would have existed in the absence of such clauses. This is because such warranties or clauses generally extend the usual liability of the architect. They impose guarantees in respect of work done, whereas usually the architect is only liable in the event he has failed to exercise reasonable care and skill.
6 Claims arising out of a survey or valuation report carried out by the insured, unless it was carried out by a qualified architect or surveyor and a disclaimer as specified by the insurer was included in the terms of appointment. The disclaimer normally

tries to exclude liability for woodwork and parts of the structure which are covered up, and high alumina cement.

7 The policy may only cover work done in the United Kingdom.

Fees recovery extension

3.13 It may be possible for the insured to extend the policy to protect the insured against costs which are necessarily incurred in recovering or attempting to recover professional fees.

4 Risk management

4.01 Architects can take steps to minimise the likelihood of claims being made against them. This is largely a matter of commonsense, but the following list may be helpful.

1 Consider the terms of your appointment carefully. Make sure fee provisions and the scope of services are clear.

2 Do not take on work which is beyond the capability of the person doing it.

3 Have a system set up to check drawings and other work before it is sent out.

4 Make sure that everyone knows when deadlines fall. Do not agree to take on projects with unrealistic deadlines.

5 Have a proper document management system.

6 Make sure you know and comply with contractual formalities. Many disputes arise when there are no proper records of variations to the works, or additional instructions.

7 Consider any third party guarantee, collateral warranty or duty of care deed very carefully, and check that it will be covered by the policy. If necessary, take legal advice.

8 Make sure any consultants or contractors have written terms of appointment and insurance.

9 Make sure that all projects are properly supervised.

10 If a project is going wrong, ensure you keep good records of what is happening.

34

Copyright

CLIVE THORNE AND AMANDA TELFER

1 The basic rules of copyright

1.01 The copyright law of the UK is contained in the Copyright, Designs and Patents Act 1988 ('the Act') and the subsidiary legislation made under that Act. Copyright exists only in material which comes within one of the categories prescribed as being capable of having copyright protection. These are as follows:

1 Literary works
2 Dramatic works
3 Musical works
4 Artistic works
5 Sound recordings
6 Films
7 Broadcasts (including electronic transmissions)
8 Typographical arrangements of published editions.

The Act describes all these copyright categories as 'works'.

Material which does not fall within one of the categories will have no copyright protection; it will not be copyright material.

1.02 Copyright subsists for defined periods which differ according to the category of work.

Following the amendment of the Act by the Duration of Copyright and Rights in Performance Regulations 1995 (SI 1995 No 3297) which came into force on 1 January 1996, the duration of copyright in each category of work can be summarized as follows:

1 Literary, dramatic, musical and artistic – which includes architectural works: 70 years from the end of the calender year in which the author died.
2 Sound recordings: 50 years from the end of the year in which they were made, or if released before the end of that period, 50 years from the end of the calendar year in which released.
3 Films: 70 years from the end of the calendar year in which the last of the principal director, the author of the screenplay, the author of the dialogue or the composer of the specially created music dies, or if there is no-one within this designated list, 50 years from the end of the year in which they were made.
4 Broadcasts and cable programmes: 50 years from the end of the calendar year in which the broadcast was made or the cable programme included in a cable programme service.
5 Typographical arrangements: 25 years from the end of the calendar year in which the edition was first published.

The basic rules of copyright

1.03 If material is entitled to copyright, the right vested in the copyright owner is that of preventing others from doing certain specified acts, called 'the restricted acts' (paragraph 2.02). The restricted acts are specified by the Act in relation to each category of work and differ for each category.

If something is done in relation to copyright material which is not one of the restricted acts specified for that type of work or an act which constitutes 'secondary infringement' and was done by a person who did not know, or had reason to believe that the act would be an infringement of copyright, there is no breach of copyright.

1.04 There are certain circumstances in which doing restricted acts without the authority of the copyright owner does not constitute breach of copyright. The most important of these general exceptions are:

1 Fair dealing (e.g. for purposes of non-commercial research, private study, criticism, or review)
2 Use of less than a substantial part of a work or incidental inclusion
3 Use for certain educational purposes
4 Use for certain library and archival purposes
5 Use in parliamentary and judicial proceedings and certain other public administration functions.

There are other important exceptions, differing according to the types of works or subject matters (for example See paragraphs 6.01 and 6.02).

1.05 In most cases the author of a work is its first owner. But there are special rules which can override this general provision (see paragraph 5 below).

1.06 There is no copyright in ideas – only in the manner of their expression.

1.07 To acquire copyright protection, works must be recorded in a material form.

1.08 Literary, dramatic, musical and artistic works must be original (i.e. have involved the use of skill and labour by the author).

1.09 The work does not have to be published, nor does it have to be registered, for it to have copyright protection.

1.10 The author or maker of the work must be a 'qualified person': basically a citizen or resident of the UK or of one of the countries which is a signatory to the Berne Copyright Convention or the Universal Copyright Convention (UCC). Alternatively, the work must have been made or published in a qualifying country, which generally speaking (although there are important exceptions for sound recordings, films, broadcasts and cable programmes) are the same countries. There are no significant countries in the copyright context which are not parties to one or the other of these conventions. China signed both Conventions in 1992.

The nature of copyright

1.11

'Copyright is a right given to or derived from works, and is not a right in novelty of ideas. It is based on the right of an author, artist or composer to prevent another person copying an original work, whether it be a book, picture or tune, which he himself has created. There is nothing in the notion of copyright to prevent a second person from producing an identical result (and himself enjoying a copyright in that work) provided it is arrived at by an independent process.'

That quotation is from the report of the Gregory Committee on Copyright Law (1952), whose recommendations formed the basis of the Copyright Act 1956.

'A writer writes an article about the making of bread. He puts words on paper. He is not entitled to a monopoly in the writing of articles about the making of bread, but the law has long recognized that he has an interest not merely in the manuscript, the words on paper which he produces, but in the skill and labour involved in the choice of words and the exact way in which he expresses his ideas by the words he chooses. If the author sells copies of his article then again a purchaser of a copy can make such use of that copy as he pleases. He can read it or sell it second-hand, if he can find anyone who will buy it. If a reader of the original article is stimulated into writing another article about bread the original author has no reason to complain. It has long been recognized that only the original author ought to have the right to reproduce the original article and sell the copies thus reproduced. If other people were free to do this they would be making a profit out of the skill and labour of the original author. It is for this reason that the law has long given to authors, for a specified term, certain exclusive rights in relation to so-called literary works. Such rights were recognized at common law at least as early as the fifteenth century'.

The latter quotation is from the report of the Whitford Committee on Copyright and Design Law (1977), upon whose recommendations the Copyright, Designs and Patents Act 1988 is largely based. These two quotations contain as clear an exposé of the nature of copyright as can be found anywhere.

As the word itself implies, 'copyright' is literally a right to prevent other people copying an original work. It should be noted that it must be an original work, not an original idea.

Intellectual property and copyright

1.12 The main difficulty in comprehending copyright seems to be the association that is made among copyright, patents, and trade marks. These diverse creatures are, for convenience, usually grouped under the headings of 'industrial property' or 'intellectual property'. Copyright certainly is a form of property, but it is arguable that it would be preferable to group copyright with passing off, breach of confidence, and invasion of privacy. Alike these causes of action the aim of copyright law is to prevent the unauthorized use of a work derived from another. In contrast, the owners of trade marks, patents and registered designs may prohibit the unauthorized use of their work even if the alleged infringement was independently created and not copied.

The sources of copyright law

1.13 Statute copyright law is now entirely contained in the Copyright, Designs and Patents Act 1988 ('the Act') as amended. There are a significant number of rules and regulations contained in statutory instruments made under the above legislation or under powers contained in the European Communities Act 1972 to bring into effect the UK's obligations under European Community Directives. In addition, certain Orders in Council extend the provisions of the Act to works originating outside the UK.

The UK is party to a number of conventions dealing with international copyright recognition and other matters of an international nature concerning copyright, of which the most important are the Berne Copyright Convention and the Universal Copyright Convention.

There is a body of case law contained in the law reports consisting of the judgments of copyright cases. Decisions on earlier legislation, the Copyright Acts of 1911 and 1956, are frequently still relevant. They are of particular importance, for example, when determining what constitutes plagiarism and where judgments on matters of degree, rather than pure construction of legislation, must be made.

The history of copyright law

1.14 Copyright effectively came into existence with the invention of printing. The first indications of copyright were the granting of licences by the Crown to printers giving them the right to print (i.e. copy) against the payment of fees to the Crown. In 1662 the Licensing Act was passed, which prohibited the printing of any book which was not licensed and registered at the Stationers Company.

The first Copyright Act was passed in 1709. This Act gave protection for printed works for only 21 years from the date of printing and unprinted works for 14 years. Again, books had to be registered at the Stationers Company.

The Copyright Act 1842 was the next important piece of legislation relating to copyright. Although it accorded copyright protection only to literary works, it laid down as the period of copyright the life of the author plus 7 years after his death, or 42 years from the date of publication, whichever should be the longer.

Architects' plans, provided they had artistic quality, first became entitled to copyright protection as artistic works under the Fine Arts Copyright Act 1862.

The Copyright Act 1911 repealed all previous copyright legislation. This Act extended copyright protection to 'architectural works of art', with the result that, as the courts held in *Meikle v Maufe* [1941] 3 All ER 144, both buildings and the plans upon which they were based were entitled to copyright protection. Plans and sketches were protected as 'literary works' and drawings as 'artistic works'. The Copyright Act 1911 was repealed by the Copyright Act 1956. Protection for works of architecture under the 1956 Act was similar to that accorded by the 1911 Act. The 1988 Act repealed the 1956 Act. It came into force on 1 August 1989.

Database right

1.15 Following the implementation of an EC Council Directive on the legal protection of databases, the Copyright Rights in Databases Regulations 1997 (SI 1997) No 3032 which came into force on 1 January 1998 created a new 'database right' which gives a certain degree of protection where there has been a 'substantial investment in obtaining, verifying or presenting the contents of the database'. A database is defined as a 'collection of independent works, data or other materials arranged in a systematic or methodical way and individually accessible by electronic or other means'. In addition, a new class of literary work, qualifying for copyright protection, has been created for databases but the originality test is stricter than for other works.

The database right can subsist whether or not the database or its contents is a copyright work. The general rule is that the right subsists for 15 years from the end of the calender year in which the database was completed and the maker of the database will be the first owner of the database right.

If a database qualifies for protection the owner can prevent third parties extracting or re-utilizing all or a substantial part of the contents of the database without consent.

The new copyright Directive

1.16 As of 30 September 2003 the Copyright European Directive, adopted to harmonize certain aspects of copyright and related rights in the information society, has been implemented into UK law. It provides greater control for authors of literary, dramatic, musical and artistic works as to how and by whom their copyright works are communicated to the public, i.e. broadcast or electronically transmitted. The Directive's primary purpose is to circumvent anti-piracy technologies, amending (inter alia) the Act's provisions in relation to fair dealing.

2 Protection under the Copyright, Designs and Patents Act 1988

2.01 Works of architecture are included in the definition of 'artistic works' for copyright purposes. Section 4 of the Act defines an 'artistic work'. In view of its importance in considering architectural copyright it is worth quoting in full:

> S.4 (1) In this Part 'artistic work' means –
>   (a) a graphic work, photograph, sculpture or collage, irrespective of artistic quality,
>   (b) a work of architecture being a building or a model for a building, or
>   (c) a work of artistic craftmanship.
>   (2) In this part – 'building' includes any fixed structure, and a part of a building or fixed structure; 'graphic work' includes
>   (a) any painting, drawing, diagram, map, chart or plan, and
>   (b) any engraving, etching, lithograph, woodcut or similar work;
>
> 'photograph' means a recording of light or other radiation on any medium on which an image is produced or from which an image may by any means be produced, and which is not part of a film; 'sculpture' includes a cast or model made for purposes of sculpture.

Works of architecture include both buildings and models for buildings. The plans, sketches, and drawings upon which works of architecture are based are also artistic works which have their own separate copyright. So also do the notes prepared by the architect, but these are protected not as artistic works but as literary works.

There is no definition of 'fixed structure' although a decision under the 1956 Act held that a garden, in that case a somewhat elaborately laid out garden, was a 'structure' and therefore a work of architecture.

A 'drawing' is not defined by the Act. The definitions of 'artistic work' and 'literary work' are so wide that they cover all the typical output of an architect's office: design sketches, blueprints, descriptive diagrams, working drawings, final drawings, artistic presentations, notes, both alphabetical and numerical and reports.

Restricted acts

2.02 As mentioned in paragraph 1.03 above, there are separate restricted acts specified in the Act in relation to each category of work. The restricted acts applicable to works of architecture are the same as those applicable to artistic works, although there are certain special exceptions (paragraph 6) from these restricted acts in relation to works of architecture. The acts restricted by the copyright in an artistic work include either directly or indirectly:

1 Copying the whole or a substantial part of the work
2 Issuing copies of the work to the public.

Secondary infringements are possessing or dealing with, or providing the means for making, what an alleged infringer knows, or has reason to believe is, an infringing copy.

Originality and artistic content

2.03 The copyright in an artistic work (for example a building, model, architectural drawing or plan) is not necessarily dependant on any aesthetic appeal nor requires any artistic character. From the few reported cases, it appears that no architect has failed to prove an infringement even though the original building was so ordinary that it might be thought inevitable that someone else would design something substantially similar.

The test for originality is a low one as was demonstrated in *Walter v Lane* [1900] AC 539, a case which it was held that a

reporter was entitled to copyright in his verbatim report of a public speech. The work must originate from the author instead of merely being copied from another work. One of the principal leading cases in the area of originality is *Interlego AG v Tyco Industries Inc* [1989] AC 217 in which it was stated that skill, labour and judgment merely in the process of copying cannot confer originality so as to give copyright protection to the copy. This is despite the fact that copying an artistic work may in fact require considerable skill.

In the case of *University of London Press Ltd v University Tutorial Press Ltd*, which concerned the copying of examination papers, the judge stated that 'the word "original" does not in this connection mean that the work must be the expression of original or inventive thought ... but that it should originate from the author'.

2.04 For architectural works, the inclusion of some distinctive design detail will make the architect's task of proving infringement much easier. In *Stovin-Bradford v Volpoint Properties Ltd* [1971] Ch 1007 the courts were influenced by the fact that although many details of the architect's drawings were not reproduced in the constructed buildings, 'a distinctive diamond-shaped feature which gave a pleasing appearance to the whole' was reproduced. In *Meikle v Maufe* the judge dismissed them as not being of artistic merit.

2.05 Some distinctive design feature may also be important when it could otherwise be proved that the person sued was without any knowledge of the plaintiff's prior design, and that he produced identical solutions because of a similarity in circumstances. In *Muller v Triborough Bridge Authority* the US Supreme Court held that a copyright of the drawing showing a novel bridge approach designed to disentangle traffic congestion was not infringed by copying, because the system of relieving traffic congestion shown embodied an idea which cannot be copyright and was the only obvious solution to the problem.

Duration of copyright

2.06 The protection of copyright in an artistic work extends for the lifetime of the artist/author and a further period of 70 years from the end of the calendar year in which he died. In the case of architectural works, this period is not affected by the fact that the work was not published during the architect's lifetime.

In the case of joint works, the 70 years begins to run from the end of the calendar year in which the last of the joint authors dies. A joint work is one in which the work is produced by the collaboration of two or more authors in which the contribution of each author is not distinct from that of the other author or authors. Thus if a building is designed by two architects, but one is exclusively responsible only for the design of the doors and windows, so that it is possible to distinguish between the contributions of the two architects it will not be a joint work.

3 Qualification

3.01 In order to qualify for copyright protection in the UK, the qualification requirements of the Act must be satisfied either as regards the author or the country in which the work was first published.

3.02 As regards authors, in the case of unpublished works, copyright will subsist only if the author was a 'qualifying person' at the time when the work was made, or, if it was being made over a period, for a substantial part of that period. In the case of a published work, the author must be a 'qualifying person' qualified at the time when the work was published, or immediately before his death (if earlier).

3.03 For copyright purposes, the expression 'qualified person' does not refer to a professional qualification, but to any British citizen, British Dependent Territories citizen, a British National (overseas), a British Overseas citizen, a British subject, or a British protected person within the meaning of the British Nationality Act 1981, or a person domiciled or resident in the UK or in another country to which the Act extends or is applied, or a body incorporated under the laws of the UK or such another country. The countries to which the Act extends or has been applied are the signatories to the Berne Copyright Convention and the Universal Copyright Convention, which includes all the major and most of the developing countries in the world.

The provision relating to corporations is not important to architects because a corporation cannot be the author of an artistic work.

3.04 As regards the country of publication, the work must have been published first in either the UK or another country to which the Act extends or has been applied, i.e. Berne Convention or UCC countries.

Publication in one country shall not be regarded as other than first publication by reason of the simultaneous publication elsewhere. Publication elsewhere within 30 days shall be regarded as simultaneous.

3.05 The Act now provides that the territorial waters of the UK shall be treated as part of the UK for copyright purposes. In addition, oil rigs and other structures which are present on the UK continental shelf for purposes directly connected with the exploration of the sea bed or the exploration of their natural resources and UK aircraft and ships are subject to UK copyright law as if they were in the UK.

4   Publication

4.01 The meaning of the word 'publication' is important as it is relevant to qualification for copyright protection and the duration of copyright. 'Publication' is defined in the Act as meaning the issue of copies to the public. In the case of literary, dramatic, musical and artistic works it includes making it available to the public by means of an electronic retrieval system.

There is a special provision in relation to architectural works. In the case of works of architecture in the form of a building or an artistic work incorporated in a building, construction of the building shall be treated as equivalent to publication of the work.

4.02 However, the issue to the public of copies of a graphic work representing, or of photographs of, a work of architecture in the form of a building, or a model for a building, does not constitute publication for the purposes of the Act. Nor does the exhibition, issuing to the public of copies of a film including the work, or the broadcasting of an artistic work constitute publication. Thus, the inclusion of a model of a building in a public exhibition such as the Royal Academy Summer Exhibition, would not amount to publication, nor would the inclusion of photographs of the model in a book.

5   Ownership

5.01 Subject to the exception for employees set out in the following paragraph, ownership of copyright in the plans resides with the architect who actually drew the plan, drawing, sketch, or diagram, and, being personal property in law, passes to its owner's personal representatives after his death, and thence as directed in his will, or, in the event of intestacy, to his next of kin. As regards the artistic copyright in the buildings or models themselves, the author and therefore *prima facie* the owner will be the person who was the effective cause of the shape and design of the building. This is most likely to be the same person as owns the copyright in the plans, but if a builder constructs the building without reference to any plans he will be the author and owner of the work of architecture.

Employees

5.02 There is, however, an important exception to this provision: the copyright in architects' drawings, buildings, or models produced by an employee in the course of his employment automatically vests in his employer, whether the latter is an architect in

partnership, a limited company, or a public authority. The copyright in work done by employees in their time and not in the course of employment vests in them. (Thomas Scott, Universal Components Ltd [2002] CHD 31/10/02) But an employer can discourage employees from accepting private commissions by providing in the contract of service – and a simple letter agreement is a contract of service – that all the copyright in the employee's work, whether produced in the course of employment or not, will vest in the employer. Section 178 of the Act provides that the words 'employed', 'employee', 'employer' and 'employment' refer to employment under a 'contract of service or apprenticeship'. Frequently architects employ independent architects and artists to carry out parts of the drawing service; increasingly persons who would appear to be employees are for a variety of reasons (not unconnected with tax and Social Security payments) engaged as self-employed sub-contractors. Such persons are rarely employed under 'a contract of service' as distinct from 'a contract for services', which is not the same thing (Chapter 2). Employer architects would be well advised to make it an express term of such a sub-contractor's appointment that any copyright arising out of his work should vest in the employing architect.

The old provisions regarding Crown copyright have been changed in the 1988 Act. The position now is that where a work is made by an officer or servant of the Crown in the course of his duties, the Crown will be the first owner of the copyright in the work.

Partners

5.03 A partner of a firm is not an 'employee' of the partnership and hence will own the legal title to a work created by him. However, if the work in question is created in the ordinary course of the partnership business and for the purposes of the partnership, the copyright in the work will be considered as a partnership asset. The legal title remains with the partner who created the work until a written assignment is executed, but the other partners have a right to apply the copyright to benefit the partnership. For the avoidance of doubt the partnership deed (Chapter 29) should set out what happens as regards ownership of copyright.

Ownership of drawings

5.04 Ownership of copyright in drawings should be distinguished from ownership of the actual pieces of paper upon which they are drawn. It is settled law that upon payment of the architect's fees the client is entitled to physical possession of all the drawings prepared at his expense. In the absence of agreement to the contrary, copyright remains with the architect who also has a lien on (right to withhold) the drawings until his fees are paid. If all copyright is assigned to the client he may make such use of it as he wishes. Architects should note that even if they have assigned the copyright, by virtue of the provisions of section 64 of the Act, they may reproduce in a subsequent work part of their own original design provided that they do not repeat or imitate the main design. This provision enables architects to repeat standard details which would otherwise pass to the client upon prior assignment of copyright.

Joint ownership

5.05 A work of joint authorship is one which results from the collaboration of two or more authors where it is not possible to distinguish the contribution of those authors. There is no requirement for the authors to have a joint intention to create the work (*Robert James Beckingham v Robert Hodgens & Others* [2003] EWCA Civ 143). The general rule, in a situation of joint authorship, is that the joint authors will be joint owners of the copyright in the work. The first instance decision of *Robin Ray v Classic FM plc* [1998] FSR 622 suggests joint authors will always hold copyright as tenants in common in equal shares (i.e. hold district severable shares that can be assigned or passed by will). However, the consensus of opinion suggests this decision is wrong and that there may be situations where joint authors will hold title as joint tenants (i.e. where one owner's share will pass automatically to the joint owner on death).

6 Exceptions from infringement of architects' copyright

Photographs, graphic works

6.01 Frequently photographs of buildings designed by architects appear as part of advertisements by the contractors who constructed the buildings. As a matter of courtesy, the contractor usually makes some acknowledgment of the design, but he is not required to do so. By section 62 of the Act, the copyright in a work of architecture is not infringed by making a graphic work representing it, making a photograph or film of it, or broadcasting or including a visual representation of it in a cable programme service. Copies of such graphic works, photographs and films can be issued to the public without infringing the copyright in the building and models of it. Making a graphic work in this sense refers to a perspective or even detailed survey of the building as built: it would remain an infringement to copy the drawing or plan from which the building was constructed.

Reconstruction

6.02 Section 65 provides that where copyright exists in a building, anything done for the purposes of reconstructing a building does not infringe copyright. There will be no infringement of the drawings or plans in accordance with which the building was, by or with the licence of the copyright owner, constructed if subsequent reconstruction of the building or part thereof is carried out by reference to original drawings or plans. This point is of particular importance in connection with the now-established 'implied licence' considered in paragraphs 8.05–8.12 below.

Fair dealing

6.03 A general defence to any alleged infringement of copyright in an artistic work is 'fair dealing' for the purpose of criticism or review, provided that there is sufficient acknowledgment. As reproduction by photograph is the most likely method of illustrating a review and as a photograph of a building is specifically exempt from infringement, this defence of 'fair dealing' would appear to be needed only in the case of drawings of buildings. A sufficient acknowledgment is an acknowledgment identifying the building by its name and location, which also identifies the name of the architect who designed it. The name of the copyright owner need not be given if he has previously required that no acknowledgment of his name should be made. As certain self-appointed groups have now taken to awarding prizes for ugliness in design, some architects might find themselves in the unusual position of wishing to have no acknowledgment made of their connection with a design, although perhaps such publicity would hardly be 'fair dealing'.

Fair dealing with an artistic work for the purposes of research for a non-commercial purpose, with a sufficient acknowledgment, is also a defence to an alleged copyright infringement. However, there are limits on how, and how many copies may be made.

6.04 Special exceptions are contained in the Act for copying for educational purposes and copying by libraries and archives and by public administration. These provisions are too detailed to be included here, and if necessary they should be specifically referred to or professional advice should be obtained.

7 Infringement

7.01 To prove infringement, a plaintiff must show:

1 Copyright subsists in his work.
2 The copyright is vested in him.
3 The alleged infringement substantially reproduces his work in material particulars.
4 The alleged infringement was copied from his work.

7.02 No action for infringement of copyright can succeed if the person who is claimed to have infringed had no knowledge of the existence of the work of the owner. In this respect it differs from patents, which must be registered but which give an absolute protection even if the person infringing a patent had no knowledge of its existence. Copyright restricts the right to copy, which presupposes some knowledge of the original by the copier. Ignorance of the fact that the work copied was the copyright owner's is not, however, a defence. It is in the nature of architects' copyright that the person allegedly infringing must have had access directly or indirectly to the drawings. Infringement can therefore take three forms, as detailed below.

Copying in the form of drawings

7.03 It is rare for drawings to be copied in every detail, and many would-be infringers of an architect's copyright believe that if details are altered, infringement is avoided. This is not so, and section 16 of the Act makes it clear that references to reproduction include reproduction of a 'substantial part'. The word 'substantial' refers to quality rather than to quantity. Reference has already been made to the distinctive diamond-shaped detail in the *Stovin-Bradford* case. It does not matter that the size of the copy may have been increased or reduced or that only a small detail of an original drawing has been copied.

Copying the drawing in the form of a building

7.04 The plans can be 'copied' in the form of a building which reproduces the plans. The leading case on this form of infringement is *Chabot v Davies* [1936] 3 All ER 221. Mr Chabot, who was not an architect but 'a designer and fixer of shop fronts and the like', prepared a drawing for the defendant, who 'was just about to open what is known as a fish and chip shop'. Mr Chabot was lucky enough to be able to prove that the contractor had actually been handed his drawing by the defendant and had made a tracing from it, but the defendant argued that a plan cannot be reproduced by a shop front but only by something in the nature of another plan. The judge held, however, that 'reproduce . . . in any material form whatsoever' must include reproduction of a drawing by the construction of an actual building based on that drawing. In *Cala Homes (South) Ltd v Alfred McAlpine East Ltd* [1995] FSR 818 the defendant had allegedly copied floor plans and hence it was difficult to see whether there had in fact been infringement. However, it was held that if it is possible to show copying whether by recreating the floor plan by measurement of the building or by reference to the plans which the defendant used to construct the building, then infringement will be established as the plans have been reproduced in a 'material form'.

Copying a building by another building

7.05 The leading case on this type of infringement and until recently on architects' copyright generally is *Meikle v Maufe* [1941] 3 All ER 144. Most architects have heard of this case, but the facts and argument bear repetition. In 1912 Heal & Son Ltd employed Smith & Brewer as architects for the building of premises on the northern part of the present site of Heal's store in Tottenham Court Road. At that time there were vague discussions about a future extension on the southern part of the site, but because of difficulties over land acquisition nothing could be done. In 1935 Heal's employed Maufe as their architect for the extension of the building. Meikle was by this time the successor in title to Smith & Brewer's copyright, and he claimed that both the extension as erected and the plans for its erection infringed the original copyright. Maufe admitted that he thought it necessary to reproduce in the southern section of the facade the features which appeared in the original northern section. His object was 'to make the new look like the old throughout nearly the whole of the Tottenham Court Road frontage'. The layout of the interiors was also substantially reproduced. The defendants put forward three arguments:

1 There could not be a separate copyright in a building as distinct from copyright in the plans on which it was based.

2 If there was a separate copyright in a building it would belong to the building contractor.

3 It was an implied term of Smith & Brewer's original engagement that Heal's should have the right to reproduce the design of the original in the extension.

7.06 The first argument failed following *Chabot v Davies*. The second argument failed because copyright protection in a building is limited to the original character or design, and in the making of such character or design the contractor plays no part. The third argument failed in this particular case as the Copyright Act 1911, under which this case was tried, provided that copyright remained with its original author, unless he had agreed to pass the right to another. Heal's contended that Smith & Brewer had impliedly consented to the reproduction of their design because they had known of the possibility of extension. The judge having heard the facts concerning the discussion about land acquisition held that he could not reasonably imply such a term in this case.

Copying a building in the form of drawings

7.07 As mentioned in paragraph 6.01, copyright in a work of architecture is not infringed by making a graphic work representing it, making a photograph or file of it, or broadcasting or including a visual representation of it in a cable programme service. In addition, once a building is erected, it is not an infringement of copyright to create and use drawings of the building to repair or reconstruct the building (see paragraph 6.02)

8 Licences

Express licence

8.01 Paragraph 6.01 of the Conditions of Engagement which appear in the RIBA Standard Form of Agreement for the Appointment of an Architect (SFA/99) states that copyright in all documents and drawings prepared by the architect remains the property of the architect. Section 91 of the Act permits prior assignment of future copyright so that client and architect can agree at the beginning of an engagement to vary the Conditions of Engagement so that the copyright which will come into existence during the commission will vest in the client.

8.02 Paragraph 6.02 of the Conditions of Engagement modifies paragraph 6.01, to give the client a licence to use the architect's design in certain circumstances.

Paragraph 6.01 entitles the client to copy and use the architect's design (including drawings, documents and bespoke software) for purposes related to the project provided that:

- The entitlement applies only to the site or part of the site to which the design relates; and
- Any fees due to the architect have been paid (NOTE: if the client is in default of payment, the architect can suspend further use of the licence on giving 7 days' notice to the client).

This entitlement applies to the operation, maintenance, repair, reinstatement, alteration, extension, promotion, leasing and sale of the works but excludes the reproduction of the architect's design for any part of any extension of the project or for any other project.

Sub-paragraph 6.2.2 provides that if permitted use occurs after the date of the last service performed under the agreement and prior to practical completion of the construction of the project the client shall:

(a) Obtain the architect's consent if the architect has not completed Detailed Proposals. The architect's consent must not be unreasonably withheld; and/or

(b) Pay a reasonable licence fee if none is agreed.

Finally, sub-paragraph 6.2.1 provides that the architect shall not be liable for the consequences of any use of any information or designs prepared by the architect except for the purposes for which they were provided.

8.03 Copyright may also be expressly assigned to the client at some later stage, but it is usual to grant a licence authorizing use of copyright subject to conditions rather than an outright assignment of all the architect's rights. An increasing number of public and commercial clients make it a condition of the architect's appointment that all copyright shall vest in the client, but the architect should not consent to this without careful thought. Following *Meikle v Maufe* it would seem reasonable that a client should not be prevented from extending a building and incorporating distinctive design features of the original building so that the two together should form one architectural unit. If the time between the original building and the extension were 23 years, as in that case, it would be restrictive to make use of copyright to force the client into employing the original architect or his successor in title. Less scrupulous clients could, however, make use of an architect's design for a small and inexpensive original building with the undisclosed intention of greatly extending the building using the same design but at no extra cost in terms of architect's fees.

8.04 So far as drawings are concerned, it must be remembered that they are the subject of copyright 'irrespective of artistic quality' so that a prior express assignment of copyright to the client could theoretically grant him copyright in respect of even the most simple standard detail contained in the drawings (but see paragraph 5.04).

Implied licence

8.05 While the RIBA Architect's Appointment contains an express licence of the architect's copyright, situations may arise where the RIBA Architect's Appointment does not form part of the contract between the architect and the client or where the terms of the RIBA Architect's Appointment do not cover particular circumstances. Problems may then arise as to what rights the client has to use the architect's drawings. As long ago as 1938, the RIBA took counsel's opinion on the theory that an architect impliedly licenses his client to make use of the architect's drawings for the purposes of construction even when the client does not employ the architect to supervise the building contract. Such an implied consent can be understood when from the beginning of the engagement the client made it clear that all he required of the architect was drawings; for if the client received the drawings and paid for them, they would be valueless unless he could use them for the purpose of construction. The courts would not allow an architect to use his copyright to prevent construction in such circumstances. Counsel advised further that even if it had originally been assumed that the architect would perform the full service and supervise construction but the client subsequently decided that he did not require supervision, an implied licence to use the copyright in the drawings would arise in the client's favour when working drawings had been completed. Counsel did not then believe that an implied licence could arise at an earlier stage, but since 1938 the extent of architects' work and its stages have increased greatly. Cumulatively detailed drawings required for outline planning consent, detailed planning consent, and Building Regulations consent all create different stages, and an implied licence can now arise earlier than was contemplated in 1938.

8.06 Before any term can be implied into a contract, the courts must consider what the parties would have decided if they had considered the question at the time they negotiated other terms of the engagement. The courts are reluctant to imply a term unless it is necessary to give efficacy to the intention of the parties. Application of these rules to an architect's engagement would suggest that it is reasonable to infer that the architect impliedly consents to the client making use of his drawings for the purpose for which they were intended. If, therefore, the nature of the engagement is not full RIBA service but, for example, obtaining outline planning permission and no more, the architect impliedly consents to the client making use of his copyright to apply for such permission. Again, if an architect is instructed to prepare drawings of a proposed alteration for submission to the client's landlord, the client may use the drawings to obtain a consent under the terms of his lease but not for any other purpose, and certainly not for the purpose of instructing a contractor to carry out the alteration work.

8.07 The whole question of implied licence has been considered by the Court of Appeal in the cases of *Blair* and *Stovin-Bradford*, both of which have been fully reported. The facts in these cases were as follows. In addition, reference should be made to *Robin Ray v Classic FM plc* mentioned earlier at paragraph 5.05 which reviewed the authorities relating to implied copyright licences in consultancy agreements.

Blair v Osborne & Tompkins

8.08 Blair was asked by his clients whether it would be possible to obtain planning consent for development at the end of his clients' garden. Having made inquiries, Blair advised that it should be possible to obtain consent for erection of two semi-detached houses. The clients instructed Blair to proceed to detailed planning consent stage and agreed to pay on the RIBA scale. The application was successful, and Blair sent the planning consent to his clients, with his account for £70 for 'taking instructions, making survey, preparing scheme and obtaining full planning consent'. As was well known to the architect, the clients did not at that stage know whether they were going to develop the land or sell it.

They paid Blair's account which he acknowledged adding 'wishing you all the best on this project' but did not employ him to do any further work because they sold the plot to a contractor/developer. They also handed over Blair's drawings to the contractor, who used his own surveyors to add the detail necessary to obtain Building Regulations consent, and this consent having been obtained the contractor erected the houses. When the architect discovered that his plans were being used he claimed that this was an infringement of his copyright. The Master of the Rolls pointed out that although the RIBA Conditions of Engagement stated that copyright remained with the architect, it was open to him to give a licence for the drawings to be used for a particular site. His Lordship was influenced by the provision in the RIBA Conditions which entitled both architect and client to terminate the engagement 'upon reasonable notice'. To his Lordship it seemed inconceivable that upon the architect withdrawing he could stop any use of the plans on the ground of infringement of copyright. It seemed equally inconceivable that he could stop their use at an earlier stage when he had done his work up to a particular point and had been paid according to the RIBA scale. Widgery LJ approved the defendant's submission that the implied licence was 'to use whatever plans had been prepared at the appropriate stage for all purposes for which they would normally be used, namely, all purposes connected with the erection of the building to which they related'. If this was not right 'the architect' could hold a client to ransom and that would be quite inconsistent with the term that the engagement could be 'put an end to at any time'. In the writer's opinion this was an unfortunate decision and went much further than was required. But it must be lived with.

Stovin-Bradford v Volpoint Properties Ltd and Another

8.09 The defendant companies, which had their own drawing office, acquired an old factory which they considered had considerable development potential, and applied for planning consent for the erection of seven large warehouses. Permission was refused, and the defendants approached Stovin-Bradford, whose work they had previously admired, explaining that they needed a plan and drawing that 'showed something which was more attractive-looking than the existing building.' What they wanted was 'a pretty picture', but because they had their own drawing office, they did not need the full services of an architect. It was accepted by the court that although the then Conditions of Engagement were not incorporated into their contract, both architect and defendants were fully aware that they existed. It was also accepted that both parties were concerned only with obtaining planning permission. As the trial judge held, the agreement reached between the parties was very simple and amounted to this: 'that Stovin-Bradford would suggest architectural improvements to the defendant's existing plan for the modification and extension of the existing building for the purpose of trying to obtain planning permission and that he would receive for this plan the sum of 100 guineas and his out-of-pocket expenses.'

1 Stovin-Bradford's original design, and warehouses built 2, 3

The drawing was produced showing an 'effect quite striking to the eye: a unification of two original structures into one with, in particular, a diamond feature in the left hand building caused by the arrangement of the roof line and the windows placed in the top part of the old portal frame building'. The plan was passed to the defendants, who made certain amendments and obtained planning permission. Stovin-Bradford had presented his account for the agreed 'nominal' 100 guineas, headed it 'Statement no. 1' and confirmed that the payment was 'for preparing sketch plans and design drawings in sufficient detail to obtain or apply for planning permission'. With commendable foresight, at the foot of the bill was typed a note saying: 'The copyright of the design remains with the architect and may not be reproduced in any form without his prior written consent'. The defendants proceeded to erect the buildings, and although many details were changed, the result incorporated the particular features of the Stovin-Bradford design to which the trial judge drew notice (**1, 2, 3**). At first instance, the trial judge held that there was an infringement and awarded £500 damages as the amount which would have been reasonably chargeable for a licence to make use of the copyright.

8.10 The Court of Appeal judgment in the Blair case having been published shortly afterwards, the defendants appealed on the ground that the Blair case was decisive authority for the view that whenever an architect prepared plans for obtaining planning permission, the client could use them for the building as he liked without further payment. This time Lord Denning, the Master of the Rolls, referred to the stages of normal service in the RIBA Conditions (now replaced by Architect's Appointment), which he defined as being: (1) plans up to an application for outline planning permission; (2) plans up to an application for detailed planning permission; (3) working drawings and specification for contractor to tender; (4) all an architect's work to completion of the building. (The author has often thought that this would be the most sensible division of the RIBA stages of normal service, but in fact the stages were not so defined in the then existing Conditions – though the stages in the current Architect's Appointment roughly correspond to this division including, for example, appraisal, strategic briefing, outline proposals, detailed proposals, tender documentation and construction to practical completion.) Again the judges referred to the provision for termination upon reasonable notice and commented that the scale charges for 'partial services' seemed to be so fixed that they contained an in-built compensation for the use of designs and drawings right through to completion of the work. Lord Denning pointed out that in the Blair case charges had been in accordance with the RIBA scale, i.e. 1/6 of the full fee. But in this case the architect had charged on 'agreed nominal fee' basis, and his fee was far less than the percentage fee (which would have been, at 1/6, some £900). The Court of Appeal confirmed that there was an infringement, that an implied licence had not arisen, and that damages of £500 were reasonable.

Conclusions

8.11 From these two decisions it would appear that charging by the RIBA scales for partial services (whether originally contemplated or brought about by a termination) will give rise to an implied licence, while charging a nominal fee will not. If the agreement between the parties is silent it is usually the case that some form of licence will be implied but the extent of that licence will depend on the facts. The RIBA Architect's Appointment provides that the client will have an express licence to use the drawings only for the specific purpose for which they were prepared, and in particular that the preparation of drawings for obtaining planning permission does not carry with it the right to use them for construction of the building without the architect's express consent (which ought not to be unreasonably withheld).

8.12 The implied licence probably includes a right to modify the plans, although the law is not settled on this point (*Hunter v Fitzroy Robinson* [1978] FSR 167). If the Architect's Appointment does not apply, the probability is that the implied licence will not be revocable by the architect even if his fees have not been paid (this point is not settled law, but see Laddie, Prescott and Vitoria, *The Modern Law of Copyright*).

Alterations to architect's drawings and works of architecture

8.13 If the client alters the plans or the completed building, the probability is that he will not thereby be in breach of the architect's copyright (*Hunter v Fitzroy Robinson*). However, the client may not 'sell or hire' buildings or plans as the unaltered work of the architect (see Section 11 below dealing with moral rights).

9 Remedies for infringement

Injunction

9.01 An injunction can be obtained to prevent the construction of a building that would infringe the copyright in another building, even if that building is part-built. Section 17 of the 1956 Act provided that no injunction could be granted after the construction of a building had started, nor could an injunction be granted to require the building (so far as it has been constructed) to be demolished. This provision was repealed by the 1988 Act and is not re-enacted in any form.

However, there is a general principle of law that an injunction will not be granted if damages are an adequate relief. It is probable that a court would, in most cases, apply this rule in the case of an injunction to prevent the construction of a building when the construction has substantially commenced. The decision of the court will depend upon all the facts and circumstances of the case.

Damages/Account of profits

9.02 Damages are available to compensate the claimant for the loss in value of the copyright resulting from the infringing action. An alternative claim to damages is an account of profits. The claimant asks for the profits that the defendant has made by the unauthorized

exploitation of the copyright. In *Chabot v Davies* the court held that the measure of damages for infringement of the designer's copyright was the amount which he might reasonably have charged for granting a licence to make use of his copyright. In *Meikle v Maufe* the court rejected an argument that the architect might reasonably claim the profit which he would have made if he had been employed to carry out the work which infringed his copyright. 'Such profits do not provide either a mathematical measure for damages or a basis upon which to estimate damages. Copyright is not the sickle which reaps an architect's profit'.

Graham J in the *Stovin-Bradford* case confirmed the licence fee basis of the two earlier cases and awarded £500 against the plaintiff's request for £1000 and the defendant's suggestion of between £10 and £20. Although this point has not been decided with reference to architect's copyright, it would appear that on general principles, exemplary damages could be awarded in addition to the licence fee where the breach was particularly flagrant.

In the case of *Potton Limited v Yorkelose Ltd* [1990] 17 FSR the defendants admitted that they had constructed 14 houses, in infringement of the plaintiffs' copyright, on a style of house named 'Grandsen'. The defendants' houses were substantial reproductions of the plaintiffs' Grandsen drawings and they had copied the drawings for obtaining outline planning permission and detailed planning permission. It was held that the plaintiffs were entitled to the profits realized on the sale of the houses, apportioned to include profits attributable to (i) the purchase, landscaping and sale of the land on which the houses were built; (ii) any increase in value of the houses during the interval between the completion of the houses and their sale; and (iii) the advertising, marketing and selling of the houses.

In the case of *Charles Church Development plc v Cronin* [1990] 17 FSR the defendants admitted that they had had a house built based on plans which were the copyright of the plaintiff. The distinction between this case and *Potton Ltd v Yorkelose Ltd* is that in the former case the houses were built for sale and had been sold, whereas in this case the house had not been sold and the plaintiffs had obtained an injunction to prevent its sale. In the former case the plaintiff sued for an account of profits. In the latter case the claim was for compensatory damages for the loss caused by the infringement. The judge held that the measure of damages was a fair fee for a licence to use the drawings, based on what an architect would have charged for the preparation of drawings. The architect's fee should be calculated on the basis that the architect would have provided the whole of the basic services – in that case 8.5% of the building costs.

Secondary losses, such as payment discounts and overdraft requirements relating to cash flow problems, caused by an infringement are too remote to merit compensation (*Claydon Architectural Metalwork Ltd v DJ Higgins & Sons Ltd* [1997] Chd 16/1/97).

9.03 The Court can award additional damages under section 97(2) of the Act in cases of flagrant infringement of copyright. In *Cala Homes v McAlpine* Laddie J said that when considering whether to award additional damages, the court must look at all the circumstances of the case. 'Although the court must have regard to the flagrancy of the infringement and the benefit accruing to the defendant, there is no requirement that both or indeed either of these features be present. It is possible to envisage cases where the infringer has gained no benefit from his infringement save for the satisfaction of spite fulfilled. In such a case, if infringement was flagrant it appears that the court might award additional damages.' Laddie J acknowledged that these damages could be 'of a punitive nature'.

More recently, the High Court in *Nottinghamshire Healthcare National Health Service Trust v News Group Newspapers Ltd* [2002] EWHC 109 held that additional damages can be awarded under section 97 of the Act in a case of deliberate or reckless infringement. However, additional damages will not be awarded if a successful claimant seeks an account of profits (*Redrow Homes Ltd v Bett Brothers Plc* [1998] HL 22/1/98).

10 Industrial designs

10.01 The law on this subject is complicated. It is not proposed to deal with this matter at length, but merely to warn architects, who may be commissioned to design articles or components capable of mass reproduction, to seek professional advice before entering into any agreement commissioning the design of such articles or components or assigning or licensing the rights therein.

Moreover, any architect who does design such articles or components should seek professional advice as to what steps should be taken to protect them. Industrial design falls mid-way between copyright (not registrable in the UK), which is concerned with 'artistic quality', and patents, which must be registered and are not concerned with artistic quality but with function and method of manufacture. The law on industrial designs was considerably changed by the 1988 Act. The present law is thus contained in the Registered Designs Act 1949 (as amended by the 1988 Act and the Registered Designs Regulations 2001 and 2003) and the 1988 Act.

Registered designs

10.02 A design of any industrial (or handicraft, which includes sculpture) item, part of an item or its ornamentation resulting from features of lines, contours, colours, shape, textures and materials, provided it is new and has individual character, may be registered at the Patent Office under the provisions of the Registered Design Act 1949, as amended by the Registered Designs Regulations 2001 and 2003.

Protection can now be granted to designs irrespective of artistic merit. Protection is not granted for features of a design that are (inter alia) not new or of individual character, are dictated by their technical function, consist of features which must be reproduced so as to permit the product to fit or connect to another ('must-fit') or conflict with an earlier design application or registration.

It is the design not the article bearing the design that is protected. Therefore, although a registered owner must specify the products to which the design will be applied or incorporated this does not limit the scope of protection, although the monopoly will be in the UK only. Advice on qualification for design registration and protection should be sought from solicitors or patent agents practising in the field of registered design.

10.03 Copyright is a negative right entitling the owner to restrain copying of the work provided the reproduction is not independently evolved. Registration of design is positive and grants to the registered owner the exclusive right to use the design, thereby entitling the owner to restrain reproduction of the design in the UK, regardless of independent creation. For this reason a registration is valid only if the design (or a variation that is wholly insignificant) has not previously been used, published or exhibited anywhere in the world. The proviso (among other express exceptions) is that the earlier design should reasonably have become known in the normal course of business to persons working in the European Economic Area and specializing in the sector concerned.

10.04 Registered design protection lasts for 5 years, on payment of fees, and is renewable up to 25 years. The owner of the registered design would normally be the original author, and therefore the copyright owner as well, but frequently manufacturers who commission a component insist upon the design being registered in their names.

10.05 A design is taken to have been used industrially for the purpose of the Registered Designs Act if it is applied to more than 50 articles.

Design right

10.06 The Act largely abolished copyright protection for most industrial designs although copyright will subsist in the design document in addition strengthened the registered design system, introduced a new unregistered right called 'design right'. 'Design' means the design of any aspect of the shape or configuration (whether internal or external) of the whole or part of an article.

The design must be original in the copyright sense and also in the sense that it is not commonplace in the relevant design field. Originality in the copyright sense has already been considered in detail but in addition the design itself must not be commonplace. One of the leading cases in this area is *Ocular Sciences Ltd v*

Aspect Vision Care Ltd [1997] RPC 289 which decided that the word 'commonplace' requires an objective assessment and is likely to cover 'any design which is trite, trivial, common-or-garden, hackneyed or of the type which would excite no peculiar attention in those in the relevant art'. The general rule (*Farmers Build Ltd v Carier Bulk Materials Handling Ltd* [1999] RPC 461 (CA)) to determine if a particular design is commonplace is whether, from the perspective of the ultimate consumer, at the time of creation the features of design are reproduced in the design of similar articles. The closer the similarity in features the more likely the design in question is 'commonplace'.

It should be noted that design right does not subsist in a method or principle of construction, nor does it subsist in surface decoration. Moreover, it does not subsist in features of shape or configuration of an article which enables the article to be connected to, or placed in, around or against, another article so that either article may perform its function; nor must it be dependent upon the appearance of another article of which the article is intended by the designer to be an integral part. This means that designs of spare parts are normally excluded from design right protection. Because design right subsists additionally to and does not replace artistic copyright, the exclusions from design right protection do not remove artistic copyright protection from, for example, surface decoration.

Design right does not subsist unless and until the design has been recorded in a design document or an article has been made to the design.

Design right expires 15 years from the end of the calendar year in which the design was first recorded in a design document or an article was made to the design. Alternatively, if articles made to the design are made available for sale or hire within 5 years from the end of that calendar year, the design right will expire 10 years from the end of the calendar year in which that first occurred. In the last 5 years of design right protection licences for the exploitation of the design must be granted (licences of right) if requested.

To qualify for design right protection the requirements set out in sections 217 to 221 of the Act must be met: these are too detailed to be set out here but have similarity to the qualification requirements described in section 3 above. However, the differences are such that reference must be made to the actual sections.

10.07 As for copyright protection, design right enables the owner to prevent unauthorized copying and other infringements. The test for infringement of design right was differentiated from the copyright test in *Woolley Jewellers Ltd v A& A Jewellery Ltd* [2002] EWCA Civ. 1119. 'There is a difference between an enquiry into whether the item copied forms a substantial part of the copyright work and an inquiry into whether the whole design containing the element copied is substantially the same design as that which enjoys design right protection'. Arden LJ went on to conclude that: 'It may not be enough to copy a part or even a substantial part. Regard has to be had to the overall design which enjoys design right'.

The provisions of the Act ensure that a claimant cannot succeed in both copyright and design right infringement claims in respect of the same acts of infringement.

Community designs

10.08 The Community Design Regulation came into force on 6 March 2002. It created the following additional European Community-wide protection for UK designs:

(a) Registered Community Designs – registration of qualifying designs entitles the owner to a monopoly against use of that design throughout the EU for a maximum of 25 years from filing. The registration process is equivalent to the UK system and can be organized via the UK Patent Office or direct with the Office of Harmonization in the Internal Market in Alicante;

(b) Unregistered Community Designs – qualifying designs automatically receive EU wide protection against copying lasting 3 years from the first public disclosure of the design in the EU.

The rules relating to the qualification for both unregistered and registered Community designs are equivalent to the rules for

UK registered designs, as outlined in paragraph 10.02 to 10.05 above. This differentiates the protection granted by virtue of the UK unregistered design right with the rights granted by the Community unregistered design right (see paragraph 10.06 above).

11 Moral rights

11.01 Moral rights of authors have existed in all continental European legal systems for many years, but the 1988 Act introduced them to UK law for the first time.

11.02 There are four basic categories of moral rights contained in the Act:

1 The right to be identified as author
2 The right to object to derogatory treatment of work
3 False attribution of work
4 The right of privacy of certain photographs and films.

11.03 Under section 77(4)(c) of the Act the author of a work of architecture in the form of a building or a model for a building, has the right to be identified whenever copies of a graphic work representing it, or of a photograph of it, are issued to the public.

Section 77(5) also provides that the author of a work of architecture in the form of a building also has the right to be identified on the building as constructed, or, where more than one building is constructed to the design, on the first to be constructed.

The right must be asserted by the author on any assignment of copyright in the work or by instrument in writing signed by the author. In the case of the public exhibition as an artistic work (for example, the inclusion of a model of a building in an exhibition), the right can be asserted by identifying the author on the original or copy of the work, or on a frame, mount or other thing to which the work is attached. If the author grants a licence to make copies of the work, then the right can be asserted for exhibitions by providing in the licence that the author must be identified on copies which are publicly exhibited.

There are certain exceptions to the right of which the most important is that it does not apply to works originally vested in the author's employer (see paragraph 5.02).

11.04 The author of a literary, dramatic, musical or artistic work has the right to object to his work being subjected to derogatory treatment. 'Treatment' means any addition to, deletion from or alteration to or adaptation of the work. The treatment is derogatory if it amounts to distortion or mutilation of the work or is otherwise prejudicial to the honour or reputation of the author.

The right in an artistic work is infringed by the commercial publication or exhibition in public of a derogatory treatment of the work, or a broadcast or the inclusion in a cable programme service of a visual image of a derogatory treatment of the work.

In the case of a work of architecture in the form of a model of a building the right is infringed by issuing copies of a graphic work representing, or of a photograph of, a derogatory treatment of the work.

However, and most importantly, the right is not infringed in the case of a work of architecture in the form of a building. But if a building is the subject of derogatory treatment, the architect is entitled to have his identification on the building as its architect removed.

In the case of works which vested originally in the author's employer the right does not apply.

11.05 In the case of a literary, dramatic, musical or artistic work, a person has the right not to have its authorship falsely attributed to him. Thus an architect can prevent a building which he has not designed being attributed to him as its architect.

11.06 The right to privacy of certain films and photographs applies only to films and photographs commissioned for private and domestic purposes and accordingly is hardly relevant here.

11.07 The rights to be identified as an author of a work and to object to derogatory treatment of a work subsist as long as copyright subsists in the work. The right to prevent false attribution continues to subsist until 20 years after a person's death.

11.08 Moral rights can be waived by an instrument in writing signed by the person entitled to the right. However, moral rights may not be assigned to a third party although they pass on death as part of the author's estate and can be disposed of by his will.

12 Law of copyright in Scotland

12.01 There is no difference between the law of copyright in Scotland and England and the new Copyright, Designs and Patents Act 1988 applies equally to both countries with the exception of section 287 and 292, which deal with Patents County Courts and section 301 which grants the Great Ormond Street Hospital permanent copyright in *Peter Pan*, all of which apply only to England.

13 Law of copyright in Northern Ireland *

13.01 The law of copyright in Northern Ireland is the same as the law of copyright in England & Wales and is contained principally in the Copyright, Patents and Designs Act 1988 which extends to Northern Ireland (see section 207).

The law is also contained in a number of UK statutory instruments which have been enacted both pursuant to powers contained in the 1988 Act and the general powers contained in the European Communities Act 1972 which permit implementation into UK law of Directives and Regulations issued by the European Union. Any such regulations apply equally in Great Britain and Northern Ireland.

* This section was written by Paul McLaughlin.

35

Architects and the law of employment

RUTH DOWNING*

Introduction

In approaching the task of revising this chapter I was struck that in its original form and layout it reflects a time when the concept of 'employment law' meant as much the law governing the relations of large trades unions and employers as the, then nascent concepts of redundancy and unfair dismissal and the newly created industrial tribunals. Equal importance was given to the law on collective labour relations as to individual rights and the common law governing individual rights was holding its own against the statutory creations of unfair dismissal and sex and race discrimination. Passing references were made to the effect of European legislation on domestic law. In the years since the last revision if far no reason other than that European Directives have been the major factor in the increase in employment legislation major additions to the chapter are necessary. As it is the chapter was silent on matters of great significance such as the Disability Discrimination Act 1995 which plainly call for inclusion.

Conscious that this chapter serves to inform architects of the basic law which affects them as employers within thier own practices and should serve to inform of them of the necessity of seeking expert advice I have endeavoured to maintain something of the familiar format, whilst alerting the reader to the enormously wider protection enjoyed by their employees.

1 Sources and institutions

1.01 Although the law of employment is a mixture of the rules developed by the common law (see Chapter 1) and those laid down by Parliament, the latter is now by far the predominant source. The domestic legislation is now further fuelled by the requirement to fulfil our obligations to Europe on social policies and matters of equality, and the effect of these Directives will be seen in most of the new rights created by the Act of Parliament or Regulations.

1.02 The basic division which can still be drawn is between the individual employment law, which is concerned with the relations between employer and employee, and the collective labour relations law, which regulates the relationship between employers and trade unions (TUs).

1.03 The basic relationship between the employer and the individual worker is defined by the contract of employment. This is the starting point for determining the rights and liabilities of parties. But as we shall see below, the last 30 years have seen the emergence of a whole range of statutory rights relating to such matters as unfair dismissal, redundancy, and maternity rights. Furthermore, it is a fundamental principle that, save in certain very exceptional

* This chapter is based on the chapter originally written for an earlier edition by Sir Patrick Elias.

cases, it is not open to the parties to contract out of these rights. They provide what is sometimes called a *floor of rights*, below which the rights of employees cannot sink. Although these rights originated in different statutes, they were first consolidated in 1978 and are now to be found in the Employment Rights Act 1996, together with the Employment Relations Act 1999, the Employment Act 2002 (*not yet in force*) and those parts of the anti-discrimition laws which bear specifically on the workplace.

1.04 It will probably be widely known that the enforcement of the individual rights of unfair dismissal and discrimination are enforced in the employment tribunal (originally the *industrial* tribunal) the composition of which is a legally qualified chairman and two lay wing members. These are nominated by the TUC and the CBI. The aim of the tribunal was always to discourage legal representation by the absence of a costs regime and by the informality of the system. The original idea was rather to see the representation of the applicant by the TU representatives and the employer by a member of the personnel staff. That is not the present situation and although many applicants and respondents do present their own cases, the complexity of the law as it has developed and the potential value of the claims, both in monetary and publicity terms, has made the presence of lawyers by far the norm.

1.05 Two further points about these tribunal hearings are worth noting. First, in most cases which go to the tribunals (notably unfair dismissals and those where discrimination is alleged) a conciliation officer seeks to bring about a settlement of the case before it is heard by the tribunal. These officers are employed by the Advisory, Conciliation and Arbitration Service (ACAS), and, like the tribunals themselves, they are to be found throughout the country. They have no power to compel anyone to discuss the case with them. But it is often advisable to do so, because a settlement can save both publicity and the costs of the action.

The second point to note about the tribunals system is that there is an appeal from the industrial tribunal, but only on a point of law, to the Employment Appeal Tribunal (EAT). Findings of fact in the Employment Tribunal cannot be interfered with by the EAT unless they are clearly perverse or cannot on any view be justified by the evidence. The EAT is technically a branch of the High Court (see Chapter 1) but is differently constituted, consisting of a judge and two others with experience in industrial relations, rather than a single judge alone. It is a much-noted anomaly of the EAT that although its role is solely to determine questions of law and not fact, the judicial president is invariably accompanied by two wing members with no legal qualification. Appeals from the EAT then go to the Court of Appeal, and any final appeal is to the House of Lords.

1.06 As has been noted, the Employment Tribunals are constituted to administer rights created by Parliament and imposed upon the relationship of employer/employee. These rights are quite separate from those rights which are created by the parties themselves and enshrined in their contract. Until 1994 an employee who wished to bring a contractual claim, for instance for wrongful dismissal, was obliged to take that type of claim to a court – either the High Court or a County Court. In 1994 tribunals were empowered to hear claims in contract for damages arising from breach of the contract of employment, or failure to pay sums due under the contract. There is a limit of £25 000 on what the tribunal can award on such a contractual claim. Claims can only be brought on the termination of the contract.

Collective labour relations law

1.07 The law regulating collective labour relations is still significantly the law of the jungle, being a power relationship. However, the law does regulate this relationship in various ways. First, it sets limits to the industrial sanctions which can lawfully be used by the parties. This area of the law is highly complex, and it is not considered further in this chapter. Second, the state provides conciliation and arbitration services (ACAS) to help promote the peaceful settlement of disputes. Finally, various rights are given to recognized trade unions, i.e. those which have been recognized by employers, and also to the officials and members of recognized trade unions (see Section 5).

2 The contract of employment

2.01 Every worker has a contract with his employer. But a distinction is drawn in law between employees and independent contractors. The former are integrated into the organization of the business, and work under what is termed a contract of service. In contrast, the latter perform a specific function and are usually in business on their own account – e.g. the plumber or window cleaner – and work under a contract for services. In borderline cases the distinction is often very difficult to draw. Also, the description which the parties choose to place on their status is not decisive, though it will be a factor to consider in a marginal case. The main importance of the distinction in the field of employment law is that only employees working under a contract of service are eligible to benefit from most of the statutory rights, e.g. unfair dismissal, redundancy, and maternity. In addition, an employer may be vicariously liable for the torts committed by his employees, but only rarely for those of independent contractors (see Chapter 3).

2.02 The test of whether an individual is indeed an employee has gone through various fashions, e.g. the control test, the organizational test. A continuing theme through all such tests has been the requirement that an employee renders the service *personally*, i.e. no substitute can be sent along by a true employee to perform the work required. The control test looked at just that, the amount and degree of control exercised by the employer, which was relevant particularly to skilled employees to whom an employer might in truth give little by way of actual instruction.

Current issues which have attracted judicial attention include the status of those who are supplied by employment agencies but who work on a long-term basis for one concern. See *Montgomery v Johnson Underwood* [2001] IRLR 269, where after 2 years' working for one business Ms Montgomery was held to be their employee and not that of the placement agency. Recent decisions have followed that line even where the contractual documents declared that there was no employment relationship between the agency and the worker, nor the placement and the worker. The other recurrent theme is that of the test of mutual obligation, that the employee owes the obligation to attend work and the employer to supply work. The test works well in circumstances where the relationship between the 'employer' and 'employee' is a more casual one in which there may be periods when the 'employee' is not called upon to do anything for the 'employer'. If there is no obligation on that person to accept any assignment, and in practise they have in the past declined the offer of work, it will be more difficult to argue that the relationship is one of employee and employer when it suits the former to do so.

2.03 The National Minimum Wage Act 1998 has introduced a further concept; that of a *worker*. The term is also used in a number of regulations granting social rights. It is far wider that that of employee and will effectively cover many of those persons who hitherto fell short of the definition while bearing the description and characteristics of independent contractor rather uneasily.

Creating the contract: control of recruitment

2.04 The basic principle is that the contract of employment is a voluntary agreement. This means that the employer can choose both with whom he will contract and the terms on which he is willing to contract. However, statute law has curbed this freedom in a number of ways. In relation to recruitment the employer can chose to employ whomsoever he likes, provided he does not refuse to recruit a person on grounds of their sex, marital status, pregnancy, race, colour, ethnic or national origins, nationality, disability or TU membership or activities. In addition the recruitment must not be offered on terms which may amount to indirect discrimination on any of the above grounds. Thus setting an upper age limit for applicants will not be unlawful, but if that would be to the detriment of a considerably larger proportion of women than men and it is to the individual's detriment because she cannot comply, e.g. she is a late starter in her career because of taking time out to raise a family, that too will be objectionable.

The interview

2.05 An employee being interviewed is under no obligation gratuitously to disclose details of his past. However, he must not misrepresent it, save that in certain exceptional cases he may lawfully be able to deny that he has committed any criminal offences if his convictions are 'spent convictions' within the meaning of the Rehabilitation of Offenders Act 1974. Whether or not a conviction is spent depends upon the nature of the offence and the period since the conviction.

The terms of contract

2.06 The basic position, consistent with the notion of freedom of contract, is that it is up to the parties to agree to the terms which will bind them. Exceptionally, terms of the agreement may be struck out as being contrary to public policy, e.g. a term in unreasonable restraint of trade (see paragraph 4.32). But generally the parties will be held to their bargain. From an employer's point of view it is sensible for all the important terms of the contract to be committed to paper and for the job to be conditional on their acceptance. This may eliminate later confusion and disagreements.

2.07 However, in the sphere of employment law the contract is not always expressly stipulated in this way. A number of points need to be noted. First, in many situations there is no real bargaining between individuals at all. The terms of employment may have been agreed between the employer and a recognized trade union negotiating collective agreements, and variations in those terms occur as the collective agreements are amended from time to time. Then the collective agreement operates as the source of the terms of the individual contract of employment. Second, once a contract of employment is agreed, the employer has a statutory obligation to provide the employee with a written statement of the particulars of his contract, and he must do this within 2 months of the employee commencing employment. Third, even where terms are expressly agreed between the parties to the contract and contained in the written particulars, they will rarely cover all the matters that will arise in the course of the employment relationship. So the express terms will have to be supplemented by implied terms. These implied terms may be usefully divided into two categories. Some will arise because of the particular relationship between the employer and the employee, and will often depend upon the customs and practices of a particular firm. For example, it may have become the practice for overtime to be worked in certain circumstances, or for employees to be more flexible in the range of tasks they perform than their specific job obligations would suggest. Once practices of this kind become reasonable, well known, and certain, they will become contractual duties. Other implied terms depend not so much on the particular employment relationship but are imposed as an incident of the general relationship between employers and employees. The judges have said that certain duties will be implied into all employment relationships, e.g. a duty on the employee not to disclose confidential information to third parties, to take reasonable care in the exercise of his duties, and to show good faith in his dealings with the employer. Likewise there are some implied duties imposed on the employer, e.g. a duty to treat the employee with respect, to take reasonable care for his health and safety, and not to act in such a way as to undermine the trust and confidence on which the contract of employment is based. This last implied term has proved of particular importance in the field of constructive dismissal (see Section 4, paragraph 4.05 below).

Equal Pay Act 1970

2.08 Although equal pay is plainly an equal opportunity issue, (see Section below) it fits into the scheme of considering the contract of employment because the legal framework is contractual, i.e. it works by importing into every contract of an equality clause. The Equal Pay Act 1970, came into force at the end of 1975. Strictly it is a misnomer, for it covers not merely pay but also all contractual terms and conditions of employment. Broadly it states that if a woman is employed on like work with a man (and this involves looking at what they actually do, and not what they might be required to do under their contracts) or on work which is rated as equivalent on a job evaluation scheme, then she is entitled to have the same terms and conditions applied to her as apply to him. An Equality Clause automatically becomes part of her contract of employment. The main exception to this is where there are differences which stem from a material difference, other than sex, between the situations of the man and the woman. It has been argued in a number of cases that the reason for the difference in pay is that market forces have required higher pay to be offered to tempt recruits to the particular job or that the pay is a historical hangover from a collective agreement. Both are potentially acceptable justifications save that the tribunal will look hard to ensure that the former, if it attracts only male applicants is not a sham, and that the latter does not simply perpetuate old inequalities of pay, particularly if they represent pay for what was and is seen as 'women's work' proof that there has been a real need to pay more money to attract employees will be acceptable.

2.09 However, if the woman is not employed on like work, she cannot complain under the Act because she considers that the differential between the respective rates of pay is too great. Indeed, in one case a woman who was a leader of a group of adventure playground workers was paid less than one of the men in the group. But the EAT held that since her job was more responsible than the man's, this meant that it was not like work, and consequently she could not claim the same pay (*Waddington v Leicester Council for Voluntary Services* [1977] 2 All ER 633)!

2.10 A woman who claims that her employer is infringing the Equal Pay Act may take a case to an employment tribunal. She may be awarded arrears of pay, but not for a period exceeding six years prior to the date on which the proceedings were instituted. Special provisions on arrear exist if the employer has concealed the facts.

Statement of the main terms of the contract

2.11 The sources of the contract of employment are so diverse that Parliament in 1963 thought it desirable that the employer should give to the employee a written statement of the principal terms. The position is now governed by the sections 1–7 of the Employment Relations Act 1996 and provides a comprehensive code. In particular there are certain details which must be provided in a 'principal statement' and then some which may be added later in the supplementary statements. It was hitherto the law that the obligation

could be fulfilled by referring the employee to other documents to ascertain these details. There is now a very limited power for the employer to refer the employee on in this way but he can do so for matters such as sick pay and pension. What the first and principal statement must contain are details of: pay, intervals at which payment will be made and hours of work. Thereafter he may give additional statements regarding grievance and disciplinary procedures, and holidays. Any changes in the terms must be notified in writing within a month of the changes happening.

2.12 However, if the employer does in fact draw up a proper written contract, this will be binding upon the employee, provided he accepts it as such. If the contract contains all the information that would have to be put in the written particulars, the latter can be dispensed with.

3 Equal opportunities

3.01 Anti-discrimination law, or what hereafter will be termed generically as 'Equal Opportunities' now plays such a far-reaching part in not just the recruitment of staff but their daily relations within the workplace and their evolving rights that it is necessary that the issue has accorded its own section. It must also be observed that it is the issues of sex, race and disability that now form such a huge part of the work of the employment tribunals that employers should be aware of the complexities of the issue. Just as the acts govern the recruitment or dismissal of staff they create and protect ongoing rights to the treatment at work, both in the promotion and the advancement of staff but also in the relations between staff and management. Claims under all these legislation can be brought during the currency of employment and the potentially destructive effect of litigation between parties who continue to work together on a daily basis during and after the hearing of such claims can readily be imagined. As an illustration of the way in which the legislation affects every stage of the employment from recruitment through to termination the Disability Discrimination Act serves as a useful illustration,

3.02 The Disability Discrimination Act 1995
Many practices will be aware of the legislation from the professional involvement in the designing and adaptation of premises. From the employment lawyers' point of view it is perhaps best to bear in mind that the tribunals are rarely troubled by claims that there is no wheelchair access or that the doors are too narrow. Indeed, many of the claims made involve applicants whose disability is not physical in origin; see for example, the leading case on the definition of disability *Goodwin v The Patent Office* [1999] IRLR 4, where the applicant was a paranoid schizophrenic. A significant number of claims involve stress-related illnesses such as depression, and statistics on the initial years of the Act reveal that back and neck problems are the most common disabilities relied upon thus far.

3.03 A person is disabled within the meaning of the Disability Discrimination Act (DDA) if they have a physical or mental impairment which has a substantial and long-term adverse effect on their ability to carry out normal day-to-day activities. The first matter of note is that the seemingly easy phrase '*normal day-to-day activities*' is itself defined by the statute. In Schedule 1 to the Act it makes clear that the impairment will only be taken to affect this ability if it affects one of a list of eight faculties; e.g., mobility, visual senses, cognitive powers, physical strength and dexterity, and the perception of physical danger. Thus it is a two-stage process: does this man's impairment, e.g. loss of an eye, affect his ability to perform the day-to-day activities (e.g. reading). That is an impairment, but is it substantial? Guidance notes appended to the DDA give examples which will fall on each side of the line and reward attention if attempting to decide if someone is indeed disabled. An inability to climb stairs would be a disability of mobility, but not if the same person could not travel in comfort in a car for more than 2 hours. An inability to carry a tray of food would be a disability but not if the only problem was not being able to carry heavy luggage.

Note also that the concept of the day-to-day activities excludes the ability to do any particular job, i.e. it is not relevant that the blind man cannot type at the same speed as a sighted man. It is also not relevant whether the disability impacts on particular hobbies or sports.

3.04 What then amounts to discrimination on grounds of disability? When such a person presents for interview or recruitment it is of course unlawful to refuse to employ him *because* he has only one eye (Section 5(1)). It is however equally discriminatory to refuse employment in circumstances where although with his disability he may not be able to perform the job, or its entire content as well as an able-bodied person, the employer unreasonably refuses to make *reasonable adjustments* to the job which would enable him to work (Section 5(2)). Note also that direct discrimination against the disabled is not, as in race and sex, a comparative issue. Thus refusal of a job to a disabled person who may require 1 day of a week to attend hospital cannot be justified on the grounds that any applicant who could only work 4 days a week would also not be selected. If the reason for absence is one relating to his disability, then without more the applicant has been treated less favourably on grounds of that disability. The onus then shifts to the employer to *justify* his need for 5 days a week attendance. That in turn triggers the question of reasonable adjustment and the employer must also show that he has a substantial reason unconnected with the disability for refusing to adjust the job to 4 days. He may be required to justify, e.g. a refusal to shift some of the duties to other staff, or to refuse to allow flexi working to catch up, or home working.

The legal requirements continue throughout employment so that adjustments must be considered at any time during the currency of the employment.

Sex discrimination

3.05 The scope of sex and race discrimination legislation covers not merely recruitment to employment but also promotion and any other non-contractual aspects of employment. For example, if the employer gives certain benefits, e.g. cheap loans or mortgages, or training opportunities, he cannot grant these on a discriminatory basis. The general comments on recruitment made above hold good. Recruitment cannot be refused because of the sex of the candidate. Conditions that impact more on women may be indirectly discriminatory; examples would be the requirement to work full time, to work in the office all the time, etc.

3.06 Exceptionally, sex discrimination is permitted where it is a genuine occupational qualification, for example on the grounds of physiology or decency. The most relevant permissible discrimination for architects is where a job is given in the UK, but it requires duties to be performed in a country whose laws and customs are such that a woman could not effectively carry out the task. Even then, it must be necessary for the employer to discriminate for this reason. So if he already employs a sufficient number of male architects to cater adequately for that particular foreign connection, this exception will not apply. Advertisements for job vacancies also need careful drafting to avoid any suggestion of unlawful discrimination.

3.07 Those who consider they have been discriminated against may complain to an employment tribunal. If the complaint is successful, the tribunal may award a declaration of the rights of the parties, an order requiring the employer to take such action as is necessary to obviate the adverse effects of the discrimination, or compensation which may include compensation for injured feelings. The legal employer is normally liable, but if the employer has taken all reasonably practical steps to eliminate the discrimination, e.g. has a clear policy and monitors it, then he can escape liability. In that case, the particular managers who discriminate will be personally liable. There is no longer any upper limit on the compensation which may be awarded.

3.08 An issue which continues to fuel litigation, not previously highlighted in this chapter is that of sexual harassment, a problem that frequently makes the newspapers and can attract large awards of compensation. The SDA contains no reference to *harassment*,

discrimination is less favourable treatment on grounds of sex, and the complainant had always to prove that she has been subjected to a detriment and would not have been treated in this way if she had not been a woman. That led to arguments that the treatment meted out to a woman was not done on sexual grounds, but pure dislike, alternatively that a man would have been treated as badly.

The situation will change although not for the SDA until October 2005. What those changes will be/can be found in the *Employers Equality (Sexual Orientation) Regulations 2002* will eventually insert into the SDA *harassment* defined as an act which is *unwanted conduct of a sexual nature or other conduct based on sex affecting the dignity of men and women at work*. The key concept is that the conduct must be 'unwanted'. The Regulations will in the meantime be the basis for outlawing harrasment on grounds of *sexual orientation* in the SDA and *race* in the RRA and came into force on 1 December 2003.

3.09 It is appropriate therefore also to mention one of the most recent changes in the equal opportunities legislation and that is in relation to discrimination not on grounds of sex *per se* but rather on grounds of *gender orientation*.

The House of Lords pronounced in late 2003 on two long running cases one involving the then policy in the Armed Forces of discharging homosexuals and the other the complaints of a lesbian teacher who was systematically abused on the basis of her sexuality. Neither claim succeeded because neither applicant could show that their relevant comparator, a lesbian solider or a male homosexual teacher, would not also have been discharged or abused. The comparison which they needed to make to succeed would have been as between a male heterosexual soldier and a female heterosexual teacher, but that would have been a *sexually* like for like and not unlawful. That position changes with the *Employment Equality (Sexual Orientation) Regulations 2003* which came into force on 1 December 2003 and the comparison will now be as between male and male or female and female but where the distinguishing feature is sexual orientation.

Race Relations Act 1976

3.10 It is also unlawful, under the Race Relations Act 1976, to discriminate on grounds of race, colour, ethnic or national origins, or nationality in respect of the terms of employment. As with sex discrimination, there is no upper limit on the compensation which may be awarded.

It was long the case that the Race Relations Act (RRA) did not protect against discrimination on the grounds of religion. The *Employer Equality (Religion or Belief) Regulations 2003*, which came into force in December 2003, now make it unlawful to discriminate on grounds relating to the religious persuasion or belief of employees.

Maternity, parental and family-related rights

3.11 All employees are now entitled to a 26-week period of Ordinary Maternity Leave (OML). In addition those who have 26 weeks employment at a date before the 15th week before the Expected Week of Childbirth (EWC) is entitled to another 26 weeks Additional Maternity Leave (AML). All terms and conditions, apart from the obligation to pay salary, remain in force. The employee is also entitled to Statuory Maternity Pay for the duration of their respective leave. It is paid at the rate of 90% of the employee's wages, subject to the current maximum of £100. A detailed consideration of the benefits' position is outside the scope of this work.

Proper notification must be given of the intention to take maternity leave and to return. In the former case it must be in writing, given no later than the 15th week before the EWC and request the starting date of the leave, which must not be earlier than 11 weeks before the EWC. The employer should then respond, within 28 days, giving the date for the ending of the leave and the return to work. Changes to that must also be notified. Exercise of the right to return notice must also be given in writing.

The timings are important, the rights new and extended, and the potential for suspicion and misunderstanding between employer and employee rife. It is imperative that guidance is taken before dealing with these rights. A failure to permit a return to work is automatically unfair and special rules apply to the situation when a redundancy arises in the absence of the employee. The matter is one which requires expert assistance to avoid problems, particularly if health problems delay the employee's ability to return to work on the originally appointed day.

3.12 New rights to reflect the government's commitment to 'family-friendly policies' should also be noted. Two new Regulations and an amendment to the ERA 1996 have introduced the right to time off work to assist with children and dependants. The *Paternity and Adoption Leave Regulations 2002* give a right to 2 weeks leave to the father of a child, which includes the partner of the mother or any person which will have responsibility for the child's upbringing. Same sex couples enjoy the same rights; 26 weeks employment is the prerequiste for the leave. The adoptive parents of a child have the similar right in respect of a newly placed child. An adoption that regularizes the position of an existing child, e.g. where the natural mother and new partner adopt her child is not covered.

The *Maternity and Parental Leave Regulations 1999* also create rights in respect of older children, up to the age of 5 years (or 18 years if the child is disabled). The employee must have worked for 1 year to acquire the rights and may claim a maximum of 13 weeks leave in respect of any one child (i.e. 26 weeks for twins) and 18 weeks if the child is disabled. The request must be made 21 days in advance of the time to be taken and it is unpaid (unless the employer wishes to implement more advantageous rights). Refusal of rights can lead to a complaint to the employment tribunal. For the emergencies that family life throws up and which cannot be anticipated 21 days in advance Section 57(A) ERA 1996 has created the right for unpaid dependants' leave. This is intended to deal with illness, injury or death or less dramatically if existing arrangements for care have fallen through. The time limit for the leave is unspecified, simply what is *reasonable*. A *dependant* is widely defined as somebody in the same household, but does not include lodgers, tenants, au pairs, etc.

Finally, as noted above the early cases law on indirect discrimination centred on the requirement for full-time working which frequently impacted on mothers. The social trend towards job shares, home working, etc. is now underpinned by the *Flexible Working (Eligibility, etc.) Regulation 2002*, the *Flexible Working (Procedural Requirements) Regulations 2002* and the *Part Time Workers (Prevention of Less Favourable Treatment) Regulations 2000*. The former enable an employee with 26 weeks service and a child aged under 6 years (18 years if disabled) to request (not require) that hours be altered to accommodate them. One request per annum is permitted. The latter Regulation regularizes the position of part-time workers who must enjoy the same rights on a pro rata basis as full-time workers.

3.13 Victimization
Finally it should be noted that all the Equal Opportunities legislation contain clauses designed to protect those who seek to assert their rights from being penalized for doing so. The term *victimization* carries a technical meaning in that the employee must be able to point to the doing of a 'protected act' which triggers, or is alleged to have triggered the objectionable behaviour. The bringing of a claim in a tribunal is the obvious example but the various Acts also give protection to those who indicate their intention to do so or take preliminary steps towards enforcing their rights.

4 Dismissal

Wrongful dismissal at common law

4.01 The most significant intervention of statute law in the area of individual rights has been in relation to dismissal. At common law, provided the employer terminates the contract in accordance with its terms, the employee will have no redress. Generally this means that the employer must give the employee that notice to which he is entitled under his contract of employment. The relevant period of notice will often be specified in the contract, but if it is not, then it will be a reasonable period. However, statute law now lays down a

minimum period of notice which must be given, whatever the contract says, and that minimum period depends upon how long the employee was employed. Currently the minimum is 1 week's notice for employment of up to 2 years, and 1 week for each year of employment up to 12 years, i.e. if 2 years' employment, 2 weeks' notice; 6 years' employment, 6 weeks' notice etc. up to a maximum of 12 years. The contract may stipulate more than this, but any provision for notice of less than the minimum will not be applied. Note that this is the notice that the employer must give to the employee. It does not operate the other way. An employee with over 1 month's service must give 1 week's notice, but that is the only minimum requirement. The contract might specify a longer period which will apply if it is longer than the statutory minimum. A claim also arises when the employee believes that the conduct of his employer has been so bad that it repudiates the contract. The employee may therefore accept that repudiatory conduct and resign.

4.02 If the employer dismisses with no notice or with inadequate notice, then this is termed a 'wrongful dismissal', and the employee will have a remedy in the ordinary courts or in the employment tribunal for breach of contract. Because a claim for wrongful dismissal is a contractual claim, the employer is entitled to any of the defences available to any other defendant to such a claim. So, for example, if the employee has committed an act of gross misconduct, then the employer may rely on that misconduct as constituting a repudiation of the contract, and may lawfully consider himself discharged from his obligations under it, including his obligation to give notice (see paragraph 4.05). But the courts and the employment tribunals do not readily find that misconduct is gross. Such conduct might include dishonesty or physical violence.

Unfair dismissal

4.03 The common law, then, sees a man's job essentially in contractual terms. Provided the contract is complied with, the employee has no grounds of complaint. This means that the reason for a dismissal can rarely be questioned at common law. As long as the employer has given the required notice, it matters not whether it is because the employee is dishonest, or smokes cigarettes, or has blond hair. Managerial prerogative is left untouched. But overlaid on the contractual relationship is a set of statutory obligations which are unique to the contract of employment and which require the employer to have a fair reason for the dismissal, and to be acting reasonably in relying upon it. The basic law of unfair dismissal can be considered under the following heads.

Eligibility

4.04 The employee must be eligible to make his complaint. This means he must have 1 year continuous employment, he must be below the normal retiring age for the job. The normal retiring age is the age at which an employee can reasonably expect to be retired. If there is no such age within the undertaking the age of 65 years will apply, to men as well as women. (Note that if the employer has a different retiring age for men and women this will be invalidated and the exclusion will not apply.)

He cannot claim if he ordinarily works abroad (though if he works in various countries but his base is in Britain, he will not fall into this category); and he must present his claim within 3 months of the dismissal.

Dismissal

4.05 The employee must show that he has been dismissed. Sometimes what in form appears to be a resignation will in law constitute a dismissal (known as constructive dismissal). For example, if the employer unilaterally reduces the wages or alters the hours of work or otherwise acts in breach of contract, the employee may resign and claim that his resignation was merely a response to an act by his employer which was tantamount to a dismissal (though the dismissal is not inevitably unfair). In order to claim constructive dismissal, the act complained of must constitute a breach of contract, although an act on the part of the employer which involves destroying the trust and confidence in the employment relationship will constitute a breach of the implied term mentioned in paragraph 4.02 above, and entitle the employee to leave and claim that he has been dismissed. For instance, such conduct as falsely and without justification accusing an employee of theft, failing to support a supervisor, upbraiding a supervisor in the presence of his subordinates, and a director using intemperate language and criticizing his personal secretary in front of a third party have all been held to amount to conduct which justifies the employee leaving and claiming that he has been dismissed. Cases on constructive dismissal illustrate the important distinction between wrongful and unfair dismissal. Because constructive dismissal requires a breach of contract on the part of the employer, it is automatically wrongful. But it is not necessarily unfair because the test for fairness is a different one. Similarly, a refusal to renew a fixed-term contract will amount to a dismissal. That dismissal cannot be wrongful because a contract which comes to an end by the effluxion of time will not have been ended by any form of breach, but it may nevertheless be unfair if the decision not to renew is unreasonable (see below).

A fair reason

4.06 Once a dismissal is established, the employer must show that he has a fair reason for the dismissal. Some reasons for dismissal are, by statute, automatically unfair. These include dismissals for reasons connected with maternity, trade union membership and the assertion by the employee of health and safety or other statutory rights or for *whistle blowing* activities that is the making of a *protected disclosure*. Similarly, a number of reasons are specifically stated to be potentially fair – misconduct, capability, redundancy, the fact that a statutory provision prohibits a person from working, and any other substantial reason.

Capability covers both inherent incompetence and incapability arising from ill health. The latter may include a prolonged absence or perhaps a series of short, intermittent absences. Some other substantial reason is a residual category covering a potentially wide range of reasons. Perhaps the most important is that it may justify dismissals where the employer takes steps to protect his business interests. For example, an employer who was concerned about his employees leaving and setting up in competition decided to require them to enter into a restraint of trade agreement (see paragraph 3.35). Some employees refused to sign the agreement and were dismissed. Again, employees who are dismissed because they refuse to accept new hours of work introduced by the employer may well be found to have been fairly dismissed if the changes had been made in order to improve efficiency. A refusal to accept new arrangements is now a common basis for such dismissal.

The employer must be acting reasonably

4.07 But it is not enough simply for the employer to have a fair reason. The law requires that 'the determination of the question whether the dismissal is fair or unfair … depends on whether in the circumstances (including the size and administrative resources of the employer's undertaking) the employer acted reasonably or unreasonably in treating [the reason] as a sufficient reason for dismissing the employee' which 'shall be determined in accordance with equity and the substantial merits of the case' (ERA 1996, Section 98(4)).

Many factors may have to be considered in determining this question. The length of service of the employee, the need for the employer to act consistently, the size and resources of the company or firm will all be relevant factors. For example, a small firm cannot as readily accommodate the lengthy illness of an employee as a large organization.

Procedural factors are as important in these cases. ACAS has produced a code of practice on disciplinary matters – Disciplinary Practice and Procedures in Employment. Like other codes, it is not directly legally binding but should be taken into account in any legal proceedings before a tribunal, since it is open for a tribunal to find a dismissal for a fair reason nevertheless unfair, if it was not effected in accordance with good procedural practice.

4.08 The code emphasizes the need for warnings, a chance to state a case, and a right of appeal. That in simple terms covers the huge canon of reported cases on unfair dismissal. Most employers will have a disciplinary code which envisages a system by which errant employees receive an ascending scale of warnings; informal oral, formal oral and then, first, second and final written. That procedure will also contain the power to dismiss for gross misconduct. Gross misconduct will cover the obvious transgressions such as dishonesty, drunkenness or gross insubordination. The employer can also write into the procedure acts which are peculiarly important to his business. Similarly, an act of negligence of such magnitude that the employer cannot afford a repeat may justify immediate dismissal.

4.09 Once an employer thinks that the employee may have committed an act of misconduct that may lead to dismissal it is imperative that he engages in a proper and fair system for the determination of the guilt of the employee and to consider the appropriate response. Since the case of *British Home Stores v Burchell [1978] IRLR 379* a three-fold test has been the orthodox approach. It must be established that the employer believed in the guilt of the employee. Then the employer must show that he had reasonable grounds upon which to sustain that belief. Finally the employer must show that at the time at which he formed that belief on those grounds he must have carried out as much investigation into the matter as was reasonable in all the circumstances. The form of the investigation is not laid down nor for any hearing that takes place. In particular there is no requirement that the hearing should be quasi-judicial with cross examination of witnesses. So long as the employee has a clear understanding of the charge and an opportunity to state his case before an impartial panel, then the procedure is likely to be fair. An appeal procedure is also required and any deficiencies in the first hearing can be cured by a proper opportunity to state a case at the appeal.

4.10 The whole position regarding the procedure for dismissing will change with the coming into force, probably late in 2004 of the *Employment Act 2000* (EA 2000). It will introduce the requirement for a minimum level of dismissal and disciplinary procedures (DDPs). A failure to follow the statutory scheme will make the dismissal automatically unfair. Conversely, if that basic level is followed then a failure to follow any additional procedures which might have been necessary will not render the dismissal unfair, unless the outcome would have been different. That represents a radical departure from the current state of the law, see the succeeding paragraph for the present state of the law. As to the DDPs themselves they should not represent any radical departure from the sort of disciplinary code that one would expect to see in a reasonably well-informed business. In short the employee must be told of the charge in writing, there must be a disciplinary hearing and the employee must have sufficient time to consider the charge before he has to attend. The hearing must equally be heard reasonably promptly and without undue delay and there must be an appeal process. The other important new issue in the EA 2000 will be the encouragement to use alternative dispute resolution instead of the tribunal.

4.11 This paragraph must be read in the light of the preceding paragraph and may be largely superseded in late 2004. In the meantime, the importance of a procedure cannot be underestimated since a dismissal for a perfectly fair reason maybe still be unfair on procedural grounds. Further it is currently not open to an employer to argue that however unfair the procedure dismissal would have been inevitable. Before the decision in *Polkey v Dayton Services [1988] ICR 142*, the tribunals would not regard as unfair any dismissal where the employee would still have been dismissed. In reversing this line of authorities the House of Lords held that procedural unfairness gave the employee the right to claim a remedy for the dismissal but that the size or nature of any remedy must reflect what had been lost by the imperfect procedure. *Polkey* was a case about following the appropriate and fair procedure for selecting for redundancy. The loss caused by the unfair procedure was that the employee had been deprived of employment (and necessarily pay) for a period of weeks over which the appropriate procedure should, but was not carried out. The *Polkey* loss is therefore most commonly to be measured in terms of the weeks' pay that would otherwise have been paid during such time as would reasonably have been spend consulting, investigating, enquiring or otherwise doing what should have been done to make the procedure fair. In some cases this may call for quite a sophisticated analysis of what the employee's chances would have been of being found guilty of the alleged misconduct, or how he might have fared in a selection procedure for redundancy. Whatever changes are wrought by the EA 2000 there is likely still to be a need to look at the actual loss sustained by the employee by reason of procedural deficiencies.

4.12 Although the ACAS Code and the preceding remarks have been related to the matters of misconduct and redundancy, it will be appreciated that all situations where dismissal may follow require the employer to be fully apprised of the facts and capable of rational justification. Thus the employee whose frequent sick absences have reached an unacceptable stage cannot be treated as guilty of misconduct (unless the allegation is that the sickness is not genuine) but must be told of his employers concerns who must obtain such medical advice as will enable them to reach a view as to whether he may soon be fit to render full-time work, the employee should be invited to state his case and discuss his position. If the employer concludes that he cannot continue to employ the employee, and that is a fair reason given the nature and size of his undertaking then substantively and procedurally he is likely to have discharged his statutory obligations.

4.13 One general point in these cases is that it is not open to the tribunal to find a dismissal unfair merely because it disagrees with the employer. It must not substitute its own judgement for that of the employer. For example, in a disciplinary case a tribunal might conclude that it would probably have given a further, final warning before dismissing. But that does not necessarily make the dismissal unfair. It is often perfectly possible for there to be a number of reasonable responses to a particular situation. One employer might dismiss, another might give a final warning, yet both may be acting within the range of reasonable responses to particular conduct. Provided the tribunal finds the employer's response to be within this range of reasonable responses, it should not find the dismissal to be unfair.

Remedies

4.14 There are three remedies envisaged: reinstatement, which means the employee being given the old job back and treated in all respects as though he had never been dismissed; re-engagement, which may involve being taken back in a different job, or perhaps in the same job but without back-pay, or on slightly different terms; and finally compensation. A tribunal must consider the three remedies in the order just given. In deciding whether to order reinstatement or re-engagement, the tribunal must consider three factors: (1) whether the employee wants his job back – if not, the tribunal must go straight on to consider compensation; (2) whether it is practicable to take the employee back – and in regard to a small firm it is likely that a tribunal will find that it is not because of personality conflicts involved; and (3) whether the employee has caused or contributed to his own dismissal – if he has, at least to any significant degree, he is unlikely to be awarded his job back.

4.15 Usually employees do not want reinstatement or re-engagement, so the tribunal simply assesses compensation. However, even if reinstatement or re-engagement is ordered, the employer is not finally compelled to obey the order, though he will have to pay additional compensation if he refuses to do so. The usual compensation is made up of two elements. One is the basic award, which is calculated in essentially the same way as a redundancy payment (see paragraph 4.21). The other is the compensatory award, which is designed to take account of the actual loss suffered by the employee following from the dismissal. This will depend on such

factors as when he is likely to obtain new employment, and what he will then earn. The amount will be reduced if the employee has caused or contributed to his own dismissal, the tribunal deciding what reduction would be just and equitable in all the circumstances, e.g. the tribunal may find that the employee is 50% to blame and reduce his compensation by half. The maximum compensatory award is now £53 500. The amounts are reviewed and increased in February each year. The size of the maximum award, vastly increased in recent years permits of quite detailed assessment on both loss of earnings and pension.

Redundancy

4.16 Redundancy has already been referred to in the context of potentially fair reasons for dismissal and the *Polkey* principle. It merits a discrete section because the termination of employment by reason of redundancy remains a feature of the working life of many employees. It has an importance independent of claims before the tribunal and raises a number of legal implications for the employer. First it is necessary to identify what, in law, amounts to a redundancy.

4.17 The three main situations in which a redundancy arises are (1) where the employer closes down altogether; (2) where the employer moves the place of work (though it should be noted that the place of work is where the employee can be required to work under his contract and not where he normally works, e.g. if the contract stipulates that he can be required to work anywhere in Great Britain and the firm moves from London to Glasgow, but his job is still available in Glasgow, this is not a redundancy); and (3) where the need for employees to do a particular kind of work has ceased or diminished. It is this final category which has caused and continues to cause considerable difficulties. Note first that there may be a constant amount of *work* but that the employer may require a smaller number of employees to perform it. Controversy raged over the question whether if the work which had diminished was that work which the employee was contractually engaged to perform, or merely work which he had come to perform as a matter of fact? This controversy came to be known as the *function* test as against the *contract* test. The significance of the dispute was that an employee with a contractual job description of say, driver, but who had come effectively to operate as a warehouseman, would be redundant if the employer decided to dispense with some warehousemen if the functional test was applied, but not if the contractual test was. Thus if selected for dismissal and unhappy with the situation he could complain that he was not redundant (contractual test) and that his dismissal was not for redundancy and unfair. Conversely the employer could argue that functionally he was now a warehouseman and that the need for them had diminished. The controversy is said to have been finally determined by the House of Lords in *Murray v Foyle Meats Ltd* [1999] ICR 827, where the then Lord Chancellor Lord Irving, declared that the two tests both '*missed the point*', stressing that the key word was *attributable* and that there was no reason why a dismissal should not be attributable to a diminution in the employer's need for employees irrespective of the terms of his contract or the function which he performed.

Note also that a dismissal may look like a redundancy situation but the dismissal may be for reasons of business efficiency. It is yet a further example within employment law of a deceptively simple concept containing traps for the unwary and needing expert assistance.

Establishing a redundancy claim

4.18 It is important to note that two sorts of redundancy claims may come to a tribunal. The first is where an employee believes that he has been made redundant and is refused a redundancy payment by his former employer. Secondly, and much more commonly the employee accepts that his dismissal is by reason of redundancy but claims that the dismissal is unfair by reason of inadequate warning or consultation or that he has been unfairly selected from a group of potential candidates.

Eligibility

4.19 He must be eligible to present the claim. In order to do this he must have 1 year's employment over the age of 18, be below 65, and normally work in Great Britain. Exceptionally, although he normally works abroad, he will be entitled to claim if he is in Great Britain at the employer's request at the time of dismissal. The qualifying period of employment was reduced from 2 years to 1 year with effect from 1 June 1999.

Offers of alternative employment

4.20 The detailed requirements of warning, consultation and selection are beyond the scope of this work. A procedure must be devised which addresses the employees right to notice of the impending redundancy and that the selection of the retained employees is an objective and transparent system which will withstand scrutiny. A key concept in the redundancy process is also the offer of alternative employment. This is important for two reasons: first from the employee's point of view he is entitled to the opportunity to stay with business albeit in a different capacity. Secondly the employee's entitlement to a statutory redundancy payment will be compromised if he unreasonably refuses an offer of suitable alternative employment. The job is unlikely to be considered suitable if it means a significant loss of status or pay. Whether any refusal is reasonable will depend upon the employee's personal circumstances. However, the employee does have a trial period of up to four weeks to decide whether a job is suitable, and within that period he is working without prejudice to his redundancy claim. But, of course, if he refuses the job after the trial period, it will still be open to the employer to claim that it was suitable employment and has been unreasonably refused.

Amount

4.21 The employee's compensation depends on his age, wages at the time he was dismissed, and years of service. Broadly speaking it is ½ a week's pay for a complete year of service between the ages of 18 and 22, 1 week's pay for each year of service between 24 and 41, and 1½ weeks' pay for each complete year of service between 41 and 65. The maximum number of years that can be taken into account is 20. The week's pay is calculated from the gross figure, but is subject to a maximum (at present) of £260 per week. So the most that can be recovered under the statute is for someone with 20 years' service, all over the age of 41, who on dismissal was earning at least £260 per week gross. He will receive £260 × 20 × 1½ = £7800. Of course, employers may voluntarily pay more than the law requires, or they may be bound to pay more than the law requires by a term in the contract of employment.

4.22 Employees in their 64th year when they are dismissed have their redundancy payment reduced by 1/12 for each month of their 64th year, so that by the time they reach 65 their redundancy payment has reduced to nil. Of course this makes good sense: employees who retire do not get redundancy payments.

The redundancy fund, which used to help employers meet redundancy payments, has been abolished.

Consultation with recognized trade unions and the D of E

4.23 In addition to the consultation which the employee must engage in with the individual employees who are selected for redundancy there also exists, in certain circumstances an obligation to consult with recognized TU representatives. Although essentially a *collective labour relations*' issue, it is important that the employer proposing any large-scale redundancies, i.e. more than 20 employees, deals with this issue as well as the individual staff issues. When an employer is *proposing* to make redundant more than 20 employees he must consult least 30 days before the first dismissal is likely to take place, and if over 100 employees are affected then the period

is 90 days. The two periods laid down are the *minimum* acceptable times and consultation should start '*in good time*' and in any event within these timescales. A failure to follow the procedure and to enter into proper consultations designed to avoid if possible any redundancies, to reduce the number of any such dismissals and to mitigate the effect of dismissals can lead to the making of a *protective award*. This is a sum of money which can be a maximum of 90 days pay and will be paid in addition to any redundancy pay due to the employees. The potential penalty is large and, by definition, if payable by a firm which is facing large-scale redundancies, an unwelcome addition to their financial difficulties. Any practice anticipating such an exercise should seek expert advice and be prepared to enter into genuine consultation and discussion with TU or other works representatives, however academic an exercise this may appear.

Transfer of undertakings

4.24 The *Transfer of Undertakings (Protection of Employment) Regulations 1981 (TUPE)* naturally find their place in the consideration of redundancy and it is in the context of redundancy payments, and more particularly who paid them, that much of the early litigation concentrated. In short the regulations exist to protect the rights of the employees whose employment is transferred to another employer. The new employer stands in the shoes of the old and the terms and conditions of employment remain the same. Detailed consideration of the methods of transfer and indeed what amounts to the transfer of an 'undertaking' is beyond the scope of this work. The issues which are likely to be of most concern to employers is the situation where the transfer, usually of a business in difficulty, entails the shedding of staff with the inevitable consequence of redundancy payments.

Any dismissal which is caused by a transfer of undertaking is automatically unfair, unless it is for an *economic, technical or organizational* (ETO) reason, entailing changes to the workforce. (If it *is* for ETO then it is not automatically *fair*, the basic rules then apply for determining whether it is fair or not.) It is a question of fact whether the dismissal is connected with a transfer, it may take place some time before the transfer is effective and still be connected with the transfer, it may take place sometimes after the transfer is complete and also be connected to it. As a result of this, it is not only prudent, but very common, for the employee who is surplus to the requirements of the newly transferred undertaking to seek redundancy and/or unfair dismissal compensation from both the transferor and the transferee.

The effect of a transfer on terms and conditions and existing rights, which could include an outstanding claim against the transferor for damages for personal injuries or simply wages owed is again a matter for detailed and specialist advice. The effect on pensions and other benefits also require specialist assistance.

Fixed-term contracts

4.25 Special rules apply to fixed-term contracts. First, if a fixed-term contract is not renewed, this in law amounts to a dismissal. But it is not necessarily unfair. In particular, if the employee is taken on for a fixed period and knows in advance that his contract is likely to be temporary and will not be renewed when the fixed term expires, a refusal to renew the contract is likely to be justified. The employer will still have to show that he is acting reasonably in not renewing the contract, but that should not be too difficult in most situations.

4.26 Second, where a fixed-term contract is for a year or more, an employee may sign away his rights to unfair dismissal, i.e. he may agree in writing that he will not claim for unfair dismissal if his contract is not renewed once the fixed term ends. This is one of the exceptional cases where an agreement to sign away statutory rights is binding. But such an agreement is not binding as regards dismissals which take effect during the fixed term. It applies only to the dismissal arising from the non-renewal of the fixed term. Similarly, rights to redundancy may also be signed away, but curiously only where the fixed term is for two years or more.

4.27 This leaves the crucial question: What is a fixed-term contract? The answer is one with an ascertainable date of termination (though it is still fixed term even if the parties can terminate it earlier by giving notice). So if the contract is to last for a particular task, and it is impossible to predict how long the job will last, this is not a fixed-term contract. When it comes to an end, it terminates because the task is completed. But this in law will not constitute a dismissal. Consequently, even if the employer is acting unreasonably in not continuing to employ the employee, the latter will have no claim for unfair dismissal.

Reference

4.28 An employer is under no legal duty to provide a reference. If he does so, there are certain legal pitfalls he must take care to avoid. If the statement is untrue, it may be libellous and he could be liable in defamation. However, he will be able to rely upon the defence of qualified privilege, which means that he will not be liable unless it can be shown that the statement was inspired by malice, i.e. was deliberately false and intended to injure the employee.

4.29 An employer who hires an employee on the basis of an untrue reference may bring a legal action against the employer issuing the reference. If it is deliberately false, the liability will be for deceit. If it is negligently written, e.g. claims are made which he could have discovered were false with some inquiries, liability will probably exist for negligence mis-statement under the doctrine of *Hedley Byrne v Heller* [1964] AC 465 (see Chapter 3, Section 2).

4.30 Certainly the employer owes a duty to his former employee not to prepare a reference negligently. In *Spring v Guardian Assurance Plc* [1994] 3 WLR 354, an insurance salesman successfully sued his former employers. They had negligently provided a reference to prospective new employers who, relying on the negligent reference, had declined to employ him. Finally, if the employer dismisses an employee for misconduct or incompetence, but then proceeds to write him a glowing reference, he may find difficulty in convincing the tribunal that the reason for which he was dismissed was, in fact, the true reason.

Duties on former employees

4.31 Once the contract is terminated, this does not mean that there are no further duties imposed on the former employee. In particular, the employee is not free to divulge confidential information or trade secrets to rivals. However, he can use his own individual skill and experience, e.g. organizational ability, even though that was gained as a result of working for the former employer. But the distinction between the knowledge which can and cannot be imparted is vague.

The House of Lords has recently made clear that the ending of employment does not signal an end to the potential liability for acts of discrimination by the ex-employer. See *Rhys Harper v Relaxion Group* [2003] IRLR 484 a joint appeal in three cases on the RRA, SDA and DDA, respectively. In each case acts perpetrated after termination laid the employer open to claims. The acts might include the refusal to investigate complaints, or to do so satisfactorily, to provide a reference which was adverse or to consider reinstatement.

Restricting competition: restraint of trade

4.32 In addition, the employee may be prevented from setting up in competition with his former employer. But this will be so only if he entered into an express clause in his contract of employment which prohibited such competition. Even then, such clauses will be binding only if they are reasonable and not contrary to the public interest. They must not be drawn wider than is necessary to protect the employer's interests; otherwise they will be considered to be in unreasonable restraint of trade and therefore void. Reasonable restrictions might prevent an architect from soliciting the clients of his former employer, and they may even encompass restrictions on the employee's right to compete within a certain area for a particular time. But if the area is drawn too widely, or the duration too long, the clause will be void and unenforceable.

5 Collective labour relations law

5.01 As mentioned above, the main provisions in the area of collective labour relations law are concerned with giving certain rights to unions and their officials. However, these are in practice given only to recognized trade unions, i.e. those with which the employer is willing to negotiate.

There is once again a mechanism by which a TU can seek to enforce recognition. Since June 2000, Section 70A, TULRCA has provided a means by which the workforce can be balloted to seek views on recognition. A 40% majority in favour is required. The ballot is seen as something of a last resort with the involvment of CAC as the primary means by which some accommodation between employer and employee might be accomplished. Detailed provisions are set out in the Act but essentially the method can only be used by one union, if another has already secured rights of recognition there is no scope for the two unions battling it out by way of a ballot. If unsuccessful, a TU cannot apply again to re-start the process within 1 year. Importantly, the power does not apply to small businesses with under 21 employees. If successful the rights conferred by the recognition are limited to the negotiation over pay, holidays and hours of work.

The consequences of recognition

5.02 Once a union is recognized by an employer, the following consequences follow.

Disclosure of information

5.03 The unions have a right to receive information from the employer without which they would be impeded in collective bargaining and which it is good industrial relations practice to disclose. However, there is a wide range of exceptions, e.g. information received in confidence, or information which would damage the employer's undertakings (such as how tender prices are calculated). Some guidance can be given by the Code of Practice on Disclosure of Information produced by ACAS. It should be emphasized, though, that no information need be divulged until the recognized union asks for it.

Consultation over redundancies

5.04 As soon as the decision to make redundance has crystallized, the employer should consult with any appropriate employee representatives among the group from which the redundancy or redundancies are to be made. This consultation may be with trade union officials or employees' representatives elected for that purpose, whichever the employer chooses. The representatives may make representations upon these proposals, and the employer must in turn reply to their points, though he is not obliged to accept them.

As noted above, in the case of collective redundancies this consultation is required if it proposed to make 20 or more employees redundant within 90 days. But this period will not apply if there are special circumstances making it impossible for him to comply with it, e.g. a sudden and unforeseen loss of work. In the case of these collective redundancies, it is necessary to notify the Department of Employment.

Reasonable time off for union officials and members

5.05 Union officials have a right to reasonable time off with pay for industrial relations activities involving the employer, e.g. negotiating, handling grievances, and attending training courses connected with these matters. What is reasonable will depend upon such factors as the size of the firm, the job of the employee, and the number of other officials. Some guidance can be found in the ACAS Code of Practice on Time Off.

5.06 Union members also have a right to reasonable time off, but without pay, for trade union matters, e.g. attending union conferences. Again the ACAS Code of Practice gives some guidance, though its principal message is that it is for employers and unions themselves to negotiate what is reasonable in all circumstances.

Health and safety representatives

5.07 Recognized unions are entitled to appoint safety representatives, who have an important role to play in helping to maintain health and safety standards. This is further discussed in paragraph 6.03.

Dismissal for union membership or non-membership

5.08 Under the Trade Union and Labour Relations (Consolidation) Act 1992 it is automatically unfair to dismiss an employee because he does not belong to a particular trade union, or because he has been refused membership of any particular trade union. The closed shop – and the complicated law relating to it – are now both things of the past.

5.09 The other side of the coin is the same. It is also automatically unfair to dismiss an employee because he does belong to a union.

6 Health and safety

6.01 The health and safety of employees is governed primarily by the Health and Safety at Work Act (HSWA) 1974. This Act now receives considerable underpinning from the six sets of regulations introduced after 1992 under the umbrella of the *Management of Health and Safety at Work Regulations*. They are *The Workplace (Health, Safety and Welfare) Regulations 1992*, *The Provision and Use of Work Equipment Regulations 1992*, *The Personal Protective Equipment Regulations 1992*, *The Manual Handling Regulations 1992* and *The Health and Safety (Display Screens Equipment) Regulations 1992*.

These the regulations concentrate on aspects of work, as can be seen from their titles, e.g. manual handling, protective equipment and computers, applying the regulatory scheme across all workplaces and all trades. That represents a building upon the scheme of the HSWA, with its focus on the prevention of accidents but more significantly a final departure from the old legislative scheme where the protection enjoyed had been specific to workplaces, e.g. *The Factories Acts* or *The Offices, Shops and Railway Premises Act*, to specific trades, e.g. *The Woodworking Regulations* or even to the use of particular substances, e.g. lead or asbestos. Now the obligation e.g. to make sure that the access to premises are safe will apply across all workplaces, trades, etc.

The Health and Safety at Work Act 1974

6.02 Under the old Acts the only persons protected were those who were employed by the owner or occupier of the factory or workplace. The HSWA extended that protection by placing duties upon employers, the self-employed and persons otherwise in control of premises. (Duties are also owed by the designers, manufacturers, importers and suppliers of articles for use at work.) The duties are owed not just to employees but to any person who may be affected by work activities requiring that the employer do all that is *reasonably practicable* to ensure the health, safety and welfare of his employees. The Act also cast upon employees duties to take reasonable care for their own safety, to cooperate with employers so as to permit them to comply with their obligations and not to interfere with anything provided in pursuance of these statutory obligations. The 1992 Regulations give protection to employed and self-employed but also cast upon all those categories of people the corresponding duty to observe the requirements of the regulations.

The protection is greater also in that the duty of the employer is now less to the 'reasonably practicable' standard and more likely to be that what is provided shall be to *suitable and sufficient* level. That is almost certainly a higher level of care.

However, the key feature of the *six pack* of Regulations and the major invention is that of the *risk assessment*. Although that was foreshadowed by the HSWA 1974 with clear policies on accident prevention the risk assessment will remain the real legacy of the new statutory framework. The concentration is now firmly on prevention by a focussed assessment of what could go wrong and how it can be avoided.

Safety representatives and committees

6.03 Where the employer recognizes a trade union, that union is entitled to appoint safety representatives, who must then be consulted by the employer on health and safety matters. In addition, the safety representatives have a right to formally inspect at least once every three months those parts of the premises for which they are responsible; to investigate any reportable accidents, i.e. those that result in the employee being absent for three days or more; and to examine any documents relating to health and safety, save those for which there are specific exemptions, e.g. personal medical records. Furthermore, provided at least two safety representatives request this, the employer must set up a safety committee within three months of the request. This committee may keep under review health and safety policies and performance. The 1992 Regulations introduced extended rights on consultation with safety representatives e.g. on any matter which might substantially affect the health and safety of workers.

Enforcement of the legislation

6.04 The powers of inspectors are quite wide, appointed under the HSWA. They can enter premises uninvited at any reasonable time, require the production of records or documents which the law requires to be kept, and oblige persons to answer questions. They may prosecute in the criminal courts if they find the laws infringed. But, in addition, they can now take effective action without the need to have recourse to the courts. They may issue 'improvement' or 'prohibition' orders. The former oblige the employer to bring his place or premises up to scratch within a certain specified period. The latter actually compel him to stop using the place or premises until the necessary improvements have been made. But prohibition orders can be issued only if the inspector considers that there is a risk of serious personal injury. The employer can appeal to an industrial tribunal against these orders. An appeal suspends the operation of an improvement order until the appeal is heard, but a prohibition order continues in force pending the appeal unless the employer obtains permission to the contrary from a tribunal. Breach of either order is automatically a criminal offence. Indeed, individual managers who are knowingly parties to a breach of the prohibition order may even be sent to prison.

Reporting accidents

6.05 Every employer should keep a record of accidents at the workplace. In addition, some accidents may have to be reported to the enforcing authorities. These include fatalities and accidents involving serious personal injury, including those resulting in hospital in-patient treatment. These accidents have to be reported to the authorities by the quickest practicable means, and a written report must be sent within seven days. For other accidents, involving absences from work of three days or more, notification to the authorities is not necessary provided the employer has reasonable grounds to believe that the employee will claim industrial injury benefit. In this case the relevant information will, in any event, be sent to the Department of Works and Pensions and they will transfer it to the enforcing authorities.

Compensation for accidents at work

6.06 The legislation discussed above is designed to prevent accidents. Indeed the HSWA specifically states that it does not create any civil liability as does the *Management of Health and Safety at Work Regulations*. The remaining five of the six regulations *do* create such liability for breach of statutory duty and some commentators on the legislation take the view that any breach of the regulations will be relevant to establishing a breach of the common law duties, i.e. that the employer has been negligent e.g. in *not* carrying out a statutory risk assessment.

An employee seeking damages for injuries suffered at work can frame his care in one of the following four ways:

1 Every employer owes a common law duty to take reasonable care to ensure the safety of his employees. More specifically this requires that he should provide safe plant and appliances, adopt safe systems of work, and employ competent employees. If an accident occurs because of a breach of this duty, the employer will be liable.
2 Breaches of the Regulations will be the basis of a claim for breach of statutory duty and because of their specific and wide coverage there will be regulations apt to cover most occurences and accidents.
3 The employer may be liable under the Occupiers Liability Act 1957. This imposes a duty of care on occupiers of premises to all those lawfully entering his premises. The standard of the duty is to take all reasonable practicable steps to make the premises safe. A claim under this Act may be made by someone not employed by the occupier.
4 Where a person, whether a worker or a third party, is injured as a result of the negligence of an employee acting in the course of his employment, the employer will be vicariously liable for the injury caused. Even if he is not personally liable under items 1–3, he may still be held responsible.

Finally note that injury to an employee can be caused not just by tripping over a loose carpet or lifting a heavy weight. The law on *stress at work* continues to develop, albeit that the Court of Appeal has restricted the scope of such litigation somewhat. An employer who is alerted to the employees inability to cope with the demands of a job, or who complains of the oppressive behaviour of managers ignores such warnings at his peril. A prudent employer in the 21st century should be alive to the greater subtleties of his obligations and the need to look to employees mental as well as physical well-being.

7 Employment law in Scotland*

7.01 Employment legislation is UK based and applies to Scotland as to England and Wales. As in England an employer is required to observe the terms of the *Employment Rights Act 1996* (with amendments thereto effected by such primary legislation as the *Public Interest Disclosure Act 1988* – whistle-blowing and such secondary legislation as the *Maternity and Paternal Leave, etc. Regulations 1999*), the Sex Discrimination Act 1975, the *Race Relations Act 1976*, the *Equal Pay Act 1970*, the *Disability Discrimination Act 1995* and the *National Minimum Wage Act 1998*. The employer is also obliged to obtemper most employment law/anti-discriminatory statutory instruments, e.g. as from 1 and 2 December 2003, respectively the *Employment Equality (Sexual Orientation) Regulations 2003* and *Employment Regulations 2003* and *Employment Equality (Religion or Belief) Regulations 2003* take effect.

Any judicial forum also has to have due regard to the substantive and procedural rights of Employers and Employees in terms of the *Human Rights Act 1998*.

The common law principles derived from Scotland law are very similar to their English counterparts although in actions raised in Scotland based on the common law of contract and the potential breach thereof in an employment context Scottish Courts, in spite of the occasional judgement of the Outer House of the Court of Session to the contrary, are markedly less likely to grant an interdict, i.e. a specific order prohibiting a course of action on the employer's part (e.g. dismissal). The lead cases on Restraint of Trade are the same in England, Wales and Scotland. However as there is a slightly different view in Scotland as to the construction of contracts and the severability of clauses when orders restricting competition are granted or refused there can be differences in individual cases. A separate system of Employment Tribunals operate in Scotland with appeals initially to the Employment Appeal Tribunal (both bodies being governed by their own Regulations). Appeals lie thereafter to the Inner House of the Court of Session and for the moment to the House of Lords. As a result of the separate appellate structure occasionally the interpretation of substantive law can be different until matters are finally resolved by the supreme appellate forum.

* This section was written by Peter G. Hutchinson.

36

International work by architects

RICHARD DYTON

1 Introduction

1.01 Any international work undertaken by architects is subject to legal complications over and above those in Britain because of the different legal and insurance systems involved. However, increasingly, architects are able to work in a European and, indeed, world market and, providing appropriate legal advice is taken, the opportunities available outweigh the perceived complications.

1.02 In the following paragraphs brief summaries are given of the legal and insurance requirements of countries in which British architects find themselves involved. There are also references to the very different attitudes and cultures in those other countries which may require an increased sensitivity by British architects.

Belgium

1.03 Architects are divided into three categories: principals, civil servants and salaried architects. The architect, despite being required to supervise the building work, acts only as adviser to the client and not generally as agent. He provides designs, costings and quantities, technical drawings and supervision. Contractors and architects in Belgium are jointly responsible for major defects in buildings for a period of ten years. Following changes in the law in 1985, professional indemnity insurance is obligatory for Belgian architects and insurance companies have established a technical inspectorate to reduce the risk of major defects. Approval of a building by the technical inspectorate is usually accepted by insurance companies as evidence of satisfactory construction. The contractual liability of the architect is 10 years following the completion of the building, but in tort the normal period of limitation is 30 years. However, with regard to latent minor defects which do not fulfil the statutory 'sufficiently serious' criterion, a client may bring a claim in contract up to 30 years from handover, provided the claim is made promptly on discovery.

Denmark

1.04 It is not necessary to hold a licence to practice architecture in Denmark. It is possible to register with the Danish Professional Body 'the DAL' if the architect has the qualifications listed in the Council Directive 85/384/EEC on the mutual recognition of diplomas and certificates. The contractual limitation period for claims against the architect is 20 years. However, in principle, under the standard contract conditions, architects' liability may only extend for 5 years from handover of the building (although in private construction projects this condition may be excluded). The Danish Building Defect Fund is an independent statutory institution which aims both to prevent the occurrence of building faults and to ensure the repair of defects in buildings covered by the Fund (for a period of 20 years). A one-off premium, equivalent to 1% of the building cost, is paid by the building owner to the fund. Half of this sum is used to cover the cost of an inspection which is carried out just before the end of the 5-year period following handover. If any defects are discovered, the fund has recourse against any consultant found to be liable, including the architect under his professional indemnity policy, within this 5-year post-handover period. The remainder of the premium is used to cover the repair of any defects discovered after the five-year inspection, for up to 20 years.

France

1.05 In France the architect's profession has traditionally been regarded as artistic rather than technical. By contrast, engineers are highly trained technically and tend to perform the type of technical duties undertaken in Britain by an architect. The architects and engineers in France are assumed to be jointly responsible with the contractor for the completed development. In the event of a claim arising from a defect in the building, all the parties are normally joined in the action and responsibilities will be apportioned between them. Any contractor or designer can be held responsible for 100% of the cost of repair while investigations are carried out into the cause of the defect. Under France's Civil Code the contractual period of liability in France for claims against architects is 2 years from 'Réception' (approximately equivalent to Practical Completion) for minor repairs and 10 years for structural defects. Liability is strict in that any claim against the architect does not need to prove negligence – merely that a building is not fit for its purpose. In addition, full economic and consequential losses are recoverable both in contract and in tort. Insurance is compulsory for anyone who could be liable under the Civil Code and 'decennial' liability insurance is taken out by the employer, although any claims paid by the insurance company may be pursued against the architect since subrogation rights are rarely waived. The importance of buying the correct insurance policy should not be underestimated.

Germany

1.06 The German construction industry is the largest and fastest growing in Europe. Architects and engineers supervise the construction of a project and the architect's responsibility does not, therefore, end with the design. There is more management and administration work in their job than is the case in many of the other EU member countries. Demarcation between engineers and architects is less clear cut than in Britain. Both professionals have four to 6 years of technical training before an additional 2 years of training for each gives them their qualification to practice. For contractual claims the limitation period for an architect is 30 years, but in tort it is 3 years. The standard German architect's appointment document (the HOAC) sets a statutory minimum fee scale, although clients have devised numerous ways to circumvent the statutory minimum fees. The liability for the architect is, like

France, 'strict' in that negligence does not have to be proved, although this is normally only the case for claims of rectification of design or fee disputes. If damages are claimed, then there is a greater onus of proof upon the client. Some loss of profit is normally recoverable but not to the extent of full consequential losses as in France.

Ireland

1.07 There are no obstacles to British architects wishing to practice in Ireland as British architectural qualifications are recognized there. The duties of an architect in Ireland are similar to those existing in Britian, so that his terms of engagement will exclude him from liability in respect of work or advice provided by other professional advisers but will make him liable for errors, patent or latent, in the design for which he is responsible. Whereas in England and Wales the position of an architect's liability in negligence towards third parties has been restricted by recent case law, this is not so for Ireland, where anyone affected by the careless act of another, whose interests that other person ought reasonably to have taken into account, would be entitled to recover compensation for negligence unless there was some public policy reason why this should not be permitted.

Italy

1.08 The roles of the architect and engineer overlap considerably. Clients may appoint an architect or an engineer to a project, or alternatively a director of works who takes responsibility not only for the design, but also manages and supervises the construction. Design-and-build contracts have been particularly popular in Italy. As in France the contractual limitation period for actions against architects is 10 years. Professional indemnity insurance is not obligatory and is rarely taken out by consultants. Unusually, the construction industry in Italy is not prone to extensive litigation which is largely due to the cost and length of judicial procedures. A recent European Court of Justice decision ordered Italy to relax its laws restricting architects qualified in other EU countries from working in Italy. Italy had failed to properly implement the European Directive that relates to the mutual recognition of architectural qualifications. The requirements it put in place in relation to the documents that a non-Italian architect had to provide were too onerous. Furthermore, Italy was in breach of the general European principle of freedom to provide services because it prevented people who were trying to exercise that freedom from establishing a permanent base in Italy. A court decision like this is very expensive for a Member State. The fines imposed are hefty and daily fines can be imposed until the Member State amends its legislation appropriately. This decision should improve the ease with which architects can set up a practice in Italy.

Netherlands

1.09 In order to use the title 'architect' in the Netherlands, it is necessary to first be enlisted in the legal register (which is called the SBA). A British qualified architect can register because their qualifications are recognised in the Netherlands by virtue of the European Directive mentioned above. Liability in contract extends for 10 years from major defects. However, one important difference in the Netherlands is that the damages awarded to a plaintiff may only amount to half the designer's fees and it is possible to opt out of liability altogether as part of the contract of engagement. Given the nature of the soil in the Netherlands, demolition and piling contractors normally have direct contracts with the employer. For the same reason, many contracts will have an engineering element.

Portugal

1.10 The qualifications of British architects will be recognized in Portugal. Prior to commencing practising, it is necessary to register with the official Portuguese registration authority, the Ordem dos Arquitectos (OA). Networking is common in Portuguese business and so a contract with a local architect will be useful. The role of an architect in Portugal is unfortunately ill-defined, but a significant difference is that, for contractors, statutory liability extends only for 5 years for private works and 2 years for state works after the commissioning of a building if the contract is silent on the point. Since 1991, professional indemnity insurance is obligatory for 'designers' (including architects) involved in private construction works, such insurance being to provide cover for a 5-year post construction liability period.

Spain

1.11 The Spanish economy suffered a slump during the mid-1990s following the Seville Expo and the Barcelona Olympics but recovered towards the end of the decade. Every building project in Spain must be designed and supervised by a registered architect who is responsible for the aesthetics of the building. He undertakes to design and supervise the building, provide project documentation and prepare sub-contracts for other professionals. Spain's legal system imposes onerous legal responsibility on the design architect. It is the individual architect, rather than the firm that he works for, who is liable for the designs he prepares. For this reason, all architects in Spain carry extensive liability insurance. Architects' registration is maintained by the 17 colleges of architects, one for each autonomous community. The 'Collegio' has considerable power since each architect must be a member, the level of fees is set by the college and it also provides building permit approval. A separate 'technical architect' is responsible for supervising the technical aspects of the building and his role covers much of the work which would be carried out in the UK by a quantity surveyor. Claims against architects must be made within 10 years of the commencement of the project but this is extended to 15 years where there has been a breach of contract.

China

1.12 Most noticeably the culture affecting the industry is, not surprisingly, entirely different. For example, if the client decides to redesign at any stage in the works, then there is no cost implication for the client. A commonly used form of building contract where British architects or engineers are involved in China is the FIDIC form (see later). However, the concept of an independent consultant acting fairly between the parties is not a widely recognized concept in China. There is now a much greater scope for work in China for two reasons. Firstly, in the form of considerable preparatory works in the run up to the 2008 Olympic Games, which China will host, and secondly, following China's full membership of the World Trade Organisation (WTO) in November 2002. In the lead up to the Olympic Games, just under 40 new sporting venues will be created and improvements to airports, roads, other transport infrastructure and telecommunications will take place. Joining the WTO has removed many of the obstacles that previously existed for foreign architects wishing to work in China. Foreign architects can now take majority shareholdings in local joint ventures and in three to five years time will be able to set up wholly owned Chinese subsidiaries. Generally speaking, the potential for work is good and is assisted by the Chinese view that a project is more prestigious if a foreign architect was involved in its design.

Malaysia

1.13 Like many of the other South-east Asian countries Malaysia is experiencing a rapidly growing construction industry. No person can practise as an architect unless he is registered with the Board of Architects. Under the Malaysian Architect Act, no person other than a registered architect shall be entitled to recover in any court any charge, fee or remuneration for any professional service rendered as an architect in Malaysia. Therefore, foreign architects not registered with the Board of Architects who provide architectural services in Malaysia cannot sue the defaulting employer for payment in Malaysia. A registered architect in Malaysia is only entitled to be paid in accordance with the scale of fees set by the Board of Architects. Foreign architects can secure temporary registration if resident and possessing special expertise or forming the foreign component of a joint venture. Often the best way to proceed in Malaysia is by way of an unincorporated joint venture.

Hong Kong

1.14 Hong Kong became a Special Administrative Region of China on 1 July 1997 and English cases are still persuasive (but not binding) authorities. Law from other Commonwealth countries is also used to decide the rights and obligations of the parties. Australian cases, in particular, can prove useful as authorities, for example, in relation to the interpretation of 'pay when paid' clauses. Again, cultural differences play a significant role in the legal system and the importance of 'saving face' means that many disputes are referred to arbitration rather than litigation in order to maintain privacy. Consequently, the procedure for arbitration is particularly well established and the prominence of the Hong Kong International Arbitration Centre is an example of its importance. Whilst arbitration procedure is similar to that in the UK, it is regulated by the Hong Kong Arbitration Ordinance and the UNCITRAL United Nations model law on arbitration and procedure is often used. Architects who wish to practise in Hong Kong face a relatively straightforward procedure. To practise in Hong Kong, no permit from the Chinese government is required. However, before one can practise as an architect in Hong Kong, he must satisfy the requirements set out in the Architect Registration Ordinance such as being a member of Hong Kong Institute of Architects (HKIA) and to satisfy the Architect's Registration Board that he has one year's relevant professional experience in Hong Kong before the date of the application for registration. The contract with the employer by an architect can be made in any form or simply on the standard conditions of engagement set out in the form of Agreement between Client and Architect and Scale of Professional Charges prepared by the HKIA. In Hong Kong, the scope of works normally performed by an architect may fall into two different categories, i.e. pre-contractual and post-contractual duties. The most important of the pre-contractual duties is design. The post-contractual duties are certification, supervision and carrying out of inspections, compliance with laws and the general administration of the building contract for the employer.

USA

1.15 Apart from Europe, one potential, but as yet largely unrealized, market for British architects is the USA. Whereas in the UK the client normally engages the architect by an appointment separate from those of other consultants, in the USA it is far more common for the architect to be appointed by the client and then for the architect to sub-contract to other consultants the performance of the engineering and mechanical services. Thus the architect will assume vicarious liability for the actions of the consultants employed by him, something which the British architect is best advised to avoid.

In contrast to the UK position, there is much wider use of standard forms produced by the American Institute of Architects (AIA). The AIA produce a whole series of agreements from the 'Owner and Architect Agreement' to the main form of building contract, together with sub-contracts. These are widely accepted within the USA, although there may be slight amendments from state to state.

In the USA architects must be licensed and individual states and territories regulate entry into, and practice of, the professions within their jurisdiction. State statutes and regulations are based on the principle that practice by one who is not of proven technical and professional competence endangers the 'public's health, safety and welfare'. Licensing laws and regulations often restrict the use of the title 'architect', as well as outlining qualifications and procedures for registration as an architect, addressing any issues of reciprocity of registration with other states and defining the unlawful practice of architecture.

In a similar way, and unlike the UK, each state has its own Building Codes and these are the primary regulatory instruments for the design of buildings and structures on the site. Since local jurisdictions are authorized to adopt and enforce building regulations,

Building Codes vary among states and even among cities within the same state. There are an estimated 13 000 Building Codes in the United States. The codes cover, *inter alia*, specific design and construction requirements, permissible construction types, and egress requirements. Once a Building code has been adopted by a jurisdiction it becomes a document that holds the force of law. Violation of building codes and regulations is viewed seriously and may lead to the architect being held legally liable or his licence being revoked. Some jurisdictions allow for construction to be stopped for non-compliance and continued non-compliance may lead to a fine or a prison sentence. It is, therefore, important for an architect to establish which building codes are in force in the jurisdiction where he is working.

Another important contrast with the UK is that there are no quantity surveyors in the USA. The architect is therefore responsible for the preparation of the contract documents for approval by the client. However, as mentioned above, the standard forms produced by the AIA usually do not require modification since they are widely accepted.

It is the contractor's responsibility to quantify and estimate once the architect has produced plans and specifications. Once again, the AIA produces a guide to tendering or 'bidding' which the client and architect can use to determine to whom the contract is let. The architect's role in producing designs and plans is not greatly different from that in the UK although in the USA 'shop drawings' are produced and a contractor is given somewhat greater scope to decide how to implement those plans.

On the question of liability in general architects tend to be sued slightly more in the USA than in the UK. This may be partly because the nature of US society is more litigious and partly because up to approximately 20% of all claims against the architect are personal injury claims. This latter characteristic is because building workers tend to sue the architect as a way of increasing the amount of compensation received for physical injury (the state-run basis being a no-fault compensation scheme, known as 'Workers' Compensation Insurance'). By accepting the state-run compensation, the worker cannot pursue his employer and may look to the architect to top up his damages.

The law relating to breach of contract and negligence varies from jurisdiction to jurisdiction and the periods of time in which claims can be made against an architect are not always clear. The length of time within which an action for negligence can be brought may be as short as 4 years. For actions for breach of contract the period may be only 1 year. In some jurisdictions, time limits are not specified and the time periods themselves may start to run at different times. It is a rapidly changing area of law and, therefore, it is important that the architect seeks legal advice as to the limitation rules that apply in the particular jurisdiction in which he is working.

In relation to insurance, there are general differences between the UK and the USA. Usually, in the latter, there is only one annual aggregate of liability cover whereas in the UK it is usual for each and every claim to be covered (although this may contain a limit in aggregate and other conditions). Also, in the USA there are specific areas of exclusion from cover such as a claim relating to asbestos or pollution. UK insurers will not automatically extend cover for a UK architect to work in the USA and it may be necessary to obtain additional insurance in the USA itself.

United Arab Emirates

1.16 Despite the fact that Abu Dhabi, the capital city of the UAE, is known as the Manhattan of the Gulf and Dubai is the fastest growing commercial centre in the region, there is almost no regulation of architects or their work. Foreign architectural firms seeking a licence to work in the country are required to have a local sponsor and to submit fully attested professional qualification certificates, for all professional disciplines to the local government office responsible for issuing the licence. This is repeated each year when the trade licence is renewed. In Dubai they are required to also belong to the local Society of Engineers. Clients generally rely on the terms of their contract with the architect and professional indemnity cover is almost always required: some government institutions have been known to require that the insurance be provided through local insurance companies. The limitation period for contractual claims against the architect, if specified in the contract, is commonly 10 years but the limitation period for tortious claims is 3 years from the date the claimant becomes aware of the harmful act. In any event, no tortious claim can be brought after 15 years from the date on which the harmful act occurred. It is also worth nothing that under UAE law contractual and tortious claims cannot be brought at the same time.

Japan

1.17 Construction firms deal with about 40% of all building design in Japan via design and build style packages. Independent architectural firms of varying sizes carry out the remaining 60% of building design. In the average Japanese firm, architectural staff spend two-thirds of their time carrying out building design work and the remaining third of their time carrying out construction supervision. Sometimes these roles overlap, notably when design development continues after construction has commenced.

Contracts in Japan are interpreted in accordance with the doctrine of good faith and fair dealing. The literal meaning of a contract will not be applied if it is not in the interests of fairness to do so. Contracts are, therefore, inexact and adaptable. This is a concept that will seem alien to British architects who rely on contracts to set out their obligations in detail.

Liability for work carried out is usually shared by the design and construction teams on a project. Liability may also be shared with third parties such as insurers. An architect is only likely to be asked to assume individual responsibility for any performance failure where there is no confidence in his proposed approach to a design. After a project has been completed, the architect will usually make at least one follow-up visit to the site a year later to check that there have not been any problems post completion.

In Japan the cost of negligence/liability is more predictable because the courts tend to award smaller amounts. As a result, there is less incentive to litigate and litigation is, as a result, less frequent. It is currently rare for Japanese architects to have liability insurance which suggests that potential awards for liability are considered to be so small that the risk does not justify the expense of buying insurance premiums. However, the number of architects who carry insurance is now increasing because the number of actions against architects is also increasing. It is still the case that litigation is discouraged by the Japanese legal system as it is expensive and time consuming but as it becomes more common, more architects will invest in insurance premiums.

1.18 The larger firms of architects in the UK have already been active in seeking appointments abroad and their type of involvement will depend very much upon the role their client gives them. They may be appointed directly by the client as the main architect for the project; they may combine with a local firm of architects and form a kind of joint venture; they may establish a local office in that particular country governed by local laws; or they may simply have an advisory role either to the client or as the job architect in an otherwise uninvolved position. The Architects' Directive which was implemented in the UK in 1987 enabled British architects to practise in any other member country of the EU without restriction. In theory this sounds very simple but in practice there are still some restrictions as, for example, in Germany where foreign architects who wish to practise there must satisfy the qualification requirements to show adequate knowledge of German regulations and the language. The European Commission has struggled to force member states to implement the legislation properly. It has brought infringement proceedings against Greece and Spain and also forced Belgium and Italy to amend their legislation to give the Directive proper effect. As the harmonization process continues, the obstacles to British architects working within the European Union shall, likewise, diminish.

1.19 Although these opening paragraphs have concentrated mainly upon Europe, the Far East and the USA, the object of this chapter is to give architects a brief glimpse of some of the legal pitfalls in working abroad together with the areas where architects will need to seek specialist legal advice in relation to their employment worldwide.

The next section deals with the problem of conflicts between different jurisdictions and some examples of the different approaches used to deal with these problems.

2 Conflicts of laws

2.01 The legal problems which the architect encounters when working overseas always involve jurisdiction and proper law: do the courts of the country in which the building is constructed have jurisdiction over him and which law will be applied to resolve a dispute arising from the design and construction of the building? In particular, it is important for the architect to know whether the terms of his appointment will be recognized in another country; whether he will be able to enforce his rights against a foreign party in a foreign jurisdiction; what law will govern the performance of the architect's services; and whether the architect's insurance will cover him for work done overseas.

Jurisdiction and proper law

2.02 It is of the utmost importance that the architect gives early consideration, before the employer has retained other consultants, the Contractor or sub-contractors, to the question of jurisdiction and proper law. Even if the employer has in mind certain contractors/consultants, the architect should attempt to influence the employer in relation to the type of appointment, building contract or subcontract to be used so that its terms are familiar to the architect and so that the jurisdiction and proper law clauses throughout the contract documents are consistent.

Clearly, the choice of jurisdiction to establish where and in which type of forum disputes will be heard is an important consideration and, in such a clause, consideration should be given to such matters as which law is to be applied, convenience, reliability of the different courts, speed, costs, the location of assets, and whether the resulting judgment will travel. In some cases, the parties may prefer to contract out of the court system and have their disputes resolved privately, by arbitration. There may, however, be local law restrictions on contracting out of the jurisdiction of the courts. Where the parties are happy to litigate, it is possible to provide for exclusive jurisdiction clauses or alternatively, non-exclusive clauses which will allow the parties a choice of forum. In circumstances where there are restrictions on the parties' rights to choose jurisdiction, jurisdiction may be reserved to the local courts. For example, local statutes may prohibit choice of jurisdiction clauses in certain types of contract, or a party may have a constitutional right to be sued in the courts of his State. Furthermore, there may be treaty obligations which regulate the choice, or there may be relevant matters of local public policy. This underlines the importance of taking legal advice beforehand so that the position can be confirmed.

There should also be a 'proper' or 'governing' law clause which specifies the substantive law of the contract which will govern the parties' legal rights and obligations under the contract may be included in the jurisdiction clause but, more usually, is dealt with in a separate clause. Without such provision the Courts reach their own view on what the substantive law should be which creates uncertainty in any dispute resolution process. When there is no express choice, the English Courts (following the 1980 Rome Convention on the Law Applicable to Contractual Obligations) usually apply a choice of the law of the legal system with the closest connection to the case. Courts, for example, if asked to adjudicate on a dispute between two French parties with the subject matter in France, would apply French law on the basis that this implements the reasonable and legitimate expectations of the parties to a transaction. Although this is the principle adopted by the English courts it is far better to provide expressly in the contract for the proper law. This is because first, local courts in another jurisdiction may adopt other principles and, secondly, it does not leave the parties' intentions open and uncertain to be decided by the court. Most countries with established legal systems will apply the law chosen expressly by the parties to the contract.

Brussels Convention

2.03 The above analysis helps to answer the question, whether the terms of the architect's appointment can be made subject to a familiar jurisdiction and law despite the fact that he is working in a foreign jurisdiction and being subject to foreign laws, provided that care is taken in the drafting of the jurisdiction clause. There is, however, an important qualification to these comments, brought about by the implementation of the Brussels Convention of 1968 (as amended by various Accession Conventions) which became law in the UK from 1 January 1987. Currently, the Brussels Convention covers jurisdiction and enforcement issues in all 15 European Union states (France, Germany, Italy, Belgium, the Netherlands, Luxembourg, Denmark, Ireland, the UK, Greece, Spain, Portugal, Sweden, Austria and Finland).

The principles also extend to other countries, such as Norway under the Lugano Convention. Under the Brussels and Lugano Conventions the general rule is that persons domiciled in a particular member country must be sued in that country. Domicile is a complex concept but can be loosely equated to residence combined with a 'substantial connection' with a chosen country. For corporations domicile is associated with 'seat'. Article 17 of the Convention, however, provides that where parties agree to settle disputes under the jurisdiction of the court in a particular member country, 'that court, or those courts, shall have exclusive jurisdiction'. This overrides any local law prohibiting jurisdiction clauses but it is important that the formalities are complied with in order to give effect to Article 17. These are that the agreement confirming jurisdiction shall be in writing or evidenced in writing or in a form which accords with practices which the parties have established between themselves unless it relates to a matter involving international trade or commerce, where other rules apply. In addition, there is a strict requirement of evidence of consent by all the relevant parties.

The question of the architect suing for his fees in the context of the rules of the Brussels Convention where there is no Article 17 jurisdiction clause in the contract has been considered by the European Court of Justice in *Hassan Shenavai v Klaus Kreischer*. Here a German architect was suing a German national residing in the Netherlands for his fees. According to the Brussels Convention the general criterion for determining jurisdiction is the domicile of the defendant. However, the Court applied one of the exceptions to the Domicile rule namely that in matters relating to a contract, the defendant may also be sued in 'the courts for the place of performance of the obligation in question'. The principal obligation in question, when the proceedings were for the recovery of architects' fees, was held to be the specific contractual obligation for the defendant to pay the fee, in the Netherlands, rather than the contractual relationship as a whole. In this case the place of performance was not the place of the architect's practice nor the site of the planned building but the place where the fee was to be treated as being paid. This was held to be the residence of the client in the Netherlands. Whether that position would apply if the proper law of the contract were English is doubtful. The architect could have safeguarded himself in that case by including in the contract a jurisdiction clause providing for the courts of his choice to have jurisdiction. Although this is a relatively old case it is still good law.

The facts of the recent Scottish case *Bitwise Ltd v CPS Broadcast Products BV* (2002) were distinguished from the *Hassan Shenavai* case. The Scottish Court followed the reasoning in the earlier case by reiterating that, in order to rely on a particular performance obligation under a contract as being indicative of the jurisdiction that applied to the contract, that obligation should also form part of the basis of the claim.

2.04 Where there appears to be a conflict between, for example, the obligations of the architect as described in the appointment governed by English law, and the obligations of the architect as described in the building contract (governed by another law), the appropriate law to be applied would be determined by the particular court having jurisdiction under its domestic conflict of law principles. Thus, for example, if the dispute were to be settled in an English court, that court would be obliged to enquire with which legal system the overall transaction had its closest and most real connection.

This would determine the 'proper law' of the contract and the judges would consider a variety of circumstances, such as the nature of the contract, the customs of business, the place where the contract was made or was to be performed, the language and form of the contract, in order to determine which legal system should apply.

2.05 The second question which concerns an architect, once he has gone through the trauma and expense of pursuing, defending or counterclaiming in a dispute against a party from another jurisdiction, is whether he would be able to enforce his successful judgment against that party. All European Union countries are parties to the Brussels Convention, but outside the European Union the ease and likelihood of recognition of foreign judgments depends on whether there is an applicable treaty between the particular countries concerned, which provides for reciprocal enforcement of judgments. If such a treaty exists then, subject to various formalities, the court of one country will enforce the other country's judgment against the defendant's assets in that jurisdiction provided, normally, that the judgment is for money only. Where no mutual recognition treaty exists between the country of judgment and the desired country of execution, the process has to be started afresh in that country although in many jurisdictions the existence of a foreign judgment in relation to the same issues will operate as proof of a debt which permits a more expedited process. This matter should be dealt with by professional advisers when entering into the appointment.

For enforcement within the European Union and EFTA countries, the Brussels and Lugano Conventions are not limited to money judgments nor to final judgments. The court in which enforcement is sought has very limited powers to investigate the jurisdiction of the court which gave the judgment. In other words, it is much easier to enforce a judgment in a country within the European Union than outside it. Enforcement may only be refused on the grounds of public policy, lack of notice of proceedings, the irreconcilability of the judgment given in a dispute between the same parties in the State in which recognition is sought, irreconcilability with an earlier judgement given in a non-contracting State involving the same cause of action and between the same parties (subject to the judgement satisfying certain conditions) and certain cases involving preliminary questions as to status. The foreign European court may not question the findings of fact on which the original court based its judgment, nor can a judgment be reviewed as to its substance.

Insurance

2.06 The third question which the architect should always consider in relation to overseas work is the extent to which his insurance will cover him for breaches of duty in the particular country in which he is working. No general answer can be given to this, nor can any statement be guaranteed in the future, since insurers will take different views in relation to various countries and at different times. For example, the type of insurance available on any project carried out in France would be the decennial project insurance towards which all the construction team pay premiums. This would cover the architect for breaches of duty for up to 10 years although it may not relieve the architect altogether because there may be subrogation rights to the insurers. However, architects who wish to practise in the USA may (due, perhaps, to the increased prevalence of claims brought against the architect there) have to seek separate professional indemnity insurance with local insurers since many UK-based insurers will not extend their cover to claims arising in the USA. In any event, before undertaking any overseas work the architect should check with his professional indemnity insurers whether or not he will be covered or can obtain cover from them in respect of that work.

Contractual duties

2.07 The standard of performance which local law may impose on architects clearly depends exclusively on the law at any particular time in the country concerned, and this can only be determined through personal experience of the architect of work in the jurisdiction and by legal advice. As between the parties who are bound contractually, the architect's duties will normally be defined in the contract documents. If the local law provides that duties are owed by the architect to third parties in tort, or indeed to parties with whom he is already in contract, the standard and scope of such duties can only be determined by reference to local lawyers. The architect will normally have to ensure that there is compliance with the local building regulations, etc., although it will first be necessary to check the architect's role under the building contract to determine if it is simply to check or to ensure compliance.

Copyright

2.08 One important aspect of international work that should be considered by architects is the protection of their copyright in relation to the designs, plans and drawings which they have prepared for the overseas work. Although it may be possible to include provision in the appointment for protection of copyright vis-à-vis the client, the drawings may be used by a number of parties who may be tempted to infringe the copyright of the architect and use the designs elsewhere, without permission. The position in the majority of developed countries roughly approximates to the provisions of the Berne Convention drawn up in 1886 with the most recent revisions in Paris in 1979. The UK has acceded to these provisions in the Copyright Act 1988 as amended by the Copyright etc. & Trademarks (Offences & Enforcement) Act 2002. The Berne Convention gives protection for a minimum of the life of the author, and a post-mortem period of 50 years (although amongst EU states this period has now been increased to 70 years) and requires countries bound by it to abandon any rules of deposit or registration as a condition of copyright protection. The Berne Convention also provides for the protection of the author's moral rights, which protects the author's right to have the work attributed to his name and the right to object to derogatory treatment of the work (once the moral right has been asserted). Any country can sign up to the Berne Convention and clearly, if the architect is dealing in a country which is a signatory to the Berne Convention he is fully protected. In other countries there may be a lesser form of protection, as under the Universal Copyright Convention (UCC), which gives protection for the life of the author plus 25 years and provides for any condition of registration or deposit to be satisfied when copies bear the symbol © accompanied by the name of the copyright owner and the year of first publication of the document. The USA has ratified the Berne Convention as have a large number of non-EU countries, recent examples being Antigua and Barbuda (2000), Armenia (2000), Democratic People's Republic of Korea (2003), and Federated States of Micronesia (2003). A full list of those countries that have ratified the Convention is located at www.wipo.org/treaties/ip/berne/index.html. Where a country is a signatory of both the Berne Convention and the UCC, the Berne Convention takes precedence. Some countries belong only to the lesser of the two Conventions, i.e. the UCC. In many developing countries, such as Vietnam, no international treaty obligations subsist whatsoever and the architect will have to rely on local copyright law, if any. Local legal advice should be sought as to the means of protecting copyright and to comply with those local laws.

Commercial considerations

2.09 Finally, the architect should consider practical commercial matters, such as failure of the employer to pay fees, the country's available resource of hard currency, and exchange rate fluctuations, taking advice from persons experienced in international work who may be able to recommend suitable insurance to cover these risks, together with ECGD cover and political credit risk insurance and possibly a performance bond. In addition, if the advice of local lawyers is to be obtained, this might best be channelled through British lawyers since many foreign lawyers, such as those in Germany, are not obliged to advise on the most cost-efficient procedure in any situation.

3 FIDIC (Federation Internationale des Ingenieurs Conseils)

3.01 In 1999 the traditional FIDIC Conditions of Contract (that were embodied in the Conditions of Contract for Works of Civil Engineering Construction and known as the 'Red Book') were superseded by the FIDIC 'Conditions of Contract for Construction'. This new document is for Building and Engineering Works which have been designed by the Employer and it replaces the traditional 'Red Book'. The other traditional FIDIC Conditions of Contract were also replaced by the new Conditions in 1999. Although, quite clearly, the new FIDIC Conditions of Contract apply to duties of the engineer, the role of architect and engineer, particularly in many European countries, becomes indistinguishable, unlike the system in the UK where roles are more clearly defined. The Old Red Book will remain in use for some years to come. There are similarities between the Old Red Book and the new Conditions of Contract with some clauses being identical, however, there are also some significant changes and so, it will be necessary for architects to familiarize themselves with the new Conditions. (Note that a comparison of the Old Red Book and the 1999 Conditions is beyond the scope of this chapter). The 1999 Conditions contain three sections, namely, the General Conditions, Guidance (as to the preparation of Particular Clauses) and Forms. There are 20 clauses in the General Conditions and it is intended, but not obligatory, that these clauses are used unchanged in every project. The Particular Conditions are prepared with a specific project in mind and are additional to the General Conditions. It may be helpful to look at some of the problems which British engineers have faced when working with the FIDIC contracts and compare them with corresponding problems which may arise for the British architect if he is appointed under a normal form of RIBA appointment for a development governed by the FIDIC terms, appropriately amended. The Conditions are designed to be used extensively in building and in industrial and process engineering as well as civil engineering. It is not unreasonable to suppose, therefore, that a British architect may, if he is working abroad, be administering the project under the terms of FIDIC.

3.02 Some of the clauses which require the architect's attention are set out below. The numbering of the clauses in the new Conditions differs significantly from the numbering in the original Conditions and so, for ease of reference, the old clause numbers are included in brackets:

- **Clause 3.1 (formerly Clause 2(1)): Engineer's duties and authority** Where the architect is acting in the role of an engineer, he must pay careful attention to this clause as he may be required to obtain the Employer's approval before exercising a specified authority. The requirements of any such specified authority would be set out in the Particular Conditions. The items that require approval will generally accord with the legal code of certain countries in which the Conditions are used.
- **Clause 1.4 (formerly Clause 5(1)): Languages and law** Clearly this clause is of major significance since the contract provisions will be construed in accordance with the specified law. The language in which the contract is written is also significant, not only from the point of view of everyday administration but also from the point of view of interpretation. Very often an international contract is written in two languages, one the local tongue and one the language of the engineering consultants who drafted the contract in the first place. In these cases there is an express clause which states that in the event of conflict or ambiguity between the two versions, the language stated in the Appendix to Tender to be the 'Ruling Language' shall prevail.

  Once the law of the contract has been established, legal advice should be sought from lawyers experienced in international jurisdictional points and the local law. In addition, a translation of the contract is helpful (if not already in two versions).
- **Clause 1.5 (formerly Clause 5(2)): Ambiguities and discrepancies** This clause is important because it provides for the conditions of contract to prevail over any other document forming part

of the contract. There may be an interpretation problem existing between the 'General Conditions and the Particular Conditions (i.e. the particular sub-clauses included for the project) and, according to the order of priority given, the Particular Conditions would take precedence over the General Conditions. Particular care is required therefore, when the Particular Conditions are drafted, especially if it is intended that the General Conditions should be applicable unchanged.

- **Clause 4.1 (formerly Clause 8): Responsibility for construction and design** This clause is of importance because it sets out very clearly the division of responsibility between the contractor and the engineer or architect. The 1999 Conditions are drafted such that the engineer or architect has responsibility for the design or specification of the Permanent Works unless the Contract specifies that this is to be the Contractor's responsibility. The Contractor is not permitted to significantly alter the arrangements and methods for the execution of the works without having previously notified the Engineer.
- **Clause 4.10 (formerly Clause 11): Inspection of the site** This is not usually a function of the architect although, under the RIBA appointment, the architect can be employed to advise on the suitability of sites and to make surveys and various other investigations. Under Clause 4.10 of the new FIDIC Conditions there are certain items upon which the contractor is deemed to have obtained information by his own enquiries. Therefore it is important to determine whether such a clause has been amended in any way by the particular conditions to require the engineer or architect to provide more information than usual.

While the above focuses on the main areas, there are other clauses of importance in FIDIC but to consider such would be to go beyond the scope of this chapter. In 1999 FIDIC also published the Conditions of Contract for Plant and Design-Build, The Conditions of Contract for EPC/Turnkey Projects and The Short Form of Contract. The Plant and Design-Build and the EPC/Turnkey Projects Conditions provide for the Contractor to take responsibility for design of the project and will therefore, be of much less significance to architects. However, it is possible that the architect (as 'engineer') may be allocated the role of Employer's 'agent' and, as such, the architect does not need to act impartially but in representing the Employer's interests must act fairly and reasonably.

4 The future

4.01 As can be seen in other chapters in this book, the liability of architects is not clear-cut and is a point of constant discussion and negotiation, particularly in relation to the architect's appointment and the problems encountered by architects striving to stay within the terms of their insurance cover. In the UK this is due to the change of direction in the law relating to architects' duties. Clearly, when there is such uncertainty in our own country, that confusion can only be compounded when dealing with other jurisdictions, some based on the common law system (which is the basis of our own system) and some based on civil law systems as in many of the European countries.

4.02 The scope for work within Europe was given a substantial fillip by the enlargement of the European Community to the European Union of 15 rather than 12 States in 1995. The inclusion of Austria, Sweden and Finland represented a large increase of opportunity in Europe for UK architects. These countries are comparatively wealthy per capita and generally have large public works projects. Already UK architects have appreciated the significance of the German construction industry, which, in the eastern part of Germany grew significantly in the early 1990s. On 1 May 2004, 10 new Member States will join to the EU. The addition of Cyprus, the Czech Republic, Estonia, Hungary, Latvia, Lithuania, Malta, Poland, Slovakia and Slovenia will increase the scope for work available to UK architects on a dramatic scale. These opportunities are particularly available to the medium or larger sized UK firms because these firms should be able firstly, to analyse effectively the advertisements (including OJEU Notices) for work opportunities abroad and, secondly, to establish the necessary local link to enable compliance with local legislation. Those UK architects who most readily adapt to the changing legislation of Europe will eventually reap the rewards in terms of a much greater client base and work experience.

4.03 Elsewhere, architectural practices are increasingly looking towards the high growth economies of Asia, Thailand, Malaysia, Hong Kong and the Middle East. The main problems experienced in these locations are cultural and financial rather than legal. Increasing experience will, in time, overcome such difficulties and established firms will see the progression into China as the next step. In the USA, UK architects continue to be in demand for their particular style and, although by far the biggest problem is obtaining professional indemnity insurance, careful risk allocation in the appointment documentation increasingly enables UK insurers to extend cover for work in these territories.

37

Architects' Registration

SARAH LUPTON

1 The nature of professionalism in architecture

1.01 The concept of a professional person and an institutional profession has been continually evolving since the eighteenth century. Numerous studies of the subject have been made; the most concise appeared in 1970 as the report of the Monopolies Commission (Part 1: *The Report* A report on the general effect on the public interest of certain restrictive practices so far as they prevail in relation to the supply of professional services (Cmnd 4463). Part 2: *The Appendices* (Cmnd 4463–1)). Appendix 5 of the report provides a range of definitions and descriptions which vary considerably but there is a general acceptance that a professional person is one who offers competence and integrity of service based upon a skilled intellectual technique and an agreed code of conduct.

1.02 The early history and development of the architectural profession in Britain is analysed in Barrington Kaye, *The Development of the Architectural Profession in Britain*. In a parallel study, Architect and Patron, Frank Jenkins, analysed the development of professional relations between architects and their clients prior to the beginning of the 1960s.

1.03 The place of professionalism and the role of the professional person in a rapidly changing society has been increasingly questioned over recent years not only by society in general but also by the members of the professions. The concerns of society are reflected in the government's questioning of the role of the Architects Registration Council of the United Kingdom in the late 1980s and subsequent legislation; the concerns of the architectural profession in this period of change are reflected in the radical changes in its codes in 1981 and the on-going review of the Code by the RIBA.

2 Architects' Registration

2.01 In 1899 the first Architects' Registration bill attempted to restrict the practice of architecture to those who were formally qualified; it was rejected as were several others that followed. In 1931 the Architects (Registration) Act did not achieve the full intentions of its sponsors. It provided for the setting up of a register of architects but in merely protecting the use of title 'architect' it did not prevent others from carrying on the practice of architecture in the way that the sponsors hoped. This remains the position in the United Kingdom; it is an offence for anyone other than those on the register to use the title *architect* but anyone may design buildings, carry out project administration, and undertake all the tasks normally done by architects. The Architects (Registration) Act 1931 and the amending Acts of 1938 and 1969 provided for the setting up, maintenance, and annual publication of a Register of Architects; the maintenance of proper standards of professional conduct; and

the provision of limited financial assistance for some students. The registration body was funded by the annual registration fee of those on the register.

2.02 In the 1980s many of the professions found themselves under criticism; there was an increasing concern for consumer rights; and the role of the professional bodies as the protectors of the public interest was questioned. In the case of the architectural profession the whole basis of its statutory position under the Architects (Registration) Acts 1931 onwards was questioned; other professions in the construction industry asked why architects alone enjoyed protection of title and architects themselves questioned the value of protection of title when the function and activity was open to anyone wishing to offer their services. The Royal Institute of British Architects and other bodies also questioned the role and need for a statutory registration body. The RIBA Council, originally in favour of the dissolution of the Registration Council and the transfer of its powers to the RIBA, reversed its policy and campaigned for its retention. The government undertook an extensive consultative exercise.

2.03 In parallel with these discussions Sir Michael Latham was conducting a government-sponsored review of procurement and contractual arrangements in the construction industry and in July 1994 his final report, *Constructing the Team*, appeared. Its executive summary covered a wide range of radical recommendations some of which were to receive official support although not as many as Latham had hoped. As there was little opportunity in the crowded Parliamentary programme to introduce a Construction Bill the government took advantage of a largely non-contentious bill on housing grants to adopt its preferred recommendations from the Latham Report, as Part II of the Housing Grants, Construction and Regeneration Act 1996. Also, having made its decision on registration following the receipt of the Warne report on the future of registration it added a Part III to the same Act. Subsequently Part III of the Housing Grants, Construction and Regeneration Act 1996 was repealed in the Architects Act 1997.

2.04 The Architects Act 1997 also repealed the Architects (Registration) Act 1931, the Architects Registration Act 1938, the Architects' Qualifications (EEC Recognition) Order 1987, and the Architects' Qualifications (EC Recognition) Order 1988. The provisions of the Act are significantly different in principle and detail from those of the 1931 and 1938 legislation. In place of the large former Architects Registration Council which consisted almost exclusively of architects there is now a small Architects Registration Board (ARB) consisting of seven members elected by persons on the register and eight persons appointed by the Privy Council in consultation with the Secretary of State. As the Act specifically makes registered persons ineligible from being appointed persons there must always be a lay majority on the Board. The government's concern for the protection of the public interest is obvious as it is laudable but in some respects it emphasizes the anomalous situation in which the architect remains the only member of the construction professions to be subject to specific statutory registration.

2.05 In addition to the Board the Act makes provision for a Statutory Professional Conduct Committee which is responsible for disciplinary matters. The make-up of the Professional Conduct Committee is interesting, it comprises;

- Four elected members of the Board, including at least one whose address in the Register is in Scotland, or (if there is no elected member who is willing to act) three elected members and one registered person whose address in the Register is in Scotland.
- Three-lay members of the Board.
- Two persons nominated by the President of the Law Society.

3 Eligibility for registration

3.01 Persons are eligible for registration if they hold such qualifications and have gained such experience as the ARB may prescribe or if they have an equivalent standard of competence. For UK registration this normally means that they must pass recognized Parts 1, 2 and 3 qualifications. (A list of all the Part 1, Part 2 and Part 3 qualifications is available on the ARB website [www.arb.org.uk] or from the ARB.) In addition, applicants for registration are required to complete a minimum period of 2 years' structured and recorded architectural experience in a range of activities.

The Board's General Rule 13 states that the 2 years' practical training experience should be working under the direct supervision of an architect registered in the EU, and 12 months must be undertaken in the UK, under the direct supervision of a UK-registered person. 12 months must be undertaken after completion of a five-year course of study and award of a Part 2 qualification. These requirements can be varied by the Board, acting within guidelines published by the Board from time to time.

3.02 Under the Architects Act 1997, the ARB has the statutory responsibility for prescribing those qualifications which lead to entry onto the UK Register of Architects.

New Prescription Procedures came into place in September 2003, alongside ARB's new assessment criteria which form the basis upon which ARB makes decisions regarding prescription. Schools of architecture, and other institutions that award architectural qualifications, must now apply for and obtain the decision of the ARB as to whether those qualifications will be recognized as a prescribed qualification. The Prescription Procedures replace previous 'Procedures for Validation' published by the ARB.

In addition to the ARB prescription of qualifications, the RIBA operates a validation procedure. This is a peer review process that 'monitors schools of architecture's compliance with internationally recognized minimum standards in architectural education and encourages excellence and diversity in student achievement'. Visiting Boards, composed of experienced practising architects and academics, visit schools of architecture to assess standard of courses for exemption from the RIBA's Examinations in Architecture. Although these visits had been in the past run jointly with the ARB, under the new Prescription Procedures the ARB need no longer participate in visits to Schools of Architecture. Nevertheless the

two institutions continue to work closely in the development and monitoring of criteria for assessment and validation of courses.

3.03 Under the Architects Directive (85/384/EEC) and the Act a national of a European Economic Area (EEA) state is entitled to registration if he holds a recognized or an established EEA qualification or a relevant EEA certificate. A person who is disqualified by an EEA state is not entitled to registration; if a person becomes disqualified by another EEA state after registration the name has to be removed from the register.

In the case of overseas applicants for registration other than EEA nationals the Board usually requires them to present themselves for interview when they have the opportunity to submit evidence of qualifications and experience in support of their case; they may be required to undertake further study and examination. Overseas persons wishing to undertake further academic and professional work in the UK would be prudent to check their position with regard to registration before embarking on a course.

3.04 An application fee and an annual retention fee is payable for registration.

3.05 It is an offence to become registered or attempt to become registered by making false or fraudulent representations or declarations, the penalty for which is a fine not exceeding level 3 on the standard scale. It is also an offence for an unregistered person to practise or carry on a business under a title containing the word 'architect', the penalty for which is a fine not exceeding level 4 on the standard scale.

3.06 A person's name may be removed from the register permanently or for a period of up to 2 years if the Professional Conduct Committee makes a disciplinary order; fails to notify the registrar of a change of business address; or fails to pay the annual retention fee.

3.07 Disciplinary Orders may be made by the Professional Conduct Committee in the event of a registered person being found guilty of unacceptable professional conduct, or serious professional incompetence, or a criminal offence relevant to the fitness of the person to practise as an architect. Unacceptable professional conduct and serious professional incompetence are assessed in relation to the Code of Professional Conduct and Practice and the context of the particular circumstances of the case.

38

Professional conduct of architects

SARAH LUPTON

1 Codes of professional conduct

1.01 An agreed and enforceable code of professional conduct is an essential part of any recognized profession; it is the profession's demonstration of its commitment to the service it offers and the standards that it upholds. Codes are devised in the interests of the clients of the profession and less directly in the interests of its members through the maintenance of the status of the profession in the eyes of society. The integrity of purpose of the codes and the impartiality of their enforcement is crucial to the public's perception of the profession. The requirements of codes change and evolve in response to changing circumstances and attitudes and emerging economic, political and social pressures. They have to reflect the attitudes of the membership of the profession and the consequences of legislation and litigation but, above all, the explicit and implicit expectations of an increasingly sophisticated clientele.

1.02 Architects in the United Kingdom are subject to the Code of Conduct of the Architects Registration Board (ARB). In addition those architects who choose to join other professional bodies such as the Royal Institute of British Architects (RIBA) or the Royal Incorporation of Architects in Scotland (RIAS) become subject to their codes. Until 1998 and the advent of the ARB the codes of the Architects Registration Council (ARC) and the codes of the institutions covered similar ground. While this remains the case – indeed, the RIAS Code is now in full alignment with that of the ARB – there remain significant differences between the ARB and RIBA Codes.

1.03 The codes have both positive and negative aspects; there are essential actions that are specifically required and there are also actions which are specifically prohibited. The codes must not be regarded as a mere technical formality; they have a direct effect on practice and the ways in which an architect works. A lack of knowledge of the detailed requirements of the codes is not acceptable as a defence in the case of an alleged misdemeanour or breach of the codes; in some circumstances it could even be held to compound the offence. Lay clients are not expected to be familiar with the requirements of the codes but their architects are required to inform their clients that architects are subject to the disciplinary sanction of the ARB. It is essential that architects have available copies of all the current relevant codes of conduct for immediate reference.

1.04 The ARB Code of Conduct is primarily concerned with the protection of the interests of the public and relations between architects and their clients. The codes of the institutions are not incompatible with the ARB Code and reflect many of the same concerns.

1.05 Failure to comply with the ARB Code could result in the removal of the person's name from the register, terminating the person's right to practise under the title 'architect' and possibly leading to the person's loss of livelihood. Failure to comply with the requirements of the code of a particular institution may lead to the suspension or loss of membership but provided that the person is not in breach of the ARB Code the right to practise under the title 'architect' remains and the business may continue. There are 'unattached' architects who are eligible for institutional membership but do not take up membership, and there are a few properly qualified individuals who do not apply for registration. The extent to which a person feels that it is necessary to take up and retain the right to the title or to continue institutional membership has to be a matter for the commercial and professional judgement of the individual. There are no statutory requirements for the employment of architects in the marketplace and clients may use whomsoever they wish to prepare designs, or inspect building works. Should clients pursue such action, neither ARB nor the professional institutions have any power to address matters of complaint.

1.06 Where allegations of improper conduct also concern matters covered by the ARB Code the institutions usually delay disciplinary proceedings until the ARB's findings are known in order to avoid unnecessary expense and inconvenience for the parties. Where an allegation of a breach of one of the codes relates to court proceedings it is usual for all disciplinary proceedings to be delayed until after the court's decision but it should be noted that disciplinary proceedings are not conditional on the court's decision.

2 ARB Code of Conduct

2.01 The ARB Code of Conduct can be viewed on the ARB web site at www.arb.org.uk and is published in hard copy under the title *Architects Code: Standards of Conduct and Practice*. It comprises a single-page Introduction, a six-page statement of twelve Standards and a two-page Guidance Note. All three parts of the Code are inter-related and have to be read together. In addition to the Code the Board also publishes General Rules, Investigations Rules and Professional Conduct Committee Rules.

A breach of the Code can result in the ARB Professional Conduct Committee issuing a disciplinary order reprimanding the architect; or fining the architect; or suspending the architect's registration for a period of up to two years; or permanently erasing the architect's name from the register.

The Introduction

2.02 The overriding obligation of the Code is that the architect is expected to act competently and with integrity in carrying out professional work. The Introduction comments that the fact that a course of conduct is not specifically referred to in the code does not mean that it cannot form the basis of disciplinary proceedings: architects are expected to have regard to the spirit of the Code as much as its express terms. Conversely, it comments that not every shortcoming on the part of an architect will necessarily give rise to disciplinary proceedings (minor transgressions of the Code are not likely to prompt action unless they form part of a pattern of unacceptable professional conduct or serious professional incompetence).

Disciplinary orders may be made if an architect is convicted of a criminal offence which is relevant to the person's fitness to practise as an architect. In addition, a disciplinary order may be made against an architect if, after considering the case, the Professional Conduct Committee is satisfied the architect is guilty of:

(a) unacceptable professional conduct defined as: conduct which falls short of the standard required of a registered person; and/or
(b) serious professional incompetence which is considered to be: service which falls short of the standards required of a registered person.

The Standards

2.03 The twelve Standards have to be read in conjunction with the Introduction and the Guidance Notes. Each of the Standards is helpfully amplified and illustrated by brief notes on some applications of the Standard to which they refer. Most of the Standards concern self-evident aspects of sound business and good practice but some are less obvious but equally important; practising architects must be aware of all twelve Standards and must understand their full implications.

The importance of the Standards must not be under-estimated; the consequences of an architect's failure to understand or apply the principles of the Standards can be serious. In the following commentary the numbers in parentheses refer to the sub-clauses of the Standards.

Standard 1: Architects should at all times act with integrity and avoid any actions which are inconsistent with their professional obligations

In its stringent requirements Standard 1 of the Code embodies many of the traditional principles of professional codes of conduct especially in context of relationships between architects and their clients and between an architect and other architects.

Architects are prohibited from making, supporting or collaborating in any form of statement which is contrary to their professional opinion or which they know to be misleading, or unfair to others, or otherwise discreditable to the profession (1.1).

Architects are required to disclose in writing to a prospective client or employer any financial or personal business interest which would or could raise a conflict of interest and doubts about their integrity if not so declared (1.2).

Architects who find that their personal or professional interests are in conflict with those of the client or others are required to withdraw from the situation or to remove the source of conflict or to obtain the agreement of the parties concerned to the continuation of the engagement (1.3). Developing complexity in funding arrangements, joint venture initiatives, partnering, and non-traditional procurement procedures increases the possibilities of conflicts of interest arising, especially where circumstances change during the project.

In relation to an architectural practice architects may not be a partner, a co-director, or take up employment with a person whose name has been removed from the register or has been disqualified from membership of a recognized professional body (1.4). Surprisingly the Code makes no reference to the employment of such a person by an architect.

Architects offering or taking part in the offering of a service which combines consulting services with contracting services must make it clear to all parties in writing that their services do not incorporate the independent functions of an architect (1.5).

Standard 2: Architects should only undertake professional work for which they are able to provide adequate professional, financial and technical competence and resources

Although no prudent architect would knowingly take on work without the necessary competence and resources being available difficulties can arise in at least three ways. First, the nature of the work may not be fully apparent at the start of the project; second, the needs of the project and the nature of the work may vary during the project; and third, the circumstances of the architect's practice may change drastically during the work. It is important that the situation is continually monitored and essential that the client is immediately advised of anything that might prevent the architect from fulfilling the obligations under the Standard.

The Standard specifically permits architects to enter competitions or undertake speculative work provided that in the event of their subsequent appointment to carry out the work they have the necessary competence and resources in place (2.1).

Where work has to be done by others working under the direction of the architect the architect is responsible for ensuring that they have the necessary competence and resources to carry out the work and are properly supervised (2.2). A sole practitioner should have arrangements in place for the conduct of their business in the event of their death, incapacity or other absence from work (2.3).

Standard 3: Architects should only promote their professional services in a truthful and responsible manner

The Standard allows architects to advertise their services provided that it is not done in a manner that is untruthful or misleading and, as appropriate, conforms to the British Code of Advertising Practice and the ITC and Radio Code of Advertising Standards and Practice. The business style of the practice or service must not be misleading. (3.1, 3.2 and 3.3) Care must be taken to ensure that it is not likely to be confused with that of another practice or service.

Difficulties can arise when partnerships are dissolved, businesses are restructured, and where former partners or staff setting up new practices wish to take credit for their previous work. Ideally these matters should be covered in termination agreements but where this has not happened care must be taken to ensure that any statements made are factually correct and capable of objective justification (3.1).

Architects are required to ensure that the work of their office and any branch office in so far as it relates to architecture is under the control and management of an architect and that the identity of that architect is apparent to clients and potential clients (3.4).

Standard 4: Architects should carry out their professional work faithfully and conscientiously and with due regard to any relevant technical and professional standards

The overriding concern of practising architects must be to ensure that work is carried out with due skill, care and diligence and so far as it is practicable within the time scale and cost limits agreed with the client.

Architects, when acting between parties or giving advice, are required to exercise impartial and independent professional judgment to the best of their ability and understanding (4.1).

The requirement that architects should perform their work with due skill, care and diligence reflects the standard applied by the courts in their consideration of allegations of professional negligence (4.2).

Standard 5: In carrying out or agreeing to carry out professional work architects should pay due regard to the interests of anyone who may reasonably be expected to use or enjoy the products of their own work

The possible implications of this Standard are extremely wide-ranging although the guidance note only refers to the need to conserve and enhance the quality of the environment and its natural resources (5.1).

Standard 6: Architects should maintain their professional service and competence in areas relevant to their professional work and discharge the requirements of any engagement with commensurate knowledge and attention

This Standard reflects the policy of most professions which now require their members to undertake continuing professional development work. Failure to maintain professional competence could count against an architect in the event of that competence having to be investigated (6.1).

Standard 7: Architects should preserve the security of monies entrusted to their care in the course of their practice or business

Wherever possible architects should avoid situations in which they are required to hold monies belonging to the client, but where it cannot be avoided the requirements of the Standard should be followed in every detail, and before doing so an architect invited to manage the client's monies would be wise to take impartial advice.

A careful record of all transactions must be kept with the monies being held (where possible) in an interest-bearing account separate from any account held by the practice or the architect concerned (7.1)

The designated 'client account' must be protected with the bank being instructed in writing that the account may not be combined with other accounts or set-off against other claims (7.2).

Withdrawals may only be made from a client account on the client's instructions or on behalf of the client (7.3).

Unless otherwise agreed any interest earned has to be paid to the client (7.4).

Standard 8: Architects should not undertake professional work without adequate and appropriate professional indemnity insurance cover

The Standard draws attention to the need for insurance cover in include work outside the architect's main professional practice (8.1). It is important that practitioners obtain confirmation from their insurers that any extensions in the services provided are covered by their insurance policies.

The insurance policy must cover work undertaken by employees (8.1).

The requirement that employed architects should so far as possible ensure that professional indemnity insurance cover or other appropriate cover is provided by their employer could pose problems in practice (8.2). There is no mention of the possible consequences of an employer's default on insurance cover.

In addition to (and without limiting) the general obligation to maintain adequate insurance cover, under Standard 8.3 (introduced in 2001) architects are now required to maintain minimum cover in accordance with the Board's guidelines on professional indemnity insurance issued from time to time. If required they must provide evidence to demonstrate compliance with this Standard.

Standard 9: Architects should ensure that their personal and professional finances are managed prudently

As a statement of good intentions the Standard is inarguable but its implications in practice are hard to predict, especially where statutory insolvency procedures have been invoked. The Standard is directed against architects who may be thought to have shown a wilful disregard of their responsibilities or a lack of integrity (9.1).

Matters such as an order of bankruptcy, the liquidation of a company where an architect is a director, an accommodation arrangement with creditors, or a failure to pay a judgment debt are issues which could lead to action under the Standard.

Standard 10: Architects should promote the Standards set out in this Code

The Standard's requirement that an architect must draw attention to the apparent misconduct of fellow practitioners provoked some critical comments when it first appeared, possibly from fear of its abuse in the increasingly competitive environment of practice. Subject to any restrictions imposed by law or the courts architects are required to inform the Registrar of any serious breach of the Code which may come to their notice (10.1).

Architects are not required to report matters widely reported in the press and are cautioned against making unreasonable or vexatious reports (10.2).

The Standard accepts that an architect appointed as an arbitrator, adjudicator, mediator, conciliator or expert witness and in receipt of privileged information may have duties which take precedence over any requirements to report breaches of the Code to the Registrar (10.3).

Apart from situations concerned with the settlement of a dispute or the circumstances described in 10.3 an architect may not enter into an agreement which would prevent any party from reporting an apparent breach of the Code to the Registrar (10.4).

An architect is required to report to the Registrar within 28 days if they are convicted of an indictable offence or sentenced to imprisonment; made the subject of an order of disqualification from acting as a company director; made the subject of a bankruptcy order; or if the company of which the architect is a director is wound up other than for the purposes of amalgamation or reconstruction (10.5).

Failure to report these things to the Registrar could count against an architect in the event of disciplinary proceedings (10.6).

An architect is required to cooperate with an Investigator appointed under the Architects Act 1997. Failure to cooperate could constitute grounds for disciplinary proceedings (10.7 and 10.8). Any threat by an architect to bring defamation proceedings in an attempt to frustrate the investigation of a complaint may be regarded as unacceptable professional conduct in itself and be treated accordingly (10.9).

Standard 11: Architects should organize and manage their professional work responsibly and with regard to the interests of their clients

Architects are prohibited from undertaking professional work unless the terms of the contract have been recorded in writing specifying the scope of the work, the fee or method of calculating it, the allocation and any limitation of responsibilities, the provisions for the termination of the appointment, and any special provisions for dispute resolution (11.1). Architects are also required to have informed their client of their position under the Code (11.1). Apart from being requirements of the Code these procedures represent good practice and are obviously in the best interest of both the client and the architect.

At the end of the contract the architect is required to return to the client on request all the papers, plans and other property to which the client is legally entitled (11.2). Normally this material includes all the drawings and other documents used in the works but not the material used by the architect in the development of the design. It may be pertinent to note that although the client is entitled to the drawings and other documents on the final payment of fees and charges the copyright in the design remains with the architect, unless otherwise specifically agreed.

Architects are required to ensure that appropriate and effective internal procedures, including monitoring and review procedures, are in place and that there are sufficient suitably qualified and supervised staff to enable the delivery of an effective and efficient client service (11.3).

Architects are required to carry out their professional work without undue delay and, so far as is reasonably practicable, in accordance with any time scale and costs limits agreed with the client (11.4).

Architects are required to keep their client informed of the progress of work undertaken on their behalf and of any issue which may significantly affect its quality or cost (11.5).

Architects are required to observe the confidentiality of their client's affairs and not to disclose confidential information without the prior consent of the client or other lawful authority (11.6).

In the event of the business interests of the architect conflicting with those of the client the architect must withdraw from the appointment or remove the cause of conflict. If the architect is unsure of whether there is a conflict the matter must be referred to the client and the architect must act on the client's decision. Particular care is needed to ensure that there are no conflicts between the business and commercial interests of the client and those of the architect's partners or co-directors.

The architect also has to be aware of possible conflicts of interest between two or more clients of the practice; where this happens the architect must make the facts of the situation clear to each of the clients and act on their decisions. Where for reasons of confidentiality it is not possible to disclose the facts the architect must withdraw from one or more of the appointments. The architect must not act or continue to act while in possession of relevant confidential information concerning another client or potential client.

Standard 12: Architects should deal with disputes or complaints concerning their professional work or that of their practice or business promptly and appropriately

The requirements of the Standard are rigorous and demanding; they lay down strict procedures and time limits for dealing with complaints. The provisions of the Standard represent good practice and reflect those already included in a number of Quality Assurance Schemes.

In the case of large practices with four or more partners or directors a senior member of staff has to be designated as the person to deal with complaints initially. If the designated person cannot resolve the matter to the satisfaction of the client the complaint has to be referred to the senior partner or managing director. If the client remains unsatisfied the client has to be advised of the rights of the Board to act in such matters (12.1).

In the case of the sole practitioner or a firm of three or fewer partners or directors the complaint has to be referred to the sole practitioner, senior partner or managing director who is required to act and if unsuccessful in satisfying the client is required to advise the client of the Board's role as before (12.2).

Wherever it is thought to be appropriate the Standard encourages the use of alternative dispute resolution procedures such as arbitration or conciliation (12.3).

At every stage complaints have to be handled courteously and sympathetically in accordance with the time scale which provides for an acknowledgement of the complaint to be sent within ten days and for the complaint to be dealt with within thirty days of the receipt of the complaint. Similar time scales apply with regard to ARB correspondence concerning the complaint (12.4).

3 The RIBA Code of Professional Conduct

3.01 The latest version of the RIBA Code of Professional Conduct and Standard of Professional Performance came into effect in April 1997 incorporating the radical changes introduced in the version published in January 1981 and the Rules and Notes concerning the application of the Principles published in September 1989. The changes of 1981 reversed much of the Institute's long-established stance on professionalism. They removed the restrictions on carrying on the business of trading in land or buildings, or as property developers, auctioneers, estate agents or contractors, subcontractors, manufacturers or suppliers in or to the construction industry; permitted members to negotiate fees with potential clients and abandoned the mandatory minimum fee system; removed the ban on practising in the form of a limited liability company and extended the permitted means by which an architect might bring himself to the notice of potential clients.

In introducing the Standard of Professional Performance as part of its Code of Professional Conduct the RIBA predated the use of standards in the Code of Conduct published by the Architects

Registration Board in August 1997. Both Codes took into account the requirements of the Architects Act 1997.

In July 2003 RIBA Council agreed to a complete redrafting of its Code of Professional Conduct, which is in progress at the time of writing. The Code review coincides with a notification from the Office of Fair Trading that it considers undertakings 3.1 and 3.3 of the RIBA Code of Professional Conduct to be contrary to the Competitions Act 1998. As a result of this the RIBA Council agreed that the two undertakings should be suspended from midnight on 13 August.

3.02 The RIBA Code of Professional Conduct and Standard of Professional Performance can be viewed on the RIBA web site at www.architecture.com and is also published in hard copy. It comprises a Preface, three Principles supported by explanatory notes, a two-page statement of the Standard of Professional Performance, and a two-page set of Member's Rules for Accounts.

Preface

3.03 The Preface serves a function similar to the Introduction of the ARB Code of Conduct and should be read together with the Principles and the Standard. The Preface refers to the objectives of the RIBA, 'the advancement of architecture and the promotion of the acquirement of the knowledge of the Arts and Sciences connected therewith' and the objective of the Code of Professional Conduct, 'the promotion of the standard of professional conduct, or self-discipline, required of Members of the Royal Institute in the interests of the public'.

The Preface states that Principles are of universal application dealing with competence and integrity and the interests of the public. Members are required to act in the spirit of the Code as well as its precise terms; they are warned that a particular course of action could be regarded as a contravention of the Code even though it may not be specifically mentioned. Members are bound by the Code regardless of their field of activity, contract of employment or membership of an association; members acting through a corporate body can be held responsible for the acts of the body.

The Preface comments that in meeting their obligations under the Code members are expected to have due regard to the need to conserve and enhance the quality of the environment, its natural resources and cultural heritage. This is a slightly broader obligation than that of Note 5.1 of the ARB Standard 5.

A member found to be in breach of the Code is liable to reprimand, suspension or expulsion.

Principles

3.04 Each of the three principles is supported by a series of specific undertakings which are likely to be extended from time to time. Note 7 of the Preface makes provision for notices of changes to be published in the monthly *RIBA Journal*. It may not be a totally satisfactory way in which to give members formal notice of significant changes in the Code but it is indicative of the need for members to ensure that they are continually aware of changes in the profession.

Inevitably the RIBA Code of Professional Conduct and Standard of Professional Performance has much in common with the ARB Code of Conduct although there are some differences, many of emphasis. Members of the RIBA who are practising architects are subject to both and need to be aware of the substance of each of the codes.

The Figures in parentheses below refer to the specific undertakings.

Principle One: A member shall faithfully carry out his duties applying his knowledge and experience with efficiency and loyalty towards his client or employer, and being mindful of the interests of those who may be expected to use or enjoy the product of his work

The undertaking that a member is required to exercise his independent professional judgement impartially to the best of his ability and understanding may appear to be self-evident but as practice and construction becomes more complicated the need to emphasize its importance becomes greater (1.1).

The undertaking that members have to declare whether or not professional indemnity insurance is held before entering into an agreement is now redundant in view of the mandatory ARB PII requirement (1.2).

The undertaking requires a written agreement specifying the terms of engagement and the scope of the service, responsibilities and any limitation of liability, the method of calculation of remuneration, and the provision for termination and adjudication (1.2).

The undertaking that before accepting or continuing with any work the member ensures that he has the necessary competence and resources to provide the service is similar but more limited than that of the ARB requirement (1.3).

The work of all offices of a member must be under the control of an architect, (1.4). The architect may not transfer responsibilities or reduce the scope of services without the prior consent of the client (1.5).

The undertaking not to evade responsibilities by abandoning a commission is not specifically mentioned in the ARB Code (1.6).

Principle Two: A member shall, at all times, avoid any action or situation which is inconsistent with his professional obligations or which is likely to raise doubts about his integrity

Principle 2 is directed towards the avoidance of inconsistencies or doubts of integrity in the work of members. The principle reflects some of the concerns of Standard 1 of the ARB Code. A member has to give written notice of any matters that might give rise to conflicts of interests and doubts about integrity (2.1) and in the event of there being sources of conflict of interests that cannot be removed to withdraw from the situation unless having declared it to all the parties concerned and they agree to the member's continuation of the engagement (2.2).

The undertaking not to make a statement written or otherwise which is contrary to his knowledge or professional opinion or which he knows to be misleading or otherwise discreditable to the profession was not covered in previous versions of the RIBA Code and is not specifically mentioned elsewhere but it is implicit in that such actions could result in civil or criminal court actions which in turn might lead to disciplinary moves (2.3).

The prohibition of simultaneous practice as an independent consultant and involvement as a principal of a business trading in land or buildings, property development, auctioneering, estate agency, contracting, manufacturing, or materials supply unless the firm is clearly distinct from the architectural practice (2.4) has its roots in the code amendments of 1981 but it has been softened considerably from the time when members were required to give written notice of any such involvement to the RIBA. In their interpretation of the code practising members have to be conscious of its spirit and in particular its aim of protecting the interests of clients by making the position of the architect clear in any of the many different situations in which the architect may appear. This is emphasized in the undertaking prohibiting members from carrying out or purporting to carry out the independent functions of an architect in relation to a contract when the architect's employer is the contractor As the profession's involvement in the construction industry becomes closer, as non-conventional procurement becomes more widespread, and as contracting organizations increasingly offer the professional skills of their in-house architectural consultancy services it is essential that the architect's role and accountability are fully understood.

The undertaking not to disclose confidential information or to use it for his own benefit or that of others without the written consent of the parties concerned (2.6) is slightly wider in scope than Standard 11.6 of the ARB Code.

The undertaking not to give or accept inducements to show favour to anyone and not to allow the member's name to be used in the advertising of any service or product associated with the construction industry (2.7) is long-standing but is still needed. Many people in the marketing industry are not aware of the restrictions of the Code.

I. KAY 1799

The undertaking preventing a member from being a partner or co-director with a person whose name has been removed from the Register of Architects or has been disqualified from membership of another professional body (2.8) mirrors that of the ARB Code. Significantly neither code prevents such a person from being an employee of an architect.

The undertaking requiring a member who has been declared personally or professionally insolvent to notify the RIBA (2.10) also mirrors the requirements of the ARB Code. Undertaking 2.11 requires members to conform with the Members' Rules for Clients Accounts (see below).

Principle Three: A member shall in every circumstance conduct himself in a manner which respects the legitimate rights and interests of others

The undertakings of Principle 3 include many of the matters covered in former versions of the Code. They are largely concerned with the procedures of appointment and relations between members.

The intent of the undertaking not to offer inducements for the introduction of clients (3.1) is obvious but on occasion particular care is needed to ensure that public relations consultants engaged in the promotion of the services of a practice understand the limitations that the Code may impose on their activities.

The undertakings concerning fee negotiations (3.2 and 3.3) attempt to provide a practical approach to establishing an equitable fee basis. Members are prohibited from quoting a fee until they have received an invitation to do so and have sufficient information to enable a quotation to be prepared indicating the service to be covered by the fee (3.2). Members are prohibited from revising a fee quotation to take into account a fee quoted by another architect for the same service (3.3) (Readers should note that at the time of writing Undertakings 3.1 and 3.3 are suspended.)

The undertaking not to attempt to supplant another architect (3.4) does not prevent an architect from undertaking work in situations where another architect has an engagement with the same client but the architect must notify the other architect (3.8). The undertaking is devised in the interests of both architects but it is often misunderstood. A member engaged to give an opinion on the work of another architect must notify the architect unless it can be shown that to do so would be prejudicial to prospective or actual litigation (3.9).

Members are prohibited from entering competitions which the RIBA has declared to be unacceptable (3.5); the grounds of unacceptability usually relate to competition conditions and payment arrangements. A member appointed as competition assessor is prohibited from acting subsequently in any other capacity for the work (3.6).

A member may not maliciously or unfairly criticize or attempt to discredit another member or his work (3.7).

A member is required to acknowledge the contribution made to his work by others (3.10) but there can be many practical difficulties in its implications.

Members are required to define the conditions of employment, authority, responsibility, and liability of the architects they employ and to ensure that any professional indemnity insurers waive their subrogation rights in respect of members who are full-time employees (3.11).

Members are required to report to the RIBA any alleged breach of code of which he may become aware and assist the Royal Institute in its investigation. Disturbingly, the related undertaking that members are required to respect and maintain confidentiality in relation to matters involving alleged or proven breaches of the Code or the RIBA Standard of Professional Performance could in certain circumstances involve a breach of the ARB Code (3.13).

Members are required to report to the Royal Institute if convicted of any indictable criminal offence including a suspended sentence or court order and personal or professional disqualification from acting as a Director (3.14).

Standard of Professional Performance

3.05 The Standard of Professional Performance is devised as a level of competence which the Royal Institute requires its members and their practices to uphold in the interests of clients and the reputation of the profession. Extreme or irresponsible failure to meet the Standard could result in disciplinary action but the introductory preface to the Standard specifically states that in the event of an isolated failure to meet the Standard disciplinary proceedings would arise only in exceptional circumstances. It further states that its primary objective is to offer advice to members who may find themselves in difficulty. Although directly or indirectly there is much common ground between them the differences in intention and status of the eleven Standards of the ARB Code and the single RIBA Standard of Professional Performance have to be noted.

The RIBA Standard of Professional Performance states;

Members are required to maintain in their work and that of their practices a standard of performance which is consistent with membership of the RIBA and with proper regard for the interests both of those who commission and those who may be expected to use and enjoy the product of their work.

Members and their practices will meet the requirements of their engagements with commensurate knowledge and attention so that the quality of the professional services provided does not fall below that which could reasonably be expected of members of the Institute in good standing in the normal conduct of their business.

The Standard is supported by eight undertakings concerning the carrying out of work honestly, competently, diligently, and expeditiously in accordance with the time scale and agreed cost limits; the fulfilment of CPD obligations and when employing other members the allowance of time for them to fulfil their CPD obligations; the operation of a formal internal client's complaints procedure; the arrangement of appropriately qualified persons to run offices and to administer contracts during periods of absence; the taking of appropriate advice when needed; the sole practitioner's establishment of contacts with other members; proper regard for the experience and capability of staff when delegating responsibility; the need to ensure that untrue claims to experience are not made and that commissions are not accepted without the necessary skills and experience being available.

Members' Rules for Clients' Accounts

3.06 The detailed rules concerning the administration of client accounts are unchanged from those introduced in 1986. In meeting the requirements of prudent practice the rules satisfy the conditions of the ARB Code. Before accepting an invitation to administer an account on behalf of a client an architect should ensure that the reasons for doing so and the scope of the account are confirmed in writing and that the procedure of the rules is followed in every detail.

4 Statement of Professional Conduct of the Royal Incorporation of Architects in Scotland (RIAS)*

4.01 The Architects Act 1997 applies throughout the United Kingdom and as elsewhere an architect practising in Scotland is subject to its Code. In addition the architect members of the Royal Incorporation of Architects and architect members of the Royal Institute of British Architects are subject to their respective codes. Many architects belong to both bodies and as such are subject to requirements of all three codes.

4.02 The existence of a separate RIAS Code stems from the Incorporation's Charter of 1922 and consequent bye laws, which call for a Declaration to be made by all who join. This statement of principle is the basis against which any alleged complaint is judged. The RIAS Council has authority to publish intimations illustrating good practice behaviour and which, in the breach, require investigation and possible disciplinary sanctions. These comprise, as with RIBA: reprimand, suspension and expulsion.

4.03 It is a prerequisite of membership of RIAS that applicants demonstrate their registration with ARB. For this reason the first intimation of every Statement of Professional Conduct, published since 1982, has been to bind active architect members explicitly to the code requirements of the registration body.

Prior to the 1997 Act, the 1931 Act which governed the activity of the Architects Registration Council of the United Kingdom (ARCUK), made it difficult and cumbersome for ARCUK to deal with complaints. For this reason the RIAS published additional intimations which enabled it to address complaints effectively and efficiently in Scotland, the numbers increasing during the later 1980s and into the 1990s as consumerism advanced.

4.04 However, the possibilities of one complaint being subject to three separate sets of investigations under three distinct codes (RIAS, RIBA and ARB) was considered to be extremely undesirable. As soon as a clear and robust code emerged from ARB with its second edition in September 1999, it became possible to start to address revisions to the RIAS Code, and in particular the intimations.

At the same time arrangements were put in place to refer all serious complaints directly to ARB in recognition of its statutory role and powers.

4.05 The 1993 RIAS Statement included 16 intimations, one of which incorporated a six-point set of Client Account Rules. The intimations dealt with a range of issues including carrying Professional Indemnity Insurance and undertaking Continuing Professional Development, having proper forms of agreement in place for appointments with an architect in control. The code had attempted to deal with competitive fee tendering by referral to set procedures, and included reference to advertising, and promotion.

Reviewing the ARB Code made clear that the majority of the intimations could be swept away, as they could now be dealt with by ARB, and slight differences between Codes would cause confusion.

4.06 The January 2000 RIAS Statement therefore only included two intimations, the second of which regulated behaviour between RIAS members and 'employees, employers, professional colleagues

... and business associates'. This required members to notify another member if they had been invited or instructed to proceed with work on a project that another member had been engaged with.

Secondly, it required members not to attempt to supplant another member.

And thirdly, it required – subject to a member's right and obligations under the ARB Code – that members having any matter of complaint or protest against another member, to notify the Secretary of the Incorporation, and make no other protest.

4.07 After a further year, it became clear that ARB was not specifically concerned under its code with the specifics of the obligations related to continuing professional development. The Incorporation therefore approved a further adjustment to its Statement in February 2001 clarifying members' obligations as individuals and as employers, and emphasizing the need to record their activity.

4.08 By the summer of 2003, however, it became clear that with new forms of procurement (including on-line fee bidding) and further interest by the Office of Fair Trading in any code aspects that could inhibit competition (i.e. the curb on attempting to supplant), the supplementary intimations were no longer appropriate.

From June 2003, therefore, the RIAS Code incorporates merely the ARB Code under Intimation 1.

4.09 RIAS Council, in agreeing this step, approved plans for continuing to issue wise counsel to members on matters of behaviour, via its other organs of communication, and dealing with matters of dispute or complaint (particularly between members) through conciliation, via a panel of members with appropriate experience.

4.10 The sanction of RIAS disciplinary procedures remain in place, however, to deal with behaviour about which ARB would have no interest, as it has no consumer-related aspects, but which could be seen to be damaging the Incorporation and thus in breach of the Declaration.

4.11 At the same time, RIAS staff continue to handle a wide range of complaints from third parties – most often clients – giving advice and assistance where possible to indicate ways in which difficulties can be overcome. For any serious complaints, complainants are referred to ARB.

4.12 The RIAS Charter and bye laws have been subject also to substantial revision during 2001–2003 as a result of the realignment of roles *vis-à-vis* the RIBA, post the devolution settlement of 1999. The greater clarity between the respective roles of ARB, RIBA and RIAS is welcome, and is reflected in the current simplicity of the RIAS Statement of Professional Conduct.

4.13 The Statement of Professional Conduct:
A member shall be bound by the Declaration signed upon election and in particular of the responsibility for upholding the repute of the Royal Incorporation as a professional body and of fellow members as individuals. Actions inconsistent with the Declaration shall be held to constitute unprofessional conduct and as such will be dealt with by Council in accordance with Bye Law 16.1.

The Declaration:

> I declare that I have read the Charter and Bye Laws of the said Incorporation and the Bye Laws of my chapter, and will be governed and bound thereby, and will submit myself to every part thereof and to any alterations thereof which may hereafter be made until I have ceased to be a member: and that by every lawful means in my power I will advance the interests and objects of the said Incorporation.

4.14 Byelaw 18 clearly sets out the current position – Byelaw 18 clarifying the role of RIAS *vis-à-vis* ARB:

18   Discipline
18.1 The Council shall put in place formal procedures for handling of complaints.
18.2 Any Member contravening the Declaration signed by the Member or conducting himself or herself in a manner which in the opinion of the Special Committee of the Disciplinary Panel is derogatory to his or her professional character or engaging in any occupation which in the opinion of the Special Committee of the Disciplinary Panel is inconsistent with the profession of an architect shall following investigation and disciplinary procedures as approved by the Council from time to time be liable to reprimand, suspension or expulsion.
18.3 Where a complaint against a member is considered and determined by the Architects Registration Board or any successor to it, the Council shall be entitled to accept, adopt and apply the findings of the Architects Registration Board both in relation to the merits of the complaint and any penalty imposed as being the appropriate disposal of a complaint involving a breach of Byelaw 18.2 without holding any further enquiry or proceedings provided always that the Council shall have before it a copy certified by the Clerk or other authorised official of the Architects Registration Board of their findings. The Council shall not however be obliged if it so resolves to adopt and apply the determination of the Architects Registration Board.

5 Statement on Professional Conduct of the Royal Society of Ulster Architects (RSUA)*

5.01 The Architects Act 1997 applies throughout the United Kingdom and as elsewhere any architect practising in Northern Ireland, including one from another state which is a member of the European Economic Area (EEA), is subject to its Code which is administered by the Architects Registration Board (ARB). The term 'EEA State', is defined in section 25 of the 1997 Act.

5.02 In Northern Ireland many practising architects who are members of the RSUA are also members of the Royal Institute of British Architects (RIBA). As such they are subject to both the ARB Code of Professional Conduct and Practice, and the RIBA Code of Conduct and Standard of Professional Practice (if a member of the RIBA).

5.03 The RSUA does not have its own Code of Conduct but makes references in its Memorandum and Articles of Association, dated 1999, to the ARB Code of Conduct as the basis for its consideration of relevant matters regarding its members (Article 8 – Discipline).

5.04 Article 8.4 includes a statement advising that the President and/or Council may choose to refer relevant matters to the ARB and/or in the case of an RIBA member to that body.

5.05 Article 8.6 states that if a member is suspended or struck off the Register by ARB, or if a person who is a member by virtue of RIBA membership is suspended or expelled by that body for any reason, then he shall be suspended or have his name removed from the Society's list of members as may be applicable.

5.06 Provided they are bona-fide architects, and not masquerading as such, persons in Northern Ireland who belong to none of the professional bodies remain subject, of course, to the ARB Code.

---

* This section was written by J.R. McDaniel.

Bibliography

General construction law

Duncan Wallace, I. (1994) *Hudson's Building and Engineering Contracts* (11th edn), (1st Supplement 2003) Sweet and Maxwell, London

Lavers, A. (ed.) (1999) *Case Studies in Post-Construction Liability and Insurance*, Spon Press, London

Lloyd, H. and Bartlett, A. (eds) (2002) *Emden's Construction Law* (looseleaf) (9th edn) Butterworths Law, London

Marsden, S. and Makepeace, P. (2003) *Construction and Engineering Law: A Guide for Project Managers*, Butterworths Tolley, London

Ramsey, V. and Furst, S. (ed.) (2001) *Keating on Building Contracts* (7th edn) (1st Supplement 2003) Sweet and Maxwell, London

Uff, J. (2002) *Construction Law*, (8th edn), Sweet and Maxwell, London

General liability: contract and tort

Beale, H. (2000) *Chitty on Contracts* (28th edn) (2nd Supplement 2001) Sweet and Maxwell, London

Buckley, R. (1999) *The Modern Law of Negligence* (2nd edn), Butterworths, London

Dugdale, A. (ed.) (2001) *Clerk and Lindsell on Torts* (18th edn) (Supplement 2003) Sweet and Maxwell, London

Dugdale, A. and Stanton, K. (1998) *Professional Negligence* (3rd edn), Butterworths, London

Furmston, M. (2001), *Cheshire Fifoot and Furmston's Law of Contract* (14th edn) Butterworths Law, London

Lewison, K. (2003) *Interpretation of Contracts*, (3rd edn), Sweet and Maxwell, London

Murphy, J. (2003) *Street on Torts* (11th edn) Butterworths, London

Powell, J. Stewart, R. and Jackson, R. (2002), *Jackson and Powell on Professional Negligence* (5th edn), Sweet and Maxwell, London

Rogers, W. (2002) *Winfield and Jolowicz on Tort* (16th edn) Sweet and Maxwell, London

Treitel, G. (2003) *The Law of Contract* (11th edn), Sweet and Maxwell, London

Walton, C. and Percy, R. (2002) *Charlesworth and Percy on Negligence* (10th edn), Sweet and Maxwell, London

Construction contract law

Chappell, D. (2002) *Parris's Standard Form of Building Contract JCT 98* Blackwell Science, Oxford

Chappell, D. (2003) *Understanding JCT Standard Building Contracts* (7th edn) Spon Press, London

Hickman, D. (2000) *PFI and Construction Contracts* Sweet & Maxwell, London

Huse, J. (2002) *Understanding and Negotiating Turnkey and EPC Contracts* (2nd edn) Sweet and Maxwell, London

Jones, D. and Savage, D. (2003) *Partnering and Alliancing* LLP Professional Publishing, London

Jones, N. (1999) *Jones and Bergman's JCT Intermediate Form of Contract* Blackwell Science, Oxford

Jones, N. (2004) *The JCT Major Project Form* Blackwell Science, Oxford

Murdoch, J. and Hughes, W. (2000) *Construction Contracts: Law and Management* (3rd edn) Spon Press, London

Roe, S. and Jenkins, J. (2003) *Partnering and Alliancing in Construction Projects* Sweet & Maxwell

Woolley, R. (2000) *Find Your Way Around JCT 98* Spon Press, London

Construction contract administration and claims

Birkby, G. and Brough, P. (2002) *Construction Companion to Extensions of Time* RIBA Publications, London

Carnell, N. (2000) *Causation and Delay in Construction Disputes* Blackwell Science, Oxford

Davison, R. (2003) *Evaluating Contract Claims* Blackwell Science, Oxford

Hackett, J. (2000) *Construction Claims: Current Practice and Case Management* LLP Professional Publishing, London

Pickavance, K. (2000) *Delay and Disruption in Construction Contracts* (2nd edn) LLP Professional Publishing, London

Powell-Smith, V. and Furmston, M. (1999) *Powell-Smith and Furmston's Building Contract Casebook* Blackwell Science, Oxford

Thomas, R. (2001) *Construction Contract Claims* Palgrave (formerly Macmillan Press), Basingstoke

Dispute Resolution

Anderson, R. (2001) *Tolley's Construction Adjudication Casebook*, Tolley Publishing, London

Foskett, D. (2001) *The Law and Practice of Compromise* (5th edn) Sweet & Maxwell, London

Gould, N. (1999) *Dispute Resolution in the Construction Industry* Thomas Telford, London

Harris, B. Planterose, R. and Tecks, J. (2003) *The Arbitration Act 1996: A Commentary* (3rd Edn) Blackwell Science, Oxford

Kendall, J. (2001) *Expert Determination* (3rd edn) Sweet & Maxwell, London

Mackie, K. Miles, D. and Marsh, W. (2000) *Commercial Dispute Resolution: An ADR Practice Guide* (2nd edn) Sweet and Maxwell, London

Marshall, E (2001) *Gill: The Law of Arbitration* (4th edn) Sweet & Maxwell, London

Merkin, R. (2000) *The Arbitration Act 1996: An Annotated Guide* LLP Professional Publishing, London

Milne, M. (2001) *Principles of Arbitration* (including audio cassette) College of Estate Management, Reading

Nesic, M. and Boulle, L. (2000) *Mediation: Principles, Process, Practice* Butterworths Law, London

Redmond, J. (2001) *Adjudication in Construction Contracts* Blackwell Science, Oxford

Riches, J. and Dancaster, C. (2001) *Construction Adjudication* (2nd edn) LLP Professional Publishing, London

Sutton, D. and Gill, J. (2002) *Russell on Arbitration* (22nd edn) Sweet & Maxwell, London.

Tackaberry, J. and Marriott, A. (eds) (2003) *Bernstein's Handbook of Arbitration and Dispute Resolution Practice* (4th edn) Sweet & Maxwell, London

Architect's professional practice and liability

Cornes, D. (1994) *Design Liability in the Construction Industry* (4th edn) Blackwell Science, Oxford

Cornes, D. & Winward, R. (2002) *Winward Fearon on Collateral Warranties* (2nd edn) Blackwell Science, Oxford

Dugdale, A. and Stanton, K. (1998) *Professional Negligence* (3rd edn) Butterworths, London

Lavers, A. and Chappell, D. (2000) *A Legal Guide to the Professional Liability of Architects* (3rd edn) RIBA Books, London

Powell, J. Stewart, R. and Jackson, R. (2002) *Jackson and Powell on Professional Negligence* (5th edn), Sweet & Maxwell, London

Partnership and Company Law

Banks, R. (ed) (2002) *Lindley and Banks on Partnership* (18th edn), Sweet & Maxwell, London

Blackett-Ord, M. (2002) *The Modern Law of Partnership and Limited Liability Partnership* (2nd edn) Butterworths Law, London

Davies, P. (2003) *Gower's Principles of Modern Company Law* (7th edn), Sweet & Maxwell, London

Mayson, S. French, D. and Ryan, C. (2003) *Mayson, French and Ryan on Company Law* (20th edn) Oxford University Press, Oxford

Morse, G. (2001) *Partnership Law* (5th edn) Blackstone Press, London

Sacker, T. (ed) (2001) *Practical Partnership Agreements* (2nd edn) Jordans, Bristol

Walmsley, K. (2003) *Butterworths Company Law Handbook* Butterworths Law, London

Employment Law

Bowers, J. (2002) *Bowers on Employment Law* (6th edn) Oxford University Press, Oxford

Hammonds (2003) *Contracts of Employment* (3rd edn) Chartered Institute of Personnel and Development, Huddersfield

Hunt, M. (2002) Employment Law Made Easy (4th edn) Law Pack Publishing, London

Leighton, P. and Proctor, G. *Recruiting Within the Law* (2nd edn) Chartered Institute of Personnel and Development, Huddersfield

Pitt, G. (2003) *Employment Law* (5th edn) Sweet & Maxwell, London

Ryley, M. and Goodwyn, E. (2000) *Employment Law for the Construction Industry* Sweet & Maxwell, London

Copyright and Intellectual Property

Britta, M. and Gage, L. (2004) *Design Law: Protecting and Exploiting Rights* Law Society Publications, London

Hart, T. and Fazzani, L. (2003) *Intellectual Property Law* (3rd edn) Palgrave Macmillan, Basingstoke

Holyoak, J. and Torremans, P. (2001) *Intellectual Property Law* (3rd edn) Butterworths Law, London

Llewellyn, D. (ed) (2003) Intellectual Property *Patents, Copyrights, Trademarks and Allied Rights* (5th edn) Sweet & Maxwell, London

Land Law

Bickford-Smith, S. and Sydenham, C. (2004) *Party Walls: Law and Practice* (2nd edn) Jordans, Bristol

Chynoweth, P. (2003) *The Party Wall Casebook* Blackwell Science, Oxford

Elvin, D. and Karas, J. (2002) *Unlawful Interference with Land* (2nd edn) Sweet & Maxwell, London

Gaunt, J. and Morgan, P. (2002) *Gale on the Law of Easements* (17th edn) Sweet & Maxwell, London

Gray, K. (2000) *Elements of Land Law* (3rd edn) Butterworths Law, London

Gray, K. and Gray, S. (2003) *Butterworths CoreText: Land Law* Butterworths Law, London

Hanbury, W. (2003) *Boundary Disputes: A Practitioner's Handbook* EMIS Professional Publishing, London

Hellawell, T. (2000) *Blackstone's Guide to Contaminated Land* Blackstone Press, London

Mynors, C. (2002) *The Law of Trees and Forestry* Sweet & Maxwell, London

Oakley, A. (2002) *Megarry's Manual of the Law of Real Property* (8th edn) Sweet & Maxwell, London

Sara, C. (2002) *Boundaries and Easements* (3rd edn) Sweet & Maxwell, London

Smith, R. (2002) *Property Law* (4th edn) Longman, London

Planning and Local Government Law

Billington, J. (2002) *Means of Escape from Fire: An Illustrated Guide to the Law* Blackwell Science, Oxford

Clayden, P. (2003) *The Law of Mobile Homes and Caravans* (2nd edn) Shaw & Sons, London

Moore, V. (2002) *A Practical Approach to Planning Law* (8th edn) Oxford University Press, Oxford

Morrell, J. and Foster, R. (2001) *Local Authority Liability* (2nd edn) Jordans, Bristol

Polley, S. (2001) *Understanding the Building Regulations* (2nd edn) Spon Press, London

Telling, A. and Duxbury, R. (2002) *Planning Law and Procedure* (12th edn) Butterworths Law, London

Tricker, R. (2003) *Building Regulations in Brief* Butterworth-Heinemann, Oxford

European and EU Law

Collins, L. and Grief, N. (2003) *European Community Law in the United Kingdom* (5th edn) Butterworths Law, London

Craig, P. and DeBurca, G. (2002) *EU Law, Text Cases and Materials* (3rd edn) Oxford University Press, Oxford

Davies, K. (2003) *Understanding European Union Law* Cavendish Publishing, London

Hanlon, J. (2003) *European Community Law* (3rd edn) Sweet & Maxwell, London

Kramer, L. (2003) *EC Environmental Law* Sweet & Maxwell, London

Musker, D. (2002) *Community Design Law Principles and Practice* Sweet & Maxwell, London

Scots Law

Anderson, R. (2000) *A Practical Guide to Adjudication in Construction Matters* W. Green, Edinburgh

Davidson, F. and MacGregor, L. (2003) *Commercial Law in Scotland* W. Green, Edinburgh

Gordon, A. (2003) *Contract* (2nd edn) W. Green, Edinburgh

Macaulay, M. and Ramsay L. (2002) *Construction and Procurement Law*, W. Green, Edinburgh

MacRoberts WS. (2000) *Building & Development: Scots Law and Procedures*, W. Green, Edinburgh

McBryde, W. (2002) *The Law of Contract in Scotland* (2nd edn) W. Green, Edinburgh

Table of Statutes and Statutory Instruments

Table of European Directives

Table of Cases

Index